MW00588204

The Holy Qur'ân

ARABIC TEXT - ENGLISH TRANSLATION

This (Book) is a clear exposition (of the truth) for humankind (to follow), and a (means to) guidance, and exhortation to those who guard against evil (and are dutiful to God and people) (3:138).

AS EXPLAINED BY

'ALLÂMAH NOORUDDÎN

Rendered into English

by

AMATUL RAHMÂN 'OMAR

'ABDUL MANNÂN 'OMAR

ISBN 978-0-9766972-3-7

Library of Congress Online Catalog: LCCN 98213119

Noor Foundation International, Inc. is a non-profit and non-secterian organisation, working for the world peace through dialogue between the religions of the world.

Funds generated from dissemination of this Holy Book will be reinvested in its further publications.

1st Edition 1990	2nd Edition 1997
3rd Printing 2000	4th Printing 2001
5th Printing 2002	6th Printing 2003
7th Printing 2005	8th Printing 2008
9th Printing 2010	3rd EDITION 2013

11th REPRINT 2016

Noor Foundation International, Inc.

P. O. Box 758, Hockessin, DE 19707

(Toll Free) 888 - 937 - 2665 Tel: 302-234-8860

E-mail: alnoorfoundation@hotmail.com

noorfoundationusa@gmail.com

Website: www.islamusa.org

Available as App: **quranapp.org**

Printed in the P. R. China

THE HOLY QUR'ÂN

ARABIC TEXT AND ENGLISH TRANSLATION

Contents

About this Translation

The Holy Qur'ân

Appendices

List of Chapters (Surâhs) and Parts

ألسّورُ و ألأجزأ

List of Chapters (Surâhs)

List of Chapters (Surâhs)

List of Chapters (Surâhs) in Alphabetical Order

INTRODUCTION TO THE STUDY OF THE HOLY QUR'ÂN

هٰذَا بَيَانٌ لِّلنَّاسِ وَ هُدًى وَّ مَوْعِظَةٌ لِّلْمُتَّقِينَ ۝

This (Qur'ân) is a clear exposition (of the truth) for humankind (to follow) and a (means to) guidance, and an exhortation to those who guard against evil (and are dutiful to God and people) (3:138) .

Everything that is beautiful, everything that is meaningful and everything that brings us happiness is what this Scripture wishes us. All those right ideas, commandments, ordinances and principles which are of permanent utility to us have been incorporated in it. It is of a character unique in its grandeur and sublimity and is ultimately destined to bring the whole humanity to perfection.

This Book is a compendium of all that is good, lasting and imperishable in the teachings of former revealed Scriptures, with a good deal more which these Scriptures lacked, but which the human being needed for his spiritual, moral and mundane progress.

This book provides us guidance, answering the innate questions that press on us: What exactly is the human being? From where has he come? Where shall he go after death? What is righteousness? What is evil? How can we acquire good and shun evil? What are the physical, moral and spiritual conditions of the human being? What is his state in the Hereafter? What is the real object of his existence and what are the means of its attainment? What is the effect of actions in the present life and the life to come? What are the sources of Divine Knowledge? What is worship? How and whom we should worship? How should we organize our life? Such are the questions which demand answers, and if no convincing and decisive answer is provided, we will be in a state of moral and behavioral crisis. This Book answers such questions and much more. It gives the laws of a society and guidance for our *Nafs Ammârah* (- self that incites to evil), for our *Nafs Lawwâmah* (- self-accusing soul) and for our *Nafs Mutma'innah* (- the soul that rests in peace). It ranks amongst the greatest masterpieces of world literature whence the scholars derive their authority for meanings, grammar and syntax by referring to its verses. It is the most widely read book in the world. Its teachings formed the basis of the Islamic civilization and it still guides and inspires millions of Muslims all over the world. It is the final authority in matters of faith and practice for all Muslims and the most reliable source of information for the biography of Muhammad, the Holy Prophet of Islam *(Peace be upon him).*

NAMES OF THE HOLY BOOK

بَلْ هُوَ قُرْاٰنٌ مَّجِيْدٌ ۝

This is (also the truth) that it is a glorious Qur'ân (85:21).

Etymologically the word Qur'ân is derived from the verb *Qara'* which is translated as 'he read', 'he conveyed or delivered a message' and 'he gathered or collected together the things'. The name Qur'ân thus refers to all the three root meanings:

1. A book which is meant to be read.
2. A book which is meant to be conveyed to the humankind.
3. A book which comprehends all the truths and in which are gathered together the Divine Messages of all other books.

In the very early revelations (2:2) the Holy Writ is called *Al-Kitâb*. The word *Kitâb* is derived from the root word *Kataba* which means 'he wrote', 'he brought together' and *Al* means 'which is complete in itself.' The application of this word to the Holy Writ in the very early revelations and the use of the name shows clearly that the Qur'ân was, from the first, meant to be a complete Book, and one that existed not only in the memory of people but also in visible characters on writing material. The Holy Writ is also called Al-Dhikr - the Book which makes provisions for eminence, fame, renown, honour and reminding, and Al-Furqân (25:1) - the Book which distinguishes between right and wrong and which is divided and revealed in portions, as the root word Firqah also means portions.

There are other names by which the Holy Book is designated in the Revelation itself. It is called Al-Hikmah (17:39) - the Wisdom; Al-Hudâ (72:13) - that which guides and makes one attain the goal; Mubârak (6:93) - Blessed; Al-Mukarramah (80:13) - the Honoured; Musaddiq (6:93) - confirming (the truth of previous Scriptures); Al-Mauizah (10:57) - the Admonition; Al-'Azîz (41:41) - the Mighty; Al-Hukm (13:37) - the Judgment; Al-Shifâ (10:57) - that which heals; Al-Tanzîl (26:192) - the Revelation; Al-Rahmah (2:105) - the Mercy, Al-Rûh (42:52) - that which gives life and is living; Al-Khair (3:103) - the Goodness; Al-Bayân (3:137) - that which explains all things; Al-Ni'mat (93:11) - the Favour; Al-Burhân (4:175) - the clear Argument; Al-Qayyim (18:2) - the Maintainer; Al-Muhaimin (5:48) - the Guardian; Al-Nûr (7:157) - the Light; Al-Haq (17:81) - the Truth; Hablallâh (3:103) - the Covenant of God; Al-Mubîn (12:1) - that which explains; Al-Karîm (56:77) - the Holy; Al-Mâjîd (50:1) - the Glorious; Al-Hakîm (36:2) - the one full of Wisdom; Al-Marfû'ah (80:14) - the Exalted; Al-Mutahharah (80:14) - the Purified; Al-'Ajab (72:1:) - the Wonderful. All these names are attributes and characteristics of the Holy Qur'ân.

LANGUAGE OF THE HOLY QUR'ÂN

إِنَّآ أَنزَلْنَٰهُ قُرْءَٰنًا عَرَبِيًّا لَّعَلَّكُمْ تَعْقِلُونَ ○

We have, indeed revealed this Qur'ân which explains its object eloquently well that you may abstain (from evil) (12:2).

The Holy Qur'ân was revealed through the medium of Arabic, which, unlike Latin, old Greek, or Sanskrit, is a living language, still spoken, written and understood in several countries of the world and by millions of people. Its grammar, vocabulary, idiom, pronunciation and script remain unchanged. It claims to be the mother and source of all other languages.

The word 'ARABIYYA is derived from 'ARIBA. 'ARIB AL-BI'RU meaning 'the well containing a lot of water.' 'ARUB AL-RAJULU mean*s* 'the man spoke clearly, plainly and distinctly, he was brisk and lively'. Thus the word *'Arabiy* conveys the sense of fullness, abundance and clearness. Arabic is so called because its roots are innumerable and are full of meanings and because it is most expressive, eloquent and comprehensive. The expression QUR'ÂNAN 'ARABÎ'YAN (12:2), therefore, would mean that the Holy Qur'ân is a Book which can express its meaning in a clear, eloquent and comprehensive language (Lane).

The Arabic alphabet contains 28 letters. Each trio of letters, in any order, is capable of giving a root word. A triliteral is a very economical word. It is a golden means between a long and a short word and is easy to pronounce and hear. The triliterals are the most common words in Arabic. They are easily conjugated and are the foundation of the quadrilaterals. Arabic does not attach much importance to words containing more than three letters (Al-Khasâis, p.380.). An attempt was undertaken by Khalîl bin Ahmad (d.175 A.H.) to compile an Arabic lexicon (Kitâb al-'Ain) on the basis of permutation and combination of 28 letters of Arabic alphabet. The number of words formed ran into hundreds of thousands. So Khalîl was unable to complete the work.

All these roots are pregnant with a vast variety of meanings. 'In Arabic', says Titus Burkhardt, 'the tree of verbal forms, of derivations from certain roots is quite inexhaustible. It can always bring forth new leaves, new expressions to represent hitherto dominant variations of the basic idea or action. This explains why this Bedouin tongue was able to become the linguistic vehicle of an entire civilization, intellectually very rich and differentiated' (Art of Islam, Language and meaning, p. 43). Even the letters of Arabic possess clear and definite meaning. For instance, the letters LÂM, MÎM, KÂF in any combination, express the idea of power and strength, which is more or less common to all the words that are formed with these letters or are derived from this root. Its grammar is very advanced and an example are the ***I'râbs*** by which it can distinguish the logical categories of speech with great clarity. There is a complete order of verbs and nouns where similar verbs are mutually related with similar nouns in a scientific way. By using simple signs like Al or Tanwîn or by changing the order of words it conveys an idea which some languages may express in many sentences. Like the number and order of letters, the accent and the spelling of a word are rigidly fixed. The slightest change of accent will yield a different root and meaning. This is a marked contrast with other languages which have been reforming their spelling from time to time. Compare this aspect of Arabic spelling with the following sarcasm of Bernard Shaw. As an example of the English spelling he constructed the word Ghoti. He pointed out that the 'gh' combination was to be pronounced like the 'f' in cough; the vowel 'o' like short 'ai' in women and the'ti' combination like 'sh' in nations. He concluded that ghoti should be pronounced fish.

Another unique feature of Arabic is that it tends to express a thought twice in slightly different forms. This parallelism is often used to express completeness. In such cases we should not look for a different meaning in each half of the parallelism. Both expressions, in reality, express one truth. The repetition in the parallelism has the function of embellishing the statement, making it more beautiful for the sake of clarification and for further imprinting it on the hearer's memory. In one form of parallelism the same truth is put first in the positive and then in the negative form, this expresses the desire to exclude all other possibilities.

One way of bringing out the unity of an idea in writing is for passages to begin and end with the same thought. This form of speech is called 'Inclusions' since one particular thought or statement includes, grasps or embraces the intermediate phases. It is also known as rising constructions. We find numerous examples of such constructions in the Holy Qur'ân. The language, thus, possesses a store of words which faithfully and completely depict most subtle thought and feeling of the human being. It expresses more meaning in a few words. It is a facsimile of the book of nature as regards the names of elements, vegetables, animals, minerals, human links and numbers, and because of the richness of synonyms, it is possible for Arabic to achieve a precision of expression and thoroughness unequaled in any other language. It is the only language which can accurately describe the attributes of God.

The final revelation, the last and complete Book of God could not, possibly, have been expressed in a language of human creation. A finite mind could not make words sufficiently wide in their connotations to convey an Infinite mind. The language of the Holy Qur'ân was the only proper vehicle to convey the message coming from God, for it is imbued with qualities which lie outside all our frames of reference and all our limiting definitions, as the Qur'ân says:

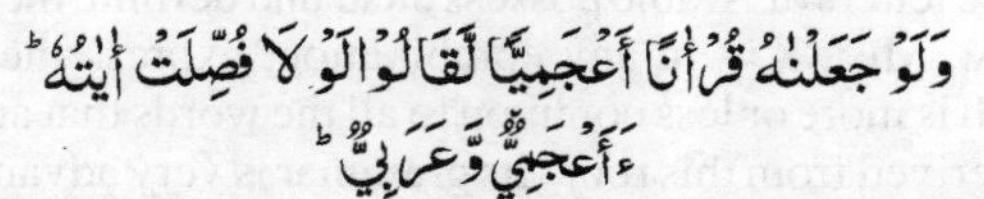

Had We made it a Qur'ân in indistinct and inexpressive language, these (faultfinders) would have surely said, 'Why has not (the subject

matter of *its verses been made clear in exposition?' What! Can indistinct and inexpressive language and an eloquently clear language (be one and the same thing) (41:44).*

DICTION OF THE QUR'ÂN

قُل لَّئِنِ اجْتَمَعَتِ الْإِنسُ وَالْجِنُّ عَلَىٰ أَن يَأْتُوا بِمِثْلِ هَٰذَا
الْقُرْآنِ لَا يَأْتُونَ بِمِثْلِهِ وَلَوْ كَانَ بَعْضُهُمْ لِبَعْضٍ ظَهِيرًا ۝

Say, 'If there should join together all human beings and the jinn to produce the like of this Qur'ân, they would never be able to produce anything like it, even though some of them might be the helpers of others' (17:88).

The style and diction of the Holy Qur'ân have been universally praised. A. J. Arberry in the preface to his translation of the Qur'ân says, 'Whenever I hear the Qur'ân chanted it is as though I am listening to music, underneath the flowing melody there is sounding all the time the insistent beat of a drum. It is like the beating of my heart.'

In the text the verses are divided according to the rhythm of the language, when a certain sound which marks the rhythm recurs there is a strong pause and the verse ends naturally, although the sentence may go on to the next verse or to several subsequent verses. 'It is inimitable symphony, the very sounds of which move men to tears and ecstasy' (M. M. Pickthall, translator's Foreword, p. 1).

E. H. Palmer says (pages lxvi - lxvii in the Introduction to his translation of the Holy Qur'ân), 'The language of the Qur'ân is universally acknowledged to be the most perfect form of Arabic speech ... the language is noble and forcible. Muhammad speaks with a living voice, his vivid word-painting brings at once before the mind the scene he describes.' The sublime simplicity, piercing force, enchanting beauty and melody of verses of the Holy Qur'ân and its poetical and spiritual aspects are not possible to be reproduced. Friend and foe alike pay ungrudging tributes to the linguistic style of the Holy Qur'ân and see in its beauty and majesty the nobility of its call, the magnanimity of its message and a sign and a miracle in this Handiwork of God.

Like everything in the nature the Holy Qur'ân has baffled all human efforts to produce another book like it (17:88). This challenge stands for all times to all people who deny the Divine origin of the Holy Qur'ân. A similar challenge is contained in verses 2:23; 10:38; 11:13; 52:33. The challenge remains unanswered to this day, as it is based on absolute truth. Whatever comes into being by exercise of God's perfect Power, whether it is a part of creation or a Book, revealed by Him, it is necessary that it should possess the quality that no one out of His creation should have the power to produce its like.

Apart from its teaching, the Holy Qur'ân has kept a permanent hold on Arabic. No other book in the world can be credited with keeping a language alive for fourteen centuries. The Qur'ân has done this. Those who have compiled books of Arabic literature admit that the language and diction of the Qur'ân surpass and excel the whole Arabic literature most preeminently. Even the Christian scholars, one and all, derive authority for their meaning, grammar and syntax by making references to the verses of the Holy Qur'ân. If the Book had been deficient and defective with regard to any of these points, they would have made it the object of their satire and rejoiced in bringing before the world its errors, weaknesses and mistakes. On the contrary, these lexicologists and writers, without any exception, acknowledge the elegance of language and eloquence of the Qur'ân. They quote its verses over and over again in support of the meaning put forth by them and thus enhance the value and worth of their own writings. No letter of it lacks wisdom, not one word is out of place or not in accord with appropriateness, and not a single phrase of it is such, as is not surely needed for the reform and spiritual uplift of humankind.

CONSISTENCY AND FREEDOM FROM CONTRADICTION

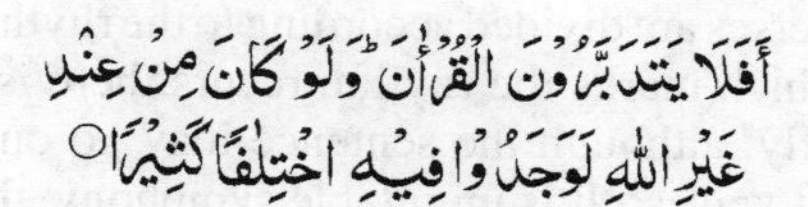

Why do they not ponder over the Qur'ân? Had it been from anyone other than Allâh, they would surely have found a good deal of inconsistency therein (4:82).

The Holy Qur'ân was revealed piecemeal and at intervals. The revelation began in 610 of the Christian era when the Holy Prophet ﷺ was 40 years of age. It was destined to continue during the twenty three years of his ministry and to end shortly before his death on June 8, 632 A.D., yet there is no inconsistency and contradiction anywhere in the Holy Book.

THE ARRANGEMENT

إِنَّ عَلَيْنَا جَمْعَهُۥ وَقُرْءَانَهُۥ

The responsibility of its collection and its arrangement lies on Us (75:17).

The word JAMA' in the verse above implies both collection and arrangement, which is a process quite different from the revelation. It is not true that the verses and chapters of the Holy Qur'ân were arranged after the death of the Holy Prophet ﷺ by someone else, or that they were arranged in the order of their lengths; the longest coming first and the shortest last. It is also wrong to say that within the chapters the passages are joined together without any regard to either chronology of revelation or similarity of subject, and that most heterogeneous materials are put together without any regard to logical sequence.

The whole Qur'ân, complete in every respect, was available in the Holy Prophet's life time (Caetani, 2:384). The Companions of the Holy Prophet say, 'We used to write down the Holy Qur'ân in the time of the Holy Prophet ﷺ' (Hâkim: Al-Mustadrik, 2:611). The arrangement of chapters and verses in the copies of the Holy Qur'ân at present in our hands does not follow the chronological order of revelation and their arrangement is TAUQIF i.e. effected by the Holy Prophet ﷺ under the guidance of Divine revelations (75:17-18). It is also said in the Holy Qur'ân:

وَرَتَّلْنَٰهُ تَرْتِيلًا

(But We have revealed it) in this manner (- piece by piece out of necessity).
And (in spite of the fact that it has not been revealed all at once,) We have arranged it in an excellent (form and order of) arrangement (and free of all contradictions) (25:32).

The concise phrase RATTALNÂ-HU-TARTÎLAN in the above verse comprises the parallel concept of putting the component parts of a thing together and arranging them well, as well as endowing it with inner consistency. The word TARTÎL refers to the measured diction and the thoughtful manner in which it ought to be enunciated. Thus, from the very first, it was meant that the verses and the chapters of the Holy Scripture should be arranged in an order different from that of their revelation, otherwise the revelation and the collection and arrangement would not have been described as two different things.

There was an arrangement followed by the Holy Prophet ﷺ and we know that many Companions of the Holy Prophet ﷺ committed the Holy Qur'ân to memory and could recite it in the recognized order as followed by the Prophet. This shows that there was a connection of its verses and chapters, and there was a recognized division of the Book and a fixed form and sequence. The chapters were distinctly marked out and their number was determined. Without a known order and sequence of verses, the Qur'ân could not have been committed to memory. The present arrangement of the Qur'ân does not differ from that followed by the Holy Prophet ﷺ. There are several sayings of the Holy Prophet ﷺ from which this can be inferred. The Holy Prophet ﷺ said, 'Whoever reads the last two verses of the chapter entitled BAQARAH on any night, they are sufficient for him' (Bukhârî; 64:12). This shows that the Holy Prophet ﷺ followed an arrangement which he had made known to his Companions. If such had not been the case he could not have referred to two verses as the 'last' two verses of a certain chapter. According to another saying of the Holy Prophet ﷺ he told his Companions to recite the first ten and last ten verses of the chapter entitled Al-KAHF at a particular occasion. Had there been no sequence of verses, 'the first ten verses and last ten verses' would have been a meaningless phrase. Not only the verses of the Holy Qur'ân but even its chapters were arranged by the Holy Prophet ﷺ himself. This is afforded by the following saying of Anas ؓ: 'At the time when the Banû Thaqîf ؓ accepted Islam I was in that delegation. The Holy Prophet ﷺ said to us, "When you people came to meet me, I was reciting my portion of the Holy Qur'ân which I used to recite daily, so I decided not to go out until I had finished it." Thereupon we questioned the Companions of the Holy Prophet ﷺ as to how they divided the Holy Qur'ân into portions for reading. They said, "We observe the following divisions, 3 chapters, 5 chapters, 7 chapters, 9 chapters, 11 chapters and 13 chapters, and all the remaining chapters beginning with chapter entitled QÂF"' (Fath al-Bârî, 9:39). This form of reading divided the Qur'ân into seven portions or Ahzâb, each portion to be recited in one day and, thus, the recital of the whole Qur'ân (114 chapters) was finished in seven days. This report of Anas ؓ shows an arrangement of chapters which is observed to this day by the whole Muslim *Ummah*. This and many other reports by the Companions of the Prophet give conclusive testimony to the fact that the form and arrangement of the chapters of the Holy Book was brought about by the Holy Prophet ﷺ himself, and that the present arrangement does not differ in the least from the original of the time of the Prophet.

The efforts of some European scholars such as Well, Nöldecke, Muir, Rodwell and others such as N. J. Dawood to rearrange the Holy Qur'ân are misleading and are unworthy of being considered as scholarly.

PRISTINE PURITY OF THE QUR'ÂN

بَلْ هُوَ قُرْاٰنٌ مَّجِيْدٌ ۙ فِيْ لَوْحٍ مَّحْفُوْظٍ ۧ

This is (also the truth) that it is a glorious Qur'ân, (Inscribed) in a Tablet well-guarded (against corruption, distortion and destruction) (85:21-22).

All the Books from God that came from time to time to every nation and to every country for human guidance have lost their purity, and man-made creeds have obscured the Words of the Lord. No religion should claim our allegiance unless its record is absolutely authentic and its Scripture undistorted. Whatever is the worth of the teachings of a religion one cannot consider or accept its claims when its very source is of a dubious character. But the Scriptures of all other religions, as admitted by their respective adherents, are wanting in genuineness.

The Qur'ân is admitted by friends and foes alike to be the very Book presented by Muhammad (peace be upon him), and it has maintained its purity all along. Amongst all the Divine Scriptures it is the only one which enjoys the distinction of having its original text intact. Contrary to the Holy Bible and the Vedas, this Holy Writ, through all the centuries since it was revealed, and all over the world and among the numerous contending sects, has maintained only one text.

It is an established fact that the present text of the Holy Qur'ân is the same that was presented by the Holy Prophet ﷺ. Every verse of it was put into writing in the lifetime of the Holy Prophet ﷺ, before his own eyes and under his orders. Since the Book was revealed in parts during a period of twenty three years, the practice was that when a verse or a part of a chapter was revealed the Holy Prophet ﷺ, under Divine guidance, specified the place of the revelation. Thus, the arrangement of verses in each chapter was entirely the work of the Holy Prophet ﷺ himself. Similarly the arrangement of the chapters *(Surâhs)* was also the work of the Holy Prophet ﷺ under Divine guidance. In one of the earliest revelations the Holy Qur'ân speaks of its collection as well as its arrangement as being a part of the Divine scheme.

THE ORIGINAL SCRIPT OF THE HOLY QUR'ÂN

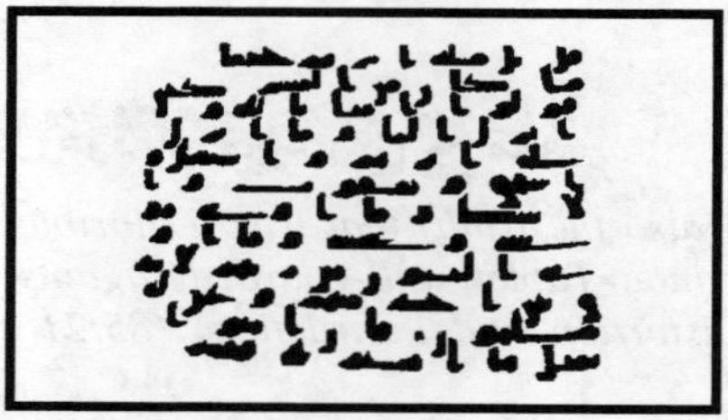

قُلْ بَلْ مِلَّةَ إِبْرٰهِمَ حَنِيفًا ۖ وَمَا كَانَ مِنَ الْمُشْرِكِينَ ﴿١٣٥﴾

قُولُوٓا ءَامَنَّا بِاللّٰهِ وَمَآ أُنْزِلَ إِلَيْنَا

وَمَآ أُنْزِلَ إِلَىٰٓ إِبْرٰهِمَ وَإِسْمٰعِيلَ

وَإِسْحٰقَ وَيَعْقُوبَ وَالْأَسْبَاطِ

وَمَآ أُوتِيَ مُوسَىٰ وَعِيسَىٰ وَمَآ

أُوتِيَ النَّبِيُّونَ مِن رَّبِّهِمْ ۚ لَا نُفَرِّقُ بَيْنَ

أَحَدٍ مِّنْهُمْ ۖ وَنَحْنُ لَهُ مُسْلِمُونَ ﴿١٣٦﴾

فَإِنْ آمَنُوا بِمِثْلِ مَآ آمَنتُم بِهِ فَقَدِ

.....Say, 'Nay, but (ours is) the faith of Abraham, the upright, and he was not of the polytheists.' Say, 'We believe in Allâh and in that (the Qur'ân) which has been revealed to us, and what was revealed to Abraham and Ismâîl and Isaac and Jacob and his children, and what was given to Moses and Jesus (we believe) in what was given to (all other) Prophets from their Lord. We (while believing in them) make no discrimination between anyone of them, and to Him do we submit ourselves entirely.' Now, if they believe just as (sincerely) as you have believed in this then ....

(2:135-137)

An image of a page from the Holy Qur'ân written about 640 A.D. (before the death of the 3rd. Caliph Osmân رض). A complete manuscript is preserved in Tashkent, Uzbekistan and another in Topekapi museum in Istanbul, Turkey. Above the old script is made readable for today's reader. *(By the courtesy of the Grand Mufti of Ma Warâ al-Nahr, Muhammad Sâddiq M. Yûsuf, Tashkent, Uzbekistan)*

FACTORS WHICH WARRANTY THE PURITY OF THE HOLY QUR'ÂN

إِنَّا نَحْنُ نَزَّلْنَا الذِّكْرَ وَإِنَّا لَهُ لَحٰفِظُونَ ۝

Verily, it was We, Ourself Who have revealed this Reminder (- the Qur'ân); and it is We Who are, most certainly, its Guardian (15:9).

God revealed the Holy Qur'ân Himself and made arrangements for its safety and security for ever. In the above verse there is attestation to the imperishable quality of the Divine Writ. This verse relates God's promise that the Qur'ân would never be corrupted and would ever remain free from all additions, diminutions and textual changes. There are many factors which warranty its purity and contribute to the safe preservation of its text, a few are summarized below:

1. PUTTING INTO WRITING:

The first and the most important point which assisted in the preservation of the text of the Holy Qur'ân is that its every verse was put into writing in the life time of the Holy Prophet ﷺ, before his own eyes. The Holy Qur'ân itself furnishes abundant evidence that it existed in a written form. Again and again the Divine Writ calls itself a AL-KITÂB, which means a book or a writing which is complete in itself. The application of the word Book to the Holy Writ also occurs in very early revelations and this use shows that the Holy Qur'ân was destined, from the very beginning, to be a complete Book. The Holy Qur'ân is also designated as Suhuf (80:13) which means written pages. There are many other references in the Holy Qur'ân showing that it will exist in a written form. It is said:

وَكِتٰبٍ مَّسْطُورٍ ۝ فِي رَقٍّ مَّنْشُورٍ ۝

And a Book inscribed - On open unrolled parchments (52:2-3).

There are also testimonies of the enemies of the Qur'ân that the Qur'ân was reduced to writing such as:

وَقَالُوٓا أَسٰطِيرُ الْأَوَّلِينَ اكْتَتَبَهَا فَهِيَ تُمْلٰى عَلَيْهِ بُكْرَةً وَّأَصِيلًا ۝

They (also) say, '(This Qur'ân consists of) fables of the ancients that he has got written down and now they are read out to him morning and evening.' (25:5).

There is a lot of historical evidence concerning the documentation of the Holy

Qur'ân. There are numerous anecdotes showing that when the Holy Prophet ﷺ received a revelation it was immediately put into writing. The general practice is described by 'Osmân رض, he says: 'It was customary with the Holy Prophet ﷺ that when any verse of the Holy Qur'ân was revealed he called one of those persons who used to write the Holy Qur'ân and said, "Write these verses in the chapter where such and such verse occur".' (Abû Dâwûd, 2:123). Zaid bin Thâbit رض who was a scribe of the Holy Prophet ﷺ and was especially appointed for writing down the revelations said, 'Whenever a revelation descended the Holy Prophet ﷺ called me and I went to him holding my pen and paper. He dictated to me first and then heard it from me and in case something was left, or some mistake was found, it was set right there and then, and afterwards it was published' (Mu'jam al-Zawâid). This shows that the Holy Qur'ân was presented to the public after it was duly written down. The Shî'a sect says that 'Alî collected the Qur'ân into a volume during the Holy Prophet's ﷺ lifetime and at his command.'

The Holy Prophet ﷺ used to say, 'Do not write from me anything except the Qur'ân.' This direction was meant as a precautionary step against any confusion with regards to the Holy Qur'ân. This saying also suggests that the Holy Prophet ﷺ took it for granted that the Holy Qur'ân was to be written down. The above conclusion is corroborated by another report from the Companions of the Prophet. They were forbidden to travel to the enemy's land with the Holy Qur'ân. This is also a conclusive proof that written copies of the Holy Qur'ân existed in abundance and Muslims were forbidden to take such copies to the enemy's country lest they should treat them with disrespect or try to make changes in them.

The Holy Prophet ﷺ was very conscious about the dictation of the Qur'ân. In a period and in circumstances when few people were able and even fewer available to read and write in the whole of Arabia, he had a sufficient number of the scribes at hand to write down the revelation of the Holy Qur'ân, as the Holy Qur'ân says:

فِي صُحُفٍ مُّكَرَّمَةٍ ۝ مَّرْفُوعَةٍ مُّطَهَّرَةٍ ۝ بِأَيْدِي سَفَرَةٍ ۝ كِرَامٍ بَرَرَةٍ ۝

(This Qur'ân is preserved) in such written leaves (of the Book) as are greatly honoured, (which are) ranked high (and) are rid of all impurities, which are in the hands of Scribes; Noble and Virtuous (80:13-16).

Sîrat al-Irâqî has named as many as forty two scribes. The well known orientalist Blachese has determined the number of these scribes to be forty one and this same number has been mentioned by Schwally who has, most probably, quoted it from Roudzât al-Ahbâb. Other books to be consulted regarding the scribes of this Divine revelation are: Ibn al-Hajr, Fath al-Bârî, Al-Jâhshiyârî, Kitâb al-Wuzarâ' wa al-Kuttâb.

The first person to write down the first revelation of the Holy Qur'ân for the Holy Prophet ﷺ was 'Osmân رض, (Ibn al-Kathîr's Fadzâil al-Qur'ân, p.5). Some

Scribes besides Zaid bin Thâbit رض, who did, by far, the greatest part of the work of writing of the Holy Qur'ân, are: Abû Bakr رض, 'Omar bin Khattâb رض, 'Alî bin Abî Tâlib رض, Zubair رض, 'Abd Allâh bin Sa'd رض, Khâlid bin Saîd رض, Abbân bin Saîd رض, Ubayya bin Ka'b رض, Mua'iqab bin Abû Fâtimah رض, 'Abd Allâh bin Arqam رض, 'Abd Allâh bin Rawaih رض. It was Hamzah bin Rabîa's رض duty to make sure that at least one or two scribes were present at all times so that no handicap, no delay, no shortcoming in any form in writing down of the revelations was caused due to the absence of the scribes.

The importance given to the writing down of the Qur'ânic revelations as they came down to the Prophet Muhammad ﷺ was so great that in the Migration of the Holy Prophet ﷺ from Makkah to the Madînah, pen, ink-pot and writing material were included in the essentials of the journey. There were many other men and women who made copies of the Holy Qur'ân for their own use. There is another real and authentic proof of committal of the Holy Qur'ân to writing and its compilation, to which Caetani says, 'The whole Qur'ân from the beginning to the end, complete in every respect, was available in the time of the Holy Prophet ﷺ (Caetani, vol 2, p384). It is in this very direction that Hârith al-Muhâsibî alludes to in his explicit account about a collection of the complete Holy Qur'ân in the household of the Holy Prophet ﷺ. This, however, was an unbound original text. Zaid bin Thâbit رض bound it together with the help of a tag made of string under the order of Abû Bakr رض.

The text of the Holy Qur'ân was also recorded in the Holy Prophet's life time on a variety of writing materials such as leather, parchment, papyrus, limestone, slates, shoulder blades, etc. (Ibn Nadîm: Kitâb Al-Fihrist; ed. G. Flugel, Leipzig 1871, p. 21; N. Abbot: The Rise of the North Arabic Script; Chicago, 1939 p. 45). A copy of the Holy Qur'ân prepared by the Holy Prophet ﷺ himself was written on a fine parchment *(Raqq)* as the Holy Qur'ân testifies in the verses 52:2-3. Among the Companions of the Prophet who had put the Holy Qur'ân in writing during his life time, the names of 'Osmân رض, 'Alî رض, 'Abd Allâh bin Mas'ûd رض, 'Abd Allâh bin 'Amar bin 'Âs رض, Sâlim رض, the freed slave of Hudhaifah, Muâdh bin Jabal رض and Ubayy bin Ka'b رض have been specifically mentioned.

Several hundred Companions of the Holy Prophet ﷺ learnt the whole Qur'ân by heart (the *Huffâz*). Some *Huffâz* were killed in the Battle of Yamâmah. 'Omar bin Khattâb رض concluded that it was not safe to depend exclusively upon those who had learnt the Qur'ân by heart and, thus, decided to take necessary steps to preserve the several copies of the Holy Qur'ân in a book form. Abû Bakr رض (the First Caliph of Prophet Muhammad ﷺ) after the death of the Prophet ﷺ, agreed to the proposal and took the task of copying of the Qur'ân in hand. He entrusted this work to Zaid bin Thâbit رض who was best qualified for this work, for he had frequently acted as an amanuensis to the Holy Prophet ﷺ, and was among the scribes, 'noble and virtuous' (80:16), and was one of those Companions of the Prophet who had learnt the Holy Qur'ân and its arrangement by heart directly from him. Moreover, he had also been present on the occasion when the Holy Prophet ﷺ had recited the whole of the completed Qur'ân, shortly, prior to his death.

'Omar رضي الله عنه publicly announced that whoever possessed any portion of the Qur'ân, received directly from the Holy Prophet ﷺ (for some Companions had written these on paper, tablets, palm-stem and shoe horn of leaf), should bring it for comparison. Zaid رضي الله عنه, with the cooperation and help of those Companions of the Holy Prophet ﷺ who had helped in the documentation of the Qur'ân and who had committed it to memory, prepared a copy of the Book. This version was checked, word by word and hyphen by hyphen, and all the written pages compared with each other for verification. Zaid رضي الله عنه would not take down any thing in his copy unless all of the sources tallied with one another and with the manuscript of the Holy Prophet ﷺ.

This copy by Zaid رضي الله عنه was kept in the custody of the Caliph of Prophet ﷺ (Abû Bakr رضي الله عنه), then in the Custody of 'Omar رضي الله عنه (second Caliph رضي الله عنه), then in the custody of learned Hafsah رضي الله عنه, wife of the Holy Prophet ﷺ and 'Omar's رضي الله عنه daughter. And it was announced that anyone who so desired, might make a copy of it or compare with it the copy he already possessed.

It is a great mistake to think that either Abû Bakr رضي الله عنه or 'Osmân رضي الله عنه was the compiler or collector of the Holy Qur'ân, though both of them did very important work in connection with the dissemination of the authentic and standard copies of the sacred text, to which everyone had access. Abû Bakr رضي الله عنه did not order Zaid bin Thâbit رضي الله عنه the writing of anything new which was not already written in the lifetime of the Holy Prophet ﷺ. 'Osmân رضي الله عنه then asked Zaid رضي الله عنه, 'Abd Allâh bin Jâbir رضي الله عنه, Sa' ad bin Al-'Âs رضي الله عنه, and 'Abdul Rahmân bin Al-Hârith رضي الله عنه to make seven copies of the one original in the custody of Hafsah رضي الله عنه daughter of ' Omar رضي الله عنه. These copies were forwarded to the chief cities of the Islamic world - Makkah, Kûfah, Basrah, Yemen, Bahrain and Damascus. One copy remained at Madînah. 'Osmân رضي الله عنه in consultation with other Companions of the Prophet also decided that the use of all other copies in any other dialect or idiom or written without proper care should be prohibited. As a precautionary measure he had all such copies burnt to foreclose any possibility of future confusion and misunderstanding. For instance, some of the Companions had noted down explanatory words and comments on the margins of their copies and it was feared that these might get mixed up with the original text of the Qur'ân. It was of course, an act of most prudent foresight to make the Holy Qur'ân safe and secure against any possible alteration in the future. The Qur'ân, which is now in the hands of all Muslims and in use all over the world is the exact copy of the Qur'ân dictated and written by the order of the Holy Prophet ﷺ before his eyes and of the copy written by the order of the first Caliph Abû Bakr رضي الله عنه, copies of which were officially sent by 'Osmân رضي الله عنه to different places. Of the copies originally made by the order of 'Osmân رضي الله عنه one can still be found in Tashkent, Uzbekistan and another in Topekapi, Turkey.

'Osmân رضي الله عنه not only sent an authenticated copy of the Qur'ân to the different centers of the Islamic world but also sent a *Qârî*, one who is well versed in the correct reading and knowledge of the Holy Qur'ân, along with it, in order to preserve the correct reading which was taught by the Holy Prophet ﷺ. When 'Osmân ؓ began to make copies of the Qur'ân from Abû Bakr's ؓ copy in the custody of Hafsah ؓ, thousands of the Companions were still living, and no change in the sequence of the verses could have remained unnoticed. There is not a slightest trace in the historical record of any form of protest or mention that anything in the text or in the arrangement was altered.

Efforts of some European scholars to prove the existence of later interpolation in the Qur'ân have failed. The utter failure of Dr. Mingana to find fault with the purity of the Qur'ânic text, on the contrary, sets the seal on the truth that among all the revealed Scriptures Qur'ân alone has remained completely immune from any interpolation or tampering. L. V. Vaglieri observes in his book 'Apology for Islam:' 'The proof of the divinity of the Qur'ân is the fact that it has been preserved intact through the ages since the time of its revelation till the present day.' In his book 'The Messenger' R. V. C. Bodley writes, 'What is important is that the Qur'ân is the only work which has survived for fourteen hundred years with an unadulterated text. Neither in the Jewish religion nor in the Christian is there anything which faintly compares to this.'

Many centuries have passed since the revelation of this wonderful Book and one can find its copies in countries which have long remained isolated from the rest of the world and among various Muslim sects, which for centuries have remained deadly enemies, yet the Holy Qur'ân has remained exactly the same unaltered Book in spite of the differences of time, lands, culture and customs. The reader can well calculate the miraculous nature of this Glorious Book of God.

2. MEMORIZING OF THE HOLY QUR'ÂN

The memorizing of the Holy Qur'ân has also assisted in the preservation of its text. Whenever any portion of the Holy Qur'ân was revealed to the Holy Prophet, he committed it to memory and continuously recited it from one end to the other. Thus, he always carried the whole of the revealed Qur'ân in his memory. The Holy Prophet ﷺ used to stress the merits of committing the Holy Qur'ân to memory so much that he said that if a person committed the Qur'ân to memory he would be saved from the torment of Hell. When he made this announcement, a large number of his Companions began to commit the Holy Qur'ân to memory. The Holy Prophet ﷺ also took pains to supervise the recitation of the Holy Qur'ân and was anxious to see that no errors crept into the process.

Since the time of 'Omar (the second Caliph), it has become customary to recite the whole text during TARÂWÎH (late night) Prayer in the month of *Ramadzân.* Memorizing of the Qur'ân is still considered highly noble, and the memorizing of the *Surâhs* and small texts is still the first stage of informal education among millions of Muslim families. No human-written book of this volume can ever be memorized wholly by any single human being, not even by its author. It is only the Holy Qur'ân that, today, stands as the singular Book memorized and recited wholly by hundreds and thousands of men, women and, even, children. It is the fulfillment of God's promise that the Holy Qur'ân is easily memorized. It is worth mentioning at this point that the author of this translation, Allâmah Nooruddîn, was the eleventh consecutive son in his family to become a 'hâfiz', (a person who memorizes and knows the whole Qur'ân by heart).

3. LIVING LANGUAGE OF THE HOLY QUR'ÂN

The third factor which assisted in the preservation of the text of the Holy Qur'ân is its language -Arabic. Arabic is a living language spoken, written and understood by millions of people, Muslims and Non-Muslims alike. Its grammar, vocabulary, idioms, pronunciation and script have remained unchanged from the time of the revelation of the Holy Qur'ân.

4. SPREAD OF THE QUR'ÂN

Another factor for the preservation of the Holy Qur'ân was that its message spread very quickly right from the start of its revelation to different regions of the world. The Holy Prophet ﷺ was still in Makkah when the Qur'ân reached the second largest city of Yathrib (Madînah) where it attracted people to read, write and learn it by heart and act upon its teachings. Thousands of Companions of the Holy Prophet ﷺ were still living when the Holy Book crossed the bounds of Arabian peninsula and reached the people living in Iraq, Iran, Palestine, Egypt, Tunis, Algiers, Morocco, Somalia, Sudan, Abbyssinia and many other parts of Africa. On the other side it travelled to central Asia, Punjâb and Sindh in the Indian subcontinent and reached as far as China and southeast Asia. This, too, was one of the means which led to the preservation of the Holy Book and made it impossible to be altered by any powerful party, a nation or a king.

5. DISSENT IN THE UMMAH

There is a famous saying of the Holy Prophet ﷺ that the difference of opinion among the people of his community (Ummah) will bring many blessings in its wake. The importance of this dissension with regard to the preservation of the Holy Qur'ân can well be judged by the fact that the Muslims fell into parties soon after the demise of the Holy Prophet ﷺ. Had one party only remained in power there was the possibility of their faith having faltered, which would have led them to bring about some changes and alterations in the Sacred Book to satisfy their ends and purposes. However, their mutual differences created a situation wherein the opposing groups kept a constant watch over one another. If one group had ever tried to effect a change in the Holy Qur'ân the other group was there to keep them in check.

6. PROTECTION OF THE UMMAH FROM GENERAL DESTRUCTION

The Muslims became a powerful nation in a very short period and, thus, the Book they carried was saved from its enemies. During the course of history, in spite of many vicissitudes of time, defeats and occupations, Muslims were saved from complete destruction. Had the Muslims been completely destroyed by universal earthly or heavenly disasters, the Holy Qur'ân would not have remained preserved. If God intends to keep His Book alive for ever, it is obvious that He will save Muslims in the future from complete destruction. What else was the cause of the destruction of the Zoroastrian Zynd and its commentary Avista, except that the followers of this religion were first attacked by Alexander and then completely wiped out by the Parthians, thus, Scriptures given to these people were all lost, without any trace. God in His Wisdom, always protected the Muslims from general destruction and if a calamity ever visited them in one part of the world, they remained safe in another and became the means of the preservation of the Holy Book.

7. THE GREAT LOVE:
The general love towards this Heavenly gift was another factor which assisted in its preservation. A Muslim, no matter how ignoble of character and averse to piety, will find that his heart is always full of reverence, respect and regard for the Glorious Qur'ân. These feelings are preserved in every believer in Islam, irrespective of his age and degree of knowledge and no one dares to bring about any change or alteration in the text of the Holy Book.

8. INIMITABILITY:
Another cause of the Holy Qur'ân being safe and secure is that no being has the ability to make even a single verse like the verses of the Qur'ân. A single word omitted from a Qur'ânic verse will cause it to lose its orderly arrangement, a word shifted from its original position, or exchanged with a synonym will have the same effect. The beauty of the verse will vanish, there will be no congruity left and the result will appear as if a fine silken brocade had been patched with a rough jute sack.

THE LASTING SCRIPTURE

وَإِن مِّن شَيْءٍ إِلَّا عِندَنَا خَزَآئِنُهُ وَمَا نُنَزِّلُهُ إِلَّا بِقَدَرٍ مَّعْلُومٍ

And there is not a thing but We have the vast treasures of it; and We do not send it down but according to a proper and prescribed measure (15:21).

The Holy Qur'ân is for all times and climes. It was not meant for a limited period. It was revealed for the good of the whole of humankind and is suited for all ages to come. It, not only has a long history but also a long future, a future which will last for ever. Those who may imagine that the Holy Qur'ân has become outmoded, is no longer needed and is of no more use, do not know what it stands for. They do not understand its real mission in human life; how it embraces the whole of human being's life and strikes a reasonable balance between different aspects of his existence. As the wonderful qualities of nature never come to an end, but appear ever fresh and new, the same is the case with this Holy Book. As the passage of time gives rise to unlimited thinking, therefore, it is necessary for a Book which claims to be Khâtam al-Kutub (the last and the perfect Book) to manifest itself in ever new forms. If it were not to meet new contingencies, it would not establish its claims.

The safeguarding of the Holy Qur'ân not only means that its text should be preserved but, also, that its benefits and influence are for all times. The Almighty has laid down in this everlasting Holy Book, some universal, all embracing and lasting principles, beyond the limits of which the varying circumstances of the human beings can never go. It has, then, left their detailed application to be determined according to changing times and the new needs arising from this change. It has, however, commanded us not to transgress the limits prescribed by these all embracing principles, as the Holy Qur'ân says:

وَتِلْكَ حُدُودُ اللّٰهِ ؕ وَمَنْ يَّتَعَدَّ حُدُودَ اللّٰهِ فَقَدْ ظَلَمَ نَفْسَهٗ

These are the limits imposed by Allâh and he that violates the limits imposed by Allâh, indeed does injustice to himself (65:1).

Thus, the Holy Qur'ân is an exposition of every spiritual truth. A storehouse of every basic principle necessary for the moral and spiritual welfare of human beings. It shows the way to all that is most upright and conformable to rectitude and benefits our individual and social life (16:89). Dr. W. Cantwell Smith writes, 'It in recent years has not moved towards a social gospel but has been a Social Gospel from the start. It has formulated a basic spiritual and social code of lasting guidance for humankind whether previously revealed or not'. Falsehood cannot approach it from fore or aft and cannot ever attain to it openly or in a stealthy manner, since it is bestowed from on high by One Who is the Wise, the Praiseworthy (41:42). Not a single truth, principle or ideal enunciated by this Book has ever been contravened or contradicted by ancient learning or by modern science. It is a storehouse of wisdom and discriminates between truth and falsehood by reasoning (25:1). Those who do not accept the Book as encompassing unlimited verities and insights do not value it as they should. The Book is living, there is internal and external evidence to show that it is not fossilized, rather, quite capable of facing the challenges of the modern world.

One may object that Islam is a religion from a Book, something fixed and final, while the soul of humanity is marching on and human knowledge is ever increasing. This is an age of rapid scientific and technological discoveries and the Qur'ân was revealed hundreds of years ago. No dead hand should be allowed to check the progress of humanity. Who can assure us that the principles and enactments which were established during a period of time long gone still have the potential for growth and renewal? Is Islam sufficiently suitable for application to other periods with different values and circumstances?

The objection seems to be sound if the religion taught in the Book is husk and gravel, a dogma, priest-craft, symbolism and ritual, if it hinges upon stories and certain supposed events in the life of its master. Then, of course, it is not a lasting religion but a superstition and a myth. It is a fog which cannot stand in the strong rays of the sun of reality and is sure to ramify into sections. Each advancement in science, culture and knowledge will shake it and its apologists will change it into something new.

The Holy Qur'ân will not change. It is from the All-Knowing, All-Wise God (11:1), Who created the human being and Who knows what suggestions the human mind makes (50:16), Who is the Originator and Nourisher to perfection of the universe, Knower of every thing. He has prescribed guidelines in the light of which the human being is free to determine his path. These are bounds set by God and he who transgresses the bounds set by God, indeed, does wrong to his own soul (65:1); as the 'word of God' and the 'work of God' should prove to be in accord.

It is a fact that Islam has not given detailed, fixed rules for all incidental questions, but only those fundamental laws which do not change, as the principles of Mathematics, Physics, Algebra and Geometry. With this comprehensiveness and elasticity the Holy Qur'ân guarantees growth and renewal of its derived subsidiary laws for ages to come. The jurists of Islam have, since then, applied the Qur'ânic verses by making analogies and deductions to enable the injunctions of the Qur'ân to answer the problems which arise in the society from time to time.

The call of the Qur'ân is to examine our stored-up resources and to acquire the knowledge of its all-embracing fundamentals before we resort to a precipitate imitation of the alien and foreign theories and laws which have no historical basis in our lives and by adopting which our individuality will be lost to the point that we will become the rear of the caravan of humanity, whereas the Holy Qur'ân calls on us to be always in its van (2:143, 3:110).

Islam allows freedom of opinion and private right of judgement. It has preached democracy in religion as well as in politics. Its laws are, no doubt, unchangeable and everlasting, but so are all such laws that rule the world and keep it healthy, morally and ethically. These laws are broad enough to cover all contingencies, however, one has to draw a line between freedom and licence.

The power of thinking is a Divine gift and to think is to differ, therefore, Islam always respected difference of opinion. 'Difference of opinion in my followers is a blessing of God', so says the Holy Prophet ﷺ, and this approval of the Holy Prophet ﷺ has opened a healthy avenue for the fair play of private judgement.

As truth is absolute; two and two never make five nor ten times ten ever make one hundred and one, so shall remain, forever, unchangeable and unalterable all those colossal and stupendous rules given in the Holy Qur'ân to govern human affairs. Adequacy can be maintained through 'Ijtihâd' (exercising judgement) and a continuously progressive interpretation of the Qur'ân from time to time in accordance with the progress of human experience. All the teachings put together make the Divine guidance contained in the Holy Qur'ân adequate for the future moral and spiritual progress of the human race for all times. A saint said once:.

'I round the globe in search of heaven did roam
returned and found my heaven was here at home'.

No doubt that it is perfectly legitimate for Muslims to borrow from other circles what is in fact already theirs by right, their 'straying camel'. But nothing that has its roots in agnosticism, or contrary to the Qur'ânic principles can be incorporated into its interpretation without poisoning the whole system.

Has Islam not had a shining record of science and civilization? Does the West not owe to Islam much of its scientific discoveries? In the fifth and the sixth Century A.D. the great civilization which had taken four thousand years to construct was on the verge of disintegration. The sanctions created by Christianity were working division and destruction instead of unity and order, at this critical time the Holy Qur'ân was an indispensable means to unite the whole known world of the East and the South. 'From a new angle', writes H.G. Wells, 'and with a fresh vigor it (the Arab mind) took up that systematic development of positive knowledge which the Greeks had begun and relinquished. If the Greek was the father, then the Arab was the foster-father of the scientific method of dealing with reality. Through the Arabs it was and not by the Latin route that the modern world received that gift of Light and Power' (The Outline of History, London, p.192).

One must study the influence and blessing of the Holy Qur'ân and appreciate the great forward leap that humanity took with its help and under its guidance and the deep abyss from the bottom of which it lifted humanity to the lofty heights of social, moral and spiritual reinforcements in every age. Through the impetus given by the Qur'ân, one of the most dynamic scientific movements in the history of exact thought began soon after the advent of Islam. This movement rapidly gained momentum and the world saw the birth of some of the greatest scientists and philosophers of all times.

'One of the most deplorable things in history', says Dr. J.W. Draper, the author of 'The Intellectual Development of Europe' 'is the systematic way in which European writers have contrived to put out of sight their scientific obligation towards the Arabs'.

Islamic history has never known such hateful organized persecution of thinkers and scholars as was conducted by the 'Inquisition Courts'. Never even for a single moment did the Qur'ân stand in the way of knowledge, science, civilization and progress. Where ever it has found its way among cultured and progressive nations, it has shown itself in complete accord with progressive tendencies and has assisted knowledge, culture and civilizations. The Holy Qur'ân says, 'Consider the flight of time. Verily, a person who is unmindful of God and higher values of this life is pursuing a losing bargain. Different, however, is the case of those who believe (in the Qur'ân) and, accordingly, do deeds of righteousness and who exhort one another to accept and preach the truth and to abide by it with patience and perseverance.' (103:1-3). Thus the passage of time has no adverse effect on the Qur'ân and its teachings.

It is because of the everlasting character of the Holy Qur'ân that the great prophecy was made that the Qur'ân will, for all times, remain safe against all attempts to destroy it and from every kind of corruption (15:9) and the selection of Arabic, which is a living language, as a vehicle for the last and everlasting Book was made.

One index of modern progress is the unprecedented divorce rate, over emphasis on sex, liquor traffic, overwhelmed mental institutions due to the ever increasing number of nervous disorder problems, criminal delinquency among teens which is reaching new heights each year, boredom, insecurity, disturbed family life and tension among vast multitudes even among those who apparently have every thing to make life worthwhile. This frame of life of the modern age needs, for its remedy, a sense of direction, a deep satisfying assurance of the meaning, purpose and aim of life itself.

Social problems, national and international, are often just personal problems writ large. The race and colour problem begins simply where one human being despises another. Employer-labor deadlocks are born of injustice or resentment in a lot of individual personal attitudes. International frictions start out as the greed of a few leaders or the personal harbored spite of many separate human beings. Hatred starts with individuals who hate, thus, the worries of society itself are, first of all, very personal problems of the people. What have science and technology done for the solution of such problems of the people? Dilemmas such as those of finance and wrong distribution of wealth are complex, knotty questions demanding abolition of interest, free enterprise, distribution of wealth after a generation and a sanction through which, at least, within 40 years, all the wealth of the over-privileged people must go to the underprivileged. These circumstances demand expert, solid thinking and cool planning according to the Qur'ân which is a tremendously constructive force in such perplexing conditions. We need smart people using their intelligence in an atmosphere made creative, sympathetic, good and Godly by the Qur'ân. Name any problem of the modern age for which there is no remedy in the Holy Qur'ân. Yes, the whole world is in a process of evolution. But all is not well with the world, it is a pattern of light and shadows, parts of which are pleasant, some definitely otherwise. However, it is not a case of 'take it or leave it' we simply have to take it because we are here and we are quite capable of improving the art of living.

The real question is whether the human being remains dominated by his animal appetite or if he controls and keeps it in check. Has he by the scientific progress gained a capacity to rise above those blind passions or is he still a mere plaything in the hands of satan and his unruly passions? If he is still no better than a mere slave to them then he is far from having achieved any real progress or advancement or

'Falâh' for which the Qur'ân was revealed. This is, indeed, a very disturbing picture of today's world. But still there is one redeeming factor, that is the Qur'ân.

It is obvious that the great merit of something is that it should fulfill the purpose for which it is fashioned and the true purpose of a Heavenly Book, and then of the Qur'ân, is to rescue humanity from a sinful life and bestow a pure life. This is the true salvation and the true 'FALÂH', as the Holy Qur'ân says:

قَدْ أَفْلَحَ مَنْ زَكّٰهَا ۝

وَقَدْ خَابَ مَنْ دَسّٰهَا ۝

'One who purifies his soul certainly succeeds.
And he, indeed, is ruined who corrupts it' (91:9,10).

Another purpose of the Qur'ân is to bestow such perfect understanding as if one can see God Who is the fountainhead of all good and joy. Love and understanding are the roots of salvation and '*Falâh*', they are the paradise on entering which all fatigue, bitterness, pain and torment is removed. Through them a person is drawn to God Who is hidden behind the beyond and He manifests Himself and informs of His existence by the affirmation 'I am present'.

Of what use is a Book which cannot clean and purify a person, bestow such pure and perfect understanding as should make one hate sins, cut asunder the sinful ego, or draw one towards God? What should a seeker after truth do with a Book which does not fill these needs? It is not the Holy Qur'ân's chief purpose to teach people subjects of secular study and to instruct them in worldly instructions, these things are only the by-products of its teachings and no present or previous Book except the Holy Qur'ân possesses this quality. Just as it is not possible that we should be able to see without eyes, in the same way it is not possible that we should be able to behold the countenance of God without the Qur'ân. It contains a large quantity of the water of life. The God, presently, is not the one who is believed in on the basis of tales and stories and who resembles a dead being; it is useless to believe in such a God. If a person follows the Holy Qur'ân truly, he would see God in this very life. It guides one towards God through reason, experience and heavenly signs in a very easy manner. A believer who acts upon its teachings does not merely contemplate like a philosopher that there ought to be a Creator of the wonderful universe but he acquires a personal insight. Diverse types of blessings descend upon him and he experiences the commandments and doctrines as realities and certainties through visions and revelation.

Every century starts a new world, therefore, the God of the Holy Qur'ân manifests new signs for each new world. At the beginning of every century God raises a Reformer as the Holy Prophet ﷺ said, 'Surely God will raise for the good of this community (of Muslims), at the commencement of every century one who will reform their religion' (AD. 36:1) i.e. a *Mujaddid*, to shed new light on the great religious truths of Islam under new circumstances. God Almighty will speak to him face to face, as is said in the Holy Qur'ân, 'Behold! As for those who say, "Our Nourisher to Perfection is God" and then remain steadfast and follow the straight path, the angels will descend upon them saying, "Have no fear nor grieve, rather, rejoice at the glad tidings of receiving the gardens of Paradise which you had been promised. We are your Patrons in the present life and in the Hereafter" (41:30,31). Again the Holy Qur'ân says, 'Allâh has promised those of you who believe and do deeds of righteousness that surely God will make them successors (vouchsafed with both spiritual and temporal leadership) on earth as He made successors from among their predecessors, and that He will surely establish for them their Faith which he has approved for them' (24:55).

And from the time of the revelation of the Qur'ân there have appeared, in every century, such men of God. On the score of such heavenly and fresh signs, the Holy Qur'ân has not been put to shame in any age. The life and blessings which were initially cultivated by Islam will remain present till the end of the world for the promotion and welfare of humankind. Is there any other Book which can produce such testimony? A living Book has always the hand of the living God at its back and such a Book is the Holy Qur'ân.

Yes the Holy Qur'ân was revealed hundreds of years ago. Today we live in a modern scientific world, but the old serpent is still alive and the ancient problems of humankind are still present, requiring a solution. Although scientific advances and inventions have provided many conveniences and lightened the human being's work, yet they have not solved the ethical and spiritual problems of the human being. When has the need ever been so vital to learn how to live unitedly, to know how to forge strong and loving family ties, to hear a powerful word of peace in a world of military attacks and nuclear nightmares, to have wholesome food, drinks and proper dress and to know where one can obtain deliverance from sin and hear the sweet voice of God? The Qur'ân tells us how such vital needs can be satisfied. The Holy Qur'ân also focuses on the very purpose of life and the ways and means to acquire it. It also provides satisfying answers to such questions as, 'Where did life come from? Why am I here? What is the purpose of my life? What does the future hold? What are the physical, moral and spiritual conditions of the human being?' The Qur'ân also provides the answers to questions about life after death and the sources of knowledge. Are such questions obsolete and their answers of no use or can we find their satisfactory answers in any other place?

Though the Holy Qur'ân gives the solution of all such problems of humanity, yet it is wonderfully laconic and concise. It has condensed the whole of its teaching in only about 1500 roots of Arabic and, thus, is a miracle in its diction and style. It is about two thirds the length of the New Testament.

Professor Hooking of Harvard University writes in his book 'The Spirit of World Policies' 'Can Islam produce fresh thinking, independent laws and relevant statutes to fit the new needs raised by modern society? Yes, and more, Islam offers humanity greater possibilities for advance than others can. In reality Islamic Shariah contains all the ingredients needed.'

In 1951 the Paris College of Law devoted a week to the study of the Islamic Canon Law. They called in experts from countries around the world. The head of the Parisian Languages Society chaired the conference and summed up at the end thus, 'Whatever our earlier ideas, about Islamic law and its rigidity or incompetence in documenting transactions we have been compelled to revise them. Let me sum up the new insight, new I think to most of us, the conference has given us in this week devoted particularly to the Islamic Canon Law. We saw in it a depth of rock-bottom principle and of particularized care which embraces humankind in its universality and is, thus, able to give an answer to all the emergencies and events of this age. In our final communique we say, "Islam's Canon Law should be made one of the formalized elements of all new international legislation to meet present day conditions, since it possesses a legal treasure of stable universal values and pronouncements to cope with the exigencies imposed by the new forums of living arising in the modern environment".'

About the vitality of Islam Bernard Shaw (1856-1950 A.D.) observes as follows: 'I have always held the religion of Muhammad in the highest estimation because of its wonderful vitality. It is the only religion which appears to me to possess that assimilation capability to the changing phase of existence which can make itself appeal to every age. I have studied him - the wonderful man - in my opinion far from being Anti-Christ, he must be called a saviour of humanity. I believe that if a man like him were to assume dictatorship of the modern world, he would succeed in solving the problems in a way that would bring it the much needed peace and happiness. I have prophesied about the faith of Muhammad that it would be acceptable to the Europe of tomorrow as it is beginning to be accepted by Europe of today'. Bernard Shaw was awarded the Noble Prize for Literature.

ONE RELIGION

شَرَعَ لَكُم مِّنَ الدِّينِ مَا وَصَّى بِهِ نُوحًا وَّ الَّذِيٓ أَوْحَيْنَآ إِلَيْكَ وَ مَا وَصَّيْنَا
بِهِۦٓ إِبْرٰهِيمَ وَ مُوسٰى وَ عِيسٰىٓ أَنْ أَقِيمُوا الدِّينَ وَ لَا تَتَفَرَّقُوا فِيهِ

He has ordained for you the same course of faith as He enjoined on Noah (to adopt), and which We have revealed to you, and it is that (same faith) which We enjoined on Abraham, Moses, Jesus, so keep the faith and do not differ in it. (He ordains you) to establish obedience (to Allâh) and not to be divided (into sects) therein.
(42:13)

The revelation of the Holy Qur'ân was not an accident, an un-connected episode in the history of people. According to the Qur'ân, Judaism, Christianity,

Hindûism, Buddhism, etc., are but different aspects of one and the same religion, which, in its original purity, was the religion of Islam (- submission to the will of God and to make peace with God and people). Noah, Abraham, Moses, Jesus, Krishna, Rama, Buddha or Confucius, all were the Prophets of God (may Allâh be pleased with them all) and were sent for the guidance of their respective people. The Qur'ân repeatedly claims to be in conformation with the truth of all faiths as the Qur'ân defines the true believers:

وَالَّذِينَ يُؤْمِنُونَ بِمَآ أُنْزِلَ إِلَيْكَ وَمَآ أُنْزِلَ مِنْ قَبْلِكَ

And who (also) believe in that (Message) which has been revealed to you
and in that which had been revealed before you (2:4).

The Qur'ân, therefore, not only recognizes the truth of all the previous Divine Books and Prophets, but also makes it obligatory for Muslims to believe in the Divine origin of their teachings and thus it takes an effective step to promote peace and harmony with the followers of other religions. The Qur'ân does not, however, mention all the Prophets by their names as it says:

وَلَقَدْ أَرْسَلْنَا رُسُلًا مِّنْ قَبْلِكَ مِنْهُم مَّنْ قَصَصْنَا
عَلَيْكَ وَمِنْهُم مَّن لَّمْ نَقْصُصْ عَلَيْكَ

And indeed We have already sent (Our) Messengers before you. There are
some of them whom We have mentioned to you and of them there are many whom We have not mentioned to you (40:78).

Thus, the Qur'ân requires not only a belief in Divine revelation to the Prophet of Islam, but belief in Divine revelation to all the Prophets sent to all nations of the world in all times. This is one of the matters relating to faith (*Îmân*) and a fundamental principle of Islam. This broad doctrine is taught repeatedly in the Qur'ân (3:184; 13:4).

Some opponents of the Qur'ân say that Muhammad wrote the Qur'ân or had it written as an imitation of the Bible or other Scriptures. This attitude is as thoughtless as saying that Jesus (peace be upon him) himself duped his contemporaries by drawing inspiration from the Hebrew Scriptures or of Buddha during his preaching. The whole of Matthew's Gospel is based on the continuation of the Old Testament and Talmud. These fault finders are blind to the fact that the source of all Divine Scriptures is the same God.

Islam is not a new faith founded by the Prophet Muhammad ﷺ but it is the same religion which was taught by all the Prophets, from Adam to Jesus (may Allâh be pleased with all of them) (cf. 22:78), as we are commanded in the Holy Qur'ân:

قُلْ آمَنَّا بِاللَّهِ وَمَا أُنزِلَ عَلَيْنَا وَمَا أُنزِلَ عَلَىٰ إِبْرَاهِيمَ وَإِسْمَاعِيلَ
وَإِسْحَاقَ وَيَعْقُوبَ وَالْأَسْبَاطِ وَمَا أُوتِيَ مُوسَىٰ وَعِيسَىٰ وَالنَّبِيُّونَ
مِن رَّبِّهِمْ لَا نُفَرِّقُ بَيْنَ أَحَدٍ مِّنْهُمْ وَنَحْنُ لَهُ مُسْلِمُونَ ۝

Say, 'We believe in Allâh and in that which has been revealed to us and in that which was revealed to Abraham, and Ismâîl and Isaac and Jacob and his children and in that which was given to Moses and Jesus and to all other Prophets from their Lord. We make no distinction between anyone of them (in believing them) and to Him alone do we submit' (3:84).

THE QU'RÂN - A NECESSITY

ظَهَرَ الْفَسَادُ فِي الْبَرِّ وَالْبَحْرِ بِمَا كَسَبَتْ أَيْدِي النَّاسِ لِيُذِيقَهُم
بَعْضَ الَّذِي عَمِلُوا لَعَلَّهُمْ يَرْجِعُونَ ۝

Disorder and corruption has prevailed on land and sea owing to the evil (deeds) which people have wrought; the result will be that He will make them taste (in this world) the fruit of some of their misdeeds, so that they may return (to the right path, giving up their evil ways) (30:41).

and, as the Book says, it is the the practice of the Creator that:

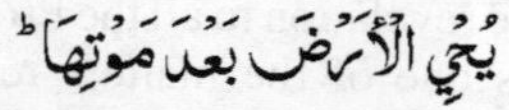

He gives life to earth after its death (30:19).

This is the major reason given by God to reveal His Book and His word through the channel of His Prophet. The Arabs questioned the necessity of a new Book in the presence of so many revealed religious and Divine Scriptures. The Qur'ân itself gives another reasons which necessitated its revelation.

1. The Qur'ân says:

وَهَٰذَا كِتَٰبٌ أَنزَلْنَٰهُ مُبَارَكٌ فَاتَّبِعُوهُ وَاتَّقُوا لَعَلَّكُمْ تُرْحَمُونَ ○ أَن
تَقُولُوٓا إِنَّمَآ أُنزِلَ الْكِتَٰبُ عَلَىٰ طَآئِفَتَيْنِ مِن قَبْلِنَا وَإِن كُنَّا عَن
دِرَاسَتِهِمْ لَغَٰفِلِينَ ○ أَوْ تَقُولُوا لَوْ أَنَّآ أُنزِلَ عَلَيْنَا الْكِتَٰبُ لَكُنَّآ أَهْدَىٰ
مِنْهُمْ فَقَدْ جَآءَكُم بَيِّنَةٌ مِّن رَّبِّكُمْ وَهُدًى وَرَحْمَةٌ

This is a (glorious) Book which We have revealed full of blessings, so follow it and guard against evil that you may be shown mercy. (We have revealed this blessed Book) lest you should say, 'The Book has only been revealed to two communities (- the Jews and the Christians) before us, and (as for us) we remained unaware of what those (Books) read.' Or lest you should say, 'Had the Book been revealed to us we would surely have been better guided than they.' Now there has certainly come to you from your Lord (in the form of the Qur'ân) a clear evidence, an excellent guidance and a great mercy (6:155-157)

2. All the previous Prophets brought certain laws of life from God, but most of these teachings had been lost owing to the vicissitudes of time. The Holy Qur'ân came and found all their Scriptures either extinct or corrupted by human interpolation. It renewed the old teachings and restored them to their original forms.

وَمَآ أَنزَلْنَا عَلَيْكَ الْكِتَٰبَ إِلَّا لِتُبَيِّنَ لَهُمُ الَّذِي اخْتَلَفُوا
فِيهِ وَهُدًى وَرَحْمَةً لِّقَوْمٍ يُؤْمِنُونَ ○

We have sent to you this perfect Book (for the purpose) that you may explain to the people things over which they differ (among themselves), and (that it may serve as) a guidance and a mercy for a people who would believe (in it) (16:64).

3. The revelation of the Holy Qur'ân is in fulfillment of the prophecies of previous Scriptures (for detailed discussion on this subject see *Fasl al-Khitâb* by Nooruddîn and *Mîthâq al-Nabiyyîn* by Abdul Haq Widyârthy). We read:

وَلَمَّا جَآءَهُمْ رَسُولٌ مِّنْ عِندِ اللَّهِ مُصَدِّقٌ لِّمَا مَعَهُمْ نَبَذَ فَرِيقٌ
مِّنَ الَّذِينَ أُوتُوا الْكِتَٰبَ كِتَٰبَ اللَّهِ وَرَآءَ ظُهُورِهِمْ كَأَنَّهُمْ لَا يَعْلَمُونَ ○

And (now) when a great Messenger (Muhammad) has come to them from Allâh confirming that (Scripture) which is with them, a party *of those who were given the Scripture cast away the Book of Allâh behind their backs, as if they know it not (2:101).*

4. The prophetic eyes of the previous Messengers foresaw that their teachings were for their particular nations and periods and that they would later suffer in purity, and that coming generations would naturally need some new and complete revelation from on High. So all of them spoke of the coming Messenger and no one among them declared that his Message was the last, complete or universal, and that it would neither disappear nor suffer from human tampering. Only the Qur'ân makes this claim. The Holy Qur'ân came with an universal mission. It repeatedly speaks of the Holy Prophet of Islam, as having been sent, as a Messenger to all humanity in the earliest as well as the latter revelations (34:28; 25:1; 21:107; 2:185). The all comprehensiveness of the Lordship of God in the very first words of the Qur'ân is in consonance with the cosmopolitan nature of the Book. The Holy Qur'ân says that God is the Nourisher to perfection of the whole world. He would not have given any special status to any person or group. The message of the Holy Qur'ân is for all human beings who stand at par under the obligation to fulfill the Divine will, and are judged on an universal scale of justice which is absolute for all people.

The universality of the Qur'ânic mission arises also from its appeal to all humankind, irrespective of descent, race, colour or cultural environment. It appeals exclusively to our reason and hence does not postulate any dogma that could be accepted on the basis of blind faith. It is the exponent of that Divine system that is impressed on the human being's nature and is the religion of every human child that is born. We read:

فَأَقِمْ وَجْهَكَ لِلدِّيْنِ حَنِيْفًا ؕ فِطْرَتَ اللّٰهِ الَّتِيْ فَطَرَ النَّاسَ عَلَيْهَا ؕ لَا
تَبْدِيْلَ لِخَلْقِ اللّٰهِ ؕ ذٰلِكَ الدِّيْنُ الْقَيِّمُ ۙ

'So pay your wholehearted attention to (the cause of) faith as one devoted (to pure faith), turning away from all that is false. (And follow) the Faith of Allâh to suit the requirements of which He has made the nature of humankind. There can be no change in the nature (of creation) which Allâh has made. That is the right and most perfect Faith' (30:30).

Equality, fraternity and liberty are fundamental to the teaching of the Qur'ân. It is only through God, Creator, Sustainer, Nourisher to perfection of all and His Word, the Qur'ân, that we shall find the road to the unification of humanity, to the brotherhood of man which knows no boundaries of colour, caste, country, language and rank. Far from being threatened by any intellectual challenge from modern civilization, the Holy Qur'ân itself might be said to constitute a serious challenge to the declining standards and values and the increasing confusion of the world.

Another factor from which the universality of the Qur'ânic mission arises is that the Holy Qur'ân is very easy to understand and to follow. God says in this Book:

وَلَقَدْ يَسَّرْنَا الْقُرْأٰنَ لِلذِّكْرِ

And indeed We made the Qur'ân easy for admonition and to understand, follow and remember (54:40).

This Book is in a language that is simple and clear. It uses only about 1500 roots of Arabic. Its language, unlike Latin, old Greek or Sanskrit, is spoken and understood by millions of people.

5. Another important object of the Holy Qur'ân is epitomized in the following verse,

لَقَدْ مَنَّ اللّٰهُ عَلَى الْمُؤْمِنِيْنَ إِذْ بَعَثَ فِيْهِمْ رَسُوْلًا مِّنْ أَنْفُسِهِمْ يَتْلُوْا عَلَيْهِمْ أٰيٰتِهٖ وَيُزَكِّيْهِمْ وَيُعَلِّمُهُمُ الْكِتٰبَ وَالْحِكْمَةَ ۚ وَإِنْ كَانُوْا مِنْ قَبْلُ لَفِيْ ضَلٰلٍ مُّبِيْنٍ ○

Verily, Allâh has bestowed a favour on the believers when He has raised amongst them a great Messenger from amongst themselves who recites to them His Messages, and purifies them and teaches them the Book and the wisdom; although before this, they were steeped in flagrant error (3:164).

This verse mentions four basic objects behind the revelation of the Holy Qur'ân,

a) To convey the signs and Messages of God.

b) To give the world a Scripture containing perfect and everlasting Law.

c) To explain the wisdom underlying these laws.

d) To lay down principles and rules of conduct which would bring about complete spiritual transformation in the lives of people, and would make its true followers a great and powerful nation, fit to lead the whole world.

These were the four objects for which Abraham prayed: 'Our Lord! Do raise among them a great Messenger from among themselves, who may recite to them Your Messages and teach them the Book and Wisdom, and may purify them. You, indeed, You are the All-Mighty, the All-Wise.' (2:129), and there is no other Book in the whole world which can fulfill these four objects.

THE PRACTICAL SYSTEM

لَيْسَ الْبِرَّ أَنْ تُوَلُّوا وُجُوهَكُمْ قِبَلَ الْمَشْرِقِ وَ الْمَغْرِبِ وَ لٰكِنَّ الْبِرَّ مَنْ
أٰمَنَ بِاللّٰهِ وَ الْيَوْمِ الْأٰخِرِ وَ الْمَلٰئِكَةِ وَ الْكِتٰبِ وَ النَّبِيّٖنَ وَ أٰتَى الْمَالَ عَلٰى
حُبِّهٖ ذَوِي الْقُرْبٰى وَ الْيَتٰمٰى وَ الْمَسٰكِيْنَ وَ ابْنَ السَّبِيْلِ وَ السَّآئِلِيْنَ
وَ فِي الرِّقَابِ وَ أَقَامَ الصَّلٰوةَ وَ أٰتَى الزَّكٰوةَ وَ الْمُوفُوْنَ بِعَهْدِهِمْ إِذَا
عٰهَدُوْا وَ الصّٰبِرِيْنَ فِي الْبَأْسَآءِ وَ الضَّرَّآءِ وَ حِيْنَ الْبَأْسِ أُولٰٓئِكَ
الَّذِيْنَ صَدَقُوْا وَ أُولٰٓئِكَ هُمُ الْمُتَّقُوْنَ ○

It is not the sole virtue that you turn your faces to the east or the west but true virtue is theirs, who believe in Allâh, the Last Day, the angels, the Book, and in the Prophets, and who give away their wealth (and substance) out of love for Him, to the near of kin, the orphans, the needy, the wayfarer and to those who ask (in charity) and in ransoming the slaves; and who observe the Prayer, who go on presenting the Zakât (- the purifying alms) and those who always fulfill their pledges and agreements when they have made one, and those who are patiently persevering in adversity and distress and (steadfast) in times of war. It is these who have proved truthful (in their promises and in their faith) and it is these who are strictly guarded against evil (2:177).

The Holy Qur'ân is not a book for dreamers and visionaries who live in Utopia, entirely divorced from the hard facts and realities of life. It is a practical system which guides us about what things to eat, how to clothe, how to wash, pray and fast. It also guides us in matters of divorce, marriage, sexuality, menstruation and hygiene. It prescribes methods of government, rules of inheritance and economics and tells us how, where, and how much to spend. There is no aspect of human life for which it has not laid down practical guidelines (for subject references see Index). It has been practised for centuries with great success and to the great astonishment of history. The Qur'ân informs us that true religions are neither theoretical nor formal, rather they are practical.

MIRROR OF THE LAWS OF NATURE

فَأَقِمْ وَجْهَكَ لِلدِّينِ حَنِيفًا ۚ فِطْرَتَ اللَّهِ الَّتِي فَطَرَ النَّاسَ عَلَيْهَا ۚ لَا تَبْدِيلَ لِخَلْقِ اللَّهِ ۚ ذَٰلِكَ الدِّينُ الْقَيِّمُ

So pay your wholehearted attention to (the cause of) faith as one devoted (to pure faith), turning away from all that is false. (And follow) the Faith of Allâh to suit the requirements of which He has made the nature of humankind. There can be no change in the nature (of creation) which Allâh has made. That is the right and most perfect Faith (30:30).

The Holy Qur'ân is the mirror of the laws of nature and their true reflection. According to the Qur'ân, Islam is a natural religion and every human being possesses it by birth, which it calls *Dîn al-Fitrah* (30:30), 'natural religion or original religion'. Qur'ânic teachings are thus easy and well suited to human requirements, needs and aspirations and are meant for the development of the innate faculties of the human being to give him a sane steadfastness against the inevitable vicissitudes of life. The faith it teaches is the voice of human nature at the deepest and most profound level of its psychological make up. To discover Islam it is necessary to delve deeply into one's nature, so it is said:

أَوَلَمْ يَتَفَكَّرُوا فِي أَنفُسِهِم

Do they never think over in their own minds (30:8)

So it was said by the Holy Prophet ﷺ: 'To understand one's Lord one must understand one's own self.' The Holy Qur'ân and the great phenomena of nature are twin manifestations of the Divine act. For the Holy Qur'ân the natural world in its totality is a vast fabric into which the signs of God are woven. It is significant that the Arabic word Ayât meaning signs is the same word that is used for the verses of the Qur'ân.

The Qur'ân does not teach us the inheritance of sin. How can it be that by the offense of one person, the whole humanity would become condemned? Each one has to bear his own burden (6:164; 17:15; 35:18; 39:2).

وَمَن يَكْسِبْ إِثْمًا فَإِنَّمَا يَكْسِبُهُ عَلَىٰ نَفْسِهِ ۚ

And whoever commits a sin deliberately, commits it only against himself (4:111).

Sin is not in the human being's nature but only an individual's acquisition after birth. Just as it is acquired, it can be purged off. Peace be on Muhammad who raised the level of humanity to the highest zenith, saying that every human being is born with a clean slate and with perfect freedom of action. He also established the principle that every human being is his own redeemer and author of his own actions and as such solely responsible for his deeds; there is nothing predestined. This was the message of salvation and *Falâh* which gave the human being a new confidence as master of his own destiny. He could apply himself with renewed vigour, confidence and determination to shape his own life in this world and in the Hereafter.

The doctrine of forgiveness of sins by God is one of the most bounteous gifts of the Prophet of Islam to humankind. Sins are temporary deviations from the right path brought about by ignorance, mistake or forgetfulness, but the human being's deeper desire - his Nafs Lawwâma (- self accusing spirit) regrets his mistake and seeks pardon from God with a contrite heart. To be broken in spirit by a sense of guilt and to seek forgiveness from God shows the innate goodness of human nature. It is wrong to say that God cannot forgive anyone's sin. God is not just a judge who cannot forgive, rather He is the Master. The Master's actions are not to be measured by mere justice.

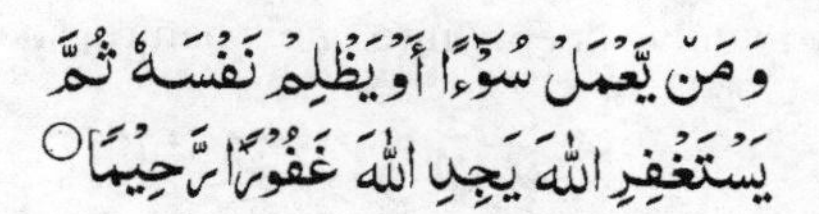

And whoever commits evil and does injustice to himself and then asks forgiveness of Allâh, will find Allâh Most Forgiving, Ever Merciful (4:110).

This Gospel of forgiveness of sins and of hope was a revolutionary message to despondent humanity condemned for ever by the guilt of original sin, reincarnation and past misdeeds. God's magnanimity to those who turn to Him for forgiveness is endless. How to acquire what our birthright gives us, avoid the degradation which our error in judgment or wrong discretion creates in us and get Falâh are clearly laid down in the pages of the Holy Qur'ân. In short, the Holy Qur'ân does not look upon people as a fallen hopeless creature, but as a perfect person capable of achieving the highest levels of righteousness.

ROLE OF REASON IN THE QUR'ÂN

يَٰأَيُّهَا النَّاسُ قَدْ جَآءَكُم بُرْهَٰنٌ مِّن رَّبِّكُمْ

O you people! a manifest Proof has indeed come to you from your Lord (4:174).

The Reason, or the Manifest Proof (*Burhân*) is one of the names which the Holy Qur'ân takes for itself. The Holy Qur'ân makes judgement on the basis of reasoning in every thing, whether it is religion, conviction or faith. Islam clearly asserts that imitation of others without reason or guidance is the prerogative of disbelievers. Nobody is a real Muslim unless he has reasoned out his religion. Thus, reason and reflection, rather than aggressiveness, are the keys to significant living.

Reason is a gift of God and it must be utilized to the full. We are not supposed to accept any thing at the expense of better judgement. Faith should not be, as the Holy Qur'ân says, a burden that we cannot intelligently bear (2:286). It is because of this fact that the Holy Book is neither dogmatic nor assertive. When it inculcates any principle or contradicts any doctrine it puts forth logical reasons to substantiate its assertions and sets forth its tenets in a way that appeal most readily to our intelligence. It repels with bright reasoning all evils that afflict people's doctrines, actions, words and works. In the course of its reasoning, physics, medicine, astronomy, mathematics, philosophy, logic, eloquence and the method of debate, all are brought into play in a most appropriate, easy and simple way. Compulsion is of no avail when logic and reason begin to rule the world. The Holy Book says the same when it lays down a golden principle in the matter of preaching its teachings. It says:

لَآ إِكْرَاهَ فِي الدِّينِ قَد تَّبَيَّنَ الرُّشْدُ مِنَ الْغَيِّ فَمَن يَكْفُرْ
بِالطَّٰغُوتِ وَيُؤْمِنۢ بِاللَّهِ فَقَدِ اسْتَمْسَكَ بِالْعُرْوَةِ الْوُثْقَىٰ لَا انفِصَامَ لَهَا

There is no compulsion of any sort in religion (as) the right way does stand obviously distinguished from the way of error. Now he that shall reject the transgressor and accepts Allâh (let such know that he) has laid hold of a support firm and strong which knows no breaking (2:256).

Thus, there is a categorical prohibition of coercion in any form that pertains to the contents of religious laws, to our attitude towards the object of our worship and everything that pertains to Faith. Forcible conversion is, under all circumstances, null and void and any attempt at forcing a person to accept Islam is a grievous sin. For this reason, the Qur'ân equates Faith with light and disbelief with darkness. The contrast is brought out to the best advantage in verses 24:35-46. These verses also cite reasons as to why force should not be used for this purpose. If the path has been clearly reasoned out and found to be the correct, there would be no point in resorting to compulsion for its acceptance. We often read verses like 27:92; 41:46 or the following:

وَقُلِ الْحَقُّ مِن رَّبِّكُمْ فَمَن شَآءَ فَلْيُؤْمِن وَمَن شَآءَ فَلْيَكْفُرْ

And say, 'It is the truth from your Lord, therefore let him who wishes (it) believe (in it) and let him who wishes (otherwise) disbelieve (in it).' (18:29)

The logic of the principle lies in the fact that there should be reasoning with every injunction. We belong to an intellectual order and cannot believe in any thing which does not come within the scope of our perception or experience, or is unable to stand the test of logic and science. If a book or a truth claims to come from God, let it prove its claim by itself and advocate its own case. Why should it rely on the advocacy, ingenuity and intelligence of others? This feature we find only in the Holy Qur'ân. Whatever this book asserts or teaches, it does not look upon its votaries to substantiate its tenets and principles. In the Holy Qur'ân one will find wisdom, logic, reasoning and constant reference to nature and history in explanation and illustration of the principles it teaches and of errors it rejects.

There are many things in nature which remain invisible. In the verse 2:3, the word Al-GHAIB does not mean imaginary and unreal things but real and verified ones, though unseen. So it is wrong to think that the Qur'ân forces some mysteries of faith upon its followers and compels them to believe blindly. AL-GHAIB signifies things which, though beyond the comprehension of our ordinary senses, can, nevertheless, be proved by reason, experience and true knowledge. The super-sensible need not necessarily be irrational. Nothing of the unseen in which the Holy Qur'ân calls upon us to believe such as God, the Angels, the Hereafter, the nature of time, are outside the scope of reason. It was because of belief in hidden realities that the followers of the Holy Qur'ân began to discover the hidden properties of things and became the forerunners in chemistry, medicine and astronomy. So AL-GHAIB denotes all those sectors or phases of reality which lie beyond the range of ordinary human perception. Nothing in the Holy Qur'ân insults intelligence, is revolting to reason or scientific sources or unable to meet the demands of rationality. It abolished dogma and made logic, mindfulness and reason the only test of religious truths. In the Holy Qur'ân Faith and Belief (*Îmân*) are spoken of as light and disbelief as darkness (2:257), and light is that which manifests hidden things. The believer in the Holy Qur'ân sets his goal much higher and tries not only to assume manifest truths but also works hard to bring out hidden truths and realities. Thus according to the Qur'ân Belief is the acceptance of a proposition as a basis for action and not just the conviction behind the truth of a guess. The Holy Prophet ﷺ said, 'Verily a human being has performed prayers, fasts and pilgrimages and given charities and done so many other good deeds, but he will be rewarded only in the proportion to the intention he employs.'

According to the Holy Qur'ân Faith (*Îmân*) does not signify a belief that cannot be translated into action and which is against reason. 'Islam stands almost alone,' says Quizot in his History of European Civilization, 'among the religions in discountenancing the reliance on tradition without argument.' God could not teach us things that did not correspond to reality and it was not possible for an affirmation contrary to the truth to be of Divine origin. In his book: Apology for Islam, L. V. Vaglieri has observed, 'On the whole we find in the Qur'ân a collection of wisdom which can be adopted by the most intelligent of men, the greatest of philosophers, and the most skillful of politicians.'

THE RELIGION OF PEACE

وَاللَّهُ يَدْعُوٓا إِلَىٰ دَارِ السَّلٰمِ ۖ وَيَهْدِي مَن يَشَآءُ
إِلَىٰ صِرٰطٍ مُّسْتَقِيمٍ ۝

Allâh invites (us all) to the abode of peace and He guides him who wishes to be guided to the exact right path leading to the goal (10:25).

The religion which the Qur'ân preaches is called Islâm (3:18), which means 'Peace', and the Book invites people to the abode of Peace (10:25). The Qur'ân does not just speak of peace but also provides us a code to achieve, establish and maintain it. A very basic announcement in the Opening Chapter (AL-FÂTIHAH) states that God is the Nourisher to perfection for all humankind and all worlds (RABB AL-'ÂLAMÎN), and that there is no claim of exclusiveness of any religious group or sect. His people benefit from His earth and from the rest of His universe, irrespective of their origin, colour or belief and His dealings with the human being in spiritual matters is also marked with the same impartiality (1:2-3). The Book mentions all the hurdles in the way of peace and tranquillity. It speaks of differences in faith, of race, in language, colour and regional patriotism (30:22) and provides guidance to remove these barriers in the path to peace. The unity of God and the unity of humankind are presented by the Qur'ân as fundamentally interconnected.

One of the basic principle that can bring about peace and unity among the nations and the religions of the world is tolerance, respect and honour towards each other's founders, saints and heroes. The Qur'ân tells us repeatedly that every nation had its Warner and these Warners are to be respected and honoured (2:4; 40:78; 42:13). India had its vedic Rishîs, Krishna, Ramachandra and Buddha, China saw its teacher in Confucious and Persia in the person of Zoroaster. As the Qur'ân says: 'There are some of them whom We have mentioned to you and of them there are some whom We have not mentioned to you' (40:78). Belief in the Divine teachings of all these Prophets is one of the fundamentals of Islamic faith (2:4). All other religions and many of their respective sects, while claiming their own Divine origin deny this privilege to other religions. The Qur'ân rejects this exclusiveness and narrowness of mind which has engendered the feeling of conceit, pride and content, and which has been disintegrating the whole fabric of human society. The Qur'ân says:

إِنَّ الَّذِينَ اٰمَنُوا وَالَّذِينَ هَادُوا وَالنَّصٰرٰى وَالصّٰبِـِٔينَ مَنْ اٰمَنَ بِاللّٰهِ
وَالْيَوْمِ الْاٰخِرِ وَعَمِلَ صٰلِحًا فَلَهُمْ أَجْرُهُمْ عِنْدَ رَبِّهِمْ وَلَا
خَوْفٌ عَلَيْهِمْ وَلَا هُمْ يَحْزَنُونَ ﴿٦٢﴾

Surely, those who (profess to) believe (in Islam), and those who follow the Jewish faith, the Christians and the Sabîans, whosoever (of these truly) believes in Allâh and the Last Day and acts righteously shall have their reward with their Lord, and shall have nothing to fear, nor shall they grieve. (2:62)

Another way of promoting peace and understanding between nations and religions of the world is the way of dialogue. The Holy Qur'ân says:

يٰٓأَهْلَ الْكِتٰبِ تَعَالَوْا إِلٰى كَلِمَةٍ سَوَآءٍ بَيْنَنَا وَبَيْنَكُمْ

O people of the Scripture! Let us agree to a proposition common to us both' (3:64).

In this verse the Qur'ân invites all the followers of Divine revelation to a dialogue based on common grounds, putting aside their mutual differences. Qur'ân, thus, does not proclaim that east is east and west is west and no understanding or union is possible between the two. The Qur'ân refutes such ideas when it says the Lord of the worlds is the same as the 'Lord of the east and of the west and of all that lies between the two' (26:28; 73:9), and again: '(He is) the Lord of the two easts and Lord of the two wests' (55:16). Therefore, the so called east and the so called west have the same God and those who claim to worship God should not act contrary to reason, wisdom and morality. As the rising and the setting of the sun on the globe of the earth, there is a rise and fall of nations. As on the globe of the earth setting point for a people is the rising point for another, the same thing happens in the histories of nations. There are innumerable risings and settings and, thus, innumerable easts and innumerable wests but nothing that is permanently east or permanently west.

JIHÂD -HOLY WAR- A MISCONCEPTION

وَجَاهِدُوا فِي اللَّهِ حَقَّ جِهَادِهِ ۚ هُوَ اجْتَبَاكُمْ وَمَا جَعَلَ
عَلَيْكُمْ فِي الدِّينِ مِنْ حَرَجٍ ۚ مِلَّةَ أَبِيكُمْ إِبْرَاهِيمَ ۚ
هُوَ سَمَّاكُمُ الْمُسْلِمِينَ مِنْ قَبْلُ وَفِي هَٰذَا

And strive your hardest to win the pleasure of Allâh, as hard a striving as is possible and as it behoves you. He has chosen you and has imposed no hardship upon you in the matter of your faith, (so follow) the creed of your father Abraham. He named you Muslims (both) before this and (again) in this (Qur'ân) (22:78).

A great misconception prevails, particularly among the Christians, propagated by their zealous missionaries, with regard to the duty of JIHÂD in Islam. Even the greatest research scholars of West have not taken pains to consult any dictionary on Arabic, or to refer to the Qur'ân to find out the meaning of the word. The word *Jihâd* according to the Arabic-English Lexicon of E. W. Lane and the great scholar of Islam Râghîb means: The use of or exerting of one's utmost powers, efforts, endeavours or ability in contending with an object of disapprobation, and this is of three kinds, namely; a visible enemy, the devil and against one's own self. All these meanings are used in the Qur'ân when a reference of JIHÂD is made.

The duty of JIHÂD is far from being synonymous with that of war, and the meaning of JIHÂD, 'the Holy war' as supposed by the western writers is unknown equally to Arabic and the fundamental teachings of the Holy Qur'ân. Even in the Traditions of the Prophet ﷺ (*Hadîth*), this word was never synonymous with 'the Holy war'. The Prophet of Islam called the greater Pilgrimage to Makkah (*Hajj*) as JIHÂD (Bukhârî 25:4). The permission to fight (22:40) under certain circumstances has no connection with the preaching of the religion by force and at no time did Islam permit the use of force for the purpose of preaching. Again the Qur'ân says: 'Strive hard with your possessions and your persons in the cause of Allâh' (9:41) and: 'Strive hard against them (the enemies of Islam, the nonbelievers) with the help of this (Qur'ân, which is full of arguments and reasoning) a mighty striving' (25:52). God expects from us a JIHÂD against our souls, against our NAFS AMMÂRAH, our commanding self which is continuously inciting us towards evil. God has not given us any permission to use any kind of force to prohibit people from going to places of worship - Churches, Synagogues and Temples - 'where the names of God are being glorified' (2:114).

WAR IN ISLAM

أُذِنَ لِلَّذِينَ يُقَٰتَلُونَ بِأَنَّهُمْ ظُلِمُوا ۚ وَإِنَّ اللَّهَ عَلَىٰ نَصْرِهِمْ
لَقَدِيرٌ ۝ الَّذِينَ أُخْرِجُوا مِن دِيَٰرِهِم بِغَيْرِ حَقٍّ إِلَّا أَن
يَقُولُوا رَبُّنَا اللَّهُ ۗ وَلَوْلَا دَفْعُ اللَّهِ النَّاسَ بَعْضَهُم بِبَعْضٍ
لَّهُدِّمَتْ صَوَٰمِعُ وَبِيَعٌ وَصَلَوَٰتٌ وَمَسَٰجِدُ يُذْكَرُ فِيهَا
اسْمُ اللَّهِ كَثِيرًا ۗ

Permission (to fight in self defence) is (now) given to those (Muslims) against whom war is waged (for no reason), because they have been done injustice to, and Allâh has indeed might and power to help them. Those who have been driven out of their homes without any just cause. Their only fault was that they said, 'Our Lord is Allâh'. If Allâh had not repelled some people by means of others, cloisters and churches and synagogues and mosques wherein the name of Allâh is mentioned very frequently, would have been razed to ground in large numbers (22:39-40).

To ensure peace we sometimes have to go to war, and the martial spirit that has been implanted by our Creator for our safety comes into play. The Qur'ân says: 'Fight in the cause of Allâh those who fight and persecute you, but commit no aggression. Surely, Allâh does not love the aggressors' (2:190). The subject is clarified further in the next verse: 'Turn them out whence they have turned you out. Killing is bad but lawlessness is even worse than carnage'. Thus, under certain circumstances war becomes indispensable. Even Jesus saw the necessity of war when he said: 'Do not think that I have come to bring peace to the world. No, I did not come to bring peace, but a sword.' (Mathew, 10:34). Islam permits fighting for two reasons:

1. To defend one's life: Senseless fighting against an enemy is to be avoided under all circumstances, for otherwise there is too much bloodshed. Other peaceful means such as migration to another country, where no persecution is expected, is to be preferred. The Prophet of Islam practiced this rule when he advised some of his followers to migrate to Abbyssinia and later he himself migrated from Makkah to Madînah.

2. To defend the land against incursions by others and to avoid persecution and lawlessness: 'Killing is bad, but lawlessness is even worse than carnage' (2:217). When the temples and churches and synagogues and mosques are razed to the ground as a result of religious persecution, defensive fighting becomes necessary. This fighting is not only to protect Muslims but also for defending the followers of other religions. It is significant to note in the verse above (22:40) that the permission to protect the mosques ranks after the places of worship of other religions. The verse also affirms the right of religious practice to followers of other religions. We fail to find any similar, clear and healthy principles of war and tolerance in other religious books. The wars of Israelites were aimed at the extinction of their enemies and sowed vengeance and rancour. Jesus left his followers in a maze regarding military matters. Christianity was all meekness and modesty as long as it was the religion of slaves and the suppressed. As soon as it secured political power, streams of blood began to flow in the name of the church. The Crusades, re-conquest of Spain, colonization and Christianizing of America and the two world wars are a few examples with no parallel in Islamic history.

The Qur'ân not only gives the conditions under which war is permitted, it also clearly defines how long and to what extent the war should be waged. Destruction of property, means of livelihood, killing of the elderly, women and children is not permitted. As soon as the enemy shows an inclination towards peace, the hostilities are to be stopped, after which all kind of hatred and feelings of vengeance must vanish (8:61).

It is not true that the battles fought by the Prophet of Islam were to spread Islam by force. Such accusations are based on ignorance and are biased. The Prophet of Islam had to fight three battles after Badr. In all these battles the very location of the battlefields and the strength of the parties were a decisive factor showing that the followers of the Prophet had chosen to fight in sheer self defence. For thirteen long years the Prophet of Islam and his followers were the victims of persecution in Makkah, so he decided to leave Makkah and migrate to Madînah. The first battle was fought at Badr which is about one hundred and twenty miles from Makkah and only sixty miles from Madînah between a force of three hundred and thirteen Muslims and a thousand Makkans. Uhud which is a suburb of Madînah, the city of refuge of the Prophet, was the scene of the second battle. The relative strength this time was about one thousand Muslims against three thousand Makkans and their allies. The third battle was an attack on the town of Madînah itself by the enemies of Islam with an army of ten thousand. These were exactly the occasions when Jesus too would have called to 'sell the clothes to purchase the sword.'

STATUS OF WOMEN ACCORDING TO THE QUR'ÂN

وَلَهُنَّ مِثْلُ الَّذِي عَلَيْهِنَّ بِالْمَعْرُوفِ

And women have their rights similar to their obligations in an equitable and just manner (2:228).

Men and women proceed from the same origin, same in nature and of the same stock (4:1). This is a clear announcement and is repeated in the verse 16:72, an announcement very different from what we read in Bible: 'Neither was the man created for the women, but the woman for the man'.

In order to raise the position of women, which had reached its lowest ebb at the time of its revelation, The Holy Qur'ân has laid down several laws pertaining to women. Chapter 4 'The Women' (AL-NISÂ') is mostly devoted to this subject. This chapter begins with the verse: 'O you people! take as a shield your Lord (the Nourisher to Perfection), Who created you from a single being. And from the same stock (from which He created the man) He created his spouse, and through them both He caused to spread a large number of men and women. O people! regard Allâh in reverence, in Whose name you appeal to one another, and (be regardful to) the ties of relationship (particularly from the female side - 4:1)'. This injunction is very comprehensive but very broad in its significance and in its application.

The Nourisher to Perfection has not preferred men to women, but has created them from the same stock and provided them both with the same capacities and capabilities, so the women are not be stigmatized for intellectual deficiency by nature and want of common sense. In matters of social status, professions, marriages and inheritance, the Holy Qur'ân gives women rights similar to those of men (2:228).

We read in the beginning pages of the Bible, on which the whole structure of Judaism and Christianity is based, the story of the Fall of man through a woman. The text in the Qur'ân relating to this account reads: "And We said, 'O Adam! dwell you and your wife in this garden and eat freely and plentifully from it as you will. But you shall not go near this tree (- evil) lest you should be of the unjust'". After some time the satan caused them both to slip from this (order of not going near evil) and, thus, brought them out of (the happy state) which they were in' (2:35-36). No sole blame falls on the woman, and the 'Adam' of the Holy Qur'ân, in order to save himself from the banishment at the expense of his wife does not say, 'The woman whom thou gavest to be with me, she gave me of the tree and I did eat'. The 'Adam' in the

Holy Qur'ân is penitent, noble and respectful towards his wife. Both of them confess their guilt when they say: "Our Lord! We have done injustice to our soul and if you do not protect us against the consequences of our faults and do not have mercy on us, we shall surely be of the losers" (7:23). What a truism which we experience in our daily lives. Every husband is an 'Adam' and every wife an 'Eve', living in the garden of their bliss, as long as they live in harmony and concord and shun evil. But no sooner do they taste the tree of evil and discord, than it causes their banishment from this happy state. This verse brings a man on the same footing as a woman.

It is not the Qur'ân that teaches us that as long as a maiden lives in the house of her father she has to be ruled by one who has the authority on her body. She is not to be bartered, nor to be given away to make up family feuds, nor to bait the enemies and be a 'snare'. She is not unclean and therefore to be brought out of the city because 'the places are holy whereunto the ark of Lord hath come'. Some saints of the mediaeval Church called the woman: 'The organ of the Devil. The instrument which the Devil used to gain possession of souls. The foundation of the arm of Devil. A scorpion ever ready to sting. The poison of an asp. The malice of dragon'. No such words about women are found in the Qur'ân or were ever heard from the lips of the Prophet of Islam. She is never a source of disgrace or shame or an object to be 'buried alive' - as practiced in the pre-Islamic Arab society.

On the contrary, the Holy Qur'ân teaches that women and men are equally indispensable for each others happiness when it says:

هُنَّ لِبَاسٌ لَّكُمْ وَ أَنْتُمْ لِبَاسٌ لَّهُنَّ

They are (a sort of) garment for you and you are
(a sort of) garment for them (2:187).

What a beautiful, suitable and befitting metaphor! As garments hide, so do wives and husbands hide each other's nakedness, their weaknesses, both physical and moral, and those places that they are ashamed of displaying to others. As clothes give comfort, protection, and grace to the body, so do wives and husbands find comfort and grace in each other's company. This 'garment' is the grace, the beauty, the embellishment.

وَ مِنْ أٰيٰتِهٖٓ أَنْ خَلَقَ لَكُمْ مِّنْ أَنْفُسِكُمْ أَزْوٰجًا لِّتَسْكُنُوٓا إِلَيْهَا
وَ جَعَلَ بَيْنَكُمْ مَّوَدَّةً وَّرَحْمَةً

And (it is one) of His signs that He has created spouses for you from
your own species that you may find comfort in them. And He has
induced mutual love and tenderness between you (30:21).

Therefore, love and kindness should be the rule and not the enforcement of authority by man, nor subservience on the part of the woman. This is the ideal of wifehood in Islam, and we have not found elsewhere a higher ideal of mutual love, affection and equality.

In the matters of marriage, divorce and inheritance women are given the same rights as men (4:7; 4:19). No guardian can force any girl into marriage without first obtaining her consent (2:19). She does not lose her identity or name after marriage and has an equal right of divorcing her husband. Accusing women and punishing them for being sexually flagrant requires producing at least four eye witnesses - a law clearly for the protection of women against false charges and accusations (4:15; 24:4). On her marriage she retains the share of her inheritance from her parents, and after marriage she acquires additional rights in the property of her husband in the form of dowry (4:24). She can enter into any financial contract (without her husband) on her own (4:4). The financial responsibility for the family lies with the men (2:228). Divorce is allowed if all conciliatory efforts fail. After the divorce no man is permitted to ask that back what he has given to his wife as dowry or as a gift, nor has he any right on the inherited property of the woman (4:20).

To have more than one wife at a time is only permitted under hard conditions and is not an injunction. The verse containing this permission (4:3) begins and ends with a capital 'if' (4:3). The permission given here is to take a second or a third or fourth wife under certain circumstances, such as wars and the consequent decimation of the male population. This permission is, thus, to provide helpless women with legal and economic protection and to save a society from adultery, street-girls, war-babies and mistresses and to provide their children legal and social protection. The permission of the first wife is absolutely necessary with whom the second wife is going to share the finances of the husband. Not only this, the husband is required to do full justice, based on equality in all matters, and if he fears he cannot do this justice, this permission to marry is no more valid. Contrary to the Jewish and the Christian laws, Qur'ân clearly allows marriages with non-Muslim women. This, too, is for the protection of women, who are given equal rights irrespective of their religion (5:5).

Decency and modesty is enjoined by Qur'ân for men as well as for women, as the following verse says: 'Tell the believers to restrain their looks (in the presence of women not closely related to them and so lawful for marriage) and guard their chastity. That is purer and best for them. Surely, Allâh is Well-Aware of what they do. And tell the believing women to restrain their looks (also in the presence of men who are not near of kin and so lawful for marriage) and guard their chastity and not to disclose their (natural and makeup) beauty except such as cannot be helped (and is apparent) and draw their head coverings over their bosoms' (24:30-31). The head covering is universally found in almost all nations of the world, however, there is no face-veil in Islam. The injunction is only to cover the bosom with a covering, and there is no such evidence that women at the time of the Prophet of Islam practised Burqua (face-veil with complete coverage of the body with the exception of the eyes) as being practiced in some societies. The Burqua system is neither of Islamic nor of Arabian origin. It is Zoroastrian in origin, later adopted by the Persians and with some modifications by the Byzantinians and the Christian nuns. This system was never adopted by a great majority of Muslim women. Qur'ân does not enjoin women any face-veil or confinement to the four walls of the house, such a practice is an expression of weakness of the men of a society.

We know from the Muslim history that women fought side by side with men, they nursed the sick and cared for the wounded. 'Â'ishah, the daughter of Abû Bakr and the wife of the Prophet ﷺ personally conducted a military action in the Battle of Jamal and commanded troops of men. The granddaughter of the Prophet Muhammad ﷺ shielded her nephew in the battle of Karbalâ. All this was not possible with Burqua. The commands in the Sûrah above are for the uplift of morality and ethics of a society and not a tactic to deprive women from the right of development of their personalities in the fields of education, professional lives and family matters. The Qur'ân has laid down no obligation or precept which could render the position of women in any way derogatory, for nowhere in the Holy Qur'ân is there any authority to deprive women from rights which men claim for themselves, and the order to practice decency and modesty is for both, men and women alike.

Following are some sayings of the Prophet of Islam about women: 'See that the women are maintained in the rights granted to them. Whoever does good to daughters will be saved from hell. Whoever looks after two girls till they come of age (of marriage) will be in the next world along with me, like my two fingers, close to each other. Shall I not point out to you the best of virtues? It is to treat tenderly your daughter when she is returned to you, having been divorced. You should not hate your wife, if you are displeased with one bad quality in her, then be pleased with another that is good. Paradise lies under the feet of your mothers'.

The concept, of some Christians, about the rights of women in Islam is based upon colossal ignorance of the teachings of the Qur'ân and Islam. History is full of innumerable instances of high cultural refinement which Muslim women attained. They have left behind noble records of righteousness, bravery and knowledge. The ladies of the Prophet's ﷺ family were noted for their learning, their virtues and strength of character. The pious Râbiah of Basrah, the scholarly Zubaidah, the wife of the caliph Hârûn al-Rashîd, Bûrân, the wife of the caliph Mâmûn, Umm al-Fazl, Mâmûn's sister and Mâmûn's daughter Umm al-Habîb are a few names known to every reader of Muslim history.

We also know that in the 11 th. century A.D. (5th after Hijrah) Fakhr al-Nisâ' lectured publicly at the cathedral Mosque of Bagdad on literature, history and poetry. Zât al-Hammâ, the lion-heart, the heroine of many battles, fought side by side with the bravest of the knights.

In all fields the All-Mighty God practices the same impartiality. We read:

وَمَنْ عَمِلَ صَٰلِحًا مِّنْ ذَكَرٍ أَوْ أُنْثَىٰ وَهُوَ مُؤْمِنٌ
فَأُولَٰئِكَ يَدْخُلُونَ الْجَنَّةَ يُرْزَقُونَ فِيهَا بِغَيْرِ حِسَابٍ ۝

But the men and women who believe and (at the same time) do righteous deeds, it is they who will enter Paradise where they will be provided for without measure (40:40).

We also read: 'Whoever acts righteously, whether male or female, and is a believer, We will certainly enable him to lead a pure life and certainly We will bestow on such their reward according to the best of their deeds' (16:97). 'Verily, Allâh has in store protection (from faults) and a great reward for the men and women who submit themselves (to the will of God), and for the men and women who believe, and for the men and women who are obedient to Allâh, and for the men and women who are true to Allâh, and for the men and women who are patiently persevering (in their faith and righteousness), and for the men and women who are humble (before God), and for the men and women who give alms, and for the men and women who fast and for the men and women who guard their chastity, and for the men and women who remember and glorify Allâh (with all His praises) again and again' (33:35). Revelation, which is God's greatest gift, is not the exclusive privilege of men and is granted equally to women just as it was granted to Prophets of God and other saints. The Holy Qur'ân cites examples of women recipients of this gift. We read about the mother of Moses in the verse 28:7 'And We revealed to the mother of Moses (saying), "Give him (- Moses) suck. But when you have fear about him (- his life) cast him (placing him in a chest) into the river and entertain no fear, nor grief (about his welfare). Verily, We shall restore him to you and shall make him (one) of the Messengers".' In the mention of Mary and the wife of Pharaoh we read in verse 66:12-13 how high a woman can rise spiritually. Mary and the wife of Pharaoh are examples for believers to follow: And Allâh compares those who believe to the wife of Pharaoh. 'Behold! She said, "My Lord! Make for me an abode in the Garden (of Paradise) close to You and deliver me from Pharaoh and his work and deliver me from the wrongdoing people".' And Allâh (next compares the believers to) Mary, the daughter of Amrân, she who took care to guard her chastity, so we breathed into him (the believer who is exemplified here) Our inspiration while she declared her faith in the revelations of her Lord and His Scriptures and she became of the devoted ones to prayers and obedient to Him (66:11-12). After reading such verses we cannot imagine that the spiritual rights of women can go any further.

THE COMPREHENSIVE BOOK AND THE PERFECT CODE

مَا فَرَّطْنَا فِي الْكِتٰبِ مِنْ شَيْءٍ

And We have neglected nothing in (Our) this perfect Book (of law) (6:38).

This Book provides us with a complete and a comprehensive code for all walks of life and lays the foundation for an ideal society. John Obertvoll says in his book 'Islam, Continuity and Change in the Modern World' (1980 ed. page 8): 'The revelation did not just define a creed or a set of beliefs, it set forth the basic blueprint by which humanity should live. In this way, the Qur'ân is the foundation for an ideal society'. No one can put forward a Divine verity which is not already contained in it. It deals exhaustively with the physical, moral and spiritual life of the individual. Its function is to spiritualize the physical side of our life or, in other words, it entwines the Here with the Hereafter. It is, thus, that every act of a follower of the Holy Qur'ân is religious, no matter how worldly it may be from someone else's point of view. J. M. Rodwell M.A. of Caius College, Cambridge in the introductory notes of his English translation of the Holy Qur'ân dated 1876 writes: 'The Qur'ân embodies much of a noble and deep moral earnestness and sententious oracular wisdom and has proved that there are elements in it on which mighty nations and conquering empires can be built.' This Book sets out in detail all knowledge of faith and teaches those means and comprehensive principles which should lead the human being not just to partial progress but to full development. It is said in the Holy Qur'ân:

وَنَزَّلْنَا عَلَيْكَ الْكِتٰبَ تِبْيٰنًا لِّكُلِّ شَيْءٍ وَّهُدًى وَّرَحْمَةً
وَّبُشْرٰى لِلْمُسْلِمِينَ

And We have revealed to you this perfect Book explaining every (basic) thing and (which serves as) a guidance and a mercy, and (gives) good tidings to those who submit (to God) (16:89) and

كِتَٰبٌ أُحْكِمَتْ ءَايَٰتُهُۥ ثُمَّ فُصِّلَتْ مِن لَّدُنْ حَكِيمٍ خَبِيرٍ

(This is) a Book, whose verses have been characterized by wisdom and they have been explained in detail. It is from One All-Wise, All-Aware (11:1).

The Holy Qur'ân is not only a comprehensive book but also perfect in its teachings:

رَسُولٌ مِّنَ ٱللَّهِ يَتْلُوا۟ صُحُفًا مُّطَهَّرَةً ۝٢ فِيهَا كُتُبٌ قَيِّمَةٌ

A Messenger from Allâh reciting (to them) written leaves of the Book, free from all impurities, consistingof eternal laws and commandments. (98:2-3)

The Holy Qur'ân provides complete guidance in all walks of life. John Davenport has observed: 'The Qur'ân is the general code of the Muslims world, a social, civil, commercial, military, judicial, penal and yet religious code'. (Apology for Muhammad).

The Holy Qur'ân is the last of the Divine Books. Perfect Law could not have been revealed in the beginning of the world, because Laws are revealed to meet and remedy evils. Religious Laws *(Sharî'at)* are gradually revealed as sins and evils grow and spread. If perfect Law had been revealed in the very beginning, detailing all the evils and sins, it would have, in a way, suggested and taught people evils and sins of which they had been ignorant. Hence, a complete and perfect Law could have only been sent down after all or most of the root evils had made their appearance. The expression KHÂTAM AL-NABIYYÎN (33:40) which has been applied to the Holy Prophet ﷺ also demands that the Book that was revealed to him should be the most perfect of all Books and it is, indeed, so.

The Holy Qur'ân says:

ٱلْيَوْمَ أَكْمَلْتُ لَكُمْ دِينَكُمْ وَأَتْمَمْتُ عَلَيْكُمْ نِعْمَتِى وَرَضِيتُ لَكُمُ ٱلْإِسْلَٰمَ دِينًا

This day have I perfected for you your faith and completed My blessings upon you and have chosen Islam for your religion (5:3).

This verse testifies to the perfection of the Qur'ân and that of Islam. The words IKMÂL (perfecting) and ITMÂM (completing) are noun-infinitives, the first relating to quality and the second to quantity. The first word shows that doctrines and commandments affecting the physical, moral and spiritual development of the human being have been perfectly embodied, while the second signifies that nothing essential has been left out. The former word pertains to injunctions relating to the physical side of the human being or his external self, while the latter relates to his spiritual side or his inner self. This verse was revealed at the 'Arafât on the afternoon of Friday, the 9th of Dhul Hijjah, 10 A.H., eighty two days before the death of the Holy Prophet. No legal injunction whatsoever was revealed after this verse.

STUDY AND UNDERSTANDING OF THE QUR'ÂN

وَرَتِّلِ الْقُرْاٰنَ تَرْتِيلًا ۝

And keep on reciting the Qur'ân distinctly and thoughtfully well (73:4).

The Holy Qur'ân has 114 Chapters (*Sûrah*) and 6348 verses. The word 'Sûrah' means 'eminence' or 'high degree' and 'step of a structure'. These Chapters are of varying length, the largest comprising 286 verses and the smallest containing only three. For the convenience of readers theologians divided the Book into 30 equal parts (*Juzz*) and each Part into four equal Sub-Parts. The longer Chapters are divided into Sections (*Rukû'*). The largest number of Sections in a Chapter is 40. Another division of the Book traceable to the Holy Prophet ﷺ himself is into seven equal Portions (*Manâzil*).

Every discipline has its own demands and the study of the Holy Qur'ân requires some rules which are to be observed.

1. To begin the reading of the Holy Qur'ân with a short prayer (16:98). The prescribed words for the prayer are: A'ÛDHUBILLAHI MIN AL - SHAITÂN AL-RAJÎM: 'I seek refuge with God from satan the rejected, (that I may not miss any teachings of the Qur'ân through weakness or negligence or prejudice, or in consequence of my sins or under the influence of evil company; and I may not fail to understand rightly any teachings of the Book, and having understood I may not relapse into ignorance)'.

2. One should read it daily, preferably at the same time and in fixed portions which one thinks that he can easily grasp. It has to be recited not only with the lips, voice and eyes but also with the best light that our intellect, heart and conscious can supply.

وَإِذَا قُرِئَ الْقُرْاٰنُ فَاسْتَمِعُوا لَهُ وَأَنْصِتُوا لَعَلَّكُمْ تُرْحَمُونَ ۝

Hence, when the Qur'ân is recited, give ear to it and keep silent (to remain attentive) so that you may be shown mercy (7:204).

The whole Qur'ân is sometimes recited in one night by some zealous individuals or groups who repair to a mosque or some other place for this purpose. It is not a right course with no authority from the Holy Qur'ân, the SUNNAH OR HADÎTH.

3. The prerequisite for understanding the Qur'ân is to study it with an open and detached mind whether or not one believes it to be a revealed Book. One should, as far as possible, free one's mind of bias in favor of or against the Qur'ân, get rid of all preconceived opinions and then approach it with the sole desire to understand. People who study it with preconceived notions read only their own ideas in its lines, and cannot grasp that which the Qur'ân wants to convey. The Qur'ân expects understanding, reflection and an open mind from those who seek to benefit from it. It is most concise in expression and furnishes many striking illustrations of condensation and economy of words. It packs volumes of meaning within the briefest compass and, thus, constantly demands intelligent reflection (4:82; 38:29).

4. The aim of the Qur'ân is to spiritualize our souls. It makes numerous statements based on historical facts, but it is not a book of history. It draws attention to different stages of the creation of the universe (7:54; 14:33; 21:28-33; 71:15-18), origin of life from water (21:30; 24:45), and of the human being (71:14; 32:7; 39:7; 40:67), but it is not a treatise on the evolution of life. It makes several references to the laws governing the wonderful system that revives the dry earth through rain (7:57), and maintains the supply of sweet and salt water in rivers and oceans (25:54; 35:12), but it is not a manual of Meteorology, Hydraulics or Ecology. It says: 'We create a human being from an extract of clay; then We reduce him to a drop of sperm (and place him) in a safe depository; Then We form the sperm into a clot; then We develop the clot into a lump of flesh; then We fashion bones out of this lump of flesh, then We clothe the bones with flesh, thereafter We evolve him into another being' (23:12-14), yet it is not a work on Obstetrics. Several of its verses contain references to the achievements in material sciences, activities in the field of trade, space research and weaponries such as: He has let the two bodies of water flow freely; they will (one day) join together. (At present) a barrier stands between them. They cannot encroach one upon the other. Pearls and corals come out of both (these seas). And to Him belong the ships raised aloft in the sea like mountain peaks (55:19-24 - a hint on the construction of Suez and Panama Canals and the huge ships crossing them). It reads further: O body of JINN (- fiery natured) and (ordinary) the people! If you have the power

and capacity to go beyond the confines of the heavens and the earth, then do go. But you will not be able to go unless you have the necessary and unusual power. Flames of fire, smoke and molten copper will be let loose upon you and you will not be able to defend yourselves (55:33), and yet the Qur'ân is not a book about material sciences, rockets, missiles or sputniks. It says that when Pharaoh Meneptah was drowning and as death overtook him, he was told: 'So, on this day We will preserve you in your body (only) that you may be a sign (to learn a lesson from) for the coming generations' (10:92). The Bible makes no mention of this, nor does any book of history, but still, the Qur'ân is not concerned with Egyptology or Archaeology. Its purpose is not to teach History, Nature, Philosophy, any other Science or Art but, as previously stated, to spiritualize our souls. It states, discusses or cites a thing only to the extent relevant to its aim and object and leaves out details as it returns to its central theme and its invitation. When the Qur'ân is studied in this light, no doubt is left that the whole Scripture is a closely reasoned argument and there is continuity of subject throughout the Book.

5. If one desires to know the Qur'ânic solution of a particular human problem, he should study the Qur'ân with a view to finding the answer to that issue. We can say, from our own experience and the experience of so many other people, that when one studies the Qur'ân with a view to researching any point one will find an answer to it therein. Many questions may arise in one's mind when proceeding through the Holy Qur'ân. The reader should note these questions and it is likely that he will find an adequate answer on the second or third reading. It is preferable that the second reading be with one's family and the third, in the company of other people.

6. The particular occasions on which particular verses were revealed shed a light on the meanings of the verses. But we must warn the readers that the sense of the term SHÂN-I-NAZÛL is not that the verses were revealed on that particular occasion, but as Shah Walî Allâh has rightly mentioned it means that the verse also applies to that occasion. To think that the verse refers only to a particular incident puts the picture out of all perspective. The Qur'ân was not revealed for a particular past and our chief interest now is to see how it can guide us in our present lives. Its meaning is manifold and whenever tested it immediately helps us. So the consideration of the historical occasion on which a particular verse is stated to have been revealed must never be allowed to obscure the underlying purpose of that verse and its inner reliance on the ethical and spiritual teachings which the Qur'ân propounds.

7. The Holy Qur'ân is a Book so full of wisdom that it has brought out the accord between the principles of spiritual and physical medicine (17:12; 41:44; 10:57). There is a deep relationship between the science of bodies and the science of religions and they conform to each other.

8. There are four SUNNÎ theological Schools or Rites. The founders of these schools are Imâm Abû Hanîfa, Imâm Mâlik, Imâm Ahmad, and Imâm Shâfi'î. The books of these schools are also very useful for understanding the Holy Qur'ân.

9. The order of arrangement of the Qur'ân - the sequence of the chapters and that of the verses is not the order in which the Qur'ân was revealed. It was arranged by the Holy Prophet ﷺ under Divine guidance according to the subject matter. Not only are the verses of the Qur'ân interrelated, but every chapter also possesses a subtle connection with the chapter preceding it. Punctuation is very useful in the study of the Qur'ân. It is an elaborate system in Arabic text which has been worked out with great care and minute attention to detail.

10. Legends in other religious Books tempted some commentators of the Holy Qur'ân to illustrate their commentaries with reference to these legends and stories (Isrâîliyyât and Qasas). These illustrations are often out of all proportion to their importance and relevance and obscure the meaning of the Holy Book. Such commentaries were, in turn, exploited by some critics of Islam who objected that Islam was built upon an imperfect knowledge of Christianity and Judaism, and that it accepted as true the legends from the Talmud, the Midrash or various fantastic schools. So during the study of the Qur'ân one must shun these Isrâîliyyâts and Qasas,

11. Any translation of the Qur'ân or a commentary should not be based upon personal opinion (T*afsîr-bir-Râiy*). Such commentary is forbidden by the Holy Prophet. He is reported to have said, 'He who interprets the Qur'ân on the basis of his opinion is in error, even if he should put forward a commentary which he considers right.'

12. It is mistakenly inferred from verse 2:106 that some of the verses of the Holy Qur'ân have been abrogated by others. This conclusion is erroneous and unwarranted. The interpretation adopted by some commentators is not based on any Qur'ânic verse or saying of the Holy Prophet ﷺ, but merely represents their own opinion and is an exploded theory; it is also totally wrong.

13. It should be borne in mind that multiplicity of meanings in the Qur'ân does not create any contradiction or generate any defect in the guidance of the Holy Book, rather the light of the greatness of the Book is enhanced by the addition of one light to another. The qualities of God's words are without limit:

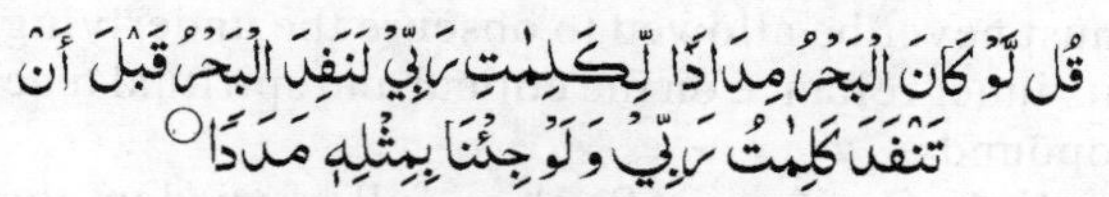

Say, "If every ocean become ink for (recording) the words and creation of my Lord, surely the oceans would be spent up before the words and creation of my Lord came to an end, even if we brought to add (therewith) as many more (oceans)" (18:109).

Then how could the Holy Qur'ân be confined to the few meanings.

14. The Holy Qur'ân draws our attention to the dangers inherent in etymological misuse. One must beware of rendering the religious terms used in the Qur'ân, such as SALÂT (Prayer), ZAKÂT (purifying alms), SOUM (Fasting), ÎMÂN (Faith), JIHÂD etc., in the meaning they acquired as Islam became institutionalized into a definite set of laws, tenets and practices. It is obvious that the Qur'ân cannot be correctly understood if we read these terms merely in the light of their literal meaning and lose sight of their ideological development, their basic purpose and the indication which they had, as intended by Him Who revealed the Book. In this respect the SUNNAH of the Messenger, peace be upon him, is the best guide.

15. It is not sufficient for an interpreter and commentator to acquire knowledge of Arabic through academic study alone and have access merely to some dictionaries and lexicons, but he must also be able to feel and hear the language as the Arabs felt and heard it at the time when the Qur'ân was being revealed.

16. The Holy Qur'ân says:

لَّا يَمَسُّهُۥٓ إِلَّا ٱلْمُطَهَّرُونَ ۝

No one can achieve true insight into it except those who are purified (by leading righteous lives) (56:79).

So another point which adds to one's understanding of the Holy Qur'ân is prayer. He who seeks to discover the true meaning and purpose of the Holy Book cannot afford to neglect supplicating to All-Knowing God for enlightenment (40:60; 29:69). Only those who lead righteous lives and achieve purity of heart are the ones granted true understanding of and insight into the real meaning of Qur'ân (56:79). For this reason the revelations, visions and explanations of the Holy Qur'ân by IMÂMS of the Era and saints are a source of profitable study of the Holy Qur'ân. We must not forget that the Imâms of the Era very often receive knowledge, truth and wisdom through revelation from God. Through these people knowledge is unveiled, the Qur'ânic wisdom made known and the knotty problems and intricate questions of that era are resolved. God, very distinctly, holds converse with them and answers their prayers so that the recipients of the revelations often think they are beholding God Himself, for God comes very close to them.

All these suggestions are intended to help in the proper study of the Holy Qur'ân. By observing these points one obtains a new kind of guidance, the Qur'ânic guidance, where every chapter and verse reveals its message.

STANDARDS FOR THE CORRECT INTERPRETATION OF THE HOLY QUR'ÂN

ثُمَّ إِنَّ عَلَيْنَا بَيَانَهُ

The responsibility of explaining it lies again on Us (75:19).

In the verses: 3:7; 7:40; 17:89; 18:54; 39:23 and 25:73 the Book itself lays down some rules which are to be adopted for its right interpretation. Some of the more important rules are given here.

1. The first standard and fundamental rule of a translation and commentary of the Holy Qur'ân should be the testimony of the Qur'ân itself. It should be remembered that the Qur'ân is not dependent upon something else for proof or disclosure of its verities. It does not comprise of any verity, commandment, prohibition or claim which is not supported by other testimonies contained in it. When we interpret a verse of the Book we should try to determine if it contains any other testimony in support of the meaning that we have adopted. If such testimony is not available and the adopted meaning contradicts the meanings of other verses then the adopted meaning is incorrect, for it is not possible to have any contradiction in the Holy Book. The verses and the words of the Qur'ân have an intimate bearing on other verses and words and they clarify and amplify one another. The Qur'ân contains its own system of check and balance. If a person finds a Qur'ânic verse to be vague or hazy in its limits or application, another verse will clarify or determinate it (vide 11:1; 25:33; read with 3:6).

2. The second standard for a correct interpretation of the Qur'ân is the Sunnah or doings of the Holy Prophet ﷺ. He translated and interpreted Qur'ânic injunctions through his actions. His sacred life is, in itself, the best commentary on the Qur'ân. We not only look to the Arabic lexicon for the interpretation of the Qur'ânic verses, but also to his life which has explained every Qur'ânic teaching by his Sunnah, a fact to which the Qur'ân has testified. Every virtue recommended or vice forbidden in it finds its illustration in his actions. So for the explanation of the Qur'ân after the Qur'ân itself we have to look to the Holy Prophet ﷺ to whom the Qur'ân was revealed. Sunnah (to give the code a practical shape), through its guidance, makes us practical followers of the Qur'ân (16:44;16:64).

3. HADÎTH or record of a saying of the Holy Prophet ﷺ is the third standard

of the correct interpretation of the Qur'ân. After the testimony of the Holy Qur'ân and the SUNNAH we have to look to the sayings of the Holy Prophet ﷺ which only explain the Qur'ân and do not abrogate it in any way. The Holy Prophet ﷺ said, 'My saying does not abrogate the Word of God, but the Word of God can abrogate my saying.'

Each Hadîth has to be supported by a chain of authorities going back to the Holy Prophet. Thus a HADÎTH consists of two parts, the chain of authorities (Sanad) followed by the substance (*Matn*). The terms Sunnah and Hadîth must be kept distinct from one another. SUNNAH properly designates the mode of action, practice and practical explanation of the Qur'ân, while Hadîth designates the narrative account and record of such action and sayings. The science of HADÎTH is considered the noblest and the most excellent after that of the Qur'ân and the SUNNAH. The Holy Prophet ﷺ himself encouraged his followers to keep and transmit his sayings. He is reported to have said, 'May God bless him who hears my words and treasures them, and understands them and spreads them.'

4. The fourth standard is the interpretation by the Companions of the Holy Prophet ﷺ. They were the first heirs of the light of the Holy Qur'ân and of its knowledge. They not only professed but practiced it. Ibn 'Omar, a well-known Companion of the Holy Prophet ﷺ once said, 'The method of our reading of the Holy Qur'ân was that we would not proceed until we had understood the verse and the deed and adapt our lives under that verse.'

5. The fifth standard is the Arabic lexicon, the lexicon that gives the meanings of the words that were understood at the time of the revelation of the Qurân. It adds to one's understanding of the Qur'ân.

SYSTEM OF TRANSLITERATION

(Pronunciation Key)

For Non-Arab readers trying to understand the correct pronunciation of Arabic words it is necessary to resort to some phonetic system of representing Arabic sounds. Changing letters into corresponding characters of another alphabet is called transliteration.

Unfortunately, there appears to be no consistent or thorough-going system in general use for anglicizing names and words written in Arabic. Furthermore, there is considerable confusion in the systems in practise. A normally authoritative and careful encyclopaedia employs, within the space of a dozen pages, three different versions of a common name like Quraish. At least three more spellings of the word are commonly used by other authors, and another twelve spellings are theoretically justifiable according to the various principles of transliteration of Arabic.

We have adopted the most recent rules of transliteration recognized by Western Orientalists, with very slight variation. However, no transliteration can exactly express the vocal difference between two languages. Besides, the inability of the characters of one language representing the exact pronunciations and sounds of another, there are specific difficulties in romanizing Arabic words. Compared to English, Arabic speech requires that the muscles of the vocal organs be kept tout which results in clearer speech, lips are much more mobile, stress is placed on producing the full sound of every word, transition from one sound to another is very rapid and vowels do not glide off into diphthong and voiced consonants.

There are some characters in Arabic alphabet such as: ث, ح, خ, ذ, غ, ع, ظ, ط, ض, ص, which have no equivalent in English. In English, the same sounds are sometimes spelt in more than one way and the same letter may be used to represent more than one sound, e.g. C represent S in face but K in cloth. Arabic spellings are much more regular and one letter or symbol represents just one sound.

In certain combinations of words, Arabic pronunciation does not follow the written characters. To this category belong all the letters known by the name of Hurûf al-Shamsiyyah and are as follows: ت tâ (t), ث thâ (th), د dâl (d), ذ dhâl (dh); ر râ (r), ز zâ (z), س sîn (s), ش shîn (sh) , ص sâd (s), ض dzâd (dz), ط tâ (t), ظ zâ (z), ل lâm (l), ن nûn (n). These are of three types:

1. Dental: Letters pronounced by applying the tongue to the teeth.
2. Sibilant: Letters having a hissing consonant sound;
3. Liquids: Letters having a flowing consonant sound.

Whenever a word beginning with one of these letters has the prefix *al* ال (representing the article 'the') the ل *(lâm, l)* is passed over in pronunciation and assimilated in the following consonant, as *al-shams* الشمس is pronounced *ash-shams* (hence the name *H̲arûf ash-Shamsiyyah*, instead of *H̲ârûf al-Shamsiyyah*). In case of remaining letters of the Arabic alphabet, which are known by the names of *H̲arûf al-Qamariyyah*, *'al* ال is pronounced fully. This merging of one letter in another (*al* in *sh* in case of *ash-Shams*) is called *idgh̲âm* (contraction of one letter into another).

This also occurs in a few other cases for which a book on Arabic grammar should be consulted. In transliteration we have followed the written form for the facility of lay-reader, writing *Al-Rah̲mân* instead of *Ar-Rah̲mân*. The system of transliteration adopted in this book is as follows:

ALPHABET	REPRESENTATION		SOUND
ا	Alif	A, a	Same as a (A) in English
ء	hamzah	'	Like *h* in honour preceded by a very slight aspira tion and a soft catch in voice.
ب	bâ	b, B	Same as *b* (B) in 'but'
ت	tâ	t, T	Softer than *t*, the Italian dental.
ث	th̲â	th̲, Th̲	Between *s* and *th* as in thing.
ج	jîm	J, J	Like 'j' in Jack.
ح	H̲	h̲, H̲	Very sharp but smooth guttural aspirate.
خ	kh̲â	kh̲, Kh̲	Like *ch* in scotch word 'loch' or as in German *ch* in 'loch' by bringing the tongue into the position of *k* as in key while pro nouncing a strong rasping *h.*

د	dâl	d, D,	Softer than *d*, the Italian dental.
ذ	dhâl	dh, Dh	Sound between *z* and th in 'that'.
ر	râ	r, R	Same as *r* in 'rain'.
ز	zâ	z, Z	Same as *z* in 'zeal'.
س	sîn	s, S	Same as *s* in 'sound'.
ش	shîn	sh, Sh	Same as *sh* in 'she'.
ص	sâd	s, S	Strongly articulated as *s* in 'kiss'.
ض	dzâd	dz, Dz	Aspirated d between *d* and *z*.
ط	tâ	t, T	Strongly articulated palatal *t*.
ظ	zâ	z, Z	Strongly articulated palatal *z*.
ع	‘ain	‘	Somewhat like a strong guttural *hamzah*.
غ	ghain	gh, Gh	Guttural *g* but soft. Requires that the throat muscles be in gargling position.
ف	fâ	f, F	Same as *f* in 'father'.
ق	qâf	q, Q	Strongly articulated guttural *k*. as in 'quail'.
ك	kâf	k, K	Same a *k* in 'king'.
ل	lâm	l, L	Same as *l* in 'lamp'.
م	mîm	m, M	Same as *m* in 'man'.
ن	nûn	n, N	Same as *n* in 'nose'.
ه	hâ	h, H	Same as *h* in 'house'.
و	wâw	w, W	Same as *w* in 'wheel'.
ي	yâ	y, Y	Same as *y* in 'yacht'.

VOWELS IN ARABIC

There are three short and three long vowels in Arabic. In all the following examples, any signs by themselves have been shown above or below a short horizontal reference line. any sign indicated above the line will always be placed over a letter and any sign below the line will always occur below the corresponding letter.

SHORT VOWELS

Fat<u>h</u>ah **َـ :** A small diagonal stroke or oblique line over a letter sounds like 'a' in 'balk' and 'u' in 'but'. It is represented by 'a' or 'A'.
Kasrah **ـِ :** A small diagonal stroke or oblique line below a letter sounds like 'i' in 'sin'. It is represented by 'i' or 'I'.
<u>Dz</u>ammah **ـُ :** A miniature or small *wâw* over a letter sounds as 'u' in 'put' or 'o' in 'so'. It is represented by 'u' or 'U'.

LONG VOWELS

Long Fat<u>h</u>ah **ـٰ :** A *fat<u>h</u>ah* in standing or upright position over a letter sounds like *'a'* 'father'. It will be written as â as in Allâh الله. It is represented by 'â' or 'Â'.
Long Kasrah **ـٖ :** A *kasrah* written perpendicularly under a letter sounds like the second 'i' in 'civilian'. It will be written as î as in *Injîl.* It is represented by 'î' or 'Î'.
Long <u>Dz</u>ammah **ـٗ :** An inverted *<u>dz</u>ammah* above the letter. It sounds like 'u' in 'ruby'. It is represented by 'û' or 'Û'.

The long vowel have three stages of which two are represented by ~ and ~. Just for an example, ' is like one 'a', ~ is like two 'aa', and ~ is like three 'aaa' and no longer then that.

> Fat<u>h</u>ah before *wâw* و is pronounced like the 'au' in 'taurat'.
> It is represented by 'au' or 'AU'.
> Fat<u>h</u>ah before *yâ* ى makes a diphthong like sound *'ai'* as 'said'.
> It is represented by 'ai' or 'AI'.

Silent *alif* after *fat<u>h</u>ah* makes a long vowel 'â' or 'Â'.
Silent *yâ* after *kasrah* makes a long vowel 'î' or 'Î'.
Silent *wâw* after *<u>dz</u>ammah* makes the long vowel 'û' or 'Û'.
Silent *wâw* after *fat<u>h</u>ah* makes the long a diphthong that sounds like the 'ou' or 'OU' as 'ou' in 'shout'.
Silent *yâ* after *fat<u>h</u>ah* makes a diphthong like *'ai'* in 'said'.

SUKÛN OR JAZM ْ :

The sign of *Jazm or Sakûn* over a letter indicates the absence of vowel sound. A letter which has this sign is called "quiescent" letter.

TANWÎN OR NUNATION:

When the signs of the short vowels (*- fat<u>h</u>ah, kasrah and <u>dz</u>ammah)* are doubled, they are pronounced with the addition of the sound of 'an', 'in' or 'un' respectively. This is called tanwîn or nunation, which takes place only at the end of indefinite nouns and adjectives. The short and long vowels at the end of a word are shown in writing as parts of the words, but the tanwîn is shown as a syllable.

- ـً *fat<u>h</u>ah tanwîn* is represented by 'an' and *pronounced as* بً as 'un' in 'sun'.
- ـٍ *kasrah tanwîn* is represented by 'in' and pronounced as بٍ as 'in' in 'fin'.
- ـٌ *<u>dz</u>ammah tanwîn* is represented by 'un' and pronounced بٌ as German name 'Gunther'.

SHADD ـّ

This sign occuring over a letter indicates the doubling of that letter's sound in pronunciation, for example, , اَبّ is اب ب where بِ is doubled and assimilated with the following ب and the sign of *shadd* is added below the *fat<u>h</u>ah.* In Allâh the stress is on the second 'l' and the first 'l' is silent.

The Roman characters in which Arabic words and names have been spelt give the sound of original only approximately. the pronounciation of which must be learnt by the ear for which we have the help of a Qârî or video and audio tapes.

SYSTEM OF PUNCTUATION
The Pause (*Waqf*)

Every language has certain rules of punctuation, of making or not making a pause in writing or speech. These rules make descriptions more accurate and statements more intelligible for the addressees.

Early Muslim scholars took great pain to put up signals and lighthouses at every rock in the way of the students, the readers and listeners of the Holy Book. They kept in view the rules of making a pause, sometimes a very short one, sometimes a little longer, sometimes not at all, and accordingly fixed certain marks to be followed. These scholars invented signs such as full-stops, colons, semicolons, commas etc. and assigned them visual forms which were abbreviations of the words whose meanings stood for various types of pauses.

1. O: A small circle O at the end of a word means that the verse has come to an end. The circle stands for an abbreviated ة of the word *waqf-tâm* which conveys that the statement is complete to the extent. A reader encountering O at the end of a verse can always stop for a complete pause. A similar pause is possible when a small ط, a small X, or a small م occur at the end of a word.

If one of the following signs: *fat<u>h</u>ah* َ, *kasrah* ِ, *<u>dz</u>ammah* ُ, *tanwîn* ً or ٍ, or *shadd* ّ are present at the last alphabet, they should be disregarded in pronunciation and the last letter should be read as if it contained the sign *of sukun* ْ.

Note the change of pronunciation of the following word: نَسْتَعِيْنُOط *(Nastaînu)* should be pronounced as نَسْتَعِيْنْO and اَحَدٌ *(A<u>h</u>adun)* as اَحَدْO *(A<u>h</u>ad)*. However a *sukun* on the last letter leaves the pronunciation unchanged if the reader decides to stop, e.g., يُوْلَدْOلا

2. While pronouncing ً form of *tanwîn* at the end of a verse; if ا *alif* or ى *Yâ* (ى without dots) occur after the letter with ً (i.e., 'an') the last letter at the time of a waqf (pause) should be pronounced with the sound of alif (i.e. 'a') and not the usual sound 'an', for example, as if followed by *Alif* at the time of *waqf* or pause. This is illustrated in the following example: O ضُحًى (7:98) would be pronounced ضُحَى <u>Dz</u>u<u>h</u>a and not <u>Dz</u>u<u>h</u>an.

3. If the last letter of a verse is *tâ marbûta* ة, it should be pronounced as if it were *hâ* ه if the reader chooses to make a stop, e.g. قُوَّةٌO should be pronounced *as Quwwah* قُوَّه. However, when the last letter is *tâ* ت it will not be changed into *hâ* ه.

Tâ marbûta ة will be pronounced as *tâ* ت when no pause is to be made at the end of a verse e.g., as in تَصْلٰى ○ نَاصِبَةٌ. Here the words will be pronounced as *Nâsibatuntaslâ* and not *Nâsibah-taslâ*.

If a letter with a *fathah tanwîn* ً is followed by *alif* without any vowel sign, this *alif* will be pronounced with the َ sound (a single *fathah*). If a letter with a *fathah tanwîn* precedes the letter *Yâ* (ى without dots) without any vowel sign, the last *Yâ* (ى without dots) will be pronounced as *alif* with a *fathah* on the preceding letter e.g.: ضُحىً will be read ضُحَا.

ع: A small *'ain* ع on the top of a circle or one standing alone within a line indicates the end of a verse along with the end of a *Sûrah.*

م: A small *mîm* م on the top of a circle or one standing alone within a line indicates a mandatory pause. Not pausing at one of these signs can alter the meaning understood by the addressees.

ط: A small *tâ* ط on top of a circle or standing alone is called *waqf-mutlaq* and indicates a pause when a sentence comes to an end but the argument continues in the next sentence.

ج: A small *jîm* ج on top of a circle or standing alone is called *waqf-jaiz.* It indicates that a pause is preferred but continuation is also allowed.

ز: A small *râ* ز on top of a circle or standing alone indicates that it is better not to make a pause at this point while reading.

ص: A small *sâd* ص on top of a circle or standing alone indicates that a reader should preferably continue without a pause, however there exists leave to make a pause. The difference between the signs *râ* and *sâd* is that in the former case it is better and preferable not to make a pause, rather go on reading by joining the words whereas in the later preference is given to making a pause while reading.

ق: A small *qâf* ق on top of a circle or standing alone indicates that a reader should not make a pause.

صل: The marks صل or Ó¼u on top of a circle or standing alone indicates that a reader may or may not stop, however it is better to join the words before and after the sign and avoid a pause.

قف: A sign of *qaff* قف or وقفة indicates that the reader need not stop.

سكتة or **س:** A sign of *sîn* س or *saktah* سكتة indicates that the reader should make a short pause but not long enough to take a breath. The difference between *qaff* and *saktah* is that one should stop longer at *qaff* قف as compared to *saktah* سكتة, but in either case not long enough to take a breath.

لا: A *lâ* لا alone within a verse strictly prohibits a pause. A *lâ* لا on the top of a circle a pause is optional. The reader can either stop or continue the reading by joining the last word before this sign and the first word of the next verse.

Difficulty may arise for a beginner if their is a *tashdîd* on the first letter after the sign. The verse will then start with a vowel-less letter or with a *nûn-qutnî* (small *nûn* ں below a letter). Thus there are three ways of making a *waqf* if *lâ* لا is on the top of a circle:

a. If the word of the verse following the above sign starts with a *tashdîd*, then either:

i. Pause at the end of the preceding verse, disregard the *tashdîd* and start the new verse in a normal way.

ii. Disregard the sign *lâ* لا above the circle and read by joining the two words on either side of this sign.

b. If the second verse begins with *Alif* ا and *lâm* ل and the third letter contains a *fat<u>h</u>ah*, then again there are two possibilities:

i. Pause at circle containing *lâ* لا, continue as if the *fat<u>h</u>ah* was on the leading *alif*.

ii. Join the two words without pausing. However if *nûn-qutnî* is found at the beginning of the second verse, followed by a letter with a *fat<u>h</u>ah*, the *nûn-qutnî* should be ignored and the verse commenced as if the leading *alif* had a *fat<u>h</u>ah*.

c. If the second verse begins with *alif* but the other conditions of the case under ii) are not fulfilled, one of the following would apply:

i. If the word before la on a circle ends with sukun, and the word after this sign has alif followed by *<u>dz</u>ammah*, read as if *<u>dz</u>ammah* is present on the leading *alif*.

ii. In case above if there is *kasrah* or *fat<u>h</u>ah* in place of *<u>dz</u>ammah*, read as if *kasrah* was under the leading *alif*.

ك: A sign of *kâ* ك means that the last encountered punctuation should again be followed. This stresses the continuity of the subject matter.

∴ : A sign of three dots (∴) is called *muânqah*. It is sometimes written as ©ج . Any word or expression marked with it can be read in continuation with the preceding or the following word.

REFERENCES

References without the name of a book are from the Holy Qur'ân. Two numbers follow such references; the first number indicates the chapter and the second is the verse which has been quoted. In references to collections of traditions, similar numbers follow the abbreviated names of the books. The first number represents the name of the book (*kitâb*), and the second number is the name of the sub-title (*bâb*).

SOME BOOKS OF REFERENCES USED IN THIS TRANSLATION FROM THE PERSONAL LIBRARY OF 'ALLAMAH NOORUDDÎN

AD.	Sunan of Abû Dâwûd Sulaimân (202-275 A.H.).
Ahmad.	Musnad of Ahmad ibn Hanbal (164-241 A.H.).
Aqrab.	Aqrab al-Muwârid by al-Khaurî al-Shartûtî.
Asâs.	Asâs al-Balâghah by Zamakhsharî.
B.	Sahîh of Al-Bukhârî (194-256 A.H.).
Bahr.	Bahr al-Muhît by Abû Hayyan al-Andulusî.
Baidzâwî.	Tafsîr by Qâdzî Abd Allâh ibn 'Omar al-Baidzâwî.
Baqâ'.	Kulliyyât Abul Baqâ'.
Dârqutnî.	Abul Hasan 'Alî (305-385 A.H.).
Dârmî.	Al-Musnad by Abû Muhammad Abd Allâh al-Dârmî (181-255 A.H.).
Ibn Hajar.	Fath al-Bârî fî Sharh Sahîh al-Bukhârî.
Ibn Jauzî.	Fath al-Mughîth.
Ibn Hishâm.	Sîrat al-Rasûl.
IJ.	Jâmi' al-Biyân fî Tafsîr al-Qur'ân by Ibn Jarîr Tabarî.
Ik.	Tafsîr Ibn Kathîr by Isma'îl ibn 'Omar ibn Kathîr.
Im.	Sunan by Muhammad ibn Yazîd ibn Mâjah Qazwînî (209-295 A.H.).
Is.	Tabaqât al-Kabîr by Muhammad ibn S'ad.
Itqân.	Itqân fî 'Ulûm al-Qur'ân by Jalâl al-Dîn Sayûtî.
Kf.	Tafsîr Kashshâf by Zamakhsharî.
Kt.	Al-Kitâb by Sîbwaih
L.	Lisân al-'Arab by Ibn Manzûr.
M.	Sahîh by Muslim ibn Hajjâj (204-261 A.H.).
Ma.	Mûwattâ' by Imâm Mâlik (17-95 A.H.).

Masûdî.	Murûj al-Dhahab.
Mi.	Miqyâs al-Lughat.
Mis.	Misbah al-Fayûmî
ML.	Maqâlât al-Islâmiyya by Ismâîl al Ash'arî.
MH.	Mustadrak of Hâkim.
Mq.	Muqaddimah by Ibn Khaldûn.
Muh.	Muhallah by Ibn Hazm
Muir.	Life of Muhammad by W. Muir.
N.	Sunan by Ahmad bin 'Alî Nasa'î (214-303 A.H.).
Q.	Qâmûs al-Muhît by Nasar al-Hurainî.
Qs.	Irshâd al-Sârî Muhammad al-Khatîb al-Qastallânî.
Qâdir	Fath al-Qâdir by Shaukânî
R.	Mufradât fî Gharâib al-Qur'ân by Abdul Qâsim Al-Husain al-Râghib.
Rd.	Radd al-Muhtâr by Ibn 'Âbidîn.
Râzî.	Tafsîr Kabîr by Râzî Fakhr al-Dîn.
RM.	Rûh al-Ma'ânî by Mahmûd al-Âlûsî.
SH.	Sharah Dîwân Hamesa by Tabrîzî.
Sihâh.	Sihâh by Ismâîl Jauharî.
T.	Tâj al-'Arûs by Murtadzâ Husainî.
Tir.	Jâmi' Tirmidhî (209-279 A.H.).
Usud.	Usud al-Ghâbah by Abû al-Husain
Z.	Zurqânî: Sharh.
ZM.	Zâd al-Ma'âd by ibn Qayyim.

ARABIC NAMES AND THEIR BIBLICAL EQUIVALENTS

Arabic Name	Biblical Form
Ayyûb	Job
Dâwûd	David
Fir'aun	Pharaoh
Hârûn	Aaron
Ibrâhîm	Abraham
Ilyâs	Elias
'Imrân	Amran
Injîl	Gospel
'Isâ	Jesus
Isẖâq	Isaac
Jâlût	Goliath
Jibrîl	Gabriel
Lûṯ	Lot
Mâjûj	Magog
Maryam	Mary
Mîkâ'il	Michael
Mûsâ	Moses
Nûh	Noah
Qârûn	Korah
Sabâ'	Shebah
Sulaimân	Solomon
Ṯâlût	Gideon or Saul
Taurât	Torah
'Uzair	Ezra
Yâjûj	Gog
Ya'qûb	Jacob
Yahûdî	Jew
Yaẖyâ	John
al-Yas'a	Elisha
Yûnus	Jonah
Zakariyyâh	Zacharias
Zulqarnain	Cyrus

سَجَدَاتُ التِّلَاوَةِ

PLACES OF PROSTRATION IN THE HOLY QUR'ÂN

موضع السّجدة	موجب السّجدة	ألآية	ألسّورة مع العدد		Chapter	(No. & Verse)
يسجدون (٢٠٦)	يسجدون	٢٠٦	٧	ألأعراف	Al-'Arâf	7:206
والأصال (١٥)	ولله يسجد	١٥	١٣	ألرّعد	Al-Ra'ad	13:15
مايؤمرون (٥٠)	ولله يسجد	٤٩	١٦	ألنّحل	Al-Nahal	16:49
خشوعا (١٠٩)	يخرّون للأذقان سجّدا	١٠٧	١٧	ألإسرآء	Al-Isrâ'	17:107
بكيّا (٥٨)	خرّوا سجّدا	٥٨	١٩	مريم	Maryam	19:58
مايشآء (١٨)	يسجد له	١٨	٢٢	ألحجّ	Al-Hajj	22:18
تفلحون (٧٧)	واسجدوا	٧٧	٢٢	ألحجّ (عند الشّافعيّ)	Al-Hajj	22:77
نفورا (٦٠)	اسجدوا	٦٠	٢٥	ألفرقان	Al-Furqân	25:60
ربّ العرش العظيم (٢٦)	ألّا يسجدوا لله	٢٥	٢٧	ألنّمل	Al-Naml	27:25
لا يستكبرون (١٥)	خرّوا سجّدا	١٥	٣٢	ألسّجدة	Al-Sajdâh	32:15
أناب (٢٤) -	وخرّ راكعا	٢٤	٣٨	صٓ (عند أبي حنيفة و مالك)	Sâd	38:24
لا يسئمون (٣٨)	واسجدوا لله	٣٧	٤١	فُصِّلت	Fussilat	41:37
واعبدوا (٦٢)	فاسجدوا	٦٢	٥٣	ألنّجم (لغير مالك)	Al-Najm	53:62
يسجدون (٢١)	يسجدون	٢١	٨٤	ألإنشقاق (لغير مالك)	Al-Inshiqaq	84:21
واقترب (١٩)	واسجد	١٩	٩٦	ألعلق (لغير مالك)	Al-'Alaq	96:19

أَلْمَنَازِلُ

PLACES OF PORTIONS (MANÂZIL) IN THE HOLY QUR'ÂN

ألجزء مع العدد		ألسّورة مع العدد		ألعدد	
..	..	ألفاتحة	١	١	Al-Fâtihah
لا يحبّ الله	٦	ألمآئدة	٥	٢	Al-Mâ'idah
يعتذرون	١١	يُونُس	١٠	٣	Yunus
سبحٰن الّذي	١٥	ألإسرآء	١٧	٤	Al-Isrâ'
وقال الّذين	١٩	ألشّعرآء	٢٦	٥	Al-Shurâ
و ما لي	٢٣	ألصّٰفّٰت	٣٧	٦	Al-Saffât
حمٓ	٢٦	قٓ	٥٠	٧	Qâf

PRAYER OF PROSTRATION

While reading the Holy Qur'ân when one reaches the places of **PROSTRATION** one must prostrate and say the following prayer.

سُبْحٰنَكَ اللّٰهُمَّ رَبَّنَا وَ بِحَمْدِكَ اللّٰهُمَّ اغْفِرْلِيْ

SUBHÂNA KA ALLÂHUMMA RABBANA
WA BI HAMDI KA ALLÂHUMMA MAGHFIRLÎ

Glory to You O Allâh!
Our Lord! And perfect and true praise belongs to You alone; O Allâh! Grant me (Your) protection.
(Bukhârì)

A SHORT REVIEW OF SOME PREVIOUS TRANSLATIONS BY NON-MUSLIMS

The scholarly concern of the Europeans with the Holy Qur'ân, most probably, began with the visit of Peter the Venerable Abbot of Cluny to Toledo in the second quarter of the 12th. Century A.D. He collected a team of men and commissioned them to produce a series of works which, together, would constitute a basis for the intellectual encounter with Islam. As part of this series, the first translation of the Holy Qur'ân into Latin was produced by an Englishman Robert of Ketton (some times mistakenly called Robertus Relenensis). The work was completed in July 1143 A.D. This translation and the companion works did not lead to any real development of scholarly Qur'ânic studies. Numerous other translations were attempted in the next centuries, but Islam was still the great enemy feared in Europe and most things written about it constituted polemics and were full of prejudice.

The surge of energy during renaissance, the invention of the printing press and advance by the Ottoman Turks into Europe combined to produce a number of works on Islam in the first half of the 16th century. These included the first printing of the Latin translation by Robert of Ketton at Bale in 1543 A.D. by Bibliander. Interest continued in the seventeenth century and among the various books to appear was a translation of the Holy Qur'ân into English in 1649 A.D. by a Scotsman Alexander Ross. He did not base his work on the Qur'ân's Arabic text, rather on a French translation, 'The Alcoran of Mahomet' by Sieu du Ryer, and it was of little use.

A certain level of scholarship was attained by George Sale, a Christian missionary. This English translation appeared in London in 1743 A.D. George Sale called the Holy Qur'ân 'so manifest a forgery' and his aim of translation was - to put it in the words of George Sale himself - '... to enable us effectually to expose the imposture,' (see 'To the Reader'; 1836 edition of the translation of the Holy Qur'ân by George Sale). In his prejudice George Sale himself forged the translation of the Holy Qur'ân. Let all readers of the Holy Qur'ân be aware of the forgeries of George Sale and not be mislead by the remarks on the cover of the loose-paper edition, 'This classical Work - the translation of the Koran by George Sale - is held to be best and most accurate.' His translation is based on the Latin translation of the Qur'ân by Marcci, the confessor of Pope Innocent XI. The object of this work, which was dedicated to the Holy Roman Emperor Leopold I, was to discredit Islam and the Qur'ân in the eyes of Europe. His translation is biased, wrong and antiquated. Al-H̲âj H̲âfiz G̲h̲ulâm Sarwar in his 'Introduction' of his translation of the Holy Qur'ân deals in detail with the forgeries of George Sale. The edition by E. M. Wherry entitled: A Comprehensive Commentary on the

Qur'ân (London 1882-86), is also based on Sale's forged translation and notes. Wherry's translation, in the words of Watt, 'is of poor quality.' (see Introduction to the Qur'ân by Bell and Watt, p. 200).

Another known English translation of the Holy Qur'ân is by J.M. Rodwell. Rodwell undertook this work in order to confuse Islam and to 'make it look like a mass of disjointed fragments.' He writes on page xxii, note of the Preface: 'A line of argument to be adopted by a Christian missionary in dealing with a Muhammadan should be, not to attack Islam as a mass of error, but to show that it contains fragments of disjointed truth - that it is based on Christianity and Judaism partially understood.' To achieve his aim he took the 114 chapters of the Holy Qur'ân, disrupted their order and rearranged them according to, what he calls, the 'chronological' order. It is like cutting a perfect human body into pieces and rearranging its bones, hair, flesh and limbs and then saying that this is a being according to his 'chronology'. The purpose of Rodwell's rearrangement is nothing but mischief and his desire to make Qur'ân 'a mass of disjointed fragments'.

E.H. Palmer is another translator of the Holy Qur'ân. Palmer took into his head that the language of Qur'ân was like the talk of an ignoramus and, thus, was to be translated as such. He says, 'The language is noble and forcible, but it is not elegant in the sense of literary refinement' (lxxvii, Introduction). Palmer, therefore, out of this bias made the style of his translation as rugged as possible. His translation, as far as the literary refinement is concerned, is the worst of all. Palmer writes in his introduction that he translated the Holy Qur'ân literally, yet he omits words, hundreds of definite and indefinite articles and other aids (e.g. and, so, that, then, therefore, but etc.) which are present in the original Arabic and are necessary for the clarity and smoothness of the style, untranslated or ignored. For further details the reader may refer to the introduction of Al-Hâj Hâfiz Ghulâm Sarwar's translation of the Holy Qur'ân.

Another well-known translation is that of Arthur J. Arberry of Cambridge. He spent a considerable time with Sher 'Ali in revising his (Sher 'Ali's) translation of the Holy Qur'ân (Holland, 1955). He first published his own translation, 'The Holy Koran, an Introduction, with Selections', in London (1953). This was an experimental translation of selected passages. It was followed in 1955 by a complete translation. His method was to put down the translation in short lines regardless of the punctuation of the text and Arabic idiom. While translating a text, it is crucial that the proper and correct punctuation methodology be adopted. The lack of due consideration to appropriate punctuation can lead to a distortion of the intended meaning of the original text. Thus, the need for due regard to correct punctuation cannot be overemphasized. Arthur J. Arberry's translation of the Holy Qur'ân is severely flawed in this respect. By incorrectly punctuating the translation, he has completely changed the meaning of the original text. The distortions in the text have been further compounded by Arberry's unique approach of arbitrarily splitting up the sentences of the original text into short disjointed phrases. This has rendered the translation incoherent and meaningless. Marshall G. S. Hodgson writes, 'Arberry's translation has two defects. The first is an unnecessary and sometimes misleading archaism, which he apparently introduced for the sake of solemnity, but which makes for a different kind of solemnity from that of the original. The second defect is that he has broken up the original into short lines which he sets off from one another on the page. These short lines do not necessarily represent precisely the units of the original. Hence the student should avoid basing any interpretation on the way Arberry has arranged them visually on the page.' (Introduction to Islamic civilization, course syllabus and selected readings. The University of Chicago, Syllabus Division, by Marshall G. S. Hodgson, September 1958).

The above remarks are just a few cursory hints to indicate how the biased critics of Islam were tempted to translate the Holy Book. We earnestly trust that the modern spirit of enquiry, scientific thought, true culture and broad-minded tolerance will prevent the acceptance of these old prejudices.

LIGHT OF THE HOLY QUR'ÂN

قَدْ جَآءَكُم مِّنَ اللهِ
نُورٌ وَّكِتٰبٌ مُّبِينٌ ﴿١٥﴾ يَّهْدِي بِهِ اللهُ مَنِ
اتَّبَعَ رِضْوٰنَهُ سُبُلَ السَّلٰمِ وَيُخْرِجُهُم مِّنَ الظُّلُمٰتِ إِلَى النُّورِ
بِإِذْنِهِ وَيَهْدِيهِمْ إِلَى صِرٰطٍ مُّسْتَقِيمٍ ﴿١٦﴾

There has come to you, indeed, from Allâh a Light and the perspicuous Book (- the Qur'ân) that distinguishes the right from the wrong. Allâh guides with this (Book) those who follow His good pleasure to the ways of peace (both physical and spiritual), and He takes them out of all kinds of darkness into the light, by His leave, and guides them along the exact right path (5:15-16).

What are the potentials of a human being? What are the limits of his reason? Is he able by himself, without the help of Revelation, to understand and explain all things, seen as well as those unseen? The Qur'ân teaches that a human being is not an animal, he is neither a god nor the personification of sin. His role is to be a vicegerent appointed by God on earth. God has bestowed on him the talents and abilities necessary for this role (95:3). Like every thing in nature, the human being enters this world pure and untainted, possessing the highest capacities and with unlimited progress before him (94:4). He is born with a natural tendency to do good and to build up his morality and spirituality on the right lines, but he has also been given a large measure of freedom of will and action to mould himself as he chooses. He has been endowed with great natural powers and creative qualities to make unlimited progress and to rise spiritually so as to become the mirror in which Divine attributes are reflected. He can reach this goal and avoid the abyss if his discretion becomes trained to work right and he receives proper guidance. The human being, having every representation of nature in him, can soar to the highest of the high, and his area of progress knows no limits. The Holy Qur'ân provides him with the light and the right guidance for his journey

The Light, characteristic of the Qur'ân, draws its true follower nearer to God. It illuminates his heart (39:22-23) and honours him with the delicious Converse with God. It discloses the dark and the hidden, and helps in the acceptance of his Prayer (40:60). It gives information of Him in Whose meeting rests the eternal salvation and happiness (89:27-30). With this Light the eye of his heart opens up and God converses with him and answers his prayers.

وَإِذَا سَأَلَكَ عِبَادِي عَنِّي فَإِنِّي قَرِيبٌ ؕ أُجِيبُ دَعْوَةَ
الدَّاعِ إِذَا دَعَانِ فَلْيَسْتَجِيبُوا لِي

And when My servants ask you concerning Me (tell them),
I am nearby indeed, I answer the prayer of the supplicant
when he prays to Me, so they should respond to My call (2:186).

The Qur'ân brings about spiritual awakening and living consciousness. He whose soul seeks the truth should arise and search for it as the means of obtaining perfect knowledge through which one can see God, and seek the mirror through which one can behold that High Being during the Converse with Him. The door of God's blessings of Converse is always open. It is open in this age, as it was open in the past. We do earnestly pray that Allâh may accept this effort of ours and make His Words clearer to the English reader than it has ever been made before, Amîn.

Amatul Rahmân 'Omar
'Abdul Mannân 'Omar
Muhabbat Sarâ - Stelleacker 18
79618 Rheinfelden - Germany
July 7, 1990

ABOUT THE TRANSLATION
AND THE TRANSLATORS

An utmost attempt has been made to make the translation as pure, simple, literal and faithful to the original Arabic text as possible. Use of archaism has been avoided which would only obscure the meaning of the Book. Clearness, ease of understanding and accuracy are the main aims of this translation. The Biblical style with 'hath', 'doth' and 'thou' forms favored by some of the predecessors has been dropped.

The use of parentheses plays a very important role in this translation. Words within parentheses are either explanations or alternative meanings of the words immediately preceding them, or they are such words which are not present in the Arabic letters, but become necessary by the rules of English grammar or Arabic idiom and leaving them out might confuse a non-Arab reader. Many of the words within parentheses may be used without any parentheses at all, for they are really part and parcel of the text. Since these words were not present in the Arabic text, it was thought prudent to put parentheses around them. It was a better way to achieve an intimate understanding of the diction of the Qur'ân. Reading without parentheses gives a very literal translation and reading with parentheses gives explanations which are most authentic and scientific, free from myths and superstitious ideas.

Footnotes have been deliberately avoided in this edition as they interrupt the smooth flow of the Book. It is a boon for those who think that a translation should not distract the reader's attention from the text to the footnotes.

There is no claim of infallibility and no claim that this translation cannot be improved further. It is not to be expected that all the transcendent excellencies and miraculous beauties of the Holy Qur'ân could be unveiled here. Many verities and beauties of the Holy Qur'ân are clothed in rich, noble, forcible and appropriate language, which not infrequently rise to a poetical sublimity and ecstasy far beyond the reach of any translation.

'Allâmah Nooruddîn

This explanation and interpretation of the Holy Qur'ân is based on 'Allâmah, Al-Hâfiz Nooruddîn's lifetime study of the Holy Qur'ân (may God be pleased with him).

About The Translators

Nooruddîn was born in Bhera (Panjab) in 1840. He received his early religious and medical education in India. He spent many years in the cities of Makkah and Madînah, where he lived in a spiritually close and long association, as a student, with scholars like Shah 'Abdul Ghanî, (grandson of Shah Wallî-Allâh Mohaddass Dehlavî) and other Islamic scholars whose daily speech mirrored the genuine spirit of Islam. While in Makkah and Madînah he was able to feel, hear, read and write Arabic prose and poetry of the time when the Qur'ân was being revealed.

Nooruddîn was a scholar and teacher of the Holy Qur'ân with international fame and recognition. His influence on the modern Islamic thought is profound and widespread. This is proven by the fact that several English translations of the Qur'ân have been done by his students under his direct or indirect influence and guidance. These include translations by Dr. Abdul Hakîm (India, 1904); Muhammad Alî (India, 1917), Sher 'Alî (Holland, 1955), Dr. Khadim Noori (Shillong - Asam, India, 1964), Malik Ghulâm Farîd (Pakistan, 1969). Khawajah Kamaluddin started the Woking Muslim Mission (London, U.K.) in 1912 A.D. under his advice, guidance and patronage.

He was one of the clearest and wisest Islamic thinkers of his age. His knowledge of the Qur'ân was vast and his learning on Islam thorough. His numerous lectures, learned sermons, eloquent orations and Qur'ânic seminars will always be remembered. He pursued a scholarly and an academic interpretation of Islam under the guiding principles of the Holy Qur'ân and the Sunnah (-Qur'ân as being understood, explained, and practiced by the Holy Prophet Muhammad[pbuh]-the last and the best of the Prophets).

He not only collected and consulted the previous translations and commentaries of the Qur'ân but also referred to the oldest and most reliable Arabic lexicons and poetry of pre-Islamic poets to ascertain the real, classical and root meanings of the Arabic words used in the Qur'ân. He had an invaluable collection of classical Islamic books in his personal library, which was 'one of the best personal Islamic libraries of the world'. *(Oriental College Magazine, Punjab University, India).*

He was aware that all the parts of the Holy Qur'ân are interconnected by a central theme, that this grand Book reflects the wisdom and unity of purpose of God and we are not permitted to make any change in the sequence of the text.

He not only followed the sober and rational approach shown by the great classical commentators like Ibn Jarîr, Ibn Kathîr, Abû Hayyân, al-Baidzâwî, Râzî, Ibn Qayyim and many others, but also his own conscious probing for the genuine. He consulted the previous Scriptures, books of Hadîth, history and jurisprudence, but never paid any attention to the mystic doctrines, Tafsîr-bir-raiy, and religious stories (Qasas). He was of the opinion that verses of the Qur'ân do not contradict each other. Hence, a Qur'ânic verse cannot be abrogated by any other Qur'ânic verse or Hadîth.

Nooruddîn was an outstanding intellectual who stands out as an extraordinary figure in the ranks of literates and religious scholars. A grand personality, purest in morals, earnest and tireless in his search for truth. His insight was deep and his observational faculties keen. There was sincerity in his word and in his writings. His veracity and enthusiasm imbued his audience with feelings akin to his own. Correctness of thought and action was always the goal of his striving. He was of healthy and firm physique and strong intellect, retentive memory, great tenacity and capacity for methodical work. Throughout his life he was strictly pious, honest and generous to the poor.

He was also a renowned physician and spent sixteen years of his life as the personal physician of the Maharaja (ruler) of Kashmir. He was of the opinion that there is a deep relationship between the principles of spiritual medicine and physical medicine. He successfully treated many serious physical diseases in the light of Qur'ânic principles and interpreted several verses of the Qur'ân by using his knowledge of medicine.

He very well knew that an important requisite for a profitable study of the Qur'ân is prayer and never neglected supplication to God whenever he had difficulty in understanding a verse. He also knew that a multiplicity of meanings of the Qur'ânic verses does not create any contradiction, the wonders of the Qur'ân are witout limit and it could not be confined to the few meanings which may be set out in a commentary. It is because of this fact that we find in his translation so many new insights and verities. However, his attemps were not against the aforementioned fundamental rules and standards for the correct interpretations of the Holy Qur'ân.

MRS. AMATUL RAHMAN 'OMAR

Handwritten notes of 'Allâmah Nooruddîn, his published Friday-Sermons and lectures on various subjects of Qur'ân; his books and Qur'ânic seminars or 'Dars' are the basis of this English translation. The Qur'ân thus explained and interpreted by him was rendered into English by his daughter-in-law Amatul Rahmân 'Omar.

Amatul Rahmân is probably the first Muslim woman in the Islamic history to translate the Holy Qur'ân in English. She earned her Masters Degree in Arabic from the University of the Panjab, Lahore, Pakistan in 1950. She was awarded several gold and silver medals from the University for her outstanding distinction and achievement in the Arabic language. She spent most part of her life in teaching Arabic and English.

She, along with her husband 'Abdul Mannân 'Omar, is also the compiler and editor of the 'commentary *(tafsîr)* of the Holy Qur'ân in English as well as Urdu language', as explained by Nooruddîn. *(Both are being readied for the press).*

'ABDUL MANNÂN 'OMAR

Amatul Ra<u>h</u>man Omar was assisted in this difficult task of translation and editing by her learned husband 'Abdul Mannân 'Omar. Because of his erudition and knowledge of Islamic studies, this fact, among many others, is a living testimony that for years he has been the Editor of the Encyclopedia of Islam (20 Volumes). He is also the author of more than hundred scholarly articles on Islam, published in the Encyclopedia of Islam.

Moreover, he is the author of "Dictionary of the Holy Qur'ân (Arabic to English)". This scholarly masterpiece combines classical Arabic dictionaries in one. This dictionary explains the real, classical, and root meanings of all the Qur'ânic words with their derivatives. It includes all 'Qur'ânic Word Index' and all 'Root Word Index'. First published in 1999.

He also had the honour of arranging, indexing, and subject-codifying, for the first time, the classical work of the orignal Musnad Imâm A<u>h</u>mad bin <u>H</u>anbal, comprising of approximately 30,000 A<u>h</u>adi<u>th</u>. The origanal work was organized according to the 'name of the narrator' narrating each <u>H</u>adi<u>th</u>, and not arranged according to the subject and topic. This new work is published under the title, "Subject Codification of the Musnad Imâm A<u>h</u>mad bin Mu<u>h</u>ammad bin <u>H</u>anbal". (10 volumes, in Arabic Only).

رَبِّ أَوْزِعْنِيٓ أَنْ أَشْكُرَ نِعْمَتَكَ الَّتِيٓ أَنْعَمْتَ عَلَيَّ وَعَلٰى وٰلِدَيَّ
وَأَنْ أَعْمَلَ صٰلِحًا تَرْضٰهُ وَأَصْلِحْ لِي فِي
ذُرِّيَّتِيٓ ۚ إِنِّي تُبْتُ إِلَيْكَ وَإِنِّي مِنَ الْمُسْلِمِينَ ﴿١٥﴾

My Lord! Rouse me up that I may give thanks for the favours You have bestowed on me and on my parents and that I may do such righteous deeds as may please You. And (my Lord!) establish righteousness among my progeny for me. To You indeed I turn penitently and I am surely of those who submit themselves (to You)' (46:15).

CHILDREN OF
AMATUL RA<u>H</u>MÂN 'OMAR AND 'ABDUL MANNÂN 'OMAR
DECEMBER 2008
The Editors

The Holy Qur'ân

Arabic Text and English Translation

PART الجُزْءُ الأَوَّلُ I

CHAPTER
1

AL-FÂTI<u>H</u>AH
(The Opening)
(Revealed before Hijrah)

سُورَةُ الفَاتِحَةِ مَكِّيَّةٌ

1. **W**ITH the name of Allâh,
the Most Gracious, the Ever Merciful,
(I commence to read the Holy Book).

بِسْمِ اللّٰهِ الرَّحْمٰنِ الرَّحِيمِ ①

2. All type of perfect and true praise belongs to Allâh alone, the Lord of the worlds,
3. The Most Gracious, the Ever Merciful,
4. Master of the Day of Requital.
5. (Lord!) You alone do we worship and You alone do we implore for help.
6. Lead us on the exact right path till we reach the goal,
7. The path of those on whom You have bestowed (Your) blessings, those who have not incurred (Your) displeasure, and those who have not gone astray.

أَلْحَمْدُ لِلّٰهِ رَبِّ الْعٰلَمِينَ ② الرَّحْمٰنِ الرَّحِيمِ ③ مٰلِكِ يَوْمِ الدِّينِ ④ إِيَّاكَ نَعْبُدُ وَ إِيَّاكَ نَسْتَعِينُ ⑤ إِهْدِنَا الصِّرٰطَ الْمُسْتَقِيمَ ⑥ صِرٰطَ الَّذِينَ أَنْعَمْتَ عَلَيْهِمْ ۵ غَيْرِ الْمَغْضُوبِ عَلَيْهِمْ وَ لَا الضَّآلِّينَ ⑦ عٌ

سُوْرَةُ الْبَقَرَةِ ٢

CHAPTER
2

AL-BAQARAH
(The Cow)
(Revealed after Hijrah)

With the name of Allâh
the Most Gracious, the Ever Merciful
(I commence to read Sûrah Al-Baqarah)

1. **A**LIF **L**ÂM **M**ÎM - I am Allâh, the All-Knowing.
2. This is the only perfect Book, wanting in naught, containing nothing doubtful, harmful or destructive, there is no false charge in it. It is a guidance for those who guard against evil;
3. Those who believe in the existence of hidden reality, which is beyond the reach of ordinary human perception and cognizance, and who observe the Prayer and spend (on others) out of that which We have provided for them,
4. And who (also) believe in that (Message) which has been revealed to you and in that which had been revealed before you, and who have firm faith in the Hereafter.

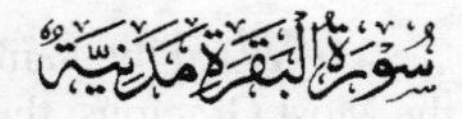

بِسْمِ اللّٰهِ الرَّحْمٰنِ الرَّحِيْمِ

الٓمٓ ﴿١﴾ ذٰلِكَ الْكِتٰبُ لَا رَيْبَ فِيْهِ
هُدًى لِّلْمُتَّقِيْنَ ﴿٢﴾ الَّذِيْنَ يُؤْمِنُوْنَ
بِالْغَيْبِ وَ يُقِيْمُوْنَ الصَّلٰوةَ وَ مِمَّا
رَزَقْنٰهُمْ يُنْفِقُوْنَ ﴿٣﴾ وَالَّذِيْنَ يُؤْمِنُوْنَ
بِمَآ أُنْزِلَ إِلَيْكَ وَ مَآ أُنْزِلَ مِنْ
قَبْلِكَ وَ بِالْأٰخِرَةِ هُمْ يُوْقِنُوْنَ ﴿٤﴾

الْجُزْءُ الْأَوَّلُ

5. It is they who follow the guidance from their Lord, and it is they alone who are successful in attaining their object in this life and in the Hereafter.
6. As for those who are bent upon denying (the truth), they would not believe, because it is all the same to them whether you warn them or do not warn them.
7. (With the result that) Allâh has set a seal upon their hearts and upon their hearing, and on their eyes is a covering. And a mighty punishment awaits them.

SECTION 2

8. THERE are some people who say, 'We believe in Allâh and the Last Day,' while they are no believers at all.
9. They abandon Allâh and those who believe, but they (as a matter of fact) only deprive themselves (of the blessings of God), and they do not perceive (it).
10. In their hearts was a disease (of hypocrisy), and Allâh has increased their disease (by making Islam triumphant). A woeful punishment awaits them because of their persistent lies.
11. When it is said to them, 'Do not disturb the peace of the land (by hypocritical tactics),' they say, 'We are simply setting things right (and so helping the cause of peace).'
12. Beware! They alone are the peace breakers, but they do not perceive (its evil consequences).
13. And when it is said to them, 'Believe as (other) people (- Companions of the Prophet) believed,' they say, 'Shall we believe as the weak-minded have believed?' Beware! It is they only who are weak-minded, but they do not know (this fact).
14. And when they meet those who have believed they say, 'We (too) have believed.' But when they are alone with their ring-leaders they say, 'We are, in reality, with you, we were simply making light of them (- the believers).'
15. Allâh will bring down disgrace upon them

أولئك على هدى من ربهم و أولئك هم
المفلحون ٥ إن الذين كفروا سواء عليهم
ءأنذرتهم أم لم تنذرهم لا يؤمنون ٦
ختم الله على قلوبهم و على سمعهم و على
أبصرهم غشوة و لهم عذاب عظيم ٧
و من الناس من يقول ءامنا بالله و باليوم
الأخر و ما هم بمؤمنين ٨ يخدعون الله
و الذين ءامنوا و ما يخدعون إلا أنفسهم
و ما يشعرون ٩ في قلوبهم مرض فزادهم
الله مرضا و لهم عذاب أليم بما كانوا
يكذبون ١٠ و إذا قيل لهم لا تفسدوا
في الأرض قالوا إنما نحن مصلحون ١١
ألا إنهم هم المفسدون و لكن لا
يشعرون ١٢ و إذا قيل لهم ءامنوا كما
ءامن الناس قالوا أنؤمن كما ءامن السفهاء
ألا إنهم هم السفهاء و لكن لا يعلمون ١٣
و إذا لقوا الذين ءامنوا قالوا ءامنا و إذا
خلوا إلى شيطينهم قالوا إنا معكم إنما
نحن مستهزءون ١٤ الله يستهزئ بهم

and will let them continue in their (ways of) transgression. They are blindly wandering.
16. It is they who have preferred misguidance to guidance, but their bargain has fetched no profit, nor are they rightly guided.
17. Their case is like the case of a person who kindled a fire (in darkness) but no sooner did it light up their surroundings than Allâh took away their light and left them in different kinds of darkness, (in a state in which) they could see nothing.
18. (They are) deaf, dumb, (and) blind, so they will not return (to the right path).
19. Or (the case of some of the hypocrites is) like (the case of those who are hit by) heavy downpour from the clouds wherein there are different kinds of darkness, thunder and lightning. They plug their ears with their fingers against the thunder-claps fearing death. And Allâh encompasses the disbelievers (to punish them).
20. The lightning (being so intensely dazzling) may well-nigh snatch away their sight. As often as it flashes for them they walk (a few steps) in it (- its light), and when it darkens against them they come to a halt. Indeed, if Allâh had so willed He would have taken away their hearing and their sight. Allâh is indeed the Possessor of power to do all that He will.

SECTION 3

21. **O** PEOPLE! Worship your Lord Who has created you as well as those before you, that you might be secure against (all sorts of) calamities.
22. (It is He) Who made for you the earth a resting place, and the heaven an edifice for protection, and caused water to pour down from the clouds. Then He brought forth therewith a great variety of fruit for your sustenance. Therefore do not set up compeers to Allâh, while you are people of knowledge!
23. And if you have any doubt as to (the truthfulness of the Qur'ân) which We have

وَيَمُدُّهُمْ فِي طُغْيَانِهِمْ يَعْمَهُونَ ﴿١٥﴾ أُولَٰئِكَ
الَّذِينَ اشْتَرَوُا الضَّلَالَةَ بِالْهُدَىٰ فَمَا رَبِحَتْ
تِجَارَتُهُمْ وَمَا كَانُوا مُهْتَدِينَ ﴿١٦﴾ مَثَلُهُمْ
كَمَثَلِ الَّذِي اسْتَوْقَدَ نَارًا فَلَمَّا أَضَاءَتْ
مَا حَوْلَهُ ذَهَبَ اللَّهُ بِنُورِهِمْ وَتَرَكَهُمْ
فِي ظُلُمَاتٍ لَا يُبْصِرُونَ ﴿١٧﴾ صُمٌّ بُكْمٌ عُمْيٌ
فَهُمْ لَا يَرْجِعُونَ ﴿١٨﴾ أَوْ كَصَيِّبٍ مِنَ السَّمَاءِ
فِيهِ ظُلُمَاتٌ وَرَعْدٌ وَبَرْقٌ يَجْعَلُونَ أَصَابِعَهُمْ
فِي آذَانِهِمْ مِنَ الصَّوَاعِقِ حَذَرَ الْمَوْتِ
وَاللَّهُ مُحِيطٌ بِالْكَافِرِينَ ﴿١٩﴾ يَكَادُ الْبَرْقُ
يَخْطَفُ أَبْصَارَهُمْ كُلَّمَا أَضَاءَ لَهُمْ مَشَوْا
فِيهِ وَإِذَا أَظْلَمَ عَلَيْهِمْ قَامُوا وَلَوْ شَاءَ اللَّهُ
لَذَهَبَ بِسَمْعِهِمْ وَأَبْصَارِهِمْ إِنَّ اللَّهَ عَلَىٰ
كُلِّ شَيْءٍ قَدِيرٌ ﴿٢٠﴾ يَا أَيُّهَا النَّاسُ اعْبُدُوا رَبَّكُمُ
الَّذِي خَلَقَكُمْ وَالَّذِينَ مِنْ قَبْلِكُمْ لَعَلَّكُمْ
تَتَّقُونَ ﴿٢١﴾ الَّذِي جَعَلَ لَكُمُ الْأَرْضَ فِرَاشًا
وَالسَّمَاءَ بِنَاءً وَأَنْزَلَ مِنَ السَّمَاءِ مَاءً فَأَخْرَجَ
بِهِ مِنَ الثَّمَرَاتِ رِزْقًا لَكُمْ فَلَا تَجْعَلُوا لِلَّهِ
أَنْدَادًا وَأَنْتُمْ تَعْلَمُونَ ﴿٢٢﴾ وَإِنْ كُنْتُمْ فِي
رَيْبٍ مِمَّا نَزَّلْنَا عَلَىٰ عَبْدِنَا فَأْتُوا بِسُورَةٍ مِنْ

ع ٣

revealed to Our servant from time to time, produce a single Sûrah (- Qur'ânic chapter) like any of (the chapters of) this, summoning (to your assistance) all your helpers (that you have) beside Allâh, if you are truthful (in your doubts),
24. But if you fail to do (so), and never shall you do (it), then guard against the Fire, the fuel of which will be human beings (who are deviating from the way of truth) and stones, (it is) prepared for the disbelievers.
25. And give good tidings to those who believe and do deeds of righteousness, that there await them Gardens from beneath which the streams flow. Every time they are given any kind of fruit from them (- the gardens) to eat, they will say, 'This is the same we were given before.' They will be given it (-the fruit) in perfect semblance (to their deeds). They shall have therein companions purified (spiritually and physically), and will abide therein forever.
26. Indeed, Allâh does not disdain to cite a parable of (a thing) even (as small as) a gnat or (of something) smaller than that. (Be it as it may) those who have believed know that this is a true (parable) from their Lord. As for those who disbelieve say, 'What could Allâh mean by (citing) such a parable?' Many does He adjudge to be erring because of these (parables) and many does He guide through them. Yet it is only the transgressors whom He adjudges to be erring because of them.
27. (Transgressors are the people) who break the covenant (they have made) with Allâh after its solemn binding, and sever the ties which Allâh has bidden to be joined and create disorder in the land. It is they who are the losers.
28. (O people!) How can you deny Allâh? When you were without life He gave you life, then He will cause you to die and again raise you to life and you shall be made to return to Him.
29. It is He Who created for your benefit all that is in the earth. Moreover He turned Himself

مِّثْلِهِۦ وَادْعُوا شُهَدَآءَكُم مِّن دُونِ اللّٰهِ
إِن كُنتُمْ صٰدِقِينَ ﴿٢٣﴾ فَإِن لَّمْ تَفْعَلُوا وَلَن
تَفْعَلُوا فَاتَّقُوا النَّارَ الَّتِي وَقُودُهَا النَّاسُ
وَالْحِجَارَةُ أُعِدَّتْ لِلْكٰفِرِينَ ﴿٢٤﴾ وَبَشِّرِ الَّذِينَ
ءَامَنُوا وَعَمِلُوا الصّٰلِحٰتِ أَنَّ لَهُمْ جَنّٰتٍ تَجْرِي
مِن تَحْتِهَا الْأَنْهٰرُ كُلَّمَا رُزِقُوا مِنْهَا مِن ثَمَرَةٍ
رِّزْقًا قَالُوا هٰذَا الَّذِي رُزِقْنَا مِن قَبْلُ
وَأُتُوا بِهِۦ مُتَشٰبِهًا وَلَهُمْ فِيهَا أَزْوٰجٌ مُّطَهَّرَةٌ
وَهُمْ فِيهَا خٰلِدُونَ ﴿٢٥﴾ إِنَّ اللّٰهَ لَا يَسْتَحْيِۦ
أَن يَضْرِبَ مَثَلًا مَّا بَعُوضَةً فَمَا فَوْقَهَا
فَأَمَّا الَّذِينَ ءَامَنُوا فَيَعْلَمُونَ أَنَّهُ الْحَقُّ مِن
رَّبِّهِمْ وَأَمَّا الَّذِينَ كَفَرُوا فَيَقُولُونَ مَاذَآ
أَرَادَ اللّٰهُ بِهٰذَا مَثَلًا يُضِلُّ بِهِۦ كَثِيرًا
وَيَهْدِي بِهِۦ كَثِيرًا وَمَا يُضِلُّ بِهِۦٓ إِلَّا
الْفٰسِقِينَ ﴿٢٦﴾ الَّذِينَ يَنقُضُونَ عَهْدَ اللّٰهِ مِنۢ
بَعْدِ مِيثٰقِهِۦ وَيَقْطَعُونَ مَآ أَمَرَ اللّٰهُ بِهِۦٓ
أَن يُوصَلَ وَيُفْسِدُونَ فِي الْأَرْضِ أُولٰٓئِكَ
هُمُ الْخٰسِرُونَ ﴿٢٧﴾ كَيْفَ تَكْفُرُونَ بِاللّٰهِ
وَكُنتُمْ أَمْوٰتًا فَأَحْيٰكُمْ ثُمَّ يُمِيتُكُمْ ثُمَّ
يُحْيِيكُمْ ثُمَّ إِلَيْهِ تُرْجَعُونَ ﴿٢٨﴾ هُوَ الَّذِي

towards the space and fashioned seven perfect heavens (- denoting the multiplicity of cosmic system). He has full knowledge of all things.

SECTION 4

30. **A**ND (recall) when your Lord said to the angels, 'I am (according to My usual practice) going to appoint a supreme religious head in the land (to convey My Message to human beings and to execute My will in the universe).' They said, 'Will You create (also) therein such (people) as will cause disorder in it and shed blood while we already glorify You with Your true praise and extol Your holiness.' He (- God) answered, 'I know that which you do not know.'
31. And He taught Adam the names, all of them, then He presented (the objects of) these names to the angels and said, 'Tell Me the names of these (things) if what you say is right.'
32. They said, 'Glory be to You, we have no knowledge except that which You have given us; You, indeed, only You are the All-Knowing, the All-Wise.'
33. He said, 'Adam! Tell them (- the angels) their names (- names of the objects).' So when he had told them their names He said, 'Did I not tell you that, indeed I know the hidden realities of the heavens and of the earth, and I know what you reveal and what you conceal.'
34. And (recall) when We said to the angels, 'Make obeisance to Adam.' So they obeyed except *Iblîs*, he refused stubbornly and waxed proud, and he was already one of the disbelievers.
35. And We said, 'O Adam! Dwell you and your wife in this garden and eat freely and plentifully from it as you will. But you shall not go near this tree (- evil) lest you should be of the unjust.'
36. After sometime the satan caused them both to slip from this (order of not going near evil)

خَلَقَ لَكُم مَّا فِي الْأَرْضِ جَمِيعًا ثُمَّ اسْتَوَىٰ
إِلَى السَّمَاءِ فَسَوَّىٰهُنَّ سَبْعَ سَمَٰوَٰتٍ وَهُوَ
بِكُلِّ شَيْءٍ عَلِيمٌ ﴿٢٩﴾ وَإِذْ قَالَ رَبُّكَ لِلْمَلَٰٓئِكَةِ
إِنِّي جَاعِلٌ فِي الْأَرْضِ خَلِيفَةً قَالُوٓا أَتَجْعَلُ
فِيهَا مَن يُفْسِدُ فِيهَا وَيَسْفِكُ الدِّمَآءَ
وَنَحْنُ نُسَبِّحُ بِحَمْدِكَ وَنُقَدِّسُ لَكَ قَالَ
إِنِّيٓ أَعْلَمُ مَا لَا تَعْلَمُونَ ﴿٣٠﴾ وَعَلَّمَ ءَادَمَ الْأَسْمَآءَ
كُلَّهَا ثُمَّ عَرَضَهُمْ عَلَى الْمَلَٰٓئِكَةِ فَقَالَ أَنۢبِـُٔونِي
بِأَسْمَآءِ هَٰٓؤُلَآءِ إِن كُنتُمْ صَٰدِقِينَ ﴿٣١﴾ قَالُوا
سُبْحَٰنَكَ لَا عِلْمَ لَنَآ إِلَّا مَا عَلَّمْتَنَآ إِنَّكَ أَنتَ
الْعَلِيمُ الْحَكِيمُ ﴿٣٢﴾ قَالَ يَٰٓـَٔادَمُ أَنۢبِئْهُم بِأَسْمَآئِهِمْ
فَلَمَّآ أَنۢبَأَهُم بِأَسْمَآئِهِمْ قَالَ أَلَمْ أَقُل لَّكُمْ
إِنِّيٓ أَعْلَمُ غَيْبَ السَّمَٰوَٰتِ وَالْأَرْضِ وَأَعْلَمُ
مَا تُبْدُونَ وَمَا كُنتُمْ تَكْتُمُونَ ﴿٣٣﴾ وَإِذْ قُلْنَا
لِلْمَلَٰٓئِكَةِ اسْجُدُوا لِءَادَمَ فَسَجَدُوٓا إِلَّآ إِبْلِيسَ
أَبَىٰ وَاسْتَكْبَرَ وَكَانَ مِنَ الْكَٰفِرِينَ ﴿٣٤﴾ وَقُلْنَا
يَٰٓـَٔادَمُ اسْكُنْ أَنتَ وَزَوْجُكَ الْجَنَّةَ وَكُلَا
مِنْهَا رَغَدًا حَيْثُ شِئْتُمَا وَلَا تَقْرَبَا هَٰذِهِ
الشَّجَرَةَ فَتَكُونَا مِنَ الظَّٰلِمِينَ ﴿٣٥﴾ فَأَزَلَّهُمَا

and thus brought them out of (the happy state) which they were in. And We said (to them), ‘Go forth, some of you are enemies of others and for you there is a sojourn in this land and a provision for a time.’

37. After that Adam received from his Lord certain (useful) commandments and He turned to him with mercy. He, indeed is Oft-returning with compassion, the Ever Merciful.

38. We said, ‘Go forth from this state, all of you, and when there comes to you a guidance from Me, then, those who follow My guidance shall have nothing to fear and nothing to grieve at.’

39. And those who disbelieve and belie Our Messages, shall be the inmates of the Fire. There they shall abide for long.

SECTION 5

40. **O** Children of Israel! Remember My blessings which I bestowed upon you and fulfill the covenant (you made) with Me, I shall fulfill the covenant (I made) with you, and Me alone you should hold in awe.

41. And believe in what I have revealed (now) confirming (the prophecies of the Scripture) which are (already) with you, and do not be the first to deny it, neither take a paltry price for My Messages, and Me alone you should take as a shield (for protection).

42. Do not confound the truth with falsehood, nor conceal the truth knowingly.

43. And observe Prayer, present *Zakât* (- purifying alms) and devote yourselves (to the service of one God) along with those who are wholly devoted (to the service of one God).

44. How is it that you enjoin others to do good and neglect your ownselves while you recite the Scripture? Do you not even (after reading the Scripture) abstain (from evils)?

45. Seek (God’s) help through perfect perseverance and Prayer, and this is indeed a very

الشيطن عنها فأخرجهما مما كانا فيه
وقلنا اهبطوا بعضكم لبعض عدو ولكم
في الأرض مستقر ومتع إلى حين ﴿٣٦﴾
فتلقى ءادم من ربه كلمت فتاب عليه
إنه هو التواب الرحيم ﴿٣٧﴾ قلنا اهبطوا منها
جميعا فإما يأتينكم مني هدى فمن تبع
هداي فلا خوف عليهم ولا هم يحزنون ﴿٣٨﴾
والذين كفروا وكذبوا بأيتنا أولئك أصحب
النار هم فيها خلدون ﴿٣٩﴾ يبني إسرءيل
اذكروا نعمتي التي أنعمت عليكم وأوفوا
بعهدي أوف بعهدكم وإيي فارهبون ﴿٤٠﴾
وءامنوا بما أنزلت مصدقا لما معكم ولا
تكونوا أول كافر به ولا تشتروا بأيتي
ثمنا قليلا وإيي فاتقون ﴿٤١﴾ ولا تلبسوا
الحق بالبطل وتكتموا الحق وأنتم تعلمون ﴿٤٢﴾
وأقيموا الصلوة وءاتوا الزكوة واركعوا مع
الركعين ﴿٤٣﴾ أتأمرون الناس بالبر وتنسون
أنفسكم وأنتم تتلون الكتب أفلا تعقلون ﴿٤٤﴾
واستعينوا بالصبر والصلوة وإنها لكبيرة

hard thing except for those who are humble.
46. Who know for certain that they will meet their Lord and that they will return to Him.

SECTION 6

47. **O** CHILDREN of Israel! Remember My blessings which I bestowed upon you and that I exalted you above (your) contemporaries.
48. And guard yourself against (the agony of) the day when no human being shall avail another in anyway, nor an intercession be accepted on anyone's behalf, nor any compensation be taken from them, nor will they be helped.
49. And (recall) when We delivered you from the people of Pharaoh who subjected you to the worst torment. They went on slaying your sons and sparing your women (to make them immodest), and indeed that was a great ordeal from your Lord.
50. And when We parted the sea for you, and rescued you and drowned the people of Pharaoh, while you were beholding.
51. And when We made an appointment with Moses (that) of (spending) forty nights, (on Mount Sinai), then you took (to worship) the (golden) calf in his absence, and you were transgressors (in doing so).
52. Yet We pardoned you after that, so that you might give thanks.
53. And (recall) when We gave Moses the Scripture and the Discrimination (- clear proof and argument to know the right from the wrong), so that you might be guided aright.
54. And when Moses said to his people, 'O my people! You have indeed done injustice to your own selves by your taking (to the worship of) the calf so (you had better) turn (penitently) to your Creator Who gradually evolves you in your being, and kill your ring leaders. That indeed will be best for you in the sight of your Creator.' (Since you did as you were told,) He turned towards you with compassion. Verily, He alone is the Oft-Returning with compassion, and is the Ever Merciful.

إِلَّا عَلَى الْخٰشِعِينَ ﴿٤٥﴾ الَّذِينَ يَظُنُّونَ أَنَّهُم
مُّلٰقُوا رَبِّهِمْ وَ أَنَّهُمْ إِلَيْهِ رٰجِعُونَ ﴿٤٦﴾ يٰبَنِي
إِسْرٰٓءِيلَ اذْكُرُوا نِعْمَتِيَ الَّتِيٓ أَنْعَمْتُ عَلَيْكُمْ
وَ أَنِّي فَضَّلْتُكُمْ عَلَى الْعٰلَمِينَ ﴿٤٧﴾ وَ اتَّقُوا يَوْمًا
لَّا تَجْزِي نَفْسٌ عَنْ نَّفْسٍ شَيْـًٔا وَّ لَا يُقْبَلُ
مِنْهَا شَفٰعَةٌ وَّ لَا يُؤْخَذُ مِنْهَا عَدْلٌ وَّ لَا هُمْ
يُنْصَرُونَ ﴿٤٨﴾ وَ إِذْ نَجَّيْنٰكُمْ مِّنْ اٰلِ فِرْعَوْنَ
يَسُومُونَكُمْ سُوٓءَ الْعَذَابِ يُذَبِّحُونَ أَبْنَآءَكُمْ
وَ يَسْتَحْيُونَ نِسَآءَكُمْ وَ فِي ذٰلِكُمْ بَلَآءٌ مِّنْ
رَّبِّكُمْ عَظِيمٌ ﴿٤٩﴾ وَ إِذْ فَرَقْنَا بِكُمُ الْبَحْرَ
فَأَنْجَيْنٰكُمْ وَ أَغْرَقْنَآ اٰلَ فِرْعَوْنَ وَ أَنْتُمْ
تَنْظُرُونَ ﴿٥٠﴾ وَ إِذْ وٰعَدْنَا مُوسٰٓى أَرْبَعِينَ لَيْلَةً
ثُمَّ اتَّخَذْتُمُ الْعِجْلَ مِنْۢ بَعْدِهِ وَ أَنْتُمْ ظٰلِمُونَ ﴿٥١﴾
ثُمَّ عَفَوْنَا عَنْكُمْ مِّنْۢ بَعْدِ ذٰلِكَ لَعَلَّكُمْ
تَشْكُرُونَ ﴿٥٢﴾ وَ إِذْ اٰتَيْنَا مُوسَى الْكِتٰبَ
وَ الْفُرْقَانَ لَعَلَّكُمْ تَهْتَدُونَ ﴿٥٣﴾ وَ إِذْ قَالَ
مُوسٰى لِقَوْمِهِ يٰقَوْمِ إِنَّكُمْ ظَلَمْتُمْ أَنْفُسَكُمْ
بِاتِّخَاذِكُمُ الْعِجْلَ فَتُوبُوٓا إِلٰى بَارِئِكُمْ فَاقْتُلُوٓا
أَنْفُسَكُمْ ذٰلِكُمْ خَيْرٌ لَّكُمْ عِنْدَ بَارِئِكُمْ
فَتَابَ عَلَيْكُمْ إِنَّهُ هُوَ التَّوَّابُ الرَّحِيمُ ﴿٥٤﴾

55. And when you had said, 'O Moses! We shall, by no means, believe you unless we see Allâh openly (face to face).' Thereupon the thunderbolt (of punishment) overtook you and you were beholding (the consequences of your conduct).

56. Then We raised you up after your (death-like) stupor, so that you might give thanks.

57. Then We outspread the cloud to be a shade over you and We supplied you Manna and Quails, (saying,) 'Eat of the good things We have provided you.' They (disobeyed and by so doing) did Us no harm but it is to their own selves that they had been doing harm.

58. And when We said, 'Enter this (near-at-hand) township and eat from it as you wish freely, and enter the gate submissively and go on praying, ("O Lord!) Relieve us of the burden of our faults." We shall (then) protect you against the evil consequences of your faults and We shall multiply the reward of those who do good to others.'

59. But those who were bent on doing wrong, gave a different version to the order that was given them, (and thus acted contrary to the Divine will). So We sent down upon those who did wrong a pestilence from heaven because they had been transgressing persistently.

SECTION 7

60. **A**ND (recall the time) when Moses prayed for water for his people and We said (to him), 'Go with your people and smite that particular rock with your staff.' So (when he did so) there gushed forth from it twelve springs so that every tribe came to know of its drinking place. (We said,) 'Eat and drink of sustenance provided by Allâh and commit not transgression in the land like peace-breakers.'

61. And when you said, 'Moses! (We are weary of one kind of food so) we will not at all remain content with one and the same food, pray,

وَ إِذْ قُلْتُمْ يٰمُوْسٰى لَنْ نُّؤْمِنَ لَكَ حَتّٰى نَرَى
اللّٰهَ جَهْرَةً فَأَخَذَتْكُمُ الصّٰعِقَةُ وَ أَنْتُمْ
تَنْظُرُوْنَ ۝٥٥ ثُمَّ بَعَثْنٰكُمْ مِّنْۢ بَعْدِ مَوْتِكُمْ
لَعَلَّكُمْ تَشْكُرُوْنَ ۝٥٦ وَ ظَلَّلْنَا عَلَيْكُمُ الْغَمَامَ
وَ أَنْزَلْنَا عَلَيْكُمُ الْمَنَّ وَ السَّلْوٰى ۖ كُلُوْا مِنْ
طَيِّبٰتِ مَا رَزَقْنٰكُمْ ۖ وَ مَا ظَلَمُوْنَا وَ لٰكِنْ كَانُوْٓا
أَنْفُسَهُمْ يَظْلِمُوْنَ ۝٥٧ وَ إِذْ قُلْنَا ادْخُلُوْا هٰذِهِ
الْقَرْيَةَ فَكُلُوْا مِنْهَا حَيْثُ شِئْتُمْ رَغَدًا
وَّ ادْخُلُوا الْبَابَ سُجَّدًا وَّ قُوْلُوْا حِطَّةٌ نَّغْفِرْ لَكُمْ
خَطٰيٰكُمْ ۚ وَ سَنَزِيْدُ الْمُحْسِنِيْنَ ۝٥٨ فَبَدَّلَ الَّذِيْنَ
ظَلَمُوْا قَوْلًا غَيْرَ الَّذِيْ قِيْلَ لَهُمْ فَأَنْزَلْنَا عَلَى
الَّذِيْنَ ظَلَمُوْا رِجْزًا مِّنَ السَّمَآءِ بِمَا كَانُوْا
يَفْسُقُوْنَ ۝٥٩ وَ إِذِ اسْتَسْقٰى مُوْسٰى لِقَوْمِهٖ فَقُلْنَا
اضْرِبْ بِّعَصَاكَ الْحَجَرَ ۖ فَانْفَجَرَتْ مِنْهُ اثْنَتَا
عَشْرَةَ عَيْنًا ۖ قَدْ عَلِمَ كُلُّ أُنَاسٍ مَّشْرَبَهُمْ ۖ
كُلُوْا وَ اشْرَبُوْا مِنْ رِّزْقِ اللّٰهِ وَ لَا تَعْثَوْا فِي
الْأَرْضِ مُفْسِدِيْنَ ۝٦٠ وَ إِذْ قُلْتُمْ يٰمُوْسٰى لَنْ
نَّصْبِرَ عَلٰى طَعَامٍ وَّاحِدٍ فَادْعُ لَنَا رَبَّكَ يُخْرِجْ

therefore, to your Lord for us that He may bring forth for us some of that which the earth produces, of its vegetables, of its cucumbers, its corn, its lentils and its onions.' He (- God) said, 'Would you take in exchange that which is inferior (- delicious food) for that which is superior (- the realisation of the noble object of your life)? (If this is so) then go to some town and you will certainly have (there) all that you have demanded.' And lo! It so happened, they were smitten with abasement and destitution and they incurred the displeasure of Allâh. That was because they denied the Messages of Allâh and sought to kill His Prophets unjustly and that was because they disobeyed and had been transgressing.

SECTION 8

62. **S**URELY, those who (profess to) believe (in Islam), and those who follow the Jewish faith, the Christians and the Sabians, whosoever (of these truly) believes in Allâh and the Last Day and acts righteously shall have their reward with their Lord, and shall have nothing to fear, nor shall they grieve.

63. And (recall, O Children of Israel!) when We took a covenant from you, (and it was the time when you were at the foot of Sinai), with (the summits of) the Mount towering above you (saying), 'Hold fast to what We have given you, and bear in mind that which is in it, so that you may guard against evil.'

64. Then, (even) after that you went back (upon your covenant). Had it not been for the grace of Allâh and His mercy upon you, you would have certainly been of the losers.

65. And indeed you have come to know (the end of) those of you who transgressed regarding the Sabbath. Thereupon We said to them, 'Be you (as) apes, despised.'

66. Thus We made this (incident) an example to learn a lesson from, for those present at the time

لَنَا مِمَّا تُنْبِتُ الْأَرْضُ مِنْ بَقْلِهَا وَ قِثَّآئِهَا
وَفُوْمِهَا وَعَدَسِهَا وَبَصَلِهَا ؕ قَالَ أَتَسْتَبْدِلُوْنَ
الَّذِيْ هُوَ أَدْنٰى بِالَّذِيْ هُوَ خَيْرٌ ؕ اِهْبِطُوْا مِصْرًا
فَإِنَّ لَكُمْ مَّا سَأَلْتُمْ ؕ وَضُرِبَتْ عَلَيْهِمُ الذِّلَّةُ
وَالْمَسْكَنَةُ ۚ وَبَآءُوْ بِغَضَبٍ مِّنَ اللّٰهِ ؕ ذٰلِكَ بِأَنَّهُمْ
كَانُوْا يَكْفُرُوْنَ بِاٰيٰتِ اللّٰهِ وَيَقْتُلُوْنَ النَّبِيّٖنَ
بِغَيْرِ الْحَقِّ ؕ ذٰلِكَ بِمَا عَصَوْا وَّكَانُوْا يَعْتَدُوْنَ ﴿٦١﴾ ع ٧ ٧
إِنَّ الَّذِيْنَ اٰمَنُوْا وَالَّذِيْنَ هَادُوْا وَالنَّصٰرٰى
وَالصّٰبِـِٔيْنَ مَنْ اٰمَنَ بِاللّٰهِ وَالْيَوْمِ الْاٰخِرِ
وَعَمِلَ صَالِحًا فَلَهُمْ أَجْرُهُمْ عِنْدَ رَبِّهِمْ ۚ وَلَا
خَوْفٌ عَلَيْهِمْ وَلَا هُمْ يَحْزَنُوْنَ ﴿٦٢﴾ وَإِذْ أَخَذْنَا
مِيْثَاقَكُمْ وَرَفَعْنَا فَوْقَكُمُ الطُّوْرَ ؕ خُذُوْا مَآ
اٰتَيْنٰكُمْ بِقُوَّةٍ وَّاذْكُرُوْا مَا فِيْهِ لَعَلَّكُمْ تَتَّقُوْنَ ﴿٦٣﴾
ثُمَّ تَوَلَّيْتُمْ مِّنْۢ بَعْدِ ذٰلِكَ ۚ فَلَوْلَا فَضْلُ اللّٰهِ
عَلَيْكُمْ وَرَحْمَتُهٗ لَكُنْتُمْ مِّنَ الْخٰسِرِيْنَ ﴿٦٤﴾
وَلَقَدْ عَلِمْتُمُ الَّذِيْنَ اعْتَدَوْا مِنْكُمْ فِي السَّبْتِ
فَقُلْنَا لَهُمْ كُوْنُوْا قِرَدَةً خٰسِـِٔيْنَ ﴿٦٥﴾ فَجَعَلْنٰهَا
نَكَالًا لِّمَا بَيْنَ يَدَيْهَا وَمَا خَلْفَهَا وَمَوْعِظَةً

(of its occurrence) and (also) for those who came after it and an admonition to all those who guard against evil.

67. (Recall) when Moses said to his people for their own good, 'Verily, Allâh commands you to slaughter a cow.' They said, 'Do you make a mockery of us?' He said, 'I seek refuge with Allâh from being (one) of the ignorant.'

68. They said, 'Pray for us to your Lord to make clear to us what (kind of a cow) it is.' He replied, 'Says He, "It indeed is a cow neither too old nor too young, (but) of middle age, in between." Now do as you are commanded.'

69. They said, 'Pray for us to your Lord to make clear to us of what colour it is.' He replied, 'Says He, "It is a cow fawn of colour, is intensely rich in tone, very pleasing to the beholders".'

70. They said, 'Pray for us to your Lord to make clear to us what it (- the cow in question) is (definitely like); for (all such) cows are much alike to us, and we shall indeed, if Allâh will, be guided to the right goal.'

71. He said, 'He (- God) says, "It is indeed a cow neither broken in to plough the land nor to water the tillage, perfectly sound (without any blemish), no spot on her", (she is of one colour).' They said, 'Now you have (after all) brought the exact truth (with the necessary description).' So they slaughtered her, though they had no mind to do it.

SECTION 9

72. **AND** (recall also) when you had (nearly) killed a (great) man (- Jesus), then you differed among yourselves respecting it (- the crucifixion). And Allâh will bring to light that (- Jesus did not die on the cross) which you had been hiding.

73. So We said, 'Judge it in the context of its other circumstances.' That is how Allâh brings the dead (for Jesus being dead to all appearances) to life, and He shows you His signs so that you may refrain (from evil).

74. Then your hearts hardened after that, so that they were (hard) like rocks or harder still; for

لِّلْمُتَّقِينَ ﴿٦٦﴾ وَإِذْ قَالَ مُوسَىٰ لِقَوْمِهِ إِنَّ اللَّهَ
يَأْمُرُكُمْ أَن تَذْبَحُوا بَقَرَةً ۖ قَالُوا أَتَتَّخِذُنَا
هُزُوًا ۖ قَالَ أَعُوذُ بِاللَّهِ أَنْ أَكُونَ مِنَ
الْجَاهِلِينَ ﴿٦٧﴾ قَالُوا ادْعُ لَنَا رَبَّكَ يُبَيِّن لَّنَا
مَا هِيَ ۚ قَالَ إِنَّهُ يَقُولُ إِنَّهَا بَقَرَةٌ لَّا فَارِضٌ
وَلَا بِكْرٌ عَوَانٌ بَيْنَ ذَٰلِكَ ۖ فَافْعَلُوا مَا تُؤْمَرُونَ ﴿٦٨﴾
قَالُوا ادْعُ لَنَا رَبَّكَ يُبَيِّن لَّنَا مَا لَوْنُهَا ۚ
قَالَ إِنَّهُ يَقُولُ إِنَّهَا بَقَرَةٌ صَفْرَاءُ فَاقِعٌ
لَّوْنُهَا تَسُرُّ النَّاظِرِينَ ﴿٦٩﴾ قَالُوا ادْعُ لَنَا رَبَّكَ
يُبَيِّن لَّنَا مَا هِيَ إِنَّ الْبَقَرَ تَشَابَهَ عَلَيْنَا
وَإِنَّا إِن شَاءَ اللَّهُ لَمُهْتَدُونَ ﴿٧٠﴾ قَالَ إِنَّهُ
يَقُولُ إِنَّهَا بَقَرَةٌ لَّا ذَلُولٌ تُثِيرُ الْأَرْضَ وَلَا
تَسْقِي الْحَرْثَ مُسَلَّمَةٌ لَّا شِيَةَ فِيهَا ۚ قَالُوا
الْآنَ جِئْتَ بِالْحَقِّ ۚ فَذَبَحُوهَا وَمَا كَادُوا
يَفْعَلُونَ ﴿٧١﴾ وَإِذْ قَتَلْتُمْ نَفْسًا فَادَّارَأْتُمْ فِيهَا ۖ
وَاللَّهُ مُخْرِجٌ مَّا كُنتُمْ تَكْتُمُونَ ﴿٧٢﴾ فَقُلْنَا
اضْرِبُوهُ بِبَعْضِهَا ۚ كَذَٰلِكَ يُحْيِي اللَّهُ الْمَوْتَىٰ
وَيُرِيكُمْ آيَاتِهِ لَعَلَّكُمْ تَعْقِلُونَ ﴿٧٣﴾ ثُمَّ قَسَتْ
قُلُوبُكُم مِّن بَعْدِ ذَٰلِكَ فَهِيَ كَالْحِجَارَةِ

ع ٨

there are rocks out of which streams come gushing forth, and there are some others out of which (some) water comes forth when they split asunder. And indeed there are some (hearts) that humble themselves for awe of Allâh. And Allâh is not at all unmindful as to what you do.
75. Do you (O Muslims!) Expect that they will believe you while (you see) there are some of them who hear the Word of Allâh and then tamper with it after having fully understood it, and they know (that this way of theirs is wrong)?
76. And when they meet those who believe they say, 'We (too) have believed.' But when they go apart one with another they say, 'Do you inform them (- the Muslims) what Allâh has disclosed to you, (- of the prophecies in your Scriptures about the Prophet), that they thereby availing themselves of it (- the Scriptures), may prevail upon you in argumentation on the authority of your Lord? Will you not, then, use your reasoning power?'
77. Do they not know that Allâh knows all that they conceal and all that they make known?
78. And (some) among them are illiterate, who do not know the Scripture except cramming it up, and are doing nothing but making conjectures.
79. Woe, therefore, to those who write the Scripture with their own hands and then say, 'This is from Allâh.' They do so that they may thereby acquire some paltry gains. Woe to them for what their hands have written (to give them out as Word of God). Again (We say), woe to them for what they do (of evil deed).
80. (Inspite of their evil doings) they say, 'The Fire (of punishment) shall not touch us except for a few days.' Say, 'Have you taken a promise (for unconditional salvation) from Allâh?' (If you have,) then Allâh will never go back upon His promise. But (is it not a fact that) you attribute to Allâh things you do not know?'
81. The truth is that, those who do evil and who are encompassed by their sins, are the inmates

أَوْ أَشَدُّ قَسْوَةً ۚ وَإِنَّ مِنَ الْحِجَارَةِ لَمَا
يَتَفَجَّرُ مِنْهُ الْأَنْهَارُ ۚ وَإِنَّ مِنْهَا لَمَا يَشَّقَّقُ
فَيَخْرُجُ مِنْهُ الْمَاءُ ۚ وَإِنَّ مِنْهَا لَمَا يَهْبِطُ
مِنْ خَشْيَةِ اللَّهِ ۗ وَمَا اللَّهُ بِغَافِلٍ عَمَّا
تَعْمَلُونَ ۞ أَفَتَطْمَعُونَ أَنْ يُؤْمِنُوا لَكُمْ
وَقَدْ كَانَ فَرِيقٌ مِنْهُمْ يَسْمَعُونَ كَلَامَ
اللَّهِ ثُمَّ يُحَرِّفُونَهُ مِنْ بَعْدِ مَا عَقَلُوهُ
وَهُمْ يَعْلَمُونَ ﴿٧٥﴾ وَإِذَا لَقُوا الَّذِينَ آمَنُوا
قَالُوا آمَنَّا ۚ وَإِذَا خَلَا بَعْضُهُمْ إِلَىٰ بَعْضٍ
قَالُوا أَتُحَدِّثُونَهُمْ بِمَا فَتَحَ اللَّهُ عَلَيْكُمْ
لِيُحَاجُّوكُمْ بِهِ عِنْدَ رَبِّكُمْ ۚ أَفَلَا تَعْقِلُونَ ﴿٧٦﴾
أَوَلَا يَعْلَمُونَ أَنَّ اللَّهَ يَعْلَمُ مَا يُسِرُّونَ وَمَا
يُعْلِنُونَ ﴿٧٧﴾ وَمِنْهُمْ أُمِّيُّونَ لَا يَعْلَمُونَ الْكِتَابَ
إِلَّا أَمَانِيَّ وَإِنْ هُمْ إِلَّا يَظُنُّونَ ﴿٧٨﴾ فَوَيْلٌ
لِلَّذِينَ يَكْتُبُونَ الْكِتَابَ بِأَيْدِيهِمْ ثُمَّ
يَقُولُونَ هَٰذَا مِنْ عِنْدِ اللَّهِ لِيَشْتَرُوا بِهِ
ثَمَنًا قَلِيلًا ۖ فَوَيْلٌ لَهُمْ مِمَّا كَتَبَتْ أَيْدِيهِمْ
وَوَيْلٌ لَهُمْ مِمَّا يَكْسِبُونَ ﴿٧٩﴾ وَقَالُوا لَنْ
تَمَسَّنَا النَّارُ إِلَّا أَيَّامًا مَعْدُودَةً ۚ قُلْ
أَتَّخَذْتُمْ عِنْدَ اللَّهِ عَهْدًا فَلَنْ يُخْلِفَ اللَّهُ
عَهْدَهُ ۖ أَمْ تَقُولُونَ عَلَى اللَّهِ مَا لَا تَعْلَمُونَ ﴿٨٠﴾
بَلَىٰ مَنْ كَسَبَ سَيِّئَةً وَأَحَاطَتْ بِهِ
خَطِيئَتُهُ فَأُولَٰئِكَ أَصْحَابُ النَّارِ ۖ هُمْ فِيهَا

of the Fire and therein they shall abide for long.

82. But those who believe and do deeds of righteousness, it is they who are the owners of Paradise, therein they shall abide forever.

SECTION 10

83. **AND** (recall) when We took a covenant from the Children of Israel, 'You shall worship none except Allâh, and do good to (your) parents and to the near of kin and the orphans and the poor (as well), and you shall speak kindly to all people and observe Prayer and present purifying alms.' But (afterwards) you all turned away (and broke your covenant) except a few of you and you are averse (to guidance and ways of virtue).

84. And (recall) when We took a covenant from you, 'You shall not shed each other's blood and you shall not expel your people from your homes.' Then you confirmed it (promising to abide by it) and you witnessed (the covenant).

85. Yet, you are the very people who (violating the terms of the covenant) slay your own people and expel a section from among you from their homes, backing up one another against them sinfully and transgressingly. And if they come to you as captives (seeking your help), you ransom them, while their very expulsion was forbidden to you. Do you believe only in a part of the Script (- covenant) while a part you deny? What is the recompense of those among you (who act like that) except disgrace in this life? And on the Day of Resurrection they shall be given over to the severest chastisement. And Allâh is not at all unmindful as to what you do.

86. It is they who have taken the present life in preference to the Hereafter, therefore the agony shall not be reduced for them, nor they shall be helped (in any other way).

SECTION 11

87. **INDEED**, We gave Moses the Scripture and sent Messengers after him in successive series. We also gave Jesus, son of Mary, clear argu-

خٰلِدُوْنَ ﴿٨١﴾ وَ الَّذِيْنَ اٰمَنُوْا وَ عَمِلُوا الصّٰلِحٰتِ
أُولٰٓئِكَ أَصْحٰبُ الْجَنَّةِ ۚ هُمْ فِيْهَا خٰلِدُوْنَ ﴿٨٢﴾
وَ إِذْ أَخَذْنَا مِيْثٰقَ بَنِيْٓ إِسْرَآءِيْلَ لَا تَعْبُدُوْنَ
إِلَّا اللّٰهَ ۟ وَ بِالْوٰلِدَيْنِ إِحْسَانًا وَّ ذِي الْقُرْبٰى
وَ الْيَتٰمٰى وَ الْمَسٰكِيْنِ وَ قُوْلُوْا لِلنَّاسِ حُسْنًا
وَّ أَقِيْمُوا الصَّلٰوةَ وَ اٰتُوا الزَّكٰوةَ ۭ ثُمَّ تَوَلَّيْتُمْ
إِلَّا قَلِيْلًا مِّنْكُمْ وَ أَنْتُمْ مُّعْرِضُوْنَ ﴿٨٣﴾ وَ إِذْ
أَخَذْنَا مِيْثٰقَكُمْ لَا تَسْفِكُوْنَ دِمَآءَكُمْ
وَ لَا تُخْرِجُوْنَ أَنْفُسَكُمْ مِّنْ دِيٰرِكُمْ ثُمَّ
أَقْرَرْتُمْ وَ أَنْتُمْ تَشْهَدُوْنَ ﴿٨٤﴾ ثُمَّ أَنْتُمْ
هٰٓؤُلَآءِ تَقْتُلُوْنَ أَنْفُسَكُمْ وَ تُخْرِجُوْنَ فَرِيْقًا
مِّنْكُمْ مِّنْ دِيٰرِهِمْ تَظٰهَرُوْنَ عَلَيْهِمْ بِالْإِثْمِ
وَ الْعُدْوَانِ ۭ وَ إِنْ يَّأْتُوْكُمْ أُسٰرٰى تُفٰدُوْهُمْ
وَ هُوَ مُحَرَّمٌ عَلَيْكُمْ إِخْرَاجُهُمْ ۭ أَفَتُؤْمِنُوْنَ
بِبَعْضِ الْكِتٰبِ وَ تَكْفُرُوْنَ بِبَعْضٍ ۚ فَمَا جَزَآءُ
مَنْ يَّفْعَلُ ذٰلِكَ مِنْكُمْ إِلَّا خِزْيٌ فِي الْحَيٰوةِ
الدُّنْيَا ۚ وَ يَوْمَ الْقِيٰمَةِ يُرَدُّوْنَ إِلٰٓى أَشَدِّ الْعَذَابِ ۭ
وَ مَا اللّٰهُ بِغٰفِلٍ عَمَّا تَعْمَلُوْنَ ﴿٨٥﴾ أُولٰٓئِكَ الَّذِيْنَ
اشْتَرَوُا الْحَيٰوةَ الدُّنْيَا بِالْاٰخِرَةِ ۡ فَلَا يُخَفَّفُ
عَنْهُمُ الْعَذَابُ وَ لَا هُمْ يُنْصَرُوْنَ ﴿٨٦﴾ وَ لَقَدْ
اٰتَيْنَا مُوْسَى الْكِتٰبَ وَ قَفَّيْنَا مِنْۢ بَعْدِهٖ
بِالرُّسُلِ ۡ وَ اٰتَيْنَا عِيْسَى ابْنَ مَرْيَمَ الْبَيِّنٰتِ

ments and strengthened him with the blessed word of God. (Is it not then unjust on your part that) whenever a Messenger came to you (O Jews!) With that (teaching) which did not suit your fancies, you behaved arrogantly? You belied some (Messengers) while others you seek to kill (even now).

88. They said, 'Our hearts are storehouse of knowledge (so that we stand in no need of further teaching).' Rather Allâh has deprived them of His mercy for their disbelief, with the result that little they believe.

89. And (now) when there has come to them the glorious Book from Allâh, fulfilling that (Prophecy) which is already with them, and previous to that they had been praying for victory over those who disbelieved, yet when that (long awaited Prophet and the Qur'ân) came to them which they recognised (also to be the truth), they disbelieved in it. (And because of this rejection) the disapproval of Allâh is the due for the disbelievers.

90. Evil is that thing they have sold themselves for that they should reject that (source of guidance) which Allâh has revealed, grudging that Allâh should send down His grace on such of His servants as He pleases. Thus they have incurred (His) displeasure after displeasure. There awaits these disbelievers a humiliating punishment.

91. When it is said to them, 'Believe in that (-the Qur'ân) which Allâh has sent down.' They say, 'We believe only in that (- the Torah) which has been sent down to us.' And they deny every thing other than that (and which has since been revealed); though it (-the Qur'ân) is the lasting truth and corroborates that which is already with them (in their own Scriptures). Say, 'Why, then, did you seek to kill the Prophets of Allâh in former times if you were (real) believers (in the former Scriptures)?'

92. Moses did come to you with clear argu-

وَأَيَّدْنَٰهُ بِرُوحِ الْقُدُسِ ۗ أَفَكُلَّمَا جَآءَكُمْ
رَسُولٌ بِمَا لَا تَهْوَىٰٓ أَنفُسُكُمُ اسْتَكْبَرْتُمْ ۚ
فَفَرِيقًا كَذَّبْتُمْ وَفَرِيقًا تَقْتُلُونَ ﴿٨٧﴾ وَقَالُوا
قُلُوبُنَا غُلْفٌ ۚ بَل لَّعَنَهُمُ اللّٰهُ بِكُفْرِهِمْ فَقَلِيلًا
مَّا يُؤْمِنُونَ ﴿٨٨﴾ وَلَمَّا جَآءَهُمْ كِتَٰبٌ مِّنْ عِنْدِ
اللّٰهِ مُصَدِّقٌ لِّمَا مَعَهُمْ وَكَانُوا مِنْ قَبْلُ
يَسْتَفْتِحُونَ عَلَى الَّذِينَ كَفَرُوا ۚ فَلَمَّا جَآءَهُم
مَّا عَرَفُوا كَفَرُوا بِهِ ۚ فَلَعْنَةُ اللّٰهِ عَلَى الْكَٰفِرِينَ ﴿٨٩﴾
بِئْسَمَا اشْتَرَوْا بِهِۦٓ أَنفُسَهُمْ أَن يَكْفُرُوا بِمَآ
أَنزَلَ اللّٰهُ بَغْيًا أَن يُنَزِّلَ اللّٰهُ مِنْ فَضْلِهِ
عَلَىٰ مَن يَشَآءُ مِنْ عِبَادِهِ ۚ فَبَآءُو بِغَضَبٍ
عَلَىٰ غَضَبٍ ۚ وَلِلْكَٰفِرِينَ عَذَابٌ مُّهِينٌ ﴿٩٠﴾
وَإِذَا قِيلَ لَهُمْ ءَامِنُوا بِمَآ أَنزَلَ اللّٰهُ قَالُوا
نُؤْمِنُ بِمَآ أُنزِلَ عَلَيْنَا وَيَكْفُرُونَ بِمَا وَرَآءَهُ ۚ
وَهُوَ الْحَقُّ مُصَدِّقًا لِّمَا مَعَهُمْ ۗ قُلْ فَلِمَ
تَقْتُلُونَ أَنۢبِيَآءَ اللّٰهِ مِنْ قَبْلُ إِنْ كُنتُم
مُّؤْمِنِينَ ﴿٩١﴾ وَلَقَدْ جَآءَكُم مُّوسَىٰ بِالْبَيِّنَٰتِ

ments yet you took to the (worship of) the calf in his absence and you were not justified in doing so.

93. And (recall) when We took a covenant from you, (while you had encamped at the foot of Sinai) with (the summits of) the Mount towering above you, (and We had said,) 'Hold fast to that which we have given you and obey.' (But) those (of you who were given this commandment) said, 'We hear and we disobey.' Their hearts were, in fact, permeated with (the love of) the calf (worship) due to their disbelief. Say, 'Evil is the way to which your faith leads you, if you are believers at all.'

94. Say, 'If the last Abode with Allâh is especially reserved for you excluding all other people, then invoke death (upon yourself standing against the Prophet of Islam) if you are on the right.'

95. But never shall they invoke it, on account of that which their own hands have sent before. Allâh knows these wrongdoers very well.

96. And you shall of course find them the greediest of all people for (this base) life and even more (greedy) than those who set up equals (to God). Each one of them would love to be granted a life of a thousand years, yet his being spared for a long life shall, by no means keep him away from the punishment. And Allâh is Watchful of all their doings.

SECTION 12

97. **S**AY, 'He who is an enemy to Gabriel, because it is he who has brought down this (Qur'ân) on your heart by the command of Allâh, and which confirms (the Scriptures) which preceded it, and is a guidance and good tidings to the believers,

98. '(Let him bear in mind that) whoever is an enemy to Allâh and His angels and His Messengers and Gabriel and Michael, then, of course, Allâh (Himself) is an enemy to such disbelievers.'

99. And We indeed have sent down to you clear

ثُمَّ اتَّخَذْتُمُ الْعِجْلَ مِنْ بَعْدِهِ وَأَنْتُمْ
ظٰلِمُونَ ﴿٩٢﴾ وَإِذْ أَخَذْنَا مِيثٰقَكُمْ وَرَفَعْنَا
فَوْقَكُمُ الطُّورَ خُذُوا مَا آتَيْنٰكُمْ بِقُوَّةٍ وَاسْمَعُوا
قَالُوا سَمِعْنَا وَعَصَيْنَا وَأُشْرِبُوا فِي قُلُوبِهِمُ
الْعِجْلَ بِكُفْرِهِمْ قُلْ بِئْسَمَا يَأْمُرُكُمْ بِهِ
إِيمٰنُكُمْ إِنْ كُنْتُمْ مُؤْمِنِينَ ﴿٩٣﴾ قُلْ إِنْ كَانَتْ
لَكُمُ الدَّارُ الْآخِرَةُ عِنْدَ اللهِ خَالِصَةً مِنْ
دُونِ النَّاسِ فَتَمَنَّوُا الْمَوْتَ إِنْ كُنْتُمْ
صٰدِقِينَ ﴿٩٤﴾ وَلَنْ يَتَمَنَّوْهُ أَبَدًا بِمَا قَدَّمَتْ
أَيْدِيهِمْ وَاللهُ عَلِيمٌ بِالظّٰلِمِينَ ﴿٩٥﴾ وَلَتَجِدَنَّهُمْ
أَحْرَصَ النَّاسِ عَلٰى حَيٰوةٍ وَمِنَ الَّذِينَ
أَشْرَكُوا يَوَدُّ أَحَدُهُمْ لَوْ يُعَمَّرُ أَلْفَ سَنَةٍ
وَمَا هُوَ بِمُزَحْزِحِهِ مِنَ الْعَذَابِ أَنْ يُعَمَّرَ
وَاللهُ بَصِيرٌ بِمَا يَعْمَلُونَ ﴿٩٦﴾ قُلْ مَنْ كَانَ
عَدُوًّا لِجِبْرِيلَ فَإِنَّهُ نَزَّلَهُ عَلٰى قَلْبِكَ بِإِذْنِ
اللهِ مُصَدِّقًا لِمَا بَيْنَ يَدَيْهِ وَهُدًى وَبُشْرٰى
لِلْمُؤْمِنِينَ ﴿٩٧﴾ مَنْ كَانَ عَدُوًّا لِلّٰهِ وَمَلٰئِكَتِهِ
وَرُسُلِهِ وَجِبْرِيلَ وَمِيكٰلَ فَإِنَّ اللهَ عَدُوٌّ
لِلْكٰفِرِينَ ﴿٩٨﴾ وَلَقَدْ أَنْزَلْنَا إِلَيْكَ آيٰتٍ بَيِّنٰتٍ

arguments which none but the disobedient reject.
100. Is it not a fact that every time they made a covenant, some of them cast it away? Rather most of them have no (true) faith.
101. And (now) when a great Messenger (Muhammad) has come to them from Allâh confirming that (Scripture) which is with them, a party of those who were given the Scripture cast away the Book of Allâh behind their backs, as if they know (it) not.
102. Moreover, they (- the Jews of the Prophet's time) pursue (the same tactics) which the rebels had followed against the empire of Solomon. And it was not Solomon that had committed breach of faith, but it was the rebels that had committed breach of faith. They (- the Jews of Madînah) teach the people the modes of intriguing; and also (pursue) that which had (once) been revealed to the two angels, Hârût and Mârût in Babylon. But these two would not teach (anything to) anyone without first declaring, 'We are but a trial (for you here), do not, therefore commit breach of faith.' So they (- the followers of Hârût and Mârût), learnt from them that (teaching) by which they made a distinction between man and his wife, (- they taught men only and not women), yet they would not harm anyone thereby (by their practice), save by the command of Allâh. But these people (- the Jews of the Prophet's time, on the contrary) are learning things that would harm them and do them no good. (They do it) even though they know that he who adopts this course will have no share (of good) in the Hereafter. Indeed, evil is that thing which they have sold themselves for. Had they but known (this fact).
103. And if these (Jews) had kept their faith and guarded against these evils, surely they would have received a better reward from Allâh. Had they but known (it).

وَمَا يَكْفُرُ بِهَآ إِلَّا الْفٰسِقُونَ ﴿٩٩﴾ أَوَكُلَّمَا
عٰهَدُوا عَهْدًا نَّبَذَهُ فَرِيقٌ مِّنْهُمْ بَلْ
أَكْثَرُهُمْ لَا يُؤْمِنُونَ ﴿١٠٠﴾ وَلَمَّا جَآءَهُمْ رَسُولٌ
مِّنْ عِنْدِ اللّٰهِ مُصَدِّقٌ لِّمَا مَعَهُمْ نَبَذَ فَرِيقٌ
مِّنَ الَّذِينَ أُوتُوا الْكِتٰبَ كِتٰبَ اللّٰهِ وَرَآءَ
ظُهُورِهِمْ كَأَنَّهُمْ لَا يَعْلَمُونَ ﴿١٠١﴾ وَاتَّبَعُوا مَا
تَتْلُوا الشَّيٰطِينُ عَلٰى مُلْكِ سُلَيْمٰنَ وَمَا
كَفَرَ سُلَيْمٰنُ وَلٰكِنَّ الشَّيٰطِينَ كَفَرُوا يُعَلِّمُونَ
النَّاسَ السِّحْرَ وَمَآ أُنْزِلَ عَلَى الْمَلَكَيْنِ
بِبَابِلَ هٰرُوتَ وَمٰرُوتَ وَمَا يُعَلِّمَانِ مِنْ
أَحَدٍ حَتّٰى يَقُولَآ إِنَّمَا نَحْنُ فِتْنَةٌ فَلَا تَكْفُرْ
فَيَتَعَلَّمُونَ مِنْهُمَا مَا يُفَرِّقُونَ بِهِ بَيْنَ الْمَرْءِ
وَزَوْجِهِ وَمَا هُمْ بِضَآرِّينَ بِهِ مِنْ أَحَدٍ
إِلَّا بِإِذْنِ اللّٰهِ وَيَتَعَلَّمُونَ مَا يَضُرُّهُمْ وَلَا
يَنْفَعُهُمْ وَلَقَدْ عَلِمُوا لَمَنِ اشْتَرٰىهُ مَا لَهُ
فِي الْأٰخِرَةِ مِنْ خَلٰقٍ وَلَبِئْسَ مَا شَرَوْا بِهِ
أَنْفُسَهُمْ لَوْ كَانُوا يَعْلَمُونَ ﴿١٠٢﴾ وَلَوْ أَنَّهُمْ ءَامَنُوا
وَاتَّقَوْا لَمَثُوبَةٌ مِّنْ عِنْدِ اللّٰهِ خَيْرٌ لَّوْ كَانُوا

SECTION 13

104. **O** YOU who believe! Say not (while addressing the Prophet), 'Râ'inâ!' (-Listen to us - a word used also for showing disrespect for the person addressed), rather say (an equivocal phrase), 'Unzurna!' (- we beg your attention), and listen to him attentively, (that you stand not in need of any such phrases that have double meanings, one in a good sense, the other in a bad one). Indeed there awaits the disbelievers a grievous punishment.

105. Neither those from among the people of the Scripture who disbelieved, nor the polytheists like that any good should be sent down to you from your Lord. But Allâh singles out for His mercy whomsoever He wishes (to receive His mercy), and Allâh is of abounding bounty.

106. Whatever Message We abrogate or abandon it, We bring a better (Message) than that or (at least) the like of it. Do you not know that Allâh is indeed Possessor of power to do all He will.

107. Do you not know that to Allâh alone belongs the sovereignty of the heavens and the earth, and that you have, apart from Allâh, neither a protecting friend, nor a helper.

108. Rather you (Jews) like to question your Messenger (unduly) as Moses was questioned before? And he who adopts disbelief instead of belief, had undoubtedly strayed from the straight direction of the path.

109. Many of the people of the Scripture would love to turn you back after your having believed, into disbelievers, out of selfish envy, and after the truth (of this Qur'ân) has become apparent to them. But pardon (them) and overlook until Allâh shall make manifest His will, indeed Allâh is Possessor of every power to do all He will.

110. And observe the Prayer and present the *Zakât* (- purifying alms) and whatever good you send forward for yourselves you will find it with Allâh. Verily, Allâh is Watchful of all that you do.

يَعْلَمُونَ ۝١٠٣ يٰٓأَيُّهَا الَّذِينَ ءَامَنُوا لَا تَقُولُوا رٰعِنَا
وَقُولُوا انْظُرْنَا وَاسْمَعُوا ۗ وَلِلْكٰفِرِينَ عَذَابٌ
أَلِيمٌ ۝١٠٤ مَا يَوَدُّ الَّذِينَ كَفَرُوا مِنْ أَهْلِ
الْكِتٰبِ وَلَا الْمُشْرِكِينَ أَنْ يُنَزَّلَ عَلَيْكُمْ
مِنْ خَيْرٍ مِنْ رَبِّكُمْ ۗ وَاللَّهُ يَخْتَصُّ بِرَحْمَتِهِ
مَنْ يَشَاءُ ۗ وَاللَّهُ ذُو الْفَضْلِ الْعَظِيمِ ۝١٠٥ مَا
نَنْسَخْ مِنْ ءَايَةٍ أَوْ نُنْسِهَا نَأْتِ بِخَيْرٍ مِنْهَآ
أَوْ مِثْلِهَا ۗ أَلَمْ تَعْلَمْ أَنَّ اللَّهَ عَلَىٰ كُلِّ شَيْءٍ
قَدِيرٌ ۝١٠٦ أَلَمْ تَعْلَمْ أَنَّ اللَّهَ لَهُ مُلْكُ السَّمٰوٰتِ
وَالْأَرْضِ ۗ وَمَا لَكُمْ مِنْ دُونِ اللَّهِ مِنْ
وَلِيٍّ وَلَا نَصِيرٍ ۝١٠٧ أَمْ تُرِيدُونَ أَنْ تَسْـَٔلُوا
رَسُولَكُمْ كَمَا سُئِلَ مُوسَىٰ مِنْ قَبْلُ ۗ
وَمَنْ يَتَبَدَّلِ الْكُفْرَ بِالْإِيمٰنِ فَقَدْ ضَلَّ
سَوَاءَ السَّبِيلِ ۝١٠٨ وَدَّ كَثِيرٌ مِنْ أَهْلِ الْكِتٰبِ
لَوْ يَرُدُّونَكُمْ مِنْ بَعْدِ إِيمٰنِكُمْ كُفَّارًا ۚ حَسَدًا
مِنْ عِنْدِ أَنْفُسِهِمْ مِنْ بَعْدِ مَا تَبَيَّنَ لَهُمُ
الْحَقُّ ۖ فَاعْفُوا وَاصْفَحُوا حَتَّىٰ يَأْتِيَ اللَّهُ بِأَمْرِهِ ۗ
إِنَّ اللَّهَ عَلَىٰ كُلِّ شَيْءٍ قَدِيرٌ ۝١٠٩ وَأَقِيمُوا الصَّلٰوةَ
وَءَاتُوا الزَّكٰوةَ ۚ وَمَا تُقَدِّمُوا لِأَنْفُسِكُمْ مِنْ خَيْرٍ
تَجِدُوهُ عِنْدَ اللَّهِ ۗ إِنَّ اللَّهَ بِمَا تَعْمَلُونَ بَصِيرٌ ۝١١٠

111. And they (- the Jews and the Christians) say (respectively about themselves), 'None shall ever enter Paradise unless he be a Jew or a Christian.' These are their wishful beliefs. Say, 'Bring forth your vivid proof (of what you state) if you are right.'

112. The truth of the matter is, whosoever submits himself entirely to Allâh and he is a doer of good to others shall have his reward with his Lord. They shall have nothing to fear and nothing to grieve at.

SECTION 14

113. **T**HE Jews say, 'The Christians have no valid ground whatsoever (for their belief),' while the Christians assert, 'The Jews have no valid ground (at all for their belief),' while they both read the same Scripture. Exactly such (ill-founded) things say those who have no knowledge. But Allâh shall judge between them on the Day of Resurrection with regard to all that about which they had been disagreeing.

114. And who can be more unjust than those who prohibit the name of Allâh from being extolled in (any of His) houses of worship and strive to ruin them. It was not proper for such, ever to enter these (places) except in fear and awe. For them is disgrace in this world, and there awaits them a severe punishment in the Hereafter.

115. And to Allâh belongs the east and the west; so whichsoever way you may turn (you will find) there is Allâh's attention. Surely, Allâh is All-Pervading, All-Knowing.

116. Moreover they (- the unjust people) say, 'Allâh has taken (to Himself) a son.' Glory be to Him. Rather, all that is in the heavens and the earth, belongs to Him. All are obedient to Him.

117. (God is) the Wonderful Originator without depending upon any matter or pattern of the heavens and the earth; and when He issues a decree He does but say to it, 'Be' and it comes to be.

118. And those who do not know (the wisdom implied in Divine revelation) say, 'Why does

وَقَالُوا لَنْ يَدْخُلَ الْجَنَّةَ إِلَّا مَنْ كَانَ هُودًا
أَوْ نَصَارَىٰ ۗ تِلْكَ أَمَانِيُّهُمْ ۗ قُلْ هَاتُوا بُرْهَانَكُمْ
إِنْ كُنْتُمْ صَادِقِينَ ﴿١١١﴾ بَلَىٰ مَنْ أَسْلَمَ وَجْهَهُ
لِلَّهِ وَهُوَ مُحْسِنٌ فَلَهُ أَجْرُهُ عِنْدَ رَبِّهِ
وَلَا خَوْفٌ عَلَيْهِمْ وَلَا هُمْ يَحْزَنُونَ ﴿١١٢﴾ وَقَالَتِ
الْيَهُودُ لَيْسَتِ النَّصَارَىٰ عَلَىٰ شَيْءٍ وَقَالَتِ
النَّصَارَىٰ لَيْسَتِ الْيَهُودُ عَلَىٰ شَيْءٍ وَهُمْ
يَتْلُونَ الْكِتَابَ ۗ كَذَٰلِكَ قَالَ الَّذِينَ لَا يَعْلَمُونَ
مِثْلَ قَوْلِهِمْ ۚ فَاللَّهُ يَحْكُمُ بَيْنَهُمْ يَوْمَ الْقِيَامَةِ
فِيمَا كَانُوا فِيهِ يَخْتَلِفُونَ ﴿١١٣﴾ وَمَنْ أَظْلَمُ
مِمَّنْ مَنَعَ مَسَاجِدَ اللَّهِ أَنْ يُذْكَرَ فِيهَا
اسْمُهُ وَسَعَىٰ فِي خَرَابِهَا ۚ أُولَٰئِكَ مَا كَانَ
لَهُمْ أَنْ يَدْخُلُوهَا إِلَّا خَائِفِينَ ۚ لَهُمْ فِي
الدُّنْيَا خِزْيٌ وَلَهُمْ فِي الْآخِرَةِ عَذَابٌ عَظِيمٌ ﴿١١٤﴾
وَلِلَّهِ الْمَشْرِقُ وَالْمَغْرِبُ ۚ فَأَيْنَمَا تُوَلُّوا فَثَمَّ
وَجْهُ اللَّهِ ۚ إِنَّ اللَّهَ وَاسِعٌ عَلِيمٌ ﴿١١٥﴾ وَقَالُوا
اتَّخَذَ اللَّهُ وَلَدًا ۗ سُبْحَانَهُ ۖ بَلْ لَهُ مَا فِي
السَّمَاوَاتِ وَالْأَرْضِ ۖ كُلٌّ لَهُ قَانِتُونَ ﴿١١٦﴾ بَدِيعُ
السَّمَاوَاتِ وَالْأَرْضِ ۖ وَإِذَا قَضَىٰ أَمْرًا فَإِنَّمَا
يَقُولُ لَهُ كُنْ فَيَكُونُ ﴿١١٧﴾ وَقَالَ الَّذِينَ لَا
يَعْلَمُونَ لَوْلَا يُكَلِّمُنَا اللَّهُ أَوْ تَأْتِينَا آيَةٌ ۗ كَذَٰلِكَ

not Allâh (Himself) speak to us or give us a (convincing) sign?' That is exactly what their predecessors had said. Their hearts have become very much alike. We have certainly made (Our) signs explicitly clear for a people who wish to be convinced.

119. Verily, We have sent you to serve all their requirements, as a Bearer of good tidings and a Warner, and you will not be called upon to account for the inmates of the flaming Fire.

120. And the Jews will never be pleased with you nor the Christians unless you follow their creed. Say, 'Allâh's guidance is the only perfect and true guidance.' If you were to follow their low desires after there has come to you this perfect knowledge, you shall have from Allâh neither a protecting friend, nor any helper.

121. They (- the true Muslims), to whom We have given the Book, follow it as it deserves to be followed. It is they who truly believe in it. And who so does not believe therein, these are they who are the utter losers.

SECTION 15

122. **O** CHILDREN of Israel! Remember My favour which I conferred upon you, and that I exalted you above all your contemporaries.

123. And guard (yourselves) against (the agony of) the day when no being shall avail another in anyway nor any compensation be accepted on anyone's behalf, nor any intercession shall be profitable to anyone nor they shall be helped.

124. (Recall) when his Lord put Abraham to test with certain commandments, so he carried them out. (God) said, 'Verily, I will make you an Imâm (- a religious leader) for the good of the people.' (Abraham) said (inquiringly), 'And from among my progeny (too, do You promise to raise leaders)?' (God) said, '(Yes, but) My (this) covenant does not embrace the wrongdoers.'

125. And when We made the House (- the *Ka'bah* at Makkah) a frequent resort for people and (a place of) peace and security, and

قَالَ الَّذِينَ مِنْ قَبْلِهِمْ مِثْلَ قَوْلِهِمْ تَشَابَهَتْ
قُلُوبُهُمْ قَدْ بَيَّنَّا الْآيَاتِ لِقَوْمٍ يُوقِنُونَ ﴿١١٨﴾ إِنَّا
أَرْسَلْنَاكَ بِالْحَقِّ بَشِيرًا وَنَذِيرًا وَلَا تُسْأَلُ
عَنْ أَصْحَابِ الْجَحِيمِ ﴿١١٩﴾ وَلَنْ تَرْضَىٰ عَنْكَ
الْيَهُودُ وَلَا النَّصَارَىٰ حَتَّىٰ تَتَّبِعَ مِلَّتَهُمْ قُلْ
إِنَّ هُدَى اللَّهِ هُوَ الْهُدَىٰ وَلَئِنِ اتَّبَعْتَ
أَهْوَاءَهُمْ بَعْدَ الَّذِي جَاءَكَ مِنَ الْعِلْمِ مَا
لَكَ مِنَ اللَّهِ مِنْ وَلِيٍّ وَلَا نَصِيرٍ ﴿١٢٠﴾ الَّذِينَ
آتَيْنَاهُمُ الْكِتَابَ يَتْلُونَهُ حَقَّ تِلَاوَتِهِ أُولَٰئِكَ
يُؤْمِنُونَ بِهِ وَمَنْ يَكْفُرْ بِهِ فَأُولَٰئِكَ هُمُ
الْخَاسِرُونَ ﴿١٢١﴾ يَا بَنِي إِسْرَائِيلَ اذْكُرُوا نِعْمَتِيَ
الَّتِي أَنْعَمْتُ عَلَيْكُمْ وَأَنِّي فَضَّلْتُكُمْ عَلَى
الْعَالَمِينَ ﴿١٢٢﴾ وَاتَّقُوا يَوْمًا لَا تَجْزِي نَفْسٌ عَنْ
نَفْسٍ شَيْئًا وَلَا يُقْبَلُ مِنْهَا عَدْلٌ وَلَا تَنْفَعُهَا
شَفَاعَةٌ وَلَا هُمْ يُنْصَرُونَ ﴿١٢٣﴾ وَإِذِ ابْتَلَىٰ إِبْرَاهِيمَ
رَبُّهُ بِكَلِمَاتٍ فَأَتَمَّهُنَّ قَالَ إِنِّي جَاعِلُكَ لِلنَّاسِ
إِمَامًا قَالَ وَمِنْ ذُرِّيَّتِي قَالَ لَا يَنَالُ
عَهْدِي الظَّالِمِينَ ﴿١٢٤﴾ وَإِذْ جَعَلْنَا الْبَيْتَ مَثَابَةً
لِلنَّاسِ وَأَمْنًا وَاتَّخِذُوا مِنْ مَقَامِ إِبْرَاهِيمَ

(We commanded), 'Take to yourselves the place of Abraham (- the *Ka'bah*) for a centre (and face towards it) during Prayer.' And We enjoined Abraham and Ismâîl, 'Purify and clean My House for those who perform the circuit (around it) and those who cleave to it for devotion and for those who bow down (before Allâh) and prostrate (to Him in Prayer).'

126. And when Abraham said (praying), 'My Lord! Make this (Makkah) a city of peace and provide its inhabitants, such of them who believe in Allâh and the Last Day, with fruits.' (God) said, 'And on him too who disbelieves I will bestow favours for a little while, then I will drive him to the punishment of the Fire. What an evil end!'

127. And when Abraham raised the foundations of the House and Ismâîl (with him, and they were praying), 'Our Lord! Accept (this service) from us, You, indeed, You are the All-Hearing, the All-Knowing.

128. 'Our Lord! Make us both submissive servants to You (alone), and (raise) from our progeny a community submissive (and preaching virtue and submissiveness) to You, and show us our ways of worship and turn to us with mercy, for only You are the Oft-Returning (with compassion), the Ever Merciful.

129. 'Our Lord! Do raise among them a great Messenger from among themselves, who may recite to them Your Messages and teach them the Book and Wisdom, and may purify them. You, indeed, You are the All-Mighty, the All-Wise.'

SECTION 16

130. **A**ND who will show aversion to Abraham's creed except he who has befooled himself. We did make him Our chosen one in this world, and surely he, in the Hereafter will surely be (counted) among the righteous.

131. When his Lord said to him, 'Submit,' he said, 'I have already submitted to the Lord of the worlds.'

132. The same (faith) did Abraham enjoin upon his sons and (so did) Jacob (saying), 'My sons!

مُصَلًّى ؕ وَعَهِدْنَآ إِلَىٰٓ إِبْرٰهٖمَ وَإِسْمٰعِيْلَ أَنْ
طَهِّرَا بَيْتِيَ لِلطَّآئِفِيْنَ وَالْعٰكِفِيْنَ وَالرُّكَّعِ
السُّجُوْدِ ﴿١٢٥﴾ وَإِذْ قَالَ إِبْرٰهٖمُ رَبِّ اجْعَلْ
هٰذَا بَلَدًا أٰمِنًا وَّارْزُقْ أَهْلَهٗ مِنَ الثَّمَرٰتِ
مَنْ أٰمَنَ مِنْهُمْ بِاللّٰهِ وَالْيَوْمِ الْأٰخِرِ ؕ قَالَ
وَمَنْ كَفَرَ فَأُمَتِّعُهٗ قَلِيْلًا ثُمَّ أَضْطَرُّهٗٓ إِلٰى
عَذَابِ النَّارِ ؕ وَبِئْسَ الْمَصِيْرُ ﴿١٢٦﴾ وَإِذْ يَرْفَعُ
إِبْرٰهٖمُ الْقَوَاعِدَ مِنَ الْبَيْتِ وَإِسْمٰعِيْلُ ؕ رَبَّنَا
تَقَبَّلْ مِنَّا ؕ إِنَّكَ أَنْتَ السَّمِيْعُ الْعَلِيْمُ ﴿١٢٧﴾ رَبَّنَا
وَاجْعَلْنَا مُسْلِمَيْنِ لَكَ وَمِنْ ذُرِّيَّتِنَآ أُمَّةً
مُّسْلِمَةً لَّكَ ۪ وَأَرِنَا مَنَاسِكَنَا وَتُبْ عَلَيْنَا ۚ
إِنَّكَ أَنْتَ التَّوَّابُ الرَّحِيْمُ ﴿١٢٨﴾ رَبَّنَا وَابْعَثْ
فِيْهِمْ رَسُوْلًا مِّنْهُمْ يَتْلُوْا عَلَيْهِمْ أٰيٰتِكَ
وَيُعَلِّمُهُمُ الْكِتٰبَ وَالْحِكْمَةَ وَيُزَكِّيْهِمْ ؕ إِنَّكَ
أَنْتَ الْعَزِيْزُ الْحَكِيْمُ ﴿١٢٩﴾ وَمَنْ يَّرْغَبُ عَنْ مِّلَّةِ
إِبْرٰهٖمَ إِلَّا مَنْ سَفِهَ نَفْسَهٗ ؕ وَلَقَدِ اصْطَفَيْنٰهُ
فِي الدُّنْيَا ۚ وَإِنَّهٗ فِي الْأٰخِرَةِ لَمِنَ الصّٰلِحِيْنَ ﴿١٣٠﴾
إِذْ قَالَ لَهٗ رَبُّهٗٓ أَسْلِمْ ۙ قَالَ أَسْلَمْتُ لِرَبِّ
الْعٰلَمِيْنَ ﴿١٣١﴾ وَوَصّٰى بِهَآ إِبْرٰهٖمُ بَنِيْهِ وَيَعْقُوْبُ ؕ

ع ٨ ١٥

Surely, Allâh has chosen for you this faith. See that when you die you are in a state of complete submission (according to His will).'

133. Were you present when death visited Jacob, and when he said to his sons, 'What (God) will you worship after me?' They replied, 'We will worship your God, the God of your fathers - Abraham, Ismâîl and Isaac, the only One God, and to Him do we submit ourselves.'

134. This was a community (preaching righteousness) which has passed away; for them is (the fruit of) what (good deeds) they performed, while for you is (the reward of) what (noble deeds) you perform. You will not be called upon to account for their deeds.

135. And they (the Jews and the Christians respectively) said, 'Be Jews or be Christians, then you shall be on the right course.' Say, 'Nay, but (ours is) the faith of Abraham, the upright, and he was not of the polytheist.'

136. Say, 'We believe in Allâh and in that (the Qur'ân) which has been revealed to us, and what was revealed to Abraham and Ismâîl and Isaac and Jacob and his children, and what was given to Moses and Jesus and (we believe) in what was given to (all other) Prophets from their Lord. We (while believing in them) make no discrimination between anyone of them, and to Him do we submit ourselves entirely.'

137. Now, if they believe just as (sincerely) as you have believed in this (Qur'ân), then, of course, they are guided aright. But if they turn back then they are only in schism, (and fighting against the truth). In that case Allâh will surely suffice you against them for He is the All-Hearing, the All-Knowing.

138. (Assume) the hues (and the attributes) of Allâh! And who is fairer than Allâh's hues (and attributes)? We are His worshippers ever.

139. Say, 'Do you dispute with us with regard to Allâh, while He is our Lord and your Lord (as well). We shall be judged by our deeds, and you

يَٰبَنِيَّ إِنَّ اللَّهَ اصْطَفَىٰ لَكُمُ الدِّينَ فَلَا تَمُوتُنَّ
إِلَّا وَأَنتُم مُّسْلِمُونَ ﴿١٣٢﴾ أَمْ كُنتُمْ شُهَدَاءَ إِذْ حَضَرَ
يَعْقُوبَ الْمَوْتُ إِذْ قَالَ لِبَنِيهِ مَا تَعْبُدُونَ مِن
بَعْدِي ۖ قَالُوا نَعْبُدُ إِلَٰهَكَ وَإِلَٰهَ آبَائِكَ إِبْرَاهِيمَ
وَإِسْمَاعِيلَ وَإِسْحَاقَ إِلَٰهًا وَاحِدًا ۚ وَنَحْنُ لَهُ
مُسْلِمُونَ ﴿١٣٣﴾ تِلْكَ أُمَّةٌ قَدْ خَلَتْ ۖ لَهَا مَا كَسَبَتْ
وَلَكُم مَّا كَسَبْتُمْ ۖ وَلَا تُسْأَلُونَ عَمَّا كَانُوا يَعْمَلُونَ ﴿١٣٤﴾
وَقَالُوا كُونُوا هُودًا أَوْ نَصَارَىٰ تَهْتَدُوا ۗ قُلْ
بَلْ مِلَّةَ إِبْرَاهِيمَ حَنِيفًا ۖ وَمَا كَانَ مِنَ
الْمُشْرِكِينَ ﴿١٣٥﴾ قُولُوا آمَنَّا بِاللَّهِ وَمَا أُنزِلَ إِلَيْنَا
وَمَا أُنزِلَ إِلَىٰ إِبْرَاهِيمَ وَإِسْمَاعِيلَ وَإِسْحَاقَ
وَيَعْقُوبَ وَالْأَسْبَاطِ وَمَا أُوتِيَ مُوسَىٰ
وَعِيسَىٰ وَمَا أُوتِيَ النَّبِيُّونَ مِن رَّبِّهِمْ لَا
نُفَرِّقُ بَيْنَ أَحَدٍ مِّنْهُمْ وَنَحْنُ لَهُ مُسْلِمُونَ ﴿١٣٦﴾
فَإِنْ آمَنُوا بِمِثْلِ مَا آمَنتُم بِهِ فَقَدِ اهْتَدَوا ۖ
وَّإِن تَوَلَّوْا فَإِنَّمَا هُمْ فِي شِقَاقٍ ۖ فَسَيَكْفِيكَهُمُ
اللَّهُ ۚ وَهُوَ السَّمِيعُ الْعَلِيمُ ﴿١٣٧﴾ صِبْغَةَ اللَّهِ ۖ
وَمَنْ أَحْسَنُ مِنَ اللَّهِ صِبْغَةً ۖ وَنَحْنُ لَهُ
عَابِدُونَ ﴿١٣٨﴾ قُلْ أَتُحَاجُّونَنَا فِي اللَّهِ وَهُوَ رَبُّنَا
وَرَبُّكُمْ وَلَنَا أَعْمَالُنَا وَلَكُمْ أَعْمَالُكُمْ وَنَحْنُ

by your deeds, and to Him alone are we sincerely devoted.

140. Do you (O Jews and the Christians!) say that Abraham, Ismâîl, Isaac, Jacob and his children were Jews or Christians? Say, 'Have you then greater knowledge or (is it) Allâh (Who knows better)?' And who is more unjust than he who conceals the testimony he has from Allâh. And Allâh is not at all unaware of what you do.'

141. These are a community (preaching righteousness) that have passed away; for them is (the good fruit of) what (good deeds) they performed, while for you is (the reward of) what (good and noble deeds) you perform. And you shall not be called to account for their deeds.

لَهُ مُخْلِصُونَ ﴿١٣٩﴾ أَمْ تَقُولُونَ إِنَّ إِبْرٰهِـمَ
وَإِسْمٰعِيلَ وَإِسْحٰقَ وَيَعْقُوبَ وَالْأَسْبَاطَ كَانُوا
هُودًا أَوْ نَصٰرٰى قُلْ ءَأَنْتُمْ أَعْلَمُ أَمِ اللّٰهُ
وَمَنْ أَظْلَمُ مِمَّنْ كَتَمَ شَهٰدَةً عِنْدَهُ مِنَ
اللّٰهِ وَمَا اللّٰهُ بِغٰفِلٍ عَمَّا تَعْمَلُونَ ﴿١٤٠﴾ تِلْكَ
أُمَّةٌ قَدْ خَلَتْ لَهَا مَا كَسَبَتْ وَلَكُمْ مَّا
كَسَبْتُمْ وَلَا تُسْـَٔلُونَ عَمَّا كَانُوا يَعْمَلُونَ ﴿١٤١﴾

PART الْجُزْءُ الثَّانِي II

SECTION 17

142. **T**HE weak-minded among the people will say, 'What has made these (Muslims) turn from their (first) *Qiblah* (- the direction they were facing in their Prayer, the holy place of worship at Jerusalem) to which they conformed (so far)?' Say, 'To Allâh belongs the east and the west, He guides him who wishes (to be guided) to the right path.'

143. And thus have We made you a nation exalted and justly balanced so that you may be a guiding example for all people (by carrying to them what you have learnt about Islam), and this perfect Messenger (of God) may be a guiding example for you. And We did not make that which you would have to be the *Qiblah* but that We might distinguish him who follows the Messenger from him who turns upon his heels. And this (change of *Qiblah*) is indeed a hard (test) except for those whom Allâh has guided aright. It was not Allâh's purpose that your faith and your worship should go in vain. Surely, Allâh is Compassionate and Ever Merciful to the people.

144. Verily, We have seen the turning of your

سَيَقُولُ السُّفَهَآءُ مِنَ النَّاسِ مَا وَلّٰهُمْ
عَنْ قِبْلَتِهِمُ الَّتِي كَانُوا عَلَيْهَا قُلْ لِّلّٰهِ
الْمَشْرِقُ وَالْمَغْرِبُ يَهْدِي مَنْ يَّشَآءُ
إِلٰى صِرٰطٍ مُّسْتَقِيمٍ ﴿١٤٢﴾ وَكَذٰلِكَ جَعَلْنٰكُمْ
أُمَّةً وَّسَطًا لِّتَكُونُوا شُهَدَآءَ عَلَى النَّاسِ
وَيَكُونَ الرَّسُولُ عَلَيْكُمْ شَهِيدًا وَمَا
جَعَلْنَا الْقِبْلَةَ الَّتِي كُنْتَ عَلَيْهَآ إِلَّا لِنَعْلَمَ
مَنْ يَّتَّبِعُ الرَّسُولَ مِمَّنْ يَّنْقَلِبُ عَلٰى
عَقِبَيْهِ وَإِنْ كَانَتْ لَكَبِيرَةً إِلَّا عَلَى
الَّذِينَ هَدَى اللّٰهُ وَمَا كَانَ اللّٰهُ لِيُضِيعَ
إِيمٰنَكُمْ إِنَّ اللّٰهَ بِالنَّاسِ لَرَءُوفٌ رَّحِيمٌ ﴿١٤٣﴾
قَدْ نَرٰى تَقَلُّبَ وَجْهِكَ فِي السَّمَآءِ فَلَنُوَلِّيَنَّكَ
قِبْلَةً تَرْضٰهَا فَوَلِّ وَجْهَكَ شَطْرَ الْمَسْجِدِ

attention (O Prophet!) repeatedly towards heaven, We will certainly give you possession of the *Qiblah* of your liking. So turn your attention in the direction of *Masjid al-Harâm* (- the Holy Mosque at Makkah) and wherever you (O Muslims!) be, turn your attentions in the direction of it. And surely those (scholars) who have been given the Scripture know for certain that this (change of *Qiblah*) is a true commandment proceeding from their Lord. And (as for the disbelievers,) Allâh is not at all unmindful as to what they do.

145. And even if you should bring to those (who went astray and) who have been given the Scripture (before you) all kinds of signs together, they would not follow your *Qiblah,* nor would you be the follower of their *Qiblah,* nor would some of them be the follower of one another's *Qiblah.* And if you (O reader!) should follow their low desires after (all) this knowledge that has come to you, then indeed, you would be of the unjust.

146. Those (of the righteous) to whom We have given the Book recognize him (- the Prophet and his truthfulness) as they recognize their own sons, but some of them do conceal the truth even though they know it.

147. It is the truth from your Lord, so (O reader!) do not be of those who doubt and so waver.

SECTION 18

148. **A**ND everyone has an ideal for which he bears up, so (your ideal should be to) vie one with another in doing all (moral and physical) good deeds. Wherever you may be, Allâh will bring you all together. Allâh indeed is the Possessor of full power to do all that He will.

149. And from wherever you (O Prophet!) may go forth keep your attention fixed in the direction of *Masjid al-Harâm* (- the Holy Mosque at Makkah) for that indeed is the true commandment proceeding from your Lord, and Allâh is not at all unaware of what you do.

150. And from wherever you come forth (for

الْحَرَامِ وَحَيْثُ مَا كُنْتُمْ فَوَلُّوا وُجُوهَكُمْ شَطْرَهُ
وَإِنَّ الَّذِينَ أُوتُوا الْكِتٰبَ لَيَعْلَمُونَ أَنَّهُ
الْحَقُّ مِنْ رَبِّهِمْ وَمَا اللّٰهُ بِغٰفِلٍ عَمَّا
يَعْمَلُونَ ﴿١٤٤﴾ وَلَئِنْ أَتَيْتَ الَّذِينَ أُوتُوا
الْكِتٰبَ بِكُلِّ آيَةٍ مَا تَبِعُوا قِبْلَتَكَ وَمَا
أَنْتَ بِتَابِعٍ قِبْلَتَهُمْ وَمَا بَعْضُهُمْ بِتَابِعٍ
قِبْلَةَ بَعْضٍ وَلَئِنِ اتَّبَعْتَ أَهْوَاءَهُمْ مِنْ
بَعْدِ مَا جَاءَكَ مِنَ الْعِلْمِ إِنَّكَ إِذًا لَمِنَ
الظّٰلِمِينَ ﴿١٤٥﴾ الَّذِينَ آتَيْنٰهُمُ الْكِتٰبَ يَعْرِفُونَهُ
كَمَا يَعْرِفُونَ أَبْنَاءَهُمْ وَإِنَّ فَرِيقًا مِنْهُمْ
لَيَكْتُمُونَ الْحَقَّ وَهُمْ يَعْلَمُونَ ﴿١٤٦﴾ الْحَقُّ
مِنْ رَبِّكَ فَلَا تَكُونَنَّ مِنَ الْمُمْتَرِينَ ﴿١٤٧﴾ ع ١٧ / ١
وَلِكُلٍّ وِجْهَةٌ هُوَ مُوَلِّيهَا فَاسْتَبِقُوا الْخَيْرٰتِ
أَيْنَ مَا تَكُونُوا يَأْتِ بِكُمُ اللّٰهُ جَمِيعًا إِنَّ
اللّٰهَ عَلَى كُلِّ شَيْءٍ قَدِيرٌ ﴿١٤٨﴾ وَمِنْ حَيْثُ
خَرَجْتَ فَوَلِّ وَجْهَكَ شَطْرَ الْمَسْجِدِ الْحَرَامِ
وَإِنَّهُ لَلْحَقُّ مِنْ رَبِّكَ وَمَا اللّٰهُ بِغٰفِلٍ عَمَّا
تَعْمَلُونَ ﴿١٤٩﴾ وَمِنْ حَيْثُ خَرَجْتَ فَوَلِّ وَجْهَكَ

saying your Prayer) turn your attention in the direction of *Masjid al-Harâm.* And wherever you may be (O Muslims!), turn your faces in the direction of it, that people may have no excuse against you, except such of those as are unjust, then do not fear them (as they follow the wrong course), but you need only stand in awe of Me. And (this command has been given to you) that I may perfect My blessings upon you and that you may attain your goal.

151. Just as (the *Ka'bah* is a means to your guidance so,) We have sent to you a great Messenger from among yourselves who recites to you Our Messages and purifies you and teaches you the Book and the Wisdom and teaches you what you did not know.

152. So glorify Me and I will grant you eminence and be thankful to Me, and be not ungrateful to Me (for My favours to you).

SECTION 19

153. **O** YOU who believe! Seek (God's) help with perfect patience and Prayer, for surely Allâh is with the patiently persevering.

154. And do not count as dead those who are killed in the cause of Allâh. Rather (they are) living, only you perceive not (their life).

155. And We will certainly reward you (after discipling you) with something after fear and hunger and some loss of substance and of lives and with fruits (of your toils). Give good tidings to the patiently preserving;

156. Who, when a calamity befalls them, say, 'Surely, we belong to Allâh and to Him, of course, we return (and in His will is our peace).'

157. It is they upon whom descend the benedictions from their Lord and His mercy, and it is they who are guided aright.

158. The *Safâ* and the *Marwah* (- the two eminences near *Ka'bah*) are certainly (two) of the symbols of Allâh, so he who is on Pilgrimage to the House or performs *'Umrah* (- a visit

شَطْرَ الْمَسْجِدِ الْحَرَامِ ۚ وَحَيْثُ مَا كُنْتُمْ
فَوَلُّوا وُجُوهَكُمْ شَطْرَهُ لِئَلَّا يَكُونَ لِلنَّاسِ
عَلَيْكُمْ حُجَّةٌ ۖ إِلَّا الَّذِينَ ظَلَمُوا مِنْهُمْ
فَلَا تَخْشَوْهُمْ وَاخْشَوْنِي ۚ وَلِأُتِمَّ نِعْمَتِي
عَلَيْكُمْ وَلَعَلَّكُمْ تَهْتَدُونَ ﴿١٥٠﴾ كَمَا أَرْسَلْنَا
فِيكُمْ رَسُولًا مِنْكُمْ يَتْلُوا عَلَيْكُمْ آيَاتِنَا
وَيُزَكِّيكُمْ وَيُعَلِّمُكُمُ الْكِتَابَ وَالْحِكْمَةَ
وَيُعَلِّمُكُمْ مَا لَمْ تَكُونُوا تَعْلَمُونَ ﴿١٥١﴾ فَاذْكُرُونِي
أَذْكُرْكُمْ وَاشْكُرُوا لِي وَلَا تَكْفُرُونِ ﴿١٥٢﴾ ع ٥ ٢
يَا أَيُّهَا الَّذِينَ آمَنُوا اسْتَعِينُوا بِالصَّبْرِ وَالصَّلَاةِ
إِنَّ اللَّهَ مَعَ الصَّابِرِينَ ﴿١٥٣﴾ وَلَا تَقُولُوا لِمَنْ
يُقْتَلُ فِي سَبِيلِ اللَّهِ أَمْوَاتٌ ۚ بَلْ أَحْيَاءٌ
وَلَٰكِنْ لَا تَشْعُرُونَ ﴿١٥٤﴾ وَلَنَبْلُوَنَّكُمْ بِشَيْءٍ
مِنَ الْخَوْفِ وَالْجُوعِ وَنَقْصٍ مِنَ الْأَمْوَالِ
وَالْأَنْفُسِ وَالثَّمَرَاتِ ۗ وَبَشِّرِ الصَّابِرِينَ ﴿١٥٥﴾
الَّذِينَ إِذَا أَصَابَتْهُمْ مُصِيبَةٌ قَالُوا إِنَّا
لِلَّهِ وَإِنَّا إِلَيْهِ رَاجِعُونَ ﴿١٥٦﴾ أُولَٰئِكَ عَلَيْهِمْ
صَلَوَاتٌ مِنْ رَبِّهِمْ وَرَحْمَةٌ ۖ وَأُولَٰئِكَ
هُمُ الْمُهْتَدُونَ ﴿١٥٧﴾ إِنَّ الصَّفَا وَالْمَرْوَةَ مِنْ
شَعَائِرِ اللَّهِ ۖ فَمَنْ حَجَّ الْبَيْتَ أَوِ اعْتَمَرَ
فَلَا جُنَاحَ عَلَيْهِ أَنْ يَطَّوَّفَ بِهِمَا ۚ وَمَنْ

to *Ka'bah*), there is no blame on him to perform *Tawâf* (- to run between) the two (eminences), and he who remains thoroughly dutiful and chooses to do good deeds spontaneously, then surely (he will find) Allâh is Appreciative and rewards every good deed done. Surely, Allâh is All-Knowing.

159. Verily, those who conceal the clear evidences and the guidance which We have revealed, after We have explained them to the people in this Book, these it is whom Allâh deprives of His mercy and also disapprove all those who can disapprove,

160. Except such (of them) as repent and mend (themselves) and declare clearly (the truth which they used to hide), it is they to whom I shall turn with mercy, for I am the Oft-Returning (with compassion and) the Ever Merciful.

161. But those who persist in disbelief and die while they are disbelievers, these are the ones upon whom be the disapproval of Allâh and of the angels and of people and (in short) of all of them.

162. They shall remain in this (state of disapproval) for long. Their punishment shall not be reduced for them, and no respite shall be given to them.

163. And your God is One God, there is no other, cannot be and will never be one worthy of worship but He, the Most Gracious, the Ever Merciful.

تَطَوَّعَ خَيْرًا فَإِنَّ اللّٰهَ شَاكِرٌ عَلِيمٌ ﴿١٥٨﴾ إِنَّ
الَّذِينَ يَكْتُمُونَ مَا أَنْزَلْنَا مِنَ الْبَيِّنٰتِ
وَالْهُدٰى مِنْ بَعْدِ مَا بَيَّنّٰهُ لِلنَّاسِ فِي
الْكِتٰبِ أُولٰٓئِكَ يَلْعَنُهُمُ اللّٰهُ وَيَلْعَنُهُمُ
اللّٰعِنُونَ ﴿١٥٩﴾ إِلَّا الَّذِينَ تَابُوا وَأَصْلَحُوا
وَبَيَّنُوا فَأُولٰٓئِكَ أَتُوبُ عَلَيْهِمْ وَأَنَا التَّوَّابُ
الرَّحِيمُ ﴿١٦٠﴾ إِنَّ الَّذِينَ كَفَرُوا وَمَاتُوا وَهُمْ
كُفَّارٌ أُولٰٓئِكَ عَلَيْهِمْ لَعْنَةُ اللّٰهِ وَالْمَلٰٓئِكَةِ
وَالنَّاسِ أَجْمَعِينَ ﴿١٦١﴾ خٰلِدِينَ فِيهَا لَا
يُخَفَّفُ عَنْهُمُ الْعَذَابُ وَلَا هُمْ يُنْظَرُونَ ﴿١٦٢﴾
وَإِلٰهُكُمْ إِلٰهٌ وّٰحِدٌ لَا إِلٰهَ إِلَّا هُوَ الرَّحْمٰنُ
الرَّحِيمُ ﴿١٦٣﴾ إِنَّ فِي خَلْقِ السَّمٰوٰتِ وَالْأَرْضِ
وَاخْتِلٰفِ الَّيْلِ وَالنَّهَارِ وَالْفُلْكِ الَّتِي
تَجْرِي فِي الْبَحْرِ بِمَا يَنْفَعُ النَّاسَ وَمَا
أَنْزَلَ اللّٰهُ مِنَ السَّمَآءِ مِنْ مَّآءٍ فَأَحْيَا بِهِ
الْأَرْضَ بَعْدَ مَوْتِهَا وَبَثَّ فِيهَا مِنْ كُلِّ
دَآبَّةٍ وَّتَصْرِيفِ الرِّيٰحِ وَالسَّحَابِ الْمُسَخَّرِ
بَيْنَ السَّمَآءِ وَالْأَرْضِ لَأٰيٰتٍ لِّقَوْمٍ يَعْقِلُونَ ﴿١٦٤﴾

SECTION 20

164. VERILY, in the creation of the heavens and the earth and in the alternation and the sequence of the night and the day and in the ships that sail in the ocean carrying the things which are useful to the people and in the water which Allâh sends down from the clouds with which He brings the dead earth in to life and (in) all sorts of crawling animals which He has spread all over it and (in) the turning about of the winds and (in) the clouds subjected to (His) law between the heavens and the earth, there are, indeed, signs for a people who use their understanding.

165. (Inspite of all these evidences in support of the unity of God) there are some people who take to themselves compeers as opposed to Allâh. They love them as they should love Allâh. But those who believe are stauncher in (their) love for Allâh. And if only those who committed this wrong could but see (the time) when they shall see the punishment, (they would realize) that the complete power only belongs to Allâh and that Allâh is Severe at inflicting the punishment.
166. (At that time) when those who were followed (- the leaders) shall disown and sever themselves from their followers and they shall see the punishment (with their own eyes) and all their ties and means shall be cut asunder.
167. And (at that time) the followers shall say, 'If we could only return (to the life of the world) we would disown them and sever ourselves from them as they disowned and severed themselves from us.' Thus Allâh will make them regret their deeds and they shall never (of themselves) get out of the Fire.

SECTION 21

168. **O** PEOPLE! Eat what is lawful and pure (of the produces) of the earth and follow not the footsteps of satan for he is your enemy severing you (from Allâh).
169. He (- satan) only bids you to indulge in evil and to (do) things foul and obscene and that you say against Allâh things you do not know.
170. And when it is said to them (- the disbelievers), 'Follow what Allâh has revealed.' They say, 'We would rather follow such things as we found our forefathers (doing and believing).' (Would they do so) even though their forefathers could not refrain (from evil), nor they could achieve their goal.
171. The case of (one that calls) those who refuse (to obey the commandments of God) is like the case of one who shouts to one (- an animal) who hears nothing, but a mere call and

وَمِنَ النَّاسِ مَنْ يَتَّخِذُ مِنْ دُونِ اللهِ
أَنْدَادًا يُحِبُّونَهُمْ كَحُبِّ اللهِ ۖ وَالَّذِينَ
آمَنُوا أَشَدُّ حُبًّا لِلَّهِ ۗ وَلَوْ يَرَى الَّذِينَ ظَلَمُوا
إِذْ يَرَوْنَ الْعَذَابَ أَنَّ الْقُوَّةَ لِلَّهِ جَمِيعًا
وَأَنَّ اللهَ شَدِيدُ الْعَذَابِ ﴿١٦٥﴾ إِذْ تَبَرَّأَ الَّذِينَ
اتُّبِعُوا مِنَ الَّذِينَ اتَّبَعُوا وَرَأَوُا الْعَذَابَ
وَتَقَطَّعَتْ بِهِمُ الْأَسْبَابُ ﴿١٦٦﴾ وَقَالَ الَّذِينَ
اتَّبَعُوا لَوْ أَنَّ لَنَا كَرَّةً فَنَتَبَرَّأَ مِنْهُمْ كَمَا
تَبَرَّءُوا مِنَّا ۗ كَذَٰلِكَ يُرِيهِمُ اللهُ أَعْمَالَهُمْ
حَسَرَاتٍ عَلَيْهِمْ ۖ وَمَا هُمْ بِخَارِجِينَ مِنَ النَّارِ ﴿١٦٧﴾ ع
يَا أَيُّهَا النَّاسُ كُلُوا مِمَّا فِي الْأَرْضِ حَلَالًا
طَيِّبًا ۖ وَلَا تَتَّبِعُوا خُطُوَاتِ الشَّيْطَانِ ۚ إِنَّهُ
لَكُمْ عَدُوٌّ مُبِينٌ ﴿١٦٨﴾ إِنَّمَا يَأْمُرُكُمْ بِالسُّوءِ
وَالْفَحْشَاءِ وَأَنْ تَقُولُوا عَلَى اللهِ مَا لَا
تَعْلَمُونَ ﴿١٦٩﴾ وَإِذَا قِيلَ لَهُمُ اتَّبِعُوا مَا أَنْزَلَ
اللهُ قَالُوا بَلْ نَتَّبِعُ مَا أَلْفَيْنَا عَلَيْهِ
آبَاءَنَا ۗ أَوَلَوْ كَانَ آبَاؤُهُمْ لَا يَعْقِلُونَ
شَيْئًا وَلَا يَهْتَدُونَ ﴿١٧٠﴾ وَمَثَلُ الَّذِينَ كَفَرُوا
كَمَثَلِ الَّذِي يَنْعِقُ بِمَا لَا يَسْمَعُ إِلَّا دُعَاءً

a cry (of a shepherd). (They are) deaf, dumb and blind, moreover they do not use their reason.

172. O you who believe! Eat of the good and pure things We have provided you with, and render thanks to Allâh, if it is He alone Whom you really worship.

173. He has forbidden you only (to eat carrion) that which dies of itself, the blood, the flesh of swine and that over (the sacrifice of) which the name of someone other than Allâh has been invoked. Yet he who is constrained (to use them) without desiring (them) nor going beyond the limits (of bare necessity), incurs no sin. Surely, Allâh is Great Protector, Ever Merciful.

174. Surely, those who hide (any part of the teaching) which Allâh has revealed in this perfect Book and take a paltry price (- worldly gains) for it, it is these who feed their bellies with nothing but fire, and Allâh will not speak to them (with affection and mercy) on the Day of Resurrection, nor He will treat them as pure, and there awaits them a grievous punishment.

175. It is these who have preferred error to guidance and punishment to protection. (The onlookers of these sufferers will say,) 'How very enduring they are at (the punishment of) the Fire!'

176. That (punishment) is because, whereas Allâh caused the perfect Book to be revealed to suit all the requirements of truth and wisdom (they have rejected it outright). Surely, those who dissented from the perfect Book have indeed gone far astray in enmity (of the truth) and in obstinacy.

SECTION 22

177. **I**T is not the sole virtue that you turn your faces to the east or the west but true virtue is theirs, who believe in Allâh, the Last Day, the angels, the Book, and in the Prophets; and who give away their wealth (and substance) out of love for Him, to the near of kin, the orphans, the needy, the wayfarer and to those who ask (in

وَنِدَاءً صُمٌّۢ بُكْمٌ عُمْيٌ فَهُمْ لَا يَعْقِلُونَ ﴿١٧١﴾
يَٰٓأَيُّهَا الَّذِينَ اٰمَنُوا كُلُوا مِنْ طَيِّبٰتِ مَا
رَزَقْنٰكُمْ وَاشْكُرُوا لِلّٰهِ إِنْ كُنْتُمْ إِيَّاهُ
تَعْبُدُونَ ﴿١٧٢﴾ إِنَّمَا حَرَّمَ عَلَيْكُمُ الْمَيْتَةَ
وَالدَّمَ وَلَحْمَ الْخِنْزِيرِ وَمَآ أُهِلَّ بِهٖ
لِغَيْرِ اللّٰهِ ۚ فَمَنِ اضْطُرَّ غَيْرَ بَاغٍ وَّلَا
عَادٍ فَلَآ إِثْمَ عَلَيْهِ ۗ إِنَّ اللّٰهَ غَفُورٌ
رَّحِيمٌ ﴿١٧٣﴾ إِنَّ الَّذِينَ يَكْتُمُونَ مَآ أَنْزَلَ
اللّٰهُ مِنَ الْكِتٰبِ وَيَشْتَرُونَ بِهٖ ثَمَنًا
قَلِيلًا ۙ أُولٰٓئِكَ مَا يَأْكُلُونَ فِي بُطُونِهِمْ
إِلَّا النَّارَ وَلَا يُكَلِّمُهُمُ اللّٰهُ يَوْمَ الْقِيٰمَةِ
وَلَا يُزَكِّيهِمْ ۚ وَلَهُمْ عَذَابٌ أَلِيمٌ ﴿١٧٤﴾ أُولٰٓئِكَ
الَّذِينَ اشْتَرَوُا الضَّلٰلَةَ بِالْهُدٰى وَالْعَذَابَ
بِالْمَغْفِرَةِ ۚ فَمَآ أَصْبَرَهُمْ عَلَى النَّارِ ﴿١٧٥﴾ ذٰلِكَ
بِأَنَّ اللّٰهَ نَزَّلَ الْكِتٰبَ بِالْحَقِّ ۗ وَإِنَّ الَّذِينَ
اخْتَلَفُوا فِي الْكِتٰبِ لَفِي شِقَاقٍ بَعِيدٍ ﴿١٧٦﴾ لَيْسَ
الْبِرَّ أَنْ تُوَلُّوا وُجُوهَكُمْ قِبَلَ الْمَشْرِقِ
وَالْمَغْرِبِ وَلٰكِنَّ الْبِرَّ مَنْ اٰمَنَ بِاللّٰهِ
وَالْيَوْمِ الْاٰخِرِ وَالْمَلٰٓئِكَةِ وَالْكِتٰبِ وَالنَّبِيّٖنَ ۚ
وَاٰتَى الْمَالَ عَلٰى حُبِّهٖ ذَوِي الْقُرْبٰى وَالْيَتٰمٰى
وَالْمَسٰكِينَ وَابْنَ السَّبِيلِ ۙ وَالسَّآئِلِينَ
وَفِي الرِّقَابِ ۚ وَأَقَامَ الصَّلٰوةَ وَاٰتَى الزَّكٰوةَ ۚ

charity) and in ransoming the slaves; and who observe the Prayer, who go on presenting the *Zakât* (- the purifying alms) and those who always fulfill their pledges and agreements when they have made one, and those who are patiently persevering in adversity and distress and (steadfast) in times of war. It is these who have proved truthful (in their promises and in their faith) and it is these who are strictly guarded against evil.

178. O you who believe! Equitable retaliation has been ordained for you in (the matter of) the slain. (Everyone shall pay for his own crime,) the freeman (murderer) for the freeman (murdered), and the slave (murderer) for the slave (murdered), and the female (murderer) for the female (murdered), but as for him who has been granted any remission by his (aggrieved) brother (or family) then pursuing (of the matter) shall be done with equity and fairness, and the payment (of the blood money) to him (the heir) should be made in a handsome manner. This is an alleviation from your Lord and a mercy. But he who exceeds the limits after this (commandment), for him is a grievous punishment.

179. O people of pure and clear wisdom! Your very life lies in (the law of) equitable retaliation, (you have been commanded) so that you may enjoy security.

180. It has been prescribed for you at the time of death to any one of you, that if the (dying) person is leaving considerable wealth behind, to make a will to his parents and the near of kin to act with equity and fairness. This is an obligation incumbent on those who guard against evil.

181. He who alters it (- the will) after he has heard it, (should know that) it is those that alter it who shall bear the burden of sin. Allâh indeed is All-Hearing, All-Knowing.

182. If anyone apprehends that the testator is partial or follows a sinful course there will be

وَالْمُوفُونَ بِعَهْدِهِمْ إِذَا عٰهَدُوا ۚ وَالصّٰبِرِينَ
فِي الْبَأْسَآءِ وَالضَّرَّآءِ وَحِينَ الْبَأْسِ ۗ أُولٰٓئِكَ
الَّذِينَ صَدَقُوا ۖ وَأُولٰٓئِكَ هُمُ الْمُتَّقُونَ ﴿١٧٧﴾ يٰٓأَيُّهَا
الَّذِينَ اٰمَنُوا كُتِبَ عَلَيْكُمُ الْقِصَاصُ فِي
الْقَتْلَى ۖ الْحُرُّ بِالْحُرِّ وَالْعَبْدُ بِالْعَبْدِ وَالْأُنْثٰى
بِالْأُنْثٰى ۚ فَمَنْ عُفِيَ لَهُ مِنْ أَخِيهِ شَيْءٌ
فَاتِّبَاعٌ بِالْمَعْرُوفِ وَأَدَآءٌ إِلَيْهِ بِإِحْسٰنٍ ۗ
ذٰلِكَ تَخْفِيفٌ مِّنْ رَّبِّكُمْ وَرَحْمَةٌ ۗ فَمَنِ
اعْتَدٰى بَعْدَ ذٰلِكَ فَلَهُ عَذَابٌ أَلِيمٌ ﴿١٧٨﴾
وَلَكُمْ فِي الْقِصَاصِ حَيٰوةٌ يّٰٓأُولِي الْأَلْبٰبِ
لَعَلَّكُمْ تَتَّقُونَ ﴿١٧٩﴾ كُتِبَ عَلَيْكُمْ إِذَا حَضَرَ
أَحَدَكُمُ الْمَوْتُ إِنْ تَرَكَ خَيْرًا ۖ الْوَصِيَّةُ
لِلْوٰلِدَيْنِ وَالْأَقْرَبِينَ بِالْمَعْرُوفِ ۚ حَقًّا عَلَى
الْمُتَّقِينَ ﴿١٨٠﴾ فَمَنْ بَدَّلَهُ بَعْدَ مَا سَمِعَهُ
فَإِنَّمَآ إِثْمُهُ عَلَى الَّذِينَ يُبَدِّلُونَهُ ۗ إِنَّ
اللّٰهَ سَمِيعٌ عَلِيمٌ ﴿١٨١﴾ فَمَنْ خَافَ مِنْ مُّوصٍ
جَنَفًا أَوْ إِثْمًا فَأَصْلَحَ بَيْنَهُمْ فَلَآ إِثْمَ

no blame on him provided he sets things right (and so brings about reconciliation) between them (- the parties concerned under the will). Surely, Allâh is Great Protector, Ever Merciful.

SECTION 23

183. **O** YOU who believe! You are bound to observe fasting as those before you (- followers of the Prophets) were bound, so that you may guard against evil.

184. (You are required to fast) for a prescribed number of days. But if anyone of you is sick or is on a journey he shall fast (to make up) the prescribed number in other days. And for those who are unable to fast is an expiation (as thanksgiving) the feeding of a poor person (daily for the days of fasting). And he who volunteers (extra) good, (will find that) it is even better for him. And that you observe fasting is better for you, if you only know.

185. The (lunar) month of *Ramadzân* is that in which the Qur'ân (started to be) revealed as a guidance for the whole of people with its clear evidences (providing comprehensive) guidance and the Discrimination (between right and wrong). Therefore he who shall witness the month, should fast (for full month) during it, but he who is sick or is on a journey shall fast (to make up) the prescribed number in other days. Allâh wishes facility for you and does not wish hardship for you. (This facility is given to you) that you may complete the number (of required fasts) and you may extol the greatness of Allâh for His having guided you, and that you may render thanks (to Him).

186. And when My servants ask you concerning Me (tell them), I am nearby indeed, I answer the prayer of the supplicant when he prays to Me, so they should respond to My call, and believe in Me (that I possess all these attributes) so that they may proceed in the right way.

187. (Though during Fasting you must abstain from all the urges of nature including the sexual urge) it is made lawful for you on the nights of the fasts to approach and lie with your

عَلَيْهِ إِنَّ اللّٰهَ غَفُوْرٌ رَّحِيْمٌ ﴿١٨٢﴾ يٰٓأَيُّهَا
الَّذِيْنَ اٰمَنُوْا كُتِبَ عَلَيْكُمُ الصِّيَامُ كَمَا
كُتِبَ عَلَى الَّذِيْنَ مِنْ قَبْلِكُمْ لَعَلَّكُمْ
تَتَّقُوْنَ ﴿١٨٣﴾ أَيَّامًا مَّعْدُوْدٰتٍ فَمَنْ كَانَ
مِنْكُمْ مَّرِيْضًا أَوْ عَلٰى سَفَرٍ فَعِدَّةٌ مِّنْ
أَيَّامٍ أُخَرَ وَعَلَى الَّذِيْنَ يُطِيْقُوْنَهٗ فِدْيَةٌ
طَعَامُ مِسْكِيْنٍ فَمَنْ تَطَوَّعَ خَيْرًا فَهُوَ
خَيْرٌ لَّهٗ وَأَنْ تَصُوْمُوْا خَيْرٌ لَّكُمْ إِنْ
كُنْتُمْ تَعْلَمُوْنَ ﴿١٨٤﴾ شَهْرُ رَمَضَانَ الَّذِيْٓ
أُنْزِلَ فِيْهِ الْقُرْاٰنُ هُدًى لِّلنَّاسِ
وَبَيِّنٰتٍ مِّنَ الْهُدٰى وَالْفُرْقَانِ فَمَنْ
شَهِدَ مِنْكُمُ الشَّهْرَ فَلْيَصُمْهُ وَمَنْ كَانَ
مَرِيْضًا أَوْ عَلٰى سَفَرٍ فَعِدَّةٌ مِّنْ أَيَّامٍ
أُخَرَ يُرِيْدُ اللّٰهُ بِكُمُ الْيُسْرَ وَلَا يُرِيْدُ
بِكُمُ الْعُسْرَ وَلِتُكْمِلُوا الْعِدَّةَ وَلِتُكَبِّرُوا
اللّٰهَ عَلٰى مَا هَدٰىكُمْ وَلَعَلَّكُمْ تَشْكُرُوْنَ ﴿١٨٥﴾
وَإِذَا سَأَلَكَ عِبَادِيْ عَنِّيْ فَإِنِّيْ قَرِيْبٌ
أُجِيْبُ دَعْوَةَ الدَّاعِ إِذَا دَعَانِ فَلْيَسْتَجِيْبُوْا
لِيْ وَلْيُؤْمِنُوْا بِيْ لَعَلَّهُمْ يَرْشُدُوْنَ ﴿١٨٦﴾ أُحِلَّ
لَكُمْ لَيْلَةَ الصِّيَامِ الرَّفَثُ إِلٰى نِسَآئِكُمْ

wives (for sexual relationship). They are (a sort of) garment for you and you are (a sort of) garment for them. Allâh knows that you have been doing injustice to yourselves (by restricting conjugal relations with your wives even at night), so He turned to you with mercy and provided you relief; now enjoy their company (at night during *Ramadzân*) and seek what Allâh has ordained for you. Eat and drink till the white streak of the dawn becomes distinct to you from the black streak (of the darkness), then complete the fast till nightfall. And you shall not lie with them (- your wives) while you perform *I'tikâf* (- while you are secluding in the mosque for prayer and devotion to God). These are the limits (imposed) by Allâh so do not approach these (limits). Thus does Allâh explains His commandments for people that they may become secure against evil.

188. Do not appropriate one another's property with iniquity (and by false means) nor seek to gain access thereby to the authorities so that you may appropriate a portion of (other) people's property by sinful means (and bribery) and that (too) knowingly (that you have no right to do so).

SECTION 24

189. **T**HEY ask you about the lunar months. Say, 'They are appointed periods of time for (general convenience of) people and for determining the time of Pilgrimage. And it is no virtue that you come into the houses from the backs of them but the true virtue is his who guards against evils. So (instead of fostering superstitious habits) you should rather enter the houses from their proper doors and take Allâh as a shield so that you may be successful.

190. And fight in the cause of Allâh those who fight and persecute you, but commit no aggression. Surely, Allâh does not love the aggressors.

191. And slay them (the aggressors against whom fighting is made incumbent) when and where you get the better of them, in disciplinary way, and turn them out whence they have turned you out. (Killing is bad but) lawlessness

هُنَّ لِبَاسٌ لَّكُمْ وَ أَنْتُمْ لِبَاسٌ لَّهُنَّ عَلِمَ
اللّٰهُ أَنَّكُمْ كُنْتُمْ تَخْتَانُونَ أَنْفُسَكُمْ فَتَابَ
عَلَيْكُمْ وَ عَفَا عَنْكُمْ فَالْـٰٔنَ بٰشِرُوهُنَّ
وَابْتَغُوا مَا كَتَبَ اللّٰهُ لَكُمْ وَ كُلُوا وَاشْرَبُوا
حَتّٰى يَتَبَيَّنَ لَكُمُ الْخَيْطُ الْأَبْيَضُ مِنَ
الْخَيْطِ الْأَسْوَدِ مِنَ الْفَجْرِ ثُمَّ أَتِمُّوا
الصِّيَامَ إِلَى الَّيْلِ وَ لَا تُبٰشِرُوهُنَّ وَ أَنْتُمْ
عٰكِفُونَ فِي الْمَسٰجِدِ تِلْكَ حُدُودُ اللّٰهِ فَلَا
تَقْرَبُوهَا كَذٰلِكَ يُبَيِّنُ اللّٰهُ أٰيٰتِهِ لِلنَّاسِ
لَعَلَّهُمْ يَتَّقُونَ ﴿١٨٧﴾ وَ لَا تَأْكُلُوا أَمْوٰلَكُمْ
بَيْنَكُمْ بِالْبٰطِلِ وَ تُدْلُوا بِهَا إِلَى الْحُكَّامِ
لِتَأْكُلُوا فَرِيقًا مِّنْ أَمْوٰلِ النَّاسِ بِالْإِثْمِ
وَ أَنْتُمْ تَعْلَمُونَ ﴿١٨٨﴾ يَسْـَٔلُونَكَ عَنِ الْأَهِلَّةِ
قُلْ هِيَ مَوٰقِيتُ لِلنَّاسِ وَ الْحَجِّ وَ لَيْسَ
الْبِرُّ بِأَنْ تَأْتُوا الْبُيُوتَ مِنْ ظُهُورِهَا
وَلٰكِنَّ الْبِرَّ مَنِ اتَّقٰى وَ أْتُوا الْبُيُوتَ مِنْ
أَبْوٰبِهَا وَ اتَّقُوا اللّٰهَ لَعَلَّكُمْ تُفْلِحُونَ ﴿١٨٩﴾
وَ قٰتِلُوا فِي سَبِيلِ اللّٰهِ الَّذِينَ يُقٰتِلُونَكُمْ
وَ لَا تَعْتَدُوا إِنَّ اللّٰهَ لَا يُحِبُّ الْمُعْتَدِينَ ﴿١٩٠﴾
وَ اقْتُلُوهُمْ حَيْثُ ثَقِفْتُمُوهُمْ وَ أَخْرِجُوهُمْ
مِّنْ حَيْثُ أَخْرَجُوكُمْ وَ الْفِتْنَةُ أَشَدُّ مِنَ

ع ٢٤

is even worse than carnage. But do not fight them in the precincts of *Masjid al-Harâm* (the Holy Mosque at Makkah) unless they fight you therein. Should they attack you (there) then slay them. This indeed is the recompense of such disbelievers.

192. But if they desist (from aggression) then, behold, Allâh is indeed Great Protector, Ever Merciful.

193. And fight them until persecution is no more and religion is (freely professed) for Allâh. But if they desist (from hostilities) then (remember) there is no punishment except against the unjust (who still persist in persecution).

194. (The violation of) a sacred month may be retaliated in the sacred month and for (the violation of) all sacred things the law of retaliation is prescribed. Then he who transgresses against you, punish him for his transgression to the extent he has transgressed against you, and take Allâh as a shield, and know that Allâh is with those who guard against evil

195. And spend in the cause of Allâh and do not cast yourselves into ruin with your own hands, and do good to others, and verily Allâh loves the doers of good to others.

196. Accomplish the *Hajj* (- the Greater Pilgrimage to Makkah) and the *'Umrah* (- the minor pilgrimage) for the sake of Allâh. But if you are kept back, then (offer) whatever sacrifice is easily available, and do not shave your heads (as is prescribed for the Pilgrims) till the offering reaches its destination (in time, or place). And whosoever of you is sick and has an ailment of his head (necessitating shaving before time) then he should make an expiation either by fasting or alms-giving or by making a sacrifice. When you are in peaceful and healthy conditions then he, who would avail himself of the *'Umrah* (- a visit to the *Ka'bah* or a minor *Hajj*) together with the *Hajj* (- the Greater Pilgrimage and thus performs *Tammattu'*) should make whatever of-

الْقَتْلِ ۚ وَلَا تُقَٰتِلُوهُمْ عِنْدَ الْمَسْجِدِ
الْحَرَامِ حَتَّىٰ يُقَٰتِلُوكُمْ فِيهِ ۖ فَإِنْ قَٰتَلُوكُمْ
فَاقْتُلُوهُمْ ۗ كَذَٰلِكَ جَزَاءُ الْكَٰفِرِينَ ﴿١٩١﴾
فَإِنِ انْتَهَوْا فَإِنَّ اللَّهَ غَفُورٌ رَحِيمٌ ﴿١٩٢﴾
وَقَٰتِلُوهُمْ حَتَّىٰ لَا تَكُونَ فِتْنَةٌ وَيَكُونَ
الدِّينُ لِلَّهِ ۖ فَإِنِ انْتَهَوْا فَلَا عُدْوَٰنَ إِلَّا
عَلَى الظَّٰلِمِينَ ﴿١٩٣﴾ الشَّهْرُ الْحَرَامُ بِالشَّهْرِ
الْحَرَامِ وَالْحُرُمَٰتُ قِصَاصٌ ۚ فَمَنِ اعْتَدَىٰ
عَلَيْكُمْ فَاعْتَدُوا عَلَيْهِ بِمِثْلِ مَا اعْتَدَىٰ
عَلَيْكُمْ ۚ وَاتَّقُوا اللَّهَ وَاعْلَمُوا أَنَّ اللَّهَ مَعَ
الْمُتَّقِينَ ﴿١٩٤﴾ وَأَنْفِقُوا فِي سَبِيلِ اللَّهِ وَلَا
تُلْقُوا بِأَيْدِيكُمْ إِلَى التَّهْلُكَةِ ۛ وَأَحْسِنُوا ۛ
إِنَّ اللَّهَ يُحِبُّ الْمُحْسِنِينَ ﴿١٩٥﴾ وَأَتِمُّوا الْحَجَّ
وَالْعُمْرَةَ لِلَّهِ ۚ فَإِنْ أُحْصِرْتُمْ فَمَا اسْتَيْسَرَ
مِنَ الْهَدْيِ ۖ وَلَا تَحْلِقُوا رُءُوسَكُمْ حَتَّىٰ
يَبْلُغَ الْهَدْيُ مَحِلَّهُ ۚ فَمَنْ كَانَ مِنْكُمْ
مَرِيضًا أَوْ بِهِ أَذًى مِنْ رَأْسِهِ فَفِدْيَةٌ
مِنْ صِيَامٍ أَوْ صَدَقَةٍ أَوْ نُسُكٍ ۚ فَإِذَا
أَمِنْتُمْ فَمَنْ تَمَتَّعَ بِالْعُمْرَةِ إِلَى الْحَجِّ
فَمَا اسْتَيْسَرَ مِنَ الْهَدْيِ ۚ فَمَنْ لَمْ يَجِدْ

fering is easily available; and whosoever finds none (for an offering) should fast for three days during (the days of) the pilgrimage and (for) seven (days) when he returns (home) - these are ten complete (days of fasting in all). This is for him whose family does not reside near the *Masjid al-Harâm* (- the Holy Mosque at Makkah). Take Allâh as a shield, and know that Allâh is Severe in retribution (if you neglect your duties).

SECTION 25

197. **T**HE months of performing the *Hajj* are well Known; so whoever undertakes to perform the *Hajj* in them (should remember that) there is (to be) no obscenity, nor abusing, nor any wrangling during the (time of) *Hajj*. And whatever good you do Allâh knows it. And take provisions for yourselves. Surely, the good of taking provision is guarding (yourselves) against the evil (of committing sin and begging). Take Me alone as (your) shield, O people of pure and clear wisdom!

198. There is no blame on you that you seek munificence from your Lord (by trading during the time of *Hajj*). When you pour forth (in large numbers) from *'Arafât* then glorify Allâh (with still more praises) near *Mash'aral-Harâm* (- Holy Mosque in *Muzdalifah*), and remember Him (with gratitude) as He has guided you, though formerly you were certainly amongst the astray.

199. And (then) proceed (to return from *'Arafât*) from where the people proceed (to come back) and seek Allâh's protection. Verily. Allâh is All Protector, Ever Merciful.

200. When you have completed the rites of devotion of the *Hajj* prescribed for you, remember Allâh with praises as your lauding of your parents or yet more earnest devout lauding. Now, there are some of people who say, 'Our Lord! Grant us all things in this (very) world,' and there is no share for such in the Hereafter.

201. And there are others among them who

فَصِيَامُ ثَلٰثَةِ أَيَّامٍ فِي الْحَجِّ وَسَبْعَةٍ إِذَا
رَجَعْتُمْ تِلْكَ عَشَرَةٌ كَامِلَةٌ ذٰلِكَ لِمَنْ
لَّمْ يَكُنْ أَهْلُهُ حَاضِرِي الْمَسْجِدِ الْحَرَامِ
وَاتَّقُوا اللّٰهَ وَاعْلَمُوا أَنَّ اللّٰهَ شَدِيدُ الْعِقَابِ ﴿١٩٦﴾
الْحَجُّ أَشْهُرٌ مَّعْلُومٰتٌ فَمَنْ فَرَضَ فِيهِنَّ
الْحَجَّ فَلَا رَفَثَ وَلَا فُسُوقَ وَلَا جِدَالَ
فِي الْحَجِّ وَمَا تَفْعَلُوا مِنْ خَيْرٍ يَعْلَمْهُ
اللّٰهُ وَتَزَوَّدُوا فَإِنَّ خَيْرَ الزَّادِ التَّقْوٰى
وَاتَّقُونِ يٰأُولِي الْأَلْبٰبِ ﴿١٩٧﴾ لَيْسَ عَلَيْكُمْ
جُنَاحٌ أَنْ تَبْتَغُوا فَضْلًا مِّنْ رَّبِّكُمْ فَإِذَا
أَفَضْتُمْ مِّنْ عَرَفٰتٍ فَاذْكُرُوا اللّٰهَ عِنْدَ
الْمَشْعَرِ الْحَرَامِ وَاذْكُرُوهُ كَمَا هَدٰىكُمْ
وَإِنْ كُنْتُمْ مِّنْ قَبْلِهِ لَمِنَ الضَّآلِّينَ ﴿١٩٨﴾ ثُمَّ
أَفِيضُوا مِنْ حَيْثُ أَفَاضَ النَّاسُ
وَاسْتَغْفِرُوا اللّٰهَ إِنَّ اللّٰهَ غَفُورٌ رَّحِيمٌ ﴿١٩٩﴾
فَإِذَا قَضَيْتُمْ مَّنٰسِكَكُمْ فَاذْكُرُوا اللّٰهَ
كَذِكْرِكُمْ آبَاءَكُمْ أَوْ أَشَدَّ ذِكْرًا فَمِنَ
النَّاسِ مَنْ يَقُولُ رَبَّنَا آتِنَا فِي الدُّنْيَا
وَمَا لَهُ فِي الْآخِرَةِ مِنْ خَلٰقٍ ﴿٢٠٠﴾ وَمِنْهُمْ

say, 'Our Lord! Grant us good in this world as well as good in the Hereafter, and guard us against the punishment of the Fire.'
202. It is they for whom there is a (very large) portion (of the reward) of what (good deeds) they have accomplished. And Allâh is Quick at reckoning.
203. Remember Allâh (at *Minâ)* with His praises during (these) days appointed (for this purpose). However if any one hastens (to leave the valley of *Minâ)* after two days there is no sin for him and if any one stays behind, it is no sin for him either. (This direction is) for him who guards against evil (under all circumstances). So take Allâh as a shield, and know that you shall all be brought together before Him.
204. Of the people there is he whose talk about the present life pleases you, and he calls Allâh to witness as to that (sincerity) which is in his heart, and yet he is of the most contentious of all the adversaries (hence your most stubborn enemy).
205. And when he is in authority, he runs about in the land (striving) to create chaos and lawlessness in it, and to destroy the tillage and the stock, but Allâh does not love disorder (and lawlessness).
206. When it is said to him, 'Take Allâh as a shield,' vain pride holds him to sin, Gehenna shall suffice him (as a reward); and how evil a resort it is!
207. Of the people there is he who sacrifices his very life seeking the pleasure of Allâh. And Allâh is very Kind and Compassionate toward such (of His) servants.
208. O you who believe! Enter into (the fold of those showing) complete submission (to Allâh) all of you, and do not follow the footsteps of satan, verily he is your enemy, severing (you from Allâh).
209. But if you slip off even after the clear proofs that have come to you, then bear in mind, that Allâh is All-Mighty, All-Wise.

مَنْ يَّقُوْلُ رَبَّنَا آتِنَا فِي الدُّنْيَا حَسَنَةً
وَّفِي الْآخِرَةِ حَسَنَةً وَّقِنَا عَذَابَ النَّارِ ﴿٢٠١﴾
أُولٰٓئِكَ لَهُمْ نَصِيبٌ مِّمَّا كَسَبُوا ۚ وَاللّٰهُ
سَرِيعُ الْحِسَابِ ﴿٢٠٢﴾ وَاذْكُرُوا اللّٰهَ فِيٓ أَيَّامٍ
مَّعْدُودٰتٍ ۚ فَمَنْ تَعَجَّلَ فِي يَوْمَيْنِ فَلَآ
إِثْمَ عَلَيْهِ ۚ وَمَنْ تَأَخَّرَ فَلَآ إِثْمَ عَلَيْهِ
لِمَنِ اتَّقٰى ۗ وَاتَّقُوا اللّٰهَ وَاعْلَمُوٓا أَنَّكُمْ إِلَيْهِ
تُحْشَرُونَ ﴿٢٠٣﴾ وَمِنَ النَّاسِ مَنْ يُّعْجِبُكَ
قَوْلُهُ فِي الْحَيٰوةِ الدُّنْيَا وَيُشْهِدُ اللّٰهَ عَلٰى
مَا فِي قَلْبِهِ ۙ وَهُوَ أَلَدُّ الْخِصَامِ ﴿٢٠٤﴾ وَإِذَا تَوَلّٰى
سَعٰى فِي الْأَرْضِ لِيُفْسِدَ فِيهَا وَيُهْلِكَ
الْحَرْثَ وَالنَّسْلَ ۗ وَاللّٰهُ لَا يُحِبُّ الْفَسَادَ ﴿٢٠٥﴾
وَإِذَا قِيلَ لَهُ اتَّقِ اللّٰهَ أَخَذَتْهُ الْعِزَّةُ
بِالْإِثْمِ فَحَسْبُهُ جَهَنَّمُ ۚ وَلَبِئْسَ الْمِهَادُ ﴿٢٠٦﴾
وَمِنَ النَّاسِ مَنْ يَّشْرِي نَفْسَهُ ابْتِغَآءَ
مَرْضَاتِ اللّٰهِ ۗ وَاللّٰهُ رَءُوفٌ بِالْعِبَادِ ﴿٢٠٧﴾ يٰٓأَيُّهَا
الَّذِينَ آمَنُوا ادْخُلُوا فِي السِّلْمِ كَآفَّةً وَلَا
تَتَّبِعُوا خُطُوٰتِ الشَّيْطٰنِ ۚ إِنَّهُ لَكُمْ عَدُوٌّ
مُّبِينٌ ﴿٢٠٨﴾ فَإِنْ زَلَلْتُمْ مِّنْ بَعْدِ مَا جَآءَتْكُمُ
الْبَيِّنٰتُ فَاعْلَمُوٓا أَنَّ اللّٰهَ عَزِيزٌ حَكِيمٌ ﴿٢٠٩﴾

210. (If the people do not believe even now,) they look for nothing but that Allâh should come to them (with the threatened punishment) in the shadows of the clouds as well as the angels (to execute His orders) and the matter be settled. And to Allâh are returned all matters (for decisions).

SECTION 26

211. **A**SK the Children of Israel how many a clear Sign did We give them. And whoever changes the favour of Allâh after it has come to him (with every convincing proof, and so makes himself deserving of punishment) he will find that Allâh is surely Severe in retribution.

212. Decked out fair is this present life (to make it appear attractive) to those who disbelieve, and they hold those who believe in condemnation. But those who guard against evil shall be (placed) above them on the Day of Resurrection. And Allâh provides (His gifts) for whom He will without reckoning and measure.

213. Humankind were (once) a single community (but they differed), so Allâh raised (His) Prophets as Bearers of good tidings and as Warners, and with them He revealed the Scriptures containing the truth, that He might judge between various people concerning all their mutual differences. But none differed therein except the very (astray) to whom it (-the Scripture) had been given, and (they differed only) after clear proofs had come to them, out of spite against one another. Now Allâh guided those who believed, by His leave, to the truth concerning which they (- the disbelievers) had differed. And Allâh guides whosoever wishes (to be guided) to the right and straight path.

214. Do you think that you will enter Paradise, while there has not yet come upon you the like of that which befell those who passed away before you? Distress and afflictions befell them, and they were made to

هَلْ يَنْظُرُونَ إِلَّآ أَنْ يَّأْتِيَهُمُ اللّٰهُ فِي ظُلَلٍ
مِّنَ الْغَمَامِ وَالْمَلٰٓئِكَةُ وَقُضِيَ الْأَمْرُ ۚ وَإِلَى
اللّٰهِ تُرْجَعُ الْأُمُورُ ﴿٢١٠﴾ سَلْ بَنِيٓ إِسْرَآءِيلَ
كَمْ أٰتَيْنٰهُمْ مِّنْ أٰيَةٍۭ بَيِّنَةٍ ۗ وَمَنْ يُّبَدِّلْ
نِعْمَةَ اللّٰهِ مِنْۢ بَعْدِ مَا جَآءَتْهُ فَإِنَّ اللّٰهَ
شَدِيدُ الْعِقَابِ ﴿٢١١﴾ زُيِّنَ لِلَّذِينَ كَفَرُوا
الْحَيٰوةُ الدُّنْيَا وَيَسْخَرُونَ مِنَ الَّذِينَ
أٰمَنُوا ۘ وَالَّذِينَ اتَّقَوْا فَوْقَهُمْ يَوْمَ الْقِيٰمَةِ ۗ
وَاللّٰهُ يَرْزُقُ مَنْ يَّشَآءُ بِغَيْرِ حِسَابٍ ﴿٢١٢﴾ كَانَ
النَّاسُ أُمَّةً وّٰحِدَةً ۖ فَبَعَثَ اللّٰهُ النَّبِيّٖنَ
مُبَشِّرِينَ وَمُنْذِرِينَ ۖ وَأَنْزَلَ مَعَهُمُ الْكِتٰبَ
بِالْحَقِّ لِيَحْكُمَ بَيْنَ النَّاسِ فِيمَا اخْتَلَفُوا
فِيهِ ۗ وَمَا اخْتَلَفَ فِيهِ إِلَّا الَّذِينَ أُوتُوهُ
مِنْۢ بَعْدِ مَا جَآءَتْهُمُ الْبَيِّنٰتُ بَغْيًۢا بَيْنَهُمْ ۚ
فَهَدَى اللّٰهُ الَّذِينَ أٰمَنُوا لِمَا اخْتَلَفُوا فِيهِ
مِنَ الْحَقِّ بِإِذْنِهِ ۗ وَاللّٰهُ يَهْدِي مَنْ يَّشَآءُ
إِلٰى صِرٰطٍ مُّسْتَقِيمٍ ﴿٢١٣﴾ أَمْ حَسِبْتُمْ أَنْ
تَدْخُلُوا الْجَنَّةَ وَلَمَّا يَأْتِكُمْ مَّثَلُ الَّذِينَ
خَلَوْا مِنْ قَبْلِكُمْ ۖ مَسَّتْهُمُ الْبَأْسَآءُ وَالضَّرَّآءُ

suffer the violent tremors, so that the Messenger and those who believed along with him spoke out, 'When (will come) the help of Allâh?' (Then they were told), 'Behold! Surely, the help of Allâh is always nearby.'
215. They question you as to what they should spend (to seek the pleasure of Allâh). Say, 'Whatever of good and abundant wealth you spend, should be for parents and near of kin, and the orphans and the needy, and the wayfarer. And whatever good you do, surely Allâh knows it fully well.'
216. Fighting has been ordained for you, though it is hard for you. But it may be that a thing is hard upon you though it is (really) good for you, and it may be that you love a thing while it is bad for you. Allâh knows (all things) while you do not know.

SECTION 27

217. **T**HEY ask you with regard to fighting in the Sacred Month. Say, 'Fighting in it is (a) grave (offence). But to bar (people) from Allâh's cause and disbelief in Him and (to hinder people from) the Holy Mosque and to turn out its people therefrom is still grave in the sight of Allâh, and persecution is all the more grave an offence than killing.' And they will not cease to fight you until they turn you back from your faith if they can. And who so from amongst you turns back from his faith, and dies while he is a disbeliever, it is they, then, whose deeds go in vain in this world and the Hereafter; and it is they who are the fellows of the Fire and therein they shall abide for long.
218. Verily, as to those who believe and those who emigrated and struggled hard in the cause of Allâh, it is they who do (rightly) hope for Allâh's mercy. And Allâh is Great Protector, Ever Merciful.
219. They ask you concerning intoxicants

وَ زُلْزِلُوا حَتّٰى يَقُولَ الرَّسُولُ وَ الَّذِينَ
اٰمَنُوا مَعَهُ مَتٰى نَصْرُ اللّٰهِ ۗ أَلَآ إِنَّ نَصْرَ
اللّٰهِ قَرِيبٌ ﴿٢١٤﴾ يَسْـَٔلُونَكَ مَاذَا يُنْفِقُونَ ۬ؕ
قُلْ مَآ أَنْفَقْتُمْ مِّنْ خَيْرٍ فَلِلْوٰلِدَيْنِ
وَالْأَقْرَبِينَ وَالْيَتٰمٰى وَالْمَسٰكِينِ وَ ابْنِ
السَّبِيلِ ۗ وَ مَا تَفْعَلُوا مِنْ خَيْرٍ فَإِنَّ اللّٰهَ
بِهٖ عَلِيمٌ ﴿٢١٥﴾ كُتِبَ عَلَيْكُمُ الْقِتَالُ وَهُوَ
كُرْهٌ لَّكُمْ ۚ وَ عَسٰٓى أَنْ تَكْرَهُوا شَيْـًٔا وَّهُوَ
خَيْرٌ لَّكُمْ ۚ وَ عَسٰٓى أَنْ تُحِبُّوا شَيْـًٔا وَّ هُوَ
شَرٌّ لَّكُمْ ۗ وَاللّٰهُ يَعْلَمُ وَأَنْتُمْ لَا تَعْلَمُونَ ﴿٢١٦﴾ ع ٢٦
يَسْـَٔلُونَكَ عَنِ الشَّهْرِ الْحَرَامِ قِتَالٍ فِيهِ ۗ
قُلْ قِتَالٌ فِيهِ كَبِيرٌ ۗ وَ صَدٌّ عَنْ سَبِيلِ
اللّٰهِ وَ كُفْرٌۢ بِهٖ وَ الْمَسْجِدِ الْحَرَامِ ۚ
وَ إِخْرَاجُ أَهْلِهٖ مِنْهُ أَكْبَرُ عِنْدَ اللّٰهِ ۚ
وَالْفِتْنَةُ أَكْبَرُ مِنَ الْقَتْلِ ۗ وَلَا يَزَالُونَ
يُقٰتِلُونَكُمْ حَتّٰى يَرُدُّوكُمْ عَنْ دِينِكُمْ إِنِ
اسْتَطٰعُوا ۗ وَ مَنْ يَّرْتَدِدْ مِنْكُمْ عَنْ دِينِهٖ
فَيَمُتْ وَ هُوَ كَافِرٌ فَأُولٰٓئِكَ حَبِطَتْ أَعْمٰلُهُمْ
فِي الدُّنْيَا وَ الْاٰخِرَةِ ۚ وَ أُولٰٓئِكَ أَصْحٰبُ النَّارِ ۚ
هُمْ فِيهَا خٰلِدُونَ ﴿٢١٧﴾ إِنَّ الَّذِينَ اٰمَنُوا
وَالَّذِينَ هَاجَرُوا وَجٰهَدُوا فِي سَبِيلِ اللّٰهِ ۙ
أُولٰٓئِكَ يَرْجُونَ رَحْمَتَ اللّٰهِ ۗ وَاللّٰهُ غَفُورٌ
رَّحِيمٌ ﴿٢١٨﴾ يَسْـَٔلُونَكَ عَنِ الْخَمْرِ وَ الْمَيْسِرِ ۗ

and games of chance. Say, 'In both of them is a great sin and both are harmful too, and they have some uses for people, but the sin inherent in them is even more serious than their usefulness.' They ask you how much they should spend (in the way of Allâh). Say, 'The surplus (- what you can spare after spending on your basic requirement).' Thus does Allâh make clear His commandments so that you may reflect -

220. Upon this world and the Hereafter. And they ask you concerning the orphans. Say, 'To set (their affairs) right (keeping in view the promotion of their welfare) is (an act of great) virtue, and if you intermix with them they are (after all) your brethren. And Allâh knows the wrongdoers from the right-doers. And if Allâh had so willed, He would certainly have made matters difficult for you. Verily, Allâh is All-Mighty, All-Wise.

221. And marry not an idolatress until she believes; while a believing maid is certainly better than an idolatress even though she may highly please you. And do not give (believing women) in marriage to idolaters until they believe. And a believing slave is better than a (free) idolater even though he may highly please you. It is they who invite to the Fire, but Allâh calls to the Paradise and to the protection by His command. He makes His Messages clear for the people so that they may take heed.

SECTION 28

222. **T**HEY ask you about (having conjugal relations during) the menstruation. Say, 'It (having conjugal relations) is harmful and a pollution, so keep aloof from women during menstruation, and do not approach them (for sexual relation) until they are thoroughly cleansed. But when they have fully cleaned themselves you may come to them as Allâh has ordained you. Verily, Allâh loves those who frequently turn (to Him)

قُلْ فِيهِمَآ إِثْمٌ كَبِيرٌ وَمَنَٰفِعُ لِلنَّاسِ
وَإِثْمُهُمَآ أَكْبَرُ مِن نَّفْعِهِمَا ۗ وَيَسْـَٔلُونَكَ
مَاذَا يُنفِقُونَ ۖ قُلِ الْعَفْوَ ۗ كَذَٰلِكَ يُبَيِّنُ
اللَّهُ لَكُمُ الْأٓيَٰتِ لَعَلَّكُمْ تَتَفَكَّرُونَ ﴿٢١٩﴾ فِي
الدُّنْيَا وَالْأٓخِرَةِ ۗ وَيَسْـَٔلُونَكَ عَنِ الْيَتَٰمَىٰ ۖ
قُلْ إِصْلَاحٌ لَّهُمْ خَيْرٌ ۖ وَإِن تُخَالِطُوهُمْ
فَإِخْوَٰنُكُمْ ۚ وَاللَّهُ يَعْلَمُ الْمُفْسِدَ مِنَ
الْمُصْلِحِ ۚ وَلَوْ شَآءَ اللَّهُ لَأَعْنَتَكُمْ ۚ إِنَّ اللَّهَ
عَزِيزٌ حَكِيمٌ ﴿٢٢٠﴾ وَلَا تَنكِحُوا الْمُشْرِكَٰتِ
حَتَّىٰ يُؤْمِنَّ ۚ وَلَأَمَةٌ مُّؤْمِنَةٌ خَيْرٌ مِّن
مُّشْرِكَةٍ وَلَوْ أَعْجَبَتْكُمْ ۗ وَلَا تُنكِحُوا
الْمُشْرِكِينَ حَتَّىٰ يُؤْمِنُوا ۚ وَلَعَبْدٌ مُّؤْمِنٌ
خَيْرٌ مِّن مُّشْرِكٍ وَلَوْ أَعْجَبَكُمْ ۗ أُولَٰٓئِكَ
يَدْعُونَ إِلَى النَّارِ ۖ وَاللَّهُ يَدْعُوٓا إِلَى
الْجَنَّةِ وَالْمَغْفِرَةِ بِإِذْنِهِ ۖ وَيُبَيِّنُ ءَايَٰتِهِۦ
لِلنَّاسِ لَعَلَّهُمْ يَتَذَكَّرُونَ ﴿٢٢١﴾ وَيَسْـَٔلُونَكَ
عَنِ الْمَحِيضِ ۖ قُلْ هُوَ أَذًى فَاعْتَزِلُوا النِّسَآءَ
فِي الْمَحِيضِ ۖ وَلَا تَقْرَبُوهُنَّ حَتَّىٰ يَطْهُرْنَ ۖ
فَإِذَا تَطَهَّرْنَ فَأْتُوهُنَّ مِنْ حَيْثُ أَمَرَكُمُ
اللَّهُ ۚ إِنَّ اللَّهَ يُحِبُّ التَّوَّٰبِينَ وَيُحِبُّ
الْمُتَطَهِّرِينَ ﴿٢٢٢﴾ نِسَآؤُكُمْ حَرْثٌ لَّكُمْ فَأْتُوا

with repentance and He loves the strivers to purification of themselves.

223. Your wives are (as) a tilth (to produce and rear children) for you, so come to your tilth when and how you like and send forward (some good) for yourselves, and take Allâh as a shield, and know that you shall meet Him, and give good tidings to the believers.

224. And make not Allâh an excuse through your oaths, that you may (thereby) abstain from doing good and from becoming secure against evil and from setting the affairs right and from making peace between various people. And Allâh is All-Hearing, All-Knowing.

225. Allâh will not call you to account for what is vain (and unintentional) in your oaths, but He calls you to account for what your minds resolve and accomplish (by intentional swearing). And Allâh is Great Protector (against faults), Highly Forbearing.

226. Those who vow (to abstain) from their wives, (the maximum) period of waiting (for them) is four months (after which divorce becomes inevitable), then if they (are reconciled within four months and) revert (to their normal relations), then, surely, Allâh is Great Protector, Ever Merciful.

227. But if they have resolved on divorce, then (they should know that) surely Allâh is All-Hearing, All-Knowing.

228. And the divorced women must keep themselves waiting for three (monthly) courses (as *'Iddat),* and it is not lawful for them to conceal what Allâh has created in their wombs, if indeed they believe in Allâh and the Last Day. And their husbands have a better right to take them back in the meanwhile, provided they desire and mean reconciliation. And women have their rights similar to (those of men and) their obligations in an equitable and just manner; yet men have a place above them. And Allâh is All-Mighty, All-Wise.

SECTION 29

229. **S**UCH a (revocable) divorce may be

حَرْثَكُمْ أَنَّىٰ شِئْتُمْ وَقَدِّمُوا لِأَنْفُسِكُمْ
وَاتَّقُوا اللَّهَ وَاعْلَمُوا أَنَّكُمْ مُلَاقُوهُ وَبَشِّرِ
الْمُؤْمِنِينَ ﴿٢٢٣﴾ وَلَا تَجْعَلُوا اللَّهَ عُرْضَةً
لِأَيْمَانِكُمْ أَنْ تَبَرُّوا وَتَتَّقُوا وَتُصْلِحُوا بَيْنَ
النَّاسِ ۗ وَاللَّهُ سَمِيعٌ عَلِيمٌ ﴿٢٢٤﴾ لَا يُؤَاخِذُكُمُ
اللَّهُ بِاللَّغْوِ فِي أَيْمَانِكُمْ وَلَٰكِنْ يُؤَاخِذُكُمْ بِمَا
كَسَبَتْ قُلُوبُكُمْ ۗ وَاللَّهُ غَفُورٌ حَلِيمٌ ﴿٢٢٥﴾ لِلَّذِينَ
يُؤْلُونَ مِنْ نِسَائِهِمْ تَرَبُّصُ أَرْبَعَةِ أَشْهُرٍ ۖ
فَإِنْ فَاءُوا فَإِنَّ اللَّهَ غَفُورٌ رَحِيمٌ ﴿٢٢٦﴾ وَإِنْ
عَزَمُوا الطَّلَاقَ فَإِنَّ اللَّهَ سَمِيعٌ عَلِيمٌ ﴿٢٢٧﴾
وَالْمُطَلَّقَاتُ يَتَرَبَّصْنَ بِأَنْفُسِهِنَّ ثَلَاثَةَ قُرُوءٍ ۚ
وَلَا يَحِلُّ لَهُنَّ أَنْ يَكْتُمْنَ مَا خَلَقَ اللَّهُ
فِي أَرْحَامِهِنَّ إِنْ كُنَّ يُؤْمِنَّ بِاللَّهِ وَالْيَوْمِ
الْآخِرِ ۚ وَبُعُولَتُهُنَّ أَحَقُّ بِرَدِّهِنَّ فِي ذَٰلِكَ
إِنْ أَرَادُوا إِصْلَاحًا ۚ وَلَهُنَّ مِثْلُ الَّذِي
عَلَيْهِنَّ بِالْمَعْرُوفِ ۚ وَلِلرِّجَالِ عَلَيْهِنَّ
دَرَجَةٌ ۗ وَاللَّهُ عَزِيزٌ حَكِيمٌ ﴿٢٢٨﴾ الطَّلَاقُ
مَرَّتَانِ ۖ فَإِمْسَاكٌ بِمَعْرُوفٍ أَوْ تَسْرِيحٌ

ع ٢٨ ٧ ١٢

(pronounced) twice, then, (after the second pronouncement) there should be either retaining (the wife) with honour and fairness or letting (her) leave with goodness. And it is not lawful for you to take (back) anything of what you have given them (your wives); however, if both (the husband and the wife) fear that they cannot abide by the injunctions of Allâh, and if you (- the Muslim community, also) fear that they cannot observe the limits (prescribed) by Allâh then there is no blame on either of them in what she gives up to redeem herself (as <u>*Khula*</u>*'*). These are the injunctions of Allâh, therefore, do not violate them; and who so violates the injunctions of Allâh, it is they who are really the wrongdoers.

230. But if he divorces her (for the third time) then she is not lawful for him after that, until she has married another husband. Now if he (- the second husband also) divorces her (of his own accord) then there is no blame on them (- the former husband and wife) to return to each other (by remarriage) provided they are sure that they will be able to abide by the injunctions of Allâh. These are the injunctions of Allâh. He makes them clear to the people who would know.

231. And when you divorce (your) women (a revocable divorce), and they approach the end of their *'Iddat* (-the prescribed period of waiting after divorce) then either retain them in an equitable manner or send them away (- freeing them) in an equitable manner. And do not retain them wrongfully that you may exceed the proper limits (and do them harm and maltreat them). And whosoever does that he has indeed done wrong and injustice to himself. Do not take Allâh's commandments in a light way; and remember Allâh's favour upon you and what He has revealed to you of the Book and the Wisdom, wherewith He exhorts you. And take Allâh as a shield and know that Allâh has perfect knowledge of everything.

SECTION 30

232. **W**HEN (some of) you divorce (their)

بِإِحۡسَٰنٍ وَلَا يَحِلُّ لَكُمۡ أَن تَأۡخُذُواْ
مِمَّآ ءَاتَيۡتُمُوهُنَّ شَيۡـًٔا إِلَّآ أَن يَخَافَآ
أَلَّا يُقِيمَا حُدُودَ ٱللَّهِ فَإِنۡ خِفۡتُمۡ أَلَّا يُقِيمَا
حُدُودَ ٱللَّهِ فَلَا جُنَاحَ عَلَيۡهِمَا فِيمَا ٱفۡتَدَتۡ
بِهِۦ تِلۡكَ حُدُودُ ٱللَّهِ فَلَا تَعۡتَدُوهَا وَمَن
يَتَعَدَّ حُدُودَ ٱللَّهِ فَأُوْلَٰٓئِكَ هُمُ ٱلظَّٰلِمُونَ ٢٢٩
فَإِن طَلَّقَهَا فَلَا تَحِلُّ لَهُۥ مِنۢ بَعۡدُ حَتَّىٰ
تَنكِحَ زَوۡجًا غَيۡرَهُۥ فَإِن طَلَّقَهَا فَلَا جُنَاحَ
عَلَيۡهِمَآ أَن يَتَرَاجَعَآ إِن ظَنَّآ أَن يُقِيمَا
حُدُودَ ٱللَّهِ وَتِلۡكَ حُدُودُ ٱللَّهِ يُبَيِّنُهَا
لِقَوۡمٖ يَعۡلَمُونَ ٢٣٠ وَإِذَا طَلَّقۡتُمُ ٱلنِّسَآءَ
فَبَلَغۡنَ أَجَلَهُنَّ فَأَمۡسِكُوهُنَّ بِمَعۡرُوفٍ
أَوۡ سَرِّحُوهُنَّ بِمَعۡرُوفٖ وَلَا تُمۡسِكُوهُنَّ
ضِرَارٗا لِّتَعۡتَدُواْ وَمَن يَفۡعَلۡ ذَٰلِكَ فَقَدۡ
ظَلَمَ نَفۡسَهُۥ وَلَا تَتَّخِذُوٓاْ ءَايَٰتِ ٱللَّهِ هُزُوٗا
وَٱذۡكُرُواْ نِعۡمَتَ ٱللَّهِ عَلَيۡكُمۡ وَمَآ
أَنزَلَ عَلَيۡكُم مِّنَ ٱلۡكِتَٰبِ وَٱلۡحِكۡمَةِ يَعِظُكُم
بِهِۦ وَٱتَّقُواْ ٱللَّهَ وَٱعۡلَمُوٓاْ أَنَّ ٱللَّهَ بِكُلِّ
شَيۡءٍ عَلِيمٞ ٢٣١ وَإِذَا طَلَّقۡتُمُ ٱلنِّسَآءَ فَبَلَغۡنَ

women (for the first or the second time) and they approach the end of the prescribed period of waiting *(- 'Iddat)* then do not prevent them from remarrying their (former) husbands when they have agreed between themselves to an equitable and decent contract. This is an exhortation for those among you who believe in Allâh and the Last Day. This is more blissful for you and purer. And Allâh knows while you do not know.

233. The mothers shall give suck to their children for two full years, (this instruction is) for him who desires to complete the (period of) suckling. And it is incumbent on the man to whom the child is born (- the father) to provide them (- the mothers) the usual maintenance and their clothing (for this period) equitably and according to usage. No soul is charged with a duty except to its capacity. Neither shall a mother be made to suffer on account of her (love for her) child, nor shall he to whom the child is born (be made to suffer) on account of his child. The (father's) heir has a like duty. However if (mother and father) both desire weaning, by mutual consent and consultation, then there is no blame on (either of) them. And if you desire to provide a wet-nurse for your children there is no blame on you, provided you hand over what you have agreed to pay equitably (and in accordance with popular usage). And keep your duty to Allâh and know that Allâh is Seer of what you do.

234. Those of you who die and leave wives behind, these (wives) should keep themselves in waiting for four months and ten days (as *'Iddat)*. So when they reach the end of their (prescribed) term (of waiting) then there is no blame on you for what they do with regard to themselves (about their remarriage) in an equitable manner. And Allâh is fully Aware of what you do.

235. There is no blame on you respecting that which you speak indirectly, regarding a proposal of marriage, to these (widowed) women

أَجَلَهُنَّ فَلَا تَعْضُلُوهُنَّ أَن يَنكِحْنَ
أَزْوَاجَهُنَّ إِذَا تَرَاضَوْا بَيْنَهُم بِالْمَعْرُوفِ ۗ ذَٰلِكَ
يُوعَظُ بِهِ مَن كَانَ مِنكُمْ يُؤْمِنُ بِاللَّهِ
وَالْيَوْمِ الْآخِرِ ۗ ذَٰلِكُمْ أَزْكَىٰ لَكُمْ وَأَطْهَرُ ۗ
وَاللَّهُ يَعْلَمُ وَأَنتُمْ لَا تَعْلَمُونَ ﴿٢٣٢﴾ وَالْوَالِدَاتُ
يُرْضِعْنَ أَوْلَادَهُنَّ حَوْلَيْنِ كَامِلَيْنِ لِمَنْ
أَرَادَ أَن يُتِمَّ الرَّضَاعَةَ ۚ وَعَلَى الْمَوْلُودِ لَهُ
رِزْقُهُنَّ وَكِسْوَتُهُنَّ بِالْمَعْرُوفِ ۚ لَا تُكَلَّفُ
نَفْسٌ إِلَّا وُسْعَهَا ۚ لَا تُضَارَّ وَالِدَةٌ بِوَلَدِهَا
وَلَا مَوْلُودٌ لَّهُ بِوَلَدِهِ ۚ وَعَلَى الْوَارِثِ مِثْلُ
ذَٰلِكَ ۗ فَإِنْ أَرَادَا فِصَالًا عَن تَرَاضٍ مِّنْهُمَا
وَتَشَاوُرٍ فَلَا جُنَاحَ عَلَيْهِمَا ۗ وَإِنْ أَرَدتُّمْ
أَن تَسْتَرْضِعُوا أَوْلَادَكُمْ فَلَا جُنَاحَ عَلَيْكُمْ
إِذَا سَلَّمْتُم مَّا آتَيْتُم بِالْمَعْرُوفِ ۗ وَاتَّقُوا
اللَّهَ وَاعْلَمُوا أَنَّ اللَّهَ بِمَا تَعْمَلُونَ بَصِيرٌ ﴿٢٣٣﴾
وَالَّذِينَ يُتَوَفَّوْنَ مِنكُمْ وَيَذَرُونَ أَزْوَاجًا
يَتَرَبَّصْنَ بِأَنفُسِهِنَّ أَرْبَعَةَ أَشْهُرٍ وَعَشْرًا ۖ
فَإِذَا بَلَغْنَ أَجَلَهُنَّ فَلَا جُنَاحَ عَلَيْكُمْ فِيمَا
فَعَلْنَ فِي أَنفُسِهِنَّ بِالْمَعْرُوفِ ۗ وَاللَّهُ بِمَا
تَعْمَلُونَ خَبِيرٌ ﴿٢٣٤﴾ وَلَا جُنَاحَ عَلَيْكُمْ فِيمَا
عَرَّضْتُم بِهِ مِنْ خِطْبَةِ النِّسَاءِ أَوْ أَكْنَنتُمْ
فِي أَنفُسِكُمْ ۚ عَلِمَ اللَّهُ أَنَّكُمْ سَتَذْكُرُونَهُنَّ
وَلَٰكِن لَّا تُوَاعِدُوهُنَّ سِرًّا إِلَّا أَن تَقُولُوا

(within their period of waiting), or whether you keep it (the proposal) hidden in your minds. Allâh knows that you will think of them, (in this connection) yet make no agreement (or promises) with them secretly, except that you say a decent word. And confirm not the marriage tie until the prescribed period of waiting reaches its end. And know that Allâh knows what is in your minds, therefore beware of Him and know that Allâh is indeed a Great Protector (against faults), Highly Forbearing.

SECTION 31

236. **T**HERE is no blame on you if you divorce women, while you have not touched them and you have not yet settled for them any marriage portion (- dowry money). But provide for them, - the affluent man according to his means and the one in straitened circumstances according to his means - a provision in an equitable manner (and in accordance with popular usage; this is) an obligation on the doers of good to others.

237. But if you divorce them before you have touched them, while you have already settled for them a marriage portion, then half of what you have settled (is due to them) unless they (-the women forgo their full due or a portion of it) or he, (the husband) in whose hand is the tie of marriage, forgoes (a portion or the full half which he is entitled to deduct and thus pays the whole dowry money), and that you (husband) forgo (and pay the whole dowry money) is nearer to becoming secure against evil. And do not neglect to do good to one another. Verily, Allâh sees well what you do.

238. Be watchful over the Prayers especially the middle (and most excellent) Prayer (which comes in the midst of rush of work and business), and do stand up before Allâh truly obedient (and in all humility).

239. And if you apprehend (any danger) then (say your Prayer) on foot or mounted, but when you are secure, then remember

قَوْلًا مَّعْرُوفًا وَلَا تَعْزِمُوا عُقْدَةَ النِّكَاحِ
حَتّٰى يَبْلُغَ الْكِتٰبُ أَجَلَهُ وَاعْلَمُوا أَنَّ اللّٰهَ
يَعْلَمُ مَا فِي أَنْفُسِكُمْ فَاحْذَرُوهُ وَاعْلَمُوا
أَنَّ اللّٰهَ غَفُورٌ حَلِيمٌ ﴿٢٣٥﴾ لَا جُنَاحَ عَلَيْكُمْ
إِنْ طَلَّقْتُمُ النِّسَاءَ مَا لَمْ تَمَسُّوهُنَّ أَوْ
تَفْرِضُوا لَهُنَّ فَرِيضَةً وَمَتِّعُوهُنَّ عَلَى
الْمُوسِعِ قَدَرُهُ وَعَلَى الْمُقْتِرِ قَدَرُهُ مَتٰعًا
بِالْمَعْرُوفِ حَقًّا عَلَى الْمُحْسِنِينَ ﴿٢٣٦﴾ وَإِنْ
طَلَّقْتُمُوهُنَّ مِنْ قَبْلِ أَنْ تَمَسُّوهُنَّ وَقَدْ
فَرَضْتُمْ لَهُنَّ فَرِيضَةً فَنِصْفُ مَا فَرَضْتُمْ
إِلَّا أَنْ يَعْفُونَ أَوْ يَعْفُوَا الَّذِي بِيَدِهِ عُقْدَةُ
النِّكَاحِ وَأَنْ تَعْفُوا أَقْرَبُ لِلتَّقْوٰى وَلَا
تَنْسَوُا الْفَضْلَ بَيْنَكُمْ إِنَّ اللّٰهَ بِمَا تَعْمَلُونَ
بَصِيرٌ ﴿٢٣٧﴾ حٰفِظُوا عَلَى الصَّلَوٰتِ وَالصَّلٰوةِ الْوُسْطٰى
وَقُومُوا لِلّٰهِ قٰنِتِينَ ﴿٢٣٨﴾ فَإِنْ خِفْتُمْ فَرِجَالًا
أَوْ رُكْبَانًا فَإِذَا أَمِنْتُمْ فَاذْكُرُوا اللّٰهَ كَمَا
عَلَّمَكُمْ مَا لَمْ تَكُونُوا تَعْلَمُونَ ﴿٢٣٩﴾ وَالَّذِينَ

Allâh in the manner He taught you (and) which (manner) you did not know (before).
240. And those of you who die and leave wives behind, there is a binding injunction (of God) for their wives for a year's maintenance without being turned out (of their homes). But if they go out (of their own accord during this period) there is no blame on you with regard to what they do about themselves in an equitable and decent manner. And Allâh is All-Mighty, All-Wise.
241. And for the divorced women (also) a provision (should be made) in a fair and equitable manner. This is an obligation binding on those who guard against evil (and have regard for duty).
242. Thus does Allâh make His commandments clear to you so that you may abstain (from evil).

SECTION 32

243. **H**AVE you not considered the case of those (Israelites) who (in their exodus) fled from their homes (in Egypt with Moses) and they were (a congregation of) thousands, for fear of death? Then Allâh said to them, 'Die', (with the result that this generation perished while wandering in the wilderness for forty years). Then (from the next generation) He revived them, (and made them inherit the Promised land). Allâh is Munificent to people; but most of the people give (Him) no thanks.
244. And fight in the cause of Allâh, and know that Allâh is All-Hearing, All-Knowing.
245. Who is there that (performs for Allâh an act of the noblest virtue and) cuts off a portion of his goodly gifts for Allâh so He multiplies it to him manifold. And Allâh receives (the sacrifices) and amplifies and to Him you shall be made to return (to get the amplified reward of your deeds).
246. Have you not considered (the case of) the Chiefs of the Children of Israel (who lived) after (the time of) Moses? When they said to a Prophet of theirs, (- Samuel), 'Appoint for us a controlling authority that we may fight in

يُتَوَفَّوْنَ مِنْكُمْ وَيَذَرُونَ أَزْوَاجًا وَصِيَّةً
لِأَزْوَاجِهِمْ مَتَاعًا إِلَى الْحَوْلِ غَيْرَ إِخْرَاجٍ
فَإِنْ خَرَجْنَ فَلَا جُنَاحَ عَلَيْكُمْ فِي مَا فَعَلْنَ
فِي أَنْفُسِهِنَّ مِنْ مَعْرُوفٍ وَاللَّهُ عَزِيزٌ حَكِيمٌ ﴿٢٤٠﴾
وَلِلْمُطَلَّقَاتِ مَتَاعٌ بِالْمَعْرُوفِ حَقًّا عَلَى
الْمُتَّقِينَ ﴿٢٤١﴾ كَذَٰلِكَ يُبَيِّنُ اللَّهُ لَكُمْ آيَاتِهِ
لَعَلَّكُمْ تَعْقِلُونَ ﴿٢٤٢﴾ أَلَمْ تَرَ إِلَى الَّذِينَ خَرَجُوا
مِنْ دِيَارِهِمْ وَهُمْ أُلُوفٌ حَذَرَ الْمَوْتِ
فَقَالَ لَهُمُ اللَّهُ مُوتُوا ثُمَّ أَحْيَاهُمْ إِنَّ اللَّهَ
لَذُو فَضْلٍ عَلَى النَّاسِ وَلَٰكِنَّ أَكْثَرَ النَّاسِ
لَا يَشْكُرُونَ ﴿٢٤٣﴾ وَقَاتِلُوا فِي سَبِيلِ اللَّهِ وَاعْلَمُوا
أَنَّ اللَّهَ سَمِيعٌ عَلِيمٌ ﴿٢٤٤﴾ مَنْ ذَا الَّذِي يُقْرِضُ
اللَّهَ قَرْضًا حَسَنًا فَيُضَاعِفَهُ لَهُ أَضْعَافًا كَثِيرَةً
وَاللَّهُ يَقْبِضُ وَيَبْسُطُ وَإِلَيْهِ تُرْجَعُونَ ﴿٢٤٥﴾
أَلَمْ تَرَ إِلَى الْمَلَإِ مِنْ بَنِي إِسْرَائِيلَ مِنْ بَعْدِ
مُوسَىٰ إِذْ قَالُوا لِنَبِيٍّ لَهُمُ ابْعَثْ لَنَا مَلِكًا
نُقَاتِلْ فِي سَبِيلِ اللَّهِ قَالَ هَلْ عَسَيْتُمْ

ع ٣١ ٧ ١٥

the cause of Allâh.' He said, 'Is it not likely, that if fighting is prescribed for you, you will not fight?' They said, 'And what reason have we that we should not fight in the cause of Allâh, and we have been indeed driven forth from our homes and (parted from) our children?' Yet, when fighting was prescribed for them, they backed out except a few of them. And Allâh knows the unjust well.

247. And their Prophet (of God) said to them, 'Verily, Allâh has appointed Tâlût (- Saul) to be a controlling authority over you.' They said, 'How can he have sovereignty over us, whereas we are better entitled to sovereignty than he, and he has not been given abundance of wealth?' He (- their Prophet of God) replied, 'Surely, Allâh has chosen him above you and He has given him a vast deal of knowledge and of bodily strength.' And Allâh gives His sovereignty to whom He wills, for Allâh is All-Embracing, All-Knowing.

248. And their Prophet (of God) said to them, 'The sign of his sovereignty is indeed that there shall come to you (in his reign) the *Tâbût* (- the heart) in which there will be *Shechinah* (- tranquillity) from your Lord and legacy (of good) left by the followers of Moses and the followers of Aaron, the angels bearing it. Verily, there is a sign for you in that, when you are true believers.'

SECTION 33

249. **S**o when Tâlût (- Saul) marched out with the forces, he said, 'Verily, Allâh is going to test you by (the ordeal of) a stream, whosoever drinks of it, he will not then belong to me, and who so does not taste it, he shall certainly belong to me, excepting him who takes (only) a handful (of water) with his hand.' But they drank of it except a few of them. So that when he had crossed it, he and those who believed along with him, they said, 'We have no power today against Jâlût (- the assailant, the Goliath) and his forces.' But those who held it as certain that they (one day) were going to meet Allâh said,

إِن كُتِبَ عَلَيْكُمُ الْقِتَالُ أَلَّا تُقَاتِلُوا ۖ قَالُوا
وَمَا لَنَا أَلَّا نُقَاتِلَ فِي سَبِيلِ اللَّهِ وَقَدْ أُخْرِجْنَا
مِن دِيَارِنَا وَأَبْنَائِنَا ۖ فَلَمَّا كُتِبَ عَلَيْهِمُ
الْقِتَالُ تَوَلَّوْا إِلَّا قَلِيلًا مِّنْهُمْ ۗ وَاللَّهُ عَلِيمٌ
بِالظَّالِمِينَ ﴿٢٤٦﴾ وَقَالَ لَهُمْ نَبِيُّهُمْ إِنَّ اللَّهَ قَدْ
بَعَثَ لَكُمْ طَالُوتَ مَلِكًا ۚ قَالُوا أَنَّىٰ يَكُونُ لَهُ
الْمُلْكُ عَلَيْنَا وَنَحْنُ أَحَقُّ بِالْمُلْكِ مِنْهُ وَلَمْ
يُؤْتَ سَعَةً مِّنَ الْمَالِ ۚ قَالَ إِنَّ اللَّهَ اصْطَفَاهُ
عَلَيْكُمْ وَزَادَهُ بَسْطَةً فِي الْعِلْمِ وَالْجِسْمِ ۖ وَاللَّهُ
يُؤْتِي مُلْكَهُ مَن يَشَاءُ ۚ وَاللَّهُ وَاسِعٌ عَلِيمٌ ﴿٢٤٧﴾
وَقَالَ لَهُمْ نَبِيُّهُمْ إِنَّ آيَةَ مُلْكِهِ أَن
يَأْتِيَكُمُ التَّابُوتُ فِيهِ سَكِينَةٌ مِّن رَّبِّكُمْ
وَبَقِيَّةٌ مِّمَّا تَرَكَ آلُ مُوسَىٰ وَآلُ هَارُونَ
تَحْمِلُهُ الْمَلَائِكَةُ ۚ إِنَّ فِي ذَٰلِكَ لَآيَةً لَّكُمْ
إِن كُنتُم مُّؤْمِنِينَ ﴿٢٤٨﴾ فَلَمَّا فَصَلَ طَالُوتُ
بِالْجُنُودِ قَالَ إِنَّ اللَّهَ مُبْتَلِيكُم بِنَهَرٍ فَمَن
شَرِبَ مِنْهُ فَلَيْسَ مِنِّي وَمَن لَّمْ يَطْعَمْهُ
فَإِنَّهُ مِنِّي إِلَّا مَنِ اغْتَرَفَ غُرْفَةً بِيَدِهِ ۚ
فَشَرِبُوا مِنْهُ إِلَّا قَلِيلًا مِّنْهُمْ ۚ فَلَمَّا جَاوَزَهُ
هُوَ وَالَّذِينَ آمَنُوا مَعَهُ قَالُوا لَا طَاقَةَ لَنَا
الْيَوْمَ بِجَالُوتَ وَجُنُودِهِ ۚ قَالَ الَّذِينَ يَظُنُّونَ
أَنَّهُم مُّلَاقُو اللَّهِ كَم مِّن فِئَةٍ قَلِيلَةٍ غَلَبَتْ

'How often a small company has triumphed over a numerous host, by the leave of Allâh! And Allâh is with the patiently-persevering.'

250. And when they confronted Jâlût (-Goliath) and his forces they said, 'Our Lord! Grant us perseverance and keep our footholds firm and help us against the disbelieving people.'

251. At last, they routed them by the leave of Allâh, and David killed Jâlût, and Allâh gave him the sovereignty and the wisdom and taught him of what He pleased. And had it not been for Allâh repelling the people - some of them by the others - the earth would have been in a state of disorder; but Allâh is full of grace to the worlds.

252. These are the Messages of Allâh, We recite them to you with the truth; and you are indeed (one) of the Messengers.

فِئَةً كَثِيرَةً بِإِذْنِ اللّٰهِ ۗ وَاللّٰهُ مَعَ الصّٰبِرِينَ ﴿٢٤٩﴾
وَلَمَّا بَرَزُوا لِجَالُوتَ وَجُنُودِهِ قَالُوا رَبَّنَا أَفْرِغْ
عَلَيْنَا صَبْرًا وَثَبِّتْ أَقْدَامَنَا وَانْصُرْنَا عَلَى
الْقَوْمِ الْكٰفِرِينَ ﴿٢٥٠﴾ فَهَزَمُوهُم بِإِذْنِ اللّٰهِ ۙ وَقَتَلَ
دَاوُدُ جَالُوتَ وَآتٰهُ اللّٰهُ الْمُلْكَ وَالْحِكْمَةَ
وَعَلَّمَهُ مِمَّا يَشَاءُ ۗ وَلَوْلَا دَفْعُ اللّٰهِ النَّاسَ
بَعْضَهُم بِبَعْضٍ لَّفَسَدَتِ الْأَرْضُ وَلٰكِنَّ اللّٰهَ
ذُو فَضْلٍ عَلَى الْعٰلَمِينَ ﴿٢٥١﴾ تِلْكَ آيٰتُ اللّٰهِ
نَتْلُوهَا عَلَيْكَ بِالْحَقِّ ۚ وَإِنَّكَ لَمِنَ الْمُرْسَلِينَ ﴿٢٥٢﴾

PART الْجُزْءُ الثَّالِثُ III

253. **W**E have made these Messengers excel one another. There are those of them to whom Allâh has spoken much, and some of them He has exalted by many degrees of rank. And We gave Jesus, son of Mary, clear arguments, and We supported him with the blessed word (of God). Had Allâh (so) willed, people (who came) after them (- the Messengers) would not have fought one another (particularly) after clear arguments had come to them, but (as it was) they differed one from another; so that some of them believed while others disbelieved. Had Allâh (so) willed they would not have fought one another. Yet Allâh does whatever He intends.

تِلْكَ الرُّسُلُ فَضَّلْنَا بَعْضَهُمْ عَلَى بَعْضٍ
مِنْهُم مَّن كَلَّمَ اللّٰهُ وَرَفَعَ بَعْضَهُمْ
دَرَجٰتٍ ۚ وَآتَيْنَا عِيسَى ابْنَ مَرْيَمَ الْبَيِّنٰتِ
وَأَيَّدْنٰهُ بِرُوحِ الْقُدُسِ ۗ وَلَوْ شَاءَ اللّٰهُ مَا
اقْتَتَلَ الَّذِينَ مِنْ بَعْدِهِم مِّنْ بَعْدِ مَا
جَاءَتْهُمُ الْبَيِّنٰتُ وَلٰكِنِ اخْتَلَفُوا فَمِنْهُم مَّنْ
آمَنَ وَمِنْهُم مَّن كَفَرَ ۚ وَلَوْ شَاءَ اللّٰهُ
مَا اقْتَتَلُوا ۟ وَلٰكِنَّ اللّٰهَ يَفْعَلُ مَا يُرِيدُ ﴿٢٥٣﴾

SECTION 34

254. **O** YOU who believe! Spend (for the cause of Allâh) out of that which We have provided you with, before there comes the Day wherein there shall be no buying and selling, nor friendship, nor intercession. Those who refuse to obey this (commandment) are

يٰأَيُّهَا الَّذِينَ آمَنُوا أَنْفِقُوا مِمَّا رَزَقْنٰكُم
مِّنْ قَبْلِ أَنْ يَأْتِيَ يَوْمٌ لَّا بَيْعٌ فِيهِ
وَلَا خُلَّةٌ وَلَا شَفٰعَةٌ ۗ وَالْكٰفِرُونَ هُمُ

the real wrongdoers (to themselves).
255. Allâh, there is no other, cannot be and will never be one worthy of worship but He, the Ever Living, Self-Subsisting and All-Sustaining. Slumber overtakes Him not, nor sleep. Whatsoever is in the heavens and whatsoever is in the earth belongs to Him. Who is there that will intercede with Him, save by His leave? He knows their future and their past; and they encompass nothing of His knowledge (of the things) except of such (things) as He (Himself) pleases (to tell). His knowledge and suzerainty extends over the heavens and the earth and the care of them both tires Him not. He is the Supreme, the Great.
256. There is no compulsion of any sort in religion (as) the right way does stand obviously distinguished from the way of error. Now he that shall reject the transgressor and accepts Allâh (let such know that he) has laid hold of a support firm and strong which knows no breaking. Allâh is All-Hearing, All-Knowing.
257. Allâh is the Patron of those who believe, He brings them out of different kinds of darkness (leading them) into light. As for those who disbelieve, their patrons are the transgressors, they bring them out of light (and lead them) into every kind of darkness. It is these who are the fellows of the Fire, therein shall they live for long.

SECTION 35

258. **H**AVE you not considered (the case of) him (- Nimrod, the then ruler of Babylon) who controversed with Abraham concerning his Lord, because Allâh had given him kingdom? When Abraham said, 'My Lord is He Who fertilizes (the earth) and causes desolation.' He (- Nimrod) replied, 'I do bring about fertility and cause desolation.' Abraham said, 'Allâh surely makes the sun rise from the east, so you should make it rise from the west.' Thereupon the one who had rejected the faith (- Nimrod) was completely confounded. Indeed, Allâh does

الظّٰلِمُوۡنَ ﴿٢٥٤﴾ اَللّٰهُ لَاۤ اِلٰهَ اِلَّا هُوَ ۚ اَلۡحَیُّ
الۡقَیُّوۡمُ ۚ لَا تَاۡخُذُهٗ سِنَةٌ وَّلَا نَوۡمٌ ؕ لَهٗ
مَا فِی السَّمٰوٰتِ وَمَا فِی الۡاَرۡضِ ؕ مَنۡ ذَا الَّذِیۡ
یَشۡفَعُ عِنۡدَهٗۤ اِلَّا بِاِذۡنِهٖ ؕ یَعۡلَمُ مَا بَیۡنَ
اَیۡدِیۡهِمۡ وَمَا خَلۡفَهُمۡ ۚ وَلَا یُحِیۡطُوۡنَ بِشَیۡءٍ
مِّنۡ عِلۡمِهٖۤ اِلَّا بِمَا شَآءَ ۚ وَسِعَ کُرۡسِیُّهُ
السَّمٰوٰتِ وَالۡاَرۡضَ ۚ وَلَا یَـُٔوۡدُهٗ حِفۡظُهُمَا ۚ
وَهُوَ الۡعَلِیُّ الۡعَظِیۡمُ ﴿٢٥٥﴾ لَاۤ اِکۡرَاهَ فِی الدِّیۡنِ
قَدۡ تَّبَیَّنَ الرُّشۡدُ مِنَ الۡغَیِّ ۚ فَمَنۡ یَّکۡفُرۡ
بِالطَّاغُوۡتِ وَیُؤۡمِنۡۢ بِاللّٰهِ فَقَدِ اسۡتَمۡسَکَ
بِالۡعُرۡوَةِ الۡوُثۡقٰی ٭ لَا انۡفِصَامَ لَهَا ؕ وَاللّٰهُ سَمِیۡعٌ
عَلِیۡمٌ ﴿٢٥٦﴾ اَللّٰهُ وَلِیُّ الَّذِیۡنَ اٰمَنُوۡا ۙ یُخۡرِجُهُمۡ
مِّنَ الظُّلُمٰتِ اِلَی النُّوۡرِ ؕ وَالَّذِیۡنَ کَفَرُوۡۤا
اَوۡلِیٰٓـُٔهُمُ الطَّاغُوۡتُ ۙ یُخۡرِجُوۡنَهُمۡ مِّنَ النُّوۡرِ
اِلَی الظُّلُمٰتِ ؕ اُولٰٓئِکَ اَصۡحٰبُ النَّارِ ۚ هُمۡ
فِیۡهَا خٰلِدُوۡنَ ﴿٢٥٧﴾ اَلَمۡ تَرَ اِلَی الَّذِیۡ حَآجَّ اِبۡرٰهٖمَ
فِیۡ رَبِّهٖۤ اَنۡ اٰتٰىهُ اللّٰهُ الۡمُلۡکَ ۘ اِذۡ قَالَ
اِبۡرٰهٖمُ رَبِّیَ الَّذِیۡ یُحۡیٖ وَیُمِیۡتُ ۙ قَالَ اَنَا
اُحۡیٖ وَاُمِیۡتُ ؕ قَالَ اِبۡرٰهٖمُ فَاِنَّ اللّٰهَ یَاۡتِیۡ
بِالشَّمۡسِ مِنَ الۡمَشۡرِقِ فَاۡتِ بِهَا مِنَ
الۡمَغۡرِبِ فَبُهِتَ الَّذِیۡ کَفَرَ ؕ وَاللّٰهُ لَا یَهۡدِی

not guide the unjust people.

259. Or consider the case of him (- Ezekiel) who passed by a town (- Jerusalem as it was left in desolation by Nebuchadnezzar) and it had fallen in upon its roofs. He said, 'When will Allâh restore this (town) to life after its destruction?' So (in his vision) Allâh kept him in a state of death for a hundred years, then He raised him (to life). Then (God) said, 'How long have you stayed (in this state of death)?' He replied, 'I may have stayed a day or a part of a day (in this state).' (God) said, '(Yes this too is correct) but (as you have witnessed in your vision) you have stayed for a hundred years. Now look at your food and drink, they have escaped the action of time, and look at your donkey (too, years have not passed over it). And (We have made you visualise all this) that We may make you a sign to the people. And look at the (dead) bones how We set them together and then clothe them with flesh.' Thus when the fact of the matter became clear to him, he said, 'I know that Allâh is the Possessor of full power to do all that He will.'

260. And (recall the time) when Abraham said, 'My Lord! Show me how You give life to the dead.' (The Lord) said, 'Do you not believe (that I can)?' He said, 'Yes I do, but (I ask this) that my mind may be at peace.' (The Lord) said, 'Take four birds and make them attached to you, then put them each on a separate hill, then call them, they will come to you swiftly. And know that Allâh is All-Mighty, All-Wise.'

SECTION 36

261. THE attribute of those who spend their wealth in the cause of Allâh is like the attribute of a grain (of corn) which sprouts seven ears, each ear bearing a hundred grains. And Allâh multiplies further for whomsoever He pleases, for Allâh is Bountiful, All-Knowing.

262. Those who spend their wealth in the cause of Allâh, then follow not up what they have

الْقَوْمَ الظَّٰلِمِينَ ﴿٢٥٨﴾ أَوْ كَالَّذِي مَرَّ عَلَىٰ قَرْيَةٍ
وَهِيَ خَاوِيَةٌ عَلَىٰ عُرُوشِهَا قَالَ أَنَّىٰ يُحْيِي
هَٰذِهِ اللَّهُ بَعْدَ مَوْتِهَا فَأَمَاتَهُ اللَّهُ مِائَةَ
عَامٍ ثُمَّ بَعَثَهُ قَالَ كَمْ لَبِثْتَ قَالَ لَبِثْتُ
يَوْمًا أَوْ بَعْضَ يَوْمٍ قَالَ بَل لَّبِثْتَ مِائَةَ
عَامٍ فَانظُرْ إِلَىٰ طَعَامِكَ وَشَرَابِكَ لَمْ
يَتَسَنَّهْ وَانظُرْ إِلَىٰ حِمَارِكَ وَلِنَجْعَلَكَ آيَةً
لِّلنَّاسِ وَانظُرْ إِلَى الْعِظَامِ كَيْفَ نُنشِزُهَا
ثُمَّ نَكْسُوهَا لَحْمًا فَلَمَّا تَبَيَّنَ لَهُ قَالَ
أَعْلَمُ أَنَّ اللَّهَ عَلَىٰ كُلِّ شَيْءٍ قَدِيرٌ ﴿٢٥٩﴾ وَإِذْ
قَالَ إِبْرَٰهِيمُ رَبِّ أَرِنِي كَيْفَ تُحْيِي الْمَوْتَىٰ
قَالَ أَوَلَمْ تُؤْمِن قَالَ بَلَىٰ وَلَٰكِن لِّيَطْمَئِنَّ
قَلْبِي قَالَ فَخُذْ أَرْبَعَةً مِّنَ الطَّيْرِ فَصُرْهُنَّ
إِلَيْكَ ثُمَّ اجْعَلْ عَلَىٰ كُلِّ جَبَلٍ مِّنْهُنَّ جُزْءًا
ثُمَّ ادْعُهُنَّ يَأْتِينَكَ سَعْيًا وَاعْلَمْ أَنَّ اللَّهَ
عَزِيزٌ حَكِيمٌ ﴿٢٦٠﴾ مَثَلُ الَّذِينَ يُنفِقُونَ
أَمْوَٰلَهُمْ فِي سَبِيلِ اللَّهِ كَمَثَلِ حَبَّةٍ أَنبَتَتْ
سَبْعَ سَنَابِلَ فِي كُلِّ سُنبُلَةٍ مِّائَةُ حَبَّةٍ
وَاللَّهُ يُضَٰعِفُ لِمَن يَشَاءُ وَاللَّهُ وَٰسِعٌ عَلِيمٌ ﴿٢٦١﴾
الَّذِينَ يُنفِقُونَ أَمْوَٰلَهُمْ فِي سَبِيلِ اللَّهِ ثُمَّ

ع ٣٥ ٣

spent with a show of obligation, nor (with) injury, they shall have their reward with their Lord. They shall have no cause of fear, nor shall they ever grieve.

263. A fair word and forbearance are better than charity followed by injury. Indeed, Allâh is Self-Sufficient (having no want), Ever Forbearing.

264. O you who believe! Do not render void your charities by (a show of) obligation and injury, like him who spends his wealth to be seen by people and does not believe in Allâh and the Last Day. So his case is like the case of a smooth rock with some soil thereon, when heavy rain hits it leaves it bare and hard. They shall not be able to gain anything of what they accomplished. And Allâh does not guide such disbelieving people to the way of success.

265. But the case of (charity on the part of) those who spend their wealth seeking the good pleasure of Allâh and for their own consolidation and with firm faith, is like the case of a garden situated on a highly fertile land. It is hit by heavy rain so it yields its fruit manifold; but even if heavy rain does not hit it then a mere drizzle (is sufficient) for it. And Allâh sees well what you do.

266. Would anyone of you wish that while he has a garden of date-palm trees and vines served with running streams, he has therein each and every kind of fruit, while he is stricken by old age and has children who are (yet) feeble, a whirlwind carrying fire should smite it (- the garden) so that it is all burnt up? (No, not at all.) Thus does Allâh explain to you His Messages so that you may give thought.

SECTION 37

267. **O** YOU who believe! Spend (for the cause of Allâh) a portion of good and pure things, that you have yourselves earned and out of that which We have produced for you from the earth. Do not intend (upon spend-

لَا يُتْبِعُونَ مَآ أَنْفَقُوا مَنًّا وَّ لَآ أَذًى لَّهُمْ
أَجْرُهُمْ عِنْدَ رَبِّهِمْ ۚ وَلَا خَوْفٌ عَلَيْهِمْ
وَلَا هُمْ يَحْزَنُونَ ﴿٢٦٢﴾ قَوْلٌ مَّعْرُوفٌ وَّمَغْفِرَةٌ
خَيْرٌ مِّنْ صَدَقَةٍ يَّتْبَعُهَآ أَذًى ۗ وَاللّٰهُ غَنِيٌّ
حَلِيمٌ ﴿٢٦٣﴾ يَٰٓأَيُّهَا الَّذِينَ أٰمَنُوا لَا تُبْطِلُوا
صَدَقٰتِكُمْ بِالْمَنِّ وَ الْأَذٰى كَالَّذِي يُنْفِقُ
مَالَهُ رِئَآءَ النَّاسِ وَ لَا يُؤْمِنُ بِاللّٰهِ
وَالْيَوْمِ الْأٰخِرِ ۗ فَمَثَلُهُ كَمَثَلِ صَفْوَانٍ عَلَيْهِ
تُرَابٌ فَأَصَابَهُ وَابِلٌ فَتَرَكَهُ صَلْدًا ۗ لَا
يَقْدِرُونَ عَلٰى شَيْءٍ مِّمَّا كَسَبُوا ۗ وَ اللّٰهُ لَا
يَهْدِي الْقَوْمَ الْكٰفِرِينَ ﴿٢٦٤﴾ وَمَثَلُ الَّذِينَ
يُنْفِقُونَ أَمْوٰلَهُمُ ابْتِغَآءَ مَرْضَاتِ اللّٰهِ
وَتَثْبِيتًا مِّنْ أَنْفُسِهِمْ كَمَثَلِ جَنَّةٍ بِرَبْوَةٍ
أَصَابَهَا وَابِلٌ فَأٰتَتْ أُكُلَهَا ضِعْفَيْنِ ۚ فَإِنْ
لَّمْ يُصِبْهَا وَابِلٌ فَطَلٌّ ۗ وَاللّٰهُ بِمَا تَعْمَلُونَ
بَصِيرٌ ﴿٢٦٥﴾ أَيَوَدُّ أَحَدُكُمْ أَنْ تَكُونَ لَهُ جَنَّةٌ
مِّنْ نَّخِيلٍ وَّأَعْنَابٍ تَجْرِي مِنْ تَحْتِهَا
الْأَنْهٰرُ لَهُ فِيهَا مِنْ كُلِّ الثَّمَرٰتِ وَأَصَابَهُ
الْكِبَرُ وَلَهُ ذُرِّيَّةٌ ضُعَفَآءُ ۖ فَأَصَابَهَآ إِعْصَارٌ
فِيهِ نَارٌ فَاحْتَرَقَتْ ۗ كَذٰلِكَ يُبَيِّنُ اللّٰهُ لَكُمُ
الْأٰيٰتِ لَعَلَّكُمْ تَتَفَكَّرُونَ ﴿٢٦٦﴾ يَٰٓأَيُّهَا الَّذِينَ
أٰمَنُوٓا أَنْفِقُوا مِنْ طَيِّبٰتِ مَا كَسَبْتُمْ وَمِمَّآ
أَخْرَجْنَا لَكُمْ مِّنَ الْأَرْضِ ۖ وَلَا تَيَمَّمُوا الْخَبِيثَ

ع ٣٦ ٤

ing) the bad and inferior. You would spend that (bad and inferior for the cause of Allâh) which you would not accept at all (for yourselves) unless you connive at it. And know that Allâh is Self-Sufficient, Ever Praiseworthy.

268. Satan threatens you with poverty and incites you to niggardliness. But Allâh promises you forgiveness from Himself and affluence. And Allâh is Bountiful, All-Knowing.

269. He grants wisdom to whomsoever He will. Indeed, he who is granted wisdom has been granted an ample good. And none would take heed except those endowed with pure and clear understanding.

270. Whatever things worthy to be spent you spend and whatever vow for the performance of non obligatory act of goodness you take, Allâh knows it well. As for wrongdoers they shall have no helpers.

271. If you give (your) alms openly it is well and good (in itself). But if you keep them secret and give them to the needy it is better for your ownselves and He will (thereby) acquit you of some of your evil deeds. Allâh is fully aware of what you do.

272. You are not responsible for their guidance to the right path but Allâh guides (him) who wishes (to be guided). (Believers!) Whatever wealth you spend (for the cause of Allâh) it is to your own good, for you do not spend (it) but to seek the good pleasure of Allâh. And whatever wealth you spend (in doing good) will be fully credited to you and you shall not be treated unjustly.

273. (These charities are meant) for those needy who are (so) confined in the way of Allâh that they are unable to move about in the land (for providing their sustenance). The person ignorant (of their condition) thinks them free from want, because of (their) abstaining (from begging). But you shall know them by their appearance (that they are in need). They do not beg of people with importunity. And whatever good thing you spend (for their help) Allâh knows it surely

مِنْهُ تُنْفِقُونَ وَلَسْتُمْ بِـَٔاخِذِيهِ إِلَّآ أَنْ
تُغْمِضُوا فِيهِ ۚ وَاعْلَمُوٓا أَنَّ اللهَ غَنِيٌّ حَمِيدٌ ﴿٢٦٧﴾
اَلشَّيْطٰنُ يَعِدُكُمُ الْفَقْرَ وَيَأْمُرُكُمْ بِالْفَحْشَآءِ ۖ
وَاللهُ يَعِدُكُمْ مَّغْفِرَةً مِّنْهُ وَفَضْلًا ۗ وَاللهُ
وٰسِعٌ عَلِيمٌ ﴿٢٦٨﴾ يُؤْتِي الْحِكْمَةَ مَنْ يَشَآءُ ۚ
وَمَنْ يُؤْتَ الْحِكْمَةَ فَقَدْ أُوتِيَ خَيْرًا كَثِيرًا ۗ
وَمَا يَذَّكَّرُ إِلَّآ أُولُوا الْأَلْبٰبِ ﴿٢٦٩﴾ وَمَآ أَنْفَقْتُمْ
مِّنْ نَّفَقَةٍ أَوْ نَذَرْتُمْ مِّنْ نَّذْرٍ فَإِنَّ اللهَ
يَعْلَمُهُ ۗ وَمَا لِلظّٰلِمِينَ مِنْ أَنْصَارٍ ﴿٢٧٠﴾ إِنْ
تُبْدُوا الصَّدَقٰتِ فَنِعِمَّا هِيَ ۚ وَإِنْ تُخْفُوهَا
وَتُؤْتُوهَا الْفُقَرَآءَ فَهُوَ خَيْرٌ لَّكُمْ ۚ وَيُكَفِّرُ
عَنْكُمْ مِّنْ سَيِّـَٔاتِكُمْ ۗ وَاللهُ بِمَا تَعْمَلُونَ
خَبِيرٌ ﴿٢٧١﴾ لَيْسَ عَلَيْكَ هُدٰىهُمْ وَلٰكِنَّ
اللهَ يَهْدِي مَنْ يَشَآءُ ۗ وَمَا تُنْفِقُوا مِنْ
خَيْرٍ فَلِأَنْفُسِكُمْ ۚ وَمَا تُنْفِقُونَ إِلَّا ابْتِغَآءَ
وَجْهِ اللهِ ۚ وَمَا تُنْفِقُوا مِنْ خَيْرٍ يُوَفَّ
إِلَيْكُمْ وَأَنْتُمْ لَا تُظْلَمُونَ ﴿٢٧٢﴾ لِلْفُقَرَآءِ الَّذِينَ
أُحْصِرُوا فِي سَبِيلِ اللهِ لَا يَسْتَطِيعُونَ ضَرْبًا
فِي الْأَرْضِ يَحْسَبُهُمُ الْجَاهِلُ أَغْنِيَآءَ مِنَ
التَّعَفُّفِ ۚ تَعْرِفُهُمْ بِسِيمٰهُمْ ۚ لَا يَسْـَٔلُونَ
النَّاسَ إِلْحَافًا ۗ وَمَا تُنْفِقُوا مِنْ خَيْرٍ

well.

SECTION 38

274. **T**HOSE who spend their wealth by night and by day (for the cause of Allâh) privately and publicly have their reward with their Lord, they shall have no cause of fear, nor shall they ever grieve.

275. Those who practice usury and interest, (their condition is such as) they will not be able to stand except like the standing of one who has lost his reason under the influence of satan. That is so because they say, 'Trade is just like usury and interest.' Whereas Allâh has made trade lawful and made interest unlawful. Then whosoever has received (this) admonition from his Lord and keeps away (from usury and interest) he may keep whatever (interest) he has taken in the past. His matter rests with Allâh. As for those who revert (to the practice of usury and interest) it is these who are the fellows of the Fire, therein shall they live for long.

276. Allâh annuls usury and interest and promotes charity. Allâh does not love any persistent and confirmed disbeliever and an arch-sinner.

277. Verily, those who believe and do deeds of righteousness and regularly observe the Prayer and go on presenting the *Zakât* shall have their reward from their Lord; they shall have no cause of fear, nor shall they ever grieve.

278. O you who believe! Take Allâh as a shield and forgo all outstanding gains from usury and interest if you are indeed believers.

279. But if you do (it) not, then beware of war from Allâh and His Messenger. But if you turn away (from such an unlawful transaction) then you shall have your principal (without interest) back. (Thus) you shall neither deal unjustly nor be dealt with unjustly.

280. If any (debtor) be in straitened circumstances there shall be respite (for him) till (his circumstances) ease. But that if you remit (the debt) by way of charity (for the sake of God), it is better for you, if you only knew.

281. And guard yourself against (the evil of)

فَإِنَّ اللّٰهَ بِهٖ عَلِيْمٌ ﴿٢٧٣﴾ اَلَّذِيْنَ يُنْفِقُوْنَ
اَمْوٰلَهُمْ بِالَّيْلِ وَالنَّهَارِ سِرًّا وَّعَلَانِيَةً
فَلَهُمْ اَجْرُهُمْ عِنْدَ رَبِّهِمْ ۚ وَلَا خَوْفٌ
عَلَيْهِمْ وَلَا هُمْ يَحْزَنُوْنَ ﴿٢٧٤﴾ اَلَّذِيْنَ يَاْكُلُوْنَ
الرِّبٰوا لَا يَقُوْمُوْنَ اِلَّا كَمَا يَقُوْمُ الَّذِيْ
يَتَخَبَّطُهُ الشَّيْطٰنُ مِنَ الْمَسِّ ؕ ذٰلِكَ بِاَنَّهُمْ
قَالُوْٓا اِنَّمَا الْبَيْعُ مِثْلُ الرِّبٰوا ۘ وَاَحَلَّ اللّٰهُ
الْبَيْعَ وَحَرَّمَ الرِّبٰوا ؕ فَمَنْ جَآءَهٗ مَوْعِظَةٌ
مِّنْ رَّبِّهٖ فَانْتَهٰى فَلَهٗ مَا سَلَفَ ؕ وَاَمْرُهٗٓ
اِلَى اللّٰهِ ؕ وَمَنْ عَادَ فَاُولٰٓئِكَ اَصْحٰبُ النَّارِ ۚ
هُمْ فِيْهَا خٰلِدُوْنَ ﴿٢٧٥﴾ يَمْحَقُ اللّٰهُ الرِّبٰوا
وَيُرْبِي الصَّدَقٰتِ ؕ وَاللّٰهُ لَا يُحِبُّ كُلَّ كَفَّارٍ
اَثِيْمٍ ﴿٢٧٦﴾ اِنَّ الَّذِيْنَ اٰمَنُوْا وَعَمِلُوا الصّٰلِحٰتِ
وَاَقَامُوا الصَّلٰوةَ وَاٰتَوُا الزَّكٰوةَ لَهُمْ اَجْرُهُمْ
عِنْدَ رَبِّهِمْ ۚ وَلَا خَوْفٌ عَلَيْهِمْ وَلَا هُمْ
يَحْزَنُوْنَ ﴿٢٧٧﴾ يٰٓاَيُّهَا الَّذِيْنَ اٰمَنُوا اتَّقُوا اللّٰهَ
وَذَرُوْا مَا بَقِيَ مِنَ الرِّبٰوٓا اِنْ كُنْتُمْ
مُّؤْمِنِيْنَ ﴿٢٧٨﴾ فَاِنْ لَّمْ تَفْعَلُوْا فَاْذَنُوْا بِحَرْبٍ
مِّنَ اللّٰهِ وَرَسُوْلِهٖ ۚ وَاِنْ تُبْتُمْ فَلَكُمْ
رُءُوْسُ اَمْوٰلِكُمْ ۚ لَا تَظْلِمُوْنَ وَلَا تُظْلَمُوْنَ ﴿٢٧٩﴾
وَاِنْ كَانَ ذُوْ عُسْرَةٍ فَنَظِرَةٌ اِلٰى مَيْسَرَةٍ ؕ
وَاَنْ تَصَدَّقُوْا خَيْرٌ لَّكُمْ اِنْ كُنْتُمْ تَعْلَمُوْنَ ﴿٢٨٠﴾

الجزء الثالث

the day when you shall be made to return to Allâh; then every soul shall be paid in full for what it has accomplished, and no injustice shall be done to them.

SECTION 39

282. **O** YOU who believe! When you transact a loan for a stipulated term, then write it down. Let a scribe write (it) in your presence in (term of) equity and fairness. The scribe shall not refuse to write down, since it is Allâh Who taught him (to write). Write he must. And let him upon whom be the liability, dictate and let him observe his duty to Allâh, his Lord, nor should he depreciate anything (what he owes) from it. But if the person upon whom the liability is, be of feeble mind or is infirm or he is incapable of dictating himself, then let some one who can watch his interests dictate in (term of) equity and fairness. And call in to witness (the transaction) two male witnesses from amongst your men. But if there be not two males (available) then let there be one male and two females such as you approve as witnesses (to bear witness), so that if either of the two women forgets then one may remind the other. And let the witnesses not refuse (to give evidence) whenever they are summoned. And never feel weary of writing it (- the transaction) down, whether it (- the debt) be small or large, along with the time of its (payment) being due. This (way) is more just in the sight of Allâh, and ensures a more upright evidence and is more likely to prevent your falling into doubts, (so write it down) except you carry ready trade and transfer the merchandise from hand to hand, in that case there shall be no blame on you that you do not write (the transaction). Yet have witnesses when you trade with one another. Let neither the scribe nor the witness be harmed, and if you do (any such thing) then that indeed, is disobedience on your part. Take Allâh as a shield (with the result that) Allâh will grant you knowledge, for Allâh has perfect knowledge of everything.

وَاتَّقُوا يَوْمًا تُرْجَعُونَ فِيهِ إِلَى اللَّهِ ثُمَّ تُوَفَّى كُلُّ نَفْسٍ مَا كَسَبَتْ وَهُمْ لَا يُظْلَمُونَ ﴿٢٨١﴾ يَا أَيُّهَا الَّذِينَ آمَنُوا إِذَا تَدَايَنْتُمْ بِدَيْنٍ إِلَى أَجَلٍ مُسَمًّى فَاكْتُبُوهُ وَلْيَكْتُبْ بَيْنَكُمْ كَاتِبٌ بِالْعَدْلِ وَلَا يَأْبَ كَاتِبٌ أَنْ يَكْتُبَ كَمَا عَلَّمَهُ اللَّهُ فَلْيَكْتُبْ وَلْيُمْلِلِ الَّذِي عَلَيْهِ الْحَقُّ وَلْيَتَّقِ اللَّهَ رَبَّهُ وَلَا يَبْخَسْ مِنْهُ شَيْئًا فَإِنْ كَانَ الَّذِي عَلَيْهِ الْحَقُّ سَفِيهًا أَوْ ضَعِيفًا أَوْ لَا يَسْتَطِيعُ أَنْ يُمِلَّ هُوَ فَلْيُمْلِلْ وَلِيُّهُ بِالْعَدْلِ وَاسْتَشْهِدُوا شَهِيدَيْنِ مِنْ رِجَالِكُمْ فَإِنْ لَمْ يَكُونَا رَجُلَيْنِ فَرَجُلٌ وَامْرَأَتَانِ مِمَّنْ تَرْضَوْنَ مِنَ الشُّهَدَاءِ أَنْ تَضِلَّ إِحْدَاهُمَا فَتُذَكِّرَ إِحْدَاهُمَا الْأُخْرَى وَلَا يَأْبَ الشُّهَدَاءُ إِذَا مَا دُعُوا وَلَا تَسْأَمُوا أَنْ تَكْتُبُوهُ صَغِيرًا أَوْ كَبِيرًا إِلَى أَجَلِهِ ذَلِكُمْ أَقْسَطُ عِنْدَ اللَّهِ وَأَقْوَمُ لِلشَّهَادَةِ وَأَدْنَى أَلَّا تَرْتَابُوا إِلَّا أَنْ تَكُونَ تِجَارَةً حَاضِرَةً تُدِيرُونَهَا بَيْنَكُمْ فَلَيْسَ عَلَيْكُمْ جُنَاحٌ أَلَّا تَكْتُبُوهَا وَأَشْهِدُوا إِذَا تَبَايَعْتُمْ وَلَا يُضَارَّ كَاتِبٌ وَلَا شَهِيدٌ وَإِنْ تَفْعَلُوا فَإِنَّهُ فُسُوقٌ بِكُمْ وَاتَّقُوا اللَّهَ وَيُعَلِّمُكُمُ اللَّهُ وَاللَّهُ بِكُلِّ شَيْءٍ عَلِيمٌ ﴿٢٨٢﴾

283. And if you be on a journey and do not find a scribe, then (let there be) a pledge with possession (of some article to secure your debt). If one of you entrusts something to another let him who is entrusted deliver his trust, and let him take Allâh, his Lord, as a shield. Do not conceal the evidence, for who so conceals it, his heart is certainly sinful. Allâh is Well-Aware of all that you do.

SECTION 40

284. **T**o Allâh belongs whatever is in the heavens and whatever is in the earth, and whether you reveal that which is in your minds or conceal it Allâh will call you to account according to it. Then He will protect whomsoever He will and will punish whomsoever He will. And Allâh is Possessor of full power to do all He will.

285. The Messenger believes in what has been revealed to him by his Lord and (so do) the faithfuls. Everyone believes in Allâh, His angels, His Books and His Messengers. (And the faithful declare,) 'We make no distinction (in believing) between any of His Messengers.' They say, '(Lord!) We have heard (Your commandments) and we are obedient. (Grant us) Your protection, Our Lord! For to You is the returning.'

286. Allâh charges no soul but to its capacity. It (- the soul) shall be paid for that which it has done (of good) and against it who has incurred (evil deliberately). (Pray,) 'Our Lord! Take us not to task if we forget or (if) we make a mistake. Our Lord! Lay not upon us the burden (of disobedience) as You laid upon those before us. Our Lord! Charge us not with the responsibility which we have not the strength to bear; therefore overlook our faults and grant us protection and have mercy on us. You are our Master, therefore help us against the disbelieving people.'

سُوْرَةُ الْبَقَرَةِ ٢

وَإِنْ كُنْتُمْ عَلَى سَفَرٍ وَلَمْ تَجِدُوا كَاتِبًا
فَرِهٰنٌ مَّقْبُوضَةٌ فَإِنْ أَمِنَ بَعْضُكُمْ بَعْضًا
فَلْيُؤَدِّ الَّذِي اؤْتُمِنَ أَمٰنَتَهُ وَلْيَتَّقِ اللهَ
رَبَّهُ وَلَا تَكْتُمُوا الشَّهٰدَةَ وَمَنْ يَّكْتُمْهَا
فَإِنَّهُ آثِمٌ قَلْبُهُ وَاللهُ بِمَا تَعْمَلُونَ عَلِيمٌ ﴿٢٨٣﴾
لِلّٰهِ مَا فِي السَّمٰوٰتِ وَمَا فِي الْأَرْضِ وَإِنْ
تُبْدُوا مَا فِي أَنْفُسِكُمْ أَوْ تُخْفُوهُ يُحَاسِبْكُمْ
بِهِ اللهُ فَيَغْفِرُ لِمَنْ يَّشَآءُ وَيُعَذِّبُ مَنْ
يَّشَآءُ وَاللهُ عَلَى كُلِّ شَيْءٍ قَدِيرٌ ﴿٢٨٤﴾ آمَنَ
الرَّسُولُ بِمَآ أُنْزِلَ إِلَيْهِ مِنْ رَّبِّهِ
وَالْمُؤْمِنُونَ كُلٌّ آمَنَ بِاللهِ وَمَلٰٓئِكَتِهِ
وَكُتُبِهِ وَرُسُلِهِ لَا نُفَرِّقُ بَيْنَ أَحَدٍ مِّنْ
رُّسُلِهِ وَقَالُوا سَمِعْنَا وَأَطَعْنَا غُفْرَانَكَ
رَبَّنَا وَإِلَيْكَ الْمَصِيرُ ﴿٢٨٥﴾ لَا يُكَلِّفُ اللهُ
نَفْسًا إِلَّا وُسْعَهَا لَهَا مَا كَسَبَتْ وَعَلَيْهَا
مَا اكْتَسَبَتْ رَبَّنَا لَا تُؤَاخِذْنَآ إِنْ نَّسِينَآ
أَوْ أَخْطَأْنَا رَبَّنَا وَلَا تَحْمِلْ عَلَيْنَآ إِصْرًا
كَمَا حَمَلْتَهُ عَلَى الَّذِينَ مِنْ قَبْلِنَا رَبَّنَا
وَلَا تُحَمِّلْنَا مَا لَا طَاقَةَ لَنَا بِهِ وَاعْفُ
عَنَّا وَاغْفِرْ لَنَا وَارْحَمْنَا أَنْتَ مَوْلٰنَا
فَانْصُرْنَا عَلَى الْقَوْمِ الْكٰفِرِينَ ﴿٢٨٦﴾

CHAPTER
3

ÂL-I-'IMRÂN
(Family of Amran)
(Revealed after Hijrah)

With the name of Allâh,
the Most Gracious, the Ever Merciful
(I commence to read Sûrah Âl-i- 'Imrân).

1. **A**LIF LÂM MÎM - I am Allâh, the All- Knowing.
2. Allâh is He. There is no other, cannot be and will never be one worthy of worship but He. He is the Living, the Self-Subsisting and All-Sustaining.
3. He has revealed to you gradually this perfect Book (-the Qur'ân) which meets all your requirements, fulfilling that (prophecies in the Scriptures) which preceded it and which still remain. He revealed the Torah and the Evangel,
4. Before this, as a guidance of the people. And He has revealed (the Qur'ân as) the Criterion of judgment (between truth and falsehood). Those who deny the revelations of Allâh there surely awaits them a severe punishment. Mighty is Allâh, the Lord of Retribution.
5. As to Allâh, verily nothing in this earth nor in the space above is hidden (from His view).
6. He it is Who fashions you in the wombs as He will. There is no other, cannot be and will never be one worthy of worship but He, the All-Mighty, the All-Wise.
7. He it is Who has revealed to you this perfect Book, some of its verses are definite and decisive. They are the basic root (conveying the established meanings) of the Book *(- Ummal Kitâb)* and other (verses) are susceptible to various interpretations. As for those in whose hearts is perversity follow (verses) that are susceptible to different interpretations, seeking (to cause) dissension and seeking an interpretation (of their own choice). But no one knows

سُورَةُ آلِ عِمْرَانَ مَدَنِيَّةٌ

بِسْمِ اللهِ الرَّحْمٰنِ الرَّحِيْمِ

الٓمٓ ﴿١﴾ اللهُ لَآ إِلٰهَ إِلَّا هُوَ الْحَيُّ الْقَيُّوْمُ ﴿٢﴾
نَزَّلَ عَلَيْكَ الْكِتٰبَ بِالْحَقِّ مُصَدِّقًا
لِّمَا بَيْنَ يَدَيْهِ وَ أَنْزَلَ التَّوْرٰىةَ
وَالْإِنْجِيْلَ ﴿٣﴾ مِنْ قَبْلُ هُدًى لِّلنَّاسِ وَأَنْزَلَ
الْفُرْقَانَ ۵ إِنَّ الَّذِيْنَ كَفَرُوْا بِاٰيٰتِ اللهِ لَهُمْ
عَذَابٌ شَدِيْدٌ وَاللهُ عَزِيْزٌ ذُو انْتِقَامٍ ﴿٤﴾
إِنَّ اللهَ لَا يَخْفٰى عَلَيْهِ شَيْءٌ فِي الْأَرْضِ
وَلَا فِي السَّمَآءِ ﴿٥﴾ هُوَ الَّذِيْ يُصَوِّرُكُمْ فِي
الْأَرْحَامِ كَيْفَ يَشَآءُ لَآ إِلٰهَ إِلَّا هُوَ الْعَزِيْزُ
الْحَكِيْمُ ﴿٦﴾ هُوَ الَّذِيْٓ أَنْزَلَ عَلَيْكَ الْكِتٰبَ مِنْهُ
اٰيٰتٌ مُّحْكَمٰتٌ هُنَّ أُمُّ الْكِتٰبِ وَأُخَرُ
مُتَشٰبِهٰتٌ فَأَمَّا الَّذِيْنَ فِيْ قُلُوْبِهِمْ زَيْغٌ
فَيَتَّبِعُوْنَ مَا تَشٰبَهَ مِنْهُ ابْتِغَآءَ الْفِتْنَةِ

its true interpretation except Allâh, and those who are firmly grounded in knowledge. They say, 'We believe in it, it is all (- the basic and decisive verses as well as the allegorical ones) from our Lord.' And none take heed except those endowed with pure and clear understanding.
8. 'Our Lord!', (they pray,) 'Let not our hearts become perverse after You have guided us, and grant us from Your Own Self special mercy, for You alone are the Most Liberal Bestower.
9. 'Our Lord! You are invariably going to assemble all humankind on the Day about (the advent of) which there is no doubt. Surely, Allâh never breaks His word.'

SECTION 2

10. **A**s to those who disbelieve, neither their possessions, nor their children shall avail them at all against (the punishment of) Allâh; and it is they that will be the fuel of the Fire.
11. (Their conduct is) like the conduct of the followers of Pharaoh and those before them. They cried lies to Our Messages, so that Allâh took them to task for their sins. Allâh is Severe in retribution.
12. Say to those who disbelieve, 'You shall soon be overcome and gathered together to be driven towards Gehenna. What an evil abode it is!'
13. There has already been for you a remarkable sign in the two armies that encountered each other (- in the Battle of *Badr*). (Behold!) One army is fighting in the cause of Allâh and the other is (an army of) disbelievers, whom they (- the Muslims) saw with their naked eyes twice as many (and not thrice as the actual figure was so that the believers did not lose their hearts). And Allâh strengthens with His help whomsoever He will. Verily, in this is a lesson for those who have eyes.
14. It has been made fairseeming to the people the love of the desired things comprising women, sons, stored up heaps of gold and

وَابْتِغَاءَ تَأْوِيلِهِ وَمَا يَعْلَمُ تَأْوِيلَهُ إِلَّا
اللَّهُ وَالرَّاسِخُونَ فِي الْعِلْمِ يَقُولُونَ آمَنَّا
بِهِ كُلٌّ مِنْ عِنْدِ رَبِّنَا وَمَا يَذَّكَّرُ إِلَّا
أُولُو الْأَلْبَابِ (٧) رَبَّنَا لَا تُزِغْ قُلُوبَنَا بَعْدَ إِذْ
هَدَيْتَنَا وَهَبْ لَنَا مِنْ لَدُنْكَ رَحْمَةً
إِنَّكَ أَنْتَ الْوَهَّابُ (٨) رَبَّنَا إِنَّكَ جَامِعُ
النَّاسِ لِيَوْمٍ لَا رَيْبَ فِيهِ إِنَّ اللَّهَ لَا يُخْلِفُ
الْمِيعَادَ (٩) إِنَّ الَّذِينَ كَفَرُوا لَنْ تُغْنِيَ
عَنْهُمْ أَمْوَالُهُمْ وَلَا أَوْلَادُهُمْ مِنَ اللَّهِ شَيْئًا
وَأُولَٰئِكَ هُمْ وَقُودُ النَّارِ (١٠) كَدَأْبِ آلِ
فِرْعَوْنَ وَالَّذِينَ مِنْ قَبْلِهِمْ كَذَّبُوا
بِآيَاتِنَا فَأَخَذَهُمُ اللَّهُ بِذُنُوبِهِمْ وَاللَّهُ
شَدِيدُ الْعِقَابِ (١١) قُلْ لِلَّذِينَ كَفَرُوا
سَتُغْلَبُونَ وَتُحْشَرُونَ إِلَىٰ جَهَنَّمَ وَبِئْسَ
الْمِهَادُ (١٢) قَدْ كَانَ لَكُمْ آيَةٌ فِي فِئَتَيْنِ
الْتَقَتَا فِئَةٌ تُقَاتِلُ فِي سَبِيلِ اللَّهِ وَأُخْرَىٰ
كَافِرَةٌ يَرَوْنَهُمْ مِثْلَيْهِمْ رَأْيَ الْعَيْنِ وَاللَّهُ
يُؤَيِّدُ بِنَصْرِهِ مَنْ يَشَاءُ إِنَّ فِي ذَٰلِكَ لَعِبْرَةً
لِأُولِي الْأَبْصَارِ (١٣) زُيِّنَ لِلنَّاسِ حُبُّ الشَّهَوَاتِ

ع ٩

silver, well-bred horses, cattle and tilth. That is the provision of the present life. Whereas with Allâh is the fairest goal (of life).

15. Say, 'Shall I inform you of something better than these? There are with their Lord Gardens served with running streams for those who become secure against evil. There they shall abide forever, and (there will be the righteous) companions perfectly purified and (above all they will enjoy) the good pleasure of Allâh.' And Allâh is Mindful of (His) servants,

16. Who say, 'Our Lord! We have certainly believed, therefore protect us against (the consequences of) our sins and save us from the punishment of the Fire.'

17. (And those who are) the patiently persevering, the truthful and the obedient, and those who spend (liberally in the cause of Allâh) and the implorers of Divine protection in the latter part of the night (and from the core of their hearts).

18. Allâh bears witness that there is no other, cannot be and will never be one worthy of worship but He, and (so do) the angels and those possessed of true knowledge, maintaining justice. There is no other, cannot be and will never be one worthy of worship but He, the All-Mighty, the All-Wise.

19. Decidedly, the true Faith acceptable to Allâh is Islam. Those who were given the Scripture were not at variance except after the knowledge had come to them; (their differences were) due to mutual envy and to spite one another. And who so denies the Messages of Allâh (should bear in mind that) then Allâh indeed is Quick at reckoning.

20. But if they dispute with you say, 'I have completely submitted myself to (the will and guidance of) Allâh and (so have) those who follow me.' And say to those who had been given the Scripture and to the unlettered, 'Have you also submitted yourselves?' Indeed, they will be following true guidance if they submit themselves (to the will of God). But if

مِنَ النِّسَآءِ وَالْبَنِينَ وَالْقَنٰطِيرِ الْمُقَنْطَرَةِ
مِنَ الذَّهَبِ وَالْفِضَّةِ وَالْخَيْلِ الْمُسَوَّمَةِ
وَالْأَنْعٰمِ وَالْحَرْثِ ذٰلِكَ مَتٰعُ الْحَيٰوةِ
الدُّنْيَا وَاللّٰهُ عِنْدَهُ حُسْنُ الْمَاٰبِ ۝ قُلْ
أَؤُنَبِّئُكُمْ بِخَيْرٍ مِّنْ ذٰلِكُمْ لِلَّذِينَ اتَّقَوْا
عِنْدَ رَبِّهِمْ جَنّٰتٌ تَجْرِي مِنْ تَحْتِهَا
الْأَنْهٰرُ خٰلِدِينَ فِيهَا وَأَزْوٰجٌ مُّطَهَّرَةٌ
وَرِضْوٰنٌ مِّنَ اللّٰهِ وَاللّٰهُ بَصِيرٌ بِالْعِبَادِ ۝١٥
الَّذِينَ يَقُولُونَ رَبَّنَا إِنَّنَا اٰمَنَّا فَاغْفِرْ لَنَا
ذُنُوبَنَا وَقِنَا عَذَابَ النَّارِ ۝١٦ اَلصّٰبِرِينَ
وَالصّٰدِقِينَ وَالْقٰنِتِينَ وَالْمُنْفِقِينَ
وَالْمُسْتَغْفِرِينَ بِالْأَسْحَارِ ۝١٧ شَهِدَ اللّٰهُ أَنَّهُ
لَا إِلٰهَ إِلَّا هُوَ وَالْمَلٰئِكَةُ وَأُولُوا الْعِلْمِ قَآئِمًا
بِالْقِسْطِ لَا إِلٰهَ إِلَّا هُوَ الْعَزِيزُ الْحَكِيمُ ۝١٨
إِنَّ الدِّينَ عِنْدَ اللّٰهِ الْإِسْلٰمُ وَمَا اخْتَلَفَ
الَّذِينَ أُوتُوا الْكِتٰبَ إِلَّا مِنْ بَعْدِ مَا
جَآءَهُمُ الْعِلْمُ بَغْيًا بَيْنَهُمْ وَمَنْ يَّكْفُرْ
بِاٰيٰتِ اللّٰهِ فَإِنَّ اللّٰهَ سَرِيعُ الْحِسَابِ ۝١٩ فَإِنْ
حَآجُّوكَ فَقُلْ أَسْلَمْتُ وَجْهِيَ لِلّٰهِ وَمَنِ
اتَّبَعَنِ وَقُلْ لِّلَّذِينَ أُوتُوا الْكِتٰبَ وَالْأُمِّيّٖنَ
ءَأَسْلَمْتُمْ فَإِنْ أَسْلَمُوا فَقَدِ اهْتَدَوْا وَإِنْ

they turn back then your responsibility is only to convey (the message). Allâh is Ever Watchful of His servants.

SECTION 3

21. **S**URELY, those who deny the Messages of Allâh and seek to kill the Prophets without a just cause and slay those among the people who enjoin equity and justice, announce to them a grievous punishment.
22. It is they whose deeds go in vain in this world and in the Hereafter, and they shall have none to help them.
23. Have you not considered (the case of) those who were given a portion of the Scripture? When they are called to the Book of Allâh (the Qur'ân) that it may judge between them, yet a party of them turn away in sheer aversion.
24. They do so because they say, 'The Fire will not (even) brush us except for a limited number of days.' (Their own lies) that they used to forge have deluded them in the matter of their faith.
25. Then how (will they fare) when We gather them together for the Day about (the advent of) which there is no doubt, and (when) every soul shall be paid in full for what it has accomplished, and they shall not be dealt with unjustly.
26. Say, 'O Allâh! The Lord of all power, You grant power to whomsoever You will and take away power from whomsoever You please, and confer honour and dignity on whomsoever You will and disgrace whomsoever You will. All good lies in Your hand. Verily, You are the Possessor of full power to do all You will,
27. 'You cause the night to merge into the day and cause the day to merge into the night, and bring forth the living from the dead and bring forth the dead from the living, and provide (all sorts of provisions) to whomsoever You will without measure.'
28. Let not the believers take the disbelievers

تَوَلَّوْا فَإِنَّمَا عَلَيْكَ الْبَلٰغُ وَ اللّٰهُ بَصِيرٌۢ
بِالْعِبَادِ ﴿٢٠﴾ إِنَّ الَّذِينَ يَكْفُرُونَ بِاٰيٰتِ
اللّٰهِ وَ يَقْتُلُونَ النَّبِيّٖنَ بِغَيْرِ حَقٍّ وَّ يَقْتُلُونَ
الَّذِينَ يَأْمُرُونَ بِالْقِسْطِ مِنَ النَّاسِ فَبَشِّرْهُمْ
بِعَذَابٍ أَلِيمٍ ﴿٢١﴾ أُولٰٓئِكَ الَّذِينَ حَبِطَتْ
أَعْمٰلُهُمْ فِي الدُّنْيَا وَ الْاٰخِرَةِ وَ مَا لَهُمْ
مِّنْ نّٰصِرِينَ ﴿٢٢﴾ أَلَمْ تَرَ إِلَى الَّذِينَ أُوتُوا
نَصِيبًا مِّنَ الْكِتٰبِ يُدْعَوْنَ إِلٰى كِتٰبِ
اللّٰهِ لِيَحْكُمَ بَيْنَهُمْ ثُمَّ يَتَوَلّٰى فَرِيقٌ مِّنْهُمْ
وَ هُمْ مُّعْرِضُونَ ﴿٢٣﴾ ذٰلِكَ بِأَنَّهُمْ قَالُوا لَنْ
تَمَسَّنَا النَّارُ إِلَّا أَيَّامًا مَّعْدُودٰتٍ وَ غَرَّهُمْ
فِي دِينِهِمْ مَّا كَانُوا يَفْتَرُونَ ﴿٢٤﴾ فَكَيْفَ إِذَا
جَمَعْنٰهُمْ لِيَوْمٍ لَّا رَيْبَ فِيهِ وَ وُفِّيَتْ كُلُّ
نَفْسٍ مَّا كَسَبَتْ وَ هُمْ لَا يُظْلَمُونَ ﴿٢٥﴾ قُلِ
اللّٰهُمَّ مٰلِكَ الْمُلْكِ تُؤْتِي الْمُلْكَ مَنْ تَشَآءُ
وَ تَنْزِعُ الْمُلْكَ مِمَّنْ تَشَآءُ وَ تُعِزُّ مَنْ تَشَآءُ
وَ تُذِلُّ مَنْ تَشَآءُ بِيَدِكَ الْخَيْرُ إِنَّكَ عَلٰى
كُلِّ شَيْءٍ قَدِيرٌ ﴿٢٦﴾ تُولِجُ الَّيْلَ فِي النَّهَارِ
وَ تُولِجُ النَّهَارَ فِي الَّيْلِ وَ تُخْرِجُ الْحَيَّ مِنَ
الْمَيِّتِ وَ تُخْرِجُ الْمَيِّتَ مِنَ الْحَيِّ وَ تَرْزُقُ
مَنْ تَشَآءُ بِغَيْرِ حِسَابٍ ﴿٢٧﴾ لَا يَتَّخِذِ الْمُؤْمِنُونَ

for allies in preference to the believers unless you very carefully guard against evil from them. Indeed he who acts likewise (in a careless manner let him remember) he has nothing to do with Allâh. And Allâh cautions you against His punishment, for to Allâh is the eventual returning.

29. Say, 'Whether you conceal that which is in your bosoms or whether you reveal it Allâh knows it, and He knows whatever is in the heavens and whatever is in the earth. Allâh is the Possessor of full power to do all that He will.'

30. (Beware of) the Day when every soul shall be confronted with what good it has done and (similarly) whatever it has done of evil. It (- the soul) will earnestly wish there would be a long distance between it and between that (evil). Allâh cautions you against His punishment. And Allâh is Most Compassionate to His servants.

SECTION 4

31. **S**AY, 'Follow me if you love Allâh, (if you do so) Allâh will love you and grant you protection from your sins. Allâh is Great Protector, Ever Merciful.'

32. Say, 'Obey Allâh and this Perfect Messenger,' but if they turn away then (remember that) Allâh does not love the disbelievers.

33. Truly, Allâh chose Adam, Noah, the family of Abraham and the family of Amran above all peoples of the time.

34. (They are) a lineage co-related with one another. Allâh is All-Hearing, All-Knowing.

35. (Allâh listened) when a woman of (the family of) Amran said, 'My Lord! I do hereby vow to You what is in my womb to be dedicated (to Your service); so do accept (it) of me. You alone are the All-Hearing, the All-Knowing.'

36. But when she gave birth to it she said, 'My Lord! I have given birth to a female.' Allâh knew best what she had given birth to, and the

الْكٰفِرِينَ أَوْلِيَآءَ مِنْ دُونِ الْمُؤْمِنِينَ ۚ
وَمَنْ يَّفْعَلْ ذٰلِكَ فَلَيْسَ مِنَ اللّٰهِ فِي شَيْءٍ
إِلَّآ أَنْ تَتَّقُوا مِنْهُمْ تُقٰةً ۗ وَيُحَذِّرُكُمُ
اللّٰهُ نَفْسَهُ ۗ وَإِلَى اللّٰهِ الْمَصِيرُ ﴿٢٨﴾ قُلْ إِنْ
تُخْفُوا مَا فِي صُدُورِكُمْ أَوْ تُبْدُوهُ يَعْلَمْهُ
اللّٰهُ ۗ وَيَعْلَمُ مَا فِي السَّمٰوٰتِ وَمَا فِي الْأَرْضِ ۗ
وَاللّٰهُ عَلٰى كُلِّ شَيْءٍ قَدِيرٌ ﴿٢٩﴾ يَوْمَ تَجِدُ
كُلُّ نَفْسٍ مَّا عَمِلَتْ مِنْ خَيْرٍ مُّحْضَرًا ۚ
وَّمَا عَمِلَتْ مِنْ سُوٓءٍ ۚ تَوَدُّ لَوْ أَنَّ بَيْنَهَا
وَبَيْنَهُ أَمَدًا بَعِيدًا ۗ وَيُحَذِّرُكُمُ اللّٰهُ
نَفْسَهُ ۗ وَاللّٰهُ رَءُوفٌ بِالْعِبَادِ ﴿٣٠﴾ قُلْ إِنْ
كُنْتُمْ تُحِبُّونَ اللّٰهَ فَاتَّبِعُونِي يُحْبِبْكُمُ اللّٰهُ
وَيَغْفِرْ لَكُمْ ذُنُوبَكُمْ ۗ وَاللّٰهُ غَفُورٌ رَّحِيمٌ ﴿٣١﴾
قُلْ أَطِيعُوا اللّٰهَ وَالرَّسُولَ ۚ فَإِنْ تَوَلَّوْا
فَإِنَّ اللّٰهَ لَا يُحِبُّ الْكٰفِرِينَ ﴿٣٢﴾ إِنَّ اللّٰهَ
اصْطَفٰىٓ أٰدَمَ وَنُوحًا وَّأٰلَ إِبْرٰهِيمَ وَأٰلَ
عِمْرٰنَ عَلَى الْعٰلَمِينَ ﴿٣٣﴾ ذُرِّيَّةً بَعْضُهَا مِنْ
بَعْضٍ ۗ وَاللّٰهُ سَمِيعٌ عَلِيمٌ ﴿٣٤﴾ إِذْ قَالَتِ
امْرَأَتُ عِمْرٰنَ رَبِّ إِنِّي نَذَرْتُ لَكَ مَا
فِي بَطْنِي مُحَرَّرًا فَتَقَبَّلْ مِنِّي ۚ إِنَّكَ أَنْتَ
السَّمِيعُ الْعَلِيمُ ﴿٣٥﴾ فَلَمَّا وَضَعَتْهَا قَالَتْ رَبِّ
إِنِّي وَضَعْتُهَآ أُنْثٰى ۗ وَاللّٰهُ أَعْلَمُ بِمَا وَضَعَتْ ۗ
وَلَيْسَ الذَّكَرُ كَالْأُنْثٰى ۚ وَإِنِّي سَمَّيْتُهَا

male (she was thinking of) was not like this female (she had brought forth). 'I have named her Mary and I do commend her to Your protection and (also) her offspring (to be saved) from satan, the accursed.'

37. So her Lord accepted her (- Mary) with a gracious acceptance and made her grow into an excellent form and assigned her to the care of Zachariah. Every time Zachariah visited her in the chamber he found with her provisions. He said, 'From where do you get all this, O Mary?' She replied (with all conscientiousness), 'It is from Allâh.' Verily, Allâh provides whomsoever He will without measure.

38. Then and there did Zachariah pray to his Lord saying, 'My Lord! Grant me, by Your Own grace, pure and pious descendant, You alone are indeed the Hearer of prayers.'

39. So the angels called to him as he stood praying in the Sanctuary, 'Allâh bears you the glad tidings of John, who shall confirm the word of God and who shall be noble, utterly chaste, a Prophet from among the righteous.'

40. 'Lord!' He said, 'How shall I have a son now that old age has already come upon me and my wife is barren?' (The Lord) said, 'Such are the ways of Allâh, He does what He will.'

41. He said, 'My Lord! Give me some instruction.' (The Lord) said, 'The instruction for you is that you shall not speak to the people for three days (and nights) except by gestures, and remember your Lord a good deal and glorify (Him) in the evening and early (in the) morning.'

SECTION 5

42. (**R**ECALL the time) when the angels said, 'O Mary! Surely Allâh has chosen you and has rid you of all impurities and has preferred you to the women of all (contemporary) people.

43. 'O Mary! Be devout to your Lord and prostrate yourself and bow along with the congregation of the worshippers of God.'

مَرْيَمَ وَإِنِّيْ أُعِيْذُهَا بِكَ وَذُرِّيَّتَهَا مِنَ
الشَّيْطٰنِ الرَّجِيْمِ ﴿٣٦﴾ فَتَقَبَّلَهَا رَبُّهَا بِقَبُوْلٍ
حَسَنٍ وَّأَنْبَتَهَا نَبَاتًا حَسَنًا ۙ وَّكَفَّلَهَا
زَكَرِيَّا ۚ كُلَّمَا دَخَلَ عَلَيْهَا زَكَرِيَّا الْمِحْرَابَ ۙ
وَجَدَ عِنْدَهَا رِزْقًا ۚ قَالَ يٰمَرْيَمُ أَنّٰى لَكِ
هٰذَا ۗ قَالَتْ هُوَ مِنْ عِنْدِ اللّٰهِ ۗ إِنَّ اللّٰهَ
يَرْزُقُ مَنْ يَّشَآءُ بِغَيْرِ حِسَابٍ ﴿٣٧﴾ هُنَالِكَ
دَعَا زَكَرِيَّا رَبَّهٗ ۚ قَالَ رَبِّ هَبْ لِيْ مِنْ
لَّدُنْكَ ذُرِّيَّةً طَيِّبَةً ۚ إِنَّكَ سَمِيْعُ الدُّعَآءِ ﴿٣٨﴾
فَنَادَتْهُ الْمَلٰٓئِكَةُ وَهُوَ قَآئِمٌ يُّصَلِّيْ فِي
الْمِحْرَابِ أَنَّ اللّٰهَ يُبَشِّرُكَ بِيَحْيٰى مُصَدِّقًا
بِكَلِمَةٍ مِّنَ اللّٰهِ وَسَيِّدًا وَّحَصُوْرًا
وَّنَبِيًّا مِّنَ الصّٰلِحِيْنَ ﴿٣٩﴾ قَالَ رَبِّ أَنّٰى يَكُوْنُ
لِيْ غُلٰمٌ وَّقَدْ بَلَغَنِيَ الْكِبَرُ وَامْرَأَتِيْ عَاقِرٌ ۗ
قَالَ كَذٰلِكَ اللّٰهُ يَفْعَلُ مَا يَشَآءُ ﴿٤٠﴾ قَالَ رَبِّ
اجْعَلْ لِّيْ آيَةً ۗ قَالَ آيَتُكَ أَلَّا تُكَلِّمَ النَّاسَ
ثَلٰثَةَ أَيَّامٍ إِلَّا رَمْزًا ۗ وَاذْكُرْ رَّبَّكَ كَثِيْرًا
وَّسَبِّحْ بِالْعَشِيِّ وَالْإِبْكَارِ ﴿٤١﴾ وَإِذْ قَالَتِ
الْمَلٰٓئِكَةُ يٰمَرْيَمُ إِنَّ اللّٰهَ اصْطَفٰكِ وَطَهَّرَكِ
وَاصْطَفٰكِ عَلٰى نِسَآءِ الْعٰلَمِيْنَ ﴿٤٢﴾ يٰمَرْيَمُ
اقْنُتِيْ لِرَبِّكِ وَاسْجُدِيْ وَارْكَعِيْ مَعَ

44. These are some of the important accounts of the things unseen We have revealed to you. You were not present with them when they (- the priests) cast their quills (to decide) as to which of them should have Mary in his charge (to arrange her marriage); and you were not with them when they (- the exalted assembly of the angels) were engaged in a discussion (over the issue of Muhammad being entrusted with the Divine mission).
45. (Recall the time) when the angels said, 'O Mary! Allâh gives you good tidings through a (prophetic) word from Him (about the birth of a son) whose name is the Messiah, Jesus, son of Mary, (he shall be) worthy of regard in this world and in the Hereafter and one of the nearest ones (to Him),
46. 'And he will speak to the people when in the cradle (- as a child) and when of old age, and shall be of the righteous.'
47. She said, 'My Lord! How can I and whence shall I have a child while no man has yet touched me (in conjugal relationship)?' (The Lord) said, 'Such are the ways of Allâh, He creates what He will. When He decrees a thing He simply commands it, "Be" and it comes to be.'
48. (The angels continued), 'And He will teach him the art of writing (and reading) and the Wisdom and the Torah and the Evangel.
49. 'And (He will appoint him) a Messenger to the Children of Israel (with the Message), "I have come to you with a sign from your Lord. (I have come so that) I determine for your benefit from clay (a person) after the manner of a bird, then I shall breathe into him (a new spirit) so that he becomes a flier (- a spiritual person) by the authority of Allâh, and I absolve the blind and the leprous, and I quicken the (spiritually) dead by the authority of Allâh, and I inform you as to what you should eat and what you should store in your houses. Behold! These facts will surely serve

الرّٰكِعِيْنَ ﴿٤٣﴾ ذٰلِكَ مِنْ اَنْۢبَآءِ الْغَيْبِ نُوْحِيْهِ
اِلَيْكَ ؕ وَ مَا كُنْتَ لَدَيْهِمْ اِذْ يُلْقُوْنَ
اَقْلَامَهُمْ اَيُّهُمْ يَكْفُلُ مَرْيَمَ ۪ وَ مَا كُنْتَ
لَدَيْهِمْ اِذْ يَخْتَصِمُوْنَ ﴿٤٤﴾ اِذْ قَالَتِ الْمَلٰٓئِكَةُ
يٰمَرْيَمُ اِنَّ اللّٰهَ يُبَشِّرُكِ بِكَلِمَةٍ مِّنْهُ ۖۗ
اسْمُهُ الْمَسِيْحُ عِيْسَى ابْنُ مَرْيَمَ وَجِيْهًا
فِي الدُّنْيَا وَ الْاٰخِرَةِ وَ مِنَ الْمُقَرَّبِيْنَ ﴿٤٥﴾
وَ يُكَلِّمُ النَّاسَ فِي الْمَهْدِ وَ كَهْلًا وَّ مِنَ
الصّٰلِحِيْنَ ﴿٤٦﴾ قَالَتْ رَبِّ اَنّٰى يَكُوْنُ لِيْ وَلَدٌ
وَّ لَمْ يَمْسَسْنِيْ بَشَرٌ ؕ قَالَ كَذٰلِكِ اللّٰهُ
يَخْلُقُ مَا يَشَآءُ ؕ اِذَا قَضٰۤى اَمْرًا فَاِنَّمَا يَقُوْلُ
لَهٗ كُنْ فَيَكُوْنُ ﴿٤٧﴾ وَ يُعَلِّمُهُ الْكِتٰبَ وَ الْحِكْمَةَ
وَ التَّوْرٰىةَ وَ الْاِنْجِيْلَ ﴿٤٨﴾ وَ رَسُوْلًا اِلٰى بَنِيْۤ
اِسْرَآءِيْلَ ۙ اَنِّيْ قَدْ جِئْتُكُمْ بِاٰيَةٍ مِّنْ
رَّبِّكُمْ ۙ اَنِّيْۤ اَخْلُقُ لَكُمْ مِّنَ الطِّيْنِ كَهَيْـَٔةِ
الطَّيْرِ فَاَنْفُخُ فِيْهِ فَيَكُوْنُ طَيْرًۢا بِاِذْنِ
اللّٰهِ ۚ وَ اُبْرِئُ الْاَكْمَهَ وَ الْاَبْرَصَ وَ اُحْيِ
الْمَوْتٰى بِاِذْنِ اللّٰهِ ۚ وَ اُنَبِّئُكُمْ بِمَا تَاْكُلُوْنَ

you as a definite sign if you are believers.

50. "And (I come) confirming that which is before me, namely the Torah, and that I declare lawful for you some of the things that had been forbidden to you. I come to you with a sign from your Lord, so take Allâh as a shield and obey me.

51. "Surely, Allâh is my Lord as well as your Lord, therefore worship Him; this is the right path".'

52. But when Jesus felt disbelief on their part (and thought his people would renounce him,) he said, 'Who are my helpers (in calling the people) towards Allâh?' The disciples said, 'We are the helpers (in the cause) of Allâh. We have believed in Allâh. Bear witness that, we are the submitting ones (to His will).'

53. (The disciples then prayed,) 'Our Lord! We believe in that which You have revealed and we follow this Messenger, so count us with the witnesses (of the truth).'

54. And they (- the persecutors of Jesus) planned (to crucify him) and Allâh planned (to save him) and Allâh is the best of the planners.

SECTION 6

55. (RECALL the time) when Allâh said, 'O Jesus! I will cause you to die a natural death, and will exalt you to Myself and I will clear you of the unchaste accusations of those who disbelieve. I am going to make your followers prevail over the disbelievers till the Day of Resurrection, then to Me (O people!) shall be your return, and I will judge all your differences.

56. 'Then as for those who disbelieve I will punish them sternly in this world and in the Hereafter and they shall have no helpers.

57. 'As for those who believe and do deeds of righteousness, He will pay them their rewards in full. Allâh loves not the unjust.'

58. That is what We recite to you; the Messages and the Reminder full of wisdom.

وَمَا تَدَّخِرُونَ فِي بُيُوتِكُمْ إِنَّ فِي ذٰلِكَ
لَآيَةً لَكُمْ إِنْ كُنْتُمْ مُؤْمِنِينَ ﴿٤٩﴾ وَمُصَدِّقًا
لِمَا بَيْنَ يَدَيَّ مِنَ التَّوْرٰىةِ وَلِأُحِلَّ لَكُمْ
بَعْضَ الَّذِي حُرِّمَ عَلَيْكُمْ وَجِئْتُكُمْ بِآيَةٍ
مِنْ رَبِّكُمْ فَاتَّقُوا اللّٰهَ وَأَطِيعُونِ ﴿٥٠﴾ إِنَّ
اللّٰهَ رَبِّي وَرَبُّكُمْ فَاعْبُدُوهُ هٰذَا صِرٰطٌ
مُسْتَقِيمٌ ﴿٥١﴾ فَلَمَّا أَحَسَّ عِيسٰى مِنْهُمُ
الْكُفْرَ قَالَ مَنْ أَنْصَارِي إِلَى اللّٰهِ قَالَ
الْحَوَارِيُّونَ نَحْنُ أَنْصَارُ اللّٰهِ آمَنَّا بِاللّٰهِ
وَاشْهَدْ بِأَنَّا مُسْلِمُونَ ﴿٥٢﴾ رَبَّنَا آمَنَّا بِمَا
أَنْزَلْتَ وَاتَّبَعْنَا الرَّسُولَ فَاكْتُبْنَا مَعَ
الشّٰهِدِينَ ﴿٥٣﴾ وَمَكَرُوا وَمَكَرَ اللّٰهُ وَاللّٰهُ
خَيْرُ الْمٰكِرِينَ ﴿٥٤﴾ إِذْ قَالَ اللّٰهُ يٰعِيسٰى إِنِّي
مُتَوَفِّيكَ وَرَافِعُكَ إِلَيَّ وَمُطَهِّرُكَ مِنَ الَّذِينَ
كَفَرُوا وَجَاعِلُ الَّذِينَ اتَّبَعُوكَ فَوْقَ الَّذِينَ
كَفَرُوا إِلَى يَوْمِ الْقِيٰمَةِ ثُمَّ إِلَيَّ مَرْجِعُكُمْ
فَأَحْكُمُ بَيْنَكُمْ فِيمَا كُنْتُمْ فِيهِ تَخْتَلِفُونَ ﴿٥٥﴾
فَأَمَّا الَّذِينَ كَفَرُوا فَأُعَذِّبُهُمْ عَذَابًا شَدِيدًا
فِي الدُّنْيَا وَالْآخِرَةِ وَمَا لَهُمْ مِنْ نٰصِرِينَ ﴿٥٦﴾
وَأَمَّا الَّذِينَ آمَنُوا وَعَمِلُوا الصّٰلِحٰتِ فَيُوَفِّيهِمْ
أُجُورَهُمْ وَاللّٰهُ لَا يُحِبُّ الظّٰلِمِينَ ﴿٥٧﴾ ذٰلِكَ
نَتْلُوهُ عَلَيْكَ مِنَ الْآيٰتِ وَالذِّكْرِ الْحَكِيمِ ﴿٥٨﴾

59. Verily, the case of Jesus is as the case of Adam in the sight of Allâh. He fashioned him out of dust, then He said to him, ‘Be’, and he came to be.
60. (O reader!) This is the real truth from your Lord, hence do not be of the disputers at all (of the facts).
61. Now who so disputes with you in this matter (of Jesus) after there has come to you true knowledge, then say (to him), ‘Come let us summon our sons and your sons, our women and your women, and our people and your people, then let us pray fervently one against the other and invoke the disapproval of Allâh upon the liars.’
62. Verily, this (which We have told) is certainly the true account. There is no other, cannot be and will never be one worthy of worship but Allâh; and surely it is Allâh Who is the All-Mighty, the All-Wise.
63. But if they turn away, then (remember that) Allâh, of course, knows the mischief-makers.

SECTION 7

64. **S**AY, ‘O people of the Scripture! Let us agree to a proposition common to us both that we worship none but Allâh and that we associate no partner with Him and that some of us shall not hold others as lords besides Allâh.’ But if they turn away (refusing) say, ‘Bear witness that we are the only submitting ones (to one God).’
65. O people of the Scripture! Why do you argue about Abraham while the Torah and the Evangel were not revealed till after him? Have you no sense?
66. Behold! You are such as have argued about that whereof you had a little knowledge, now, why do you argue about that whereof you have no knowledge at all? Indeed, Allâh knows the truth while you do not.
67. Abraham was neither a Jew nor a Christian, but he was upright who had submitted (to the

إِنَّ مَثَلَ عِيسَىٰ عِندَ اللَّهِ كَمَثَلِ آدَمَ
خَلَقَهُ مِن تُرَابٍ ثُمَّ قَالَ لَهُ كُن فَيَكُونُ ﴿٥٩﴾
الْحَقُّ مِن رَّبِّكَ فَلَا تَكُن مِّنَ الْمُمْتَرِينَ ﴿٦٠﴾
فَمَنْ حَاجَّكَ فِيهِ مِن بَعْدِ مَا جَاءَكَ مِنَ
الْعِلْمِ فَقُلْ تَعَالَوْا نَدْعُ أَبْنَاءَنَا وَأَبْنَاءَكُمْ
وَنِسَاءَنَا وَنِسَاءَكُمْ وَأَنفُسَنَا وَأَنفُسَكُمْ
ثُمَّ نَبْتَهِلْ فَنَجْعَل لَّعْنَتَ اللَّهِ عَلَى
الْكَاذِبِينَ ﴿٦١﴾ إِنَّ هَٰذَا لَهُوَ الْقَصَصُ الْحَقُّ
وَمَا مِنْ إِلَٰهٍ إِلَّا اللَّهُ وَإِنَّ اللَّهَ لَهُوَ الْعَزِيزُ
الْحَكِيمُ ﴿٦٢﴾ فَإِن تَوَلَّوْا فَإِنَّ اللَّهَ عَلِيمٌ
بِالْمُفْسِدِينَ ﴿٦٣﴾ قُلْ يَا أَهْلَ الْكِتَابِ تَعَالَوْا
إِلَىٰ كَلِمَةٍ سَوَاءٍ بَيْنَنَا وَبَيْنَكُمْ أَلَّا نَعْبُدَ
إِلَّا اللَّهَ وَلَا نُشْرِكَ بِهِ شَيْئًا وَلَا يَتَّخِذَ
بَعْضُنَا بَعْضًا أَرْبَابًا مِّن دُونِ اللَّهِ فَإِن
تَوَلَّوْا فَقُولُوا اشْهَدُوا بِأَنَّا مُسْلِمُونَ ﴿٦٤﴾
يَا أَهْلَ الْكِتَابِ لِمَ تُحَاجُّونَ فِي إِبْرَاهِيمَ
وَمَا أُنزِلَتِ التَّوْرَاةُ وَالْإِنجِيلُ إِلَّا مِن
بَعْدِهِ أَفَلَا تَعْقِلُونَ ﴿٦٥﴾ هَا أَنتُمْ هَٰؤُلَاءِ
حَاجَجْتُمْ فِيمَا لَكُم بِهِ عِلْمٌ فَلِمَ
تُحَاجُّونَ فِيمَا لَيْسَ لَكُم بِهِ عِلْمٌ
وَاللَّهُ يَعْلَمُ وَأَنتُمْ لَا تَعْلَمُونَ ﴿٦٦﴾ مَا كَانَ
إِبْرَاهِيمُ يَهُودِيًّا وَلَا نَصْرَانِيًّا وَلَٰكِن
كَانَ حَنِيفًا مُّسْلِمًا وَمَا كَانَ مِنَ

ع ١٤

will of God), and he was not one of the polytheists.

68. The people nearest to Abraham are surely those who followed him (in the days of his prophethood) and this Prophet and those who believe (in him). Indeed, Allâh is the Patron of the believers.

69. (Believers!) A section of the people of the Scripture would fain lead you astray, but it is only the people like themselves that they lead astray, only they perceive not.

70. O people of the Scripture! Why do you deny the revelations of Allâh while you are witnessing (their truth)?

71. O people of the Scripture! Why do you confound the truth with falsehood and conceal the truth and that (too) deliberately?

SECTION 8

72. **A** SECTION of the people of the Scripture said (to their companions in confidence), 'Avow belief in that (- the Qur'ân) which has been revealed to the believers, in the early hours of the day and deny (it) in the latter part of it, so that they (- the newly converted Muslims) may return (to disbelief),

73. 'Yet avow this belief only for the sake of those who follow your creed.' Say, 'Surely, the true guidance is Allâh's guidance', (and they also said, 'Do not believe,) that anyone will ever be given the like of that (gift of prophethood) which you have been given, or that they will ever be able to prevail upon you in argument before your Lord.' Say, 'Eminence (of prophethood and sovereignty) is entirely in the hands of Allâh. He confers it to whomsoever He will.' And Allâh is All-Embracing, All-Knowing.

74. Allâh has singled out for His grace (of the bestowal of Divine revelation) one whom He has pleased, for Allâh is the Lord of great eminence.

75. And among the people of the Scripture there is he if you trust him with a huge treasure he will surrender it to you; yet there is another

الْمُشْرِكِينَ ﴿٦٧﴾ إِنَّ أَوْلَى النَّاسِ بِإِبْرَاهِيمَ
لَلَّذِينَ اتَّبَعُوهُ وَهَٰذَا النَّبِيُّ وَالَّذِينَ
آمَنُوا ۗ وَاللَّهُ وَلِيُّ الْمُؤْمِنِينَ ﴿٦٨﴾ وَدَّتْ
طَائِفَةٌ مِنْ أَهْلِ الْكِتَابِ لَوْ يُضِلُّونَكُمْ
وَمَا يُضِلُّونَ إِلَّا أَنْفُسَهُمْ وَمَا يَشْعُرُونَ ﴿٦٩﴾
يَا أَهْلَ الْكِتَابِ لِمَ تَكْفُرُونَ بِآيَاتِ اللَّهِ
وَأَنْتُمْ تَشْهَدُونَ ﴿٧٠﴾ يَا أَهْلَ الْكِتَابِ لِمَ
تَلْبِسُونَ الْحَقَّ بِالْبَاطِلِ وَتَكْتُمُونَ الْحَقَّ
وَأَنْتُمْ تَعْلَمُونَ ﴿٧١﴾ وَقَالَتْ طَائِفَةٌ مِنْ
أَهْلِ الْكِتَابِ آمِنُوا بِالَّذِي أُنْزِلَ عَلَى
الَّذِينَ آمَنُوا وَجْهَ النَّهَارِ وَاكْفُرُوا آخِرَهُ
لَعَلَّهُمْ يَرْجِعُونَ ﴿٧٢﴾ وَلَا تُؤْمِنُوا إِلَّا لِمَنْ
تَبِعَ دِينَكُمْ قُلْ إِنَّ الْهُدَىٰ هُدَى
اللَّهِ أَنْ يُؤْتَىٰ أَحَدٌ مِثْلَ مَا أُوتِيتُمْ أَوْ
يُحَاجُّوكُمْ عِنْدَ رَبِّكُمْ ۗ قُلْ إِنَّ الْفَضْلَ
بِيَدِ اللَّهِ يُؤْتِيهِ مَنْ يَشَاءُ ۗ وَاللَّهُ وَاسِعٌ
عَلِيمٌ ﴿٧٣﴾ يَخْتَصُّ بِرَحْمَتِهِ مَنْ يَشَاءُ ۗ
وَاللَّهُ ذُو الْفَضْلِ الْعَظِيمِ ﴿٧٤﴾ وَمِنْ أَهْلِ
الْكِتَابِ مَنْ إِنْ تَأْمَنْهُ بِقِنْطَارٍ يُؤَدِّهِ
إِلَيْكَ وَمِنْهُمْ مَنْ إِنْ تَأْمَنْهُ بِدِينَارٍ

ع ٨ ١٥

among them that if you entrust him with a single dinâr he will not surrender it to you unless you keep on pressing him. They do that because they say, 'We are not liable to be called to account in the matter of the unlettered (- not of Jewish race),' and they tell a lie in the name of Allâh deliberately.

76. Nay (they will indeed be called to account). Yet who so discharges his obligations and guards against evil, (he will find that) Allâh, In fact, loves those who guard against evil.

77. (On the contrary) those who take paltry gains for (shaking off their) covenant with Allâh and their oaths, it is these for whom there shall be no big share in the Hereafter, Allâh will never speak to them (lovingly) nor look at them (with affection) on the Day of Resurrection, nor will He treat them as pure; there awaits them a woeful punishment.

78. There are some among them who twist their tongues while reciting their Scripture that you may think that (what they recite) is a part of the Scripture, whilst it is no part of the Scripture and they say, 'This is from Allâh,' whereas it is not from Allâh. They tell a lie in the name of Allâh deliberately.

79. It is not given to a human being that Allâh should give him the Book, the sovereignty and the prophethood and then he should say to the people, 'Be servants to me beside Allâh.' He would rather say, 'Be you the sole devotees of (Allâh) the Lord, for you teach the Book and because you study (it).'

80. Nor would (it be possible for him that) he bid you take the angels and Prophets as your lords. Would he bid you disbelieve after you have submitted yourselves (to the will of God)?

SECTION 9

81. (**R**ECALL the time) when Allâh bound (the people) to a covenant through the Prophets (saying), 'Indeed, whatever I have vouchsafed to you of the Book and the Wisdom, and then

لَا يُؤَدِّهِۦٓ إِلَيْكَ إِلَّا مَا دُمْتَ عَلَيْهِ قَآئِمًا ۗ ذَٰلِكَ
بِأَنَّهُمْ قَالُوا۟ لَيْسَ عَلَيْنَا فِى ٱلْأُمِّيِّـۧنَ سَبِيلٌ
وَيَقُولُونَ عَلَى ٱللَّهِ ٱلْكَذِبَ وَهُمْ يَعْلَمُونَ ٧٥
بَلَىٰ مَنْ أَوْفَىٰ بِعَهْدِهِۦ وَٱتَّقَىٰ فَإِنَّ ٱللَّهَ
يُحِبُّ ٱلْمُتَّقِينَ ٧٦ إِنَّ ٱلَّذِينَ يَشْتَرُونَ
بِعَهْدِ ٱللَّهِ وَأَيْمَٰنِهِمْ ثَمَنًا قَلِيلًا أُو۟لَٰٓئِكَ
لَا خَلَٰقَ لَهُمْ فِى ٱلْءَاخِرَةِ وَلَا يُكَلِّمُهُمُ
ٱللَّهُ وَلَا يَنظُرُ إِلَيْهِمْ يَوْمَ ٱلْقِيَٰمَةِ وَلَا
يُزَكِّيهِمْ وَلَهُمْ عَذَابٌ أَلِيمٌ ٧٧ وَإِنَّ
مِنْهُمْ لَفَرِيقًا يَلْوُۥنَ أَلْسِنَتَهُم بِٱلْكِتَٰبِ
لِتَحْسَبُوهُ مِنَ ٱلْكِتَٰبِ وَمَا هُوَ مِنَ
ٱلْكِتَٰبِ وَيَقُولُونَ هُوَ مِنْ عِندِ ٱللَّهِ
وَمَا هُوَ مِنْ عِندِ ٱللَّهِ وَيَقُولُونَ عَلَى ٱللَّهِ
ٱلْكَذِبَ وَهُمْ يَعْلَمُونَ ٧٨ مَا كَانَ
لِبَشَرٍ أَن يُؤْتِيَهُ ٱللَّهُ ٱلْكِتَٰبَ وَٱلْحُكْمَ
وَٱلنُّبُوَّةَ ثُمَّ يَقُولَ لِلنَّاسِ كُونُوا۟
عِبَادًا لِّى مِن دُونِ ٱللَّهِ وَلَٰكِن كُونُوا۟
رَبَّٰنِيِّـۧنَ بِمَا كُنتُمْ تُعَلِّمُونَ ٱلْكِتَٰبَ وَبِمَا
كُنتُمْ تَدْرُسُونَ ٧٩ وَلَا يَأْمُرَكُمْ أَن
تَتَّخِذُوا۟ ٱلْمَلَٰٓئِكَةَ وَٱلنَّبِيِّـۧنَ أَرْبَابًا ۗ
أَيَأْمُرُكُم بِٱلْكُفْرِ بَعْدَ إِذْ أَنتُم مُّسْلِمُونَ ٨٠ ع ٩ ١٦
وَإِذْ أَخَذَ ٱللَّهُ مِيثَٰقَ ٱلنَّبِيِّـۧنَ لَمَآ ءَاتَيْتُكُم
مِّن كِتَٰبٍ وَحِكْمَةٍ ثُمَّ جَآءَكُمْ رَسُولٌ

there comes to you a Messenger fulfilling that which is with you, you shall surely believe in him and have to help him.' (The Lord further) said, 'Do you agree and do you undertake the heavy responsibility of My covenant on these (terms)?' They said, 'We do agree.' (God) said, 'Bear witness to it and I am with you among the witnesses.'

82. Now those who turn away (and break their pledge) after this, will be the real transgressors.

83. Do they then seek a creed other than Allâh's while all those that are in the heavens and on the earth submit to Him willingly or unwillingly, and to Him they shall be made to return?

84. Say, 'We believe in Allâh and in that which has been revealed to us and in that which was revealed to Abraham and Ismâîl and Isaac and Jacob and his children and in that which was given to Moses and Jesus and to all other Prophets from their Lord. We make no distinction between anyone of them (in believing them) and to Him alone do we submit.'

85. And whosoever seeks a faith other then Islam (- complete submission to the will of God,) it will never be accepted from him, and he shall be of the losers in the Hereafter.

86. How is Allâh to guide a people who renounce their faith after having accepted it and after testifying to the truth of the Messenger and after clear and sound proofs had come to them? And Allâh never guides a people who cannot discriminate between right and wrong.

87. It is these whose recompense is that the disapproval of Allâh shall be upon them, and that of the angels and of people, all together.

88. They shall abide there for long, their punishment shall not be reduced, nor shall they be reprieved;

89. Except those who repent after this and make amends, (such will find that) surely Allâh is Great Protector, Ever Merciful.

90. Verily, those who chose disbelief after they

مُّصَدِّقٌ لِّمَا مَعَكُمْ لَتُؤْمِنُنَّ بِهِۦ وَلَتَنصُرُنَّهُۥ
قَالَ ءَأَقْرَرْتُمْ وَأَخَذْتُمْ عَلَىٰ ذَٰلِكُمْ إِصْرِى
قَالُوٓا أَقْرَرْنَا ۚ قَالَ فَاشْهَدُوا وَأَنَا مَعَكُم
مِّنَ الشَّٰهِدِينَ ﴿٨١﴾ فَمَن تَوَلَّىٰ بَعْدَ ذَٰلِكَ
فَأُولَٰٓئِكَ هُمُ الْفَٰسِقُونَ ﴿٨٢﴾ أَفَغَيْرَ دِينِ اللَّهِ
يَبْغُونَ وَلَهُۥٓ أَسْلَمَ مَن فِى السَّمَٰوَٰتِ
وَالْأَرْضِ طَوْعًا وَكَرْهًا وَإِلَيْهِ يُرْجَعُونَ ﴿٨٣﴾
قُلْ ءَامَنَّا بِاللَّهِ وَمَآ أُنزِلَ عَلَيْنَا وَمَآ
أُنزِلَ عَلَىٰٓ إِبْرَٰهِيمَ وَإِسْمَٰعِيلَ وَإِسْحَٰقَ
وَيَعْقُوبَ وَالْأَسْبَاطِ وَمَآ أُوتِىَ مُوسَىٰ
وَعِيسَىٰ وَالنَّبِيُّونَ مِن رَّبِّهِمْ لَا نُفَرِّقُ
بَيْنَ أَحَدٍ مِّنْهُمْ وَنَحْنُ لَهُۥ مُسْلِمُونَ ﴿٨٤﴾
وَمَن يَبْتَغِ غَيْرَ الْإِسْلَٰمِ دِينًا فَلَن
يُقْبَلَ مِنْهُ وَهُوَ فِى الْأٰخِرَةِ مِنَ
الْخَٰسِرِينَ ﴿٨٥﴾ كَيْفَ يَهْدِى اللَّهُ قَوْمًا
كَفَرُوا بَعْدَ إِيمَٰنِهِمْ وَشَهِدُوٓا أَنَّ الرَّسُولَ
حَقٌّ وَجَآءَهُمُ الْبَيِّنَٰتُ ۚ وَاللَّهُ لَا يَهْدِى
الْقَوْمَ الظَّٰلِمِينَ ﴿٨٦﴾ أُولَٰٓئِكَ جَزَآؤُهُمْ أَنَّ
عَلَيْهِمْ لَعْنَةَ اللَّهِ وَالْمَلَٰٓئِكَةِ وَالنَّاسِ
أَجْمَعِينَ ﴿٨٧﴾ خَٰلِدِينَ فِيهَا ۚ لَا يُخَفَّفُ
عَنْهُمُ الْعَذَابُ وَلَا هُمْ يُنظَرُونَ ﴿٨٨﴾ إِلَّا
الَّذِينَ تَابُوا مِنْ بَعْدِ ذَٰلِكَ وَأَصْلَحُوا
فَإِنَّ اللَّهَ غَفُورٌ رَّحِيمٌ ﴿٨٩﴾ إِنَّ الَّذِينَ كَفَرُوا

had believed and then go on increasing in disbelief, their repentance shall not be accepted and these are the people who are completely lost.

91. Verily, as to those who have disbelieved and die while they are disbelievers, there shall not be accepted from anyone of them (even) an earthful of gold if he would ransom himself thereby. There awaits them a woeful punishment, they shall have no helpers (either).

بَعْدَ إِيمَٰنِهِمْ ثُمَّ ازْدَادُوا كُفْرًا لَّن تُقْبَلَ
تَوْبَتُهُمْ ۚ وَأُولَٰٓئِكَ هُمُ الضَّآلُّونَ ﴿٩٠﴾ إِنَّ
الَّذِينَ كَفَرُوا وَمَاتُوا وَهُمْ كُفَّارٌ
فَلَن يُقْبَلَ مِنْ أَحَدِهِم مِّلْءُ الْأَرْضِ
ذَهَبًا وَلَوِ افْتَدَىٰ بِهِۦٓ ۗ أُولَٰٓئِكَ لَهُمْ
عَذَابٌ أَلِيمٌ وَمَا لَهُم مِّن نَّٰصِرِينَ ﴿٩١﴾

PART الجزء الرابع IV

SECTION 10

92. **N**ever shall you attain the highest state of virtue unless you spend (in the cause of Allâh) out of that which you love; and whatever you spend, Allâh, indeed, knows it well.

93. All the (pure) food (which is lawful in Islam) was lawful for the Children of Israel except what Israel forbade himself before the advent of Torah. Say, 'Bring then the Torah and read it, if you are right (in your assertions).'

94. Now, whoso forges a lie against Allâh after that, it is they who are the unjust.

95 Say, '(Now that it has been proved that) Allâh has declared the truth, therefore follow the creed of Abraham, the upright, and he was not of the polytheists.

96. Verily, the first House founded for the good of humankind is the one at Bakkah (- the valley of Makkah). (It is the House) full of blessings and a means of guidance for all the peoples.

97. Therein are clear Memorials: (The first is) the Place where Abraham stood for prayers *(- Maqâm Ibrahîm)*; (secondly,) whosoever enters it (- the valley of Bakkah) is in a state of

لَن تَنَالُوا الْبِرَّ حَتَّىٰ تُنفِقُوا مِمَّا
تُحِبُّونَ ۚ وَمَا تُنفِقُوا مِن شَيْءٍ فَإِنَّ اللَّهَ
بِهِۦ عَلِيمٌ ﴿٩٢﴾ كُلُّ الطَّعَامِ كَانَ حِلًّا لِّبَنِيٓ
إِسْرَٰٓءِيلَ إِلَّا مَا حَرَّمَ إِسْرَٰٓءِيلُ عَلَىٰ
نَفْسِهِۦ مِن قَبْلِ أَن تُنَزَّلَ التَّوْرَىٰةُ ۗ قُلْ
فَأْتُوا بِالتَّوْرَىٰةِ فَاتْلُوهَآ إِن كُنتُمْ صَٰدِقِينَ ﴿٩٣﴾
فَمَنِ افْتَرَىٰ عَلَى اللَّهِ الْكَذِبَ مِنۢ بَعْدِ
ذَٰلِكَ فَأُولَٰٓئِكَ هُمُ الظَّٰلِمُونَ ﴿٩٤﴾ قُلْ صَدَقَ
اللَّهُ ۗ فَاتَّبِعُوا مِلَّةَ إِبْرَٰهِيمَ حَنِيفًا ۖ وَمَا
كَانَ مِنَ الْمُشْرِكِينَ ﴿٩٥﴾ إِنَّ أَوَّلَ بَيْتٍ
وُضِعَ لِلنَّاسِ لَلَّذِي بِبَكَّةَ مُبَارَكًا
وَهُدًى لِّلْعَٰلَمِينَ ﴿٩٦﴾ فِيهِ ءَايَٰتٌۢ بَيِّنَٰتٌ مَّقَامُ
إِبْرَٰهِيمَ ۖ وَمَن دَخَلَهُۥ كَانَ ءَامِنًا ۗ وَلِلَّهِ

peace and security; (thirdly,) Pilgrimage to the House *(- Ka'bah)* is due to Allâh from everyone of humankind who is (physically, financially and in many other ways) able and has the means to make the journey thereto. And whosoever disobeys (let him remember that) Allâh is Independent of the worlds.

98. Say, 'O you people of the Scripture! Why do you deny the Messages of Allâh, while Allâh is Witness to all that you do.'

99. Say, 'O people of the Scripture! Why do you hinder him who believes, from (following) the path of Allâh? You try to seek crookedness in it, while you yourselves are witnesses (to its truth). And Allâh is not at all unmindful of what you do.'

100. O you who believe! If you obey a section of those who have been given the Scripture, they will turn you back into disbelievers after your having believed.

101. And how would you disbelieve while the Messages of Allâh are rehearsed to you, and His Messenger is present in your midst. And whosoever holds fast to Allâh is indeed guided on to the exact right path.

SECTION 11

102. **O** YOU who believe! Observe your duty to Allâh as it ought to be observed, and let not death overtake you unless you be in a state of complete submission (to your Lord).

103. Hold fast to the means of access to Allâh all together, and do not be disunited, and remember Allâh's favours to you, when you were enemies one to another. He united your hearts in love so that by His grace you became brethren. And you were on the brink of a pit of fire, He saved you therefrom. Thus does Allâh explain to you His Messages and miracles that you may be guided aright.

104. And let there always be a community (of such people) among you who should call people to goodness and enjoin equity and forbid evil. It

على الناس حج البيت من استطاع إليه
سبيلا ۚ ومن كفر فإن الله غني عن
العلمين ﴿٩٧﴾ قل يأهل الكتب لم تكفرون
بايت الله ۖ والله شهيد على ما تعملون ﴿٩٨﴾
قل يأهل الكتب لم تصدون عن سبيل
الله من ءامن تبغونها عوجا وأنتم شهداء ۗ
وما الله بغفل عما تعملون ﴿٩٩﴾ يأيها الذين
ءامنوا إن تطيعوا فريقا من الذين أوتوا
الكتب يردوكم بعد إيمنكم كفرين ﴿١٠٠﴾
وكيف تكفرون وأنتم تتلى عليكم
ءايت الله وفيكم رسوله ۗ ومن يعتصم
بالله فقد هدي إلى صرط مستقيم ﴿١٠١﴾
يأيها الذين ءامنوا اتقوا الله حق تقاته
ولا تموتن إلا وأنتم مسلمون ﴿١٠٢﴾
واعتصموا بحبل الله جميعا ولا تفرقوا ۚ
واذكروا نعمت الله عليكم إذ كنتم
أعداء فألف بين قلوبكم فأصبحتم
بنعمته إخونا وكنتم على شفا حفرة
من النار فأنقذكم منها ۗ كذلك يبين
الله لكم ءايته لعلكم تهتدون ﴿١٠٣﴾ ولتكن
منكم أمة يدعون إلى الخير ويأمرون
بالمعروف وينهون عن المنكر ۚ وأولئك

ع ١٠

is these who shall attain to their goal.

105. And do not be like those who were disunited and fell into variance after clear proofs had come to them. It is these for whom a great punishment awaits.

106. On the day when some faces shall be lit up by happiness and some faces shall be clouded because of sorrow. (It will be said to) those whose faces are clouded, 'Is it not (true) that you disbelieved after your belief? Taste now, the punishment because you disbelieved.'

107. And as for those whose faces shall be lit up, they shall come under the mercy of Allâh, and in it they shall abide forever.

108. Such are the revelations of Allâh comprising the truth. We rehearse them to you. And Allâh means no injustice to (any of His) creatures.

109. And to Allâh belongs whatsoever is in the heavens and whatsoever is in the earth, and all matters stand referred to Allâh.

SECTION 12

110. **Y**OU are the noblest people raised up for the good of humankind. You enjoin equity and forbid evil, and you believe truly in Allâh. Had the people of the Scripture (also) believed, it would surely have been best for them. Some of them are believers, yet most of them are disobedient.

111. They shall do you no harm except a trifling hurt, and if they fight you, they will show you their backs (and flee), they shall never be helped then.

112. Smitten are they with ignominy wherever they are found unless they have a bond (of protection) from Allâh, or a bond (of security) from the people. They have incurred the displeasure of Allâh and have been condemned to humiliation. That is so because they would disbelieve in the Messages of Allâh and would

هُمُ الْمُفْلِحُوْنَ ﴿١٠٤﴾ وَلَا تَكُوْنُوْا كَالَّذِيْنَ
تَفَرَّقُوْا وَ اخْتَلَفُوْا مِنْۢ بَعْدِ مَا جَآءَهُمُ
الْبَيِّنٰتُ ؕ وَ اُولٰٓئِكَ لَهُمْ عَذَابٌ عَظِيْمٌ ﴿١٠٥﴾ يَّوْمَ
تَبْيَضُّ وُجُوْهٌ وَّ تَسْوَدُّ وُجُوْهٌ ۚ فَاَمَّا الَّذِيْنَ
اسْوَدَّتْ وُجُوْهُهُمْ ۟ اَكَفَرْتُمْ بَعْدَ اِيْمَانِكُمْ
فَذُوْقُوا الْعَذَابَ بِمَا كُنْتُمْ تَكْفُرُوْنَ ﴿١٠٦﴾
وَاَمَّا الَّذِيْنَ ابْيَضَّتْ وُجُوْهُهُمْ فَفِيْ رَحْمَةِ
اللّٰهِ ؕ هُمْ فِيْهَا خٰلِدُوْنَ ﴿١٠٧﴾ تِلْكَ اٰيٰتُ اللّٰهِ
نَتْلُوْهَا عَلَيْكَ بِالْحَقِّ ؕ وَمَا اللّٰهُ يُرِيْدُ ظُلْمًا
لِّلْعٰلَمِيْنَ ﴿١٠٨﴾ وَلِلّٰهِ مَا فِي السَّمٰوٰتِ وَمَا فِي
الْاَرْضِ ؕ وَاِلَى اللّٰهِ تُرْجَعُ الْاُمُوْرُ ﴿١٠٩﴾ كُنْتُمْ
خَيْرَ اُمَّةٍ اُخْرِجَتْ لِلنَّاسِ تَاْمُرُوْنَ
بِالْمَعْرُوْفِ وَتَنْهَوْنَ عَنِ الْمُنْكَرِ وَتُؤْمِنُوْنَ
بِاللّٰهِ ؕ وَلَوْ اٰمَنَ اَهْلُ الْكِتٰبِ لَكَانَ خَيْرًا
لَّهُمْ ؕ مِنْهُمُ الْمُؤْمِنُوْنَ وَاَكْثَرُهُمُ الْفٰسِقُوْنَ ﴿١١٠﴾
لَنْ يَّضُرُّوْكُمْ اِلَّآ اَذًى ؕ وَاِنْ يُّقَاتِلُوْكُمْ
يُوَلُّوْكُمُ الْاَدْبَارَ ۟ ثُمَّ لَا يُنْصَرُوْنَ ﴿١١١﴾ ضُرِبَتْ
عَلَيْهِمُ الذِّلَّةُ اَيْنَ مَا ثُقِفُوْٓا اِلَّا بِحَبْلٍ مِّنَ
اللّٰهِ وَحَبْلٍ مِّنَ النَّاسِ وَبَآءُوْ بِغَضَبٍ
مِّنَ اللّٰهِ وَضُرِبَتْ عَلَيْهِمُ الْمَسْكَنَةُ ؕ ذٰلِكَ
بِاَنَّهُمْ كَانُوْا يَكْفُرُوْنَ بِاٰيٰتِ اللّٰهِ وَيَقْتُلُوْنَ
الْاَنْۢبِيَآءَ بِغَيْرِ حَقٍّ ؕ ذٰلِكَ بِمَا عَصَوْا وَّكَانُوْا

seek to kill the Prophets without any just cause. And that is so because they rebelled and had been transgressing as usual.

113. They (- the people of the Scripture) are not all alike. Among these people of the Scripture there are some upright people. They rehearse the Message of Allâh in the hours of the night and they prostrate themselves (in His worship).

114. They believe in Allâh and the Last Day and enjoin good and forbid evil, and they vie one with another in (doing) good deeds. And it is these who are of the truly righteous.

115. And whatever good they do, they shall not be denied its due recognition. And Allâh knows well those who guard against evil.

116. Verily, as to those who disbelieve, neither their possessions nor their children shall avail them aught against (the punishment of) Allâh. And it is they who are the fellows of the Fire, therein shall they live long.

117. That which they spend for the present life bears likeness with the wind wherein is freezing cold which smites the tilth of the people who have done injustice to themselves, so it destroys it. Allâh does no injustice to them but they wrong themselves.

118. O you who believe! Do not hold other people as confidants of your secrets to the exclusion of your own (honest) folk. Such people shall not be remiss to corrupt you; they love all that by which you get into trouble. Gross hatred has already expressed itself through (the utterances of) their mouths and what their hearts conceal is far worse. Now We have explained the Messages fully to you if you would only understand.

119. Behold! You are those who love them while they do not love you, though you believe in every (Divine) Book, in the whole of it. And when they meet you they say, 'We believe,' and when they are alone they bite their fingertips

يَعْتَدُوْنَ ﴿١١٢﴾ لَيْسُوْا سَوَآءً ۭ مِنْ اَهْلِ الْكِتٰبِ
اُمَّةٌ قَآىِٕمَةٌ يَّتْلُوْنَ اٰيٰتِ اللّٰهِ اٰنَآءَ الَّيْلِ
وَهُمْ يَسْجُدُوْنَ ﴿١١٣﴾ يُؤْمِنُوْنَ بِاللّٰهِ وَالْيَوْمِ
الْاٰخِرِ وَيَاْمُرُوْنَ بِالْمَعْرُوْفِ وَيَنْهَوْنَ
عَنِ الْمُنْكَرِ وَيُسٰرِعُوْنَ فِي الْخَيْرٰتِ ۭ
وَاُولٰۗىِٕكَ مِنَ الصّٰلِحِيْنَ ﴿١١٤﴾ وَمَا يَفْعَلُوْا مِنْ
خَيْرٍ فَلَنْ يُّكْفَرُوْهُ ۭ وَاللّٰهُ عَلِيْمٌۢ بِالْمُتَّقِيْنَ ﴿١١٥﴾
اِنَّ الَّذِيْنَ كَفَرُوْا لَنْ تُغْنِيَ عَنْهُمْ اَمْوٰلُهُمْ
وَلَآ اَوْلٰدُهُمْ مِّنَ اللّٰهِ شَيْـًٔا ۭ وَاُولٰۗىِٕكَ
اَصْحٰبُ النَّارِ ۚ هُمْ فِيْهَا خٰلِدُوْنَ ﴿١١٦﴾ مَثَلُ
مَا يُنْفِقُوْنَ فِيْ هٰذِهِ الْحَيٰوةِ الدُّنْيَا كَمَثَلِ
رِيْحٍ فِيْهَا صِرٌّ اَصَابَتْ حَرْثَ قَوْمٍ ظَلَمُوْٓا
اَنْفُسَهُمْ فَاَهْلَكَتْهُ ۭ وَمَا ظَلَمَهُمُ اللّٰهُ وَلٰكِنْ
اَنْفُسَهُمْ يَظْلِمُوْنَ ﴿١١٧﴾ يٰٓاَيُّهَا الَّذِيْنَ اٰمَنُوْا لَا
تَتَّخِذُوْا بِطَانَةً مِّنْ دُوْنِكُمْ لَا يَاْلُوْنَكُمْ
خَبَالًا ۭ وَدُّوْا مَا عَنِتُّمْ ۚ قَدْ بَدَتِ الْبَغْضَاۗءُ
مِنْ اَفْوَاهِهِمْ ښ وَمَا تُخْفِيْ صُدُوْرُهُمْ اَكْبَرُ ۭ
قَدْ بَيَّنَّا لَكُمُ الْاٰيٰتِ اِنْ كُنْتُمْ تَعْقِلُوْنَ ﴿١١٨﴾
هٰٓاَنْتُمْ اُولَاۗءِ تُحِبُّوْنَهُمْ وَلَا يُحِبُّوْنَكُمْ
وَتُؤْمِنُوْنَ بِالْكِتٰبِ كُلِّهٖ ۚ وَاِذَا لَقُوْكُمْ
قَالُوْٓا اٰمَنَّا ښ وَاِذَا خَلَوْا عَضُّوْا عَلَيْكُمُ

out of rage against you. Say, 'Perish in your rage. Surely, Allâh knows the inmost secrets of your hearts.'

120. If anything good contacts you, it hurts them, but if an evil afflicts you, they rejoice thereat. However, if you patiently persevere and ward off evil, their machination will do you no harm at all. Verily, Allâh encompasses all their activities.

SECTION 13

121. AND (recall the time) when you (O Prophet!) went forth early in the morning from your family assigning to the believers their battle-posts (in the Battle of *Uhud*). And Allâh is All- Hearing, All-Knowing.

122. When two groups from among you (- the two clans of *Banû Hârithah and Banû Salamah*) were disposed to show cowardliness. And Allâh was the Protecting friend of them both, and in Allâh the believers should put their trust.

123. Surely, Allâh had already helped you at (the Battle of) *Badr* while you were utterly weak, therefore take Allâh as a shield so that (He may bless you and) you may give Him thanks.

124. (Recall the time) when you said to the believers, 'Does it not suffice you that your Lord should reinforce you with three thousand angels sent down (by Him)?

125. 'Indeed (it does); and if you patiently persevere and guard against evil and they (- the enemies) come upon you suddenly and in hot haste of theirs, your Lord will reinforce you with five thousand swooping and havoc-making angels.'

126. And Allâh meant not this (help by the angels) except as good tidings (of victory) for you, and to set your hearts at ease therewith. There is no real help and victory except from Allâh alone, the All-Mighty, the All-Wise.

127. (God will do accordingly at *Uhud)* with the result that He may cut of a section of those

الْأَنَامِلَ مِنَ الْغَيْظِ قُلْ مُوتُوا بِغَيْظِكُمْ
إِنَّ اللَّهَ عَلِيمٌ بِذَاتِ الصُّدُورِ ﴿١١٩﴾ إِنْ
تَمْسَسْكُمْ حَسَنَةٌ تَسُؤْهُمْ وَإِنْ تُصِبْكُمْ
سَيِّئَةٌ يَفْرَحُوا بِهَا وَإِنْ تَصْبِرُوا وَتَتَّقُوا
لَا يَضُرُّكُمْ كَيْدُهُمْ شَيْئًا إِنَّ اللَّهَ بِمَا
يَعْمَلُونَ مُحِيطٌ ﴿١٢٠﴾ وَإِذْ غَدَوْتَ مِنْ أَهْلِكَ
تُبَوِّئُ الْمُؤْمِنِينَ مَقَاعِدَ لِلْقِتَالِ وَاللَّهُ
سَمِيعٌ عَلِيمٌ ﴿١٢١﴾ إِذْ هَمَّتْ طَائِفَتَانِ مِنْكُمْ
أَنْ تَفْشَلَا وَاللَّهُ وَلِيُّهُمَا وَعَلَى اللَّهِ
فَلْيَتَوَكَّلِ الْمُؤْمِنُونَ ﴿١٢٢﴾ وَلَقَدْ نَصَرَكُمُ
اللَّهُ بِبَدْرٍ وَأَنْتُمْ أَذِلَّةٌ فَاتَّقُوا اللَّهَ
لَعَلَّكُمْ تَشْكُرُونَ ﴿١٢٣﴾ إِذْ تَقُولُ لِلْمُؤْمِنِينَ
أَلَنْ يَكْفِيَكُمْ أَنْ يُمِدَّكُمْ رَبُّكُمْ بِثَلَاثَةِ
آلَافٍ مِنَ الْمَلَائِكَةِ مُنْزَلِينَ ﴿١٢٤﴾ بَلَى إِنْ
تَصْبِرُوا وَتَتَّقُوا وَيَأْتُوكُمْ مِنْ فَوْرِهِمْ
هَٰذَا يُمْدِدْكُمْ رَبُّكُمْ بِخَمْسَةِ آلَافٍ مِنَ
الْمَلَائِكَةِ مُسَوِّمِينَ ﴿١٢٥﴾ وَمَا جَعَلَهُ اللَّهُ إِلَّا
بُشْرَىٰ لَكُمْ وَلِتَطْمَئِنَّ قُلُوبُكُمْ بِهِ
وَمَا النَّصْرُ إِلَّا مِنْ عِنْدِ اللَّهِ الْعَزِيزِ
الْحَكِيمِ ﴿١٢٦﴾ لِيَقْطَعَ طَرَفًا مِنَ الَّذِينَ كَفَرُوا

who disbelieve and their leaders and vanquish others with humiliation so that they might go back utterly frustrated.

128. (O Prophet!) You have no say whatsoever in the matter, (it is up to Him alone) whether He turns towards them with mercy or punishes them because they are certainly wrongdoers.

129. And to Allâh belongs whatsoever is in the heavens and whatsoever is in the earth. He protects (against sins) whom He will and punishes whom He will. Allâh is Great Protector, Ever Merciful.

SECTION 14

130. **O** YOU who believe! Do not practise usury and interest involving multiple additions, and keep your duty to Allâh and take Him as a shield so that you may prosper.

131. Be on your guard against the Fire which has been prepared for the disbelievers.

132. And obey Allâh and this Messenger that you may be shown mercy.

133. Wing your way to the protection of your Lord and to the Paradise whose expanse is as (vast as) the heavens and the earth. It is prepared for those who become secure against evil;

134. Those who spend (in the cause of Allâh) in prosperity and adversity and those who suppress anger and pardon (the offences of) the people. And Allâh loves such doers of good to others,

135. And those who when they commit any act of indecency or do injustice to themselves remember Allâh and implore (Him for) protection against their sins - and who can protect against sins except Allâh? - And they do not deliberately persist in doing wrong.

136. It is these whose reward is protection from their Lord, and Gardens served with running streams, therein they shall live forever. How excellent is the reward of the painstaking (in

أَوْ يَكْبِتَهُمْ فَيَنقَلِبُوا خَائِبِينَ ﴿١٢٧﴾ لَيْسَ لَكَ
مِنَ الْأَمْرِ شَيْءٌ أَوْ يَتُوبَ عَلَيْهِمْ أَوْ
يُعَذِّبَهُمْ فَإِنَّهُمْ ظَالِمُونَ ﴿١٢٨﴾ وَلِلَّهِ مَا فِي
السَّمَاوَاتِ وَمَا فِي الْأَرْضِ ۚ يَغْفِرُ لِمَن
يَشَاءُ وَيُعَذِّبُ مَن يَشَاءُ ۚ وَاللَّهُ غَفُورٌ
رَّحِيمٌ ﴿١٢٩﴾ يَا أَيُّهَا الَّذِينَ آمَنُوا لَا تَأْكُلُوا
الرِّبَا أَضْعَافًا مُّضَاعَفَةً ۖ وَاتَّقُوا اللَّهَ لَعَلَّكُمْ
تُفْلِحُونَ ﴿١٣٠﴾ وَاتَّقُوا النَّارَ الَّتِي أُعِدَّتْ
لِلْكَافِرِينَ ﴿١٣١﴾ وَأَطِيعُوا اللَّهَ وَالرَّسُولَ لَعَلَّكُمْ
تُرْحَمُونَ ﴿١٣٢﴾ وَسَارِعُوا إِلَىٰ مَغْفِرَةٍ مِّن رَّبِّكُمْ
وَجَنَّةٍ عَرْضُهَا السَّمَاوَاتُ وَالْأَرْضُ أُعِدَّتْ
لِلْمُتَّقِينَ ﴿١٣٣﴾ الَّذِينَ يُنفِقُونَ فِي السَّرَّاءِ
وَالضَّرَّاءِ وَالْكَاظِمِينَ الْغَيْظَ وَالْعَافِينَ
عَنِ النَّاسِ ۗ وَاللَّهُ يُحِبُّ الْمُحْسِنِينَ ﴿١٣٤﴾
وَالَّذِينَ إِذَا فَعَلُوا فَاحِشَةً أَوْ ظَلَمُوا
أَنفُسَهُمْ ذَكَرُوا اللَّهَ فَاسْتَغْفَرُوا لِذُنُوبِهِمْ
وَمَن يَغْفِرُ الذُّنُوبَ إِلَّا اللَّهُ وَلَمْ يُصِرُّوا عَلَىٰ
مَا فَعَلُوا وَهُمْ يَعْلَمُونَ ﴿١٣٥﴾ أُولَٰئِكَ جَزَاؤُهُم
مَّغْفِرَةٌ مِّن رَّبِّهِمْ وَجَنَّاتٌ تَجْرِي مِن

the right direction).

137. Surely, there have been diverse dispensations before you, so travel in the land and see how evil was the fate of those who cried lies (to the Prophets).

138. This (Qur'ân) is a clear exposition (of the truth) for humankind (to follow) and a (means to) guidance, and an exhortation to those who guard against evil (and are dutiful to God and people).

139. Therefore slacken not, nor grieve, and when you are true believers you shall certainly be the triumphant.

140. If you have received an outer injury (in the Battle of *Uhud),* surely, the (disbelieving) people have already received a similar injury (in the same battle) - these days of vicissitudes are those which We cause to alternate among the people, (it is so that you may be admonished) and that (among other things), Allâh may distinguish those who (really) believe and so that He may raise martyrs from among you; and Allâh does not love the unjust.

141. And (it is) so that Allâh may purge all the impurities of those who (truly) believe and so that He may wipe off the disbelievers gradually.

142. Do you suppose that you would enter Paradise while Allâh has not yet distinguished those of you who strive hard (in the cause of Allâh) and has not yet distinguished the patiently persevering.

143. And you used to long for *(Jihâd* and a martyr's) death before you met it, but now you have seen it and you will see yet (many more wonders happen).

SECTION 15

144. AND Muhammad is but a Messenger. Surely, all Messengers have passed away before him. Would you recant if he dies or be killed. And

تَحْتِهَا الْأَنْهٰرُ خٰلِدِينَ فِيهَا ۚ وَ نِعْمَ
أَجْرُ الْعٰمِلِينَ ﴿١٣٦﴾ قَدْ خَلَتْ مِنْ قَبْلِكُمْ
سُنَنٌ فَسِيرُوا فِي الْأَرْضِ فَانْظُرُوا كَيْفَ
كَانَ عٰقِبَةُ الْمُكَذِّبِينَ ﴿١٣٧﴾ هٰذَا بَيَانٌ
لِّلنَّاسِ وَ هُدًى وَّ مَوْعِظَةٌ لِّلْمُتَّقِينَ ﴿١٣٨﴾
وَ لَا تَهِنُوا وَ لَا تَحْزَنُوا وَ أَنْتُمُ الْأَعْلَوْنَ
إِنْ كُنْتُمْ مُّؤْمِنِينَ ﴿١٣٩﴾ إِنْ يَّمْسَسْكُمْ
قَرْحٌ فَقَدْ مَسَّ الْقَوْمَ قَرْحٌ مِّثْلُهُ ۚ
وَ تِلْكَ الْأَيَّامُ نُدَاوِلُهَا بَيْنَ النَّاسِ ۚ
وَ لِيَعْلَمَ اللّٰهُ الَّذِينَ اٰمَنُوا وَ يَتَّخِذَ مِنْكُمْ
شُهَدَآءَ ۚ وَ اللّٰهُ لَا يُحِبُّ الظّٰلِمِينَ ﴿١٤٠﴾
وَ لِيُمَحِّصَ اللّٰهُ الَّذِينَ اٰمَنُوا وَ يَمْحَقَ
الْكٰفِرِينَ ﴿١٤١﴾ أَمْ حَسِبْتُمْ أَنْ تَدْخُلُوا
الْجَنَّةَ وَ لَمَّا يَعْلَمِ اللّٰهُ الَّذِينَ جٰهَدُوا
مِنْكُمْ وَ يَعْلَمَ الصّٰبِرِينَ ﴿١٤٢﴾ وَ لَقَدْ كُنْتُمْ
تَمَنَّوْنَ الْمَوْتَ مِنْ قَبْلِ أَنْ تَلْقَوْهُ فَقَدْ
رَأَيْتُمُوهُ وَ أَنْتُمْ تَنْظُرُونَ ﴿١٤٣﴾ وَ مَا مُحَمَّدٌ
إِلَّا رَسُولٌ ۚ قَدْ خَلَتْ مِنْ قَبْلِهِ الرُّسُلُ ۚ
أَفَإِنْ مَّاتَ أَوْ قُتِلَ انْقَلَبْتُمْ عَلٰى أَعْقٰبِكُمْ ۚ

he who recants shall do no harm at all to Allâh, and Allâh will certainly reward the grateful.
145. Nor can a living being die save by the leave of Allâh - a decree with a prescribed term. And he who desires the reward (for his deeds) of this world, We grant him thereof; and he who desires the reward of the Hereafter, We will grant him thereof. And We will certainly reward the grateful.
146. There has been many a Prophet beside whom many worshippers of the Lord fought. They were neither unnerved on account of all that befell them in the cause of Allâh, nor did they weaken, nor did they show inconsistency (against their adversary). Allâh certainly loves such patiently-persevering ones.
147. Their word (of prayer) was only that they said, 'Our Lord! Grant us protection against the consequences of our sins and our excesses in our conduct, and make our foothold firm, and grant us victory over the disbelieving people.'
148. So Allâh granted them the reward of this world as also an excellent reward of the Hereafter. And Allâh loves the doers of good to others.

SECTION 16

149. **O** YOU who believe! If you obey those who have disbelieved, they will make you turn apostates so that you will become losers.
150. Nay, (you do not have to do this for) Allâh is your Patron and Protector and He is the best of the helpers.
151. We shall certainly strike terror into the hearts of those who have disbelieved, because they have associated with Allâh that for which He has sent down no authority, their abode is the Fire and how dismal is the lodging of the wrongdoers!
152. And certainly Allâh had made good His promise to you when you were slaying them to

وَمَنْ يَّنْقَلِبْ عَلٰى عَقِبَيْهِ فَلَنْ يَّضُرَّ اللّٰهَ
شَيْـًٔا ۗ وَسَيَجْزِي اللّٰهُ الشّٰكِرِيْنَ ﴿١٤٤﴾ وَمَا
كَانَ لِنَفْسٍ اَنْ تَمُوْتَ اِلَّا بِاِذْنِ اللّٰهِ كِتٰبًا
مُّؤَجَّلًا ۗ وَمَنْ يُّرِدْ ثَوَابَ الدُّنْيَا نُؤْتِهٖ
مِنْهَا ۚ وَمَنْ يُّرِدْ ثَوَابَ الْاٰخِرَةِ نُؤْتِهٖ
مِنْهَا ۗ وَسَنَجْزِي الشّٰكِرِيْنَ ﴿١٤٥﴾ وَكَاَيِّنْ مِّنْ
نَّبِيٍّ قٰتَلَ مَعَهٗ رِبِّيُّوْنَ كَثِيْرٌ ۚ فَمَا وَهَنُوْا
لِمَآ اَصَابَهُمْ فِيْ سَبِيْلِ اللّٰهِ وَمَا ضَعُفُوْا
وَمَا اسْتَكَانُوْا ۗ وَاللّٰهُ يُحِبُّ الصّٰبِرِيْنَ ﴿١٤٦﴾
وَمَا كَانَ قَوْلَهُمْ اِلَّآ اَنْ قَالُوْا رَبَّنَا اغْفِرْ لَنَا
ذُنُوْبَنَا وَاِسْرَافَنَا فِيْٓ اَمْرِنَا وَثَبِّتْ اَقْدَامَنَا
وَانْصُرْنَا عَلَى الْقَوْمِ الْكٰفِرِيْنَ ﴿١٤٧﴾ فَاٰتٰىهُمُ
اللّٰهُ ثَوَابَ الدُّنْيَا وَحُسْنَ ثَوَابِ الْاٰخِرَةِ ۗ
وَاللّٰهُ يُحِبُّ الْمُحْسِنِيْنَ ﴿١٤٨﴾ يٰٓاَيُّهَا الَّذِيْنَ
اٰمَنُوْٓا اِنْ تُطِيْعُوا الَّذِيْنَ كَفَرُوْا يَرُدُّوْكُمْ
عَلٰٓى اَعْقَابِكُمْ فَتَنْقَلِبُوْا خٰسِرِيْنَ ﴿١٤٩﴾ بَلِ اللّٰهُ
مَوْلٰىكُمْ ۚ وَهُوَ خَيْرُ النّٰصِرِيْنَ ﴿١٥٠﴾ سَنُلْقِيْ
فِيْ قُلُوْبِ الَّذِيْنَ كَفَرُوا الرُّعْبَ بِمَآ
اَشْرَكُوْا بِاللّٰهِ مَا لَمْ يُنَزِّلْ بِهٖ سُلْطٰنًا ۚ
وَمَاْوٰىهُمُ النَّارُ ۗ وَبِئْسَ مَثْوَى الظّٰلِمِيْنَ ﴿١٥١﴾
وَلَقَدْ صَدَقَكُمُ اللّٰهُ وَعْدَهٗٓ اِذْ تَحُسُّوْنَهُمْ
بِاِذْنِهٖ ۚ حَتّٰٓى اِذَا فَشِلْتُمْ وَتَنَازَعْتُمْ فِي

pieces by His leave (in the Battle of *Uhud)*, until, when you became lax and disagreed among yourselves about the (implications of the) order (of the Prophet), and you disobeyed (your leader *Abdullah bin Jubair),* after He had brought that (victory) which you desired within your sight (He withdrew His help from you). There were some among you who desired the present life and among you were those who desired the life to come. Then He turned you away from (gaining clear victory over) them (- the enemy), that He might reveal your (true) selves. Yet He surely pardoned you. Allâh is Gracious to the believers.

153. When you were going hard and far (in pursuit of the enemy in the Battle of *Uhud)* and you would not cast even a side-glance at and wait for anyone while the Messenger was calling out to you from your rear (to come back). So He gave you greater sorrow (which proved unreal later on) in place of the sorrow (you had already) in order that you should not grieve over what you had missed (of clear victory) nor over what befell you (of the hardships). And Allâh is Well-Aware of what you do.

154. Then, after the sorrow He sent down tranquility upon you - a slumber which overwhelmed a party of you, while another party (of the hypocrites) whom their own personal interests had made anxious, entertained unjustly false notions about Allâh like the false notions (they used to bear in the days) of ignorance. They said, 'Have we any authority in (the execution of) the matter (of administration)?' Say, 'The whole authority rests with Allâh.' They hide in their minds (- thoughts) which they would not disclose to you. They say, 'If we had any authority in (the execution of) the matter (of administration) we would not have been killed here.' Say, 'Even if you had been confined in your homes, surely those who were ordained to be slain would have, nevertheless, gone forth to the places where they were destined to fall. And (all this that took place in the Battle of *Uhud* was) that Allâh might reveal

الْأَمْرِ وَعَصَيْتُم مِّن بَعْدِ مَا أَرَاكُم مَّا
تُحِبُّونَ ۚ مِنكُم مَّن يُرِيدُ الدُّنْيَا وَمِنكُم
مَّن يُرِيدُ الْآخِرَةَ ۚ ثُمَّ صَرَفَكُمْ عَنْهُمْ
لِيَبْتَلِيَكُمْ ۖ وَلَقَدْ عَفَا عَنكُمْ ۗ وَاللَّهُ ذُو
فَضْلٍ عَلَى الْمُؤْمِنِينَ ﴿١٥٢﴾ إِذْ تُصْعِدُونَ
وَلَا تَلْوُونَ عَلَىٰ أَحَدٍ وَالرَّسُولُ يَدْعُوكُمْ
فِي أُخْرَاكُمْ فَأَثَابَكُمْ غَمًّا بِغَمٍّ لِّكَيْلَا
تَحْزَنُوا عَلَىٰ مَا فَاتَكُمْ وَلَا مَا أَصَابَكُمْ ۗ
وَاللَّهُ خَبِيرٌ بِمَا تَعْمَلُونَ ﴿١٥٣﴾ ثُمَّ أَنزَلَ عَلَيْكُم
مِّن بَعْدِ الْغَمِّ أَمَنَةً نُّعَاسًا يَغْشَىٰ طَائِفَةً
مِّنكُمْ ۖ وَطَائِفَةٌ قَدْ أَهَمَّتْهُمْ أَنفُسُهُمْ
يَظُنُّونَ بِاللَّهِ غَيْرَ الْحَقِّ ظَنَّ الْجَاهِلِيَّةِ ۖ
يَقُولُونَ هَل لَّنَا مِنَ الْأَمْرِ مِن شَيْءٍ ۗ
قُلْ إِنَّ الْأَمْرَ كُلَّهُ لِلَّهِ ۗ يُخْفُونَ فِي أَنفُسِهِم
مَّا لَا يُبْدُونَ لَكَ ۖ يَقُولُونَ لَوْ كَانَ لَنَا مِنَ
الْأَمْرِ شَيْءٌ مَّا قُتِلْنَا هَاهُنَا ۗ قُل لَّوْ كُنتُمْ
فِي بُيُوتِكُمْ لَبَرَزَ الَّذِينَ كُتِبَ عَلَيْهِمُ

what was in your hearts and so that He might purge what was in your minds. And Allâh knows well what is in the minds (of the people).

155. Surely, those of you who turned their backs on the day when two armies met (in the battlefield of *Uhud)* it was satan indeed who sought to seduce them (to do so) without any intention on their part because of certain other doings of theirs, and most certainly Allâh has already pardoned them. Verily, Allâh is Great Protector, Ever Forbearing.

SECTION 17

156. **O** YOU who believe! Do not be like those who have concealed (the truth) and who say of their brethren when they (- the latter) travel in the land or go forth on any campaign (and fall martyrs), 'Had they been with us they would not have died or been killed.' They say it so that Allâh makes this a cause of intense regret in their hearts. (The fact, however, is that) it is Allâh Who gives life and causes death. Allâh sees well all what you do.

157. And if you are killed (in the cause of Allâh) or you die, surely (you will find that) the protection from Allâh and (His) mercy (which fall to your lot) are far better than what they (- who have concealed the truth) amass.

158. Indeed, whether you die or be killed, verily you shall be gathered together and brought before Allâh.

159. So (O Prophet!) it is owing to the great mercy of Allâh that you are gentle towards them. Had you been harsh, hard-hearted, they would have certainly dispersed from around you; hence pardon them and ask protection for them, and consult them in matters (of administration), and when you are determined (after due consultation), put your trust in Allâh. Verily, Allâh loves those who put their trust in Him.

160. If Allâh goes on helping you there is none

الْقَتْلُ إِلَىٰ مَضَاجِعِهِمْ ۖ وَلِيَبْتَلِيَ اللَّهُ مَا فِي
صُدُورِكُمْ وَلِيُمَحِّصَ مَا فِي قُلُوبِكُمْ ۗ وَاللَّهُ
عَلِيمٌ بِذَاتِ الصُّدُورِ ﴿١٥٤﴾ إِنَّ الَّذِينَ
تَوَلَّوْا مِنكُمْ يَوْمَ الْتَقَى الْجَمْعَانِ إِنَّمَا
اسْتَزَلَّهُمُ الشَّيْطَانُ بِبَعْضِ مَا كَسَبُوا ۖ وَلَقَدْ
عَفَا اللَّهُ عَنْهُمْ ۗ إِنَّ اللَّهَ غَفُورٌ حَلِيمٌ ﴿١٥٥﴾
يَا أَيُّهَا الَّذِينَ آمَنُوا لَا تَكُونُوا كَالَّذِينَ
كَفَرُوا وَقَالُوا لِإِخْوَانِهِمْ إِذَا ضَرَبُوا فِي
الْأَرْضِ أَوْ كَانُوا غُزًّى لَّوْ كَانُوا عِندَنَا مَا
مَاتُوا وَمَا قُتِلُوا لِيَجْعَلَ اللَّهُ ذَٰلِكَ حَسْرَةً
فِي قُلُوبِهِمْ ۗ وَاللَّهُ يُحْيِي وَيُمِيتُ ۗ وَاللَّهُ بِمَا
تَعْمَلُونَ بَصِيرٌ ﴿١٥٦﴾ وَلَئِن قُتِلْتُمْ فِي سَبِيلِ
اللَّهِ أَوْ مُتُّمْ لَمَغْفِرَةٌ مِّنَ اللَّهِ وَرَحْمَةٌ
خَيْرٌ مِّمَّا يَجْمَعُونَ ﴿١٥٧﴾ وَلَئِن مُّتُّمْ أَوْ
قُتِلْتُمْ لَإِلَى اللَّهِ تُحْشَرُونَ ﴿١٥٨﴾ فَبِمَا رَحْمَةٍ
مِّنَ اللَّهِ لِنتَ لَهُمْ ۖ وَلَوْ كُنتَ فَظًّا غَلِيظَ
الْقَلْبِ لَانفَضُّوا مِنْ حَوْلِكَ ۖ فَاعْفُ عَنْهُمْ
وَاسْتَغْفِرْ لَهُمْ وَشَاوِرْهُمْ فِي الْأَمْرِ ۖ فَإِذَا
عَزَمْتَ فَتَوَكَّلْ عَلَى اللَّهِ ۚ إِنَّ اللَّهَ يُحِبُّ
الْمُتَوَكِّلِينَ ﴿١٥٩﴾ إِن يَنصُرْكُمُ اللَّهُ فَلَا غَالِبَ

to overcome you and if He forsakes you, then, who is there that will help you besides Him. Let the believers put their trust in Allâh alone.

161. It is not possible for a Prophet to be guilty of a breach of trust, but whoever (else) is guilty of a breach of a trust he will have to bring forth that about which he had been guilty, on the Day of Resurrection when every soul shall be paid in full for what it has accomplished, and they shall not be done any injustice.

162. Can the person who (always) follows the good pleasure of Allâh be like the person who has incurred the displeasure of Allâh and whose abode is Gehenna? What an evil destined abode it is!

163. They (- the believers and the Prophets) have exalted degrees of rank of grace with Allâh. And Allâh sees well of all that they do.

164. Verily, Allâh has bestowed a favour on the believers when He has raised amongst them a great Messenger from amongst themselves who recites to them His Messages, and purifies them and teaches them the Book and the wisdom; although before this, they were steeped in flagrant error.

165. (So what) when you suffered a loss (at the Battle of *Uhud)* you had already inflicted a loss (upon your enemy) twice as heavy as that (at the Battle of *Badr)*, you (began to) say, 'Whence is this?' Say, 'It is of your own making.' Surely, Allâh is the Possessor of full power to do all that He will.

166. And that which befell you on the day when the two armies met (at *Uhud),* was so by the leave of Allâh, and (it happened thus) so that He might distinguish the believers,

167. And that He might distinguish those who practise hypocrisy. Indeed, it was said to them (- the hypocrites), 'Come forward, fight in the cause of Allâh, or at least help the defences.' They said, 'If we but knew that it would be a fight we would surely follow you, (but the Muslims were going to a sure destruction).' On that day, they were nearer to

لَكُمۡ وَإِنۡ يَّخۡذُلۡكُمۡ فَمَنۡ ذَا الَّذِيۡ يَنۡصُرُكُمۡ
مِّنۡۢ بَعۡدِهٖ ؕ وَعَلَى اللّٰهِ فَلۡيَتَوَكَّلِ الۡمُؤۡمِنُوۡنَ ﴿١٦٠﴾
وَمَا كَانَ لِنَبِيٍّ أَنۡ يَّغُلَّ ؕ وَمَنۡ يَّغۡلُلۡ
يَأۡتِ بِمَا غَلَّ يَوۡمَ الۡقِيٰمَةِ ۚ ثُمَّ تُوَفّٰى
كُلُّ نَفۡسٍ مَّا كَسَبَتۡ وَهُمۡ لَا يُظۡلَمُوۡنَ ﴿١٦١﴾
أَفَمَنِ اتَّبَعَ رِضۡوَانَ اللّٰهِ كَمَنۡۢ بَآءَ بِسَخَطٍ
مِّنَ اللّٰهِ وَمَأۡوٰهُ جَهَنَّمُ ؕ وَبِئۡسَ الۡمَصِيۡرُ ﴿١٦٢﴾
هُمۡ دَرَجٰتٌ عِنۡدَ اللّٰهِ ؕ وَاللّٰهُ بَصِيۡرٌۢ بِمَا
يَعۡمَلُوۡنَ ﴿١٦٣﴾ لَقَدۡ مَنَّ اللّٰهُ عَلَى الۡمُؤۡمِنِيۡنَ
إِذۡ بَعَثَ فِيۡهِمۡ رَسُوۡلًا مِّنۡ أَنۡفُسِهِمۡ يَتۡلُوۡا
عَلَيۡهِمۡ أٰيٰتِهٖ وَيُزَكِّيۡهِمۡ وَيُعَلِّمُهُمُ الۡكِتٰبَ
وَالۡحِكۡمَةَ ۚ وَإِنۡ كَانُوۡا مِنۡ قَبۡلُ لَفِيۡ ضَلٰلٍ
مُّبِيۡنٍ ﴿١٦٤﴾ أَوَلَمَّآ أَصَابَتۡكُمۡ مُّصِيۡبَةٌ قَدۡ أَصَبۡتُمۡ
مِّثۡلَيۡهَا ۙ قُلۡتُمۡ أَنّٰى هٰذَا ؕ قُلۡ هُوَ مِنۡ عِنۡدِ
أَنۡفُسِكُمۡ ؕ إِنَّ اللّٰهَ عَلٰى كُلِّ شَيۡءٍ قَدِيۡرٌ ﴿١٦٥﴾ وَمَآ
أَصَابَكُمۡ يَوۡمَ الۡتَقَى الۡجَمۡعٰنِ فَبِإِذۡنِ اللّٰهِ
وَلِيَعۡلَمَ الۡمُؤۡمِنِيۡنَ ﴿١٦٦﴾ وَلِيَعۡلَمَ الَّذِيۡنَ نَافَقُوۡا ۖۚ
وَقِيۡلَ لَهُمۡ تَعَالَوۡا قٰتِلُوۡا فِيۡ سَبِيۡلِ اللّٰهِ أَوِ
ادۡفَعُوۡا ؕ قَالُوۡا لَوۡ نَعۡلَمُ قِتَالًا لَّاتَّبَعۡنٰكُمۡ ؕ هُمۡ
لِلۡكُفۡرِ يَوۡمَئِذٍ أَقۡرَبُ مِنۡهُمۡ لِلۡإِيۡمٰنِ ۚ يَقُوۡلُوۡنَ

ع

disbelief than to belief. They say with their mouths that which is not in their minds. And Allâh knows best all that they conceal.

168. It is these who said of their brethren whilst they (themselves) stayed behind (declining the field), 'If they had obeyed us, they would not have been killed.' Say, 'Then avert death from yourselves if you are right.'

169. And think not of those who have been killed in the cause of Allâh as dead. Nay, they are alive, enjoying the company of their (Ever- Living) Lord and well provided (as they deserve to be for an everlasting life);

170. Jubilant because of that which Allâh has given them out of His grace. They are receiving glad tidings also about those (believers similar to themselves) who are still left behind them (in this world) and have not yet joined them, that they shall have no cause of fear, nor shall they grieve, (rather they will be victorious and will see the promises of Allâh fulfilled).

171. And they (- the martyrs) are also receiving glad tidings (that those who have been left behind in the world are happy) because of the favours of Allâh and (His) great bounty and that Allâh does not suffer the reward of the believers to be lost.

SECTION 18

172. **THOSE** who responded to the call of Allâh and the Messenger after they had received an injury (at *U<u>h</u>ud),* for those amongst them who did their duty well and warded off evil (by pursuing the enemy forces the next day up to *<u>H</u>amrâ'al-Asad,* a place near Madînah), there awaits a great reward.

173. Those to whom (at the time of the expedition of *Badr al-Sug<u>h</u>râ)* people said, 'People have assembled against you, so fear them.' But this (threat of danger) increased their faith and they said, 'Allâh is Sufficient for us, and He is an excellent Disposer of affairs'.

174. Hence they returned with a mighty

بِأَفْوَٰهِهِم مَّا لَيْسَ فِي قُلُوبِهِمْ وَاللَّهُ أَعْلَمُ
بِمَا يَكْتُمُونَ ﴿١٦٧﴾ الَّذِينَ قَالُوا لِإِخْوَانِهِمْ وَقَعَدُوا
لَوْ أَطَاعُونَا مَا قُتِلُوا قُلْ فَادْرَءُوا عَنْ أَنفُسِكُمُ
الْمَوْتَ إِن كُنتُمْ صَٰدِقِينَ ﴿١٦٨﴾ وَلَا تَحْسَبَنَّ
الَّذِينَ قُتِلُوا فِي سَبِيلِ اللَّهِ أَمْوَٰتًا بَلْ
أَحْيَاءٌ عِندَ رَبِّهِمْ يُرْزَقُونَ ﴿١٦٩﴾ فَرِحِينَ بِمَا
آتَىٰهُمُ اللَّهُ مِن فَضْلِهِ وَيَسْتَبْشِرُونَ بِالَّذِينَ
لَمْ يَلْحَقُوا بِهِم مِّنْ خَلْفِهِمْ أَلَّا خَوْفٌ عَلَيْهِمْ
وَلَا هُمْ يَحْزَنُونَ ﴿١٧٠﴾ يَسْتَبْشِرُونَ بِنِعْمَةٍ
مِّنَ اللَّهِ وَفَضْلٍ وَأَنَّ اللَّهَ لَا يُضِيعُ أَجْرَ
الْمُؤْمِنِينَ ﴿١٧١﴾ الَّذِينَ اسْتَجَابُوا لِلَّهِ وَالرَّسُولِ
مِن بَعْدِ مَا أَصَابَهُمُ الْقَرْحُ لِلَّذِينَ أَحْسَنُوا
مِنْهُمْ وَاتَّقَوْا أَجْرٌ عَظِيمٌ ﴿١٧٢﴾ الَّذِينَ قَالَ لَهُمُ
النَّاسُ إِنَّ النَّاسَ قَدْ جَمَعُوا لَكُمْ فَاخْشَوْهُمْ
فَزَادَهُمْ إِيمَٰنًا وَقَالُوا حَسْبُنَا اللَّهُ وَنِعْمَ
الْوَكِيلُ ﴿١٧٣﴾ فَانقَلَبُوا بِنِعْمَةٍ مِّنَ اللَّهِ وَفَضْلٍ

ع ١٧/٨

blessing from Allâh and a great bounty. They suffered no harm whatsoever, and they followed the good pleasure of Allâh. Indeed, Allâh is the Possessor of great bounty.

175. (Now you have come to know that) it is satan, in fact, who merely threatens through his friends, so do not fear them, rather fear Me, if you are (true) believers.

176. And do not let those who vie one with another in (following the ways of) disbelief grieve you. Surely, they shall not be able to do the slightest harm to Allâh. It is Allâh's will to assign them no portion in the Hereafter. Rather, there awaits them a great punishment.

177. Those who preferred disbelief to belief will not be able to do the least harm to Allâh. A grievous punishment awaits them.

178. And do not let those who disbelieve think that the respite We give them is good for them. Surely, We grant them respite but they do not avail it, with the result that they add to their sins. A humiliating punishment awaits them.

179. And Allâh is not going to leave (you), the believers, as you are, unless He has distinguished the corrupt from the good. Nor is Allâh going to reveal fully to (everyone of) you, the unseen; but Allâh chooses (for His Messages) such of His Messengers as He will. Believe, therefore in Allâh and His Messengers; and (remember) if you believe (truly) and guard against evil then there is for you a great reward.

180. And do not let those, who behave niggardly in (spending) what Allâh has granted them of His bounty, think that it is good for them, nay it is bad for them. They shall certainly have the things they were niggardly about, hung about their necks like halters on the Day of Resurrection. And to Allâh belongs the heritage of the heavens and the earth. Indeed, Allâh is Well-Aware of all that you do.

SECTION 19

181. **ALLÂH** has most certainly heard the words

لَمْ يَمْسَسْهُمْ سُوْٓءٌ وَّاتَّبَعُوْا رِضْوٰنَ اللّٰهِ ۭ
وَاللّٰهُ ذُوْ فَضْلٍ عَظِيْمٍ ﴿١٧٤﴾ اِنَّمَا ذٰلِكُمُ الشَّيْطٰنُ
يُخَوِّفُ اَوْلِيَآءَهٗ ۠ فَلَا تَخَافُوْهُمْ وَخَافُوْنِ
اِنْ كُنْتُمْ مُّؤْمِنِيْنَ ﴿١٧٥﴾ وَلَا يَحْزُنْكَ الَّذِيْنَ
يُسٰرِعُوْنَ فِي الْكُفْرِ ۚ اِنَّهُمْ لَنْ يَّضُرُّوا اللّٰهَ
شَيْـًٔا ۭ يُرِيْدُ اللّٰهُ اَلَّا يَجْعَلَ لَهُمْ حَظًّا فِي
الْاٰخِرَةِ ۚ وَلَهُمْ عَذَابٌ عَظِيْمٌ ﴿١٧٦﴾ اِنَّ الَّذِيْنَ
اشْتَرَوُا الْكُفْرَ بِالْاِيْمٰنِ لَنْ يَّضُرُّوا اللّٰهَ
شَيْـًٔا ۚ وَلَهُمْ عَذَابٌ اَلِيْمٌ ﴿١٧٧﴾ وَلَا يَحْسَبَنَّ
الَّذِيْنَ كَفَرُوْا اَنَّمَا نُمْلِيْ لَهُمْ خَيْرٌ لِّاَنْفُسِهِمْ ۭ
اِنَّمَا نُمْلِيْ لَهُمْ لِيَزْدَادُوْا اِثْمًا ۚ وَلَهُمْ عَذَابٌ
مُّهِيْنٌ ﴿١٧٨﴾ مَا كَانَ اللّٰهُ لِيَذَرَ الْمُؤْمِنِيْنَ عَلٰى
مَآ اَنْتُمْ عَلَيْهِ حَتّٰى يَمِيْزَ الْخَبِيْثَ مِنَ
الطَّيِّبِ ۭ وَمَا كَانَ اللّٰهُ لِيُطْلِعَكُمْ عَلَى
الْغَيْبِ وَلٰكِنَّ اللّٰهَ يَجْتَبِيْ مِنْ رُّسُلِهٖ
مَنْ يَّشَآءُ ۠ فَاٰمِنُوْا بِاللّٰهِ وَرُسُلِهٖ ۚ وَاِنْ
تُؤْمِنُوْا وَتَتَّقُوْا فَلَكُمْ اَجْرٌ عَظِيْمٌ ﴿١٧٩﴾ وَلَا
يَحْسَبَنَّ الَّذِيْنَ يَبْخَلُوْنَ بِمَآ اٰتٰىهُمُ اللّٰهُ
مِنْ فَضْلِهٖ هُوَ خَيْرًا لَّهُمْ ۭ بَلْ هُوَ شَرٌّ لَّهُمْ ۭ
سَيُطَوَّقُوْنَ مَا بَخِلُوْا بِهٖ يَوْمَ الْقِيٰمَةِ ۭ
وَلِلّٰهِ مِيْرَاثُ السَّمٰوٰتِ وَالْاَرْضِ ۭ وَاللّٰهُ بِمَا
تَعْمَلُوْنَ خَبِيْرٌ ﴿١٨٠﴾ لَقَدْ سَمِعَ اللّٰهُ قَوْلَ الَّذِيْنَ

ع ١٨ ٩

of those who said, 'Allâh is poor and we are rich.' Certainly We shall record what they say and their efforts towards seeking to kill the Prophets unjustly. And We shall say (at the time of retribution), 'Taste (now) the punishment of burning.

182. 'This (punishment) is because of that which your own hands have sent forward,' and the fact is that Allâh is not at all unjust to His servants.

183. (These are the very Jews) who said, 'Surely, Allâh has enjoined us not to believe in any Messenger unless He brings us an offering which is consumed by the fire (in accordance with mosaic law).' Say, 'Surely Messengers have come to you before me with clear signs and with that of which you speak. Why, then did you seek to kill them if you have been right (in your demand)?'

184. But if they cry lies to you (you need not be disheartened) even so lies were cried to many Messengers before you, who came with clear signs, with the Books full of wisdom and with the glorious Scripture.

185. Every living being is destined to taste death. And you shall, verily, be paid in full your rewards on the Day of Resurrection. Then whoso is removed away from the Fire and is admitted to Paradise, he has, of course, successfully attained his goal. And the life of this world is nothing but a vain provision (causing negligence).

186. You shall, certainly, be tried in your substance and lives and you shall certainly hear from those who were given the Scripture before you and from those who set up equals (to God) a good deal of hurtful abuse. But if you are patiently persevering and guard against evil, then this (attitude) is worth being followed with constancy and firm determination.

187. Recall the time when Allâh took a covenant from those who were given the Scripture

قَالُوٓا إِنَّ اللّٰهَ فَقِيرٌ وَّنَحْنُ أَغْنِيَآءُ سَنَكْتُبُ
مَا قَالُوا وَقَتْلَهُمُ الْأَنْبِيَآءَ بِغَيْرِ حَقٍّ
وَّنَقُولُ ذُوقُوا عَذَابَ الْحَرِيقِ ﴿١٨١﴾ ذٰلِكَ بِمَا
قَدَّمَتْ أَيْدِيكُمْ وَأَنَّ اللّٰهَ لَيْسَ بِظَلَّامٍ
لِّلْعَبِيدِ ﴿١٨٢﴾ أَلَّذِينَ قَالُوٓا إِنَّ اللّٰهَ عَهِدَ إِلَيْنَآ
أَلَّا نُؤْمِنَ لِرَسُولٍ حَتّٰى يَأْتِيَنَا بِقُرْبَانٍ
تَأْكُلُهُ النَّارُ قُلْ قَدْ جَآءَكُمْ رُسُلٌ مِّنْ قَبْلِي
بِالْبَيِّنٰتِ وَبِالَّذِي قُلْتُمْ فَلِمَ قَتَلْتُمُوهُمْ
إِنْ كُنْتُمْ صٰدِقِينَ ﴿١٨٣﴾ فَإِنْ كَذَّبُوكَ فَقَدْ
كُذِّبَ رُسُلٌ مِّنْ قَبْلِكَ جَآءُو بِالْبَيِّنٰتِ
وَالزُّبُرِ وَالْكِتٰبِ الْمُنِيرِ ﴿١٨٤﴾ كُلُّ نَفْسٍ ذَآئِقَةُ
الْمَوْتِ وَإِنَّمَا تُوَفَّوْنَ أُجُورَكُمْ يَوْمَ الْقِيٰمَةِ
فَمَنْ زُحْزِحَ عَنِ النَّارِ وَأُدْخِلَ الْجَنَّةَ
فَقَدْ فَازَ وَمَا الْحَيٰوةُ الدُّنْيَآ إِلَّا مَتٰعُ
الْغُرُورِ ﴿١٨٥﴾ لَتُبْلَوُنَّ فِيٓ أَمْوٰلِكُمْ
وَأَنْفُسِكُمْ وَلَتَسْمَعُنَّ مِنَ الَّذِينَ أُوتُوا
الْكِتٰبَ مِنْ قَبْلِكُمْ وَمِنَ الَّذِينَ أَشْرَكُوٓا
أَذًى كَثِيرًا وَإِنْ تَصْبِرُوا وَتَتَّقُوا فَإِنَّ
ذٰلِكَ مِنْ عَزْمِ الْأُمُورِ ﴿١٨٦﴾ وَإِذْ أَخَذَ اللّٰهُ
مِيثَاقَ الَّذِينَ أُوتُوا الْكِتٰبَ لَتُبَيِّنُنَّهُ

that, 'You must explain (the teachings of) this (Scripture) to the people and not conceal it.' But they threw it away behind their backs, and accepted a paltry price for it. How evil is that which they have chosen!

188. You should not think - indeed you should not think that those who exult in what they have brought about, and love to be praised for what they have not done, are secure from punishment; rather a woeful punishment awaits them.

189. The sovereignty of the heavens and the earth belongs to Allâh alone, and Allâh is the Possessor of full power to do all that He will.

SECTION 20

190. SURELY, in the creation of the heavens and the earth and (in) the alternation of the night and the day there are many signs for people of pure and clear understanding.

191. These are the persons who remember Allâh standing, and sitting and (lying) on their sides and reflect upon the creation of the heavens and the earth (and say,) 'Our Lord! You have not created (all) this in vain. Glory be to You, save us from the punishment of the Fire.

192. 'Our Lord! Whomsoever You cause to enter the Fire, You have truly disgraced him, and there will be none to help these unjust.

193. 'Our Lord! Certainly, we heard a crier calling to the Faith, saying, "Believe in your Lord," and we have believed. Our Lord! Protect us against our sins and rid us of our evils and cause us to die (and after death count us) with the virtuous.

194. 'Our Lord! Grant us what You have promised us through Your Messengers and do not disgrace us on the Day of Resurrection. Surely, You do not break Your promise.'

195. Their Lord then, accepted their prayer for them (saying), 'I will not, most certainly suffer the deed of any doer (of good) from among

لِلنَّاسِ وَلَا تَكْتُمُونَهُۥ فَنَبَذُوهُ وَرَآءَ
ظُهُورِهِمْ وَاشْتَرَوْا بِهِۦ ثَمَنًا قَلِيلًا
فَبِئْسَ مَا يَشْتَرُونَ ﴿١٨٧﴾ لَا تَحْسَبَنَّ الَّذِينَ
يَفْرَحُونَ بِمَآ أَتَوا وَّيُحِبُّونَ أَن يُحْمَدُوا
بِمَا لَمْ يَفْعَلُوا فَلَا تَحْسَبَنَّهُم بِمَفَازَةٍ
مِّنَ الْعَذَابِ وَلَهُمْ عَذَابٌ أَلِيمٌ ﴿١٨٨﴾
وَلِلَّهِ مُلْكُ السَّمٰوٰتِ وَالْأَرْضِ وَاللَّهُ عَلٰى
كُلِّ شَيْءٍ قَدِيرٌ ﴿١٨٩﴾ إِنَّ فِي خَلْقِ السَّمٰوٰتِ
وَالْأَرْضِ وَاخْتِلٰفِ الَّيْلِ وَالنَّهَارِ لَأٰيٰتٍ
لِّأُولِي الْأَلْبٰبِ ﴿١٩٠﴾ الَّذِينَ يَذْكُرُونَ اللَّهَ
قِيٰمًا وَقُعُودًا وَعَلٰى جُنُوبِهِمْ وَيَتَفَكَّرُونَ
فِي خَلْقِ السَّمٰوٰتِ وَالْأَرْضِ رَبَّنَا مَا
خَلَقْتَ هٰذَا بٰطِلًا سُبْحٰنَكَ فَقِنَا عَذَابَ
النَّارِ ﴿١٩١﴾ رَبَّنَآ إِنَّكَ مَن تُدْخِلِ النَّارَ
فَقَدْ أَخْزَيْتَهُۥ وَمَا لِلظّٰلِمِينَ مِنْ أَنْصَارٍ ﴿١٩٢﴾
رَبَّنَآ إِنَّنَا سَمِعْنَا مُنَادِيًا يُنَادِي لِلْإِيمٰنِ
أَنْ ءَامِنُوا بِرَبِّكُمْ فَـَٔامَنَّا رَبَّنَا فَاغْفِرْ لَنَا
ذُنُوبَنَا وَكَفِّرْ عَنَّا سَيِّـَٔاتِنَا وَتَوَفَّنَا مَعَ الْأَبْرَارِ ﴿١٩٣﴾
رَبَّنَا وَءَاتِنَا مَا وَعَدْتَّنَا عَلٰى رُسُلِكَ وَلَا
تُخْزِنَا يَوْمَ الْقِيٰمَةِ إِنَّكَ لَا تُخْلِفُ الْمِيعَادَ ﴿١٩٤﴾
فَاسْتَجَابَ لَهُمْ رَبُّهُمْ أَنِّي لَآ أُضِيعُ عَمَلَ
عٰمِلٍ مِّنْكُم مِّنْ ذَكَرٍ أَوْ أُنْثٰى بَعْضُكُم

you, whether male or female, to be lost; the one of you being as the other. Hence those who have emigrated, and have been driven out of their homes, and have been persecuted in My cause, and who have fought and been killed, surely I will absolve them of their evils and will, of course, admit them into Gardens served with running streams, a reward from Allâh. And Allâh, with Him is the fairest reward (to offer).

196. Do not let the moving about in the land, of those who have disbelieved, deceive you.

197. (It is) a brief provision, then Gehenna shall be their abode. What an evil place of rest!

198. But those who took their Lord as a shield shall have Gardens served with running streams, therein shall they live foever, an entertainment from Allâh Himself; and that which is with Allâh is better still for the virtuous.

199. There are some among the people of the Scripture who believe in Allâh and in that which has been revealed to you and in that which has been revealed to them, humbling themselves before Allâh, they barter not the Messages of Allâh for a paltry price, it is these whose reward is due with their Lord. Indeed, Allâh is Swift in reckoning.

200. O you who believe! Be patiently persevering and strive to excel (the disbelievers) in being patiently persevering and guard (the frontiers) and ward off evil and keep your duty to Allâh, so that you may attain your goal.

مِّنْ بَعْضٍ ۚ فَالَّذِينَ هَاجَرُوا وَأُخْرِجُوا مِنْ
دِيَارِهِمْ وَأُوذُوا فِي سَبِيلِي وَقَاتَلُوا وَقُتِلُوا
لَأُكَفِّرَنَّ عَنْهُمْ سَيِّئَاتِهِمْ وَلَأُدْخِلَنَّهُمْ جَنَّاتٍ
تَجْرِي مِنْ تَحْتِهَا الْأَنْهَارُ ثَوَابًا مِّنْ عِنْدِ
اللَّهِ ۗ وَاللَّهُ عِنْدَهُ حُسْنُ الثَّوَابِ ﴿١٩٥﴾ لَا
يَغُرَّنَّكَ تَقَلُّبُ الَّذِينَ كَفَرُوا فِي الْبِلَادِ ﴿١٩٦﴾
مَتَاعٌ قَلِيلٌ ثُمَّ مَأْوَاهُمْ جَهَنَّمُ ۚ وَبِئْسَ
الْمِهَادُ ﴿١٩٧﴾ لَٰكِنِ الَّذِينَ اتَّقَوْا رَبَّهُمْ لَهُمْ
جَنَّاتٌ تَجْرِي مِنْ تَحْتِهَا الْأَنْهَارُ خَالِدِينَ
فِيهَا نُزُلًا مِّنْ عِنْدِ اللَّهِ ۗ وَمَا عِنْدَ اللَّهِ
خَيْرٌ لِّلْأَبْرَارِ ﴿١٩٨﴾ وَإِنَّ مِنْ أَهْلِ الْكِتَابِ
لَمَنْ يُؤْمِنُ بِاللَّهِ وَمَا أُنْزِلَ إِلَيْكُمْ وَمَا
أُنْزِلَ إِلَيْهِمْ خَاشِعِينَ لِلَّهِ لَا يَشْتَرُونَ
بِآيَاتِ اللَّهِ ثَمَنًا قَلِيلًا ۗ أُولَٰئِكَ لَهُمْ أَجْرُهُمْ
عِنْدَ رَبِّهِمْ ۗ إِنَّ اللَّهَ سَرِيعُ الْحِسَابِ ﴿١٩٩﴾
يَا أَيُّهَا الَّذِينَ آمَنُوا اصْبِرُوا وَصَابِرُوا
وَرَابِطُوا وَاتَّقُوا اللَّهَ لَعَلَّكُمْ تُفْلِحُونَ ﴿٢٠٠﴾

سُورَةُ النِّسَاءِ ٤

CHAPTER
4

AL-NISÂ'
(The Women)
(Revealed after Hijrah)

With the name of Allâh,
the Most Gracious, the Ever Merciful
(I commence to read Sûrah Al-Nisâ').

1. **O** YOU people! Take as a shield your Lord Who created you from a single being. And from the same stock (from which He created the man) He created his spouse, and through them both He caused to spread a large number of men and women. O people! Regard Allâh with reverence in Whose name you appeal to one another, and (be regardful to) the ties of relationship (particularly from the female side). Verily, Allâh ever keeps watch over you.

2. And give the orphans their property and substitute not (your) worthless things for (their) good ones, nor consume their property mingling it along with your own property, for this indeed is a great sin.

3. And if (you wish to marry them and) you fear that you will not be able to do justice to the orphan girls then (marry them not, rather) marry of women (other than these) as may be agreeable to you, (you may marry) two or three or four (provided you do justice to them), but if you fear that you will not be able to deal (with all of them) equitably then (confine yourselves only to) one, or (you may marry) that whom your right hands possess (- your female captives of war). That is the best way to avoid doing injustice.

4. And give the women their dowers unasked, willingly and as agreed gift. But if they be pleased to remit you a portion thereof, of their own free will, then take it with grace and pleasure.

سُورَةُ النِّسَاءِ مَدَنِيَّةٌ

بِسْمِ اللّٰهِ الرَّحْمٰنِ الرَّحِيْمِ

يَاَيُّهَا النَّاسُ اتَّقُوْا رَبَّكُمُ الَّذِيْ خَلَقَكُمْ
مِّنْ نَّفْسٍ وَّاحِدَةٍ وَّخَلَقَ مِنْهَا زَوْجَهَا
وَبَثَّ مِنْهُمَا رِجَالًا كَثِيْرًا وَّنِسَآءً وَاتَّقُوا
اللّٰهَ الَّذِيْ تَسَآءَلُوْنَ بِهٖ وَالْاَرْحَامَ اِنَّ
اللّٰهَ كَانَ عَلَيْكُمْ رَقِيْبًا ﴿١﴾ وَاٰتُوا الْيَتٰمٰٓى
اَمْوٰلَهُمْ وَلَا تَتَبَدَّلُوا الْخَبِيْثَ بِالطَّيِّبِ
وَلَا تَاْكُلُوْٓا اَمْوٰلَهُمْ اِلٰٓى اَمْوٰلِكُمْ اِنَّهٗ كَانَ
حُوْبًا كَبِيْرًا ﴿٢﴾ وَاِنْ خِفْتُمْ اَلَّا تُقْسِطُوْا فِي
الْيَتٰمٰى فَانْكِحُوْا مَا طَابَ لَكُمْ مِّنَ النِّسَآءِ
مَثْنٰى وَثُلٰثَ وَرُبٰعَ فَاِنْ خِفْتُمْ اَلَّا تَعْدِلُوْا
فَوَاحِدَةً اَوْ مَا مَلَكَتْ اَيْمَانُكُمْ ذٰلِكَ اَدْنٰٓى اَلَّا
تَعُوْلُوْا ﴿٣﴾ وَاٰتُوا النِّسَآءَ صَدُقٰتِهِنَّ نِحْلَةً
فَاِنْ طِبْنَ لَكُمْ عَنْ شَيْءٍ مِّنْهُ نَفْسًا
فَكُلُوْهُ هَنِيْٓئًا مَّرِيْٓئًا ﴿٤﴾ وَلَا تُؤْتُوا السُّفَهَآءَ

الجزء الرابع

5. And do not make over to the weak of understanding your property which Allâh has made a means of subsistence for you, but provide for them (their maintenance) and clothe them out of its profits and speak to them words of kind advice.

6. And keep on testing the orphans until they attain the (age of) marriage, then if you perceive in them sound judgment deliver to them their property and do not consume it extravagantly and hastily as they grow up (fearing lest they should claim it when they attain the age of marriage). And let him (- the guardian) who can afford to do without, let him avoid remuneration, but he who is needy may charge reasonable remuneration with equity. And when you hand over to them (- the orphans) their property let there be some witnesses to attest. And Allâh is enough as a Reckoner (and call you to account).

7. (As the basis of law of inheritance,) for men is a share in (the property) that the parents and near relations leave behind and the women shall have a share in (the property) that the parents and the near relations leave behind, whether it (- property) be small or large, a determined share (ordained by Allâh).

8. And when there are present at the division (of the heritage other) relatives and the orphans and the needy, then give them something out of it and speak to them kind words.

9. And let the persons (who divide the heritage) be afraid of Allâh, for if they leave behind them (their own) weak offspring they would be anxious on their account. Let them, therefore, keep their duty to Allâh and let them say the right thing.

10. Verily, those who consume the property of the orphans unjustly, as a matter of fact, feed their bellies with fire; and they shall certainly burn in a blazing fire.

SECTION 2

11. **A**LLÂH prescribes (the following) law (of

سورة النساء ٤

أمولكم التي جعل الله لكم قيما وارزقوهم
فيها واكسوهم وقولوا لهم قولا
معروفا ٥ وابتلوا اليتمى حتى إذا بلغوا
النكاح فإن أنستم منهم رشدا
فادفعوا إليهم أمولهم ولا تأكلوها إسرافا
وبدارا أن يكبروا ومن كان غنيا
فليستعفف ومن كان فقيرا فليأكل
بالمعروف فإذا دفعتم إليهم أمولهم
فأشهدوا عليهم وكفى بالله حسيبا ٦
للرجال نصيب مما ترك الولدان
والأقربون وللنساء نصيب مما ترك
الولدان والأقربون مما قل منه أو
كثر نصيبا مفروضا ٧ وإذا حضر القسمة
أولوا القربى واليتمى والمسكين فارزقوهم
منه وقولوا لهم قولا معروفا ٨ وليخش
الذين لو تركوا من خلفهم ذرية
ضعفا خافوا عليهم فليتقوا الله وليقولوا
قولا سديدا ٩ إن الذين يأكلون
أمول اليتمى ظلما إنما يأكلون في
بطونهم نارا وسيصلون سعيرا ١٠ يوصيكم

ع ١٢

inheritance) for your children. For male is the equal of the portion of two females; but if they be all females (two or) more than two, for them is two thirds of what he (- the deceased) has left; and if there be only one, for her is the half and for his parents, for each one of the two is a sixth of what he has left, if he (- the deceased) has a child; but if he has no child and his parents only be his heirs, then for the mother is one third (and the rest two thirds is for the father); but if there be (in addition to his parents) his brothers (and sisters) then there is one sixth for the mother after (the payment of) any bequest he may have bequeathed or (still more important) of any debt (- bequests made by the testator and his debts shall however be satisfied first). Your fathers and your children, you do not know which of them deserve better to benefit from you. (This) fixing (of portions) is from Allâh. Surely, Allâh is All-Knowing, All-Wise.

12. And for you is half of that which your wives leave behind, if they have no child; but if they have a child, then for you is one fourth of what they leave behind, after (the payment of) any bequest they may have bequeathed or (still more important) of any (of their) debt. And for them (- your wives) is one fourth of what you leave behind if you have no child; but if you leave a child, then, for them is an eighth of what you leave after (the payment of) any bequest you have bequeathed or (still more important) of any debt. And if there be a man or a woman whose heritage is to be divided and he (or she - the deceased) has no child and he (or she) has (left behind) a brother or a sister then for each one of the twain is a sixth; but if they be more than one then they are (equal) sharers in one third after the payment of any bequest bequeathed or (still more important) of any debt (provided such bequest made by the testator and the debt) shall be without (any intent of)

اللهُ فِيٓ أَوْلٰدِكُمْ لِلذَّكَرِ مِثْلُ حَظِّ الْأُنْثَيَيْنِ
فَإِنْ كُنَّ نِسَآءً فَوْقَ اثْنَتَيْنِ فَلَهُنَّ
ثُلُثَا مَا تَرَكَ وَ إِنْ كَانَتْ وٰحِدَةً فَلَهَا
النِّصْفُ وَلِأَبَوَيْهِ لِكُلِّ وٰحِدٍ مِّنْهُمَا
السُّدُسُ مِمَّا تَرَكَ إِنْ كَانَ لَهُ وَلَدٌ
فَإِنْ لَّمْ يَكُنْ لَّهُ وَلَدٌ وَّ وَرِثَهُ أَبَوٰهُ
فَلِأُمِّهِ الثُّلُثُ فَإِنْ كَانَ لَهُ إِخْوَةٌ
فَلِأُمِّهِ السُّدُسُ مِنْ بَعْدِ وَصِيَّةٍ يُّوصِي
بِهَآ أَوْ دَيْنٍ ءَابَآؤُكُمْ وَ أَبْنَآؤُكُمْ لَا
تَدْرُونَ أَيُّهُمْ أَقْرَبُ لَكُمْ نَفْعًا فَرِيضَةً
مِّنَ اللهِ إِنَّ اللهَ كَانَ عَلِيمًا حَكِيمًا ﴿١١﴾
وَلَكُمْ نِصْفُ مَا تَرَكَ أَزْوٰجُكُمْ إِنْ لَّمْ
يَكُنْ لَّهُنَّ وَلَدٌ فَإِنْ كَانَ لَهُنَّ وَلَدٌ
فَلَكُمُ الرُّبُعُ مِمَّا تَرَكْنَ مِنْ بَعْدِ
وَصِيَّةٍ يُّوصِينَ بِهَآ أَوْ دَيْنٍ وَ لَهُنَّ
الرُّبُعُ مِمَّا تَرَكْتُمْ إِنْ لَّمْ يَكُنْ لَّكُمْ
وَلَدٌ فَإِنْ كَانَ لَكُمْ وَلَدٌ فَلَهُنَّ الثُّمُنُ
مِمَّا تَرَكْتُمْ مِّنْ بَعْدِ وَصِيَّةٍ تُوصُونَ
بِهَآ أَوْ دَيْنٍ وَ إِنْ كَانَ رَجُلٌ يُّورَثُ
كَلٰلَةً أَوِ امْرَأَةٌ وَّ لَهُ أَخٌ أَوْ أُخْتٌ
فَلِكُلِّ وٰحِدٍ مِّنْهُمَا السُّدُسُ فَإِنْ كَانُوٓا
أَكْثَرَ مِنْ ذٰلِكَ فَهُمْ شُرَكَآءُ فِي الثُّلُثِ
مِنْ بَعْدِ وَصِيَّةٍ يُّوصٰى بِهَآ أَوْ دَيْنٍ
غَيْرَ مُضَآرٍّ وَصِيَّةً مِّنَ اللهِ وَ اللهُ عَلِيمٌ

being harmful (to the interests of the heirs). This is an injunction from Allâh, and Allâh is All-Knowing, Most Forbearing.

13. These are the limits (of the law imposed) by Allâh, and who obeys Allâh and His Messenger He will admit them into Gardens served with running streams; therein they shall abide forever; and that is a great achievement.

14. But whoso disobeys Allâh and His Messenger and transgresses the limits imposed by Him He will make him enter Fire where he shall abide long, and for him is a humiliating punishment.

SECTION 3

15. **A**s to those of your women who commit sexual perversity, call in four of you to witness against them, and if they bear witness then confine them to their houses, until death overtakes them or Allâh makes for them a way out.

16. And if two of your males commit the same (act of indecency), then punish them both, so if they repent and amend (keeping their conduct good) then turn aside from them, verily Allâh is Oft-Returning (with compassion), Ever Merciful.

17. Verily, Allâh undertakes to accept the repentance of only those who do evil through lack of knowledge, then repent soon after. Such are the person towards whom Allâh turns with mercy. And Allâh is All-Knowing, All-Wise.

18. But repentance is of no avail to those who go on doing evil deeds until, when death visits one of them, he says, 'I do repent now,' nor it is of any use to those who die whilst they are disbelievers. It is for such people that We have prepared a woeful punishment.

19. O you who believe! It is not lawful for you to treat women (of your deceased relatives) as inherited property by force, nor should you detain them that you may take away part of that which you have given them, except that they

حَلِيمٌ ﴿١٢﴾ تِلْكَ حُدُودُ اللَّهِ ۚ وَمَنْ يُطِعِ اللَّهَ
وَرَسُولَهُ يُدْخِلْهُ جَنَّاتٍ تَجْرِي مِنْ
تَحْتِهَا الْأَنْهَارُ خَالِدِينَ فِيهَا ۚ وَذَٰلِكَ
الْفَوْزُ الْعَظِيمُ ﴿١٣﴾ وَمَنْ يَعْصِ اللَّهَ وَرَسُولَهُ
وَيَتَعَدَّ حُدُودَهُ يُدْخِلْهُ نَارًا خَالِدًا
فِيهَا وَلَهُ عَذَابٌ مُهِينٌ ﴿١٤﴾ وَاللَّاتِي يَأْتِينَ
الْفَاحِشَةَ مِنْ نِسَائِكُمْ فَاسْتَشْهِدُوا عَلَيْهِنَّ
أَرْبَعَةً مِنْكُمْ ۖ فَإِنْ شَهِدُوا فَأَمْسِكُوهُنَّ
فِي الْبُيُوتِ حَتَّىٰ يَتَوَفَّاهُنَّ الْمَوْتُ أَوْ
يَجْعَلَ اللَّهُ لَهُنَّ سَبِيلًا ﴿١٥﴾ وَاللَّذَانِ
يَأْتِيَانِهَا مِنْكُمْ فَآذُوهُمَا ۖ فَإِنْ تَابَا
وَأَصْلَحَا فَأَعْرِضُوا عَنْهُمَا ۗ إِنَّ اللَّهَ كَانَ
تَوَّابًا رَحِيمًا ﴿١٦﴾ إِنَّمَا التَّوْبَةُ عَلَى اللَّهِ
لِلَّذِينَ يَعْمَلُونَ السُّوءَ بِجَهَالَةٍ ثُمَّ
يَتُوبُونَ مِنْ قَرِيبٍ فَأُولَٰئِكَ يَتُوبُ
اللَّهُ عَلَيْهِمْ ۗ وَكَانَ اللَّهُ عَلِيمًا حَكِيمًا ﴿١٧﴾
وَلَيْسَتِ التَّوْبَةُ لِلَّذِينَ يَعْمَلُونَ السَّيِّئَاتِ
حَتَّىٰ إِذَا حَضَرَ أَحَدَهُمُ الْمَوْتُ قَالَ إِنِّي
تُبْتُ الْآنَ وَلَا الَّذِينَ يَمُوتُونَ وَهُمْ
كُفَّارٌ ۚ أُولَٰئِكَ أَعْتَدْنَا لَهُمْ عَذَابًا
أَلِيمًا ﴿١٨﴾ يَا أَيُّهَا الَّذِينَ آمَنُوا لَا يَحِلُّ لَكُمْ
أَنْ تَرِثُوا النِّسَاءَ كَرْهًا ۖ وَلَا تَعْضُلُوهُنَّ
لِتَذْهَبُوا بِبَعْضِ مَا آتَيْتُمُوهُنَّ إِلَّا أَنْ

commit flagrant indecency. But consort with them in peace. Then if you have a dislike for them, it may be that you dislike a thing but Allâh has placed a good deal of good in it.

20. And if you desire to take one wife in place of (another) wife and you have given one of them a huge treasure, then take nothing from that which you have given. Would you take it by false accusation and by committing an open sin?

21. And how can you take it when you have already lain with one another and they (- your wives) have bound you down to a firm and solemn covenant (by marriage)?

22. And marry not those women whom your fathers had married, except what had already passed (- you shall not be called to account for what you did in the past, only you have to divorce them now); for it is a thing highly indecent and repugnant and an evil practice.

SECTION 4

23. **F**ORBIDDEN to you (for marriage) are your mothers, your daughters, your sisters, your paternal aunts, and your maternal aunts, and the daughters of a brother, and the daughters of a sister, and your (foster) mothers who have given suck to you, and your foster sisters, and the mothers of your wives, and your stepdaughters who are being brought up under your care and have been born of your wives (by their former husbands,) unto whom you have gone in, but if you have not gone in unto them (- their mothers), then there is no blame on you (in marrying their daughters), and the wives of your sons who are from your own loins; and (it is forbidden to you) to keep in wedlock two sisters (at one and the same time), except what has already passed, (you have to divorce one of them). Surely, Allâh is Most Protector (against faults), Ever Merciful.

يَّأْتِينَ بِفَٰحِشَةٍ مُّبَيِّنَةٍ ۚ وَعَاشِرُوهُنَّ
بِالْمَعْرُوفِ ۚ فَإِن كَرِهْتُمُوهُنَّ فَعَسَىٰ
أَن تَكْرَهُوا شَيْـًٔا وَيَجْعَلَ اللَّهُ فِيهِ
خَيْرًا كَثِيرًا ﴿١٩﴾ وَإِنْ أَرَدتُّمُ اسْتِبْدَالَ
زَوْجٍ مَّكَانَ زَوْجٍ وَآتَيْتُمْ إِحْدَاهُنَّ
قِنطَارًا فَلَا تَأْخُذُوا مِنْهُ شَيْـًٔا ۚ
أَتَأْخُذُونَهُ بُهْتَانًا وَإِثْمًا مُّبِينًا ﴿٢٠﴾
وَكَيْفَ تَأْخُذُونَهُ وَقَدْ أَفْضَىٰ بَعْضُكُمْ
إِلَىٰ بَعْضٍ وَأَخَذْنَ مِنكُم مِّيثَاقًا غَلِيظًا ﴿٢١﴾
وَلَا تَنكِحُوا مَا نَكَحَ آبَاؤُكُم مِّنَ النِّسَاءِ
إِلَّا مَا قَدْ سَلَفَ ۚ إِنَّهُ كَانَ فَاحِشَةً وَمَقْتًا
وَسَاءَ سَبِيلًا ﴿٢٢﴾ حُرِّمَتْ عَلَيْكُمْ أُمَّهَاتُكُمْ
وَبَنَاتُكُمْ وَأَخَوَاتُكُمْ وَعَمَّاتُكُمْ وَخَالَاتُكُمْ
وَبَنَاتُ الْأَخِ وَبَنَاتُ الْأُخْتِ وَأُمَّهَاتُكُمُ اللَّاتِي
أَرْضَعْنَكُمْ وَأَخَوَاتُكُم مِّنَ الرَّضَاعَةِ وَأُمَّهَاتُ
نِسَائِكُمْ وَرَبَائِبُكُمُ اللَّاتِي فِي حُجُورِكُم مِّن
نِّسَائِكُمُ اللَّاتِي دَخَلْتُم بِهِنَّ فَإِن لَّمْ
تَكُونُوا دَخَلْتُم بِهِنَّ فَلَا جُنَاحَ عَلَيْكُمْ
وَحَلَائِلُ أَبْنَائِكُمُ الَّذِينَ مِنْ أَصْلَابِكُمْ
وَأَن تَجْمَعُوا بَيْنَ الْأُخْتَيْنِ إِلَّا مَا
قَدْ سَلَفَ ۗ إِنَّ اللَّهَ كَانَ غَفُورًا رَّحِيمًا ﴿٢٣﴾

PART الجزء الخامس V

سورة النساء ٤

24. **AND** (you are also forbidden to marry) already married women who are in a wedlock. Yet those (captives in war) whom your right hands possess (are permitted to you for marriage even if not formally divorced by their former husbands, since their captivity is equivalent to divorce). This is the law prescribed to you by Allâh. All (women) beyond those (mentioned above) are lawful to you, provided you seek (their hands) by means of your wealth (- by granting dowers), marrying them properly and not (committing fornication) to pursue your lust. You shall, for the benefits you draw from them (by regular marriage), pay them (- your wives) such of their dowers as have been fixed. There is, however, no blame on you (in increasing or decreasing the amount of dower) which you (- husband and wife) mutually agree upon, after it has been (once) fixed. Surely, Allâh is All-Knowing, All-Wise.

25. And those of you who have not the means (- social or financial) to marry free believing women (may marry) such of your believing bonds women as your right hands own (by being captives in war). Allâh knows very well (the state of) your faith, you are all (sprung) one from another, so marry them with the permission of their guardians and give them their dowers with equity, they being properly married, not (committing fornication), to pursue their lust nor taking secret paramours. And if after they are married they commit adultery then they incur (the punishment of fifty strips which is) half of that (punishment prescribed) for free women. This (permission to marry a bonds woman) is for him among you who fears (that otherwise he will fall into) sin. But it is better for you to exercise restraint. Allâh is, indeed, Great Protector, Ever Merciful.

وَّالْمُحْصَنٰتُ مِنَ النِّسَآءِ إِلَّا مَا مَلَكَتْ
أَيْمٰنُكُمْ كِتٰبَ اللّٰهِ عَلَيْكُمْ وَأُحِلَّ لَكُمْ مَّا
وَرَآءَ ذٰلِكُمْ أَنْ تَبْتَغُوْا بِأَمْوٰلِكُمْ مُّحْصِنِيْنَ
غَيْرَ مُسٰفِحِيْنَ فَمَا اسْتَمْتَعْتُمْ بِهٖ مِنْهُنَّ
فَأْتُوْهُنَّ أُجُوْرَهُنَّ فَرِيْضَةً وَلَا جُنَاحَ
عَلَيْكُمْ فِيْمَا تَرٰضَيْتُمْ بِهٖ مِنْ بَعْدِ
الْفَرِيْضَةِ إِنَّ اللّٰهَ كَانَ عَلِيْمًا حَكِيْمًا ﴿٢٤﴾
وَمَنْ لَّمْ يَسْتَطِعْ مِنْكُمْ طَوْلًا أَنْ يَّنْكِحَ
الْمُحْصَنٰتِ الْمُؤْمِنٰتِ فَمِنْ مَّا مَلَكَتْ
أَيْمٰنُكُمْ مِّنْ فَتَيٰتِكُمُ الْمُؤْمِنٰتِ وَاللّٰهُ أَعْلَمُ
بِإِيْمٰنِكُمْ بَعْضُكُمْ مِّنْ بَعْضٍ فَانْكِحُوْهُنَّ
بِإِذْنِ أَهْلِهِنَّ وَأٰتُوْهُنَّ أُجُوْرَهُنَّ بِالْمَعْرُوْفِ
مُحْصَنٰتٍ غَيْرَ مُسٰفِحٰتٍ وَّلَا مُتَّخِذٰتِ
أَخْدَانٍ فَإِذَا أُحْصِنَّ فَإِنْ أَتَيْنَ بِفٰحِشَةٍ
فَعَلَيْهِنَّ نِصْفُ مَا عَلَى الْمُحْصَنٰتِ مِنَ
الْعَذَابِ ذٰلِكَ لِمَنْ خَشِيَ الْعَنَتَ مِنْكُمْ
وَأَنْ تَصْبِرُوْا خَيْرٌ لَّكُمْ وَاللّٰهُ غَفُوْرٌ

SECTION 5

26. ALLÂH desires to make clear (His commandments) to you, and guide you to the (righteous) ways of your predecessors, and to turn to you with mercy. Verily, Allâh is All-Knowing, All-Wise.

27. Whereas Allâh desires to turn to you with mercy, those who follow (the dictates of their) lusts want you to drift far away (from the right path).

28. Allâh desires that He should lighten (the burden of bindings on) you, for a human being has been created weak.

29. O you who believe! Do not consume your (- one another's) property amongst yourselves by unlawful means, rather it be a trade based on free mutual consent. And do not kill your people. Surely, Allâh has been Ever Merciful to you.

30. But whoever does any such thing aggressively and unjustly, We shall certainly cast him into Fire. And this is ever easy for Allâh.

31. If you keep away from major prohibitions (to you), We will wipe off your preliminary evil (inclinations) and We will admit you to a place and state of great honour.

32. And do not covet the favours which Allâh has bestowed on some of you to excel others. Men shall have the share of the fruit of their labour, and for women is the share of the fruit of their labour. You had better seek from Allâh His bounty. Verily, Allâh has perfect knowledge of all things.

33. We have appointed heirs to everyone respecting that which the parents and the near relatives leave behind. And those with whom you have entered into a solemn covenant (- the husband and wife), so give them their due. Surely, Allâh is ever a Witness over everything.

SECTION 6

34. MEN are the full maintainers of women,

رَّحِيمٌ ﴿٢٥﴾ يُرِيدُ اللَّهُ لِيُبَيِّنَ لَكُمْ وَيَهْدِيَكُمْ
سُنَنَ الَّذِينَ مِن قَبْلِكُمْ وَيَتُوبَ عَلَيْكُمْ
وَاللَّهُ عَلِيمٌ حَكِيمٌ ﴿٢٦﴾ وَاللَّهُ يُرِيدُ أَن يَتُوبَ
عَلَيْكُمْ وَيُرِيدُ الَّذِينَ يَتَّبِعُونَ الشَّهَوَاتِ
أَن تَمِيلُوا مَيْلًا عَظِيمًا ﴿٢٧﴾ يُرِيدُ اللَّهُ أَن
يُخَفِّفَ عَنكُمْ وَخُلِقَ الْإِنسَانُ ضَعِيفًا ﴿٢٨﴾
يَا أَيُّهَا الَّذِينَ آمَنُوا لَا تَأْكُلُوا أَمْوَالَكُم
بَيْنَكُم بِالْبَاطِلِ إِلَّا أَن تَكُونَ تِجَارَةً عَن
تَرَاضٍ مِّنكُمْ وَلَا تَقْتُلُوا أَنفُسَكُمْ إِنَّ
اللَّهَ كَانَ بِكُمْ رَحِيمًا ﴿٢٩﴾ وَمَن يَفْعَلْ ذَٰلِكَ
عُدْوَانًا وَظُلْمًا فَسَوْفَ نُصْلِيهِ نَارًا وَكَانَ
ذَٰلِكَ عَلَى اللَّهِ يَسِيرًا ﴿٣٠﴾ إِن تَجْتَنِبُوا كَبَائِرَ
مَا تُنْهَوْنَ عَنْهُ نُكَفِّرْ عَنكُمْ سَيِّئَاتِكُمْ
وَنُدْخِلْكُم مُّدْخَلًا كَرِيمًا ﴿٣١﴾ وَلَا تَتَمَنَّوْا
مَا فَضَّلَ اللَّهُ بِهِ بَعْضَكُمْ عَلَىٰ بَعْضٍ
لِّلرِّجَالِ نَصِيبٌ مِّمَّا اكْتَسَبُوا وَلِلنِّسَاءِ
نَصِيبٌ مِّمَّا اكْتَسَبْنَ وَاسْأَلُوا اللَّهَ مِن
فَضْلِهِ إِنَّ اللَّهَ كَانَ بِكُلِّ شَيْءٍ عَلِيمًا ﴿٣٢﴾
وَلِكُلٍّ جَعَلْنَا مَوَالِيَ مِمَّا تَرَكَ الْوَالِدَانِ
وَالْأَقْرَبُونَ وَالَّذِينَ عَقَدَتْ أَيْمَانُكُمْ
فَآتُوهُمْ نَصِيبَهُمْ إِنَّ اللَّهَ كَانَ عَلَىٰ كُلِّ
شَيْءٍ شَهِيدًا ﴿٣٣﴾ الرِّجَالُ قَوَّامُونَ عَلَى النِّسَاءِ

because Allâh has made one of them excel the other, and because men spend out of their wealth on them. So virtuous women are those who are obedient (to Allâh) and guard (their own chastity as well as the rights and secrets of their husbands even) in (their) absence, as Allâh has guarded (the women's rights). As for those women (on whose part) you apprehend disobedience and bad behavior, you may admonish them (first lovingly) and (then) refuse to share their beds with them and (as a last resort) punish them (mildly). If they, then, obey you, you shall seek no other way against them. Indeed, Allâh alone is High, (and) Great.
35. But if you apprehend a breach between the two (- a man and his wife) then appoint one arbiter from his people and one arbiter from her people; if the two have a mind to effect reconciliation, Allâh will bring it about between them. Verily, Allâh is All-Knowing, All-Aware.
36. And worship Allâh and associate naught with Him, and be good to parents and near of kin and orphans and the needy and to the neighbour who is related to you and the neighbour who is an alien and to the companion by (your) side and the wayfarer and those whom your right hands possess. Surely, Allâh does not love those who are arrogant, (and) boastful.
37. Regarding those who practise niggardliness and counsel human beings to be niggardly and conceal that which Allâh has given them out of His bounty and grace, We have in store a humiliating punishment for such thankless people;
38. As well as for those who spend their wealth for public show and do not believe in Allâh and the Last Day. And whoso has satan for his companion (let him bear in mind that) an evil companion he is.
39. Why, what (harm) could come to them if they believed in Allâh and in the Last Day and spent from that which Allâh had provided

بِمَا فَضَّلَ اللّٰهُ بَعْضَهُمْ عَلٰى بَعْضٍ وَّ بِمَآ
أَنْفَقُوْا مِنْ أَمْوٰلِهِمْ ۚ فَالصّٰلِحٰتُ قٰنِتٰتٌ
حٰفِظٰتٌ لِّلْغَيْبِ بِمَا حَفِظَ اللّٰهُ ۚ وَالّٰتِيْ
تَخَافُوْنَ نُشُوْزَهُنَّ فَعِظُوْهُنَّ وَاهْجُرُوْهُنَّ
فِي الْمَضَاجِعِ وَاضْرِبُوْهُنَّ ۚ فَإِنْ أَطَعْنَكُمْ
فَلَا تَبْغُوْا عَلَيْهِنَّ سَبِيْلًا ۗ إِنَّ اللّٰهَ كَانَ
عَلِيًّا كَبِيْرًا ﴿٣٤﴾ وَإِنْ خِفْتُمْ شِقَاقَ بَيْنِهِمَا
فَابْعَثُوْا حَكَمًا مِّنْ أَهْلِهٖ وَحَكَمًا مِّنْ
أَهْلِهَا ۚ إِنْ يُّرِيْدَآ إِصْلٰحًا يُّوَفِّقِ اللّٰهُ بَيْنَهُمَا ۗ
إِنَّ اللّٰهَ كَانَ عَلِيْمًا خَبِيْرًا ﴿٣٥﴾ وَاعْبُدُوا اللّٰهَ
وَلَا تُشْرِكُوْا بِهٖ شَيْئًا وَّ بِالْوٰلِدَيْنِ إِحْسٰنًا
وَّبِذِي الْقُرْبٰى وَالْيَتٰمٰى وَالْمَسٰكِيْنِ وَالْجَارِ ذِي
الْقُرْبٰى وَالْجَارِ الْجُنُبِ وَالصَّاحِبِ بِالْجَنْۢبِ
وَابْنِ السَّبِيْلِ ۙ وَمَا مَلَكَتْ أَيْمٰنُكُمْ ۗ إِنَّ
اللّٰهَ لَا يُحِبُّ مَنْ كَانَ مُخْتَالًا فَخُوْرًا ﴿٣٦﴾
الَّذِيْنَ يَبْخَلُوْنَ وَيَأْمُرُوْنَ النَّاسَ بِالْبُخْلِ
وَيَكْتُمُوْنَ مَآ اٰتٰهُمُ اللّٰهُ مِنْ فَضْلِهٖ ۗ
وَأَعْتَدْنَا لِلْكٰفِرِيْنَ عَذَابًا مُّهِيْنًا ﴿٣٧﴾ وَالَّذِيْنَ
يُنْفِقُوْنَ أَمْوٰلَهُمْ رِئَآءَ النَّاسِ وَلَا يُؤْمِنُوْنَ
بِاللّٰهِ وَلَا بِالْيَوْمِ الْاٰخِرِ ۗ وَمَنْ يَّكُنِ
الشَّيْطٰنُ لَهٗ قَرِيْنًا فَسَآءَ قَرِيْنًا ﴿٣٨﴾ وَمَاذَا
عَلَيْهِمْ لَوْ اٰمَنُوْا بِاللّٰهِ وَالْيَوْمِ الْاٰخِرِ وَأَنْفَقُوْا
مِمَّا رَزَقَهُمُ اللّٰهُ ۗ وَكَانَ اللّٰهُ بِهِمْ عَلِيْمًا ﴿٣٩﴾

them? Indeed, Allâh knows them full well.

40. Verily, Allâh does not do injustice not (even) so much as the weight of an atom; and if there be a single good deed He multiplies it and gives from Himself a great reward.

41. How then (shall these wrongdoers fare) when We call a witness from every nation and when We call you (O Prophet!) to stand witness over these (followers of yours)?

42. On that day those who disbelieved and disobeyed the Messenger would wish that the earth were made level with them. They shall not be able to conceal anything from Allâh.

SECTION 7

43. **O** YOU who believe! Do not go near Prayer when you are not in full possession of your senses, until you understand all that you say (in your Prayers); nor (occupy yourselves in Prayer) when you are unclean (and under an obligation to have a bath) until you have bathed yourselves. But (you can do without a bath) when you are travelling along a way. If you are taken ill or (are) on a journey, or if one of you comes from the privy, or you have had (sexual) contact with women and you find no water (for bathing or ablution) then have recourse to pure and clean dust and wipe your faces and your hands (therewith). Indeed, Allâh is Most Benign, Great Protector.

44. Have you not considered (the case of) those who were given a portion of the Scripture? They prefer to go astray and desire that you too should go astray from the right path.

45. And Allâh knows your enemies full well. And Allâh suffices as a Patron, and Allâh suffices as a Helper.

46. (These enemies of yours are) of those who are judaised. They tear the words from their context and say, 'We hear and we disobey,' and (say), 'Lend us an ear, O you to whom no one would lend an ear!' and (say,) 'Râ'inâ', giving

إِنَّ اللَّهَ لَا يَظْلِمُ مِثْقَالَ ذَرَّةٍ وَإِن تَكُ
حَسَنَةً يُضَٰعِفْهَا وَيُؤْتِ مِن لَّدُنْهُ أَجْرًا
عَظِيمًا ﴿٤٠﴾ فَكَيْفَ إِذَا جِئْنَا مِن كُلِّ أُمَّةٍ
بِشَهِيدٍ وَجِئْنَا بِكَ عَلَىٰ هَٰٓؤُلَآءِ شَهِيدًا ﴿٤١﴾
يَوْمَئِذٍ يَوَدُّ الَّذِينَ كَفَرُوا وَعَصَوُا الرَّسُولَ لَوْ
تُسَوَّىٰ بِهِمُ الْأَرْضُ وَلَا يَكْتُمُونَ اللَّهَ حَدِيثًا ﴿٤٢﴾
يَٰٓأَيُّهَا الَّذِينَ ءَامَنُوا لَا تَقْرَبُوا الصَّلَوٰةَ وَأَنتُمْ
سُكَٰرَىٰ حَتَّىٰ تَعْلَمُوا مَا تَقُولُونَ وَلَا جُنُبًا
إِلَّا عَابِرِي سَبِيلٍ حَتَّىٰ تَغْتَسِلُوا وَإِن
كُنتُم مَّرْضَىٰٓ أَوْ عَلَىٰ سَفَرٍ أَوْ جَآءَ أَحَدٌ
مِّنكُم مِّنَ الْغَآئِطِ أَوْ لَٰمَسْتُمُ النِّسَآءَ فَلَمْ
تَجِدُوا مَآءً فَتَيَمَّمُوا صَعِيدًا طَيِّبًا فَامْسَحُوا
بِوُجُوهِكُمْ وَأَيْدِيكُمْ إِنَّ اللَّهَ كَانَ
عَفُوًّا غَفُورًا ﴿٤٣﴾ أَلَمْ تَرَ إِلَى الَّذِينَ أُوتُوا
نَصِيبًا مِّنَ الْكِتَٰبِ يَشْتَرُونَ الضَّلَٰلَةَ
وَيُرِيدُونَ أَن تَضِلُّوا السَّبِيلَ ﴿٤٤﴾ وَاللَّهُ أَعْلَمُ
بِأَعْدَآئِكُمْ وَكَفَىٰ بِاللَّهِ وَلِيًّا وَكَفَىٰ بِاللَّهِ
نَصِيرًا ﴿٤٥﴾ مِّنَ الَّذِينَ هَادُوا يُحَرِّفُونَ الْكَلِمَ
عَن مَّوَاضِعِهِ وَيَقُولُونَ سَمِعْنَا وَعَصَيْنَا
وَاسْمَعْ غَيْرَ مُسْمَعٍ وَرَٰعِنَا لَيًّا بِأَلْسِنَتِهِمْ

a slight twist to their tongues (while pronouncing the word and thereby) slandering the true meanings (and thus making a play with the word) and seeking to injure the Faith. It would have been better and more upright on their part to have said, 'We hear and we obey;' and 'Lend us an ear;' and 'Unzurnâ' (we beg your attention)'. Allâh has disapproved of them because of their disbelief so that they will not believe, excepting a few (of them).

47. O you who have been given the Scripture! Believe in (the Qur'ân) which We have now revealed fulfilling such (prophecies) as you have, before We make extinct and destroy some of your leaders and deprive them of their glory or We condemn them as We condemned the people of the Sabbath (breakers); and (remember) the decree of Allâh is bound to be executed.

48. Surely, Allâh does not forgive (unless the sinner turns to Him with repentance) that a partner be associated with Him but He forgives everything short of it to whomsoever He will. And whoso associates a partner with Allâh has indeed committed a very great sin.

49. Have you not considered those who assert themselves to be pure? Nay, only Allâh purifies whom He will; and they shall not be treated unjustly, not even a whit.

50. Behold! How they forge lies against Allâh, and sufficient is that as a very flagrant sin (to prove their sinfulness).

SECTION 8

51. **H**AVE you not considered the case of those who were given a portion of the Scripture? They believe in nonsensical things devoid of good and follow those who transgress, and they say of those who disbelieve, 'These are better guided in the (right) way than those who believe (in Islam).'

52. It is these whom Allâh has deprived of His blessings, and he whom Allâh deprives of His

وَطَعْنًا فِي الدِّيْنِ ۖ وَلَوْ أَنَّهُمْ قَالُوْا سَمِعْنَا
وَأَطَعْنَا وَاسْمَعْ وَانْظُرْنَا لَكَانَ خَيْرًا لَّهُمْ
وَأَقْوَمَ ۙ وَلٰكِنْ لَّعَنَهُمُ اللّٰهُ بِكُفْرِهِمْ فَلَا
يُؤْمِنُوْنَ إِلَّا قَلِيْلًا ﴿٤٦﴾ يٰٓأَيُّهَا الَّذِيْنَ أُوْتُوا
الْكِتٰبَ اٰمِنُوْا بِمَا نَزَّلْنَا مُصَدِّقًا لِّمَا مَعَكُمْ
مِّنْ قَبْلِ أَنْ نَّطْمِسَ وُجُوْهًا فَنَرُدَّهَا عَلٰٓى
أَدْبَارِهَآ أَوْ نَلْعَنَهُمْ كَمَا لَعَنَّآ أَصْحٰبَ
السَّبْتِ ۖ وَكَانَ أَمْرُ اللّٰهِ مَفْعُوْلًا ﴿٤٧﴾ إِنَّ اللّٰهَ
لَا يَغْفِرُ أَنْ يُّشْرَكَ بِهٖ وَيَغْفِرُ مَا دُوْنَ
ذٰلِكَ لِمَنْ يَّشَآءُ ۚ وَمَنْ يُّشْرِكْ بِاللّٰهِ فَقَدِ
افْتَرٰٓى إِثْمًا عَظِيْمًا ﴿٤٨﴾ أَلَمْ تَرَ إِلَى الَّذِيْنَ
يُزَكُّوْنَ أَنْفُسَهُمْ ۚ بَلِ اللّٰهُ يُزَكِّيْ مَنْ يَّشَآءُ
وَلَا يُظْلَمُوْنَ فَتِيْلًا ﴿٤٩﴾ اُنْظُرْ كَيْفَ يَفْتَرُوْنَ
عَلَى اللّٰهِ الْكَذِبَ ۖ وَكَفٰى بِهٖٓ إِثْمًا مُّبِيْنًا ﴿٥٠﴾ ع ٨
أَلَمْ تَرَ إِلَى الَّذِيْنَ أُوْتُوْا نَصِيْبًا مِّنَ الْكِتٰبِ
يُؤْمِنُوْنَ بِالْجِبْتِ وَالطّٰغُوْتِ وَيَقُوْلُوْنَ
لِلَّذِيْنَ كَفَرُوْا هٰٓؤُلَآءِ أَهْدٰى مِنَ الَّذِيْنَ
اٰمَنُوْا سَبِيْلًا ﴿٥١﴾ أُولٰٓئِكَ الَّذِيْنَ لَعَنَهُمُ اللّٰهُ
وَمَنْ يَّلْعَنِ اللّٰهُ فَلَنْ تَجِدَ لَهٗ نَصِيْرًا ﴿٥٢﴾

blessings, you will never find for him any helper.

53. They have no share in the kingdom. If they had they would not give the people (even so much as) the little groove in a date-stone.

54. Or do they feel jealous of the people for which Allâh has granted them out of His bounty and grace? (Let them remember) We surely gave the Children of Abraham the Scripture and the Wisdom, and We also gave them a grand kingdom.

55. There are some among them who believe in it (- the Qur'ân) and there are others among them who turn away from it, and Gehenna shall suffice for burning (those who turn away).

56. We shall soon cast into Fire all those who deny Our Messages. As often as their skins are burnt up We will replace them with other (new) skins that they may (continually) taste (agony of) punishment. Surely, Allâh is All-Mighty, All-Wise.

57. And those who believe and do righteous deeds We shall certainly admit them to Gardens served with running streams. They shall abide therein forever. There shall be for them (to keep their company) therein, (spiritually and physically) purified companions, and We shall admit them to (a place of) thick and pleasant shades (of Our mercy and protection).

58. Surely, Allâh commands you to make over the trusts (such as the affairs of the state) to those who are competent to it, and that when you judge between the people you should judge with justice. That which Allâh exhorts you to do is best indeed. Allâh is All-Hearing, All-Seeing.

59. O you who believe! Obey Allâh and obey (His) Messenger and those who are in authority among you (to decide your affairs). And should you differ among yourselves in anything, refer it to Allâh and His Messenger (and judge according to their teachings), if

أَمْ لَهُمْ نَصِيبٌ مِّنَ الْمُلْكِ فَإِذًا لَّا يُؤْتُونَ
النَّاسَ نَقِيرًا ﴿٥٣﴾ أَمْ يَحْسُدُونَ النَّاسَ
عَلَىٰ مَا آتَاهُمُ اللَّهُ مِن فَضْلِهِ ۖ فَقَدْ آتَيْنَا
آلَ إِبْرَاهِيمَ الْكِتَابَ وَالْحِكْمَةَ وَآتَيْنَاهُم
مُّلْكًا عَظِيمًا ﴿٥٤﴾ فَمِنْهُم مَّنْ آمَنَ بِهِ وَمِنْهُم
مَّن صَدَّ عَنْهُ ۚ وَكَفَىٰ بِجَهَنَّمَ سَعِيرًا ﴿٥٥﴾
إِنَّ الَّذِينَ كَفَرُوا بِآيَاتِنَا سَوْفَ نُصْلِيهِمْ
نَارًا كُلَّمَا نَضِجَتْ جُلُودُهُم بَدَّلْنَاهُمْ
جُلُودًا غَيْرَهَا لِيَذُوقُوا الْعَذَابَ ۗ إِنَّ اللَّهَ كَانَ
عَزِيزًا حَكِيمًا ﴿٥٦﴾ وَالَّذِينَ آمَنُوا وَعَمِلُوا
الصَّالِحَاتِ سَنُدْخِلُهُمْ جَنَّاتٍ تَجْرِي مِن
تَحْتِهَا الْأَنْهَارُ خَالِدِينَ فِيهَا أَبَدًا ۖ لَّهُمْ
فِيهَا أَزْوَاجٌ مُّطَهَّرَةٌ ۖ وَنُدْخِلُهُمْ ظِلًّا
ظَلِيلًا ﴿٥٧﴾ إِنَّ اللَّهَ يَأْمُرُكُمْ أَن تُؤَدُّوا
الْأَمَانَاتِ إِلَىٰ أَهْلِهَا وَإِذَا حَكَمْتُم بَيْنَ
النَّاسِ أَن تَحْكُمُوا بِالْعَدْلِ ۚ إِنَّ اللَّهَ نِعِمَّا
يَعِظُكُم بِهِ ۗ إِنَّ اللَّهَ كَانَ سَمِيعًا بَصِيرًا ﴿٥٨﴾ يَا أَيُّهَا
الَّذِينَ آمَنُوا أَطِيعُوا اللَّهَ وَأَطِيعُوا الرَّسُولَ
وَأُولِي الْأَمْرِ مِنكُمْ ۖ فَإِن تَنَازَعْتُمْ فِي شَيْءٍ
فَرُدُّوهُ إِلَى اللَّهِ وَالرَّسُولِ إِن كُنتُمْ
تُؤْمِنُونَ بِاللَّهِ وَالْيَوْمِ الْآخِرِ ۚ ذَٰلِكَ خَيْرٌ

indeed you believe in Allâh and the Last Day. That is (in your) best (interest) and most commendable in the long run.

SECTION 9

60. **H**AVE you not considered the case of those who assert that they believe in what has been revealed to you and what has been revealed before you? On the contrary they desire to refer (their disputes) for judgment to the transgressor, whereas they were commanded to reject him, and satan desires to lead them astray to a far off straying.
61. And when it is said to them, 'Come to (follow) that which Allâh has revealed and to the perfect Messenger;' you can see the hypocrites turn away from you with aversion.
62. Then how is it that when a calamity befalls them because of their own misdoings they come to you swearing by Allâh (saying), 'We meant nothing but to do good and (to effect) concord and reconciliation?'
63. It is they of whom Allâh knows what is in their hearts. So turn aside from them, and admonish them and speak to them with regard to their own selves an effective word.
64. And We have sent no Messenger but that he should be obeyed by the leave of Allâh. Had they, when they had acted contrary to their own interests, come to you and sought the protection of Allâh, and had this perfect Messenger (also) sought protection for them they would have surely found Allâh Oft-Returning with compassion, Ever Merciful.
65. But no, (not so as they have asserted,) by your Lord! They are no believers at all unless they refer all their disputes (that arise between them) to you for judgment, then they do not find any demur in their minds about the propriety of your judgment, and they submit (to your decisions) with entire submission.
66. If We had made it binding on them, 'Lay

وَأَحْسَنُ تَأْوِيلًا ﴿٥٩﴾ أَلَمْ تَرَ إِلَى الَّذِينَ
يَزْعُمُونَ أَنَّهُمْ ءَامَنُوا بِمَا أُنْزِلَ إِلَيْكَ وَمَا
أُنْزِلَ مِنْ قَبْلِكَ يُرِيدُونَ أَنْ يَتَحَاكَمُوا
إِلَى الطَّٰغُوتِ وَقَدْ أُمِرُوا أَنْ يَكْفُرُوا بِهِۦ
وَيُرِيدُ الشَّيْطَٰنُ أَنْ يُضِلَّهُمْ ضَلَٰلًا بَعِيدًا ﴿٦٠﴾
وَإِذَا قِيلَ لَهُمْ تَعَالَوْا إِلَىٰ مَا أَنْزَلَ اللَّهُ
وَإِلَى الرَّسُولِ رَأَيْتَ الْمُنَٰفِقِينَ يَصُدُّونَ
عَنْكَ صُدُودًا ﴿٦١﴾ فَكَيْفَ إِذَا أَصَٰبَتْهُمْ
مُّصِيبَةٌ بِمَا قَدَّمَتْ أَيْدِيهِمْ ثُمَّ جَاءُوكَ
يَحْلِفُونَ بِاللَّهِ إِنْ أَرَدْنَا إِلَّا إِحْسَٰنًا وَتَوْفِيقًا ﴿٦٢﴾
أُولَٰئِكَ الَّذِينَ يَعْلَمُ اللَّهُ مَا فِي قُلُوبِهِمْ
فَأَعْرِضْ عَنْهُمْ وَعِظْهُمْ وَقُلْ لَّهُمْ فِيٓ
أَنْفُسِهِمْ قَوْلًا بَلِيغًا ﴿٦٣﴾ وَمَا أَرْسَلْنَا مِنْ
رَّسُولٍ إِلَّا لِيُطَاعَ بِإِذْنِ اللَّهِ وَلَوْ أَنَّهُمْ إِذْ
ظَّلَمُوٓا أَنْفُسَهُمْ جَاءُوكَ فَاسْتَغْفَرُوا اللَّهَ
وَاسْتَغْفَرَ لَهُمُ الرَّسُولُ لَوَجَدُوا اللَّهَ تَوَّابًا
رَّحِيمًا ﴿٦٤﴾ فَلَا وَرَبِّكَ لَا يُؤْمِنُونَ حَتَّىٰ
يُحَكِّمُوكَ فِيمَا شَجَرَ بَيْنَهُمْ ثُمَّ لَا يَجِدُوا
فِيٓ أَنْفُسِهِمْ حَرَجًا مِّمَّا قَضَيْتَ وَيُسَلِّمُوا
تَسْلِيمًا ﴿٦٥﴾ وَلَوْ أَنَّا كَتَبْنَا عَلَيْهِمْ أَنِ اقْتُلُوٓا
أَنْفُسَكُمْ أَوِ اخْرُجُوا مِنْ دِيَٰرِكُمْ مَّا فَعَلُوهُ

down your lives or go out of your homes,' they would not have done it, excepting a few of them. And if they had done what they are exhorted to do, it would surely have been better for them and conducive to a greater strength (in their faith);

67. And in that case We could certainly have bestowed upon them from Ourself a great reward;

68. And We would have surely guided them in the exact right path.

69. And those who obey Allâh and this perfect Messenger, it is these who are with those upon whom Allâh has bestowed His blessings (in this life and the Hereafter) - the Prophets, the Truthful (in their belief, words and deeds), and the Bearers of Testimony (to the truth of the religion of Allâh by their words and deeds), as well as the Martyrs, and the Righteous (who stick to the right course under all circumstances), and how excellent companions they are!

70. This is the grace from Allâh (if such companions are available). And Allâh suffices as One Who is All Knowing.

SECTION 10

71. **O** YOU who believe! Take your precautions always by way of security, then either march forward in separate companies or march forward in a body (according to the requirement of the war situation).

72. And indeed there is among you who tarries behind (and does not leave to fight in the cause of Allâh). Then, if a calamity befalls you, he says, 'Allâh has been gracious to me, indeed, since I was not present with them.'

73. And if some good fortune comes to you from Allâh he would cry, as if there were no friendship between you and him, 'Would that I had been with them, had it been so I should have indeed achieved a great success.'

74. Let those, who would prefer the Hereafter to the present life, fight in the cause of Allâh.

إِلَّا قَلِيلٌ مِّنْهُمْ وَ لَوْ أَنَّهُمْ فَعَلُوا مَا
يُوعَظُونَ بِهِ لَكَانَ خَيْرًا لَّهُمْ وَ أَشَدَّ
تَثْبِيتًا ﴿٦٦﴾ وَّإِذًا لَّأٰتَيْنٰهُم مِّن لَّدُنَّا أَجْرًا
عَظِيمًا ﴿٦٧﴾ وَّ لَهَدَيْنٰهُمْ صِرٰطًا مُّسْتَقِيمًا ﴿٦٨﴾
وَ مَن يُّطِعِ اللهَ وَ الرَّسُولَ فَأُولٰٓئِكَ مَعَ
الَّذِينَ أَنْعَمَ اللهُ عَلَيْهِم مِّنَ النَّبِيّٖنَ
وَ الصِّدِّيقِينَ وَ الشُّهَدَآءِ وَ الصّٰلِحِينَ
وَ حَسُنَ أُولٰٓئِكَ رَفِيقًا ﴿٦٩﴾ ذٰلِكَ الْفَضْلُ مِنَ
اللهِ وَ كَفٰى بِاللهِ عَلِيمًا ﴿٧٠﴾ يٰٓأَيُّهَا الَّذِينَ
أٰمَنُوا خُذُوا حِذْرَكُمْ فَانْفِرُوا ثُبَاتٍ أَوِ
انْفِرُوا جَمِيعًا ﴿٧١﴾ وَ إِنَّ مِنْكُمْ لَمَن لَّيُبَطِّئَنَّ
فَإِنْ أَصٰبَتْكُم مُّصِيبَةٌ قَالَ قَدْ أَنْعَمَ
اللهُ عَلَيَّ إِذْ لَمْ أَكُن مَّعَهُمْ شَهِيدًا ﴿٧٢﴾
وَ لَئِنْ أَصٰبَكُمْ فَضْلٌ مِّنَ اللهِ لَيَقُولَنَّ كَأَن
لَّمْ تَكُنْ بَيْنَكُمْ وَ بَيْنَهُ مَوَدَّةٌ يٰلَيْتَنِي
كُنْتُ مَعَهُمْ فَأَفُوزَ فَوْزًا عَظِيمًا ﴿٧٣﴾ فَلْيُقٰتِلْ
فِي سَبِيلِ اللهِ الَّذِينَ يَشْرُونَ الْحَيٰوةَ الدُّنْيَا
بِالْأٰخِرَةِ وَ مَن يُّقٰتِلْ فِي سَبِيلِ اللهِ
فَيُقْتَلْ أَوْ يَغْلِبْ فَسَوْفَ نُؤْتِيهِ أَجْرًا
عَظِيمًا ﴿٧٤﴾ وَ مَا لَكُمْ لَا تُقٰتِلُونَ فِي سَبِيلِ

And whoso fights in the cause of Allâh and is killed or conquers, We shall soon grant him a great reward.

75. What (excuse) have you (to offer) that you would not fight in the cause of Allâh and for (the rescue of) the weak and the down-trodden men and women and the children who all say, 'Our Lord! Take us out of this town of which the people are tyrants, and grant us a defender who comes from You and a helper by Your Own grace.'

76. Those who believe fight in the cause of Allâh, and those who choose disbelief fight in the cause of the transgressor; fight you, therefore, against the friends of satan, surely, the stratagem of satan is ever weak.

SECTION 11

77. **H**AVE you not considered those to whom it was said, 'Withhold your hands (from fighting) and keep up Prayer and go on presenting the *Zakât?'* But now when fighting has been made binding upon them, a section of them (- the hypocrites) begin to fear the people as they should fear Allâh or with a still stronger fear and they say, 'Our Lord! Why have You made fighting binding upon us? Would You not defer us to a near term (and grant us a little respite).' Say, 'The enjoyment of this world is short (and negligible its pleasures) and the Hereafter is better for him who guards against evil and keeps his duty to Allâh, and you shall not be done injustice to, not even a whit.'

78. Death will overtake you wherever you may be, even if you be in strongly built castles. And if any good occurs to them (-to the hypocrites) they say, 'This is from Allâh' and if evil befalls them they say, 'This is from you.' Say, 'Everything is from Allâh.' What is the matter with these people that they hardly understand (anything)?

79. Whatever of good comes to you (O people!)

اللّٰهِ وَ الْمُسْتَضْعَفِيْنَ مِنَ الرِّجَالِ وَ النِّسَآءِ
وَ الْوِلْدَانِ الَّذِيْنَ يَقُوْلُوْنَ رَبَّنَآ أَخْرِجْنَا
مِنْ هٰذِهِ الْقَرْيَةِ الظَّالِمِ أَهْلُهَا وَ اجْعَلْ
لَّنَا مِنْ لَّدُنْكَ وَلِيًّا وَّ اجْعَلْ لَّنَا مِنْ لَّدُنْكَ
نَصِيْرًا ﴿٧٥﴾ اَلَّذِيْنَ اٰمَنُوْا يُقَاتِلُوْنَ فِيْ سَبِيْلِ
اللّٰهِ وَ الَّذِيْنَ كَفَرُوْا يُقَاتِلُوْنَ فِيْ سَبِيْلِ
الطَّاغُوْتِ فَقَاتِلُوْٓا أَوْلِيَآءَ الشَّيْطٰنِ إِنَّ كَيْدَ
الشَّيْطٰنِ كَانَ ضَعِيْفًا ﴿٧٦﴾ أَلَمْ تَرَ إِلَى الَّذِيْنَ ع ٧
قِيْلَ لَهُمْ كُفُّوْٓا أَيْدِيَكُمْ وَ أَقِيْمُوا الصَّلٰوةَ
وَ اٰتُوا الزَّكٰوةَ فَلَمَّا كُتِبَ عَلَيْهِمُ الْقِتَالُ إِذَا
فَرِيْقٌ مِّنْهُمْ يَخْشَوْنَ النَّاسَ كَخَشْيَةِ اللّٰهِ
أَوْ أَشَدَّ خَشْيَةً وَ قَالُوْا رَبَّنَا لِمَ كَتَبْتَ
عَلَيْنَا الْقِتَالَ لَوْلَآ أَخَّرْتَنَآ إِلٰٓى أَجَلٍ قَرِيْبٍ
قُلْ مَتَاعُ الدُّنْيَا قَلِيْلٌ وَ الْاٰخِرَةُ خَيْرٌ لِّمَنِ
اتَّقٰى وَ لَا تُظْلَمُوْنَ فَتِيْلًا ﴿٧٧﴾ أَيْنَمَا تَكُوْنُوْا
يُدْرِكْكُّمُ الْمَوْتُ وَ لَوْ كُنْتُمْ فِيْ بُرُوْجٍ
مُّشَيَّدَةٍ وَ إِنْ تُصِبْهُمْ حَسَنَةٌ يَّقُوْلُوْا
هٰذِهٖ مِنْ عِنْدِ اللّٰهِ وَ إِنْ تُصِبْهُمْ سَيِّئَةٌ
يَّقُوْلُوْا هٰذِهٖ مِنْ عِنْدِكَ قُلْ كُلٌّ مِّنْ
عِنْدِ اللّٰهِ فَمَالِ هٰٓؤُلَآءِ الْقَوْمِ لَا يَكَادُوْنَ
يَفْقَهُوْنَ حَدِيْثًا ﴿٧٨﴾ مَآ أَصَابَكَ مِنْ حَسَنَةٍ

is from Allâh and whatever of evil befalls you is from your ownselves. And We have sent you (O Muhammad!) as a great Messenger for the good of all humankind, and Allâh suffices as a witness.

80. He that obeys this perfect Messenger, surely, has obeyed Allâh. As for those who turn away, then, We have not sent you as a guardian over them (so as to be held accountable for their actions).

81. And they (- the hypocrites) say (in your presence), '(We stand for) obedience,' but when they sally forth from your presence, a party of them spend the night scheming contrary to what you say, and Allâh is keeping a record of whatever they scheme by night. So turn away from them and put (your) trust in Allâh, and Allâh suffices as a Disposer of affairs.

82. Why do they not ponder over the Qur'ân? Had it been from anyone other than Allâh, they would surely have found a good deal of inconsistency therein.

83. And when there comes to them news (a mere rumour), be it a matter of peace or of fear, they spread it around. But had they referred it to the perfect Messenger and to those in authority among them, surely those of them who can illicit (the truth) from it would have understood it (and could make correct deductions). And had it not been for the grace of Allâh upon you and His mercy you would all have followed satan, excepting a few.

84. (Prophet!) Fight, therefore, in the cause of Allâh, you are made responsible only for your ownself, and urge on the faithful (to fight a war in self-defence). It may be, Allâh will restrain the fury of those who have chosen disbelief. Allâh is mightier in prowess and stronger in inflicting exemplary punishment.

85. And he who participates with others in doing good (to others, and intercedes for a righteous cause) there shall be for him a share

فَمِنَ اللَّهِ وَمَآ أَصَابَكَ مِنْ سَيِّئَةٍ فَمِن
نَّفْسِكَ وَأَرْسَلْنَكَ لِلنَّاسِ رَسُولًا وَكَفَى
بِاللَّهِ شَهِيدًا ﴿٧٩﴾ مَّنْ يُطِعِ الرَّسُولَ فَقَدْ
أَطَاعَ اللَّهَ وَمَنْ تَوَلَّى فَمَآ أَرْسَلْنَكَ عَلَيْهِمْ
حَفِيظًا ﴿٨٠﴾ وَيَقُولُونَ طَاعَةٌ فَإِذَا بَرَزُوا مِنْ
عِنْدِكَ بَيَّتَ طَآئِفَةٌ مِّنْهُمْ غَيْرَ الَّذِي
تَقُولُ وَاللَّهُ يَكْتُبُ مَا يُبَيِّتُونَ فَأَعْرِضْ
عَنْهُمْ وَتَوَكَّلْ عَلَى اللَّهِ وَكَفَى بِاللَّهِ
وَكِيلًا ﴿٨١﴾ أَفَلَا يَتَدَبَّرُونَ الْقُرْءَانَ وَلَوْ كَانَ
مِنْ عِنْدِ غَيْرِ اللَّهِ لَوَجَدُوا فِيهِ اخْتِلَفًا
كَثِيرًا ﴿٨٢﴾ وَإِذَا جَآءَهُمْ أَمْرٌ مِّنَ الْأَمْنِ أَوِ
الْخَوْفِ أَذَاعُوا بِهِ وَلَوْ رَدُّوهُ إِلَى الرَّسُولِ
وَإِلَى أُولِي الْأَمْرِ مِنْهُمْ لَعَلِمَهُ الَّذِينَ
يَسْتَنْبِطُونَهُ مِنْهُمْ وَلَوْلَا فَضْلُ اللَّهِ عَلَيْكُمْ
وَرَحْمَتُهُ لَاتَّبَعْتُمُ الشَّيْطَنَ إِلَّا قَلِيلًا ﴿٨٣﴾
فَقَتِلْ فِي سَبِيلِ اللَّهِ لَا تُكَلَّفُ إِلَّا نَفْسَكَ
وَحَرِّضِ الْمُؤْمِنِينَ عَسَى اللَّهُ أَنْ يَكُفَّ
بَأْسَ الَّذِينَ كَفَرُوا وَاللَّهُ أَشَدُّ بَأْسًا
وَأَشَدُّ تَنْكِيلًا ﴿٨٤﴾ مَّنْ يَشْفَعْ شَفَعَةً حَسَنَةً
يَكُنْ لَّهُ نَصِيبٌ مِّنْهَا وَمَنْ يَشْفَعْ شَفَعَةً

in its credit, and he who participates with anyone in doing evil (and intercedes for a wrongful cause), has a like portion in its evil consequences. And Allâh controls the distribution of all things.

86. And whenever you are greeted with a prayer greet with a better prayer or (at least) return the same. Verily, Allâh takes account of everything.

87. Allâh is He, there is no other, cannot be and will never be one worthy of worship but He. He will most certainly (continue to) assemble you till the Day of Resurrection, there is no doubt about (the advent of) it; and there is none more truthful to his word than Allâh.

SECTION 12

88. **H**ow is it then with you, that you are divided into two parties regarding the hypocrites, while Allâh has overthrown them for (the sins) which they committed knowingly? Do you desire to guide him whom Allâh has forsaken? And he whom Allâh forsakes you shall not find for him a way (of his deliverance).

89. They would like you to reject the faith as they have done themselves, that you may be all alike; therefore, make no friends with them until they emigrate in the cause of Allâh. But if they turn back (to hostility), then capture them and kill them wherever you find them, and do not take anyone of them as a friend or as a helper.

90. Different, however, is the case of those who join a people with whom you have a pact, or of those who come over to you whilst their hearts are constricted from fighting against you or fighting against their (own) people. If Allâh had so willed He would have given them power over you, then they certainly would have fought against you. Hence if they leave you alone and do not fight against you but make you an offer of peace then Allâh allows you no way (of fighting) against them.

91. You will find others (among these hypocrites) who desire to be secure from you as well

سَيِّئَةً يَّكُن لَّهُ كِفْلٌ مِّنْهَا وَكَانَ اللّٰهُ
عَلٰى كُلِّ شَيْءٍ مُّقِيتًا ﴿٨٥﴾ وَإِذَا حُيِّيتُم بِتَحِيَّةٍ
فَحَيُّوا بِأَحْسَنَ مِنْهَا أَوْ رُدُّوهَا إِنَّ اللّٰهَ كَانَ
عَلٰى كُلِّ شَيْءٍ حَسِيبًا ﴿٨٦﴾ اَللّٰهُ لَا إِلٰهَ إِلَّا هُوَ
لَيَجْمَعَنَّكُمْ إِلٰى يَوْمِ الْقِيٰمَةِ لَا رَيْبَ فِيهِ
وَمَنْ أَصْدَقُ مِنَ اللّٰهِ حَدِيثًا ﴿٨٧﴾ فَمَا لَكُمْ
فِي الْمُنٰفِقِينَ فِئَتَيْنِ وَاللّٰهُ أَرْكَسَهُم بِمَا
كَسَبُوا أَتُرِيدُونَ أَن تَهْدُوا مَنْ أَضَلَّ
اللّٰهُ وَمَن يُّضْلِلِ اللّٰهُ فَلَن تَجِدَ لَهُ
سَبِيلًا ﴿٨٨﴾ وَدُّوا لَوْ تَكْفُرُونَ كَمَا كَفَرُوا
فَتَكُونُونَ سَوَاءً فَلَا تَتَّخِذُوا مِنْهُمْ أَوْلِيَاءَ
حَتّٰى يُهَاجِرُوا فِي سَبِيلِ اللّٰهِ فَإِن تَوَلَّوْا
فَخُذُوهُمْ وَاقْتُلُوهُمْ حَيْثُ وَجَدْتُّمُوهُمْ
وَلَا تَتَّخِذُوا مِنْهُمْ وَلِيًّا وَّلَا نَصِيرًا ﴿٨٩﴾ إِلَّا
الَّذِينَ يَصِلُونَ إِلٰى قَوْمٍ بَيْنَكُمْ وَبَيْنَهُم
مِّيثٰقٌ أَوْ جَاءُوكُمْ حَصِرَتْ صُدُورُهُمْ أَن
يُّقٰتِلُوكُمْ أَوْ يُقٰتِلُوا قَوْمَهُمْ وَلَوْ شَاءَ اللّٰهُ
لَسَلَّطَهُمْ عَلَيْكُمْ فَلَقٰتَلُوكُمْ فَإِنِ اعْتَزَلُوكُمْ
فَلَمْ يُقٰتِلُوكُمْ وَأَلْقَوْا إِلَيْكُمُ السَّلَمَ فَمَا
جَعَلَ اللّٰهُ لَكُمْ عَلَيْهِمْ سَبِيلًا ﴿٩٠﴾ سَتَجِدُونَ

as safe from their own people. But whenever they are made to have a recourse to hostility (towards the Muslims) they fall headlong into it (as if under compulsion). Therefore if they do not leave you alone, nor make an offer of peace to you nor withhold their hands (from being hostile), then capture them and kill them wherever you find them. And it is these against whom We have given you absolute authority.

SECTION 13

92. **I**T is not befitting for a believer to kill another believer except (what happens) by mistake; and he who kills a believer by mistake let him set a believing captive of war free and pay blood-money to be handed over to the heirs of the deceased, unless they (- the heirs) forgo it as a free-will offering. But if he (- the slain) is a believer belonging to people hostile to you, then there is still only the (penance of) freeing a believing captive of war; and if he (- the slain) belongs to a people with whom you have a pact, then there is the payment of blood-money, to be handed over to his heirs and (also) the freeing of a believing captive of war; but he who does not find (the means to set free a captive of war,) shall fast two consecutive months, a method of penance (devised) by Allâh. And Allâh is All-Knowing, All-Wise.

93. And whoever kills a believer intentionally, his recompense is Gehenna, he shall abide therein. Allâh has shown His displeasure against him and has (also) deprived him of His blessings and prepared for him a great punishment.

94. O you who believe! When you set forth in the cause of Allâh, then make proper investigations (before you dub anyone as a disbeliever), and do not say to him who offers you 'Salâm', (- peace, the Muslim salutation to show himself thereby a Muslim,) 'You are not a believer.' You seek the transitory goods of this life, but Allâh has good things in plenty with Him.

آخَرِينَ يُرِيدُونَ أَنْ يَأْمَنُوكُمْ وَيَأْمَنُوا
قَوْمَهُمْ كُلَّ مَا رُدُّوا إِلَى الْفِتْنَةِ أُرْكِسُوا
فِيهَا فَإِنْ لَمْ يَعْتَزِلُوكُمْ وَيُلْقُوا إِلَيْكُمُ
السَّلَمَ وَيَكُفُّوا أَيْدِيَهُمْ فَخُذُوهُمْ
وَاقْتُلُوهُمْ حَيْثُ ثَقِفْتُمُوهُمْ وَأُولَٰئِكُمْ
جَعَلْنَا لَكُمْ عَلَيْهِمْ سُلْطَانًا مُبِينًا ﴿٩١﴾ وَمَا كَانَ
لِمُؤْمِنٍ أَنْ يَقْتُلَ مُؤْمِنًا إِلَّا خَطَأً وَمَنْ
قَتَلَ مُؤْمِنًا خَطَأً فَتَحْرِيرُ رَقَبَةٍ مُؤْمِنَةٍ
وَدِيَةٌ مُسَلَّمَةٌ إِلَىٰ أَهْلِهِ إِلَّا أَنْ يَصَّدَّقُوا
فَإِنْ كَانَ مِنْ قَوْمٍ عَدُوٍّ لَكُمْ وَهُوَ مُؤْمِنٌ
فَتَحْرِيرُ رَقَبَةٍ مُؤْمِنَةٍ وَإِنْ كَانَ مِنْ
قَوْمٍ بَيْنَكُمْ وَبَيْنَهُمْ مِيثَاقٌ فَدِيَةٌ مُسَلَّمَةٌ
إِلَىٰ أَهْلِهِ وَتَحْرِيرُ رَقَبَةٍ مُؤْمِنَةٍ فَمَنْ لَمْ
يَجِدْ فَصِيَامُ شَهْرَيْنِ مُتَتَابِعَيْنِ تَوْبَةً
مِنَ اللَّهِ وَكَانَ اللَّهُ عَلِيمًا حَكِيمًا ﴿٩٢﴾ وَمَنْ
يَقْتُلْ مُؤْمِنًا مُتَعَمِّدًا فَجَزَاؤُهُ جَهَنَّمُ
خَالِدًا فِيهَا وَغَضِبَ اللَّهُ عَلَيْهِ وَلَعَنَهُ
وَأَعَدَّ لَهُ عَذَابًا عَظِيمًا ﴿٩٣﴾ يَا أَيُّهَا الَّذِينَ
آمَنُوا إِذَا ضَرَبْتُمْ فِي سَبِيلِ اللَّهِ فَتَبَيَّنُوا
وَلَا تَقُولُوا لِمَنْ أَلْقَىٰ إِلَيْكُمُ السَّلَامَ لَسْتَ
مُؤْمِنًا تَبْتَغُونَ عَرَضَ الْحَيَاةِ الدُّنْيَا
فَعِنْدَ اللَّهِ مَغَانِمُ كَثِيرَةٌ كَذَٰلِكَ كُنْتُمْ
مِنْ قَبْلُ فَمَنَّ اللَّهُ عَلَيْكُمْ فَتَبَيَّنُوا إِنَّ

You were such (disbelievers) before that (you accepted Islam), but Allâh has conferred His special favour on you, hence do make proper investigations. Surely, Allâh is Well-Aware of what you do.

95. Such of the believers as stay (at home) excepting the disabled ones, and those who strive in the cause of Allâh with their substance and their lives, are not equal. Allâh has exalted in rank those who strive (in His cause) with their substance and their lives above those who stay (at home), and yet to each one Allâh has promised good but Allâh has indeed granted eminence to those who strive (in His cause) over those who stay (at home) by giving them much better reward.

96. (It will consist of) exalted ranks bestowed by Him and (His) protection and mercy, for Allâh is Great Protector, Ever Merciful.

SECTION 14

97. **S**URELY, the angels will ask those whom they cause to die while they were acting unjustly towards themselves (by prolonging their stay in the land of the disbelievers and thus transgressing against their own souls), 'What circumstances were you in (that you did not avow Islâm openly)?' They will reply, 'We were treated as weak in the country (to express our belief).' They (- the angels) will say, 'Was not Allâh's earth spacious enough for you to have emigrated therein?' It is these whose abode shall be Gehenna and an evil destination it is!

98. Different however is the case of those (actually) weak - men, women and children, who can find no device, nor means (to emigrate).

99. As to these Allâh may pardon them (for their helplessness), for Allâh is the Effacer of sins, Most Forgiving.

100. And whoso emigrates in the cause of Allâh will find in the earth an abundant place of

سُورَةُ النِّسَاءِ ٤

اللّٰهَ كَانَ بِمَا تَعۡمَلُونَ خَبِيرًا ﴿٩٤﴾ لَا يَسۡتَوِي
الۡقٰعِدُونَ مِنَ الۡمُؤۡمِنِينَ غَيۡرُ أُولِي الضَّرَرِ
وَالۡمُجٰهِدُونَ فِي سَبِيلِ اللّٰهِ بِأَمۡوٰلِهِمۡ
وَأَنۡفُسِهِمۡ فَضَّلَ اللّٰهُ الۡمُجٰهِدِينَ بِأَمۡوٰلِهِمۡ
وَأَنۡفُسِهِمۡ عَلَى الۡقٰعِدِينَ دَرَجَةً وَكُلًّا
وَعَدَ اللّٰهُ الۡحُسۡنٰى وَفَضَّلَ اللّٰهُ الۡمُجٰهِدِينَ
عَلَى الۡقٰعِدِينَ أَجۡرًا عَظِيمًا ﴿٩٥﴾ دَرَجٰتٍ مِّنۡهُ
وَمَغۡفِرَةً وَرَحۡمَةً وَكَانَ اللّٰهُ غَفُورًا
رَّحِيمًا ﴿٩٦﴾ إِنَّ الَّذِينَ تَوَفّٰهُمُ الۡمَلٰٓئِكَةُ
ظَالِمِيٓ أَنۡفُسِهِمۡ قَالُوا فِيمَ كُنۡتُمۡ قَالُوا
كُنَّا مُسۡتَضۡعَفِينَ فِي الۡأَرۡضِ قَالُوٓا أَلَمۡ
تَكُنۡ أَرۡضُ اللّٰهِ وٰسِعَةً فَتُهَاجِرُوا فِيهَا
فَأُولٰٓئِكَ مَأۡوٰهُمۡ جَهَنَّمُ وَسَآءَتۡ مَصِيرًا ﴿٩٧﴾
إِلَّا الۡمُسۡتَضۡعَفِينَ مِنَ الرِّجَالِ وَالنِّسَآءِ
وَالۡوِلۡدٰنِ لَا يَسۡتَطِيعُونَ حِيلَةً وَلَا
يَهۡتَدُونَ سَبِيلًا ﴿٩٨﴾ فَأُولٰٓئِكَ عَسَى اللّٰهُ أَنۡ
يَعۡفُوَ عَنۡهُمۡ وَكَانَ اللّٰهُ عَفُوًّا غَفُورًا ﴿٩٩﴾
وَمَنۡ يُهَاجِرۡ فِي سَبِيلِ اللّٰهِ يَجِدۡ فِي الۡأَرۡضِ
مُرٰغَمًا كَثِيرًا وَسَعَةً وَمَنۡ يَخۡرُجۡ مِنۡ
بَيۡتِهِ مُهَاجِرًا إِلَى اللّٰهِ وَرَسُولِهِ ثُمَّ

ع ١٣ ١٠

refuge and plenty of resources. And whoso sets forth from his home, emigrating in the cause of Allâh and His Messenger, then death overtakes him, he shall have his reward with Allâh for sure. Allâh is Great Protector, Ever Merciful.

SECTION 15

101. AND when you are journeying in the land there is no blame on you that you shorten the Prayer, if you fear that those who disbelieve may give you trouble. Verily, the disbelievers are your open enemies.

102. And (Prophet!) when you are amongst them (- the Muslims in the battlefield) leading the Prayer for them (in the time of fear,) let a party of them join you in Prayer retaining their arms. When they have performed their prostrations (and their one *Rak'at* is over) let them take their positions at the rear of the main body (for protection); and let another party who have not yet said Prayer come forward and join Prayer with you, taking their necessary precautions of defence and retaining their arms. Those who have disbelieved would wish you to be heedless of your arms and stores so that they may fall upon you united and all of a sudden. And there is no blame on you if you are suffering inconvenience on account of rain or if you are taken ill, that you lay aside your arms (relieving yourselves), but (even then) you must take your necessary precautions of defence. Verily, Allâh has prepared a humiliating punishment for the disbelievers.

103. And when you have finished the Prayer, then remember Allâh standing and sitting, and (lying) on your sides (in short in all positions and in all conditions). And when you feel secure (from danger) then observe Prayer (in the normal prescribed form). Verily, Prayer is enjoined on the believers (to be performed) at the fixed times.

104. And do not be slack in pursuing these (hostile) people. If you have suffered hard-

يُدْرِكْهُ الْمَوْتُ فَقَدْ وَقَعَ أَجْرُهُ عَلَى اللَّهِ ۗ
وَكَانَ اللَّهُ غَفُورًا رَّحِيمًا ﴿١٠٠﴾ وَإِذَا ضَرَبْتُمْ
فِي الْأَرْضِ فَلَيْسَ عَلَيْكُمْ جُنَاحٌ أَن تَقْصُرُوا
مِنَ الصَّلَوٰةِ ۖ إِنْ خِفْتُمْ أَن يَفْتِنَكُمُ الَّذِينَ
كَفَرُوا ۚ إِنَّ الْكَٰفِرِينَ كَانُوا لَكُمْ عَدُوًّا
مُّبِينًا ﴿١٠١﴾ وَإِذَا كُنتَ فِيهِمْ فَأَقَمْتَ لَهُمُ
الصَّلَوٰةَ فَلْتَقُمْ طَآئِفَةٌ مِّنْهُم مَّعَكَ
وَلْيَأْخُذُوا أَسْلِحَتَهُمْ فَإِذَا سَجَدُوا
فَلْيَكُونُوا مِن وَرَآئِكُمْ وَلْتَأْتِ طَآئِفَةٌ
أُخْرَىٰ لَمْ يُصَلُّوا فَلْيُصَلُّوا مَعَكَ وَلْيَأْخُذُوا
حِذْرَهُمْ وَأَسْلِحَتَهُمْ ۗ وَدَّ الَّذِينَ كَفَرُوا لَوْ
تَغْفُلُونَ عَنْ أَسْلِحَتِكُمْ وَأَمْتِعَتِكُمْ فَيَمِيلُونَ
عَلَيْكُم مَّيْلَةً وَٰحِدَةً ۚ وَلَا جُنَاحَ عَلَيْكُمْ
إِن كَانَ بِكُمْ أَذًى مِّن مَّطَرٍ أَوْ كُنتُم
مَّرْضَىٰ أَن تَضَعُوا أَسْلِحَتَكُمْ ۖ وَخُذُوا حِذْرَكُمْ
إِنَّ اللَّهَ أَعَدَّ لِلْكَٰفِرِينَ عَذَابًا مُّهِينًا ﴿١٠٢﴾ فَإِذَا
قَضَيْتُمُ الصَّلَوٰةَ فَاذْكُرُوا اللَّهَ قِيَٰمًا وَقُعُودًا
وَعَلَىٰ جُنُوبِكُمْ ۚ فَإِذَا اطْمَأْنَنتُمْ فَأَقِيمُوا
الصَّلَوٰةَ ۚ إِنَّ الصَّلَوٰةَ كَانَتْ عَلَى الْمُؤْمِنِينَ
كِتَٰبًا مَّوْقُوتًا ﴿١٠٣﴾ وَلَا تَهِنُوا فِي ابْتِغَآءِ

ships they (too) have suffered as you did but (the superiority you have over them is that) you hope from Allâh what they do not. And Allâh is All-Knowing, All-Wise.

SECTION 16

105. **W**E have surely revealed to you this perfect Book comprising the truth, that you judge between the people (enlightened) by that knowledge which Allâh has given you, and do not become a partisan of the dishonest.
106. And seek protection of Allâh. Verily, Allâh is Great Protector, Ever Merciful.
107. And do not plead on behalf of those who act dishonestly towards themselves. Surely, Allâh does not love him who is given to dishonest ways, (and is) a great sinner.
108. They seek to hide (their crimes) from the people, but they cannot hide from Allâh; and He is present with them when they pass the night in holding discourses which does not please Him. And Allâh encompasses all that they do (until He puts an end to their evil ways).
109. Behold! You are of those who may plead on their behalf in the present life. But who will plead on their behalf with Allâh on the Day of Resurrection, or who will be a disposer of their affairs?
110. And whoever commits evil and does injustice to himself and then asks forgiveness of Allâh, will find Allâh Most Forgiving, Ever Merciful.
111. And whoever commits a sin deliberately, commits it only against himself. Allâh is All-Knowing, All-Wise.
112. But one who commits a fault or a sin and imputes it to an innocent person (for the sake of his own defence), he certainly bears the burden of calumny along with that of a flagrant sin.

SECTION 17

113. (**P**ROPHET!) A party of those (who are false to themselves) had certainly made up their minds to ruin you, but for the grace of Allâh and

الْقَوْمِ إِنْ تَكُونُوا تَأْلَمُونَ فَإِنَّهُمْ
يَأْلَمُونَ كَمَا تَأْلَمُونَ وَتَرْجُونَ مِنَ اللَّهِ
مَا لَا يَرْجُونَ وَكَانَ اللَّهُ عَلِيمًا حَكِيمًا ﴿١٠٤﴾
إِنَّا أَنْزَلْنَا إِلَيْكَ الْكِتَابَ بِالْحَقِّ لِتَحْكُمَ
بَيْنَ النَّاسِ بِمَا أَرَاكَ اللَّهُ وَلَا تَكُنْ
لِلْخَائِنِينَ خَصِيمًا ﴿١٠٥﴾ وَاسْتَغْفِرِ اللَّهَ إِنَّ
اللَّهَ كَانَ غَفُورًا رَحِيمًا ﴿١٠٦﴾ وَلَا تُجَادِلْ
عَنِ الَّذِينَ يَخْتَانُونَ أَنْفُسَهُمْ إِنَّ اللَّهَ
لَا يُحِبُّ مَنْ كَانَ خَوَّانًا أَثِيمًا ﴿١٠٧﴾
يَسْتَخْفُونَ مِنَ النَّاسِ وَلَا يَسْتَخْفُونَ
مِنَ اللَّهِ وَهُوَ مَعَهُمْ إِذْ يُبَيِّتُونَ مَا لَا
يَرْضَى مِنَ الْقَوْلِ وَكَانَ اللَّهُ بِمَا يَعْمَلُونَ
مُحِيطًا ﴿١٠٨﴾ هَا أَنْتُمْ هَؤُلَاءِ جَادَلْتُمْ عَنْهُمْ
فِي الْحَيَاةِ الدُّنْيَا فَمَنْ يُجَادِلُ اللَّهَ عَنْهُمْ
يَوْمَ الْقِيَامَةِ أَمْ مَنْ يَكُونُ عَلَيْهِمْ وَكِيلًا ﴿١٠٩﴾
وَمَنْ يَعْمَلْ سُوءًا أَوْ يَظْلِمْ نَفْسَهُ ثُمَّ
يَسْتَغْفِرِ اللَّهَ يَجِدِ اللَّهَ غَفُورًا رَحِيمًا ﴿١١٠﴾
وَمَنْ يَكْسِبْ إِثْمًا فَإِنَّمَا يَكْسِبُهُ عَلَى
نَفْسِهِ وَكَانَ اللَّهُ عَلِيمًا حَكِيمًا ﴿١١١﴾
وَمَنْ يَكْسِبْ خَطِيئَةً أَوْ إِثْمًا ثُمَّ يَرْمِ
بِهِ بَرِيئًا فَقَدِ احْتَمَلَ بُهْتَانًا وَإِثْمًا
مُبِينًا ﴿١١٢﴾ وَلَوْلَا فَضْلُ اللَّهِ عَلَيْكَ
وَرَحْمَتُهُ لَهَمَّتْ طَائِفَةٌ مِنْهُمْ أَنْ يُضِلُّوكَ

الجزء الخامس

His mercy upon you, they ruin none but themselves, and they can do you no harm. And Allâh has revealed to you this perfect Book and the Wisdom and has taught you that which you did not know. Allâh's favour upon you is great indeed (and you enjoy His protection in temporal as well as in spiritual matters).

114. There is no good in many of their secret conferences. But (good lies only in the secret deliberations of) those who enjoin charity, equitable dealings or making peace between people. And whoso does that, seeking the pleasure of Allâh, We shall soon bestow a great reward on him.

115. And as to him who opposes the Messenger in a hostile manner after true guidance has become clear to him, and follows a way other than that of the believers, We will let him pursue the way which he is (himself) pursuing, and shall cast him into Gehenna, and an evil destination it is!

SECTION 18

116. **A**LLÂH does not forgive (without repentance on the part of the sinner) that a partner be associated with Him though He forgives everything short of that to whomsoever He will. And he who associates a partner with Allâh has strayed, indeed, a far off straying.

117. Whatever they (- the polytheists) call on besides Him are none but lifeless objects (and false deities). In fact, they call on none but satan, the rebellious,

118. Whom Allâh has deprived of His blessings and who had said, 'I will certainly take from Your servants an appointed portion,

119. 'And certainly, I will lead them astray and assuredly I will arouse vain desires in them, and I will incite them (to polytheistic practices) and they will slit the ears of cattle (as a mark of their dedication to their deities), and I will most assuredly make them change (for the worse,) the things created by Allâh.' And he who takes this satan to him for a friend rather than Allâh,

وَمَا يُضِلُّونَ إِلَّآ أَنْفُسَهُمْ وَمَا يَضُرُّونَكَ
مِنْ شَيْءٍ ۚ وَأَنْزَلَ اللَّهُ عَلَيْكَ الْكِتٰبَ
وَالْحِكْمَةَ وَعَلَّمَكَ مَا لَمْ تَكُنْ تَعْلَمُ ۚ
وَكَانَ فَضْلُ اللَّهِ عَلَيْكَ عَظِيمًا ﴿١١٣﴾ لَا خَيْرَ
فِي كَثِيرٍ مِّنْ نَّجْوٰىهُمْ إِلَّا مَنْ أَمَرَ بِصَدَقَةٍ
أَوْ مَعْرُوفٍ أَوْ إِصْلَاحٍ بَيْنَ النَّاسِ ۚ
وَمَنْ يَّفْعَلْ ذٰلِكَ ابْتِغَآءَ مَرْضَاتِ اللَّهِ
فَسَوْفَ نُؤْتِيهِ أَجْرًا عَظِيمًا ﴿١١٤﴾ وَمَنْ
يُّشَاقِقِ الرَّسُولَ مِنْ بَعْدِ مَا تَبَيَّنَ لَهُ
الْهُدٰى وَيَتَّبِعْ غَيْرَ سَبِيلِ الْمُؤْمِنِينَ
نُوَلِّهِ مَا تَوَلّٰى وَنُصْلِهِ جَهَنَّمَ ۖ وَسَآءَتْ
مَصِيرًا ﴿١١٥﴾ إِنَّ اللَّهَ لَا يَغْفِرُ أَنْ يُّشْرَكَ بِهِ
وَيَغْفِرُ مَا دُونَ ذٰلِكَ لِمَنْ يَّشَآءُ ۚ وَمَنْ
يُّشْرِكْ بِاللَّهِ فَقَدْ ضَلَّ ضَلٰلًا بَعِيدًا ﴿١١٦﴾
إِنْ يَّدْعُونَ مِنْ دُونِهِ إِلَّآ إِنٰثًا ۚ وَإِنْ
يَّدْعُونَ إِلَّا شَيْطٰنًا مَّرِيدًا ﴿١١٧﴾ لَّعَنَهُ اللَّهُ ۘ
وَقَالَ لَأَتَّخِذَنَّ مِنْ عِبَادِكَ نَصِيبًا
مَّفْرُوضًا ﴿١١٨﴾ وَلَأُضِلَّنَّهُمْ وَلَأُمَنِّيَنَّهُمْ
وَلَاٰمُرَنَّهُمْ فَلَيُبَتِّكُنَّ اٰذَانَ الْأَنْعٰمِ
وَلَاٰمُرَنَّهُمْ فَلَيُغَيِّرُنَّ خَلْقَ اللَّهِ ۚ وَمَنْ
يَّتَّخِذِ الشَّيْطٰنَ وَلِيًّا مِّنْ دُونِ اللَّهِ فَقَدْ

has of course suffered an evident loss.

120. He (- satan) holds out promises to them and arouses false hopes in them. But satan promises nothing but vain things to them.

121. It is these (- his dupes) whose abode is Gehenna and they shall find no way of escape from it.

122. And those who believe and do deeds of righteousness We will certainly admit them into Gardens served with running streams, there they shall abide forever. Allâh's promise is unfailing. And who is more truthful than Allâh in word.

123. (O people!) It (- the salvation) shall not be according to your vain desires, nor according to the vain desires of the people of the Scripture. He who does evil shall be recompensed accordingly, and he shall find for himself no patron nor a helper besides Allâh.

124. But whosoever does deeds of righteousness be it male or female, provided he (or she) is a believer, it is these, then who shall enter Paradise and shall not be treated unjustly even (so much as) the groove in a date-stone.

125. And who is better in faith than one who submits his whole attention to Allâh and he is a doer of good to others and follows the religion of Abraham, the upright? And Allâh had taken Abraham for a special friend.

126. And to Allâh belongs whatever is in the heavens and whatever is in the earth. And Allâh encompasses each and everything.

SECTION 19

127. **A**ND they seek your ruling with regard to (marrying) women (having no husbands). Say, 'Allâh gives you His ruling about them and He reminds you the ruling as has (already) been mentioned to you in this Book regarding women without husbands (- widows, divorced, or yet to be married) to whom you do not give their rights prescribed for them, yet you feel inclined

خَسِرَ خُسْرَانًا مُّبِينًا ﴿١١٩﴾ يَعِدُهُمْ وَيُمَنِّيهِمْ
وَمَا يَعِدُهُمُ الشَّيْطَٰنُ إِلَّا غُرُورًا ﴿١٢٠﴾ أُولَٰٓئِكَ
مَأْوَىٰهُمْ جَهَنَّمُ وَلَا يَجِدُونَ عَنْهَا مَحِيصًا ﴿١٢١﴾
وَالَّذِينَ ءَامَنُوا وَعَمِلُوا الصَّٰلِحَٰتِ سَنُدْخِلُهُمْ
جَنَّٰتٍ تَجْرِي مِن تَحْتِهَا الْأَنْهَٰرُ خَٰلِدِينَ
فِيهَآ أَبَدًا ۖ وَعْدَ اللَّهِ حَقًّا ۚ وَمَنْ أَصْدَقُ
مِنَ اللَّهِ قِيلًا ﴿١٢٢﴾ لَّيْسَ بِأَمَانِيِّكُمْ وَلَآ
أَمَانِيِّ أَهْلِ الْكِتَٰبِ ۗ مَن يَعْمَلْ سُوٓءًا يُجْزَ
بِهِۦ وَلَا يَجِدْ لَهُۥ مِن دُونِ اللَّهِ وَلِيًّا وَلَا
نَصِيرًا ﴿١٢٣﴾ وَمَن يَعْمَلْ مِنَ الصَّٰلِحَٰتِ مِن
ذَكَرٍ أَوْ أُنثَىٰ وَهُوَ مُؤْمِنٌ فَأُولَٰٓئِكَ يَدْخُلُونَ
الْجَنَّةَ وَلَا يُظْلَمُونَ نَقِيرًا ﴿١٢٤﴾ وَمَنْ أَحْسَنُ
دِينًا مِّمَّنْ أَسْلَمَ وَجْهَهُۥ لِلَّهِ وَهُوَ مُحْسِنٌ
وَاتَّبَعَ مِلَّةَ إِبْرَٰهِيمَ حَنِيفًا ۗ وَاتَّخَذَ اللَّهُ
إِبْرَٰهِيمَ خَلِيلًا ﴿١٢٥﴾ وَلِلَّهِ مَا فِي السَّمَٰوَٰتِ
وَمَا فِي الْأَرْضِ ۚ وَكَانَ اللَّهُ بِكُلِّ شَيْءٍ
مُّحِيطًا ﴿١٢٦﴾ وَيَسْتَفْتُونَكَ فِي النِّسَآءِ ۖ قُلِ اللَّهُ
يُفْتِيكُمْ فِيهِنَّ وَمَا يُتْلَىٰ عَلَيْكُمْ فِي
الْكِتَٰبِ فِي يَتَٰمَى النِّسَآءِ الَّتِي لَا تُؤْتُونَهُنَّ
مَا كُتِبَ لَهُنَّ وَتَرْغَبُونَ أَن تَنكِحُوهُنَّ

to get them in marriage (with a mind to take over their belongings) and (the ruling is also regarding) the helpless children. (He enjoins you to) stand firm in observing equity towards the orphans. And (remember) whatever good you do Allâh knows it very well.

128. And if a woman fears high-handedness or indifference on the part of her husband then there is no blame on them both that they may be amicably reconciled to each other and reconciliation is the best. And covetousness and greed is ever present in human minds, but if you do good and guard against (this) evil, (you will find) then Allâh is Well-Aware of what you do.

129. It is not within your power (as far as natural feelings of love and devotion are concerned,) to maintain perfect balance between wives (and to treat them with equal justice) even though you be ever so eager; but do not incline with a total inclination (towards one so that you completely sever your relations with the other) so as to leave her like some thing suspended (as virtually deserted). And if you keep things right and guard against evil, then surely Allâh is Great Protector, Ever Merciful.

130. And if they (-the husband and the wife) choose to separate (through divorce obtained by either of them), Allâh will make both independent and free from want out of His bounty. And Allâh is All Bountiful, Ever-Wise.

131. And to Allâh belongs whatever is in the heavens and whatever is in the earth. And We enjoined those who were given the Scripture before you and (We enjoin) you also to take Allâh as a shield and keep your duty to Him; but if you disobey, then (remember that) to Allâh belongs whatever is in the heavens and whatever is in the earth. And Allâh is Self-Sufficient, Praiseworthy.

132. And to Allâh belongs whatever is in the heavens and whatever is in the earth and Sufficient is Allâh as Disposer of affairs.

133. If He so will He can make you pass away, O people! and bring another people (in

والمستضعفين من الولدان وأن تقوموا
لليتمى بالقسط وما تفعلوا من خير فإن
الله كان به عليما ﴿١٢٧﴾ وإن امرأة خافت
من بعلها نشوزا أو إعراضا فلا جناح
عليهما أن يصلحا بينهما صلحا والصلح
خير وأحضرت الأنفس الشح وإن
تحسنوا وتتقوا فإن الله كان بما تعملون
خبيرا ﴿١٢٨﴾ ولن تستطيعوا أن تعدلوا بين
النساء ولو حرصتم فلا تميلوا كل
الميل فتذروها كالمعلقة وإن تصلحوا
وتتقوا فإن الله كان غفورا رحيما ﴿١٢٩﴾
وإن يتفرقا يغن الله كلا من سعته
وكان الله وسعا حكيما ﴿١٣٠﴾ ولله ما في السموت
وما في الأرض ولقد وصينا الذين أوتوا
الكتب من قبلكم وإياكم أن اتقوا الله
وإن تكفروا فإن لله ما في السموت وما
في الأرض وكان الله غنيا حميدا ﴿١٣١﴾ ولله
ما في السموت وما في الأرض وكفى
بالله وكيلا ﴿١٣٢﴾ إن يشأ يذهبكم أيها

your stead), and Allâh is Possessor of power to do all this.

134. Whosoever seeks the reward of this world let him know that the reward of this world and (that of) the Hereafter is with Allâh. Allâh is All-Hearing, All-Seeing.

SECTION 20

135. **O** YOU who believe! Be strict observers of justice, bearers of true evidence for the sake of Allâh, even though it be against yourselves or (against your) parents or near of kin; (let neither of the parties) whether (the one against whom or the one in favour of whom you bear evidence) be rich or poor (weigh with yourself). (Bear in mind) Allâh is more regardful of them both (than you are), therefore, do not follow your low desires in order to be able to do justice. And if you distort or evade (true evidence) remember Allâh is Well-Aware of what you do.

136. O you who believe! Maintain faith in Allâh and in His Messenger and in this perfect Book which He has revealed to His perfect Messenger and in the Scripture He revealed before. And whoso denies Allâh and His angels and His Books and His Messengers and the Last Day, he has indeed strayed far away (from the truth).

137. Verily, those who believed and then disbelieved, again believed, again disbelieved and then became worse in disbelief, it is not for Allâh to pardon them, nor to guide them in the (right) way (to make them successful).

138. Tell the hypocrites clearly that a woeful punishment awaits them.

139. Do those who hold the disbelievers for friends to the exclusion of the believers, seek honour at their hands? Let them remember that all honour truly belongs to Allâh alone.

140. And He has already revealed to you in this Book (the commandment) that when you

النَّاسُ وَيَأْتِ بِآخَرِينَ ۚ وَكَانَ اللَّهُ عَلَىٰ
ذَٰلِكَ قَدِيرًا ﴿١٣٣﴾ مَنْ كَانَ يُرِيدُ ثَوَابَ الدُّنْيَا
فَعِنْدَ اللَّهِ ثَوَابُ الدُّنْيَا وَالْآخِرَةِ ۚ وَكَانَ
اللَّهُ سَمِيعًا بَصِيرًا ﴿١٣٤﴾ يَا أَيُّهَا الَّذِينَ آمَنُوا
كُونُوا قَوَّامِينَ بِالْقِسْطِ شُهَدَاءَ لِلَّهِ وَلَوْ
عَلَىٰ أَنْفُسِكُمْ أَوِ الْوَالِدَيْنِ وَالْأَقْرَبِينَ ۚ إِنْ
يَكُنْ غَنِيًّا أَوْ فَقِيرًا فَاللَّهُ أَوْلَىٰ بِهِمَا ۖ فَلَا
تَتَّبِعُوا الْهَوَىٰ أَنْ تَعْدِلُوا ۚ وَإِنْ تَلْوُوا أَوْ
تُعْرِضُوا فَإِنَّ اللَّهَ كَانَ بِمَا تَعْمَلُونَ خَبِيرًا ﴿١٣٥﴾
يَا أَيُّهَا الَّذِينَ آمَنُوا آمِنُوا بِاللَّهِ وَرَسُولِهِ
وَالْكِتَابِ الَّذِي نَزَّلَ عَلَىٰ رَسُولِهِ وَالْكِتَابِ
الَّذِي أَنْزَلَ مِنْ قَبْلُ ۚ وَمَنْ يَكْفُرْ بِاللَّهِ
وَمَلَائِكَتِهِ وَكُتُبِهِ وَرُسُلِهِ وَالْيَوْمِ الْآخِرِ
فَقَدْ ضَلَّ ضَلَالًا بَعِيدًا ﴿١٣٦﴾ إِنَّ الَّذِينَ آمَنُوا
ثُمَّ كَفَرُوا ثُمَّ آمَنُوا ثُمَّ كَفَرُوا ثُمَّ ازْدَادُوا
كُفْرًا لَمْ يَكُنِ اللَّهُ لِيَغْفِرَ لَهُمْ وَلَا
لِيَهْدِيَهُمْ سَبِيلًا ﴿١٣٧﴾ بَشِّرِ الْمُنَافِقِينَ بِأَنَّ
لَهُمْ عَذَابًا أَلِيمًا ﴿١٣٨﴾ الَّذِينَ يَتَّخِذُونَ
الْكَافِرِينَ أَوْلِيَاءَ مِنْ دُونِ الْمُؤْمِنِينَ ۚ
أَيَبْتَغُونَ عِنْدَهُمُ الْعِزَّةَ فَإِنَّ الْعِزَّةَ لِلَّهِ
جَمِيعًا ﴿١٣٩﴾ وَقَدْ نَزَّلَ عَلَيْكُمْ فِي الْكِتَابِ أَنْ
إِذَا سَمِعْتُمْ آيَاتِ اللَّهِ يُكْفَرُ بِهَا وَيُسْتَهْزَأُ

hear Allâh's Messages being denied and being ridiculed you should not sit with such (absurd people) unless they engage in a topic other than that, for in case (you do not leave their company) you will be indeed like them. Allâh is going to assemble the hypocrites and the disbelievers in Gehenna one and all.
141. Those (- hypocrites) who await (news) about you, then if you win a victory by the grace of Allâh they say, 'Is it not that we were with you (and on your side)? But should there be for the disbelievers a share of it they will say (to them), 'Did we not goad you to wage war; and did we not save you from the harm of the faithful?' Then Allâh will judge between you on the Day of Resurrection; and Allâh will never let the disbelievers have a way (to prevail) against the believers.

SECTION 21

142. **V**ERILY, the hypocrites abandon Allâh but He will abandon them. And when they stand up for Prayer they stand listlessly to show off to the people (that they worship) yet they remember Allâh but little.
143. Wavering between that (- disbelief and belief), belonging neither to these nor to those. And he whom Allâh causes to be ruined, you shall not find a way (of escape) for him.
144. O you who believe! Do not take disbelievers for friends to the exclusion of believers. Do you mean to provide Allâh with clear plea against yourselves.
145. The hypocrites shall surely be in the lowest reaches of the Fire. You shall never find any helper for them.
146. Yet such of these (- hypocrites) who turn with sincere repentance and amend (themselves) and hold fast to Allâh and become sincere in their allegiance to Allâh, it is these who are with the believers and Allâh will soon grant these believers a great reward.
147. What Allâh has to do with punishing you if you be grateful (to Him) and believe (in Him). Allâh is Ever Appreciating, All-Knowing.

بِهَا فَلَا تَقْعُدُوا مَعَهُمْ حَتّٰى يَخُوضُوا فِي
حَدِيثٍ غَيْرِهٖٓ ۖ إِنَّكُمْ إِذًا مِّثْلُهُمْ ۗ إِنَّ اللّٰهَ
جَامِعُ الْمُنٰفِقِينَ وَالْكٰفِرِينَ فِي جَهَنَّمَ
جَمِيعًا ﴿١٤٠﴾ الَّذِينَ يَتَرَبَّصُونَ بِكُمْ ۚ فَإِنْ كَانَ
لَكُمْ فَتْحٌ مِّنَ اللّٰهِ قَالُوٓا أَلَمْ نَكُنْ مَّعَكُمْ ۖ
وَإِنْ كَانَ لِلْكٰفِرِينَ نَصِيبٌ ۙ قَالُوٓا أَلَمْ
نَسْتَحْوِذْ عَلَيْكُمْ وَنَمْنَعْكُمْ مِّنَ الْمُؤْمِنِينَ ۗ
فَاللّٰهُ يَحْكُمُ بَيْنَكُمْ يَوْمَ الْقِيٰمَةِ ۗ وَلَنْ
يَّجْعَلَ اللّٰهُ لِلْكٰفِرِينَ عَلَى الْمُؤْمِنِينَ سَبِيلًا ﴿١٤١﴾
إِنَّ الْمُنٰفِقِينَ يُخٰدِعُونَ اللّٰهَ وَهُوَ خٰدِعُهُمْ ۚ
وَإِذَا قَامُوٓا إِلَى الصَّلٰوةِ قَامُوا كُسَالٰى ۙ
يُرَآءُونَ النَّاسَ وَلَا يَذْكُرُونَ اللّٰهَ إِلَّا
قَلِيلًا ﴿١٤٢﴾ مُّذَبْذَبِينَ بَيْنَ ذٰلِكَ ۖ لَآ إِلٰى هٰٓؤُلَآءِ
وَلَآ إِلٰى هٰٓؤُلَآءِ ۗ وَمَنْ يُّضْلِلِ اللّٰهُ فَلَنْ تَجِدَ
لَهٗ سَبِيلًا ﴿١٤٣﴾ يٰٓأَيُّهَا الَّذِينَ اٰمَنُوا لَا تَتَّخِذُوا
الْكٰفِرِينَ أَوْلِيَآءَ مِنْ دُونِ الْمُؤْمِنِينَ ۗ
أَتُرِيدُونَ أَنْ تَجْعَلُوا لِلّٰهِ عَلَيْكُمْ سُلْطٰنًا
مُّبِينًا ﴿١٤٤﴾ إِنَّ الْمُنٰفِقِينَ فِي الدَّرْكِ الْأَسْفَلِ
مِنَ النَّارِ ۚ وَلَنْ تَجِدَ لَهُمْ نَصِيرًا ﴿١٤٥﴾ إِلَّا الَّذِينَ
تَابُوا وَأَصْلَحُوا وَاعْتَصَمُوا بِاللّٰهِ وَأَخْلَصُوا
دِينَهُمْ لِلّٰهِ فَأُولٰٓئِكَ مَعَ الْمُؤْمِنِينَ ۗ وَسَوْفَ
يُؤْتِ اللّٰهُ الْمُؤْمِنِينَ أَجْرًا عَظِيمًا ﴿١٤٦﴾ مَا
يَفْعَلُ اللّٰهُ بِعَذَابِكُمْ إِنْ شَكَرْتُمْ
وَاٰمَنْتُمْ ۚ وَكَانَ اللّٰهُ شَاكِرًا عَلِيمًا ﴿١٤٧﴾

148. ALLÂH does not like the public utterance of the hurtful speech, except (it is by) one who has been done injustice to. And Allâh is All-Hearing, All-Knowing.

149. If you do a good deed openly or do it in private or pardon an injury (done to you) remember Allâh is Ever Pardoning, All-Powerful.

150. Verily, those who disbelieve in Allâh and His Messengers, (or while believing) choose to make a distinction between Allâh and His Messengers, and say, 'We believe in some and disbelieve in others,' intending to strike a course in between,

151. It is these who are veritable disbelievers and We have prepared a humiliating punishment for such disbelievers.

152. (On the other hand) those who believe in Allâh and (all of) His Messengers and (while believing) make no distinction between any of them, it is to these whom He will soon give their rewards. Indeed, Allâh is Great Protector, Ever Merciful.

SECTION 22

153. THE people of the Scripture ask you to bring down upon them a Book from the heaven. They made a (more wicked and) greater demand than that from Moses, when they said, 'Show us Allâh openly (face to face);' then a destructive punishment overtook them for their wrongdoing. Then they took the calf (for worship) after clear commandments had come to them, but We pardoned (them) even that. And We gave Moses an undisputed authority.

154. And We raised the Mount above them while taking their covenant (at the foot of the Mount), and We said to them, 'Enter the gate (of the town) submissively,' and We said to them, 'Do not violate the (law of) Sabbath.' And We took from them a solemn covenant.

155. Then because of their breaking their

لَا يُحِبُّ اللَّهُ الْجَهْرَ بِالسُّوءِ مِنَ الْقَوْلِ
إِلَّا مَن ظُلِمَ ۚ وَكَانَ اللَّهُ سَمِيعًا عَلِيمًا ﴿١٤٨﴾
إِن تُبْدُوا خَيْرًا أَوْ تُخْفُوهُ أَوْ تَعْفُوا عَن سُوءٍ
فَإِنَّ اللَّهَ كَانَ عَفُوًّا قَدِيرًا ﴿١٤٩﴾ إِنَّ الَّذِينَ
يَكْفُرُونَ بِاللَّهِ وَرُسُلِهِ وَيُرِيدُونَ أَن
يُفَرِّقُوا بَيْنَ اللَّهِ وَرُسُلِهِ وَيَقُولُونَ
نُؤْمِنُ بِبَعْضٍ وَنَكْفُرُ بِبَعْضٍ وَيُرِيدُونَ
أَن يَتَّخِذُوا بَيْنَ ذَٰلِكَ سَبِيلًا ﴿١٥٠﴾ أُولَٰئِكَ
هُمُ الْكَافِرُونَ حَقًّا ۚ وَأَعْتَدْنَا لِلْكَافِرِينَ
عَذَابًا مُّهِينًا ﴿١٥١﴾ وَالَّذِينَ آمَنُوا بِاللَّهِ
وَرُسُلِهِ وَلَمْ يُفَرِّقُوا بَيْنَ أَحَدٍ مِّنْهُمْ أُولَٰئِكَ
سَوْفَ يُؤْتِيهِمْ أُجُورَهُمْ ۗ وَكَانَ اللَّهُ
غَفُورًا رَّحِيمًا ﴿١٥٢﴾ يَسْأَلُكَ أَهْلُ الْكِتَابِ أَن
تُنَزِّلَ عَلَيْهِمْ كِتَابًا مِّنَ السَّمَاءِ ۚ فَقَدْ سَأَلُوا
مُوسَىٰ أَكْبَرَ مِن ذَٰلِكَ فَقَالُوا أَرِنَا اللَّهَ
جَهْرَةً فَأَخَذَتْهُمُ الصَّاعِقَةُ بِظُلْمِهِمْ ۚ ثُمَّ
اتَّخَذُوا الْعِجْلَ مِن بَعْدِ مَا جَاءَتْهُمُ
الْبَيِّنَاتُ فَعَفَوْنَا عَن ذَٰلِكَ ۚ وَآتَيْنَا مُوسَىٰ
سُلْطَانًا مُّبِينًا ﴿١٥٣﴾ وَرَفَعْنَا فَوْقَهُمُ الطُّورَ
بِمِيثَاقِهِمْ وَقُلْنَا لَهُمُ ادْخُلُوا الْبَابَ سُجَّدًا
وَقُلْنَا لَهُمْ لَا تَعْدُوا فِي السَّبْتِ وَأَخَذْنَا
مِنْهُم مِّيثَاقًا غَلِيظًا ﴿١٥٤﴾ فَبِمَا نَقْضِهِم

covenant and their denial of the Messages of Allâh and their antagonising the Prophets without a just cause and their saying, 'Our hearts are uncircumcised (and so cannot hear).' Nay, (the truth however is) Allâh has set a seal upon their hearts because of their disbelief so that they believe but a little.

156. And (The Lord has done this) because of their denying (Jesus) and because of their uttering a great calumny against Mary,

157. And because of their (falsely) claiming, 'We did kill the Messiah, Jesus, son of Mary, the (false) Messenger of Allâh,' whereas they killed him not, nor did they cause his death by crucifixion, but he was made to them to resemble (one crucified to death). Verily, those who differ therein are certainly in (a state of) confusion about it. They have no definite knowledge of the matter but are only following a conjecture. They did not kill him, this much is certain (and thus could not prove the Christ as accursed).

158. Rather Allâh exalted him with all honour to His presence. And Allâh is All-Mighty, All-Wise.

159. And there is none from among the people of the Scripture (- the Jews and the Christians) but most certainly will believe in this (incident, that Jesus died on the cross) before his death, (while as a matter of fact they have no sure knowledge about Jesus dying on the cross). And on the Day of Resurrection he (- Jesus) will be a witness against them.

160. Then (by way of punishing them) on account of the transgression of those who judaised, We made unlawful to them certain of the good and pure things which had been allowed to them before, and that too on account of their causing hindrances to many (people, and their own staying away) from Allâh's way;

161. And (also on account of) their taking interest and usury though they were forbidden it, and because of their misappropriating people's

مِّيثَٰقَهُمْ وَكُفْرِهِم بِـَٔايَٰتِ ٱللَّهِ وَقَتْلِهِمُ
ٱلْأَنۢبِيَآءَ بِغَيْرِ حَقٍّ وَقَوْلِهِمْ قُلُوبُنَا غُلْفٌۢ
بَلْ طَبَعَ ٱللَّهُ عَلَيْهَا بِكُفْرِهِمْ فَلَا يُؤْمِنُونَ
إِلَّا قَلِيلًا ﴿١٥٥﴾ وَبِكُفْرِهِمْ وَقَوْلِهِمْ عَلَىٰ مَرْيَمَ
بُهْتَٰنًا عَظِيمًا ﴿١٥٦﴾ وَقَوْلِهِمْ إِنَّا قَتَلْنَا
ٱلْمَسِيحَ عِيسَى ٱبْنَ مَرْيَمَ رَسُولَ ٱللَّهِ
وَمَا قَتَلُوهُ وَمَا صَلَبُوهُ وَلَٰكِن شُبِّهَ لَهُمْ
وَإِنَّ ٱلَّذِينَ ٱخْتَلَفُوا۟ فِيهِ لَفِى شَكٍّ مِّنْهُ
مَا لَهُم بِهِۦ مِنْ عِلْمٍ إِلَّا ٱتِّبَاعَ ٱلظَّنِّ
وَمَا قَتَلُوهُ يَقِينًۢا ﴿١٥٧﴾ بَل رَّفَعَهُ ٱللَّهُ إِلَيْهِ
وَكَانَ ٱللَّهُ عَزِيزًا حَكِيمًا ﴿١٥٨﴾ وَإِن مِّنْ أَهْلِ
ٱلْكِتَٰبِ إِلَّا لَيُؤْمِنَنَّ بِهِۦ قَبْلَ مَوْتِهِۦ
وَيَوْمَ ٱلْقِيَٰمَةِ يَكُونُ عَلَيْهِمْ شَهِيدًا ﴿١٥٩﴾ فَبِظُلْمٍ
مِّنَ ٱلَّذِينَ هَادُوا۟ حَرَّمْنَا عَلَيْهِمْ طَيِّبَٰتٍ
أُحِلَّتْ لَهُمْ وَبِصَدِّهِمْ عَن سَبِيلِ ٱللَّهِ
كَثِيرًا ﴿١٦٠﴾ وَأَخْذِهِمُ ٱلرِّبَوٰا۟ وَقَدْ نُهُوا۟ عَنْهُ
وَأَكْلِهِمْ أَمْوَٰلَ ٱلنَّاسِ بِٱلْبَٰطِلِ وَأَعْتَدْنَا

belongings. And We have prepared a woeful punishment for those among them who disbelieve.

162. But those from among them who are firmly grounded in knowledge and the faithful who believe in that (Divine Message) which has been revealed to you and that which was revealed before you, and (especially) the observers of Prayers, and those who go on presenting the *Zakât,* and believe in Allâh and the Last Day, it is they We will certainly bestow on them a great reward.

SECTION 23

163. **S**URELY, We have sent down (Our) revelation to you as We sent it down to Noah and the Prophets (who came) after him, and We sent revelation to Abraham, Ismâîl, Isaac, Jacob and his children and to Jesus, Job, Jonah, Aaron and Solomon. And We gave David a Scripture.

164. And (there are some) Messengers whom We have mentioned to you before and (many) Messengers We have not mentioned them to you, and Allâh spoke (to you as He spoke) to Moses in explicit words at great length.

165. All these Messengers (were) Bearers of good tidings (to the believers) and Warners (to the disbelievers, and were sent) so that people may have no plea against Allâh after (the advent of) the Messengers. And Allâh is All-Mighty, All-Wise.

166. (They deny the Qur'ân) but Allâh (Himself) bears witness through His revelation to you that He has revealed it (- the Qur'ân pregnant) with His knowledge, and the angels bear witness (as well). Yet Allâh suffices for a Witness.

167. Those who disbelieve and hinder (others) from (following) Allâh's way, have indeed strayed, a far off straying.

168. Those who have disbelieved and have associated partners with Him, it is not for Allâh to protect them, nor will He show them any way

169. Other than the way leading to Gehenna, wherein they shall live for long; indeed that

لِلْكٰفِرِيْنَ مِنْهُمْ عَذَابًا أَلِيْمًا ﴿١٦١﴾ لٰكِنِ الرّٰسِخُوْنَ
فِي الْعِلْمِ مِنْهُمْ وَ الْمُؤْمِنُوْنَ يُؤْمِنُوْنَ بِمَآ
أُنْزِلَ إِلَيْكَ وَ مَآ أُنْزِلَ مِنْ قَبْلِكَ وَ الْمُقِيْمِيْنَ
الصَّلٰوةَ وَ الْمُؤْتُوْنَ الزَّكٰوةَ وَ الْمُؤْمِنُوْنَ بِاللّٰهِ
وَ الْيَوْمِ الْأٰخِرِ أُولٰٓئِكَ سَنُؤْتِيْهِمْ أَجْرًا
عَظِيْمًا ﴿١٦٢﴾ إِنَّآ أَوْحَيْنَآ إِلَيْكَ كَمَآ أَوْحَيْنَآ إِلٰى
نُوْحٍ وَّ النَّبِيّٖنَ مِنْ بَعْدِهٖ وَ أَوْحَيْنَآ إِلٰٓى
إِبْرٰهِيْمَ وَ إِسْمٰعِيْلَ وَ إِسْحٰقَ وَ يَعْقُوْبَ
وَ الْأَسْبَاطِ وَ عِيْسٰى وَ أَيُّوْبَ وَ يُوْنُسَ
وَ هٰرُوْنَ وَ سُلَيْمٰنَ وَ أٰتَيْنَا دَاوٗدَ زَبُوْرًا ﴿١٦٣﴾
وَ رُسُلًا قَدْ قَصَصْنٰهُمْ عَلَيْكَ مِنْ قَبْلُ
وَ رُسُلًا لَّمْ نَقْصُصْهُمْ عَلَيْكَ وَ كَلَّمَ اللّٰهُ
مُوْسٰى تَكْلِيْمًا ﴿١٦٤﴾ رُسُلًا مُّبَشِّرِيْنَ وَ مُنْذِرِيْنَ
لِئَلَّا يَكُوْنَ لِلنَّاسِ عَلَى اللّٰهِ حُجَّةٌۢ بَعْدَ
الرُّسُلِ وَ كَانَ اللّٰهُ عَزِيْزًا حَكِيْمًا ﴿١٦٥﴾ لٰكِنِ
اللّٰهُ يَشْهَدُ بِمَآ أَنْزَلَ إِلَيْكَ أَنْزَلَهٗ بِعِلْمِهٖ
وَ الْمَلٰٓئِكَةُ يَشْهَدُوْنَ وَ كَفٰى بِاللّٰهِ شَهِيْدًا ﴿١٦٦﴾
إِنَّ الَّذِيْنَ كَفَرُوْا وَ صَدُّوْا عَنْ سَبِيْلِ اللّٰهِ
قَدْ ضَلُّوْا ضَلٰلًا بَعِيْدًا ﴿١٦٧﴾ إِنَّ الَّذِيْنَ كَفَرُوْا
وَ ظَلَمُوْا لَمْ يَكُنِ اللّٰهُ لِيَغْفِرَ لَهُمْ وَ لَا
لِيَهْدِيَهُمْ طَرِيْقًا ﴿١٦٨﴾ إِلَّا طَرِيْقَ جَهَنَّمَ خٰلِدِيْنَ

would be easy for Allâh.

170. O people! This Messenger has indeed come to you with the truth from your Lord, so believe, it will be better for you. But if you disbelieve know that whatever is in the heavens and in the earth belongs to Him. Allâh is ever All-Knowing, All-Wise.

171. O people of the Scripture! Do not go beyond the limits (of propriety) in the matter of your religion, nor say anything regarding Allâh except that which is perfectly true. The Messiah, Jesus, son of Mary was only a Messenger of Allâh, and (a fulfillment of) His word which He communicated to Mary, and a mercy from Him. Believe, therefore, in Allâh and in all His Messengers, and do not say, '(There are) three (Gods).' Refrain (from following this doctrine) it will be better for you. Verily, Allâh is the One and only worthy of worship. He is Holy. Far above having a son. To Him belongs whatever is in the heavens and whatever is in the earth. And Allâh suffices as a Disposer of affairs.

SECTION 24

172. **T**HE Messiah never disdains to be (looked upon as) a servant of Allâh, nor do the angels who are nearest (to Him consider the fact degrading for themselves). And whoever disdains from His service (and worship) and behaves arrogantly, (the day will come when) He will gather them all together to Himself.

173. (On that Day) as to those who believed and did deeds of righteousness, He will give them their rewards in full and will add to them even more out of His bounty. But as for those who disdained (to worship God) and acted arrogantly, He will inflict a woeful punishment on them all. And apart from Allâh they will find for themselves no patron nor helper.

174. O you people! A manifest proof has indeed come to you from your Lord, and We have sent down a clear light to you which distinguishes (the right from the wrong).

فِيهَآ أَبَدًا ۚ وَ كَانَ ذٰلِكَ عَلَى اللّٰهِ يَسِيرًا ﴿١٦٩﴾
يٰٓأَيُّهَا النَّاسُ قَدْ جَآءَكُمُ الرَّسُولُ بِالْحَقِّ
مِنْ رَّبِّكُمْ فَأٰمِنُوا خَيْرًا لَّكُمْ ۚ وَ إِنْ تَكْفُرُوا
فَإِنَّ لِلّٰهِ مَا فِي السَّمٰوٰتِ وَ الْأَرْضِ ۚ وَ كَانَ
اللّٰهُ عَلِيمًا حَكِيمًا ﴿١٧٠﴾ يٰٓأَهْلَ الْكِتٰبِ لَا تَغْلُوا
فِي دِينِكُمْ وَ لَا تَقُولُوا عَلَى اللّٰهِ إِلَّا الْحَقَّ ۚ
إِنَّمَا الْمَسِيحُ عِيسَى ابْنُ مَرْيَمَ رَسُولُ
اللّٰهِ وَ كَلِمَتُهٗٓ ۚ أَلْقٰهَآ إِلٰى مَرْيَمَ وَ رُوحٌ
مِّنْهُ ۫ فَأٰمِنُوا بِاللّٰهِ وَ رُسُلِهٖ ۚ وَ لَا تَقُولُوا
ثَلٰثَةٌ ۚ اِنْتَهُوا خَيْرًا لَّكُمْ ۚ إِنَّمَا اللّٰهُ إِلٰهٌ
وّٰحِدٌ ۚ سُبْحٰنَهٗٓ أَنْ يَّكُونَ لَهٗ وَلَدٌ ۘ لَهٗ مَا
فِي السَّمٰوٰتِ وَ مَا فِي الْأَرْضِ ۚ وَ كَفٰى بِاللّٰهِ
وَكِيلًا ﴿١٧١﴾ لَنْ يَّسْتَنْكِفَ الْمَسِيحُ أَنْ يَّكُونَ
عَبْدًا لِّلّٰهِ وَ لَا الْمَلٰٓئِكَةُ الْمُقَرَّبُونَ ۚ وَ مَنْ
يَّسْتَنْكِفْ عَنْ عِبَادَتِهٖ وَ يَسْتَكْبِرْ
فَسَيَحْشُرُهُمْ إِلَيْهِ جَمِيعًا ﴿١٧٢﴾ فَأَمَّا الَّذِينَ
أٰمَنُوا وَ عَمِلُوا الصّٰلِحٰتِ فَيُوَفِّيهِمْ أُجُورَهُمْ
وَ يَزِيدُهُمْ مِّنْ فَضْلِهٖ ۚ وَ أَمَّا الَّذِينَ اسْتَنْكَفُوا
وَ اسْتَكْبَرُوا فَيُعَذِّبُهُمْ عَذَابًا أَلِيمًا ۙ وَّ لَا
يَجِدُونَ لَهُمْ مِّنْ دُونِ اللّٰهِ وَلِيًّا وَّ لَا
نَصِيرًا ﴿١٧٣﴾ يٰٓأَيُّهَا النَّاسُ قَدْ جَآءَكُمْ بُرْهٰنٌ
مِّنْ رَّبِّكُمْ وَ أَنْزَلْنَآ إِلَيْكُمْ نُورًا مُّبِينًا ﴿١٧٤﴾

175. Now as to those who believe in Allâh and hold fast to Him, He will surely admit them to His mercy and to (His) grace and will guide them along a straight and right path (leading) to Himself.

176. They ask you of your ruling (in the matter of inheritance of a *kalâlah*). Say, 'Allâh gives you His ruling concerning *kalâlah* (- one who has neither parents left nor a child).' If a man dies (and) he has no child but leaves (only) a sister (behind), then she shall inherit half of what he leaves. Likewise he (- the brother who is *kalâlah)* shall inherit her (whole property) if she (- the sister) has no child (and dies). But if there be two sisters (or more) then they shall receive two third of what he (- brother who is *kalâlah)* leaves. And if they (- the survivors) be brethren, men and women, then for the male is the equal of the portion of two females. Allâh makes (His commandments) clear to you lest you should err. And Allâh knows all things well.

فَأَمَّا الَّذِينَ آمَنُوا بِاللَّهِ وَاعْتَصَمُوا بِهِ
فَسَيُدْخِلُهُمْ فِي رَحْمَةٍ مِّنْهُ وَفَضْلٍ
وَيَهْدِيهِمْ إِلَيْهِ صِرَاطًا مُّسْتَقِيمًا ﴿١٧٥﴾ يَسْتَفْتُونَكَ
قُلِ اللَّهُ يُفْتِيكُمْ فِي الْكَلَالَةِ ۚ إِنِ امْرُؤٌا
هَلَكَ لَيْسَ لَهُ وَلَدٌ وَلَهُ أُخْتٌ فَلَهَا نِصْفُ
مَا تَرَكَ ۚ وَهُوَ يَرِثُهَا إِن لَّمْ يَكُن لَّهَا وَلَدٌ ۚ
فَإِن كَانَتَا اثْنَتَيْنِ فَلَهُمَا الثُّلُثَانِ مِمَّا
تَرَكَ ۚ وَإِن كَانُوا إِخْوَةً رِّجَالًا وَنِسَاءً
فَلِلذَّكَرِ مِثْلُ حَظِّ الْأُنثَيَيْنِ ۗ يُبَيِّنُ اللَّهُ
لَكُمْ أَن تَضِلُّوا ۗ وَاللَّهُ بِكُلِّ شَيْءٍ عَلِيمٌ ﴿١٧٦﴾

CHAPTER
5

سُورَةُ المَائِدَةِ مَدَنِيَّةٌ

AL-MÂ'IDAH
(The Table Spread with Food)
(Revealed after Hijrah)

With the name of Allâh,
the Most Gracious, the Ever Merciful
(I commence to read Sûrah Al-Mâ'idah).

بِسْمِ اللَّهِ الرَّحْمَٰنِ الرَّحِيمِ

1. **O** YOU who believe! Abide by all (your) obligations. All quadrupeds (of the class) of cattle (and feeding on plants) are made lawful to you (for food) other than those which are enumerated to you (as forbidden). Yet you are forbidden (to kill) game whilst in a pilgrim's garb or in the Sacred Precincts. Verily, Allâh decrees what He intends.

2. O you who believe! Do not desecrate the symbols (that lead to the knowledge and

يَا أَيُّهَا الَّذِينَ آمَنُوا أَوْفُوا بِالْعُقُودِ ۚ
أُحِلَّتْ لَكُم بَهِيمَةُ الْأَنْعَامِ إِلَّا مَا يُتْلَىٰ
عَلَيْكُمْ غَيْرَ مُحِلِّي الصَّيْدِ وَأَنتُمْ حُرُمٌ ۗ
إِنَّ اللَّهَ يَحْكُمُ مَا يُرِيدُ ﴿١﴾ يَا أَيُّهَا الَّذِينَ

realisation) of Allâh, nor any sacred month, nor the animals brought as an offering, nor those animals wearing necklaces (as a mark of sacrifice during the *Hajj),* nor those (Pilgrims) repairing to the Sacred House, seeking favour and grace of their Lord and (His) good pleasure. And when you are free from Pilgrimage, having taken off the Pilgrims garb and are off the Sacred Precincts you may go hunting. And do not let the enmity of a people (and your grievances) that they hindered you from the *Masjid al-Harâm* (- Holy Mosque at Makkah) incite you to transgression (against them). Help one another in righteousness and in warding off evil, but do not help one another to commit sin and transgression, and take Allâh as a shield. Surely, Allâh is Severe in retribution.

3. You are forbidden (to take for food) an animal which dies of itself (a carrion), and the blood (poured forth), also the flesh of swine, and that which is immolated in the name of anyone other than Allâh, and that which has been strangled, and that which has been beaten to death, and that which has been killed by a fall, and that which has been gored to death, and that of which a wild beast has eaten, except what you have duly slaughtered (before its expiry). And (also forbidden to you is) that which has been slaughtered at altars (set up for false deities), and (you are also not permitted) that you seek to know your lot by the divining arrows. These are all acts of disobedience. This day have those who disbelieve despaired of (harming) your Faith. So do not hold them in awe but stand in awe of Me. This day have I perfected for you your faith and completed My blessings upon you and have chosen Islam for your Faith (so abide by all these limits imposed upon you with regard to taking your food); but he who is forced by extreme hunger without being wilfully inclined to sin then, surely (he will find that) Allâh is Great Protector, Ever Merciful.

4. They ask you what is made lawful for them. Say, 'All good and pure things are made lawful

آمَنُوا لَا تُحِلُّوا شَعَائِرَ اللَّهِ وَلَا الشَّهْرَ الْحَرَامَ
وَلَا الْهَدْيَ وَلَا الْقَلَائِدَ وَلَا آمِّينَ الْبَيْتَ
الْحَرَامَ يَبْتَغُونَ فَضْلًا مِنْ رَبِّهِمْ وَرِضْوَانًا
وَإِذَا حَلَلْتُمْ فَاصْطَادُوا وَلَا يَجْرِمَنَّكُمْ
شَنَآنُ قَوْمٍ أَنْ صَدُّوكُمْ عَنِ الْمَسْجِدِ
الْحَرَامِ أَنْ تَعْتَدُوا وَتَعَاوَنُوا عَلَى الْبِرِّ
وَالتَّقْوَى وَلَا تَعَاوَنُوا عَلَى الْإِثْمِ وَالْعُدْوَانِ
وَاتَّقُوا اللَّهَ إِنَّ اللَّهَ شَدِيدُ الْعِقَابِ ﴿٢﴾
حُرِّمَتْ عَلَيْكُمُ الْمَيْتَةُ وَالدَّمُ وَلَحْمُ
الْخِنْزِيرِ وَمَا أُهِلَّ لِغَيْرِ اللَّهِ بِهِ
وَالْمُنْخَنِقَةُ وَالْمَوْقُوذَةُ وَالْمُتَرَدِّيَةُ وَالنَّطِيحَةُ
وَمَا أَكَلَ السَّبُعُ إِلَّا مَا ذَكَّيْتُمْ وَمَا ذُبِحَ
عَلَى النُّصُبِ وَأَنْ تَسْتَقْسِمُوا بِالْأَزْلَامِ
ذَٰلِكُمْ فِسْقٌ الْيَوْمَ يَئِسَ الَّذِينَ كَفَرُوا
مِنْ دِينِكُمْ فَلَا تَخْشَوْهُمْ وَاخْشَوْنِ الْيَوْمَ
أَكْمَلْتُ لَكُمْ دِينَكُمْ وَأَتْمَمْتُ عَلَيْكُمْ
نِعْمَتِي وَرَضِيتُ لَكُمُ الْإِسْلَامَ دِينًا فَمَنِ
اضْطُرَّ فِي مَخْمَصَةٍ غَيْرَ مُتَجَانِفٍ لِإِثْمٍ
فَإِنَّ اللَّهَ غَفُورٌ رَحِيمٌ ﴿٣﴾ يَسْأَلُونَكَ مَاذَا

for you. Also (made lawful) is the game held down by those birds and beasts of prey which you have trained, provided you set them at it to catch (it living) for you, (without their own eating from it after killing it), since you train them according to the knowledge Allâh has given you. So eat of that which they hold down for you and pronounce thereon the name of Allâh (while slaughtering it or while sending the hunting creatures after it). And take Allâh as a shield. Surely, Allâh is Swift in reckoning.
5. This day all good and pure things have been made lawful for you. And the food of those who have been given the Scripture is lawful for you (provided the food does not include anything forbidden in Islam), and your food is lawful for them. And (lawful for you for marriage are) the chaste women from among the believing women and chaste women from among those who have been given the Scripture before you, provided that you pay them their dowers (to live with them) after contracting valid marriage, not committing fornication, nor seeking secret love affairs by taking secret paramours. And whoever denies the commandments of (the true) faith, no doubt (he will find) his deeds have gone in vain and he will be of the losers in the Hereafter.

SECTION 2

6. **O** YOU who believe! When you get up for Prayer (perform the ablution, so as to) wash your faces and your hands up to the elbows, and pass your (wet) hands over your heads (for *masah*), and (wash) your feet up to the ankles. And if you are under an obligation to perform a bath, then wash yourselves thoroughly clean by a bath. But if you have been taken ill or on a journey (while under obligation to take a bath) or one of you comes from the privy, or you have had (sexual) contact with women and you do not find water, then have recourse to clean pure dust and wipe your faces and your

أُحِلَّ لَهُمْ قُلْ أُحِلَّ لَكُمُ الطَّيِّبٰتُ وَمَا
عَلَّمْتُم مِّنَ الْجَوَارِحِ مُكَلِّبِينَ تُعَلِّمُونَهُنَّ
مِمَّا عَلَّمَكُمُ اللّٰهُ فَكُلُوا مِمَّا أَمْسَكْنَ عَلَيْكُمْ
وَاذْكُرُوا اسْمَ اللّٰهِ عَلَيْهِ وَاتَّقُوا اللّٰهَ إِنَّ
اللّٰهَ سَرِيعُ الْحِسَابِ ④ اَلْيَوْمَ أُحِلَّ لَكُمُ
الطَّيِّبٰتُ وَطَعَامُ الَّذِينَ أُوتُوا الْكِتٰبَ حِلٌّ
لَّكُمْ وَطَعَامُكُمْ حِلٌّ لَّهُمْ وَالْمُحْصَنٰتُ
مِنَ الْمُؤْمِنٰتِ وَالْمُحْصَنٰتُ مِنَ الَّذِينَ
أُوتُوا الْكِتٰبَ مِن قَبْلِكُمْ إِذَا آتَيْتُمُوهُنَّ
أُجُورَهُنَّ مُحْصِنِينَ غَيْرَ مُسٰفِحِينَ وَلَا
مُتَّخِذِي أَخْدَانٍ وَمَن يَكْفُرْ بِالْإِيمٰنِ
فَقَدْ حَبِطَ عَمَلُهُ وَهُوَ فِي الْآخِرَةِ مِنَ
الْخٰسِرِينَ ⑤ يٰأَيُّهَا الَّذِينَ آمَنُوا إِذَا قُمْتُمْ
إِلَى الصَّلٰوةِ فَاغْسِلُوا وُجُوهَكُمْ وَأَيْدِيَكُمْ
إِلَى الْمَرَافِقِ وَامْسَحُوا بِرُءُوسِكُمْ وَأَرْجُلَكُمْ
إِلَى الْكَعْبَيْنِ وَإِن كُنتُمْ جُنُبًا فَاطَّهَّرُوا
وَإِن كُنتُم مَّرْضَى أَوْ عَلَى سَفَرٍ أَوْ جَاءَ أَحَدٌ
مِّنكُم مِّنَ الْغَائِطِ أَوْ لٰمَسْتُمُ النِّسَاءَ فَلَمْ

ع ٥

hands with it (as *Tayammum).* Allâh does not intend to impose any impediments on you, but He intends to purify you (internally and externally) and complete His blessings upon you so that you may give (Him) thanks.

7. And (O Muslims!) Remember Allâh's favour which rests upon you (in the form of the Qur'ân) and (to abide by its teachings) His covenant to which He has bound you, when you said, 'We hear (your commandments) and we obey (them).' And take Allâh as a shield. Verily, Allâh knows well what is in the inmost depths of the minds.

8. O you who believe! Be steadfast, upholders of the right for the cause of Allâh, bearers of true witness in equity, and do not let the enmity of a people move you at all to act otherwise than equitably. Be equitable (always); that is nearer to being secure against evil, and take Allâh as a shield. Surely, Allâh is Well-Aware of what you do.

9. Allâh has promised protection and a great reward for those who believe and do deeds of righteousness.

10. But as to those who disbelieve and reject Our Messages it is these who are the fellows of the blazing Fire.

11. O you who believe! Remember Allâh's favour upon you when a people had made up their minds to lay their hands on you, but He withheld their hands from you; and take Allâh as a shield. The believers should then put (their) trust in Allâh.

SECTION 3

12. **A**ND Allâh, indeed, took a covenant from the Children of Israel, and We raised twelve chieftains from among them. And Allâh said, 'Surely, I am with you. If you observe prayer and present the *Zakât* (purifying-dues) and believe in My Messengers and lend them support in a respectful manner, and perform an act of virtue and cut off a portion of your goodly

تَجِدُوا مَاءً فَتَيَمَّمُوا صَعِيدًا طَيِّبًا فَامْسَحُوا
بِوُجُوهِكُمْ وَأَيْدِيكُم مِّنْهُ مَا يُرِيدُ اللّٰهُ
لِيَجْعَلَ عَلَيْكُم مِّنْ حَرَجٍ وَّلٰكِن يُّرِيدُ
لِيُطَهِّرَكُمْ وَلِيُتِمَّ نِعْمَتَهُ عَلَيْكُمْ لَعَلَّكُمْ
تَشْكُرُونَ ⑥ وَاذْكُرُوا نِعْمَةَ اللّٰهِ عَلَيْكُمْ
وَمِيثَاقَهُ الَّذِي وَاثَقَكُم بِهِ إِذْ قُلْتُمْ سَمِعْنَا
وَأَطَعْنَا وَاتَّقُوا اللّٰهَ إِنَّ اللّٰهَ عَلِيمٌ بِذَاتِ
الصُّدُورِ ⑦ يٰأَيُّهَا الَّذِينَ آمَنُوا كُونُوا
قَوّٰمِينَ لِلّٰهِ شُهَدَاءَ بِالْقِسْطِ وَلَا يَجْرِمَنَّكُمْ
شَنَآنُ قَوْمٍ عَلَىٰ أَلَّا تَعْدِلُوا اعْدِلُوا هُوَ
أَقْرَبُ لِلتَّقْوَىٰ وَاتَّقُوا اللّٰهَ إِنَّ اللّٰهَ خَبِيرٌ
بِمَا تَعْمَلُونَ ⑧ وَعَدَ اللّٰهُ الَّذِينَ آمَنُوا
وَعَمِلُوا الصّٰلِحٰتِ لَهُم مَّغْفِرَةٌ وَّأَجْرٌ عَظِيمٌ ⑨
وَالَّذِينَ كَفَرُوا وَكَذَّبُوا بِآيٰتِنَا أُولٰئِكَ
أَصْحٰبُ الْجَحِيمِ ⑩ يٰأَيُّهَا الَّذِينَ آمَنُوا
اذْكُرُوا نِعْمَتَ اللّٰهِ عَلَيْكُمْ إِذْ هَمَّ قَوْمٌ
أَن يَّبْسُطُوا إِلَيْكُمْ أَيْدِيَهُمْ فَكَفَّ أَيْدِيَهُمْ
عَنكُمْ وَاتَّقُوا اللّٰهَ وَعَلَى اللّٰهِ فَلْيَتَوَكَّلِ
الْمُؤْمِنُونَ ⑪ وَلَقَدْ أَخَذَ اللّٰهُ مِيثَاقَ بَنِي
إِسْرٰٓءِيلَ وَبَعَثْنَا مِنْهُمُ اثْنَيْ عَشَرَ نَقِيبًا
وَقَالَ اللّٰهُ إِنِّي مَعَكُمْ لَئِنْ أَقَمْتُمُ الصَّلٰوةَ

ع ٣

gifts for (the cause of) Allâh, I will certainly absolve you of your sins and will surely admit you to Gardens served with running streams. But if anyone of you disbelieves after that surely he has strayed away from the right way.
13. So on account of their breaking their covenant We deprived them of Our blessings, and We let their hearts become hardened. Now they pervert the words from their proper context (of the Divine Book) and (in doing so) they have abandoned a good portion of what they were (reminded of and) exhorted with. And you will never cease to discover one dishonesty (or the other) on their part, with the exception of a few of them; so pardon them and pass (them) over. Verily, Allâh loves the doers of good to others.
14. We took the covenant of those (also) who say, 'We are Christians;' but they have abandoned a good portion of what they were (reminded of and) exhorted with. So We have kindled enmity and hatred between (various sects of) them till the Day of Resurrection. And Allâh will soon inform them of all their machination.
15. O people of the Scripture! Our Messenger, who has come to you, unfolds many teachings of the Scripture which you had kept hidden, and many a thing he passes over. There has come to you, indeed, from Allâh a Light and the perspicuous Book (- the Qur'ân) that distinguishes the right from the wrong.
16. Allâh guides with this (Book) those who follow His good pleasure to the ways of peace (both physical and spiritual), and He takes them out of all kinds of darkness into the light, by His leave, and guides them along the exact right path.
17. They have only disbelieved who say, 'Verily, Allâh - He is the Messiah, son of Mary.' Say, 'Who then had any power to stand in the way of Allâh when He intended to put an end

وَ أَتَيْتُمُ الزَّكٰوةَ وَ أٰمَنْتُمْ بِرُسُلِي
وَعَزَّرْتُمُوهُمْ وَأَقْرَضْتُمُ اللّٰهَ قَرْضًا حَسَنًا
لَأُكَفِّرَنَّ عَنْكُمْ سَيِّاٰتِكُمْ وَ لَأُدْخِلَنَّكُمْ
جَنّٰتٍ تَجْرِي مِنْ تَحْتِهَا الْأَنْهٰرُ فَمَنْ
كَفَرَ بَعْدَ ذٰلِكَ مِنْكُمْ فَقَدْ ضَلَّ سَوَآءَ
السَّبِيلِ ﴿١٢﴾ فَبِمَا نَقْضِهِمْ مِّيثٰقَهُمْ لَعَنّٰهُمْ
وَجَعَلْنَا قُلُوبَهُمْ قٰسِيَةً يُحَرِّفُونَ الْكَلِمَ
عَنْ مَّوَاضِعِهِ وَنَسُوا حَظًّا مِّمَّا ذُكِّرُوا بِهِ
وَلَا تَزَالُ تَطَّلِعُ عَلٰى خَآئِنَةٍ مِّنْهُمْ إِلَّا
قَلِيلًا مِّنْهُمْ فَاعْفُ عَنْهُمْ وَ اصْفَحْ إِنَّ
اللّٰهَ يُحِبُّ الْمُحْسِنِينَ ﴿١٣﴾ وَ مِنَ الَّذِينَ
قَالُوا إِنَّا نَصٰرٰى أَخَذْنَا مِيثٰقَهُمْ فَنَسُوا
حَظًّا مِّمَّا ذُكِّرُوا بِهِ فَأَغْرَيْنَا بَيْنَهُمُ
الْعَدَاوَةَ وَ الْبَغْضَآءَ إِلٰى يَوْمِ الْقِيٰمَةِ
وَسَوْفَ يُنَبِّئُهُمُ اللّٰهُ بِمَا كَانُوا يَصْنَعُونَ ﴿١٤﴾
يٰٓأَهْلَ الْكِتٰبِ قَدْ جَآءَكُمْ رَسُولُنَا يُبَيِّنُ
لَكُمْ كَثِيرًا مِّمَّا كُنْتُمْ تُخْفُونَ مِنَ الْكِتٰبِ
وَيَعْفُوا عَنْ كَثِيرٍ قَدْ جَآءَكُمْ مِّنَ اللّٰهِ
نُورٌ وَّ كِتٰبٌ مُّبِينٌ ﴿١٥﴾ يَّهْدِي بِهِ اللّٰهُ مَنِ
اتَّبَعَ رِضْوٰنَهُ سُبُلَ السَّلٰمِ وَ يُخْرِجُهُمْ
مِّنَ الظُّلُمٰتِ إِلَى النُّورِ بِإِذْنِهِ وَيَهْدِيهِمْ
إِلٰى صِرٰطٍ مُّسْتَقِيمٍ ﴿١٦﴾ لَقَدْ كَفَرَ الَّذِينَ
قَالُوا إِنَّ اللّٰهَ هُوَ الْمَسِيحُ ابْنُ مَرْيَمَ قُلْ

to the Messiah, son of Mary, and his mother, and all those that were in the earth?' And to Allâh belongs the sovereignty of the heavens and the earth and all that lies between the two. He creates what He will, for He is the Possessor of full power to do all that He will.

18. The Jews and the Christians say (in respect of their respective selves), 'We are the sons of Allâh, and His loved ones.' Say, 'Why then does He punish you for your sins? Nay, you are but human beings like many of His creation.' He protects whom He will and punishes whom He will. To Allâh belongs the sovereignty of the heavens and the earth and all that lies between the two and to Him is the (final) return (of all).

19. O people of the Scripture! There has already come to you Our Messenger who makes things clear to you after a break in the series of Messengers lest you should say, 'There has not come to us any Bearer of good tidings, nor a Warner.' Now there has, indeed, come to you a Bearer of good tidings and a Warner. And Allâh is the Possessor of full power to do all that He will.

SECTION 4

20. **A**ND (recall the time) when Moses said to his people, 'O my people! Remember Allâh's blessings upon you when He raised Prophets among you and made you masters of your own affairs, and He gave you what He has not given to any other of your contemporary peoples.

21. 'O my people, enter the Holy Land which Allâh has ordained for you, and turn not on your backs, for then you turn losers.'

22. They said, 'O Moses! Surely there are in that (land) arrogant and exceedingly powerful people and we shall never enter it until they depart from it, but if they depart from it, then we will certainly enter (it).'

23. (Thereupon) two men (- Joshua and Caleb) from among those who feared (their Lord) and

فَمَنْ يَّمْلِكُ مِنَ اللّٰهِ شَيْـًٔا إِنْ أَرَادَ أَنْ
يُّهْلِكَ الْمَسِيْحَ ابْنَ مَرْيَمَ وَأُمَّهٗ وَمَنْ
فِي الْأَرْضِ جَمِيْعًا ۭ وَلِلّٰهِ مُلْكُ السَّمٰوٰتِ
وَالْأَرْضِ وَمَا بَيْنَهُمَا ۭ يَخْلُقُ مَا يَشَآءُ ۭ
وَاللّٰهُ عَلٰى كُلِّ شَيْءٍ قَدِيْرٌ ﴿١٧﴾ وَقَالَتِ الْيَهُوْدُ
وَالنَّصٰرٰى نَحْنُ أَبْنٰٓؤُا اللّٰهِ وَأَحِبّٰٓؤُهٗ ۭ قُلْ
فَلِمَ يُعَذِّبُكُمْ بِذُنُوْبِكُمْ ۭ بَلْ أَنْتُمْ بَشَرٌ
مِّمَّنْ خَلَقَ ۭ يَغْفِرُ لِمَنْ يَّشَآءُ وَيُعَذِّبُ مَنْ
يَّشَآءُ ۭ وَلِلّٰهِ مُلْكُ السَّمٰوٰتِ وَالْأَرْضِ وَمَا
بَيْنَهُمَا ۡ وَإِلَيْهِ الْمَصِيْرُ ﴿١٨﴾ يٰٓأَهْلَ الْكِتٰبِ
قَدْ جَآءَكُمْ رَسُوْلُنَا يُبَيِّنُ لَكُمْ عَلٰى فَتْرَةٍ
مِّنَ الرُّسُلِ أَنْ تَقُوْلُوْا مَا جَآءَنَا مِنْۢ بَشِيْرٍ
وَّلَا نَذِيْرٍ ۡ فَقَدْ جَآءَكُمْ بَشِيْرٌ وَّنَذِيْرٌ ۭ
وَاللّٰهُ عَلٰى كُلِّ شَيْءٍ قَدِيْرٌ ﴿١٩﴾ وَإِذْ قَالَ مُوْسٰى
لِقَوْمِهٖ يٰقَوْمِ اذْكُرُوْا نِعْمَةَ اللّٰهِ عَلَيْكُمْ
إِذْ جَعَلَ فِيْكُمْ أَنْبِيَآءَ وَجَعَلَكُمْ مُّلُوْكًا ۖ
وَّاٰتٰىكُمْ مَّا لَمْ يُؤْتِ أَحَدًا مِّنَ الْعٰلَمِيْنَ ﴿٢٠﴾
يٰقَوْمِ ادْخُلُوا الْأَرْضَ الْمُقَدَّسَةَ الَّتِيْ كَتَبَ
اللّٰهُ لَكُمْ وَلَا تَرْتَدُّوْا عَلٰٓى أَدْبَارِكُمْ فَتَنْقَلِبُوْا
خٰسِرِيْنَ ﴿٢١﴾ قَالُوْا يٰمُوْسٰٓى إِنَّ فِيْهَا قَوْمًا
جَبَّارِيْنَ ۖ وَإِنَّا لَنْ نَّدْخُلَهَا حَتّٰى يَخْرُجُوْا
مِنْهَا ۚ فَإِنْ يَّخْرُجُوْا مِنْهَا فَإِنَّا دٰخِلُوْنَ ﴿٢٢﴾

on whom Allâh had bestowed His blessings said, 'Enter the gate (of the city advancing) against them, for when once you have entered it you shall surely be victorious, and in Allâh you should put your trust when you are believers (in Him).'

24. They said, 'O Moses! We will, certainly, never enter it so long as they are therein, so go forth you and your Lord, then fight (there) you two, surely, we will sit down here (and watch).'

25. (Moses) said, 'My Lord! Surely, I have no control but on myself and my brother (Aaron), therefore bring about separation between us and these disobedient people.'

26. (God) said, 'Verily, it (- the Holy Land) is forbidden to them for forty years. They shall wander about in the earth distracted and in confusion, so grieve not over these disobedient people.'

SECTION 5

27. **A**ND relate to them with the truth the great news of the two sons of Adam, when they (each) made an offering, and it was accepted from one of them and was not accepted from the other. (The latter whose offering was not accepted, out of jealousy for the other) said, 'I will slay you.' He replied, '(How can I be held responsible for the rejection of your offering;) Allâh accepts only from those who become secure against evil,

28. 'Should you lay your hand on me to kill me, I am not at all going to lay my hand on you to kill you. I do fear Allâh, the Lord of the worlds;

29. 'I would rather like you to bear (the burden of) the sin (committed) against me (- the sin of the murder), and (that of) your own sin (committed previously due to which your offering was not accepted), and thus you would become of the fellows of the Fire.' Such indeed is the recompense of the wrongdoers.

30. But (the baser instincts of) his mind prompted him (whose offering was not accepted) to kill

قال رجلان من الذين يخافون أنعم
الله عليهما ادخلوا عليهم الباب فإذا
دخلتموه فإنكم غلبون وعلى الله فتوكلوا
إن كنتم مؤمنين ﴿٢٣﴾ قالوا يموسى إنا لن
ندخلها أبدا ما داموا فيها فاذهب أنت
وربك فقتلا إنا ههنا قعدون ﴿٢٤﴾ قال
رب إني لا أملك إلا نفسي وأخي فافرق
بيننا وبين القوم الفسقين ﴿٢٥﴾ قال فإنها
محرمة عليهم أربعين سنة يتيهون
في الأرض فلا تأس على القوم الفسقين ﴿٢٦﴾
واتل عليهم نبأ ابني آدم بالحق إذ قربا
قربانا فتقبل من أحدهما ولم يتقبل
من الآخر قال لأقتلنك قال إنما يتقبل
الله من المتقين ﴿٢٧﴾ لئن بسطت إلي يدك
لتقتلني ما أنا بباسط يدي إليك لأقتلك
إني أخاف الله رب العلمين ﴿٢٨﴾ إني أريد
أن تبوأ بإثمي وإثمك فتكون من
أصحب النار وذلك جزؤا الظلمين ﴿٢٩﴾

his brother (whose offering was accepted), so he killed him, wherefore he became one of the losers.
31. Then Allâh sent a raven which scratched into the earth so as to show him how he might cover his brother's dead body. He said, 'Woe is me! Am I unable to be even like this raven so that I may cover the dead body of my brother?' And he became one of the remorseful.
32. Because of this (incident) We laid down for the Children of Israel that he who kills a human being - unless it be for (murdering) a person or for (reforming) disorder in the country, it is as if he has killed the entire human race. And whoso saves a (human) life it is as if he has saved the entire humankind. Certainly, Our Messengers had already come to them with clear arguments, yet (even after that) many of them were certainly those who committed excesses in the land.
33. The only recompense of those who make war against Allâh and His Messenger and who strive hard to create disorder in the land, is (according to the nature of the crime) that they be executed or crucified to death, or that their hands and feet be cut off on account of their opposition, or their (free) movement in the land be banned (by exile or imprisonment). This would mean ignominy for them in this world and there awaits them in the Hereafter a severe punishment.
34. Different, however, is the case of those (criminals) who turn with repentance before you overpower them. And know that, surely, Allâh is Great Protector, Ever Merciful.

SECTION 6

35. **O** YOU who believe! Take Allâh as a shield and seek means of nearness to Him, and struggle for His cause, so that you may attain your goal.
36. As for those who disbelieve even if they come to possess all that is in the earth and as much more (to offer) that they might redeem themselves therewith from the punishment of the Day of Resurrection, it would not be

فَطَوَّعَتْ لَهُ نَفْسُهُ قَتْلَ أَخِيهِ فَقَتَلَهُ
فَأَصْبَحَ مِنَ الْخٰسِرِينَ ﴿٣٠﴾ فَبَعَثَ اللّٰهُ غُرَابًا
يَّبْحَثُ فِي الْأَرْضِ لِيُرِيَهُ كَيْفَ يُوٰرِي
سَوْءَةَ أَخِيهِ قَالَ يٰوَيْلَتٰٓى أَعَجَزْتُ أَنْ
أَكُونَ مِثْلَ هٰذَا الْغُرَابِ فَأُوٰرِيَ سَوْءَةَ
أَخِي فَأَصْبَحَ مِنَ النّٰدِمِينَ ﴿٣١﴾ مِنْ أَجْلِ
ذٰلِكَ كَتَبْنَا عَلٰى بَنِيٓ إِسْرَآءِيلَ أَنَّهُ مَنْ
قَتَلَ نَفْسًا بِغَيْرِ نَفْسٍ أَوْ فَسَادٍ فِي الْأَرْضِ
فَكَأَنَّمَا قَتَلَ النَّاسَ جَمِيعًا وَمَنْ أَحْيَاهَا
فَكَأَنَّمَا أَحْيَا النَّاسَ جَمِيعًا وَلَقَدْ جَآءَتْهُمْ
رُسُلُنَا بِالْبَيِّنٰتِ ثُمَّ إِنَّ كَثِيرًا مِّنْهُمْ بَعْدَ
ذٰلِكَ فِي الْأَرْضِ لَمُسْرِفُونَ ﴿٣٢﴾ إِنَّمَا جَزٰٓؤُا
الَّذِينَ يُحَارِبُونَ اللّٰهَ وَرَسُولَهُ وَيَسْعَوْنَ
فِي الْأَرْضِ فَسَادًا أَنْ يُّقَتَّلُوٓا أَوْ يُصَلَّبُوٓا
أَوْ تُقَطَّعَ أَيْدِيهِمْ وَأَرْجُلُهُمْ مِّنْ خِلٰفٍ
أَوْ يُنْفَوْا مِنَ الْأَرْضِ ذٰلِكَ لَهُمْ خِزْيٌ فِي
الدُّنْيَا وَلَهُمْ فِي الْأٰخِرَةِ عَذَابٌ عَظِيمٌ ﴿٣٣﴾
إِلَّا الَّذِينَ تَابُوا مِنْ قَبْلِ أَنْ تَقْدِرُوا
عَلَيْهِمْ فَاعْلَمُوٓا أَنَّ اللّٰهَ غَفُورٌ رَّحِيمٌ ﴿٣٤﴾
يٰٓأَيُّهَا الَّذِينَ أٰمَنُوا اتَّقُوا اللّٰهَ وَابْتَغُوٓا إِلَيْهِ
الْوَسِيلَةَ وَجٰهِدُوا فِي سَبِيلِهِ لَعَلَّكُمْ
تُفْلِحُونَ ﴿٣٥﴾ إِنَّ الَّذِينَ كَفَرُوا لَوْ أَنَّ لَهُمْ
مَّا فِي الْأَرْضِ جَمِيعًا وَّمِثْلَهُ مَعَهُ لِيَفْتَدُوا

accepted from them. There awaits them a grievous punishment.

37. They would wish to come out of the Fire but they will not be able to come out of it (of themselves). There awaits them a long-lasting punishment.

38. And as for the man addicted to theft and the woman addicted to theft, cut off their hands in retribution of (the crime) that they have committed - an exemplary punishment from Allâh. And Allâh is All-Mighty, All-Wise.

39. But whoso turns in repentance after his committing an unjust deed and reforms (himself) then surely Allâh will turn to him with mercy. Verily, Allâh is Great Protector, Ever Merciful.

40. Do you not know that Allâh is He to Whom belongs the sovereignty of the heavens and the earth? He punishes whom He will and protects whom He will. And Allâh is the Possessor of full power to do all that He will.

41. O Messenger! Let not those who vie with one another in (spreading) disbelief, those of them who say with their mouths, 'we believe', but their hearts believe not, and those of them who judaised, grieve you. They are the acceptors of falsehood and are those who listen for conveying to other people who have not yet come to you. They tear the words (of God) from their proper places (and pervert the meanings thereof and) say, 'If you are given this (sort of commandment) accept it and if you are not given this, then be careful.' And he (on) whom Allâh desires (to inflict) His punishment, you can do nothing to save him from (the punishment of) Allâh. It is these whose hearts Allâh has not been pleased to purify. Ignominy is their lot in this world, and there awaits them in the Hereafter a great punishment.

42. (They are) habitual listeners to falsehood, too much given to eat things forbidden. If they come to you (seeking your judgment) judge between them or turn aside from them. If you turn aside from them, they shall do you no harm

بِهٖ مِنْ عَذَابِ يَوْمِ الْقِيٰمَةِ مَا تُقُبِّلَ
مِنْهُمْ وَلَهُمْ عَذَابٌ أَلِيمٌ ﴿٣٦﴾ يُرِيدُونَ
أَنْ يَخْرُجُوا مِنَ النَّارِ وَمَا هُمْ بِخٰرِجِينَ
مِنْهَا وَلَهُمْ عَذَابٌ مُّقِيمٌ ﴿٣٧﴾ وَالسَّارِقُ
وَالسَّارِقَةُ فَاقْطَعُوٓا أَيْدِيَهُمَا جَزَآءًۢ بِمَا
كَسَبَا نَكٰلًا مِّنَ اللّٰهِ وَاللّٰهُ عَزِيزٌ حَكِيمٌ ﴿٣٨﴾
فَمَنْ تَابَ مِنْۢ بَعْدِ ظُلْمِهٖ وَأَصْلَحَ فَإِنَّ
اللّٰهَ يَتُوبُ عَلَيْهِ إِنَّ اللّٰهَ غَفُورٌ رَّحِيمٌ ﴿٣٩﴾
أَلَمْ تَعْلَمْ أَنَّ اللّٰهَ لَهٗ مُلْكُ السَّمٰوٰتِ
وَالْأَرْضِ يُعَذِّبُ مَنْ يَّشَآءُ وَيَغْفِرُ لِمَنْ
يَّشَآءُ وَاللّٰهُ عَلٰى كُلِّ شَيْءٍ قَدِيرٌ ﴿٤٠﴾ يٰٓأَيُّهَا
الرَّسُولُ لَا يَحْزُنْكَ الَّذِينَ يُسٰرِعُونَ
فِي الْكُفْرِ مِنَ الَّذِينَ قَالُوٓا أٰمَنَّا بِأَفْوٰهِهِمْ
وَلَمْ تُؤْمِنْ قُلُوبُهُمْ وَمِنَ الَّذِينَ هَادُوا
سَمّٰعُونَ لِلْكَذِبِ سَمّٰعُونَ لِقَوْمٍ أٰخَرِينَ
لَمْ يَأْتُوكَ يُحَرِّفُونَ الْكَلِمَ مِنْۢ بَعْدِ
مَوَاضِعِهٖ يَقُولُونَ إِنْ أُوتِيتُمْ هٰذَا
فَخُذُوهُ وَإِنْ لَّمْ تُؤْتَوْهُ فَاحْذَرُوا وَمَنْ
يُّرِدِ اللّٰهُ فِتْنَتَهٗ فَلَنْ تَمْلِكَ لَهٗ مِنَ اللّٰهِ
شَيْـًٔا أُولٰٓئِكَ الَّذِينَ لَمْ يُرِدِ اللّٰهُ أَنْ يُّطَهِّرَ
قُلُوبَهُمْ لَهُمْ فِي الدُّنْيَا خِزْيٌ وَّلَهُمْ فِي
الْأٰخِرَةِ عَذَابٌ عَظِيمٌ ﴿٤١﴾ سَمّٰعُونَ لِلْكَذِبِ

at all. But if you judge, then judge between them with justice, for surely Allâh loves the just.

43. And how should they appoint you their judge whilst they have with them the Torah which contains the law (and judgment) of Allâh. Yet they turn their backs even after that (you judge between them). And such people are not true believers (neither in the Qur'ân nor in the Torah).

SECTION 7

44. **V**ERILY, it is We Who revealed Torah wherein there was guidance and light. According to it the Prophets, who submitted themselves (to Us), did judge for those who judaised and (so also did) the teachers of Divine knowledge, and those learned (in the Law); (they did it) because they were required to preserve some of the Scripture of Allâh and (because) they stood guardians over it. Hence hold not people in awe but stand in awe of Me and do not barter away My Messages for a trifling gain. And he who does not judge according to that (law) which Allâh has revealed, it is these who are the real disbelievers.

45. And therein We laid down (the following law) for them (- the Jews); life for life and eye for eye, and nose for nose, and ear for ear, and tooth for tooth and for (other) injuries an equitable retaliation. But he who chooses to forgo (the right) thereto for the sake of Allâh, it shall be an expiation of sins for him. And whoever does not judge according to (the law) which Allâh has revealed, these it is who are the very unjust.

46. And We sent Jesus, son of Mary, in the footsteps of these (Prophets), fulfilling that which was (revealed) before him, of the Torah, and We gave him the Evangel which contained guidance and light, fulfilling that which was (revealed) before it, of the Torah, and was a (means of) guidance and an exhortation for

أَكّٰلُونَ لِلسُّحْتِ ۚ فَإِنْ جَآءُوكَ فَاحْكُمْ
بَيْنَهُمْ أَوْ أَعْرِضْ عَنْهُمْ ۚ وَإِنْ تُعْرِضْ
عَنْهُمْ فَلَنْ يَّضُرُّوكَ شَيْئًا ۚ وَإِنْ حَكَمْتَ
فَاحْكُمْ بَيْنَهُمْ بِالْقِسْطِ ۚ إِنَّ اللّٰهَ يُحِبُّ
الْمُقْسِطِينَ ﴿٤٢﴾ وَكَيْفَ يُحَكِّمُونَكَ وَعِنْدَهُمُ
التَّوْرٰىةُ فِيهَا حُكْمُ اللّٰهِ ثُمَّ يَتَوَلَّوْنَ مِنْ
بَعْدِ ذٰلِكَ ۚ وَمَآ أُولٰٓئِكَ بِالْمُؤْمِنِينَ ﴿٤٣﴾ إِنَّآ
أَنْزَلْنَا التَّوْرٰىةَ فِيهَا هُدًى وَّنُورٌ ۚ يَحْكُمُ
بِهَا النَّبِيُّونَ الَّذِينَ أَسْلَمُوا لِلَّذِينَ هَادُوا
وَالرَّبّٰنِيُّونَ وَالْأَحْبَارُ بِمَا اسْتُحْفِظُوا مِنْ
كِتٰبِ اللّٰهِ وَكَانُوا عَلَيْهِ شُهَدَآءَ ۚ فَلَا تَخْشَوُا
النَّاسَ وَاخْشَوْنِ وَلَا تَشْتَرُوا بِأٰيٰتِي ثَمَنًا
قَلِيلًا ۚ وَمَنْ لَّمْ يَحْكُمْ بِمَآ أَنْزَلَ اللّٰهُ
فَأُولٰٓئِكَ هُمُ الْكٰفِرُونَ ﴿٤٤﴾ وَكَتَبْنَا عَلَيْهِمْ
فِيهَآ أَنَّ النَّفْسَ بِالنَّفْسِ وَالْعَيْنَ بِالْعَيْنِ
وَالْأَنْفَ بِالْأَنْفِ وَالْأُذُنَ بِالْأُذُنِ وَالسِّنَّ
بِالسِّنِّ وَالْجُرُوحَ قِصَاصٌ ۚ فَمَنْ تَصَدَّقَ
بِهِ فَهُوَ كَفَّارَةٌ لَّهُ ۚ وَمَنْ لَّمْ يَحْكُمْ بِمَآ
أَنْزَلَ اللّٰهُ فَأُولٰٓئِكَ هُمُ الظّٰلِمُونَ ﴿٤٥﴾ وَقَفَّيْنَا
عَلٰٓى أٰثٰرِهِمْ بِعِيسَى ابْنِ مَرْيَمَ مُصَدِّقًا
لِّمَا بَيْنَ يَدَيْهِ مِنَ التَّوْرٰىةِ ۖ وَأٰتَيْنٰهُ
الْإِنْجِيلَ فِيهِ هُدًى وَّنُورٌ وَّمُصَدِّقًا لِّمَا

those who guard against evil.

47. And let the followers of the Evangel judge according to what Allâh has revealed therein. And indeed those who do not judge according to what Allâh has revealed it is these who are the real disobedient.

48. And We have revealed to you this perfect Book comprising the truth and wisdom, fulfilling (the prophecies of) the Scripture which was present before it and stands as a guardian over it, then judge between them according to that which Allâh has revealed (of the Qur'ân), and do not deviate from the truth that has come to you in order to follow their low desires. For each one of you did We prescribe a spiritual law and a well-defined way (- a code in secular matters). And if Allâh had so willed He might have made you all one community (by force), but He wishes to show your perfection (the capacities and capabilities) that He has endowed you with. Therefore vie one with another in (doing) good deeds. To Allâh is the return of you all, then He will inform you as to that wherein you were at variance.

49. And (We have revealed this perfect Book to you) that you judge between them according to that (law) which Allâh has revealed and do not follow their low desires, rather be on your guard against them lest they should (tempt you and) cause you fall into trouble due to some part of (the commandments) that Allâh has revealed to you. If they turn back (showing disregard to Our revelations), know that Allâh intends to punish them for some of their sins. Indeed, a large number of human beings are certainly disobedient.

50. Do they seek to enforce the law of (the days of) ignorance? And who is better than Allâh in giving judgment for a people who are convinced (of their faith)?

SECTION 8

51. **O** YOU who believe! Do not take those

بَيْنَ يَدَيْهِ مِنَ التَّوْرٰىةِ وَ هُدًى وَّ مَوْعِظَةً
لِّلْمُتَّقِينَ ﴿٤٦﴾ وَلْيَحْكُمْ أَهْلُ الْإِنْجِيلِ بِمَآ
أَنْزَلَ اللهُ فِيهِ ۗ وَ مَنْ لَّمْ يَحْكُمْ بِمَآ أَنْزَلَ
اللهُ فَأُولٰٓئِكَ هُمُ الْفٰسِقُونَ ﴿٤٧﴾ وَ أَنْزَلْنَآ إِلَيْكَ
الْكِتٰبَ بِالْحَقِّ مُصَدِّقًا لِّمَا بَيْنَ يَدَيْهِ
مِنَ الْكِتٰبِ وَ مُهَيْمِنًا عَلَيْهِ فَاحْكُمْ
بَيْنَهُمْ بِمَآ أَنْزَلَ اللهُ وَ لَا تَتَّبِعْ أَهْوَآءَهُمْ
عَمَّا جَآءَكَ مِنَ الْحَقِّ ۗ لِكُلٍّ جَعَلْنَا مِنْكُمْ
شِرْعَةً وَّ مِنْهَاجًا ۗ وَ لَوْ شَآءَ اللهُ لَجَعَلَكُمْ
أُمَّةً وّٰحِدَةً وَّ لٰكِنْ لِّيَبْلُوَكُمْ فِي مَآ
أٰتٰىكُمْ فَاسْتَبِقُوا الْخَيْرٰتِ ۗ إِلَى اللهِ مَرْجِعُكُمْ
جَمِيعًا فَيُنَبِّئُكُمْ بِمَا كُنْتُمْ فِيهِ تَخْتَلِفُونَ ﴿٤٨﴾
وَ أَنِ احْكُمْ بَيْنَهُمْ بِمَآ أَنْزَلَ اللهُ وَ لَا
تَتَّبِعْ أَهْوَآءَهُمْ وَ احْذَرْهُمْ أَنْ يَّفْتِنُوكَ
عَنْ بَعْضِ مَآ أَنْزَلَ اللهُ إِلَيْكَ ۗ فَإِنْ تَوَلَّوْا
فَاعْلَمْ أَنَّمَا يُرِيدُ اللهُ أَنْ يُّصِيبَهُمْ بِبَعْضِ
ذُنُوبِهِمْ ۗ وَ إِنَّ كَثِيرًا مِّنَ النَّاسِ لَفٰسِقُونَ ﴿٤٩﴾
أَفَحُكْمَ الْجٰهِلِيَّةِ يَبْغُونَ ۗ وَ مَنْ أَحْسَنُ
مِنَ اللهِ حُكْمًا لِّقَوْمٍ يُّوقِنُونَ ﴿٥٠﴾ يٰٓأَيُّهَا

particular (type of) Jews and Christians (who are enemies of Islam) for allies. They are allies of one to another (when against you), and whoso from amongst you takes them for allies, is indeed one of them. Verily, Allâh does not guide the unjust people to attain their goal.

52. Now you shall see those in whose hearts is a disease (of hypocrisy) vying one with another towards them (- those Jews and those Christians to take them for allies). They say, 'We are afraid lest a misfortune should befall us.' But it is well nigh that Allâh will bring about a victory or some other (more remarkable) event (in favour of Islam) from Himself; then they will become more remorseful (and ashamed) for what they secretly harboured in their minds.

53. And those who have believed will say (at that time), 'Are these they who swore by Allâh their most solemn oaths that they were surely with you?' Their deeds have gone waste (and their machination failed), so that they have become the losers.

54. O you who believe! If anyone of you should renounce his Faith (let him remember that) Allâh will bring forth (in his stead) a people (more zealous in faith) whom He will love and who will love Him, who will be kind and humble towards the believers, and mighty and firm against the disbelievers. They will strive hard in the cause of Allâh and will not fear the reproach of any faultfinder. (Remember) these (virtues) are (to be attained through) Allâh's bounty which He bestows upon whomsoever He will. And Allâh is Bountiful, All-Knowing.

55. Your real ally is only Allâh, and His Messenger, and those who believe, who observe Prayer and present the *Zakât,* and they bow down (in obedience to Allâh).

56. And whoso takes for his allies Allâh and His Messenger and those who believe, (let him know that surely such a one is the party of Allâh) and it is the party of Allâh that is truly triumphant.

الَّذِينَ آمَنُوا لَا تَتَّخِذُوا الْيَهُودَ وَالنَّصَارَىٰ
أَوْلِيَاءَ بَعْضُهُمْ أَوْلِيَاءُ بَعْضٍ وَمَنْ يَتَوَلَّهُمْ
مِنْكُمْ فَإِنَّهُ مِنْهُمْ إِنَّ اللَّهَ لَا يَهْدِي
الْقَوْمَ الظَّالِمِينَ ﴿٥١﴾ فَتَرَى الَّذِينَ فِي قُلُوبِهِمْ
مَرَضٌ يُسَارِعُونَ فِيهِمْ يَقُولُونَ نَخْشَىٰ
أَنْ تُصِيبَنَا دَائِرَةٌ فَعَسَى اللَّهُ أَنْ يَأْتِيَ
بِالْفَتْحِ أَوْ أَمْرٍ مِنْ عِنْدِهِ فَيُصْبِحُوا عَلَىٰ
مَا أَسَرُّوا فِي أَنْفُسِهِمْ نَادِمِينَ ﴿٥٢﴾ وَيَقُولُ الَّذِينَ
آمَنُوا أَهَٰؤُلَاءِ الَّذِينَ أَقْسَمُوا بِاللَّهِ جَهْدَ أَيْمَانِهِمْ
إِنَّهُمْ لَمَعَكُمْ حَبِطَتْ أَعْمَالُهُمْ فَأَصْبَحُوا خَاسِرِينَ ﴿٥٣﴾
يَا أَيُّهَا الَّذِينَ آمَنُوا مَنْ يَرْتَدَّ مِنْكُمْ عَنْ
دِينِهِ فَسَوْفَ يَأْتِي اللَّهُ بِقَوْمٍ يُحِبُّهُمْ
وَيُحِبُّونَهُ أَذِلَّةٍ عَلَى الْمُؤْمِنِينَ أَعِزَّةٍ عَلَى
الْكَافِرِينَ يُجَاهِدُونَ فِي سَبِيلِ اللَّهِ وَلَا
يَخَافُونَ لَوْمَةَ لَائِمٍ ذَٰلِكَ فَضْلُ اللَّهِ
يُؤْتِيهِ مَنْ يَشَاءُ وَاللَّهُ وَاسِعٌ عَلِيمٌ ﴿٥٤﴾
إِنَّمَا وَلِيُّكُمُ اللَّهُ وَرَسُولُهُ وَالَّذِينَ آمَنُوا
الَّذِينَ يُقِيمُونَ الصَّلَاةَ وَيُؤْتُونَ الزَّكَاةَ
وَهُمْ رَاكِعُونَ ﴿٥٥﴾ وَمَنْ يَتَوَلَّ اللَّهَ وَرَسُولَهُ
وَالَّذِينَ آمَنُوا فَإِنَّ حِزْبَ اللَّهِ هُمُ الْغَالِبُونَ ﴿٥٦﴾

SECTION 9

57. **O** YOU who believe! Do not make those who take your religion lightly and consider it worthless, from among those who were given the Scripture before you and the other infidels, your allies. And keep your duty to Allâh if you are (true) believers.

58. And when you call (the people) to Prayer, they take it lightly and consider it worthless. They do so because they are a people who do not understand.

59. Say, 'O People of the Scripture! Do you find fault with us only because we believe in Allâh and in that which has been revealed to us, and in that which was revealed before (us)? Whereas most of you are disobedient (to God).'

60. Say, 'Shall I inform you of those who shall receive from Allâh a recompense worse than that of those (who try to find fault with Us)? They are those whom Allâh has deprived of His blessings and upon whom He brought His displeasure and indignation and of whom He has made (as) apes and swine and who serve the transgressor (- the devil). It is these who are indeed worse-placed and farther astray from the right path.'

61. And when they come to you they say, 'We believe,' while, in fact, they enter without faith and go out without it. And Allâh knows best all they conceal.

62. And you will find many of them vying one with another in committing sin and transgression and being too much given to eat things forbidden. How evil is that which they practise!

63. Why do not the teachers of divine knowledge and those learned in the Law prohibit them from their blasphemous talk and deeds and their being too much given to eating things forbidden? Evil indeed is their machination.

64. And the Jews said, 'Allâh's hand is fettered (from assisting the helpless Muslims).' Fettered are their own hands (from assisting the

سُوْرَةُ الْمَآئِدَةِ ٥

يٰۤاَيُّهَا الَّذِيْنَ اٰمَنُوْا لَا تَتَّخِذُوا الَّذِيْنَ اتَّخَذُوْا
دِيْنَكُمْ هُزُوًا وَّلَعِبًا مِّنَ الَّذِيْنَ اُوْتُوا الْكِتٰبَ
مِنْ قَبْلِكُمْ وَالْكُفَّارَ اَوْلِيَآءَ ۚ وَاتَّقُوا اللّٰهَ اِنْ
كُنْتُمْ مُّؤْمِنِيْنَ ﴿٥٧﴾ وَاِذَا نَادَيْتُمْ اِلَى الصَّلٰوةِ
اتَّخَذُوْهَا هُزُوًا وَّلَعِبًا ؕ ذٰلِكَ بِاَنَّهُمْ قَوْمٌ
لَّا يَعْقِلُوْنَ ﴿٥٨﴾ قُلْ يٰۤاَهْلَ الْكِتٰبِ هَلْ
تَنْقِمُوْنَ مِنَّاۤ اِلَّاۤ اَنْ اٰمَنَّا بِاللّٰهِ وَمَاۤ اُنْزِلَ
اِلَيْنَا وَمَاۤ اُنْزِلَ مِنْ قَبْلُ وَاَنَّ اَكْثَرَكُمْ
فٰسِقُوْنَ ﴿٥٩﴾ قُلْ هَلْ اُنَبِّئُكُمْ بِشَرٍّ مِّنْ
ذٰلِكَ مَثُوْبَةً عِنْدَ اللّٰهِ ؕ مَنْ لَّعَنَهُ اللّٰهُ
وَغَضِبَ عَلَيْهِ وَجَعَلَ مِنْهُمُ الْقِرَدَةَ
وَالْخَنَازِيْرَ وَعَبَدَ الطَّاغُوْتَ ؕ اُولٰٓئِكَ شَرٌّ
مَّكَانًا وَّاَضَلُّ عَنْ سَوَآءِ السَّبِيْلِ ﴿٦٠﴾ وَاِذَا
جَآءُوْكُمْ قَالُوْۤا اٰمَنَّا وَقَدْ دَّخَلُوْا بِالْكُفْرِ
وَهُمْ قَدْ خَرَجُوْا بِهٖ ؕ وَاللّٰهُ اَعْلَمُ بِمَا
كَانُوْا يَكْتُمُوْنَ ﴿٦١﴾ وَتَرٰى كَثِيْرًا مِّنْهُمْ يُسَارِعُوْنَ
فِي الْاِثْمِ وَالْعُدْوَانِ وَاَكْلِهِمُ السُّحْتَ ؕ
لَبِئْسَ مَا كَانُوْا يَعْمَلُوْنَ ﴿٦٢﴾ لَوْلَا يَنْهٰىهُمُ
الرَّبّٰنِيُّوْنَ وَالْاَحْبَارُ عَنْ قَوْلِهِمُ الْاِثْمَ
وَاَكْلِهِمُ السُّحْتَ ؕ لَبِئْسَ مَا كَانُوْا
يَصْنَعُوْنَ ﴿٦٣﴾ وَقَالَتِ الْيَهُوْدُ يَدُ اللّٰهِ مَغْلُوْلَةٌ ؕ
غُلَّتْ اَيْدِيْهِمْ وَلُعِنُوْا بِمَا قَالُوْا ۘ بَلْ

enemies of Islam), and they are deprived of blessings of Allâh for what they said. Nay, (the truth of the matter is that) both His hands are wide open (and free). He spends as He pleases. And that which has been revealed to you from your Lord will most surely increase many of them in inordinate rebellion and in disbelief. And We have kindled enmity and hatred among them till the Day of Resurrection. Every time they kindle a fire for war, Allâh puts it out, but they strive to create disorder in the land, whereas Allâh does not like the creators of disorder.

65. And if the people of the Scripture had only believed and guarded against evil, We would surely have absolved them of their sins and We would surely make them enter Gardens of bliss.

66. If they had only observed the Torah and the Evangel and that which has been revealed to them (now) from their Lord, they would surely have eaten (of good things) from above them and from under their feet, (thus would have enjoyed the boons of the heaven and the earth). Though there is amongst them a community who is moderate (and of balanced mind), yet a large number of them are such that evil are their deeds.

SECTION 10

67. **O** MESSENGER! Convey (to the people the entire message) well that has been revealed to you from your Lord; and if you do it not, you have not (at all) conveyed His message as it ought to have been. And Allâh will protect you from all (the onslaughts of) people (on your life). Verily, Allâh will not let the disbelieving people have their way.

68. Say, 'O People of the Scripture! You stand nowhere unless you observe the Torah and the Evangel and that (- Qur'ân) which has (now) been revealed to you from your Lord.' And certainly that which has been revealed to you from your Lord will increase many of them in

يَدَاهُ مَبْسُوطَتَانِ يُنْفِقُ كَيْفَ يَشَآءُ
وَلَيَزِيدَنَّ كَثِيرًا مِّنْهُم مَّآ أُنْزِلَ إِلَيْكَ
مِن رَّبِّكَ طُغْيَانًا وَكُفْرًا وَأَلْقَيْنَا بَيْنَهُمُ
الْعَدَاوَةَ وَالْبَغْضَآءَ إِلَى يَوْمِ الْقِيٰمَةِ كُلَّمَآ
أَوْقَدُوا نَارًا لِّلْحَرْبِ أَطْفَأَهَا اللّٰهُ
وَيَسْعَوْنَ فِي الْأَرْضِ فَسَادًا وَاللّٰهُ لَا يُحِبُّ
الْمُفْسِدِينَ ﴿٦٤﴾ وَلَوْ أَنَّ أَهْلَ الْكِتٰبِ ءَامَنُوا
وَاتَّقَوْا لَكَفَّرْنَا عَنْهُمْ سَيِّاٰتِهِمْ وَلَأَدْخَلْنٰهُمْ
جَنّٰتِ النَّعِيمِ ﴿٦٥﴾ وَلَوْ أَنَّهُمْ أَقَامُوا التَّوْرٰىةَ
وَالْإِنْجِيلَ وَمَآ أُنْزِلَ إِلَيْهِم مِّن رَّبِّهِمْ
لَأَكَلُوا مِنْ فَوْقِهِمْ وَمِنْ تَحْتِ أَرْجُلِهِمْ
مِنْهُمْ أُمَّةٌ مُّقْتَصِدَةٌ وَكَثِيرٌ مِّنْهُمْ
ع سَآءَ مَا يَعْمَلُونَ ﴿٦٦﴾ يٰٓأَيُّهَا الرَّسُولُ بَلِّغْ
مَآ أُنْزِلَ إِلَيْكَ مِن رَّبِّكَ وَإِن لَّمْ
تَفْعَلْ فَمَا بَلَّغْتَ رِسَالَتَهُ وَاللّٰهُ يَعْصِمُكَ
مِنَ النَّاسِ إِنَّ اللّٰهَ لَا يَهْدِي الْقَوْمَ
الْكٰفِرِينَ ﴿٦٧﴾ قُلْ يٰٓأَهْلَ الْكِتٰبِ لَسْتُمْ
عَلَى شَيْءٍ حَتّٰى تُقِيمُوا التَّوْرٰىةَ وَالْإِنْجِيلَ
وَمَآ أُنْزِلَ إِلَيْكُم مِّن رَّبِّكُمْ وَلَيَزِيدَنَّ
كَثِيرًا مِّنْهُم مَّآ أُنْزِلَ إِلَيْكَ مِن
رَّبِّكَ طُغْيَانًا وَكُفْرًا فَلَا تَأْسَ

ordinate rebellion and disbelief; so do not grieve for the disbelieving people.

69. Verily, those who have believed and those who judaised and the Sabians and the Christians, whosoever believes in Allâh and the Last Day and does righteous deeds, they shall have no cause of fear nor shall they ever grieve.

70. Surely, We took a covenant from the Children of Israel and We sent Messengers to them. Every time there came to them a Messenger with that (Message) which did not suit their fanciful desires, (they defied him so that) some they treated as liars and others they sought to kill.

71. And they thought there would be no punishment (for them) so they willfully became blind and deaf; (then they sought Allâh's pardon) then Allâh turned to them (with mercy with the advent of Jesus), yet again many of them became blind and deaf. And Allâh is Watchful of what they do.

72. Indeed, they have disbelieved who say, 'Allâh - He is the Messiah, son of Mary,' whereas the Messiah (himself) said, 'O Children of Israel! Worship Allâh Who is my Lord and your Lord.' Surely whoso associates partners with Allâh, him has Allâh forbidden Paradise, and his resort will be the Fire and these transgressors shall have no helpers.

73. Most certainly, they have disbelieved who say, 'Allâh is the third of the three.' But in fact there is no other, cannot be and will never be one worthy of worship except One God. And if they refrain not from what they say, there shall certainly befall those who disbelieve from among them, a grievous punishment.

74. Will they not turn with repentance to Allâh and seek His protection, while Allâh is Great Protector, Ever Merciful?

75. The Messiah, son of Mary, was only a Messenger, all the Messengers have (like him) passed away before him, his mother was a

عَلَى الْقَوْمِ الْكَافِرِينَ ﴿٦٨﴾ إِنَّ الَّذِينَ آمَنُوا
وَالَّذِينَ هَادُوا وَالصَّابِئُونَ وَالنَّصَارَىٰ
مَنْ آمَنَ بِاللَّهِ وَالْيَوْمِ الْآخِرِ وَعَمِلَ
صَالِحًا فَلَا خَوْفٌ عَلَيْهِمْ وَلَا هُمْ
يَحْزَنُونَ ﴿٦٩﴾ لَقَدْ أَخَذْنَا مِيثَاقَ بَنِي
إِسْرَائِيلَ وَأَرْسَلْنَا إِلَيْهِمْ رُسُلًا
كُلَّمَا جَاءَهُمْ رَسُولٌ بِمَا لَا تَهْوَىٰ
أَنْفُسُهُمْ فَرِيقًا كَذَّبُوا وَفَرِيقًا يَقْتُلُونَ ﴿٧٠﴾
وَحَسِبُوا أَلَّا تَكُونَ فِتْنَةٌ فَعَمُوا وَصَمُّوا
ثُمَّ تَابَ اللَّهُ عَلَيْهِمْ ثُمَّ عَمُوا وَصَمُّوا
كَثِيرٌ مِنْهُمْ وَاللَّهُ بَصِيرٌ بِمَا يَعْمَلُونَ ﴿٧١﴾
لَقَدْ كَفَرَ الَّذِينَ قَالُوا إِنَّ اللَّهَ هُوَ
الْمَسِيحُ ابْنُ مَرْيَمَ وَقَالَ الْمَسِيحُ
يَا بَنِي إِسْرَائِيلَ اعْبُدُوا اللَّهَ رَبِّي
وَرَبَّكُمْ إِنَّهُ مَنْ يُشْرِكْ بِاللَّهِ فَقَدْ حَرَّمَ
اللَّهُ عَلَيْهِ الْجَنَّةَ وَمَأْوَاهُ النَّارُ وَمَا
لِلظَّالِمِينَ مِنْ أَنْصَارٍ ﴿٧٢﴾ لَقَدْ كَفَرَ الَّذِينَ
قَالُوا إِنَّ اللَّهَ ثَالِثُ ثَلَاثَةٍ وَمَا مِنْ
إِلَٰهٍ إِلَّا إِلَٰهٌ وَاحِدٌ وَإِنْ لَمْ يَنْتَهُوا
عَمَّا يَقُولُونَ لَيَمَسَّنَّ الَّذِينَ كَفَرُوا
مِنْهُمْ عَذَابٌ أَلِيمٌ ﴿٧٣﴾ أَفَلَا يَتُوبُونَ إِلَى
اللَّهِ وَيَسْتَغْفِرُونَهُ وَاللَّهُ غَفُورٌ رَحِيمٌ ﴿٧٤﴾
مَا الْمَسِيحُ ابْنُ مَرْيَمَ إِلَّا رَسُولٌ قَدْ
خَلَتْ مِنْ قَبْلِهِ الرُّسُلُ وَأُمُّهُ صِدِّيقَةٌ
كَانَا يَأْكُلَانِ الطَّعَامَ انْظُرْ كَيْفَ نُبَيِّنُ

highly truthful woman. They both used to eat food. See how We explain the arguments for their good, yet see, how they are turned away (from the truth).

76. Say, 'Do you worship beside Allâh that which has no power over doing you any harm or good?' As for Allâh, He is the All-Hearing, the All-Knowing.

77. Say, 'O People of the Scripture! Do not exaggerate in (the matter of) your religion falsely and unjustly, nor follow the fancies of a people who had gone astray before (you) and had led many astray, and (now again) who have strayed away from the right path.

SECTION 11

78. **T**HOSE who disbelieved among the Children of Israel were deprived of the blessings of God (firstly) by the tongue of David and (then by) Jesus, son of Mary. That was so because they rebelled and used to transgress.

79. They did not prohibit one another from hateful things they committed. How evil were the practices they used to follow!

80. You will find many of them allying (themselves) with those who disbelieve. Evil is that which they have sent forward for themselves (to the effect) that Allâh is displeased with them and in this punishment they shall abide.

81. And if they had believed in Allâh and this perfect Prophet and (in) what has been revealed to him, they would not have taken them for allies; but (they do so for) many of them are disobedient.

82. You shall certainly find the Jews and those who associate partners with Allâh the most vehement of the people in enmity against those who believe, and you shall certainly find those who say, 'We are Christians,' the nearest in friendship towards those who believe. That is so because there are savants and monks amongst them and because they are not haughty.

لَهُمُ الْآيٰتِ ثُمَّ انْظُرْ أَنّٰى يُؤْفَكُونَ ﴿٧٥﴾
قُلْ أَتَعْبُدُونَ مِنْ دُونِ اللّٰهِ مَا لَا يَمْلِكُ
لَكُمْ ضَرًّا وَّلَا نَفْعًا ۚ وَاللّٰهُ هُوَ السَّمِيعُ
الْعَلِيمُ ﴿٧٦﴾ قُلْ يٰأَهْلَ الْكِتٰبِ لَا تَغْلُوا
فِي دِينِكُمْ غَيْرَ الْحَقِّ وَلَا تَتَّبِعُوا
أَهْوَاءَ قَوْمٍ قَدْ ضَلُّوا مِنْ قَبْلُ وَأَضَلُّوا
كَثِيرًا وَّضَلُّوا عَنْ سَوَاءِ السَّبِيلِ ﴿٧٧﴾ ع ١١ ١٤
لُعِنَ الَّذِينَ كَفَرُوا مِنْ بَنِي إِسْرٰٓءِيلَ
عَلٰى لِسَانِ دَاوُدَ وَعِيسَى ابْنِ مَرْيَمَ ۚ
ذٰلِكَ بِمَا عَصَوْا وَّكَانُوا يَعْتَدُونَ ﴿٧٨﴾
كَانُوا لَا يَتَنَاهَوْنَ عَنْ مُّنْكَرٍ فَعَلُوهُ ۚ
لَبِئْسَ مَا كَانُوا يَفْعَلُونَ ﴿٧٩﴾ تَرٰى كَثِيرًا
مِّنْهُمْ يَتَوَلَّوْنَ الَّذِينَ كَفَرُوا ۚ لَبِئْسَ
مَا قَدَّمَتْ لَهُمْ أَنْفُسُهُمْ أَنْ سَخِطَ اللّٰهُ
عَلَيْهِمْ وَفِي الْعَذَابِ هُمْ خٰلِدُونَ ﴿٨٠﴾
وَلَوْ كَانُوا يُؤْمِنُونَ بِاللّٰهِ وَالنَّبِيِّ وَمَا أُنْزِلَ
إِلَيْهِ مَا اتَّخَذُوهُمْ أَوْلِيَاءَ وَلٰكِنَّ
كَثِيرًا مِّنْهُمْ فٰسِقُونَ ﴿٨١﴾ لَتَجِدَنَّ أَشَدَّ
النَّاسِ عَدٰوَةً لِّلَّذِينَ أٰمَنُوا الْيَهُودَ
وَالَّذِينَ أَشْرَكُوا ۚ وَلَتَجِدَنَّ أَقْرَبَهُمْ
مَّوَدَّةً لِّلَّذِينَ أٰمَنُوا الَّذِينَ قَالُوا
إِنَّا نَصٰرٰى ۚ ذٰلِكَ بِأَنَّ مِنْهُمْ قِسِّيسِينَ
وَرُهْبَانًا وَّأَنَّهُمْ لَا يَسْتَكْبِرُونَ ﴿٨٢﴾

PART الجزء السابع VII

83. AND when they hear that (Divine Message) which has been revealed to this perfect Messenger you will find their eyes overflow with tears because of the truth they have recognised. They say, 'Our Lord! We believe, so count us among the witnesses (to the truth).'
84. (They add,) 'What excuse do we have to disbelieve in Allâh and (in) the truth that has come to us while we earnestly desire that our Lord should count us with the righteous people?'
85. Therefore Allâh will reward them for what they said, with Gardens served with running streams, they shall abide therein forever. Such indeed is the reward of the doers of good to others.
86. But those who have disbelieved and cried lies to Our Messages, it is these who are the fellows of the blazing Fire.

SECTION 12

87. O YOU who believe! Do not forbid yourselves good and pure things which Allâh has made lawful for you, and do not transgress. Verily, Allâh does not like the transgressors.
88. And eat of what Allâh has provided you of (things) lawful, good and pure. And take Allâh as a shield, in whom you repose your faith.
89. Allâh will not call you to account for (such of) your oaths as are vain, but He will call you to account for (breaking) the oaths which you take in earnest (for doing a thing or not doing it). The expiation for breaking such an oath is the feeding of ten needy persons (the average food) as you feed your own families with, or provide them with clothes, or liberating of someone (from the yoke of slavery or debt etc.). But whoever does not find (the means to do any of these), then he shall fast for three days. That is how you expiate your oaths when

وَإِذَا سَمِعُوا مَا أُنْزِلَ إِلَى الرَّسُولِ تَرَى
أَعْيُنَهُمْ تَفِيضُ مِنَ الدَّمْعِ مِمَّا عَرَفُوا
مِنَ الْحَقِّ يَقُولُونَ رَبَّنَا آمَنَّا فَاكْتُبْنَا مَعَ
الشّٰهِدِينَ ﴿٨٣﴾ وَمَا لَنَا لَا نُؤْمِنُ بِاللّٰهِ وَمَا
جَاءَنَا مِنَ الْحَقِّ وَنَطْمَعُ أَنْ يُدْخِلَنَا رَبُّنَا
مَعَ الْقَوْمِ الصّٰلِحِينَ ﴿٨٤﴾ فَأَثٰبَهُمُ اللّٰهُ بِمَا
قَالُوا جَنّٰتٍ تَجْرِي مِنْ تَحْتِهَا الْأَنْهٰرُ
خٰلِدِينَ فِيهَا وَذٰلِكَ جَزَاءُ الْمُحْسِنِينَ ﴿٨٥﴾
وَالَّذِينَ كَفَرُوا وَكَذَّبُوا بِـَٔايٰتِنَا أُولٰٓئِكَ
أَصْحٰبُ الْجَحِيمِ ﴿٨٦﴾ يٰٓأَيُّهَا الَّذِينَ آمَنُوا لَا ع ٩
تُحَرِّمُوا طَيِّبٰتِ مَا أَحَلَّ اللّٰهُ لَكُمْ وَلَا
تَعْتَدُوا إِنَّ اللّٰهَ لَا يُحِبُّ الْمُعْتَدِينَ ﴿٨٧﴾ وَكُلُوا
مِمَّا رَزَقَكُمُ اللّٰهُ حَلٰلًا طَيِّبًا وَاتَّقُوا اللّٰهَ
الَّذِي أَنْتُمْ بِهِ مُؤْمِنُونَ ﴿٨٨﴾ لَا يُؤَاخِذُكُمُ
اللّٰهُ بِاللَّغْوِ فِي أَيْمٰنِكُمْ وَلٰكِنْ يُؤَاخِذُكُمْ
بِمَا عَقَّدْتُمُ الْأَيْمٰنَ فَكَفّٰرَتُهُ إِطْعَامُ
عَشَرَةِ مَسٰكِينَ مِنْ أَوْسَطِ مَا تُطْعِمُونَ
أَهْلِيكُمْ أَوْ كِسْوَتُهُمْ أَوْ تَحْرِيرُ رَقَبَةٍ فَمَنْ
لَمْ يَجِدْ فَصِيَامُ ثَلٰثَةِ أَيَّامٍ ذٰلِكَ كَفّٰرَةُ
أَيْمٰنِكُمْ إِذَا حَلَفْتُمْ وَاحْفَظُوا أَيْمٰنَكُمْ

you have sworn them solemnly (and then break them). But do guard your oaths. Thus does Allâh explain to you His commandments so that you may give (Him) thanks.

90. O you who believe! Intoxicants and games of chance, and alters set up for false deities and divining arrows are only abominations, some of satan's handiworks, therefore shun each one (of these abominations) so that you may attain your goal.

91. Satan only intends to precipitate enmity and hatred between you by means of intoxicants and games of chance and to stop you from the remembrance of Allâh and from (observing your) Prayer. Will you not then be the abstainer (therefrom)?

92. Obey Allâh and obey this perfect Messenger and be on your guard (against disobeying them), but if you turn away, then bear in mind that Our Messenger is responsible only for the conveyance (of the Message) in clear terms.

93. There is no blame on those who believe and do deeds of righteousness for what they have eaten (before the prohibition came), provided they guard against (prohibited things in future) and are steadfast in their faith, and do deeds of righteousness and provided they guard against evil (as a duty to themselves); and provided further that they take (God) as a shield, and do good to others (as their duty to their fellow-beings). And Allâh loves the doers of good to others.

SECTION 13

94. **O** YOU who believe! Allâh is going to try you regarding something of the game which is within the reach of your hands and your lances. Allâh will do it so that He may distinguish those who stand in awe of Allâh even unseen. But he that transgresses even after that (warning) shall receive a grievous punishment.

95. O you who believe! Kill no game while you are in a pilgrim's garb or in the Sacred Precincts. And whosoever amongst you kills it

كَذٰلِكَ يُبَيِّنُ اللّٰهُ لَكُمْ اٰيٰتِهٖ لَعَلَّكُمْ
تَشْكُرُوْنَ ﴿٨٩﴾ يٰٓاَيُّهَا الَّذِيْنَ اٰمَنُوْٓا اِنَّمَا الْخَمْرُ
وَالْمَيْسِرُ وَالْاَنْصَابُ وَالْاَزْلَامُ رِجْسٌ مِّنْ
عَمَلِ الشَّيْطٰنِ فَاجْتَنِبُوْهُ لَعَلَّكُمْ تُفْلِحُوْنَ ﴿٩٠﴾
اِنَّمَا يُرِيْدُ الشَّيْطٰنُ اَنْ يُّوْقِعَ بَيْنَكُمُ الْعَدَاوَةَ
وَالْبَغْضَآءَ فِي الْخَمْرِ وَالْمَيْسِرِ وَيَصُدَّكُمْ
عَنْ ذِكْرِ اللّٰهِ وَعَنِ الصَّلٰوةِ ۚ فَهَلْ اَنْتُمْ
مُّنْتَهُوْنَ ﴿٩١﴾ وَاَطِيْعُوا اللّٰهَ وَاَطِيْعُوا الرَّسُوْلَ
وَاحْذَرُوْا ۚ فَاِنْ تَوَلَّيْتُمْ فَاعْلَمُوْٓا اَنَّمَا عَلٰى
رَسُوْلِنَا الْبَلٰغُ الْمُبِيْنُ ﴿٩٢﴾ لَيْسَ عَلَى الَّذِيْنَ
اٰمَنُوْا وَعَمِلُوا الصّٰلِحٰتِ جُنَاحٌ فِيْمَا طَعِمُوْٓا
اِذَا مَا اتَّقَوْا وَّاٰمَنُوْا وَعَمِلُوا الصّٰلِحٰتِ ثُمَّ
اتَّقَوْا وَّاٰمَنُوْا ثُمَّ اتَّقَوْا وَّاَحْسَنُوْا ۗ وَاللّٰهُ
يُحِبُّ الْمُحْسِنِيْنَ ﴿٩٣﴾ يٰٓاَيُّهَا الَّذِيْنَ اٰمَنُوْا ع
لَيَبْلُوَنَّكُمُ اللّٰهُ بِشَيْءٍ مِّنَ الصَّيْدِ تَنَالُهٗٓ
اَيْدِيْكُمْ وَرِمَاحُكُمْ لِيَعْلَمَ اللّٰهُ مَنْ يَّخَافُهٗ
بِالْغَيْبِ ۚ فَمَنِ اعْتَدٰى بَعْدَ ذٰلِكَ فَلَهٗ
عَذَابٌ اَلِيْمٌ ﴿٩٤﴾ يٰٓاَيُّهَا الَّذِيْنَ اٰمَنُوْا لَا
تَقْتُلُوا الصَّيْدَ وَاَنْتُمْ حُرُمٌ ۗ وَمَنْ قَتَلَهٗ

intentionally he shall recompense by sacrificing a domestic cattle, the like of the animal he has killed, the same to be determined by two just persons from among you, and (the same) to be brought as an offering to the *Ka'bah,* or the expiation (of his sin) is the feeding of a number of needy persons, or the equivalent in fasting, so that he may suffer the penalty of his deed. Allâh has pardoned whatever might have happened in the past, and whoso does it again Allâh will punish him (for his offence), for Mighty is Allâh, Lord of retribution.

96. It is made lawful for you (even when you are in a Pilgrim's garb to hunt) the game of the sea (and water) and to eat its food; a provision for you and for the travellers (who can make it a provision for their way), but unlawful for you is the game of the land as long as you are in a Pilgrim's garb or in the Sacred Precincts. Keep your duty to Allâh, to Whom you shall be gathered.

97. Allâh has made the *Ka'bah*, the Holy House (at Makkah) to serve as an anchor (-a means of support) and a means of uplifting for humankind, and also (each) sacred month and animals brought as an offering and animals wearing necklaces (meant for sacrifice during the *Hajj).* He has done this that you may know that Allâh knows all that lies in the heavens and all that lies in the earth, and that Allâh has complete knowledge of all things.

98. You should know that Allâh is Severe at retribution and that (at the same time) Allâh is Great Protector, Ever Merciful.

99. This perfect Messenger is responsible only for the conveyance (of the Message). And Allâh knows all that you reveal and all that you conceal.

100. Say, 'The bad and impure, and the good and pure are not alike even though the abundance of the bad and impure may charm you.' Take Allâh, therefore, as a shield (seeking refuge in Him), O you people of pure and clear under-

مِنكُم مُّتَعَمِّدًا فَجَزَآءٌ مِّثْلُ مَا قَتَلَ مِنَ
النَّعَمِ يَحْكُمُ بِهِ ذَوَا عَدْلٍ مِّنكُمْ هَدْيًا
بَٰلِغَ الْكَعْبَةِ أَوْ كَفَّٰرَةٌ طَعَامُ مَسَٰكِينَ أَوْ
عَدْلُ ذَٰلِكَ صِيَامًا لِّيَذُوقَ وَبَالَ أَمْرِهِ
عَفَا اللَّهُ عَمَّا سَلَفَ وَمَنْ عَادَ فَيَنتَقِمُ
اللَّهُ مِنْهُ وَاللَّهُ عَزِيزٌ ذُو انتِقَامٍ ﴿٩٥﴾ أُحِلَّ
لَكُمْ صَيْدُ الْبَحْرِ وَطَعَامُهُ مَتَٰعًا لَّكُمْ
وَلِلسَّيَّارَةِ وَحُرِّمَ عَلَيْكُمْ صَيْدُ الْبَرِّ مَا
دُمْتُمْ حُرُمًا وَاتَّقُوا اللَّهَ الَّذِي إِلَيْهِ
تُحْشَرُونَ ﴿٩٦﴾ جَعَلَ اللَّهُ الْكَعْبَةَ الْبَيْتَ الْحَرَامَ
قِيَٰمًا لِّلنَّاسِ وَالشَّهْرَ الْحَرَامَ وَالْهَدْيَ
وَالْقَلَٰٓئِدَ ذَٰلِكَ لِتَعْلَمُوا أَنَّ اللَّهَ يَعْلَمُ مَا
فِي السَّمَٰوَٰتِ وَمَا فِي الْأَرْضِ وَأَنَّ اللَّهَ بِكُلِّ
شَيْءٍ عَلِيمٌ ﴿٩٧﴾ اعْلَمُوا أَنَّ اللَّهَ شَدِيدُ
الْعِقَابِ وَأَنَّ اللَّهَ غَفُورٌ رَّحِيمٌ ﴿٩٨﴾ مَا عَلَى
الرَّسُولِ إِلَّا الْبَلَٰغُ وَاللَّهُ يَعْلَمُ مَا تُبْدُونَ
وَمَا تَكْتُمُونَ ﴿٩٩﴾ قُل لَّا يَسْتَوِي الْخَبِيثُ
وَالطَّيِّبُ وَلَوْ أَعْجَبَكَ كَثْرَةُ الْخَبِيثِ فَاتَّقُوا

standing! so that you may attain the goal.

SECTION 14

101. **O** YOU who believe! Do not inquire into (the details of Divine Laws on many) things which, if explained to you, would cause you trouble, though if you ask about them while the Qur'ân is being revealed, they will be explained to you; (yet) Allâh has passed over this (detailed mentioning on purpose), for Allâh is Great Protector, Ever Forbearing.

102. A people before you asked questions about such (details and) then they became disbelievers therein.

103. Allâh has not instituted (superstition like those of) any *Bahîrah* (- an animal having her ear slit and let loose for free pasture, dedicated to some god, their milk was not used, nor their back, nor their meat); or *Sâ'ibah* (- an animal having given birth to ten females, liberated to pasture where she would, not be ridden, nor milk drunk except by her young); or *Wasîlah* (- an animal which gave birth to seven females consecutively and at the seventh birth she bore a pair male and female. Each of the latter was let loose and the milk of the animal drunk by men only and not by women;) or *Hâmi* (- an animal that is left at liberty without being made use of in any way whatsoever). But those who disbelieve have fabricated a lie (by such superstitious dedications) in the name of Allâh. Most of them cannot refrain (from such polytheistic superstitions).

104. And when it is said to them, 'Come to what Allâh has revealed and to this perfect Messenger.' They say, 'Sufficient for us is that (tradition) wherein we have found our forefathers.' What! (would they follow them blindly) even though their forefathers had no knowledge whatsoever and had no guidance?

105. O you who believe! (take care of yourselves for) upon you is the responsibility of

اللهَ يَاُولِي الْأَلْبٰبِ لَعَلَّكُمْ تُفْلِحُوْنَ ﴿١٠٠﴾ يَاَيُّهَا
الَّذِيْنَ اٰمَنُوْا لَا تَسْـَٔلُوْا عَنْ اَشْيَآءَ اِنْ
تُبْدَ لَكُمْ تَسُؤْكُمْ وَ اِنْ تَسْـَٔلُوْا عَنْهَا حِيْنَ
يُنَزَّلُ الْقُرْاٰنُ تُبْدَ لَكُمْ عَفَا اللهُ عَنْهَا
وَ اللهُ غَفُوْرٌ حَلِيْمٌ ﴿١٠١﴾ قَدْ سَاَلَهَا قَوْمٌ مِّنْ
قَبْلِكُمْ ثُمَّ اَصْبَحُوْا بِهَا كٰفِرِيْنَ ﴿١٠٢﴾ مَا جَعَلَ
اللهُ مِنْۢ بَحِيْرَةٍ وَّ لَا سَآئِبَةٍ وَّ لَا وَصِيْلَةٍ
وَّ لَا حَامٍ وَّ لٰكِنَّ الَّذِيْنَ كَفَرُوْا يَفْتَرُوْنَ
عَلَى اللهِ الْكَذِبَ وَ اَكْثَرُهُمْ لَا يَعْقِلُوْنَ ﴿١٠٣﴾
وَ اِذَا قِيْلَ لَهُمْ تَعَالَوْا اِلٰى مَآ اَنْزَلَ اللهُ
وَ اِلَى الرَّسُوْلِ قَالُوْا حَسْبُنَا مَا وَجَدْنَا
عَلَيْهِ اٰبَآءَنَا اَوَ لَوْ كَانَ اٰبَآؤُهُمْ لَا يَعْلَمُوْنَ
شَيْـًٔا وَّ لَا يَهْتَدُوْنَ ﴿١٠٤﴾ يَاَيُّهَا الَّذِيْنَ اٰمَنُوْا

your ownselves. He who has gone astray can do you no harm provided you are rightly guided. Towards Allâh is the final return of you all, then will He inform you as to what you have been doing.

106. O you who believe! When death comes to one of you (and you wish to make your will) let there be present among you, at the time of making the will, two just persons from among you or two others from among the outsiders, in case you are journeying in the country and the calamity of death overtakes you. In case you doubt (their honesty in giving evidence), you shall detain both (the witnesses) after Prayer, then let them both swear by Allâh (and bear witness) saying, 'We will accept for this (- our oath) no price; (we will bear true evidence) even though he (in whose favour or against we bear evidence) be near of kin, nor will we hide the testimony (enjoined to be borne uprightly) by Allâh, for if we do so, we shall certainly be among the sinners.'

107. But if it be discovered that these two have become guilty of sin, then let two others stand in their place from among those (heirs) against whom the (former) two (witnesses) who were in a better position (to give true evidence) are sinfully deposed, and the two (latter witnesses) swear by Allâh (saying), 'Surely, our testimony is truer than the testimony of those two and we have not exceeded the bounds of justice (in bearing the evidence) for, in that case, we shall certainly be of the wrongdoers.'

108. This way is more likely to ensure that they (- the witnesses) will give the testimony in its true form and nature or at least they will be afraid that other oaths will be taken after their oaths (to counter them). Therefore take Allâh as a shield and listen (to Him) for Allâh guides not the disobedient people to the ways of success.

عَلَيْكُمْ أَنْفُسَكُمْ ۚ لَا يَضُرُّكُمْ مَّنْ ضَلَّ إِذَا
اهْتَدَيْتُمْ ۚ إِلَى اللّٰهِ مَرْجِعُكُمْ جَمِيعًا
فَيُنَبِّئُكُمْ بِمَا كُنْتُمْ تَعْمَلُونَ ﴿١٠٥﴾ يٰأَيُّهَا
الَّذِينَ اٰمَنُوا شَهٰدَةُ بَيْنِكُمْ إِذَا حَضَرَ
أَحَدَكُمُ الْمَوْتُ حِينَ الْوَصِيَّةِ اثْنٰنِ
ذَوَا عَدْلٍ مِّنْكُمْ أَوْ اٰخَرٰنِ مِنْ غَيْرِكُمْ
إِنْ أَنْتُمْ ضَرَبْتُمْ فِي الْأَرْضِ فَأَصٰبَتْكُمْ
مُّصِيبَةُ الْمَوْتِ ۚ تَحْبِسُونَهُمَا مِنْ بَعْدِ
الصَّلٰوةِ فَيُقْسِمٰنِ بِاللّٰهِ إِنِ ارْتَبْتُمْ لَا
نَشْتَرِي بِهٖ ثَمَنًا وَّلَوْ كَانَ ذَا قُرْبٰى ۙ وَلَا
نَكْتُمُ شَهٰدَةَ ۙ اللّٰهِ إِنَّآ إِذًا لَّمِنَ الْأٰثِمِينَ ﴿١٠٦﴾
فَإِنْ عُثِرَ عَلٰى أَنَّهُمَا اسْتَحَقَّآ إِثْمًا فَاٰخَرٰنِ
يَقُومٰنِ مَقَامَهُمَا مِنَ الَّذِينَ اسْتَحَقَّ عَلَيْهِمُ
الْأَوْلَيٰنِ فَيُقْسِمٰنِ بِاللّٰهِ لَشَهٰدَتُنَآ أَحَقُّ
مِنْ شَهٰدَتِهِمَا وَمَا اعْتَدَيْنَا ۖ إِنَّآ إِذًا
لَّمِنَ الظّٰلِمِينَ ﴿١٠٧﴾ ذٰلِكَ أَدْنٰى أَنْ يَّأْتُوا
بِالشَّهٰدَةِ عَلٰى وَجْهِهَآ أَوْ يَخَافُوٓا أَنْ تُرَدَّ
أَيْمٰنٌ بَعْدَ أَيْمٰنِهِمْ ۚ وَاتَّقُوا اللّٰهَ وَاسْمَعُوا ۚ
وَاللّٰهُ لَا يَهْدِي الْقَوْمَ الْفٰسِقِينَ ﴿١٠٨﴾ يَوْمَ

ع

SECTION 15

109. (IMAGINE) the day when Allâh will gather together all the Messengers and ask, 'What response did you receive?' They will say, 'We have no real knowledge (about the minds of the people), surely it is You alone Who have true and perfect knowledge of all things unseen.'

110. (Again imagine) when Allâh said, 'O Jesus, son of Mary! Remember My blessing upon you and upon your mother, how I strengthened you with the holy revelation. You spoke to the people (when you were) in the cradle and when of old age, and how I taught you the Scripture and the wisdom and the Torah and the Evangel, and how you determined from clay the likeness of a bird by My leave, then you breathed into it (a new spirit) then it became a soaring being by My leave, and by My leave you absolved the blind, the leprous, and by My leave you raised the (spiritually or nearly) dead to life, and how I warded off the Children of Israel from (putting) you (to death). It was the time when you came to them with clear arguments, but those among them who disbelieved had said, "This is naught but a hoax cutting (us) off (from the nation)".

111. 'And how I revealed to the disciples to believe in Me and in My Messenger, and they said, "We believe, and (O God!) bear witness that we are the submitting ones".'

112. (Recall the time) when the disciples said, 'O Jesus, son of Mary! Would your Lord consent to send down to us a table spread with a sure and lasting food from heaven?' He said, 'Keep your duty to Allâh, if you are true believers.'

113. They said, 'We desire that we may eat of it and that our hearts be at rest and that we may know that you have indeed spoken the truth to us and that we may be among the witnesses thereto.'

114. Jesus, son of Mary, prayed, 'O Allâh! Our Lord! Send down to us a table spread with a sure and lasting food from heaven that it may be

يَجْمَعُ اللّٰهُ الرُّسُلَ فَيَقُوْلُ مَاذَآ أُجِبْتُمْ ۖ
قَالُوْا لَا عِلْمَ لَنَا ۖ إِنَّكَ أَنْتَ عَلّٰمُ الْغُيُوْبِ ﴿١٠٩﴾
إِذْ قَالَ اللّٰهُ يٰعِيْسَى ابْنَ مَرْيَمَ اذْكُرْ
نِعْمَتِيْ عَلَيْكَ وَعَلٰى وٰلِدَتِكَ ۘ إِذْ أَيَّدْتُّكَ
بِرُوْحِ الْقُدُسِ ۙ تُكَلِّمُ النَّاسَ فِي الْمَهْدِ
وَكَهْلًا ۚ وَإِذْ عَلَّمْتُكَ الْكِتٰبَ وَالْحِكْمَةَ
وَالتَّوْرٰىةَ وَالْإِنْجِيْلَ ۚ وَإِذْ تَخْلُقُ مِنَ
الطِّيْنِ كَهَيْـَٔةِ الطَّيْرِ بِإِذْنِيْ فَتَنْفُخُ فِيْهَا
فَتَكُوْنُ طَيْرًا بِإِذْنِيْ وَتُبْرِئُ الْأَكْمَهَ
وَالْأَبْرَصَ بِإِذْنِيْ ۚ وَإِذْ تُخْرِجُ الْمَوْتٰى بِإِذْنِيْ ۚ
وَإِذْ كَفَفْتُ بَنِيْٓ إِسْرَآءِيْلَ عَنْكَ إِذْ جِئْتَهُمْ
بِالْبَيِّنٰتِ فَقَالَ الَّذِيْنَ كَفَرُوْا مِنْهُمْ إِنْ
هٰذَآ إِلَّا سِحْرٌ مُّبِيْنٌ ﴿١١٠﴾ وَإِذْ أَوْحَيْتُ إِلَى
الْحَوَارِيّٖنَ أَنْ اٰمِنُوْا بِيْ وَبِرَسُوْلِيْ ۚ قَالُوْٓا
اٰمَنَّا وَاشْهَدْ بِأَنَّنَا مُسْلِمُوْنَ ﴿١١١﴾ إِذْ قَالَ
الْحَوَارِيُّوْنَ يٰعِيْسَى ابْنَ مَرْيَمَ هَلْ يَسْتَطِيْعُ
رَبُّكَ أَنْ يُّنَزِّلَ عَلَيْنَا مَآئِدَةً مِّنَ السَّمَآءِ ۖ
قَالَ اتَّقُوا اللّٰهَ إِنْ كُنْتُمْ مُّؤْمِنِيْنَ ﴿١١٢﴾ قَالُوْا
نُرِيْدُ أَنْ نَّأْكُلَ مِنْهَا وَتَطْمَئِنَّ قُلُوْبُنَا
وَنَعْلَمَ أَنْ قَدْ صَدَقْتَنَا وَنَكُوْنَ عَلَيْهَا مِنَ
الشّٰهِدِيْنَ ﴿١١٣﴾ قَالَ عِيْسَى ابْنُ مَرْيَمَ اللّٰهُمَّ
رَبَّنَآ أَنْزِلْ عَلَيْنَا مَآئِدَةً مِّنَ السَّمَآءِ تَكُوْنُ

سُوۡرَةُ الۡمَآئِدَةِ ٥

to us a (source of) festival ever recurring, to the first of us and to the last of us and (serve as) a sign from You and provide sustenance for us, for You are the Best of Providers of sustenance.'

115. Allâh said, 'I will surely be (always) sending it (- the food) down to you but whosoever shows ingratitude afterwards, I will surely punish him with a punishment which I will give to no one else in the whole world.'

SECTION 16

116. AND when Allâh said, 'O Jesus, son of Mary! Did you say to the people, "Take me and my mother for two gods beside Allâh?"' He (- Jesus) replied, 'Glory be to You! It was not possible and proper for me to say a thing to which I had no right. If I had said it, you would indeed have known it, (for) you know all that is in my mind but I do not know what is in Yours. It is You alone Who truly know all things unseen.

117. 'I said nothing to them except that what You had commanded me, "Worship Allâh, My Lord as well as your Lord". I was a witness over them (only) so long as I remained among them but ever since You caused me to die, You Yourself have been the Watcher over them and You are the Witness to everything.

118. 'If You punish them, then surely they are Your servants and if You pardon them, You surely are the All-Mighty, the All-Wise.'

119. Allâh said, 'This is the day when their truth shall benefit the truthful. They shall have Gardens served with running streams (to keep them green and flourishing); there they shall live forever and ever. Allâh is well pleased with them and they are well pleased with Him. That indeed is the greatest triumph.'

120. To Allâh belongs the sovereignty of the heavens and the earth and whatever lies in them, and He is the Possessor of full power to do all that He will.

لَنَا عِيدًا لِّأَوَّلِنَا وَ أٰخِرِنَا وَ أٰيَةً مِّنْكَ
وَارْزُقْنَا وَأَنْتَ خَيْرُ الرّٰزِقِينَ ﴿١١٤﴾ قَالَ اللّٰهُ إِنِّي
مُنَزِّلُهَا عَلَيْكُمْ فَمَنْ يَّكْفُرْ بَعْدُ مِنْكُمْ فَإِنِّيٓ
أُعَذِّبُهٗ عَذَابًا لَّآ أُعَذِّبُهٗٓ أَحَدًا مِّنَ الْعٰلَمِينَ ﴿١١٥﴾
وَإِذْ قَالَ اللّٰهُ يٰعِيسَى ابْنَ مَرْيَمَ ءَأَنْتَ
قُلْتَ لِلنَّاسِ اتَّخِذُونِي وَأُمِّيَ إِلٰهَيْنِ مِنْ
دُونِ اللّٰهِ قَالَ سُبْحٰنَكَ مَا يَكُونُ لِيٓ أَنْ
أَقُولَ مَا لَيْسَ لِي بِحَقٍّ إِنْ كُنْتُ قُلْتُهٗ
فَقَدْ عَلِمْتَهٗ تَعْلَمُ مَا فِي نَفْسِي وَلَآ أَعْلَمُ
مَا فِي نَفْسِكَ إِنَّكَ أَنْتَ عَلّٰمُ الْغُيُوبِ ﴿١١٦﴾ مَا
قُلْتُ لَهُمْ إِلَّا مَآ أَمَرْتَنِي بِهٖٓ أَنِ اعْبُدُوا
اللّٰهَ رَبِّي وَرَبَّكُمْ وَكُنْتُ عَلَيْهِمْ شَهِيدًا مَّا
دُمْتُ فِيهِمْ فَلَمَّا تَوَفَّيْتَنِي كُنْتَ أَنْتَ
الرَّقِيبَ عَلَيْهِمْ وَأَنْتَ عَلٰى كُلِّ شَيْءٍ
شَهِيدٌ ﴿١١٧﴾ إِنْ تُعَذِّبْهُمْ فَإِنَّهُمْ عِبَادُكَ وَإِنْ
تَغْفِرْ لَهُمْ فَإِنَّكَ أَنْتَ الْعَزِيزُ الْحَكِيمُ ﴿١١٨﴾
قَالَ اللّٰهُ هٰذَا يَوْمُ يَنْفَعُ الصّٰدِقِينَ صِدْقُهُمْ
لَهُمْ جَنّٰتٌ تَجْرِي مِنْ تَحْتِهَا الْأَنْهٰرُ خٰلِدِينَ
فِيهَآ أَبَدًا رَضِيَ اللّٰهُ عَنْهُمْ وَرَضُوا عَنْهُ
ذٰلِكَ الْفَوْزُ الْعَظِيمُ ﴿١١٩﴾ لِلّٰهِ مُلْكُ السَّمٰوٰتِ
وَالْأَرْضِ وَمَا فِيهِنَّ وَهُوَ عَلٰى كُلِّ شَيْءٍ قَدِيرٌ ﴿١٢٠﴾

الْجُزْءُ السَّابِعُ

CHAPTER
6

AL-AN'ÂM
(The Cattle)
(Revealed Before Hijrah)

With the name of Allâh,
the Most Gracious, the Ever Merciful
(I commence to read Sûrah Al-An'âm).

1. **A**LL type of perfect and true praise belongs to Allâh Who created the heavens and the earth and brought into being all kinds of darkness and the light. Yet, inspite of this, those who disbelieve ascribe equals to their Lord.

2. It is He Who created you from clay, then He determined a term (of this life); and there is (yet another) term (of the life of the Hereafter) stated with Him, still you dispute (being doubtful about the Resurrection).

3. And He is Allâh Who alone (exercises every authority) in the heavens and in the earth. He knows you inside and outside, and He knows what you accomplish (by way of your deeds, good or bad).

4. (And as for the people) there comes to them no Message of the Messages of their Lord but they turn away from it.

5. So they have already cried lies to this perfect truth when it came to them, but soon there shall come to them the news of (the fulfillment of the prophecies) that they have been taking very lightly.

6. Have these people not considered how many generations We destroyed before them to whom We had given so firm a hold and power on the earth, such a firm hold as We have not given you? And We sent clouds over them pouring down abundant rain, and We caused rivers to flow subject to their command and control. Yet

سُوۡرَةُ الۡاَنۡعَامِ مَكِّيَّةٌ

بِسۡمِ اللّٰهِ الرَّحۡمٰنِ الرَّحِيۡمِ

اَلۡحَمۡدُ لِلّٰهِ الَّذِيۡ خَلَقَ السَّمٰوٰتِ وَ الۡاَرۡضَ
وَ جَعَلَ الظُّلُمٰتِ وَ النُّوۡرَ ؕ ثُمَّ الَّذِيۡنَ كَفَرُوۡا
بِرَبِّهِمۡ يَعۡدِلُوۡنَ ﴿١﴾ هُوَ الَّذِيۡ خَلَقَكُمۡ مِّنۡ
طِيۡنٍ ثُمَّ قَضٰۤى اَجَلًا ؕ وَ اَجَلٌ مُّسَمًّى عِنۡدَهٗ
ثُمَّ اَنۡتُمۡ تَمۡتَرُوۡنَ ﴿٢﴾ وَ هُوَ اللّٰهُ فِي السَّمٰوٰتِ
وَ فِي الۡاَرۡضِ ؕ يَعۡلَمُ سِرَّكُمۡ وَ جَهۡرَكُمۡ
وَ يَعۡلَمُ مَا تَكۡسِبُوۡنَ ﴿٣﴾ وَ مَا تَاۡتِيۡهِمۡ مِّنۡ اٰيَةٍ
مِّنۡ اٰيٰتِ رَبِّهِمۡ اِلَّا كَانُوۡا عَنۡهَا مُعۡرِضِيۡنَ ﴿٤﴾
فَقَدۡ كَذَّبُوۡا بِالۡحَقِّ لَمَّا جَآءَهُمۡ ؕ فَسَوۡفَ
يَاۡتِيۡهِمۡ اَنۡۢبٰٓؤُا مَا كَانُوۡا بِهٖ يَسۡتَهۡزِءُوۡنَ ﴿٥﴾
اَلَمۡ يَرَوۡا كَمۡ اَهۡلَكۡنَا مِنۡ قَبۡلِهِمۡ مِّنۡ
قَرۡنٍ مَّكَّنّٰهُمۡ فِي الۡاَرۡضِ مَا لَمۡ نُمَكِّنۡ لَّكُمۡ
وَ اَرۡسَلۡنَا السَّمَآءَ عَلَيۡهِمۡ مِّدۡرَارًا ۪ وَّ جَعَلۡنَا
الۡاَنۡهٰرَ تَجۡرِيۡ مِنۡ تَحۡتِهِمۡ فَاَهۡلَكۡنٰهُمۡ

We destroyed them owing to their sins and raised other generations after them.

7. And if We had sent down to you a book (written) on parchment and they had touched it with their own hands, (even then) those who have disbelieved would have invariably said, 'This is nothing but a fascinating device to cut off (from the people).'

8. And they said, '(If the Prophet is true and sincere in his claim) why has not an angel been sent down to (help) him?' But if We had sent down an angel the matter would have been decided, then they would not have been respited.

9. And had We appointed him (- this Messenger) from among the angels, We would surely have made him (appear as) a man and (even in that case) We would have obscured that which they are themselves obscuring now.

10. (O Muhammad!) Certainly Messengers have been treated scornfully before you but that (prophecy of the ultimate success of the Messenger) which they held in scorn recoiled on those who had held (the prophecy) in scorn.

بِذُنُوبِهِمْ وَأَنْشَأْنَا مِنْ بَعْدِهِمْ قَرْنًا آخَرِينَ ۝٦
وَلَوْ نَزَّلْنَا عَلَيْكَ كِتَابًا فِي قِرْطَاسٍ فَلَمَسُوهُ
بِأَيْدِيهِمْ لَقَالَ الَّذِينَ كَفَرُوا إِنْ هَٰذَا إِلَّا
سِحْرٌ مُبِينٌ ۝٧ وَقَالُوا لَوْلَا أُنْزِلَ عَلَيْهِ مَلَكٌ
وَلَوْ أَنْزَلْنَا مَلَكًا لَقُضِيَ الْأَمْرُ ثُمَّ لَا
يُنْظَرُونَ ۝٨ وَلَوْ جَعَلْنَاهُ مَلَكًا لَجَعَلْنَاهُ رَجُلًا
وَلَلَبَسْنَا عَلَيْهِمْ مَا يَلْبِسُونَ ۝٩ وَلَقَدِ
اسْتُهْزِئَ بِرُسُلٍ مِنْ قَبْلِكَ فَحَاقَ بِالَّذِينَ
سَخِرُوا مِنْهُمْ مَا كَانُوا بِهِ يَسْتَهْزِئُونَ ۝١٠ قُلْ
سِيرُوا فِي الْأَرْضِ ثُمَّ انْظُرُوا كَيْفَ كَانَ
عَاقِبَةُ الْمُكَذِّبِينَ ۝١١ قُلْ لِمَنْ مَا فِي السَّمَاوَاتِ
وَالْأَرْضِ قُلْ لِلَّهِ كَتَبَ عَلَىٰ نَفْسِهِ الرَّحْمَةَ
لَيَجْمَعَنَّكُمْ إِلَىٰ يَوْمِ الْقِيَامَةِ لَا رَيْبَ فِيهِ
الَّذِينَ خَسِرُوا أَنْفُسَهُمْ فَهُمْ لَا يُؤْمِنُونَ ۝١٢
وَلَهُ مَا سَكَنَ فِي اللَّيْلِ وَالنَّهَارِ وَهُوَ

ع ٧

SECTION 2

11. SAY, 'Go about in the land and see how (evil) was the end of those who treated (the Prophets) as liars.'

12. Ask (them), 'To whom belongs all that lies in the heavens and in the earth?' Then (since they will not be able to answer), say, '(It belongs) to Allâh.' He has taken upon Himself (the rule of) mercy (so He does not take the sinners to task immediately). He will continue to assemble you together till the Day of Resurrection. There is no doubt in it. Yet those who have lost their souls will not believe.

13. To Him belongs whatever exists in the darkness of the night and (whatever dwells in) the light of the day. And He is the All-Hearing, the All-Knowing.

14. Say, 'Shall I take to myself a patron other

than Allâh, the Originator of the heavens and the earth? It is He Who feeds but is fed by none.' Say, 'I have surely been commanded that I be the first of those who submit (to God).' (It has been said to them,) 'Be not of those who associate partners with Allâh.'

15. Say, 'If I disobey my Lord, I fear the punishment of the dreadful Day.'

16. He, from whomsoever this (punishment) is averted on that Day, (God) indeed has mercy on him, an obvious achievement is that!

17. If Allâh afflicts you with some harm, then no one can remove it but He. But if He bestows upon you a favour, remember that He is the Possessor of every power to do all that He will.

18. And He is the All-Dominant over His servants. And He is the All-Wise, the All-Aware.

19. Ask, 'Who is the best (witness) in respect of bearing testimony?' Say, 'It is Allâh, He is Witness between me and you, and this Qur'ân has been revealed to me so that I may thereby warn you and all those whom it may reach (against the evil consequences of disbelief and misdeeds).' What (do you say)? Do you in fact bear witness that there are other gods besides Allâh? Say, 'I do not bear witness thereto.' Say (moreover), 'The fact is that He is the One and Only God; and surely I am sick and quit all those whom you associate (with Him).'

20. Those whom We have given this perfect Book recognise him (- the Prophet Muhammad) as they recognise their own sons. Yet those who have lost their souls will not believe.

SECTION 3

21. **W**HO is more unjust than he who forges a lie in the name of Allâh or who cries lies to His Messages. Verily, such wrongdoers will never attain the goal.

22. (Beware of) the Day when We shall gather them all together, then We shall say to those who associate partners (with Us), 'Where are (now) your associate-gods about whom you

السَّمِيعُ الْعَلِيمُ (١٣) قُلْ أَغَيْرَ اللّٰهِ أَتَّخِذُ وَلِيًّا
فَاطِرِ السَّمٰوٰتِ وَالْأَرْضِ وَهُوَ يُطْعِمُ وَلَا
يُطْعَمُ قُلْ إِنِّيٓ أُمِرْتُ أَنْ أَكُونَ أَوَّلَ مَنْ
أَسْلَمَ وَلَا تَكُونَنَّ مِنَ الْمُشْرِكِينَ (١٤) قُلْ
إِنِّيٓ أَخَافُ إِنْ عَصَيْتُ رَبِّي عَذَابَ يَوْمٍ
عَظِيمٍ (١٥) مَنْ يُصْرَفْ عَنْهُ يَوْمَئِذٍ فَقَدْ
رَحِمَهُ وَذٰلِكَ الْفَوْزُ الْمُبِينُ (١٦) وَإِنْ
يَمْسَسْكَ اللّٰهُ بِضُرٍّ فَلَا كَاشِفَ لَهُ إِلَّا
هُوَ وَإِنْ يَمْسَسْكَ بِخَيْرٍ فَهُوَ عَلٰى كُلِّ
شَيْءٍ قَدِيرٌ (١٧) وَهُوَ الْقَاهِرُ فَوْقَ عِبَادِهِ
وَهُوَ الْحَكِيمُ الْخَبِيرُ (١٨) قُلْ أَيُّ شَيْءٍ أَكْبَرُ
شَهٰدَةً قُلِ اللّٰهُ شَهِيدٌ بَيْنِي وَبَيْنَكُمْ
وَأُوحِيَ إِلَيَّ هٰذَا الْقُرْاٰنُ لِأُنْذِرَكُمْ بِهِ وَمَنْ
بَلَغَ أَئِنَّكُمْ لَتَشْهَدُونَ أَنَّ مَعَ اللّٰهِ اٰلِهَةً
أُخْرٰى قُلْ لَّآ أَشْهَدُ قُلْ إِنَّمَا هُوَ إِلٰهٌ
وّٰحِدٌ وَّإِنَّنِي بَرِيٓءٌ مِّمَّا تُشْرِكُونَ (١٩) اَلَّذِينَ
اٰتَيْنٰهُمُ الْكِتٰبَ يَعْرِفُونَهُ كَمَا يَعْرِفُونَ
أَبْنَآءَهُمُ الَّذِينَ خَسِرُوٓا أَنْفُسَهُمْ فَهُمْ
لَا يُؤْمِنُونَ (٢٠) وَمَنْ أَظْلَمُ مِمَّنِ افْتَرٰى
عَلَى اللّٰهِ كَذِبًا أَوْ كَذَّبَ بِاٰيٰتِهِ إِنَّهُ لَا يُفْلِحُ
الظّٰلِمُونَ (٢١) وَيَوْمَ نَحْشُرُهُمْ جَمِيعًا ثُمَّ نَقُولُ

ع ٢ / ٨

used to assert (as gods)?'

23. (On that Day) they would have no excuse, but that they would say, 'By Allâh, Our Lord, we were never polytheists.'

24. Look! How they lie against themselves, and those (associate-gods) which they used to forge shall fail them.

25. Some of these (disbelievers pretend to) listen to you but We have put veils over their hearts (due to their own hard-heartedness) that they do not understand and there is heaviness in their ears (to listen to the truth). Even if they see every sign (of Ours), they would not believe therein; (their hard-heartedness has reached) such an extent that when they come to you, they dispute with you. Those who disbelieve say, 'This (Qur'ân) is nothing but fables of the ancients.'

26. They deter (others) from (believing in) this (Qur'ân) and (themselves too) keep away from it, yet it is their own ruin that they bring about (by such things), only they do not perceive (it).

27. Could you but see (them) when they are made to stand before the Fire (making a full appraisal of it). They will say then, 'Oh! Would that we could be sent back (to have a chance to mend our ways), then we would not cry lies to the revelations of our Lord and would be of the believers.'

28. Nay, it is only that this (- treachery of theirs) which they had been hiding before, must have (now) become obvious to them. Yet, even though if they were sent back they would again return to that which they were prohibited from. They are most certainly liars.

29. And they say, 'There is no life beyond this our present life. And we shall never be raised again.'

30. And could you but see when they are made to stand before their Lord, (He) will say, 'Is not this (Resurrection) true?' They shall say, 'Yes, indeed, by Our Lord, it is!' He will say, 'Suffer then the punishment as a result of your disbelief.'

لِلَّذِينَ أَشْرَكُوا أَيْنَ شُرَكَاؤُكُمُ الَّذِينَ كُنتُمْ
تَزْعُمُونَ ﴿٢٢﴾ ثُمَّ لَمْ تَكُن فِتْنَتُهُمْ إِلَّا أَن قَالُوا
وَاللَّهِ رَبِّنَا مَا كُنَّا مُشْرِكِينَ ﴿٢٣﴾ انظُرْ كَيْفَ
كَذَبُوا عَلَىٰ أَنفُسِهِمْ وَضَلَّ عَنْهُم مَّا كَانُوا
يَفْتَرُونَ ﴿٢٤﴾ وَمِنْهُم مَّن يَسْتَمِعُ إِلَيْكَ
وَجَعَلْنَا عَلَىٰ قُلُوبِهِمْ أَكِنَّةً أَن يَفْقَهُوهُ وَفِي
آذَانِهِمْ وَقْرًا وَإِن يَرَوْا كُلَّ آيَةٍ لَّا يُؤْمِنُوا
بِهَا حَتَّىٰ إِذَا جَاءُوكَ يُجَادِلُونَكَ يَقُولُ
الَّذِينَ كَفَرُوا إِنْ هَٰذَا إِلَّا أَسَاطِيرُ الْأَوَّلِينَ ﴿٢٥﴾
وَهُمْ يَنْهَوْنَ عَنْهُ وَيَنْأَوْنَ عَنْهُ وَإِن
يُهْلِكُونَ إِلَّا أَنفُسَهُمْ وَمَا يَشْعُرُونَ ﴿٢٦﴾ وَلَوْ
تَرَىٰ إِذْ وُقِفُوا عَلَى النَّارِ فَقَالُوا يَا لَيْتَنَا نُرَدُّ
وَلَا نُكَذِّبَ بِآيَاتِ رَبِّنَا وَنَكُونَ مِنَ الْمُؤْمِنِينَ ﴿٢٧﴾
بَلْ بَدَا لَهُم مَّا كَانُوا يُخْفُونَ مِن قَبْلُ وَلَوْ
رُدُّوا لَعَادُوا لِمَا نُهُوا عَنْهُ وَإِنَّهُمْ لَكَاذِبُونَ ﴿٢٨﴾
وَقَالُوا إِنْ هِيَ إِلَّا حَيَاتُنَا الدُّنْيَا وَمَا نَحْنُ
بِمَبْعُوثِينَ ﴿٢٩﴾ وَلَوْ تَرَىٰ إِذْ وُقِفُوا عَلَىٰ رَبِّهِمْ
قَالَ أَلَيْسَ هَٰذَا بِالْحَقِّ قَالُوا بَلَىٰ وَرَبِّنَا

SECTION 4

31. **T**HOSE who cried lies to (the news of) meeting Allâh have indeed suffered a loss; (they will go on denying it) until the Hour (of Resurrection) overtakes them unaware. They will then say, 'Woe to us, for our neglecting it (- the Hour, in our life).' And they shall be bearing the burdens (of their sins) on their backs. Behold! How evil is the burden they shall bear.
32. The life of this world is nought but a futile and frivolous thing causing diversion (from God). And certainly, the last abode is the best for those who guard against evil. Have you no sense?
33. We know full well that what they say (by way of denying Our Messages) grieves you, yet surely it is not you that they cry lies to, but it is the Messages of Allâh that these wrongdoers are deliberately rejecting.
34. Indeed, Messengers have already been cried lies to even before you, but they patiently persevered inspite of their having been rejected and persecuted till Our help came to them. None can alter the decrees of Allâh. There has already come to you some of the news of the Messengers (gone before).
35. If their (- of the disbelievers) turning away in aversion is hard on you (to bear) then you may, if you can, seek a tunnel into the earth or a ladder into the heaven and then bring them some sign (to bring all to guidance); but if Allâh had willed, He could surely have brought them all together (by force) to the guidance, so do not be of those who lack knowledge.
36. Only those who listen respond (to the truth). And as for the (spiritually) dead Allâh will raise them to life (after their being buried in graves,) they shall then be made to return to Him.
37. And they say, 'Why has not a sign (asked for) been revealed to him by his Lord?' Say, 'Surely, Allâh has power and is Appraiser (as to how and when) to send down a sign, but most

قَالَ فَذُوقُوا الْعَذَابَ بِمَا كُنْتُمْ تَكْفُرُونَ ﴿٣٠﴾
قَدْ خَسِرَ الَّذِينَ كَذَّبُوا بِلِقَاءِ اللّٰهِ حَتّٰى إِذَا
جَاءَتْهُمُ السَّاعَةُ بَغْتَةً قَالُوا يٰحَسْرَتَنَا عَلٰى
مَا فَرَّطْنَا فِيهَا وَهُمْ يَحْمِلُونَ أَوْزَارَهُمْ عَلٰى
ظُهُورِهِمْ أَلَا سَاءَ مَا يَزِرُونَ ﴿٣١﴾ وَمَا الْحَيٰوةُ
الدُّنْيَا إِلَّا لَعِبٌ وَلَهْوٌ وَلَلدَّارُ الْأٰخِرَةُ خَيْرٌ
لِلَّذِينَ يَتَّقُونَ أَفَلَا تَعْقِلُونَ ﴿٣٢﴾ قَدْ نَعْلَمُ إِنَّهُ
لَيَحْزُنُكَ الَّذِي يَقُولُونَ فَإِنَّهُمْ لَا يُكَذِّبُونَكَ
وَلٰكِنَّ الظّٰلِمِينَ بِأٰيٰتِ اللّٰهِ يَجْحَدُونَ ﴿٣٣﴾ وَلَقَدْ
كُذِّبَتْ رُسُلٌ مِنْ قَبْلِكَ فَصَبَرُوا عَلٰى مَا
كُذِّبُوا وَأُوذُوا حَتّٰى أَتٰىهُمْ نَصْرُنَا وَلَا
مُبَدِّلَ لِكَلِمٰتِ اللّٰهِ وَلَقَدْ جَاءَكَ مِنْ نَبَإِى
الْمُرْسَلِينَ ﴿٣٤﴾ وَإِنْ كَانَ كَبُرَ عَلَيْكَ إِعْرَاضُهُمْ
فَإِنِ اسْتَطَعْتَ أَنْ تَبْتَغِيَ نَفَقًا فِي الْأَرْضِ أَوْ
سُلَّمًا فِي السَّمَاءِ فَتَأْتِيَهُمْ بِأٰيَةٍ وَلَوْ شَاءَ
اللّٰهُ لَجَمَعَهُمْ عَلَى الْهُدٰى فَلَا تَكُونَنَّ مِنَ
الْجٰهِلِينَ ﴿٣٥﴾ إِنَّمَا يَسْتَجِيبُ الَّذِينَ يَسْمَعُونَ
وَالْمَوْتٰى يَبْعَثُهُمُ اللّٰهُ ثُمَّ إِلَيْهِ يُرْجَعُونَ ﴿٣٦﴾
وَقَالُوا لَوْلَا نُزِّلَ عَلَيْهِ أٰيَةٌ مِنْ رَبِّهِ قُلْ

of them know (it) not.'

38. There is no terrestrial creature (that crawls) in the earth nor a bird that flies (in the air) with its two wings but (they are) creatures like you, (all subject to the Divine laws). We have neglected nothing in (Our) this perfect Book (of law). Then to their Lord shall they all be gathered.

39. And those who cry lies to Our signs are deaf and dumb, (groping) in utter darkness. Allâh allows to perish whom He will. And whom He will, He sets on the right and exact path.

40. Say, 'Do you ever consider if the punishment of Allâh comes upon you or the (promised) Hour overtakes you, will you (then) call upon (any god) other than Allâh, if what you say be true?

41. 'Nay, but you will call upon Him alone, then He will, if He please, relieve (you) of that distress for (the removal of) which you called upon Him; and you will abandon those (false gods) which you associate with Him.'

SECTION 5

42. **W**E have already sent (Messengers) towards the communities before you, then (on their rejecting the Messengers) We afflicted them with destitution, calamities and adversities so that they might become humble (before Us).

43. Why did they not then, when Our punishment overtook them, grow humble? (It was for the fact that) their hearts had hardened and satan had made their deeds seem fair to them.

44. Then, when they abandoned that whereof they had been reminded, We opened to them the gates of everything. Until when they began to boast over what they were given, We seized them unawares; then behold! they were in sore despair (of all good).

45. In this way the last remnants of these people who had acted wrongfully were completely rooted out. (So it proved that) all perfect and true praise belongs to Allâh, the

إِنَّ اللهَ قَادِرٌ عَلَىٰ أَنْ يُنَزِّلَ ءَايَةً وَّلٰكِنَّ
أَكْثَرَهُمْ لَا يَعْلَمُونَ ﴿٣٧﴾ وَمَا مِنْ دَآبَّةٍ فِي
الْأَرْضِ وَلَا طٰٓئِرٍ يَطِيرُ بِجَنَاحَيْهِ إِلَّآ أُمَمٌ
أَمْثَالُكُمْ مَا فَرَّطْنَا فِي الْكِتٰبِ مِنْ شَيْءٍ ثُمَّ
إِلَىٰ رَبِّهِمْ يُحْشَرُونَ ﴿٣٨﴾ وَالَّذِينَ كَذَّبُوا بِأٰيٰتِنَا
صُمٌّ وَّبُكْمٌ فِي الظُّلُمٰتِ مَنْ يَشَإِ اللهُ يُضْلِلْهُ
وَمَنْ يَشَأْ يَجْعَلْهُ عَلَىٰ صِرٰطٍ مُّسْتَقِيمٍ ﴿٣٩﴾ قُلْ
أَرَءَيْتَكُمْ إِنْ أَتٰىكُمْ عَذَابُ اللهِ أَوْ أَتَتْكُمُ
السَّاعَةُ أَغَيْرَ اللهِ تَدْعُونَ إِنْ كُنْتُمْ
صٰدِقِينَ ﴿٤٠﴾ بَلْ إِيَّاهُ تَدْعُونَ فَيَكْشِفُ مَا
تَدْعُونَ إِلَيْهِ إِنْ شَآءَ وَتَنْسَوْنَ مَا تُشْرِكُونَ ﴿٤١﴾ ع ١١ ١٠
وَلَقَدْ أَرْسَلْنَآ إِلَىٰٓ أُمَمٍ مِّنْ قَبْلِكَ فَأَخَذْنٰهُمْ
بِالْبَأْسَآءِ وَالضَّرَّآءِ لَعَلَّهُمْ يَتَضَرَّعُونَ ﴿٤٢﴾ فَلَوْلَآ
إِذْ جَآءَهُمْ بَأْسُنَا تَضَرَّعُوا وَلٰكِنْ قَسَتْ قُلُوبُهُمْ
وَزَيَّنَ لَهُمُ الشَّيْطٰنُ مَا كَانُوا يَعْمَلُونَ ﴿٤٣﴾ فَلَمَّا
نَسُوا مَا ذُكِّرُوا بِهِ فَتَحْنَا عَلَيْهِمْ أَبْوٰبَ كُلِّ
شَيْءٍ حَتَّىٰٓ إِذَا فَرِحُوا بِمَآ أُوتُوٓا أَخَذْنٰهُمْ
بَغْتَةً فَإِذَا هُمْ مُّبْلِسُونَ ﴿٤٤﴾ فَقُطِعَ دَابِرُ

Lord of all the worlds.

46. Say, 'Have you ever considered if Allâh were to take away your hearing and your sight and set a seal upon your hearts, what god other than Allâh can restore these (boons) to you?' See how We expound (multiple) arguments in diverse ways. Yet they turn away thereafter.

47. Say, 'Did you ever consider if Allâh's punishment were to overtake you unaware or (after) manifest (warnings), would any be destroyed except the wrongdoing people?'

48. And We send not the Messengers but as Bearers of good tidings (to believers and doers of good) and as Warners (to disbelievers and evil doers) then whosoever believes and mends his ways will have no cause of fear, nor shall they grieve.

49. But those who cry lies to Our Messages shall be punished because of their disobedience.

50. Say, 'I do not say to you that with me are the treasures of Allâh, nor do I know the unseen; and I do not say to you (that) I am an angel. I indeed follow only what is revealed to me.' Say, 'Can a blind person and one gifted with sight be alike?' Will you not even then give thought?

SECTION 6

51. **S**o warn by means of this (Qur'ân) those who fear that they shall be gathered to their Lord, besides whom they have neither a protector nor any intercessor, so (warn them) that they may guard against evil.

52. And do not drive away those who call upon their Lord morning and evening seeking His pleasure. No responsibility lies on you on their account and no responsibility whatsoever lies on them on your account that you should drive them away. In case (you do it) you would be counted as the unjust.

53. In this way have We made a distinction in some of them from the other with the result that

الْقَوْمِ الَّذِينَ ظَلَمُوا ۚ وَالْحَمْدُ لِلَّهِ رَبِّ
الْعَلَمِينَ ﴿٤٥﴾ قُلْ أَرَءَيْتُمْ إِنْ أَخَذَ اللَّهُ سَمْعَكُمْ
وَأَبْصَرَكُمْ وَخَتَمَ عَلَى قُلُوبِكُمْ مَّنْ إِلَهٌ
غَيْرُ اللَّهِ يَأْتِيكُمْ بِهِ ۗ أَنْظُرْ كَيْفَ نُصَرِّفُ
الْأَيَتِ ثُمَّ هُمْ يَصْدِفُونَ ﴿٤٦﴾ قُلْ أَرَءَيْتَكُمْ
إِنْ أَتَكُمْ عَذَابُ اللَّهِ بَغْتَةً أَوْ جَهْرَةً هَلْ
يُهْلَكُ إِلَّا الْقَوْمُ الظَّلِمُونَ ﴿٤٧﴾ وَمَا نُرْسِلُ
الْمُرْسَلِينَ إِلَّا مُبَشِّرِينَ وَمُنْذِرِينَ ۚ فَمَنْ
أَمَنَ وَأَصْلَحَ فَلَا خَوْفٌ عَلَيْهِمْ وَلَا هُمْ
يَحْزَنُونَ ﴿٤٨﴾ وَالَّذِينَ كَذَّبُوا بِأَيَتِنَا يَمَسُّهُمُ
الْعَذَابُ بِمَا كَانُوا يَفْسُقُونَ ﴿٤٩﴾ قُلْ لَا أَقُولُ
لَكُمْ عِنْدِي خَزَائِنُ اللَّهِ وَلَا أَعْلَمُ الْغَيْبَ
وَلَا أَقُولُ لَكُمْ إِنِّي مَلَكٌ ۚ إِنْ أَتَّبِعُ إِلَّا مَا
يُوحَى إِلَيَّ ۚ قُلْ هَلْ يَسْتَوِي الْأَعْمَى وَالْبَصِيرُ
أَفَلَا تَتَفَكَّرُونَ ﴿٥٠﴾ وَأَنْذِرْ بِهِ الَّذِينَ يَخَافُونَ
أَنْ يُحْشَرُوا إِلَى رَبِّهِمْ لَيْسَ لَهُمْ مِّنْ دُونِهِ
وَلِيٌّ وَلَا شَفِيعٌ لَّعَلَّهُمْ يَتَّقُونَ ﴿٥١﴾ وَلَا تَطْرُدِ
الَّذِينَ يَدْعُونَ رَبَّهُمْ بِالْغَدَوةِ وَالْعَشِيِّ
يُرِيدُونَ وَجْهَهُ ۖ مَا عَلَيْكَ مِنْ حِسَابِهِمْ مِّنْ
شَيْءٍ وَمَا مِنْ حِسَابِكَ عَلَيْهِمْ مِّنْ شَيْءٍ
فَتَطْرُدَهُمْ فَتَكُونَ مِنَ الظَّلِمِينَ ﴿٥٢﴾ وَكَذَلِكَ

ع

they say, 'Are these the ones whom Allâh has favoured (by choosing them) from among us?' Does not Allâh know best the grateful?
54. When those who believe in Our Messages come to you, say, 'Peace be upon you. Your Lord has taken upon Himself (the rule of) mercy, so that whoso from among you commits evil through lack of knowledge then turns (for mercy towards his Lord) thereafter and mends his ways, then (his Lord forgives him because) He is Great Protector, Ever Merciful.'
55. That is how We expound Our arguments (that you may seek Allâh's mercy) and that the way of those who cut their ties (with God) may be exposed.

SECTION 7

56. **S**AY, 'I am strictly forbidden to worship those (false gods) whom you call upon besides Allâh.' Say, 'I do not follow your caprices. In that case I would have certainly become lost, and I would not have been of the guided ones.'
57. Say, 'Surely, I take my stand upon clear guidance from my Lord while you have cried lies to it. I have no power over that (punishment) which you seek to hasten before its (fixed) time. The judgment rests with none but Allâh. He declares the true judgment and He is the Best of deciders (as to whom, when and how to punish).'
58. Say, 'If I had power over that which you seek to hasten before its (appointed) time, the matter would have been decided between you and me. And Allâh knows best the unjust (and He also knows when to punish them).'
59. All the treasures of the unseen lie at His disposal. No one knows them but He; He knows whatsoever is in the land and in the sea. There falls not a single leaf but He knows it, nor is there a grain in the dark beds of the earth, nor anything fresh or dry but all is recorded in a clear book (- in God's perfect knowledge).

فَتَنَّا بَعْضَهُمْ بِبَعْضٍ لِّيَقُوْلُوْٓا اَهٰٓؤُلَآءِ مَنَّ اللّٰهُ
عَلَيْهِمْ مِّنْۢ بَيْنِنَا ؕ اَلَيْسَ اللّٰهُ بِاَعْلَمَ بِالشّٰكِرِيْنَ ﴿۵۳﴾
وَ اِذَا جَآءَكَ الَّذِيْنَ يُؤْمِنُوْنَ بِاٰيٰتِنَا فَقُلْ سَلٰمٌ
عَلَيْكُمْ كَتَبَ رَبُّكُمْ عَلٰى نَفْسِهِ الرَّحْمَةَ ۙ اَنَّهٗ
مَنْ عَمِلَ مِنْكُمْ سُوْٓءًۢا بِجَهَالَةٍ ثُمَّ تَابَ مِنْۢ
بَعْدِهٖ وَ اَصْلَحَ فَاَنَّهٗ غَفُوْرٌ رَّحِيْمٌ ﴿۵۴﴾ وَ كَذٰلِكَ
نُفَصِّلُ الْاٰيٰتِ وَ لِتَسْتَبِيْنَ سَبِيْلُ الْمُجْرِمِيْنَ ﴿۵۵﴾
قُلْ اِنِّيْ نُهِيْتُ اَنْ اَعْبُدَ الَّذِيْنَ تَدْعُوْنَ مِنْ
دُوْنِ اللّٰهِ ؕ قُلْ لَّآ اَتَّبِعُ اَهْوَآءَكُمْ ۙ قَدْ ضَلَلْتُ
اِذًا وَّ مَآ اَنَا مِنَ الْمُهْتَدِيْنَ ﴿۵۶﴾ قُلْ اِنِّيْ عَلٰى
بَيِّنَةٍ مِّنْ رَّبِّيْ وَ كَذَّبْتُمْ بِهٖ ؕ مَا عِنْدِيْ مَا
تَسْتَعْجِلُوْنَ بِهٖ ؕ اِنِ الْحُكْمُ اِلَّا لِلّٰهِ ؕ يَقُصُّ
الْحَقَّ وَ هُوَ خَيْرُ الْفٰصِلِيْنَ ﴿۵۷﴾ قُلْ لَّوْ اَنَّ عِنْدِيْ
مَا تَسْتَعْجِلُوْنَ بِهٖ لَقُضِيَ الْاَمْرُ بَيْنِيْ وَ بَيْنَكُمْ ؕ
وَ اللّٰهُ اَعْلَمُ بِالظّٰلِمِيْنَ ﴿۵۸﴾ وَ عِنْدَهٗ مَفَاتِحُ
الْغَيْبِ لَا يَعْلَمُهَآ اِلَّا هُوَ ؕ وَ يَعْلَمُ مَا فِي الْبَرِّ
وَ الْبَحْرِ ؕ وَ مَا تَسْقُطُ مِنْ وَّرَقَةٍ اِلَّا يَعْلَمُهَا وَ لَا

60. It is He Who takes your soul by night (in sleep) and He knows what you have done by day, yet He raises you up therein that the term stated (for your life) may be completed. Then to Him is your return, then He will inform you plainly about your deeds.

SECTION 8

61. **A**ND He is the All-Dominant over His servants, and He goes on sending guardians to watch over you. When death comes to one of you, Our messengers (- the angels) take away his soul. They neglect (their duty) in no way.
62. Then they shall all be made to return to Allâh, their Master the only True One. Surely, His is the judgment, He is the Swiftest of the reckoners.
63. Say, 'Who delivers you from the horrors of the land and the sea when you call upon Him in humility and in open supplication (saying), "If He delivers us from this (hardship) we shall ever be grateful (to Him)?"'
64. Say, 'It is Allâh who delivers you from these (horrors) and from every calamity, still you associate partners (with Him).'
65. Say, 'He has power to send upon you a calamity from above and from beneath your feet or He may throw you into confusion by making you confront with conflicting parties, and make you taste the dissension (and violence) of one another.' Behold! How We explain Our Messages in different ways so that they may give thought.
66. Your people have cried lies to this (Qur'ân), though it is the truth. Say, 'I am not responsible for your affairs.'
67. For (the fulfillment of) every prophecy there is an appointed time, and it will not go beyond that, and soon you will come to know (its truth).
68. And when you see those who engage in vain discourse about Our Messages, turn away from

حَبَّةٍ فِي ظُلُمٰتِ الْأَرْضِ وَلَا رَطْبٍ وَّلَا يَابِسٍ إِلَّا
فِي كِتٰبٍ مُّبِينٍ ﴿٥٩﴾ وَهُوَ الَّذِي يَتَوَفّٰكُمْ بِالَّيْلِ
وَيَعْلَمُ مَا جَرَحْتُمْ بِالنَّهَارِ ثُمَّ يَبْعَثُكُمْ فِيهِ
لِيُقْضٰى أَجَلٌ مُّسَمًّى ثُمَّ إِلَيْهِ مَرْجِعُكُمْ ثُمَّ
يُنَبِّئُكُمْ بِمَا كُنْتُمْ تَعْمَلُونَ ﴿٦٠﴾ وَهُوَ الْقَاهِرُ
فَوْقَ عِبَادِهِ وَيُرْسِلُ عَلَيْكُمْ حَفَظَةً حَتّٰى
إِذَا جَآءَ أَحَدَكُمُ الْمَوْتُ تَوَفَّتْهُ رُسُلُنَا وَهُمْ
لَا يُفَرِّطُونَ ﴿٦١﴾ ثُمَّ رُدُّوا إِلَى اللّٰهِ مَوْلٰهُمُ الْحَقِّ
أَلَا لَهُ الْحُكْمُ وَهُوَ أَسْرَعُ الْحٰسِبِينَ ﴿٦٢﴾ قُلْ
مَنْ يُّنَجِّيكُمْ مِّنْ ظُلُمٰتِ الْبَرِّ وَالْبَحْرِ تَدْعُونَهُ
تَضَرُّعًا وَّخُفْيَةً لَئِنْ أَنْجٰنَا مِنْ هٰذِهِ لَنَكُونَنَّ
مِنَ الشّٰكِرِينَ ﴿٦٣﴾ قُلِ اللّٰهُ يُنَجِّيكُمْ مِّنْهَا وَمِنْ
كُلِّ كَرْبٍ ثُمَّ أَنْتُمْ تُشْرِكُونَ ﴿٦٤﴾ قُلْ هُوَ الْقَادِرُ
عَلٰى أَنْ يَّبْعَثَ عَلَيْكُمْ عَذَابًا مِّنْ فَوْقِكُمْ أَوْ مِنْ
تَحْتِ أَرْجُلِكُمْ أَوْ يَلْبِسَكُمْ شِيَعًا وَّيُذِيقَ
بَعْضَكُمْ بَأْسَ بَعْضٍ انْظُرْ كَيْفَ نُصَرِّفُ الْأٰيٰتِ
لَعَلَّهُمْ يَفْقَهُونَ ﴿٦٥﴾ وَكَذَّبَ بِهِ قَوْمُكَ وَهُوَ الْحَقُّ
قُلْ لَّسْتُ عَلَيْكُمْ بِوَكِيلٍ ﴿٦٦﴾ لِكُلِّ نَبَإٍ مُّسْتَقَرٌّ

ع ٥ ١٣

them, until they engage in a topic other than that. And if satan should make you forget this (advice of Ours), then sit no more, after (its) recollection, with such wrongdoers.

69. Those who guard against evil are not in the least accountable for these (evildoers). They are only to admonish (them) so that they may too guard against evil.

70. And leave alone those who take their religion as a futile and frivolous thing causing diversion (from Allâh). Present life has beguiled them, therefore go on admonishing (such people) by means of this (Qur'ân) lest a soul should be consigned to perdition because of its misdeeds. There is no patron for it (- the soul) apart from Allâh, nor intercessor, and even if it may offer every compensation it will not be accepted from it. It is these who are destroyed for what they accomplished. There awaits them a drink of boiling water and a grievous punishment because they disbelieved.

SECTION 9

71. **S**AY, 'Shall we call, besides Allâh, upon that which can neither profit us nor harm us (by itself), and shall we be turned back on our heels (and led astray) after Allâh has guided us, like one whom the evil ones have made to follow his caprices (leaving him) utterly bewildered in the land; (whilst) he has companions who call him to the guidance (of Allâh, saying), "Come to us".' Say, 'Verily, Allâh's guidance is the only perfect guidance. And we are commanded (by Him) to submit to the Lord of all the worlds.'

72. 'And (we are also commanded by Him,) "Observe Prayer and take Him as a shield. And it is He to Whom you shall all be gathered".'

73. It is He Who has created the heavens and the earth to suit the requirements of truth and wisdom. The day He says, 'Be', it (- the Resurrection) shall come to be. His Word is bound to be carried out. To Him belongs the

وَسَوْفَ تَعْلَمُوْنَ ﴿٦٧﴾ وَإِذَا رَأَيْتَ الَّذِيْنَ يَخُوْضُوْنَ
فِيْٓ اٰيٰتِنَا فَأَعْرِضْ عَنْهُمْ حَتّٰى يَخُوْضُوْا فِيْ حَدِيْثٍ
غَيْرِهٖ ؕ وَإِمَّا يُنْسِيَنَّكَ الشَّيْطٰنُ فَلَا تَقْعُدْ
بَعْدَ الذِّكْرٰى مَعَ الْقَوْمِ الظّٰلِمِيْنَ ﴿٦٨﴾ وَمَا عَلَى
الَّذِيْنَ يَتَّقُوْنَ مِنْ حِسَابِهِمْ مِّنْ شَيْءٍ وَّلٰكِنْ
ذِكْرٰى لَعَلَّهُمْ يَتَّقُوْنَ ﴿٦٩﴾ وَذَرِ الَّذِيْنَ اتَّخَذُوْا
دِيْنَهُمْ لَعِبًا وَّلَهْوًا وَّغَرَّتْهُمُ الْحَيٰوةُ الدُّنْيَا
وَذَكِّرْ بِهٖٓ أَنْ تُبْسَلَ نَفْسٌۢ بِمَا كَسَبَتْ ۖ لَيْسَ
لَهَا مِنْ دُوْنِ اللّٰهِ وَلِيٌّ وَّلَا شَفِيْعٌ ۚ وَإِنْ تَعْدِلْ
كُلَّ عَدْلٍ لَّا يُؤْخَذْ مِنْهَا ؕ أُولٰٓئِكَ الَّذِيْنَ أُبْسِلُوْا
بِمَا كَسَبُوْا ۚ لَهُمْ شَرَابٌ مِّنْ حَمِيْمٍ وَّعَذَابٌ
أَلِيْمٌۢ بِمَا كَانُوْا يَكْفُرُوْنَ ﴿٧٠﴾ قُلْ أَنَدْعُوْا مِنْ
دُوْنِ اللّٰهِ مَا لَا يَنْفَعُنَا وَلَا يَضُرُّنَا وَنُرَدُّ عَلٰٓى
أَعْقَابِنَا بَعْدَ إِذْ هَدٰىنَا اللّٰهُ كَالَّذِي اسْتَهْوَتْهُ
الشَّيٰطِيْنُ فِي الْأَرْضِ حَيْرَانَ ۠ لَهٗٓ أَصْحٰبٌ
يَدْعُوْنَهٗٓ إِلَى الْهُدَى ائْتِنَا ؕ قُلْ إِنَّ هُدَى اللّٰهِ
هُوَ الْهُدٰى ؕ وَأُمِرْنَا لِنُسْلِمَ لِرَبِّ الْعٰلَمِيْنَ ﴿٧١﴾
وَأَنْ أَقِيْمُوا الصَّلٰوةَ وَاتَّقُوْهُ ؕ وَهُوَ الَّذِيْٓ إِلَيْهِ
تُحْشَرُوْنَ ﴿٧٢﴾ وَهُوَ الَّذِيْ خَلَقَ السَّمٰوٰتِ
وَالْأَرْضَ بِالْحَقِّ ؕ وَيَوْمَ يَقُوْلُ كُنْ فَيَكُوْنُ ۚ

sovereignty on the day when the trumpet will be blown (for spiritual awakening in this world and for physical Resurrection in the Hereafter). He is the Knower of all the hidden realities and the seen. And He is the All-Wise, the All-Aware.

74. (Recall the time) when Abraham said to his sire Azar, 'Do you worship idols as gods? Surely, I see you and your people (steeped) in clear error.'

75. Thus (for his pure and noble nature) We have been showing Abraham, the sole kingdom (of Ours) of the heavens and the earth (to grant him an insight into the Divine laws of nature). And (We did it) that he might be of those who are firmly convinced.

76. Then (after being convinced of Our unity once on the occasion of a debate on the topic) when the night darkened over him, he saw a planet. He said (on seeing it to the idol-worshippers), 'Is this my Lord (as you assert)?' But when it set he said, 'I do not love the setting ones (to accept as my God).'

77. Then when he saw the moon rise with spreading light he said (to the people), 'Is this my Lord (as you assert)?' But when it set he said, 'Had my Lord not guided me aright I would have, invariably, been of the people who have gone astray.'

78. And when he saw the sun rise with spreading light (he said to them), 'Is this my Lord (as you assert, as) this is the biggest? But when it (also) set he said, 'O my people! I am surely (sick and) quit of that you associate (with Him).

79. 'Surely, I have turned myself with devotion and in a most upright manner to Him Who originated the heavens and the earth. I have never been of the polytheists.'

80. His people tried to overpower him in argument, he said, 'Do you argue with me regarding Allâh, when He (Himself) has already guided me aright? And I fear not, in anyway, the things you worship besides Him,

قَوْلُهُ الْحَقُّ ۚ وَلَهُ الْمُلْكُ يَوْمَ يُنفَخُ فِي الصُّورِ ۚ
عَالِمُ الْغَيْبِ وَالشَّهَادَةِ ۚ وَهُوَ الْحَكِيمُ الْخَبِيرُ ﴿٧٣﴾
وَإِذْ قَالَ إِبْرَاهِيمُ لِأَبِيهِ آزَرَ أَتَتَّخِذُ أَصْنَامًا
آلِهَةً ۖ إِنِّي أَرَاكَ وَقَوْمَكَ فِي ضَلَالٍ مُّبِينٍ ﴿٧٤﴾
وَكَذَٰلِكَ نُرِي إِبْرَاهِيمَ مَلَكُوتَ السَّمَاوَاتِ
وَالْأَرْضِ وَلِيَكُونَ مِنَ الْمُوقِنِينَ ﴿٧٥﴾ فَلَمَّا جَنَّ
عَلَيْهِ اللَّيْلُ رَأَىٰ كَوْكَبًا ۖ قَالَ هَٰذَا رَبِّي ۖ فَلَمَّا أَفَلَ
قَالَ لَا أُحِبُّ الْآفِلِينَ ﴿٧٦﴾ فَلَمَّا رَأَى الْقَمَرَ بَازِغًا
قَالَ هَٰذَا رَبِّي ۖ فَلَمَّا أَفَلَ قَالَ لَئِن لَّمْ يَهْدِنِي
رَبِّي لَأَكُونَنَّ مِنَ الْقَوْمِ الضَّالِّينَ ﴿٧٧﴾ فَلَمَّا رَأَى
الشَّمْسَ بَازِغَةً قَالَ هَٰذَا رَبِّي هَٰذَا أَكْبَرُ ۖ
فَلَمَّا أَفَلَتْ قَالَ يَا قَوْمِ إِنِّي بَرِيءٌ مِّمَّا تُشْرِكُونَ ﴿٧٨﴾
إِنِّي وَجَّهْتُ وَجْهِيَ لِلَّذِي فَطَرَ السَّمَاوَاتِ
وَالْأَرْضَ حَنِيفًا ۖ وَمَا أَنَا مِنَ الْمُشْرِكِينَ ﴿٧٩﴾
وَحَاجَّهُ قَوْمُهُ ۚ قَالَ أَتُحَاجُّونِّي فِي اللَّهِ وَقَدْ

unless it is my Lord Who wills some (harm to me, it is a different) thing. My Lord comprehends all things in His knowledge. Will you not even then take admonition?

81. 'How (and why) should I fear (the things) that you associate with Him, while you are not afraid that you have associated those things with Allâh for (the worship of) which He has given you no authority?' Which of the two parties then (of the monotheists and polytheists) is better entitled to security (and salvation) if you truly know?

82. It is only those who believe and have not polluted their faith with associating partners with Allâh, to whom belongs peace (and salvation). It is these alone who are rightly guided.

SECTION 10

83. **T**HAT was Our argument with which We equipped Abraham against his people. We raise, in degrees of rank, whom We will. Verily, your Lord is All-Wise, All-Knowing.

84. And We granted him Isaac and Jacob, each one We guided aright, and Noah did We guide before, And of his descendants, We guided David, Solomon, Job, Joseph, Moses and Aaron. In this way do We reward the performers of good to others.

85. And (We guided) Zachariah, John, Jesus and Elias, everyone (of them) was of the righteous.

86. And (We also guided) Ismâîl and Elisha and Jonah and Lot - and everyone did We exalt above their people.

87. And (We exalted men) from among their fathers and their descendants and their brethren. We chose them and We guided them along the exact right path.

88. That is the guidance of Allâh, He guides by it such of His servants as He will. But if they had

هَدٰىنِ وَلَآ أَخَافُ مَا تُشْرِكُونَ بِهِۦٓ إِلَّآ أَن
يَشَآءَ رَبِّي شَيْـًٔا وَسِعَ رَبِّي كُلَّ شَيْءٍ عِلْمًا
أَفَلَا تَتَذَكَّرُونَ ﴿٨٠﴾ وَكَيْفَ أَخَافُ مَآ أَشْرَكْتُمْ
وَلَا تَخَافُونَ أَنَّكُمْ أَشْرَكْتُم بِاللّٰهِ مَا لَمْ يُنَزِّلْ
بِهِۦ عَلَيْكُمْ سُلْطٰنًا فَأَيُّ الْفَرِيقَيْنِ أَحَقُّ بِالْأَمْنِ
إِن كُنتُمْ تَعْلَمُونَ ﴿٨١﴾ الَّذِينَ ءَامَنُوا وَلَمْ يَلْبِسُوٓا
إِيمٰنَهُم بِظُلْمٍ أُولٰٓئِكَ لَهُمُ الْأَمْنُ وَهُم
مُّهْتَدُونَ ﴿٨٢﴾ وَتِلْكَ حُجَّتُنَآ ءَاتَيْنٰهَآ إِبْرٰهِيمَ عَلٰى
قَوْمِهِۦ نَرْفَعُ دَرَجٰتٍ مَّن نَّشَآءُ إِنَّ رَبَّكَ حَكِيمٌ
عَلِيمٌ ﴿٨٣﴾ وَوَهَبْنَا لَهُۥٓ إِسْحٰقَ وَيَعْقُوبَ كُلًّا
هَدَيْنَا وَنُوحًا هَدَيْنَا مِن قَبْلُ وَمِن ذُرِّيَّتِهِۦ
دَاوُۥدَ وَسُلَيْمٰنَ وَأَيُّوبَ وَيُوسُفَ وَمُوسٰى وَهٰرُونَ
وَكَذٰلِكَ نَجْزِي الْمُحْسِنِينَ ﴿٨٤﴾ وَزَكَرِيَّا وَيَحْيٰى
وَعِيسٰى وَإِلْيَاسَ كُلٌّ مِّنَ الصّٰلِحِينَ ﴿٨٥﴾
وَإِسْمٰعِيلَ وَالْيَسَعَ وَيُونُسَ وَلُوطًا وَكُلًّا
فَضَّلْنَا عَلَى الْعٰلَمِينَ ﴿٨٦﴾ وَمِنْ ءَابَآئِهِمْ وَذُرِّيّٰتِهِمْ
وَإِخْوٰنِهِمْ وَاجْتَبَيْنٰهُمْ وَهَدَيْنٰهُمْ إِلٰى صِرٰطٍ

ع ١٢ ٩ ١٥

associated partners (with Him in their worship), surely all their deeds would have gone in vain.

89. It is these (Messengers) to whom We gave the Scripture, the decisive authority and the prophethood. But if these (the so-called preservers of the Book) reject these (blissful things - the Book, the authority and the prophecy, it matters little) for We have now entrusted them to a people (- the Muslims) who are not at all ungrateful for these (blessings).

90. It is these whom Allâh has guided; so follow their guidance. Say, 'I ask you no reward for bringing this (guidance). This is nought but a reminder for all the worlds.'

SECTION 11

91. **T**HEY (- the deniers) have not appreciated Allâh with the true honour due to Him when they said, 'Allâh has not revealed anything to any human being.' Say, 'Who had revealed the Scripture which Moses brought; a light and guidance for the people, (though) you render it as scraps of paper, (some of) which you show while the major portion you hide, whereas you have been taught (through) that which you did not know, neither you, nor your forefathers?' Say, 'Allâh (revealed it).' Then leave them amusing themselves in their vain discourse.

92. And (similar to the Torah is) this splendid Book which We have revealed, full of blessings, completing (in a comprehensive form all the Divine Messages) which were before it, and (is revealed) that you may warn (the people of) this centre of cities (- the Makkans) and (the people of the places) all around it (- the people of the whole world). And those who believe in the Hereafter believe also in this (Qur'ân), and they are most careful about (performing) their Prayer.

93. Who is more unjust than the person who fabricates a lie in the name of Allâh deliberately or says, 'A revelation has been sent to me,' while nothing has been revealed to him, and the

مُسْتَقِيمٍ ﴿٨٧﴾ ذٰلِكَ هُدَى اللّٰهِ يَهْدِي بِهٖ مَنْ
يَّشَآءُ مِنْ عِبَادِهٖ ۚ وَلَوْ أَشْرَكُوا لَحَبِطَ عَنْهُمْ
مَّا كَانُوا يَعْمَلُونَ ﴿٨٨﴾ أُولٰٓئِكَ الَّذِينَ أٰتَيْنٰهُمُ
الْكِتٰبَ وَالْحُكْمَ وَالنُّبُوَّةَ ۚ فَإِنْ يَّكْفُرْ بِهَا هٰٓؤُلَآءِ
فَقَدْ وَكَّلْنَا بِهَا قَوْمًا لَّيْسُوا بِهَا بِكٰفِرِينَ ﴿٨٩﴾
أُولٰٓئِكَ الَّذِينَ هَدَى اللّٰهُ فَبِهُدٰىهُمُ اقْتَدِهْ ۗ
قُلْ لَّآ أَسْئَلُكُمْ عَلَيْهِ أَجْرًا ۚ إِنْ هُوَ إِلَّا ذِكْرٰى
لِلْعٰلَمِينَ ﴿٩٠﴾ ع ٨/١٦ وَمَا قَدَرُوا اللّٰهَ حَقَّ قَدْرِهٖٓ إِذْ قَالُوا
مَآ أَنْزَلَ اللّٰهُ عَلٰى بَشَرٍ مِّنْ شَيْءٍ ۗ قُلْ مَنْ أَنْزَلَ
الْكِتٰبَ الَّذِي جَآءَ بِهٖ مُوسٰى نُورًا وَّهُدًى
لِّلنَّاسِ تَجْعَلُونَهٗ قَرَاطِيسَ تُبْدُونَهَا وَتُخْفُونَ
كَثِيرًا ۚ وَعُلِّمْتُمْ مَّا لَمْ تَعْلَمُوٓا أَنْتُمْ وَلَآ أٰبَآؤُكُمْ ۖ
قُلِ اللّٰهُ ۙ ثُمَّ ذَرْهُمْ فِي خَوْضِهِمْ يَلْعَبُونَ ﴿٩١﴾
وَهٰذَا كِتٰبٌ أَنْزَلْنٰهُ مُبٰرَكٌ مُّصَدِّقُ الَّذِي
بَيْنَ يَدَيْهِ وَلِتُنْذِرَ أُمَّ الْقُرٰى وَمَنْ حَوْلَهَا ۚ
وَالَّذِينَ يُؤْمِنُونَ بِالْأٰخِرَةِ يُؤْمِنُونَ بِهٖ وَهُمْ
عَلٰى صَلَاتِهِمْ يُحَافِظُونَ ﴿٩٢﴾ وَمَنْ أَظْلَمُ مِمَّنِ

person who says, 'I will (also) bring down the like what Allâh has sent down?' Could you but see the wrongdoers when they are in the agonies of death and when the angels would lay down their hands on them saying, 'Give up your souls. This day you shall be given a disgraceful punishment on account of that falsehood which you uttered regarding Allâh wrongfully and (because) you disdained His revelations.'
94. (God will say on that day,) 'How is it that you have come to Us all alone as We created you in the first instance and you have left that which We put in your charge (in the world) behind yourselves, and We do not see with you your intercessors whom you (falsely) asserted that they were (Our) partisans in (the disposal of) matters relating to you. Indeed the ties between you (and your false deities) are now cut off and the things you falsely asserted (to be gods) have failed you.'

SECTION 12

95. **V**ERILY, it is Allâh Who splits the (seed) grains and (fruit) stones. He brings forth the living out of the lifeless and He brings forth the lifeless out of the living. Such is Allâh, wherefore then are you turned back.
96. He is the cleaver of the daybreak (from the dark of the night), and He has made the night for rest, and the sun and the moon for reckoning (of time). That is the decree of the All-Mighty, the All-Knowing.
97. It is He Who has made the stars for you that you may follow the right course with their help in the darkness of the land and the sea. We have certainly explained (Our) commandments in detail for a people who would know.
98. It is He Who has evolved you from one living entity, then (He provided for you) a permanent abode (from the grave to the final abode of bliss) and a temporary lodging (from the loins of the father to the grave).

افۡتَرٰى عَلَى اللّٰهِ كَذِبًا اَوۡ قَالَ اُوۡحِيَ اِلَيَّ وَلَمۡ يُوۡحَ
اِلَيۡهِ شَيۡءٌ وَّمَنۡ قَالَ سَاُنۡزِلُ مِثۡلَ مَاۤ اَنۡزَلَ
اللّٰهُ ؕ وَلَوۡ تَرٰۤى اِذِ الظّٰلِمُوۡنَ فِىۡ غَمَرٰتِ الۡمَوۡتِ
وَالۡمَلٰٓئِكَةُ بَاسِطُوۡۤا اَيۡدِيۡهِمۡ ۚ اَخۡرِجُوۡۤا اَنۡفُسَكُمۡ ؕ
اَلۡيَوۡمَ تُجۡزَوۡنَ عَذَابَ الۡهُوۡنِ بِمَا كُنۡتُمۡ تَقُوۡلُوۡنَ
عَلَى اللّٰهِ غَيۡرَ الۡحَقِّ وَكُنۡتُمۡ عَنۡ اٰيٰتِهٖ تَسۡتَكۡبِرُوۡنَ ﴿٩٣﴾
وَلَقَدۡ جِئۡتُمُوۡنَا فُرَادٰى كَمَا خَلَقۡنٰكُمۡ اَوَّلَ مَرَّةٍ
وَّتَرَكۡتُمۡ مَّا خَوَّلۡنٰكُمۡ وَرَآءَ ظُهُوۡرِكُمۡ ۚ وَمَا نَرٰى
مَعَكُمۡ شُفَعَآءَكُمُ الَّذِيۡنَ زَعَمۡتُمۡ اَنَّهُمۡ فِيۡكُمۡ
شُرَكٰٓؤُا ؕ لَقَدۡ تَّقَطَّعَ بَيۡنَكُمۡ وَضَلَّ عَنۡكُمۡ مَّا كُنۡتُمۡ
تَزۡعُمُوۡنَ ﴿٩٤﴾ اِنَّ اللّٰهَ فَالِقُ الۡحَبِّ وَالنَّوٰى ؕ يُخۡرِجُ
الۡحَىَّ مِنَ الۡمَيِّتِ وَمُخۡرِجُ الۡمَيِّتِ مِنَ الۡحَىِّ ؕ
ذٰلِكُمُ اللّٰهُ فَاَنّٰى تُؤۡفَكُوۡنَ ﴿٩٥﴾ فَالِقُ الۡاِصۡبَاحِ ۚ
وَجَعَلَ الَّيۡلَ سَكَنًا وَّالشَّمۡسَ وَالۡقَمَرَ حُسۡبَانًا ؕ
ذٰلِكَ تَقۡدِيۡرُ الۡعَزِيۡزِ الۡعَلِيۡمِ ﴿٩٦﴾ وَهُوَ الَّذِىۡ جَعَلَ
لَكُمُ النُّجُوۡمَ لِتَهۡتَدُوۡا بِهَا فِىۡ ظُلُمٰتِ الۡبَرِّ
وَالۡبَحۡرِ ؕ قَدۡ فَصَّلۡنَا الۡاٰيٰتِ لِقَوۡمٍ يَّعۡلَمُوۡنَ ﴿٩٧﴾
وَهُوَ الَّذِىۡۤ اَنۡشَاَكُمۡ مِّنۡ نَّفۡسٍ وَّاحِدَةٍ فَمُسۡتَقَرٌّ

ع ١٢ ١٧

Verily. We have explained (Our) signs in detail for a people who would understand.
99. It is We Who pour down water from the clouds and then We bring forth every kind of vegetation, then We bring forth therefrom green foliage from which We produce clustered grain. And (We bring forth) from the date-palm out of its spathes bunches (of dates) hanging low and (We bring forth) gardens of vines and olives and pomegranate - similar (in kind) yet dissimilar (from one another in variety). Look at them when they bear fruit and look also how they ripen. Verily, in all this there are signs for a people who would believe.
100. Yet they ascribe to Allâh as (His) associates the *jinns*, although He has created them also. And they falsely ascribe to Him sons and daughters without any knowledge. Glory be to Him. And He is far beyond and above all the things that they attribute (to Him).

SECTION 13

101. **H**E is Wonderful and Primary Originator of the heavens and the earth! How (and whence) can there be a son for Him, when He has no consort? He has created all things and He has perfect knowledge of everything.
102. Such is Allâh, your Lord. There is no other, cannot be and will never be one worthy of worship but He, the Creator of all things; therefore worship Him, for He is the Disposer of all affairs.
103. The physical vision comprehends Him not, but He comprehends all visions, He is the All-Subtle Being (incomprehensible and imperceptible), the All-Aware.
104. (Say,) 'There has already come to you enlightenment and clear proofs from your Lord, then whosoever sees clearly (and is enlightened), it is for his own good, and whosoever chooses to remain blind, it is to

وَّ مُسْتَوْدَعٌ قَدْ فَصَّلْنَا الْأٰيٰتِ لِقَوْمٍ يَّفْقَهُوْنَ ﴿٩٨﴾
وَ هُوَ الَّذِيْٓ أَنْزَلَ مِنَ السَّمَآءِ مَآءً فَأَخْرَجْنَا
بِهٖ نَبَاتَ كُلِّ شَيْءٍ فَأَخْرَجْنَا مِنْهُ خَضِرًا
نُّخْرِجُ مِنْهُ حَبًّا مُّتَرَاكِبًا وَ مِنَ النَّخْلِ مِنْ
طَلْعِهَا قِنْوَانٌ دَانِيَةٌ وَّ جَنّٰتٍ مِّنْ أَعْنَابٍ
وَّ الزَّيْتُوْنَ وَ الرُّمَّانَ مُشْتَبِهًا وَّ غَيْرَ مُتَشَابِهٍ
أُنْظُرُوْٓا إِلٰى ثَمَرِهٖٓ إِذَآ أَثْمَرَ وَ يَنْعِهٖ إِنَّ فِيْ
ذٰلِكُمْ لَأٰيٰتٍ لِّقَوْمٍ يُّؤْمِنُوْنَ ﴿٩٩﴾ وَ جَعَلُوْا لِلّٰهِ
شُرَكَآءَ الْجِنَّ وَ خَلَقَهُمْ وَ خَرَقُوْا لَهٗ بَنِيْنَ
وَ بَنٰتٍۭ بِغَيْرِ عِلْمٍ سُبْحٰنَهٗ وَ تَعٰلٰى عَمَّا
يَصِفُوْنَ ﴿١٠٠﴾ بَدِيْعُ السَّمٰوٰتِ وَ الْأَرْضِ أَنّٰى
يَكُوْنُ لَهٗ وَلَدٌ وَّ لَمْ تَكُنْ لَّهٗ صٰحِبَةٌ
وَ خَلَقَ كُلَّ شَيْءٍ وَ هُوَ بِكُلِّ شَيْءٍ عَلِيْمٌ ﴿١٠١﴾
ذٰلِكُمُ اللّٰهُ رَبُّكُمْ لَآ إِلٰهَ إِلَّا هُوَ خَالِقُ كُلِّ شَيْءٍ
فَاعْبُدُوْهُ وَ هُوَ عَلٰى كُلِّ شَيْءٍ وَّكِيْلٌ ﴿١٠٢﴾ لَا
تُدْرِكُهُ الْأَبْصٰرُ وَ هُوَ يُدْرِكُ الْأَبْصٰرَ وَ هُوَ
اللَّطِيْفُ الْخَبِيْرُ ﴿١٠٣﴾ قَدْ جَآءَكُمْ بَصَآئِرُ مِنْ
رَّبِّكُمْ فَمَنْ أَبْصَرَ فَلِنَفْسِهٖ وَ مَنْ عَمِيَ

ع ١٢ ٦ ١٨

his own loss. I am not a guardian over you (as I should ward off all evil by force).'

105. Thus do We explain Our revelations in diverse ways (that the truth might become evident), but (its one result is) that they (- the disbelievers) will say (to the Prophet), 'You have learnt well and diligently (from previous Scripture);' but (We vary the revelations) that it may be a clear explanation from us to the people who have knowledge.

106. Follow what has been revealed to you from your Lord, there is no other, cannot be and will never be one worthy of worship but He; and turn away from the polytheists.

107. If Allâh had (enforced) His will, they would not have associated partners with Him. And We have not made you a guardian over them, nor are you a disposer of their affairs.

108. Do not revile those whom they call upon besides Allâh, lest they should revile Allâh transgressingly (and) through lack of knowledge. Just as We made their deeds fair-seeming to them so have We made to each people fair-seeming what they do. Then to their Lord is their return, so He will inform them as to what they have been doing.

109. And they swear by Allâh their most solemn oaths that if there comes to them a (particular) sign they would invariably believe in it. Say, '(Not to speak of a single sign) there are indeed many signs with Allâh, but what is there to assure you that when that (sign) comes, even then, they will not believe.'

110. We shall confound their hearts and their eyes, since they did not believe in it (- God's signs) in the first instance, and We shall leave them alone wandering blindly in their transgression.

فَعَلَيْهَا ۚ وَمَآ أَنَا۠ عَلَيْكُم بِحَفِيظٍ ﴿١٠٤﴾ وَكَذٰلِكَ
نُصَرِّفُ الْأٓيٰتِ وَلِيَقُولُوا دَرَسْتَ وَلِنُبَيِّنَهُ
لِقَوْمٍ يَعْلَمُونَ ﴿١٠٥﴾ اتَّبِعْ مَآ أُوحِيَ إِلَيْكَ
مِن رَّبِّكَ ۖ لَآ إِلٰهَ إِلَّا هُوَ ۖ وَأَعْرِضْ عَنِ
الْمُشْرِكِينَ ﴿١٠٦﴾ وَلَوْ شَآءَ اللّٰهُ مَآ أَشْرَكُوا ۗ
وَمَا جَعَلْنٰكَ عَلَيْهِمْ حَفِيظًا ۖ وَمَآ أَنْتَ عَلَيْهِم
بِوَكِيلٍ ﴿١٠٧﴾ وَلَا تَسُبُّوا الَّذِينَ يَدْعُونَ مِن
دُونِ اللّٰهِ فَيَسُبُّوا اللّٰهَ عَدْوًا بِغَيْرِ عِلْمٍ ۗ
كَذٰلِكَ زَيَّنَّا لِكُلِّ أُمَّةٍ عَمَلَهُمْ ثُمَّ
إِلَىٰ رَبِّهِم مَّرْجِعُهُمْ فَيُنَبِّئُهُم بِمَا كَانُوا
يَعْمَلُونَ ﴿١٠٨﴾ وَأَقْسَمُوا بِاللّٰهِ جَهْدَ أَيْمٰنِهِمْ
لَئِن جَآءَتْهُمْ ءَايَةٌ لَّيُؤْمِنُنَّ بِهَا ۚ قُلْ
إِنَّمَا الْأٓيٰتُ عِندَ اللّٰهِ ۖ وَمَا يُشْعِرُكُمْ
أَنَّهَآ إِذَا جَآءَتْ لَا يُؤْمِنُونَ ﴿١٠٩﴾ وَنُقَلِّبُ
أَفْـِٔدَتَهُمْ وَأَبْصٰرَهُمْ كَمَا لَمْ يُؤْمِنُوا بِهِ
أَوَّلَ مَرَّةٍ وَنَذَرُهُمْ فِي طُغْيٰنِهِمْ يَعْمَهُونَ ﴿١١٠﴾

ع ١٣

SECTION 14

111. **E**VEN if We should send down the angels to them, and the dead should speak to them, and even if We should bring all things together face to face (to them), they would not believe unless Allâh had (enforced) His will. The thing is that most of them persist in ignorance.

112. And in the same manner have We made the evil ones from among (ordinary) human beings and the *jinns* enemies to every prophet; some of them suggest one to another gilded speech to beguile (them). Had your Lord (enforced) His will, they would not have done so; so leave them alone with what they forge;

113. And the result (of their so doing) is that the hearts of those who do not believe in the Hereafter are inclined to it (- their guile), and they take pleasure therein and they continue committing their (evil) deeds as they are doing.

114. (Say,) 'What! Shall I seek for a judge (to decide between us) other than Allâh, when it is He, Who has revealed to you this perfect Book clearly explained?' And those to whom We have given this Book know that it is revealed by your Lord with all the requirements of truth and wisdom, so be not of the disputers.

115. The (prophetic) word of your Lord is bound to be fulfilled in truth and justice. There is no one who can change His words. He is the All-Hearing, the All-Knowing.

116. Should you obey the majority of those on earth, they would lead you astray from Allâh's way. They follow nothing but mere surmise and they do nothing but make conjectures.

117. Surely He, Your Lord, knows best who goes astray from His way; as He knows best the rightly guided.

118. So (do not follow those who go astray, and) eat of that over which the name of Allâh

وَلَوْ أَنَّنَا نَزَّلْنَا إِلَيْهِمُ الْمَلٰٓئِكَةَ وَكَلَّمَهُمُ
الْمَوْتٰى وَحَشَرْنَا عَلَيْهِمْ كُلَّ شَيْءٍ قُبُلًا
مَّا كَانُوا لِيُؤْمِنُوٓا إِلَّآ أَنْ يَشَآءَ اللّٰهُ وَلٰكِنَّ
أَكْثَرَهُمْ يَجْهَلُونَ ﴿١١١﴾ وَكَذٰلِكَ جَعَلْنَا لِكُلِّ
نَبِيٍّ عَدُوًّا شَيٰطِينَ الْإِنْسِ وَالْجِنِّ يُوحِي
بَعْضُهُمْ إِلٰى بَعْضٍ زُخْرُفَ الْقَوْلِ غُرُورًا
وَلَوْ شَآءَ رَبُّكَ مَا فَعَلُوهُ فَذَرْهُمْ وَمَا
يَفْتَرُونَ ﴿١١٢﴾ وَلِتَصْغٰٓى إِلَيْهِ أَفْـِٔدَةُ الَّذِينَ
لَا يُؤْمِنُونَ بِالْاٰخِرَةِ وَلِيَرْضَوْهُ وَلِيَقْتَرِفُوا
مَا هُمْ مُّقْتَرِفُونَ ﴿١١٣﴾ أَفَغَيْرَ اللّٰهِ أَبْتَغِي حَكَمًا
وَّهُوَ الَّذِيٓ أَنْزَلَ إِلَيْكُمُ الْكِتٰبَ مُفَصَّلًا
وَالَّذِينَ اٰتَيْنٰهُمُ الْكِتٰبَ يَعْلَمُونَ أَنَّهُ
مُنَزَّلٌ مِّنْ رَّبِّكَ بِالْحَقِّ فَلَا تَكُونَنَّ
مِنَ الْمُمْتَرِينَ ﴿١١٤﴾ وَتَمَّتْ كَلِمَتُ رَبِّكَ
صِدْقًا وَّعَدْلًا لَا مُبَدِّلَ لِكَلِمٰتِهِ وَهُوَ
السَّمِيعُ الْعَلِيمُ ﴿١١٥﴾ وَإِنْ تُطِعْ أَكْثَرَ مَنْ
فِي الْأَرْضِ يُضِلُّوكَ عَنْ سَبِيلِ اللّٰهِ إِنْ
يَتَّبِعُونَ إِلَّا الظَّنَّ وَإِنْ هُمْ إِلَّا يَخْرُصُونَ ﴿١١٦﴾
إِنَّ رَبَّكَ هُوَ أَعْلَمُ مَنْ يَضِلُّ عَنْ سَبِيلِهِ
وَهُوَ أَعْلَمُ بِالْمُهْتَدِينَ ﴿١١٧﴾ فَكُلُوا مِمَّا

has been pronounced, if you are indeed believers in His Messages.

119. What reason have you that you do not eat of that over which Allâh's name has been pronounced, whilst He has already explained to you the things He has forbidden to you, excepting that which you are constrained to (eat out of necessity). And surely many mislead (others) by following their own fancies due to lack of knowledge. Verily, your Lord knows best these transgressors.

120. Refrain from sin in form and in spirit (both). Verily, those who commit sins deliberately shall be repaid according to the deeds committed by them.

121. And do not eat of that on which Allâh's name has not been pronounced, for it is the sure (product of) disobedience. Certainly, the evil ones suggest their friends to dispute with you, and if you obey them, you shall invariably become polytheists.

SECTION 15

122. **C**AN he, who was lifeless (before) and to whom We gave life and We provided for him a light whereby he moves about among the people, be like the person whose condition is (as one) consigned to thick darkness from whence he cannot emerge? Thus the deeds of the disbelievers are made fair-seeming to them (by satan);

123. Similarly have We made the leaders in every town the guilty ones, (because their doings seem fair to them) with the result that they intrigue therein; but little do they understand that, (as a matter of fact,) they intrigue only against themselves.

124. And when there comes to them a (Divine) Message they say, 'We will never believe unless we ourselves are given the like of what has been given to the Messengers of Allâh.' Allâh knows best whom to entrust His Messengership. Surely, humiliation and severe and disgraceful

ذُكِرَ اسْمُ اللّٰهِ عَلَيْهِ إِنْ كُنْتُمْ بِاٰيٰتِهٖ
مُؤْمِنِيْنَ ﴿١١٨﴾ وَمَا لَكُمْ أَلَّا تَأْكُلُوْا مِمَّا ذُكِرَ
اسْمُ اللّٰهِ عَلَيْهِ وَقَدْ فَصَّلَ لَكُمْ مَّا حَرَّمَ
عَلَيْكُمْ إِلَّا مَا اضْطُرِرْتُمْ إِلَيْهِ ۖ وَإِنَّ كَثِيْرًا
لَّيُضِلُّوْنَ بِأَهْوَآئِهِمْ بِغَيْرِ عِلْمٍ ۗ إِنَّ رَبَّكَ
هُوَ أَعْلَمُ بِالْمُعْتَدِيْنَ ﴿١١٩﴾ وَذَرُوْا ظَاهِرَ الْإِثْمِ
وَبَاطِنَهٗ ۗ إِنَّ الَّذِيْنَ يَكْسِبُوْنَ الْإِثْمَ
سَيُجْزَوْنَ بِمَا كَانُوْا يَقْتَرِفُوْنَ ﴿١٢٠﴾ وَلَا
تَأْكُلُوْا مِمَّا لَمْ يُذْكَرِ اسْمُ اللّٰهِ عَلَيْهِ
وَإِنَّهٗ لَفِسْقٌ ۗ وَإِنَّ الشَّيٰطِيْنَ لَيُوْحُوْنَ
إِلٰى أَوْلِيَآئِهِمْ لِيُجٰدِلُوْكُمْ ۚ وَإِنْ أَطَعْتُمُوْهُمْ
إِنَّكُمْ لَمُشْرِكُوْنَ ﴿١٢١﴾ أَوَمَنْ كَانَ مَيْتًا
فَأَحْيَيْنٰهُ وَجَعَلْنَا لَهٗ نُوْرًا يَّمْشِيْ بِهٖ فِي
النَّاسِ كَمَنْ مَّثَلُهٗ فِي الظُّلُمٰتِ لَيْسَ
بِخَارِجٍ مِّنْهَا ۗ كَذٰلِكَ زُيِّنَ لِلْكٰفِرِيْنَ مَا
كَانُوْا يَعْمَلُوْنَ ﴿١٢٢﴾ وَكَذٰلِكَ جَعَلْنَا فِيْ كُلِّ
قَرْيَةٍ أَكٰبِرَ مُجْرِمِيْهَا لِيَمْكُرُوْا فِيْهَا ۗ وَمَا
يَمْكُرُوْنَ إِلَّا بِأَنْفُسِهِمْ وَمَا يَشْعُرُوْنَ ﴿١٢٣﴾
وَإِذَا جَآءَتْهُمْ اٰيَةٌ قَالُوْا لَنْ نُّؤْمِنَ حَتّٰى
نُؤْتٰى مِثْلَ مَآ أُوْتِيَ رُسُلُ اللّٰهِ ۘ اَللّٰهُ أَعْلَمُ
حَيْثُ يَجْعَلُ رِسَالَتَهٗ ۗ سَيُصِيْبُ الَّذِيْنَ
أَجْرَمُوْا صَغَارٌ عِنْدَ اللّٰهِ وَعَذَابٌ شَدِيْدٌ

punishment from Allâh shall befall those who cut off their ties (with Him) because of their intrigues (against Our Prophets).

125. But as to whom Allâh intends to guide He opens his bosom to Islam and as to him whom He allows to go astray He makes his bosom close and constricted, so that he feels as though he were climbing up the heights. Just as Allâh does this He lays ignominy on those who do not believe.

126. And this path (of Islam) is an exact right path (leading) to your Lord. We have indeed explained the Messages (of truth) in detail for a people who would accept admonition.

127. There awaits with their Lord an abode of peace, and He is their Patron because of their (righteous) deeds.

128. Beware of the day when He will gather them all together (and say), 'O multitude of *jinn!* You made a great many of the (ordinary) people subservient to yourselves (in disobedience).' And their votaries from the people will say, 'Our Lord! Some of us benefited one from another but (at last) we have reached the end of the (appointed) term which You determined for us.' He will then say, 'The Fire is your lodging, therein to abide, unless Allâh wills (otherwise).' Verily, your Lord is All-Wise, All-Knowing.

129. In the like manner do We let some of the unjust have power one over another because of their (wrongful) deeds.

SECTION 16

130. '**O** MULTITUDE of *jinn* (- fiery natured, haughty) and (ordinary) peoples! Did there come to you no Messengers from among yourselves who related to you My Messages and warned you that you would face this your day?' They will say, '(Yes,) we bear witness against ourselves.' And the present life has beguiled them. And they will bear witness against themselves (on that day) that they were disbelievers.

131. This (sending of the Messengers) is because

بِمَا كَانُوا يَمْكُرُونَ ﴿١٢٤﴾ فَمَن يُرِدِ اللَّهُ أَن
يَهْدِيَهُ يَشْرَحْ صَدْرَهُ لِلْإِسْلَامِ وَمَن يُرِدْ
أَن يُضِلَّهُ يَجْعَلْ صَدْرَهُ ضَيِّقًا حَرَجًا كَأَنَّمَا
يَصَّعَّدُ فِي السَّمَاءِ كَذَٰلِكَ يَجْعَلُ اللَّهُ الرِّجْسَ
عَلَى الَّذِينَ لَا يُؤْمِنُونَ ﴿١٢٥﴾ وَهَٰذَا صِرَاطُ
رَبِّكَ مُسْتَقِيمًا قَدْ فَصَّلْنَا الْآيَاتِ لِقَوْمٍ
يَذَّكَّرُونَ ﴿١٢٦﴾ لَهُمْ دَارُ السَّلَامِ عِندَ رَبِّهِمْ
وَهُوَ وَلِيُّهُم بِمَا كَانُوا يَعْمَلُونَ ﴿١٢٧﴾ وَيَوْمَ
يَحْشُرُهُمْ جَمِيعًا يَا مَعْشَرَ الْجِنِّ قَدِ
اسْتَكْثَرْتُم مِّنَ الْإِنسِ وَقَالَ أَوْلِيَاؤُهُم
مِّنَ الْإِنسِ رَبَّنَا اسْتَمْتَعَ بَعْضُنَا بِبَعْضٍ
وَبَلَغْنَا أَجَلَنَا الَّذِي أَجَّلْتَ لَنَا قَالَ النَّارُ
مَثْوَاكُمْ خَالِدِينَ فِيهَا إِلَّا مَا شَاءَ اللَّهُ إِنَّ
رَبَّكَ حَكِيمٌ عَلِيمٌ ﴿١٢٨﴾ وَكَذَٰلِكَ نُوَلِّي بَعْضَ
الظَّالِمِينَ بَعْضًا بِمَا كَانُوا يَكْسِبُونَ ﴿١٢٩﴾
يَا مَعْشَرَ الْجِنِّ وَالْإِنسِ أَلَمْ يَأْتِكُمْ رُسُلٌ
مِّنكُمْ يَقُصُّونَ عَلَيْكُمْ آيَاتِي وَيُنذِرُونَكُمْ
لِقَاءَ يَوْمِكُمْ هَٰذَا قَالُوا شَهِدْنَا عَلَىٰ أَنفُسِنَا
وَغَرَّتْهُمُ الْحَيَاةُ الدُّنْيَا وَشَهِدُوا عَلَىٰ
أَنفُسِهِمْ أَنَّهُمْ كَانُوا كَافِرِينَ ﴿١٣٠﴾ ذَٰلِكَ أَن لَّمْ

your Lord destroys no township unjustly whilst their inhabitants are unwarned.
132. And for all are (fixed different) degrees (of rank) in accordance with their deeds. Your Lord is not at all unaware of what they do.
133. Your Lord is Self-Sufficient, Lord of mercy. If He will, He may do away with you (O disbelievers!) and replace you with such others as He will, just as He evolved you from the seeds of other people.
134. Verily, that punishment which you are promised must come to pass and you cannot frustrate (His plans).
135. Say, 'O my people! Go on working according to (the utmost of) your capacities and positions. Surely, I am doing (my best)! Soon you shall come to know for whom is the (best) reward of this abode.' Anyhow, the wrongdoers never attain their goal.
136. They allocate to Allâh a portion out of what He has produced of the tillage and the cattle, and they say, 'This is for Allâh,' - according to their fancies - 'and this is (set apart) for our gods (we associate with Allâh).' Then what is for their associate-gods never goes over to Allâh, but what is (set apart) for Allâh does (often) go over to their associate-gods. How ill they judge!
137. Just (as their associate-gods turned the polytheists away from Allâh) so did they make (even so monstrous a deed as) the killing of their children seem fair to a large number of the polytheists, with the result that they ruin them and that they obscure for them their religion. And if Allâh had (enforced) His will they would not have done so, so leave them alone and that what they forge.
138. And they say (according to their fancies), 'Such and such cattle and tillage are secure; (since their use is forbidden for others,) none shall eat them except whom we please.' So they assert - there are some cattle whose backs have been forbidden (for use), and some cattle over

يَكُنۡ رَّبُّكَ مُهۡلِكَ الۡقُرٰى بِظُلۡمٍ وَّ اَهۡلُهَا
غٰفِلُوۡنَ ﴿١٣١﴾ وَ لِكُلٍّ دَرَجٰتٌ مِّمَّا عَمِلُوۡا ؕ وَ مَا
رَبُّكَ بِغٰفِلٍ عَمَّا يَعۡمَلُوۡنَ ﴿١٣٢﴾ وَ رَبُّكَ الۡغَنِيُّ
ذُو الرَّحۡمَةِ ؕ اِنۡ يَّشَاۡ يُذۡهِبۡكُمۡ وَ يَسۡتَخۡلِفۡ
مِنۡۢ بَعۡدِكُمۡ مَّا يَشَآءُ كَمَاۤ اَنۡشَاَكُمۡ مِّنۡ
ذُرِّيَّةِ قَوۡمٍ اٰخَرِيۡنَ ﴿١٣٣﴾ اِنَّ مَا تُوۡعَدُوۡنَ لَاٰتٍ
وَّ مَاۤ اَنۡتُمۡ بِمُعۡجِزِيۡنَ ﴿١٣٤﴾ قُلۡ يٰقَوۡمِ اعۡمَلُوۡا
عَلٰى مَكَانَتِكُمۡ اِنِّىۡ عَامِلٌ ۚ فَسَوۡفَ تَعۡلَمُوۡنَ
مَنۡ تَكُوۡنُ لَهٗ عٰقِبَةُ الدَّارِ ؕ اِنَّهٗ لَا يُفۡلِحُ
الظّٰلِمُوۡنَ ﴿١٣٥﴾ وَ جَعَلُوۡا لِلّٰهِ مِمَّا ذَرَاَ مِنَ
الۡحَرۡثِ وَ الۡاَنۡعَامِ نَصِيۡبًا فَقَالُوۡا هٰذَا لِلّٰهِ
بِزَعۡمِهِمۡ وَ هٰذَا لِشُرَكَآئِنَا ۚ فَمَا كَانَ
لِشُرَكَآئِهِمۡ فَلَا يَصِلُ اِلَى اللّٰهِ ۚ وَ مَا كَانَ
لِلّٰهِ فَهُوَ يَصِلُ اِلٰى شُرَكَآئِهِمۡ ؕ سَآءَ مَا
يَحۡكُمُوۡنَ ﴿١٣٦﴾ وَ كَذٰلِكَ زَيَّنَ لِكَثِيۡرٍ مِّنَ
الۡمُشۡرِكِيۡنَ قَتۡلَ اَوۡلٰدِهِمۡ شُرَكَآؤُهُمۡ
لِيُرۡدُوۡهُمۡ وَ لِيَلۡبِسُوۡا عَلَيۡهِمۡ دِيۡنَهُمۡ ؕ وَ لَوۡ
شَآءَ اللّٰهُ مَا فَعَلُوۡهُ فَذَرۡهُمۡ وَ مَا يَفۡتَرُوۡنَ ﴿١٣٧﴾
وَ قَالُوۡا هٰذِهٖۤ اَنۡعَامٌ وَّ حَرۡثٌ حِجۡرٌ ۖ لَّا
يَطۡعَمُهَاۤ اِلَّا مَنۡ نَّشَآءُ بِزَعۡمِهِمۡ وَ اَنۡعَامٌ
حُرِّمَتۡ ظُهُوۡرُهَا وَ اَنۡعَامٌ لَّا يَذۡكُرُوۡنَ

which they would not pronounce the name of Allâh. (They do all this) forging a lie against Him (that such practices are by His will). Soon He will surely punish them for the lies they have forged.

139. They further say, 'That (the young one) which is (living) in the womb of such and such cattle is exclusively reserved for our males and is forbidden to our spouses, but if it be stillborn then they are (all) partakers of it.' He will surely repay them with punishment for their (false) specification. Surely, He is All-Wise, All-Knowing.

140. Certainly, they suffer a loss (those) who kill their children in folly (and) ignorance, and forbid (themselves) what Allâh has provided for them; forging lies in the name of Allâh. They have indeed gone astray and they are not rightly guided.

SECTION 17

141. **A**ND He it is Who evolved gardens trellised and untrellised, and the date-palms, and the cornfields whose produce and fruits are of diverse kinds and tastes, and oil producing plants, and pomegranates; similar (in kind) yet dissimilar (in variety). Eat of the fruit of each when it yields fruit, and render thereof His due (in charity) on the day of harvesting, and do not exceed the bounds. Verily, He loves not those who exceed the bounds.

142. (He it is Who created some) of the cattle for carrying burdens and some (like sheep and goat) are too low (to carry burdens but fit for slaughter). Eat of what Allâh has provided for you and do not follow in the footsteps of satan, for he is indeed an enemy disuniting you (from Allâh).

143. And (of cattle slaughtered for food, He has created) eight (heads in four) pairs, the pair of sheep, the pair of goats. Say, 'Is it the two males He has made unlawful, or the two females, or

اسْمَ اللهِ عَلَيْهَا افْتِرَآءً عَلَيْهِ سَيَجْزِيهِمْ
بِمَا كَانُوا يَفْتَرُونَ ﴿١٣٨﴾ وَقَالُوا مَا فِي بُطُونِ
هٰذِهِ الْأَنْعٰمِ خَالِصَةٌ لِّذُكُورِنَا وَمُحَرَّمٌ
عَلٰٓى أَزْوٰجِنَا وَإِنْ يَّكُنْ مَّيْتَةً فَهُمْ فِيهِ
شُرَكَآءُ سَيَجْزِيهِمْ وَصْفَهُمْ إِنَّهُ حَكِيمٌ
عَلِيمٌ ﴿١٣٩﴾ قَدْ خَسِرَ الَّذِينَ قَتَلُوا أَوْلٰدَهُمْ
سَفَهًا بِغَيْرِ عِلْمٍ وَحَرَّمُوا مَا رَزَقَهُمُ اللهُ
افْتِرَآءً عَلَى اللهِ قَدْ ضَلُّوا وَمَا كَانُوا
مُهْتَدِينَ ﴿١٤٠﴾ وَهُوَ الَّذِيٓ أَنْشَأَ جَنّٰتٍ مَّعْرُوشٰتٍ
وَّغَيْرَ مَعْرُوشٰتٍ وَّالنَّخْلَ وَالزَّرْعَ مُخْتَلِفًا
أُكُلُهُ وَالزَّيْتُونَ وَالرُّمَّانَ مُتَشٰبِهًا وَّغَيْرَ
مُتَشٰبِهٍ كُلُوا مِنْ ثَمَرِهٖٓ إِذَآ أَثْمَرَ وَأٰتُوا
حَقَّهُ يَوْمَ حَصَادِهٖ وَلَا تُسْرِفُوا إِنَّهُ لَا
يُحِبُّ الْمُسْرِفِينَ ﴿١٤١﴾ وَمِنَ الْأَنْعٰمِ حَمُولَةً
وَّفَرْشًا كُلُوا مِمَّا رَزَقَكُمُ اللهُ وَلَا تَتَّبِعُوا
خُطُوٰتِ الشَّيْطٰنِ إِنَّهُ لَكُمْ عَدُوٌّ مُّبِينٌ ﴿١٤٢﴾
ثَمٰنِيَةَ أَزْوٰجٍ مِنَ الضَّأْنِ اثْنَيْنِ وَمِنَ
الْمَعْزِ اثْنَيْنِ قُلْ ءٰٓالذَّكَرَيْنِ حَرَّمَ أَمِ

is it that (young) which the wombs of the two females contain (which He has forbidden)? Expound to me (the case) with (sure) knowledge if you are in the right.'

144. And (He created) the pair of camels and the pair of cows. Say, 'Is it the two males that He has made unlawful or the two females or is it that which the wombs of the two females contain (which He has forbidden)? Or were you present when Allâh enjoined this (unlawfulness and lawfulness) on you?' Who is more unjust than he who forges a lie against Allâh deliberately that he may lead the people astray without having any knowledge. Verily, Allâh does not guide the unjust people.

SECTION 18

145. **S**ay, 'I find nothing in what Allâh has revealed to me that forbids the people to eat anything except it be that which dies of itself, or blood poured forth, or flesh of swine; for (all) this is unclean, or (I find that thing forbidden) what is profane, which has been sacrificed in other than Allâh's name, yet he who is constrained (to eat any of them), having no desire (for that) and having no intention to exceed the limit, (will find that) surely your Lord is Great Protector, Ever Merciful.

146. And as for those who judaised, We forbade them every animal having claws, We forbade them the fat of the oxen and that of the goats (and of the sheep) except that (fat) which their backs or entrails bear or which cleaves to a bone. That is how We punished them for their transgression; and We are always true to Our words.

147. And if they cry lies to you then say to them, 'Your Lord is the Lord of All-Embracing Mercy; but His punishment cannot be averted from the guilty people.'

148. Now those who associate partners (with Allâh) say, 'If Allâh had (so) willed we would not have associated partners (with Him), nor would have our forefathers, nor would we have

الأنثيين أما اشتملت عليه أرحام
الأنثيين نبئوني بعلم إن كنتم صدقين ﴿١٤٣﴾
ومن الإبل اثنين ومن البقر اثنين قل
ءالذكرين حرم أم الأنثيين أما اشتملت
عليه أرحام الأنثيين أم كنتم شهداء إذ
وصىكم الله بهذا فمن أظلم ممن افترى
على الله كذبا ليضل الناس بغير علم
إن الله لا يهدي القوم الظلمين ﴿١٤٤﴾ قل لا
أجد في ما أوحي إلي محرما على طاعم
يطعمه إلا أن يكون ميتة أو دما مسفوحا
أو لحم خنزير فإنه رجس أو فسقا أهل
لغير الله به فمن اضطر غير باغ ولا عاد
فإن ربك غفور رحيم ﴿١٤٥﴾ وعلى الذين هادوا
حرمنا كل ذي ظفر ومن البقر والغنم
حرمنا عليهم شحومهما إلا ما حملت
ظهورهما أو الحوايا أو ما اختلط بعظم
ذلك جزينهم ببغيهم وإنا لصدقون ﴿١٤٦﴾
فإن كذبوك فقل ربكم ذو رحمة وسعة
ولا يرد بأسه عن القوم المجرمين ﴿١٤٧﴾
سيقول الذين أشركوا لو شاء الله ما أشركنا

ع ٤

made anything unlawful (of our own);' just as (they deny you) their predecessors cried lies (to their apostles of God) until they suffered Our punishment. Say, 'Have you any knowledge (about it)? Then present it before us. You follow naught but mere conjectures, and you do nothing but tell lies.'
149. Say, 'Then with Allâh is the conclusive argument. Had He (enforced) His will, He would have surely guided you all.'
150. Say, 'Bring your witnesses who can testify that Allâh has forbidden the thing (you forbid yourselves).' Then supposing they testify this, do not bear them out, nor follow the caprice of those who treat Our Messages as lies and who do not believe in the Hereafter and who set up equals to their Lord.

SECTION 19

151. **S**AY, 'Come, I will rehearse to you what your Lord has made binding on you; it is that you shall associate not any thing as partner with Him, and that you shall be good to parents, and that you waste not your children because of poverty. It is We Who make provisions for you as well for them too. (Allâh has also enjoined upon you that you) approach not indecencies, whether open or hidden, and that you kill no soul which Allâh has made sacred, except in the cause of justice.' This has He enjoined you with, so that you may (learn to) abstain (from evil).
152. And (He has enjoined you) that you do not approach the property of an orphan except in the fairest manner; until he attains his maturity, and give full measure and weight with equity. We charge no soul except to its capacity, and that when you speak (giving your verdict), observe justice even though the person concerned be a relative (of yours), and fulfill the covenant (you made) with Allâh. That is what He enjoins upon you so that you may take heed,
153. And (the Lord says,) 'This is My exact right path, so follow it, and follow not (diverse)

وَلَآ أٰبَآؤُنَا وَلَا حَرَّمْنَا مِنْ شَيْءٍ كَذٰلِكَ
كَذَّبَ الَّذِينَ مِنْ قَبْلِهِمْ حَتّٰى ذَاقُوا بَأْسَنَا
قُلْ هَلْ عِنْدَكُمْ مِّنْ عِلْمٍ فَتُخْرِجُوهُ لَنَا إِنْ
تَتَّبِعُونَ إِلَّا الظَّنَّ وَإِنْ أَنْتُمْ إِلَّا تَخْرُصُونَ ﴿١٤٨﴾
قُلْ فَلِلّٰهِ الْحُجَّةُ الْبٰلِغَةُ فَلَوْ شَآءَ لَهَدٰىكُمْ
أَجْمَعِينَ ﴿١٤٩﴾ قُلْ هَلُمَّ شُهَدَآءَكُمُ الَّذِينَ
يَشْهَدُونَ أَنَّ اللّٰهَ حَرَّمَ هٰذَا فَإِنْ شَهِدُوا
فَلَا تَشْهَدْ مَعَهُمْ وَلَا تَتَّبِعْ أَهْوَآءَ الَّذِينَ
كَذَّبُوا بِأٰيٰتِنَا وَالَّذِينَ لَا يُؤْمِنُونَ بِالْأٰخِرَةِ
وَهُمْ بِرَبِّهِمْ يَعْدِلُونَ ﴿١٥٠﴾ قُلْ تَعَالَوْا أَتْلُ مَا
حَرَّمَ رَبُّكُمْ عَلَيْكُمْ أَلَّا تُشْرِكُوا بِهِ شَيْـًٔا
وَبِالْوٰلِدَيْنِ إِحْسٰنًا وَلَا تَقْتُلُوٓا أَوْلٰدَكُمْ
مِّنْ إِمْلٰقٍ نَحْنُ نَرْزُقُكُمْ وَإِيَّاهُمْ وَلَا
تَقْرَبُوا الْفَوٰحِشَ مَا ظَهَرَ مِنْهَا وَمَا بَطَنَ
وَلَا تَقْتُلُوا النَّفْسَ الَّتِي حَرَّمَ اللّٰهُ إِلَّا بِالْحَقِّ
ذٰلِكُمْ وَصّٰكُمْ بِهِ لَعَلَّكُمْ تَعْقِلُونَ ﴿١٥١﴾ وَلَا
تَقْرَبُوا مَالَ الْيَتِيمِ إِلَّا بِالَّتِي هِيَ أَحْسَنُ
حَتّٰى يَبْلُغَ أَشُدَّهُ وَأَوْفُوا الْكَيْلَ وَالْمِيزَانَ
بِالْقِسْطِ لَا نُكَلِّفُ نَفْسًا إِلَّا وُسْعَهَا وَإِذَا
قُلْتُمْ فَاعْدِلُوا وَلَوْ كَانَ ذَا قُرْبٰى وَبِعَهْدِ
اللّٰهِ أَوْفُوا ذٰلِكُمْ وَصّٰكُمْ بِهِ لَعَلَّكُمْ
تَذَكَّرُونَ ﴿١٥٢﴾ وَأَنَّ هٰذَا صِرٰطِي مُسْتَقِيمًا

ع ١٨ ٥

ways, lest they should deviate you away from His (straight) way.' That is what He enjoins you with, that you may guard against evil.

154. And behold! We gave Moses the Scripture to complete (Our favours) upon him who did good to others and is righteous, and to explain everything worth explaining and as a guidance and a mercy, so that the people may believe in that they will meet their Lord.

155. And (similarly) this is a (glorious) Book which We have revealed full of blessings, so follow it and guard against evil that you may be shown mercy.

SECTION 20

156. (**W**E have revealed this blessed Book) lest you should say, 'The Book has only been revealed to two communities (- the Jews and the Christians) before us, and (as for us) we remained unaware of what those (Books) read.'

157. Or lest you should say, 'Had the Book been revealed to us we would surely have been better guided than they.' Now there has certainly come to you from your Lord (in the form of the Qur'ân) a clear evidence, an excellent guidance and a great mercy. Who then, is more unjust than he who cries lies to the revelations of Allâh and turns away from them? We will certainly award those who turn away from Our revelations an awful punishment, because of their having turned away.

158. Do they await only that the angels should come to them (with wars), or that (complete destruction from) your Lord should come (upon them), or that some of the signs of your Lord should visit them (with earthly calamities). The day when some of the signs of your Lord shall come, no soul, that did not believe earlier or accomplished some good deeds through (his) belief, will ever benefit by his faith. Say, 'Wait, we too are waiting.'

159. Verily, those who have caused a split in their religion and became (divided into) sects

فاتبعوه ولا تتبعوا السبل فتفرق بكم
عن سبيله ذلكم وصىكم به لعلكم
تتقون ﴿١٥٣﴾ ثم آتينا موسى الكتب تماما
على الذي أحسن وتفصيلا لكل شيء
وهدى ورحمة لعلهم بلقاء ربهم
يؤمنون ﴿١٥٤﴾ وهذا كتب أنزلنه مبارك
فاتبعوه واتقوا لعلكم ترحمون ﴿١٥٥﴾ أن
تقولوا إنما أنزل الكتب على طائفتين
من قبلنا وإن كنا عن دراستهم لغفلين ﴿١٥٦﴾
أو تقولوا لو أنا أنزل علينا الكتب لكنا
أهدى منهم فقد جاءكم بينة من
ربكم وهدى ورحمة فمن أظلم ممن
كذب بآيت الله وصدف عنها سنجزي
الذين يصدفون عن آيتنا سوء العذاب
بما كانوا يصدفون ﴿١٥٧﴾ هل ينظرون إلا
أن تأتيهم الملئكة أو يأتي ربك أو يأتي
بعض آيت ربك يوم يأتي بعض آيت
ربك لا ينفع نفسا إيمنها لم تكن آمنت
من قبل أو كسبت في إيمنها خيرا
قل انتظروا إنا منتظرون ﴿١٥٨﴾ إن الذين

you have no concern whatsoever with them. Their case will come before Allâh, then He will (judge it) and will fully inform them of what they have been doing.

160. Whosoever does good shall be repaid tenfold, but he who commits evil shall be recompensed only in proportion (to the evil done), and they shall not be dealt with unjustly.

161. Say, 'As for me, surely my Lord has guided me to the exact straight path, the ever true faith, the creed of Abraham the upright, and he was not of the polytheists.'

162. Say, 'Surely, my Prayer and my sacrifice and my living and my dying are (all) for the sake of Allâh, the Lord of the worlds.

163. No associate-partner has He, and so am I ordained, and I am the first of the submitting ones (to Allâh).'

164. Say, 'Shall I seek a Lord other than Allâh whilst He is the Lord of all things?' And no soul does anything (evil) but only against itself; no soul that bears a burden shall bear the burden of another. Then to your Lord is your return and He will fully inform you about that (truth) wherein you have been disagreeing.

165. And He it is Who has made you successors (of others and rulers) of the land, and He has exalted some of you over the others in degrees (of rank) so that He may try you by that which He has given you. Surely, your Lord is Quick at retribution; and He is all the same, Great Protector, Ever Merciful.

فَرَّقُوا دِينَهُمْ وَكَانُوا شِيَعًا لَّسْتَ مِنْهُمْ
فِي شَيْءٍ إِنَّمَا أَمْرُهُمْ إِلَى اللَّهِ ثُمَّ يُنَبِّئُهُم
بِمَا كَانُوا يَفْعَلُونَ ﴿١٥٩﴾ مَن جَاءَ بِالْحَسَنَةِ
فَلَهُ عَشْرُ أَمْثَالِهَا وَمَن جَاءَ بِالسَّيِّئَةِ
فَلَا يُجْزَىٰ إِلَّا مِثْلَهَا وَهُمْ لَا يُظْلَمُونَ ﴿١٦٠﴾
قُلْ إِنَّنِي هَدَانِي رَبِّي إِلَىٰ صِرَاطٍ مُّسْتَقِيمٍ
دِينًا قِيَمًا مِّلَّةَ إِبْرَاهِيمَ حَنِيفًا وَمَا
كَانَ مِنَ الْمُشْرِكِينَ ﴿١٦١﴾ قُلْ إِنَّ صَلَاتِي
وَنُسُكِي وَمَحْيَايَ وَمَمَاتِي لِلَّهِ رَبِّ
الْعَالَمِينَ ﴿١٦٢﴾ لَا شَرِيكَ لَهُ وَبِذَٰلِكَ أُمِرْتُ
وَأَنَا أَوَّلُ الْمُسْلِمِينَ ﴿١٦٣﴾ قُلْ أَغَيْرَ اللَّهِ
أَبْغِي رَبًّا وَهُوَ رَبُّ كُلِّ شَيْءٍ وَلَا
تَكْسِبُ كُلُّ نَفْسٍ إِلَّا عَلَيْهَا وَلَا تَزِرُ
وَازِرَةٌ وِزْرَ أُخْرَىٰ ثُمَّ إِلَىٰ رَبِّكُم مَّرْجِعُكُمْ
فَيُنَبِّئُكُم بِمَا كُنتُمْ فِيهِ تَخْتَلِفُونَ ﴿١٦٤﴾
وَهُوَ الَّذِي جَعَلَكُمْ خَلَائِفَ الْأَرْضِ وَرَفَعَ
بَعْضَكُمْ فَوْقَ بَعْضٍ دَرَجَاتٍ لِّيَبْلُوَكُمْ
فِي مَا آتَاكُمْ إِنَّ رَبَّكَ سَرِيعُ الْعِقَابِ
وَإِنَّهُ لَغَفُورٌ رَّحِيمٌ ﴿١٦٥﴾

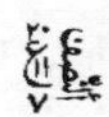

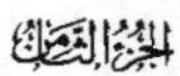

CHAPTER
7

سُورَةُ الأَعرَافِ ٧

AL-A'RÂF
(The Elevated Places)
(Revealed before Hijrah)

With the name of Allâh,
the Most Gracious, the Ever Merciful
(I commence to read Sûrah Al-A'râf)

1. ALIF LÂM MÎM SÂD - I am Allâh, the Best Knower, the Most Truthful.
2. (This Qur'ân is) a (glorious) Book revealed to you that you may warn (the erring) therewith, and (that it may be) a source of eminence and honour to the believers. Let there be no constriction in your mind on this account.
3. (People!) Follow (the Message) which has been revealed to you by your Lord and follow no patrons (as you assume them to be), apart from Allâh. How little heed you pay to admonition!
4. So many a (rebellious) township have We caused to be ruined; so Our punishment visited them by night or while they were taking their midday rest;
5. So that their cry meant nothing when Our punishment came upon them except that they (apologisingly) said, 'Truly we were wrongdoing people.'
6. We will then invariably question those to whom (the Messages) were sent and We will certainly question (also) the Messengers.
7. We will certainly relate to them (true facts) with exact details, having full knowledge of them, for We were never absent (from them when it came to pass).
8. On that day the weighing (- the judging of deeds) will be just and true, then he whose scales (of good deeds) are heavy, it is these only who shall attain their goal.
9. And those whose scales are light (and their

سُورَةُ الأَعْرَافِ مَكِّيَّةٌ

بِسْمِ اللهِ الرَّحْمٰنِ الرَّحِيْمِ

الٓمٓصٓ ① كِتٰبٌ أُنْزِلَ إِلَيْكَ فَلَا يَكُنْ فِي
صَدْرِكَ حَرَجٌ مِّنْهُ لِتُنْذِرَ بِهٖ وَذِكْرٰى
لِلْمُؤْمِنِيْنَ ② إِتَّبِعُوْا مَآ أُنْزِلَ إِلَيْكُمْ مِّنْ
رَّبِّكُمْ وَلَا تَتَّبِعُوْا مِنْ دُوْنِهٖٓ أَوْلِيَآءَ
قَلِيْلًا مَّا تَذَكَّرُوْنَ ③ وَكَمْ مِّنْ قَرْيَةٍ
أَهْلَكْنٰهَا فَجَآءَهَا بَأْسُنَا بَيٰتًا أَوْ هُمْ
قَآئِلُوْنَ ④ فَمَا كَانَ دَعْوٰىهُمْ إِذْ جَآءَهُمْ
بَأْسُنَآ إِلَّآ أَنْ قَالُوْٓا إِنَّا كُنَّا ظٰلِمِيْنَ ⑤
فَلَنَسْـَٔلَنَّ الَّذِيْنَ أُرْسِلَ إِلَيْهِمْ وَلَنَسْـَٔلَنَّ
الْمُرْسَلِيْنَ ⑥ فَلَنَقُصَّنَّ عَلَيْهِمْ بِعِلْمٍ وَّمَا
كُنَّا غَآئِبِيْنَ ⑦ وَالْوَزْنُ يَوْمَئِذِنِ الْحَقُّ
فَمَنْ ثَقُلَتْ مَوٰزِيْنُهٗ فَأُولٰٓئِكَ هُمُ
الْمُفْلِحُوْنَ ⑧ وَمَنْ خَفَّتْ مَوٰزِيْنُهٗ فَأُولٰٓئِكَ

deeds of little account), it is they who have made their souls suffer losses because they have been unjust with regard to Our Messages.
10. (People!) We have indeed established you in the earth (giving you power therein), and provided for you therein (various) means of subsistence. How little thanks you give!

SECTION 2

11. **W**E did determine you, then We gave you shape, then said to the angels, 'Make submission to (the Children of) Adam,' so they all submitted. But *Iblîs* (did not), he would not be of those who submit.
12. (God) said, 'What prevented you from submitting when I commanded you (to submit)?' (*Iblîs*) said, 'I am better than he (- the human being). You created me from fire whereas You created him from clay.'
13. (God) said, 'Get down from this (haughty state) for it is not proper for you to behave proudly here, so be gone. Surely, you are of those who have agreed to remain in an abject position.'
14. He (- *Iblîs*, in impertinent defiance) said, 'Grant me respite till the day when they are raised up again.'
15. (God) said, 'Surely, you are of those (already) given respite.'
16. (*Iblîs*) said, 'Now, since You have adjudged me to be perverted and lost, I will assuredly lie in wait for them (- the Children of Adam) on the straight and exact path that leads to You.
17. 'There will I come upon them from their front and from their backs and from their right and from their left so that You will not find most of them grateful (to You).'
18. (God) said, 'Get out from this (state), despised and driven away. Be sure, whosoever of these (human beings) follows you I will certainly fill Gehenna with you all.'
19. And (We said), 'O Adam! Dwell you and your wife in this garden, then eat you both

الَّذِينَ خَسِرُوٓا أَنفُسَهُم بِمَا كَانُوا بِـَٔايٰتِنَا
يَظْلِمُونَ ﴿٩﴾ وَلَقَدْ مَكَّنّٰكُمْ فِي الْأَرْضِ
وَجَعَلْنَا لَكُمْ فِيهَا مَعٰيِشَ قَلِيلًا مَّا تَشْكُرُونَ ﴿١٠﴾ ع ٢ / ٨
وَلَقَدْ خَلَقْنٰكُمْ ثُمَّ صَوَّرْنٰكُمْ ثُمَّ قُلْنَا
لِلْمَلٰٓئِكَةِ اسْجُدُوا لِـَٔادَمَ فَسَجَدُوٓا إِلَّآ
إِبْلِيسَ لَمْ يَكُن مِّنَ السّٰجِدِينَ ﴿١١﴾ قَالَ
مَا مَنَعَكَ أَلَّا تَسْجُدَ إِذْ أَمَرْتُكَ قَالَ
أَنَا خَيْرٌ مِّنْهُ خَلَقْتَنِي مِن نَّارٍ وَّخَلَقْتَهُ
مِن طِينٍ ﴿١٢﴾ قَالَ فَاهْبِطْ مِنْهَا فَمَا يَكُونُ
لَكَ أَن تَتَكَبَّرَ فِيهَا فَاخْرُجْ إِنَّكَ مِنَ
الصّٰغِرِينَ ﴿١٣﴾ قَالَ أَنظِرْنِيٓ إِلٰى يَوْمِ يُبْعَثُونَ ﴿١٤﴾
قَالَ إِنَّكَ مِنَ الْمُنظَرِينَ ﴿١٥﴾ قَالَ فَبِمَآ
أَغْوَيْتَنِي لَأَقْعُدَنَّ لَهُمْ صِرٰطَكَ الْمُسْتَقِيمَ ﴿١٦﴾
ثُمَّ لَـَٔاتِيَنَّهُم مِّنۢ بَيْنِ أَيْدِيهِمْ وَمِنْ خَلْفِهِمْ
وَعَنْ أَيْمٰنِهِمْ وَعَن شَمَآئِلِهِمْ وَلَا تَجِدُ
أَكْثَرَهُمْ شٰكِرِينَ ﴿١٧﴾ قَالَ اخْرُجْ مِنْهَا مَذْءُومًا
مَّدْحُورًا لَّمَن تَبِعَكَ مِنْهُمْ لَأَمْلَأَنَّ جَهَنَّمَ
مِنكُمْ أَجْمَعِينَ ﴿١٨﴾ وَيٰٓـَٔادَمُ اسْكُنْ أَنتَ وَزَوْجُكَ

when and where you like but do not (even) approach this tree or you both will become of the transgressors.'

20. Then satan made an evil suggestion to them both, with the result that their shortcomings which were hidden from them, became manifest to them, and he said, 'Your Lord forbade you from this tree only lest you should become angels or become of the immortals.'

21. And he ardently swore to them both (saying), 'Most certainly, I am one of your sincere advisers.'

22. Thus he led them on the way of guile and deceit. And when they tasted of the tree (and committed the things forbidden to them), their shortcomings became manifest to them. They (in order to cover themselves) began to stick the leaves of the garden over themselves and their Lord called out to them both (saying,) 'Did I not forbid you from (approaching) that tree, and tell you that satan is to you an enemy disuniting (from Me)?'

23. Both of them said, 'Our Lord! We have done injustice to our souls, and if You do not protect us (against the consequences of our faults) and do not have mercy on us, we shall surely be of the losers.'

24. (God) said, 'Get down (from this land). Some of you are (indeed) enemies of others, and there will be for you on this earth a habitation and (enjoyment of) provision for a while.'

25. And (He added), 'In this (very universe) you shall live and therein you shall die and from it you shall be brought forth (in the Hereafter).'

SECTION 3

26. **O** CHILDREN of Adam! We have given you a raiment that covers your nakedness and is a source of (your) elegance and protection. Yet the raiment that guards against evils, that is the

الْجَنَّةَ فَكُلَا مِنْ حَيْثُ شِئْتُمَا وَ لَا تَقْرَبَا
هٰذِهِ الشَّجَرَةَ فَتَكُونَا مِنَ الظّٰلِمِينَ ﴿١٩﴾
فَوَسْوَسَ لَهُمَا الشَّيْطٰنُ لِيُبْدِيَ لَهُمَا مَا وٗرِيَ
عَنْهُمَا مِنْ سَوْءٰتِهِمَا وَ قَالَ مَا نَهٰكُمَا
رَبُّكُمَا عَنْ هٰذِهِ الشَّجَرَةِ إِلَّآ أَنْ تَكُونَا
مَلَكَيْنِ أَوْ تَكُونَا مِنَ الْخٰلِدِينَ ﴿٢٠﴾ وَ قَاسَمَهُمَآ
إِنِّي لَكُمَا لَمِنَ النّٰصِحِينَ ﴿٢١﴾ فَدَلّٰىهُمَا بِغُرُورٍ
فَلَمَّا ذَاقَا الشَّجَرَةَ بَدَتْ لَهُمَا سَوْءٰتُهُمَا
وَ طَفِقَا يَخْصِفٰنِ عَلَيْهِمَا مِنْ وَّرَقِ الْجَنَّةِ
وَ نَادٰىهُمَا رَبُّهُمَآ أَلَمْ أَنْهَكُمَا عَنْ تِلْكُمَا
الشَّجَرَةِ وَ أَقُلْ لَّكُمَآ إِنَّ الشَّيْطٰنَ لَكُمَا
عَدُوٌّ مُّبِينٌ ﴿٢٢﴾ قَالَا رَبَّنَا ظَلَمْنَآ أَنْفُسَنَا
وَ إِنْ لَّمْ تَغْفِرْ لَنَا وَ تَرْحَمْنَا لَنَكُونَنَّ مِنَ
الْخٰسِرِينَ ﴿٢٣﴾ قَالَ اهْبِطُوا بَعْضُكُمْ لِبَعْضٍ
عَدُوٌّ وَ لَكُمْ فِي الْأَرْضِ مُسْتَقَرٌّ وَّ مَتٰعٌ إِلٰى
حِينٍ ﴿٢٤﴾ قَالَ فِيهَا تَحْيَوْنَ وَ فِيهَا تَمُوتُونَ
وَ مِنْهَا تُخْرَجُونَ ﴿٢٥﴾ يٰبَنِيٓ أٰدَمَ قَدْ أَنْزَلْنَا
عَلَيْكُمْ لِبَاسًا يُّوٰرِي سَوْءٰتِكُمْ وَ رِيشًا
وَ لِبَاسُ التَّقْوٰى ذٰلِكَ خَيْرٌ ذٰلِكَ مِنْ أٰيٰتِ

best (of robes). That is one of the commandments of Allâh so that they may attain eminence.

27. O Children of Adam! Do not let satan put you in trouble (in the same way) as he turned your parents out of the garden, stripping them of their raiment (of innocence) with the result that their shortcomings were made manifest to them both. Verily, he (- satan) sees you, he and his tribe, in such a way as you see them not. Verily, We have made satans friends of those who do not believe.

28. And when they (- the disbelievers) commit an act of indecency, they say, 'We found our forefathers (practising) on it, and it is Allâh Who has enjoined it upon us.' Say, 'Surely, Allâh never enjoins indecencies. Do you attribute to Allâh what you do not know (that it is from Him).'

29. Say, 'My Lord has ordained to be equitable, and to keep your attention upright towards Him always in (your) every Prayer, and to call upon Him exclusively bearing true faith in Him. As He brought you into being (in the first instance) so shall you return (to Him again).'

30. There is a party whom He has guided aright, but there is another party, straying has become an established fact with them. Verily, they have taken the evil ones for friends to the exclusion of Allâh, yet they deem they are rightly guided.

31. O Children of Adam! Look to your elegance (by dressing properly) at every time and place of worship, and eat and drink but exceed not the bounds, for He does not love those who exceed the bounds.

SECTION 4

32. SAY, 'Who has made unlawful Allâh's beautiful things of adornment and elegance which He has produced for His servants and the delicious and pure things of (His) providing?' Say, 'They are primarily meant for the believers (and for the disbelievers too) in this present life (but) exclusively for (the believers) on

اللهِ لَعَلَّهُمْ يَذَّكَّرُونَ ﴿٢٦﴾ يٰبَنِيٓ ءَادَمَ لَا
يَفْتِنَنَّكُمُ الشَّيْطٰنُ كَمَآ أَخْرَجَ أَبَوَيْكُم مِّنَ
الْجَنَّةِ يَنْزِعُ عَنْهُمَا لِبَاسَهُمَا لِيُرِيَهُمَا سَوْءٰتِهِمَا ؕ
إِنَّهُ يَرٰىكُمْ هُوَ وَقَبِيلُهُ مِنْ حَيْثُ لَا
تَرَوْنَهُمْ ؕ إِنَّا جَعَلْنَا الشَّيٰطِينَ أَوْلِيَآءَ لِلَّذِينَ
لَا يُؤْمِنُونَ ﴿٢٧﴾ وَإِذَا فَعَلُوا فٰحِشَةً قَالُوا وَجَدْنَا
عَلَيْهَآ ءَابَآءَنَا وَاللهُ أَمَرَنَا بِهَا ؕ قُلْ إِنَّ اللهَ
لَا يَأْمُرُ بِالْفَحْشَآءِ ؕ أَتَقُولُونَ عَلَى اللهِ مَا لَا
تَعْلَمُونَ ﴿٢٨﴾ قُلْ أَمَرَ رَبِّي بِالْقِسْطِ ۟ وَأَقِيمُوا
وُجُوهَكُمْ عِنْدَ كُلِّ مَسْجِدٍ وَّادْعُوهُ مُخْلِصِينَ
لَهُ الدِّينَ ؕ كَمَا بَدَأَكُمْ تَعُودُونَ ﴿٢٩﴾ فَرِيقًا
هَدٰى وَفَرِيقًا حَقَّ عَلَيْهِمُ الضَّلٰلَةُ ؕ إِنَّهُمُ
اتَّخَذُوا الشَّيٰطِينَ أَوْلِيَآءَ مِنْ دُونِ اللهِ
وَيَحْسَبُونَ أَنَّهُم مُّهْتَدُونَ ﴿٣٠﴾ يٰبَنِيٓ ءَادَمَ خُذُوا
زِينَتَكُمْ عِنْدَ كُلِّ مَسْجِدٍ وَّكُلُوا وَاشْرَبُوا
وَلَا تُسْرِفُوا ۚ إِنَّهُ لَا يُحِبُّ الْمُسْرِفِينَ ﴿٣١﴾ ع
قُلْ مَنْ حَرَّمَ زِينَةَ اللهِ الَّتِيٓ أَخْرَجَ لِعِبَادِهِ
وَالطَّيِّبٰتِ مِنَ الرِّزْقِ ؕ قُلْ هِيَ لِلَّذِينَ ءَامَنُوا
فِي الْحَيٰوةِ الدُّنْيَا خَالِصَةً يَّوْمَ الْقِيٰمَةِ ؕ

the Day of Resurrection.' In this way do We explain the Messages for a people who would know.

33. Say, 'Verily, My Lord has forbidden all (acts of) indecency, open and hidden, and every (kind of) sin and aggression, which is never justifiable; and (He forbids you also) to associate with Allâh that for which He has sent down no authority, and to say concerning Allâh that which you do not know (that it is in fact said by Him).'

34. For (the end of) every nation there is a term fixed, so that when their term comes, they cannot delay a single moment (to avoid it) nor can they get ahead (of it to escape from it).

35. O Children of Adam! Whenever there come to you Messengers from amongst yourselves relating to you My Messages, then whosoever (by accepting them) becomes secure against evil and amends, there shall remain no fear on them nor shall they grieve.

36. But those who cry lies to Our Messages and turn away from them disdainfully, it is they who are the fellows of the Fire, where they shall abide till long.

37. Who is more unjust than he who forges a lie in the name of Allâh or cries lies to His Messages. It is these who shall continue to have their lot of the Book as ordained (by Allâh) until (there comes the time) when Our messengers (- the angels) come to them to take away their souls. They (- the angels) will say, 'Where is (now) that which you used to call upon besides Allâh?' They will reply, 'They are lost to us', and they will bear witness against themselves that they were disbelievers.

38. He (- God) will say, 'Enter into the Fire along with the communities that have passed away before you, from among the *jinns* and ordinary people.' Every time a (new) community enters it, it curses its sister (evildoing community), until when they have all followed

كَذٰلِكَ نُفَصِّلُ الْأٰيٰتِ لِقَوْمٍ يَّعْلَمُوْنَ ﴿٣٢﴾ قُلْ
إِنَّمَا حَرَّمَ رَبِّيَ الْفَوٰحِشَ مَا ظَهَرَ مِنْهَا
وَ مَا بَطَنَ وَ الْإِثْمَ وَ الْبَغْيَ بِغَيْرِ الْحَقِّ وَ أَنْ
تُشْرِكُوْا بِاللّٰهِ مَا لَمْ يُنَزِّلْ بِهٖ سُلْطٰنًا وَّ أَنْ
تَقُوْلُوْا عَلَى اللّٰهِ مَا لَا تَعْلَمُوْنَ ﴿٣٣﴾ وَ لِكُلِّ أُمَّةٍ
أَجَلٌ فَإِذَا جَآءَ أَجَلُهُمْ لَا يَسْتَأْخِرُوْنَ سَاعَةً
وَّ لَا يَسْتَقْدِمُوْنَ ﴿٣٤﴾ يٰبَنِيْٓ أٰدَمَ إِمَّا يَأْتِيَنَّكُمْ
رُسُلٌ مِّنْكُمْ يَقُصُّوْنَ عَلَيْكُمْ أٰيٰتِيْ فَمَنِ اتَّقٰى
وَ أَصْلَحَ فَلَا خَوْفٌ عَلَيْهِمْ وَ لَا هُمْ يَحْزَنُوْنَ ﴿٣٥﴾
وَ الَّذِيْنَ كَذَّبُوْا بِأٰيٰتِنَا وَ اسْتَكْبَرُوْا عَنْهَآ
أُولٰٓئِكَ أَصْحٰبُ النَّارِ هُمْ فِيْهَا خٰلِدُوْنَ ﴿٣٦﴾
فَمَنْ أَظْلَمُ مِمَّنِ افْتَرٰى عَلَى اللّٰهِ كَذِبًا أَوْ
كَذَّبَ بِأٰيٰتِهٖ أُولٰٓئِكَ يَنَالُهُمْ نَصِيْبُهُمْ مِّنَ
الْكِتٰبِ حَتّٰٓى إِذَا جَآءَتْهُمْ رُسُلُنَا يَتَوَفَّوْنَهُمْ
قَالُوْٓا أَيْنَ مَا كُنْتُمْ تَدْعُوْنَ مِنْ دُوْنِ اللّٰهِ
قَالُوْا ضَلُّوْا عَنَّا وَ شَهِدُوْا عَلٰٓى أَنْفُسِهِمْ أَنَّهُمْ
كَانُوْا كٰفِرِيْنَ ﴿٣٧﴾ قَالَ ادْخُلُوْا فِيْٓ أُمَمٍ قَدْ خَلَتْ
مِنْ قَبْلِكُمْ مِّنَ الْجِنِّ وَ الْإِنْسِ فِي النَّارِ كُلَّمَا
دَخَلَتْ أُمَّةٌ لَّعَنَتْ أُخْتَهَا حَتّٰٓى إِذَا ادَّارَكُوْا
فِيْهَا جَمِيْعًا قَالَتْ أُخْرٰىهُمْ لِأُولٰىهُمْ رَبَّنَا هٰٓؤُلَآءِ

one another into it, the last of them will say with regard to the first of them (-the leaders), 'Our Lord! These led us astray so give them punishment of the Fire over and over again.' He will say, 'Everyone is having (his punishment) over and over again, but you do not know (about one another).'

39. And the first of them, (- their leaders) will say to the last of them (- the followers), '(If we are to blame), you (too) are no better than we. Suffer therefore, the punishment of your (evil) deeds.'

SECTION 5

40. **B**E sure, those who cry lies to Our Messages and turn away from them disdainfully, the gates of the (spiritual) firmament shall not be opened for them, nor shall they enter Paradise until a camel passes through the eye of a needle. In this way do We award punishment to those who cut their ties (with Allâh).

41. They shall have Gehenna for their bed and above them awnings (of fire for cover), and thus do We requite the wrongdoers.

42. (As for) those who believe and do deeds of righteousness - We charge no soul except according to its capacity. It is these who are the rightful owners of Paradise where they shall abide forever.

43. We shall strip their hearts of whatever rancour there may be (for others). They shall have streams rolling at their feet, and they shall say, 'All perfect and true praise belongs to Allâh Who guided us to attain to this (Paradise). We could never have been led aright (to this) if Allâh had not guided us. The Messengers of Our Lord did come (to us) with the truth.' It will be proclaimed to them, 'This is the very Paradise which you are made to inherit as a reward of your (good) deeds.'

44. The owners of Paradise will call out to the

أَضَلُّونَا فَـَٔاتِهِمْ عَذَابًا ضِعْفًا مِّنَ النَّارِ ۖ قَالَ
لِكُلٍّ ضِعْفٌ وَلَٰكِن لَّا تَعْلَمُونَ ﴿٣٨﴾ وَقَالَتْ
أُولَىٰهُمْ لِأُخْرَىٰهُمْ فَمَا كَانَ لَكُمْ عَلَيْنَا مِن
فَضْلٍ فَذُوقُوا الْعَذَابَ بِمَا كُنتُمْ تَكْسِبُونَ ﴿٣٩﴾
إِنَّ الَّذِينَ كَذَّبُوا بِـَٔايَاتِنَا وَاسْتَكْبَرُوا عَنْهَا لَا
تُفَتَّحُ لَهُمْ أَبْوَابُ السَّمَاءِ وَلَا يَدْخُلُونَ
الْجَنَّةَ حَتَّىٰ يَلِجَ الْجَمَلُ فِي سَمِّ الْخِيَاطِ ۚ
وَكَذَٰلِكَ نَجْزِي الْمُجْرِمِينَ ﴿٤٠﴾ لَهُم مِّن جَهَنَّمَ
مِهَادٌ وَمِن فَوْقِهِمْ غَوَاشٍ ۚ وَكَذَٰلِكَ نَجْزِي
الظَّالِمِينَ ﴿٤١﴾ وَالَّذِينَ آمَنُوا وَعَمِلُوا الصَّالِحَاتِ
لَا نُكَلِّفُ نَفْسًا إِلَّا وُسْعَهَا أُولَٰئِكَ أَصْحَابُ
الْجَنَّةِ ۖ هُمْ فِيهَا خَالِدُونَ ﴿٤٢﴾ وَنَزَعْنَا مَا فِي
صُدُورِهِم مِّنْ غِلٍّ تَجْرِي مِن تَحْتِهِمُ الْأَنْهَارُ ۖ
وَقَالُوا الْحَمْدُ لِلَّهِ الَّذِي هَدَانَا لِهَٰذَا وَمَا
كُنَّا لِنَهْتَدِيَ لَوْلَا أَنْ هَدَانَا اللَّهُ ۖ لَقَدْ
جَاءَتْ رُسُلُ رَبِّنَا بِالْحَقِّ ۖ وَنُودُوا أَن تِلْكُمُ
الْجَنَّةُ أُورِثْتُمُوهَا بِمَا كُنتُمْ تَعْمَلُونَ ﴿٤٣﴾
وَنَادَىٰ أَصْحَابُ الْجَنَّةِ أَصْحَابَ النَّارِ أَن قَدْ

fellows of the Fire, 'We have found, what Our Lord had promised, to be true. Have you (too) found what your Lord had promised (to you) to be true?' They will say, 'Yes.' Then a herald will proclaim amongst them, 'Let the disapproval of Allâh be on these wrongdoers

45. 'Who hinder (the people) from Allâh's way and seek to make it (look as) crooked, and who are disbelievers in the Hereafter.'

46. And between the two (- the Fire and the Paradise) is a barrier, and on the elevated places there shall be men (like the Prophets and other exalted spiritual dignitaries) who will recognise everyone by his appearance. And they shall call out to the (prospective) inmates of Paradise, 'Peace be on you!' These (prospective inmates of Paradise) will not have (yet) entered therein, though they will be hoping (for this entry).

47. And when their eyes are turned towards the fellows of the Fire, they will say, 'Our Lord! Place us not with these wrongdoing people.'

SECTION 6

48. **T**HE occupants of the elevated places will call out to certain men (from the fellows of the Fire), whom they will recognise by their appearance, 'Behold! Neither your multitude nor that (amassing) in which you took pride have been of any avail to you.

49. 'Are these (owners of Paradise) the ones about whom you swore that Allâh would not extend His mercy to them?' (Allâh has ordered them,) 'Enter Paradise! No fear shall remain on you, nor ever shall you grieve.'

50. Now the fellows of the Fire will call out to the owners of Paradise, 'Pour down upon us some water or (give us) some of that which Allâh has provided for you.' They will say, 'Allâh has forbidden them both to the disbelievers;

51. 'Those who took their faith for a futile and frivolous thing causing diversion (from Allâh), they were beguiled by the worldly life.' (And

وَجَدْنَا مَا وَعَدَنَا رَبُّنَا حَقًّا فَهَلْ وَجَدْتُّمْ مَّا وَعَدَ
رَبُّكُمْ حَقًّا قَالُوْا نَعَمْ فَاَذَّنَ مُؤَذِّنٌۢ بَيْنَهُمْ
اَنْ لَّعْنَةُ اللّٰهِ عَلَى الظّٰلِمِيْنَ ﴿٤٤﴾ الَّذِيْنَ يَصُدُّوْنَ
عَنْ سَبِيْلِ اللّٰهِ وَ يَبْغُوْنَهَا عِوَجًا وَ هُمْ بِالْاٰخِرَةِ
كٰفِرُوْنَ ﴿٤٥﴾ وَ بَيْنَهُمَا حِجَابٌ وَ عَلَى الْاَعْرَافِ
رِجَالٌ يَّعْرِفُوْنَ كُلًّا بِسِيْمٰىهُمْ وَ نَادَوْا اَصْحٰبَ
الْجَنَّةِ اَنْ سَلٰمٌ عَلَيْكُمْ لَمْ يَدْخُلُوْهَا وَ هُمْ
يَطْمَعُوْنَ ﴿٤٦﴾ وَ اِذَا صُرِفَتْ اَبْصٰرُهُمْ تِلْقَآءَ
اَصْحٰبِ النَّارِ قَالُوْا رَبَّنَا لَا تَجْعَلْنَا مَعَ الْقَوْمِ
الظّٰلِمِيْنَ ﴿٤٧﴾ وَ نَادٰۤى اَصْحٰبُ الْاَعْرَافِ رِجَالًا
يَّعْرِفُوْنَهُمْ بِسِيْمٰىهُمْ قَالُوْا مَاۤ اَغْنٰى عَنْكُمْ
جَمْعُكُمْ وَ مَا كُنْتُمْ تَسْتَكْبِرُوْنَ ﴿٤٨﴾ اَهٰۤؤُلَآءِ
الَّذِيْنَ اَقْسَمْتُمْ لَا يَنَالُهُمُ اللّٰهُ بِرَحْمَةٍ
اُدْخُلُوا الْجَنَّةَ لَا خَوْفٌ عَلَيْكُمْ وَ لَاۤ اَنْتُمْ
تَحْزَنُوْنَ ﴿٤٩﴾ وَ نَادٰۤى اَصْحٰبُ النَّارِ اَصْحٰبَ
الْجَنَّةِ اَنْ اَفِيْضُوْا عَلَيْنَا مِنَ الْمَآءِ اَوْ مِمَّا
رَزَقَكُمُ اللّٰهُ قَالُوْا اِنَّ اللّٰهَ حَرَّمَهُمَا عَلَى
الْكٰفِرِيْنَ ﴿٥٠﴾ الَّذِيْنَ اتَّخَذُوْا دِيْنَهُمْ لَهْوًا
وَّ لَعِبًا وَّ غَرَّتْهُمُ الْحَيٰوةُ الدُّنْيَا فَالْيَوْمَ

ع ٦ ١٢

God will say,) 'So on this day We shall forsake them as they forsook (the idea of) the meeting of this day of theirs, and as they denied Our Messages deliberately.

52. 'Although We had brought them a Book which We had made clear with knowledge, as a guidance and as a mercy for a people who believe.'

53. Do these (disbelievers) just await the final sequel (of the warning) thereof? The day its final sequel comes, those who had forsaken it before (in this life) would say, 'The Messengers of our Lord did indeed come with the truth. Have we (now) any intercessors so that they may intercede for us? Or could we be sent back so that we might act otherwise than we used to act?' They have indeed ruined their souls and that which they used to forge has failed them.

SECTION 7

54. **A**s a matter of fact your Lord is Allâh, Who created the heavens and the earth in six aeons and at the same time He is well established on the Throne of Authority. He covers the night with the day which follows (the night) incessantly. And He created the sun and the moon and the stars all subservient (to humankind) by His command. Beware! His is all, the creation and the command. Blessed be Allâh, Lord of the worlds.

55. Call upon your Lord with humility and open supplication. In fact He does not love the transgressors.

56. And do not create disorder in the land after the fair ordering thereof and call on Him with fear (of His displeasure) and with hope (of His mercy). Surely the mercy of Allâh is always close to the doers of good to others.

57. He it is Who sends the winds as good tidings heralding His mercy, till when they (those winds) bear heavy clouds, find them light, We drive (the clouds) to a dead land, then We make it rain, then We bring forth (from the

نَنْسٰهُمْ كَمَا نَسُوْا لِقَآءَ يَوْمِهِمْ هٰذَا وَ مَا
كَانُوْا بِاٰيٰتِنَا يَجْحَدُوْنَ ﴿٥١﴾ وَ لَقَدْ جِئْنٰهُمْ
بِكِتٰبٍ فَصَّلْنٰهُ عَلٰى عِلْمٍ هُدًى وَّ رَحْمَةً
لِّقَوْمٍ يُّؤْمِنُوْنَ ﴿٥٢﴾ هَلْ يَنْظُرُوْنَ إِلَّا تَأْوِيْلَهٗ
يَوْمَ يَأْتِيْ تَأْوِيْلُهٗ يَقُوْلُ الَّذِيْنَ نَسُوْهُ مِنْ
قَبْلُ قَدْ جَآءَتْ رُسُلُ رَبِّنَا بِالْحَقِّ فَهَلْ
لَّنَا مِنْ شُفَعَآءَ فَيَشْفَعُوْا لَنَآ أَوْ نُرَدُّ فَنَعْمَلَ
غَيْرَ الَّذِيْ كُنَّا نَعْمَلُ قَدْ خَسِرُوْٓا أَنْفُسَهُمْ
وَ ضَلَّ عَنْهُمْ مَّا كَانُوْا يَفْتَرُوْنَ ﴿٥٣﴾ إِنَّ رَبَّكُمُ
اللّٰهُ الَّذِيْ خَلَقَ السَّمٰوٰتِ وَ الْأَرْضَ فِيْ سِتَّةِ
أَيَّامٍ ثُمَّ اسْتَوٰى عَلَى الْعَرْشِ يُغْشِي الَّيْلَ
النَّهَارَ يَطْلُبُهٗ حَثِيْثًا وَّ الشَّمْسَ وَ الْقَمَرَ
وَ النُّجُوْمَ مُسَخَّرٰتٍ بِأَمْرِهٖ أَلَا لَهُ الْخَلْقُ
وَ الْأَمْرُ تَبٰرَكَ اللّٰهُ رَبُّ الْعٰلَمِيْنَ ﴿٥٤﴾ اُدْعُوْا
رَبَّكُمْ تَضَرُّعًا وَّ خُفْيَةً إِنَّهٗ لَا يُحِبُّ
الْمُعْتَدِيْنَ ﴿٥٥﴾ وَ لَا تُفْسِدُوْا فِي الْأَرْضِ بَعْدَ
إِصْلٰحِهَا وَ ادْعُوْهُ خَوْفًا وَّ طَمَعًا إِنَّ رَحْمَتَ
اللّٰهِ قَرِيْبٌ مِّنَ الْمُحْسِنِيْنَ ﴿٥٦﴾ وَ هُوَ الَّذِيْ
يُرْسِلُ الرِّيٰحَ بُشْرًا بَيْنَ يَدَيْ رَحْمَتِهٖ
حَتّٰى إِذَآ أَقَلَّتْ سَحَابًا ثِقَالًا سُقْنٰهُ لِبَلَدٍ
مَّيِّتٍ فَأَنْزَلْنَا بِهِ الْمَآءَ فَأَخْرَجْنَا بِهٖ مِنْ
كُلِّ الثَّمَرٰتِ كَذٰلِكَ نُخْرِجُ الْمَوْتٰى لَعَلَّكُمْ

dead land) by means of that (water) all manner of fruit; that is how We will bring forth the dead so that you may achieve eminence and honour.

58. And (as for) the fertile land, its vegetation comes forth (flourishing and well) by the leave of its Lord, and that (land) which is inferior (its herbage) comes forth but scantily and (that too) defective. That is how We expound (Our) Messages in diverse ways for a people who give thanks.

SECTION 8

59. **W**E sent Noah to his people and he said, 'O my people! Worship Allâh, there is no one worthy of worship for you other than He. Surely, I fear lest there should befall you the punishment of an awful Day.'

60. The chiefs of his people said, 'Surely, we see you steeped in evident error.'

61. He said, 'O my people! I am in no error, (nor am I lost), rather I am Messenger from the Lord of the worlds.

62. 'I deliver to you the Messages of my Lord, and I advise you sincerely, for I know from Allâh what you do not know.

63. 'Well, does it make you wonder that an exhortation, leading to eminence and honour, has come to you from your Lord through a man from among you, so that he may warn you, and so that you may become secure against evil, and that you may be shown mercy?'

64. But they (to whom he delivered His Messages) cried lies to him, so We rescued him and those with him in the Ark (from the deluge), and We drowned those who cried lies to Our Messages. They were certainly a (spiritually) blind people.

SECTION 9

65. **A**ND to 'Âd (We sent) their brother Hûd. He said, 'O my people! Worship Allâh, you have no deity other than He; will you not then guard against evil?'

66. The unbelieving chiefs of his people said,

تَذَكَّرُونَ ﴿٥٧﴾ وَالْبَلَدُ الطَّيِّبُ يَخْرُجُ نَبَاتُهُ
بِإِذْنِ رَبِّهِ ۚ وَالَّذِي خَبُثَ لَا يَخْرُجُ إِلَّا
نَكِدًا ۚ كَذَٰلِكَ نُصَرِّفُ الْآيَاتِ لِقَوْمٍ يَشْكُرُونَ ﴿٥٨﴾
لَقَدْ أَرْسَلْنَا نُوحًا إِلَىٰ قَوْمِهِ فَقَالَ يَٰقَوْمِ
اعْبُدُوا اللَّهَ مَا لَكُم مِّنْ إِلَٰهٍ غَيْرُهُ ۖ إِنِّي أَخَافُ
عَلَيْكُمْ عَذَابَ يَوْمٍ عَظِيمٍ ﴿٥٩﴾ قَالَ الْمَلَأُ
مِن قَوْمِهِ إِنَّا لَنَرَاكَ فِي ضَلَالٍ مُّبِينٍ ﴿٦٠﴾
قَالَ يَٰقَوْمِ لَيْسَ بِي ضَلَالَةٌ وَلَٰكِنِّي رَسُولٌ
مِّن رَّبِّ الْعَالَمِينَ ﴿٦١﴾ أُبَلِّغُكُمْ رِسَالَاتِ رَبِّي
وَأَنصَحُ لَكُمْ وَأَعْلَمُ مِنَ اللَّهِ مَا لَا
تَعْلَمُونَ ﴿٦٢﴾ أَوَعَجِبْتُمْ أَن جَاءَكُمْ ذِكْرٌ
مِّن رَّبِّكُمْ عَلَىٰ رَجُلٍ مِّنكُمْ لِيُنذِرَكُمْ
وَلِتَتَّقُوا وَلَعَلَّكُمْ تُرْحَمُونَ ﴿٦٣﴾ فَكَذَّبُوهُ
فَأَنجَيْنَاهُ وَالَّذِينَ مَعَهُ فِي الْفُلْكِ
وَأَغْرَقْنَا الَّذِينَ كَذَّبُوا بِآيَاتِنَا ۚ إِنَّهُمْ
كَانُوا قَوْمًا عَمِينَ ﴿٦٤﴾ وَإِلَىٰ عَادٍ أَخَاهُمْ
هُودًا ۗ قَالَ يَٰقَوْمِ اعْبُدُوا اللَّهَ مَا لَكُم
مِّنْ إِلَٰهٍ غَيْرُهُ ۚ أَفَلَا تَتَّقُونَ ﴿٦٥﴾ قَالَ الْمَلَأُ
الَّذِينَ كَفَرُوا مِن قَوْمِهِ إِنَّا لَنَرَاكَ

'We surely see you in folly and in fact we deem you one of the liars.'

67. He said, 'O my people! There is no foolishness in me, on the contrary I am a Messenger from the Lord of the worlds.

68. 'I deliver to you the Messages of my Lord and I am to you a counselor, sincere and trustworthy.

69. 'Do you wonder that an exhortation, leading to eminence and honour, should come to you from your Lord, through a man from among you so that he may warn you? Remember (His favour) when He made you (- the *Adites)* rulers after the people of Noah and increased you vastly in respect of (your bodily) constitution (by making you stout and strong and tall), remember then the favours of Allâh so that you may attain the goal.'

70. They said, 'Have you come to us that we may worship Allâh alone and renounce that which our fathers worshipped? Bring down on us the punishment you threaten us with, if you are of the truthful.'

71. He said, 'There has already fallen upon you the punishment and the displeasure from your Lord. Would you dispute with me regarding mere names (of your false gods) which you have coined, you and your fathers, names in support of which Allâh has sent down no authority? (If so) then wait (for the consequences), I too, am with you, among those who wait.'

72. So We, in Our mercy, saved him and his companions, and We rooted out the last remnants of those who cried lies to Our Messages, for they would not believe.

SECTION 10

73. **A**ND to Thamûd (We sent) their brother Sâlih. He said, 'O my people! Worship Allâh, you have no other god than Him. A clear proof has already come to you from your Lord. Here

فِي سَفَاهَةٍ وَإِنَّا لَنَظُنُّكَ مِنَ الْكَٰذِبِينَ ﴿٦٦﴾
قَالَ يَٰقَوْمِ لَيْسَ بِي سَفَاهَةٌ وَلَٰكِنِّي
رَسُولٌ مِّن رَّبِّ الْعَٰلَمِينَ ﴿٦٧﴾ أُبَلِّغُكُمْ رِسَٰلَٰتِ
رَبِّي وَأَنَا لَكُمْ نَاصِحٌ أَمِينٌ ﴿٦٨﴾ أَوَعَجِبْتُمْ
أَن جَآءَكُمْ ذِكْرٌ مِّن رَّبِّكُمْ عَلَىٰ رَجُلٍ
مِّنكُمْ لِيُنذِرَكُمْ وَاذْكُرُوٓا إِذْ جَعَلَكُمْ
خُلَفَآءَ مِنۢ بَعْدِ قَوْمِ نُوحٍ وَزَادَكُمْ فِي
الْخَلْقِ بَصْطَةً فَاذْكُرُوٓا ءَالَآءَ اللَّهِ لَعَلَّكُمْ
تُفْلِحُونَ ﴿٦٩﴾ قَالُوٓا أَجِئْتَنَا لِنَعْبُدَ اللَّهَ وَحْدَهُ
وَنَذَرَ مَا كَانَ يَعْبُدُ ءَابَآؤُنَا فَأْتِنَا بِمَا
تَعِدُنَآ إِن كُنتَ مِنَ الصَّٰدِقِينَ ﴿٧٠﴾ قَالَ قَدْ
وَقَعَ عَلَيْكُم مِّن رَّبِّكُمْ رِجْسٌ وَغَضَبٌ
أَتُجَٰدِلُونَنِي فِيٓ أَسْمَآءٍ سَمَّيْتُمُوهَآ أَنتُمْ
وَءَابَآؤُكُم مَّا نَزَّلَ اللَّهُ بِهَا مِن سُلْطَٰنٍ
فَانتَظِرُوٓا إِنِّي مَعَكُم مِّنَ الْمُنتَظِرِينَ ﴿٧١﴾
فَأَنجَيْنَٰهُ وَالَّذِينَ مَعَهُۥ بِرَحْمَةٍ مِّنَّا
وَقَطَعْنَا دَابِرَ الَّذِينَ كَذَّبُوا بِـَٔايَٰتِنَا
وَمَا كَانُوا مُؤْمِنِينَ ﴿٧٢﴾ وَإِلَىٰ ثَمُودَ
أَخَاهُمْ صَٰلِحًا قَالَ يَٰقَوْمِ اعْبُدُوا اللَّهَ
مَا لَكُم مِّنْ إِلَٰهٍ غَيْرُهُۥ قَدْ جَآءَتْكُم
بَيِّنَةٌ مِّن رَّبِّكُمْ هَٰذِهِۦ نَاقَةُ اللَّهِ
لَكُمْ ءَايَةً فَذَرُوهَا تَأْكُلْ فِيٓ أَرْضِ
اللَّهِ وَلَا تَمَسُّوهَا بِسُوٓءٍ فَيَأْخُذَكُمْ عَذَابٌ

is a she-camel (let loose for the cause) of Allâh, a sign for you. Let her alone to pasture in Allâh's land and do her no harm or a woeful punishment shall overtake you.

74. 'And recall (His favour) when He made you (- Thamûd) the ruler after 'Âd and assigned you abode in the land after your sufferings. You build castles in its plains, and hewed houses out of the mountains. Remember, therefore, the favours of Allâh and do not commit mischief in the land, (acting as) creators of disorder.'

75. The chieftains of his people who considered themselves strong and great said to those who were reckoned weak, to those of them who had believed, 'Are you sure that Sâlih is one sent from his Lord?' They replied, 'Surely, we are believers in that (Message) he has been sent with.'

76. Those who considered themselves great and strong said (scornfully), 'Lo! We are disbelievers in that which you believe in.'

77. So they hamstrung the she-camel and flouted the commandment of their Lord and said, 'O Sâlih! Bring down on us the punishment you used to threatens us with, if you are really one of the sent ones (by God).'

78. So the earthquake seized them and the morning found them lying prostrate on the ground in their habitations.

79. Then he (- Sâlih) turned away from them and said, (lamenting upon their disaster), 'O my people! I delivered to you the Messages of my Lord and offered you sincere advice but you do not like sincere counsellors.'

80. And (We sent) Lot, (and recall) when he said to his people, 'Do you commit such abomination (of sodomy) as is unprecedent and unsurpassed in the whole world?

81. 'You indeed approach men rather than (your) women to satisfy your lust. The fact is that you are a people who transgress all limits.'

82. His people had no reply to make but that

أَلِيمٌ ﴿٧٣﴾ وَاذْكُرُوٓا إِذْ جَعَلَكُمْ خُلَفَآءَ
مِنۢ بَعْدِ عَادٍ وَبَوَّأَكُمْ فِي الْأَرْضِ
تَتَّخِذُونَ مِنْ سُهُولِهَا قُصُورًا وَتَنْحِتُونَ
الْجِبَالَ بُيُوتًا فَاذْكُرُوٓا ءَالَآءَ اللَّهِ
وَلَا تَعْثَوْا فِي الْأَرْضِ مُفْسِدِينَ ﴿٧٤﴾ قَالَ الْمَلَأُ
الَّذِينَ اسْتَكْبَرُوا مِنْ قَوْمِهِ لِلَّذِينَ
اسْتُضْعِفُوا لِمَنْ ءَامَنَ مِنْهُمْ أَتَعْلَمُونَ
أَنَّ صٰلِحًا مُّرْسَلٌ مِّنْ رَّبِّهِ قَالُوٓا إِنَّا
بِمَآ أُرْسِلَ بِهِ مُؤْمِنُونَ ﴿٧٥﴾ قَالَ الَّذِينَ
اسْتَكْبَرُوٓا إِنَّا بِالَّذِيٓ ءَامَنْتُمْ بِهِ كٰفِرُونَ ﴿٧٦﴾
فَعَقَرُوا النَّاقَةَ وَعَتَوْا عَنْ أَمْرِ رَبِّهِمْ
وَقَالُوا يٰصٰلِحُ ائْتِنَا بِمَا تَعِدُنَآ إِنْ
كُنْتَ مِنَ الْمُرْسَلِينَ ﴿٧٧﴾ فَأَخَذَتْهُمُ
الرَّجْفَةُ فَأَصْبَحُوا فِي دَارِهِمْ جٰثِمِينَ ﴿٧٨﴾
فَتَوَلّٰى عَنْهُمْ وَقَالَ يٰقَوْمِ لَقَدْ أَبْلَغْتُكُمْ
رِسَالَةَ رَبِّي وَنَصَحْتُ لَكُمْ وَلٰكِنْ لَّا
تُحِبُّونَ النّٰصِحِينَ ﴿٧٩﴾ وَلُوطًا إِذْ قَالَ
لِقَوْمِهِٓ أَتَأْتُونَ الْفٰحِشَةَ مَا سَبَقَكُمْ
بِهَا مِنْ أَحَدٍ مِّنَ الْعٰلَمِينَ ﴿٨٠﴾ إِنَّكُمْ
لَتَأْتُونَ الرِّجَالَ شَهْوَةً مِّنْ دُونِ
النِّسَآءِ بَلْ أَنْتُمْ قَوْمٌ مُّسْرِفُونَ ﴿٨١﴾
وَمَا كَانَ جَوَابَ قَوْمِهِٓ إِلَّآ أَنْ قَالُوٓا
أَخْرِجُوهُمْ مِّنْ قَرْيَتِكُمْ إِنَّهُمْ أُنَاسٌ

they said (to one another), 'Turn them (- Lot and his followers) out of your township, for they are a people who show off to be pure.'
83. And We saved him and his followers, except his wife who chose to be of those who stayed behind.
84. And We pelted (the rest of) them with a severe rain (- a rain of stones due to volcanic eruption combined with an earthquake). Behold! How (evil) was the end of those who cut off their ties (with Allâh).

SECTION 11

85. AND to (the people of) Midian (We sent) their brother Shu'aib. He said, 'O my people! Worship Allâh for you have no one worthy of worship other than Him. A clear proof (to this effect) has already come to you from your Lord, so give full measure and (full) weight, and do not cheat people of their goods, nor create disorder in the land after the fair ordering therein. This indeed is best for you, if you are true believers.
86. 'And do not sit in every path holding out threats (to the wayfarers), and turning those who believe in Him, away from the path of Allâh and seeking to make it (appear as) crooked. And remember (His favours) when you were but a few then He multiplied you. Behold! What was the end of the spreaders of corruption.
87. 'And if there be a party of you who believes in what I am sent with, and a party who does not believe then wait with patience until Allâh judges between us, for He is the Best of Judges.'

يَتَطَهَّرُونَ ﴿٨٢﴾ فَأَنْجَيْنٰهُ وَأَهْلَهٗٓ إِلَّا
امْرَأَتَهٗ ۖ كَانَتْ مِنَ الْغٰبِرِيْنَ ﴿٨٣﴾
وَأَمْطَرْنَا عَلَيْهِمْ مَّطَرًا ۖ فَانْظُرْ كَيْفَ
كَانَ عٰقِبَةُ الْمُجْرِمِيْنَ ﴿٨٤﴾ وَإِلٰى مَدْيَنَ
أَخَاهُمْ شُعَيْبًا ۗ قَالَ يٰقَوْمِ اعْبُدُوا اللّٰهَ
مَا لَكُمْ مِّنْ إِلٰهٍ غَيْرُهٗ ۗ قَدْ جَآءَتْكُمْ
بَيِّنَةٌ مِّنْ رَّبِّكُمْ فَأَوْفُوا الْكَيْلَ
وَالْمِيْزَانَ وَلَا تَبْخَسُوا النَّاسَ
أَشْيَآءَهُمْ وَلَا تُفْسِدُوْا فِي الْأَرْضِ
بَعْدَ إِصْلٰحِهَا ۗ ذٰلِكُمْ خَيْرٌ لَّكُمْ إِنْ
كُنْتُمْ مُّؤْمِنِيْنَ ﴿٨٥﴾ وَلَا تَقْعُدُوْا بِكُلِّ
صِرٰطٍ تُوْعِدُوْنَ وَتَصُدُّوْنَ عَنْ سَبِيْلِ
اللّٰهِ مَنْ اٰمَنَ بِهٖ وَتَبْغُوْنَهَا عِوَجًا ۚ
وَاذْكُرُوْٓا إِذْ كُنْتُمْ قَلِيْلًا فَكَثَّرَكُمْ
وَانْظُرُوْا كَيْفَ كَانَ عٰقِبَةُ الْمُفْسِدِيْنَ ﴿٨٦﴾
وَإِنْ كَانَ طَآئِفَةٌ مِّنْكُمْ اٰمَنُوْا
بِالَّذِيْٓ أُرْسِلْتُ بِهٖ وَطَآئِفَةٌ
لَّمْ يُؤْمِنُوْا فَاصْبِرُوْا حَتّٰى يَحْكُمَ
اللّٰهُ بَيْنَنَا ۚ وَهُوَ خَيْرُ الْحٰكِمِيْنَ ﴿٨٧﴾

ع ١٢ ١٧

PART الجزء التاسع IX

سورة الأعراف ٧

88. THE chiefs who considered themselves strong and great among his people said, 'We will certainly turn you O Shu‘aib! and also those who believe with you, out of our township or else you (all) shall have to revert to our creed.' He said, 'What! (shall we be forced to accept your creed) even though we are unwilling (at heart)?

89. 'We should indeed be forging a lie against Allâh, if we revert to your creed after Allâh has delivered us from it, and it is in no way possible for us to revert thereto unless Allâh, our Lord, should (so) will. Our Lord comprehends all things in His knowledge. In Allâh alone do we put our trust, (so Him do we beseech,) "O our Lord! Decide between us and our people rightly for You are the Best of all Who open (the truth)".'

90. The chiefs who had disbelieved from among his people then said, 'If you follow Shu‘aib you shall then, truly be the losers.'

91. Then they were caught in an earthquake and the morning found them lying prostrate on the ground in their habitations.

92. Those who cried lies to Shu‘aib became (so extinct) as though they had never dwelt therein. Those alone who had cried lies to Shu‘aib were the losers.

93. So he turned away from them and said, 'O my people! I did deliver to you the Messages of my Lord and I did offer you sincere advice; how can I lament over a disbelieving people.'

SECTION 12

94. AND never did We send any Prophet to any township but We afflicted its people with destitution (from Our blessings) and with tribulations so that they might grow humble (before the Almighty).

95. Then We brought comfort (for them) in place of (their) distress until they grew in

قَالَ الْمَلَأُ الَّذِينَ اسْتَكْبَرُوا مِنْ قَوْمِهِ
لَنُخْرِجَنَّكَ يٰشُعَيْبُ وَالَّذِينَ اٰمَنُوا مَعَكَ
مِنْ قَرْيَتِنَا أَوْ لَتَعُودُنَّ فِي مِلَّتِنَا ۚ قَالَ
أَوَلَوْ كُنَّا كٰرِهِينَ ﴿٨٨﴾ قَدِ افْتَرَيْنَا عَلَى
اللّٰهِ كَذِبًا إِنْ عُدْنَا فِي مِلَّتِكُمْ بَعْدَ إِذْ
نَجّٰىنَا اللّٰهُ مِنْهَا ۚ وَمَا يَكُونُ لَنَا أَنْ
نَعُودَ فِيهَا إِلَّا أَنْ يَشَاءَ اللّٰهُ رَبُّنَا ۚ وَسِعَ
رَبُّنَا كُلَّ شَيْءٍ عِلْمًا ۚ عَلَى اللّٰهِ تَوَكَّلْنَا ۚ
رَبَّنَا افْتَحْ بَيْنَنَا وَبَيْنَ قَوْمِنَا بِالْحَقِّ
وَأَنْتَ خَيْرُ الْفٰتِحِينَ ﴿٨٩﴾ وَقَالَ الْمَلَأُ الَّذِينَ
كَفَرُوا مِنْ قَوْمِهِ لَئِنِ اتَّبَعْتُمْ شُعَيْبًا
إِنَّكُمْ إِذًا لَّخٰسِرُونَ ﴿٩٠﴾ فَأَخَذَتْهُمُ الرَّجْفَةُ
فَأَصْبَحُوا فِي دَارِهِمْ جٰثِمِينَ ﴿٩١﴾ الَّذِينَ كَذَّبُوا
شُعَيْبًا كَأَنْ لَمْ يَغْنَوْا فِيهَا ۚ الَّذِينَ كَذَّبُوا
شُعَيْبًا كَانُوا هُمُ الْخٰسِرِينَ ﴿٩٢﴾ فَتَوَلّٰى عَنْهُمْ
وَقَالَ يٰقَوْمِ لَقَدْ أَبْلَغْتُكُمْ رِسٰلٰتِ رَبِّي
وَنَصَحْتُ لَكُمْ ۚ فَكَيْفَ أٰسٰى عَلٰى قَوْمٍ كٰفِرِينَ ﴿٩٣﴾
وَمَا أَرْسَلْنَا فِي قَرْيَةٍ مِّنْ نَّبِيٍّ إِلَّا أَخَذْنَا
أَهْلَهَا بِالْبَأْسَاءِ وَالضَّرَّاءِ لَعَلَّهُمْ يَضَّرَّعُونَ ﴿٩٤﴾
ثُمَّ بَدَّلْنَا مَكَانَ السَّيِّئَةِ الْحَسَنَةَ حَتّٰى

affluence, (number and excess) and said, 'Surely, tribulations and prosperity visited our fathers (also, so it is a normal course of events).' So We seized them unawares while they perceived not (the peril they were in).
96. And if the people of the townships had believed and guarded against transgression, We would invariably have opened for them (the gates of) blessings of the heaven and the earth, but they cried lies (to the Prophets), so We punished them on account of what they used to accomplish.
97. Do the people of these townships feel secure against the coming of Our punishment upon them by night while they are asleep?
98. And do the people of these townships feel secure against the coming of Our punishment upon them in the early part of the forenoon while they are engaged in futile and frivolous (worldly) pursuits?
99. Do they feel secure from the design of Allâh? No one at all feels secure from Allâh's design, except the people who are (doomed to be) losers.

SECTION 13

100 **D**OES it not serve as guidance to those who have inherited the earth from its (previous) occupants that, if We will, We can afflict them (with some punishment) for their sins and put a seal upon their hearts, so that they will not be able to listen (to some guiding advice).
101. Such were the (people of) townships, We have related to you some of their news. Their Messengers did indeed come to them with clear proofs but they would not believe because they had cried lies (to them) in the beginning. That is how Allâh seals up the hearts of the disbelievers.
102. We did not find in most of them any (regard for the observance of their) covenant; indeed, We found most of them disobedient (and transgressors).
103. Then after these (Messengers), We sent

عَفَوْا وَّ قَالُوْا قَدْ مَسَّ اٰبَآءَنَا الضَّرَّآءُ
وَالسَّرَّآءُ فَاَخَذْنٰهُمْ بَغْتَةً وَّهُمْ لَا يَشْعُرُوْنَ ﴿۹۵﴾
وَلَوْ اَنَّ اَهْلَ الْقُرٰٓى اٰمَنُوْا وَاتَّقَوْا لَفَتَحْنَا
عَلَيْهِمْ بَرَكٰتٍ مِّنَ السَّمَآءِ وَالْاَرْضِ وَلٰكِنْ
كَذَّبُوْا فَاَخَذْنٰهُمْ بِمَا كَانُوْا يَكْسِبُوْنَ ﴿۹۶﴾
اَفَاَمِنَ اَهْلُ الْقُرٰٓى اَنْ يَّاْتِيَهُمْ بَاْسُنَا
بَيَاتًا وَّهُمْ نَآئِمُوْنَ ﴿۹۷﴾ اَوَاَمِنَ اَهْلُ الْقُرٰٓى
اَنْ يَّاْتِيَهُمْ بَاْسُنَا ضُحًى وَّهُمْ يَلْعَبُوْنَ ﴿۹۸﴾
اَفَاَمِنُوْا مَكْرَ اللّٰهِ فَلَا يَاْمَنُ مَكْرَ اللّٰهِ اِلَّا
الْقَوْمُ الْخٰسِرُوْنَ ﴿۹۹﴾ اَوَلَمْ يَهْدِ لِلَّذِيْنَ
يَرِثُوْنَ الْاَرْضَ مِنْۢ بَعْدِ اَهْلِهَآ اَنْ لَّوْ
نَشَآءُ اَصَبْنٰهُمْ بِذُنُوْبِهِمْ وَنَطْبَعُ عَلٰى قُلُوْبِهِمْ
فَهُمْ لَا يَسْمَعُوْنَ ﴿۱۰۰﴾ تِلْكَ الْقُرٰى نَقُصُّ
عَلَيْكَ مِنْ اَنْۢبَآئِهَا وَلَقَدْ جَآءَتْهُمْ رُسُلُهُمْ
بِالْبَيِّنٰتِ فَمَا كَانُوْا لِيُؤْمِنُوْا بِمَا كَذَّبُوْا
مِنْ قَبْلُ كَذٰلِكَ يَطْبَعُ اللّٰهُ عَلٰى قُلُوْبِ
الْكٰفِرِيْنَ ﴿۱۰۱﴾ وَمَا وَجَدْنَا لِاَكْثَرِهِمْ مِّنْ
عَهْدٍ وَاِنْ وَّجَدْنَآ اَكْثَرَهُمْ لَفٰسِقِيْنَ ﴿۱۰۲﴾
ثُمَّ بَعَثْنَا مِنْۢ بَعْدِهِمْ مُّوْسٰى بِاٰيٰتِنَآ اِلٰى

Moses with Our signs to Pharaoh and his chiefs, but they did injustice to these (signs by denying them), now see how (bad) was the end of the mischief-makers.

104. And Moses said, 'O Pharaoh! Truly, I am a Messenger from the Lord of the worlds;

105. 'I stand upon it (-the Prophethood), worthy to say nothing (in the name) of Allâh but the truth. I have indeed brought to you a clear proof (of my truthfulness) from your Lord, therefore let the Children of Israel go with me.'

106. (Pharaoh) said, 'If you have indeed come with a sign, then bring it forth, if you are of the truthful.'

107. So he (- Moses) flung down his staff, and behold! it was a serpent, plainly visible.

108. And he drew forth his hand then lo! it was shining white (-blemishless) for the beholders.

SECTION 14

109. **T**he chiefs of Pharaoh's people said (to each other), 'This (fellow here) is most surely a skilled sorcerer,

110. 'Who desires to turn you out from your land, now what do you advise?'

111. (After their deliberations) they said (to Pharaoh), 'Put him and his brother off a while and send to the cities heralds,

112. 'Who would (collect and) bring to you every skilled sorcerer.'

113. And the (most reputed) sorcerers came to Pharaoh. They said, 'We shall indeed be richly rewarded if we be the prevailing ones?'

114. (Pharaoh) said, 'Yes, and you shall also be even of those drawn near and close (to me).'

115. They said, 'Moses! Either you present (first what you have), or shall we be the (first) ones to present?'

116. (Moses) said, 'You may present (first, what you have).' And when they presented (their devices) they cast a spell on the peoples' eyes and sought to strike awe into them and they

فِرۡعَوۡنَ وَ مَلَاۡئِهٖ فَظَلَمُوۡا بِهَا ۚ فَانۡظُرۡ كَيۡفَ
كَانَ عٰقِبَةُ الۡمُفۡسِدِيۡنَ ﴿١٠٣﴾ وَ قَالَ مُوۡسٰى
يٰفِرۡعَوۡنُ اِنِّيۡ رَسُوۡلٌ مِّنۡ رَّبِّ الۡعٰلَمِيۡنَ ﴿١٠٤﴾
حَقِيۡقٌ عَلٰۤى اَنۡ لَّاۤ اَقُوۡلَ عَلَى اللّٰهِ اِلَّا الۡحَقَّ ؕ
قَدۡ جِئۡتُكُمۡ بِبَيِّنَةٍ مِّنۡ رَّبِّكُمۡ فَاَرۡسِلۡ
مَعِيَ بَنِيۡۤ اِسۡرَآءِيۡلَ ﴿١٠٥﴾ قَالَ اِنۡ كُنۡتَ
جِئۡتَ بِاٰيَةٍ فَاۡتِ بِهَاۤ اِنۡ كُنۡتَ مِنَ
الصّٰدِقِيۡنَ ﴿١٠٦﴾ فَاَلۡقٰى عَصَاهُ فَاِذَا هِيَ ثُعۡبَانٌ
مُّبِيۡنٌ ﴿١٠٧﴾ وَّ نَزَعَ يَدَهٗ فَاِذَا هِيَ بَيۡضَآءُ
لِلنّٰظِرِيۡنَ ﴿١٠٨﴾ قَالَ الۡمَلَاُ مِنۡ قَوۡمِ فِرۡعَوۡنَ
اِنَّ هٰذَا لَسٰحِرٌ عَلِيۡمٌ ﴿١٠٩﴾ يُّرِيۡدُ اَنۡ يُّخۡرِجَكُمۡ
مِّنۡ اَرۡضِكُمۡ ۚ فَمَاذَا تَاۡمُرُوۡنَ ﴿١١٠﴾ قَالُوۡۤا
اَرۡجِهۡ وَ اَخَاهُ وَ اَرۡسِلۡ فِي الۡمَدَآئِنِ حٰشِرِيۡنَ ﴿١١١﴾
يَاۡتُوۡكَ بِكُلِّ سٰحِرٍ عَلِيۡمٍ ﴿١١٢﴾ وَ جَآءَ السَّحَرَةُ
فِرۡعَوۡنَ قَالُوۡۤا اِنَّ لَنَا لَاَجۡرًا اِنۡ كُنَّا نَحۡنُ
الۡغٰلِبِيۡنَ ﴿١١٣﴾ قَالَ نَعَمۡ وَ اِنَّكُمۡ لَمِنَ الۡمُقَرَّبِيۡنَ ﴿١١٤﴾
قَالُوۡا يٰمُوۡسٰۤى اِمَّاۤ اَنۡ تُلۡقِيَ وَ اِمَّاۤ اَنۡ نَّكُوۡنَ
نَحۡنُ الۡمُلۡقِيۡنَ ﴿١١٥﴾ قَالَ اَلۡقُوۡا ۚ فَلَمَّاۤ اَلۡقَوۡا
سَحَرُوۡۤا اَعۡيُنَ النَّاسِ وَ اسۡتَرۡهَبُوۡهُمۡ وَ جَآءُوۡ

came out with a mighty enchantment.
117. And We sent a revelation to Moses (saying), 'Cast your staff (now).' Then it began to destroy (as he did it) all their lying show.
118. So was the truth established and all their efforts (to frustrate it) proved vain.
119. Thus they (-Pharaoh and his people) were vanquished then and there, and they went back humiliated.
120. And the sorcerers were impelled (by divine mercy) to fall down prostrate.
121. They (-the sorcerers) said, 'We believe in the Lord of the Worlds;
122. 'The Lord of Moses and Aaron.'
123. Pharaoh said, 'Dared you believe in Him before I gave you permission? Surely, this is some secret device which you have devised in this (central) city that you may expel from it its inhabitants. You shall come to know then (the consequence of your doings) very soon.
124. 'I will certainly have your hands and your feet cut off on alternate sides on account of (your) disobedience, then will I crucify you to death one and all (making your death all the more painful.')
125. They, (however, remained firm and) said, '(Never mind) we have all to return to our Lord after all.
126. 'And you find no fault in us but that we have believed in the signs of our Lord when they came to us (and we pray to Him), "Our Lord! Pour forth upon us patience and perseverance and grant that we die in a state of complete submission (to You)".'

SECTION 15

127. **T**HEN the chiefs of the people of Pharaoh said (to Pharaoh), 'Will you leave Moses and his people (free) to create disorder in the land and to desert you and your gods?' He said, 'We shall certainly go on gradually killing their sons and will let their women live, (seeking to make them immodest). Surely, we are dominant over them.'
128. Moses said to his people, 'Pray to Allâh

بِسِحۡرٍ عَظِيمٍ ۞ وَأَوۡحَيۡنَآ إِلَىٰ مُوسَىٰٓ أَنۡ
أَلۡقِ عَصَاكَ ۖ فَإِذَا هِيَ تَلۡقَفُ مَا يَأۡفِكُونَ ﴿١١٧﴾
فَوَقَعَ الۡحَقُّ وَبَطَلَ مَا كَانُوا يَعۡمَلُونَ ﴿١١٨﴾
فَغُلِبُوا هُنَالِكَ وَانۡقَلَبُوا صٰغِرِينَ ﴿١١٩﴾ وَأُلۡقِيَ
السَّحَرَةُ سٰجِدِينَ ﴿١٢٠﴾ قَالُوٓا ءَامَنَّا بِرَبِّ
الۡعٰلَمِينَ ﴿١٢١﴾ رَبِّ مُوسَىٰ وَهٰرُونَ ﴿١٢٢﴾ قَالَ
فِرۡعَوۡنُ ءَامَنۡتُمۡ بِهِۦ قَبۡلَ أَنۡ ءَاذَنَ لَكُمۡ ۖ إِنَّ
هٰذَا لَمَكۡرٌ مَّكَرۡتُمُوهُ فِي الۡمَدِينَةِ لِتُخۡرِجُوا
مِنۡهَآ أَهۡلَهَا ۖ فَسَوۡفَ تَعۡلَمُونَ ﴿١٢٣﴾ لَأُقَطِّعَنَّ
أَيۡدِيَكُمۡ وَأَرۡجُلَكُمۡ مِّنۡ خِلٰفٍ ثُمَّ
لَأُصَلِّبَنَّكُمۡ أَجۡمَعِينَ ﴿١٢٤﴾ قَالُوٓا إِنَّآ إِلَىٰ رَبِّنَا
مُنۡقَلِبُونَ ﴿١٢٥﴾ وَمَا تَنۡقِمُ مِنَّآ إِلَّآ أَنۡ ءَامَنَّا
بِـَٔايٰتِ رَبِّنَا لَمَّا جَآءَتۡنَا ۚ رَبَّنَآ أَفۡرِغۡ عَلَيۡنَا
صَبۡرًا وَتَوَفَّنَا مُسۡلِمِينَ ﴿١٢٦﴾ وَقَالَ الۡمَلَأُ
مِنۡ قَوۡمِ فِرۡعَوۡنَ أَتَذَرُ مُوسَىٰ وَقَوۡمَهُۥ لِيُفۡسِدُوا
فِي الۡأَرۡضِ وَيَذَرَكَ وَءَالِهَتَكَ ۚ قَالَ سَنُقَتِّلُ
أَبۡنَآءَهُمۡ وَنَسۡتَحۡيِۦ نِسَآءَهُمۡ وَإِنَّا فَوۡقَهُمۡ

ع ٤٨

imploring Him for help and be patiently persevering. Verily, the earth belongs to Allâh. He gives it as a heritage to such of His servants as He will, and the (happy) end is for those who become secure against evil and keep their duty (to Allâh).

129. They (- the persons of superficial thinking of the children of Israel) said, 'We were persecuted before you came to us and (are being persecuted) even after you have come to us.' (Moses) said, 'It is well nigh that your Lord will destroy your enemy and make you rulers in the (promised) land and then He will see how you act.'

SECTION 16

130. **A**ND We, surely, seized Pharaoh's followers with years of drought and scarcity of fruits and children so that they might take heed.

131. But when something good came their way, they said, 'This is ours (as we deserved it),' and if something adverse befell them they would attribute their ill luck to Moses and his companions. Beware! Surely, their deeds are (recorded) with Allâh but most of them do not know (this).

132. And they said (to Moses), 'Whatsoever sign you may bring to us to cast a spell upon us with it, we will not be believers in you at all.'

133. Then We sent upon them widespread death and destruction (caused by storms, epidemics,) and the locusts, the lice, the frogs and the blood (-wars); signs (all) distinct and well defined, but they continued to behave arrogantly for they were a people who had cut off their ties (with God).

134. And whenever a punishment fell upon them they said, 'O Moses! Pray for us to your Lord invoking the promise He has made to you. If you avert the punishment from us we will certainly believe in you, and we will let the Children of Israel go with you.'

قٰهِرُونَ ﴿١٢٧﴾ قَالَ مُوسٰى لِقَوْمِهِ اسْتَعِينُوا
بِاللّٰهِ وَاصْبِرُوا ۚ إِنَّ الْأَرْضَ لِلّٰهِ ۙ يُورِثُهَا
مَنْ يَشَاءُ مِنْ عِبَادِهِ ۖ وَالْعٰقِبَةُ لِلْمُتَّقِينَ ﴿١٢٨﴾
قَالُوا أُوذِينَا مِنْ قَبْلِ أَنْ تَأْتِيَنَا وَمِنْ
بَعْدِ مَا جِئْتَنَا ۚ قَالَ عَسٰى رَبُّكُمْ أَنْ يُهْلِكَ
عَدُوَّكُمْ وَيَسْتَخْلِفَكُمْ فِي الْأَرْضِ فَيَنْظُرَ
كَيْفَ تَعْمَلُونَ ﴿١٢٩﴾ وَلَقَدْ أَخَذْنَا آلَ فِرْعَوْنَ
بِالسِّنِينَ وَنَقْصٍ مِنَ الثَّمَرٰتِ لَعَلَّهُمْ
يَذَّكَّرُونَ ﴿١٣٠﴾ فَإِذَا جَاءَتْهُمُ الْحَسَنَةُ قَالُوا
لَنَا هٰذِهِ ۖ وَإِنْ تُصِبْهُمْ سَيِّئَةٌ يَطَّيَّرُوا
بِمُوسٰى وَمَنْ مَعَهُ ۗ أَلَا إِنَّمَا طٰئِرُهُمْ عِنْدَ
اللّٰهِ وَلٰكِنَّ أَكْثَرَهُمْ لَا يَعْلَمُونَ ﴿١٣١﴾ وَقَالُوا
مَهْمَا تَأْتِنَا بِهِ مِنْ آيَةٍ لِتَسْحَرَنَا بِهَا فَمَا
نَحْنُ لَكَ بِمُؤْمِنِينَ ﴿١٣٢﴾ فَأَرْسَلْنَا عَلَيْهِمُ
الطُّوفَانَ وَالْجَرَادَ وَالْقُمَّلَ وَالضَّفَادِعَ
وَالدَّمَ آيٰتٍ مُفَصَّلٰتٍ فَاسْتَكْبَرُوا وَكَانُوا
قَوْمًا مُجْرِمِينَ ﴿١٣٣﴾ وَلَمَّا وَقَعَ عَلَيْهِمُ الرِّجْزُ
قَالُوا يٰمُوسَى ادْعُ لَنَا رَبَّكَ بِمَا عَهِدَ
عِنْدَكَ ۖ لَئِنْ كَشَفْتَ عَنَّا الرِّجْزَ لَنُؤْمِنَنَّ
لَكَ وَلَنُرْسِلَنَّ مَعَكَ بَنِي إِسْرٰٓءِيلَ ﴿١٣٤﴾

135. But no sooner did We avert that punishment from them up to a (scheduled) term which they were to reach (in all events) than they at once broke their promise.
136. We then inflicted (the last) punishment on them; We drowned them in the sea for they had cried lies to Our Messages and were heedless of them.
137. And We made the people who were deemed weak (and were oppressed) inherit the eastern and western parts of the (promised) land which We had blessed. Thus was fulfilled the most gracious word of your Lord in favour of the Children of Israel, for they had patiently persevered; and We annihilated all that Pharaoh and his people had wrought and what they had erected.
138. And We brought the Children of Israel across the sea. Then they came to a people who clung to some idols they had (for worship). They said, 'O Moses! Make for us a god like the gods they have.' He (-Moses) said, 'You are a foolish people who act through lack of knowledge.
139. 'Verily, as to these (idolaters) that (cult of idolatry) wherein they are engrossed is doomed to be shattered and utterly vain is all that they are doing.'
140. (Moses) added, 'Am I to seek for you a god other than Allâh? Whereas He has made you excel the peoples of your time.
141. 'And (recall the word of God) when (He said), "We rescued you from Pharaoh's people, who subjected you to the worst torment, they gradually went on killing your sons and let your women live (and thus sought to make them immodest). And in this indeed was a great ordeal from your Lord".'

SECTION 17

142. **A**ND We made an appointment with Moses for thirty nights (and days to pray in solitude) which We supplemented with another ten (to receive the Law) so that the period appointed by his Lord came to be full forty nights (and

فلما كشفنا عنهم الرجز إلى أجل هم
بلغوه إذا هم ينكثون ﴿١٣٥﴾ فانتقمنا منهم
فأغرقنهم في اليم بأنهم كذبوا بايتنا
وكانوا عنها غفلين ﴿١٣٦﴾ وأورثنا القوم
الذين كانوا يستضعفون مشرق الأرض
ومغربها التي بركنا فيها وتمت
كلمت ربك الحسنى على بني إسراءيل
بما صبروا ودمرنا ما كان يصنع
فرعون وقومه وما كانوا يعرشون ﴿١٣٧﴾
وجوزنا ببني إسراءيل البحر فأتوا على
قوم يعكفون على أصنام لهم قالوا
يموسى اجعل لنا إلها كما لهم ءالهة
قال إنكم قوم تجهلون ﴿١٣٨﴾ إن هؤلاء متبر
ما هم فيه وبطل ما كانوا يعملون ﴿١٣٩﴾
قال أغير الله أبغيكم إلها وهو فضلكم
على العلمين ﴿١٤٠﴾ وإذ أنجينكم من ءال
فرعون يسومونكم سوء العذاب يقتلون
أبناءكم ويستحيون نساءكم وفي ذلكم
بلاء من ربكم عظيم ﴿١٤١﴾ ووعدنا موسى
ثلثين ليلة وأتممنها بعشر فتم ميقت
ربه أربعين ليلة وقال موسى لأخيه
هرون اخلفني في قومي وأصلح ولا تتبع

days). (When leaving) Moses said to his brother Aaron, 'Act for me (taking my place) in my absence among my people and reform and manage (them) well and do not follow the way of those who create disorder.'

143. And when Moses came at the time and place appointed by Us, and his Lord spoke to him, he said, 'My Lord! Reveal yourself to me that I may look at you.' He said, 'You cannot stand My revelation. Yet look at the mountain, and if it stands firm in its place, (only) then you shall stand My revelation.' Then when his Lord manifested His glory to the mountain, He sent it crashing down into pieces and Moses fell down unconscious, so that when he recovered he said, 'Glory be to You! I turn towards You and I am the first to believe.'

144. He said, 'O Moses! Verily, I have preferred you to all the people (of your time) by (entrusting you with) My Messages and by My discourse (with you), so take (firm hold of that) what I have given you and be of the grateful.'

145. And We preserved (in writing) for him on the Tablets all kinds of precepts and clear details of everything (which the Children of Israel needed). Then (We bade him), 'Hold them fast and bid your people to carry out its best (teachings in its true significance). I will soon show you people the resort of the transgressors.' (- This nation will become corrupt and will meet an evil end.)

146. I shall soon turn away from My Messages those who behave haughtily in the land without any justification. Even if they witness every (possible) sign they will not believe therein and even if they see the path of rectitude they will not adopt it as (their) way; but if they see the way of error and falsehood they will adopt it as (their) way. This (state of theirs) is because they cried lies to Our Messages and they were heedless to them.

147. And those who cry lies to Our Messages and the meeting of the Hereafter, vain and void are their deeds. They shall only be recom-

سَبِيلَ الْمُفْسِدِينَ ﴿١٤٢﴾ وَلَمَّا جَاءَ مُوسَىٰ
لِمِيقَاتِنَا وَكَلَّمَهُ رَبُّهُ قَالَ رَبِّ أَرِنِي أَنظُرْ
إِلَيْكَ ۚ قَالَ لَن تَرَانِي وَلَٰكِنِ انظُرْ إِلَى الْجَبَلِ
فَإِنِ اسْتَقَرَّ مَكَانَهُ فَسَوْفَ تَرَانِي ۚ فَلَمَّا
تَجَلَّىٰ رَبُّهُ لِلْجَبَلِ جَعَلَهُ دَكًّا وَخَرَّ مُوسَىٰ
صَعِقًا ۚ فَلَمَّا أَفَاقَ قَالَ سُبْحَانَكَ تُبْتُ إِلَيْكَ
وَأَنَا أَوَّلُ الْمُؤْمِنِينَ ﴿١٤٣﴾ قَالَ يَا مُوسَىٰ إِنِّي
اصْطَفَيْتُكَ عَلَى النَّاسِ بِرِسَالَاتِي وَبِكَلَامِي
فَخُذْ مَا آتَيْتُكَ وَكُن مِّنَ الشَّاكِرِينَ ﴿١٤٤﴾
وَكَتَبْنَا لَهُ فِي الْأَلْوَاحِ مِن كُلِّ شَيْءٍ
مَّوْعِظَةً وَتَفْصِيلًا لِّكُلِّ شَيْءٍ فَخُذْهَا
بِقُوَّةٍ وَأْمُرْ قَوْمَكَ يَأْخُذُوا بِأَحْسَنِهَا ۚ
سَأُرِيكُمْ دَارَ الْفَاسِقِينَ ﴿١٤٥﴾ سَأَصْرِفُ
عَنْ آيَاتِيَ الَّذِينَ يَتَكَبَّرُونَ فِي الْأَرْضِ
بِغَيْرِ الْحَقِّ وَإِن يَرَوْا كُلَّ آيَةٍ لَّا يُؤْمِنُوا
بِهَا وَإِن يَرَوْا سَبِيلَ الرُّشْدِ لَا يَتَّخِذُوهُ
سَبِيلًا وَإِن يَرَوْا سَبِيلَ الْغَيِّ يَتَّخِذُوهُ
سَبِيلًا ۚ ذَٰلِكَ بِأَنَّهُمْ كَذَّبُوا بِآيَاتِنَا وَكَانُوا
عَنْهَا غَافِلِينَ ﴿١٤٦﴾ وَالَّذِينَ كَذَّبُوا بِآيَاتِنَا

pensed according to (the nature of) their deeds.

SECTION 18

148. **A**nd the people of Moses in his absence, made out of their ornaments a calf; a mere frame (of saffron hue), with a lowing sound. Could they not see that it neither spoke to them, nor guided them to any way? Yet they took it (for god to worship) and became wrongdoers.
149. And when (the magic spell was broken) they were smitten with remorse and realised that they had indeed gone astray, they said, ‘Unless our Lord have mercy on us and protect us (against the consequences of our sins) we shall surely be of the losers.’
150. And when Moses returned to his people indignant and sorrowful he said, ‘How evil is that (course) which you adopted in my place in my absence! Did you seek to hasten on the command of your Lord (for punishment)?’ And he put down the Tablets and caught hold of his brother (Aaron, who was entrusted to carry out Moses’ mission in his absence) by the head, pulling him towards himself. He (- Aaron) said, ‘Son of my Mother! Surely (I am not to be blamed for it), these people deemed me weak and were about to kill me. Therefore let not the enemies rejoice over my misery and count me not with these idolaters.’
151. He (- Moses) said, ‘My Lord! Protect me and my brother and admit us to Your mercy. You are indeed the Most Merciful of those who show mercy.’

SECTION 19

152. (**T**HE Lord said in answer to Moses’ supplications,) ‘The displeasure of their Lord and disgrace in the present life shall surely overtake those who took the calf (for worship).’ That is how do We repay the forgers of lies with punishment.
153. But those who do evil deeds and turn with repentance thereafter and believe truly (shall find that) your Lord, after this (change in them) is indeed Great Protector, Ever Merciful.

وَلِقَآءِ الْأٰخِرَةِ حَبِطَتْ أَعْمٰلُهُمْ هَلْ يُجْزَوْنَ
إِلَّا مَا كَانُوْا يَعْمَلُوْنَ ﴿١٤٧﴾ وَاتَّخَذَ قَوْمُ مُوْسٰى
مِنْۢ بَعْدِهٖ مِنْ حُلِيِّهِمْ عِجْلًا جَسَدًا لَّهٗ
خُوَارٌ أَلَمْ يَرَوْا أَنَّهٗ لَا يُكَلِّمُهُمْ وَلَا
يَهْدِيْهِمْ سَبِيْلًا ۘ اِتَّخَذُوْهُ وَكَانُوْا ظٰلِمِيْنَ ﴿١٤٨﴾
وَلَمَّا سُقِطَ فِيْٓ أَيْدِيْهِمْ وَرَأَوْا أَنَّهُمْ قَدْ
ضَلُّوْا قَالُوْا لَئِنْ لَّمْ يَرْحَمْنَا رَبُّنَا وَيَغْفِرْ لَنَا
لَنَكُوْنَنَّ مِنَ الْخٰسِرِيْنَ ﴿١٤٩﴾ وَلَمَّا رَجَعَ مُوْسٰى
إِلٰى قَوْمِهٖ غَضْبٰنَ أَسِفًا قَالَ بِئْسَمَا
خَلَفْتُمُوْنِيْ مِنْۢ بَعْدِيْ أَعَجِلْتُمْ أَمْرَ
رَبِّكُمْ وَأَلْقَى الْأَلْوَاحَ وَأَخَذَ بِرَأْسِ أَخِيْهِ
يَجُرُّهٗٓ إِلَيْهِ قَالَ ابْنَ أُمَّ إِنَّ الْقَوْمَ
اسْتَضْعَفُوْنِيْ وَكَادُوْا يَقْتُلُوْنَنِيْ فَلَا تُشْمِتْ
بِيَ الْأَعْدَآءَ وَلَا تَجْعَلْنِيْ مَعَ الْقَوْمِ الظّٰلِمِيْنَ ﴿١٥٠﴾
قَالَ رَبِّ اغْفِرْ لِيْ وَلِأَخِيْ وَأَدْخِلْنَا فِيْ
رَحْمَتِكَ وَأَنْتَ أَرْحَمُ الرّٰحِمِيْنَ ﴿١٥١﴾ إِنَّ الَّذِيْنَ
اتَّخَذُوا الْعِجْلَ سَيَنَالُهُمْ غَضَبٌ مِّنْ
رَّبِّهِمْ وَذِلَّةٌ فِي الْحَيٰوةِ الدُّنْيَا وَكَذٰلِكَ
نَجْزِي الْمُفْتَرِيْنَ ﴿١٥٢﴾ وَالَّذِيْنَ عَمِلُوا السَّيِّاٰتِ
ثُمَّ تَابُوْا مِنْۢ بَعْدِهَا وَأٰمَنُوْٓا إِنَّ رَبَّكَ

154. When the anger of Moses calmed down, he took up the Tablets. These inscriptions contained guidance and mercy for all those who hold their Lord in awe (with every care).
155. Now Moses selected from his people seventy men (to take with him) to Our appointed place and time, but when the earthquake seized them he said, 'My Lord! If You so willed You could have destroyed them as well as me before (this). But would You destroy us on account of that which the foolish among us have done? This (matter of the calf) is nothing but (an ordeal from You) that You may distinguish the good from the bad (of us). You adjudge, by such means, to be astray whomsoever You will and You guide whomsoever You will. You are our Patron, protect us therefore, and have mercy on us, for You are the Best of Protectors (against the consequence of our faults).
156. 'And ordain for us what is good in this world and in the Hereafter for to You alone we turn (repenting).' He (the Almighty) said, 'As for My punishment, I inflict on whom I will, but My mercy embraces all things. So I will ordain it for those who guard against evil and spend in charity, and for those who believe in Our Messages;
157. 'Those who follow this perfect Messenger, the Arab Prophet whom they find described in the Torah and the Evangel which are with them, who enjoins upon them that which is right and forbids them that which is wrong, and who makes lawful for them all the pure and good things, and makes unlawful all the impure and bad things, and who relieves them of their heavy burdens and shackles that weigh them down. Indeed those who believe in him and honour him and serve him and follow the light that has been sent down with him, it is these who will attain their goal.'

مِنْ بَعْدِهَا لَغَفُورٌ رَّحِيمٌ ﴿١٥٣﴾ وَلَمَّا سَكَتَ
عَن مُّوسَى الْغَضَبُ أَخَذَ الْأَلْوَاحَ وَفِي
نُسْخَتِهَا هُدًى وَرَحْمَةٌ لِّلَّذِينَ هُمْ لِرَبِّهِمْ
يَرْهَبُونَ ﴿١٥٤﴾ وَاخْتَارَ مُوسَى قَوْمَهُ سَبْعِينَ
رَجُلًا لِّمِيقَاتِنَا فَلَمَّا أَخَذَتْهُمُ الرَّجْفَةُ قَالَ
رَبِّ لَوْ شِئْتَ أَهْلَكْتَهُم مِّن قَبْلُ وَإِيَّايَ
أَتُهْلِكُنَا بِمَا فَعَلَ السُّفَهَاءُ مِنَّا إِنْ هِيَ إِلَّا
فِتْنَتُكَ تُضِلُّ بِهَا مَن تَشَاءُ وَتَهْدِي مَن
تَشَاءُ أَنتَ وَلِيُّنَا فَاغْفِرْ لَنَا وَارْحَمْنَا وَأَنتَ
خَيْرُ الْغَافِرِينَ ﴿١٥٥﴾ ۞ وَاكْتُبْ لَنَا فِي هَٰذِهِ الدُّنْيَا
حَسَنَةً وَفِي الْآخِرَةِ إِنَّا هُدْنَا إِلَيْكَ قَالَ
عَذَابِي أُصِيبُ بِهِ مَنْ أَشَاءُ وَرَحْمَتِي
وَسِعَتْ كُلَّ شَيْءٍ فَسَأَكْتُبُهَا لِلَّذِينَ يَتَّقُونَ
وَيُؤْتُونَ الزَّكَاةَ وَالَّذِينَ هُم بِآيَاتِنَا
يُؤْمِنُونَ ﴿١٥٦﴾ الَّذِينَ يَتَّبِعُونَ الرَّسُولَ النَّبِيَّ
الْأُمِّيَّ الَّذِي يَجِدُونَهُ مَكْتُوبًا عِندَهُمْ
فِي التَّوْرَاةِ وَالْإِنجِيلِ يَأْمُرُهُم بِالْمَعْرُوفِ
وَيَنْهَاهُمْ عَنِ الْمُنكَرِ وَيُحِلُّ لَهُمُ الطَّيِّبَاتِ
وَيُحَرِّمُ عَلَيْهِمُ الْخَبَائِثَ وَيَضَعُ عَنْهُمْ إِصْرَهُمْ
وَالْأَغْلَالَ الَّتِي كَانَتْ عَلَيْهِمْ فَالَّذِينَ آمَنُوا
بِهِ وَعَزَّرُوهُ وَنَصَرُوهُ وَاتَّبَعُوا النُّورَ الَّذِي

SECTION 20

158. **S**AY, 'O people! I am a Messenger to you all from Allâh to whom belongs the kingdom of the heavens and the earth. There is no other, cannot be and will never be One worthy of worship but He, Who gives life and causes death, so believe in Allâh and in His Messenger, the Arab, the Prophet who believes in Allâh and in (all) His words, and follow him so that you may be rightly guided so as to reach the goal.'

159. There is a community among the people of Moses who guide (the people) to the truth and with it they dispense justice.

160. We divided them (- the people of Moses) into twelve tribes according to the ancestral lineage (to which they belonged). And We sent Our revelation to Moses when his people asked of him (something) to drink (saying), 'Strike that rock with your staff.' Then (as he did), there gushed out from it twelve springs, so that all the people now knew their (respective) drinking place. And We outspread the rain clouds to be a shade over them and We sent down for them Manna and quails (saying), 'Eat of the pure things wherewith We have provided you.' And they did us no harm (when they went wrong) but it was to themselves that they had been doing harm.

161. And (recall the time) when it was said to them, 'Dwell in this township (-Ya<u>th</u>rib) and eat therefrom when you will and pray, "Relieve us of the burden of our sins," and enter its gate submissively. (If you do so) We will protect you against (the consequences of) your sins. We shall multiply the reward of the doers of excellent deeds.'

162. But those amongst them who were unjust changed the word to something different from that which they were told. So We sent down upon them unavoidable punishment from heaven because they had always been wrongdoers.

أُنْزِلَ مَعَهُ أُولَٰٓئِكَ هُمُ الْمُفْلِحُونَ ﴿١٥٧﴾ قُلْ
يَٰٓأَيُّهَا النَّاسُ إِنِّي رَسُولُ اللَّهِ إِلَيْكُمْ جَمِيعًا
الَّذِي لَهُ مُلْكُ السَّمَٰوَٰتِ وَالْأَرْضِ لَآ إِلَٰهَ
إِلَّا هُوَ يُحْيِۦ وَيُمِيتُ فَـَٔامِنُوا بِاللَّهِ وَرَسُولِهِ
النَّبِيِّ الْأُمِّيِّ الَّذِي يُؤْمِنُ بِاللَّهِ وَكَلِمَٰتِهِۦ
وَاتَّبِعُوهُ لَعَلَّكُمْ تَهْتَدُونَ ﴿١٥٨﴾ وَمِنْ قَوْمِ مُوسَىٰٓ
أُمَّةٌ يَهْدُونَ بِالْحَقِّ وَبِهِۦ يَعْدِلُونَ ﴿١٥٩﴾
وَقَطَّعْنَٰهُمُ اثْنَتَيْ عَشْرَةَ أَسْبَاطًا أُمَمًا
وَأَوْحَيْنَآ إِلَىٰ مُوسَىٰٓ إِذِ اسْتَسْقَىٰهُ قَوْمُهُۥٓ
أَنِ اضْرِب بِّعَصَاكَ الْحَجَرَ فَانْبَجَسَتْ
مِنْهُ اثْنَتَا عَشْرَةَ عَيْنًا قَدْ عَلِمَ كُلُّ
أُنَاسٍ مَّشْرَبَهُمْ وَظَلَّلْنَا عَلَيْهِمُ الْغَمَٰمَ
وَأَنْزَلْنَا عَلَيْهِمُ الْمَنَّ وَالسَّلْوَىٰ كُلُوا
مِنْ طَيِّبَٰتِ مَا رَزَقْنَٰكُمْ وَمَا ظَلَمُونَا
وَلَٰكِنْ كَانُوٓا أَنْفُسَهُمْ يَظْلِمُونَ ﴿١٦٠﴾ وَإِذْ قِيلَ
لَهُمُ اسْكُنُوا هَٰذِهِ الْقَرْيَةَ وَكُلُوا مِنْهَا
حَيْثُ شِئْتُمْ وَقُولُوا حِطَّةٌ وَادْخُلُوا
الْبَابَ سُجَّدًا نَّغْفِرْ لَكُمْ خَطِيٓـَٰٔتِكُمْ
سَنَزِيدُ الْمُحْسِنِينَ ﴿١٦١﴾ فَبَدَّلَ الَّذِينَ
ظَلَمُوا مِنْهُمْ قَوْلًا غَيْرَ الَّذِي قِيلَ
لَهُمْ فَأَرْسَلْنَا عَلَيْهِمْ رِجْزًا مِّنَ السَّمَآءِ

SECTION 21

163. **A**ND ask them as to (what happened to the people of) the township (- Eila) which was on the seashore (of the Red Sea) when they profaned the Sabbath. On the day of their Sabbath their fish appeared to them in shoals upon shoals on the surface (of the water), but on the day when they did not observe the Sabbath (and fishing was open), it did not appear to them. Thus did We go on making a distinction between the good and the evil ones of them by means of their acts of disobedience.

164. And (ask them what happened to those people) when a section from amongst them said (to another section), 'Why do you admonish a people whom Allâh is going to destroy completely, or whom He is going to punish with a severe punishment?' They answered, 'We do it so that it may serve as an excuse (to be absolved from blame) before your Lord and that they may become secure (against the punishment).'

165. But when they disregarded the warning that had been given them, We saved those who forbade evil and We seized those who did wrong, with a serious punishment of extreme destitution because they were exceeding the bounds of obedience.

166. So when they insolently refused to keep away from that which they were forbidden, We condemned them to be (as) apes despised.

167. And (imagine the time) when your Lord proclaimed (to the Children of Israel) that He would certainly continue to subject them, till the Day of Resurrection, to the people who would afflict them with the worst torment. Verily, your Lord is Quick to punish the evil but He is (all the same) Great Protector, Ever Merciful.

168. And We broke them up into (separate) sections of peoples on the earth, of which some are the righteous and some otherwise, and We went on distinguishing the good among them

ع ١٠ بما كانوا يظلمون ﴿١٦٢﴾ وسئلهم عن القرية
التي كانت حاضرة البحر إذ يعدون
في السبت إذ تأتيهم حيتانهم يوم
سبتهم شرعا ويوم لا يسبتون لا
تأتيهم كذلك نبلوهم بما كانوا
يفسقون ﴿١٦٣﴾ وإذ قالت أمة منهم لم
تعظون قوما الله مهلكهم أو معذبهم
عذابا شديدا قالوا معذرة إلى ربكم
ولعلهم يتقون ﴿١٦٤﴾ فلما نسوا ما ذكروا
به أنجينا الذين ينهون عن السوء
وأخذنا الذين ظلموا بعذاب بئيس بما
كانوا يفسقون ﴿١٦٥﴾ فلما عتوا عن ما نهوا
عنه قلنا لهم كونوا قردة خسئين ﴿١٦٦﴾
وإذ تأذن ربك ليبعثن عليهم إلى يوم
القيمة من يسومهم سوء العذاب إن
ربك لسريع العقاب وإنه لغفور
رحيم ﴿١٦٧﴾ وقطعنهم في الأرض أمما

from the evil ones, through prosperity and adversity (both) so that they might turn (to Us).

169. Then there succeeded them an evil generation who having inherited the Scripture (of Moses), go on taking the paltry goods of this base (life) and say, 'We shall surely be protected.' And if the like of these goods (again) come their way, they will take them (and sin persistently). Were they not bound to the covenant mentioned in the Scripture that they would not say of Allâh anything but the truth? And they have read for themselves what it (- the Scripture) contains. And the abode of the Hereafter is better only for those who become secure against evil. Have you then no sense?

170. And (as to) those who hold fast to the Scripture and establish worship, (let them bear in mind that) We will not at all allow the reward of those who set things right to be lost.

171. And (make them recall the time) when We shook (due to the quake) the mount (Sinai) above them, as though it were to be a shade above them (like a wall) and they thought it was about to fall on them. (We said,) 'Hold fast to that which We have given you and remember its contents that you might become secure against evil.'

SECTION 22

172. **B**EHOLD! When your Lord brings forth from Adam's children - from their loins, their offspring, and makes them bear witness to themselves when He says, 'Am I not your Lord Who sustains you?' They say (in evidence which human nature itself bears), 'Yes we bear witness (to it and acknowledge it).' (Allâh does that) lest you should say on the Day of Resurrection, 'Surely, we were unaware of this (that You are our Lord).'

173. Or (lest) you should say, 'It were only our forefathers who associated partners (with God) in the past and we only happened to be their children who came after them (to follow in their footsteps). Will You then destroy us for

مِنْهُمُ الصّٰلِحُونَ وَ مِنْهُمْ دُونَ ذٰلِكَ
وَبَلَوْنٰهُم بِالْحَسَنٰتِ وَالسَّيِّاٰتِ لَعَلَّهُمْ
يَرْجِعُونَ ﴿١٦٨﴾ فَخَلَفَ مِنْ بَعْدِهِمْ خَلْفٌ
وَّرِثُوا الْكِتٰبَ يَأْخُذُونَ عَرَضَ هٰذَا الْأَدْنٰى
وَيَقُولُونَ سَيُغْفَرُ لَنَا ۚ وَ إِنْ يَأْتِهِمْ عَرَضٌ
مِّثْلُهُ يَأْخُذُوهُ ۚ أَلَمْ يُؤْخَذْ عَلَيْهِم مِّيثٰقُ
الْكِتٰبِ أَنْ لَّا يَقُولُوا عَلَى اللّٰهِ إِلَّا الْحَقَّ
وَدَرَسُوا مَا فِيهِ ۗ وَ الدَّارُ الْأٰخِرَةُ خَيْرٌ
لِّلَّذِينَ يَتَّقُونَ ۗ أَفَلَا تَعْقِلُونَ ﴿١٦٩﴾ وَ الَّذِينَ
يُمَسِّكُونَ بِالْكِتٰبِ وَ أَقَامُوا الصَّلٰوةَ ۗ
إِنَّا لَا نُضِيعُ أَجْرَ الْمُصْلِحِينَ ﴿١٧٠﴾ وَ إِذْ نَتَقْنَا
الْجَبَلَ فَوْقَهُمْ كَأَنَّهُ ظُلَّةٌ وَّ ظَنُّوا أَنَّهُ
وَاقِعٌ بِهِمْ ۚ خُذُوا مَا أٰتَيْنٰكُم بِقُوَّةٍ
وَّاذْكُرُوا مَا فِيهِ لَعَلَّكُمْ تَتَّقُونَ ﴿١٧١﴾ وَإِذْ
أَخَذَ رَبُّكَ مِنْ بَنِىٓ أٰدَمَ مِنْ ظُهُورِهِمْ
ذُرِّيَّتَهُمْ وَ أَشْهَدَهُمْ عَلٰىٓ أَنْفُسِهِمْ أَلَسْتُ
بِرَبِّكُمْ ۗ قَالُوا بَلٰى ۛ شَهِدْنَا ۛ أَنْ تَقُولُوا
يَوْمَ الْقِيٰمَةِ إِنَّا كُنَّا عَنْ هٰذَا غٰفِلِينَ ﴿١٧٢﴾
أَوْ تَقُولُوٓا إِنَّمَآ أَشْرَكَ أٰبَآؤُنَا مِنْ قَبْلُ

ع ٢١ ١١

the vain doings of the perpetrators of falsehood?'

174. And in this manner do We explain the Messages in detail (in order that they may give up evil ways) and that they may turn (to us).

175. And relate to them the news of him to whom We gave Our commandments but he withdrew himself therefrom, the satan followed him with the result that he became one of those led astray (and became a pervert).

176. Had We so willed We would have exalted him (in ranks) thereby (- by means of these Our commandments), but he remained inclined to (the material things of) this world and followed his low desires. His case therefore is like that of a dog, if you bear down upon it, it lolls its tongue out or if you leave it alone, it still lolls out its tongue. Such is the case with the people who cry lies to Our commandments; (they do not give up their evil ways whether you warn them or not). So narrate to them the account (of the people of old) that they may reflect.

177. Sad is the case of the people who cry lies to Our commandments and it is their own selves that they have wronged.

178. Those alone are rightly guided to whom Allâh shows guidance, but whom He adjudges to be astray and leaves them in error, it is these who are the losers.

179. And, verily, We have created many of the *jinns* and the ordinary people whose end is Gehenna. They have hearts wherewith they do not understand and they have eyes but they do not see with them (the truth), and they have ears but they do not hear (the Messages) with them. They are like cattle, nay, they are (even) worse. It is these who are utterly heedless (to the warnings).

180. And to Allâh alone belong all the fairest and most perfect attributes, so call on Him by these, and leave alone those who deviate from the right way with respect to His attributes (and violate their sanctity). They shall be repaid with punishment for their (evil)

وَكُنَّا ذُرِّيَّةً مِّنْ بَعْدِهِمْ أَفَتُهْلِكُنَا
بِمَا فَعَلَ الْمُبْطِلُونَ ﴿١٧٣﴾ وَكَذٰلِكَ نُفَصِّلُ
الْأٰيٰتِ وَلَعَلَّهُمْ يَرْجِعُونَ ﴿١٧٤﴾ وَاتْلُ عَلَيْهِمْ
نَبَأَ الَّذِيٓ أٰتَيْنٰهُ أٰيٰتِنَا فَانْسَلَخَ مِنْهَا
فَأَتْبَعَهُ الشَّيْطٰنُ فَكَانَ مِنَ الْغَاوِينَ ﴿١٧٥﴾
وَلَوْ شِئْنَا لَرَفَعْنٰهُ بِهَا وَلٰكِنَّهُ أَخْلَدَ
إِلَى الْأَرْضِ وَاتَّبَعَ هَوٰىهُ فَمَثَلُهُ كَمَثَلِ
الْكَلْبِ إِنْ تَحْمِلْ عَلَيْهِ يَلْهَثْ أَوْ
تَتْرُكْهُ يَلْهَثْ ذٰلِكَ مَثَلُ الْقَوْمِ الَّذِينَ
كَذَّبُوا بِأٰيٰتِنَا فَاقْصُصِ الْقَصَصَ لَعَلَّهُمْ
يَتَفَكَّرُونَ ﴿١٧٦﴾ سَآءَ مَثَلًا الْقَوْمُ الَّذِينَ كَذَّبُوا
بِأٰيٰتِنَا وَأَنْفُسَهُمْ كَانُوا يَظْلِمُونَ ﴿١٧٧﴾ مَنْ
يَهْدِ اللهُ فَهُوَ الْمُهْتَدِي وَمَنْ يُضْلِلْ
فَأُولٰٓئِكَ هُمُ الْخٰسِرُونَ ﴿١٧٨﴾ وَلَقَدْ ذَرَأْنَا
لِجَهَنَّمَ كَثِيرًا مِّنَ الْجِنِّ وَالْإِنْسِ لَهُمْ
قُلُوبٌ لَّا يَفْقَهُونَ بِهَا وَلَهُمْ أَعْيُنٌ لَّا
يُبْصِرُونَ بِهَا وَلَهُمْ أٰذَانٌ لَّا يَسْمَعُونَ بِهَا
أُولٰٓئِكَ كَالْأَنْعٰمِ بَلْ هُمْ أَضَلُّ أُولٰٓئِكَ
هُمُ الْغٰفِلُونَ ﴿١٧٩﴾ وَلِلّٰهِ الْأَسْمَآءُ الْحُسْنٰى
فَادْعُوهُ بِهَا وَذَرُوا الَّذِينَ يُلْحِدُونَ فِيٓ

deeds.

181. And of those whom We have created are a community who give true guidance to the truth and who dispense justice therewith.

SECTION 23

182. **A**ND (as for) those who cry lies to Our Messages We shall lead them (to destruction) step by step, in a manner unknown to them.

183. And I give them respite, My device is very strong and sure.

184. Have they not reflected (so that they may see) that their comrade (Muhammad) has no vestige of insanity but is a plain warner?

185. Have they not pondered over the sovereignty of the heavens and the earth and everything that Allâh has created? And (have they not looked into the fact) that it may be their (own) term (of destruction) has already drawn nigh? In what announcement other than this (Prophet and the self-evident Qur'ân) will they believe?

186. Whomsoever Allâh adjudges to be astray and leaves in error, there can be no guide for him. And He leaves them (alone) in their transgression (blindly) wandering in distraction.

187. They ask you about the Hour, when it will come to pass. Say, 'Surely, the knowledge thereof is with my Lord. He alone will reveal it at its proper time. It shall be heavy on the heavens and on the earth. It shall not come upon you but all of a sudden.' They ask you (about it) as if you were curiously solicitous about it (from Allâh). Say, 'The knowledge of it is only with Allâh, but most people do not know (this fact).'

188. Say, 'I have no power over (bringing) any gain or (avoiding) any harm to myself save to the extent that Allâh will. And had I known the unseen I would surely have secured a great deal of good (for myself) and no harm would ever have come to me. I am only a warner (to the wicked) and a bearer of good tidings (to the people who believe).

أَسْمَآئِهٖ ؕ سَيُجْزَوْنَ مَا كَانُوْا يَعْمَلُوْنَ ﴿۱۸۰﴾ وَمِمَّنْ
خَلَقْنَآ أُمَّةٌ يَّهْدُوْنَ بِالْحَقِّ وَبِهٖ يَعْدِلُوْنَ ﴿۱۸۱﴾
وَالَّذِيْنَ كَذَّبُوْا بِاٰيٰتِنَا سَنَسْتَدْرِجُهُمْ مِّنْ
حَيْثُ لَا يَعْلَمُوْنَ ﴿۱۸۲﴾ وَأُمْلِيْ لَهُمْ ؕ إِنَّ كَيْدِيْ
مَتِيْنٌ ﴿۱۸۳﴾ أَوَلَمْ يَتَفَكَّرُوْا مَا بِصَاحِبِهِمْ مِّنْ
جِنَّةٍ ؕ إِنْ هُوَ إِلَّا نَذِيْرٌ مُّبِيْنٌ ﴿۱۸۴﴾ أَوَلَمْ
يَنْظُرُوْا فِيْ مَلَكُوْتِ السَّمٰوٰتِ وَالْأَرْضِ
وَمَا خَلَقَ اللّٰهُ مِنْ شَيْءٍ وَّأَنْ عَسٰٓى أَنْ
يَّكُوْنَ قَدِ اقْتَرَبَ أَجَلُهُمْ ۚ فَبِأَيِّ حَدِيْثٍ
بَعْدَهٗ يُؤْمِنُوْنَ ﴿۱۸۵﴾ مَنْ يُّضْلِلِ اللّٰهُ فَلَا
هَادِيَ لَهٗ ؕ وَيَذَرُهُمْ فِيْ طُغْيَانِهِمْ يَعْمَهُوْنَ ﴿۱۸۶﴾
يَسْـَٔلُوْنَكَ عَنِ السَّاعَةِ أَيَّانَ مُرْسٰهَا ؕ قُلْ
إِنَّمَا عِلْمُهَا عِنْدَ رَبِّيْ ۚ لَا يُجَلِّيْهَا لِوَقْتِهَآ
إِلَّا هُوَ ؕ ثَقُلَتْ فِي السَّمٰوٰتِ وَالْأَرْضِ ؕ لَا
تَأْتِيْكُمْ إِلَّا بَغْتَةً ؕ يَسْـَٔلُوْنَكَ كَأَنَّكَ حَفِيٌّ
عَنْهَا ؕ قُلْ إِنَّمَا عِلْمُهَا عِنْدَ اللّٰهِ وَلٰكِنَّ
أَكْثَرَ النَّاسِ لَا يَعْلَمُوْنَ ﴿۱۸۷﴾ قُلْ لَّآ أَمْلِكُ
لِنَفْسِيْ نَفْعًا وَّلَا ضَرًّا إِلَّا مَا شَآءَ اللّٰهُ ؕ وَلَوْ
كُنْتُ أَعْلَمُ الْغَيْبَ لَاسْتَكْثَرْتُ مِنَ الْخَيْرِ ۚ
وَمَا مَسَّنِيَ السُّوْٓءُ ۚ إِنْ أَنَا إِلَّا نَذِيْرٌ
وَّبَشِيْرٌ لِّقَوْمٍ يُّؤْمِنُوْنَ ﴿۱۸۸﴾ هُوَ الَّذِيْ خَلَقَكُمْ

SECTION 24

189. **I**T is He Who has created you from one living entity, and from the same stock (that He created a human being) He brought into being his mate that he might find comfort in her. When he covers her (in conjugal relationship) she conceives a light burden and carries it about, then when she grows heavy (with the child), they both pray to Allâh, their Lord, (saying) 'If You give us a good one (- a child with a sound mind in a sound body), we shall surely be of the grateful (to you).'

190. But when He gives them a good (child), they both ascribe to Him associates in respect of (the birth of) that (child) which He has given them. Allâh is Highly Exalted far above the things they associate (with Him).

191. Do they associate (with Him as partners) those who create nothing but are themselves created.

192. And they (the associated gods) will have no power to give them (who associate partners with Allâh) any help, nor can they help themselves (but will themselves perish).

193. And if you (O Polytheists!) invite these (associated gods) for (your) guidance, they will not respond to you. It makes no difference to you whether you call them or you remain silent.

194. Verily, those whom you call on beside Allâh are (merely helpless maids or) servants like yourselves. (If it is not so then) call on them, they should then make a response to you if you are right.

195. Have these (false gods) feet with which they walk, or have they hands with which they hold, or have they eyes with which they see, or have they ears with which they hear? Say, 'Call upon your associate gods, then contrive you all against me and give me no respite, (yet you will see that I am triumphant because)

196. 'Verily, My Protecting-Friend is Allâh who has revealed this perfect Book and He takes into (His) protection all the righteous.

197. 'And those whom you call upon besides Him have no power to help you, nor can they

مِّن نَّفْسٍ وَّٰحِدَةٍ وَّجَعَلَ مِنْهَا زَوْجَهَا
لِيَسْكُنَ إِلَيْهَا فَلَمَّا تَغَشَّىٰهَا حَمَلَتْ حَمْلًا
خَفِيفًا فَمَرَّتْ بِهِ فَلَمَّا أَثْقَلَت دَّعَوَا اللَّهَ رَبَّهُمَا
لَئِنْ ءَاتَيْتَنَا صَٰلِحًا لَّنَكُونَنَّ مِنَ الشَّٰكِرِينَ ﴿١٨٩﴾
فَلَمَّا ءَاتَىٰهُمَا صَٰلِحًا جَعَلَا لَهُ شُرَكَاءَ فِيمَا
ءَاتَىٰهُمَا فَتَعَٰلَى اللَّهُ عَمَّا يُشْرِكُونَ ﴿١٩٠﴾ أَيُشْرِكُونَ
مَا لَا يَخْلُقُ شَيْـًٔا وَهُمْ يُخْلَقُونَ ﴿١٩١﴾ وَلَا
يَسْتَطِيعُونَ لَهُمْ نَصْرًا وَلَا أَنفُسَهُمْ
يَنصُرُونَ ﴿١٩٢﴾ وَإِن تَدْعُوهُمْ إِلَى الْهُدَىٰ
لَا يَتَّبِعُوكُمْ سَوَاءٌ عَلَيْكُمْ أَدَعَوْتُمُوهُمْ أَمْ
أَنتُمْ صَٰمِتُونَ ﴿١٩٣﴾ إِنَّ الَّذِينَ تَدْعُونَ مِن
دُونِ اللَّهِ عِبَادٌ أَمْثَالُكُمْ فَادْعُوهُمْ
فَلْيَسْتَجِيبُوا لَكُمْ إِن كُنتُمْ صَٰدِقِينَ ﴿١٩٤﴾
أَلَهُمْ أَرْجُلٌ يَمْشُونَ بِهَا أَمْ لَهُمْ أَيْدٍ
يَبْطِشُونَ بِهَا أَمْ لَهُمْ أَعْيُنٌ يُبْصِرُونَ
بِهَا أَمْ لَهُمْ ءَاذَانٌ يَسْمَعُونَ بِهَا قُلِ
ادْعُوا شُرَكَاءَكُمْ ثُمَّ كِيدُونِ فَلَا تُنظِرُونِ ﴿١٩٥﴾
إِنَّ وَلِـِّۧيَ اللَّهُ الَّذِي نَزَّلَ الْكِتَٰبَ وَهُوَ
يَتَوَلَّى الصَّٰلِحِينَ ﴿١٩٦﴾ وَالَّذِينَ تَدْعُونَ مِن
دُونِهِ لَا يَسْتَطِيعُونَ نَصْرَكُمْ وَلَا أَنفُسَهُمْ

help themselves.'

198. And if you call these (polytheists) to guidance they will not even be able to hear (you speak). And though you see them (as if they are) looking at you while (as a matter of fact) they do not see (anything being absent minded as they are).

199. Take to forgiveness and ever forbear and enjoin (the doing of) good and turn away from (those who intentionally want to remain) ignorant.

200. Should any imputation from satan (who spreads reports for sowing dissension) afflict you then seek refuge in Allâh. He is indeed All-Hearing, All-Knowing.

201. Verily, (as for) those who (really wish to) guard (against calamities) when some (enraging) suggestion from satan assails them, they remember (Allâh and His guidance), then behold, they begin to see (things in their true light).

202. And their brethren (the human associates of satan) draw them into error and they do not relax (in their evil designs).

203. And when you do not bring to them a (fresh) revelation they say, 'Why do you not forge a verse (and invent it as a revelation)?' Say, 'I only follow what is revealed to me by my Lord. These (Qur'ânic verses) are enlightening (and) proofs from your Lord and source of guidance and mercy (of Allâh) for a people who would believe,

204. Hence, when the Qur'ân is recited, give ear to it and keep silent (to remain attentive) so that you may be shown mercy.

205. Keep on remembering Your Lord in your mind with humility and awe and in a voice not loud, in the mornings and the evenings, and do not be of the heedless.

206. Verily, those who are near to your Lord (and feel His presence with them) do not wax too proud to worship Him but they glorify Him and prostrate themselves in obedience to Him.

[PROSTRATION]

يَنصُرُونَ ﴿١٩٧﴾ وَإِن تَدْعُوهُمْ إِلَى الْهُدَىٰ لَا
يَسْمَعُوا وَتَرَاهُمْ يَنظُرُونَ إِلَيْكَ وَهُمْ
لَا يُبْصِرُونَ ﴿١٩٨﴾ خُذِ الْعَفْوَ وَأْمُرْ بِالْعُرْفِ
وَأَعْرِضْ عَنِ الْجَاهِلِينَ ﴿١٩٩﴾ وَإِمَّا يَنزَغَنَّكَ
مِنَ الشَّيْطَانِ نَزْغٌ فَاسْتَعِذْ بِاللَّهِ إِنَّهُ سَمِيعٌ
عَلِيمٌ ﴿٢٠٠﴾ إِنَّ الَّذِينَ اتَّقَوْا إِذَا مَسَّهُمْ طَيِفٌ
مِّنَ الشَّيْطَانِ تَذَكَّرُوا فَإِذَا هُم مُّبْصِرُونَ ﴿٢٠١﴾
وَإِخْوَانُهُمْ يَمُدُّونَهُمْ فِي الْغَيِّ ثُمَّ لَا
يُقْصِرُونَ ﴿٢٠٢﴾ وَإِذَا لَمْ تَأْتِهِم بِآيَةٍ قَالُوا
لَوْلَا اجْتَبَيْتَهَا قُلْ إِنَّمَا أَتَّبِعُ مَا يُوحَىٰ إِلَيَّ
مِن رَّبِّي هَٰذَا بَصَائِرُ مِن رَّبِّكُمْ وَهُدًى
وَرَحْمَةٌ لِّقَوْمٍ يُؤْمِنُونَ ﴿٢٠٣﴾ وَإِذَا قُرِئَ
الْقُرْآنُ فَاسْتَمِعُوا لَهُ وَأَنصِتُوا لَعَلَّكُمْ
تُرْحَمُونَ ﴿٢٠٤﴾ وَاذْكُر رَّبَّكَ فِي نَفْسِكَ
تَضَرُّعًا وَخِيفَةً وَدُونَ الْجَهْرِ مِنَ الْقَوْلِ
بِالْغُدُوِّ وَالْآصَالِ وَلَا تَكُن مِّنَ الْغَافِلِينَ ﴿٢٠٥﴾
إِنَّ الَّذِينَ عِندَ رَبِّكَ لَا يَسْتَكْبِرُونَ عَنْ
عِبَادَتِهِ وَيُسَبِّحُونَهُ وَلَهُ يَسْجُدُونَ ۩ ﴿٢٠٦﴾ السجدة

CHAPTER
8

سُورَةُ الأَنفَالِ ٨

AL-ANFÂL
(The Voluntary Gifts)
(Revealed after Hijrah)

With the name of Allâh,
the most Gracious, the Ever Merciful
(I commence to read Sûrah Al-Anfâl).

1. **P**EOPLE ask you about the voluntary gifts (for the advancement of the cause of Allâh). Say, 'The voluntary gifts are at the disposal of Allâh and His Messenger (to administer). So take Allâh as a shield and reconcile your mutual differences and obey Allâh and His Messenger if you are (true) believers.

2. Verily, the (true) believers are only those whose hearts tremble when the name of Allâh is mentioned before them, and when His Messages are recited to them, it increases them in faith and in their Lord only do they put their trust;

3. Who observe Prayer and go on spending from that which We have provided for them.

4. It is these who are the believers in truth. There awaits them with their Lord exalted degrees (of rank) as well as (His) protection and an honourable provision.

5. (This reward is) because your Lord brought you forth from your house (for the Battle of *Badr*) for a righteous purpose, even though a party of the believers considered it very difficult.

6. These (disbelievers) disputed with you concerning the truth (of Islam) after it had been made clear (by signs and proofs). (On being invited to accept Islam they were behaving) as though they were being driven towards death, but they will actually be facing death very soon.

7. And (O Companions of the Prophet! recall the time) when Allâh promised you (victory

سُورَةُ الأَنفَالِ مَدَنِيَّةٌ

بِسْمِ اللّٰهِ الرَّحْمٰنِ الرَّحِيْمِ

يَسْـَٔلُوْنَكَ عَنِ الْأَنْفَالِ ؕ قُلِ الْأَنْفَالُ لِلّٰهِ
وَالرَّسُوْلِ ۚ فَاتَّقُوا اللّٰهَ وَأَصْلِحُوْا ذَاتَ
بَيْنِكُمْ ۪ وَأَطِيْعُوا اللّٰهَ وَرَسُوْلَهٗٓ إِنْ كُنْتُمْ
مُّؤْمِنِيْنَ ﴿١﴾ إِنَّمَا الْمُؤْمِنُوْنَ الَّذِيْنَ إِذَا
ذُكِرَ اللّٰهُ وَجِلَتْ قُلُوْبُهُمْ وَإِذَا تُلِيَتْ
عَلَيْهِمْ أٰيٰتُهٗ زَادَتْهُمْ إِيْمٰنًا وَّعَلٰى رَبِّهِمْ
يَتَوَكَّلُوْنَ ﴿٢﴾ الَّذِيْنَ يُقِيْمُوْنَ الصَّلٰوةَ
وَمِمَّا رَزَقْنٰهُمْ يُنْفِقُوْنَ ﴿٣﴾ أُولٰٓئِكَ هُمُ
الْمُؤْمِنُوْنَ حَقًّا ؕ لَهُمْ دَرَجٰتٌ عِنْدَ رَبِّهِمْ
وَمَغْفِرَةٌ وَّرِزْقٌ كَرِيْمٌ ﴿٤﴾ كَمَآ أَخْرَجَكَ
رَبُّكَ مِنْۢ بَيْتِكَ بِالْحَقِّ وَإِنَّ فَرِيْقًا
مِّنَ الْمُؤْمِنِيْنَ لَكٰرِهُوْنَ ﴿٥﴾ يُجٰدِلُوْنَكَ
فِي الْحَقِّ بَعْدَ مَا تَبَيَّنَ كَأَنَّمَا يُسَاقُوْنَ
إِلَى الْمَوْتِ وَهُمْ يَنْظُرُوْنَ ﴿٦﴾ وَإِذْ يَعِدُكُمُ

الْجُزْءُ التَّاسِعُ

over) one of the two (enemy) parties; (the well-equipped Makkan army and the other ill-equipped caravan from Syria), that it should be yours (for fighting against), while you wanted the unarmed party to fall into your hands (to get an easy victory), but Allâh wanted to establish the truth by fulfilling His words (of prophecy) and to cut off the very root of the disbelievers;
8. So that He might establish the truth and wipe out the falsehood, though those who had cut their ties with Allâh considered it hard.
9. (Recall the time) when you (O Companions of the Prophet!) implored your Lord to aid you in distress, and He responded to you (saying), 'I shall reinforce you with a thousand of the angels coming in continuous succession.'
10. And Allâh made this (coming of the angels) only as good tidings (of your victory) and (that was) so that your hearts might thereby be at rest, for (in any case) victory comes only by the help of Allâh. Verily, Allâh is All-Mighty, All-Wise.

SECTION 2

11. (**R**ECALL the time) when He caused a sort of slumber to prevail upon you to give you a sense of peaceful security from Himself, and He sent down upon you water from the clouds that He might thereby purify you and remove from you the scourge of satan, that He might strengthen your hearts and thereby make your feet firm and strong.
12. (It was the time) when your Lord revealed to the angels (to convey to the believers), 'I am with you;' (and He commanded the angels) to make those who believe stand firm and fast, and '(O believers!) I will indeed strike terror into the hearts of those who disbelieve. So smite on (your enemy's) necks and above these (- on their heads) and strike off all their fingertips.'
13. This (punishment) is (given them) because they have cut themselves off from Allâh and His Messenger, and whosoever opposes Allâh

اللّٰهُ إِحْدَى الطَّآئِفَتَيْنِ أَنَّهَا لَكُمْ وَتَوَدُّونَ
أَنَّ غَيْرَ ذَاتِ الشَّوْكَةِ تَكُونُ لَكُمْ
وَيُرِيدُ اللّٰهُ أَنْ يُحِقَّ الْحَقَّ بِكَلِمٰتِهِ وَيَقْطَعَ
دَابِرَ الْكٰفِرِينَ ⑦ لِيُحِقَّ الْحَقَّ وَيُبْطِلَ
الْبٰطِلَ وَلَوْ كَرِهَ الْمُجْرِمُونَ ⑧ إِذْ تَسْتَغِيثُونَ
رَبَّكُمْ فَاسْتَجَابَ لَكُمْ أَنِّي مُمِدُّكُمْ بِأَلْفٍ
مِّنَ الْمَلٰٓئِكَةِ مُرْدِفِينَ ⑨ وَمَا جَعَلَهُ اللّٰهُ
إِلَّا بُشْرٰى وَلِتَطْمَئِنَّ بِهِ قُلُوبُكُمْ وَمَا
النَّصْرُ إِلَّا مِنْ عِنْدِ اللّٰهِ إِنَّ اللّٰهَ عَزِيزٌ
حَكِيمٌ ⑩ إِذْ يُغَشِّيكُمُ النُّعَاسَ أَمَنَةً مِّنْهُ
وَيُنَزِّلُ عَلَيْكُمْ مِّنَ السَّمَآءِ مَآءً
لِّيُطَهِّرَكُمْ بِهِ وَيُذْهِبَ عَنْكُمْ رِجْزَ
الشَّيْطٰنِ وَلِيَرْبِطَ عَلٰى قُلُوبِكُمْ وَيُثَبِّتَ
بِهِ الْأَقْدَامَ ⑪ إِذْ يُوحِي رَبُّكَ إِلَى الْمَلٰٓئِكَةِ
أَنِّي مَعَكُمْ فَثَبِّتُوا الَّذِينَ أٰمَنُوا سَأُلْقِي
فِي قُلُوبِ الَّذِينَ كَفَرُوا الرُّعْبَ فَاضْرِبُوا
فَوْقَ الْأَعْنَاقِ وَاضْرِبُوا مِنْهُمْ كُلَّ
بَنَانٍ ⑫ ذٰلِكَ بِأَنَّهُمْ شَآقُّوا اللّٰهَ وَرَسُولَهُ
وَمَنْ يُشَاقِقِ اللّٰهَ وَرَسُولَهُ فَإِنَّ اللّٰهَ

and His Messenger, as its result Allâh (too) is Severe in punishment (to such).

14. That is (your punishment), so suffer some of it (in this life), and (know) that (in the Hereafter) there awaits the disbelievers the torment of the Fire.

15. O you who believe! When you meet those who disbelieve in battle array, do not show them your backs.

16. And he that shows his back to them at such a time, unless he is maneuvering in warfare or as a measure to rally to another company, has truly incurred the displeasure of Allâh, and his refuge is Gehenna. What an evil destined end it is!

17. Therefore (in this war O Muslims!) you killed them not. (As a matter of fact) it was Allâh Who killed them. And (O Prophet!) it was not you who threw (a handful of small stones) when you did (apparently) throw them (towards the enemy) but it was Allâh Who threw (that He might vanquish your enemies) and that He might confer on the believers from Himself a bounteous favour. Verily, Allâh is All-Hearing, All-Knowing.

18. That is (what happened at the Battle of Badr), and (know for the future too) that Allâh will always go on thwarting the (war) strategies of the disbelievers.

19. If you (O disbelievers!) sought a decision then such a decision (in the form of the results of the Battle of *Badr*) has of course come to you. And if you (now) desist (from persecuting the believers), it is better for you. And if you return (to hostilities), We too will return (to their help), and your hosts, though they may be numerous, will be of no avail to you; and (know) that Allâh is with the believers.

SECTION 3

20. **O** YOU who believe! Obey Allâh and His Messenger and do not turn away from him

سُورَةُ الْأَنْفَالِ ٨

شَدِيدُ الْعِقَابِ ﴿١٣﴾ ذَٰلِكُمْ فَذُوقُوهُ
وَأَنَّ لِلْكَٰفِرِينَ عَذَابَ النَّارِ ﴿١٤﴾ يَٰأَيُّهَا الَّذِينَ
ءَامَنُوا إِذَا لَقِيتُمُ الَّذِينَ كَفَرُوا زَحْفًا
فَلَا تُوَلُّوهُمُ الْأَدْبَارَ ﴿١٥﴾ وَمَنْ يُوَلِّهِمْ
يَوْمَئِذٍ دُبُرَهُ إِلَّا مُتَحَرِّفًا لِقِتَالٍ أَوْ مُتَحَيِّزًا
إِلَىٰ فِئَةٍ فَقَدْ بَاءَ بِغَضَبٍ مِنَ اللَّهِ وَمَأْوَاهُ
جَهَنَّمُ وَبِئْسَ الْمَصِيرُ ﴿١٦﴾ فَلَمْ تَقْتُلُوهُمْ
وَلَٰكِنَّ اللَّهَ قَتَلَهُمْ وَمَا رَمَيْتَ إِذْ رَمَيْتَ
وَلَٰكِنَّ اللَّهَ رَمَىٰ وَلِيُبْلِيَ الْمُؤْمِنِينَ مِنْهُ
بَلَاءً حَسَنًا إِنَّ اللَّهَ سَمِيعٌ عَلِيمٌ ﴿١٧﴾
ذَٰلِكُمْ وَأَنَّ اللَّهَ مُوهِنُ كَيْدِ الْكَٰفِرِينَ ﴿١٨﴾
إِنْ تَسْتَفْتِحُوا فَقَدْ جَاءَكُمُ الْفَتْحُ وَإِنْ
تَنْتَهُوا فَهُوَ خَيْرٌ لَكُمْ وَإِنْ تَعُودُوا نَعُدْ
وَلَنْ تُغْنِيَ عَنْكُمْ فِئَتُكُمْ شَيْئًا وَلَوْ كَثُرَتْ
وَأَنَّ اللَّهَ مَعَ الْمُؤْمِنِينَ ﴿١٩﴾ يَٰأَيُّهَا الَّذِينَ
ءَامَنُوا أَطِيعُوا اللَّهَ وَرَسُولَهُ وَلَا تَوَلَّوْا عَنْهُ

ع ٢ ١٦

whilst you hear (him speak).
21. And be not like those who say, 'We listen' while they do not listen and do not accept.
22. Surely, the worst of animal that walk or crawl in the sight of Allâh are those that are deaf and dumb and who are devoid of understanding.
23. Had Allâh found any good in them, He would have certainly made them listen (to the Qur'ân). And if (in the present situation) He makes them listen, they will turn away and they are averse.
24. O you who believe! Respond to Allâh and the Messenger when he calls you to that which will give you life and know that Allâh intervenes between a person and (the inclinations of) his heart and that it is He to Whom you shall all be gathered (after having been raised to life).
25. And guard against an affliction which surely will not afflict only those of you in particular who have acted unjustly (but it will involve others also who are inclined towards them); and know that Allâh is Severe in requiting.
26. And (recall the time) when you were only a few and were looked upon as weak in the land, you were afraid lest the people should take you by storm, but He provided you refuge (in Madînah) and strengthened you with His help and provided you with good and pure things so that you might give thanks.
27. O you who believe! Do not be dishonest to Allâh and His Messenger, nor betray your trusts knowingly.
28. And bear in mind that your possessions and your children are but an ordeal and it is Allâh alone with Whom there is a mighty reward.

SECTION 4

29. **O** YOU who believe! If you take Allâh as a shield He will grant you Discrimination (between right and wrong as is the Battle of

وَأَنْتُمْ تَسْمَعُونَ ﴿٢٠﴾ وَلَا تَكُونُوا كَالَّذِينَ
قَالُوا سَمِعْنَا وَهُمْ لَا يَسْمَعُونَ ﴿٢١﴾ إِنَّ شَرَّ
الدَّوَآبِّ عِنْدَ اللّٰهِ الصُّمُّ الْبُكْمُ الَّذِينَ
لَا يَعْقِلُونَ ﴿٢٢﴾ وَلَوْ عَلِمَ اللّٰهُ فِيهِمْ خَيْرًا
لَّأَسْمَعَهُمْ وَلَوْ أَسْمَعَهُمْ لَتَوَلَّوْا وَّهُمْ
مُّعْرِضُونَ ﴿٢٣﴾ يٰٓأَيُّهَا الَّذِينَ أٰمَنُوا اسْتَجِيبُوا
لِلّٰهِ وَلِلرَّسُولِ إِذَا دَعَاكُمْ لِمَا يُحْيِيكُمْ
وَاعْلَمُوٓا أَنَّ اللّٰهَ يَحُولُ بَيْنَ الْمَرْءِ
وَقَلْبِهِ وَأَنَّهُ إِلَيْهِ تُحْشَرُونَ ﴿٢٤﴾ وَاتَّقُوا
فِتْنَةً لَّا تُصِيبَنَّ الَّذِينَ ظَلَمُوا مِنْكُمْ
خَاصَّةً وَاعْلَمُوٓا أَنَّ اللّٰهَ شَدِيدُ الْعِقَابِ ﴿٢٥﴾
وَاذْكُرُوٓا إِذْ أَنْتُمْ قَلِيلٌ مُّسْتَضْعَفُونَ
فِي الْأَرْضِ تَخَافُونَ أَنْ يَتَخَطَّفَكُمُ النَّاسُ
فَأٰوٰىكُمْ وَأَيَّدَكُمْ بِنَصْرِهِ وَرَزَقَكُمْ مِّنَ
الطَّيِّبٰتِ لَعَلَّكُمْ تَشْكُرُونَ ﴿٢٦﴾ يٰٓأَيُّهَا الَّذِينَ
أٰمَنُوا لَا تَخُونُوا اللّٰهَ وَالرَّسُولَ وَتَخُونُوٓا
أَمٰنٰتِكُمْ وَأَنْتُمْ تَعْلَمُونَ ﴿٢٧﴾ وَاعْلَمُوٓا أَنَّمَا
أَمْوٰلُكُمْ وَأَوْلٰدُكُمْ فِتْنَةٌ وَّأَنَّ اللّٰهَ عِنْدَهُ
أَجْرٌ عَظِيمٌ ﴿٢٨﴾ يٰٓأَيُّهَا الَّذِينَ أٰمَنُوٓا إِنْ تَتَّقُوا
اللّٰهَ يَجْعَلْ لَّكُمْ فُرْقَانًا وَّيُكَفِّرْ عَنْكُمْ

Badr) and rid you of all your evil thoughts and deeds, and will protect you (against their adverse consequences), for Allâh is Possessor of great bounties.

30. And (O Prophet! recall the time) when those who disbelieved plotted (evil) against you, (and when so devised) they might confine you or kill you or turn you out. And even now they are devising (means and methods to harm you), and Allâh also devised (to counteract their evil designs); and Allâh is the Best of devisers.

31. And when Our verses are recited to them they say, 'We have already heard (them before). If We so wish, we could certainly compose the like of this. These are nothing but fables of the former peoples.'

32. And (recall the time) when they said, 'O Allâh! If this (faith of Islam) indeed be the truth revealed by You, then rain down upon us stones from heaven, or bring down upon us (some other) grievous punishment.'

33. Allâh was not going to punish them so long as you (O Prophet!) were among them, nor would He punish them while they were seeking His protection.

34. But what plea have they (now) that Allâh should not punish them when they keep (His worshippers) back from the Holy Mosque (at Makkah), whilst they are not (fit to be) its (true) trustees. Its (true) trustees are only those who have become secure against evil but most of these (disbelievers) know not (this fact).

35. (How can they be the trustees of the Holy Mosque as) their prayer at the House is nothing but (sacrilegious activities like) whistling and clapping of hands. (O disbelievers! you asked for punishment) therefore suffer the punishment (at the Battle of Badr) on account of your disbelief.

36. Those who disbelieve spend their possessions to hinder (the people) from the way of Allâh. They will surely continue to spend it

سَيِّئَاتِكُمْ وَيَغْفِرْ لَكُمْ ۗ وَاللَّهُ ذُو الْفَضْلِ
الْعَظِيمِ ﴿٢٩﴾ وَإِذْ يَمْكُرُ بِكَ الَّذِينَ كَفَرُوا
لِيُثْبِتُوكَ أَوْ يَقْتُلُوكَ أَوْ يُخْرِجُوكَ ۚ وَيَمْكُرُونَ
وَيَمْكُرُ اللَّهُ ۖ وَاللَّهُ خَيْرُ الْمَاكِرِينَ ﴿٣٠﴾
وَإِذَا تُتْلَىٰ عَلَيْهِمْ آيَاتُنَا قَالُوا قَدْ سَمِعْنَا لَوْ
نَشَاءُ لَقُلْنَا مِثْلَ هَٰذَا ۙ إِنْ هَٰذَا إِلَّا أَسَاطِيرُ
الْأَوَّلِينَ ﴿٣١﴾ وَإِذْ قَالُوا اللَّهُمَّ إِنْ كَانَ
هَٰذَا هُوَ الْحَقَّ مِنْ عِنْدِكَ فَأَمْطِرْ
عَلَيْنَا حِجَارَةً مِنَ السَّمَاءِ أَوِ ائْتِنَا
بِعَذَابٍ أَلِيمٍ ﴿٣٢﴾ وَمَا كَانَ اللَّهُ لِيُعَذِّبَهُمْ
وَأَنْتَ فِيهِمْ ۚ وَمَا كَانَ اللَّهُ مُعَذِّبَهُمْ
وَهُمْ يَسْتَغْفِرُونَ ﴿٣٣﴾ وَمَا لَهُمْ أَلَّا يُعَذِّبَهُمُ
اللَّهُ وَهُمْ يَصُدُّونَ عَنِ الْمَسْجِدِ الْحَرَامِ
وَمَا كَانُوا أَوْلِيَاءَهُ ۚ إِنْ أَوْلِيَاؤُهُ إِلَّا
الْمُتَّقُونَ وَلَٰكِنَّ أَكْثَرَهُمْ لَا يَعْلَمُونَ ﴿٣٤﴾
وَمَا كَانَ صَلَاتُهُمْ عِنْدَ الْبَيْتِ إِلَّا
مُكَاءً وَتَصْدِيَةً ۚ فَذُوقُوا الْعَذَابَ
بِمَا كُنْتُمْ تَكْفُرُونَ ﴿٣٥﴾ إِنَّ الَّذِينَ
كَفَرُوا يُنْفِقُونَ أَمْوَالَهُمْ لِيَصُدُّوا عَنْ

thereafter. Then, in the long run, (this expenditure) will be to them a (source of) regret and after that they shall be overcome. Such of them who persist in disbelief shall be gathered into Gehenna;

37. So that Allâh may distinguish and separate the impure from the pure and (in doing so) He will pile the impure one upon another, then He will huddle them all together, then He will consign them (-the huddled pile) to Gehenna. Such, in fact, are the very losers.

SECTION 5

38. **S**AY to these who disbelieve that if they desist (now from persecuting the Muslims) they will be protected against the past (misdeeds), but if they revert (to their old ways of mischief), then the example of their predecessors has already gone before (and they will meet the same doom).

39. And (O Muslims!) fight them until there is no more persecution (in the name of religion) and adopting a (certain) religion is wholly for the sake of Allâh, but if they desist, then surely Allâh is Watchful of what they do (and they will not be done injustice to).

40. But if they turn back (and refuse all these terms and fight you) then know that Allâh is your Protecting friend, what an excellent Protecting Friend! and what an excellent Helper!

سَبِيلِ اللّٰهِ ۚ فَسَيُنْفِقُونَهَا ثُمَّ تَكُونُ
عَلَيْهِمْ حَسْرَةً ثُمَّ يُغْلَبُونَ ۚ وَ الَّذِينَ
كَفَرُوٓا إِلَىٰ جَهَنَّمَ يُحْشَرُونَ ﴿٣٦﴾ لِيَمِيزَ
اللّٰهُ الْخَبِيثَ مِنَ الطَّيِّبِ وَ يَجْعَلَ
الْخَبِيثَ بَعْضَهُ عَلَىٰ بَعْضٍ فَيَرْكُمَهُ جَمِيعًا
فَيَجْعَلَهُ فِي جَهَنَّمَ ۚ أُولٰٓئِكَ هُمُ الْخٰسِرُونَ ﴿٣٧﴾ ع ٩/١٨
قُلْ لِلَّذِينَ كَفَرُوٓا إِنْ يَنْتَهُوا يُغْفَرْ
لَهُمْ مَا قَدْ سَلَفَ ۚ وَ إِنْ يَعُودُوا فَقَدْ
مَضَتْ سُنَّتُ الْأَوَّلِينَ ﴿٣٨﴾ وَ قٰتِلُوهُمْ حَتّٰى
لَا تَكُونَ فِتْنَةٌ وَ يَكُونَ الدِّينُ كُلُّهُ
لِلّٰهِ ۚ فَإِنِ انْتَهَوْا فَإِنَّ اللّٰهَ بِمَا يَعْمَلُونَ
بَصِيرٌ ﴿٣٩﴾ وَ إِنْ تَوَلَّوْا فَاعْلَمُوٓا أَنَّ اللّٰهَ
مَوْلٰىكُمْ ۚ نِعْمَ الْمَوْلٰى وَ نِعْمَ النَّصِيرُ ﴿٤٠﴾

PART الجزء العاشر X

سورة الأنفال ٨

41. AND know that whatever you acquire on winning a victory, a fifth of it belongs to Allâh, to the Messenger and to the kindred and the orphan, and the needy and the wayfarer; (this you must observe) if you believe in Allâh and in what We sent down upon Our servant on the Day of Discrimination (between the truth and the falsehood), the day the two armies encountered each other (at the Battle of *Badr*). Indeed, Allâh is Possessor of power to do all He will.

42. When (on that day) you were on the nearer end (-the side nearer to Madînah of the valley of *Badr*) and those (of the hostile forces of disbelievers) were at its farther end (- the side which was farther from Madînah) and the caravan (of the *Quraish* from Syria) was on a level lower than yours (- towards the sea-coast). And had you made a mutual appointment beforehand (as to when and where to meet the foe) you would have differed with regard to the place and time of the appointment, (but the encounter did take place), that Allâh brought about that which was already decreed (by Him), so that he who had (already spiritually) perished on the altar of reason might perish (physically also), and he who has (already spiritually) come to life through a clear sign might live (physically also). Most surely, Allâh is All-Hearing, All-Knowing.

43. (Prophet! recall the time) when Allâh showed these (disbelievers) to you in your dream to be only a few, and had He shown them to you as many (O believers!) You would surely have been demoralised and would have disputed one with another about the matter (of waging war), but Allâh saved (you). Indeed, He has the best knowledge of that which is in (your) hearts.

44. And when you encountered (them), He made them appear as a few in your eyes and He made you appear as a few in their eyes, in order that Allâh might bring about the thing that had already been decreed. And to Allâh all matters stand

وَاعْلَمُوٓا أَنَّمَا غَنِمْتُم مِّن شَيْءٍ فَأَنَّ
لِلّٰهِ خُمُسَهُ وَلِلرَّسُولِ وَلِذِي الْقُرْبٰى
وَالْيَتٰمٰى وَالْمَسٰكِينِ وَابْنِ السَّبِيلِ إِن
كُنتُمْ ءَامَنتُم بِاللّٰهِ وَمَآ أَنْزَلْنَا عَلٰى عَبْدِنَا
يَوْمَ الْفُرْقَانِ يَوْمَ الْتَقَى الْجَمْعَانِ وَاللّٰهُ
عَلٰى كُلِّ شَيْءٍ قَدِيرٌ ﴿٤١﴾ إِذْ أَنْتُم بِالْعُدْوَةِ
الدُّنْيَا وَهُم بِالْعُدْوَةِ الْقُصْوٰى وَالرَّكْبُ
أَسْفَلَ مِنكُمْ وَلَوْ تَوَاعَدتُّمْ لَاخْتَلَفْتُمْ
فِي الْمِيعٰدِ وَلٰكِن لِّيَقْضِيَ اللّٰهُ أَمْرًا كَانَ
مَفْعُولًا لِّيَهْلِكَ مَنْ هَلَكَ عَنْ بَيِّنَةٍ
وَّيَحْيٰى مَنْ حَيَّ عَنْ بَيِّنَةٍ وَإِنَّ اللّٰهَ
لَسَمِيعٌ عَلِيمٌ ﴿٤٢﴾ إِذْ يُرِيكَهُمُ اللّٰهُ فِي
مَنَامِكَ قَلِيلًا وَلَوْ أَرٰىكَهُمْ كَثِيرًا لَّفَشِلْتُمْ
وَلَتَنٰزَعْتُمْ فِي الْأَمْرِ وَلٰكِنَّ اللّٰهَ سَلَّمَ إِنَّهُ
عَلِيمٌ بِذَاتِ الصُّدُورِ ﴿٤٣﴾ وَإِذْ يُرِيكُمُوهُمْ
إِذِ الْتَقَيْتُمْ فِيٓ أَعْيُنِكُمْ قَلِيلًا وَّيُقَلِّلُكُمْ

referred (for decision).

SECTION 6

45. **O** YOU who believe! When you encounter a host, remain steadfast, and remember Allâh much that you may triumph.

46. And obey Allâh and His Messenger and dispute not with one another or you will be demoralised and your strength will depart (from you) and do persevere, for Allâh is surely with the patiently persevering ones.

47. And be not like those who marched forth from their homes (at the time of Battle of *Badr*) boastfully and making an ostentatious display of themselves to the people, and who hindered (the people) from following the path of Allâh. And Allâh is the Destroyer of whatever they do (against Islam).

48. And (recall the time) when satan made their deeds fair-seeming to them and said, 'Today none among the people shall overpower you, for surely, I am your protecting helper.' But when the two hosts came face to face with each other, he (- satan) retraced his steps and said, 'Surely I have nothing to do with you, I see that which you do not see. I am surely afraid of Allâh, for Allâh is Severe in requital.'

SECTION 7

49. (**T**HIS was the time) when the hypocrites and those who carried in their hearts a disease were saying, 'Their religion has deluded these (Muslims).' But (the truth of the matter is that) who so puts his trust in Allâh finds that surely Allâh is All-Mighty, All-Wise.

50. Could you but see the angels carrying away the souls of those who disbelieve, smiting their faces and their backs (saying), 'Suffer the punishment of burning.

51. 'This (punishment) is because of (the deeds) which your (own) hands have sent forward and

فِيٓ أَعۡيُنِهِمۡ لِيَقۡضِيَ ٱللَّهُ أَمۡرٗا كَانَ مَفۡعُولٗاۗ
وَإِلَى ٱللَّهِ تُرۡجَعُ ٱلۡأُمُورُ ٤٤ يَٰٓأَيُّهَا ٱلَّذِينَ
ءَامَنُوٓاْ إِذَا لَقِيتُمۡ فِئَةٗ فَٱثۡبُتُواْ وَٱذۡكُرُواْ
ٱللَّهَ كَثِيرٗا لَّعَلَّكُمۡ تُفۡلِحُونَ ٤٥ وَأَطِيعُواْ
ٱللَّهَ وَرَسُولَهُۥ وَلَا تَنَٰزَعُواْ فَتَفۡشَلُواْ
وَتَذۡهَبَ رِيحُكُمۡۖ وَٱصۡبِرُوٓاْۚ إِنَّ ٱللَّهَ مَعَ
ٱلصَّٰبِرِينَ ٤٦ وَلَا تَكُونُواْ كَٱلَّذِينَ خَرَجُواْ
مِن دِيَٰرِهِم بَطَرٗا وَرِئَآءَ ٱلنَّاسِ
وَيَصُدُّونَ عَن سَبِيلِ ٱللَّهِۚ وَٱللَّهُ بِمَا
يَعۡمَلُونَ مُحِيطٞ ٤٧ وَإِذۡ زَيَّنَ لَهُمُ ٱلشَّيۡطَٰنُ
أَعۡمَٰلَهُمۡ وَقَالَ لَا غَالِبَ لَكُمُ ٱلۡيَوۡمَ مِنَ
ٱلنَّاسِ وَإِنِّي جَارٞ لَّكُمۡۖ فَلَمَّا تَرَآءَتِ
ٱلۡفِئَتَانِ نَكَصَ عَلَىٰ عَقِبَيۡهِ وَقَالَ إِنِّي
بَرِيٓءٞ مِّنكُمۡ إِنِّيٓ أَرَىٰ مَا لَا تَرَوۡنَ
إِنِّيٓ أَخَافُ ٱللَّهَۚ وَٱللَّهُ شَدِيدُ ٱلۡعِقَابِ ٤٨
إِذۡ يَقُولُ ٱلۡمُنَٰفِقُونَ وَٱلَّذِينَ فِي قُلُوبِهِم
مَّرَضٌ غَرَّ هَٰٓؤُلَآءِ دِينُهُمۡۗ وَمَن يَتَوَكَّلۡ
عَلَى ٱللَّهِ فَإِنَّ ٱللَّهَ عَزِيزٌ حَكِيمٞ ٤٩ وَلَوۡ
تَرَىٰٓ إِذۡ يَتَوَفَّى ٱلَّذِينَ كَفَرُواْ ٱلۡمَلَٰٓئِكَةُ
يَضۡرِبُونَ وُجُوهَهُمۡ وَأَدۡبَٰرَهُمۡ
وَذُوقُواْ عَذَابَ ٱلۡحَرِيقِ ٥٠ ذَٰلِكَ بِمَا قَدَّمَتۡ

(know) Allâh is by no means unjust to His servants.'

52. (Their ways are) like the ways of the followers of Pharaoh and those before them. They disbelieved in the Messages of Allâh, so Allâh seized them for their sins. Mighty is Allâh and Severe in punishing (the evil done).

53. It happened thus because Allâh is One Who would never withdraw a favour which He has conferred on a people until they themselves change their own state of mind, and that is because Allâh is (all the same) All-Hearing, All-Knowing.

54. Just as it happened to the followers of Pharaoh and those before them (so the same fate will meet them) for they had cried lies to the commandments of their Lord. So We destroyed them on account of their sins, and We drowned the followers of Pharaoh because they were all wrongdoers.

55. Surely, the worst of beasts in the sight of Allâh are those who denied to believe (in the truth in the first instance) so they would not believe;

56. (Particularly) those with whom you entered into a pact, but every time they break their pact and they do not guard (against breach of trusts).

57. Therefore if you find these (breakers of trust) in battle array, then (by inflicting an exemplary punishment upon them) disperse those behind them so that they may be admonished.

58. And if you fear (and have reasons to fear) treachery from a people, then annul (their pact) on terms of equality. Indeed, Allâh loves not the treacherous.

SECTION 8

59. **A**ND let not those who disbelieve think that they have outstripped (Us). They shall not be able to frustrate (Our purpose).

60. (Believers! It is your duty also that you) keep prepared to meet them with whatever you can afford of armed force and of mounted

سُورَةُ الْأَنْفَالِ ٨

أَيْدِيكُمْ وَأَنَّ اللَّهَ لَيْسَ بِظَلَّامٍ
لِّلْعَبِيدِ ﴿٥١﴾ كَدَأْبِ آلِ فِرْعَوْنَ وَالَّذِينَ
مِن قَبْلِهِمْ كَفَرُوا بِآيَاتِ اللَّهِ فَأَخَذَهُمُ
اللَّهُ بِذُنُوبِهِمْ إِنَّ اللَّهَ قَوِيٌّ شَدِيدُ
الْعِقَابِ ﴿٥٢﴾ ذَٰلِكَ بِأَنَّ اللَّهَ لَمْ يَكُ مُغَيِّرًا
نِّعْمَةً أَنْعَمَهَا عَلَىٰ قَوْمٍ حَتَّىٰ يُغَيِّرُوا مَا
بِأَنفُسِهِمْ وَأَنَّ اللَّهَ سَمِيعٌ عَلِيمٌ ﴿٥٣﴾ كَدَأْبِ
آلِ فِرْعَوْنَ وَالَّذِينَ مِن قَبْلِهِمْ كَذَّبُوا
بِآيَاتِ رَبِّهِمْ فَأَهْلَكْنَاهُم بِذُنُوبِهِمْ
وَأَغْرَقْنَا آلَ فِرْعَوْنَ وَكُلٌّ كَانُوا
ظَالِمِينَ ﴿٥٤﴾ إِنَّ شَرَّ الدَّوَابِّ عِندَ اللَّهِ
الَّذِينَ كَفَرُوا فَهُمْ لَا يُؤْمِنُونَ ﴿٥٥﴾ الَّذِينَ
عَاهَدتَّ مِنْهُمْ ثُمَّ يَنقُضُونَ عَهْدَهُمْ
فِي كُلِّ مَرَّةٍ وَهُمْ لَا يَتَّقُونَ ﴿٥٦﴾ فَإِمَّا
تَثْقَفَنَّهُمْ فِي الْحَرْبِ فَشَرِّدْ بِهِم مَّنْ
خَلْفَهُمْ لَعَلَّهُمْ يَذَّكَّرُونَ ﴿٥٧﴾ وَإِمَّا تَخَافَنَّ
مِن قَوْمٍ خِيَانَةً فَانبِذْ إِلَيْهِمْ عَلَىٰ
سَوَاءٍ إِنَّ اللَّهَ لَا يُحِبُّ الْخَائِنِينَ ﴿٥٨﴾ وَلَا
يَحْسَبَنَّ الَّذِينَ كَفَرُوا سَبَقُوا إِنَّهُمْ
لَا يُعْجِزُونَ ﴿٥٩﴾ وَأَعِدُّوا لَهُم مَّا اسْتَطَعْتُم
مِّن قُوَّةٍ وَمِن رِّبَاطِ الْخَيْلِ تُرْهِبُونَ

pickets at the frontier, to strike terror thereby into the hearts of the enemies of Allâh and your enemies and such others besides them that you do not know, (but) Allâh knows them. And whatever you spend in the cause of Allâh, shall be repaid to you in full and you will not be dealt with unjustly.

61. And if they incline towards peace, you should also incline towards it and put your trust in Allâh. Surely, it is He Who is All-Hearing, All-Knowing.

62. But if they intend to desert you, (remember that) Allâh surely suffices you. It is He Who has strengthened you with His help and with the believers;

63. And He has united their (- believers') hearts in mutual affection. Had you spent all that is in the earth you could not have united their hearts so, but Allâh united their hearts in mutual affection. He is indeed All-Mighty, All-Wise.

64. O Prophet! Allâh is sufficient for you and for the believers who follow you.

SECTION 9

65. **O** PROPHET! Urge the believers frequently and strongly to (defensive) fighting. If there be of you twenty steadfast, they shall overcome two hundred and if there be a hundred of you they shall overcome a thousand of those who disbelieve, because these are a people devoid of understanding.

66. For the present Allâh has lightened your burden, for He knows that there is yet some weakness in you, thus, if there be of you one hundred persevering and steadfast persons they shall (still) overcome (at least) two hundred and if there be a thousand of you they shall overcome two thousand by the leave of Allâh. And Allâh is with the steadfast.

67. It does not behove a Prophet to keep captives unless he has triumphed after a regular bloody fighting in the land. (If you take captives without warfare,) you desire the temporary and

بِهٖ عَدُوَّ اللّٰهِ وَ عَدُوَّكُمْ وَ اٰخَرِيْنَ
مِنْ دُوْنِهِمْ ۚ لَا تَعْلَمُوْنَهُمْ ۚ اَللّٰهُ يَعْلَمُهُمْ ۚ
وَ مَا تُنْفِقُوْا مِنْ شَيْءٍ فِيْ سَبِيْلِ اللّٰهِ
يُوَفَّ اِلَيْكُمْ وَ اَنْتُمْ لَا تُظْلَمُوْنَ ۞ وَ اِنْ
جَنَحُوْا لِلسَّلْمِ فَاجْنَحْ لَهَا وَ تَوَكَّلْ عَلَى
اللّٰهِ ۭ اِنَّهٗ هُوَ السَّمِيْعُ الْعَلِيْمُ ﴿٦١﴾ وَ اِنْ
يُّرِيْدُوْٓا اَنْ يَّخْدَعُوْكَ فَاِنَّ حَسْبَكَ اللّٰهُ ۭ
هُوَ الَّذِيْٓ اَيَّدَكَ بِنَصْرِهٖ وَ بِالْمُؤْمِنِيْنَ ﴿٦٢﴾
وَ اَلَّفَ بَيْنَ قُلُوْبِهِمْ ۭ لَوْ اَنْفَقْتَ مَا فِي
الْاَرْضِ جَمِيْعًا مَّآ اَلَّفْتَ بَيْنَ قُلُوْبِهِمْ
وَ لٰكِنَّ اللّٰهَ اَلَّفَ بَيْنَهُمْ ۭ اِنَّهٗ عَزِيْزٌ
حَكِيْمٌ ﴿٦٣﴾ يٰٓاَيُّهَا النَّبِيُّ حَسْبُكَ اللّٰهُ وَ مَنِ
اتَّبَعَكَ مِنَ الْمُؤْمِنِيْنَ ﴿٦٤﴾ يٰٓاَيُّهَا النَّبِيُّ
حَرِّضِ الْمُؤْمِنِيْنَ عَلَى الْقِتَالِ ۭ اِنْ يَّكُنْ
مِّنْكُمْ عِشْرُوْنَ صٰبِرُوْنَ يَغْلِبُوْا مِائَتَيْنِ ۚ
وَ اِنْ يَّكُنْ مِّنْكُمْ مِّائَةٌ يَّغْلِبُوْٓا اَلْفًا
مِّنَ الَّذِيْنَ كَفَرُوْا بِاَنَّهُمْ قَوْمٌ لَّا يَفْقَهُوْنَ ﴿٦٥﴾
اَلْـٰٔنَ خَفَّفَ اللّٰهُ عَنْكُمْ وَ عَلِمَ اَنَّ فِيْكُمْ
ضَعْفًا ۭ فَاِنْ يَّكُنْ مِّنْكُمْ مِّائَةٌ صَابِرَةٌ
يَّغْلِبُوْا مِائَتَيْنِ ۚ وَ اِنْ يَّكُنْ مِّنْكُمْ اَلْفٌ
يَّغْلِبُوْٓا اَلْفَيْنِ بِاِذْنِ اللّٰهِ ۭ وَ اللّٰهُ مَعَ الصّٰبِرِيْنَ ﴿٦٦﴾
مَا كَانَ لِنَبِيٍّ اَنْ يَّكُوْنَ لَهٗٓ اَسْرٰى حَتّٰى
يُثْخِنَ فِي الْاَرْضِ ۭ تُرِيْدُوْنَ عَرَضَ الدُّنْيَا ۤ

frail goods of this world, while Allâh desires (for you the good of) the Hereafter. And Allâh is All-Mighty, All-Wise.

68. Had there not been a prior decree (of a war at *Badr*) from Allâh you would certainly have come to grief as a result of that which you were going to undertake (by attacking the caravan of *Quraish* from Syria).

69. So eat (and spend) of that which you have acquired after winning the war as is lawful, good and pure, and take Allâh as a shield, for Allâh is Great Protector, Ever Merciful.

SECTION 10

70. **P**ROPHET! Say to those captives (of war) who are in your custody, 'If Allâh finds any good in your heart, He will give you even better than that which has been taken away from you (as ransom) and will protect you (against your sins), for Allâh is Great Protector, Ever Merciful,

71. But if they intend to play false with you, (remember that) they were false to Allâh before, but He delivered them into your control. And Allâh is All-Knowing, All-Wise.

72. Surely, those who have believed and have emigrated and strove hard with their possessions and their persons in the cause of Allâh (- the *Muhâjirs*), and who have given (them) refuge and helped (- the *Ansâr*), are friends one to another. But you are not responsible for the protection of those who have believed but have not emigrated until they do emigrate. However if they seek your help in (the matter of) faith, then it is binding upon you to help them except against a people between whom and yourselves is a treaty. Indeed, Allâh knows well all that you do.

73. And (as for) those who disbelieve, they are friends one to another. Hence if you (O Muslims!) do not act (as has been ordained for you to help one another) there will be persecution and great corruption in the land.

74. And those who have believed and emigrated

وَاللّٰهُ يُرِيدُ الْأٰخِرَةَ ۗ وَاللّٰهُ عَزِيزٌ حَكِيمٌ ﴿٦٧﴾
لَوْلَا كِتٰبٌ مِّنَ اللّٰهِ سَبَقَ لَمَسَّكُمْ فِيمَآ
أَخَذْتُمْ عَذَابٌ عَظِيمٌ ﴿٦٨﴾ فَكُلُوا مِمَّا
غَنِمْتُمْ حَلٰلًا طَيِّبًا ۖ وَّاتَّقُوا اللّٰهَ ۗ إِنَّ اللّٰهَ
غَفُورٌ رَّحِيمٌ ﴿٦٩﴾ يٰٓأَيُّهَا النَّبِيُّ قُلْ لِّمَنْ فِيٓ
أَيْدِيكُمْ مِّنَ الْأَسْرٰٓى إِنْ يَّعْلَمِ اللّٰهُ فِي
قُلُوبِكُمْ خَيْرًا يُّؤْتِكُمْ خَيْرًا مِّمَّآ أُخِذَ مِنْكُمْ
وَيَغْفِرْ لَكُمْ ۗ وَاللّٰهُ غَفُورٌ رَّحِيمٌ ﴿٧٠﴾ وَإِنْ
يُّرِيدُوا خِيَانَتَكَ فَقَدْ خَانُوا اللّٰهَ مِنْ قَبْلُ
فَأَمْكَنَ مِنْهُمْ ۗ وَاللّٰهُ عَلِيمٌ حَكِيمٌ ﴿٧١﴾
إِنَّ الَّذِينَ أٰمَنُوا وَهَاجَرُوا وَجٰهَدُوا بِأَمْوٰلِهِمْ
وَأَنْفُسِهِمْ فِي سَبِيلِ اللّٰهِ وَالَّذِينَ أٰوَوْا
وَّنَصَرُوٓا أُولٰٓئِكَ بَعْضُهُمْ أَوْلِيَآءُ بَعْضٍ ۗ وَالَّذِينَ
أٰمَنُوا وَلَمْ يُهَاجِرُوا مَا لَكُمْ مِّنْ وَّلٰيَتِهِمْ
مِّنْ شَيْءٍ حَتّٰى يُهَاجِرُوا ۚ وَإِنِ اسْتَنْصَرُوكُمْ
فِي الدِّينِ فَعَلَيْكُمُ النَّصْرُ إِلَّا عَلٰى قَوْمٍ
بَيْنَكُمْ وَبَيْنَهُمْ مِّيثٰقٌ ۗ وَاللّٰهُ بِمَا تَعْمَلُونَ
بَصِيرٌ ﴿٧٢﴾ وَالَّذِينَ كَفَرُوا بَعْضُهُمْ أَوْلِيَآءُ
بَعْضٍ ۗ إِلَّا تَفْعَلُوهُ تَكُنْ فِتْنَةٌ فِي الْأَرْضِ
وَفَسَادٌ كَبِيرٌ ﴿٧٣﴾ وَالَّذِينَ أٰمَنُوا وَهَاجَرُوا

ع ٩ ٥

and strove hard for the cause of Allâh, and those who have given (them) refuge and have helped, it is these indeed who are the true believers. For them is (His) protection (against sins) and an honourable provision (from Him).
75. And (even) those who have believed afterwards, and emigrated and strove hard jointly with you for the cause of Allâh, they of course belong to you. And (as to) blood relations they are nearer one to another (to inheritance) according to the law of Allâh. Surely, Allâh has perfect knowledge of everything.

وَجٰهَدُوا فِي سَبِيلِ اللّٰهِ وَالَّذِينَ ءَاوَوا
وَّنَصَرُوٓا أُولٰٓئِكَ هُمُ الْمُؤْمِنُونَ حَقًّا لَهُم
مَّغْفِرَةٌ وَرِزْقٌ كَرِيمٌ ﴿٧٤﴾ وَالَّذِينَ ءَامَنُوا مِنْ
بَعْدُ وَهَاجَرُوا وَجٰهَدُوا مَعَكُمْ فَأُولٰٓئِكَ
مِنكُمْ وَأُولُوا الْأَرْحَامِ بَعْضُهُمْ أَوْلَىٰ بِبَعْضٍ
فِي كِتٰبِ اللّٰهِ إِنَّ اللّٰهَ بِكُلِّ شَيْءٍ عَلِيمٌ ﴿٧٥﴾

CHAPTER 9

AL-TAUBAH
(The Repentance)
(Revealed after Hijrah)

سُورَةُ التَّوْبَةِ مَدَنِيَّةٌ

1. (**T**HIS is) a declaration of complete absolution on the part of Allâh and His Messenger (from all obligations) to those of the polytheists with whom you had entered into a treaty (but they broke it repeatedly).
2. So you may go about (freely O you breakers of the treaties!) in the land for four months (since the date of this declaration), and know that you cannot frustrate (the will of) Allâh, and (know) that Allâh will humiliate the disbelievers.
3. And this is a proclamation from Allâh and His Messenger to the people on the occasion of the Greater Pilgrimage (on the day of Sacrifice) that Allâh and His Messenger owe no obligation to these polytheists. If you (O polytheists!) turn to Him in repentance it is better for you. But if you turn away then know that you cannot frustrate (the will of) Allâh. And proclaim (O Prophet!) the news of a grievous punishment to

بَرَآءَةٌ مِّنَ اللّٰهِ وَرَسُولِهِۦٓ إِلَى الَّذِينَ
عٰهَدتُّم مِّنَ الْمُشْرِكِينَ ﴿١﴾ فَسِيحُوا فِي
الْأَرْضِ أَرْبَعَةَ أَشْهُرٍ وَاعْلَمُوٓا أَنَّكُمْ
غَيْرُ مُعْجِزِي اللّٰهِ وَأَنَّ اللّٰهَ مُخْزِي
الْكٰفِرِينَ ﴿٢﴾ وَأَذٰنٌ مِّنَ اللّٰهِ وَرَسُولِهِۦٓ
إِلَى النَّاسِ يَوْمَ الْحَجِّ الْأَكْبَرِ أَنَّ اللّٰهَ
بَرِيٓءٌ مِّنَ الْمُشْرِكِينَ وَرَسُولُهُۥ فَإِنْ
تُبْتُمْ فَهُوَ خَيْرٌ لَّكُمْ وَإِنْ تَوَلَّيْتُمْ فَاعْلَمُوٓا
أَنَّكُمْ غَيْرُ مُعْجِزِي اللّٰهِ وَبَشِّرِ الَّذِينَ

these disbelievers;

4. Excepting those of the polytheists with whom you have entered into a treaty (and) who subsequently did not fail you in any manner, nor did they back up anyone against you. So abide by the treaty you had entered with them to the end of the term you have fixed with them. Allâh, surely loves those who keep their duty.

5. But when the prohibited (four) months (when no attack on the breakers of the treaties was permissible) have expired, slay such polytheists (who broke their treaties) wherever you find them and capture them and besiege them and lie in wait for them in every place from which it is possible to perceive the enemy and watch their movements. But if they turn in repentance and keep up Prayer and go on presenting the *Zakât,* leave their path free. Indeed, Allâh is Great Protector, Ever Merciful.

6. And if any of the polytheists seeks your protection, grant him protection so that he may hear the word of Allâh, then conduct him to a place where he feels himself safe and secure. That (treatment) is (to be meted out to them) because they are a people who have no knowledge (of Islam).

SECTION 2

7. **T**HERE can be no treaty (on the part) of these Polytheists (after their repeated violations of the same) in the sight of Allâh and His Messenger. This, however, does not apply to those with whom you entered into a treaty near the Holy Mosque (at Makkah). So long as they keep true to (the treaty for) you, you should also keep true (in maintaining the treaty) for them. Allâh, surely, loves those who become secure (against the breach of trusts).

8. How (can there be a treaty with deliberate violators of agreements) while, if they get the better of you they would respect no bond, nor words of honour in dealing with you. They would try to please you with (mere words of) their mouths whereas their hearts dissent (from

كَفَرُوا بِعَذَابٍ أَلِيمٍ ③ إِلَّا الَّذِينَ عٰهَدْتُم
مِّنَ الْمُشْرِكِينَ ثُمَّ لَمْ يَنقُصُوكُمْ شَيْئًا
وَّلَمْ يُظٰهِرُوا عَلَيْكُمْ أَحَدًا فَأَتِمُّوا إِلَيْهِمْ
عَهْدَهُمْ إِلَىٰ مُدَّتِهِمْ ۚ إِنَّ اللَّهَ يُحِبُّ
الْمُتَّقِينَ ④ فَإِذَا انسَلَخَ الْأَشْهُرُ الْحُرُمُ
فَاقْتُلُوا الْمُشْرِكِينَ حَيْثُ وَجَدتُّمُوهُمْ
وَخُذُوهُمْ وَاحْصُرُوهُمْ وَاقْعُدُوا لَهُمْ كُلَّ
مَرْصَدٍ ۚ فَإِن تَابُوا وَأَقَامُوا الصَّلٰوةَ وَآتَوُا
الزَّكٰوةَ فَخَلُّوا سَبِيلَهُمْ ۚ إِنَّ اللَّهَ غَفُورٌ
رَّحِيمٌ ⑤ وَإِنْ أَحَدٌ مِّنَ الْمُشْرِكِينَ اسْتَجَارَكَ
فَأَجِرْهُ حَتَّىٰ يَسْمَعَ كَلٰمَ اللَّهِ ثُمَّ أَبْلِغْهُ
مَأْمَنَهُ ۚ ذٰلِكَ بِأَنَّهُمْ قَوْمٌ لَّا يَعْلَمُونَ ⑥ ع
كَيْفَ يَكُونُ لِلْمُشْرِكِينَ عَهْدٌ عِندَ اللَّهِ
وَعِندَ رَسُولِهِ إِلَّا الَّذِينَ عٰهَدتُّمْ عِندَ
الْمَسْجِدِ الْحَرَامِ ۖ فَمَا اسْتَقٰمُوا لَكُمْ
فَاسْتَقِيمُوا لَهُمْ ۚ إِنَّ اللَّهَ يُحِبُّ الْمُتَّقِينَ ⑦
كَيْفَ وَإِن يَظْهَرُوا عَلَيْكُمْ لَا يَرْقُبُوا فِيكُمْ
إِلًّا وَلَا ذِمَّةً ۚ يُرْضُونَكُم بِأَفْوٰهِهِمْ وَتَأْبَىٰ

what they say), and most of them are perfidious.
9. They have preferred paltry gains (- this world) to the revelations of Allâh and thus have turned (people) away from His path. Surely, evil is what they do!
10. They observe no bond nor any word of honour while dealing with one who trusts (them). It is these who are the transgressors.
11. But if (even) such (sworn antagonists) turn in repentance and keep up Prayer and go on presenting the *Zakât,* they are your brethren in faith. And We explain the commandments in detail for a people who know.
12. And if they break their oaths after (they have ratified) their pledge and revile and commit aggression against your Faith, then fight such leaders of disbelief that they may desist. Indeed, solemn (binding) oaths have no value with them.
13. Will you not fight a people who have broken their solemn oaths and proposed to turn out the Messenger and were the first to commence (the fight) against you. Are you afraid of them? Nay, Allâh is more worthy that you should stand in awe of Him if you be (true) believers.
14. Fight them, Allâh will punish them at your hands and humiliate them and will grant you victory over them, and He will heal (the agonies of) the minds of a believing people.
15. And He may take away the suppressed rage of their (- the disbeliever's) hearts. And Allâh turns (with mercy) to him who wishes (Him to turn to him with grace). Verily, Allâh is All-Knowing, All-Wise.
16. Do you think that you will be left (alone in peace) while Allâh has not yet distinguished those who strove hard (for His cause) from among you and who have taken no protecting friend apart from Allâh and His Messenger and the believers? Allâh is Well-Aware of what you do.

SECTION 3

17. **I**T is not for the polytheists to keep the mosques of Allâh in a good and flourishing state

سُورَةُ التَّوْبَةِ ٩

قُلُوبُهُمْ وَأَكْثَرُهُمْ فٰسِقُونَ ﴿٨﴾ إِشْتَرَوْا
بِأٰيٰتِ اللّٰهِ ثَمَنًا قَلِيلًا فَصَدُّوا عَنْ سَبِيلِهِ
إِنَّهُمْ سَاءَ مَا كَانُوا يَعْمَلُونَ ﴿٩﴾ لَا يَرْقُبُونَ
فِي مُؤْمِنٍ إِلًّا وَلَا ذِمَّةً وَأُولٰٓئِكَ هُمُ
الْمُعْتَدُونَ ﴿١٠﴾ فَإِنْ تَابُوا وَأَقَامُوا الصَّلٰوةَ
وَأٰتَوُا الزَّكٰوةَ فَإِخْوٰنُكُمْ فِي الدِّينِ
وَنُفَصِّلُ الْأٰيٰتِ لِقَوْمٍ يَعْلَمُونَ ﴿١١﴾ وَإِنْ نَّكَثُوا
أَيْمٰنَهُمْ مِّنْ بَعْدِ عَهْدِهِمْ وَطَعَنُوا فِي
دِينِكُمْ فَقٰتِلُوا أَيِمَّةَ الْكُفْرِ إِنَّهُمْ لَا
أَيْمٰنَ لَهُمْ لَعَلَّهُمْ يَنْتَهُونَ ﴿١٢﴾ أَلَا تُقٰتِلُونَ
قَوْمًا نَّكَثُوا أَيْمٰنَهُمْ وَهَمُّوا بِإِخْرَاجِ الرَّسُولِ وَهُمْ
بَدَءُوكُمْ أَوَّلَ مَرَّةٍ أَتَخْشَوْنَهُمْ فَاللّٰهُ أَحَقُّ
أَنْ تَخْشَوْهُ إِنْ كُنْتُمْ مُّؤْمِنِينَ ﴿١٣﴾ قٰتِلُوهُمْ
يُعَذِّبْهُمُ اللّٰهُ بِأَيْدِيكُمْ وَيُخْزِهِمْ وَيَنْصُرْكُمْ
عَلَيْهِمْ وَيَشْفِ صُدُورَ قَوْمٍ مُّؤْمِنِينَ ﴿١٤﴾
وَيُذْهِبْ غَيْظَ قُلُوبِهِمْ وَيَتُوبُ اللّٰهُ عَلٰى
مَنْ يَشَاءُ وَاللّٰهُ عَلِيمٌ حَكِيمٌ ﴿١٥﴾ أَمْ
حَسِبْتُمْ أَنْ تُتْرَكُوا وَلَمَّا يَعْلَمِ اللّٰهُ
الَّذِينَ جٰهَدُوا مِنْكُمْ وَلَمْ يَتَّخِذُوا مِنْ
دُونِ اللّٰهِ وَلَا رَسُولِهِ وَلَا الْمُؤْمِنِينَ
ع ٨ وَلِيجَةً وَاللّٰهُ خَبِيرٌ بِمَا تَعْمَلُونَ ﴿١٦﴾ مَا
كَانَ لِلْمُشْرِكِينَ أَنْ يَعْمُرُوا مَسٰجِدَ اللّٰهِ
شٰهِدِينَ عَلٰى أَنْفُسِهِمْ بِالْكُفْرِ أُولٰٓئِكَ

الجزء العاشر

while they bear witness to their own disbelief. It is these whose deeds have all gone in vain and in the Fire they shall abide.

18. He alone keeps the mosques of Allâh in a good and flourishing state who believes in Allâh and the Last Day and observes Prayer and goes on presenting the *Zakât* and holds none but Allâh in awe. Therefore it is these alone who are likely to be among those who attain true guidance.

19. Do you hold the giving of drink to the Pilgrims and keeping the Holy Mosque in a good and flourishing state as equal to (the deeds of) him who believes in Allâh and the Last Day and strives hard in the cause of Allâh? They are not equal in the sight of Allâh. Allâh guides not to ultimate success the people who have no sense of proportion.

20. Those who believe and emigrate (for the sake of God) and strive hard for the cause of Allâh with their possessions and their persons, have the highest rank with Allâh and it is these who are the triumphant.

21. Their Lord gives them good tidings of great mercy from Him and of good pleasure and of Gardens obtaining lasting and abundant bliss for them.

22. They shall abide therein for ever and ever. Indeed Allâh is He with Whom there awaits a great reward (for them).

23. O you who believe! Take not your fathers and brothers for allies, if they prefer disbelief to belief. And whoever of you ally themselves with them, it is then these who are the real wrongdoers.

24. Say, 'If your fathers and your sons and your brethren and your mates and your kinsfolk and the belongings you have acquired and the trade, the slump of which you fear and the homes you love are dearer to you than Allâh and His Messenger and striving hard for the cause of Allâh, then wait till Allâh brings about His

سُورَةُ التَّوۡبَةِ ٩

حَبِطَتۡ أَعۡمَٰلُهُمۡ وَفِي النَّارِ هُمۡ
خَٰلِدُونَ ١٧ إِنَّمَا يَعۡمُرُ مَسَٰجِدَ اللَّهِ مَنۡ
ءَامَنَ بِاللَّهِ وَالۡيَوۡمِ الۡأٓخِرِ وَأَقَامَ الصَّلَوٰةَ
وَءَاتَى الزَّكَوٰةَ وَلَمۡ يَخۡشَ إِلَّا اللَّهَ فَعَسَىٰٓ
أُوْلَٰٓئِكَ أَن يَكُونُواْ مِنَ الۡمُهۡتَدِينَ ١٨
أَجَعَلۡتُمۡ سِقَايَةَ الۡحَآجِّ وَعِمَارَةَ الۡمَسۡجِدِ
الۡحَرَامِ كَمَنۡ ءَامَنَ بِاللَّهِ وَالۡيَوۡمِ الۡأٓخِرِ
وَجَٰهَدَ فِي سَبِيلِ اللَّهِۚ لَا يَسۡتَوُۥنَ
عِندَ اللَّهِۗ وَاللَّهُ لَا يَهۡدِي الۡقَوۡمَ
الظَّٰلِمِينَ ١٩ الَّذِينَ ءَامَنُواْ وَهَاجَرُواْ
وَجَٰهَدُواْ فِي سَبِيلِ اللَّهِ بِأَمۡوَٰلِهِمۡ
وَأَنفُسِهِمۡ أَعۡظَمُ دَرَجَةً عِندَ اللَّهِۚ وَأُوْلَٰٓئِكَ
هُمُ الۡفَآئِزُونَ ٢٠ يُبَشِّرُهُمۡ رَبُّهُم بِرَحۡمَةٖ
مِّنۡهُ وَرِضۡوَٰنٖ وَجَنَّٰتٖ لَّهُمۡ فِيهَا نَعِيمٞ
مُّقِيمٌ ٢١ خَٰلِدِينَ فِيهَآ أَبَدًاۚ إِنَّ اللَّهَ
عِندَهُۥٓ أَجۡرٌ عَظِيمٞ ٢٢ يَٰٓأَيُّهَا الَّذِينَ ءَامَنُواْ
لَا تَتَّخِذُوٓاْ ءَابَآءَكُمۡ وَإِخۡوَٰنَكُمۡ أَوۡلِيَآءَ
إِنِ اسۡتَحَبُّواْ الۡكُفۡرَ عَلَى الۡإِيمَٰنِۚ وَمَن
يَتَوَلَّهُم مِّنكُمۡ فَأُوْلَٰٓئِكَ هُمُ الظَّٰلِمُونَ ٢٣
قُلۡ إِن كَانَ ءَابَآؤُكُمۡ وَأَبۡنَآؤُكُمۡ
وَإِخۡوَٰنُكُمۡ وَأَزۡوَٰجُكُمۡ وَعَشِيرَتُكُمۡ
وَأَمۡوَٰلٌ اقۡتَرَفۡتُمُوهَا وَتِجَٰرَةٞ تَخۡشَوۡنَ
كَسَادَهَا وَمَسَٰكِنُ تَرۡضَوۡنَهَآ أَحَبَّ
إِلَيۡكُم مِّنَ اللَّهِ وَرَسُولِهِۦ وَجِهَادٖ فِي

judgment. Indeed, Allâh guides no sinful people to success.

SECTION 4

25. **A**LLÂH has already helped you on many a battle field and on the day of (the battle of) *Hunain* when your multitude made you feel proud but it availed you nought and the land with all its spaciousness became straitened for you then you turned back retreating.
26. Then Allâh sent down His *Shechinah* (- peace of mind and tranquility) upon His Messenger and upon the believers and He sent down troops which were not visible to you and He punished those who disbelieved. And such is the recompense of the disbelievers.
27. Yet after this (punishment) Allâh will turn (with His mercy) to him who wishes (Him to turn to him with His grace), for Allâh is Great Protector, Ever Merciful.
28. O you who believe! The polytheists are (spiritually) altogether unclean, so they shall not come near the Holy Mosque after this year of theirs. And if you fear (this will spell) poverty (for you) then (rest contented) Allâh will soon make you rich out of His bounty if He will. Verily, Allâh is All-Knowing, All-Wise.
29. Fight against such of the people who despite having been given the Scripture do not (really) believe in Allâh and the Last Day, and who do not hold unlawful what Allâh and His Messenger have declared to be unlawful, and do not subscribe to the true faith, until they pay the *Jizyah* (- the commutation tax), provided they can afford it, and they are content with their state of subjection (having become incorporated in the Islamic government).

SECTION 5

30. **T**HERE are some of the Jews who say, 'Ezra is the son of Allâh,' while the Christians say, 'The Messiah is the son of Allâh.' These are mere words that they speak. They only imitate

سُورَةُ التَّوْبَةِ ٩

سَبِيلِهِ فَتَرَبَّصُوا حَتَّى يَأْتِيَ اللَّهُ بِأَمْرِهِ
وَاللَّهُ لَا يَهْدِي الْقَوْمَ الْفَسِقِينَ ﴿٢٤﴾ لَقَدْ
نَصَرَكُمُ اللَّهُ فِي مَوَاطِنَ كَثِيرَةٍ وَيَوْمَ
حُنَيْنٍ إِذْ أَعْجَبَتْكُمْ كَثْرَتُكُمْ فَلَمْ تُغْنِ
عَنْكُمْ شَيْئًا وَضَاقَتْ عَلَيْكُمُ الْأَرْضُ
بِمَا رَحُبَتْ ثُمَّ وَلَّيْتُمْ مُدْبِرِينَ ﴿٢٥﴾ ثُمَّ
أَنْزَلَ اللَّهُ سَكِينَتَهُ عَلَى رَسُولِهِ وَعَلَى
الْمُؤْمِنِينَ وَأَنْزَلَ جُنُودًا لَمْ تَرَوْهَا
وَعَذَّبَ الَّذِينَ كَفَرُوا وَذَلِكَ جَزَاءُ
الْكَفِرِينَ ﴿٢٦﴾ ثُمَّ يَتُوبُ اللَّهُ مِنْ بَعْدِ ذَلِكَ
عَلَى مَنْ يَشَاءُ وَاللَّهُ غَفُورٌ رَحِيمٌ ﴿٢٧﴾ يَأَيُّهَا
الَّذِينَ آمَنُوا إِنَّمَا الْمُشْرِكُونَ نَجَسٌ
فَلَا يَقْرَبُوا الْمَسْجِدَ الْحَرَامَ بَعْدَ عَامِهِمْ
هَذَا وَإِنْ خِفْتُمْ عَيْلَةً فَسَوْفَ يُغْنِيكُمُ
اللَّهُ مِنْ فَضْلِهِ إِنْ شَاءَ إِنَّ اللَّهَ عَلِيمٌ
حَكِيمٌ ﴿٢٨﴾ قَتِلُوا الَّذِينَ لَا يُؤْمِنُونَ بِاللَّهِ
وَلَا بِالْيَوْمِ الْآخِرِ وَلَا يُحَرِّمُونَ مَا
حَرَّمَ اللَّهُ وَرَسُولُهُ وَلَا يَدِينُونَ دِينَ
الْحَقِّ مِنَ الَّذِينَ أُوتُوا الْكِتَبَ حَتَّى
يُعْطُوا الْجِزْيَةَ عَنْ يَدٍ وَهُمْ صَغِرُونَ ﴿٢٩﴾
وَقَالَتِ الْيَهُودُ عُزَيْرٌ ابْنُ اللَّهِ وَقَالَتِ
النَّصَرَى الْمَسِيحُ ابْنُ اللَّهِ ذَلِكَ قَوْلُهُمْ

the words of the infidels of old. Allâh assail them! Wither they are deluded away!

31. They have taken their learned men and their monks for lords apart from Allâh, and (similarly they have taken) the Messiah, son of Mary, whilst they were enjoined to worship none but One God. There is no other, cannot be and will never be One worthy of worship but He. Too glorified is He for what they associate (with Him).

32. They seek to put out the light of Allâh with (the breath of) their mouths, but Allâh disdains every other thing save that He will perfect His light; however much the disbelievers may consider (it) hard.

33. It is He Who sent His Messenger with the guidance and the Faith of Truth that He may make it triumph over every (other) faith, even though the polytheists consider (it) hard.

34. O you who believe! Many of the learned men (of the Jews) and the (Christian) monks wrongfully appropriate the belongings of the people and turn (the people) away from, and themselves forsake the path of Allâh. Give the news of woeful punishment to them and to those who treasure gold and silver and do not spend it in the cause of Allâh.

35. The day (will come) when these (treasures) shall be heated in the Fire of Gehenna and their foreheads and their sides and their backs be branded with it; (and it shall be said to them,) 'This is what you hoarded up for yourselves, therefore suffer (now the punishment) for what you have been (unlawfully) treasuring up.

36. Verily, the number of months with Allâh is twelve months (in a year) according to the law of Allâh since the day He created the heavens and the earth. Of these four (months) are sacred *(- Rajab, Muharram, Dhul-Qa'dah and Dhul-Hijjah)*. That is the established law. Do not do injustice to yourselves (by waging wars) during these (sacred months). And fight the polytheists all together (in your defence) just as they fight you all together. And know that

بِأَفْوَٰهِهِمْ يُضَٰهِـُٔونَ قَوْلَ الَّذِينَ كَفَرُوا
مِن قَبْلُ قَٰتَلَهُمُ اللَّهُ أَنَّىٰ يُؤْفَكُونَ ﴿٣٠﴾
اتَّخَذُوٓا أَحْبَارَهُمْ وَرُهْبَٰنَهُمْ أَرْبَابًا مِّن
دُونِ اللَّهِ وَالْمَسِيحَ ابْنَ مَرْيَمَ وَمَآ
أُمِرُوٓا إِلَّا لِيَعْبُدُوٓا إِلَٰهًا وَٰحِدًا لَّآ إِلَٰهَ
إِلَّا هُوَ سُبْحَٰنَهُۥ عَمَّا يُشْرِكُونَ ﴿٣١﴾ يُرِيدُونَ
أَن يُطْفِـُٔوا نُورَ اللَّهِ بِأَفْوَٰهِهِمْ وَيَأْبَى اللَّهُ
إِلَّآ أَن يُتِمَّ نُورَهُۥ وَلَوْ كَرِهَ الْكَٰفِرُونَ ﴿٣٢﴾
هُوَ الَّذِيٓ أَرْسَلَ رَسُولَهُۥ بِالْهُدَىٰ وَدِينِ
الْحَقِّ لِيُظْهِرَهُۥ عَلَى الدِّينِ كُلِّهِۦ وَلَوْ
كَرِهَ الْمُشْرِكُونَ ﴿٣٣﴾ يَٰٓأَيُّهَا الَّذِينَ ءَامَنُوٓا
إِنَّ كَثِيرًا مِّنَ الْأَحْبَارِ وَالرُّهْبَانِ لَيَأْكُلُونَ
أَمْوَٰلَ النَّاسِ بِالْبَٰطِلِ وَيَصُدُّونَ عَن
سَبِيلِ اللَّهِ وَالَّذِينَ يَكْنِزُونَ الذَّهَبَ
وَالْفِضَّةَ وَلَا يُنفِقُونَهَا فِي سَبِيلِ اللَّهِ
فَبَشِّرْهُم بِعَذَابٍ أَلِيمٍ ﴿٣٤﴾ يَوْمَ يُحْمَىٰ
عَلَيْهَا فِي نَارِ جَهَنَّمَ فَتُكْوَىٰ بِهَا جِبَاهُهُمْ
وَجُنُوبُهُمْ وَظُهُورُهُمْ هَٰذَا مَا كَنَزْتُمْ
لِأَنفُسِكُمْ فَذُوقُوا مَا كُنتُمْ تَكْنِزُونَ ﴿٣٥﴾
إِنَّ عِدَّةَ الشُّهُورِ عِندَ اللَّهِ اثْنَا عَشَرَ شَهْرًا
فِي كِتَٰبِ اللَّهِ يَوْمَ خَلَقَ السَّمَٰوَٰتِ
وَالْأَرْضَ مِنْهَآ أَرْبَعَةٌ حُرُمٌ ذَٰلِكَ الدِّينُ
الْقَيِّمُ فَلَا تَظْلِمُوا فِيهِنَّ أَنفُسَكُمْ

نصف

Allâh is indeed with those who become secure against evil.

37. The postponement (of a sacred month to some other month) is an excess (committed in the days of) disbelief; the disbelievers are led astray by this (practice). They hold it lawful (for waging a war) one year and forbid it another year, thus adjusting the term of the ban prescribed by Allâh and making lawful what Allâh has made unlawful. The evil of their deeds has been made (by satan) fair-seeming to them. And Allâh guides not the disbelieving people in the ways of success.

SECTION 6

38. **O** YOU (the so-called) believers! What (excuse) have you that when it is said to you to go forth for the cause of Allâh (to *Tabûk*) you incline heavily towards the earth. Would you be contented with the present life in preference to the Hereafter? (If it is so then remember that) the provision of this present life, as compared with the Hereafter, is but little.

39. If you do not go forth on the expedition, He will make you endure a grievous suffering and will choose instead of you a people better than you and you will do Him no harm at all. For Allâh is Possessor of every power to do all He will.

40. If you do not help him (- the Prophet), then (know) Allâh has already helped him when those who disbelieved turned him out (from Makkah with only one companion); he being the second of the two when they were both in the cave (of Thaur); and when he said to his companion *(- Abû Bakr)*, 'Grieve not (about me). Surely, Allâh is with us.' Then Allâh sent down His *Shechinah* (- peace and tranquility) upon him, and helped him with troops which were not visible to you, and He humbled the word of those who disbelieved to the lowest, and it is the word of Allâh alone which is the supermost (and so prevails). Allâh is All-

وَقَٰتِلُوا الْمُشْرِكِينَ كَآفَّةً كَمَا يُقَٰتِلُونَكُمْ
كَآفَّةً ۚ وَاعْلَمُوٓا أَنَّ اللَّهَ مَعَ الْمُتَّقِينَ ﴿٣٦﴾
إِنَّمَا النَّسِيٓءُ زِيَادَةٌ فِي الْكُفْرِ يُضَلُّ
بِهِ الَّذِينَ كَفَرُوا يُحِلُّونَهُۥ عَامًا وَيُحَرِّمُونَهُۥ
عَامًا لِّيُوَاطِـُٔوا عِدَّةَ مَا حَرَّمَ اللَّهُ فَيُحِلُّوا
مَا حَرَّمَ اللَّهُ ۚ زُيِّنَ لَهُمْ سُوٓءُ أَعْمَٰلِهِمْ ۗ
وَاللَّهُ لَا يَهْدِي الْقَوْمَ الْكَٰفِرِينَ ﴿٣٧﴾ يَٰٓأَيُّهَا
الَّذِينَ ءَامَنُوا مَا لَكُمْ إِذَا قِيلَ لَكُمُ انفِرُوا
فِي سَبِيلِ اللَّهِ اثَّاقَلْتُمْ إِلَى الْأَرْضِ ۚ أَرَضِيتُم
بِالْحَيَوٰةِ الدُّنْيَا مِنَ الْءَاخِرَةِ ۚ فَمَا مَتَٰعُ
الْحَيَوٰةِ الدُّنْيَا فِي الْءَاخِرَةِ إِلَّا قَلِيلٌ ﴿٣٨﴾ إِلَّا
تَنفِرُوا يُعَذِّبْكُمْ عَذَابًا أَلِيمًا
وَيَسْتَبْدِلْ قَوْمًا غَيْرَكُمْ وَلَا تَضُرُّوهُ
شَيْـًٔا ۗ وَاللَّهُ عَلَىٰ كُلِّ شَيْءٍ قَدِيرٌ ﴿٣٩﴾ إِلَّا
تَنصُرُوهُ فَقَدْ نَصَرَهُ اللَّهُ إِذْ أَخْرَجَهُ
الَّذِينَ كَفَرُوا ثَانِيَ اثْنَيْنِ إِذْ هُمَا
فِي الْغَارِ إِذْ يَقُولُ لِصَٰحِبِهِۦ لَا تَحْزَنْ إِنَّ
اللَّهَ مَعَنَا ۖ فَأَنزَلَ اللَّهُ سَكِينَتَهُۥ عَلَيْهِ
وَأَيَّدَهُۥ بِجُنُودٍ لَّمْ تَرَوْهَا وَجَعَلَ كَلِمَةَ
الَّذِينَ كَفَرُوا السُّفْلَىٰ ۗ وَكَلِمَةُ اللَّهِ هِيَ

Mighty, All-Wise.

41. Go forth (all whether) light (- being ill-equipped) or heavy (- being well-equipped) and strive hard with your possessions and your persons in the cause of Allâh. That is better for you, if only you knew (your own gain or loss).

42. Had it been an immediate gain and a short journey these (hypocrites) would certainly have followed you, but the hard journey seemed too distant to them, still they will swear (after your successful return) by Allâh (saying), 'If only we could, we would surely have marched forth with you.' They spell their own ruin, Allâh knows well that they are liars.

SECTION 7

43. **A**LLÂH set your affairs aright (and brought honour and glory to you since you pardoned the hypocrites). Why did you give them leave (to stay behind)? (You should not have given them leave) until you had clearly known those who spoke the truth (and offered genuine excuses) and you had come to know the liars.

44. Those who believe in Allâh and the Last Day do not beg leave of you (to be excused) from striving hard with their possessions and their persons. And Allâh is Well-Aware of those who keep their duty (to Him).

45. They alone will beg leave of you who do not believe in Allâh and the Last Day and whose hearts are full of doubts, so overwhelmed by their doubts they waver.

46. If they had (really) intended to go forth they would certainly have made some preparations (for the expedition), but Allâh disliked their attending (to their duty) and He held them back and it was said (to them), 'Remain back with those who stay behind.'

47. Had they set forth with you (O believers!) they would have only added to your trouble, and

الْعُلْيَا ۗ وَاللَّهُ عَزِيزٌ حَكِيمٌ ﴿٤٠﴾ انْفِرُوا خِفَافًا
وَثِقَالًا وَجَاهِدُوا بِأَمْوَالِكُمْ وَأَنْفُسِكُمْ
فِي سَبِيلِ اللَّهِ ۚ ذَٰلِكُمْ خَيْرٌ لَكُمْ إِنْ كُنْتُمْ
تَعْلَمُونَ ﴿٤١﴾ لَوْ كَانَ عَرَضًا قَرِيبًا وَسَفَرًا
قَاصِدًا لَاتَّبَعُوكَ وَلَٰكِنْ بَعُدَتْ عَلَيْهِمُ
الشُّقَّةُ ۚ وَسَيَحْلِفُونَ بِاللَّهِ لَوِ اسْتَطَعْنَا
لَخَرَجْنَا مَعَكُمْ يُهْلِكُونَ أَنْفُسَهُمْ
وَاللَّهُ يَعْلَمُ إِنَّهُمْ لَكَاذِبُونَ ﴿٤٢﴾ عَفَا اللَّهُ
عَنْكَ لِمَ أَذِنْتَ لَهُمْ حَتَّىٰ يَتَبَيَّنَ لَكَ
الَّذِينَ صَدَقُوا وَتَعْلَمَ الْكَاذِبِينَ ﴿٤٣﴾ لَا
يَسْتَأْذِنُكَ الَّذِينَ يُؤْمِنُونَ بِاللَّهِ وَالْيَوْمِ
الْآخِرِ أَنْ يُجَاهِدُوا بِأَمْوَالِهِمْ وَأَنْفُسِهِمْ
وَاللَّهُ عَلِيمٌ بِالْمُتَّقِينَ ﴿٤٤﴾ إِنَّمَا يَسْتَأْذِنُكَ
الَّذِينَ لَا يُؤْمِنُونَ بِاللَّهِ وَالْيَوْمِ الْآخِرِ
وَارْتَابَتْ قُلُوبُهُمْ فَهُمْ فِي رَيْبِهِمْ
يَتَرَدَّدُونَ ﴿٤٥﴾ وَلَوْ أَرَادُوا الْخُرُوجَ لَأَعَدُّوا
لَهُ عُدَّةً وَلَٰكِنْ كَرِهَ اللَّهُ انْبِعَاثَهُمْ
فَثَبَّطَهُمْ وَقِيلَ اقْعُدُوا مَعَ الْقَاعِدِينَ ﴿٤٦﴾
لَوْ خَرَجُوا فِيكُمْ مَا زَادُوكُمْ إِلَّا خَبَالًا

they would have moved about hurriedly in your midst seeking to create disruption among you, and there are some spies in your midst who would have listened to them on their (- your enemies) behalf. And Allâh is Well-Aware of these wrongdoers.

48. They already sought to create dissension before this and they had been meditating plots to upset your plans till the truth became manifest and the decree of Allâh prevailed, though they considered (it) hard.

49. And among these (hypocrites) are those who said (to you), 'Grant us leave (to stay behind) and spare us the trial.' Behold! They have already fallen into the trial. And certainly Gehenna encompasses the disbelievers (for punishing them).

50. If good befalls you it grieves them, but if some hardship afflicts you they say, 'We had indeed taken our precautions beforehand,' and they turn away rejoicing.

51. Say, 'Nothing will afflict us but what Allâh has ordained for us, He is our Patron.' And in Allâh let the believers put their trust.

52. Say, 'You only await for us one of the two good things (- victory or martyrdom), while we await for you (one of two evils to befall) that Allâh will afflict you with punishment either from Himself or at our hands. Wait then, we are (also) waiting with you (as to our respective ends).

53. Say, 'Whether you spend willingly or unwillingly, this (- your charity) shall never be accepted from you, for you are indeed a people ever disobedient.'

54. And nothing prevents their contributions from being accepted except that they (practically) disbelieve in Allâh and His Messenger and they perform not the Prayer but lazily and they spend not (in the cause of Allâh) but reluctantly.

وَلَأَوْضَعُوا خِلٰلَكُمْ يَبْغُونَكُمُ الْفِتْنَةَ
وَفِيكُمْ سَمّٰعُونَ لَهُمْ ۗ وَاللّٰهُ عَلِيمٌۢ بِالظّٰلِمِينَ ﴿٤٧﴾
لَقَدِ ابْتَغَوُا الْفِتْنَةَ مِنْ قَبْلُ وَقَلَّبُوا
لَكَ الْأُمُورَ حَتّٰى جَآءَ الْحَقُّ وَظَهَرَ أَمْرُ
اللّٰهِ وَهُمْ كٰرِهُونَ ﴿٤٨﴾ وَمِنْهُمْ مَّنْ يَقُولُ
ائْذَنْ لِّي وَلَا تَفْتِنِّي ۚ أَلَا فِي الْفِتْنَةِ
سَقَطُوا ۗ وَإِنَّ جَهَنَّمَ لَمُحِيطَةٌۢ بِالْكٰفِرِينَ ﴿٤٩﴾
إِنْ تُصِبْكَ حَسَنَةٌ تَسُؤْهُمْ ۚ وَإِنْ
تُصِبْكَ مُصِيبَةٌ يَقُولُوا قَدْ أَخَذْنَا أَمْرَنَا
مِنْ قَبْلُ وَيَتَوَلَّوْا وَّهُمْ فَرِحُونَ ﴿٥٠﴾ قُلْ لَّنْ
يُصِيبَنَا إِلَّا مَا كَتَبَ اللّٰهُ لَنَا ۚ هُوَ مَوْلٰنَا ۚ
وَعَلَى اللّٰهِ فَلْيَتَوَكَّلِ الْمُؤْمِنُونَ ﴿٥١﴾ قُلْ
هَلْ تَرَبَّصُونَ بِنَا إِلَّا إِحْدَى الْحُسْنَيَيْنِ ۖ
وَنَحْنُ نَتَرَبَّصُ بِكُمْ أَنْ يُصِيبَكُمُ اللّٰهُ
بِعَذَابٍ مِّنْ عِنْدِهِ أَوْ بِأَيْدِينَا ۖ فَتَرَبَّصُوا
إِنَّا مَعَكُمْ مُّتَرَبِّصُونَ ﴿٥٢﴾ قُلْ أَنْفِقُوا طَوْعًا
أَوْ كَرْهًا لَّنْ يُتَقَبَّلَ مِنْكُمْ ۖ إِنَّكُمْ كُنْتُمْ
قَوْمًا فٰسِقِينَ ﴿٥٣﴾ وَمَا مَنَعَهُمْ أَنْ تُقْبَلَ
مِنْهُمْ نَفَقٰتُهُمْ إِلَّا أَنَّهُمْ كَفَرُوا بِاللّٰهِ
وَبِرَسُولِهِ وَلَا يَأْتُونَ الصَّلٰوةَ إِلَّا وَهُمْ

55. So let not their riches nor their children make you wonder. Allâh only intends to punish them therewith in the present life and (that) their souls may depart while they are disbelievers.
56. And they swear by Allâh that they indeed belong to you, but they do not belong to you, on the other hand they are too timid a people (to appear in their true colours).
57. Could they find a shelter or some caverns or any (other) place to enter into, they would certainly have turned thereto rushing headlong (for it).
58. And some of these (hypocrites) are those who find fault with you in the (distribution of) charities. If they are given a share out of it, they are pleased, but if they are not given any share out of it, they at once feel offended.
59. (It would have been better for them) if they had been well content with what Allâh and His Messenger had given them, and had said, 'Sufficient for us is Allâh. Allâh will grant us out of His bounty and so will His Messenger. Surely, to Allâh alone do we turn in supplication.'

SECTION 8

60. **C**OMPULSORY charities (- *Zakât*) are meant for the destitute and the needy, and for its functionaries, and (for) those whose hearts require to be consoled (in all sincerity), and for the emancipation of the slaves, and for (the relief of) those in debt, and (for spending) in the cause of Allâh, and for the wayfarer. (This is) an obligation imposed by Allâh, for Allâh is All-Knowing, All-Wise.
61. And among these (hypocrites) are those who talk ill of the Prophet and say, 'He gives ear to all.' Say, 'His giving ear to all is to your own good. He believes in Allâh and trusts the faithful, and he is a great mercy for those of you who believe.' And there awaits a grievous punishment for those who talk ill of the Messenger of Allâh.
62. They swear by Allâh to you to please you

سُورَةُ التَّوْبَةِ ٩

كُسَالَىٰ وَلَا يُنفِقُونَ إِلَّا وَهُمْ كَٰرِهُونَ ﴿٥٤﴾
فَلَا تُعْجِبْكَ أَمْوَٰلُهُمْ وَلَا أَوْلَٰدُهُمْ إِنَّمَا
يُرِيدُ اللَّهُ لِيُعَذِّبَهُم بِهَا فِي الْحَيَوٰةِ الدُّنْيَا
وَتَزْهَقَ أَنفُسُهُمْ وَهُمْ كَٰفِرُونَ ﴿٥٥﴾
وَيَحْلِفُونَ بِاللَّهِ إِنَّهُمْ لَمِنكُمْ وَمَا هُم
مِّنكُمْ وَلَٰكِنَّهُمْ قَوْمٌ يَفْرَقُونَ ﴿٥٦﴾ لَوْ يَجِدُونَ
مَلْجَـًٔا أَوْ مَغَٰرَٰتٍ أَوْ مُدَّخَلًا لَّوَلَّوْا إِلَيْهِ
وَهُمْ يَجْمَحُونَ ﴿٥٧﴾ وَمِنْهُم مَّن يَلْمِزُكَ فِي
الصَّدَقَٰتِ فَإِنْ أُعْطُوا مِنْهَا رَضُوا وَإِن لَّمْ
يُعْطَوْا مِنْهَا إِذَا هُمْ يَسْخَطُونَ ﴿٥٨﴾ وَلَوْ أَنَّهُمْ
رَضُوا مَا آتَاهُمُ اللَّهُ وَرَسُولُهُ وَقَالُوا
حَسْبُنَا اللَّهُ سَيُؤْتِينَا اللَّهُ مِن فَضْلِهِ
وَرَسُولُهُ إِنَّا إِلَى اللَّهِ رَٰغِبُونَ ﴿٥٩﴾ إِنَّمَا الصَّدَقَٰتُ
لِلْفُقَرَاءِ وَالْمَسَٰكِينِ وَالْعَٰمِلِينَ عَلَيْهَا
وَالْمُؤَلَّفَةِ قُلُوبُهُمْ وَفِي الرِّقَابِ وَالْغَٰرِمِينَ
وَفِي سَبِيلِ اللَّهِ وَابْنِ السَّبِيلِ فَرِيضَةً
مِّنَ اللَّهِ وَاللَّهُ عَلِيمٌ حَكِيمٌ ﴿٦٠﴾ وَمِنْهُمُ
الَّذِينَ يُؤْذُونَ النَّبِيَّ وَيَقُولُونَ هُوَ أُذُنٌ
قُلْ أُذُنُ خَيْرٍ لَّكُمْ يُؤْمِنُ بِاللَّهِ وَيُؤْمِنُ
لِلْمُؤْمِنِينَ وَرَحْمَةٌ لِّلَّذِينَ آمَنُوا مِنكُمْ
وَالَّذِينَ يُؤْذُونَ رَسُولَ اللَّهِ لَهُمْ عَذَابٌ

(O believers!). If they were true believers they should realize that Allâh, as well as His Messenger, is more worthy that they should please Him (with their belief in the truth and their righteous deeds).

63. Have they not (yet) known that whosoever opposes Allâh and His Messenger merits, of course, the Fire of Gehenna wherein he shall abide? That is the great humiliation indeed!

64. Some of the hypocrites (only pretend to) fear that a *Sûrah* might be revealed to them (-the believers) against them, that may acquaint them of what is hidden in their (- hypocrites') minds. Say, 'Take it lightly (if you must), Allâh will surely bring to light what you (simply pretend to) fear (about being disclosed).'

65. And if you (thereupon) ask them (to explain their conduct) they will certainly say, 'We were talking idly and just making a jest.' Say, 'Is it of (the Almighty Being like) Allâh and His revelations and His Messenger that you (dare to) talk so lightly (could you find none else for the purpose!).

66. 'Make no (false) excuses (now), you have certainly disbelieved after your confession of belief. Even if We forgive one party of you, We will punish the (people of the) other party for they are steeped in sin.'

SECTION 9

67. **T**HE hypocrites, both men and women, are all (strictly) alike. They enjoin the wrong and forbid the right and withhold their hands (from spending for the cause of Allâh). They have forsaken Allâh, so He (too) has forsaken them. It is the hypocrites who have truly been the rebellious.

68. Allâh has promised the hypocrites, both men and women, and the disbelievers, the Fire of Gehenna; they shall abide therein. It is sufficient for them. Allâh has rejected them. And for them there awaits a long-lasting punishment.

69. (Say to hypocrites,) 'You are like your predecessors. (But) they were mightier than

سُورَةُ التَّوْبَةِ ٩

أَلِيمٌ ﴿٦١﴾ يَحْلِفُونَ بِاللَّهِ لَكُمْ لِيُرْضُوكُمْ
وَاللَّهُ وَرَسُولُهُ أَحَقُّ أَنْ يُرْضُوهُ إِنْ كَانُوا
مُؤْمِنِينَ ﴿٦٢﴾ أَلَمْ يَعْلَمُوا أَنَّهُ مَنْ يُحَادِدِ
اللَّهَ وَرَسُولَهُ فَأَنَّ لَهُ نَارَ جَهَنَّمَ خَالِدًا
فِيهَا ذَٰلِكَ الْخِزْيُ الْعَظِيمُ ﴿٦٣﴾ يَحْذَرُ الْمُنَافِقُونَ
أَنْ تُنَزَّلَ عَلَيْهِمْ سُورَةٌ تُنَبِّئُهُمْ بِمَا فِي
قُلُوبِهِمْ قُلِ اسْتَهْزِءُوا إِنَّ اللَّهَ مُخْرِجٌ مَا
تَحْذَرُونَ ﴿٦٤﴾ وَلَئِنْ سَأَلْتَهُمْ لَيَقُولُنَّ إِنَّمَا
كُنَّا نَخُوضُ وَنَلْعَبُ قُلْ أَبِاللَّهِ وَآيَاتِهِ
وَرَسُولِهِ كُنْتُمْ تَسْتَهْزِءُونَ ﴿٦٥﴾ لَا تَعْتَذِرُوا
قَدْ كَفَرْتُمْ بَعْدَ إِيمَانِكُمْ إِنْ نَعْفُ عَنْ
طَائِفَةٍ مِنْكُمْ نُعَذِّبْ طَائِفَةً بِأَنَّهُمْ كَانُوا
مُجْرِمِينَ ﴿٦٦﴾ الْمُنَافِقُونَ وَالْمُنَافِقَاتُ بَعْضُهُمْ
مِنْ بَعْضٍ يَأْمُرُونَ بِالْمُنْكَرِ وَيَنْهَوْنَ
عَنِ الْمَعْرُوفِ وَيَقْبِضُونَ أَيْدِيَهُمْ نَسُوا
اللَّهَ فَنَسِيَهُمْ إِنَّ الْمُنَافِقِينَ هُمُ الْفَاسِقُونَ ﴿٦٧﴾
وَعَدَ اللَّهُ الْمُنَافِقِينَ وَالْمُنَافِقَاتِ وَالْكُفَّارَ
نَارَ جَهَنَّمَ خَالِدِينَ فِيهَا هِيَ حَسْبُهُمْ
وَلَعَنَهُمُ اللَّهُ وَلَهُمْ عَذَابٌ مُقِيمٌ ﴿٦٨﴾ كَالَّذِينَ

you in strength and richer in possessions and children. Then they enjoyed their lot for a short time; so you too have enjoyed your lot as your predecessors enjoyed theirs. And you indulged in idle talk as they did (but remember), it is these whose deeds have gone in vain in this world and the Hereafter, and it is these who are completely lost.'

70. Have they not heard the news of their predecessors, of the people of Noah, 'Âd and Thamûd and of the people of Abraham and of the dwellers of Midian, and of the cities (of Sodom and Gomorrah) which were overthrown? There had come to them their Messengers (of God) with clear proofs (but they denied them and suffered the consequences thereof). So it was not Allâh Who dealt with them unjustly but they did injustice to themselves.

71. And the believing men and women both are friends one of another. They enjoin the right and forbid the wrong and observe Prayer and go on presenting the *Zakât* and obey Allâh and His Messenger. It is these on whom Allâh will certainly have mercy. Surely, Allâh is All-Mighty, All-Wise.

72. Allâh has promised the believing men and women both, Gardens served with running streams, they shall abide therein; and (He has also promised them) delightful and goodly dwelling places in Gardens of Eternity. And Allâh's good pleasure is the greatest (blessing) of all. That is the most sublime achievement.

SECTION 10

73. **O** PROPHET! Strive hard against the disbelievers and the hypocrites and remain strictly firm against them. Their abode is Gehenna. What an evil resort it is!

74. These (hypocrites) swear by Allâh that they have said nothing (wrong), whereas they had certainly spoken the word of blasphemy and took to the ways of disbelief after their having

مِنْ قَبْلِكُمْ كَانُوٓا أَشَدَّ مِنْكُمْ قُوَّةً
وَأَكْثَرَ أَمْوَٰلًا وَأَوْلَٰدًا فَاسْتَمْتَعُوا
بِخَلَٰقِهِمْ فَاسْتَمْتَعْتُمْ بِخَلَٰقِكُمْ كَمَا
اسْتَمْتَعَ الَّذِينَ مِنْ قَبْلِكُمْ بِخَلَٰقِهِمْ
وَخُضْتُمْ كَالَّذِي خَاضُوا أُولَٰٓئِكَ
حَبِطَتْ أَعْمَٰلُهُمْ فِي الدُّنْيَا وَالْأٰخِرَةِ
وَأُولَٰٓئِكَ هُمُ الْخَٰسِرُونَ ﴿٦٩﴾ أَلَمْ يَأْتِهِمْ
نَبَأُ الَّذِينَ مِنْ قَبْلِهِمْ قَوْمِ نُوحٍ وَعَادٍ
وَثَمُودَ وَقَوْمِ إِبْرٰهِيمَ وَأَصْحَٰبِ
مَدْيَنَ وَالْمُؤْتَفِكَٰتِ أَتَتْهُمْ رُسُلُهُمْ
بِالْبَيِّنَٰتِ فَمَا كَانَ اللّٰهُ لِيَظْلِمَهُمْ
وَلَٰكِنْ كَانُوٓا أَنْفُسَهُمْ يَظْلِمُونَ ﴿٧٠﴾
وَالْمُؤْمِنُونَ وَالْمُؤْمِنَٰتُ بَعْضُهُمْ أَوْلِيَآءُ
بَعْضٍ يَأْمُرُونَ بِالْمَعْرُوفِ وَيَنْهَوْنَ
عَنِ الْمُنْكَرِ وَيُقِيمُونَ الصَّلٰوةَ وَيُؤْتُونَ
الزَّكٰوةَ وَيُطِيعُونَ اللّٰهَ وَرَسُولَهُ أُولَٰٓئِكَ
سَيَرْحَمُهُمُ اللّٰهُ إِنَّ اللّٰهَ عَزِيزٌ حَكِيمٌ ﴿٧١﴾
وَعَدَ اللّٰهُ الْمُؤْمِنِينَ وَالْمُؤْمِنَٰتِ جَنّٰتٍ
تَجْرِي مِنْ تَحْتِهَا الْأَنْهٰرُ خٰلِدِينَ
فِيهَا وَمَسٰكِنَ طَيِّبَةً فِي جَنّٰتِ عَدْنٍ
وَرِضْوَانٌ مِّنَ اللّٰهِ أَكْبَرُ ذٰلِكَ هُوَ الْفَوْزُ
الْعَظِيمُ ﴿٧٢﴾ يٰٓأَيُّهَا النَّبِيُّ جٰهِدِ الْكُفَّارَ
وَالْمُنٰفِقِينَ وَاغْلُظْ عَلَيْهِمْ وَمَأْوٰىهُمْ
جَهَنَّمُ وَبِئْسَ الْمَصِيرُ ﴿٧٣﴾ يَحْلِفُونَ بِاللّٰهِ
مَا قَالُوا وَلَقَدْ قَالُوا كَلِمَةَ الْكُفْرِ

ع ٩ ١٥

embraced Islam, and they meditated that which they could never attain. And they cherished hatred (against believers) for no other reason but that Allâh and His Messenger had enriched them out of His bounty, If they repent it would be good for them, but if they remain averse Allâh will punish them with a grievous punishment in this world and in the Hereafter, and they shall find neither a patron nor a helper in the entire land.

75. Some among them are those who made a covenant with Allâh (saying), 'If He grants us of His bounty we would most assuredly give alms and be certainly of the righteous (after reforming ourselves).

76. But when He granted them of His bounty they hoarded it and they went back (upon their covenant) and they were averse (to righteousness).

77. Consequently He has punished them by infesting their hearts with hypocrisy lasting till the day they shall meet Him. (This was) because they broke their word to Allâh which they had given Him and because they indulged in lies.

78. Have they not known (yet) that Allâh is aware of their hidden thoughts and their private counsels and that Allâh is fully Aware of all hidden realities?

79. (It is the hypocrites) who find fault with those of the believers who give alms voluntarily and freely and deride such believers who find nothing (to contribute) except their service (or the meager fruit of their toil). Allâh shall look down upon them (for their derision) and for them is a grievous punishment.

80. (It makes no difference to them) whether you ask protection (of God from sins) for these (hypocrites) or you do not ask protection for them. Even if you ask protection for them seventy times Allâh will never protect them (against the consequences of their sins). That is because they disbelieved in Allâh and His Messenger, and Allâh guides no perfidious people

وَكَفَرُوا بَعْدَ إِسْلَٰمِهِمْ وَهَمُّوا بِمَا لَمْ يَنَالُوا
وَمَا نَقَمُوٓا إِلَّآ أَنْ أَغْنَىٰهُمُ اللَّهُ وَرَسُولُهُۥ
مِنْ فَضْلِهِۦ فَإِنْ يَتُوبُوا يَكُ خَيْرًا لَّهُمْ
وَإِنْ يَتَوَلَّوْا يُعَذِّبْهُمُ اللَّهُ عَذَابًا أَلِيمًا
فِي الدُّنْيَا وَالْأٰخِرَةِ وَمَا لَهُمْ فِي الْأَرْضِ
مِنْ وَّلِيٍّ وَّلَا نَصِيرٍ ﴿٧٤﴾ وَمِنْهُمْ مَّنْ عٰهَدَ
اللَّهَ لَئِنْ أٰتٰنَا مِنْ فَضْلِهِۦ لَنَصَّدَّقَنَّ
وَلَنَكُونَنَّ مِنَ الصّٰلِحِينَ ﴿٧٥﴾ فَلَمَّآ أٰتٰهُمْ
مِّنْ فَضْلِهِۦ بَخِلُوا بِهِۦ وَتَوَلَّوْا وَّهُمْ
مُّعْرِضُونَ ﴿٧٦﴾ فَأَعْقَبَهُمْ نِفَاقًا فِي قُلُوبِهِمْ
إِلَىٰ يَوْمِ يَلْقَوْنَهُۥ بِمَآ أَخْلَفُوا اللَّهَ مَا
وَعَدُوهُ وَبِمَا كَانُوا يَكْذِبُونَ ﴿٧٧﴾ أَلَمْ
يَعْلَمُوٓا أَنَّ اللَّهَ يَعْلَمُ سِرَّهُمْ وَنَجْوٰهُمْ
وَأَنَّ اللَّهَ عَلّٰمُ الْغُيُوبِ ﴿٧٨﴾ الَّذِينَ يَلْمِزُونَ
الْمُطَّوِّعِينَ مِنَ الْمُؤْمِنِينَ فِي الصَّدَقٰتِ
وَالَّذِينَ لَا يَجِدُونَ إِلَّا جُهْدَهُمْ
فَيَسْخَرُونَ مِنْهُمْ سَخِرَ اللَّهُ مِنْهُمْ
وَلَهُمْ عَذَابٌ أَلِيمٌ ﴿٧٩﴾ إِسْتَغْفِرْ لَهُمْ أَوْ
لَا تَسْتَغْفِرْ لَهُمْ إِنْ تَسْتَغْفِرْ لَهُمْ
سَبْعِينَ مَرَّةً فَلَنْ يَغْفِرَ اللَّهُ لَهُمْ

(in the ways of success).

SECTION 11

81. **T**HOSE who were left behind (in the *Tabûk* expedition because of their making false excuses) rejoiced in their staying (at home) behind the Messenger of Allâh. They found it hard to strive with their possessions and their persons in the cause of Allâh. And they said (one to another), 'Go not forth to fight in the heat.' Say, 'The fire of Gehenna is even more intense in heat.' If only they could understand (it).

82. (Well!) Let them laugh a little (now) as they have to weep much more to recompense for what they have wrought.

83. Should Allâh bring you (safe and sound) back (from *Tabûk* expedition) and you meet a party of them (- the hypocrites), and they ask leave of you to go forth (to join the next expedition with you) say, 'You shall never go forth with me, nor ever fight an enemy with me. You chose to stay (at home) the first time, now stay with those who remain behind.'

84. Nor shall you ever offer (*Janâzah* or a funeral) Prayer for any one of them who dies, nor stand by the grave of any one of them (to pray), for they disbelieved in Allâh and His Messenger and died while they were (still) disobedient.

85. And let not their possessions and their children cause you to wonder. Allâh only intends to punish them in this life through them (their possessions and children), and that their souls depart while they are still disbelievers.

86. And when a Sûrah (- Qur'ânic chapter) is revealed (enjoining), 'Believe in Allâh and strive along with His Messenger (in the cause of Allâh) even the well-to-do among them ask leave of you and say, 'Leave us alone to be with those who stay (at home).'

ذَٰلِكَ بِأَنَّهُمْ كَفَرُوا بِاللَّهِ وَرَسُولِهِ
وَاللَّهُ لَا يَهْدِي الْقَوْمَ الْفَاسِقِينَ ﴿٨٠﴾ فَرِحَ
الْمُخَلَّفُونَ بِمَقْعَدِهِمْ خِلَافَ رَسُولِ
اللَّهِ وَكَرِهُوا أَنْ يُجَاهِدُوا بِأَمْوَالِهِمْ
وَأَنْفُسِهِمْ فِي سَبِيلِ اللَّهِ وَقَالُوا لَا
تَنْفِرُوا فِي الْحَرِّ ۗ قُلْ نَارُ جَهَنَّمَ أَشَدُّ
حَرًّا ۚ لَوْ كَانُوا يَفْقَهُونَ ﴿٨١﴾ فَلْيَضْحَكُوا
قَلِيلًا وَلْيَبْكُوا كَثِيرًا ۚ جَزَاءً بِمَا
كَانُوا يَكْسِبُونَ ﴿٨٢﴾ فَإِنْ رَجَعَكَ اللَّهُ
إِلَىٰ طَائِفَةٍ مِنْهُمْ فَاسْتَأْذَنُوكَ لِلْخُرُوجِ
فَقُلْ لَنْ تَخْرُجُوا مَعِيَ أَبَدًا وَلَنْ تُقَاتِلُوا
مَعِيَ عَدُوًّا ۖ إِنَّكُمْ رَضِيتُمْ بِالْقُعُودِ
أَوَّلَ مَرَّةٍ فَاقْعُدُوا مَعَ الْخَالِفِينَ ﴿٨٣﴾ وَلَا
تُصَلِّ عَلَىٰ أَحَدٍ مِنْهُمْ مَاتَ أَبَدًا
وَلَا تَقُمْ عَلَىٰ قَبْرِهِ ۖ إِنَّهُمْ كَفَرُوا بِاللَّهِ
وَرَسُولِهِ وَمَاتُوا وَهُمْ فَاسِقُونَ ﴿٨٤﴾ وَلَا
تُعْجِبْكَ أَمْوَالُهُمْ وَأَوْلَادُهُمْ ۚ إِنَّمَا يُرِيدُ
اللَّهُ أَنْ يُعَذِّبَهُمْ بِهَا فِي الدُّنْيَا
وَتَزْهَقَ أَنْفُسُهُمْ وَهُمْ كَافِرُونَ ﴿٨٥﴾
وَإِذَا أُنْزِلَتْ سُورَةٌ أَنْ آمِنُوا بِاللَّهِ
وَجَاهِدُوا مَعَ رَسُولِهِ اسْتَأْذَنَكَ أُولُو
الطَّوْلِ مِنْهُمْ وَقَالُوا ذَرْنَا نَكُنْ

87. They are pleased to be (counted) with the misbehaved and worthless (folk) and a seal has been set upon their hearts so that they do not understand.

88. But the Messenger and those who believed with him strove hard (in the cause of Allâh) with their possessions and their persons, it is these who shall have all the good things and it is these who shall attain their goal.

89. Allâh has provided them Gardens served with running streams (to keep them green and flourishing). Therein they shall abide. That is the sublime achievement.

SECTION 12

90. **A**ND those who make false excuses from among the Arabs of the desert, came (with the request) that leave (- to stay away from defensive fighting) might be given them. And those who made false promises to Allâh and His Messenger stayed (at home). There shall befall those who stuck to disbelief from among them a grievous punishment.

91. (For being unable to proceed on to defensive fighting) no blame lies on the weak, nor on the sick, nor on those who find nothing that they could spend, provided they are sincere and true to Allâh and His Messenger. There is no way (of reproach) against the doers of good to others. And Allâh is Great Protector, Ever Merciful.

92. Nor (a blame lies) on those whom when they came to you (Prophet! with the request) that you should mount them, you said, 'I find not whereon I may mount you.' They then turned away (helpless as they were) while their eyes were overflowing with tears of grief because they could find nothing that they could spend.

93. Blame shall lie only on those who beg leave of you though they are rich. They have chosen to be (numbered) with the misbehaved and worthless (folk). And Allâh has set a seal upon their hearts so that they are not aware (of their loss).

مَعَ الْقٰعِدِينَ ﴿٨٦﴾ رَضُوا بِأَنْ يَكُونُوا
مَعَ الْخَوَالِفِ وَطُبِعَ عَلٰى قُلُوبِهِمْ فَهُمْ
لَا يَفْقَهُونَ ﴿٨٧﴾ لٰكِنِ الرَّسُولُ وَالَّذِينَ
اٰمَنُوا مَعَهُ جٰهَدُوا بِأَمْوٰلِهِمْ
وَأَنْفُسِهِمْ وَأُولٰٓئِكَ لَهُمُ الْخَيْرٰتُ
وَأُولٰٓئِكَ هُمُ الْمُفْلِحُونَ ﴿٨٨﴾ أَعَدَّ اللّٰهُ لَهُمْ
جَنّٰتٍ تَجْرِي مِنْ تَحْتِهَا الْأَنْهٰرُ خٰلِدِينَ
فِيهَا ذٰلِكَ الْفَوْزُ الْعَظِيمُ ﴿٨٩﴾ وَجَآءَ
الْمُعَذِّرُونَ مِنَ الْأَعْرَابِ لِيُؤْذَنَ لَهُمْ
وَقَعَدَ الَّذِينَ كَذَبُوا اللّٰهَ وَرَسُولَهُ
سَيُصِيبُ الَّذِينَ كَفَرُوا مِنْهُمْ عَذَابٌ
أَلِيمٌ ﴿٩٠﴾ لَيْسَ عَلَى الضُّعَفَآءِ وَلَا عَلَى
الْمَرْضٰى وَلَا عَلَى الَّذِينَ لَا يَجِدُونَ
مَا يُنْفِقُونَ حَرَجٌ إِذَا نَصَحُوا لِلّٰهِ
وَرَسُولِهِ مَا عَلَى الْمُحْسِنِينَ مِنْ سَبِيلٍ
وَاللّٰهُ غَفُورٌ رَّحِيمٌ ﴿٩١﴾ وَلَا عَلَى الَّذِينَ
إِذَا مَآ أَتَوْكَ لِتَحْمِلَهُمْ قُلْتَ لَآ أَجِدُ
مَآ أَحْمِلُكُمْ عَلَيْهِ تَوَلَّوْا وَّأَعْيُنُهُمْ
تَفِيضُ مِنَ الدَّمْعِ حَزَنًا أَلَّا يَجِدُوا مَا
يُنْفِقُونَ ﴿٩٢﴾ إِنَّمَا السَّبِيلُ عَلَى الَّذِينَ
يَسْتَـْٔذِنُونَكَ وَهُمْ أَغْنِيَآءُ رَضُوا بِأَنْ
يَكُونُوا مَعَ الْخَوَالِفِ وَطَبَعَ اللّٰهُ
عَلٰى قُلُوبِهِمْ فَهُمْ لَا يَعْلَمُونَ ﴿٩٣﴾

PART الجزء الحادي عشر XI

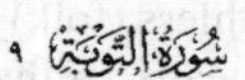

94. **T**HESE (hypocrites) will make (false) excuses to you when you return to them (after the expedition to *Tabûk*. You should at that time) say (to them), 'Make no excuses, we shall never believe you; Allâh has already fully informed us of all the facts relating to you. Allâh will (henceforth) watch your conduct and (so will) His Messenger. Then (at length) you will be brought before Him Who knows the hidden as well as the manifest realities He will then inform you fully about your deeds.'

95. When you go back to them they will certainly swear to you by Allâh (that they had a genuine excuse) so that you may leave them alone (without reproaching them). So leave them alone. Surely, they are altogether unclean and their resort is Gehenna; a deserving recompense for what they want to do.

96. They will swear to you that you may be pleased with them; but even if you are pleased with them (they should know that) Allâh will not be pleased with the disobedient people.

97. The (disbelievers among the) Arabs of the desert are the most stubborn in disbelief and hypocrisy and the most prone not to know the limits of (law) which Allâh has revealed to His Messenger. And Allâh is All-Knowing, All-Wise.

98. And some of the Arabs of the desert regard whatever they spend (in the cause of Allâh) as an undue fine, and they wait for the calamities to (befall) you. On themselves (shall fall) an even worse calamity. And Allâh is All-Hearing, All-Knowing.

99. And some of the Arabs of the desert are such as believe in Allâh and the Last Day and regard whatever they spend (in the cause of Allâh) as means of bringing themselves close to Allâh and (of earning) the blessings of the Messenger. Listen, it is surely a means of bringing them

يعتذرون إليكم إذا رجعتم إليهم
قل لا تعتذروا لن نؤمن لكم قد نبأنا
الله من أخباركم وسيرى الله عملكم
ورسوله ثم تردون إلى علم الغيب
والشهادة فينبئكم بما كنتم تعملون ﴿٩٤﴾
سيحلفون بالله لكم إذا انقلبتم إليهم
لتعرضوا عنهم فأعرضوا عنهم إنهم
رجس ومأوىهم جهنم جزاء بما كانوا
يكسبون ﴿٩٥﴾ يحلفون لكم لترضوا عنهم
فإن ترضوا عنهم فإن الله لا يرضى عن
القوم الفسقين ﴿٩٦﴾ الأعراب أشد كفرا
ونفاقا وأجدر ألا يعلموا حدود ما أنزل
الله على رسوله والله عليم حكيم ﴿٩٧﴾
ومن الأعراب من يتخذ ما ينفق مغرما
ويتربص بكم الدوائر عليهم دائرة
السوء والله سميع عليم ﴿٩٨﴾ ومن الأعراب
من يؤمن بالله واليوم الآخر ويتخذ
ما ينفق قربت عند الله وصلوت الرسول

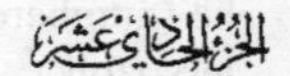

close (to Him). Allâh will certainly admit them to His mercy. Surely, Allâh is Great Protector, Ever Merciful.

SECTION 13

100. AND (as for) the foremost (in spiritual rank, outstripping others in faith and righteous actions) and the first (to embrace Islam) from among the Emigrants and the Helpers and those who followed their example in the best possible manner, Allâh is well-pleased with them and they are well-pleased with Him, He has provided for them Gardens served with running streams (to keep them green and flourishing). They will abide therein forever. That indeed is the most sublime achievement.
101. Some of the Arabs of the desert living around you and some of the people of Madînah (also) are hypocrites. They persist in and are habituated to hypocrisy, you know them not, but We know them. We will punish them again and again (in this life), then they shall be made to revert to a greater punishment (in the Hereafter).
102. And there are others, (among those who stayed behind), who have confessed their faults, they have linked up one good deed with another which is bad, (so their deeds are both good and bad). Allâh is likely to turn to them with mercy. Verily, Allâh is Great Protector, Ever Merciful.
103. (Prophet!) Take a portion of their possessions as *Zakât* so that you may thereby purify them (of their evils) and enhance them in their virtuous deeds, and pray for them, your prayer is indeed a (source of) solace for them. And Allâh is All-Hearing, All-Knowing.
104. Do they not know that Allâh is He Who accepts repentance from His servants and accepts their alms and that Allâh is He Who is Oft-Returning (with compassion), Ever Merciful?
105. And say, 'Go on doing (as you like), Allâh will surely keep an eye on your deeds and (so

أَلَآ إِنَّهَا قُرْبَةٌ لَّهُمْ سَيُدْخِلُهُمُ اللَّهُ فِي
رَحْمَتِهِ إِنَّ اللَّهَ غَفُورٌ رَّحِيمٌ ﴿٩٩﴾ وَالسَّٰبِقُونَ
الْأَوَّلُونَ مِنَ الْمُهَٰجِرِينَ وَالْأَنصَارِ وَالَّذِينَ
اتَّبَعُوهُم بِإِحْسَٰنٍ رَّضِيَ اللَّهُ عَنْهُمْ
وَرَضُوا عَنْهُ وَأَعَدَّ لَهُمْ جَنَّٰتٍ تَجْرِي
تَحْتَهَا الْأَنْهَٰرُ خَٰلِدِينَ فِيهَا أَبَدًا ذَٰلِكَ
الْفَوْزُ الْعَظِيمُ ﴿١٠٠﴾ وَمِمَّنْ حَوْلَكُم مِّنَ
الْأَعْرَابِ مُنَٰفِقُونَ وَمِنْ أَهْلِ الْمَدِينَةِ
مَرَدُوا عَلَى النِّفَاقِ لَا تَعْلَمُهُمْ نَحْنُ
نَعْلَمُهُمْ سَنُعَذِّبُهُم مَّرَّتَيْنِ ثُمَّ يُرَدُّونَ
إِلَىٰ عَذَابٍ عَظِيمٍ ﴿١٠١﴾ وَءَاخَرُونَ اعْتَرَفُوا
بِذُنُوبِهِمْ خَلَطُوا عَمَلًا صَٰلِحًا وَءَاخَرَ سَيِّئًا
عَسَى اللَّهُ أَن يَتُوبَ عَلَيْهِمْ إِنَّ اللَّهَ غَفُورٌ
رَّحِيمٌ ﴿١٠٢﴾ خُذْ مِنْ أَمْوَٰلِهِمْ صَدَقَةً تُطَهِّرُهُمْ
وَتُزَكِّيهِم بِهَا وَصَلِّ عَلَيْهِمْ إِنَّ صَلَوٰتَكَ
سَكَنٌ لَّهُمْ وَاللَّهُ سَمِيعٌ عَلِيمٌ ﴿١٠٣﴾ أَلَمْ
يَعْلَمُوا أَنَّ اللَّهَ هُوَ يَقْبَلُ التَّوْبَةَ عَنْ
عِبَادِهِ وَيَأْخُذُ الصَّدَقَٰتِ وَأَنَّ اللَّهَ هُوَ
التَّوَّابُ الرَّحِيمُ ﴿١٠٤﴾ وَقُلِ اعْمَلُوا فَسَيَرَى

ع ١٣

will) His Messenger and the believers, and you will surely be brought back to Him Who knows the hidden and the manifest realities, then He will tell you all that you have been doing.

106. And there are (yet) others (among those who stayed behind and whose case has been deferred and) who are made to wait for the decree of Allâh. May be He punishes them or may be He turns to them (with mercy). Allâh is All-Knowing, All-Wise.

107. And (there are among the hypocrites) those who have built a mosque to cause harm (to Islam) and to promote disbelief and in order to cause discord among the believers, and to provide a hiding place for him who had already made war against Allâh and His Messenger. And they will certainly swear (saying), 'We meant nothing but good (in building the mosque).' But Allâh bears witness that they are certainly liars.

108. (Prophet!) Never shall you stand in that (mosque for prayer). Certainly, the mosque which was founded upon piety (and observance of duty) from the (very) first day is more worthy that you stand (for Prayer) therein. In this (mosque) there are men (performers of Prayers) who love to become purified; and Allâh loves those who purify themselves externally and internally.

109. Is he, who founded his edifice on taking Allâh as a shield and (on) His good pleasure, better or he who founded his edifice on the brink of a hollowed and crumbling water-worn bank so that it toppled along with him into the Fire of Gehenna? And Allâh guides not the wrongdoing people (to the ways of success).

110. This building of theirs which they have built will never cease to rankle in their hearts unless their hearts are torn to pieces (with anguish and repentance). And Allâh is All-Knowing, All-Wise.

اللهُ عَمَلَكُمْ وَرَسُولُهُ وَالْمُؤْمِنُونَ
وَسَتُرَدُّونَ إِلَىٰ عَلِمِ الْغَيْبِ وَالشَّهَٰدَةِ
فَيُنَبِّئُكُم بِمَا كُنتُمْ تَعْمَلُونَ ﴿١٠٥﴾ وَءَاخَرُونَ
مُرْجَوْنَ لِأَمْرِ اللهِ إِمَّا يُعَذِّبُهُمْ وَإِمَّا
يَتُوبُ عَلَيْهِمْ وَاللهُ عَلِيمٌ حَكِيمٌ ﴿١٠٦﴾ وَالَّذِينَ
اتَّخَذُوا مَسْجِدًا ضِرَارًا وَكُفْرًا وَتَفْرِيقًا
بَيْنَ الْمُؤْمِنِينَ وَإِرْصَادًا لِّمَنْ حَارَبَ
اللهَ وَرَسُولَهُ مِن قَبْلُ وَلَيَحْلِفُنَّ إِنْ
أَرَدْنَا إِلَّا الْحُسْنَىٰ وَاللهُ يَشْهَدُ إِنَّهُمْ
لَكَٰذِبُونَ ﴿١٠٧﴾ لَا تَقُمْ فِيهِ أَبَدًا لَّمَسْجِدٌ
أُسِّسَ عَلَى التَّقْوَىٰ مِنْ أَوَّلِ يَوْمٍ أَحَقُّ
أَن تَقُومَ فِيهِ فِيهِ رِجَالٌ يُحِبُّونَ أَن
يَتَطَهَّرُوا وَاللهُ يُحِبُّ الْمُطَّهِّرِينَ ﴿١٠٨﴾ أَفَمَنْ
أَسَّسَ بُنْيَٰنَهُ عَلَىٰ تَقْوَىٰ مِنَ اللهِ
وَرِضْوَٰنٍ خَيْرٌ أَم مَّنْ أَسَّسَ بُنْيَٰنَهُ عَلَىٰ
شَفَا جُرُفٍ هَارٍ فَانْهَارَ بِهِ فِي نَارِ جَهَنَّمَ
وَاللهُ لَا يَهْدِي الْقَوْمَ الظَّٰلِمِينَ ﴿١٠٩﴾ لَا يَزَالُ
بُنْيَٰنُهُمُ الَّذِي بَنَوْا رِيبَةً فِي قُلُوبِهِمْ إِلَّا أَن
تَقَطَّعَ قُلُوبُهُمْ وَاللهُ عَلِيمٌ حَكِيمٌ ﴿١١٠﴾ إِنَّ

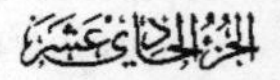

SECTION 14

111. **A**LLÂH has indeed purchased from the believers their persons and their possessions. Theirs, in return, is the (Heavenly) Garden; they fight in the cause of Allâh, so they slay and are slain, an unfailing promise (that He has made) binding upon Himself (as mentioned) in the Torah and the Evangel and the Qur'ân. And who is more faithful and true to his covenant than Allâh? (Believers!) Rejoice over the bargain you have made with Him and this indeed is a great achievement.

112. (These believers are) those who turn to Allâh (in repentance), who worship Him, who praise Him, who fast, who bow down (before Him), who prostrate themselves (in Prayer), who enjoin what is right and forbid what is wrong and who keep the limits set by Allâh. Proclaim to such believers good tidings (of untold gifts in the Heavenly Garden).

113. It is not (proper) for the Prophet and those who believe that they should pray for protection for the polytheists (who have died without repentance) even if they be their near kinsmen, after it has become clear to them that they are the fellows of the flaming Fire.

114. And Abraham's praying for protection for his (idolatrous) sire was only because of a promise he had made to him, but when it became clear to him that he (- his sire) was an enemy to Allâh, he (- Abraham) dissociated himself from him. Abraham was, as a matter of fact, soft of heart (and) forbearing.

115. It is not for Allâh to condemn a people as lost after He has guided them, unless He has made clear to them the things they ought to guard against. Surely, Allâh has full knowledge of everything.

116. Verily, it is Allâh to Whom belongs the kingdom of the heavens and the earth. He gives life and causes death. And you have, apart from Allâh, no friend nor helper.

117. Certainly, Allâh has turned with mercy to

اللهَ اشْتَرٰى مِنَ الْمُؤْمِنِيْنَ أَنْفُسَهُمْ
وَأَمْوٰلَهُمْ بِأَنَّ لَهُمُ الْجَنَّةَ يُقٰتِلُوْنَ فِيْ
سَبِيْلِ اللهِ فَيَقْتُلُوْنَ وَيُقْتَلُوْنَ وَعْدًا
عَلَيْهِ حَقًّا فِي التَّوْرٰىةِ وَالْإِنْجِيْلِ وَالْقُرْاٰنِ
وَمَنْ أَوْفٰى بِعَهْدِهٖ مِنَ اللهِ فَاسْتَبْشِرُوْا
بِبَيْعِكُمُ الَّذِيْ بَايَعْتُمْ بِهٖ وَذٰلِكَ هُوَ
الْفَوْزُ الْعَظِيْمُ ﴿١١١﴾ اَلتّٰٓئِبُوْنَ الْعٰبِدُوْنَ
الْحٰمِدُوْنَ السّٰٓئِحُوْنَ الرّٰكِعُوْنَ السّٰجِدُوْنَ
الْاٰمِرُوْنَ بِالْمَعْرُوْفِ وَالنَّاهُوْنَ عَنِ
الْمُنْكَرِ وَالْحٰفِظُوْنَ لِحُدُوْدِ اللهِ وَبَشِّرِ
الْمُؤْمِنِيْنَ ﴿١١٢﴾ مَا كَانَ لِلنَّبِيِّ وَالَّذِيْنَ اٰمَنُوْٓا
أَنْ يَّسْتَغْفِرُوْا لِلْمُشْرِكِيْنَ وَلَوْ كَانُوْٓا
أُولِيْ قُرْبٰى مِنْ بَعْدِ مَا تَبَيَّنَ لَهُمْ أَنَّهُمْ
أَصْحٰبُ الْجَحِيْمِ ﴿١١٣﴾ وَمَا كَانَ اسْتِغْفَارُ
إِبْرٰهِيْمَ لِأَبِيْهِ إِلَّا عَنْ مَّوْعِدَةٍ وَّعَدَهَآ
إِيَّاهُ فَلَمَّا تَبَيَّنَ لَهٗٓ أَنَّهٗ عَدُوٌّ لِّلّٰهِ تَبَرَّأَ
مِنْهُ إِنَّ إِبْرٰهِيْمَ لَأَوَّاهٌ حَلِيْمٌ ﴿١١٤﴾ وَمَا كَانَ
اللهُ لِيُضِلَّ قَوْمًا بَعْدَ إِذْ هَدٰىهُمْ حَتّٰى
يُبَيِّنَ لَهُمْ مَّا يَتَّقُوْنَ إِنَّ اللهَ بِكُلِّ شَيْءٍ
عَلِيْمٌ ﴿١١٥﴾ إِنَّ اللهَ لَهٗ مُلْكُ السَّمٰوٰتِ
وَالْأَرْضِ يُحْيٖ وَيُمِيْتُ وَمَا لَكُمْ مِّنْ
دُوْنِ اللهِ مِنْ وَّلِيٍّ وَّلَا نَصِيْرٍ ﴿١١٦﴾ لَقَدْ تَّابَ

the Prophet and to the Emigrants and the Helpers who stood by him in the hour of distress (- in the expedition to *Tabûk*) after the hearts of some of the people were about to swerve (from the duty). Again He turned to them with mercy. In fact, He is towards them Most-Loving, Ever Merciful.

118. And (He also turned with mercy) to the three (Companions of the Prophet, *Ka'b* son of *Mâlik, Hilâl* son of *'Umayyah* and *Murârah* son of *Rabî'ah); whose* case was deferred (for decree of Allâh), until the earth, for (all) its spaciousness became narrow for them, and their lives (also) became unbearable for them, and they were convinced that there was no refuge (to escape the punishment) from Allâh save in Him. Then He turned to them with mercy that they might also turn (with repentance to Him). Surely, it is Allâh Who is the Oft-Returning with compassion, the Ever Merciful.

SECTION 15

119. **O** YOU who believe! Keep your duty to Allâh and be with the truthful.

120. It was not proper for the people of Madînah and (for) the Arabs of the desert (who live) around them to have stayed back from the Messenger of Allâh (at the time of expedition to *Tabûk*) nor (was it proper for them) to have preferred their own lives to his. That is because they suffer no thirst, nor fatigue, nor hunger in Allâh's way nor do they make a journey which enrages the disbelievers, nor do they gain an advantage over an enemy, but a righteous deed is credited to their account (in the record of their deeds) because of it. Verily, Allâh suffers not the reward of the doers of good to be lost.

121. Nor do they spend any sum, little or much, nor do they traverse a valley (during their *Jihâd* expedition) but it is recorded to their account, that Allâh may award them the highest (reward) for their deeds.

122. It is not possible for the believers to go forth (from their homes learning for religious

الله على النبي والمهجرين والأنصار الذين
اتبعوه في ساعة العسرة من بعد ما كاد
يزيغ قلوب فريق منهم ثم تاب عليهم
إنه بهم رءوف رحيم ﴿١١٧﴾ وعلى الثلثة
الذين خلفوا حتى إذا ضاقت عليهم
الأرض بما رحبت وضاقت عليهم أنفسهم
وظنوا أن لا ملجأ من الله إلا إليه ثم
تاب عليهم ليتوبوا إن الله هو التواب
الرحيم ﴿١١٨﴾ يأيها الذين ءامنوا اتقوا الله ع ٨ ٣
وكونوا مع الصدقين ﴿١١٩﴾ ما كان لأهل
المدينة ومن حولهم من الأعراب
أن يتخلفوا عن رسول الله ولا يرغبوا
بأنفسهم عن نفسه ذلك بأنهم لا
يصيبهم ظمأ ولا نصب ولا مخمصة
في سبيل الله ولا يطـون موطئا يغيظ
الكفار ولا ينالون من عدو نيلا إلا
كتب لهم به عمل صلح إن الله لا
يضيع أجر المحسنين ﴿١٢٠﴾ ولا ينفقون
نفقة صغيرة ولا كبيرة ولا يقطعون
واديا إلا كتب لهم ليجزيهم الله أحسن
ما كانوا يعملون ﴿١٢١﴾ وما كان المؤمنون

learning) all together. Then, why should not a party from every section of them go forth, that they may (learn and) become well-versed in religion, and may warn their people when they return (home) to them, so that they too may guard against (unislamic ways of life).

SECTION 16

123. **O** YOU who believe! Fight such of the disbelievers as dwell near to you and let them find firmness in you and know that Allâh is with those who become secure against evil.

124. And whenever a *Sûrah* is revealed there are some of these (hypocrites) who say (scornfully), 'Which one of you has this (chapter) increased in faith?' As for the believers it (- the revelation of the chapter) does certainly increase their faith and they do rejoice (therefore).

125. But (as regards) those in whose heart is a disease (of hypocrisy), it (- every new revelation of a chapter) certainly adds more uncleanness to their previous uncleanness and they die while they are still disbelievers.

126. Do they not see that they are tried every year once or twice. Still they do not repent nor would they take heed.

127. And whenever a *Sûrah* is revealed, these (hypocrites) look one at another (as if to ask), 'Is anyone watching you?' Then they turn away. Allâh has turned away their hearts (from the Light) because they are a people devoid of understanding.

128. (People!) Certainly, there has come to you a Messenger from among yourselves; your sufferings tell hard upon him; he is ardently desirous of your (welfare) and (he is) very loving and merciful to the believers.

129. But if they turn their backs (upon you) say, 'Allâh is sufficient for me. There is no other, cannot be and will never be one worthy of worship but He, in Him do I put my trust, and He is the Lord of the Mighty throne.'

لِيَنفِرُوا كَافَّةً فَلَوْلَا نَفَرَ مِن كُلِّ فِرْقَةٍ
مِّنْهُمْ طَائِفَةٌ لِّيَتَفَقَّهُوا فِي الدِّينِ وَلِيُنذِرُوا
قَوْمَهُمْ إِذَا رَجَعُوا إِلَيْهِمْ لَعَلَّهُمْ يَحْذَرُونَ ﴿١٢٢﴾
يَا أَيُّهَا الَّذِينَ آمَنُوا قَاتِلُوا الَّذِينَ يَلُونَكُم
مِّنَ الْكُفَّارِ وَلْيَجِدُوا فِيكُمْ غِلْظَةً وَاعْلَمُوا
أَنَّ اللَّهَ مَعَ الْمُتَّقِينَ ﴿١٢٣﴾ وَإِذَا مَا أُنزِلَتْ سُورَةٌ
فَمِنْهُم مَّن يَقُولُ أَيُّكُمْ زَادَتْهُ هَٰذِهِ إِيمَانًا
فَأَمَّا الَّذِينَ آمَنُوا فَزَادَتْهُمْ إِيمَانًا وَهُمْ
يَسْتَبْشِرُونَ ﴿١٢٤﴾ وَأَمَّا الَّذِينَ فِي قُلُوبِهِم
مَّرَضٌ فَزَادَتْهُمْ رِجْسًا إِلَىٰ رِجْسِهِمْ وَمَاتُوا
وَهُمْ كَافِرُونَ ﴿١٢٥﴾ أَوَلَا يَرَوْنَ أَنَّهُمْ يُفْتَنُونَ
فِي كُلِّ عَامٍ مَّرَّةً أَوْ مَرَّتَيْنِ ثُمَّ لَا يَتُوبُونَ
وَلَا هُمْ يَذَّكَّرُونَ ﴿١٢٦﴾ وَإِذَا مَا أُنزِلَتْ سُورَةٌ
نَّظَرَ بَعْضُهُمْ إِلَىٰ بَعْضٍ هَلْ يَرَاكُم مِّنْ
أَحَدٍ ثُمَّ انصَرَفُوا صَرَفَ اللَّهُ قُلُوبَهُم
بِأَنَّهُمْ قَوْمٌ لَّا يَفْقَهُونَ ﴿١٢٧﴾ لَقَدْ جَاءَكُمْ
رَسُولٌ مِّنْ أَنفُسِكُمْ عَزِيزٌ عَلَيْهِ مَا عَنِتُّمْ
حَرِيصٌ عَلَيْكُم بِالْمُؤْمِنِينَ رَءُوفٌ رَّحِيمٌ ﴿١٢٨﴾
فَإِن تَوَلَّوْا فَقُلْ حَسْبِيَ اللَّهُ لَا إِلَٰهَ إِلَّا هُوَ
عَلَيْهِ تَوَكَّلْتُ وَهُوَ رَبُّ الْعَرْشِ الْعَظِيمِ ﴿١٢٩﴾

CHAPTER
10

سُوْرَةُ يُوْنُسَ ١٠

YÛNUS
(Jonah)
(Revealed before Hijrah)

With the name of Allâh,
the Most Gracious, the Ever Merciful
(I commence to read Sûrah Yûnus).

1. ALIF LÂM RÂ - I am Allâh, the All-Seeing. These are the verses of the perfect Book (which is) full of wisdom.

2. Is this a (matter of) wonder for the people that We have sent Our revelation to a man from among themselves (saying), 'Warn the people (against the evils of disbelief and sin) and give glad tidings to those who believe that they stand on a strong and honourable footing with their Lord?' The disbelievers say, 'Certainly, this (man) is an evident enchanter.'

3. Verily, your Lord is Allâh Who created the heavens and the earth in six aeons and (at the same time) He is well-established on the Throne (of authority). He regulates all affairs. As an intercessor, there can be none (to intercede with Him) save after His leave. Such is Allâh, your Lord, so worship Him. Will you not, then, mind?

4. To Him is the return of you all (eventual). (This) promise of Allâh is certain to be true. He it is Who originates the creation, then He reproduces it, so that He may justly reward those who believe and do deeds of righteousness. And those who disbelieve, they shall have a drink of boiling water and a grievous punishment, because of their disbelieving.

5. He it is Who made the sun (radiate) brilliant light and the moon (reflect) a lustre, and fixed for it (each one of them) stages according to an estimated measure that you might know the

سُوْرَةُ يُوْنُسَ مَكِّيَّةٌ

بِسْمِ اللّٰهِ الرَّحْمٰنِ الرَّحِيْمِ

الٓرٰ تِلْكَ اٰيٰتُ الْكِتٰبِ الْحَكِيْمِ ① أَكَانَ
لِلنَّاسِ عَجَبًا أَنْ أَوْحَيْنَآ إِلٰى رَجُلٍ مِّنْهُمْ
أَنْ أَنْذِرِ النَّاسَ وَ بَشِّرِ الَّذِيْنَ اٰمَنُوْٓا
أَنَّ لَهُمْ قَدَمَ صِدْقٍ عِنْدَ رَبِّهِمْ قَالَ
الْكٰفِرُوْنَ إِنَّ هٰذَا لَسٰحِرٌ مُّبِيْنٌ ② إِنَّ
رَبَّكُمُ اللّٰهُ الَّذِيْ خَلَقَ السَّمٰوٰتِ وَ الْأَرْضَ
فِيْ سِتَّةِ أَيَّامٍ ثُمَّ اسْتَوٰى عَلَى الْعَرْشِ
يُدَبِّرُ الْأَمْرَ مَا مِنْ شَفِيْعٍ إِلَّا مِنْ بَعْدِ
إِذْنِهٖ ذٰلِكُمُ اللّٰهُ رَبُّكُمْ فَاعْبُدُوْهُ أَفَلَا
تَذَكَّرُوْنَ ③ إِلَيْهِ مَرْجِعُكُمْ جَمِيْعًا وَعْدَ
اللّٰهِ حَقًّا إِنَّهٗ يَبْدَؤُا الْخَلْقَ ثُمَّ يُعِيْدُهٗ
لِيَجْزِيَ الَّذِيْنَ اٰمَنُوْا وَ عَمِلُوا الصّٰلِحٰتِ
بِالْقِسْطِ وَ الَّذِيْنَ كَفَرُوْا لَهُمْ شَرَابٌ مِّنْ
حَمِيْمٍ وَّ عَذَابٌ أَلِيْمٌ بِمَا كَانُوْا يَكْفُرُوْنَ ④
هُوَ الَّذِيْ جَعَلَ الشَّمْسَ ضِيَآءً وَّ الْقَمَرَ
نُوْرًا وَّ قَدَّرَهٗ مَنَازِلَ لِتَعْلَمُوْا عَدَدَ السِّنِيْنَ

counting (and number) of the years and the reckoning (of time). Allâh created all this only to suit the requirements of truth and wisdom. He explains in detail these signs for a people who would know.
6. Certainly, in the alternation of night and day and in all that Allâh has created in the heavens and the earth there are sure signs for a people who guard against evil.
7. Verily, those who fear not the meeting with Us, nor do they cherish a hope (for the same) and are pleased to choose the life of this world and feel contented therewith, and (similarly) those who are heedless of Our signs,
8. It is these indeed whose resort is the Fire, because of their (such) deeds.
9. As to those who believe and do deeds of righteousness, their Lord shall lead them, because of their faith, into Gardens of bliss served with running streams (to keep them green and flourishing).
10. Their prayer therein will be, 'Glory be to You, O Allâh!' And their greeting therein (to each other) shall be 'Peace!' And the conclusion of their prayer will be, 'All type of perfect and true praise belongs to Allâh the Lord of the worlds.'

SECTION 2

11. **I**F Allâh were to hasten on the evil for the people (as a consequence of their evil actions), just as they would seek to hasten on (for themselves) the good, (the end of) their term (of life) would certainly have been brought upon them (forthwith). But We leave alone those who fear not the meeting with Us, nor do they cherish any hope (for the same). They are wandering distractedly in their transgression.
12. When a person is in a certain affliction he calls on Us (lying) on his sides, or sitting or standing; but when We remove his affliction he passes on (with his face turned away) as if he had never called on Us for (the removal of) the affliction that befell him. Thus it is that their (base) doings are made fair seeming to these

وَالْحِسَابَ مَا خَلَقَ اللّٰهُ ذٰلِكَ إِلَّا بِالْحَقِّ
يُفَصِّلُ الْأٰيٰتِ لِقَوْمٍ يَّعْلَمُوْنَ ⑤ إِنَّ فِي
اخْتِلٰفِ الَّيْلِ وَالنَّهَارِ وَمَا خَلَقَ اللّٰهُ فِي
السَّمٰوٰتِ وَالْأَرْضِ لَأٰيٰتٍ لِّقَوْمٍ يَّتَّقُوْنَ ⑥
إِنَّ الَّذِيْنَ لَا يَرْجُوْنَ لِقَآءَنَا وَرَضُوْا
بِالْحَيٰوةِ الدُّنْيَا وَاطْمَأَنُّوْا بِهَا وَالَّذِيْنَ
هُمْ عَنْ أٰيٰتِنَا غٰفِلُوْنَ ⑦ أُولٰٓئِكَ مَأْوٰىهُمُ
النَّارُ بِمَا كَانُوْا يَكْسِبُوْنَ ⑧ إِنَّ الَّذِيْنَ أٰمَنُوْا
وَعَمِلُوا الصّٰلِحٰتِ يَهْدِيْهِمْ رَبُّهُمْ بِإِيْمٰنِهِمْ
تَجْرِيْ مِنْ تَحْتِهِمُ الْأَنْهٰرُ فِيْ جَنّٰتِ النَّعِيْمِ ⑨
دَعْوٰىهُمْ فِيْهَا سُبْحٰنَكَ اللّٰهُمَّ وَتَحِيَّتُهُمْ
فِيْهَا سَلٰمٌ وَأٰخِرُ دَعْوٰىهُمْ أَنِ الْحَمْدُ لِلّٰهِ
رَبِّ الْعٰلَمِيْنَ ⑩ وَلَوْ يُعَجِّلُ اللّٰهُ لِلنَّاسِ
الشَّرَّ اسْتِعْجَالَهُمْ بِالْخَيْرِ لَقُضِيَ إِلَيْهِمْ
أَجَلُهُمْ فَنَذَرُ الَّذِيْنَ لَا يَرْجُوْنَ لِقَآءَنَا فِيْ
طُغْيٰنِهِمْ يَعْمَهُوْنَ ⑪ وَإِذَا مَسَّ الْإِنْسٰنَ
الضُّرُّ دَعَانَا لِجَنْۢبِهٖٓ أَوْ قَاعِدًا أَوْ قَآئِمًا
فَلَمَّا كَشَفْنَا عَنْهُ ضُرَّهٗ مَرَّ كَأَنْ لَّمْ
يَدْعُنَآ إِلٰى ضُرٍّ مَّسَّهٗ كَذٰلِكَ زُيِّنَ

extravagant people.

13. And We certainly destroyed several generations before you when they went wrong inspite of the fact that there had come to them their Messengers (of God) with clear proofs but they would not believe. Just (as We repaid them) so We repay all such guilty people (with punishment).

14. Then We made you inherit the land after these (generations) that We might see how you would act.

15. When Our clear verses are recited to them, those who fear not the meeting with Us, nor do they cherish any hope (for the same,) say, 'Bring a Qur'ân other than this one or (at least) make some changes in it.' Say (to them), 'It is not for me to introduce changes in it of my own accord. I follow nothing but what is revealed to me. Truly if I disobey my Lord I fear the punishment of a great (dreadful) Day.'

16. Say, 'Had Allâh (so) willed (that He should replace the teachings of the Qur'ân with some other teachings), I should not have recited this (Qur'ân) to you, nor would He have made it known to you. I had indeed lived among you a (whole) lifetime before this (claim to Prophethood. Was not my truthfulness undisputed?). Will you not then refrain (from opposing me)?'

17. Who is then more unjust than he who forges a lie in the name of Allâh or cries lies to His Messages? It is but certain that the guilty shall never attain their goal.

18. And (some) people worship, apart from Allâh, things that can neither harm them (of their own accord) nor can help them. They say, 'These are our intercessors with Allâh.' Say, 'Do you (presume to) inform Allâh of the things of whose existence in the heavens or in the earth He does not know?' Glory be to Him! High be He, exalted above (all the things) they associate (with Him).

19. And humankind were but a single nation, then they fell into variance. Had it not been for a word (-the postponement of their punishment,

سُورَةُ يُونُسَ ١٠

لِلْمُسْرِفِينَ مَا كَانُوا يَعْمَلُونَ ﴿١٢﴾ وَلَقَدْ أَهْلَكْنَا
الْقُرُونَ مِنْ قَبْلِكُمْ لَمَّا ظَلَمُوا وَجَاءَتْهُمْ
رُسُلُهُمْ بِالْبَيِّنَاتِ وَمَا كَانُوا لِيُؤْمِنُوا كَذَلِكَ
نَجْزِي الْقَوْمَ الْمُجْرِمِينَ ﴿١٣﴾ ثُمَّ جَعَلْنَاكُمْ
خَلَائِفَ فِي الْأَرْضِ مِنْ بَعْدِهِمْ لِنَنْظُرَ
كَيْفَ تَعْمَلُونَ ﴿١٤﴾ وَإِذَا تُتْلَى عَلَيْهِمْ آيَاتُنَا
بَيِّنَاتٍ قَالَ الَّذِينَ لَا يَرْجُونَ لِقَاءَنَا ائْتِ
بِقُرْآنٍ غَيْرِ هَذَا أَوْ بَدِّلْهُ قُلْ مَا يَكُونُ
لِي أَنْ أُبَدِّلَهُ مِنْ تِلْقَاءِ نَفْسِي إِنْ أَتَّبِعُ
إِلَّا مَا يُوحَى إِلَيَّ إِنِّي أَخَافُ إِنْ عَصَيْتُ
رَبِّي عَذَابَ يَوْمٍ عَظِيمٍ ﴿١٥﴾ قُلْ لَوْ شَاءَ اللَّهُ
مَا تَلَوْتُهُ عَلَيْكُمْ وَلَا أَدْرَاكُمْ بِهِ فَقَدْ
لَبِثْتُ فِيكُمْ عُمُرًا مِنْ قَبْلِهِ أَفَلَا تَعْقِلُونَ ﴿١٦﴾
فَمَنْ أَظْلَمُ مِمَّنِ افْتَرَى عَلَى اللَّهِ كَذِبًا أَوْ
كَذَّبَ بِآيَاتِهِ إِنَّهُ لَا يُفْلِحُ الْمُجْرِمُونَ ﴿١٧﴾
وَيَعْبُدُونَ مِنْ دُونِ اللَّهِ مَا لَا يَضُرُّهُمْ وَلَا
يَنْفَعُهُمْ وَيَقُولُونَ هَؤُلَاءِ شُفَعَاؤُنَا عِنْدَ
اللَّهِ قُلْ أَتُنَبِّئُونَ اللَّهَ بِمَا لَا يَعْلَمُ فِي
السَّمَاوَاتِ وَلَا فِي الْأَرْضِ سُبْحَانَهُ وَتَعَالَى
عَمَّا يُشْرِكُونَ ﴿١٨﴾ وَمَا كَانَ النَّاسُ إِلَّا أُمَّةً

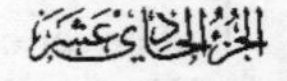

see 8:33) that preceded from your Lord (as His promise), the issue wherein they disagreed would have (long been) decided between them.
20. And they say, 'Why is not a (decisive) sign (of destruction) sent down to him from his Lord?' Say then, 'The hidden reality (will come to pass. The knowledge of it) belongs to Allâh alone, so wait (for the time ordained). Surely, I am with you among those who wait.'

SECTION 3

21. **W**HEN We show mercy to people after adversity has visited them, they at once start scheming (devices) against Our revelations. Say, 'Allâh is Quicker at scheming (counter-devices). Indeed Our messengers (- the angels appointed for the purpose) are recording all that you devise.
22. He it is Who enables you to journey through the land and on the sea. When you are on the ships, and these (means of transport) with those (on board) sail with a fair breeze, while they are taking a joyful pride in them, a violent wind overtakes them, wave (after wave) surges on them from every side, and they feel sure that they are caught in a disaster, (then) they call upon Allâh with a sincere faith in Him (saying), 'If You deliver us from this (calamity) we will certainly be of the thankful.'
23. Nevertheless when He delivers them, behold! they begin to commit excesses in the land for no just reason. O people! Your excesses will only recoil upon your ownselves. Have a temporary enjoyment of the life of this world, then to Us shall be your return (and) then We will tell you all that you have been doing.
24. The life of this world is simply like water. We send it down from the clouds so that the produce of the earth, whereof people and cattle eat, grows with this (water) abundantly until when the earth (by means of it) receives its excellent ornature and has decked itself fairly

وٰحِدَةً فَاخْتَلَفُوا ۚ وَلَوْلَا كَلِمَةٌ سَبَقَتْ
مِنْ رَّبِّكَ لَقُضِيَ بَيْنَهُمْ فِيمَا فِيهِ يَخْتَلِفُونَ ﴿١٩﴾
وَيَقُولُونَ لَوْلَا أُنْزِلَ عَلَيْهِ اٰيَةٌ مِّنْ رَّبِّهِ
فَقُلْ إِنَّمَا الْغَيْبُ لِلّٰهِ فَانْتَظِرُوا إِنِّي مَعَكُمْ
مِّنَ الْمُنْتَظِرِينَ ﴿٢٠﴾ وَإِذَا أَذَقْنَا النَّاسَ رَحْمَةً
مِّنْ بَعْدِ ضَرَّاءَ مَسَّتْهُمْ إِذَا لَهُمْ مَّكْرٌ فِي
اٰيَاتِنَا ۚ قُلِ اللّٰهُ أَسْرَعُ مَكْرًا ۚ إِنَّ رُسُلَنَا
يَكْتُبُونَ مَا تَمْكُرُونَ ﴿٢١﴾ هُوَ الَّذِي يُسَيِّرُكُمْ
فِي الْبَرِّ وَالْبَحْرِ ۖ حَتّٰى إِذَا كُنْتُمْ فِي الْفُلْكِ
وَجَرَيْنَ بِهِمْ بِرِيحٍ طَيِّبَةٍ وَّفَرِحُوا بِهَا
جَاءَتْهَا رِيحٌ عَاصِفٌ وَّجَاءَهُمُ الْمَوْجُ مِنْ
كُلِّ مَكَانٍ وَّظَنُّوا أَنَّهُمْ أُحِيطَ بِهِمْ دَعَوُا
اللّٰهَ مُخْلِصِينَ لَهُ الدِّينَ ۚ لَئِنْ أَنْجَيْتَنَا
مِنْ هٰذِهِ لَنَكُونَنَّ مِنَ الشّٰكِرِينَ ﴿٢٢﴾ فَلَمَّا
أَنْجٰهُمْ إِذَا هُمْ يَبْغُونَ فِي الْأَرْضِ بِغَيْرِ
الْحَقِّ ۗ يٰأَيُّهَا النَّاسُ إِنَّمَا بَغْيُكُمْ عَلٰى أَنْفُسِكُمْ
مَّتٰعَ الْحَيٰوةِ الدُّنْيَا ثُمَّ إِلَيْنَا مَرْجِعُكُمْ
فَنُنَبِّئُكُمْ بِمَا كُنْتُمْ تَعْمَلُونَ ﴿٢٣﴾ إِنَّمَا مَثَلُ
الْحَيٰوةِ الدُّنْيَا كَمَاءٍ أَنْزَلْنٰهُ مِنَ السَّمَاءِ فَاخْتَلَطَ

beautiful and its owners feel sure that they are its masters, unexpectedly We command its destruction either by night or by day, so We render it a field that is mown down as though nothing had existed there the day before. Thus do We explain in detail the signs for a people who reflect.

25. Allâh invites (us all) to the abode of peace and He guides him who wishes to be guided to the exact right path leading to the goal.

26. There shall be the fairest reward and (yet) a good deal more (of blessings) for those who do good to others. Neither gloom (of sorrow) nor (traces of) ignominy shall overspread their faces. It is these who are the (rightful) owners of the Paradise, there they shall abide forever.

27. And (as for) those who knowingly committed evil deeds, they shall be punished in measure with the evil done and ignominy shall cover them. They shall have none to protect them against (the punishment of) Allâh. And (they shall look) as if their faces have been covered with patches of night with no light. It is these who are the fellows of the Fire, they shall abide in it for long.

28. And (imagine) the day when We shall muster all the people together, then We shall say to those who associated partners (with God), 'Keep to your places (in Gehenna) you and your (associated) partners (with God).' Then We shall separate them thoroughly one from another, and their (associated) partners (with God) will say (to them), 'Surely, it was not us that you worshipped;

29. 'So (this day) Allâh suffices as a witness between us and you. We were surely quite ignorant of all that you worshipped.'

30. At that time every soul shall find explicitly that what it had done in the past and they will be brought back before Allâh, their True Patron, and all that they used to forge shall be

بِهِ نَبَاتُ الْأَرْضِ مِمَّا يَأْكُلُ النَّاسُ وَالْأَنْعَٰمُ
حَتَّىٰٓ إِذَآ أَخَذَتِ الْأَرْضُ زُخْرُفَهَا وَازَّيَّنَتْ
وَظَنَّ أَهْلُهَآ أَنَّهُمْ قَٰدِرُونَ عَلَيْهَآ أَتَىٰهَآ
أَمْرُنَا لَيْلًا أَوْ نَهَارًا فَجَعَلْنَٰهَا حَصِيدًا كَأَن
لَّمْ تَغْنَ بِالْأَمْسِ كَذَٰلِكَ نُفَصِّلُ الْأَيَٰتِ
لِقَوْمٍ يَتَفَكَّرُونَ ﴿٢٤﴾ وَاللَّهُ يَدْعُوٓا إِلَىٰ دَارِ
السَّلَٰمِ وَيَهْدِي مَن يَشَآءُ إِلَىٰ صِرَٰطٍ
مُّسْتَقِيمٍ ﴿٢٥﴾ لِّلَّذِينَ أَحْسَنُوا الْحُسْنَىٰ
وَزِيَادَةٌ وَلَا يَرْهَقُ وُجُوهَهُمْ قَتَرٌ وَلَا ذِلَّةٌ
أُولَٰٓئِكَ أَصْحَٰبُ الْجَنَّةِ هُمْ فِيهَا خَٰلِدُونَ ﴿٢٦﴾
وَالَّذِينَ كَسَبُوا السَّيِّـَٔاتِ جَزَآءُ سَيِّئَةٍ
بِمِثْلِهَا وَتَرْهَقُهُمْ ذِلَّةٌ مَّا لَهُم مِّنَ اللَّهِ
مِنْ عَاصِمٍ كَأَنَّمَآ أُغْشِيَتْ وُجُوهُهُمْ
قِطَعًا مِّنَ الَّيْلِ مُظْلِمًا أُولَٰٓئِكَ أَصْحَٰبُ
النَّارِ هُمْ فِيهَا خَٰلِدُونَ ﴿٢٧﴾ وَيَوْمَ نَحْشُرُهُمْ
جَمِيعًا ثُمَّ نَقُولُ لِلَّذِينَ أَشْرَكُوا مَكَانَكُمْ
أَنتُمْ وَشُرَكَآؤُكُمْ فَزَيَّلْنَا بَيْنَهُمْ وَقَالَ
شُرَكَآؤُهُم مَّا كُنتُمْ إِيَّانَا تَعْبُدُونَ ﴿٢٨﴾ فَكَفَىٰ
بِاللَّهِ شَهِيدًا بَيْنَنَا وَبَيْنَكُمْ إِن كُنَّا عَنْ
عِبَادَتِكُمْ لَغَٰفِلِينَ ﴿٢٩﴾ هُنَالِكَ تَبْلُوا كُلُّ نَفْسٍ

lost to them.

SECTION 4

31. **A**SK, 'Who provides you sustenance from the heaven and the earth? Or who controls hearing and sight? And who brings forth the living out of the dead and brings forth the dead out of the living? And who directs and regulates all the affairs (of the universe)?' They will certainly say thereupon, 'It is Allâh.' Then say, 'Will you not even then guard against evil (doings).

32. 'Such, then, is Allâh, your true Lord; so what (would you have) after (discarding) the truth save perdition? Wither are you being turned away (from the truth)?'

33. Just as (He is your true Lord), the verdict of your Lord shall be confirmed against those who rebel, because they do not believe.

34. Say, 'Is there anyone of your (associated) partners (with God) who starts the cycle of creation and then continues it?' Say, 'It is Allâh Who starts the cycle of creation and then continues it. Wither then are you being deviated away (from the truth)?'

35. Ask, 'Is there any of your (associated) partners (with God) who leads to the truth?' Say, 'It is Allâh alone Who leads to the truth. Is then He Who leads to the truth more worthy to be followed or he (assumed to be god) that cannot find the way (himself) unless he be guided? What, then, is the matter with you? How do you judge?'

36. And most of them follow nothing but mere conjecture whereas, by no means, can a conjecture do away with the need of the truth. The fact is, Allâh is Well-Aware of what they do.

37. This Qur'ân is not such as could have been devised (by anyone), besides Allâh. On the contrary (Allâh has revealed it as) a confirmation of all the previous Scriptures and is a clear and detailed explanation of the divine Law. It is wanting in nought, containing nothing doubt-

مَّآ أَسْلَفَتْ وَرُدُّوٓا إِلَى اللهِ مَوْلٰهُمُ الْحَقِّ
وَضَلَّ عَنْهُم مَّا كَانُوا يَفْتَرُونَ ﴿٣٠﴾ قُلْ مَن
يَرْزُقُكُم مِّنَ السَّمَآءِ وَالْأَرْضِ أَمَّن
يَمْلِكُ السَّمْعَ وَالْأَبْصٰرَ وَمَن يُخْرِجُ
الْحَيَّ مِنَ الْمَيِّتِ وَيُخْرِجُ الْمَيِّتَ مِنَ الْحَيِّ
وَمَن يُدَبِّرُ الْأَمْرَ ۚ فَسَيَقُولُونَ اللهُ ۚ فَقُلْ
أَفَلَا تَتَّقُونَ ﴿٣١﴾ فَذٰلِكُمُ اللهُ رَبُّكُمُ الْحَقُّ ۚ فَمَا
ذَا بَعْدَ الْحَقِّ إِلَّا الضَّلٰلُ ۚ فَأَنّٰى تُصْرَفُونَ ﴿٣٢﴾
كَذٰلِكَ حَقَّتْ كَلِمَتُ رَبِّكَ عَلَى الَّذِينَ
فَسَقُوٓا أَنَّهُمْ لَا يُؤْمِنُونَ ﴿٣٣﴾ قُلْ هَلْ مِن
شُرَكَآئِكُم مَّن يَبْدَؤُا الْخَلْقَ ثُمَّ يُعِيدُهٗ ۚ
قُلِ اللهُ يَبْدَؤُا الْخَلْقَ ثُمَّ يُعِيدُهٗ فَأَنّٰى
تُؤْفَكُونَ ﴿٣٤﴾ قُلْ هَلْ مِن شُرَكَآئِكُم مَّن
يَهْدِيٓ إِلَى الْحَقِّ ۚ قُلِ اللهُ يَهْدِي لِلْحَقِّ ۚ
أَفَمَن يَهْدِيٓ إِلَى الْحَقِّ أَحَقُّ أَن يُتَّبَعَ
أَمَّن لَّا يَهِدِّيٓ إِلَّآ أَن يُهْدٰى ۚ فَمَا لَكُمْ
كَيْفَ تَحْكُمُونَ ﴿٣٥﴾ وَمَا يَتَّبِعُ أَكْثَرُهُمْ إِلَّا
ظَنًّا ۚ إِنَّ الظَّنَّ لَا يُغْنِي مِنَ الْحَقِّ شَيْئًا ۚ
إِنَّ اللهَ عَلِيمٌ بِمَا يَفْعَلُونَ ﴿٣٦﴾ وَمَا كَانَ
هٰذَا الْقُرْاٰنُ أَن يُفْتَرٰى مِن دُونِ اللهِ
وَلٰكِن تَصْدِيقَ الَّذِي بَيْنَ يَدَيْهِ

ful, disturbing, harmful or destructive and there is no false charge in it. (It proceeds) from the Lord of the worlds.

38. And yet they say, 'He has forged it.' Then produce a (single) chapter like it, calling upon whomsoever you can (for your help), apart from Allâh, if you are truthful (in your this assertion).

39. Nay, (the thing is that) they have cried lies to that the (full) knowledge of which they could not comprehend and whose (true) significance has not yet been explained to them. Their predecessors cried lies (to the truth) just in the same manner. But behold, how was the end of the wrong doers!

40. There are some who will believe in this (Qur'ân) and there are others among them who will never believe therein, and your Lord knows very well those who act wrongfully.

SECTION 5

41. IF they still cry lies to you, say (to them), 'I will reap the fruit of my actions (useful or harmful as it is) and you will reap the fruit of yours. You are not to blame for what I do, and I am not responsible to account for what you do.

42. And some of them (appear to) give ear to you. Can you make the deaf hear, even though they would not (care to) perceive (in order to be guided aright)?

43. And some of them (appear to) look at you, but can you guide the blind even though they would not care to see (the right guidance)?

44. Verily, Allâh does no injustice to the people at all but the people do injustice to themselves.

45. And on the day when He shall gather them all together (they will feel) as if they had not lived (in this world) but for a fraction of a day. They will recognise (the repentance of) one another. Losers, indeed, were those who denied the (truth of the) meeting with Allâh and would

وَتَفْصِيلَ الْكِتَٰبِ لَا رَيْبَ فِيهِ مِن رَّبِّ
الْعَٰلَمِينَ ﴿٣٧﴾ أَمْ يَقُولُونَ افْتَرَىٰهُ قُلْ فَأْتُوا
بِسُورَةٍ مِّثْلِهِ وَادْعُوا مَنِ اسْتَطَعْتُم مِّن
دُونِ اللَّهِ إِن كُنتُمْ صَٰدِقِينَ ﴿٣٨﴾ بَلْ كَذَّبُوا
بِمَا لَمْ يُحِيطُوا بِعِلْمِهِ وَلَمَّا يَأْتِهِمْ تَأْوِيلُهُ
كَذَٰلِكَ كَذَّبَ الَّذِينَ مِن قَبْلِهِمْ فَانظُرْ
كَيْفَ كَانَ عَٰقِبَةُ الظَّٰلِمِينَ ﴿٣٩﴾ وَمِنْهُم مَّن
يُؤْمِنُ بِهِ وَمِنْهُم مَّن لَّا يُؤْمِنُ بِهِ
وَرَبُّكَ أَعْلَمُ بِالْمُفْسِدِينَ ﴿٤٠﴾ وَإِن كَذَّبُوكَ ع
فَقُل لِّي عَمَلِي وَلَكُمْ عَمَلُكُمْ أَنتُم بَرِيـُٔونَ
مِمَّا أَعْمَلُ وَأَنَا بَرِيٓءٌ مِّمَّا تَعْمَلُونَ ﴿٤١﴾
وَمِنْهُم مَّن يَسْتَمِعُونَ إِلَيْكَ أَفَأَنتَ تُسْمِعُ الصُّمَّ
وَلَوْ كَانُوا لَا يَعْقِلُونَ ﴿٤٢﴾ وَمِنْهُم مَّن يَنظُرُ إِلَيْكَ
أَفَأَنتَ تَهْدِي الْعُمْيَ وَلَوْ كَانُوا لَا يُبْصِرُونَ ﴿٤٣﴾
إِنَّ اللَّهَ لَا يَظْلِمُ النَّاسَ شَيْـًٔا وَلَٰكِنَّ النَّاسَ
أَنفُسَهُمْ يَظْلِمُونَ ﴿٤٤﴾ وَيَوْمَ يَحْشُرُهُمْ كَأَن
لَّمْ يَلْبَثُوا إِلَّا سَاعَةً مِّنَ النَّهَارِ يَتَعَارَفُونَ
بَيْنَهُمْ قَدْ خَسِرَ الَّذِينَ كَذَّبُوا بِلِقَاءِ اللَّهِ

not receive (true) guidance.
46. And We shall show you (O Muhammad! the visitation on them of) some of that (punishment) with which We have threatened these (disbelievers) before We cause you to die. Anyhow they shall all have to return to Us. Moreover Allâh is Witness to all that they do.
47. And for every nation there is a Messenger. So when their Messenger (of God) comes, the issue between them is judged with all fairness, and they are not done injustice to.
48. And they say, 'Tell if you are truthful, when this promise is to be fulfilled?'
49. Say, 'I have no power to hurt or to do good to myself. It shall happen as Allâh will. There is a term appointed for every nation (for the recompense of their actions). When their term comes they cannot remain behind (it) a single moment (to escape from it), nor can they get ahead (of it to avoid it).'
50. Say, 'Tell me, if His punishment overtakes you (unexpectedly) by night or by day. How can those who cut off their ties (with Allâh) hasten away (to escape) from it?
51. 'Will you then believe in it when this (punishment) has (actually) befallen (you)? (It will be useless then and you will be told), "Now (you believe!) whereas you were keen on hastening it on before the appointed time".'
52. At that time it will be said to the wrong doers, 'Suffer the abiding punishment. You are only repaid (with punishment) for those actions of yours that you deliberately committed.'
53. They inquire of you (to inform them), 'Is this (warning about punishment) certain to be true?' Say, 'Yes, by my Lord! It is most surely bound to be true. You cannot frustrate Him (in His purpose in order to avert it).'

SECTION 6

54. **AND** if every soul that has committed wrong had all the treasures of the earth, it would surely offer (the whole of) it to ransom

وما كانوا مهتدين ﴿٤٥﴾ وإما نرينك بعض
الذي نعدهم أو نتوفينك فإلينا مرجعهم
ثم الله شهيد على ما يفعلون ﴿٤٦﴾ ولكل أمة
رسول فإذا جاء رسولهم قضي بينهم بالقسط
وهم لا يظلمون ﴿٤٧﴾ ويقولون متى هذا الوعد
إن كنتم صادقين ﴿٤٨﴾ قل لا أملك لنفسي
ضرا ولا نفعا إلا ما شاء الله لكل أمة
أجل إذا جاء أجلهم فلا يستأخرون
ساعة ولا يستقدمون ﴿٤٩﴾ قل أرأيتم إن
أتاكم عذابه بياتا أو نهارا ماذا يستعجل
منه المجرمون ﴿٥٠﴾ أثم إذا ما وقع آمنتم
به آلآن وقد كنتم به تستعجلون ﴿٥١﴾
ثم قيل للذين ظلموا ذوقوا عذاب الخلد
هل تجزون إلا بما كنتم تكسبون ﴿٥٢﴾
ويستنبئونك أحق هو قل إي وربي إنه
لحق وما أنتم بمعجزين ﴿٥٣﴾ ولو أن لكل
نفس ظلمت ما في الأرض لافتدت به

ع٦

(itself) therewith. And they will express (their) hidden remorse (and repent) when they see the punishment; but the matter will be judged between them equitably and no injustice shall be done to them.

55. Behold! Whatever is in the heavens and the earth belongs to Allâh. Behold! Surely Allâh's promise is true, though most of them do not know (this truth).

56. It is He Who gives life and causes death and to Him you shall all be made to return.

57. O people! There has come to you an exhortation (to do away with your weaknesses) from your Lord and a cure for whatever (disease) is in your hearts, and (a Book full of) excellent guidance and a mercy, (and full of blessings) to the believers (in the ultimate form of the Qur'ân).

58. Say, 'All this (revelation of the Qur'ân) is through the grace of Allâh and His mercy. In this, therefore, let them rejoice, (because) this (Qur'ân) is better than all that they hoard.'

59. Say, 'Have you considered that, out of the provisions Allâh has provided for you, you have classified by yourselves some as unlawful and some lawful?' Say, 'Has Allâh given you leave (to do so) or do you forge lies in the name of Allâh?'

60. What do those, who forge lies in the name of Allâh, think of the Day of Resurrection? Surely, Allâh is Gracious towards humankind but most of them do not thank (Him).

SECTION 7

61. **A**ND (O Prophet!) in whatever state you may be and whatever portion of the Qur'ân you recite that is from Him, and (O people!) you do no work but We are watching over you when you are engrossed therein. There does not escape from your Lord even so much as an atom's weight in the earth or in the heavens, neither is there anything smaller than that nor greater but

وَأَسَرُّوا النَّدَامَةَ لَمَّا رَأَوُا الْعَذَابَ ۚ وَقُضِيَ
بَيْنَهُم بِالْقِسْطِ وَهُمْ لَا يُظْلَمُونَ ﴿٥٤﴾ أَلَآ إِنَّ
لِلَّهِ مَا فِي السَّمٰوٰتِ وَالْأَرْضِ ۗ أَلَآ إِنَّ
وَعْدَ اللَّهِ حَقٌّ وَّلٰكِنَّ أَكْثَرَهُمْ لَا يَعْلَمُونَ ﴿٥٥﴾
هُوَ يُحْيِ وَيُمِيتُ وَإِلَيْهِ تُرْجَعُونَ ﴿٥٦﴾ يٰٓأَيُّهَا
النَّاسُ قَدْ جَآءَتْكُم مَّوْعِظَةٌ مِّن رَّبِّكُمْ
وَشِفَآءٌ لِّمَا فِي الصُّدُورِ ۙ وَهُدًى وَّرَحْمَةٌ
لِّلْمُؤْمِنِينَ ﴿٥٧﴾ قُلْ بِفَضْلِ اللَّهِ وَبِرَحْمَتِهِ
فَبِذٰلِكَ فَلْيَفْرَحُوا ۖ هُوَ خَيْرٌ مِّمَّا يَجْمَعُونَ ﴿٥٨﴾
قُلْ أَرَءَيْتُم مَّآ أَنْزَلَ اللَّهُ لَكُم مِّن رِّزْقٍ
فَجَعَلْتُم مِّنْهُ حَرَامًا وَّحَلٰلًا ۖ قُلْ ءَآللَّهُ أَذِنَ
لَكُمْ أَمْ عَلَى اللَّهِ تَفْتَرُونَ ﴿٥٩﴾ وَمَا ظَنُّ الَّذِينَ
يَفْتَرُونَ عَلَى اللَّهِ الْكَذِبَ يَوْمَ الْقِيٰمَةِ ۖ إِنَّ
اللَّهَ لَذُو فَضْلٍ عَلَى النَّاسِ وَلٰكِنَّ أَكْثَرَهُمْ
لَا يَشْكُرُونَ ﴿٦٠﴾ ع وَمَا تَكُونُ فِي شَأْنٍ وَّمَا
تَتْلُوا مِنْهُ مِن قُرْءَانٍ وَّلَا تَعْمَلُونَ مِنْ
عَمَلٍ إِلَّا كُنَّا عَلَيْكُمْ شُهُودًا إِذْ تُفِيضُونَ
فِيهِ ۚ وَمَا يَعْزُبُ عَن رَّبِّكَ مِن مِّثْقَالِ ذَرَّةٍ
فِي الْأَرْضِ وَلَا فِي السَّمَآءِ وَلَآ أَصْغَرَ مِنْ

it is recorded in a plain book (of divine law and is governed thereby).

62. Behold! The friends of Allâh, neither fear shall overwhelm them, nor shall they (ever) remain in grief.

63. (It is) those who believed and ever kept on guarding against evil.

64. They shall have glad tidings (for they commune with their Lord) in the present life and (also) in the Hereafter. There is no changing the words of Allâh; that indeed is the supreme achievement.

65. And do not let their (-your opponents' hostile) words grieve you, (because) all power belongs to Allâh. He is the All-Hearing, the All-Knowing.

66. Behold! Surely to Allâh belongs whoever is in the heavens and whoever is on the earth. Those who call on gods other than Allâh (as a matter of fact) do not follow their (associated) partners (with Allâh), they follow nothing but (their own) surmises and they do nothing but conjecture.

67. It is He Who made for you the night (dark) so that you may rest in it, and (Who) made the day full of light (that you may work in it). Surely, in this there are many signs for the people who would listen (to the Messages of God).

68. (Some of) these people (have gone so far as to) say, 'Allâh has taken to Him a son?' Holy is He! He is Self-Sufficient. Whatever is in the heavens and whatever is in the earth belongs to Him. You have no authority for (attributing) this (to Him). Do you attribute to Allâh what you do not know (yourselves)?

69. Say, 'Surely, those who forge a lie in the name of Allâh will never attain the goal.'

70. (They will have) some provision (to enjoy) in this world then to Us shall be their return, then We shall make them suffer a terrible punishment because of their hiding (the truth)

ذٰلِكَ وَلَآ أَكْبَرَ إِلَّا فِي كِتٰبٍ مُّبِينٍ ﴿٦١﴾ أَلَآ
إِنَّ أَوْلِيَآءَ اللّٰهِ لَا خَوْفٌ عَلَيْهِمْ وَلَا هُمْ
يَحْزَنُونَ ﴿٦٢﴾ الَّذِينَ أٰمَنُوا وَكَانُوا يَتَّقُونَ ﴿٦٣﴾
لَهُمُ الْبُشْرٰى فِي الْحَيٰوةِ الدُّنْيَا وَفِي
الْأٰخِرَةِ لَا تَبْدِيلَ لِكَلِمٰتِ اللّٰهِ ذٰلِكَ
هُوَ الْفَوْزُ الْعَظِيمُ ﴿٦٤﴾ وَلَا يَحْزُنْكَ قَوْلُهُمْ
إِنَّ الْعِزَّةَ لِلّٰهِ جَمِيعًا هُوَ السَّمِيعُ الْعَلِيمُ ﴿٦٥﴾
أَلَآ إِنَّ لِلّٰهِ مَنْ فِي السَّمٰوٰتِ وَمَنْ فِي الْأَرْضِ
وَمَا يَتَّبِعُ الَّذِينَ يَدْعُونَ مِنْ دُونِ اللّٰهِ
شُرَكَآءَ إِنْ يَتَّبِعُونَ إِلَّا الظَّنَّ وَإِنْ هُمْ
إِلَّا يَخْرُصُونَ ﴿٦٦﴾ هُوَ الَّذِي جَعَلَ لَكُمُ الَّيْلَ
لِتَسْكُنُوا فِيهِ وَالنَّهَارَ مُبْصِرًا إِنَّ فِي ذٰلِكَ
لَأٰيٰتٍ لِّقَوْمٍ يَسْمَعُونَ ﴿٦٧﴾ قَالُوا اتَّخَذَ اللّٰهُ
وَلَدًا سُبْحٰنَهُ هُوَ الْغَنِيُّ لَهُ مَا فِي السَّمٰوٰتِ
وَمَا فِي الْأَرْضِ إِنْ عِنْدَكُمْ مِّنْ سُلْطٰنٍ
بِهٰذَآ أَتَقُولُونَ عَلَى اللّٰهِ مَا لَا تَعْلَمُونَ ﴿٦٨﴾
قُلْ إِنَّ الَّذِينَ يَفْتَرُونَ عَلَى اللّٰهِ الْكَذِبَ
لَا يُفْلِحُونَ ﴿٦٩﴾ مَتٰعٌ فِي الدُّنْيَا ثُمَّ إِلَيْنَا
مَرْجِعُهُمْ ثُمَّ نُذِيقُهُمُ الْعَذَابَ الشَّدِيدَ

and because they continue to disbelieve.

SECTION 8

71. **R**ELATE to them (some of) the life-events of Noah, because he (also) had said to his people, 'O my people! If my station (with God) and my reminding you (of your duty to God) through the Messages of Allâh is hard upon you, (you should bear in mind that as for me) I put my trust in Allâh. (And on your part you should) decide upon your course of action (mustering all your resources to gain success), and call your allies to your help, then do not let your designs be vague to you, then carry them out against me and give me no respite.

72. 'But if you turn back (you will suffer for it). I have asked of you no reward (for any of my services to you). My reward lies with Allâh alone. And I have been commanded to be of those who fully resign themselves (to Him).'

73. But still they cried lies to him. So We saved him (-Noah) and all those who were with him in the Ark and We made them rulers while We drowned those who had cried lies to Our Messages. Behold then, how evil was the end of those who had been warned (beforehand).

74. Then We sent after him (-Noah, many) Messengers to their (respective) people and they brought them clear proofs; but they would not believe (in them), because they had already cried lies to them. In this way We seal the hearts of the transgressors (because of their own stubborn and unjustified refusal to listen).

75. Then We sent after them Moses and Aaron with Our signs to Pharaoh and his chiefs, but they behaved arrogantly. And they were a people who had cut off their ties (with Allâh).

76. And when there came to them the truth from Us, they said, 'This is, of course, enchantment creating dissension.'

77. Moses said, 'Is that how you talk of the truth when it has come to you? Can this be an enchantment, whereas the enchanters never

بِمَا كَانُوا يَكْفُرُونَ ﴿٧٠﴾ وَاتْلُ عَلَيْهِمْ نَبَأَ نُوحٍ
إِذْ قَالَ لِقَوْمِهِ يَٰقَوْمِ إِن كَانَ كَبُرَ عَلَيْكُم
مَّقَامِي وَتَذْكِيرِي بِآيَٰتِ اللَّهِ فَعَلَى اللَّهِ
تَوَكَّلْتُ فَأَجْمِعُوا أَمْرَكُمْ وَشُرَكَاءَكُمْ ثُمَّ
لَا يَكُنْ أَمْرُكُمْ عَلَيْكُمْ غُمَّةً ثُمَّ اقْضُوا إِلَيَّ
وَلَا تُنظِرُونِ ﴿٧١﴾ فَإِن تَوَلَّيْتُمْ فَمَا سَأَلْتُكُم
مِّنْ أَجْرٍ إِنْ أَجْرِيَ إِلَّا عَلَى اللَّهِ وَأُمِرْتُ
أَنْ أَكُونَ مِنَ الْمُسْلِمِينَ ﴿٧٢﴾ فَكَذَّبُوهُ فَنَجَّيْنَٰهُ
وَمَن مَّعَهُ فِي الْفُلْكِ وَجَعَلْنَٰهُمْ خَلَٰٓئِفَ
وَأَغْرَقْنَا الَّذِينَ كَذَّبُوا بِآيَٰتِنَا فَانظُرْ كَيْفَ
كَانَ عَٰقِبَةُ الْمُنذَرِينَ ﴿٧٣﴾ ثُمَّ بَعَثْنَا مِنْ
بَعْدِهِ رُسُلًا إِلَىٰ قَوْمِهِمْ فَجَاءُوهُم بِالْبَيِّنَٰتِ
فَمَا كَانُوا لِيُؤْمِنُوا بِمَا كَذَّبُوا بِهِ مِن قَبْلُ
كَذَٰلِكَ نَطْبَعُ عَلَىٰ قُلُوبِ الْمُعْتَدِينَ ﴿٧٤﴾ ثُمَّ
بَعَثْنَا مِنْ بَعْدِهِم مُّوسَىٰ وَهَٰرُونَ إِلَىٰ فِرْعَوْنَ
وَمَلَإِيْهِ بِآيَٰتِنَا فَاسْتَكْبَرُوا وَكَانُوا قَوْمًا
مُّجْرِمِينَ ﴿٧٥﴾ فَلَمَّا جَاءَهُمُ الْحَقُّ مِنْ عِندِنَا
قَالُوا إِنَّ هَٰذَا لَسِحْرٌ مُّبِينٌ ﴿٧٦﴾ قَالَ مُوسَىٰ
أَتَقُولُونَ لِلْحَقِّ لَمَّا جَاءَكُمْ أَسِحْرٌ هَٰذَا وَلَا

attain their goal?'

78. They said, 'Have you come to us that you may turn us away from what we found our forefathers practising and to make sure that you two reign supreme in the land? But (remember) we will not believe in either of you at all.'

79. And Pharaoh said (to his people), 'Bring every skilled sorcerer to me.'

80. Now when the sorcerers came, Moses said to them, 'Present whatever you have to present.'

81. Then, when they had presented (what they would present), Moses said, 'What you have brought is a mere deception. Allâh will soon render it void (because) Allâh does not at all allow the machination of the mischief-makers to thrive.

82. 'And Allâh will establish the truth by dint of His decrees even though the guilty may find (it) hard.'

SECTION 9

83. **N**ONE, however, but a few youths from among his people accepted Moses (while others held back), for fear of Pharaoh and their chiefs lest he should persecute them. And surely Pharaoh was ever a tyrant in the land and truthfully he was of those who committed excesses (and high-handedness).

84. And Moses said, 'O my people! Put your trust in Allâh, if you have (really) believed in Him (and) if you have (truly) submitted (to His will).'

85. Thereupon they said, 'In Allâh alone do we put our trust. Our Lord! Do not make us a target of persecution of the wrongdoing people.

86. 'And deliver us by your mercy from (the evil designs of) the disbelieving people.'

87. And We spoke to Moses and his brother (Aaron saying), 'You both should prepare lodging for your people (bringing them together from different parts of the country) in the central town (of Egypt) and make your houses so as to face one another and perform worship.' And (We also revealed to them to) proclaim

يفلح السحرون ﴿٧٧﴾ قالوا أجئتنا لتلفتنا عما
وجدنا عليه ءاباءنا وتكون لكما الكبرياء
في الأرض وما نحن لكما بمؤمنين ﴿٧٨﴾
وقال فرعون ائتوني بكل سحر عليم ﴿٧٩﴾
فلما جاء السحرة قال لهم موسى ألقوا ما
أنتم ملقون ﴿٨٠﴾ فلما ألقوا قال موسى ما جئتم
به السحر إن الله سيبطله إن الله لا
يصلح عمل المفسدين ﴿٨١﴾ ويحق الله الحق
بكلمته ولو كره المجرمون ﴿٨٢﴾ فما ءامن
لموسى إلا ذرية من قومه على خوف من
فرعون وملإيهم أن يفتنهم وإن فرعون
لعال في الأرض وإنه لمن المسرفين ﴿٨٣﴾
وقال موسى يقوم إن كنتم ءامنتم بالله
فعليه توكلوا إن كنتم مسلمين ﴿٨٤﴾ فقالوا
على الله توكلنا ربنا لا تجعلنا فتنة
للقوم الظلمين ﴿٨٥﴾ ونجنا برحمتك من
القوم الكفرين ﴿٨٦﴾ وأوحينا إلى موسى
وأخيه أن تبوءا لقومكما بمصر بيوتا
واجعلوا بيوتكم قبلة وأقيموا الصلوة

ع ١٣

good tidings (of success) to the believers.
88. And Moses said (praying and Aaron joined him in prayer), 'Our Lord! You have given Pharaoh and his chiefs pomp and wealth in the present life with the result, Our Lord! That they lead people astray from Your path. Our Lord! Destroy their wealth and attack their hearts, so that they believe not until they see the grievous punishment.'
89. (The Lord) said, 'The prayer of you both has been accepted, so remain you two steadfast and follow not the way of those who do not know.'
90. And We brought the Children of Israel across the sea, and Pharaoh and his legion pursued them in wanton aggression and for no justified cause till when he (Pharaoh) was about to be drowned, he cried, 'I (confess and) believe that there is no one worthy of worship but He in Whom the Children of Israel have believed in, and I am of those who submit (to Him).'
91. (The Lord) said, 'What! (do you remember) now (while dying), whereas you had (always) disobeyed before (this), and you had been of the miscreants!
92. 'So, on this day We will preserve you in your body (only) that you may be a sign (to learn a lesson from) for the coming generations, though most of the people are quite heedless of Our signs.'

SECTION 10

93. **A**ND We assigned to the Children of Israel an excellent place to settle (in Palestine), and We provided them with good and pure things; and they differed not (among themselves) until there had come to them true knowledge. Surely, your Lord will, on the Day of Resurrection, settle the issue between them concerning which they differ (now).
94. And if you (O reader!) are in doubt regard-

وَبَشِّرِ الْمُؤْمِنِينَ ﴿٨٧﴾ وَقَالَ مُوسَىٰ رَبَّنَا إِنَّكَ
آتَيْتَ فِرْعَوْنَ وَمَلَأَهُ زِينَةً وَأَمْوَالًا فِي
الْحَيَاةِ الدُّنْيَا رَبَّنَا لِيُضِلُّوا عَنْ سَبِيلِكَ
رَبَّنَا اطْمِسْ عَلَىٰ أَمْوَالِهِمْ وَاشْدُدْ عَلَىٰ
قُلُوبِهِمْ فَلَا يُؤْمِنُوا حَتَّىٰ يَرَوُا الْعَذَابَ
الْأَلِيمَ ﴿٨٨﴾ قَالَ قَدْ أُجِيبَتْ دَعْوَتُكُمَا فَاسْتَقِيمَا
وَلَا تَتَّبِعَانِّ سَبِيلَ الَّذِينَ لَا يَعْلَمُونَ ﴿٨٩﴾
وَجَاوَزْنَا بِبَنِي إِسْرَائِيلَ الْبَحْرَ فَأَتْبَعَهُمْ فِرْعَوْنُ
وَجُنُودُهُ بَغْيًا وَعَدْوًا حَتَّىٰ إِذَا أَدْرَكَهُ الْغَرَقُ
قَالَ آمَنْتُ أَنَّهُ لَا إِلَٰهَ إِلَّا الَّذِي آمَنَتْ
بِهِ بَنُو إِسْرَائِيلَ وَأَنَا مِنَ الْمُسْلِمِينَ ﴿٩٠﴾
آلْآنَ وَقَدْ عَصَيْتَ قَبْلُ وَكُنْتَ مِنَ
الْمُفْسِدِينَ ﴿٩١﴾ فَالْيَوْمَ نُنَجِّيكَ بِبَدَنِكَ
لِتَكُونَ لِمَنْ خَلْفَكَ آيَةً ۚ وَإِنَّ كَثِيرًا
مِنَ النَّاسِ عَنْ آيَاتِنَا لَغَافِلُونَ ﴿٩٢﴾ وَلَقَدْ بَوَّأْنَا
بَنِي إِسْرَائِيلَ مُبَوَّأَ صِدْقٍ وَرَزَقْنَاهُمْ مِنَ
الطَّيِّبَاتِ فَمَا اخْتَلَفُوا حَتَّىٰ جَاءَهُمُ الْعِلْمُ
إِنَّ رَبَّكَ يَقْضِي بَيْنَهُمْ يَوْمَ الْقِيَامَةِ فِيمَا كَانُوا فِيهِ
يَخْتَلِفُونَ ﴿٩٣﴾ فَإِنْ كُنْتَ فِي شَكٍّ مِمَّا أَنْزَلْنَا

ing that which We have revealed to you, ask those who have read this Book (- the Qur'ân) before you. (They will tell you that) there has, in fact, come to you the perfect truth from your Lord, so be not of the contenders at all.

95. And be not of those who cry lies to the Messages of Allâh, for then you shall be of the losers.

96. Verily, those against whom the verdict (of punishment) of your Lord has been confirmed will not believe,

97. Till they see the grievous punishment, even though they have witnessed every (kind of) sign.

98. Why was there no community other than the people of Jonah who should have believed (as a whole), so that their belief would have done them good? (If it had been so it would have been much better), for when they (-the people of Jonah) believed, We spared them a humiliating punishment in the present life and We gave them provision (to avail themselves therefrom) for a time.

99. And if your Lord had (enforced) His will those who are on the earth would have believed one and all. Would you then constrain the people to become believers (while Allâh has not forced them to believe)?

100. Indeed, no one can believe save by the leave of Allâh. Yet He will inflict (His) punishment on those who would not refrain (from evil).

101. Say, 'Behold (the miracles) which are happening in the heavens and the earth (in support of the Prophet Muhammad,) though, (it is true at the same time) that signs and warnings are of no good to a people who do not believe (owing to obstinacy and ignorance).

102. They only wait for the like of the calamities (to be repeated) as were suffered by those

إِلَيْكَ فَسْـَٔلِ الَّذِينَ يَقْرَءُونَ الْكِتٰبَ مِنْ
قَبْلِكَ لَقَدْ جَآءَكَ الْحَقُّ مِنْ رَّبِّكَ فَلَا تَكُونَنَّ
مِنَ الْمُمْتَرِينَ ﴿٩٤﴾ وَلَا تَكُونَنَّ مِنَ الَّذِينَ
كَذَّبُوا بِأٰيٰتِ اللهِ فَتَكُونَ مِنَ الْخٰسِرِينَ ﴿٩٥﴾
إِنَّ الَّذِينَ حَقَّتْ عَلَيْهِمْ كَلِمَتُ رَبِّكَ لَا
يُؤْمِنُونَ ﴿٩٦﴾ وَلَوْ جَآءَتْهُمْ كُلُّ أٰيَةٍ حَتّٰى يَرَوُا
الْعَذَابَ الْأَلِيمَ ﴿٩٧﴾ فَلَوْلَا كَانَتْ قَرْيَةٌ
أٰمَنَتْ فَنَفَعَهَآ إِيمٰنُهَآ إِلَّا قَوْمَ يُونُسَ
لَمَّآ أٰمَنُوا كَشَفْنَا عَنْهُمْ عَذَابَ الْخِزْيِ
فِي الْحَيٰوةِ الدُّنْيَا وَمَتَّعْنٰهُمْ إِلٰى حِينٍ ﴿٩٨﴾
وَلَوْ شَآءَ رَبُّكَ لَأٰمَنَ مَنْ فِي الْأَرْضِ كُلُّهُمْ
جَمِيعًا أَفَأَنْتَ تُكْرِهُ النَّاسَ حَتّٰى يَكُونُوا
مُؤْمِنِينَ ﴿٩٩﴾ وَمَا كَانَ لِنَفْسٍ أَنْ تُؤْمِنَ
إِلَّا بِإِذْنِ اللهِ وَيَجْعَلُ الرِّجْسَ عَلَى الَّذِينَ
لَا يَعْقِلُونَ ﴿١٠٠﴾ قُلِ انْظُرُوا مَاذَا فِي السَّمٰوٰتِ
وَالْأَرْضِ وَمَا تُغْنِي الْأٰيٰتُ وَالنُّذُرُ
عَنْ قَوْمٍ لَّا يُؤْمِنُونَ ﴿١٠١﴾ فَهَلْ يَنْتَظِرُونَ

who passed away before them. Say, 'Wait then (and) I am with you among those who wait.'
103. Then (when the punishment descends, We shall destroy the evildoers, but) We shall save Our Messengers and those who believed. Thus (does it always happen), We have made it binding upon Ourselves to save the believers.

SECTION 11

104. SAY, 'O you people! If you are in doubt regarding my creed, then (be sure that) I do not worship those whom you worship apart from Allâh, but I worship Allâh (alone), Who causes you to die. And I have been commanded that I should be of the believers.
105. 'And (I have also been commanded to convey to you God's Message), "Devote your attention to the true faith in an upright manner, and be not of the polytheists.
106. "And do not call upon, apart from Allâh any other that can neither do good to you, nor can harm you (of his own) for if you do so you shall certainly be of the unjust".'
107. And if Allâh afflicts you with harm, none can remove it but He, and if He desires any good for you, none can stop His bounty. He bestows it on whomsoever of His servants He wishes. And He is the Great Protector, the Ever Merciful.
108. Say, 'O you people! There has come to you the truth from your Lord, so whosoever follows guidance follows it only for (the good of) his own soul, and he who goes astray, only goes astray against it. And I am not responsible for you.
109. And follow that which is revealed to you and patiently persevere till Allâh gives His judgment, for He is the Best of judges.

سورة يونس ١٠

إلا مثل أيام الذين خلوا من قبلهم
قل فانتظروا إني معكم من المنتظرين ﴿١٠٢﴾
ثم ننجي رسلنا والذين آمنوا كذلك
حقا علينا ننج المؤمنين ﴿١٠٣﴾ قل يأيها
الناس إن كنتم في شك من ديني فلا
أعبد الذين تعبدون من دون الله
ولكن أعبد الله الذي يتوفىكم وأمرت
أن أكون من المؤمنين ﴿١٠٤﴾ وأن أقم
وجهك للدين حنيفا ولا تكونن من
المشركين ﴿١٠٥﴾ ولا تدع من دون الله ما
لا ينفعك ولا يضرك فإن فعلت فإنك
إذا من الظلمين ﴿١٠٦﴾ وإن يمسسك الله بضر
فلا كاشف له إلا هو وإن يردك بخير فلا
راد لفضله يصيب به من يشاء من عباده
وهو الغفور الرحيم ﴿١٠٧﴾ قل يأيها الناس
قد جاءكم الحق من ربكم فمن
اهتدى فإنما يهتدي لنفسه ومن
ضل فإنما يضل عليها وما أنا عليكم
بوكيل ﴿١٠٨﴾ واتبع ما يوحى إليك واصبر
حتى يحكم الله وهو خير الحكمين ﴿١٠٩﴾

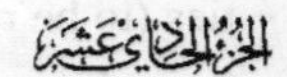

CHAPTER
11

سُورَةُ هُودٍ ١١

HÛD
(Hûd)
(Revealed before Hijrah)

سُورَةُ هُودٍ مَكِّيَّةٌ

With the name of Allâh,
the Most Gracious, the Ever Merciful
(I commence to read Sûrah Hûd).

بِسْمِ اللّٰهِ الرَّحْمٰنِ الرَّحِيمِ

1. ALIF LÂM RÂ - I am Allâh, the All-Seeing. (This is) a Book, whose verses have been characterised by wisdom and they have been explained in detail. It is from One All-Wise, All-Aware (God).

2. (Say, O Prophet!) 'You worship none but Allâh, (and) I am indeed to you a Warner (warning you against the evil consequences of disbelief and evil doings), and a Bearer of good tidings (to the righteous) from Him.

3. 'And that you seek the protection of your Lord (against your faults) and then turn to Him (in repentance). He will provide for you a goodly provision (in this life) till an appointed term. And He will grant of His abounding bounty to every one possessed of abundant merit. And if you turn away, then surely I fear the punishment of a great (dreadful) Day for you.

4. 'To Allâh is your return and He is the Possessor of full power to do all that He will.'

5. Behold! They fold up their bosoms (refusing to accept the truth with open minds and in an effort) that they may hide (their enmity and hatred) from Him. Behold! Even (as they try to hide their true selves) when they wrap themselves in their garments (so that they might not see Divine signs, nor hear His Messages), He knows what they conceal and what they reveal. He is Well-Aware of what is in the (depths of their) hearts.

الٓرٰ كِتٰبٌ أُحْكِمَتْ ءَايٰتُهُۥ ثُمَّ فُصِّلَتْ مِن
لَّدُنْ حَكِيمٍ خَبِيرٍ ﴿١﴾ أَلَّا تَعْبُدُوٓا إِلَّا اللّٰهَ
إِنَّنِي لَكُم مِّنْهُ نَذِيرٌ وَبَشِيرٌ ﴿٢﴾ وَأَنِ
اسْتَغْفِرُوا رَبَّكُمْ ثُمَّ تُوبُوٓا إِلَيْهِ يُمَتِّعْكُم مَّتٰعًا
حَسَنًا إِلَىٰٓ أَجَلٍ مُّسَمًّى وَيُؤْتِ كُلَّ ذِي
فَضْلٍ فَضْلَهُۥ وَإِن تَوَلَّوْا فَإِنِّيٓ أَخَافُ عَلَيْكُمْ
عَذَابَ يَوْمٍ كَبِيرٍ ﴿٣﴾ إِلَى اللّٰهِ مَرْجِعُكُمْ
وَهُوَ عَلَىٰ كُلِّ شَيْءٍ قَدِيرٌ ﴿٤﴾ أَلَآ إِنَّهُمْ يَثْنُونَ
صُدُورَهُمْ لِيَسْتَخْفُوا مِنْهُ أَلَا حِينَ
يَسْتَغْشُونَ ثِيَابَهُمْ يَعْلَمُ مَا يُسِرُّونَ
وَمَا يُعْلِنُونَ إِنَّهُۥ عَلِيمٌۢ بِذَاتِ الصُّدُورِ ﴿٥﴾

الجزء الحادي عشر

PART الجزء الثاني عشر XII

سورة هود ١١

6. **T**HERE is not a single moving creature on the earth but its sustenance rests with Allâh. He knows its permanent lodging place and its temporary sojourn. Everyone is governed by a clear law.

7. And it is He Who created the heavens and the earth in six aeons and His Throne (of power ever) rests on water (to which the life is due), that He might show whoever of you is best in deeds and conduct. And if you were to say (to them), 'You are indeed going to be raised after death,' those who disbelieve will certainly say, 'This is naught but an obvious hoax.'

8. In fact, if We defer the punishment from them till a reckoned time they would certainly ask, 'What is that which withholds it?' Behold! The day this (punishment) befalls them, it shall not be such as to be averted from them. And that (punishment) which they used to hold in scorn, shall overwhelm them.

SECTION 2

9. **A**ND if We bestow upon a human being mercy from Us and then withdraw it from him, he is totally despairing (and) completely ungrateful.

10. And if We confer upon him (Our) blessings after adversity has afflicted him, he will certainly say, 'Gone are all my woes (now).' He is, of course, exultant and boastful (over a little favour).

11. Such, however, is not the case with those who steadfastly persevere (in virtues) and do deeds of righteousness. It is these for whom there awaits protection and a great reward.

12. (The disbelievers vainly hope that) you may omit a part of the revelations made to you; and that you will be distressed and worried because of the fact that they say, 'Why has not a treasure been sent down to him, or why

وَمَا مِن دَآبَّةٍ فِي الْأَرْضِ إِلَّا عَلَى اللَّهِ رِزْقُهَا وَيَعْلَمُ مُسْتَقَرَّهَا وَمُسْتَوْدَعَهَا كُلٌّ فِي كِتَٰبٍ مُّبِينٍ ﴿٦﴾ وَهُوَ الَّذِي خَلَقَ السَّمَٰوَٰتِ وَالْأَرْضَ فِي سِتَّةِ أَيَّامٍ وَكَانَ عَرْشُهُ عَلَى الْمَاءِ لِيَبْلُوَكُمْ أَيُّكُمْ أَحْسَنُ عَمَلًا وَلَئِن قُلْتَ إِنَّكُم مَّبْعُوثُونَ مِن بَعْدِ الْمَوْتِ لَيَقُولَنَّ الَّذِينَ كَفَرُوا إِنْ هَٰذَا إِلَّا سِحْرٌ مُّبِينٌ ﴿٧﴾ وَلَئِنْ أَخَّرْنَا عَنْهُمُ الْعَذَابَ إِلَىٰ أُمَّةٍ مَّعْدُودَةٍ لَّيَقُولُنَّ مَا يَحْبِسُهُ أَلَا يَوْمَ يَأْتِيهِمْ لَيْسَ مَصْرُوفًا عَنْهُمْ وَحَاقَ بِهِم مَّا كَانُوا بِهِ يَسْتَهْزِءُونَ ﴿٨﴾ وَلَئِنْ أَذَقْنَا الْإِنسَٰنَ مِنَّا رَحْمَةً ثُمَّ نَزَعْنَٰهَا مِنْهُ إِنَّهُ لَيَـُٔوسٌ كَفُورٌ ﴿٩﴾ وَلَئِنْ أَذَقْنَٰهُ نَعْمَاءَ بَعْدَ ضَرَّاءَ مَسَّتْهُ لَيَقُولَنَّ ذَهَبَ السَّيِّـَٔاتُ عَنِّي إِنَّهُ لَفَرِحٌ فَخُورٌ ﴿١٠﴾ إِلَّا الَّذِينَ صَبَرُوا وَعَمِلُوا الصَّٰلِحَٰتِ أُولَٰئِكَ لَهُم مَّغْفِرَةٌ وَأَجْرٌ كَبِيرٌ ﴿١١﴾ فَلَعَلَّكَ تَارِكٌ بَعْضَ مَا يُوحَىٰ إِلَيْكَ وَضَائِقٌ بِهِ صَدْرُكَ أَن يَقُولُوا لَوْلَا أُنزِلَ عَلَيْهِ كَنزٌ أَوْ جَاءَ مَعَهُ مَلَكٌ إِنَّمَا أَنتَ نَذِيرٌ وَاللَّهُ عَلَىٰ

has no angel come with him?' (This is far from you that you do such things,) for you are only a Warner (against the evil consequences of disbelief and rebellion), and Allâh is Guardian over every thing.

13. Do they say, 'He has forged this (Qur'ân)?' Say (to them in reply), 'If you are truthful (in your objection then) bring ten forged chapters like it, calling upon whom you can (for your help) apart from Allâh.'

14. But if they do not respond to you, then know that this (Qur'ân) which has been revealed is (replete) with (that which is only within) Allâh's knowledge and that there is no other, cannot be and will never be one worthy of worship save Him. Will you then be the submitting ones (after knowing all this)?

15. Those who desire (the provisions of) this present life and its ornature, We will repay them in full (the reward) for their deeds in this (very life) and they will be made to suffer no loss therein.

16. It is these for whom waits nothing in the Hereafter but the Fire. And all that they do for the sake of this (life) shall come to naught (in the next) and all their activities shall prove vain and futile.

17. How can he, who stands upon a clear proof from his Lord and (to testify to whose truth) a witness from Him follows him and (to witness whom) he is preceded by the Book of Moses, which was a guide and a mercy, (be an impostor)? Those (who keep in view all these clear proofs from their Lord) believe in him (-this Messenger of God). And whoever of these parties disbelieves in him, the Fire is his promised place. So (O reader!) be you not in doubt about this (Qur'ân). It is indeed the Truth. It is from your Lord, but most people do not believe.

18. And who is more unjust than those who forge lies in the name of Allâh. They shall be produced before their Lord and the witnesses will all say, 'These are they who lied against their Lord.' Beware! The disapproval of Allâh lies upon the

كُلِّ شَيْءٍ وَكِيلٌ ﴿١٢﴾ أَمْ يَقُولُونَ افْتَرَىٰهُ
قُلْ فَأْتُوا بِعَشْرِ سُوَرٍ مِّثْلِهِ مُفْتَرَيَٰتٍ
وَادْعُوا مَنِ اسْتَطَعْتُم مِّن دُونِ اللَّهِ إِن
كُنتُمْ صَٰدِقِينَ ﴿١٣﴾ فَإِلَّمْ يَسْتَجِيبُوا لَكُمْ
فَاعْلَمُوا أَنَّمَا أُنزِلَ بِعِلْمِ اللَّهِ وَأَن لَّا
إِلَٰهَ إِلَّا هُوَ فَهَلْ أَنتُم مُّسْلِمُونَ ﴿١٤﴾ مَن
كَانَ يُرِيدُ الْحَيَوٰةَ الدُّنْيَا وَزِينَتَهَا نُوَفِّ إِلَيْهِمْ
أَعْمَٰلَهُمْ فِيهَا وَهُمْ فِيهَا لَا يُبْخَسُونَ ﴿١٥﴾
أُولَٰئِكَ الَّذِينَ لَيْسَ لَهُمْ فِي الْأٰخِرَةِ إِلَّا
النَّارُ وَحَبِطَ مَا صَنَعُوا فِيهَا وَبَٰطِلٌ مَّا
كَانُوا يَعْمَلُونَ ﴿١٦﴾ أَفَمَن كَانَ عَلَىٰ بَيِّنَةٍ مِّن
رَّبِّهِ وَيَتْلُوهُ شَاهِدٌ مِّنْهُ وَمِن قَبْلِهِ
كِتَٰبُ مُوسَىٰ إِمَامًا وَرَحْمَةً أُولَٰئِكَ يُؤْمِنُونَ
بِهِ وَمَن يَكْفُرْ بِهِ مِنَ الْأَحْزَابِ فَالنَّارُ
مَوْعِدُهُ فَلَا تَكُ فِي مِرْيَةٍ مِّنْهُ إِنَّهُ الْحَقُّ
مِن رَّبِّكَ وَلَٰكِنَّ أَكْثَرَ النَّاسِ لَا يُؤْمِنُونَ ﴿١٧﴾
وَمَنْ أَظْلَمُ مِمَّنِ افْتَرَىٰ عَلَى اللَّهِ كَذِبًا
أُولَٰئِكَ يُعْرَضُونَ عَلَىٰ رَبِّهِمْ وَيَقُولُ الْأَشْهَٰدُ
هَٰؤُلَاءِ الَّذِينَ كَذَبُوا عَلَىٰ رَبِّهِمْ أَلَا لَعْنَةُ

unjust,

19. Those who keep (the people) away from the path of Allâh and seek to paint it as crooked, it is these who are the disbelievers in the Hereafter.

20. Such cannot frustrate (God's designs) in the land nor is there any protecting friend for them apart from Allâh. They shall have their punishment doubled. They could neither bear to hear (the truth) nor did they see (it).

21. It is these who have suffered a loss in respect of their own souls and that (false deities) which they forged have failed them.

22. No doubt, it is these who shall be the worst losers in the Hereafter.

23. Verily, those who believe and do deeds of righteousness and humble themselves before their Lord, it is these who are the owners of Paradise, they shall abide in it.

24. The case of these two groups (of disbelievers and believers) is like (the case of) the blind and the deaf (on the one hand) and the seeing and the hearing (on the other). Can the case of the two be alike? Will you not even then take heed?

SECTION 3

25. **A**ND (similar were the circumstances when) We sent Noah to his people (and he said), 'Verily, I am a plain Warner to you.

26. '(And my Message is) that you worship none but Allâh; otherwise I fear lest there should overtake you the punishment of a woeful day.'

27. Thereupon the chiefs of his people who had disbelieved said, 'We find you but a human being like ourselves, and we find none have followed you except those who are the meanest of us, having only superficial views. And we find you (and your followers) possessing no superiority over us. Rather we take you all to be liars.'

28. He said, 'O my people, have you considered that if I stand on a clear proof from my

اللهِ عَلَى الظّٰلِمِينَ ﴿١٨﴾ الَّذِينَ يَصُدُّونَ عَنْ
سَبِيلِ اللهِ وَيَبْغُونَهَا عِوَجًا ۚ وَهُمْ بِالْآخِرَةِ
هُمْ كٰفِرُونَ ﴿١٩﴾ أُولٰٓئِكَ لَمْ يَكُونُوا مُعْجِزِينَ
فِي الْأَرْضِ وَمَا كَانَ لَهُمْ مِنْ دُونِ اللهِ
مِنْ أَوْلِيَاءَ ۘ يُضٰعَفُ لَهُمُ الْعَذَابُ ۚ مَا كَانُوا
يَسْتَطِيعُونَ السَّمْعَ وَمَا كَانُوا يُبْصِرُونَ ﴿٢٠﴾
أُولٰٓئِكَ الَّذِينَ خَسِرُوٓا أَنْفُسَهُمْ وَضَلَّ
عَنْهُمْ مَا كَانُوا يَفْتَرُونَ ﴿٢١﴾ لَا جَرَمَ أَنَّهُمْ
فِي الْآخِرَةِ هُمُ الْأَخْسَرُونَ ﴿٢٢﴾ إِنَّ الَّذِينَ
آمَنُوا وَعَمِلُوا الصّٰلِحٰتِ وَأَخْبَتُوٓا إِلٰى رَبِّهِمْ
أُولٰٓئِكَ أَصْحٰبُ الْجَنَّةِ ۚ هُمْ فِيهَا خٰلِدُونَ ﴿٢٣﴾
مَثَلُ الْفَرِيقَيْنِ كَالْأَعْمٰى وَالْأَصَمِّ وَالْبَصِيرِ
وَالسَّمِيعِ ۚ هَلْ يَسْتَوِيٰنِ مَثَلًا ۚ أَفَلَا تَذَكَّرُونَ ﴿٢٤﴾ ع
وَلَقَدْ أَرْسَلْنَا نُوحًا إِلٰى قَوْمِهِ ۖ إِنِّي لَكُمْ
نَذِيرٌ مُبِينٌ ﴿٢٥﴾ أَنْ لَا تَعْبُدُوٓا إِلَّا اللهَ ۖ إِنِّيٓ
أَخَافُ عَلَيْكُمْ عَذَابَ يَوْمٍ أَلِيمٍ ﴿٢٦﴾ فَقَالَ
الْمَلَأُ الَّذِينَ كَفَرُوا مِنْ قَوْمِهِ مَا نَرٰىكَ
إِلَّا بَشَرًا مِثْلَنَا وَمَا نَرٰىكَ اتَّبَعَكَ إِلَّا الَّذِينَ
هُمْ أَرَاذِلُنَا بَادِيَ الرَّأْيِ ۚ وَمَا نَرٰى لَكُمْ
عَلَيْنَا مِنْ فَضْلٍ بَلْ نَظُنُّكُمْ كٰذِبِينَ ﴿٢٧﴾
قَالَ يٰقَوْمِ أَرَءَيْتُمْ إِنْ كُنْتُ عَلٰى بَيِّنَةٍ مِنْ

Lord and He has conferred upon me a great mercy (- Prophethood) from Himself and it has been obscured to you, shall we thrust it upon you (to accept) while you are averse to it?

29. 'And O my people! I ask you in return for this (- my teaching) no wealth. My reward is due only from Allâh. I am not at all one to drive away those who believe, for they are going to meet their Lord (to be blessed) and I see you are a people who are acting through lack of knowledge.

30. 'And O my people! Who would save me from (the punishment of) Allâh if I were to drive them away? Will you not then consider?

31. 'And I do not say to you that I possess the treasures of Allâh, nor that I know the hidden realities, nor do I say that I am an angel, nor do I say concerning those whom your eyes despise that Allâh will not grant them any good. Allâh knows best whatever is in their minds. I shall indeed be of the unjust (if I say anything of the kind).'

32. They said, 'Noah! You have disputed with us long and have disputed with us many a time; bring down on us now that (punishment) you threaten us with, if you are of the truthful ones.'

33. He said, 'Allâh alone will bring it down on you if He will and you cannot frustrate Him (in His purpose).

34. 'And my sincere counsel will do you no good, choose as I may to counsel you in case Allâh intends to destroy you. (All the same,) He is your Lord and to Him you shall be made to return.'

35. Or do they say, 'He (- Muhammad) has forged it.' Say (O Muhammad!), 'If I have forged it then on me will be the penalty of my crime and I am quit of (all the responsibilities of) the sin you commit (by denying me).'

SECTION 4

36. **A**ND it was revealed to Noah, 'No one of your people besides those who have so far

رَبِّيْ وَ اٰتٰىنِيْ رَحْمَةً مِّنْ عِنْدِهٖ فَعُمِّيَتْ
عَلَيْكُمْ ؕ اَنُلْزِمُكُمُوْهَا وَ اَنْتُمْ لَهَا كٰرِهُوْنَ ﴿٢٨﴾
وَ يٰقَوْمِ لَاۤ اَسْـَٔلُكُمْ عَلَيْهِ مَالًا ؕ اِنْ اَجْرِيَ
اِلَّا عَلَى اللّٰهِ وَ مَاۤ اَنَا بِطَارِدِ الَّذِيْنَ اٰمَنُوْا ؕ
اِنَّهُمْ مُّلٰقُوْا رَبِّهِمْ وَ لٰكِنِّيْۤ اَرٰىكُمْ قَوْمًا
تَجْهَلُوْنَ ﴿٢٩﴾ وَ يٰقَوْمِ مَنْ يَّنْصُرُنِيْ مِنَ اللّٰهِ اِنْ
طَرَدْتُّهُمْ ؕ اَفَلَا تَذَكَّرُوْنَ ﴿٣٠﴾ وَ لَاۤ اَقُوْلُ لَكُمْ
عِنْدِيْ خَزَآئِنُ اللّٰهِ وَ لَاۤ اَعْلَمُ الْغَيْبَ وَ لَاۤ
اَقُوْلُ اِنِّيْ مَلَكٌ وَّ لَاۤ اَقُوْلُ لِلَّذِيْنَ تَزْدَرِيْۤ
اَعْيُنُكُمْ لَنْ يُّؤْتِيَهُمُ اللّٰهُ خَيْرًا ؕ اَللّٰهُ اَعْلَمُ
بِمَا فِيْۤ اَنْفُسِهِمْ ۚۖ اِنِّيْۤ اِذًا لَّمِنَ الظّٰلِمِيْنَ ﴿٣١﴾
قَالُوْا يٰنُوْحُ قَدْ جٰدَلْتَنَا فَاَكْثَرْتَ جِدَالَنَا
فَاْتِنَا بِمَا تَعِدُنَاۤ اِنْ كُنْتَ مِنَ الصّٰدِقِيْنَ ﴿٣٢﴾
قَالَ اِنَّمَا يَاْتِيْكُمْ بِهِ اللّٰهُ اِنْ شَآءَ وَ مَاۤ
اَنْتُمْ بِمُعْجِزِيْنَ ﴿٣٣﴾ وَ لَا يَنْفَعُكُمْ نُصْحِيْۤ اِنْ
اَرَدْتُّ اَنْ اَنْصَحَ لَكُمْ اِنْ كَانَ اللّٰهُ يُرِيْدُ
اَنْ يُّغْوِيَكُمْ ؕ هُوَ رَبُّكُمْ ۟ وَ اِلَيْهِ تُرْجَعُوْنَ ﴿٣٤﴾
اَمْ يَقُوْلُوْنَ افْتَرٰىهُ ؕ قُلْ اِنِ افْتَرَيْتُهٗ فَعَلَيَّ
اِجْرَامِيْ وَ اَنَا بَرِيْٓءٌ مِّمَّا تُجْرِمُوْنَ ﴿٣٥﴾ وَ اُوْحِيَ
اِلٰى نُوْحٍ اَنَّهٗ لَنْ يُّؤْمِنَ مِنْ قَوْمِكَ اِلَّا مَنْ

believed, will henceforth believe, therefore grieve not over what they have been doing.

37. 'And build the Ark under Our eyes and in accordance with Our revelation, and address not (to plead with) Me in favour of those who act unjustly. Verily, they are doomed to be drowned.'

38. And he set himself to making the Ark and every time the chiefs of his people passed by him they looked down upon him, (thereupon) he said, 'Surely, we (in our turn) will look down on you just as you look down (on us now).

39. 'You shall soon know for yourself who it is who will be overtaken by the punishment that will disgrace him, and on whom descends a long lasting penalty.'

40. (Thus it was) till Our command (about the punishment) came and waters of the springs (of the valley) swelled and gushed forth, We said, 'Embark in it two of every kind (needed) male and female and (all the members of) your family except those about the destruction of whom (Our) verdict has already been announced and (embark in it) also those who believe.' Yet there had not believed in him excepting a few.

41. And (Noah) said, 'Embark in it. With the name of Allâh and His help be its course and its mooring. Surely, my Lord is indeed Great Protector, Ever Merciful.'

42. Now this (Ark) moved carrying them amidst waves as (high as) mountains. And Noah called out to his son who was (standing) aloof, 'My dear son, embark with us and do not be with the disbelievers.'

43. He said, 'I shall betake myself to a mountain for refuge which will protect me from this water.' (Noah) said, 'There is no protection (for anyone) this day, from the decree of Allâh (about this punishment), but he (will be safe) on whom He has mercy.' And (lo!) a wave separated the two so he (- Noah's son) was among the drowned.

44. And it was said, 'O earth! Swallow back

قَدْ ءَامَنَ فَلَا تَبْتَئِسْ بِمَا كَانُوا يَفْعَلُونَ ﴿٣٦﴾
وَاصْنَعِ الْفُلْكَ بِأَعْيُنِنَا وَوَحْيِنَا وَلَا تُخَاطِبْنِي
فِي الَّذِينَ ظَلَمُوا إِنَّهُمْ مُّغْرَقُونَ ﴿٣٧﴾ وَيَصْنَعُ
الْفُلْكَ وَكُلَّمَا مَرَّ عَلَيْهِ مَلَأٌ مِّنْ قَوْمِهِ
سَخِرُوا مِنْهُ قَالَ إِنْ تَسْخَرُوا مِنَّا فَإِنَّا نَسْخَرُ
مِنْكُمْ كَمَا تَسْخَرُونَ ﴿٣٨﴾ فَسَوْفَ تَعْلَمُونَ مَنْ
يَأْتِيهِ عَذَابٌ يُخْزِيهِ وَيَحِلُّ عَلَيْهِ عَذَابٌ
مُّقِيمٌ ﴿٣٩﴾ حَتَّى إِذَا جَاءَ أَمْرُنَا وَفَارَ التَّنُّورُ
قُلْنَا احْمِلْ فِيهَا مِنْ كُلٍّ زَوْجَيْنِ اثْنَيْنِ
وَأَهْلَكَ إِلَّا مَنْ سَبَقَ عَلَيْهِ الْقَوْلُ وَمَنْ ءَامَنَ
وَمَا ءَامَنَ مَعَهُ إِلَّا قَلِيلٌ ﴿٤٠﴾ وَقَالَ ارْكَبُوا
فِيهَا بِسْمِ اللَّهِ مَجْرِىٰهَا وَمُرْسٰىهَا إِنَّ رَبِّي
لَغَفُورٌ رَّحِيمٌ ﴿٤١﴾ وَهِيَ تَجْرِي بِهِمْ فِي مَوْجٍ
كَالْجِبَالِ وَنَادَىٰ نُوحٌ ابْنَهُ وَكَانَ فِي مَعْزِلٍ
يٰبُنَيَّ ارْكَبْ مَّعَنَا وَلَا تَكُنْ مَّعَ الْكٰفِرِينَ ﴿٤٢﴾
قَالَ سَاٰوِي إِلَىٰ جَبَلٍ يَعْصِمُنِي مِنَ الْمَاءِ
قَالَ لَا عَاصِمَ الْيَوْمَ مِنْ أَمْرِ اللَّهِ إِلَّا مَنْ
رَّحِمَ وَحَالَ بَيْنَهُمَا الْمَوْجُ فَكَانَ مِنَ
الْمُغْرَقِينَ ﴿٤٣﴾ وَقِيلَ يٰأَرْضُ ابْلَعِي مَاءَكِ

your water, and O cloud! Abate and stop (pouring).' So the water was made to subside and the matter was decided. And this (Ark) came to rest on (the mount) Al-Jûdî. And the word went forth, 'Away with the unjust people!'

45. And Noah called to his Lord and said , 'My Lord! My son belongs to my family and surely your promise is (also) true; yet you are the Most Just of the judges.'

46. (The Lord) said, 'He decidedly does not belong to your family as he is given to unrighteous conduct, so do not ask of Me that of which you have no knowledge. I advise you not to be of those wanting in knowledge.'

47. He said, 'My Lord! I beg You to protect me that I should ask You that of which I have no knowledge. And unless You forgive me and have mercy on me I shall be of the losers.'

48. There came the command, 'Noah! Descend (from the Ark) with peace from Us and (varied) blessings (We shall bestow) on you and upon peoples (to be born) of those with you. There shall be other peoples whom We shall grant provisions (of this world for a time), then they will receive from Us a grievous punishment (as a result of their transgression).'

49. These (announcements full of warnings) are some of the important news of the hidden realities We have revealed them to you. You did not know them, neither you, nor your people before this. Therefore, persevere (in doing good), for those who become secure against evil shall surely have the (good and successful) end.

SECTION 5

50. AND (We sent) to (the tribe of) 'Âd, their kinsman Hûd (as a Messenger). He said, 'My people! Worship Allâh (alone). You have no one worthy of worship other than He. You are but fabricators (of lies by assigning partners with Him in His sovereignty).

51. 'My people! I ask of you no reward for this (teaching). My reward is not due but from

وَ يٰسَمَآءُ أَقْلِعِي وَ غِيضَ الْمَآءُ وَ قُضِيَ الْأَمْرُ
وَ اسْتَوَتْ عَلَى الْجُودِيِّ وَ قِيلَ بُعْدًا لِّلْقَوْمِ
الظّٰلِمِينَ ﴿٤٤﴾ وَ نَادٰى نُوحٌ رَّبَّهٗ فَقَالَ رَبِّ
إِنَّ ابْنِي مِنْ أَهْلِي وَ إِنَّ وَعْدَكَ الْحَقُّ وَ أَنْتَ
أَحْكَمُ الْحٰكِمِينَ ﴿٤٥﴾ قَالَ يٰنُوحُ إِنَّهٗ لَيْسَ مِنْ
أَهْلِكَ إِنَّهٗ عَمَلٌ غَيْرُ صٰلِحٍ فَلَا تَسْئَلْنِ
مَا لَيْسَ لَكَ بِهٖ عِلْمٌ إِنِّيٓ أَعِظُكَ أَنْ تَكُونَ
مِنَ الْجٰهِلِينَ ﴿٤٦﴾ قَالَ رَبِّ إِنِّيٓ أَعُوذُ بِكَ أَنْ
أَسْئَلَكَ مَا لَيْسَ لِي بِهٖ عِلْمٌ وَ إِلَّا تَغْفِرْ لِي
وَ تَرْحَمْنِيٓ أَكُنْ مِّنَ الْخٰسِرِينَ ﴿٤٧﴾ قِيلَ يٰنُوحُ
اهْبِطْ بِسَلٰمٍ مِّنَّا وَ بَرَكٰتٍ عَلَيْكَ وَ عَلٰٓى أُمَمٍ
مِّمَّنْ مَّعَكَ وَ أُمَمٌ سَنُمَتِّعُهُمْ ثُمَّ يَمَسُّهُمْ
مِّنَّا عَذَابٌ أَلِيمٌ ﴿٤٨﴾ تِلْكَ مِنْ أَنْبَآءِ الْغَيْبِ
نُوحِيهَآ إِلَيْكَ مَا كُنْتَ تَعْلَمُهَآ أَنْتَ وَ لَا
قَوْمُكَ مِنْ قَبْلِ هٰذَا فَاصْبِرْ إِنَّ الْعٰقِبَةَ
لِلْمُتَّقِينَ ﴿٤٩﴾ وَ إِلٰى عَادٍ أَخَاهُمْ هُودًا قَالَ
يٰقَوْمِ اعْبُدُوا اللّٰهَ مَا لَكُمْ مِّنْ إِلٰهٍ غَيْرُهٗ
إِنْ أَنْتُمْ إِلَّا مُفْتَرُونَ ﴿٥٠﴾ يٰقَوْمِ لَآ أَسْئَلُكُمْ

Him Who created me. Will you not then understand?

52. 'And my people! Seek protection of your Lord, and turn to Him in repentance. (If you do so) He will send clouds over you pouring down abundance of rain, and He will add more strength to your (present) strength. And do not turn away (from Him) as those who sever their ties (with God).'

53. They said, 'O Hûd, you have brought us no clear proof (about your truthfulness), and we will not forsake our gods (merely) for your saying, nor are we going to be believers in you at all.

54. 'All that we can say is that some of our gods have smitten you with evil (rendering you insane).' (Hûd) said, 'Surely I call Allâh to witness; and do you also bear witness that I have nothing to do with the gods you associate (with Allâh)

55. 'Apart from Him, so you and all (your gods) together devise concerted plans against me and give me no respite.

56. 'I have definitely put my trust in Allâh, (Who is) my Lord and your Lord. There is no living and moving creature but He holds its forelock, (having absolute power over it). Surely, right and just are the ways of my Lord.

57. 'If you turn away (from Him, remember that) I have fully conveyed to you that (Message) I have been sent with to you. (If you do not accept it,) my Lord will replace you with another people to be rulers. And you shall be able to do Him no harm at all. Surely, my Lord is Preserver of all things.'

58. And when Our command (about the punishment) came, We saved Hûd and those who believed with him by a special mercy from us. And We delivered them from a severe torment.

59. And such were 'Âd, they deliberately denied the commandments of their Lord and

سُورَةُ هُودٍ ١١

عَلَيْهِ أَجْرًا إِنْ أَجْرِيَ إِلَّا عَلَى الَّذِي فَطَرَنِي
أَفَلَا تَعْقِلُونَ ﴿٥١﴾ وَيَٰقَوْمِ اسْتَغْفِرُوا رَبَّكُمْ ثُمَّ
تُوبُوا إِلَيْهِ يُرْسِلِ السَّمَاءَ عَلَيْكُم مِّدْرَارًا
وَيَزِدْكُمْ قُوَّةً إِلَىٰ قُوَّتِكُمْ وَلَا تَتَوَلَّوْا مُجْرِمِينَ ﴿٥٢﴾
قَالُوا يَٰهُودُ مَا جِئْتَنَا بِبَيِّنَةٍ وَمَا نَحْنُ بِتَارِكِي
آلِهَتِنَا عَن قَوْلِكَ وَمَا نَحْنُ لَكَ بِمُؤْمِنِينَ ﴿٥٣﴾
إِن نَّقُولُ إِلَّا اعْتَرَاكَ بَعْضُ آلِهَتِنَا بِسُوءٍ
قَالَ إِنِّي أُشْهِدُ اللَّهَ وَاشْهَدُوا أَنِّي بَرِيءٌ مِّمَّا
تُشْرِكُونَ ﴿٥٤﴾ مِن دُونِهِ فَكِيدُونِي جَمِيعًا ثُمَّ
لَا تُنظِرُونِ ﴿٥٥﴾ إِنِّي تَوَكَّلْتُ عَلَى اللَّهِ رَبِّي
وَرَبِّكُم مَّا مِن دَابَّةٍ إِلَّا هُوَ آخِذٌ بِنَاصِيَتِهَا
إِنَّ رَبِّي عَلَىٰ صِرَاطٍ مُّسْتَقِيمٍ ﴿٥٦﴾ فَإِن تَوَلَّوْا فَقَدْ
أَبْلَغْتُكُم مَّا أُرْسِلْتُ بِهِ إِلَيْكُمْ وَيَسْتَخْلِفُ
رَبِّي قَوْمًا غَيْرَكُمْ وَلَا تَضُرُّونَهُ شَيْئًا إِنَّ
رَبِّي عَلَىٰ كُلِّ شَيْءٍ حَفِيظٌ ﴿٥٧﴾ وَلَمَّا جَاءَ أَمْرُنَا
نَجَّيْنَا هُودًا وَالَّذِينَ آمَنُوا مَعَهُ بِرَحْمَةٍ مِّنَّا
وَنَجَّيْنَاهُم مِّنْ عَذَابٍ غَلِيظٍ ﴿٥٨﴾ وَتِلْكَ عَادٌ
جَحَدُوا بِآيَاتِ رَبِّهِمْ وَعَصَوْا رُسُلَهُ وَاتَّبَعُوا

disobeyed His Messengers and followed the bidding of every haughty enemy (of truth).

60. And there was sent following them a curse in this world and on the Day of Resurrection (they will meet the same fate). Behold! (the tribe of) 'Âd behaved ungratefully towards their Lord (by denying His favours). Look! Destruction is decreed for 'Âd, the people of Hûd.

SECTION 6

61. **A**ND to the tribe of Thamûd (We sent as a Messenger) their kinsman Sâlih. He said, 'My people! Worship Allâh, you have no One worthy of worship other than He. It is He Who brought you forth from the earth and made you dwell therein. So seek protection of Him and turn to Him in repentance. Verily, my Lord is Nigh, Responsive (to prayers).'

62. They said, 'Sâlih! You have hitherto been among us as one in whom we placed our hopes. Do you forbid us to worship what our forefathers have been worshipping? And as a matter of fact we are in disquieting doubt about that (faith) you call us to.'

63. He said, 'My people! Have you considered that if (in my claim to Prophethood) I stand on a clear proof from my Lord and He has granted me Mercy (- Prophethood) from Himself, who then will help (to save) me against (the punishment of) Allâh if I disobey Him? For then you will increase me in nothing but in leading me to loss.

64. 'My people! This is a she-camel appointed by Allâh as a sign for you; so leave her alone to pasture on Allâh's earth and afflict her not with any harm or an imminent torment shall seize you.'

65. But they hamstrung her, so that he (- Sâlih) said, 'You shall enjoy the provision of Allâh in your worldly abodes only for (another) three days. This is a promise which will never prove false.'

أَمْرَ كُلِّ جَبَّارٍ عَنِيدٍ ﴿٥٩﴾ وَأُتْبِعُوا فِي هَٰذِهِ
الدُّنْيَا لَعْنَةً وَيَوْمَ الْقِيَامَةِ ۗ أَلَا إِنَّ عَادًا
كَفَرُوا رَبَّهُمْ ۗ أَلَا بُعْدًا لِعَادٍ قَوْمِ هُودٍ ﴿٦٠﴾
وَإِلَىٰ ثَمُودَ أَخَاهُمْ صَالِحًا ۚ قَالَ يَا قَوْمِ اعْبُدُوا
اللَّهَ مَا لَكُمْ مِنْ إِلَٰهٍ غَيْرُهُ ۖ هُوَ أَنْشَأَكُمْ
مِنَ الْأَرْضِ وَاسْتَعْمَرَكُمْ فِيهَا فَاسْتَغْفِرُوهُ
ثُمَّ تُوبُوا إِلَيْهِ ۚ إِنَّ رَبِّي قَرِيبٌ مُجِيبٌ ﴿٦١﴾
قَالُوا يَا صَالِحُ قَدْ كُنْتَ فِينَا مَرْجُوًّا قَبْلَ هَٰذَا
أَتَنْهَانَا أَنْ نَعْبُدَ مَا يَعْبُدُ آبَاؤُنَا وَإِنَّنَا لَفِي
شَكٍّ مِمَّا تَدْعُونَا إِلَيْهِ مُرِيبٍ ﴿٦٢﴾ قَالَ يَا قَوْمِ
أَرَأَيْتُمْ إِنْ كُنْتُ عَلَىٰ بَيِّنَةٍ مِنْ رَبِّي
وَآتَانِي مِنْهُ رَحْمَةً فَمَنْ يَنْصُرُنِي مِنَ اللَّهِ إِنْ
عَصَيْتُهُ ۖ فَمَا تَزِيدُونَنِي غَيْرَ تَخْسِيرٍ ﴿٦٣﴾
وَيَا قَوْمِ هَٰذِهِ نَاقَةُ اللَّهِ لَكُمْ آيَةً فَذَرُوهَا
تَأْكُلْ فِي أَرْضِ اللَّهِ وَلَا تَمَسُّوهَا بِسُوءٍ
فَيَأْخُذَكُمْ عَذَابٌ قَرِيبٌ ﴿٦٤﴾ فَعَقَرُوهَا فَقَالَ
تَمَتَّعُوا فِي دَارِكُمْ ثَلَاثَةَ أَيَّامٍ ۖ ذَٰلِكَ وَعْدٌ
غَيْرُ مَكْذُوبٍ ﴿٦٥﴾ فَلَمَّا جَاءَ أَمْرُنَا نَجَّيْنَا صَالِحًا

66. And when Our command (about punishment) came (to pass), We saved Sâlih and with him the believers by a (special) mercy from Us and (We saved them) from the ignominy of that day. Surely, All-Powerful is your Lord (and) All Mighty.
67. And a thunderbolt (caused by an earthquake) seized those who had acted unjustly. And the next morning found them lying prostrate in their habitations,
68. As if they had never dwelt in them. Behold! The Thamûd behaved ungratefully to their Lord (denying His favours upon them). So away with (the tribe of) Thamûd!

SECTION 7

69. AND certainly, Our messengers came to Abraham with good tidings. They said, '(We bid you) peace.' He said, 'Peace be (on you too) always.' And he lost no time in bringing them a roasted calf.
70. But when he saw that their hands did not extend to that (meal) he considered it strange on their part and apprehended evil from them. They said, 'Have no fear for we have been sent to the people of Lot.'
71. And his wife was standing (nearby) and she too was inspired with awe. So we gave her good tidings of (the birth of) Isaac and after Isaac of (his son) Jacob.
72. She said, 'O wonder for me! Shall I bear a child while I am a very old woman and this husband of mine (also) a very old man? This is a wonderful thing indeed!'
73. They (- Our messengers) said, 'Do you marvel at the decree of Allâh? Members of this house! The mercy of Allâh and His blessings are upon you. Surely, He is the Lord of all praise, Owner of all glory.'
74. And when awe departed from Abraham and the good tidings came to him, he started pleading with Us for the people of Lot.
75. Surely, Abraham was gentle, tenderhearted and oft-returning (to Us).
76. (Thereupon We said to him,) 'Abraham!

وَّ الَّذِينَ آمَنُوا مَعَهُ بِرَحْمَةٍ مِّنَّا وَمِنْ خِزْيِ
يَوْمِئِذٍ إِنَّ رَبَّكَ هُوَ الْقَوِيُّ الْعَزِيزُ ﴿٦٦﴾ وَأَخَذَ
الَّذِينَ ظَلَمُوا الصَّيْحَةُ فَأَصْبَحُوا فِي دِيَارِهِمْ
جَاثِمِينَ ﴿٦٧﴾ كَأَن لَّمْ يَغْنَوْا فِيهَا أَلَا إِنَّ ثَمُودَ
كَفَرُوا رَبَّهُمْ أَلَا بُعْدًا لِّثَمُودَ ﴿٦٨﴾ وَلَقَدْ جَاءَتْ
رُسُلُنَا إِبْرَاهِيمَ بِالْبُشْرَىٰ قَالُوا سَلَامًا قَالَ
سَلَامٌ فَمَا لَبِثَ أَن جَاءَ بِعِجْلٍ حَنِيذٍ ﴿٦٩﴾ فَلَمَّا
رَأَىٰ أَيْدِيَهُمْ لَا تَصِلُ إِلَيْهِ نَكِرَهُمْ وَأَوْجَسَ
مِنْهُمْ خِيفَةً قَالُوا لَا تَخَفْ إِنَّا أُرْسِلْنَا إِلَىٰ
قَوْمِ لُوطٍ ﴿٧٠﴾ وَامْرَأَتُهُ قَائِمَةٌ فَضَحِكَتْ
فَبَشَّرْنَاهَا بِإِسْحَاقَ وَمِن وَرَاءِ إِسْحَاقَ
يَعْقُوبَ ﴿٧١﴾ قَالَتْ يَا وَيْلَتَىٰ أَأَلِدُ وَأَنَا عَجُوزٌ
وَهَٰذَا بَعْلِي شَيْخًا إِنَّ هَٰذَا لَشَيْءٌ عَجِيبٌ ﴿٧٢﴾
قَالُوا أَتَعْجَبِينَ مِنْ أَمْرِ اللَّهِ رَحْمَتُ اللَّهِ
وَبَرَكَاتُهُ عَلَيْكُمْ أَهْلَ الْبَيْتِ إِنَّهُ حَمِيدٌ
مَّجِيدٌ ﴿٧٣﴾ فَلَمَّا ذَهَبَ عَنْ إِبْرَاهِيمَ الرَّوْعُ
وَجَاءَتْهُ الْبُشْرَىٰ يُجَادِلُنَا فِي قَوْمِ لُوطٍ ﴿٧٤﴾ إِنَّ
إِبْرَاهِيمَ لَحَلِيمٌ أَوَّاهٌ مُّنِيبٌ ﴿٧٥﴾ يَا إِبْرَاهِيمُ

Turn away from this (pleading now), for your Lords command has decidedly come. They are certainly going to receive a punishment that cannot be averted.'

77. And when Our messengers came to Lot he was grieved on their account and felt helpless on their behalf (- of his people, for he had no means to protect them) and he said, 'This is a distressful and hard day.'

78. And (on hearing the news of the strangers' arrival) his people came (as if) driven on towards him and before this they were given to evil practices. He said, 'My people! These are my daughters. They can be purer (guarantee against any conspiracy on my part) for you and take Allâh as a shield (against His punishment) and do not disgrace me in the matter of my guests. Is there not among you any right-minded man?'

79. They said, 'You certainly know we have no claim on your daughters, and you know well what we want (from you about the strangers).'

80. He said, 'Would that I had power to deal with you, rather I should betake myself for refuge to a strong support (of God).'

81. (The messengers) said, 'Lot! We are messengers of your Lord. They shall not at all reach you, so set forth (from here) with your family in the latter part of the night and let not anyone of you look about, but your wife (will not obey). Surely, she shall be smitten by that calamity which is going to smite the rest of them; the appointed time of theirs is the morning. Is not the morning nigh?'

82. So when Our command (about the punishment) came to pass we turned those (townships) upside down and We rained upon them, layer upon layer, with many stones of petrified clay,

83. Ear-marked (for them) by (the decree of) your Lord. And this (sort of punishment) is not far from the unjust people (of the opponents of the Prophet).

أَعْرِضْ عَنْ هَٰذَا ۚ إِنَّهُ قَدْ جَاءَ أَمْرُ رَبِّكَ
وَإِنَّهُمْ آتِيهِمْ عَذَابٌ غَيْرُ مَرْدُودٍ ﴿٧٦﴾ وَلَمَّا
جَاءَتْ رُسُلُنَا لُوطًا سِيءَ بِهِمْ وَضَاقَ بِهِمْ
ذَرْعًا وَقَالَ هَٰذَا يَوْمٌ عَصِيبٌ ﴿٧٧﴾ وَجَاءَهُ
قَوْمُهُ يُهْرَعُونَ إِلَيْهِ ۖ وَمِنْ قَبْلُ كَانُوا
يَعْمَلُونَ السَّيِّئَاتِ ۚ قَالَ يَٰقَوْمِ هَٰؤُلَاءِ بَنَاتِي
هُنَّ أَطْهَرُ لَكُمْ ۖ فَاتَّقُوا اللَّهَ وَلَا تُخْزُونِ فِي
ضَيْفِي ۖ أَلَيْسَ مِنْكُمْ رَجُلٌ رَشِيدٌ ﴿٧٨﴾ قَالُوا
لَقَدْ عَلِمْتَ مَا لَنَا فِي بَنَاتِكَ مِنْ حَقٍّ ۚ
وَإِنَّكَ لَتَعْلَمُ مَا نُرِيدُ ﴿٧٩﴾ قَالَ لَوْ أَنَّ لِي بِكُمْ
قُوَّةً أَوْ آوِي إِلَىٰ رُكْنٍ شَدِيدٍ ﴿٨٠﴾ قَالُوا يَٰلُوطُ
إِنَّا رُسُلُ رَبِّكَ لَنْ يَصِلُوا إِلَيْكَ ۖ فَأَسْرِ
بِأَهْلِكَ بِقِطْعٍ مِنَ اللَّيْلِ وَلَا يَلْتَفِتْ مِنْكُمْ
أَحَدٌ إِلَّا امْرَأَتَكَ ۖ إِنَّهُ مُصِيبُهَا مَا أَصَابَهُمْ ۚ
إِنَّ مَوْعِدَهُمُ الصُّبْحُ ۚ أَلَيْسَ الصُّبْحُ بِقَرِيبٍ ﴿٨١﴾
فَلَمَّا جَاءَ أَمْرُنَا جَعَلْنَا عَٰلِيَهَا سَافِلَهَا وَأَمْطَرْنَا
عَلَيْهَا حِجَارَةً مِنْ سِجِّيلٍ مَنْضُودٍ ﴿٨٢﴾ مُسَوَّمَةً
عِنْدَ رَبِّكَ ۖ وَمَا هِيَ مِنَ الظَّٰلِمِينَ بِبَعِيدٍ ﴿٨٣﴾

SECTION 8

84. AND to Midian (We sent) their kinsman Shu'aib (as a Messenger). He said, 'My people! Worship Allâh, you have no one worthy of worship other than He. And give not short measure and (short) weight. (Today) I see you in (a state of) prosperity. But (for tomorrow) I fear lest there should befall you the punishment of a (dreadful) day that encompasses all (for destruction).

85. 'And my people! Give true measure and full weight with equity and defraud not people of their possession and commit not inequity in the land as peace-breakers.

86. 'The residue left to you by Allâh (after your paying the dues of others) is better for you, if you are true believers. Yet I am not a guardian over you.'

87. They said, 'O Shu'aib! Does your prayer enjoin you that we should give up what our fathers worshipped or (does it bid you) that we cease to do with our possessions as we like? You, (O Shu'aib!) are you (so to say,) the only intelligent and the right-directing one?'

88. He said, 'My people! What do you think? While I stand (by His grace) on a clear proof from my Lord, (then why should not I guide people to the path of peace?), He has provided me from Himself with a goodly and honest livelihood (I cannot therefore be dishonest to Him). I have no intention to practise contrary to you the very thing which I forbid you to do. All that I desire is to set things right as far as I can. There is no power in me to do something (for setting things right) except through the help of Allâh. In Him do I put my trust and to Him do I always turn.

89. 'And my people! Let not your breach with and hostility towards me make you guilty, so that there may befall you the like of that calamity which befell the people of Noah, and the people of Hûd and the people of Sâlih. And the people of Lot are not far off from you. (You should ponder over their destruction and learn a lesson therefrom.)

وَإِلَىٰ مَدْيَنَ أَخَاهُمْ شُعَيْبًا ۚ قَالَ يَٰقَوْمِ
اعْبُدُوا اللَّهَ مَا لَكُم مِّنْ إِلَٰهٍ غَيْرُهُ ۖ وَلَا
تَنقُصُوا الْمِكْيَالَ وَالْمِيزَانَ ۚ إِنِّي أَرَاكُم بِخَيْرٍ
وَإِنِّي أَخَافُ عَلَيْكُمْ عَذَابَ يَوْمٍ مُّحِيطٍ ﴿٨٤﴾
وَيَٰقَوْمِ أَوْفُوا الْمِكْيَالَ وَالْمِيزَانَ بِالْقِسْطِ
وَلَا تَبْخَسُوا النَّاسَ أَشْيَاءَهُمْ وَلَا تَعْثَوْا فِي
الْأَرْضِ مُفْسِدِينَ ﴿٨٥﴾ بَقِيَّتُ اللَّهِ خَيْرٌ لَّكُمْ إِن
كُنتُم مُّؤْمِنِينَ ۚ وَمَا أَنَا عَلَيْكُم بِحَفِيظٍ ﴿٨٦﴾ قَالُوا
يَٰشُعَيْبُ أَصَلَوٰتُكَ تَأْمُرُكَ أَن نَّتْرُكَ مَا يَعْبُدُ
آبَاؤُنَا أَوْ أَن نَّفْعَلَ فِي أَمْوَٰلِنَا مَا نَشَٰٓؤُا ۖ
إِنَّكَ لَأَنتَ الْحَلِيمُ الرَّشِيدُ ﴿٨٧﴾ قَالَ يَٰقَوْمِ
أَرَءَيْتُمْ إِن كُنتُ عَلَىٰ بَيِّنَةٍ مِّن رَّبِّي
وَرَزَقَنِي مِنْهُ رِزْقًا حَسَنًا ۚ وَمَا أُرِيدُ أَنْ
أُخَالِفَكُمْ إِلَىٰ مَا أَنْهَاكُمْ عَنْهُ ۚ إِنْ أُرِيدُ
إِلَّا الْإِصْلَٰحَ مَا اسْتَطَعْتُ ۚ وَمَا تَوْفِيقِي إِلَّا
بِاللَّهِ ۚ عَلَيْهِ تَوَكَّلْتُ وَإِلَيْهِ أُنِيبُ ﴿٨٨﴾ وَيَٰقَوْمِ
لَا يَجْرِمَنَّكُمْ شِقَاقِي أَن يُصِيبَكُم مِّثْلُ مَا
أَصَابَ قَوْمَ نُوحٍ أَوْ قَوْمَ هُودٍ أَوْ قَوْمَ
صَٰلِحٍ ۚ وَمَا قَوْمُ لُوطٍ مِّنكُم بِبَعِيدٍ ﴿٨٩﴾

90. 'And seek protection of your Lord and turn to Him (in repentance). Verily, my Lord is Ever Merciful, Most-Loving.'
91. They said, 'Shu'aib! We do not understand much of what you say and truly we find you a weakling among us. And had it not been (a consideration) for your tribe, we would surely have stoned you to death. And you occupy no strong and respectable position at all as compared with us.'
92. He said, 'My people! Does my tribe occupy stronger and more respectable position with you than Allâh? And (He has occupied no importance in your eyes that) you have cast Him behind your backs neglected. Surely, my Lord encompasses all your activities (in His knowledge).
93. 'And my people! Do your worst, I (too) am doing (my best). You will soon know who is overtaken by a punishment that will disgrace him, and who it is that is a liar. And be on watch, I shall be with you watching.'
94. And when Our command (about the punishment) came We saved Shu'aib and with him the believers by Our mercy, and the calamity seized those who had acted unjustly so that the morning found them lying prostrate in their habitations;
95. (They were so destroyed and desolated) as if they had never dwelt there. So away with Midian; even as Thamûd were done away.

SECTION 9

96. AND surely We sent Moses with Our signs and manifest strong arguments,
97. To Pharaoh and the nobles of his court, but they carried out Pharaoh's bidding; whereas the bidding of Pharaoh was not at all right directed.
98. He (- Pharaoh) will lead his people on the Day of Resurrection and will land them down into the Fire, and evil is the arriving place to be arrived at (by them).
99. There was sent following after them a curse in this (life) and on the Day of Resurrec-

وَاسْتَغْفِرُوا رَبَّكُمْ ثُمَّ تُوبُوا إِلَيْهِ إِنَّ رَبِّي
رَحِيمٌ وَدُودٌ ﴿٩٠﴾ قَالُوا يٰشُعَيْبُ مَا نَفْقَهُ كَثِيرًا
مِمَّا تَقُولُ وَإِنَّا لَنَرٰىكَ فِينَا ضَعِيفًا وَلَوْلَا
رَهْطُكَ لَرَجَمْنٰكَ وَمَا أَنْتَ عَلَيْنَا بِعَزِيزٍ ﴿٩١﴾
قَالَ يٰقَوْمِ أَرَهْطِي أَعَزُّ عَلَيْكُمْ مِنَ اللّٰهِ
وَاتَّخَذْتُمُوهُ وَرَاءَكُمْ ظِهْرِيًّا إِنَّ رَبِّي بِمَا
تَعْمَلُونَ مُحِيطٌ ﴿٩٢﴾ وَيٰقَوْمِ اعْمَلُوا عَلٰى مَكَانَتِكُمْ
إِنِّي عٰمِلٌ سَوْفَ تَعْلَمُونَ مَنْ يَأْتِيهِ عَذَابٌ
يُخْزِيهِ وَمَنْ هُوَ كٰذِبٌ وَارْتَقِبُوا إِنِّي مَعَكُمْ
رَقِيبٌ ﴿٩٣﴾ وَلَمَّا جَاءَ أَمْرُنَا نَجَّيْنَا شُعَيْبًا
وَالَّذِينَ أٰمَنُوا مَعَهُ بِرَحْمَةٍ مِنَّا وَأَخَذَتِ
الَّذِينَ ظَلَمُوا الصَّيْحَةُ فَأَصْبَحُوا فِي دِيٰرِهِمْ
جٰثِمِينَ ﴿٩٤﴾ كَأَنْ لَمْ يَغْنَوْا فِيهَا أَلَا بُعْدًا
لِمَدْيَنَ كَمَا بَعِدَتْ ثَمُودُ ﴿٩٥﴾ وَلَقَدْ أَرْسَلْنَا
مُوسٰى بِأٰيٰتِنَا وَسُلْطٰنٍ مُبِينٍ ﴿٩٦﴾ إِلٰى فِرْعَوْنَ
وَمَلَإِيْهِ فَاتَّبَعُوا أَمْرَ فِرْعَوْنَ وَمَا أَمْرُ
فِرْعَوْنَ بِرَشِيدٍ ﴿٩٧﴾ يَقْدُمُ قَوْمَهُ يَوْمَ الْقِيٰمَةِ
فَأَوْرَدَهُمُ النَّارَ وَبِئْسَ الْوِرْدُ الْمَوْرُودُ ﴿٩٨﴾
وَأُتْبِعُوا فِي هٰذِهِ لَعْنَةً وَيَوْمَ الْقِيٰمَةِ بِئْسَ

ع ١٢ ٨

tion (they shall be the victims of it too). Evil is the gift which shall be given (them)!

100. That is a part of the important news of the (ruined) townships (of the past), We relate them to you. Some of these (cities) still exist while others have been mown down (and perished).

101. We did no wrong to them (- their inhabitants) but they wronged themselves. And when their Lord's command (about their punishment) came to pass, their gods, whom they called upon apart from Allâh, were of no avail to them. In fact, they added nothing to them except (leading them to) destruction.

102. Such is the punishing grasp of your Lord when He takes to task the peoples of the townships (after bringing home to them the truth) while they are steeped in wrongdoings. Surely, painful is His punishing grasp (and) severe.

103. In fact, there is in that a sign (to learn a lesson from) for him who fears the punishment of the Hereafter. That is a day on which the whole of humankind is to be gathered together and that is a day to be witnessed (by all, to be sure).

104. And We defer it not but for a computed term.

105. The day it comes, no soul shall speak save by His leave; (on that day) some will turn out wretched and (others) fortunate.

106. As for the wretched, they shall be in the Fire, where they shall moan and cry,

107. And they shall abide therein, unless your Lord otherwise will, so long as the heavens and the earth (thereof) endure. Surely your Lord does bring about very well what He intends (to do).

108. As for those who turn out fortunate they shall be in Paradise. They will abide therein so long as the heavens and the earth (thereof) endure, unless your Lord otherwise will. This

سُورَةُ هُودٍ ١١

الرِّفْدُ الْمَرْفُودُ ﴿٩٩﴾ ذَٰلِكَ مِنْ أَنْبَاءِ الْقُرَىٰ نَقُصُّهُ
عَلَيْكَ مِنْهَا قَائِمٌ وَحَصِيدٌ ﴿١٠٠﴾ وَمَا ظَلَمْنَاهُمْ وَلَٰكِنْ
ظَلَمُوا أَنْفُسَهُمْ فَمَا أَغْنَتْ عَنْهُمْ آلِهَتُهُمُ
الَّتِي يَدْعُونَ مِنْ دُونِ اللَّهِ مِنْ شَيْءٍ لَمَّا
جَاءَ أَمْرُ رَبِّكَ وَمَا زَادُوهُمْ غَيْرَ تَتْبِيبٍ ﴿١٠١﴾
وَكَذَٰلِكَ أَخْذُ رَبِّكَ إِذَا أَخَذَ الْقُرَىٰ وَهِيَ
ظَالِمَةٌ إِنَّ أَخْذَهُ أَلِيمٌ شَدِيدٌ ﴿١٠٢﴾ إِنَّ فِي
ذَٰلِكَ لَآيَةً لِمَنْ خَافَ عَذَابَ الْآخِرَةِ ذَٰلِكَ
يَوْمٌ مَجْمُوعٌ لَهُ النَّاسُ وَذَٰلِكَ يَوْمٌ مَشْهُودٌ ﴿١٠٣﴾
وَمَا نُؤَخِّرُهُ إِلَّا لِأَجَلٍ مَعْدُودٍ ﴿١٠٤﴾ يَوْمَ يَأْتِ
لَا تَكَلَّمُ نَفْسٌ إِلَّا بِإِذْنِهِ فَمِنْهُمْ شَقِيٌّ
وَسَعِيدٌ ﴿١٠٥﴾ فَأَمَّا الَّذِينَ شَقُوا فَفِي النَّارِ لَهُمْ
فِيهَا زَفِيرٌ وَشَهِيقٌ ﴿١٠٦﴾ خَالِدِينَ فِيهَا مَا
دَامَتِ السَّمَاوَاتُ وَالْأَرْضُ إِلَّا مَا شَاءَ
رَبُّكَ إِنَّ رَبَّكَ فَعَّالٌ لِمَا يُرِيدُ ﴿١٠٧﴾ وَأَمَّا
الَّذِينَ سُعِدُوا فَفِي الْجَنَّةِ خَالِدِينَ فِيهَا
مَا دَامَتِ السَّمَاوَاتُ وَالْأَرْضُ إِلَّا مَا شَاءَ

الجزء الثاني عشر

is a gift that shall never be cut off.
109. So (O people!) have no doubt about the (falsehood of) gods of those (polytheistic) people. They worship (these gods) only because their fathers worshipped (them) before (them), and We shall surely pay them their dues in full, undiminished.

SECTION 10

110. AND We gave Moses the Book, but differences arose about it and had it not been for a word (- promise of mercy) that had gone forth from your Lord the issue between them (- the believers and the disbelievers) must have been decided (long before) and (now) they (- the disbelievers) are in a disquieting doubt about it (- the Qur'ân).
111. Your Lord will certainly repay them all in full (the reward of) their deeds (when they will be presented before Him); for He is Well-Aware of all what they do.
112. So stand you upright, as you have been commanded, and (also) those who (have left their evil ways and) turned to Allâh (in repentance) and joined you. Do not exceed the bounds (set by Allâh, O people!). He indeed is Observer of your deeds.
113. Do not incline towards those who have committed wrong; lest the Fire (of Gehenna) should reach you while you shall find none to protect you, apart from Allâh, nor shall you be helped.
114. And observe Prayer at the two ends of the day and in some early hours of the night. Surely, the good deeds wipe out the evil ones. That is a reminder for those who would remember.
115. And be you patiently persevering, for surely Allâh suffers not the reward of the doers of good to others to go waste.
116. Why, then, were there not among the generations that preceded you persons pos-

سُورَةُ هُودٍ ١١

رَبُّكَ ۗ عَطَآءً غَيْرَ مَجْذُوذٍ ﴿١٠٨﴾ فَلَا تَكُ فِي
مِرْيَةٍ مِّمَّا يَعْبُدُ هَٰٓؤُلَآءِ ۚ مَا يَعْبُدُونَ إِلَّا
كَمَا يَعْبُدُ ءَابَآؤُهُم مِّن قَبْلُ ۚ وَإِنَّا لَمُوَفُّوهُمْ
نَصِيبَهُمْ غَيْرَ مَنقُوصٍ ﴿١٠٩﴾ وَلَقَدْ ءَاتَيْنَا مُوسَى
الْكِتَٰبَ فَاخْتُلِفَ فِيهِ ۗ وَلَوْلَا كَلِمَةٌ سَبَقَتْ
مِن رَّبِّكَ لَقُضِيَ بَيْنَهُمْ ۚ وَإِنَّهُمْ لَفِي شَكٍّ
مِّنْهُ مُرِيبٍ ﴿١١٠﴾ وَإِنَّ كُلًّا لَّمَّا لَيُوَفِّيَنَّهُمْ رَبُّكَ
أَعْمَٰلَهُمْ ۚ إِنَّهُۥ بِمَا يَعْمَلُونَ خَبِيرٌ ﴿١١١﴾ فَاسْتَقِمْ
كَمَآ أُمِرْتَ وَمَن تَابَ مَعَكَ وَلَا تَطْغَوْا ۚ
إِنَّهُۥ بِمَا تَعْمَلُونَ بَصِيرٌ ﴿١١٢﴾ وَلَا تَرْكَنُوٓا إِلَى
الَّذِينَ ظَلَمُوا فَتَمَسَّكُمُ النَّارُ وَمَا لَكُم مِّن
دُونِ اللَّهِ مِنْ أَوْلِيَآءَ ثُمَّ لَا تُنصَرُونَ ﴿١١٣﴾
وَأَقِمِ الصَّلَوٰةَ طَرَفَيِ النَّهَارِ وَزُلَفًا مِّنَ الَّيْلِ ۚ
إِنَّ الْحَسَنَٰتِ يُذْهِبْنَ السَّيِّـَٔاتِ ۚ ذَٰلِكَ
ذِكْرَىٰ لِلذَّٰكِرِينَ ﴿١١٤﴾ وَاصْبِرْ فَإِنَّ اللَّهَ لَا
يُضِيعُ أَجْرَ الْمُحْسِنِينَ ﴿١١٥﴾ فَلَوْلَا كَانَ مِنَ

الجزء الثاني عشر

sessed of excellence who would forbid the perpetration of evil in the land. But there were only a few of those (who acted righteously and) whom We had saved from among them. And (all others) who had committed wrong pursued that (wanton) ease and plenty they were afforded with (and this led to their rebellion and disobedience), and they became those who cut off their ties (with Allâh).
117. And your Lord is not the One Who would destroy the townships unjustly (simply for their disbelief) while the inhabitants thereof (live in peace and) set things right.
118. Had your Lord (enforced) His will He would have certainly made the whole of humankind one community, but (since He did not like to enforce His will upon people) they would not cease to differ.
119. Different, however, is the case of those on whom your Lord has had mercy. Indeed, it is for (the bestowal of mercy) that He has created them; yet (this) word of your Lord, 'Verily I will fill Gehenna with the (rebellious) *jinn* and (ordinary) people all together,' has perfectly come true.
120. And all that We relate to you of the important news of the Messengers is to make your heart firm and strong thereby. And there has come to you, implied in these (news) the truth, an exhortation, and a reminder for the believers.
121. And say to those who do not believe, 'Do your worst, we too are doing (Our best).
122. 'And you may await (our end), we (too) are awaiting (yours).'
123. To Allâh belongs the hidden realities of the heavens and the earth. To Him all matters stand referred. So worship Him and put your trust in Him; for your Lord is not at all unmindful of what you do.

الْقُرُونِ مِنْ قَبْلِكُمْ أُولُوا بَقِيَّةٍ يَنْهَوْنَ عَنِ
الْفَسَادِ فِي الْأَرْضِ إِلَّا قَلِيلًا مِمَّنْ أَنْجَيْنَا
مِنْهُمْ ۗ وَاتَّبَعَ الَّذِينَ ظَلَمُوا مَا أُتْرِفُوا فِيهِ
وَكَانُوا مُجْرِمِينَ ﴿١١٦﴾ وَمَا كَانَ رَبُّكَ لِيُهْلِكَ
الْقُرَىٰ بِظُلْمٍ وَأَهْلُهَا مُصْلِحُونَ ﴿١١٧﴾ وَلَوْ شَاءَ
رَبُّكَ لَجَعَلَ النَّاسَ أُمَّةً وَاحِدَةً ۖ وَلَا يَزَالُونَ
مُخْتَلِفِينَ ﴿١١٨﴾ إِلَّا مَنْ رَحِمَ رَبُّكَ ۚ وَلِذَٰلِكَ
خَلَقَهُمْ ۗ وَتَمَّتْ كَلِمَةُ رَبِّكَ لَأَمْلَأَنَّ
جَهَنَّمَ مِنَ الْجِنَّةِ وَالنَّاسِ أَجْمَعِينَ ﴿١١٩﴾
وَكُلًّا نَقُصُّ عَلَيْكَ مِنْ أَنْبَاءِ الرُّسُلِ مَا
نُثَبِّتُ بِهِ فُؤَادَكَ ۚ وَجَاءَكَ فِي هَٰذِهِ
الْحَقُّ وَمَوْعِظَةٌ وَذِكْرَىٰ لِلْمُؤْمِنِينَ ﴿١٢٠﴾
وَقُلْ لِلَّذِينَ لَا يُؤْمِنُونَ اعْمَلُوا عَلَىٰ مَكَانَتِكُمْ
إِنَّا عَامِلُونَ ﴿١٢١﴾ وَانْتَظِرُوا إِنَّا مُنْتَظِرُونَ ﴿١٢٢﴾
وَلِلَّهِ غَيْبُ السَّمَاوَاتِ وَالْأَرْضِ وَإِلَيْهِ
يُرْجَعُ الْأَمْرُ كُلُّهُ فَاعْبُدْهُ وَتَوَكَّلْ
عَلَيْهِ ۚ وَمَا رَبُّكَ بِغَافِلٍ عَمَّا تَعْمَلُونَ ﴿١٢٣﴾

CHAPTER
12

سُورَةُ يُوسُفَ ١٢

YÛSUF
(Joseph)
(Revealed before Hijrah)

With the name of Allâh,
the Most Gracious, the Ever Merciful
(I commence to read Sûrah Yûsuf).

1. ALIF LÂM RÂ - I am Allâh, the All-Seeing. These are the verses of the perfect Book, containing luminous (truths) that tell the right from the wrong.
2. We have, indeed revealed this Qur'ân which explains its object eloquently well that you may abstain (from evils).
3. We narrate (rightly) to you with the best explanation because We revealed to you this Qur'ân; otherwise you were of those not possessed of the (requisite) knowledge before this.
4. (Remember the time) when Joseph said to his father, 'My dear father! I have seen (in a vision) eleven stars and the sun and the moon. I saw them falling down prostrate (before God) because of me.'
5. He said, 'My dear son! Relate not your vision to your brothers lest they should intrigue against you, for satan is to a human being an enemy disuniting.
6. 'And thus (shall it be as He has shown you in this vision). Your Lord will make you His chosen one and impart you knowledge of the true interpretation of (Divine) sayings and will perfect His favours upon you and upon the family of Jacob, just as He perfected it formerly upon two of your forefathers - Abraham and Isaac. Verily, your Lord is All-Knowing, All-Wise.'

SECTION 2

7. THE fact is that there are many signs in (the account of) Joseph and his brothers for the

سُورَةُ يُوسُفَ مَكِّيَّةٌ

بِسْمِ اللَّهِ الرَّحْمَٰنِ الرَّحِيمِ

الٓر تِلْكَ ءَايَٰتُ الْكِتَٰبِ الْمُبِينِ ١ إِنَّآ
أَنزَلْنَٰهُ قُرْءَٰنًا عَرَبِيًّا لَّعَلَّكُمْ تَعْقِلُونَ ٢
نَحْنُ نَقُصُّ عَلَيْكَ أَحْسَنَ الْقَصَصِ بِمَآ
أَوْحَيْنَآ إِلَيْكَ هَٰذَا الْقُرْءَانَ وَإِن كُنتَ
مِن قَبْلِهِۦ لَمِنَ الْغَٰفِلِينَ ٣ إِذْ قَالَ يُوسُفُ
لِأَبِيهِ يَٰٓأَبَتِ إِنِّي رَأَيْتُ أَحَدَ عَشَرَ كَوْكَبًا
وَالشَّمْسَ وَالْقَمَرَ رَأَيْتُهُمْ لِي سَٰجِدِينَ ٤
قَالَ يَٰبُنَيَّ لَا تَقْصُصْ رُءْيَاكَ عَلَىٰٓ إِخْوَتِكَ
فَيَكِيدُوا لَكَ كَيْدًا إِنَّ الشَّيْطَٰنَ لِلْإِنسَٰنِ
عَدُوٌّ مُّبِينٌ ٥ وَكَذَٰلِكَ يَجْتَبِيكَ رَبُّكَ
وَيُعَلِّمُكَ مِن تَأْوِيلِ الْأَحَادِيثِ وَيُتِمُّ نِعْمَتَهُۥ
عَلَيْكَ وَعَلَىٰٓ ءَالِ يَعْقُوبَ كَمَآ أَتَمَّهَا عَلَىٰٓ
أَبَوَيْكَ مِن قَبْلُ إِبْرَٰهِيمَ وَإِسْحَٰقَ إِنَّ
رَبَّكَ عَلِيمٌ حَكِيمٌ ٦ لَقَدْ كَانَ فِي يُوسُفَ ع

الجزء الثاني عشر

inquirers (about the prophethood of Muhammad and about his opponents).

8. (Recall) when they (- brothers of Joseph) said (to one another), 'Surely, Joseph and his brother (Benjamin) are dearer to our father than we are, though we are a formidable party. Surely, our father is cherishing a love that has gone too far.

9. 'So you (had better either) kill Joseph or remove him to some distant land. (In this way) your father's favour will be exclusively yours. After that you can (repent and) become a pious people.'

10. (At this) a speaker among them said, 'If you are bent upon doing something at all, do not kill Joseph but put him into the dark depths of the dry well; (perhaps) some caravan of travellers may pick him out.'

11. (On making this resolution) they (went to their father and) said, 'Our father! Why do you not trust us with regard to Joseph, while, as a matter of fact, we are his sincere well-wishers?

12. 'Send him forth with us (for an outing) tomorrow, that he may enjoy himself and play. Surely, we will keep guard over him.'

13. He said, 'It worries me that you should take him away. Moreover, I fear lest a wolf should devour him while you are heedless of him.'

14. They said, 'If the wolf were to devour him inspite of the fact we are a formidable party, in that case we shall be indeed losers.'

15. So when (after forcing their father) they took him away and agreed to put him into the depths of a dry well (and carried their plan out), We revealed to him (- Joseph), 'You shall certainly tell them (one day) of this (treacherous) doing of theirs while they perceive not.'

16. And they came weeping to their father at nightfall.

17. They said, 'Our father! We went forth racing one with another and left Joseph (behind) with our belongings and the wolf devoured him. But

وَإِخْوَتِهِۦٓ ءَايَٰتٌ لِّلسَّآئِلِينَ ۞٧ إِذْ قَالُوا
لَيُوسُفُ وَأَخُوهُ أَحَبُّ إِلَىٰٓ أَبِينَا مِنَّا
وَنَحْنُ عُصْبَةٌ إِنَّ أَبَانَا لَفِي ضَلَٰلٍ مُّبِينٍ ٨
اقْتُلُوا يُوسُفَ أَوِ اطْرَحُوهُ أَرْضًا يَخْلُ لَكُمْ
وَجْهُ أَبِيكُمْ وَتَكُونُوا مِنۢ بَعْدِهِۦ قَوْمًا
صَٰلِحِينَ ٩ قَالَ قَآئِلٌ مِّنْهُمْ لَا تَقْتُلُوا
يُوسُفَ وَأَلْقُوهُ فِي غَيَٰبَتِ الْجُبِّ يَلْتَقِطْهُ
بَعْضُ السَّيَّارَةِ إِن كُنتُمْ فَٰعِلِينَ ١٠ قَالُوا
يَٰٓأَبَانَا مَا لَكَ لَا تَأْمَنَّا عَلَىٰ يُوسُفَ وَإِنَّا
لَهُۥ لَنَٰصِحُونَ ١١ أَرْسِلْهُ مَعَنَا غَدًا يَرْتَعْ
وَيَلْعَبْ وَإِنَّا لَهُۥ لَحَٰفِظُونَ ١٢ قَالَ إِنِّي لَيَحْزُنُنِيٓ
أَن تَذْهَبُوا بِهِۦ وَأَخَافُ أَن يَأْكُلَهُ الذِّئْبُ
وَأَنتُمْ عَنْهُ غَٰفِلُونَ ١٣ قَالُوا لَئِنْ أَكَلَهُ
الذِّئْبُ وَنَحْنُ عُصْبَةٌ إِنَّآ إِذًا لَّخَٰسِرُونَ ١٤
فَلَمَّا ذَهَبُوا بِهِۦ وَأَجْمَعُوٓا أَن يَجْعَلُوهُ فِي
غَيَٰبَتِ الْجُبِّ وَأَوْحَيْنَآ إِلَيْهِ لَتُنَبِّئَنَّهُم
بِأَمْرِهِمْ هَٰذَا وَهُمْ لَا يَشْعُرُونَ ١٥ وَجَآءُو
أَبَاهُمْ عِشَآءً يَبْكُونَ ١٦ قَالُوا يَٰٓأَبَانَآ إِنَّا
ذَهَبْنَا نَسْتَبِقُ وَتَرَكْنَا يُوسُفَ عِندَ مَتَٰعِنَا

you would never believe us though we be the truthful ones.'

18. And (to assure their father) they came (to him) with (stains of) false blood on his (- Joseph's) shirt. He (- Jacob) said, 'This is not true, but you yourselves have made a (malicious) thing seem fair to you. So (now showing) patience is befitting (for me). And it is Allâh (alone) Whose help can be sought to avert what you describe.'

19. (Now) there came a caravan of travellers and they sent their water-drawer (to fetch water) and he let down his bucket (into the well). And behold! He cried, 'Oh, glad tidings, here is a young boy.' So they (- Joseph's brothers) presented him (in this way) as (if) a piece of merchandise, and Allâh was Well-Aware of their doings.

20. And they (- the brothers of Joseph) sold him, (claiming him to be their slave, to the travellers) for a trifling price - a few *dirhams* (- silver coins), and they were not (even) desirous of it.

SECTION 3

21. AND (Joseph was taken to Egypt and resold there;) the man from Egypt who bought him (from the travellers) said to his wife, 'Make his stay honourable. He may prove useful to us or we may adopt him as a son.' In this way did We grant Joseph an honourable position in the country and (We did it) that We might impart to him knowledge of the interpretation of some (Divine) sayings. And Allâh has full power over His decree, but most people do not know (this).

22. And when he attained his (age of) full strength, We granted him judgment and knowledge, and thus do We reward the doers of good deeds to others.

23. Now the woman in whose house he was (putting up) sought to seduce him against his will and she bolted the doors well and said, 'Now come, I am ready to receive you.' He (- Joseph) said, '(How can it be possible,) I

فَأَكَلَهُ الذِّئْبُ ۚ وَمَا أَنتَ بِمُؤْمِنٍ لَّنَا
وَلَوْ كُنَّا صَادِقِينَ ﴿١٧﴾ وَجَاءُو عَلَىٰ قَمِيصِهِ
بِدَمٍ كَذِبٍ ۚ قَالَ بَلْ سَوَّلَتْ لَكُمْ أَنفُسُكُمْ
أَمْرًا ۖ فَصَبْرٌ جَمِيلٌ ۖ وَاللَّهُ الْمُسْتَعَانُ عَلَىٰ
مَا تَصِفُونَ ﴿١٨﴾ وَجَاءَتْ سَيَّارَةٌ فَأَرْسَلُوا
وَارِدَهُمْ فَأَدْلَىٰ دَلْوَهُ ۖ قَالَ يَا بُشْرَىٰ هَٰذَا
غُلَامٌ ۚ وَأَسَرُّوهُ بِضَاعَةً ۚ وَاللَّهُ عَلِيمٌ بِمَا
يَعْمَلُونَ ﴿١٩﴾ وَشَرَوْهُ بِثَمَنٍ بَخْسٍ دَرَاهِمَ
مَعْدُودَةٍ وَكَانُوا فِيهِ مِنَ الزَّاهِدِينَ ﴿٢٠﴾
وَقَالَ الَّذِي اشْتَرَاهُ مِن مِّصْرَ لِامْرَأَتِهِ
أَكْرِمِي مَثْوَاهُ عَسَىٰ أَن يَنفَعَنَا أَوْ نَتَّخِذَهُ
وَلَدًا ۚ وَكَذَٰلِكَ مَكَّنَّا لِيُوسُفَ فِي الْأَرْضِ
وَلِنُعَلِّمَهُ مِن تَأْوِيلِ الْأَحَادِيثِ ۚ وَاللَّهُ
غَالِبٌ عَلَىٰ أَمْرِهِ وَلَٰكِنَّ أَكْثَرَ النَّاسِ لَا
يَعْلَمُونَ ﴿٢١﴾ وَلَمَّا بَلَغَ أَشُدَّهُ آتَيْنَاهُ حُكْمًا
وَعِلْمًا ۚ وَكَذَٰلِكَ نَجْزِي الْمُحْسِنِينَ ﴿٢٢﴾ وَرَاوَدَتْهُ
الَّتِي هُوَ فِي بَيْتِهَا عَن نَّفْسِهِ وَغَلَّقَتِ الْأَبْوَابَ
وَقَالَتْ هَيْتَ لَكَ ۚ قَالَ مَعَاذَ اللَّهِ ۖ إِنَّهُ رَبِّي

seek refuge with Allâh, He alone is my Lord. He has made my stay (with you) honourable. Verily, the wrong doers never flourish.'

24. And she made up her mind with regard to him, and he made up his mind with regard to her (and would have fallen into her snares as the temptations were so strong) if he had not seen the manifest evidence of his Lord. (It happened thus) so that We might turn away from him every evil and indecency. Surely, he was one of Our purified servants.

25. And both of them ran for the door, one trying to outdo the other. And (in the struggle) she tore his shirt from behind. They encountered her husband (all of a sudden) by the door. She said, 'There can be no punishment less than imprisonment or some other painful torture for the man who intended evil with your wife.'

26. He (- Joseph) said, 'No, (it is not so as she describes but) she it was who sought to seduce me against my will.' Now a (learned) witness of her own family bore a (circumstantial) evidence (saying), 'If his shirt has been torn from the front then she speaks the truth and he is of the liars.

27. 'But if his shirt has been torn from behind then she is a liar and he speaks the truth.'

28. So when he (- her husband) saw his shirt torn from behind, he (at once understood the truth of the matter and) said (to his wife), 'This is surely a (deceiving) device which you women practise. Your (cunning) device is indeed great.'

29. (Turning to Joseph) he said, 'Joseph! Leave the matter alone and you (- woman) seek forgiveness for your sin. It is you, of course who are at fault.'

SECTION 4

30. **A**ND the women talked in the city, 'The wife of the 'Azîz (- Potiphar, the captain of king's guard) seeks to seduce her young slave against his will. His love has indeed penetrated deep in her heart. Indeed we see her in

أَحۡسَنَ مَثۡوَايَ ۖ إِنَّهُۥ لَا يُفۡلِحُ الظّٰلِمُوۡنَ ﴿٢٣﴾
وَلَقَدۡ هَمَّتۡ بِهٖ ۚ وَهَمَّ بِهَا لَوۡلَآ أَنۡ رَّأٰ
بُرۡهٰنَ رَبِّهٖ ۚ كَذٰلِكَ لِنَصۡرِفَ عَنۡهُ السُّوۡٓءَ
وَالۡفَحۡشَآءَ ۚ إِنَّهُۥ مِنۡ عِبَادِنَا الۡمُخۡلَصِيۡنَ ﴿٢٤﴾
وَاسۡتَبَقَا الۡبَابَ وَقَدَّتۡ قَمِيۡصَهُۥ مِنۡ دُبُرٍ
وَّأَلۡفَيَا سَيِّدَهَا لَدَا الۡبَابِ ۚ قَالَتۡ مَا جَزَآءُ
مَنۡ أَرَادَ بِأَهۡلِكَ سُوۡٓءًا إِلَّآ أَنۡ يُّسۡجَنَ أَوۡ
عَذَابٌ أَلِيۡمٌ ﴿٢٥﴾ قَالَ هِيَ رَاوَدَتۡنِيۡ عَنۡ نَّفۡسِيۡ
وَشَهِدَ شَاهِدٌ مِّنۡ أَهۡلِهَا ۚ إِنۡ كَانَ
قَمِيۡصُهُۥ قُدَّ مِنۡ قُبُلٍ فَصَدَقَتۡ وَهُوَ مِنَ
الۡكٰذِبِيۡنَ ﴿٢٦﴾ وَإِنۡ كَانَ قَمِيۡصُهُۥ قُدَّ مِنۡ
دُبُرٍ فَكَذَبَتۡ وَهُوَ مِنَ الصّٰدِقِيۡنَ ﴿٢٧﴾ فَلَمَّا
رَأٰ قَمِيۡصَهُۥ قُدَّ مِنۡ دُبُرٍ قَالَ إِنَّهُۥ مِنۡ
كَيۡدِكُنَّ ۖ إِنَّ كَيۡدَكُنَّ عَظِيۡمٌ ﴿٢٨﴾ يُوۡسُفُ
أَعۡرِضۡ عَنۡ هٰذَا ۚ وَاسۡتَغۡفِرِيۡ لِذَنۡۢبِكِ ۚ
إِنَّكِ كُنۡتِ مِنَ الۡخٰطِـِٔيۡنَ ﴿٢٩﴾ وَقَالَ نِسۡوَةٌ
فِي الۡمَدِيۡنَةِ امۡرَأَتُ الۡعَزِيۡزِ تُرَاوِدُ فَتٰهَا

ع ٣ ١٤

obvious error (in going too far in her love).'

31. And when she heard of their sly whisperings (and taunting remarks), she sent for them and prepared a repast for them, then (on the women's arrival) she gave to each one of them a knife (to eat fruit therewith) and said (to Joseph then), 'Come forth in their presence.' So when they saw him they found him a dignified personality and cut their hands (through wonder and) said, 'Glory be to Allâh! He is not a human being. He is but a noble angel.'

32. She said, 'So (you have seen) this is he about whom you blamed me. I did seek to seduce him against his will, but he preserved himself (from sin), yet (I tell him aloud) if he does not do what I bid him, he shall certainly be imprisoned, and he shall indeed be of the humiliated ones.'

33. (Hearing this) he (- Joseph) said, 'My Lord, the prison is more to my liking than that to which they call me to, and unless you turn away their guile from me I might yield to their allurement and be of those devoid of knowledge.'

34. So his Lord accepted his prayer and turned away their (- women's) guile from him. Verily, He is All-Hearing, All-Knowing.

35. Then it occurred to them (-the companions of the 'Azîz) after they had examined all the circumstances and signs (of Joseph's innocence) that they had better imprison him for a time. (So Joseph was consigned to the prison.)

SECTION 5

36. AND with him there entered the prison two young men (- the butler and the baker of the king). One of them said to him, 'I see myself (in a dream) pressing grapes.' And the other said, 'I see myself carrying upon my head bread of which the birds are eating. Inform us of the interpretation of these (dreams) for we surely find you of the doers of good to others.'

37. He said, '(Do not worry,) I shall inform you of the interpretation of these (dreams) before the meal you two are given comes to

عَنْ نَّفْسِهٖ قَدْ شَغَفَهَا حُبًّا إِنَّا لَنَرٰىهَا فِي
ضَلٰلٍ مُّبِينٍ ۝٣٠ فَلَمَّا سَمِعَتْ بِمَكْرِهِنَّ
أَرْسَلَتْ إِلَيْهِنَّ وَأَعْتَدَتْ لَهُنَّ مُتَّكَـًٔا
وَّءَاتَتْ كُلَّ وٰحِدَةٍ مِّنْهُنَّ سِكِّينًا وَّقَالَتِ
اخْرُجْ عَلَيْهِنَّ فَلَمَّا رَأَيْنَهٗٓ أَكْبَرْنَهٗ
وَقَطَّعْنَ أَيْدِيَهُنَّ وَقُلْنَ حٰشَ لِلّٰهِ مَا هٰذَا
بَشَرًا إِنْ هٰذَآ إِلَّا مَلَكٌ كَرِيمٌ ۝٣١ قَالَتْ
فَذٰلِكُنَّ الَّذِي لُمْتُنَّنِي فِيهِ وَلَقَدْ
رٰوَدْتُّهٗ عَنْ نَّفْسِهٖ فَاسْتَعْصَمَ وَلَئِنْ لَّمْ
يَفْعَلْ مَآ ءَامُرُهٗ لَيُسْجَنَنَّ وَلَيَكُونًا
مِّنَ الصّٰغِرِينَ ۝٣٢ قَالَ رَبِّ السِّجْنُ أَحَبُّ
إِلَيَّ مِمَّا يَدْعُونَنِيٓ إِلَيْهِ وَإِلَّا تَصْرِفْ
عَنِّي كَيْدَهُنَّ أَصْبُ إِلَيْهِنَّ وَأَكُنْ
مِّنَ الْجٰهِلِينَ ۝٣٣ فَاسْتَجَابَ لَهٗ رَبُّهٗ فَصَرَفَ
عَنْهُ كَيْدَهُنَّ إِنَّهٗ هُوَ السَّمِيعُ الْعَلِيمُ ۝٣٤
ثُمَّ بَدَا لَهُمْ مِّنْ بَعْدِ مَا رَأَوُا الْأٰيٰتِ
لَيَسْجُنُنَّهٗ حَتّٰى حِينٍ ۝٣٥ وَدَخَلَ مَعَهُ
السِّجْنَ فَتَيَانِ قَالَ أَحَدُهُمَآ إِنِّيٓ أَرٰىنِيٓ أَعْصِرُ
خَمْرًا وَقَالَ الْأٰخَرُ إِنِّيٓ أَرٰىنِيٓ أَحْمِلُ فَوْقَ
رَأْسِي خُبْزًا تَأْكُلُ الطَّيْرُ مِنْهُ نَبِّئْنَا بِتَأْوِيلِهٖ
إِنَّا نَرٰىكَ مِنَ الْمُحْسِنِينَ ۝٣٦ قَالَ لَا يَأْتِيكُمَا

you. This (my ability to interpret, you should bear in mind) is a part of that knowledge which my Lord has imparted to me. I have indeed renounced the creed of the people who do not believe in Allâh and who, moreover, are disbelievers in the Hereafter.

38. 'And I have followed the creed of my fathers, Abraham, Isaac and Jacob. It is not proper for us to associate anything as a partner with Allâh. That (He taught us unity of God) is entirely due to Allâh's grace upon us and upon (other) people. But most people do not render thanks (for this blessing).

39. 'My two fellow-prisoners! What is better? Diverse and numerous gods or Allâh, the One, the Most Supreme?

40. 'You worship nothing, apart from Him but some mere (imaginary) names coined by you and by your fathers. Allâh has sent down no authority for (worshipping) that. The judgment rests with Allâh alone. He has commanded that you shall worship none but Him alone. That is the right (and lasting) faith yet most people know (it) not.

41. 'My two fellow-prisoners! As for one of you, he will pour out wine for his lord to drink and as for the other, he shall be crucified so that the birds will eat (flesh) from off his head. The matter about which you inquired stands decreed.'

42. And he said to the one of the two whom he knew would be released, 'Mention me to your lord.' But satan made him (-the released person) forget to mention (Joseph) to his lord so that he (- Joseph) remained confined in the prison for a few years.

SECTION 6

43. **N**ow (it so happened that one day) the king said, 'I saw (in a dream) seven fat kine which seven lean ones were eating, and seven green ears of corn and (as many) others withered. You nobles of the court! Explain to me the

طَعَامٌ تُرْزَقَانِهِ إِلَّا نَبَّأْتُكُمَا بِتَأْوِيلِهِ قَبْلَ أَنْ يَأْتِيَكُمَا ۚ ذٰلِكُمَا مِمَّا عَلَّمَنِي رَبِّي ۚ إِنِّي تَرَكْتُ مِلَّةَ قَوْمٍ لَّا يُؤْمِنُونَ بِاللهِ وَهُمْ بِالْآخِرَةِ هُمْ كٰفِرُونَ ﴿٣٧﴾ وَاتَّبَعْتُ مِلَّةَ آبَاءِي إِبْرٰهِيمَ وَإِسْحٰقَ وَيَعْقُوبَ ۚ مَا كَانَ لَنَا أَنْ نُّشْرِكَ بِاللهِ مِنْ شَيْءٍ ۚ ذٰلِكَ مِنْ فَضْلِ اللهِ عَلَيْنَا وَعَلَى النَّاسِ وَلٰكِنَّ أَكْثَرَ النَّاسِ لَا يَشْكُرُونَ ﴿٣٨﴾ يٰصٰحِبَيِ السِّجْنِ ءَأَرْبَابٌ مُّتَفَرِّقُونَ خَيْرٌ أَمِ اللهُ الْوٰحِدُ الْقَهَّارُ ﴿٣٩﴾ مَا تَعْبُدُونَ مِنْ دُونِهِ إِلَّا أَسْمَاءً سَمَّيْتُمُوهَا أَنْتُمْ وَآبَاؤُكُمْ مَّا أَنْزَلَ اللهُ بِهَا مِنْ سُلْطٰنٍ ۚ إِنِ الْحُكْمُ إِلَّا لِلّٰهِ ۚ أَمَرَ أَلَّا تَعْبُدُوا إِلَّا إِيَّاهُ ۚ ذٰلِكَ الدِّينُ الْقَيِّمُ وَلٰكِنَّ أَكْثَرَ النَّاسِ لَا يَعْلَمُونَ ﴿٤٠﴾ يٰصٰحِبَيِ السِّجْنِ أَمَّا أَحَدُكُمَا فَيَسْقِي رَبَّهُ خَمْرًا ۖ وَأَمَّا الْآخَرُ فَيُصْلَبُ فَتَأْكُلُ الطَّيْرُ مِنْ رَّأْسِهِ ۚ قُضِيَ الْأَمْرُ الَّذِي فِيهِ تَسْتَفْتِيٰنِ ﴿٤١﴾ وَقَالَ لِلَّذِي ظَنَّ أَنَّهُ نَاجٍ مِّنْهُمَا اذْكُرْنِي عِنْدَ رَبِّكَ فَأَنْسٰهُ الشَّيْطٰنُ ذِكْرَ رَبِّهِ فَلَبِثَ فِي السِّجْنِ بِضْعَ سِنِينَ ﴿٤٢﴾ وَقَالَ الْمَلِكُ إِنِّي أَرٰى

ع ٧ ١٥

real significance of my dream if you can interpret dreams.'

44. They said, '(These are) confused dreams and we do not know the interpretation of such confused dreams.'

45 And of the two (prisoners) the one who had got his release and who (now) recalled (Joseph) to his mind after a long time, said, 'I will inform you of its (true) interpretation, therefore send me (for the purpose to Joseph in prison).'

46 (So he went to Joseph in the prison and exclaimed,) 'Joseph, O the man of truth! Explain to us the (real) significance of (a dream in which) seven fat kine which seven lean ones devour; and (of) seven green ears of corn and as many others withered, so that I may return to the people and they may know (the interpretation and thereby your exalted position).'

47. He (- Joseph) replied, 'You shall sow for seven years working hard and continuously and let what you have harvested remain in its ear excepting a little whereof you may eat.

48. 'Then there shall follow seven (years of famine) of great severity (and) these (years) shall consume all the stores you have laid by in advance for them except a little which you may have preserved.

49. 'Then, thereafter shall come a year of rains in which people shall be relieved and in which (season) they will press (fruit and seeds).'

SECTION 7

50. **A**ND the King (after hearing the interpretation by Joseph) said, 'Bring him to me!' But when the messengers came to him he said, 'Go back to your lord and ask him (on my behalf), 'How does the matter (deserving of your attention) stands with regard to the women who cut their hands; for my Lord has full knowledge of their crafty designs.'

51. (The king then sent for the ladies and to them) he said, 'What was that important matter

سَبۡعَ بَقَرٰتٍ سِمَانٍ يَّأۡكُلُهُنَّ سَبۡعٌ
عِجَافٌ وَّسَبۡعَ سُنۡبُلٰتٍ خُضۡرٍ وَّأُخَرَ
يٰبِسٰتٍ ۖ يٰۤأَيُّهَا الۡمَلَأُ أَفۡتُونِي فِي رُءۡيَايَ
إِنۡ كُنۡتُمۡ لِلرُّءۡيَا تَعۡبُرُونَ ﴿٤٣﴾ قَالُوۡا أَضۡغٰثُ
أَحۡلٰمٍ ۚ وَمَا نَحۡنُ بِتَأۡوِيلِ الۡأَحۡلٰمِ بِعٰلِمِينَ ﴿٤٤﴾
وَقَالَ الَّذِي نَجَا مِنۡهُمَا وَادَّكَرَ بَعۡدَ أُمَّةٍ
أَنَا أُنَبِّئُكُمۡ بِتَأۡوِيلِهِ فَأَرۡسِلُونِ ﴿٤٥﴾ يُوسُفُ
أَيُّهَا الصِّدِّيقُ أَفۡتِنَا فِي سَبۡعِ بَقَرٰتٍ سِمَانٍ
يَّأۡكُلُهُنَّ سَبۡعٌ عِجَافٌ وَّسَبۡعِ سُنۡبُلٰتٍ
خُضۡرٍ وَّأُخَرَ يٰبِسٰتٍ ۙ لَّعَلِّيۤ أَرۡجِعُ إِلَى
النَّاسِ لَعَلَّهُمۡ يَعۡلَمُونَ ﴿٤٦﴾ قَالَ تَزۡرَعُونَ
سَبۡعَ سِنِينَ دَأَبًا ۚ فَمَا حَصَدۡتُّمۡ فَذَرُوهُ
فِي سُنۡبُلِهِۦٓ إِلَّا قَلِيلًا مِّمَّا تَأۡكُلُونَ ﴿٤٧﴾ ثُمَّ
يَأۡتِي مِنۡ بَعۡدِ ذٰلِكَ سَبۡعٌ شِدَادٌ يَّأۡكُلۡنَ
مَا قَدَّمۡتُمۡ لَهُنَّ إِلَّا قَلِيلًا مِّمَّا تُحۡصِنُونَ ﴿٤٨﴾
ثُمَّ يَأۡتِي مِنۡ بَعۡدِ ذٰلِكَ عَامٌ فِيهِ يُغَاثُ
النَّاسُ وَفِيهِ يَعۡصِرُونَ ﴿٤٩﴾ وَقَالَ الۡمَلِكُ
ائۡتُونِي بِهِۦ ۚ فَلَمَّا جَآءَهُ الرَّسُولُ قَالَ
ارۡجِعۡ إِلَى رَبِّكَ فَسۡئَلۡهُ مَا بَالُ النِّسۡوَةِ الّٰتِي
قَطَّعۡنَ أَيۡدِيَهُنَّ ۖ إِنَّ رَبِّي بِكَيۡدِهِنَّ عَلِيمٌ ﴿٥٠﴾
قَالَ مَا خَطۡبُكُنَّ إِذۡ رٰوَدۡتُّنَّ يُوسُفَ عَنۡ

(in reality) that you had in view when you sought to seduce Joseph against his will?' They said, 'He kept away (from committing sin) for the sake of Allâh. We did not perceive the least evil (intention) on his part.' The wife of the 'Azîz said, 'Now the truth has come to light (at last). It was I who sought to seduce him against his will and most surely he is of the truthful.'

52. (When the news was brought to Joseph he said,) 'This (course of action I adopted) so that he (- the 'Azîz) might know that I had not betrayed him in (his) absence and that Allâh suffers not the device of the unfaithful to succeed.'

نَفْسِهِ قُلْنَ حَاشَ لِلَّهِ مَا عَلِمْنَا عَلَيْهِ مِنْ
سُوءٍ قَالَتِ امْرَأَتُ الْعَزِيزِ الْآنَ حَصْحَصَ
الْحَقُّ أَنَا رَاوَدْتُهُ عَنْ نَفْسِهِ وَإِنَّهُ لَمِنَ
الصَّادِقِينَ ﴿٥١﴾ ذَلِكَ لِيَعْلَمَ أَنِّي لَمْ أَخُنْهُ
بِالْغَيْبِ وَأَنَّ اللَّهَ لَا يَهْدِي كَيْدَ الْخَائِنِينَ ﴿٥٢﴾

PART الجزء الثالث عشر XIII

53. 'YET I do not hold myself to be free from weakness, for the Commanding Self is surely prone to enjoin evil, except on whom my Lord has mercy. My Lord is of course Protector (against sins), Ever Merciful.'

54. And the king said, 'Bring him to me. I will make him my special attache.' And when he (- Joseph came and) spoke to him, he (- the king) said, 'From this day you hold a (notable) position of honour (and) trust with us.'

55. (Joseph) said, 'Appoint me over the treasures (- granaries and stores) of the land, for I am a careful keeper and possessed of knowledge (of the job).'

56. That is how We granted Joseph high power in the country. He wielded authority therein wherever he chose. We bestow Our mercy on whomsoever We will and We suffer not the reward of the doers of excellent deeds to be lost.

57. Yet those who believe and have been guarding against sin and dutiful, shall have a much better reward in the Hereafter.

وَمَا أُبَرِّئُ نَفْسِي إِنَّ النَّفْسَ لَأَمَّارَةٌ
بِالسُّوءِ إِلَّا مَا رَحِمَ رَبِّي إِنَّ رَبِّي غَفُورٌ
رَحِيمٌ ﴿٥٣﴾ وَقَالَ الْمَلِكُ ائْتُونِي بِهِ أَسْتَخْلِصْهُ
لِنَفْسِي فَلَمَّا كَلَّمَهُ قَالَ إِنَّكَ الْيَوْمَ لَدَيْنَا
مَكِينٌ أَمِينٌ ﴿٥٤﴾ قَالَ اجْعَلْنِي عَلَى خَزَائِنِ
الْأَرْضِ إِنِّي حَفِيظٌ عَلِيمٌ ﴿٥٥﴾ وَكَذَلِكَ مَكَّنَّا
لِيُوسُفَ فِي الْأَرْضِ يَتَبَوَّأُ مِنْهَا حَيْثُ
يَشَاءُ نُصِيبُ بِرَحْمَتِنَا مَنْ نَشَاءُ وَلَا نُضِيعُ
أَجْرَ الْمُحْسِنِينَ ﴿٥٦﴾ وَلَأَجْرُ الْآخِرَةِ خَيْرٌ
لِلَّذِينَ آمَنُوا وَكَانُوا يَتَّقُونَ ﴿٥٧﴾ وَجَاءَ إِخْوَةُ

ع ٨

SECTION 8

58. AND (in the years of famine) Joseph's brothers came (from Kin'ân to Egypt) and they

presented themselves to him. But though he knew them they recognized him not.
59. When he had provided them with their provision he said, '(When you come next) bring me your brother from your father's side. Do you not see that I give full measure (of corn) and I am the best of hosts?
60. 'But if you do not bring him to me, there shall be no more measure (of corn) for you from me, nor shall you find access to me.'
61. They said, 'We will certainly persuade his father to part with him and we are sure to do (it).'
62. And he said to his servants, 'Put their cash (they paid for the corn) in their saddle-bags,' (and to himself,) 'that they may recognize it (as benevolence) when they return to their family and perhaps they may come back (with his brother on this account).'
63. So when they returned to their father they said, 'Our father! (a further) measure (of corn) has been denied us (unless we take our brother Benjamin with us), therefore send our brother with us that we may have (our) measure (of corn) and we will surely be able to take (due) care of him.'
64. (Jacob) said, 'Shall I trust you with him as I trusted you with his brother before? (I would rather trust Allâh.) Allâh is the best Guardian and He is the Most Merciful of those who show mercy.'
65. And when they unpacked their goods they found their cash (too) returned to them. They said, 'Our father! What more should we desire? Here is our cash returned to us. And (if Benjamin accompanies us we will make the best use of it,) we will bring food for our family and we will take care of our brother, and we shall have the measure of a camel-load in addition. That measure of corn (we have already brought) is a light one (and so little and insufficient).
66. He said, 'Never will I send him with you until you give me a solemn pledge in the name

يوسف فدخلوا عليه فعرفهم وهم له
منكرون ٥٨ ولما جهزهم بجهازهم قال
ائتوني بأخ لكم من أبيكم ألا ترون أني
أوفي الكيل وأنا خير المنزلين ٥٩ فإن لم
تأتوني به فلا كيل لكم عندي ولا
تقربون ٦٠ قالوا سنراود عنه أباه وإنا
لفاعلون ٦١ وقال لفتيانه اجعلوا بضاعتهم
في رحالهم لعلهم يعرفونها إذا انقلبوا
إلى أهلهم لعلهم يرجعون ٦٢ فلما رجعوا
إلى أبيهم قالوا يأبانا منع منا الكيل
فأرسل معنا أخانا نكتل وإنا له
لحافظون ٦٣ قال هل آمنكم عليه إلا كما
أمنتكم على أخيه من قبل فالله خير
حافظا وهو أرحم الرحمين ٦٤ ولما فتحوا
متاعهم وجدوا بضاعتهم ردت إليهم قالوا
يأبانا ما نبغي هذه بضاعتنا ردت إلينا
ونمير أهلنا ونحفظ أخانا ونزداد كيل
بعير ذلك كيل يسير ٦٥ قال لن أرسله

of Allâh that you shall surely bring him to me unless it be that you yourselves are beset with difficult circumstances.' When they had given him their solemn pledge he said, 'Allâh shall be Guardian over what we have agreed.'

67. And he also said (on their departure), 'My sons! (reaching Egypt) enter (the city) not by one gate rather enter (it) by different gates. Yet I can avail you naught against (the decree of) Allâh. The decision only rests with Allâh. In Him do I put my trust and in Him let all who would trust, put their trust (in the like manner).'

68. And when they entered the city after the manner their father had bidden them (Jacob's object was achieved but) it could not at all help them against the decree of Allâh. All that it came to was that Jacob's desire he had in his mind was (thus) satisfied (and his purpose achieved) and he was surely possessed of knowledge because We had imparted full knowledge to him. But most people do not know (these things).

SECTION 9

69. **W**HEN they entered upon Joseph he betook his brother to himself for restful lodging (making him his personal guest). He (- Joseph) said (to Benjamin), 'I am your (real) brother (Joseph), so now do not grieve over what they (- our other brothers) have been doing.'

70. When he had provided them with their provision (to set on a return journey), someone put a drinking cup in the saddle-bag of his brother (Benjamin). Then (it so happened that) a crier called, 'O (men of) the caravan carrying the corn! You are most surely thieves.'

71. They (- men of the caravan) said turning towards them (- the heralds), 'What is it that you are missing?'

72. They said, 'We find the king's measuring vessel missing' and (added), 'Whoever restores it shall receive a camel-load (of corn as a

مَعَكُمْ حَتّٰى تُؤْتُوْنِ مَوْثِقًا مِّنَ اللّٰهِ لَتَأْتُنَّنِيْ
بِهٖٓ إِلَّآ أَنْ يُّحَاطَ بِكُمْ ۚ فَلَمَّآ أٰتَوْهُ مَوْثِقَهُمْ
قَالَ اللّٰهُ عَلٰى مَا نَقُوْلُ وَكِيْلٌ ﴿٦٦﴾ وَقَالَ
يٰبَنِيَّ لَا تَدْخُلُوْا مِنْۢ بَابٍ وّٰحِدٍ وَّادْخُلُوْا
مِنْ أَبْوٰبٍ مُّتَفَرِّقَةٍ ۖ وَمَآ أُغْنِيْ عَنْكُمْ مِّنَ
اللّٰهِ مِنْ شَيْءٍ ۖ إِنِ الْحُكْمُ إِلَّا لِلّٰهِ ۖ عَلَيْهِ
تَوَكَّلْتُ ۖ وَعَلَيْهِ فَلْيَتَوَكَّلِ الْمُتَوَكِّلُوْنَ ﴿٦٧﴾
وَلَمَّا دَخَلُوْا مِنْ حَيْثُ أَمَرَهُمْ أَبُوْهُمْ ۖ مَا
كَانَ يُغْنِيْ عَنْهُمْ مِّنَ اللّٰهِ مِنْ شَيْءٍ إِلَّا
حَاجَةً فِيْ نَفْسِ يَعْقُوْبَ قَضٰهَا ۖ وَإِنَّهٗ
لَذُوْ عِلْمٍ لِّمَا عَلَّمْنٰهُ وَلٰكِنَّ أَكْثَرَ النَّاسِ لَا
يَعْلَمُوْنَ ﴿٦٨﴾ وَلَمَّا دَخَلُوْا عَلٰى يُوْسُفَ أٰوٰى
إِلَيْهِ أَخَاهُ قَالَ إِنِّيْٓ أَنَا أَخُوْكَ فَلَا تَبْتَئِسْ
بِمَا كَانُوْا يَعْمَلُوْنَ ﴿٦٩﴾ فَلَمَّا جَهَّزَهُمْ بِجَهَازِهِمْ
جَعَلَ السِّقَايَةَ فِيْ رَحْلِ أَخِيْهِ ثُمَّ أَذَّنَ
مُؤَذِّنٌ أَيَّتُهَا الْعِيْرُ إِنَّكُمْ لَسٰرِقُوْنَ ﴿٧٠﴾ قَالُوْا
وَأَقْبَلُوْا عَلَيْهِمْ مَّاذَا تَفْقِدُوْنَ ﴿٧١﴾ قَالُوْا
نَفْقِدُ صُوَاعَ الْمَلِكِ وَلِمَنْ جَآءَ بِهٖ حِمْلُ

reward),' (and one of them said), 'I am surely responsible for it.'
73. They replied, 'By Allâh, you know well that we did not come to commit mischief in this country, nor are we (professional) thieves.'
74. They (- the Egyptians) said, 'What shall be the punishment for this (theft) if you are (proved to be) liars?'
75. They replied, 'The punishment for this is that he in whose saddle-bag this (vessel) is found shall himself be the penalty for it (and so he himself shall be confiscated as its forfeit). This is how we punish the wrong doers.'
76. Then he (- the king's herald) began (the search) with the sacks of others before (he came to) the sack of his (- Joseph's) brother (Benjamin). (Finding the vessel therein) he brought it out of his brother's sack. That is how We contrived for Joseph (to keep Benjamin with him, otherwise) he could not have taken his brother according to the king's law. Yet it came about as Allâh willed. We raise in degrees (of rank) whomsoever We will. And over and above every possessor of knowledge there is One (Almighty God), Who is All-Knowing.
77. (Joseph's brothers) said, 'If he has stolen, (no wonder) a brother of his had (also) committed theft before (this).' But Joseph kept it secret in his heart and did not disclose it to them. He (simply) said, 'You are a worse case and Allâh knows best what you are alleging.'
78. (Brothers of Joseph) said, 'O noble chief! Surely he has an old father, advanced in years, so retain one of us in his place. Surely, we see you to be of the doers of good (to all).'
79. He said, 'God forbid that we take anyone except the one with whom we found our property, for (otherwise) we would, of course, be unjust.'

SECTION 10

80. **W**HEN they were despaired of (moving) him, they retired to confer together in private. One of their leaders said, 'Are you not aware that your father has bound you to a solemn

بَعِيرٍ وَأَنَا بِهِ زَعِيمٌ ﴿٧٢﴾ قَالُوا تَاللَّهِ لَقَدْ عَلِمْتُم مَّا جِئْنَا لِنُفْسِدَ فِي الْأَرْضِ وَمَا كُنَّا سَارِقِينَ ﴿٧٣﴾ قَالُوا فَمَا جَزَاؤُهُ إِن كُنتُمْ كَاذِبِينَ ﴿٧٤﴾ قَالُوا جَزَاؤُهُ مَن وُجِدَ فِي رَحْلِهِ فَهُوَ جَزَاؤُهُ ۚ كَذَٰلِكَ نَجْزِي الظَّالِمِينَ ﴿٧٥﴾ فَبَدَأَ بِأَوْعِيَتِهِمْ قَبْلَ وِعَاءِ أَخِيهِ ثُمَّ اسْتَخْرَجَهَا مِن وِعَاءِ أَخِيهِ ۚ كَذَٰلِكَ كِدْنَا لِيُوسُفَ ۖ مَا كَانَ لِيَأْخُذَ أَخَاهُ فِي دِينِ الْمَلِكِ إِلَّا أَن يَشَاءَ اللَّهُ ۚ نَرْفَعُ دَرَجَاتٍ مَّن نَّشَاءُ ۗ وَفَوْقَ كُلِّ ذِي عِلْمٍ عَلِيمٌ ﴿٧٦﴾ قَالُوا إِن يَسْرِقْ فَقَدْ سَرَقَ أَخٌ لَّهُ مِن قَبْلُ ۚ فَأَسَرَّهَا يُوسُفُ فِي نَفْسِهِ وَلَمْ يُبْدِهَا لَهُمْ ۚ قَالَ أَنتُمْ شَرٌّ مَّكَانًا ۖ وَاللَّهُ أَعْلَمُ بِمَا تَصِفُونَ ﴿٧٧﴾ قَالُوا يَا أَيُّهَا الْعَزِيزُ إِنَّ لَهُ أَبًا شَيْخًا كَبِيرًا فَخُذْ أَحَدَنَا مَكَانَهُ ۖ إِنَّا نَرَاكَ مِنَ الْمُحْسِنِينَ ﴿٧٨﴾ قَالَ مَعَاذَ اللَّهِ أَن نَّأْخُذَ إِلَّا مَن وَجَدْنَا مَتَاعَنَا عِندَهُ إِنَّا إِذًا لَّظَالِمُونَ ﴿٧٩﴾ فَلَمَّا اسْتَيْأَسُوا مِنْهُ خَلَصُوا نَجِيًّا ۖ قَالَ كَبِيرُهُمْ أَلَمْ تَعْلَمُوا

pledge in the name of Allâh? And how before this, you fell short of your duty in respect of Joseph? Never will I, therefore, leave this land until my father gives me permission or Allâh, Who is the best of Judges, decides (the matter) for me.

81. 'Return all of you to your father and say, "Our father! Your son has committed the theft, and we say no more than what we know (and we did not witness him stealing), and we could not be guardians over what was unseen (by us).

82. "And you may inquire of (the inhabitants of) the city we were in, and of (the people of) the caravan carrying the corn we accompanied. We speak nothing but the truth".'

83. (So when, reaching home Jacob's sons gave all this information to him, Jacob) said, 'Nay, it is not so, rather your (baser) selves have embellished to you an other (abominable) thing. So (now showing) patience is befitting. It is not far from (the grace of) Allâh to bring them all to me for He is indeed the All-Knowing, the All-Wise.'

84. And he turned away from them and said, 'O my grief for Joseph!' And his eyes were drowned (with tears) for the pangs of grief and he was suppressing (his sorrow).

85. They said, 'By Allâh! You will not cease mentioning Joseph until you are consumed away (for some disease) or become of the perished.'

86. He replied, 'I complain of my anguish and of my sorrow to Allâh alone. I know from Allâh what you do not know.

87. 'Go, my sons, and make a thorough search for Joseph and his brother. Do not despair of Allâh's soothing mercy. Verily, none but the people who deny (the truth) can ever lose hope of Allâh's soothing mercy.'

88. And when they (- Joseph's brothers) came again before him (- Joseph) they said, 'O noble chief! Distress and poverty (due to famine) has befallen us and our family. We have brought

أَنَّ أَبَاكُمْ قَدْ أَخَذَ عَلَيْكُم مَّوْثِقًا مِّنَ اللَّهِ
وَمِن قَبْلُ مَا فَرَّطتُمْ فِي يُوسُفَ فَلَنْ أَبْرَحَ
الْأَرْضَ حَتَّىٰ يَأْذَنَ لِي أَبِي أَوْ يَحْكُمَ اللَّهُ
لِي وَهُوَ خَيْرُ الْحَٰكِمِينَ ٨٠ ارْجِعُوا إِلَىٰ أَبِيكُمْ
فَقُولُوا يَٰأَبَانَا إِنَّ ابْنَكَ سَرَقَ وَمَا شَهِدْنَا
إِلَّا بِمَا عَلِمْنَا وَمَا كُنَّا لِلْغَيْبِ حَٰفِظِينَ ٨١
وَسْـَٔلِ الْقَرْيَةَ الَّتِي كُنَّا فِيهَا وَالْعِيرَ
الَّتِي أَقْبَلْنَا فِيهَا ۖ وَإِنَّا لَصَٰدِقُونَ ٨٢ قَالَ
بَلْ سَوَّلَتْ لَكُمْ أَنفُسُكُمْ أَمْرًا ۖ فَصَبْرٌ
جَمِيلٌ ۖ عَسَى اللَّهُ أَن يَأْتِيَنِي بِهِمْ جَمِيعًا ۚ
إِنَّهُ هُوَ الْعَلِيمُ الْحَكِيمُ ٨٣ وَتَوَلَّىٰ عَنْهُمْ
وَقَالَ يَٰأَسَفَىٰ عَلَىٰ يُوسُفَ وَابْيَضَّتْ عَيْنَاهُ
مِنَ الْحُزْنِ فَهُوَ كَظِيمٌ ٨٤ قَالُوا تَاللَّهِ تَفْتَؤُا
تَذْكُرُ يُوسُفَ حَتَّىٰ تَكُونَ حَرَضًا أَوْ تَكُونَ
مِنَ الْهَٰلِكِينَ ٨٥ قَالَ إِنَّمَا أَشْكُوا بَثِّي
وَحُزْنِي إِلَى اللَّهِ وَأَعْلَمُ مِنَ اللَّهِ مَا لَا تَعْلَمُونَ ٨٦
يَٰبَنِيَّ اذْهَبُوا فَتَحَسَّسُوا مِن يُوسُفَ وَأَخِيهِ
وَلَا تَا۟يْـَٔسُوا مِن رَّوْحِ اللَّهِ ۖ إِنَّهُ لَا يَا۟يْـَٔسُ
مِن رَّوْحِ اللَّهِ إِلَّا الْقَوْمُ الْكَٰفِرُونَ ٨٧ فَلَمَّا
دَخَلُوا عَلَيْهِ قَالُوا يَٰأَيُّهَا الْعَزِيزُ مَسَّنَا
وَأَهْلَنَا الضُّرُّ وَجِئْنَا بِبِضَٰعَةٍ مُّزْجَىٰةٍ فَأَوْفِ

only a scanty amount of money. Give us (nonetheless) full measure (of corn) and show us charity. Surely, Allâh rewards the charitable.'

89. (Joseph) said, 'Are you aware what you did to Joseph and his brother (- Benjamin to involve him in trouble) in your ignorance?'

90. They (were startled and) said, 'Are you (Joseph)? Yes you are Joseph indeed!' He said, '(Yes) I am Joseph, and this is my brother (Benjamin), Allâh has indeed been gracious to us. As a matter of fact, he who guards against evil (seeking refuge in Him) and patiently perseveres, will find that Allâh suffers not the reward of the doers of good to others to be lost.'

91. They said, 'By Allâh, Allâh has surely exalted you above us and we have indeed been guilty.'

92. (Joseph) said, 'No reproach (from me shall be) on you this day. May Allâh forgive you; He is the Most Merciful of those who show mercy.

93. 'Go with this my shirt and lay it before my father he will come to know (the whole affair and as well believe). And bring to me the whole of your family.'

SECTION 11

94. **S**o when the caravan with the corn departed (from Egypt) their father said (in Kin'ân), 'If you do not pronounce my judgment to be weak and unsound (let me tell you that) I do scent the power of Joseph.'

95. They (- people of Joseph's household) said, 'By Allâh! You are (still) suffering from your old delusion.'

96. And when the bearer of the happy tidings came (to Jacob) he laid it (- the shirt) before him and he became enlightened (about the true state of affairs), he said, 'Did I not tell you I know from Allâh what you do not know.'

97. They said, 'Our father! Pray that our sins are forgiven to us, for certainly we have been sinful.'

98. He (- Jacob) said, 'I will certainly pray to my Lord to forgive you. Surely, He is the Most

لَنَا الْكَيْلَ وَتَصَدَّقْ عَلَيْنَا ۖ إِنَّ اللَّهَ يَجْزِي
الْمُتَصَدِّقِينَ ﴿٨٨﴾ قَالَ هَلْ عَلِمْتُم مَّا فَعَلْتُم
بِيُوسُفَ وَأَخِيهِ إِذْ أَنتُمْ جَاهِلُونَ ﴿٨٩﴾ قَالُوا
أَإِنَّكَ لَأَنتَ يُوسُفُ ۖ قَالَ أَنَا يُوسُفُ وَهَٰذَا
أَخِي ۖ قَدْ مَنَّ اللَّهُ عَلَيْنَا ۖ إِنَّهُ مَن يَتَّقِ
وَيَصْبِرْ فَإِنَّ اللَّهَ لَا يُضِيعُ أَجْرَ الْمُحْسِنِينَ ﴿٩٠﴾
قَالُوا تَاللَّهِ لَقَدْ آثَرَكَ اللَّهُ عَلَيْنَا وَإِن كُنَّا
لَخَاطِئِينَ ﴿٩١﴾ قَالَ لَا تَثْرِيبَ عَلَيْكُمُ الْيَوْمَ ۖ
يَغْفِرُ اللَّهُ لَكُمْ ۖ وَهُوَ أَرْحَمُ الرَّاحِمِينَ ﴿٩٢﴾
اذْهَبُوا بِقَمِيصِي هَٰذَا فَأَلْقُوهُ عَلَىٰ وَجْهِ
أَبِي يَأْتِ بَصِيرًا وَأْتُونِي بِأَهْلِكُمْ أَجْمَعِينَ ﴿٩٣﴾
وَلَمَّا فَصَلَتِ الْعِيرُ قَالَ أَبُوهُمْ إِنِّي لَأَجِدُ
رِيحَ يُوسُفَ ۖ لَوْلَا أَن تُفَنِّدُونِ ﴿٩٤﴾ قَالُوا
تَاللَّهِ إِنَّكَ لَفِي ضَلَالِكَ الْقَدِيمِ ﴿٩٥﴾ فَلَمَّا أَن
جَاءَ الْبَشِيرُ أَلْقَاهُ عَلَىٰ وَجْهِهِ فَارْتَدَّ بَصِيرًا ۖ
قَالَ أَلَمْ أَقُل لَّكُمْ إِنِّي أَعْلَمُ مِنَ اللَّهِ
مَا لَا تَعْلَمُونَ ﴿٩٦﴾ قَالُوا يَا أَبَانَا اسْتَغْفِرْ لَنَا
ذُنُوبَنَا إِنَّا كُنَّا خَاطِئِينَ ﴿٩٧﴾ قَالَ سَوْفَ

Forgiving, the Ever Merciful.'

99. And when they all came to Joseph he betook his parents to himself for a restful lodging (making them his personal guests) and said, 'Enter the city, if Allâh will, you shall always be safe and secure.'

100. And he took his parents to the royal court and they all fell down prostrate (before God) because of him and he said, 'My father! This is the real fulfillment of my vision of old. My Lord has made it come true. He has been gracious to me, indeed, when he released me out of the prison and brought you from the desert. (This all happened) after satan had stirred up discord between me and my brothers. Surely, my Lord is Benignant to whomsoever He pleases. He it is, Who is the All-Knowing, the All-Wise.'

101. (Addressing his Lord, Joseph then said,) 'My Lord! You have bestowed a part of the sovereignty upon me and it is You Who have imparted me true knowledge of the significance of (divine) sayings. O You, the Originator of the heavens and the earth! You alone are my Patron in this world and the Hereafter. Let it be that I die in a state of complete submission (to You), let it be that I join the righteous.'

102. (Prophet!) This (narrative) is a part of the important news of the hidden realities which We reveal to you. You were not present with these (enemies of yours) when they agreed upon their plan (against you) and they are (still) hatching subtle plots.

103. And many people, even though you ardently desire (it), will not at all believe.

104. While you ask from them no wages for it (-bringing this teaching contained in the Qur'ân). On the other hand this (Qur'ân) is but (a source of) eminence and glory for all humankind.

SECTION 12

105. **A**ND many are the signs in the heavens and the earth, which they pass by turning away

سُورَةُ يُوسُفَ ١٢

أَسْتَغْفِرُ لَكُمْ رَبِّيٓ ۖ إِنَّهُۥ هُوَ ٱلْغَفُورُ ٱلرَّحِيمُ ﴿٩٨﴾
فَلَمَّا دَخَلُوا۟ عَلَىٰ يُوسُفَ ءَاوَىٰٓ إِلَيْهِ أَبَوَيْهِ
وَقَالَ ٱدْخُلُوا۟ مِصْرَ إِن شَآءَ ٱللَّهُ ءَامِنِينَ ﴿٩٩﴾
وَرَفَعَ أَبَوَيْهِ عَلَى ٱلْعَرْشِ وَخَرُّوا۟ لَهُۥ سُجَّدًا ۖ
وَقَالَ يَٰٓأَبَتِ هَٰذَا تَأْوِيلُ رُءْيَٰىَ مِن قَبْلُ
قَدْ جَعَلَهَا رَبِّي حَقًّا ۖ وَقَدْ أَحْسَنَ بِيٓ إِذْ
أَخْرَجَنِي مِنَ ٱلسِّجْنِ وَجَآءَ بِكُم مِّنَ ٱلْبَدْوِ
مِنۢ بَعْدِ أَن نَّزَغَ ٱلشَّيْطَٰنُ بَيْنِي وَبَيْنَ
إِخْوَتِيٓ ۚ إِنَّ رَبِّي لَطِيفٌ لِّمَا يَشَآءُ ۚ إِنَّهُۥ هُوَ
ٱلْعَلِيمُ ٱلْحَكِيمُ ﴿١٠٠﴾ رَبِّ قَدْ ءَاتَيْتَنِي مِنَ
ٱلْمُلْكِ وَعَلَّمْتَنِي مِن تَأْوِيلِ ٱلْأَحَادِيثِ ۚ
فَاطِرَ ٱلسَّمَٰوَٰتِ وَٱلْأَرْضِ أَنتَ وَلِيِّۦ فِي
ٱلدُّنْيَا وَٱلْءَاخِرَةِ ۖ تَوَفَّنِي مُسْلِمًا وَأَلْحِقْنِي
بِٱلصَّٰلِحِينَ ﴿١٠١﴾ ذَٰلِكَ مِنْ أَنۢبَآءِ ٱلْغَيْبِ نُوحِيهِ
إِلَيْكَ ۖ وَمَا كُنتَ لَدَيْهِمْ إِذْ أَجْمَعُوٓا۟ أَمْرَهُمْ
وَهُمْ يَمْكُرُونَ ﴿١٠٢﴾ وَمَآ أَكْثَرُ ٱلنَّاسِ وَلَوْ
حَرَصْتَ بِمُؤْمِنِينَ ﴿١٠٣﴾ وَمَا تَسْـَٔلُهُمْ عَلَيْهِ
مِنْ أَجْرٍ ۚ إِنْ هُوَ إِلَّا ذِكْرٌ لِّلْعَٰلَمِينَ ﴿١٠٤﴾ ع ١١ ٥
وَكَأَيِّن مِّنْ ءَايَةٍ فِي ٱلسَّمَٰوَٰتِ وَٱلْأَرْضِ

الجزء الثالث عشر

(arrogantly) from them.
106. In fact, most of them believe not in Allâh without (at the same time) ascribing partners (to Him).
107. Do they then, feel secure from the coming of an overwhelming punishment on them from Allâh, or the sudden coming of the Hour upon them, taking them unaware.
108. Say, 'This is my path. I call to Allâh. I am on sure knowledge verifiable by reason and (so are) those who follow me. (I believe that) Holy is Allâh. I am not of the polytheists.'
109. And We sent none (as Messengers) before you but they were men from among the people of the townships to whom We revealed (Our will). Have they not then journeyed in the land and seen how was the end of their predecessors? Indeed, the abode of the Hereafter holds out better promises for those who guard against evil and keep their duty. Will you not then refrain (from disbelief and unrighteous deeds)?
110. (It always happened with the previous Messengers as well, they went on with their teachings) till when those Messengers despaired (of believing on the part of their people) and they (the people of their nation) thought that they have been told only lies (in the name of revelations), Our help reached these (Messengers) suddenly, delivering those whom We pleased. Surely, Our punishment is not averted from the people who sever their ties (with Us).
111. Most assuredly the narratives of the people (gone by) contain lessons for the people possessed of pure and clear understanding. This (Qur'ân) is no forged narrative. It is a fulfillment of those (prophecies contained in the Scriptures) which were before it and is a detailed exposition of all things, and a guide, and a mercy to a people who believe.

يَمُرُّونَ عَلَيْهَا وَهُمْ عَنْهَا مُعْرِضُونَ ﴿١٠٥﴾
وَمَا يُؤْمِنُ أَكْثَرُهُمْ بِاللهِ إِلَّا وَهُمْ
مُّشْرِكُونَ ﴿١٠٦﴾ أَفَأَمِنُوٓا أَنْ تَأْتِيَهُمْ غَٰشِيَةٌ
مِّنْ عَذَابِ اللهِ أَوْ تَأْتِيَهُمُ السَّاعَةُ بَغْتَةً
وَّهُمْ لَا يَشْعُرُونَ ﴿١٠٧﴾ قُلْ هَٰذِهِۦ سَبِيلِيٓ
أَدْعُوٓا إِلَى اللهِ عَلَىٰ بَصِيرَةٍ أَنَا۠ وَمَنِ اتَّبَعَنِي
وَسُبْحَٰنَ اللهِ وَمَآ أَنَا۠ مِنَ الْمُشْرِكِينَ ﴿١٠٨﴾
وَمَآ أَرْسَلْنَا مِنْ قَبْلِكَ إِلَّا رِجَالًا نُّوحِيٓ
إِلَيْهِم مِّنْ أَهْلِ الْقُرَىٰ أَفَلَمْ يَسِيرُوا
فِي الْأَرْضِ فَيَنْظُرُوا كَيْفَ كَانَ عَٰقِبَةُ
الَّذِينَ مِنْ قَبْلِهِمْ وَلَدَارُ الْأَخِرَةِ خَيْرٌ
لِّلَّذِينَ اتَّقَوْا أَفَلَا تَعْقِلُونَ ﴿١٠٩﴾ حَتَّىٰٓ إِذَا
اسْتَيْـَٔسَ الرُّسُلُ وَظَنُّوٓا أَنَّهُمْ قَدْ
كُذِبُوا جَآءَهُمْ نَصْرُنَا فَنُجِّيَ مَنْ نَّشَآءُ
وَلَا يُرَدُّ بَأْسُنَا عَنِ الْقَوْمِ الْمُجْرِمِينَ ﴿١١٠﴾
لَقَدْ كَانَ فِي قَصَصِهِمْ عِبْرَةٌ لِّأُولِي
الْأَلْبَٰبِ مَا كَانَ حَدِيثًا يُفْتَرَىٰ
وَلَٰكِنْ تَصْدِيقَ الَّذِي بَيْنَ يَدَيْهِ
وَتَفْصِيلَ كُلِّ شَيْءٍ وَّهُدًى وَّرَحْمَةً
لِّقَوْمٍ يُؤْمِنُونَ ﴿١١١﴾

CHAPTER
13

سُورَةُ الرَّعْدِ ١٣

AL-RA'D
(The Thunder)
(Revealed after Hijrah)

With the name of Allâh,
the Most Gracious, the Ever Merciful
(I commence to read Sûrah Al-Ra'd).

1. ALIF LÂM MÎM RÂ - I am Allâh, the Best Knowing, the All-Seeing. These are the verses of the perfect Book, and that which has been revealed to you by your Lord is the complete truth. But most people do not (still) believe (in it).
2. Allâh is He Who raised up the heavens without any pillars that you can see, and He occupied the throne (of sovereignty). And He made the sun and the moon subservient (to you), each one of these (planets) pursues its course for a specified term. He regulates all affairs (of this universe). He explains in detail His Messages so that you may have firm conviction of the meeting with your Lord.
3. And it is He Who drew forth the earth (from another heavenly body) and made it productive and fertile by means of particles (of other planets), and made firm mountains and rivers on it. He has grown therein fruit of every kind in a pair comprising both sexes (the male stamens and the female pistils). He causes the night to cover the day. Behold! In all this there are signs for a people who reflect.
4. And in the earth are (diverse) tracts side by side, and (in them there are) gardens of vines and (different kinds of) cornfields and date-palms; growing in clusters (many together from one root) and (others) growing separately from different roots. They are all watered with the same water, yet We make some of them excel others in (respect of) bearing fruit and (their) tastes. Behold! In all this, there are signs

سُورَةُ الرَّعْدِ مَدَنِيَّةٌ

بِسْمِ اللّٰهِ الرَّحْمٰنِ الرَّحِيْمِ

الٓمّٓرٰ قف تِلْكَ اٰيٰتُ الْكِتٰبِ ؕ وَ الَّذِيْٓ اُنْزِلَ
اِلَيْكَ مِنْ رَّبِّكَ الْحَقُّ وَ لٰكِنَّ اَكْثَرَ النَّاسِ
لَا يُؤْمِنُوْنَ ① اَللّٰهُ الَّذِيْ رَفَعَ السَّمٰوٰتِ
بِغَيْرِ عَمَدٍ تَرَوْنَهَا ثُمَّ اسْتَوٰى عَلَى الْعَرْشِ
وَ سَخَّرَ الشَّمْسَ وَ الْقَمَرَ ؕ كُلٌّ يَّجْرِيْ
لِاَجَلٍ مُّسَمًّى ؕ يُدَبِّرُ الْاَمْرَ يُفَصِّلُ الْاٰيٰتِ
لَعَلَّكُمْ بِلِقَآءِ رَبِّكُمْ تُوْقِنُوْنَ ② وَ هُوَ الَّذِيْ
مَدَّ الْاَرْضَ وَ جَعَلَ فِيْهَا رَوَاسِيَ وَ اَنْهٰرًا ؕ
وَ مِنْ كُلِّ الثَّمَرٰتِ جَعَلَ فِيْهَا زَوْجَيْنِ
اثْنَيْنِ يُغْشِي الَّيْلَ النَّهَارَ ؕ اِنَّ فِيْ ذٰلِكَ
لَاٰيٰتٍ لِّقَوْمٍ يَّتَفَكَّرُوْنَ ③ وَ فِي الْاَرْضِ
قِطَعٌ مُّتَجٰوِرٰتٌ وَّ جَنّٰتٌ مِّنْ اَعْنَابٍ وَّ زَرْعٌ
وَّ نَخِيْلٌ صِنْوَانٌ وَّ غَيْرُ صِنْوَانٍ يُّسْقٰى بِمَآءٍ
وَّاحِدٍ قف وَ نُفَضِّلُ بَعْضَهَا عَلٰى بَعْضٍ فِي الْاُكُلِ ؕ

(to recognize their Lord) for a people who use their understanding.

5. And (you, O reader! are right) if you would wonder (at the disbelievers for) wondrous indeed are their words: 'Is it true that we shall be raised to a new creation when we are reduced to dust (after death?).' These are the ones who disbelieve in their Lord and these are the ones who shall have halters around their necks. They shall be the fellows of the Fire wherein they shall abide.

6. They want you to hasten on (their) punishment in preference to (your doing them) good, whereas there has already been awarded (to the people) before them exemplary punishment. Verily, your Lord is full of forgiveness to humankind despite their unjust doings, yet your Lord is (likewise) Strict in inflicting punishment.

7. And those who disbelieve say, 'Why has no sign (of destruction) been sent down to him from his Lord?' While you are nought but a Warner and a Guide for every people.

SECTION 2

8. **ALLÂH** knows what every female carries and (He knows) what the wombs miscarry and what they nourish and help to grow. He has the (proper and fixed) measure of everything.

9. (He is the) Knower of the hidden realities and the visible, the Incomparably Great, the Most Exalted.

10. He among you, who conceals his thoughts and he who speaks them aloud, and (also) he who lurks by night and he who goes forth (openly) by day are all alike (in His knowledge).

11. He (- the Messenger) has companies (of angels) successively ranged before him and behind him. They guard him by the command of Allâh. Verily, Allâh does not change the condition of a people until they (first) change their ways and their minds. When Allâh decides

سُورَةُ الرَّعۡدِ ١٣

إِنَّ فِي ذَٰلِكَ لَأٓيَٰتٍ لِّقَوۡمٍ يَعۡقِلُونَ ۝٤ وَإِن تَعۡجَبۡ فَعَجَبٌ قَوۡلُهُمۡ أَءِذَا كُنَّا تُرَٰبًا أَءِنَّا لَفِي خَلۡقٍ جَدِيدٍۗ أُوْلَٰٓئِكَ ٱلَّذِينَ كَفَرُواْ بِرَبِّهِمۡۖ وَأُوْلَٰٓئِكَ ٱلۡأَغۡلَٰلُ فِيٓ أَعۡنَاقِهِمۡۖ وَأُوْلَٰٓئِكَ أَصۡحَٰبُ ٱلنَّارِۖ هُمۡ فِيهَا خَٰلِدُونَ ۝٥ وَيَسۡتَعۡجِلُونَكَ بِٱلسَّيِّئَةِ قَبۡلَ ٱلۡحَسَنَةِ وَقَدۡ خَلَتۡ مِن قَبۡلِهِمُ ٱلۡمَثُلَٰتُۗ وَإِنَّ رَبَّكَ لَذُو مَغۡفِرَةٍ لِّلنَّاسِ عَلَىٰ ظُلۡمِهِمۡۖ وَإِنَّ رَبَّكَ لَشَدِيدُ ٱلۡعِقَابِ ۝٦ وَيَقُولُ ٱلَّذِينَ كَفَرُواْ لَوۡلَآ أُنزِلَ عَلَيۡهِ ءَايَةٌ مِّن رَّبِّهِۦٓۗ إِنَّمَآ أَنتَ مُنذِرٌۖ وَلِكُلِّ قَوۡمٍ هَادٍ ۝٧ ٱللَّهُ يَعۡلَمُ مَا تَحۡمِلُ كُلُّ أُنثَىٰ وَمَا تَغِيضُ ٱلۡأَرۡحَامُ وَمَا تَزۡدَادُۖ وَكُلُّ شَيۡءٍ عِندَهُۥ بِمِقۡدَارٍ ۝٨ عَٰلِمُ ٱلۡغَيۡبِ وَٱلشَّهَٰدَةِ ٱلۡكَبِيرُ ٱلۡمُتَعَالِ ۝٩ سَوَآءٌ مِّنكُم مَّنۡ أَسَرَّ ٱلۡقَوۡلَ وَمَن جَهَرَ بِهِۦ وَمَنۡ هُوَ مُسۡتَخۡفِۭ بِٱلَّيۡلِ وَسَارِبُۢ بِٱلنَّهَارِ ۝١٠ لَهُۥ مُعَقِّبَٰتٌ مِّنۢ بَيۡنِ يَدَيۡهِ وَمِنۡ خَلۡفِهِۦ يَحۡفَظُونَهُۥ مِنۡ أَمۡرِ ٱللَّهِۗ إِنَّ ٱللَّهَ لَا يُغَيِّرُ مَا بِقَوۡمٍ حَتَّىٰ يُغَيِّرُواْ مَا

upon punishing a people there is no averting it. (At that time) they have no helping friend apart from Him.

12. He it is, Who shows you the lightning to induce fear and to inspire hope (in you); and (it is He) Who raises the heavy clouds.

13. And the thunder glorifies Him with His true praise and (so do) the angels in awe of Him. He sends the thunderbolts and therewith smites whom He will. Yet they dispute about Allâh, though He is Mighty in prowess.

14. He alone deserves being called upon (in prayer). Those they call upon, apart from Him, give them no response whatsoever, but (these polytheists pray to them) like one who stretches forth both of his hands towards the water (wishing) that it may reach his mouth while it never reaches it. And the call of the disbelievers is nought but in vain.

15. All those that are in the heavens and on the earth submit to Allâh alone; whether they choose to obey willingly or not, and likewise do their shadows, in the mornings and evenings, (and they are all subject to the divine law (- His law of nature).

[PROSTRATION]

16. Ask (them), 'Who is the Lord of the heavens and the earth?' (They will not be able to answer it, therefore) say, 'It is Allâh.' Say (again), 'Have you, even then, taken, apart from Him (such other) helpers as have no power to receive good or avoid harm even for themselves?' Say, 'Is the blind person as good as the person who can see? Or are the different kinds of darkness the same as the light? Or have they ascribed to Allâh associate partners who have created the things as He has created, with the result that the two creations look similar to them?' Say, 'Allâh (alone) is the Creator of all things and He is the One, the Most Supreme.'

17. He sends down some water from the clouds so that the water courses flow up to their capacity, and the torrent carries (on its surface)

بِأَنْفُسِهِمْ ۗ وَإِذَآ أَرَادَ اللّٰهُ بِقَوْمٍ سُوْٓءًا
فَلَا مَرَدَّ لَهٗ ۚ وَمَا لَهُمْ مِّنْ دُوْنِهٖ مِنْ
وَّالٍ ١١ هُوَ الَّذِيْ يُرِيْكُمُ الْبَرْقَ خَوْفًا
وَّطَمَعًا وَّيُنْشِئُ السَّحَابَ الثِّقَالَ ١٢ وَيُسَبِّحُ
الرَّعْدُ بِحَمْدِهٖ وَالْمَلٰٓئِكَةُ مِنْ خِيْفَتِهٖ ۚ
وَيُرْسِلُ الصَّوٰعِقَ فَيُصِيْبُ بِهَا مَنْ يَّشَآءُ
وَهُمْ يُجٰدِلُوْنَ فِي اللّٰهِ ۚ وَهُوَ شَدِيْدُ
الْمِحَالِ ١٣ لَهٗ دَعْوَةُ الْحَقِّ ۗ وَالَّذِيْنَ يَدْعُوْنَ
مِنْ دُوْنِهٖ لَا يَسْتَجِيْبُوْنَ لَهُمْ بِشَيْءٍ إِلَّا
كَبٰسِطِ كَفَّيْهِ إِلَى الْمَآءِ لِيَبْلُغَ فَاهُ وَمَا هُوَ
بِبٰلِغِهٖ ۗ وَمَا دُعَآءُ الْكٰفِرِيْنَ إِلَّا فِيْ ضَلٰلٍ ١٤
وَلِلّٰهِ يَسْجُدُ مَنْ فِي السَّمٰوٰتِ وَالْأَرْضِ طَوْعًا
وَّكَرْهًا وَّظِلٰلُهُمْ بِالْغُدُوِّ وَالْأٰصَالِ ١٥ السجدة قُلْ
مَنْ رَّبُّ السَّمٰوٰتِ وَالْأَرْضِ ۗ قُلِ اللّٰهُ ۗ
قُلْ أَفَاتَّخَذْتُمْ مِّنْ دُوْنِهٖٓ أَوْلِيَآءَ لَا يَمْلِكُوْنَ
لِأَنْفُسِهِمْ نَفْعًا وَّلَا ضَرًّا ۗ قُلْ هَلْ يَسْتَوِي
الْأَعْمٰى وَالْبَصِيْرُ ۙ أَمْ هَلْ تَسْتَوِي الظُّلُمٰتُ
وَالنُّوْرُ ۚ أَمْ جَعَلُوْا لِلّٰهِ شُرَكَآءَ خَلَقُوْا كَخَلْقِهٖ
فَتَشَابَهَ الْخَلْقُ عَلَيْهِمْ ۗ قُلِ اللّٰهُ خٰلِقُ كُلِّ
شَيْءٍ وَّهُوَ الْوٰحِدُ الْقَهَّارُ ١٦ أَنْزَلَ مِنَ السَّمَآءِ
مَآءً فَسَالَتْ أَوْدِيَةٌۢ بِقَدَرِهَا فَاحْتَمَلَ

swelling foam. And out of that (metal) which the people heat in the fire seeking to make ornaments and other articles a similar foam rises to (the surface of) it. In this way does Allâh illustrate truth and falsehood. As for the foam it goes away as (does all) dross, but as to that which does good to humankind it stays in the earth. That is how Allâh sets forth excellent description of things.

18. There is an everlasting good (in store) for those who respond to the call of their Lord. And (as for) those who do not respond to His call, even though they had possessed all that is on the earth and as much more, they would certainly offer it to ransom (themselves) with it. It is these for whom an evil reckoning awaits and their refuge is Gehenna. What a wretched place to rest!

SECTION 3

19. **H**ow can then he, who knows that what has been revealed to you from your Lord, is the truth, be like the person who is blind? Only those possessed of pure and clear understanding do give thought.

20. These are the persons who fulfill the covenant (they made) with Allâh and do not break their solemn pledge.

21. These are the persons who keep the ties (of love and relationship) Allâh has commanded to be kept, who hold their Lord in awe and who dread the evil reckoning.

22. And these are the persons who patiently persevere (in virtues and in guarding against evil), seek the favour of their Lord, and observe Prayer, and who spend of what We have provided them, secretly and openly, and who avert evil (by repaying it) with good. It is these who shall have the best end of the (present) abode -

23. Everlasting Gardens of Paradise where they themselves, and (also) such of them as are righteous and fit (for earning a place in Heaven) from among their fathers and their spouses and

السَّيْلُ زَبَدًا رَّابِيًا ۚ وَمِمَّا يُوقِدُونَ عَلَيْهِ
فِي النَّارِ ابْتِغَاءَ حِلْيَةٍ أَوْ مَتَاعٍ زَبَدٌ مِّثْلُهُ ۚ كَذَٰلِكَ
يَضْرِبُ اللَّهُ الْحَقَّ وَالْبَاطِلَ ۚ فَأَمَّا الزَّبَدُ
فَيَذْهَبُ جُفَاءً ۖ وَأَمَّا مَا يَنفَعُ النَّاسَ
فَيَمْكُثُ فِي الْأَرْضِ ۚ كَذَٰلِكَ يَضْرِبُ اللَّهُ
الْأَمْثَالَ ﴿١٧﴾ لِلَّذِينَ اسْتَجَابُوا لِرَبِّهِمُ الْحُسْنَىٰ ۚ
وَالَّذِينَ لَمْ يَسْتَجِيبُوا لَهُ لَوْ أَنَّ لَهُم مَّا فِي
الْأَرْضِ جَمِيعًا وَمِثْلَهُ مَعَهُ لَافْتَدَوْا بِهِ ۚ
أُولَٰئِكَ لَهُمْ سُوءُ الْحِسَابِ ۚ وَمَأْوَاهُمْ جَهَنَّمُ ۖ
وَبِئْسَ الْمِهَادُ ﴿١٨﴾ أَفَمَن يَعْلَمُ أَنَّمَا أُنزِلَ
إِلَيْكَ مِن رَّبِّكَ الْحَقُّ كَمَنْ هُوَ أَعْمَىٰ ۚ إِنَّمَا
يَتَذَكَّرُ أُولُو الْأَلْبَابِ ﴿١٩﴾ الَّذِينَ يُوفُونَ بِعَهْدِ
اللَّهِ وَلَا يَنقُضُونَ الْمِيثَاقَ ﴿٢٠﴾ وَالَّذِينَ
يَصِلُونَ مَا أَمَرَ اللَّهُ بِهِ أَن يُوصَلَ وَيَخْشَوْنَ
رَبَّهُمْ وَيَخَافُونَ سُوءَ الْحِسَابِ ﴿٢١﴾ وَالَّذِينَ
صَبَرُوا ابْتِغَاءَ وَجْهِ رَبِّهِمْ وَأَقَامُوا الصَّلَوٰةَ
وَأَنفَقُوا مِمَّا رَزَقْنَٰهُمْ سِرًّا وَعَلَانِيَةً
وَيَدْرَءُونَ بِالْحَسَنَةِ السَّيِّئَةَ أُولَٰئِكَ لَهُمْ
عُقْبَى الدَّارِ ﴿٢٢﴾ جَنَّٰتُ عَدْنٍ يَدْخُلُونَهَا

their children shall enter. And angels shall attend on them from every door (saying),
24. 'Peace be ever upon you because you patiently persevered (in virtues and guarded against sin).' How excellent and blissful is the reward of this abode in the Hereafter!
25. But as for those who break the covenant (they made) with Allâh after having ratified it, and sever the ties Allâh has commanded to be kept and disturb the peace of the country. It is these on whom lies the disapproval (of Allâh) and they shall have an evil end of this abode.
26. Allâh amplifies the means of livelihood for such of (His) people as He will and straitens them (for such of them as He will). (Some) people are happy with the present life whereas the present life, as compared with the Hereafter, is but a fleeting (and insignificant) enjoyment.

SECTION 4

27. AND those who disbelieve say, 'Why has no sign (of the destruction of his opponents) been revealed to this (Prophet) from his Lord?' Say, 'Verily, Allâh lets him go astray who wishes (to be left in error) and guides to Himself (only) those who turn again and again (to Him);
28. 'Those who believe and whose hearts find peace in the remembrance of Allâh. Look! It is in the remembrance of Allâh alone that the hearts really find peace;
29. 'Those who believe and do deeds of righteousness, an enviable state (of bliss) is theirs (in this world), and an excellent and blissful place of return (awaits them in the Hereafter).'
30. It is therefore, We have sent you to a people before whom other peoples have passed away, so that you may recite to them that (Qur'ân) which We have revealed to you, Yet they disbelieve in (God) the Most Gracious. Say, 'He is my Lord, there is no other, cannot be and will never be one worthy of worship but He. In Him do I put my trust and to Him is my

وَمَنْ صَلَحَ مِنْ أٰبَآئِهِمْ وَ أَزْوٰجِهِمْ وَذُرِّيّٰتِهِمْ
وَ الْمَلٰٓئِكَةُ يَدْخُلُونَ عَلَيْهِمْ مِّنْ كُلِّ بَابٍ ﴿٢٣﴾
سَلٰمٌ عَلَيْكُمْ بِمَا صَبَرْتُمْ فَنِعْمَ عُقْبَى الدَّارِ ﴿٢٤﴾
وَ الَّذِينَ يَنْقُضُونَ عَهْدَ اللّٰهِ مِنْ بَعْدِ
مِيثٰقِهِ وَ يَقْطَعُونَ مَآ أَمَرَ اللّٰهُ بِهِۦٓ أَنْ
يُّوصَلَ وَ يُفْسِدُونَ فِي الْأَرْضِ أُولٰٓئِكَ لَهُمُ
اللَّعْنَةُ وَ لَهُمْ سُوٓءُ الدَّارِ ﴿٢٥﴾ اَللّٰهُ يَبْسُطُ الرِّزْقَ
لِمَنْ يَّشَآءُ وَ يَقْدِرُ وَ فَرِحُوا بِالْحَيٰوةِ الدُّنْيَا
وَ مَا الْحَيٰوةُ الدُّنْيَا فِي الْأٰخِرَةِ إِلَّا مَتٰعٌ ﴿٢٦﴾
وَ يَقُولُ الَّذِينَ كَفَرُوا لَوْلَآ أُنْزِلَ عَلَيْهِ أٰيَةٌ
مِّنْ رَّبِّهِ قُلْ إِنَّ اللّٰهَ يُضِلُّ مَنْ يَّشَآءُ
وَ يَهْدِيٓ إِلَيْهِ مَنْ أَنَابَ ﴿٢٧﴾ الَّذِينَ أٰمَنُوا
وَ تَطْمَئِنُّ قُلُوبُهُمْ بِذِكْرِ اللّٰهِ أَلَا بِذِكْرِ
اللّٰهِ تَطْمَئِنُّ الْقُلُوبُ ﴿٢٨﴾ اَلَّذِينَ أٰمَنُوا وَ عَمِلُوا
الصّٰلِحٰتِ طُوبٰى لَهُمْ وَ حُسْنُ مَاٰبٍ ﴿٢٩﴾ كَذٰلِكَ
أَرْسَلْنٰكَ فِيٓ أُمَّةٍ قَدْ خَلَتْ مِنْ قَبْلِهَآ أُمَمٌ
لِّتَتْلُوَا عَلَيْهِمُ الَّذِيٓ أَوْحَيْنَآ إِلَيْكَ وَ هُمْ
يَكْفُرُونَ بِالرَّحْمٰنِ قُلْ هُوَ رَبِّي لَآ إِلٰهَ إِلَّا

complete return.'

31. Had there been a Qur'ân whereby mountains could be moved, or whereby the earth could be torn asunder, or whereby the dead could be made to speak (it is this very Qur'ân indeed). Behold! The commandment and all power belongs to Allâh. Have not those who believe realized yet that if Allâh had (enforced) His will He would have indeed guided all humankind. And as for those who disbelieve, one calamity or the other will continue to befall them owing to their (evil) activities till you come to alight in their neighborhood, until the promise of Allâh (about the conquest of Makkah) comes to pass. Verily, Allâh will not fail (this) promise (of His).

SECTION 5

32. AND surely Messengers before you were treated scornfully. But (at first) I granted respite to those who disbelieved, after that I took them to task; and (behold) how (exemplary) was then My punishment.

33. How shall He Who stands (watchful) over each and every soul as to what it accomplishes (let them go unpunished inspite of His knowledge)? And yet they ascribe to Allâh several partners. Say, '(Would) you name their attributes; and would you inform Him of something important which is on the earth but unknown to Him, or are these merely empty (and false) words?' Nay, the fact of the matter is that their designing and their activities are made fair-seeming to the disbelievers (by satan), and they have been barred from the (right) path. And he whom Allâh forsakes has no guide.

34. They are doomed to punishment in the present life (and the next). But the punishment of the Hereafter will of course, be graver still. They will have no saviour at all from (the punishment of) Allâh.

35. The likeness of (the Garden of) Paradise which has been promised to those who become

سُورَةُ الرَّعْدِ ١٣

هُوَ عَلَيْهِ تَوَكَّلْتُ وَإِلَيْهِ مَتَابِ ﴿٣٠﴾ وَلَوْ أَنَّ
قُرْءَانًا سُيِّرَتْ بِهِ الْجِبَالُ أَوْ قُطِّعَتْ بِهِ
الْأَرْضُ أَوْ كُلِّمَ بِهِ الْمَوْتَىٰ بَل لِّلَّهِ الْأَمْرُ
جَمِيعًا أَفَلَمْ يَايْـَٔسِ الَّذِينَ ءَامَنُوا أَن لَّوْ
يَشَاءُ اللَّهُ لَهَدَى النَّاسَ جَمِيعًا وَلَا يَزَالُ
الَّذِينَ كَفَرُوا تُصِيبُهُم بِمَا صَنَعُوا قَارِعَةٌ
أَوْ تَحُلُّ قَرِيبًا مِّن دَارِهِمْ حَتَّىٰ يَأْتِيَ وَعْدُ
اللَّهِ إِنَّ اللَّهَ لَا يُخْلِفُ الْمِيعَادَ ﴿٣١﴾ وَلَقَدِ
اسْتُهْزِئَ بِرُسُلٍ مِّن قَبْلِكَ فَأَمْلَيْتُ لِلَّذِينَ
كَفَرُوا ثُمَّ أَخَذْتُهُمْ فَكَيْفَ كَانَ عِقَابِ ﴿٣٢﴾
أَفَمَنْ هُوَ قَائِمٌ عَلَىٰ كُلِّ نَفْسٍ بِمَا كَسَبَتْ
وَجَعَلُوا لِلَّهِ شُرَكَاءَ قُلْ سَمُّوهُمْ أَمْ تُنَبِّئُونَهُ
بِمَا لَا يَعْلَمُ فِي الْأَرْضِ أَمْ بِظَاهِرٍ مِّنَ الْقَوْلِ
بَلْ زُيِّنَ لِلَّذِينَ كَفَرُوا مَكْرُهُمْ وَصُدُّوا
عَنِ السَّبِيلِ وَمَن يُضْلِلِ اللَّهُ فَمَا لَهُ مِنْ
هَادٍ ﴿٣٣﴾ لَهُمْ عَذَابٌ فِي الْحَيَوٰةِ الدُّنْيَا وَلَعَذَابُ
الْأَخِرَةِ أَشَقُّ وَمَا لَهُم مِّنَ اللَّهِ مِن وَاقٍ ﴿٣٤﴾
مَثَلُ الْجَنَّةِ الَّتِي وُعِدَ الْمُتَّقُونَ تَجْرِي مِنْ

secure against sin and are dutiful is that (of a garden) served with running streams (to keep it green and flourishing). It has everlasting fruit and (so will be) its shade. Such is the end of those who guard against sins but the end of disbelievers is the Fire.

36. And those to whom We have given the insight of the Book (- the Qur'ân) rejoice at what has been revealed to you. But there are some factions (of other religions) who deny some of its parts. Say, 'I have only been commanded to worship Allâh and not to associate (anything) with Him. To Him do I call (you) and to Him is my return.'

37. (Just as We revealed other Scriptures) so have We revealed it (- the Qur'ân) as a clear judgment (couched) in Arabic and if you (O reader!) were to follow their vain desires after the knowledge has come to you, you will have not a single helper nor a saviour against (the punishment of) Allâh.

SECTION 6

38. **A**ND most surely, We sent before you many Messengers and We gave them wives and children. Yet it was not possible for a Messenger to bring a sign but by Allâh's command. For everything that has an appointed term, there is a (divine) law (to regulate it).

39. Allâh repeals (the law relating to punishment) what He will and He establishes and confirms (what He pleases) and with Him is the source and origin of all laws and commandments.

40. We will indeed let you witness (O Muhammad! the realisation of) some of the punishments with which We threaten them (- the disbelievers) with before We cause you to die. You are responsible only for the delivery (of the Message) and the reckoning is Our Own responsibility.

41. Do they not see that We are invading the land (of disbelief and are gradually) reducing and curtailing it from its sides? Allâh judges the

سُوْرَةُ الرَّعْدِ ١٣

تَحْتِهَا الْأَنْهٰرُ ؕ أُكُلُهَا دَآئِمٌ وَّ ظِلُّهَا ؕ تِلْكَ
عُقْبَى الَّذِيْنَ اتَّقَوْا ۖ وَّعُقْبَى الْكٰفِرِيْنَ النَّارُ ﴿٣٥﴾
وَالَّذِيْنَ أٰتَيْنٰهُمُ الْكِتٰبَ يَفْرَحُوْنَ بِمَآ أُنْزِلَ
إِلَيْكَ وَمِنَ الْأَحْزَابِ مَنْ يُّنْكِرُ بَعْضَهٗ ؕ قُلْ
إِنَّمَآ أُمِرْتُ أَنْ أَعْبُدَ اللّٰهَ وَلَآ أُشْرِكَ بِهٖ ؕ
إِلَيْهِ أَدْعُوْا وَإِلَيْهِ مَاٰبِ ﴿٣٦﴾ وَكَذٰلِكَ أَنْزَلْنٰهُ
حُكْمًا عَرَبِيًّا ؕ وَلَئِنِ اتَّبَعْتَ أَهْوَآءَهُمْ بَعْدَ
مَا جَآءَكَ مِنَ الْعِلْمِ ۙ مَا لَكَ مِنَ اللّٰهِ مِنْ
وَّلِيٍّ وَّلَا وَاقٍ ﴿٣٧﴾ وَلَقَدْ أَرْسَلْنَا رُسُلًا مِّنْ
قَبْلِكَ وَجَعَلْنَا لَهُمْ أَزْوَاجًا وَّذُرِّيَّةً ؕ وَمَا
كَانَ لِرَسُوْلٍ أَنْ يَّأْتِيَ بِاٰيَةٍ إِلَّا بِإِذْنِ اللّٰهِ ؕ
لِكُلِّ أَجَلٍ كِتَابٌ ﴿٣٨﴾ يَمْحُوا اللّٰهُ مَا يَشَآءُ
وَيُثْبِتُ ۖ وَعِنْدَهٗٓ أُمُّ الْكِتٰبِ ﴿٣٩﴾ وَإِنْ مَّا
نُرِيَنَّكَ بَعْضَ الَّذِيْ نَعِدُهُمْ أَوْ نَتَوَفَّيَنَّكَ
فَإِنَّمَا عَلَيْكَ الْبَلٰغُ وَعَلَيْنَا الْحِسَابُ ﴿٤٠﴾
أَوَلَمْ يَرَوْا أَنَّا نَأْتِي الْأَرْضَ نَنْقُصُهَا مِنْ
أَطْرَافِهَا ؕ وَاللّٰهُ يَحْكُمُ لَا مُعَقِّبَ لِحُكْمِهٖ ؕ

الجزء الثالث عشر

matter, there is none to reverse His judgment. Swift is He at calling to account.
42. And their predecessors did devise plans (against the truth) but all effective devising (and the success) of the plans rests with Allâh. He knows what every person accomplishes. The disbelievers will soon come to know who will gain the (good and successful) end of this abode.
43. And those who disbelieve say, 'You are not a sent one (of God)'. Say, 'Allâh suffices as a Witness between me and you, and (so are) those who possess knowledge of the Divine Book.'

وَهُوَ سَرِيعُ الْحِسَابِ ﴿٤١﴾ وَقَدْ مَكَرَ الَّذِينَ
مِنْ قَبْلِهِمْ فَلِلّٰهِ الْمَكْرُ جَمِيعًا يَعْلَمُ مَا
تَكْسِبُ كُلُّ نَفْسٍ وَسَيَعْلَمُ الْكُفّٰرُ لِمَنْ
عُقْبَى الدَّارِ ﴿٤٢﴾ وَيَقُولُ الَّذِينَ كَفَرُوا لَسْتَ
مُرْسَلًا قُلْ كَفٰى بِاللّٰهِ شَهِيدًا بَيْنِي
وَبَيْنَكُمْ وَمَنْ عِنْدَهُ عِلْمُ الْكِتٰبِ ﴿٤٣﴾

CHAPTER
14

IBRÂHÎM
(Abraham)
(Revealed before Hijrah)

سُورَةُ إِبْرٰهِيمَ مَكِّيَّةٌ

With the name of Allâh,
the Most Gracious, the Ever Merciful
(I commence to read Sûrah Ibrâhîm).

بِسْمِ اللّٰهِ الرَّحْمٰنِ الرَّحِيمِ

1. ALIF LÂM RÂ - I am Allâh, the All-Seeing. (This is) a great Book which We have revealed to you that you may bring humankind, by the leave of their Lord, out of different kinds of darkness into light, to the path of the All-Mighty, the Praiseworthy,
2. (To the path of) Allâh, to Whom belongs all that is in the heavens and all that is in the earth. And woe to the disbelievers for a dreadful punishment (that will befall them)!
3. Such as prefer the present life to the Hereafter, and forsake the path of Allâh and hinder (the people) from it, and try to paint it as crooked, seeking to undertake it by remaining crooked. It is these who have gone far off in error.
4. And We sent no Messenger but (he spoke) in

الٓرٰ كِتٰبٌ أَنْزَلْنٰهُ إِلَيْكَ لِتُخْرِجَ النَّاسَ
مِنَ الظُّلُمٰتِ إِلَى النُّورِ بِإِذْنِ رَبِّهِمْ إِلٰى
صِرٰطِ الْعَزِيزِ الْحَمِيدِ ﴿١﴾ اللّٰهِ الَّذِي لَهُ مَا
فِي السَّمٰوٰتِ وَمَا فِي الْأَرْضِ وَوَيْلٌ لِّلْكٰفِرِينَ
مِنْ عَذَابٍ شَدِيدٍ ﴿٢﴾ الَّذِينَ يَسْتَحِبُّونَ
الْحَيٰوةَ الدُّنْيَا عَلَى الْآخِرَةِ وَيَصُدُّونَ عَنْ
سَبِيلِ اللّٰهِ وَيَبْغُونَهَا عِوَجًا أُولٰٓئِكَ فِي

the language of his people so that he might make (all Our Messages) clear to them, yet Allâh leaves in error those who wish to remain in error and guides him who wishes to be guided (to the right path). And He is the All-Mighty, the All-Wise.

5. And We sent Moses with Our signs saying, 'Bring forth your people from different kinds of darkness into light and remind them of Allâh's favours and punishments. Behold! There are signs in these (narratives) for every patiently persevering and grateful person.'

6. And (call to mind) when Moses said to his people, 'Remember Allâh's blessings upon you, when He delivered you from the people of Pharaoh, who afflicted you with painful sufferings and slew your sons and spared your women to make them immodest and in that (deliverance) there was a great reward from your Lord.

SECTION 2

7. **A**ND (recall) when your Lord made it known (to you), 'If you indeed be thankful, I will bestow more (favours) on you, but if you are ungrateful, (you will find that) My punishment is of course most severe.'

8. Moses said, 'If you turn ungrateful, you and everyone on this earth altogether (remember that) Allâh stands in need of no thanks. Verily, Allâh is Self-Sufficient, Praiseworthy (in His Own right).

9. Has not the important news come to you of your predecessors, the people of Noah, (the tribes of) 'Âd and <u>Th</u>amûd and those who came after them. None knows them (now) but Allâh. Their Messengers (of God) came to them with clear proofs, but they put their hands again and again on their mouths (showing great resentment and out of rage) saying, 'We have already rejected that (revelation) you have been sent with and in fact we are in disquieting doubt as to that (faith) you call us to.'

10. Their Messengers (of God) said, 'Is there

ضَلٰلٍۭ بَعِيۡدٍ ﴿٣﴾ وَ مَاۤ اَرۡسَلۡنَا مِنۡ رَّسُوۡلٍ اِلَّا
بِلِسَانِ قَوۡمِهٖ لِيُبَيِّنَ لَهُمۡ ؕ فَيُضِلُّ اللّٰهُ مَنۡ
يَّشَآءُ وَ يَهۡدِيۡ مَنۡ يَّشَآءُ ؕ وَ هُوَ الۡعَزِيۡزُ
الۡحَكِيۡمُ ﴿٤﴾ وَ لَقَدۡ اَرۡسَلۡنَا مُوۡسٰى بِاٰيٰتِنَاۤ
اَنۡ اَخۡرِجۡ قَوۡمَكَ مِنَ الظُّلُمٰتِ اِلَى النُّوۡرِ ۬ۙ
وَ ذَكِّرۡهُمۡ بِاَيّٰىمِ اللّٰهِ ؕ اِنَّ فِيۡ ذٰلِكَ لَاٰيٰتٍ
لِّكُلِّ صَبَّارٍ شَكُوۡرٍ ﴿٥﴾ وَ اِذۡ قَالَ مُوۡسٰى لِقَوۡمِهِ
اذۡكُرُوۡا نِعۡمَةَ اللّٰهِ عَلَيۡكُمۡ اِذۡ اَنۡجٰىكُمۡ مِّنۡ
اٰلِ فِرۡعَوۡنَ يَسُوۡمُوۡنَكُمۡ سُوۡٓءَ الۡعَذَابِ
وَ يُذَبِّحُوۡنَ اَبۡنَآءَكُمۡ وَ يَسۡتَحۡيُوۡنَ نِسَآءَكُمۡ ؕ
وَ فِيۡ ذٰلِكُمۡ بَلَآءٌ مِّنۡ رَّبِّكُمۡ عَظِيۡمٌ ﴿٦﴾ وَ اِذۡ
تَاَذَّنَ رَبُّكُمۡ لَئِنۡ شَكَرۡتُمۡ لَاَزِيۡدَنَّكُمۡ
وَ لَئِنۡ كَفَرۡتُمۡ اِنَّ عَذَابِيۡ لَشَدِيۡدٌ ﴿٧﴾ وَ قَالَ
مُوۡسٰۤى اِنۡ تَكۡفُرُوۡۤا اَنۡتُمۡ وَ مَنۡ فِي الۡاَرۡضِ جَمِيۡعًا ۙ
فَاِنَّ اللّٰهَ لَغَنِيٌّ حَمِيۡدٌ ﴿٨﴾ اَلَمۡ يَاۡتِكُمۡ نَبَؤُا
الَّذِيۡنَ مِنۡ قَبۡلِكُمۡ قَوۡمِ نُوۡحٍ وَّ عَادٍ
وَّ ثَمُوۡدَ ۬ؕ وَ الَّذِيۡنَ مِنۡۢ بَعۡدِهِمۡ ؕۛ لَا يَعۡلَمُهُمۡ
اِلَّا اللّٰهُ ؕ جَآءَتۡهُمۡ رُسُلُهُمۡ بِالۡبَيِّنٰتِ فَرَدُّوۡۤا
اَيۡدِيَهُمۡ فِيۡۤ اَفۡوَاهِهِمۡ وَ قَالُوۡۤا اِنَّا كَفَرۡنَا
بِمَاۤ اُرۡسِلۡتُمۡ بِهٖ وَ اِنَّا لَفِيۡ شَكٍّ مِّمَّا
تَدۡعُوۡنَنَاۤ اِلَيۡهِ مُرِيۡبٍ ﴿٩﴾ قَالَتۡ رُسُلُهُمۡ

any doubt about Allâh, the Originator of the heavens and the earth? He calls you (to Himself) that He may protect you against your sins and grant you respite till an appointed time (to the end of your lives).' They said, 'You are nothing but a human being like ourselves. You desire to stop us from (worshipping) that our fathers have been worshipping; so you better bring us some manifest authority.'

11. Their Messengers (of God) said to them, 'It is true we are nothing but human beings like yourselves but Allâh shows (His) favours (by sending revelations and prophethood) to such of His servants as He will. It is not (possible) for us to bring you an authority except by the leave of Allâh. (We put our trust in Him) and in Allâh (alone) should the believers put their trust.

12. 'And why should we not put our trust in Allâh while He has guided us in our ways? We will surely endure patiently all persecutions you have subjected us to. So in Allâh alone let those put their trust who have learnt to put their trust in Him.'

SECTION 3

13. **A**ND those who disbelieved, then said to their Messengers (of God), 'We will, assuredly, turn you out of our country or you will have to return to our creed.' Then did their Lord send (His) revelation to them (- the Messengers) saying, 'We will invariably destroy these wrong doers.

14. 'And We will surely make you occupy the country after them. That (promise) shall hold good for everyone of him who fears to stand before My tribunal and fears My threatful warning.'

15. They sought a judgment, (but when it came) every haughty person (and) enemy (of truth) met with no success (and was utterly disappointed).

16. Gehenna lies before him where he shall be made to drink boiling and repulsive water.

17. He will try to sip it but shall not be able to

أَفِي اللّٰهِ شَكٌّ فَاطِرِ السَّمٰوٰتِ وَ الْأَرْضِ ۖ
يَدْعُوكُمْ لِيَغْفِرَ لَكُمْ مِّنْ ذُنُوبِكُمْ وَيُؤَخِّرَكُمْ
إِلَىٰٓ أَجَلٍ مُّسَمًّى ۚ قَالُوٓا إِنْ أَنْتُمْ إِلَّا بَشَرٌ
مِّثْلُنَا ۖ تُرِيدُونَ أَنْ تَصُدُّونَا عَمَّا كَانَ
يَعْبُدُ ءَابَآؤُنَا فَأْتُونَا بِسُلْطٰنٍ مُّبِينٍ ﴿١٠﴾ قَالَتْ
لَهُمْ رُسُلُهُمْ إِنْ نَّحْنُ إِلَّا بَشَرٌ مِّثْلُكُمْ
وَلٰكِنَّ اللّٰهَ يَمُنُّ عَلٰى مَنْ يَّشَآءُ مِنْ عِبَادِهٖ ۖ
وَ مَا كَانَ لَنَآ أَنْ نَّأْتِيَكُمْ بِسُلْطٰنٍ إِلَّا بِإِذْنِ
اللّٰهِ ۚ وَعَلَى اللّٰهِ فَلْيَتَوَكَّلِ الْمُؤْمِنُونَ ﴿١١﴾ وَمَا
لَنَآ أَلَّا نَتَوَكَّلَ عَلَى اللّٰهِ وَ قَدْ هَدٰىنَا سُبُلَنَا ۚ
وَلَنَصْبِرَنَّ عَلٰى مَآ ءَاذَيْتُمُونَا ۚ وَعَلَى اللّٰهِ
فَلْيَتَوَكَّلِ الْمُتَوَكِّلُونَ ﴿١٢﴾ وَقَالَ الَّذِينَ كَفَرُوا
لِرُسُلِهِمْ لَنُخْرِجَنَّكُمْ مِّنْ أَرْضِنَآ أَوْ لَتَعُودُنَّ
فِي مِلَّتِنَا ۖ فَأَوْحٰىٓ إِلَيْهِمْ رَبُّهُمْ لَنُهْلِكَنَّ
الظّٰلِمِينَ ﴿١٣﴾ وَلَنُسْكِنَنَّكُمُ الْأَرْضَ مِنْۢ
بَعْدِهِمْ ۚ ذٰلِكَ لِمَنْ خَافَ مَقَامِي وَخَافَ
وَعِيدِ ﴿١٤﴾ وَاسْتَفْتَحُوا وَخَابَ كُلُّ جَبَّارٍ
عَنِيدٍ ﴿١٥﴾ مِّنْ وَّرَآئِهٖ جَهَنَّمُ وَيُسْقٰى مِنْ مَّآءٍ

ع ٢ / ١٤

swallow it easily, and death shall come to him from every quarter; yet he shall not die. Moreover he shall see before him further harsh doom.

18. The works of those who disbelieve in (the Messages and blessings of) their Lord, are like ashes on which the wind blows violently on a tempestuous day. They shall have no power to reap the fruit of their deeds. That is indeed an extremely ruinous error.

19. Have you (O reader!) not considered that Allâh created the heavens and the earth to suit the requirements of truth and wisdom. If He (so) will, He can do away with you and bring forth a new creation.

20. And that is not at all difficult for Allâh.

21. (Beware of the Day when) the people shall appear before Allâh in a body so that the weak shall say to those who considered themselves great, 'We were your followers definitely. Can you not help (to save) us (today) in any manner against the punishment of Allâh?' They will reply, 'Had Allâh guided us (to a way of deliverance) we would have surely guided you. It makes no difference for us (now) whether we show impatience or remain patient. There is no way of escape for us (this day).'

SECTION 4

22. **W**HEN the judgment (of God) has been passed (and matter decided), satan will say (to these people), 'Verily, Allâh made you a true promise, and I (also) made you a promise but I failed you. I had no authority over you, however, I called you and you obeyed me. Therefore blame me not (now) but you should blame your ownselves. I can render you no help, nor can you render me any help. In as much as your associating me as partner (with God), I have already declared that I have nothing to do with it. As for the wrong doers, there awaits them a grievous punishment.'

23. But those who believe and do righteous deeds shall be made to enter Gardens served with

صَدِيدٍ ﴿١٦﴾ يَتَجَرَّعُهُ وَلَا يَكَادُ يُسِيغُهُ وَيَأْتِيهِ
الْمَوْتُ مِنْ كُلِّ مَكَانٍ وَمَا هُوَ بِمَيِّتٍ
وَمِنْ وَرَائِهِ عَذَابٌ غَلِيظٌ ﴿١٧﴾ مَثَلُ الَّذِينَ كَفَرُوا
بِرَبِّهِمْ أَعْمَالُهُمْ كَرَمَادٍ اشْتَدَّتْ بِهِ الرِّيحُ
فِي يَوْمٍ عَاصِفٍ لَا يَقْدِرُونَ مِمَّا كَسَبُوا
عَلَى شَيْءٍ ذَلِكَ هُوَ الضَّلَالُ الْبَعِيدُ ﴿١٨﴾ أَلَمْ تَرَ
أَنَّ اللَّهَ خَلَقَ السَّمَاوَاتِ وَالْأَرْضَ بِالْحَقِّ
إِنْ يَشَأْ يُذْهِبْكُمْ وَيَأْتِ بِخَلْقٍ جَدِيدٍ ﴿١٩﴾
وَمَا ذَلِكَ عَلَى اللَّهِ بِعَزِيزٍ ﴿٢٠﴾ وَبَرَزُوا لِلَّهِ
جَمِيعًا فَقَالَ الضُّعَفَاءُ لِلَّذِينَ اسْتَكْبَرُوا
إِنَّا كُنَّا لَكُمْ تَبَعًا فَهَلْ أَنْتُمْ مُغْنُونَ عَنَّا
مِنْ عَذَابِ اللَّهِ مِنْ شَيْءٍ قَالُوا لَوْ هَدَانَا
اللَّهُ لَهَدَيْنَاكُمْ سَوَاءٌ عَلَيْنَا أَجَزِعْنَا أَمْ
صَبَرْنَا مَا لَنَا مِنْ مَحِيصٍ ﴿٢١﴾ وَقَالَ الشَّيْطَانُ
لَمَّا قُضِيَ الْأَمْرُ إِنَّ اللَّهَ وَعَدَكُمْ وَعْدَ
الْحَقِّ وَوَعَدْتُكُمْ فَأَخْلَفْتُكُمْ وَمَا كَانَ
لِيَ عَلَيْكُمْ مِنْ سُلْطَانٍ إِلَّا أَنْ دَعَوْتُكُمْ
فَاسْتَجَبْتُمْ لِي فَلَا تَلُومُونِي وَلُومُوا أَنْفُسَكُمْ
مَا أَنَا بِمُصْرِخِكُمْ وَمَا أَنْتُمْ بِمُصْرِخِيَّ
إِنِّي كَفَرْتُ بِمَا أَشْرَكْتُمُونِ مِنْ قَبْلُ
إِنَّ الظَّالِمِينَ لَهُمْ عَذَابٌ أَلِيمٌ ﴿٢٢﴾ وَأُدْخِلَ

ع ٤ ١٥

running streams (to keep them green and flourishing). There they shall abide in forever by the leave of their Lord. Their greeting therein shall be, 'Peace.'

24. Have you (O reader!) not considered how Allâh compares a holy word to a good tree whose (each) root is firm and whose (every) branch (spreads out) to the very sky.

25. This (tree) goes on bringing forth its fruit at all times by the leave of its Lord. And Allâh gives excellent descriptions (of things) for the people so that they may take heed.

26. And the likeness of an evil word is as an evil tree which can be uprooted from above the earth; it has no stability.

27. Allâh strengthens those who have believed with the (true) word firmly established, (both) in the present life and in the Hereafter. Allâh perishes the wrongdoers and Allâh does whatever He will.

SECTION 5

28. **H**AVE you not seen those who have done away with Allâh's favour for (their) ingratitude. They have landed their people into the abode of ruin -

29. In Gehenna; they shall enter it. What a wretched place to settle in!

30. And they set up compeers to Allâh to lead (people) astray from His path, say, '(Well) enjoy yourselves a while; you are heading towards the Fire.'

31. Say to My servants who have believed, to observe Prayer and to spend secretly and openly out of that We have provided for them, before there comes the day (of reckoning) when neither bargaining, nor fast-friendship shall help them (to get salvation).

32. Allâh is He Who created the heavens and the earth and He causes water to come down from the clouds and He brings forth fruits therewith to be your sustenance. He has made subservient to you the ships that they may sail through the sea by His leave and He has made subservient to you the rivers (also).

الَّذِينَ ءَامَنُوا وَعَمِلُوا الصَّٰلِحَٰتِ جَنَّٰتٍ
تَجْرِي مِنْ تَحْتِهَا الْأَنْهَٰرُ خَٰلِدِينَ فِيهَا
بِإِذْنِ رَبِّهِمْ تَحِيَّتُهُمْ فِيهَا سَلَٰمٌ ﴿٢٣﴾ أَلَمْ
تَرَ كَيْفَ ضَرَبَ اللَّهُ مَثَلًا كَلِمَةً طَيِّبَةً
كَشَجَرَةٍ طَيِّبَةٍ أَصْلُهَا ثَابِتٌ وَفَرْعُهَا
فِي السَّمَاءِ ﴿٢٤﴾ تُؤْتِي أُكُلَهَا كُلَّ حِينٍ بِإِذْنِ
رَبِّهَا وَيَضْرِبُ اللَّهُ الْأَمْثَالَ لِلنَّاسِ
لَعَلَّهُمْ يَتَذَكَّرُونَ ﴿٢٥﴾ وَمَثَلُ كَلِمَةٍ
خَبِيثَةٍ كَشَجَرَةٍ خَبِيثَةٍ اجْتُثَّتْ مِنْ فَوْقِ
الْأَرْضِ مَا لَهَا مِنْ قَرَارٍ ﴿٢٦﴾ يُثَبِّتُ اللَّهُ
الَّذِينَ ءَامَنُوا بِالْقَوْلِ الثَّابِتِ فِي الْحَيَوٰةِ
الدُّنْيَا وَفِي الْآخِرَةِ وَيُضِلُّ اللَّهُ الظَّٰلِمِينَ وَ
يَفْعَلُ اللَّهُ مَا يَشَاءُ ﴿٢٧﴾ أَلَمْ تَرَ إِلَى الَّذِينَ
بَدَّلُوا نِعْمَتَ اللَّهِ كُفْرًا وَأَحَلُّوا قَوْمَهُمْ
دَارَ الْبَوَارِ ﴿٢٨﴾ جَهَنَّمَ يَصْلَوْنَهَا وَبِئْسَ
الْقَرَارُ ﴿٢٩﴾ وَجَعَلُوا لِلَّهِ أَنْدَادًا لِيُضِلُّوا عَنْ
سَبِيلِهِ قُلْ تَمَتَّعُوا فَإِنَّ مَصِيرَكُمْ إِلَى
النَّارِ ﴿٣٠﴾ قُلْ لِعِبَادِيَ الَّذِينَ ءَامَنُوا يُقِيمُوا
الصَّلَوٰةَ وَيُنْفِقُوا مِمَّا رَزَقْنَٰهُمْ سِرًّا وَعَلَانِيَةً
مِنْ قَبْلِ أَنْ يَأْتِيَ يَوْمٌ لَا بَيْعٌ فِيهِ وَلَا
خِلَٰلٌ ﴿٣١﴾ اللَّهُ الَّذِي خَلَقَ السَّمَٰوَٰتِ وَالْأَرْضَ
وَأَنْزَلَ مِنَ السَّمَاءِ مَاءً فَأَخْرَجَ بِهِ مِنَ
الثَّمَرَٰتِ رِزْقًا لَكُمْ وَسَخَّرَ لَكُمُ الْفُلْكَ
لِتَجْرِيَ فِي الْبَحْرِ بِأَمْرِهِ وَسَخَّرَ لَكُمُ الْأَنْهَٰرَ ﴿٣٢﴾

33. And He has made subservient to you the sun and the moon, both moving constantly (according to some fixed laws), and He has made subservient to you the night and the day.
34. He has given you of all that you wanted of Him (by your natural demand). And if you try to count Allâh's bounties, you will not be able to number them. Surely, a human being is very unjust, very ungrateful.

SECTION 6

35. (RECALL the time) when Abraham said, 'My Lord, make this (would be) city (of Makkah) secure and a haven of peace, and keep me and my children away from worshipping idols.
36. 'My Lord! A large number of people has gone astray because of these (idols) to be sure. Then whoso follows me he is certainly of me. As for the person who disobeys me, (I can say only,) You are indeed Great Protector (against faults), Ever Merciful.
37. 'Our Lord! I have settled some of my children in an uncultivable valley (of Makkah), in the vicinity of your Holy House. Our Lord! (I have done) so that they may observe Prayer. Then make the hearts of the people incline towards them and provide them with fruits so that they may always give thanks.
38. 'Our Lord! You know all that we keep secret and all that we make known. There is nothing either on the earth or in the heaven that may be hidden from Allâh.
39. 'All true and perfect praise belongs to Allâh Who has given me despite my old age (two sons) - Ismâîl and Isaac. My Lord is of course, the Hearer of prayers.
40. 'My Lord! Make me a constant and steadfast observer of Prayer and my children (as well). Our Lord! (bestow Your Grace on us) and accept my prayer.
41. 'Our Lord! Protect me, my parents and the believers, against faults on the day when the

وَسَخَّرَ لَكُمُ الشَّمْسَ وَالْقَمَرَ دَآئِبَيْنِ ۚ
وَسَخَّرَ لَكُمُ الَّيْلَ وَالنَّهَارَ ﴿٣٣﴾ وَاٰتٰكُم
مِّنْ كُلِّ مَا سَأَلْتُمُوهُ ۚ وَإِنْ تَعُدُّوا نِعْمَتَ
اللّٰهِ لَا تُحْصُوهَا ۗ إِنَّ الْإِنْسٰنَ لَظَلُومٌ
كَفَّارٌ ﴿٣٤﴾ وَإِذْ قَالَ إِبْرٰهِيمُ رَبِّ اجْعَلْ
هٰذَا الْبَلَدَ اٰمِنًا وَّاجْنُبْنِي وَبَنِيَّ أَنْ نَّعْبُدَ
الْأَصْنَامَ ﴿٣٥﴾ رَبِّ إِنَّهُنَّ أَضْلَلْنَ كَثِيرًا مِّنَ
النَّاسِ ۚ فَمَنْ تَبِعَنِي فَإِنَّهُ مِنِّي ۚ وَمَنْ
عَصَانِي فَإِنَّكَ غَفُورٌ رَّحِيمٌ ﴿٣٦﴾ رَبَّنَا إِنِّي
أَسْكَنْتُ مِنْ ذُرِّيَّتِي بِوَادٍ غَيْرِ ذِي زَرْعٍ
عِنْدَ بَيْتِكَ الْمُحَرَّمِ ۙ رَبَّنَا لِيُقِيمُوا الصَّلٰوةَ
فَاجْعَلْ أَفْئِدَةً مِّنَ النَّاسِ تَهْوِي إِلَيْهِمْ
وَارْزُقْهُمْ مِّنَ الثَّمَرٰتِ لَعَلَّهُمْ يَشْكُرُونَ ﴿٣٧﴾
رَبَّنَا إِنَّكَ تَعْلَمُ مَا نُخْفِي وَمَا نُعْلِنُ ۗ وَمَا
يَخْفٰى عَلَى اللّٰهِ مِنْ شَيْءٍ فِي الْأَرْضِ وَلَا
فِي السَّمَآءِ ﴿٣٨﴾ اَلْحَمْدُ لِلّٰهِ الَّذِي وَهَبَ لِي
عَلَى الْكِبَرِ إِسْمٰعِيلَ وَإِسْحٰقَ ۚ إِنَّ رَبِّي
لَسَمِيعُ الدُّعَآءِ ﴿٣٩﴾ رَبِّ اجْعَلْنِي مُقِيمَ الصَّلٰوةِ
وَمِنْ ذُرِّيَّتِي ۖ رَبَّنَا وَتَقَبَّلْ دُعَآءِ ﴿٤٠﴾ رَبَّنَا
اغْفِرْ لِي وَلِوٰلِدَيَّ وَلِلْمُؤْمِنِينَ يَوْمَ يَقُومُ

reckoning takes place.'

SECTION 7

42. **A**ND (O reader!) do not think that Allâh is unaware of all that these wrongdoers do. He only defers their punishment to the day when the eyes (of the people) will fixedly stare (in horror).
43. They will be running in panic with their necks outstretched and heads erect, they will not be able to wink their eyes, and their hearts (utterly) void (of courage and hope).
44. Warn these people of the day when the (threatened) punishment overtakes them, and those who are unjust will say, 'Our Lord! Grant us respite for a short term, we will respond to Your call and follow the Messengers.' (It will be said to them), 'Did you not swear before now (that) you would never have a fall?
45. '(You said this though) you occupied the dwelling places of those who had wronged themselves and it had been clear to you how We had dealt with them (- the unjust). We have set forth all these descriptions for you clearly.'
46. They have (already) hatched their plots. But even though they have plots that can move mountains, Allâh has power over (rendering) their plots (ineffective).
47. So (O reader!) do not think that Allâh is going to break His Promise He made to His Messengers. Allâh is All-Mighty, Lord of retribution.
48. Beware of the day when this earth will be changed into another earth and the heavens (as well shall be superseded by other heavens) and they (- all people) shall appear before Allâh, the One, the Most Supreme.
49. And on that day you shall see these guilty bound together in chains.
50. Pitch will form their raiments and the fire shall envelop their faces;
51. (This will be) so that Allâh may reward every soul according to his deeds. Verily, Allâh

ع ٧ ١٨

الْحِسَابُ ﴿٤١﴾ وَلَا تَحْسَبَنَّ اللّٰهَ غٰفِلًا عَمَّا
يَعْمَلُ الظّٰلِمُوْنَ ۬ؕ اِنَّمَا يُؤَخِّرُهُمْ لِيَوْمٍ
تَشْخَصُ فِيْهِ الْاَبْصَارُ ﴿٤٢﴾ مُهْطِعِيْنَ مُقْنِعِيْ
رُءُوْسِهِمْ لَا يَرْتَدُّ اِلَيْهِمْ طَرْفُهُمْ ۚ وَاَفْـِٕدَتُهُمْ
هَوَآءٌ ﴿٤٣﴾ وَاَنْذِرِ النَّاسَ يَوْمَ يَاْتِيْهِمُ الْعَذَابُ
فَيَقُوْلُ الَّذِيْنَ ظَلَمُوْا رَبَّنَآ اَخِّرْنَآ اِلٰٓى اَجَلٍ
قَرِيْبٍ ۙ نُّجِبْ دَعْوَتَكَ وَنَتَّبِعِ الرُّسُلَ ؕ
اَوَلَمْ تَكُوْنُوْٓا اَقْسَمْتُمْ مِّنْ قَبْلُ مَا لَكُمْ مِّنْ
زَوَالٍ ﴿٤٤﴾ وَّسَكَنْتُمْ فِيْ مَسٰكِنِ الَّذِيْنَ
ظَلَمُوْٓا اَنْفُسَهُمْ وَتَبَيَّنَ لَكُمْ كَيْفَ فَعَلْنَا
بِهِمْ وَضَرَبْنَا لَكُمُ الْاَمْثَالَ ﴿٤٥﴾ وَقَدْ مَكَرُوْا
مَكْرَهُمْ وَعِنْدَ اللّٰهِ مَكْرُهُمْ ؕ وَاِنْ كَانَ
مَكْرُهُمْ لِتَزُوْلَ مِنْهُ الْجِبَالُ ﴿٤٦﴾ فَلَا
تَحْسَبَنَّ اللّٰهَ مُخْلِفَ وَعْدِهٖ رُسُلَهٗ ؕ اِنَّ
اللّٰهَ عَزِيْزٌ ذُو انْتِقَامٍ ﴿٤٧﴾ يَوْمَ تُبَدَّلُ الْاَرْضُ
غَيْرَ الْاَرْضِ وَالسَّمٰوٰتُ وَبَرَزُوْا لِلّٰهِ
الْوَاحِدِ الْقَهَّارِ ﴿٤٨﴾ وَتَرَى الْمُجْرِمِيْنَ يَوْمَئِذٍ
مُّقَرَّنِيْنَ فِي الْاَصْفَادِ ﴿٤٩﴾ سَرَابِيْلُهُمْ مِّنْ
قَطِرَانٍ وَّتَغْشٰى وُجُوْهَهُمُ النَّارُ ﴿٥٠﴾ لِيَجْزِيَ
اللّٰهُ كُلَّ نَفْسٍ مَّا كَسَبَتْ ؕ اِنَّ اللّٰهَ

is Swift at reckoning.
52. This (Qur'ân) is a Message to, (and sufficient to meet all the requirements of) all humankind. (It has other aims to serve,) and that they may be warned thereby, and that they may know that He is the only One God, and that those possessed of pure knowledge may take heed.

سَرِيعُ الْحِسَابِ ﴿٥١﴾ هَٰذَا بَلَٰغٌ لِّلنَّاسِ
وَلِيُنذَرُوا بِهِ وَلِيَعْلَمُوا أَنَّمَا هُوَ إِلَٰهٌ
وَاحِدٌ وَلِيَذَّكَّرَ أُولُوا الْأَلْبَابِ ﴿٥٢﴾

CHAPTER 15

AL-HIJR
(The Rock)
(Revealed before Hijrah)

سُورَةُ الْحِجْرِ مَكِّيَّةٌ

With the name of Allâh,
the Most Gracious, the Ever Merciful
(I commence to read Sûrah Al-Hijr).

بِسْمِ اللَّهِ الرَّحْمَٰنِ الرَّحِيمِ

1. **A**LIF LÂM RÂ - I am Allâh, the All-Seeing. These are the verses of the perfect Book and of the Qur'ân, that distinguishes the right from the wrong.

الٓر تِلْكَ آيَاتُ الْكِتَابِ وَقُرْآنٍ مُّبِينٍ ﴿١﴾

PART الْجُزْءُ الرَّابِعَ عَشَرَ XIV

2. **O**FTEN those who disbelieve (in the verses of this perfect Book) would wish they had been Muslims.
3. Leave them alone to eat and enjoy themselves and let vain hopes beguile them, but they will soon know (the reality).
4. And never did We destroy a township but it had a decree made known.
5. No people can outstrip its term and none can ever remain behind.
6. And they say, 'O you to whom this Reminder (- the Qur'ân) has been revealed! You are a mad

رُبَمَا يَوَدُّ الَّذِينَ كَفَرُوا لَوْ كَانُوا
مُسْلِمِينَ ﴿٢﴾ ذَرْهُمْ يَأْكُلُوا وَيَتَمَتَّعُوا وَيُلْهِهِمُ
الْأَمَلُ فَسَوْفَ يَعْلَمُونَ ﴿٣﴾ وَمَا أَهْلَكْنَا
مِن قَرْيَةٍ إِلَّا وَلَهَا كِتَابٌ مَّعْلُومٌ ﴿٤﴾ مَا
تَسْبِقُ مِنْ أُمَّةٍ أَجَلَهَا وَمَا يَسْتَأْخِرُونَ ﴿٥﴾
وَقَالُوا يَا أَيُّهَا الَّذِي نُزِّلَ عَلَيْهِ الذِّكْرُ

man indeed.

7. 'Why do you not bring the angels (for punishment) to us, if you are of the truthful?'

8. We send no angels until (the punishment becomes) rightly due and (when once We do send them) these (disbelievers) will not be the respited ones.

9. Verily, it was We, We Ourself Who have revealed this Reminder (- the Qur'ân); and it is We Who are, most certainly, its Guardian.

10. Indeed, We sent (Messengers) before you to the sects of the former peoples,

11. Yet not a single Messenger ever came to them but they treated him scornfully.

12. (Just as We made this a habit with the peoples gone by,) so do We cause this (tendency of scornful treatment) enter the minds of these people who sever their ties (with God).

13. They will not believe in this (Qur'ân), though the precedence of the former peoples has already gone (before them showing how the opposition of truth makes them deserving of the punishment of God).

14. And if We opened to them a gate of the heaven and they (-the angels) began ascending through it,

15. Even then these people would surely say, 'Our eyes have only been dazed; rather We are a bewitched people.'

SECTION 2

16. **W**E have indeed set up constellations in the heaven, and We have decked it fair for the beholders,

17. And We have guarded it against (the intrusion of) every rebellious rejected satan.

18. As to one who wishes to steal a hearing (of the revelation to distort it) a bright fiery flame pursues him.

19. We have spread out and put fertilizers in the earth from outside, and set up firm mountains therein, and We have caused to grow upon it

سُوْرَةُ الْحِجْرِ ١٥

إِنَّكَ لَمَجْنُونٌ ﴿٦﴾ لَوْ مَا تَأْتِينَا بِالْمَلَٰٓئِكَةِ
إِنْ كُنْتَ مِنَ الصّٰدِقِينَ ﴿٧﴾ مَا نُنَزِّلُ
الْمَلَٰٓئِكَةَ إِلَّا بِالْحَقِّ وَمَا كَانُوٓا إِذًا
مُّنْظَرِينَ ﴿٨﴾ إِنَّا نَحْنُ نَزَّلْنَا الذِّكْرَ وَإِنَّا
لَهُ لَحٰفِظُونَ ﴿٩﴾ وَلَقَدْ أَرْسَلْنَا مِنْ قَبْلِكَ
فِي شِيَعِ الْأَوَّلِينَ ﴿١٠﴾ وَمَا يَأْتِيهِمْ مِّنْ
رَّسُولٍ إِلَّا كَانُوا بِهِ يَسْتَهْزِءُونَ ﴿١١﴾ كَذٰلِكَ
نَسْلُكُهُ فِي قُلُوبِ الْمُجْرِمِينَ ﴿١٢﴾ لَا يُؤْمِنُونَ
بِهِ وَقَدْ خَلَتْ سُنَّةُ الْأَوَّلِينَ ﴿١٣﴾ وَلَوْ فَتَحْنَا
عَلَيْهِمْ بَابًا مِّنَ السَّمَآءِ فَظَلُّوا فِيهِ
يَعْرُجُونَ ﴿١٤﴾ لَقَالُوٓا إِنَّمَا سُكِّرَتْ أَبْصٰرُنَا
بَلْ نَحْنُ قَوْمٌ مَّسْحُورُونَ ﴿١٥﴾ وَلَقَدْ جَعَلْنَا
فِي السَّمَآءِ بُرُوجًا وَّزَيَّنّٰهَا لِلنّٰظِرِينَ ﴿١٦﴾
وَحَفِظْنٰهَا مِنْ كُلِّ شَيْطٰنٍ رَّجِيمٍ ﴿١٧﴾ إِلَّا
مَنِ اسْتَرَقَ السَّمْعَ فَأَتْبَعَهُ شِهَابٌ مُّبِينٌ ﴿١٨﴾
وَالْأَرْضَ مَدَدْنٰهَا وَأَلْقَيْنَا فِيهَا رَوَاسِيَ

ع ٥

الجزء الرابع عشر

every suitable thing in due proportion.
20. And We have provided in it means of livelihood for you and even for (all) others whom it is not for you to provide.
21. And there is not a thing but We have the vast treasures of it; and We do not send it down but according to a proper and prescribed measure.
22. And We send impregnating winds and pour water from the clouds and give it to you to drink. You are not the ones to store it up.
23. And surely it is We, Ourself Who give life and cause death; and it is We Who are the (sole) survivors (after every thing perishes).
24. And indeed We know those among you who are the foremost in accepting the truth, and We indeed know those who are the laggards.
25. And certainly it is your Lord Who will gather them together; verily, He is All-Wise, All-Knowing.

SECTION 3

26. **S**URELY, We created human being from dry ringing clay, (transformed) from black mud moulded into shape.
27. And We created the *jinn* before (him) from the fire of intensely hot wind.
28. And (recall the time) when your Lord said to the angels, 'I am, indeed, going to create a human being from dry ringing clay (formed) from black mud, moulded into shape.
29. 'So when I have shaped him in perfection and have breathed My revelation into him, fall you down in submission to him.'
30. And (when He created the human being,) the angels submitted, all of them together.
31. But *Iblîs* (though he was separately bidden to do the same, did not). He stubbornly refused to be with those who submit.
32. (Lord) said, '*Iblîs!* What is (the reason) with you that you would not be with those who submit?'
33. He replied, 'I would never submit to a

وَأَنْۢبَتْنَا فِيهَا مِنْ كُلِّ شَيْءٍ مَّوْزُونٍ ۝١٩
وَجَعَلْنَا لَكُمْ فِيهَا مَعٰيِشَ وَمَنْ لَّسْتُمْ لَهُ
بِرٰزِقِينَ ۝٢٠ وَإِنْ مِّنْ شَيْءٍ إِلَّا عِنْدَنَا
خَزَآئِنُهُ وَمَا نُنَزِّلُهُ إِلَّا بِقَدَرٍ مَّعْلُومٍ ۝٢١
وَأَرْسَلْنَا الرِّيٰحَ لَوٰقِحَ فَأَنْزَلْنَا مِنَ السَّمَآءِ
مَآءً فَأَسْقَيْنٰكُمُوهُ وَمَآ أَنْتُمْ لَهُ بِخٰزِنِينَ ۝٢٢
وَإِنَّا لَنَحْنُ نُحْيِ وَنُمِيتُ وَنَحْنُ الْوٰرِثُونَ ۝٢٣
وَلَقَدْ عَلِمْنَا الْمُسْتَقْدِمِينَ مِنْكُمْ وَلَقَدْ
عَلِمْنَا الْمُسْتَـْٔخِرِينَ ۝٢٤ وَإِنَّ رَبَّكَ هُوَ
يَحْشُرُهُمْ إِنَّهُ حَكِيمٌ عَلِيمٌ ۝٢٥ وَلَقَدْ
خَلَقْنَا الْإِنْسٰنَ مِنْ صَلْصٰلٍ مِّنْ حَمَإٍ
مَّسْنُونٍ ۝٢٦ وَالْجَآنَّ خَلَقْنٰهُ مِنْ قَبْلُ
مِنْ نَّارِ السَّمُومِ ۝٢٧ وَإِذْ قَالَ رَبُّكَ لِلْمَلٰٓئِكَةِ
إِنِّي خٰلِقٌۢ بَشَرًا مِّنْ صَلْصٰلٍ مِّنْ حَمَإٍ
مَّسْنُونٍ ۝٢٨ فَإِذَا سَوَّيْتُهُ وَنَفَخْتُ فِيهِ
مِنْ رُّوحِي فَقَعُوا لَهُ سٰجِدِينَ ۝٢٩ فَسَجَدَ
الْمَلٰٓئِكَةُ كُلُّهُمْ أَجْمَعُونَ ۝٣٠ إِلَّآ إِبْلِيسَ
أَبٰىٓ أَنْ يَكُونَ مَعَ السّٰجِدِينَ ۝٣١ قَالَ يٰٓإِبْلِيسُ
مَا لَكَ أَلَّا تَكُونَ مَعَ السّٰجِدِينَ ۝٣٢ قَالَ لَمْ

ع ٢

human being whom You have created from dry ringing clay (formed) from black mud, moulded into shape.'

34. (Lord) said, '(If it is so) then get out from this (state), for, surely, you are rejected.

35. 'And of course (My) disapproval shall be on you till the Day of Requital.'

36. He said, 'My Lord, then grant me respite till the day when these (human beings) shall be raised (to spiritual life).'

37. (Lord) said, 'You are indeed of those already granted respite,

38. 'Till the day of which the time is known (to Me).'

39. He said, 'My Lord! Since You have condemned me as astray (and erring), I will surely make (evil of straying from the straight path) fair-seeming to them (as long as they stay) on the earth; I shall seduce them all,

40. 'Except your (sincere) servants from among them; (Your) chosen and purified ones, (whom I shall not be able to seduce).'

41. (Lord) said, 'The path (that My sincere servants follow) leads straight to Me.

42. 'As for My servants, you have no authority over them. Different, however, is the case of such of the deviators who (choose to) follow you.

43. 'And, of course, Gehenna is the promised place for such of them all.

44. 'It has seven gates. Each gate shall have an assigned portion of them (who have gone astray).

SECTION 4

45. 'SURELY, those who guard against evil and are dutiful (to Me and humankind) shall live amidst gardens and fountains.

46. '(It will be said to them,) "Enter therein (to live) in peace (and be) secure".'

47. And We shall remove every vestige of rancour that may be in their hearts. They will be like brothers (seated cheerfully) on raised

أَكُن لِّأَسْجُدَ لِبَشَرٍ خَلَقْتَهُ مِن صَلْصَٰلٍ
مِّنْ حَمَإٍ مَّسْنُونٍ ﴿٣٣﴾ قَالَ فَاخْرُجْ مِنْهَا
فَإِنَّكَ رَجِيمٌ ﴿٣٤﴾ وَإِنَّ عَلَيْكَ اللَّعْنَةَ إِلَىٰ
يَوْمِ الدِّينِ ﴿٣٥﴾ قَالَ رَبِّ فَأَنظِرْنِي إِلَىٰ يَوْمِ
يُبْعَثُونَ ﴿٣٦﴾ قَالَ فَإِنَّكَ مِنَ الْمُنظَرِينَ ﴿٣٧﴾ إِلَىٰ
يَوْمِ الْوَقْتِ الْمَعْلُومِ ﴿٣٨﴾ قَالَ رَبِّ بِمَا أَغْوَيْتَنِي
لَأُزَيِّنَنَّ لَهُمْ فِي الْأَرْضِ وَلَأُغْوِيَنَّهُمْ
أَجْمَعِينَ ﴿٣٩﴾ إِلَّا عِبَادَكَ مِنْهُمُ الْمُخْلَصِينَ ﴿٤٠﴾
قَالَ هَٰذَا صِرَاطٌ عَلَيَّ مُسْتَقِيمٌ ﴿٤١﴾ إِنَّ عِبَادِي
لَيْسَ لَكَ عَلَيْهِمْ سُلْطَٰنٌ إِلَّا مَنِ اتَّبَعَكَ
مِنَ الْغَاوِينَ ﴿٤٢﴾ وَإِنَّ جَهَنَّمَ لَمَوْعِدُهُمْ
أَجْمَعِينَ ﴿٤٣﴾ لَهَا سَبْعَةُ أَبْوَٰبٍ لِّكُلِّ بَابٍ
مِّنْهُمْ جُزْءٌ مَّقْسُومٌ ﴿٤٤﴾ إِنَّ الْمُتَّقِينَ فِي
جَنَّٰتٍ وَعُيُونٍ ﴿٤٥﴾ ادْخُلُوهَا بِسَلَٰمٍ ءَامِنِينَ ﴿٤٦﴾
وَنَزَعْنَا مَا فِي صُدُورِهِم مِّنْ غِلٍّ إِخْوَٰنًا

couches (of happiness), face to face.
48. They shall suffer no fatigue, nor shall they ever be ejected from there.
49. (O Prophet!) Give My servants the important news that I - I alone - am most certainly the One Great Protector, the Ever Merciful.
50. And (also tell them) that My punishment is a very grievous one.
51. And (also) give them the important news about Abraham's guests.
52. When they entered upon him and greeted him saying, 'Peace (be upon you)' he answered, 'We feel afraid of you.'
53. They said, 'Have no fear, we give you good tidings of (the birth of) a son endowed with knowledge.'
54. He (-Abraham) said, 'Do you give me the good tidings inspite of the fact that old age has come upon me. So on what (basis) are you giving (me this) good tidings.'
55. They said, 'We give you good tidings on the basis of (the revelation of) truth; therefore do not be of the despairing ones (of the mercy of Allâh).'
56. He said, 'And who despairs of the mercy of his Lord, but the erring ones?'
57. He added, 'O you messengers! What is your real business then?'
58. They said, 'We have been sent to (destroy) a guilty people.
59. 'Excepting the followers of Lot (because they are not guilty). We shall invariably deliver them all.
60. 'Excepting his wife, (of whom God says,) "We have decided that she (will not accompany those ordained to be delivered but) shall be really of those staying behind".'

SECTION 5

61. **W**HEN the messengers came to Lot (and his) followers,
62. (Lot) said, 'Surely, you are an unknown people, I apprehend evil from you (because of your coming).'

عَلَىٰ سُرُرٍ مُّتَقَٰبِلِينَ ﴿٤٧﴾ لَا يَمَسُّهُمْ فِيهَا
نَصَبٌ وَمَا هُم مِّنْهَا بِمُخْرَجِينَ ﴿٤٨﴾ نَبِّئْ
عِبَادِيٓ أَنِّيٓ أَنَا الْغَفُورُ الرَّحِيمُ ﴿٤٩﴾ وَأَنَّ
عَذَابِي هُوَ الْعَذَابُ الْأَلِيمُ ﴿٥٠﴾ وَنَبِّئْهُمْ
عَن ضَيْفِ إِبْرَٰهِيمَ ﴿٥١﴾ إِذْ دَخَلُوا عَلَيْهِ
فَقَالُوا سَلَٰمًا قَالَ إِنَّا مِنكُمْ وَجِلُونَ ﴿٥٢﴾
قَالُوا لَا تَوْجَلْ إِنَّا نُبَشِّرُكَ بِغُلَٰمٍ عَلِيمٍ ﴿٥٣﴾
قَالَ أَبَشَّرْتُمُونِي عَلَىٰٓ أَن مَّسَّنِيَ الْكِبَرُ
فَبِمَ تُبَشِّرُونَ ﴿٥٤﴾ قَالُوا بَشَّرْنَٰكَ بِالْحَقِّ
فَلَا تَكُن مِّنَ الْقَٰنِطِينَ ﴿٥٥﴾ قَالَ وَمَن
يَقْنَطُ مِن رَّحْمَةِ رَبِّهِۦٓ إِلَّا الضَّآلُّونَ ﴿٥٦﴾ قَالَ
فَمَا خَطْبُكُمْ أَيُّهَا الْمُرْسَلُونَ ﴿٥٧﴾ قَالُوٓا إِنَّآ
أُرْسِلْنَآ إِلَىٰ قَوْمٍ مُّجْرِمِينَ ﴿٥٨﴾ إِلَّآ ءَالَ لُوطٍ
إِنَّا لَمُنَجُّوهُمْ أَجْمَعِينَ ﴿٥٩﴾ إِلَّا امْرَأَتَهُۥ قَدَّرْنَآ
إِنَّهَا لَمِنَ الْغَٰبِرِينَ ﴿٦٠﴾ فَلَمَّا جَآءَ ءَالَ لُوطٍ
الْمُرْسَلُونَ ﴿٦١﴾ قَالَ إِنَّكُمْ قَوْمٌ مُّنكَرُونَ ﴿٦٢﴾

63. They said, '(You need no apprehensions.) But we have come to you with (the news of) that (punishment) about (the truth of) which they doubted.
64. 'And we have come to you with sure news and most certainly we are truthful;
65. 'So set forth (from here) with your people in the (latter) part of the night and yourself following in their wake. Let none of you look about (and lag behind) but proceed to where you are commanded.'
66. And We appraised him (-Lot) with certainty of this decree that the roots (and last remnants) of these people are to be cut off when they rise at dawn.
67. And the residents of the city came rejoicing (to the house of Lot).
68. (Lot) said, 'Surely, these are my guests, therefore do not put me to shame (by your disrespectful behaviour towards them).
69. 'And keep your duty to Allâh and disgrace me not.'
70. They said, 'Have we not told you not to entertain (all sorts of unknown) people?'
71. He said, 'Here are my daughters (as hostages to serve as a guarantee that the strangers will not make a mischief), if you must do something (to make any investigation against me).'
72. (Prophet!) By your (holy) life and by your true faith these (your opponents) are (also) wandering distractedly in a fit of frenzy.
73. Then a dreadful punishment overtook these (opponents of Lot) at sunrise.
74. We turned it (- the city) upside down, and rained upon the people petrified hard stones of clay (constantly).
75. Surely, in this (narrative) there are many signs for such as can interpret (signs).
76. And (the ruins of) these (townships) lie on a road that still exists (right on the highway between Arabia and Syria).

قالوا بل جئنك بما كانوا فيه يمترون ﴿٦٣﴾
و أتينك بالحق و إنا لصدقون ﴿٦٤﴾ فأسر
بأهلك بقطع من اليل و اتبع أدبرهم
و لا يلتفت منكم أحد و امضوا حيث
تؤمرون ﴿٦٥﴾ و قضينا إليه ذلك الأمر أن
دابر هؤلاء مقطوع مصبحين ﴿٦٦﴾ وجاء
أهل المدينة يستبشرون ﴿٦٧﴾ قال إن
هؤلاء ضيفي فلا تفضحون ﴿٦٨﴾ واتقوا الله
ولا تخزون ﴿٦٩﴾ قالوا أولم ننهك عن
العلمين ﴿٧٠﴾ قال هؤلاء بناتي إن كنتم
فعلين ﴿٧١﴾ لعمرك إنهم لفي سكرتهم
يعمهون ﴿٧٢﴾ فأخذتهم الصيحة مشرقين ﴿٧٣﴾
فجعلنا عليها سافلها و أمطرنا عليهم
حجارة من سجيل ﴿٧٤﴾ إن في ذلك لأيت
للمتوسمين ﴿٧٥﴾ و إنها لبسبيل مقيم ﴿٧٦﴾

77. Behold! In this (narration) is indeed a sign for the believers.
78. Certainly, the dwellers of the thicket (of Midian) were (also) a wrong doing people.
79. Therefore We inflicted punishment on them; and (the ruins of) both their cities (-the city of Sodomites and the city of Aikah) lie indeed on the open highway (traversed by the caravans from Hijâz to Syria).

SECTION 6

80. AND the dwellers of the Hijr (- a township of Thamûd lying between Tabûk and Madînah, also) cried lies to the Messengers.
81. And We gave them Our commandments but they were averse to them.
82. And they (in search of a life of peace and security,) used to hew some parts of the mountains into houses feeling secure (therein).
83. But the dreadful punishment overtook them in the morning.
84. So that all that they had accomplished was of no avail to them.
85. And We have not created the heavens and the earth and all that is between the two but to suit the requirements of truth and wisdom. And the (threatened) Hour (of punishment) is sure to come. So turn away from them with goodly grace.
86. Surely, it is your Lord Who is the Great Creator, the Possessor of perfect knowledge.
87. And in fact We have given you the seven oft-recited (verses of *Sûrah Al-Fâtihah*) and the Grand Qur'ân.
88. Extend not your eyes desirously towards the fleeting enjoyments We have bestowed on some classes (of people) among them, nor grieve over (this destruction of) them and be kind and gentle to the believers,
89. And proclaim, 'I am, indeed, the plain Warner (promised by God).'
90. Since We (have decided to) send down (this revelation full of warnings) to those who have formed themselves into factions by

إِنَّ فِي ذَٰلِكَ لَأٓيَةً لِّلْمُؤْمِنِينَ ﴿٧٧﴾ وَإِن كَانَ
أَصْحَٰبُ الْأَيْكَةِ لَظَٰلِمِينَ ﴿٧٨﴾ فَانتَقَمْنَا مِنْهُمْ
وَإِنَّهُمَا لَبِإِمَامٍ مُّبِينٍ ﴿٧٩﴾ وَلَقَدْ كَذَّبَ
أَصْحَٰبُ الْحِجْرِ الْمُرْسَلِينَ ﴿٨٠﴾ وَءَاتَيْنَٰهُمْ ءَايَٰتِنَا
فَكَانُوا عَنْهَا مُعْرِضِينَ ﴿٨١﴾ وَكَانُوا يَنْحِتُونَ
مِنَ الْجِبَالِ بُيُوتًا ءَامِنِينَ ﴿٨٢﴾ فَأَخَذَتْهُمُ
الصَّيْحَةُ مُصْبِحِينَ ﴿٨٣﴾ فَمَآ أَغْنَىٰ عَنْهُم مَّا
كَانُوا يَكْسِبُونَ ﴿٨٤﴾ وَمَا خَلَقْنَا السَّمَٰوَٰتِ
وَالْأَرْضَ وَمَا بَيْنَهُمَآ إِلَّا بِالْحَقِّ وَإِنَّ
السَّاعَةَ لَأٓتِيَةٌ فَاصْفَحِ الصَّفْحَ الْجَمِيلَ ﴿٨٥﴾
إِنَّ رَبَّكَ هُوَ الْخَلَّٰقُ الْعَلِيمُ ﴿٨٦﴾ وَلَقَدْ ءَاتَيْنَٰكَ
سَبْعًا مِّنَ الْمَثَانِي وَالْقُرْءَانَ الْعَظِيمَ ﴿٨٧﴾ لَا
تَمُدَّنَّ عَيْنَيْكَ إِلَىٰ مَا مَتَّعْنَا بِهِۦٓ أَزْوَٰجًا
مِّنْهُمْ وَلَا تَحْزَنْ عَلَيْهِمْ وَاخْفِضْ جَنَاحَكَ
لِلْمُؤْمِنِينَ ﴿٨٨﴾ وَقُلْ إِنِّيٓ أَنَا النَّذِيرُ الْمُبِينُ ﴿٨٩﴾
كَمَآ أَنزَلْنَا عَلَى الْمُقْتَسِمِينَ ﴿٩٠﴾ الَّذِينَ جَعَلُوا

taking oaths (against you).
91. And who have pronounced the Qur'ân to be a pack of lies.
92. So by your Lord, We will surely question them all,
93. About their (mis)deeds.
94. Therefore declare openly what you are commanded (to deliver) and turn away from the polytheists.
95. We do suffice you (to punish) those who treat (you) scornfully.
96. Who set up an other god beside Allâh; but they shall soon come to know (the consequences).
97. And We know, indeed, that your mind is distressed because of (polytheistic things) that they say,
98. So (the remedy of this distress is that you) glorify your Lord with all His true praise and be of those who prostrate themselves (before Him).
99. And go on worshipping your Lord until there comes to you that which is certain (and you breathe your last).

الْقُرْاٰنَ عِضِيْنَ ﴿٩١﴾ فَوَرَبِّكَ لَنَسْـَٔلَنَّهُمْ
أَجْمَعِيْنَ ﴿٩٢﴾ عَمَّا كَانُوْا يَعْمَلُوْنَ ﴿٩٣﴾ فَاصْدَعْ
بِمَا تُؤْمَرُ وَأَعْرِضْ عَنِ الْمُشْرِكِيْنَ ﴿٩٤﴾
إِنَّا كَفَيْنٰكَ الْمُسْتَهْزِءِيْنَ ﴿٩٥﴾ الَّذِيْنَ يَجْعَلُوْنَ
مَعَ اللّٰهِ إِلٰهًا اٰخَرَ فَسَوْفَ يَعْلَمُوْنَ ﴿٩٦﴾
وَلَقَدْ نَعْلَمُ أَنَّكَ يَضِيْقُ صَدْرُكَ بِمَا
يَقُوْلُوْنَ ﴿٩٧﴾ فَسَبِّحْ بِحَمْدِ رَبِّكَ وَكُنْ
مِّنَ السّٰجِدِيْنَ ﴿٩٨﴾ وَاعْبُدْ رَبَّكَ حَتّٰى
يَأْتِيَكَ الْيَقِيْنُ ﴿٩٩﴾

CHAPTER
16

AL-NAHL
(The Bee)
(Revealed before Hijrah)

سُوْرَةُ النَّحْلِ مَكِّيَّةٌ

With the name of Allâh,
the Most Gracious, the Ever Merciful
(I commence to read Sûrah Al-Nahl).

بِسْمِ اللّٰهِ الرَّحْمٰنِ الرَّحِيْمِ

1. **T**HE command of Allâh (regarding the punishment to the disbelievers) has come, therefore you need not seek to expedite it before its appointed time; and He is beyond and far above (all the things) they associate (with Him).
2. He sends down the angels with the revelation by His command to such of His servants as He

أَتٰى أَمْرُ اللّٰهِ فَلَا تَسْتَعْجِلُوْهُ سُبْحٰنَهٗ
وَتَعٰلٰى عَمَّا يُشْرِكُوْنَ ﴿١﴾ يُنَزِّلُ الْمَلٰٓئِكَةَ

will, (saying,) ' Warn the people that there is no other, cannot be and will never be one worthy of worship but I, therefore take (only) Me as a shield.

3. 'He has created the heavens and the earth to suit the requirements of truth and wisdom. He is beyond and far above (all) the things they associate (with Him).'

4. He has created human being from a mere drop of fluid, (a small life germ) then look! What a perspicuous and sound debater he has turned out to be.

5. And the cattle (too) He has created; they provide you with the things giving warmth and (various) other benefits, and through some of these (cattle) you obtain your food.

6. And in them there is for you provision of graceful beauty (and a matter of pride and honour), when you bring them home in the evening and when you drive them out to pasture in the morning.

7. And it is (these cattle) that carry your heavy loads to lands that you could never reach except by putting yourselves to great hardships. Indeed, your Lord is Most Compassionate, Ever Merciful.

8. And (He has created) horses, mules and donkeys that you may ride them and look graceful. And He will yet create (for you) things of which (today) you have no knowledge.

9. And (because He is our Creator) upon Allâh lies (the responsibility of) leading to the right path, for there are some (paths) deviating (from the right and moderate course and so they lead astray). And if He had (enforced) His will, He would have guided you all.

SECTION 2

10. **He** it is Who poured down water from the clouds for you. It provides you with drink; it produces the plants on which you pasture (your

بِالرُّوحِ مِنْ أَمْرِهِ عَلَىٰ مَنْ يَشَاءُ مِنْ
عِبَادِهِ أَنْ أَنْذِرُوا أَنَّهُ لَا إِلَٰهَ إِلَّا أَنَا
فَاتَّقُونِ ② خَلَقَ السَّمَٰوٰتِ وَالْأَرْضَ بِالْحَقِّ
تَعَٰلَىٰ عَمَّا يُشْرِكُونَ ③ خَلَقَ الْإِنْسَٰنَ مِنْ
نُطْفَةٍ فَإِذَا هُوَ خَصِيمٌ مُبِينٌ ④ وَالْأَنْعَٰمَ
خَلَقَهَا لَكُمْ فِيهَا دِفْءٌ وَمَنَٰفِعُ وَمِنْهَا
تَأْكُلُونَ ⑤ وَلَكُمْ فِيهَا جَمَالٌ حِينَ تُرِيحُونَ
وَحِينَ تَسْرَحُونَ ⑥ وَتَحْمِلُ أَثْقَالَكُمْ إِلَىٰ
بَلَدٍ لَمْ تَكُونُوا بَٰلِغِيهِ إِلَّا بِشِقِّ الْأَنْفُسِ
إِنَّ رَبَّكُمْ لَرَءُوفٌ رَحِيمٌ ⑦ وَالْخَيْلَ
وَالْبِغَالَ وَالْحَمِيرَ لِتَرْكَبُوهَا وَزِينَةً
وَيَخْلُقُ مَا لَا تَعْلَمُونَ ⑧ وَعَلَى اللَّهِ قَصْدُ
السَّبِيلِ وَمِنْهَا جَائِرٌ وَلَوْ شَاءَ لَهَدَٰكُمْ
أَجْمَعِينَ ⑨ هُوَ الَّذِي أَنْزَلَ مِنَ السَّمَاءِ

ع ٩ ٧

herds of cattle).
11. He thereby grows for you the crops (of corn) and olives and date-palms and vines and all kinds of other fruit. Surely, in that there is a sign for a people who reflect.
12. And He has made subservient to you the night and the day and the sun and the moon. And (similarly) the stars (too) are made subservient to you by His command. Surely, in that there are many a sign for a people who make use of their understanding.
13. And (consider over) that what He has created for you in the earth which is of varying colours and qualities. Verily, in that is, of course, a sign for a people who take heed.
14. And He it is Who has made subservient (to you) the sea that you may eat of its fresh flesh (of fish), and may bring forth out of it (precious and beautiful things of) ornaments for your wear. And you see the ships cleaving through it. (They do so that you may journey with ease) and that you may seek of His bounty (in other ways) and that you may render thanks (to Him).
15. And He has placed firm mountains in the earth lest it shall quake and that they may be a source of benefit and provision of food for you, and (has made) rivers (flow on it), and many routes that you may take the right way to reach your goal.
16. And (He has established many other) landmarks as well; (it is by these) and by the stars (too) that the people can follow the right direction.
17. Can He then Who creates (out of nothing) be like those who can create nought? Will you not then take heed?
18. If you count Allâh's blessings and bounties (upon you, they are so many that) you will never be able to number them. Most surely, Allâh is Great Protector, Ever Merciful.
19. Allâh knows all that you conceal and all that

مَاءً لَّكُم مِّنْهُ شَرَابٌ وَّ مِنْهُ شَجَرٌ فِيهِ
تُسِيمُونَ ١٠ يُنْبِتُ لَكُم بِهِ الزَّرْعَ وَ الزَّيْتُونَ
وَ النَّخِيلَ وَ الْأَعْنَٰبَ وَ مِن كُلِّ الثَّمَرَٰتِ
إِنَّ فِي ذَٰلِكَ لَأٓيَةً لِّقَوْمٍ يَتَفَكَّرُونَ ١١
وَسَخَّرَ لَكُمُ الَّيْلَ وَ النَّهَارَ وَ الشَّمْسَ وَ الْقَمَرَ
وَ النُّجُومُ مُسَخَّرَٰتٌ بِأَمْرِهِ إِنَّ فِي ذَٰلِكَ
لَأٓيَٰتٍ لِّقَوْمٍ يَعْقِلُونَ ١٢ وَ مَا ذَرَأَ لَكُمْ
فِي الْأَرْضِ مُخْتَلِفًا أَلْوَٰنُهُ إِنَّ فِي ذَٰلِكَ
لَأٓيَةً لِّقَوْمٍ يَذَّكَّرُونَ ١٣ وَ هُوَ الَّذِي سَخَّرَ
الْبَحْرَ لِتَأْكُلُوا مِنْهُ لَحْمًا طَرِيًّا وَّ تَسْتَخْرِجُوا
مِنْهُ حِلْيَةً تَلْبَسُونَهَا وَ تَرَى الْفُلْكَ مَوَاخِرَ
فِيهِ وَ لِتَبْتَغُوا مِن فَضْلِهِ وَ لَعَلَّكُمْ
تَشْكُرُونَ ١٤ وَ أَلْقَىٰ فِي الْأَرْضِ رَوَٰسِيَ أَن
تَمِيدَ بِكُمْ وَ أَنْهَٰرًا وَّ سُبُلًا لَّعَلَّكُمْ
تَهْتَدُونَ ١٥ وَ عَلَٰمَٰتٍ وَ بِالنَّجْمِ هُمْ
يَهْتَدُونَ ١٦ أَفَمَن يَخْلُقُ كَمَن لَّا يَخْلُقُ
أَفَلَا تَذَكَّرُونَ ١٧ وَ إِن تَعُدُّوا نِعْمَةَ اللَّهِ
لَا تُحْصُوهَا إِنَّ اللَّهَ لَغَفُورٌ رَّحِيمٌ ١٨ وَ اللَّهُ

you profess and do openly.

20. And the things whom they call upon apart from Allâh can create nothing. Rather they are themselves created.

21. They are dead, not alive. And they do not perceive when they shall be raised (to life again).

SECTION 3

22. **Y**OUR God is One God. But as for those who do not believe in the Hereafter, their hearts are strangers (to the truth), and they are full of vanity.

23. As a matter of fact, Allâh knows what they conceal and all that they profess and do openly. Surely, He does not love such vain persons at all.

24. And when these (disbelievers) are asked, 'What is (in your opinion) that which your Lord has sent down?' They say, 'They are (mere) stories of the ancients.'

25. (They say it) with the result that they will bear their own burdens in full on the Day of Resurrection and (also) a portion of the burdens of those (who are) without knowledge and whom they are leading astray (because of their ignorance). Look! How evil is the burden which they bear!

SECTION 4

26. **T**HEIR predecessors did (also) hatch schemes (against the Prophets), Allâh struck at the very root of their foundations, so that the roof fell down from above them and the punishment came upon them from quarters they did not perceive.

27. (That is not all,) then on the Day of Resurrection He will disgrace them and will say, 'Where are My (so called) partners (associated with Me by you), for whose sake you used to oppose (My Prophets and the believers in truth).' At that time those who have been given the knowledge would say, 'Surely, this day disgrace and calamity shall be the lot of the disbelievers.'

يعلم ما تسرون وما تعلنون (١٩) والذين
يدعون من دون الله لا يخلقون شيئا
وهم يخلقون (٢٠) أموات غير أحياء وما
يشعرون أيان يبعثون (٢١) إلهكم إله
واحد فالذين لا يؤمنون بالآخرة
قلوبهم منكرة وهم مستكبرون (٢٢)
لا جرم أن الله يعلم ما يسرون وما
يعلنون إنه لا يحب المستكبرين (٢٣)
وإذا قيل لهم ماذا أنزل ربكم قالوا
أساطير الأولين (٢٤) ليحملوا أوزارهم
كاملة يوم القيمة ومن أوزار الذين
يضلونهم بغير علم ألا ساء ما يزرون (٢٥)
قد مكر الذين من قبلهم فأتى الله
بنينهم من القواعد فخر عليهم السقف
من فوقهم وأتىهم العذاب من حيث
لا يشعرون (٢٦) ثم يوم القيمة يخزيهم
ويقول أين شركاءي الذين كنتم
تشاقون فيهم قال الذين أوتوا العلم
إن الخزي اليوم والسوء على الكفرين (٢٧)

28. Those whom the angels cause to die while they are (still engrossed) in doing wrong to themselves; (when they are on the point of death) they will offer submission (saying), 'We used to do no evil.' (The angels will say,) 'It is not as you say. Surely, Allâh knows well all that you have been doing.
29. 'Therefore enter the gates of Gehenna to abide therein.' Evil indeed is the abode of those whose hearts are full of vanity and pride.
30. And (when) it is said to those who guarded against evil, 'What (do you think) is that which your Lord has revealed?' They said, 'The best.' There is a good reward in this world for those who do good but the abode of the Hereafter they shall have is indeed far better. How excellent is the abode of those who become secure against evil!
31. (These abodes) they shall enter (are) Gardens of Eternity, served with running streams (to keep them green and flourishing). They shall have therein all that they desire. That is how Allâh rewards those who become secure against evil.
32. Those (are happy indeed) whom the angels cause to die while they are pure saying, 'Peace be upon you! Enter Paradise because of those (noble deeds) you have been doing.'
33. These (disbelievers) only wait for the angels to descend upon them (with the punishment), or that the decisive decree of your Lord should come to pass. Their predecessors acted in a (wrong) way as they do. Allâh did not deal with them unjustly but they have been doing injustice to themselves.
34. So that the evil consequences of their deeds afflicted them. And (that punishment) which they used to look down upon encompassed them.

SECTION 5

35. **T**HOSE who associated partners (with Allâh) said (also), 'Had Allâh so willed, neither we nor our fathers would have worshipped

سُوْرَةُ النَّحْلِ ١٦

الَّذِيْنَ تَتَوَفّٰهُمُ الْمَلٰٓئِكَةُ ظَالِمِيْٓ اَنْفُسِهِمْ ص
فَاَلْقَوُا السَّلَمَ مَا كُنَّا نَعْمَلُ مِنْ سُوْٓءٍ ط
بَلٰٓى اِنَّ اللّٰهَ عَلِيْمٌ بِمَا كُنْتُمْ تَعْمَلُوْنَ ﴿٢٨﴾
فَادْخُلُوْٓا اَبْوَابَ جَهَنَّمَ خٰلِدِيْنَ فِيْهَا ط
فَلَبِئْسَ مَثْوَى الْمُتَكَبِّرِيْنَ ﴿٢٩﴾ وَقِيْلَ لِلَّذِيْنَ
اتَّقَوْا مَاذَآ اَنْزَلَ رَبُّكُمْ ط قَالُوْا خَيْرًا ط
لِلَّذِيْنَ اَحْسَنُوْا فِيْ هٰذِهِ الدُّنْيَا حَسَنَةٌ ط
وَلَدَارُ الْاٰخِرَةِ خَيْرٌ ط وَلَنِعْمَ دَارُ الْمُتَّقِيْنَ ﴿٣٠﴾
جَنّٰتُ عَدْنٍ يَّدْخُلُوْنَهَا تَجْرِيْ مِنْ تَحْتِهَا
الْاَنْهٰرُ لَهُمْ فِيْهَا مَا يَشَآءُوْنَ ط كَذٰلِكَ
يَجْزِي اللّٰهُ الْمُتَّقِيْنَ ﴿٣١﴾ الَّذِيْنَ تَتَوَفّٰهُمُ
الْمَلٰٓئِكَةُ طَيِّبِيْنَ يَقُوْلُوْنَ سَلٰمٌ عَلَيْكُمُ
ادْخُلُوا الْجَنَّةَ بِمَا كُنْتُمْ تَعْمَلُوْنَ ﴿٣٢﴾ هَلْ
يَنْظُرُوْنَ اِلَّآ اَنْ تَأْتِيَهُمُ الْمَلٰٓئِكَةُ اَوْ
يَأْتِيَ اَمْرُ رَبِّكَ ط كَذٰلِكَ فَعَلَ الَّذِيْنَ مِنْ
قَبْلِهِمْ ط وَمَا ظَلَمَهُمُ اللّٰهُ وَلٰكِنْ كَانُوْٓا
اَنْفُسَهُمْ يَظْلِمُوْنَ ﴿٣٣﴾ فَاَصَابَهُمْ سَيِّاٰتُ مَا
ع عَمِلُوْا وَحَاقَ بِهِمْ مَّا كَانُوْا بِهٖ يَسْتَهْزِءُوْنَ ﴿٣٤﴾
وَقَالَ الَّذِيْنَ اَشْرَكُوْا لَوْ شَآءَ اللّٰهُ مَا عَبَدْنَا

anything apart from Him, nor would we have forbidden anything without (sanction from) Him.' Their predecessors acted as they do. But there is no other responsibility upon the Messengers except the delivery (of the Message) in plain terms.

36. And We raised a Messenger among every community (teaching,) 'Worship Allâh and shun the transgressor (- satan).' Thus there were some among them whom Allâh guided and there were some among them who were condemned to be lost. So travel in the land and behold how evil was the end of those who cried lies (to the truth).

37. (Prophet!) If you are solicitous of their guidance, then (know that) Allâh never guides those who lead (others) astray (knowingly), and they shall have no helpers (to protect them against the evil consequences of their deeds).

38. And they have sworn by Allâh their most earnest oaths that Allâh will not raise the dead to life. Why not? It is a promise binding (in accordance with His will) upon Him. (He has guaranteed it,) but most people do not know (this true fact).

39. (It is a fact that He will raise the dead to life) so that He may make plain to them the things over which they were at variance (in the present life), and so that the disbelievers may know that they were truly liars.

40. Our word to a thing when We intend it (to come into being) is only that We say to it, 'Be' and it comes to be.

SECTION 6

41. **W**E will certainly provide a goodly abode in this world for those who emigrated (from their homes) in the cause of Allâh after they were dealt with unjustly. And truly the reward (that they shall have) in the Hereafter is greater still. If the disbelievers but knew (it would have been much better for them).

مِنْ دُونِهِ مِنْ شَيْءٍ نَحْنُ وَ لَآ ءَابَآؤُنَا
وَلَا حَرَّمْنَا مِنْ دُونِهِ مِنْ شَيْءٍ كَذٰلِكَ
فَعَلَ الَّذِينَ مِنْ قَبْلِهِمْ فَهَلْ عَلَى الرُّسُلِ
إِلَّا الْبَلٰغُ الْمُبِينُ ﴿٣٥﴾ وَلَقَدْ بَعَثْنَا فِي كُلِّ
أُمَّةٍ رَّسُولًا أَنِ اعْبُدُوا اللّٰهَ وَ اجْتَنِبُوا
الطّٰغُوتَ فَمِنْهُمْ مَّنْ هَدَى اللّٰهُ وَمِنْهُمْ
مَّنْ حَقَّتْ عَلَيْهِ الضَّلٰلَةُ فَسِيرُوا فِي الْأَرْضِ
فَانْظُرُوا كَيْفَ كَانَ عٰقِبَةُ الْمُكَذِّبِينَ ﴿٣٦﴾
إِنْ تَحْرِصْ عَلٰى هُدٰىهُمْ فَإِنَّ اللّٰهَ لَا يَهْدِي
مَنْ يُّضِلُّ وَمَا لَهُمْ مِّنْ نّٰصِرِينَ ﴿٣٧﴾ وَأَقْسَمُوا
بِاللّٰهِ جَهْدَ أَيْمٰنِهِمْ لَا يَبْعَثُ اللّٰهُ مَنْ
يَّمُوتُ بَلٰى وَعْدًا عَلَيْهِ حَقًّا وَّلٰكِنَّ أَكْثَرَ
النَّاسِ لَا يَعْلَمُونَ ﴿٣٨﴾ لِيُبَيِّنَ لَهُمُ الَّذِي
يَخْتَلِفُونَ فِيهِ وَلِيَعْلَمَ الَّذِينَ كَفَرُوا
أَنَّهُمْ كَانُوا كٰذِبِينَ ﴿٣٩﴾ إِنَّمَا قَوْلُنَا لِشَيْءٍ إِذَآ
أَرَدْنٰهُ أَنْ نَّقُولَ لَهُ كُنْ فَيَكُونُ ﴿٤٠﴾ وَالَّذِينَ
هَاجَرُوا فِي اللّٰهِ مِنْ بَعْدِ مَا ظُلِمُوا لَنُبَوِّئَنَّهُمْ فِي
الدُّنْيَا حَسَنَةً وَلَأَجْرُ الْآخِرَةِ أَكْبَرُ لَوْ

42. These are those (emigrants) who patiently persevered and put their trust in their Lord (alone).
43. And we sent not (as Messengers) before you but they were men to whom We revealed (Our teachings). So ask the people of the Reminder (- the Qur'ân), if you do not know.
44. (We sent these above mentioned men) with clear proofs and Scriptures. And (similarly now) We have revealed to you the Reminder that you may explain to humankind (the commandments) that have been sent down to them so that they may ponder and reflect (over it).
45. Do they, who have been hatching evil plots (against you), feel secure that Allâh will not abase them in this very earth and that punishment will not befall them from quarters they perceive not.
46. Or (do they feel secure) that He will not seize them in their going to and fro so that they shall not be able to frustrate (Him in His designs and plans).
47. Or it may be that He will take them to task through (a process of) gradual diminution (until disbelief is completely annihilated)? For surely your Lord is All-Compassionate, Ever Merciful.
48. Have they not considered that the shadow of everything which Allâh has created shift from the right and from the left, prostrating themselves to Allâh (in obedience to His laws) in humble supplication?
49. All that is in the heavens and on the earth of the crawling and moving creatures and the angels (too), make obeisance to Allâh and they do not disdain (to worship Him).
50. They fear (disobedience to) their Lord above them, and do whatever they are commanded.

[PROSTRATION]

SECTION 7

51. **A**LLÂH has said, 'Take not to you two gods (to worship) He is the only One God. Therefore

كَانُوا يَعۡلَمُونَ ﴿٤١﴾ الَّذِينَ صَبَرُوا وَعَلَىٰ رَبِّهِمۡ
يَتَوَكَّلُونَ ﴿٤٢﴾ وَمَا أَرۡسَلۡنَا مِن قَبۡلِكَ إِلَّا
رِجَالًا نُّوحِيٓ إِلَيۡهِمۡ فَسۡـَٔلُوٓا أَهۡلَ الذِّكۡرِ
إِن كُنتُمۡ لَا تَعۡلَمُونَ ﴿٤٣﴾ بِالۡبَيِّنٰتِ وَالزُّبُرِ
وَأَنزَلۡنَآ إِلَيۡكَ الذِّكۡرَ لِتُبَيِّنَ لِلنَّاسِ مَا
نُزِّلَ إِلَيۡهِمۡ وَلَعَلَّهُمۡ يَتَفَكَّرُونَ ﴿٤٤﴾ أَفَأَمِنَ
الَّذِينَ مَكَرُوا السَّيِّـَٔاتِ أَن يَخۡسِفَ اللَّهُ
بِهِمُ الۡأَرۡضَ أَوۡ يَأۡتِيَهُمُ الۡعَذَابُ مِنۡ حَيۡثُ
لَا يَشۡعُرُونَ ﴿٤٥﴾ أَوۡ يَأۡخُذَهُمۡ فِي تَقَلُّبِهِمۡ فَمَا هُم
بِمُعۡجِزِينَ ﴿٤٦﴾ أَوۡ يَأۡخُذَهُمۡ عَلَىٰ تَخَوُّفٍ فَإِنَّ
رَبَّكُمۡ لَرَءُوفٌ رَّحِيمٌ ﴿٤٧﴾ أَوَلَمۡ يَرَوۡا إِلَىٰ مَا
خَلَقَ اللَّهُ مِن شَيۡءٍ يَتَفَيَّؤُا ظِلٰلُهُۥ عَنِ
الۡيَمِينِ وَالشَّمَآئِلِ سُجَّدًا لِّلَّهِ وَهُمۡ
دٰخِرُونَ ﴿٤٨﴾ وَلِلَّهِ يَسۡجُدُ مَا فِي السَّمٰوٰتِ
وَمَا فِي الۡأَرۡضِ مِن دَآبَّةٍ وَالۡمَلٰٓئِكَةُ وَهُمۡ
لَا يَسۡتَكۡبِرُونَ ﴿٤٩﴾ يَخَافُونَ رَبَّهُم مِّن فَوۡقِهِمۡ
وَيَفۡعَلُونَ مَا يُؤۡمَرُونَ ﴿٥٠﴾ السجدة وَقَالَ اللَّهُ لَا

stand in awe of Me and (I repeat) Me alone.

52. All that is in the heavens and on the earth belongs to Him. Obedience is due to Him forever. Will you still take something other than Allâh as (your) shield?

53. And whatever blessings you have, come from Allâh. And when affliction befalls you it is to Him that you cry (for redress).

54. Yet as soon as He removes the affliction from you some among you (begin to) associate (others as) partners with their Lord (in His worship),

55. With the result that they show ingratitude for the favours which We have bestowed upon them. Well, enjoy yourselves a little, for soon you will know (the evil consequences of your ingratitude).

56. And they set apart (for the false gods) a portion of that (gift) We have provided them with, about (the reality of) which they know not. By Allâh, you will be called upon to account for all that you have forged.

57. And they assign daughters to Allâh; Holy is He, whereas they (wish to) have for themselves what they desire.

58. When one of them is given the tidings (of the birth) of a female, his face clouds up and darkens (in sorrow) and he is full of grief and anger suppressed up.

59. He hides himself (in shame) from the people because of the (so called) bad news he has received, (considering) whether he should keep her (alive) inspite of disgrace, or commit her somewhere in the dust. Look! Evil (in every way) is the judgment they make.

60. Evil (in every way) is the state of those who do not believe in the Hereafter; while sublime are the attributes of Allâh (in every respect). And He is the All-Mighty, All-Wise.

SECTION 8

61. **A**ND if Allâh were to seize the people (immediately) for their (committing) injus-

تَتَّخِذُوْٓا اِلٰهَيْنِ اثْنَيْنِ ۚ اِنَّمَا هُوَ اِلٰهٌ وَّاحِدٌ
فَاِيَّايَ فَارْهَبُوْنِ ﴿٥١﴾ وَلَهٗ مَا فِي السَّمٰوٰتِ
وَالْاَرْضِ وَلَهُ الدِّيْنُ وَاصِبًا ۭ اَفَغَيْرَ اللّٰهِ
تَتَّقُوْنَ ﴿٥٢﴾ وَمَا بِكُمْ مِّنْ نِّعْمَةٍ فَمِنَ اللّٰهِ
ثُمَّ اِذَا مَسَّكُمُ الضُّرُّ فَاِلَيْهِ تَجْــَٔرُوْنَ ﴿٥٣﴾
ثُمَّ اِذَا كَشَفَ الضُّرَّ عَنْكُمْ اِذَا فَرِيْقٌ
مِّنْكُمْ بِرَبِّهِمْ يُشْرِكُوْنَ ﴿٥٤﴾ لِيَكْفُرُوْا بِمَآ
اٰتَيْنٰهُمْ ۭ فَتَمَتَّعُوْا ۣ فَسَوْفَ تَعْلَمُوْنَ ﴿٥٥﴾
وَيَجْعَلُوْنَ لِمَا لَا يَعْلَمُوْنَ نَصِيْبًا مِّمَّا رَزَقْنٰهُمْ
تَاللّٰهِ لَتُسْــَٔلُنَّ عَمَّا كُنْتُمْ تَفْتَرُوْنَ ﴿٥٦﴾
وَيَجْعَلُوْنَ لِلّٰهِ الْبَنٰتِ سُبْحٰنَهٗ ۙ وَلَهُمْ مَّا
يَشْتَهُوْنَ ﴿٥٧﴾ وَاِذَا بُشِّرَ اَحَدُهُمْ بِالْاُنْثٰى
ظَلَّ وَجْهُهٗ مُسْوَدًّا وَّهُوَ كَظِيْمٌ ﴿٥٨﴾ يَتَوَارٰى
مِنَ الْقَوْمِ مِنْ سُوْۗءِ مَا بُشِّرَ بِهٖ ۭ اَيُمْسِكُهٗ
عَلٰي هُوْنٍ اَمْ يَدُسُّهٗ فِي التُّرَابِ ۭ اَلَا سَاۗءَ
مَا يَحْكُمُوْنَ ﴿٥٩﴾ لِلَّذِيْنَ لَا يُؤْمِنُوْنَ بِالْاٰخِرَةِ
مَثَلُ السَّوْءِ ۚ وَلِلّٰهِ الْمَثَلُ الْاَعْلٰى ۭ وَهُوَ
الْعَزِيْزُ الْحَكِيْمُ ﴿٦٠﴾ وَلَوْ يُؤَاخِذُ اللّٰهُ النَّاسَ

ع ٧ ١٣

tice (and their ascribing partners with Him), He would not leave any (unjust and polytheistic) living and crawling creature on the face of the earth, but He gives them respite till an appointed term. So when their time (of punishment) comes, they cannot delay (it) by a single moment (and escape it), nor can they go ahead (of it to save themselves from it).
62. And they ascribe to Allâh what they dislike (for themselves), nevertheless their tongues utter the lie that they shall have the best of every thing (in the Hereafter). As a matter of fact there awaits them the Fire, and indeed they are the ones to be sent (therein) in advance and abandoned.
63. By Allâh! We did send (Messengers) to (all) nations before you but (it so happened that) satan made their (evil) deeds fair-seeming to them. So he is their (- disbelievers') patron (again) this day, and there awaits them a grievous punishment.
64. We have sent to you this perfect Book (for no other purpose) but that you may explain to the people things over which they differ (among themselves), and (that it may serve as) a guidance and a mercy for a people who would believe (in it).
65. And Allâh has sent down water (of Divine revelation) from above and with it He has given life to (the whole of) earth after its death. Surely, there is a sign in this for a people who would listen (to the truth).

SECTION 9

66. **A**ND most surely, you have an evidence in the cattle (also, which should lead you from ignorance to knowledge). We feed you with pure milk which lies in their bellies; betwixt the faeces and the blood, (which is) agreeable and sweet for those who drink (it).
67. And (We feed you with the) fruits of the date-palms and the vine (too); you obtain from it intoxicants and wholesome food. In that there is a remarkable sign for a people

بِظُلْمِهِم مَّا تَرَكَ عَلَيْهَا مِن دَآبَّةٍ وَّلٰكِن
يُؤَخِّرُهُمْ إِلَىٰٓ أَجَلٍ مُّسَمًّى ۚ فَإِذَا جَآءَ أَجَلُهُمْ
لَا يَسْتَـْٔخِرُونَ سَاعَةً وَّلَا يَسْتَقْدِمُونَ ﴿٦١﴾
وَيَجْعَلُونَ لِلّٰهِ مَا يَكْرَهُونَ وَتَصِفُ
أَلْسِنَتُهُمُ الْكَذِبَ أَنَّ لَهُمُ الْحُسْنٰى ۖ لَا جَرَمَ
أَنَّ لَهُمُ النَّارَ وَأَنَّهُم مُّفْرَطُونَ ﴿٦٢﴾ تَاللّٰهِ
لَقَدْ أَرْسَلْنَآ إِلَىٰٓ أُمَمٍ مِّن قَبْلِكَ فَزَيَّنَ
لَهُمُ الشَّيْطٰنُ أَعْمٰلَهُمْ فَهُوَ وَلِيُّهُمُ الْيَوْمَ
وَلَهُمْ عَذَابٌ أَلِيمٌ ﴿٦٣﴾ وَمَآ أَنزَلْنَا عَلَيْكَ
الْكِتٰبَ إِلَّا لِتُبَيِّنَ لَهُمُ الَّذِي اخْتَلَفُوا
فِيهِ ۙ وَهُدًى وَرَحْمَةً لِّقَوْمٍ يُؤْمِنُونَ ﴿٦٤﴾
وَاللّٰهُ أَنزَلَ مِنَ السَّمَآءِ مَآءً فَأَحْيَا بِهِ
الْأَرْضَ بَعْدَ مَوْتِهَا ۚ إِنَّ فِي ذٰلِكَ لَأٰيَةً
لِّقَوْمٍ يَسْمَعُونَ ﴿٦٥﴾ وَإِنَّ لَكُمْ فِي الْأَنْعٰمِ
لَعِبْرَةً ۖ نُّسْقِيكُم مِّمَّا فِي بُطُونِهِ مِنۢ
بَيْنِ فَرْثٍ وَدَمٍ لَّبَنًا خَالِصًا سَآئِغًا
لِّلشّٰرِبِينَ ﴿٦٦﴾ وَمِن ثَمَرٰتِ النَّخِيلِ

who make use of their understanding.
68. And your Lord inspired the bees (saying), 'Make your hives in the hills and in the trees and in the trellises which the people erect,
69. 'Then eat of every (kind of) fruit and follow the ways (and laws) of your Lord as that have been made easy (for you).' There comes forth from their insides a fine fluid of varying hues which is a cure for the people. In fact, in this there is a sign for a people who reflect.
70. Allâh has created you, then He causes you to die; and there are some of you who are driven to the worst part of life (-very advanced old age), with the result that he knows nothing after (having had) knowledge. Verily, Allâh is All-Knowing, All-Powerful.

SECTION 10

71. **A**ND Allâh has given to some of you better means of sustenance than to others; but the preferred ones would not give away and restore to their bondsmen their (share of) sustenance, even though they are equal (sharers) with them. Do they then deny the bounty of Allâh?
72. And Allâh has made for you mates from your own species and has given you sons, (daughters) and grandchildren from your mates and has provided you with good and pure things. Will the people still believe in vain and false things and deny the blessing of Allâh?
73. And they worship, apart from Allâh, such things as possess no authority to grant them any provision from the heavens and the earth, nor can they (ever) have such power in fact.
74. So coin not similitudes to Allâh. Allâh knows (its evil) and you do not know.
75. Allâh sets forth (for your knowledge) an excellent description of a slave who is owned (by another), (and) who has no power over anything. On the other hand there is another (a free man) whom We have provided with goodly

وَ الْاَعْنٰبِ تَتَّخِذُوْنَ مِنْهُ سَكَرًا وَّ رِزْقًا
حَسَنًا ۭ اِنَّ فِيْ ذٰلِكَ لَاٰيَةً لِّقَوْمٍ يَّعْقِلُوْنَ ﴿٦٧﴾
وَ اَوْحٰى رَبُّكَ اِلَى النَّحْلِ اَنِ اتَّخِذِيْ مِنَ
الْجِبَالِ بُيُوْتًا وَّ مِنَ الشَّجَرِ وَ مِمَّا يَعْرِشُوْنَ ﴿٦٨﴾
ثُمَّ كُلِيْ مِنْ كُلِّ الثَّمَرٰتِ فَاسْلُكِيْ سُبُلَ
رَبِّكِ ذُلُلًا ۭ يَخْرُجُ مِنْۢ بُطُوْنِهَا شَرَابٌ
مُّخْتَلِفٌ اَلْوَانُهٗ فِيْهِ شِفَآءٌ لِّلنَّاسِ ۭ اِنَّ فِيْ
ذٰلِكَ لَاٰيَةً لِّقَوْمٍ يَّتَفَكَّرُوْنَ ﴿٦٩﴾ وَ اللّٰهُ خَلَقَكُمْ
ثُمَّ يَتَوَفّٰىكُمْ ۟ۙ وَ مِنْكُمْ مَّنْ يُّرَدُّ اِلٰۤى اَرْذَلِ
الْعُمُرِ لِكَيْ لَا يَعْلَمَ بَعْدَ عِلْمٍ شَيْـًٔا ۭ اِنَّ اللّٰهَ
عَلِيْمٌ قَدِيْرٌ ﴿٧٠﴾ وَ اللّٰهُ فَضَّلَ بَعْضَكُمْ عَلٰى
بَعْضٍ فِي الرِّزْقِ ۚ فَمَا الَّذِيْنَ فُضِّلُوْا بِرَآدِّيْ
رِزْقِهِمْ عَلٰى مَا مَلَكَتْ اَيْمٰنُهُمْ فَهُمْ فِيْهِ
سَوَآءٌ ۭ اَفَبِنِعْمَةِ اللّٰهِ يَجْحَدُوْنَ ﴿٧١﴾ وَ اللّٰهُ
جَعَلَ لَكُمْ مِّنْ اَنْفُسِكُمْ اَزْوَاجًا وَّ جَعَلَ لَكُمْ
مِّنْ اَزْوٰجِكُمْ بَنِيْنَ وَ حَفَدَةً وَّ رَزَقَكُمْ
مِّنَ الطَّيِّبٰتِ ۭ اَفَبِالْبٰطِلِ يُؤْمِنُوْنَ وَ بِنِعْمَتِ
اللّٰهِ هُمْ يَكْفُرُوْنَ ﴿٧٢﴾ وَ يَعْبُدُوْنَ مِنْ دُوْنِ
اللّٰهِ مَا لَا يَمْلِكُ لَهُمْ رِزْقًا مِّنَ السَّمٰوٰتِ
وَ الْاَرْضِ شَيْـًٔا وَّ لَا يَسْتَطِيْعُوْنَ ﴿٧٣﴾ فَلَا
تَضْرِبُوْا لِلّٰهِ الْاَمْثَالَ ۭ اِنَّ اللّٰهَ يَعْلَمُ وَ اَنْتُمْ
لَا تَعْلَمُوْنَ ﴿٧٤﴾ ضَرَبَ اللّٰهُ مَثَلًا عَبْدًا مَّمْلُوْكًا

ع ٩ ١٥

provision from Ourself and he spends out of it secretly and openly (in Our cause). Can they both be alike? (No, not at all.) All true and perfect praise belongs to Allâh, but the thing is, most of these people do not know.

76. And Allâh sets forth an excellent description of (other) two men. One of them is dumb and has no power over anything and he is a useless burden on his master; wherever he sends him he fetches no good. Can he be like the man who enjoins justice and who follows the exact right path? (No, not at all.)

SECTION 11

77. **A**ND to Allâh belongs (the knowledge of) the hidden realities of the heavens and the earth, and the matter of the (coming of the promised) Hour is just like the twinkling of an eye. May be, it is nearer still. Behold! Allâh is Possessor of every power (to do) all He will.

78. And Allâh brought you forth from the wombs of your mothers, while you were void of all knowledge, He gave you ears, eyes and hearts, so that you might render (Him) thanks.

79. Have they not seen the birds held under subjection (while flying) in the vault of the heaven? None withholds them (from falling down) but Allâh. In this there are signs for a people who believe.

80. Allâh has made your houses a place of rest (for you), and He has (also) made for you of the skins of the cattle houses (of tents) which you find light (to carry) at the time of your journey and useful at the time when you halt. And out of their wool and their furs and their hair, (He has supplied you with) household goods and (other) articles of temporary use and utility.

81. And Allâh has provided you shelter from the sun in the things that He has created, He has made places of retreat in the mountains and He has made for you such garments as protect you from heat (and cold) and coats of mail to

لَا يَقْدِرُ عَلٰى شَيْءٍ وَّ مَنْ رَّزَقْنٰهُ مِنَّا رِزْقًا
حَسَنًا فَهُوَ يُنْفِقُ مِنْهُ سِرًّا وَّ جَهْرًا هَلْ
يَسْتَوٗنَ اَلْحَمْدُ لِلّٰهِ بَلْ أَكْثَرُهُمْ لَا
يَعْلَمُوْنَ ﴿٧٥﴾ وَ ضَرَبَ اللّٰهُ مَثَلًا رَّجُلَيْنِ
أَحَدُهُمَآ أَبْكَمُ لَا يَقْدِرُ عَلٰى شَيْءٍ وَّ هُوَ
كَلٌّ عَلٰى مَوْلٰىهُ أَيْنَمَا يُوَجِّهْهُ لَا يَأْتِ بِخَيْرٍ
هَلْ يَسْتَوِي هُوَ وَ مَنْ يَأْمُرُ بِالْعَدْلِ
وَ هُوَ عَلٰى صِرٰطٍ مُّسْتَقِيْمٍ ﴿٧٦﴾ وَ لِلّٰهِ غَيْبُ
السَّمٰوٰتِ وَ الْأَرْضِ وَ مَآ أَمْرُ السَّاعَةِ إِلَّا
كَلَمْحِ الْبَصَرِ أَوْ هُوَ أَقْرَبُ إِنَّ اللّٰهَ عَلٰى
كُلِّ شَيْءٍ قَدِيْرٌ ﴿٧٧﴾ وَ اللّٰهُ أَخْرَجَكُمْ مِّنْ بُطُوْنِ
أُمَّهٰتِكُمْ لَا تَعْلَمُوْنَ شَيْـًٔا وَّ جَعَلَ لَكُمُ
السَّمْعَ وَ الْأَبْصٰرَ وَ الْأَفْـِٔدَةَ لَعَلَّكُمْ تَشْكُرُوْنَ ﴿٧٨﴾
أَلَمْ يَرَوْا إِلَى الطَّيْرِ مُسَخَّرٰتٍ فِي جَوِّ السَّمَآءِ
مَا يُمْسِكُهُنَّ إِلَّا اللّٰهُ إِنَّ فِي ذٰلِكَ لَأٰيٰتٍ
لِّقَوْمٍ يُّؤْمِنُوْنَ ﴿٧٩﴾ وَ اللّٰهُ جَعَلَ لَكُمْ مِّنْ
بُيُوْتِكُمْ سَكَنًا وَّ جَعَلَ لَكُمْ مِّنْ جُلُوْدِ
الْأَنْعٰمِ بُيُوْتًا تَسْتَخِفُّوْنَهَا يَوْمَ ظَعْنِكُمْ
وَ يَوْمَ إِقَامَتِكُمْ وَ مِنْ أَصْوَافِهَا وَ أَوْبَارِهَا
وَ أَشْعَارِهَآ أَثٰثًا وَّ مَتٰعًا إِلٰى حِيْنٍ ﴿٨٠﴾ وَ اللّٰهُ
جَعَلَ لَكُمْ مِّمَّا خَلَقَ ظِلٰلًا وَّ جَعَلَ لَكُمْ

guard you in intensity of your wars. (Just as He has given you these things,) thus does He complete His favours upon you that you may submit (wholly to Him).

82. But if still these (opponents) turn away, you should know that upon you is (only the responsibility of) delivery (of the divine Message) in plain terms.

83. They recognize the bounty of Allâh, yet they deny it. Most of them have no sense of gratitude (for His favours).

SECTION 12

84. **A**ND (beware of) the day when We shall raise a witness from every nation, then those who were ungrateful shall not be given leave (to make amends) nor shall they be afforded an opportunity to approach the threshold (of God) to offer a plea or an excuse (and thus solicit His good will).

85. And when those who behaved unjustly actually face the punishment (in the Hereafter), it shall neither be reduced for them (after that) nor shall they be given respite.

86. And when those who associate partners (with God) will see their associate-gods they will say, 'Our Lord! These are partners associated with You by us, whom we used to call upon instead of You.' But they (-the so-called partners) will retort them with the words, 'Most surely, you are liars.'

87. And on that day they shall tender submission to Allâh, and all that they used to forge shall forsake them.

88. (As to) those who disbelieve and hinder (the people) from Allâh's way, We shall enhance many times over their punishment because of the evil they wrought.

89. (Beware of) the day when We shall raise from every people a witness who shall hail from among themselves and who shall testify against them. And We shall bring you (O

سُورَةُ النَّحۡلِ ١٦

مِّنَ الۡجِبَالِ اَكۡنَانًا وَّجَعَلَ لَكُمۡ سَرَابِيۡلَ
تَقِيۡكُمُ الۡحَرَّ وَسَرَابِيۡلَ تَقِيۡكُمۡ بَاۡسَكُمۡ
كَذٰلِكَ يُتِمُّ نِعۡمَتَهٗ عَلَيۡكُمۡ لَعَلَّكُمۡ
تُسۡلِمُوۡنَ ﴿٨١﴾ فَاِنۡ تَوَلَّوۡا فَاِنَّمَا عَلَيۡكَ
الۡبَلٰغُ الۡمُبِيۡنُ ﴿٨٢﴾ يَعۡرِفُوۡنَ نِعۡمَتَ اللّٰهِ
ثُمَّ يُنۡكِرُوۡنَهَا وَاَكۡثَرُهُمُ الۡكٰفِرُوۡنَ ﴿٨٣﴾
وَيَوۡمَ نَبۡعَثُ مِنۡ كُلِّ اُمَّةٍ شَهِيۡدًا ثُمَّ لَا
يُؤۡذَنُ لِلَّذِيۡنَ كَفَرُوۡا وَلَا هُمۡ يُسۡتَعۡتَبُوۡنَ ﴿٨٤﴾
وَاِذَا رَاَ الَّذِيۡنَ ظَلَمُوا الۡعَذَابَ فَلَا يُخَفَّفُ
عَنۡهُمۡ وَلَا هُمۡ يُنۡظَرُوۡنَ ﴿٨٥﴾ وَاِذَا رَاَ الَّذِيۡنَ
اَشۡرَكُوۡا شُرَكَآءَهُمۡ قَالُوۡا رَبَّنَا هٰٓؤُلَآءِ شُرَكَآؤُنَا
الَّذِيۡنَ كُنَّا نَدۡعُوۡا مِنۡ دُوۡنِكَ فَاَلۡقَوۡا اِلَيۡهِمُ
الۡقَوۡلَ اِنَّكُمۡ لَكٰذِبُوۡنَ ﴿٨٦﴾ وَاَلۡقَوۡا اِلَى اللّٰهِ
يَوۡمَئِذِ السَّلَمَ وَضَلَّ عَنۡهُمۡ مَّا كَانُوۡا
يَفۡتَرُوۡنَ ﴿٨٧﴾ اَلَّذِيۡنَ كَفَرُوۡا وَصَدُّوۡا عَنۡ
سَبِيۡلِ اللّٰهِ زِدۡنٰهُمۡ عَذَابًا فَوۡقَ الۡعَذَابِ
بِمَا كَانُوۡا يُفۡسِدُوۡنَ ﴿٨٨﴾ وَيَوۡمَ نَبۡعَثُ فِىۡ كُلِّ

Muhammad!) as a witness against (all) these. And (that is why) We have revealed to you this perfect Book explaining every (basic) thing and (which serves as) a guidance and a mercy, and (gives) good tidings to those who submit (to God).

SECTION 13

90. **A**LLÂH enjoins justice and the doing of good to others and giving like kindred and He forbids indecencies and manifest evil and transgression. He admonishes you that you may take heed and attain eminence.
91. And keep your covenant with Allâh when you have once made any covenant (with Him). And do not break your oaths once you have ratified them, while you have already made Allâh your surety. Verily, Allâh knows how you conduct yourselves.
92. And be not like the woman who breaks her yarn after spinning it strong with hard labour into thread. You use your oaths to deceive one another (for fear) lest one nation should become more powerful than the other nation. Surely, Allâh tries you thereby and on the Day of Resurrection will make clear to you all the things about which you had been differing (from one another).
93. Had Allâh (enforced) His will He would surely have made you (all) one nation (following one and the same faith). But He leaves in error him who wishes (to remain so) and guides him who wishes (to be guided). And you shall surely be called upon to account for your deeds and conduct.
94. Do not use your oaths to deceive one another or you will lose your foothold (again) after having gained stability and you will suffer evil consequences for your barring (the people) from (following) Allâh's way and for forsaking the path of Allâh and you shall receive great punishment.

أُمَّةٍ شَهِيدًا عَلَيْهِم مِّنْ أَنفُسِهِمْ وَجِئْنَا
بِكَ شَهِيدًا عَلَىٰ هَٰٓؤُلَآءِ ۚ وَنَزَّلْنَا عَلَيْكَ
الْكِتَٰبَ تِبْيَٰنًا لِّكُلِّ شَيْءٍ وَهُدًى وَرَحْمَةً
وَبُشْرَىٰ لِلْمُسْلِمِينَ ۞ إِنَّ اللَّهَ يَأْمُرُ بِالْعَدْلِ
وَالْإِحْسَٰنِ وَإِيتَآئِ ذِي الْقُرْبَىٰ وَيَنْهَىٰ
عَنِ الْفَحْشَآءِ وَالْمُنكَرِ وَالْبَغْيِ ۚ يَعِظُكُمْ
لَعَلَّكُمْ تَذَكَّرُونَ ﴿٩٠﴾ وَأَوْفُوا بِعَهْدِ اللَّهِ إِذَا
عَٰهَدتُّمْ وَلَا تَنقُضُوا الْأَيْمَٰنَ بَعْدَ تَوْكِيدِهَا
وَقَدْ جَعَلْتُمُ اللَّهَ عَلَيْكُمْ كَفِيلًا ۚ إِنَّ اللَّهَ
يَعْلَمُ مَا تَفْعَلُونَ ﴿٩١﴾ وَلَا تَكُونُوا كَالَّتِي
نَقَضَتْ غَزْلَهَا مِن بَعْدِ قُوَّةٍ أَنكَٰثًا ۖ
تَتَّخِذُونَ أَيْمَٰنَكُمْ دَخَلًا بَيْنَكُمْ أَن تَكُونَ
أُمَّةٌ هِيَ أَرْبَىٰ مِنْ أُمَّةٍ ۚ إِنَّمَا يَبْلُوكُمُ اللَّهُ
بِهِ ۚ وَلَيُبَيِّنَنَّ لَكُمْ يَوْمَ الْقِيَٰمَةِ مَا كُنتُمْ
فِيهِ تَخْتَلِفُونَ ﴿٩٢﴾ وَلَوْ شَآءَ اللَّهُ لَجَعَلَكُمْ
أُمَّةً وَٰحِدَةً وَلَٰكِن يُضِلُّ مَن يَشَآءُ
وَيَهْدِي مَن يَشَآءُ ۚ وَلَتُسْـَٔلُنَّ عَمَّا كُنتُمْ
تَعْمَلُونَ ﴿٩٣﴾ وَلَا تَتَّخِذُوٓا أَيْمَٰنَكُمْ دَخَلًا
بَيْنَكُمْ فَتَزِلَّ قَدَمٌ بَعْدَ ثُبُوتِهَا وَتَذُوقُوا
السُّوٓءَ بِمَا صَدَدتُّمْ عَن سَبِيلِ اللَّهِ ۖ

ع ٦/١٨

95. And do not sell the covenant you made with Allâh for a paltry price (-worldly gains). That reward (of righteousness) which is with Allâh is better for you, if only you knew.
96. (Did you but know) that which is with you shall pass away (being transitory) but that which is with Allâh is enduring and will last. And We will certainly give those who patiently persevere their reward according to the best of their deeds.
97. Whoever acts righteously, whether male or female, and is a believer, We will certainly enable him lead a pure life and surely We will bestow on such their reward according to the best of their deeds.
98. And when you recite the Qur'ân, seek refuge with Allâh from satan, the rejected.
99. Surely, he has no authority over those who believe and put their trust in their Lord.
100. His authority is over those only who take him as their friend and who associate partners with Him (under his influence).

SECTION 14

101. **A**ND Allâh knows very well the need of what He reveals, yet when We replace a revelation with another revelation they say (to you), 'You are only a fabricator (of lies).' The truth is, however, that most of them know nothing.
102. Say, 'The Spirit of Holiness has brought this (Qur'ân) down from your Lord to suit the requirement of truth and wisdom, (Allâh has revealed it) so that He may strengthen those who believe in their faith and so that (this may serve as) a guidance and good tidings for Muslims.
103. And We know fully well what they say (by way of objection) that this (Qur'ân) is (not revealed by God but it is) only what a human being instructs to him (- to Muhammad). But (strange it is) that the tongue of him to whom they (unjustly) allude (of making this insinu-

وَلَكُمْ عَذَابٌ عَظِيمٌ ﴿٩٤﴾ وَلَا تَشْتَرُوا بِعَهْدِ
اللَّهِ ثَمَنًا قَلِيلًا ۚ إِنَّمَا عِنْدَ اللَّهِ هُوَ خَيْرٌ
لَكُمْ إِنْ كُنْتُمْ تَعْلَمُونَ ﴿٩٥﴾ مَا عِنْدَكُمْ
يَنْفَدُ وَمَا عِنْدَ اللَّهِ بَاقٍ ۗ وَلَنَجْزِيَنَّ الَّذِينَ
صَبَرُوا أَجْرَهُمْ بِأَحْسَنِ مَا كَانُوا يَعْمَلُونَ ﴿٩٦﴾
مَنْ عَمِلَ صَالِحًا مِنْ ذَكَرٍ أَوْ أُنْثَىٰ وَهُوَ
مُؤْمِنٌ فَلَنُحْيِيَنَّهُ حَيَاةً طَيِّبَةً ۖ وَلَنَجْزِيَنَّهُمْ
أَجْرَهُمْ بِأَحْسَنِ مَا كَانُوا يَعْمَلُونَ ﴿٩٧﴾ فَإِذَا
قَرَأْتَ الْقُرْآنَ فَاسْتَعِذْ بِاللَّهِ مِنَ الشَّيْطَانِ
الرَّجِيمِ ﴿٩٨﴾ إِنَّهُ لَيْسَ لَهُ سُلْطَانٌ عَلَى الَّذِينَ
آمَنُوا وَعَلَىٰ رَبِّهِمْ يَتَوَكَّلُونَ ﴿٩٩﴾ إِنَّمَا سُلْطَانُهُ
عَلَى الَّذِينَ يَتَوَلَّوْنَهُ وَالَّذِينَ هُمْ بِهِ
مُشْرِكُونَ ﴿١٠٠﴾ وَإِذَا بَدَّلْنَا آيَةً مَكَانَ
آيَةٍ ۙ وَاللَّهُ أَعْلَمُ بِمَا يُنَزِّلُ قَالُوا إِنَّمَا
أَنْتَ مُفْتَرٍ ۚ بَلْ أَكْثَرُهُمْ لَا يَعْلَمُونَ ﴿١٠١﴾
قُلْ نَزَّلَهُ رُوحُ الْقُدُسِ مِنْ رَبِّكَ بِالْحَقِّ
لِيُثَبِّتَ الَّذِينَ آمَنُوا وَهُدًى وَبُشْرَىٰ
لِلْمُسْلِمِينَ ﴿١٠٢﴾ وَلَقَدْ نَعْلَمُ أَنَّهُمْ يَقُولُونَ
إِنَّمَا يُعَلِّمُهُ بَشَرٌ ۗ لِسَانُ الَّذِي يُلْحِدُونَ

ation) is foreign and wanting in clearness, whereas the language of this (Qur'ân) is chaste Arabic, plain and clear.
104. Surely, Allâh will not guide those (to success) who do not believe in the Messages of Allâh (intentionally). There awaits them a grievous punishment.
105. It is only those who do not believe in Allâh's Messages, who forge lies. And it is they who are the liars themselves.
106. Those who disbelieve in Allâh after they have believed in Him - but not those who are compelled (to recant) while their hearts find peace (and are firm) in the faith - (and) those who accept disbelief from the core of their hearts shall incur the displeasure of Allâh and shall receive a stern punishment.
107. That is because they have preferred the present life to the Hereafter and because Allâh does not guide the disbelieving people (to their goal).
108. It is these people on whose hearts, hearing and eyes Allâh has set a seal (for their disbelief). And it is these people who are really heedless.
109. Undoubtedly, it is they who will be the very losers in the Hereafter.
110. Again those who emigrated (from their homes) after they had been persecuted and strove hard (in the cause of Allâh) and patiently persevered, will ultimately find that your Lord, yes, your own Lord is indeed Great Protector, Ever Merciful (to them).

SECTION 15

111. (**T**HE perfect manifestation of such a recompense will be) on the day when every soul shall come pleading for (protection for) itself, and every soul shall be repaid in full for its deeds and they shall, in no way, be dealt with unjustly.
112. And Allâh sets-forth an excellent description of a township (-Makkah). It enjoyed a state of security and peace. It received its provi-

إِلَيْهِ أَعْجَمِيٌّ وَهَٰذَا لِسَانٌ عَرَبِيٌّ مُّبِينٌ ﴿١٠٣﴾
إِنَّ الَّذِينَ لَا يُؤْمِنُونَ بِآيَاتِ اللَّهِ لَا يَهْدِيهِمُ
اللَّهُ وَلَهُمْ عَذَابٌ أَلِيمٌ ﴿١٠٤﴾ إِنَّمَا يَفْتَرِي
الْكَذِبَ الَّذِينَ لَا يُؤْمِنُونَ بِآيَاتِ اللَّهِ ۖ
وَأُولَٰئِكَ هُمُ الْكَاذِبُونَ ﴿١٠٥﴾ مَن كَفَرَ
بِاللَّهِ مِن بَعْدِ إِيمَانِهِ إِلَّا مَنْ أُكْرِهَ
وَقَلْبُهُ مُطْمَئِنٌّ بِالْإِيمَانِ وَلَٰكِن مَّن شَرَحَ
بِالْكُفْرِ صَدْرًا فَعَلَيْهِمْ غَضَبٌ مِّنَ اللَّهِ ۖ
وَلَهُمْ عَذَابٌ عَظِيمٌ ﴿١٠٦﴾ ذَٰلِكَ بِأَنَّهُمُ
اسْتَحَبُّوا الْحَيَاةَ الدُّنْيَا عَلَى الْآخِرَةِ
وَأَنَّ اللَّهَ لَا يَهْدِي الْقَوْمَ الْكَافِرِينَ ﴿١٠٧﴾ أُولَٰئِكَ
الَّذِينَ طَبَعَ اللَّهُ عَلَىٰ قُلُوبِهِمْ وَسَمْعِهِمْ
وَأَبْصَارِهِمْ ۖ وَأُولَٰئِكَ هُمُ الْغَافِلُونَ ﴿١٠٨﴾ لَا
جَرَمَ أَنَّهُمْ فِي الْآخِرَةِ هُمُ الْخَاسِرُونَ ﴿١٠٩﴾
ثُمَّ إِنَّ رَبَّكَ لِلَّذِينَ هَاجَرُوا مِن بَعْدِ
مَا فُتِنُوا ثُمَّ جَاهَدُوا وَصَبَرُوا إِنَّ رَبَّكَ
مِن بَعْدِهَا لَغَفُورٌ رَّحِيمٌ ﴿١١٠﴾ يَوْمَ تَأْتِي
كُلُّ نَفْسٍ تُجَادِلُ عَن نَّفْسِهَا وَتُوَفَّىٰ كُلُّ
نَفْسٍ مَّا عَمِلَتْ وَهُمْ لَا يُظْلَمُونَ ﴿١١١﴾
وَضَرَبَ اللَّهُ مَثَلًا قَرْيَةً كَانَتْ آمِنَةً

sion in plenty from every quarter. But (it so happened) that it began to show ingratitude for the bounties of Allâh. So Allâh made (the citizens of) it taste a pall of hunger and fear (which covered it like a garment -the conditions of famine and war prevailed there) because of what its citizens had wrought.

113. And certainly there had come to them a (great) Messenger from among their own men, but they cried lies to him so the (promised) punishment overtook them while they were behaving transgressingly.

114. So (believers!) eat of the lawful, good and pure things Allâh has provided you and give thanks for Allâh's bounty, if it is, in fact, Him that you worship.

115. He has made unlawful for you only carrion (that which dies of itself), blood (flowed out), the flesh of swine and that which has been sacrificed in some other name than Allâh's. But he who is constrained (to do this) not desiring it and having no intention either to disobey or to exceed the limits (of necessity), will find that Allâh surely is Great Protector, Ever Merciful.

116. And do not say because of the lies which your tongues utter, 'This is lawful and that is unlawful,' lest you should forge a lie against Allâh. Those who forge lies against Allâh will never attain the goal.

117. (Though in forging lies) they may enjoy themselves for a brief spell in this life, yet a grievous punishment awaits them (in the Hereafter).

118. We have already made unlawful to those (also) who judaised, all that We have related to you already. And We did not deal with them unjustly. Rather they wronged themselves.

119. Again, those who commit evil in ignorance and then after that turn to Him in repentance and mend their ways, will find that surely after that, (for those who repent) your Lord is Great Protector, Ever Merciful.

مُّطْمَئِنَّةً يَّأْتِيهَا رِزْقُهَا رَغَدًا مِّنْ كُلِّ
مَكَانٍ فَكَفَرَتْ بِأَنْعُمِ اللّٰهِ فَأَذَاقَهَا اللّٰهُ
لِبَاسَ الْجُوعِ وَالْخَوْفِ بِمَا كَانُوا يَصْنَعُونَ ﴿١١٢﴾
وَلَقَدْ جَاءَهُمْ رَسُولٌ مِّنْهُمْ فَكَذَّبُوهُ
فَأَخَذَهُمُ الْعَذَابُ وَهُمْ ظٰلِمُونَ ﴿١١٣﴾ فَكُلُوا
مِمَّا رَزَقَكُمُ اللّٰهُ حَلٰلًا طَيِّبًا وَّاشْكُرُوا
نِعْمَتَ اللّٰهِ إِنْ كُنْتُمْ إِيَّاهُ تَعْبُدُونَ ﴿١١٤﴾
إِنَّمَا حَرَّمَ عَلَيْكُمُ الْمَيْتَةَ وَالدَّمَ
وَلَحْمَ الْخِنْزِيرِ وَمَا أُهِلَّ لِغَيْرِ اللّٰهِ بِهِ ۚ
فَمَنِ اضْطُرَّ غَيْرَ بَاغٍ وَّلَا عَادٍ فَإِنَّ اللّٰهَ
غَفُورٌ رَّحِيمٌ ﴿١١٥﴾ وَلَا تَقُولُوا لِمَا تَصِفُ
أَلْسِنَتُكُمُ الْكَذِبَ هٰذَا حَلٰلٌ وَّهٰذَا حَرَامٌ
لِّتَفْتَرُوا عَلَى اللّٰهِ الْكَذِبَ ۗ إِنَّ الَّذِينَ
يَفْتَرُونَ عَلَى اللّٰهِ الْكَذِبَ لَا يُفْلِحُونَ ﴿١١٦﴾
مَتٰعٌ قَلِيلٌ ۖ وَّلَهُمْ عَذَابٌ أَلِيمٌ ﴿١١٧﴾
وَعَلَى الَّذِينَ هَادُوا حَرَّمْنَا مَا قَصَصْنَا عَلَيْكَ
مِنْ قَبْلُ ۚ وَمَا ظَلَمْنٰهُمْ وَلٰكِنْ كَانُوا
أَنْفُسَهُمْ يَظْلِمُونَ ﴿١١٨﴾ ثُمَّ إِنَّ رَبَّكَ لِلَّذِينَ
عَمِلُوا السُّوءَ بِجَهٰلَةٍ ثُمَّ تَابُوا مِنْ بَعْدِ
ذٰلِكَ وَأَصْلَحُوا إِنَّ رَبَّكَ مِنْ بَعْدِهَا

SECTION 16

120. **T**HE truth of the matter is that Abraham was a paragon of virtue; obedient to Allâh, upright, and he was not of the polytheists,
121. Highly thankful for His favours. He chose him and guided him on to the exact right path.
122. And We granted him great success (and all comforts) of this life, and in the Hereafter he is most surely among the righteous.
123. Again, (Prophet! to complete Our favours on Abraham) We have revealed to you (saying), 'Follow the creed of Abraham (who was an) upright, (devotee of God) and was not of the polytheists.'
124. The (punishment for profaning the) Sabbath was made to recoil on those only who were at odds over it, and your Lord will surely judge between them concerning all their differences on the Day of Resurrection.
125. (Prophet!) Call the people to the way of your Lord with wisdom and goodly and kind exhortation, and argue with them in the most pleasant and best manner. Surely, your Lord knows very well who has gone astray from His path, and He knows very well the guided ones to the right path.
126. (Believers!) If you have to punish (the oppressors) then punish them to the extent you have been persecuted. But if you endure patiently, remember it is far better for the patiently persevering.
127. And be patiently-persevering. Verily, you can exercise patient endurance only with (the help of) Allâh. Do not grieve at their state, nor feel distressed on account of their intrigues (out of enmity for you).
128. Allâh is, of course, with those who guard against evil, and those who are doers of good to others.

سُورَةُ النَّحْلِ ١٦

لَغَفُورٌ رَّحِيمٌ ﴿١١٩﴾ إِنَّ إِبْرَٰهِيمَ كَانَ ع ٩ ٢١
أُمَّةً قَانِتًا لِّلَّهِ حَنِيفًا وَلَمْ يَكُ مِنَ
الْمُشْرِكِينَ ﴿١٢٠﴾ شَاكِرًا لِّأَنْعُمِهِ اجْتَبَىٰهُ
وَهَدَىٰهُ إِلَىٰ صِرَٰطٍ مُّسْتَقِيمٍ ﴿١٢١﴾ وَءَاتَيْنَٰهُ
فِي الدُّنْيَا حَسَنَةً وَإِنَّهُ فِي الْأٓخِرَةِ لَمِنَ
الصَّٰلِحِينَ ﴿١٢٢﴾ ثُمَّ أَوْحَيْنَآ إِلَيْكَ أَنِ
اتَّبِعْ مِلَّةَ إِبْرَٰهِيمَ حَنِيفًا وَمَا كَانَ
مِنَ الْمُشْرِكِينَ ﴿١٢٣﴾ إِنَّمَا جُعِلَ السَّبْتُ
عَلَى الَّذِينَ اخْتَلَفُوا فِيهِ وَإِنَّ رَبَّكَ
لَيَحْكُمُ بَيْنَهُمْ يَوْمَ الْقِيَٰمَةِ فِيمَا
كَانُوا فِيهِ يَخْتَلِفُونَ ﴿١٢٤﴾ ادْعُ إِلَىٰ سَبِيلِ
رَبِّكَ بِالْحِكْمَةِ وَالْمَوْعِظَةِ الْحَسَنَةِ
وَجَٰدِلْهُم بِالَّتِي هِيَ أَحْسَنُ إِنَّ رَبَّكَ
هُوَ أَعْلَمُ بِمَن ضَلَّ عَن سَبِيلِهِ وَهُوَ
أَعْلَمُ بِالْمُهْتَدِينَ ﴿١٢٥﴾ وَإِنْ عَاقَبْتُمْ
فَعَاقِبُوا بِمِثْلِ مَا عُوقِبْتُم بِهِ وَلَئِن
صَبَرْتُمْ لَهُوَ خَيْرٌ لِّلصَّٰبِرِينَ ﴿١٢٦﴾ وَاصْبِرْ
وَمَا صَبْرُكَ إِلَّا بِاللَّهِ وَلَا تَحْزَنْ
عَلَيْهِمْ وَلَا تَكُ فِي ضَيْقٍ مِّمَّا
يَمْكُرُونَ ﴿١٢٧﴾ إِنَّ اللَّهَ مَعَ الَّذِينَ اتَّقَوا
وَّالَّذِينَ هُم مُّحْسِنُونَ ﴿١٢٨﴾ ع ١٦ ٢٢

الجزء الرابع عشر

CHAPTER
17

سُورَةُ الإِسْرَاءِ ١٧

ISRÂ'
(The Night-Journey)
(Revealed before Hijrah)

With the name of Allâh,
the Most Gracious, the Ever Merciful
(I commence to read Sûrah Al-Isrâ').

PART الجزء الخامس عشر XV

سُورَةُ الإِسْرَاءِ مَكِّيَّةٌ

بِسْمِ اللهِ الرَّحْمٰنِ الرَّحِيْمِ

1. **G**LORY be to Him Who carried His servant by night from the Holy Mosque (at Makkah) to the Distant Mosque (at Jerusalem), the precincts of which (too) We have blessed, that We might show him some of Our signs. In fact, He alone is the All-Hearing, the All-Seeing.
2. And (similarly) We gave Moses the Scripture and We made it a guidance for the Children of Israel, saying, 'Take no (one as) disposer of affairs apart from Me.
3. 'O You the progeny of those whom We bore (in the Ark) with Noah (to protect them from the deluge)!' He was indeed a grateful servant (of Ours).
4. And in the Scripture We have conveyed to the Children of Israel with certainty (saying), 'Twice you shall create disorder in the land and shall surely become exceedingly overbearing and arrogant.'
5. So when (*in 588 B.C.* the time for) the first of the two warnings came, We roused against you, (O Children of Israel! Some of) Our servants possessed of great valour and might in warfare, and they penetrated into the innermost recesses of your country and habitations. Indeed, it was a warning (about the punish-

سُبْحٰنَ الَّذِيٓ أَسْرٰى بِعَبْدِهٖ لَيْلًا مِّنَ
الْمَسْجِدِ الْحَرَامِ إِلَى الْمَسْجِدِ الْأَقْصَا الَّذِي
بٰرَكْنَا حَوْلَهٗ لِنُرِيَهٗ مِنْ أٰيٰتِنَا ۚ إِنَّهٗ هُوَ
السَّمِيعُ الْبَصِيرُ ﴿١﴾ وَأٰتَيْنَا مُوسَى الْكِتٰبَ
وَجَعَلْنٰهُ هُدًى لِّبَنِيٓ إِسْرٰٓءِيلَ أَلَّا
تَتَّخِذُوا مِنْ دُونِي وَكِيلًا ﴿٢﴾ ذُرِّيَّةَ مَنْ
حَمَلْنَا مَعَ نُوحٍ ۚ إِنَّهٗ كَانَ عَبْدًا شَكُورًا ﴿٣﴾
وَقَضَيْنَآ إِلٰى بَنِيٓ إِسْرٰٓءِيلَ فِي الْكِتٰبِ
لَتُفْسِدُنَّ فِي الْأَرْضِ مَرَّتَيْنِ وَلَتَعْلُنَّ عُلُوًّا
كَبِيرًا ﴿٤﴾ فَإِذَا جَآءَ وَعْدُ أُولٰىهُمَا بَعَثْنَا عَلَيْكُمْ
عِبَادًا لَّنَآ أُولِي بَأْسٍ شَدِيدٍ فَجَاسُوا

ment) of Allâh bound to be carried out.

6. Then We gave you back the power to prevail over these (enemies of yours through *Cyrus* and *Zerubbabel*), and We helped you with (various) possessions and sons and We increased your manpower (militarily).

7. (We said,) 'If you did good, you did it for your ownselves, and if you did evil it was only to the same end.' So when (the time for carrying out) the latter warning came (We raised certain other people - Romans under *Titus* in *70 A.D.*, against you to destroy your glory), so that they might do evil to (you and) your leading men and invade and enter the Mosque (at Jerusalem) in the same way as others (of your enemies) had invaded and entered it the first time, and so that they might destroy utterly all that they had conquered.

8. Still it is well-nigh that your Lord will again have mercy on you, (through Islam) but if you return (to mischief, We warn,) We too will return (to Our punishment), We have made Gehenna a prison-house for the ungrateful.

9. This Qur'ân, assuredly, guides to that which is most upright and gives to the believers, who do righteous deeds, the glad tidings that there awaits them a great reward,

10. And (also warns) that We have grievous punishment in store for those who do not believe in the Hereafter.

SECTION 2

11. As it is (many a time) a human being prays and calls for evil to himself as he ought to pray and call for good. Human being is ever extremely hasty.

12. And We have made the night and the day (such as they became) two signs, (in a way that) We obliterated the sign of the night (- darkness of ignorance and disbelief) and We displayed the sign of the day as sight - giving that you may seek the bounty of your Lord and that you

خِلَٰلَ الدِّيَارِ وَكَانَ وَعْدًا مَّفْعُولًا ﴿٥﴾ ثُمَّ
رَدَدْنَا لَكُمُ الْكَرَّةَ عَلَيْهِمْ وَأَمْدَدْنَٰكُم
بِأَمْوَٰلٍ وَبَنِينَ وَجَعَلْنَٰكُمْ أَكْثَرَ نَفِيرًا ﴿٦﴾
إِنْ أَحْسَنتُمْ أَحْسَنتُمْ لِأَنفُسِكُمْ وَإِنْ
أَسَأْتُمْ فَلَهَا فَإِذَا جَآءَ وَعْدُ الْأٓخِرَةِ لِيَسُـٔوا
وُجُوهَكُمْ وَلِيَدْخُلُوا الْمَسْجِدَ كَمَا دَخَلُوهُ
أَوَّلَ مَرَّةٍ وَلِيُتَبِّرُوا مَا عَلَوْا تَتْبِيرًا ﴿٧﴾ عَسَىٰ
رَبُّكُمْ أَن يَرْحَمَكُمْ وَإِنْ عُدتُّمْ عُدْنَا
وَجَعَلْنَا جَهَنَّمَ لِلْكَٰفِرِينَ حَصِيرًا ﴿٨﴾ إِنَّ هَٰذَا
الْقُرْءَانَ يَهْدِي لِلَّتِي هِيَ أَقْوَمُ وَيُبَشِّرُ
الْمُؤْمِنِينَ الَّذِينَ يَعْمَلُونَ الصَّٰلِحَٰتِ أَنَّ
لَهُمْ أَجْرًا كَبِيرًا ﴿٩﴾ وَأَنَّ الَّذِينَ لَا يُؤْمِنُونَ
ع ١ بِالْأٓخِرَةِ أَعْتَدْنَا لَهُمْ عَذَابًا أَلِيمًا ﴿١٠﴾ وَيَدْعُ
الْإِنسَٰنُ بِالشَّرِّ دُعَآءَهُ بِالْخَيْرِ وَكَانَ
الْإِنسَٰنُ عَجُولًا ﴿١١﴾ وَجَعَلْنَا الَّيْلَ وَالنَّهَارَ
ءَايَتَيْنِ فَمَحَوْنَا ءَايَةَ الَّيْلِ وَجَعَلْنَا ءَايَةَ النَّهَارِ
مُبْصِرَةً لِّتَبْتَغُوا فَضْلًا مِّن رَّبِّكُمْ وَلِتَعْلَمُوا
عَدَدَ السِّنِينَ وَالْحِسَابَ وَكُلَّ شَيْءٍ

may learn (from the alternation of night and day) the computation of years and (the science of) all sorts of counting and measuring. We have clearly explained every thing (and all knowledge of Faith) in detail.

13. And every human being We have made his deeds cling to his neck and on the Day of Resurrection We shall bring out for him a book (recording all his deeds) which he will find wide open.

14. (It will be said to him,) 'Read your book. Sufficient is your own conscience this day as a reckoner against you.'

15. He who follows the right way follows it to his own good and he who goes astray, surely, he goes astray to his own loss. And no soul that bears the burden shall bear the burden of another. And We never punish unless We have sent a Messenger.

16. And when We intend to destroy a township, We (first) address Our command to its lawless people who lead lazy lives (to show obedience), but they revolt therein so that it stands condemned and We destroy it with an utter destruction.

17. (In accordance with this rule of Ours) We have destroyed many a generation after Noah. And your Lord suffices as One Who is Aware and Beholder of the sins of His servants.

18. For him who desires the present (transitory) life (only) We shall hasten an immediate reward for him in this very life (giving) what We will to whom We will. But We have prepared Gehenna for him, he shall enter it, condemned and rejected.

19. As for those who choose the Hereafter and strive for it, the striving that is its due, and are believers, it is these whose striving shall find favour (with their Lord).

20. To all of them, these (who hanker after this world) as well as those (whose choice is the life to come) We render aid, (and this is) out of the bounty of your Lord; the bounty of your Lord is not confined (to any one section

سُورَةُ الْإِسْرَاءِ ١٧

فَصَّلْنٰهُ تَفْصِيلًا ﴿١٢﴾ وَكُلَّ إِنْسٰنٍ أَلْزَمْنٰهُ
طٰٓئِرَهُۥ فِي عُنُقِهِۦ ۖ وَنُخْرِجُ لَهُۥ يَوْمَ الْقِيٰمَةِ
كِتٰبًا يَلْقٰهُ مَنْشُورًا ﴿١٣﴾ اِقْرَأْ كِتٰبَكَ ۖ كَفٰى
بِنَفْسِكَ الْيَوْمَ عَلَيْكَ حَسِيبًا ﴿١٤﴾ مَنِ اهْتَدٰى
فَإِنَّمَا يَهْتَدِي لِنَفْسِهِۦ ۖ وَمَنْ ضَلَّ فَإِنَّمَا
يَضِلُّ عَلَيْهَا ۚ وَلَا تَزِرُ وَازِرَةٌ وِزْرَ أُخْرٰى ۗ
وَمَا كُنَّا مُعَذِّبِينَ حَتّٰى نَبْعَثَ رَسُولًا ﴿١٥﴾
وَإِذَآ أَرَدْنَآ أَنْ نُهْلِكَ قَرْيَةً أَمَرْنَا مُتْرَفِيهَا
فَفَسَقُوا فِيهَا فَحَقَّ عَلَيْهَا الْقَوْلُ فَدَمَّرْنٰهَا تَدْمِيرًا ﴿١٦﴾
وَكَمْ أَهْلَكْنَا مِنَ الْقُرُونِ مِنْۢ بَعْدِ نُوحٍ ۗ
وَكَفٰى بِرَبِّكَ بِذُنُوبِ عِبَادِهِۦ خَبِيرًۢا بَصِيرًا ﴿١٧﴾
مَنْ كَانَ يُرِيدُ الْعَاجِلَةَ عَجَّلْنَا لَهُۥ فِيهَا مَا
نَشَآءُ لِمَنْ نُرِيدُ ثُمَّ جَعَلْنَا لَهُۥ جَهَنَّمَ يَصْلٰىهَا
مَذْمُومًا مَدْحُورًا ﴿١٨﴾ وَمَنْ أَرَادَ الْأٰخِرَةَ
وَسَعٰى لَهَا سَعْيَهَا وَهُوَ مُؤْمِنٌ فَأُولٰٓئِكَ كَانَ
سَعْيُهُمْ مَشْكُورًا ﴿١٩﴾ كُلًّا نُمِدُّ هٰٓؤُلَآءِ وَهٰٓؤُلَآءِ
مِنْ عَطَآءِ رَبِّكَ ۚ وَمَا كَانَ عَطَآءُ رَبِّكَ

الجزء الخامس عشر

of the people).

21. Behold! How We have exalted some of them over others (in the present life), yet the Hereafter holds out greater degrees of rank and (confers) greater merits and excellence.

22. Do not set up another god with Allâh, lest you remain debased and forsaken.

SECTION 3

23. **Y**OUR Lord has enjoined you to worship none but Him and to be good to parents. If either or both attain old age (while living) with you, never say to them, 'Fie!' (- any word expressive of disgust or dislike), nor reproach them (by your action). Rather address them with kind and respectful words (always).

24. And lower to them the wings of submissiveness out of tenderness (treating them with humility and compassion). And say (praying for them), 'My Lord! Have mercy upon them just as they nourished and brought me up as a child.'

25. Your Lord knows very well what is in your minds. If (He will find that) you are righteous, surely, He is a great Protector of those who turn to Him (for forgiveness) again and again.

26. And give to the near of kin and the needy, and the wayfarer their dues, and do not squander (your wealth) wastefully.

27. Certainly, the squanderers are like satans and satan is always ungrateful to his Lord.

28. If you have to turn away from them seeking the mercy from your Lord that you hope for, even then speak to them a kind word.

29. And do not keep your hand shackled to your neck (out of miserliness), nor stretch it out to an entire stretching (extravagantly), lest you sit down reproached (incurring blame) and exhausted (on becoming penniless).

30. Surely, your Lord multiplies His provisions and means of livelihood for such of His people as He will and He measures it out (justly), for He is Well-Aware and Seeing of

مَحْظُورًا ﴿٢٠﴾ اُنْظُرْ كَيْفَ فَضَّلْنَا بَعْضَهُمْ عَلٰى
بَعْضٍ ۚ وَلَلْاٰخِرَةُ اَكْبَرُ دَرَجٰتٍ وَّاَكْبَرُ
تَفْضِيلًا ﴿٢١﴾ لَا تَجْعَلْ مَعَ اللّٰهِ اِلٰهًا اٰخَرَ فَتَقْعُدَ
مَذْمُومًا مَّخْذُولًا ﴿٢٢﴾ وَقَضٰى رَبُّكَ اَلَّا تَعْبُدُوٓا
اِلَّآ اِيَّاهُ وَبِالْوٰلِدَيْنِ اِحْسٰنًا ۚ اِمَّا يَبْلُغَنَّ
عِنْدَكَ الْكِبَرَ اَحَدُهُمَآ اَوْ كِلٰهُمَا فَلَا تَقُلْ
لَّهُمَآ اُفٍّ وَّلَا تَنْهَرْهُمَا وَقُلْ لَّهُمَا قَوْلًا
كَرِيمًا ﴿٢٣﴾ وَاخْفِضْ لَهُمَا جَنَاحَ الذُّلِّ مِنَ
الرَّحْمَةِ وَقُلْ رَّبِّ ارْحَمْهُمَا كَمَا رَبَّيٰنِي
صَغِيرًا ﴿٢٤﴾ رَبُّكُمْ اَعْلَمُ بِمَا فِي نُفُوسِكُمْ ۚ اِنْ
تَكُونُوا صٰلِحِينَ فَاِنَّهٗ كَانَ لِلْاَوّٰبِينَ غَفُورًا ﴿٢٥﴾
وَاٰتِ ذَا الْقُرْبٰى حَقَّهٗ وَالْمِسْكِينَ وَابْنَ
السَّبِيلِ وَلَا تُبَذِّرْ تَبْذِيرًا ﴿٢٦﴾ اِنَّ الْمُبَذِّرِينَ
كَانُوٓا اِخْوٰنَ الشَّيٰطِينِ ۚ وَكَانَ الشَّيْطٰنُ
لِرَبِّهٖ كَفُورًا ﴿٢٧﴾ وَاِمَّا تُعْرِضَنَّ عَنْهُمُ ابْتِغَآءَ
رَحْمَةٍ مِّنْ رَّبِّكَ تَرْجُوهَا فَقُلْ لَّهُمْ قَوْلًا
مَّيْسُورًا ﴿٢٨﴾ وَلَا تَجْعَلْ يَدَكَ مَغْلُولَةً اِلٰى
عُنُقِكَ وَلَا تَبْسُطْهَا كُلَّ الْبَسْطِ فَتَقْعُدَ
مَلُومًا مَّحْسُورًا ﴿٢٩﴾ اِنَّ رَبَّكَ يَبْسُطُ الرِّزْقَ
لِمَنْ يَّشَآءُ وَيَقْدِرُ ۚ اِنَّهٗ كَانَ بِعِبَادِهٖ خَبِيرًا

ع ٢

(the true needs of) His people inside out.

SECTION 4

31. **A**ND do not kill your children for fear of want. It is We Who provide for them as well as for you. Indeed, the killing of them is a great sin.
32. And Keep away from adultery and fornication; surely, it is an abominable act and an (extremely) evil practice.
33. And do not kill anyone, the sanctity of which Allâh has upheld (and has forbidden you to slay) except for a just cause. And We have given, of course, to the heir of the person who is killed unjustly the right (to demand retribution or to forgive). But let him not exceed the (prescribed) limits in killing (the murderer) because he is indeed helped (and protected by law).
34. And go not near (to utilize) the property of an orphan, except in the fairest manner and intention (in favour of the orphan) until he attains his (age of) full strength, (when the property is to be returned to him,) and fulfill (your) agreements, (for every) agreement is certainly questioned about and has to be accounted for.
35. And give full measure when you measure out, and weigh with a right (and even) balance. That is best and most commendable in the long run.
36. And do not follow and utter that of which you have no knowledge. Surely, the ear and eye and the heart, all of these, shall be called upon to account (for it).
37. And do not walk haughtily in the land, for you cannot (thus) rend the earth asunder, nor can you match the mountains in height.
38. All these (doings) are such that the evil in them is simply hateful in the sight of your Lord.
39. These (teachings) are a part of the wisdom which your Lord has revealed to you and (the basis of all these acts of righteousness is that you) set up no other god beside Allâh, lest you be cast into Gehenna condemned, rejected.
40. (Disbelievers!) Has your Lord favoured

سُورَةُ الإِسْرَاءِ ١٧

ع ٤ ٣

بَصِيرًا ﴿٣٠﴾ وَلَا تَقْتُلُوٓا أَوْلَٰدَكُمْ خَشْيَةَ إِمْلَٰقٍ
نَّحْنُ نَرْزُقُهُمْ وَإِيَّاكُمْ إِنَّ قَتْلَهُمْ كَانَ
خِطْـًٔا كَبِيرًا ﴿٣١﴾ وَلَا تَقْرَبُوا الزِّنَىٰٓ إِنَّهُۥ كَانَ
فَٰحِشَةً وَسَآءَ سَبِيلًا ﴿٣٢﴾ وَلَا تَقْتُلُوا النَّفْسَ
الَّتِي حَرَّمَ اللَّهُ إِلَّا بِالْحَقِّ وَمَن قُتِلَ
مَظْلُومًا فَقَدْ جَعَلْنَا لِوَلِيِّهِۦ سُلْطَٰنًا فَلَا
يُسْرِف فِّي الْقَتْلِ إِنَّهُۥ كَانَ مَنصُورًا ﴿٣٣﴾ وَلَا
تَقْرَبُوا مَالَ الْيَتِيمِ إِلَّا بِالَّتِي هِيَ أَحْسَنُ
حَتَّىٰ يَبْلُغَ أَشُدَّهُۥ وَأَوْفُوا بِالْعَهْدِ إِنَّ
الْعَهْدَ كَانَ مَسْـُٔولًا ﴿٣٤﴾ وَأَوْفُوا الْكَيْلَ إِذَا
كِلْتُمْ وَزِنُوا بِالْقِسْطَاسِ الْمُسْتَقِيمِ ذَٰلِكَ
خَيْرٌ وَأَحْسَنُ تَأْوِيلًا ﴿٣٥﴾ وَلَا تَقْفُ مَا لَيْسَ
لَكَ بِهِۦ عِلْمٌ إِنَّ السَّمْعَ وَالْبَصَرَ وَالْفُؤَادَ
كُلُّ أُولَٰٓئِكَ كَانَ عَنْهُ مَسْـُٔولًا ﴿٣٦﴾ وَلَا تَمْشِ
فِي الْأَرْضِ مَرَحًا إِنَّكَ لَن تَخْرِقَ الْأَرْضَ
وَلَن تَبْلُغَ الْجِبَالَ طُولًا ﴿٣٧﴾ كُلُّ ذَٰلِكَ كَانَ
سَيِّئُهُۥ عِندَ رَبِّكَ مَكْرُوهًا ﴿٣٨﴾ ذَٰلِكَ مِمَّآ
أَوْحَىٰٓ إِلَيْكَ رَبُّكَ مِنَ الْحِكْمَةِ وَلَا تَجْعَلْ
مَعَ اللَّهِ إِلَٰهًا ءَاخَرَ فَتُلْقَىٰ فِي جَهَنَّمَ مَلُومًا
مَّدْحُورًا ﴿٣٩﴾ أَفَأَصْفَٰكُمْ رَبُّكُم بِالْبَنِينَ

you with sons and chosen for Himself daughters from among the angels? Surely, most grievous is the blasphemy you utter.

سُورَةُ الْإِسْرَاءِ ١٧

SECTION 5

41. **A**ND certainly, in this Qur'ân, We have explained (for the people the truth) in a variety of forms that they may take heed and become great. But (their condition is such that) it increases them only in aversion.

42. Say, 'Had there been other gods as they allege beside Him (- the One God), in that case these (polytheists) would have certainly sought out (by their help) a way to the Lord of the Mighty throne.

43. Glory be to Him! And far High indeed be He exalted above the things these (polytheists) say.

44. The seven heavens, the earth and all those inhabiting them extol His glory. In fact, there is not even a single thing but glorifies Him with His true and perfect praise, but you do not understand their glorification. Verily, Most Forbearing is He, Great Protector.

45. And when you recite the Qur'ân, We place between you and those who do not believe in the Hereafter, an impregnable screen,

46. And We cover their hearts with veils and plug their ears with something heavy, lest they should understand it. And when you mention the name of your Lord Who is the Only One, in the Qur'ân, they turn their backs (on it) in aversion.

47. We know very well the purpose of their listening when they listen to you (and the purpose with which they confer) when they confer in private (and) when the unjust say, 'You follow none but a man who is defrauded and deprived of reason.'

48. Behold! How they coin similitudes to depict you, as a result of which they have gone astray; so they will not be able to find

وَاتَّخَذَ مِنَ الْمَلٰٓئِكَةِ إِنٰثًا إِنَّكُمْ لَتَقُولُونَ
قَوْلًا عَظِيمًا ﴿٤٠﴾ وَلَقَدْ صَرَّفْنَا فِي هٰذَا الْقُرْاٰنِ
لِيَذَّكَّرُوا وَمَا يَزِيدُهُمْ إِلَّا نُفُورًا ﴿٤١﴾ قُلْ لَّوْ
كَانَ مَعَهُۥٓ ءَالِهَةٌ كَمَا يَقُولُونَ إِذًا لَّابْتَغَوْا
إِلٰى ذِي الْعَرْشِ سَبِيلًا ﴿٤٢﴾ سُبْحٰنَهُۥ وَتَعٰلٰى
عَمَّا يَقُولُونَ عُلُوًّا كَبِيرًا ﴿٤٣﴾ تُسَبِّحُ لَهُ السَّمٰوٰتُ
السَّبْعُ وَالْأَرْضُ وَمَنْ فِيهِنَّ وَإِنْ مِّنْ
شَيْءٍ إِلَّا يُسَبِّحُ بِحَمْدِهٖ وَلٰكِنْ لَّا تَفْقَهُونَ
تَسْبِيحَهُمْ إِنَّهُۥ كَانَ حَلِيمًا غَفُورًا ﴿٤٤﴾ وَإِذَا
قَرَأْتَ الْقُرْاٰنَ جَعَلْنَا بَيْنَكَ وَبَيْنَ الَّذِينَ
لَا يُؤْمِنُونَ بِالْاٰخِرَةِ حِجَابًا مَّسْتُورًا ﴿٤٥﴾
وَّجَعَلْنَا عَلٰى قُلُوبِهِمْ أَكِنَّةً أَنْ يَّفْقَهُوهُ وَفِيٓ
اٰذَانِهِمْ وَقْرًا وَإِذَا ذَكَرْتَ رَبَّكَ فِي الْقُرْاٰنِ
وَحْدَهُۥ وَلَّوْا عَلٰىٓ أَدْبٰرِهِمْ نُفُورًا ﴿٤٦﴾ نَحْنُ أَعْلَمُ
بِمَا يَسْتَمِعُونَ بِهٖٓ إِذْ يَسْتَمِعُونَ إِلَيْكَ وَإِذْ هُمْ
نَجْوٰىٓ إِذْ يَقُولُ الظّٰلِمُونَ إِنْ تَتَّبِعُونَ إِلَّا رَجُلًا
مَّسْحُورًا ﴿٤٧﴾ اُنْظُرْ كَيْفَ ضَرَبُوا لَكَ الْأَمْثَالَ

الجزء الخامس عشر

a way (of their salvation).
49. And they (also) say, 'What! When we are reduced to bones and (that too) broken particles (of dust) shall we then be really raised again to a new life?'
50. Say, 'Yes, even if you be reduced to stones or iron,
51. 'Or some other creation yet more hard (that you can possibly conceive) in your mind, (even then you shall be raised to a new life).' Thereupon they will say, 'Who will restore us (to life)?' Say, 'The same Who originated you the first time.' At this, then, they will shake their heads at you (expressing wonder and disbelief in being raised) and will say, 'When will it come to pass?' Say, 'May be it is near.'
52. (This promise will be fulfilled) on the day when He will call you forth, then you will respond (to Him) saying His praises and you will think that you have tarried (in the world) only for a little while.

SECTION 6

53. **A**ND say to My servants that they should speak only what is gracious, for satan (is keen to) provoke discord among them. Satan indeed is an enemy to the people, disuniting (one another).
54. Your Lord knows you best. He will have mercy on you if He will or He will punish you if He will. And We have not sent you to be a disposer of their affairs (authorising you to punish them or reward them).
55. And your Lord knows best those that are in the heavens and on the earth. And most surely We have exalted some of the Prophets above others, and it is We Who gave David the *Zabûr* (- the Psalms).
56. Say, 'Call upon those whom you assert (to be gods) apart from Him, then (you will realize) they have no power to rid you of affliction nor to avert (it) or transfer it to others.'
57. Those whom they call upon (apart from

فَضَلُّوْا فَلَا يَسْتَطِيْعُوْنَ سَبِيْلًا ﴿٤٨﴾ وَقَالُوْٓا ءَاِذَا
كُنَّا عِظَامًا وَّرُفَاتًا ءَاِنَّا لَمَبْعُوْثُوْنَ خَلْقًا جَدِيْدًا ﴿٤٩﴾
قُلْ كُوْنُوْا حِجَارَةً اَوْ حَدِيْدًا ﴿٥٠﴾ اَوْ خَلْقًا مِّمَّا
يَكْبُرُ فِيْ صُدُوْرِكُمْ فَسَيَقُوْلُوْنَ مَنْ يُّعِيْدُنَا
قُلِ الَّذِيْ فَطَرَكُمْ اَوَّلَ مَرَّةٍ فَسَيُنْغِضُوْنَ
اِلَيْكَ رُءُوْسَهُمْ وَيَقُوْلُوْنَ مَتٰى هُوَ قُلْ عَسٰٓى
اَنْ يَّكُوْنَ قَرِيْبًا ﴿٥١﴾ يَوْمَ يَدْعُوْكُمْ فَتَسْتَجِيْبُوْنَ
بِحَمْدِهٖ وَتَظُنُّوْنَ اِنْ لَّبِثْتُمْ اِلَّا قَلِيْلًا ﴿٥٢﴾
وَقُلْ لِّعِبَادِيْ يَقُوْلُوا الَّتِيْ هِيَ اَحْسَنُ اِنَّ
الشَّيْطٰنَ يَنْزَغُ بَيْنَهُمْ اِنَّ الشَّيْطٰنَ كَانَ
لِلْاِنْسٰنِ عَدُوًّا مُّبِيْنًا ﴿٥٣﴾ رَبُّكُمْ اَعْلَمُ بِكُمْ
اِنْ يَّشَاْ يَرْحَمْكُمْ اَوْ اِنْ يَّشَاْ يُعَذِّبْكُمْ وَمَآ
اَرْسَلْنٰكَ عَلَيْهِمْ وَكِيْلًا ﴿٥٤﴾ وَرَبُّكَ اَعْلَمُ بِمَنْ
فِي السَّمٰوٰتِ وَالْاَرْضِ وَلَقَدْ فَضَّلْنَا بَعْضَ
النَّبِيّٖنَ عَلٰى بَعْضٍ وَّاٰتَيْنَا دَاوٗدَ زَبُوْرًا ﴿٥٥﴾ قُلِ
ادْعُوا الَّذِيْنَ زَعَمْتُمْ مِّنْ دُوْنِهٖ فَلَا يَمْلِكُوْنَ
كَشْفَ الضُّرِّ عَنْكُمْ وَلَا تَحْوِيْلًا ﴿٥٦﴾ اُولٰٓئِكَ
الَّذِيْنَ يَدْعُوْنَ يَبْتَغُوْنَ اِلٰى رَبِّهِمُ الْوَسِيْلَةَ

Him, thinking them to be a means of gaining nearness to God,) themselves seek nearness to their Lord and solicit His favour (even) those of them who are nearest (to God are still competing to be closer to Him) and hope for His mercy and fear His punishment. As a matter of fact the punishment of your Lord is a thing to beware of.

58. And there is no township but We shall destroy it or We shall subject it to a severe chastisement before the Day of Resurrection. That is written down in the book (- in the knowledge of God).

59. And nothing could prevent Us from going on sending (Our) signs though the former people cried lies to them. And We gave to Thamûd the she-camel as an enlightenment and an eye opener, but they dealt with her unjustly. And We do not send (Our) signs except to warn the people (against the evil consequences of disbelief and transgression).

60. And (Prophet! recall the time) when We said to you, 'Surely, your Lord has encompassed all people (for destruction) and has power over them (still they remained indifferent).' We made the vision which We showed you (being carried to Jerusalem from Makkah by night) and also the tree (- evil word; see 14:26) disapproved of in the Qur'ân, a means of distinction between the good and the bad for the people. (Despite the fact that) We have been warning them (by sending Our signs), this (warning from Us) only leads them to unrestrained inordinacy.

SECTION 7

61. **A**ND (recall the time) when We said to the angels, 'Submit to Adam!' Then they all submitted. But *Iblîs* (who too was told to do the same, did not), he said, 'Shall I submit to one whom You have created out of clay?'

62. And he added, 'What do You think? This is he whom You have honoured and placed above me. If You grant me respite till the Day

أَيُّهُمْ أَقْرَبُ وَيَرْجُونَ رَحْمَتَهُ وَيَخَافُونَ
عَذَابَهُ إِنَّ عَذَابَ رَبِّكَ كَانَ مَحْذُورًا ﴿٥٧﴾
وَإِنْ مِنْ قَرْيَةٍ إِلَّا نَحْنُ مُهْلِكُوهَا قَبْلَ يَوْمِ
الْقِيَامَةِ أَوْ مُعَذِّبُوهَا عَذَابًا شَدِيدًا كَانَ
ذَٰلِكَ فِي الْكِتَابِ مَسْطُورًا ﴿٥٨﴾ وَمَا مَنَعَنَا أَنْ
نُرْسِلَ بِالْآيَاتِ إِلَّا أَنْ كَذَّبَ بِهَا الْأَوَّلُونَ
وَآتَيْنَا ثَمُودَ النَّاقَةَ مُبْصِرَةً فَظَلَمُوا بِهَا
وَمَا نُرْسِلُ بِالْآيَاتِ إِلَّا تَخْوِيفًا ﴿٥٩﴾ وَإِذْ قُلْنَا
لَكَ إِنَّ رَبَّكَ أَحَاطَ بِالنَّاسِ وَمَا جَعَلْنَا
الرُّؤْيَا الَّتِي أَرَيْنَاكَ إِلَّا فِتْنَةً لِلنَّاسِ وَالشَّجَرَةَ
الْمَلْعُونَةَ فِي الْقُرْآنِ وَنُخَوِّفُهُمْ فَمَا يَزِيدُهُمْ
إِلَّا طُغْيَانًا كَبِيرًا ﴿٦٠﴾ وَإِذْ قُلْنَا لِلْمَلَائِكَةِ اسْجُدُوا
لِآدَمَ فَسَجَدُوا إِلَّا إِبْلِيسَ قَالَ أَأَسْجُدُ
لِمَنْ خَلَقْتَ طِينًا ﴿٦١﴾ قَالَ أَرَأَيْتَكَ هَٰذَا الَّذِي
كَرَّمْتَ عَلَيَّ لَئِنْ أَخَّرْتَنِ إِلَىٰ يَوْمِ الْقِيَامَةِ لَأَحْتَنِكَنَّ

of Resurrection, I will most certainly bring his progeny under my sway, having overpowered them, I shall destroy them for sure, except a few.'

63. 'Be gone!' said He; 'As for those of them who follow you, Gehenna is the recompense of you all, an ample recompense.

64. 'And beguile whomsoever of them you can with your speech and rally your horsemen against them, and your foot men (- fast riders and slow walkers in disobedience, with all your might) and share with them their wealth and children and hold out promises to them (what you like).' Indeed, satan promises them nothing but mere fraud.

65. 'As to My true servants, you shall have certainly no authority over them. And sufficient is your Lord as Disposer of affairs.'

66. Your Lord is He Who drives the ships on the sea for you that you may seek of His bounty. He is certainly Ever Merciful to you.

67. And when you encounter some distress on the sea, (at that time all) those (gods) whom you call upon are lost (to you), but not He. Yet when He brings you safe to the land, you turn away (from Him). Of course, such a person is very ungrateful.

68. Do you then feel secure that He will not humiliate you in the side of the land and make you sink (in the earth on the side of) the shore, or send against you a violent squall of pebbles. For (if He does) you shall find none responsible to protect and help you.

69. Or do you feel secure and have made sure that He will (not) send you back in it (- the sea) a second time (and) then send against you a fierce storm blast and drown you because of your ingratitude, for (if He does), you will find no helper in the matter for yourselves to protect you against Us.

70. And most surely We have made the Children of Adam greatly honoured and have carried them over land and sea, and We have

ذُرِّيَّتَهُۥٓ إِلَّا قَلِيلًا ﴿٦٢﴾ قَالَ اذْهَبْ فَمَن تَبِعَكَ
مِنْهُمْ فَإِنَّ جَهَنَّمَ جَزَآؤُكُمْ جَزَآءً مَّوْفُورًا ﴿٦٣﴾
وَاسْتَفْزِزْ مَنِ اسْتَطَعْتَ مِنْهُم بِصَوْتِكَ
وَأَجْلِبْ عَلَيْهِم بِخَيْلِكَ وَرَجِلِكَ وَشَارِكْهُمْ
فِي الْأَمْوَٰلِ وَالْأَوْلَٰدِ وَعِدْهُمْ ۚ وَمَا يَعِدُهُمُ
الشَّيْطَٰنُ إِلَّا غُرُورًا ﴿٦٤﴾ إِنَّ عِبَادِي لَيْسَ لَكَ
عَلَيْهِمْ سُلْطَٰنٌ ۚ وَكَفَىٰ بِرَبِّكَ وَكِيلًا ﴿٦٥﴾ رَّبُّكُمُ
الَّذِي يُزْجِي لَكُمُ الْفُلْكَ فِي الْبَحْرِ لِتَبْتَغُوا مِن
فَضْلِهِۦٓ ۚ إِنَّهُۥ كَانَ بِكُمْ رَحِيمًا ﴿٦٦﴾ وَإِذَا مَسَّكُمُ
الضُّرُّ فِي الْبَحْرِ ضَلَّ مَن تَدْعُونَ إِلَّآ إِيَّاهُ ۖ
فَلَمَّا نَجَّىٰكُمْ إِلَى الْبَرِّ أَعْرَضْتُمْ ۚ وَكَانَ
الْإِنسَٰنُ كَفُورًا ﴿٦٧﴾ أَفَأَمِنتُمْ أَن يَخْسِفَ بِكُمْ
جَانِبَ الْبَرِّ أَوْ يُرْسِلَ عَلَيْكُمْ حَاصِبًا ثُمَّ
لَا تَجِدُوا لَكُمْ وَكِيلًا ﴿٦٨﴾ أَمْ أَمِنتُمْ أَن
يُعِيدَكُمْ فِيهِ تَارَةً أُخْرَىٰ فَيُرْسِلَ عَلَيْكُمْ
قَاصِفًا مِّنَ الرِّيحِ فَيُغْرِقَكُم بِمَا كَفَرْتُمْ ۙ ثُمَّ
لَا تَجِدُوا لَكُمْ عَلَيْنَا بِهِۦ تَبِيعًا ﴿٦٩﴾ وَلَقَدْ
كَرَّمْنَا بَنِيٓ ءَادَمَ وَحَمَلْنَٰهُمْ فِي الْبَرِّ وَالْبَحْرِ

provided them with good and pure things and have distinctly exalted them far above most of Our creation.

SECTION 8

71. (BEWARE of) the day when We shall call all people along with their leaders. Now whoever is given his book (- recording his deeds) in his right hand, such will read their book (eagerly) and they will not be dealt with unjustly in the least.
72. But whoever remained (spiritually) blind in this world shall also be blind in the Hereafter. Rather he will be even farther removed from the right path.
73. And they had spared nothing in causing you (the severest) affliction with the purpose to turn you away from the revelations given to you, that you might forge in Our name something different from that which We have revealed to you. In that case they would surely have taken you for a special friend.
74. And if We had not made you firm and steadfast, you might have inclined towards them a little.
75. In that case (if you had been one to forge a lie against Us) We would have made you taste multiple sufferings in this life and multiple sufferings in death, (and) then you would have found for yourself no helper against Us. (But you remained steadfast).
76. They had spared nothing in unsettling you from the land (of Makkah), with the result that they drive you out from it. But in that case they (themselves) would not have stayed after you except for a little while.
77. Such (has been Our) practice with those of Our Messengers whom We sent before you and you will find no change in Our practice.

SECTION 9

78. OBSERVE Prayer at the declining and paling of the sun, on to the complete darkness

وَرَزَقْنٰهُم مِّنَ الطَّيِّبٰتِ وَ فَضَّلْنٰهُمْ عَلٰى كَثِيرٍ
مِّمَّنْ خَلَقْنَا تَفْضِيلًا ﴿٧٠﴾ يَوْمَ نَدْعُوا كُلَّ أُنَاسٍ
بِإِمٰمِهِمْ فَمَنْ أُوتِيَ كِتٰبَهُ بِيَمِينِهِ فَأُولٰٓئِكَ
يَقْرَءُونَ كِتٰبَهُمْ وَ لَا يُظْلَمُونَ فَتِيلًا ﴿٧١﴾ وَمَن
كَانَ فِي هٰذِهِ أَعْمٰى فَهُوَ فِي الْأٰخِرَةِ أَعْمٰى
وَأَضَلُّ سَبِيلًا ﴿٧٢﴾ وَ إِن كَادُوا لَيَفْتِنُونَكَ
عَنِ الَّذِي أَوْحَيْنَا إِلَيْكَ لِتَفْتَرِيَ عَلَيْنَا
غَيْرَهُ ۖ وَ إِذًا لَّاتَّخَذُوكَ خَلِيلًا ﴿٧٣﴾ وَ لَوْ لَا
أَن ثَبَّتْنٰكَ لَقَدْ كِدتَّ تَرْكَنُ إِلَيْهِمْ شَيْـًٔا
قَلِيلًا ﴿٧٤﴾ إِذًا لَّأَذَقْنٰكَ ضِعْفَ الْحَيٰوةِ وَ ضِعْفَ
الْمَمَاتِ ثُمَّ لَا تَجِدُ لَكَ عَلَيْنَا نَصِيرًا ﴿٧٥﴾
وَ إِن كَادُوا لَيَسْتَفِزُّونَكَ مِنَ الْأَرْضِ لِيُخْرِجُوكَ
مِنْهَا وَ إِذًا لَّا يَلْبَثُونَ خِلٰفَكَ إِلَّا قَلِيلًا ﴿٧٦﴾
سُنَّةَ مَن قَدْ أَرْسَلْنَا قَبْلَكَ مِن رُّسُلِنَا
وَ لَا تَجِدُ لِسُنَّتِنَا تَحْوِيلًا ﴿٧٧﴾ أَقِمِ الصَّلٰوةَ
لِدُلُوكِ الشَّمْسِ إِلٰى غَسَقِ الَّيْلِ وَ قُرْءَانَ

(in diverse hours) of the night, and recite the Qur'ân at dawn. Verily, the regular recital (of the Qur'ân) at dawn is (specially) acceptable (to God) and witnessed (by the angels).

79. And remain awake for it (- the recitation of the Qur'ân and Prayer) for a part of the night after having risen from sleep as a supererogatory service for you. Thus it may be that your Lord will raise you to a laudable exalted position.

80. And say (in Prayer), 'My Lord, grant that when I enter (wherever You take me to while migrating) I enter with truth (in every way) and when I depart, I depart with truth, and grant me by Your grace authoritative help (which should sustain me in my activities).'

81. And say, 'Truth has come and falsehood has vanished away.' Falsehood is indeed ever bound to vanish away.

82. And We are gradually revealing of the Qur'ân (that teaching) which is (the cause of) healing and mercy for the believers. But this (revelation) only leads the unjust persons from loss to loss.

83. And when We bestow favours on a human being, he turns away and withdraws himself aside, but when evil overtakes him he is given to despair.

84. Say, 'Everyone acts after his own way and fashion and your Lord knows very well who is best guided in the right path.'

SECTION 10

85. **A**ND they question you about the revelation, and the human soul. Say, 'The revelation and the soul is by the command of my Lord, (because) little is the knowledge there of that you have been given.'

86. Had We so willed We could surely take away that which We have revealed to you. If We did so you could find none to plead your cause (to restore it to you) against Our will.

سورة الإسراء ١٧

الفجر إن قرءان الفجر كان مشهودا ﴿٧٨﴾
ومن الّيل فتهجد به نافلة لك عسى أن
يبعثك ربك مقاما محمودا ﴿٧٩﴾ وقل رب
أدخلني مدخل صدق وأخرجني مخرج
صدق واجعل لي من لدنك سلطنا نصيرا ﴿٨٠﴾
وقل جاء الحق وزهق البطل إن البطل
كان زهوقا ﴿٨١﴾ وننزل من القرءان ما هو
شفاء ورحمة للمؤمنين ولا يزيد الظلمين
إلا خسارا ﴿٨٢﴾ وإذا أنعمنا على الإنسن أعرض
ونا بجانبه وإذا مسه الشر كان يؤسا ﴿٨٣﴾
قل كل يعمل على شاكلته فربكم أعلم
بمن هو أهدى سبيلا ﴿٨٤﴾ ويسئلونك عن
الروح قل الروح من أمر ربي وما أوتيتم
من العلم إلا قليلا ﴿٨٥﴾ ولئن شئنا لنذهبن
بالذي أوحينا إليك ثم لا تجد لك به
علينا وكيلا ﴿٨٦﴾ إلا رحمة من ربك إن

ع ٩

الجزء الخامس عشر

87. But (it is) the special mercy from your Lord (that He will not do so); His grace and favour upon you is very great in fact.

88. Say, 'If there should join together all human beings and the *jinn* to produce the like of this Qur'ân, they would never be able to produce anything like it, even though some of them might be the helpers of others.'

89. And in this Qur'ân We have explained in various ways and forms all kinds of rare things of exquisite beauty to humankind but most people choose to reject everything except (following the way of) disbelief.

90. And they say, 'We will never believe unless you cause a spring to gush forth for us from the earth,

91. 'Or there be a garden of date-palms and vines for you, and you cause the streams to gush forth abundantly in its midst,

92. 'Or, as you assert (and claim that it shall happen), cause the heaven to fall down upon us in fragments, or bring Allâh and the angels face to face with us,

93. 'Or, there be a house made of gold for you, or you ascend into the heaven; but we will not believe in your ascending till you bring down to us a book that we can read.' (Say), 'Glory be to my Lord! I am not but a human being (sent as) a Messenger.'

SECTION 11

94. **A**ND nothing has prevented the people from believing when the guidance came to them except their sayings, 'Has Allâh raised a human being (like us) as a Messenger?'

95. Say, 'Had there been angels on the earth (in place of human beings) walking about secure and sound We (too) would have invariably sent down an angel from heaven as a Messenger to them.'

96. Say, 'Allâh suffices as a witness between me and you. Surely, He is Ever Aware of and sees His servants full well.'

97. He whom Allâh guides (to the straight and

سُورَةُ الْإِسْرَاءِ ١٧

فَضْلَهُ كَانَ عَلَيْكَ كَبِيرًا ﴿٨٧﴾ قُل لَّئِنِ اجْتَمَعَتِ
الْإِنسُ وَالْجِنُّ عَلَىٰ أَن يَأْتُوا بِمِثْلِ هَٰذَا
الْقُرْآنِ لَا يَأْتُونَ بِمِثْلِهِ وَلَوْ كَانَ بَعْضُهُمْ
لِبَعْضٍ ظَهِيرًا ﴿٨٨﴾ وَلَقَدْ صَرَّفْنَا لِلنَّاسِ فِي
هَٰذَا الْقُرْآنِ مِن كُلِّ مَثَلٍ فَأَبَىٰ أَكْثَرُ
النَّاسِ إِلَّا كُفُورًا ﴿٨٩﴾ وَقَالُوا لَن نُّؤْمِنَ لَكَ
حَتَّىٰ تَفْجُرَ لَنَا مِنَ الْأَرْضِ يَنبُوعًا ﴿٩٠﴾ أَوْ
تَكُونَ لَكَ جَنَّةٌ مِّن نَّخِيلٍ وَعِنَبٍ فَتُفَجِّرَ
الْأَنْهَٰرَ خِلَالَهَا تَفْجِيرًا ﴿٩١﴾ أَوْ تُسْقِطَ السَّمَاءَ كَمَا
زَعَمْتَ عَلَيْنَا كِسَفًا أَوْ تَأْتِيَ بِاللَّهِ وَالْمَلَٰئِكَةِ
قَبِيلًا ﴿٩٢﴾ أَوْ يَكُونَ لَكَ بَيْتٌ مِّن زُخْرُفٍ أَوْ
تَرْقَىٰ فِي السَّمَاءِ وَلَن نُّؤْمِنَ لِرُقِيِّكَ حَتَّىٰ
تُنَزِّلَ عَلَيْنَا كِتَٰبًا نَّقْرَؤُهُ قُلْ سُبْحَانَ رَبِّي
هَلْ كُنتُ إِلَّا بَشَرًا رَّسُولًا ﴿٩٣﴾ وَمَا مَنَعَ النَّاسَ
أَن يُؤْمِنُوا إِذْ جَاءَهُمُ الْهُدَىٰ إِلَّا أَن قَالُوا
أَبَعَثَ اللَّهُ بَشَرًا رَّسُولًا ﴿٩٤﴾ قُل لَّوْ كَانَ فِي
الْأَرْضِ مَلَٰئِكَةٌ يَمْشُونَ مُطْمَئِنِّينَ لَنَزَّلْنَا
عَلَيْهِم مِّنَ السَّمَاءِ مَلَكًا رَّسُولًا ﴿٩٥﴾ قُلْ كَفَىٰ
بِاللَّهِ شَهِيدًا بَيْنِي وَبَيْنَكُمْ إِنَّهُ كَانَ
بِعِبَادِهِ خَبِيرًا بَصِيرًا ﴿٩٦﴾ وَمَن يَهْدِ اللَّهُ فَهُوَ

ع ١٠

right path) is the only one rightly guided, but those whom He abandons to perish, you will find no protecting friends for them apart from Him. And We shall gather them on the Day of Resurrection (dragging them) on their faces. They shall be blind, dumb and deaf. Gehenna is their resort. As often as it (- the flames of the Hell-Fire) abate, We shall add (fuel) to the blaze for them.

98. Such shall be their recompense because they rejected Our commandments and said, 'Shall we really be raised up as a new creation when (after our death) we are reduced to mere bones and broken particles (of dust).

99. Have they not seen that Allâh, Who created the heavens and the earth, has the power to create their like? And He has appointed for them a term, no doubt about it. Yet the unjust would reject everything except (following in the way of) disbelief.

100. Say, 'Even if you possessed all the treasures of the mercy and blessings of my Lord yet you would hold (them) back for fear of depleting, for a human being is very niggardly indeed.'

SECTION 12

101. **A**ND most certainly, We gave Moses nine clear signs. So ask the Children of Israel (about it). When he (- Moses) came to them, Pharaoh said to him, 'Moses! I think you to be under a spell and a victim of deception.'

102. He said, 'You know fully well that none other but the Lord of the heavens and the earth has revealed these signs as (means of) enlightenment. Surely, I believe you, O Pharaoh! To be doomed to perish.'

103. So he resolved to weaken them by humiliating them in and thus scare them out of the country; but We drowned him and those with him, one and all.

104. And We said after (it was all over with Pharaoh), to the Children of Israel, 'Settle

الْمُهْتَدِ ۚ وَمَنْ يُّضْلِلْ فَلَنْ تَجِدَ لَهُمْ أَوْلِيَآءَ
مِنْ دُونِهِ ۚ وَنَحْشُرُهُمْ يَوْمَ الْقِيٰمَةِ عَلٰى
وُجُوهِهِمْ عُمْيًا وَّبُكْمًا وَّصُمًّا ۚ مَأْوٰىهُمْ
جَهَنَّمُ ۚ كُلَّمَا خَبَتْ زِدْنٰهُمْ سَعِيرًا ﴿٩٧﴾ ذٰلِكَ
جَزَآؤُهُمْ بِأَنَّهُمْ كَفَرُوا بِأٰيٰتِنَا وَقَالُوٓا ءَإِذَا كُنَّا
عِظٰمًا وَّرُفٰتًا ءَإِنَّا لَمَبْعُوثُونَ خَلْقًا جَدِيدًا ﴿٩٨﴾
أَوَلَمْ يَرَوْا أَنَّ اللّٰهَ الَّذِي خَلَقَ السَّمٰوٰتِ
وَالْأَرْضَ قَادِرٌ عَلٰٓى أَنْ يَّخْلُقَ مِثْلَهُمْ وَجَعَلَ
لَهُمْ أَجَلًا لَّا رَيْبَ فِيهِ ۚ فَأَبَى الظّٰلِمُونَ إِلَّا
كُفُورًا ﴿٩٩﴾ قُلْ لَّوْ أَنْتُمْ تَمْلِكُونَ خَزَآئِنَ
رَحْمَةِ رَبِّيٓ إِذًا لَّأَمْسَكْتُمْ خَشْيَةَ الْإِنْفَاقِ ۚ
وَكَانَ الْإِنْسٰنُ قَتُورًا ﴿١٠٠﴾ وَلَقَدْ أٰتَيْنَا مُوسٰى
تِسْعَ أٰيٰتٍۭ بَيِّنٰتٍ فَسْـَٔلْ بَنِيٓ إِسْرَآءِيلَ إِذْ
جَآءَهُمْ فَقَالَ لَهُ فِرْعَوْنُ إِنِّي لَأَظُنُّكَ يٰمُوسٰى
مَسْحُورًا ﴿١٠١﴾ قَالَ لَقَدْ عَلِمْتَ مَآ أَنْزَلَ هٰٓؤُلَآءِ
إِلَّا رَبُّ السَّمٰوٰتِ وَالْأَرْضِ بَصَآئِرَ ۚ وَإِنِّي
لَأَظُنُّكَ يٰفِرْعَوْنُ مَثْبُورًا ﴿١٠٢﴾ فَأَرَادَ أَنْ
يَّسْتَفِزَّهُمْ مِّنَ الْأَرْضِ فَأَغْرَقْنٰهُ وَمَنْ مَّعَهُ
جَمِيعًا ﴿١٠٣﴾ وَّقُلْنَا مِنْۢ بَعْدِهِ لِبَنِيٓ إِسْرَآءِيلَ
اسْكُنُوا الْأَرْضَ فَإِذَا جَآءَ وَعْدُ الْأٰخِرَةِ جِئْنَا

down occupying the (promised) land (of Palestine). When the time of fulfillment of the second Prophecy comes, We shall bring you back gathering you (from various lands).'

105. We revealed it (- the Qur'ân) to suit all the requirement of truth and wisdom and it has come down (to you) with truth and wisdom. (Prophet!) We have sent you (on one hand) as a Bearer of good tidings and as a Warner (on the other).

106. We have divided this Qur'ân into distinct chapters and have revealed it in stages that you may recite it to humankind at intervals and (that is why) We have revealed it piece by piece, and in stages.

107. Say, 'You may believe in it (- the Qur'ân) or you may not believe, those who have been given the (spiritual) knowledge before it (- its revelation) fall down on their faces prostrating submissively (before their Lord) when it is recited to them.'

108. And they say, 'Glory be to Our Lord! The promise of our Lord is really bound to be fulfilled.'

109. They fall down on their faces weeping and (as they listen to the divine words) it adds to their humility.

[PROSTRATION]

110. Say, 'Call upon (Him by the name of) Allâh or call upon (Him by the name of) *Al-Rahmân* (the Most Gracious). (In short) call upon Him by whichsoever name you like, all beautiful names belong to Him (- the One God). And utter not your prayer in a loud voice nor utter it in too low tones (completely concealing it) but seek a middle course.'

111. And say, 'All true and perfect praise belongs to Allâh Who has not taken to Himself a son, and Who has no associate-partner in His kingdom, nor has He any helper because of any weakness. And extol His glory with repeated glorification.'

سُوْرَةُ الْاِسْرَآءِ ١٧

بِكُمْ لَفِيْفًا ﴿١٠٤﴾ وَ بِالْحَقِّ اَنْزَلْنٰهُ وَ بِالْحَقِّ نَزَلَ
وَ مَآ اَرْسَلْنٰكَ اِلَّا مُبَشِّرًا وَّ نَذِيْرًا ﴿١٠٥﴾ وَ قُرْاٰنًا
فَرَقْنٰهُ لِتَقْرَاَهٗ عَلَى النَّاسِ عَلٰى مُكْثٍ
وَّ نَزَّلْنٰهُ تَنْزِيْلًا ﴿١٠٦﴾ قُلْ اٰمِنُوْا بِهٖٓ اَوْ لَا تُؤْمِنُوْا
اِنَّ الَّذِيْنَ اُوْتُوا الْعِلْمَ مِنْ قَبْلِهٖٓ اِذَا يُتْلٰى
عَلَيْهِمْ يَخِرُّوْنَ لِلْاَذْقَانِ سُجَّدًا ﴿١٠٧﴾ وَّ يَقُوْلُوْنَ
سُبْحٰنَ رَبِّنَآ اِنْ كَانَ وَعْدُ رَبِّنَا لَمَفْعُوْلًا ﴿١٠٨﴾
وَ يَخِرُّوْنَ لِلْاَذْقَانِ يَبْكُوْنَ وَ يَزِيْدُهُمْ
خُشُوْعًا ﴿١٠٩﴾ قُلِ ادْعُوا اللّٰهَ اَوِ ادْعُوا الرَّحْمٰنَ
اَيًّا مَّا تَدْعُوْا فَلَهُ الْاَسْمَآءُ الْحُسْنٰى وَ لَا
تَجْهَرْ بِصَلَاتِكَ وَ لَا تُخَافِتْ بِهَا وَ ابْتَغِ
بَيْنَ ذٰلِكَ سَبِيْلًا ﴿١١٠﴾ وَ قُلِ الْحَمْدُ لِلّٰهِ الَّذِيْ
لَمْ يَتَّخِذْ وَلَدًا وَّ لَمْ يَكُنْ لَّهٗ شَرِيْكٌ فِي الْمُلْكِ
وَ لَمْ يَكُنْ لَّهٗ وَلِيٌّ مِّنَ الذُّلِّ وَ كَبِّرْهُ تَكْبِيْرًا ﴿١١١﴾

الجزء الخامس عشر

CHAPTER
18

سُوْرَةُ الْكَهْفِ ١٨

AL-KAHF

(The Place of Refuge)

(Revealed before Hijrah)

سُوْرَةُ الْكَهْفِ مَكِّيَّةٌ

With the name of Allâh,
the Most Gracious, the Ever Merciful
(I commence to read Sûrah Al-Kahf).

بِسْمِ اللّٰهِ الرَّحْمٰنِ الرَّحِيْمِ

1. **A**LL type of true and perfect praise belongs to Allâh Who has revealed this perfect Book to His servant, and has not assigned to it any crookedness.
2. (He has made it) rightly directing, that it may warn (the disbelievers) of a severe calamity (coming) from Him and that it may give good tidings to the believers who do deeds of righteousness, that there awaits them a (place of) goodly reward,
3. Wherein they shall stay forever.
4. And that it may warn those who say, 'Allâh has begotten a son.'
5. (This is absolutely wrong.) They have no real knowledge of Him, nor (had) their fathers. Grievous is the word that comes out of their mouths. They speak naught but a lie.
6. Will you worry yourself to death sorrowing after them, if they do not believe in this (great) discourse (- the Qur'ân).
7. Verily, We have made all that is on the earth as an embellishment for it, that We may try them as to which of them is the most excellent in (respect of) performing the noblest deeds.
8. Yet it is We Who shall (one day) reduce all that is on it to a barren soil.

الْحَمْدُ لِلّٰهِ الَّذِيْٓ أَنْزَلَ عَلٰى عَبْدِهِ الْكِتٰبَ
وَلَمْ يَجْعَلْ لَّهٗ عِوَجًا ١ قَيِّمًا لِّيُنْذِرَ بَأْسًا
شَدِيْدًا مِّنْ لَّدُنْهُ وَيُبَشِّرَ الْمُؤْمِنِيْنَ الَّذِيْنَ
يَعْمَلُوْنَ الصّٰلِحٰتِ أَنَّ لَهُمْ أَجْرًا حَسَنًا ٢
مّٰكِثِيْنَ فِيْهِ أَبَدًا ٣ وَّيُنْذِرَ الَّذِيْنَ قَالُوا
اتَّخَذَ اللّٰهُ وَلَدًا ٤ مَا لَهُمْ بِهٖ مِنْ عِلْمٍ
وَّلَا لِاٰبَآئِهِمْ كَبُرَتْ كَلِمَةً تَخْرُجُ مِنْ
أَفْوٰهِهِمْ إِنْ يَّقُوْلُوْنَ إِلَّا كَذِبًا ٥ فَلَعَلَّكَ
بٰخِعٌ نَّفْسَكَ عَلٰٓى اٰثٰرِهِمْ إِنْ لَّمْ يُؤْمِنُوْا بِهٰذَا
الْحَدِيْثِ أَسَفًا ٦ إِنَّا جَعَلْنَا مَا عَلَى الْأَرْضِ
زِيْنَةً لَّهَا لِنَبْلُوَهُمْ أَيُّهُمْ أَحْسَنُ عَمَلًا ٧
وَإِنَّا لَجٰعِلُوْنَ مَا عَلَيْهَا صَعِيْدًا جُرُزًا ٨

9. Do you think that the People of the Place of Refuge and of the Inscriptions were a wonder among Our signs.
10. (Recall the time) when the young men betook themselves to the Place of Refuge and said (in prayer), 'Our Lord! Grant us mercy from Yourself and provide for us right course in our affair (setting all things right for us).'
11. So We sealed up their ears (to cut them off from the outside world) in their Place of Refuge for (only) a number of years.
12. Then We raised them up (for making certain efforts) that We might distinguish as to which of the two groups had made better use of the time they had stayed there according to its rightful requirement.

SECTION 2

13. **W**E relate to you their true story. They were a few young men who believed in their Lord and whom We had led from guidance to guidance.
14. And We strengthened their hearts when they stood up (in the cause of God) and (said), 'Our Lord is the Lord of the heavens and the earth. Never shall we call upon any god apart from Him (for in that case) we would certainly be uttering a preposterous thing far from the truth.
15. 'These people of ours have taken to them (for worship) other gods apart from Him. Why do they not bring any clear proof and authority in support (of their belief). (In fact they have no such proof,) Who can be more unjust than the person who forges a lie against Allâh?'
16. (They said one to another), 'So (now) when you have left them and that which they worship apart from Allâh, you should take shelter in the Place of Refuge. (If you do so) your Lord will extend to you His mercy and will provide some ease for you in (this) affair of yours.'

سُورَةُ الْكَهْفِ ١٨

أَمْ حَسِبْتَ أَنَّ أَصْحٰبَ الْكَهْفِ وَالرَّقِيمِ
كَانُوا مِنْ ءَايٰتِنَا عَجَبًا ﴿٩﴾ إِذْ أَوَى الْفِتْيَةُ إِلَى
الْكَهْفِ فَقَالُوا رَبَّنَا ءَاتِنَا مِنْ لَّدُنْكَ رَحْمَةً
وَّهَيِّئْ لَنَا مِنْ أَمْرِنَا رَشَدًا ﴿١٠﴾ فَضَرَبْنَا عَلَى
ءَاذَانِهِمْ فِي الْكَهْفِ سِنِينَ عَدَدًا ﴿١١﴾ ثُمَّ
بَعَثْنٰهُمْ لِنَعْلَمَ أَيُّ الْحِزْبَيْنِ أَحْصٰى لِمَا
لَبِثُوا أَمَدًا ﴿١٢﴾ نَحْنُ نَقُصُّ عَلَيْكَ نَبَأَهُمْ
بِالْحَقِّ إِنَّهُمْ فِتْيَةٌ ءَامَنُوا بِرَبِّهِمْ
وَزِدْنٰهُمْ هُدًى ﴿١٣﴾ وَرَبَطْنَا عَلَى قُلُوبِهِمْ إِذْ
قَامُوا فَقَالُوا رَبُّنَا رَبُّ السَّمٰوٰتِ وَالْأَرْضِ
لَنْ نَّدْعُوَا مِنْ دُونِهِ إِلٰهًا لَّقَدْ قُلْنَا إِذًا
شَطَطًا ﴿١٤﴾ هٰؤُلَاءِ قَوْمُنَا اتَّخَذُوا مِنْ دُونِهِ
ءَالِهَةً لَوْلَا يَأْتُونَ عَلَيْهِمْ بِسُلْطٰنٍ بَيِّنٍ
فَمَنْ أَظْلَمُ مِمَّنِ افْتَرٰى عَلَى اللهِ كَذِبًا ﴿١٥﴾
وَإِذِ اعْتَزَلْتُمُوهُمْ وَمَا يَعْبُدُونَ إِلَّا اللهَ
فَأْوُا إِلَى الْكَهْفِ يَنْشُرْ لَكُمْ رَبُّكُمْ مِنْ
رَّحْمَتِهِ وَيُهَيِّئْ لَكُمْ مِنْ أَمْرِكُمْ مِرْفَقًا ﴿١٦﴾

ع ٢ ١٣

17. And (O people!) you could see the sun when it rose, inclining to the right of their (spacious) Place of Refuge, and when it set declining to their left, while they were in the open space of this (refuge of theirs); this was one of the signs of Allâh. He alone is rightly guided whom Allâh guides. As for the person whom He forsakes, you will find no helper, no guide, for him.

SECTION 3

18. You might think them wary while they are dormant and asleep. We shall make them turn over (now) to the right and (then) to the left while their dog is (present with them) stretching its paws forward on the threshold in the courtyard. If you had become aware of their (true) state you would have turned back from them in fright and you would have surely been filled with great awe of them.

19. And (just as We made them dormant) We raised them (to life from the state of lethargy). So that they questioned one another. One of them asked, 'How long have you remained (dormant)?' (Some of them) said, 'We have remained (in this state of inactivity) a day or a part of a day.' (Others) said, 'Only your Lord knows best (the time) you have remained so. Now send one of you with these silver coins of yours to the city, he should see which of its (inhabitants) has the best and purest food and let him bring for you provisions from it. And let him be courteous and let him not at all apprise anyone about you.

20. '(For) if they come to know of you they will condemn you or make you revert to their faith (by force) and in that case (that you revert to their faith), you will never attain your goal and prosper ever.'

21. That is how We let (other people) know about them (- their intentions and the real state of their affairs), that people might know that the promise of Allâh is true and that as to the (coming of the promised) hour there is no

وَتَرَى الشَّمْسَ إِذَا طَلَعَت تَّزَٰوَرُ عَنْ
كَهْفِهِمْ ذَاتَ الْيَمِينِ وَإِذَا غَرَبَت تَّقْرِضُهُمْ
ذَاتَ الشِّمَالِ وَهُمْ فِي فَجْوَةٍ مِّنْهُ ذَٰلِكَ
مِنْ ءَايَٰتِ اللَّهِ مَن يَهْدِ اللَّهُ فَهُوَ الْمُهْتَدِ
وَمَن يُضْلِلْ فَلَن تَجِدَ لَهُ وَلِيًّا مُّرْشِدًا ﴿١٧﴾
وَتَحْسَبُهُمْ أَيْقَاظًا وَهُمْ رُقُودٌ وَنُقَلِّبُهُمْ
ذَاتَ الْيَمِينِ وَذَاتَ الشِّمَالِ وَكَلْبُهُم
بَٰسِطٌ ذِرَاعَيْهِ بِالْوَصِيدِ لَوِ اطَّلَعْتَ عَلَيْهِمْ
لَوَلَّيْتَ مِنْهُمْ فِرَارًا وَلَمُلِئْتَ مِنْهُمْ رُعْبًا ﴿١٨﴾
وَكَذَٰلِكَ بَعَثْنَٰهُمْ لِيَتَسَاءَلُوا بَيْنَهُمْ
قَالَ قَائِلٌ مِّنْهُمْ كَمْ لَبِثْتُمْ قَالُوا
لَبِثْنَا يَوْمًا أَوْ بَعْضَ يَوْمٍ قَالُوا رَبُّكُمْ
أَعْلَمُ بِمَا لَبِثْتُمْ فَابْعَثُوا أَحَدَكُم بِوَرِقِكُمْ
هَٰذِهِ إِلَى الْمَدِينَةِ فَلْيَنظُرْ أَيُّهَا أَزْكَىٰ
طَعَامًا فَلْيَأْتِكُم بِرِزْقٍ مِّنْهُ وَلْيَتَلَطَّفْ
وَلَا يُشْعِرَنَّ بِكُمْ أَحَدًا ﴿١٩﴾ إِنَّهُمْ إِن يَظْهَرُوا
عَلَيْكُمْ يَرْجُمُوكُمْ أَوْ يُعِيدُوكُمْ فِي مِلَّتِهِمْ
وَلَن تُفْلِحُوا إِذًا أَبَدًا ﴿٢٠﴾ وَكَذَٰلِكَ أَعْثَرْنَا
عَلَيْهِمْ لِيَعْلَمُوا أَنَّ وَعْدَ اللَّهِ حَقٌّ وَأَنَّ

doubt about it. And (recall the time) when the people (that followed) argued among themselves about their affairs and they said, 'Build a monument over them;' their Lord knows them best. Those (of them) who won their point said, 'We will certainly build a mosque (- place of worship) over them.'

22. Guessing at random (- about them) some say, '(They were) three, their dog being the fourth,' while others say, '(They were) five and their dog being the sixth.' Yet there are others who say, '(They were) seven and their dog being the eighth.' Say, 'My Lord knows best their real number. None knows them except a few.' So do not argue about them save with arguing on known premise (which is) overpowering and seek no legal order concerning them from anyone of them, (from those who make random guesses).

SECTION 4

23. **A**ND never say of anything, 'I am going to do it tomorrow,'

24. Unless (you add to it) 'God willing.' And remember your Lord whenever you forget (and make a mistake) and say, 'I hope my Lord will guide me to a course even shorter than this to the right path (leading to success).

25. And they (- the early Christians) stayed in this Place of Refuge three hundred years and extended (their stay) another nine (years).

26. Say, 'Allâh knows best how long they stayed. To Him belong the hidden realities in the heavens and the earth. How clear He sees and how well He hears! They have no helper beside Him. He lets none associate with Him and share His judgment.

27. And recite (to these people) what is revealed to you of the commandment of your Lord. There is none who can change His words, and you will find no refuge apart from Him.

28. And keep yourself attached to those who call upon their Lord morning and evening, constantly seeking His pleasure, and do not let

الساعة لا ريب فيها إذ يتنازعون
بينهم أمرهم فقالوا ابنوا عليهم بنيانا
ربهم أعلم بهم قال الذين غلبوا على
أمرهم لنتخذن عليهم مسجدا ﴿٢١﴾ سيقولون
ثلاثة رابعهم كلبهم ويقولون خمسة
سادسهم كلبهم رجما بالغيب ويقولون
سبعة وثامنهم كلبهم قل ربي أعلم بعدتهم
ما يعلمهم إلا قليل فلا تمار فيهم إلا مراء
ظاهرا ولا تستفت فيهم منهم أحدا ﴿٢٢﴾ ولا
تقولن لشايء إني فاعل ذلك غدا ﴿٢٣﴾ إلا أن
يشاء الله واذكر ربك إذا نسيت وقل عسى
أن يهدين ربي لأقرب من هذا رشدا ﴿٢٤﴾
ولبثوا في كهفهم ثلث مائة سنين وازدادوا
تسعا ﴿٢٥﴾ قل الله أعلم بما لبثوا له غيب
السموت والأرض أبصر به وأسمع ما
لهم من دونه من ولي ولا يشرك في
حكمه أحدا ﴿٢٦﴾ واتل ما أوحي إليك من
كتاب ربك لا مبدل لكلمته ولن تجد
من دونه ملتحدا ﴿٢٧﴾ واصبر نفسك مع الذين
يدعون ربهم بالغدوة والعشي يريدون

ع ٣ ١٥

your eyes turn away from them to pursue the glamour of the present life and do not follow him whose heart We have declared unmindful of Our remembrance; who follows his evil inclinations, and whose affair exceeds all legitimate limits.

29. And say, 'It is the truth from your Lord, therefore let him who wishes (it) believe (in it) and let him who wishes (otherwise) disbelieve (in it).' (But let everyone remember,) We have prepared for the unjust a fire whose (flaming) enclosure will surround (and fumes envelope) them. If they cry for water, they shall be helped with water (boiling) like molten lead, which will scald their faces. How dreadful the drink and how dismal is (the Fire as) a resting place!

30. But those who believe and do deeds of righteousness (should know that) We surely do not suffer the reward of those who do good deeds to be lost.

31. It is these for whom there await the Gardens of Eternity served with running streams (to keep them green and flourishing). There they shall be adorned with bracelets of gold and wear green robes of fine silk and rich brocade. They will be reclining in these (Gardens) upon raised couches. How excellent the reward! And how beautiful the resting place!

SECTION 5

32. **A**ND relate to these (opponents of yours) the parable (and description of the conditions) of two men. We had provided to one of them two vine-gardens which We fenced with date-palms and We placed cornfields between the two.

33. Each of the two gardens brought forth its fruit (in abundance); failing not the least in them. And We had made a stream to flow (as well) in between the two.

34. Thus he (- the owner) had an abundance of fruit (and substances of diverse kinds). So he

وجهه ولا تعد عيناك عنهم تريد زينة الحيوة
الدنيا ولا تطع من أغفلنا قلبه عن ذكرنا
واتبع هوىه وكان أمره فرطا ﴿٢٨﴾ وقل الحق
من ربكم فمن شاء فليؤمن ومن شاء
فليكفر إنا أعتدنا للظلمين نارا أحاط بهم
سرادقها وإن يستغيثوا يغاثوا بماء كالمهل
يشوي الوجوه بئس الشراب وساءت مرتفقا ﴿٢٩﴾
إن الذين ءامنوا وعملوا الصلحت إنا لا
نضيع أجر من أحسن عملا ﴿٣٠﴾ أولئك لهم
جنت عدن تجري من تحتهم الأنهر يحلون
فيها من أساور من ذهب ويلبسون ثيابا
خضرا من سندس وإستبرق متكئين
فيها على الأرائك نعم الثواب وحسنت
مرتفقا ﴿٣١﴾ واضرب لهم مثلا رجلين جعلنا
لأحدهما جنتين من أعنب وحففنهما
بنخل وجعلنا بينهما زرعا ﴿٣٢﴾ كلتا الجنتين
ءاتت أكلها ولم تظلم منه شيئا وفجرنا
خللهما نهرا ﴿٣٣﴾ وكان له ثمر فقال لصحبه

said to his companion (- the other man) while he was arguing (boastfully and vainly) with him, 'I am richer than you in wealth and mightier in respect of manpower.'

35. And (it so happened that) he entered his garden while he was unjust to his own soul. He said, (to his companion), 'I do not think that this wealth will ever perish.

36. 'And I do not think that the (promised) Hour (of Resurrection) will ever come. But if I am ever made to return to my Lord I will certainly find (there) an even better resort than this.'

37. His companion said to him, while he was arguing with him, 'Do you disbelieve in Him Who created you (first) from dust and then from a sperm drop, then He fashioned you into a (perfect) man.

38. 'But as for myself (I believe that) He, Allâh alone is my Lord, and I will associate none with my Lord.

39. 'And why did you not say when you entered your garden, "(Only) that which Allâh wills (comes to pass)", for power belongs only to Allâh; though you see me inferior to yourself in riches and children,

40. 'There is every hope that my Lord will give me a garden better than yours and He may visit this (garden of yours) with thunderbolts from above, so that it is turned into a barren waste.

41. 'Or its water may be drained (into the earth) so that you will not be able to find it.'

42. Now (it came to pass that) his fruit (and substance) was utterly destroyed and while it (-the vine garden) lay toppled over on its trellises, he began to wring his hands on account of what he had spent on it and said, 'Would that I had associated none with my Lord.'

43. But (then) there was no party left to defend him against Allâh, nor could he defend himself, (for it was Allâh alone Who could help him).

44. At such a time (it is thus established that) protection belongs only to Allâh (and help

وَهُوَ يُحَاوِرُهُۥٓ أَنَا۠ أَكْثَرُ مِنكَ مَالًا وَأَعَزُّ نَفَرًا ﴿٣٤﴾
وَدَخَلَ جَنَّتَهُۥ وَهُوَ ظَالِمٌ لِّنَفْسِهِۦ قَالَ مَآ
أَظُنُّ أَن تَبِيدَ هَٰذِهِۦٓ أَبَدًا ﴿٣٥﴾ وَمَآ أَظُنُّ
ٱلسَّاعَةَ قَآئِمَةً وَلَئِن رُّدِدتُّ إِلَىٰ رَبِّي
لَأَجِدَنَّ خَيْرًا مِّنْهَا مُنقَلَبًا ﴿٣٦﴾ قَالَ لَهُۥ صَاحِبُهُۥ
وَهُوَ يُحَاوِرُهُۥٓ أَكَفَرْتَ بِٱلَّذِي خَلَقَكَ مِن
تُرَابٍ ثُمَّ مِن نُّطْفَةٍ ثُمَّ سَوَّىٰكَ رَجُلًا ﴿٣٧﴾
لَّٰكِنَّا۠ هُوَ ٱللَّهُ رَبِّي وَلَآ أُشْرِكُ بِرَبِّيٓ أَحَدًا ﴿٣٨﴾
وَلَوْلَآ إِذْ دَخَلْتَ جَنَّتَكَ قُلْتَ مَا شَآءَ ٱللَّهُ
لَا قُوَّةَ إِلَّا بِٱللَّهِ إِن تَرَنِ أَنَا۠ أَقَلَّ مِنكَ
مَالًا وَوَلَدًا ﴿٣٩﴾ فَعَسَىٰ رَبِّيٓ أَن يُؤْتِيَنِ خَيْرًا
مِّن جَنَّتِكَ وَيُرْسِلَ عَلَيْهَا حُسْبَانًا مِّنَ
ٱلسَّمَآءِ فَتُصْبِحَ صَعِيدًا زَلَقًا ﴿٤٠﴾ أَوْ يُصْبِحَ
مَآؤُهَا غَوْرًا فَلَن تَسْتَطِيعَ لَهُۥ طَلَبًا ﴿٤١﴾
وَأُحِيطَ بِثَمَرِهِۦ فَأَصْبَحَ يُقَلِّبُ كَفَّيْهِ عَلَىٰ مَآ
أَنفَقَ فِيهَا وَهِيَ خَاوِيَةٌ عَلَىٰ عُرُوشِهَا وَيَقُولُ
يَٰلَيْتَنِي لَمْ أُشْرِكْ بِرَبِّيٓ أَحَدًا ﴿٤٢﴾ وَلَمْ تَكُن
لَّهُۥ فِئَةٌ يَنصُرُونَهُۥ مِن دُونِ ٱللَّهِ وَمَا كَانَ
مُنتَصِرًا ﴿٤٣﴾ هُنَالِكَ ٱلْوَلَٰيَةُ لِلَّهِ ٱلْحَقِّ هُوَ خَيْرٌ

comes from Him alone), the true (God), He is the Best in respect of rewarding and the Best in respect of bringing about good results.

SECTION 6

45. **A**ND give them the similitude of the life of this world. It is like water which We send down from the clouds, so the vegetation and plants of the earth flourish with it. And then it turns into chaff which the winds scatter about. Behold! Allâh is the Holder of all power over what He will.

46. Wealth and children are an adornment of the life of this world. But with regard to (immediate) reward, ever-abiding righteous deeds are the best in the sight of your Lord, they (also) promise the best hope (in respect of the future).

47. And beware of the day when We shall set the mountains in motion and make them vanish and you shall find (the nations of) the earth march forth (against one another), and We shall gather all peoples together and We shall leave none of them behind.

48. And they shall be presented before your Lord ranged in rows, (and it will be said to them,) 'Now certainly you have come to Us (no better than) We created you the first time. But you had thought that We would appoint for you no time for the fulfillment of (Our) promise.'

49. And (on that day) the record (of their deeds) will be exhibited (before them), and you will see those who cut off their ties (with Allâh) fearful as to that which is (recorded) in it. They will say, 'Woe to us! What sort of record is this! It leaves out neither a small thing nor a great one but has recounted everything.' And they will find all they did confronting (them) and your Lord does injustice to no one ever.

SECTION 7

50. **A**ND (recall the time) when We said to the angels, 'Submit to Adam.' So they all submitted (bowing), but *Iblîs* (did not); he was one

ثوابا وخير عقبا ﴿٤٤﴾ واضرب لهم مثل الحيوة
الدنيا كماء أنزلنه من السماء فاختلط به
نبات الأرض فأصبح هشيما تذروه
الريح وكان الله على كل شيء مقتدرا ﴿٤٥﴾
المال والبنون زينة الحيوة الدنيا
والبقيت الصلحت خير عند ربك ثوابا
وخير أملا ﴿٤٦﴾ ويوم نسير الجبال وترى
الأرض بارزة وحشرنهم فلم نغادر منهم
أحدا ﴿٤٧﴾ وعرضوا على ربك صفا لقد
جئتمونا كما خلقنكم أول مرة بل زعمتم
ألن نجعل لكم موعدا ﴿٤٨﴾ ووضع الكتب
فترى المجرمين مشفقين مما فيه
ويقولون يويلتنا مال هذا الكتب لا يغادر
صغيرة ولا كبيرة إلا أحصها ووجدوا
ما عملوا حاضرا ولا يظلم ربك أحدا ﴿٤٩﴾
وإذ قلنا للملئكة اسجدوا لأدم فسجدوا
إلا إبليس كان من الجن ففسق عن أمر

of the *jinn*, he disobeyed the command of his Lord. (People!) Would you (then) take him and his progeny (and cohorts) for friends rather than Me while they are your enemies? How evil is the substitute (of God) the unjust have chosen!

51. I did not call them (- *Iblîs* and his cohorts) to make them witness and to help at (the time of) the creation of the heavens and the earth nor at (the time of) their own creation. I would never take those who lead (others) astray for (My) helpers.

52. And (beware of) the day when He will say, 'Call on My (so called) partners about whom you had many pretensions.' Thereupon they will call on them but they will give them no answer, and We shall make their association with them a (cause of their) perdition.

53. And those who cut off their ties (with Allâh) will see the fire and realize that they are going to fall into it, and they shall find no way of escape from it.

SECTION 8

54. **A**ND We have explained in various ways in this Qur'ân every kind of excellent thing for the good of the people; but of all things human being is the most contentious.

55. Unless the precedence of the ancients should be repeated in their case or the punishment should stare them in the face, there is nothing to hinder people from believing in the guidance when it comes to them and from seeking protection and pardon of their Lord.

56. And We send no Apostles but as Bearers of good tidings (to the obedient on the one hand) and as Warners (to the disobedient on the other). And those who disbelieve contend by means of falsehood that they may refute the truth thereby. And they scoff at My commandments and (the punishment) of which they had been warned.

57. And who is more unjust than he who is reminded of the Messages of his Lord but he

رَبِّهِ ۗ أَفَتَتَّخِذُونَهُ وَذُرِّيَّتَهُ أَوْلِيَاءَ مِنْ
دُونِي وَهُمْ لَكُمْ عَدُوٌّ ۚ بِئْسَ لِلظَّالِمِينَ بَدَلًا ﴿٥٠﴾
مَا أَشْهَدْتُهُمْ خَلْقَ السَّمَاوَاتِ وَالْأَرْضِ وَلَا
خَلْقَ أَنْفُسِهِمْ وَمَا كُنْتُ مُتَّخِذَ الْمُضِلِّينَ
عَضُدًا ﴿٥١﴾ وَيَوْمَ يَقُولُ نَادُوا شُرَكَائِيَ الَّذِينَ
زَعَمْتُمْ فَدَعَوْهُمْ فَلَمْ يَسْتَجِيبُوا لَهُمْ وَجَعَلْنَا
بَيْنَهُمْ مَوْبِقًا ﴿٥٢﴾ وَرَأَى الْمُجْرِمُونَ النَّارَ فَظَنُّوا
أَنَّهُمْ مُوَاقِعُوهَا وَلَمْ يَجِدُوا عَنْهَا مَصْرِفًا ﴿٥٣﴾ ع ١٩
وَلَقَدْ صَرَّفْنَا فِي هَٰذَا الْقُرْآنِ لِلنَّاسِ مِنْ
كُلِّ مَثَلٍ ۚ وَكَانَ الْإِنْسَانُ أَكْثَرَ شَيْءٍ جَدَلًا ﴿٥٤﴾
وَمَا مَنَعَ النَّاسَ أَنْ يُؤْمِنُوا إِذْ جَاءَهُمُ الْهُدَىٰ
وَيَسْتَغْفِرُوا رَبَّهُمْ إِلَّا أَنْ تَأْتِيَهُمْ سُنَّةُ
الْأَوَّلِينَ أَوْ يَأْتِيَهُمُ الْعَذَابُ قُبُلًا ﴿٥٥﴾ وَمَا نُرْسِلُ
الْمُرْسَلِينَ إِلَّا مُبَشِّرِينَ وَمُنْذِرِينَ ۚ وَيُجَادِلُ
الَّذِينَ كَفَرُوا بِالْبَاطِلِ لِيُدْحِضُوا بِهِ الْحَقَّ
وَاتَّخَذُوا آيَاتِي وَمَا أُنْذِرُوا هُزُوًا ﴿٥٦﴾ وَمَنْ أَظْلَمُ
مِمَّنْ ذُكِّرَ بِآيَاتِ رَبِّهِ فَأَعْرَضَ عَنْهَا وَنَسِيَ مَا

turns away from them and forgets what he has forwarded with his own hands (to be stored). In fact We have placed veils upon their hearts which prevent them from understanding it (- the Qur'ân) and in their ears is (created) heaviness (so that they have turned deaf). You call them to the right path as you may they will never follow the right course and accept guidance.

58. Your Lord is All-Protecting, Full of mercy. If He were to take them to task for all that they have done He would certainly have hastened for them the punishment. Yet there is a time appointed for them. They will never find an escape from it.

59. And these are townships (of the people committed to punishment), We destroyed them when they committed inequities and wrong. And We appointed a fixed time for their destruction.

SECTION 9

60. **A**ND (recall the time) when Moses said to his (sincere) young (comrade), 'I will not stop till I reach the confluence of the two rivers (the Niles at Khartoum); even if I must have to go on (journeying) for years.'

61. But when they reached the confluence (where the two rivers met) they forgot (all about) their fish (which they had brought with them) so that it took its way straight into the river burrowing (in to it).

62. And when they had gone further he said to his (sincere) young (comrade), 'Bring us our breakfast; indeed the journey of today has been very tiring for us.'

63. He (- the young comrade) replied, 'Did you see (what happened) when we betook ourselves to the rock for shelter, I forgot (all about) the fish; and none but satan made me forget to mention this (to you) and behold! it made its way into the river. What a wonder (that I should thus forget)!

64. (Moses) said, 'That is (the place) which we have been seeking.' So both of them

قدمت يداه إنا جعلنا على قلوبهم أكنة
أن يفقهوه وفي آذانهم وقرا وإن تدعهم
إلى الهدى فلن يهتدوا إذا أبدا ٥٧ وربك
الغفور ذو الرحمة لو يؤاخذهم بما كسبوا
لعجل لهم العذاب بل لهم موعد لن يجدوا
من دونه موئلا ٥٨ وتلك القرى أهلكناهم
لما ظلموا وجعلنا لمهلكهم موعدا ٥٩ وإذ
قال موسى لفتاه لا أبرح حتى أبلغ مجمع
البحرين أو أمضي حقبا ٦٠ فلما بلغا مجمع
بينهما نسيا حوتهما فاتخذ سبيله في البحر
سربا ٦١ فلما جاوزا قال لفتاه آتنا غداءنا
لقد لقينا من سفرنا هذا نصبا ٦٢ قال
أرأيت إذ أوينا إلى الصخرة فإني نسيت
الحوت وما أنسانيه إلا الشيطان أن
أذكره واتخذ سبيله في البحر عجبا ٦٣
قال ذلك ما كنا نبغ فارتدا على

ع

returned retracing their steps.

65. So that they found a (noble and great) servant of Ours to whom We had granted mercy from Us and whom We had taught (great) Knowledge from Ourself.

66. Moses said to him, 'May I follow you so that you may teach me (some of) the ways of rectitude which you have been taught?'

67. He (- the great man) said, '(Yes, but) while keeping company with me you will never be able to bear (and keep company) with me in patience,

68. 'And how can you have patience about things the knowledge of which you do not comprehend.'

69. (Moses) said, 'You will find me patient, God willing, and I shall not disobey you in any matter.'

70. He (- the great man) said, 'Well, if you would follow me, (mind that) you shall ask me no question about anything unless I myself broach the subject to you.'

SECTION 10

71. **S**o both of them set out until when they embarked in a boat he scuttled it. (Thereupon Moses) said, 'Have you scuttled it that you may drown (its) occupants? It is indeed a strangely grievous thing you have done.'

72. He replied, 'Did I not say that you would not be able to bear with me (and keep company with me patiently).'

73. (Moses) said, 'Do not take me to task for what I forgot; do not be too hard on me for this lapse of mine.'

74. Then they both set out again till when they met a boy, he (- the great man) slew him. (At this Moses) said, 'Why have you slain an innocent person without (his having slain) any one. Most certainly, it is a strangely wondrous act you have committed.'

أَثَارِهِمَا قَصَصًا ﴿٦٤﴾ فَوَجَدَا عَبْدًا مِّنْ عِبَادِنَا
آتَيْنَاهُ رَحْمَةً مِّنْ عِنْدِنَا وَعَلَّمْنَاهُ مِن
لَّدُنَّا عِلْمًا ﴿٦٥﴾ قَالَ لَهُ مُوسَى هَلْ أَتَّبِعُكَ عَلَى
أَن تُعَلِّمَنِ مِمَّا عُلِّمْتَ رُشْدًا ﴿٦٦﴾ قَالَ إِنَّكَ
لَن تَسْتَطِيعَ مَعِيَ صَبْرًا ﴿٦٧﴾ وَكَيْفَ تَصْبِرُ
عَلَى مَا لَمْ تُحِطْ بِهِ خُبْرًا ﴿٦٨﴾ قَالَ سَتَجِدُنِي
إِن شَاءَ اللهُ صَابِرًا وَلَا أَعْصِي لَكَ أَمْرًا ﴿٦٩﴾
قَالَ فَإِنِ اتَّبَعْتَنِي فَلَا تَسْأَلْنِي عَن
شَيْءٍ حَتَّى أُحْدِثَ لَكَ مِنْهُ ذِكْرًا ﴿٧٠﴾
فَانْطَلَقَا حَتَّى إِذَا رَكِبَا فِي السَّفِينَةِ
خَرَقَهَا قَالَ أَخَرَقْتَهَا لِتُغْرِقَ أَهْلَهَا
لَقَدْ جِئْتَ شَيْئًا إِمْرًا ﴿٧١﴾ قَالَ أَلَمْ أَقُلْ
إِنَّكَ لَن تَسْتَطِيعَ مَعِيَ صَبْرًا ﴿٧٢﴾ قَالَ
لَا تُؤَاخِذْنِي بِمَا نَسِيتُ وَلَا تُرْهِقْنِي
مِنْ أَمْرِي عُسْرًا ﴿٧٣﴾ فَانْطَلَقَا حَتَّى إِذَا
لَقِيَا غُلَامًا فَقَتَلَهُ قَالَ أَقَتَلْتَ نَفْسًا
زَكِيَّةً بِغَيْرِ نَفْسٍ لَقَدْ جِئْتَ شَيْئًا نُكْرًا ﴿٧٤﴾

PART الجزء السادس عشر XVI

سورة الكهف ١٨

75. **H**E (- the great divine being) said, 'Did I not tell you that you would not certainly be able to bear with me patiently?'

76. (Moses) said, 'If I question you about anything after this keep me in your company no more, for (in that case) you shall have reached the extent of being excused by me (- I shall have no excuse to offer).'

77. So both of them again set out till when they came upon the inhabitants of a town they asked them for food, but they refused to entertain them as guests. Then they found therein (- the town) a wall which was on the point of falling down and he (- the divine being) repaired it. (Moses) said, 'If you had wanted, you could have charged for it.'

78. (The divine being thereupon) said, 'This is the parting (of the ways) between me and you. Now I shall tell you the significance of that with which you could not have patience:

79. 'As for the boat it belonged to (certain) poor people who worked on the river, and in their rear there was a (brutal) king who seized every (good) boat by force, so I chose to damage it (the boat).

80. 'And as for the boy, his parents were believers and we feared that he should involve them in trouble through transgression and disbelief,

81. 'So we desired that their Lord should give them in his place (a child) superior to him in virtue and purity and more regardful to attend to the right of relationships.

82. 'As for the wall it belonged to two orphan boys of the town and under this (wall there) was a treasure belonging to them and their father had been a righteous man. So your Lord desired that they should attain their (age of) full strength and then take out their treasure; a mercy from your Lord, and I did not do it of my own accord, (whatever I did was the will of the Lord). This is the significance of that which

قَالَ أَلَمْ أَقُل لَّكَ إِنَّكَ لَن تَسْتَطِيعَ
مَعِيَ صَبْرًا ﴿٧٥﴾ قَالَ إِن سَأَلْتُكَ عَن شَيْءٍ
بَعْدَهَا فَلَا تُصَاحِبْنِي قَدْ بَلَغْتَ مِن لَّدُنِّي
عُذْرًا ﴿٧٦﴾ فَانطَلَقَا حَتَّىٰ إِذَا أَتَيَا أَهْلَ قَرْيَةٍ
اسْتَطْعَمَا أَهْلَهَا فَأَبَوْا أَن يُضَيِّفُوهُمَا فَوَجَدَا
فِيهَا جِدَارًا يُرِيدُ أَن يَنقَضَّ فَأَقَامَهُ قَالَ
لَوْ شِئْتَ لَتَّخَذْتَ عَلَيْهِ أَجْرًا ﴿٧٧﴾ قَالَ هَٰذَا
فِرَاقُ بَيْنِي وَبَيْنِكَ سَأُنَبِّئُكَ بِتَأْوِيلِ
مَا لَمْ تَسْتَطِع عَّلَيْهِ صَبْرًا ﴿٧٨﴾ أَمَّا السَّفِينَةُ
فَكَانَتْ لِمَسَاكِينَ يَعْمَلُونَ فِي الْبَحْرِ فَأَرَدتُّ
أَنْ أَعِيبَهَا وَكَانَ وَرَاءَهُم مَّلِكٌ يَأْخُذُ كُلَّ
سَفِينَةٍ غَصْبًا ﴿٧٩﴾ وَأَمَّا الْغُلَامُ فَكَانَ أَبَوَاهُ
مُؤْمِنَيْنِ فَخَشِينَا أَن يُرْهِقَهُمَا طُغْيَانًا
وَكُفْرًا ﴿٨٠﴾ فَأَرَدْنَا أَن يُبْدِلَهُمَا رَبُّهُمَا خَيْرًا مِّنْهُ
زَكَاةً وَأَقْرَبَ رُحْمًا ﴿٨١﴾ وَأَمَّا الْجِدَارُ فَكَانَ
لِغُلَامَيْنِ يَتِيمَيْنِ فِي الْمَدِينَةِ وَكَانَ تَحْتَهُ
كَنزٌ لَّهُمَا وَكَانَ أَبُوهُمَا صَالِحًا فَأَرَادَ رَبُّكَ
أَن يَبْلُغَا أَشُدَّهُمَا وَيَسْتَخْرِجَا كَنزَهُمَا
رَحْمَةً مِّن رَّبِّكَ وَمَا فَعَلْتُهُ عَنْ أَمْرِي

الجزء السادس عشر

you were not able to bear with patience.'

SECTION 11

83. AND they ask you about Dhul-Qarnain (- Cyrus of Persia). Say, 'I will just recite to you (in the word of Lord) some of his account,'
84. Verily, We granted him authority on the earth, (his empire extended from Persia to the Black Sea on one side and from Asia Minor to Afghanistan and Baluchistan on the other) and provided him with all sorts of means.
85. Then (it so happened that) he launched out on a (particular) course (to the western part of his empire).
86. So that when he reached (the land of) the setting of the sun, (the western most part of his empire,) he found it (- the sun) disappearing (as if) in a vast muddy pool of murky water (- the Black Sea), and close to it he found a certain people. We said, 'Dhul-Qarnain! you may either punish (them) or treat them with kindness. (They being at your disposal.)'
87. He said, '(Well) as for him who transgresses and does wrong we shall certainly punish him, then will he be produced before his Lord Who will inflict upon him a dreadful punishment.
88. 'But as for him who submits and believes and acts righteously, there is for him a handsome reward (with his Lord) and we shall speak to him easy (words) of our command (dealing indulgently with him).'
89. Then he launched out on (another) course (to the eastern part of his empire).
90. So that when he reached the land of the rising of the sun (- eastern most point of his empire) he found it rising on a people for whom We had provided no shelter against it (- the sun).
91. That is how (it was). As for him, We alone had full knowledge of all that he had with him.
92. Then he launched out on (yet another)

ع ١٢

ذٰلِكَ تَأْوِيلُ مَا لَمْ تَسْطِع عَّلَيْهِ صَبْرًا ﴿٨٢﴾
وَيَسْـَٔلُونَكَ عَنْ ذِي الْقَرْنَيْنِ قُلْ سَأَتْلُوا
عَلَيْكُم مِّنْهُ ذِكْرًا ﴿٨٣﴾ إِنَّا مَكَّنَّا لَهُۥ فِي الْأَرْضِ
وَأٰتَيْنٰهُ مِنْ كُلِّ شَيْءٍ سَبَبًا ﴿٨٤﴾ فَأَتْبَعَ سَبَبًا ﴿٨٥﴾
حَتّٰى إِذَا بَلَغَ مَغْرِبَ الشَّمْسِ وَجَدَهَا تَغْرُبُ
فِي عَيْنٍ حَمِئَةٍ وَّوَجَدَ عِنْدَهَا قَوْمًا قُلْنَا يٰذَا
الْقَرْنَيْنِ إِمَّآ أَنْ تُعَذِّبَ وَ إِمَّآ أَنْ تَتَّخِذَ
فِيهِمْ حُسْنًا ﴿٨٦﴾ قَالَ أَمَّا مَنْ ظَلَمَ فَسَوْفَ
نُعَذِّبُهُۥ ثُمَّ يُرَدُّ إِلٰى رَبِّهِۦ فَيُعَذِّبُهُۥ عَذَابًا
نُّكْرًا ﴿٨٧﴾ وَ أَمَّا مَنْ أٰمَنَ وَعَمِلَ صٰلِحًا فَلَهُۥ
جَزَآءً الْحُسْنٰى وَسَنَقُولُ لَهُۥ مِنْ أَمْرِنَا
يُسْرًا ﴿٨٨﴾ ثُمَّ أَتْبَعَ سَبَبًا ﴿٨٩﴾ حَتّٰى إِذَا بَلَغَ
مَطْلِعَ الشَّمْسِ وَجَدَهَا تَطْلُعُ عَلٰى قَوْمٍ لَّمْ
نَجْعَل لَّهُم مِّنْ دُونِهَا سِتْرًا ﴿٩٠﴾ كَذٰلِكَ
وَقَدْ أَحَطْنَا بِمَا لَدَيْهِ خُبْرًا ﴿٩١﴾ ثُمَّ أَتْبَعَ

course (to the northern part of his empire, - to the territory between the Caspian Sea and the Caucasian Mountains).

93. So that when he reached a place (- Derbent) between two barriers (on one side the Caspian Sea and on the other the Caucasian mountains) he found in their vicinity a people who could hardly understand speech (in his Persian language).

94. They said, 'Dhul-Qarnain! Gog and Magog (-respectively the ancestors of the present Teutonic and Slavonic races) are playing havoc in this country. Shall we pay you tribute on condition that you set up a barrier between us and them?'

95. He said, 'The power which my Lord has endowed me with about this is better (than this your tribute), you (only) help me with (your resources and human endeavour of physical) strength. I will raise a rampart between you and them.'

96. (Then he said,) 'Bring me ingots of iron.' (So that when all was provided for and) he had filled the space between the two barriers, he said, 'Now blow (with your bellows).' (They blew) till when he had made it (- the ignots red hot as) fire, he said, 'Bring me molten copper that I may pour (it) thereon.'

97. So (there was built the rampart which) they (- Gog and Magog) could neither scale nor they had the strength to cause a breach through it.

98. He said (thereupon), 'This (rampart signifies) a great mercy of my Lord. But when the promise of my Lord (about the spread of the tentacles of Gog and Magog all over the world) shall come to pass, He will raise it to the ground (crumbling it to pieces), and the promise of my Lord is certainly true.'

99. And We shall leave them (- Gog and Magog) alone at that time surging as waves (in furious attacks) one over another. And the trumpet shall be blown. Then shall We gather

سَبَبًا ﴿٩٢﴾ حَتّٰىٓ إِذَا بَلَغَ بَيْنَ السَّدَّيْنِ وَجَدَ
مِنْ دُوْنِهِمَا قَوْمًا لَّا يَكَادُوْنَ يَفْقَهُوْنَ
قَوْلًا ﴿٩٣﴾ قَالُوْا يٰذَا الْقَرْنَيْنِ إِنَّ يَأْجُوْجَ
وَمَأْجُوْجَ مُفْسِدُوْنَ فِي الْأَرْضِ فَهَلْ نَجْعَلُ
لَكَ خَرْجًا عَلٰٓى أَنْ تَجْعَلَ بَيْنَنَا وَبَيْنَهُمْ
سَدًّا ﴿٩٤﴾ قَالَ مَا مَكَّنِّيْ فِيْهِ رَبِّيْ خَيْرٌ
فَأَعِيْنُوْنِيْ بِقُوَّةٍ أَجْعَلْ بَيْنَكُمْ وَبَيْنَهُمْ
رَدْمًا ﴿٩٥﴾ اٰتُوْنِيْ زُبَرَ الْحَدِيْدِ حَتّٰىٓ إِذَا سَاوٰى
بَيْنَ الصَّدَفَيْنِ قَالَ انْفُخُوْا حَتّٰىٓ إِذَا جَعَلَهٗ
نَارًا قَالَ اٰتُوْنِيْٓ أُفْرِغْ عَلَيْهِ قِطْرًا ﴿٩٦﴾ فَمَا
اسْطَاعُوْٓا أَنْ يَّظْهَرُوْهُ وَمَا اسْتَطَاعُوْا لَهٗ نَقْبًا ﴿٩٧﴾
قَالَ هٰذَا رَحْمَةٌ مِّنْ رَّبِّيْ فَإِذَا جَآءَ وَعْدُ
رَبِّيْ جَعَلَهٗ دَكَّآءَ وَكَانَ وَعْدُ رَبِّيْ حَقًّا ﴿٩٨﴾
وَتَرَكْنَا بَعْضَهُمْ يَوْمَئِذٍ يَّمُوْجُ فِيْ بَعْضٍ

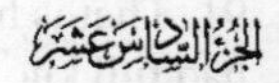

them all together.

100. And We shall (in a way) present hell on that day, face to face to the disbelievers,

101. Those (of them) whose eyes were under a cover (not heeding) My Reminder, and they could not even afford to hear (to the voice of truth).

SECTION 12

102. **D**o those disbelievers think, even then, that they can take My servants as patrons to My exclusion? (Let them know) surely We have prepared Gehenna for the disbelievers as an entertainment.

103. Say, 'Shall We inform you of those whose deeds shall spell their utter loss?'

104. (They are) those whose efforts are (all) lost in (pursuit of things relating to) the life of this world, yet they think they are doing works of good manufacturing.

105. It is these who disbelieve in and deny the Messages of Allâh and the meeting with Him. So their deeds have gone vain, and on the Day of Resurrection We shall assign them no weight.

106. That is their recompense, Gehenna, because they disbelieved and they looked down upon My signs and My Messengers.

107. Those who believe and do deeds of righteousness, will have Gardens of Paradise for an entertainment and an abode;

108. Wherein they shall abide for ever, having no desire to be removed from there.

109. Say, 'If every ocean became ink for (recording) the words and creation of my Lord, surely, the oceans would be spent up before the words and creation of my Lord came to an end, even if we brought to add (therewith) as many more (oceans).

110. Say, 'I am but a human being like you. It has been revealed to me that your God is only One God. So let him who hopes to meet his Lord do deeds of righteousness and let him associate no one in the worship of his Lord.

وَنُفِخَ فِي الصُّوْرِ فَجَمَعْنٰهُمْ جَمْعًا ﴿٩٩﴾ وَّعَرَضْنَا
جَهَنَّمَ يَوْمَئِذٍ لِّلْكٰفِرِيْنَ عَرْضًا ﴿١٠٠﴾ الَّذِيْنَ
كَانَتْ أَعْيُنُهُمْ فِيْ غِطَآءٍ عَنْ ذِكْرِيْ
وَكَانُوْا لَا يَسْتَطِيْعُوْنَ سَمْعًا ﴿١٠١﴾ أَفَحَسِبَ الَّذِيْنَ
كَفَرُوْٓا أَنْ يَّتَّخِذُوْا عِبَادِيْ مِنْ دُوْنِيْٓ أَوْلِيَآءَ
إِنَّآ أَعْتَدْنَا جَهَنَّمَ لِلْكٰفِرِيْنَ نُزُلًا ﴿١٠٢﴾ قُلْ
هَلْ نُنَبِّئُكُمْ بِالْأَخْسَرِيْنَ أَعْمَالًا ﴿١٠٣﴾ أَلَّذِيْنَ
ضَلَّ سَعْيُهُمْ فِي الْحَيٰوةِ الدُّنْيَا وَهُمْ
يَحْسَبُوْنَ أَنَّهُمْ يُحْسِنُوْنَ صُنْعًا ﴿١٠٤﴾ أُولٰٓئِكَ
الَّذِيْنَ كَفَرُوْا بِاٰيٰتِ رَبِّهِمْ وَلِقَآئِهٖ فَحَبِطَتْ
أَعْمٰلُهُمْ فَلَا نُقِيْمُ لَهُمْ يَوْمَ الْقِيٰمَةِ وَزْنًا ﴿١٠٥﴾
ذٰلِكَ جَزَآؤُهُمْ جَهَنَّمُ بِمَا كَفَرُوْا وَاتَّخَذُوْٓا
اٰيٰتِيْ وَرُسُلِيْ هُزُوًا ﴿١٠٦﴾ إِنَّ الَّذِيْنَ اٰمَنُوْا
وَعَمِلُوا الصّٰلِحٰتِ كَانَتْ لَهُمْ جَنّٰتُ الْفِرْدَوْسِ
نُزُلًا ﴿١٠٧﴾ خٰلِدِيْنَ فِيْهَا لَا يَبْغُوْنَ عَنْهَا حِوَلًا ﴿١٠٨﴾
قُلْ لَّوْ كَانَ الْبَحْرُ مِدَادًا لِّكَلِمٰتِ رَبِّيْ
لَنَفِدَ الْبَحْرُ قَبْلَ أَنْ تَنْفَدَ كَلِمٰتُ رَبِّيْ
وَلَوْ جِئْنَا بِمِثْلِهٖ مَدَدًا ﴿١٠٩﴾ قُلْ إِنَّمَآ أَنَا
بَشَرٌ مِّثْلُكُمْ يُوْحٰٓى إِلَيَّ أَنَّمَآ إِلٰهُكُمْ إِلٰهٌ وَّاحِدٌ
فَمَنْ كَانَ يَرْجُوْا لِقَآءَ رَبِّهٖ فَلْيَعْمَلْ عَمَلًا
صٰلِحًا وَّلَا يُشْرِكْ بِعِبَادَةِ رَبِّهٖٓ أَحَدًا ﴿١١٠﴾

CHAPTER
19

سُورَةُ مَرۡيَمَ ١٩

MARYAM
(Mary)
(Revealed before Hijrah)

سُوۡرَةُ مَرۡيَمَ مَكِّيَّةٌ

With the name of Allâh,
the Most Gracious, the Ever Merciful
(I commence to read Sûrah Maryam).

بِسۡمِ اللّٰهِ الرَّحۡمٰنِ الرَّحِيۡمِ

1. KÂF HÂ YÂ 'AIN SÂD - Allâh is sufficient for all, and He is the True Guide, Bestower of mercy and security and blessings, the All-Knowing, the Supermost, Truthful.
2. (This is) an account of the mercy of your Lord (shown) to His servant Zachariah,
3. When he called upon his God, crying aloud (in humble supplication).
4. He said (praying), 'My Lord! now the very bones within me have waxed feeble and the hair of (my) head are all gray and hoary, my Lord! never have I been (hitherto) deprived of a favourable response to my prayer to You.
5. 'I fear (for the unrighteousness of) my kinsfolk after me, and my wife is barren. Grant me by Your (special) grace a (pious and righteous) successor,
6. 'Who may be an heir to me and inherit (the divine blessings promised to) the House of Jacob and make him, my Lord! well-pleasing (to You).'
7. (God accepted his prayer and said,) 'Zachariah! We give you the glad tidings of (the birth of) a son, named Yahyâ (- John, - who will live long). We have made none like him (in your house) before this.'
8. He (- Zachariah) said, 'My Lord! how shall I beget a son when my wife is barren and I have

كٓهٰيٰعٓصٓ ① ذِكۡرُ رَحۡمَتِ رَبِّكَ عَبۡدَهٗ
زَكَرِيَّآ ② إِذۡ نَادٰى رَبَّهٗ نِدَآءً خَفِيًّا ③ قَالَ
رَبِّ إِنِّيۡ وَهَنَ الۡعَظۡمُ مِنِّيۡ وَاشۡتَعَلَ الرَّأۡسُ
شَيۡبًا وَّلَمۡ أَكُنۡۢ بِدُعَآئِكَ رَبِّ شَقِيًّا ④
وَإِنِّيۡ خِفۡتُ الۡمَوَالِيَ مِنۡ وَّرَآءِيۡ وَكَانَتِ
امۡرَأَتِيۡ عَاقِرًا فَهَبۡ لِيۡ مِنۡ لَّدُنۡكَ وَلِيًّا ⑤
يَّرِثُنِيۡ وَيَرِثُ مِنۡ اٰلِ يَعۡقُوۡبَ ۖ وَاجۡعَلۡهُ
رَبِّ رَضِيًّا ⑥ يٰزَكَرِيَّآ إِنَّا نُبَشِّرُكَ بِغُلٰمِۣ
اسۡمُهٗ يَحۡيٰى ۙ لَمۡ نَجۡعَلۡ لَّهٗ مِنۡ قَبۡلُ سَمِيًّا ⑦
قَالَ رَبِّ أَنّٰى يَكُوۡنُ لِيۡ غُلٰمٌ وَّكَانَتِ امۡرَأَتِيۡ

(already) reached the extreme (limit of) old age?'
9. (The Lord) said, 'So shall it be,' and (the angel bearing the revelation) said, 'Your Lord says, "It is easy for Me, and behold, I have created you before this whereas you (too) were nothing".'
10. He (- Zachariah) said, 'My Lord! appoint for me a commandment.' (The Lord) said, 'The commandment for you is that you shall not speak to people for three successive (days and) nights, being in sound health.
11. Then he (- Zachariah) went forth to his people from the Sanctuary and told them in a low voice and by signs, to glorify (their Lord) morning and evening.
12. (We said to John,) 'Yahyâ! hold fast the (divine) Book.' And while he was yet a child We gave him wisdom,
13. And tenderheartedness and purity by Our (special) grace. He was one who carefully guarded against evil.
14. And (he was) dutiful towards his parents and he was neither arrogant nor rebellious.
15. Blessed was he the day he was born and the day he died and (peace will be upon him) the day he will be raised to life (again).

SECTION 2

16. **A**ND give an account of Mary in this Book when she withdrew from her people to an eastern spacious place (of the temple).
17. Then she screened herself off from them. Then We sent to her Our (angel of) revelation and he presented himself to her in the form of a perfect and well-proportioned man.
18. Mary said, 'I invoke the Most Gracious (God) to defend me from you. If you guard the least against evil (leave me alone).'
19. He said, 'I am but a messenger of your

عَاقِرًا وَّقَدْ بَلَغْتُ مِنَ الْكِبَرِ عِتِيًّا ﴿٨﴾ قَالَ
كَذٰلِكَ قَالَ رَبُّكَ هُوَ عَلَيَّ هَيِّنٌ وَّقَدْ
خَلَقْتُكَ مِنْ قَبْلُ وَلَمْ تَكُ شَيْـًٔا ﴿٩﴾ قَالَ
رَبِّ اجْعَلْ لِّيْٓ اٰيَةً قَالَ اٰيَتُكَ اَلَّا تُكَلِّمَ
النَّاسَ ثَلٰثَ لَيَالٍ سَوِيًّا ﴿١٠﴾ فَخَرَجَ عَلٰى قَوْمِهٖ
مِنَ الْمِحْرَابِ فَاَوْحٰٓى اِلَيْهِمْ اَنْ سَبِّحُوْا
بُكْرَةً وَّعَشِيًّا ﴿١١﴾ يٰيَحْيٰى خُذِ الْكِتٰبَ بِقُوَّةٍ
وَاٰتَيْنٰهُ الْحُكْمَ صَبِيًّا ﴿١٢﴾ وَّحَنَانًا مِّنْ لَّدُنَّا
وَزَكٰوةً وَكَانَ تَقِيًّا ﴿١٣﴾ وَّبَرًّا بِوَالِدَيْهِ وَلَمْ
يَكُنْ جَبَّارًا عَصِيًّا ﴿١٤﴾ وَسَلٰمٌ عَلَيْهِ يَوْمَ وُلِدَ
وَيَوْمَ يَمُوْتُ وَيَوْمَ يُبْعَثُ حَيًّا ﴿١٥﴾ وَاذْكُرْ ع
فِي الْكِتٰبِ مَرْيَمَ اِذِ انْتَبَذَتْ مِنْ اَهْلِهَا
مَكَانًا شَرْقِيًّا ﴿١٦﴾ فَاتَّخَذَتْ مِنْ دُوْنِهِمْ
حِجَابًا فَاَرْسَلْنَآ اِلَيْهَا رُوْحَنَا فَتَمَثَّلَ لَهَا
بَشَرًا سَوِيًّا ﴿١٧﴾ قَالَتْ اِنِّيْٓ اَعُوْذُ بِالرَّحْمٰنِ
مِنْكَ اِنْ كُنْتَ تَقِيًّا ﴿١٨﴾ قَالَ اِنَّمَآ اَنَا رَسُوْلُ

Lord. I give you (glad tidings of) a most pure son.'

20. She said, 'How can I bear a son while no man (has married me and) has yet touched me, nor have I been unchaste.'

21. (The angel) said, 'So the fact is (just as you describe). Your Lord has said, "It is easy for Me. (We shall do it) so that We make him a sign and a (source of) blessing from Us for the people. It is a matter ordained".'

22. She (- Mary) conceived him (- the child) and withdrew with him to a remote place.

23. (At the time of the delivery of the child) the throes of child birth drove her to the trunk of the palm-tree. She said, 'Oh! would that I had become unconscious before this and had become a thing gone and forgotten.'

24. Then a voice called her from the side of the slope by her (saying), 'Do not grieve, your Lord has placed a rivulet on the side of the slope by you (and a chief of the nation has been born to you).

25. 'Shake the branch of the palm-tree, drawing it towards you, it will cause fresh and ripe dates to fall upon you.

26. 'Eat therefore and drink and be happy. Then if you see any human being tell (him), "I have vowed a fast to the Gracious God so I will not speak to any human being today".'

27. (When Jesus grew up) she took him to her people carrying him on a mount. They said, 'Mary! you have brought a strange thing.

28. 'O sister of Aaron! your father was not a bad man, nor was your mother unchaste.'

29. Thereupon she pointed to him (- her son Jesus meaning thereby that he will answer them). They said, 'How should we speak to one who was (till recently) a child in the cradle?'

30. (It came to pass that the son of Mary) said, 'I am indeed a servant of Allâh, He has given me the Book, and made me a Prophet.

31. 'And He has made me blessed wherever I

سُورَةُ مَرْيَمَ ١٩

رَبِّكِ ۖ لِأَهَبَ لَكِ غُلَامًا زَكِيًّا ﴿١٩﴾ قَالَتْ أَنَّىٰ
يَكُونُ لِي غُلَامٌ وَلَمْ يَمْسَسْنِي بَشَرٌ وَلَمْ
أَكُ بَغِيًّا ﴿٢٠﴾ قَالَ كَذَٰلِكِ قَالَ رَبُّكِ هُوَ عَلَيَّ
هَيِّنٌ ۖ وَلِنَجْعَلَهُ آيَةً لِّلنَّاسِ وَرَحْمَةً مِّنَّا ۚ
وَكَانَ أَمْرًا مَّقْضِيًّا ﴿٢١﴾ فَحَمَلَتْهُ فَانتَبَذَتْ
بِهِ مَكَانًا قَصِيًّا ﴿٢٢﴾ فَأَجَاءَهَا الْمَخَاضُ إِلَىٰ
جِذْعِ النَّخْلَةِ قَالَتْ يَا لَيْتَنِي مِتُّ قَبْلَ
هَٰذَا وَكُنتُ نَسْيًا مَّنسِيًّا ﴿٢٣﴾ فَنَادَاهَا مِن
تَحْتِهَا أَلَّا تَحْزَنِي قَدْ جَعَلَ رَبُّكِ تَحْتَكِ
سَرِيًّا ﴿٢٤﴾ وَهُزِّي إِلَيْكِ بِجِذْعِ النَّخْلَةِ تُسَاقِطْ
عَلَيْكِ رُطَبًا جَنِيًّا ﴿٢٥﴾ فَكُلِي وَاشْرَبِي وَقَرِّي
عَيْنًا ۖ فَإِمَّا تَرَيِنَّ مِنَ الْبَشَرِ أَحَدًا فَقُولِي
إِنِّي نَذَرْتُ لِلرَّحْمَٰنِ صَوْمًا فَلَنْ أُكَلِّمَ
الْيَوْمَ إِنسِيًّا ﴿٢٦﴾ فَأَتَتْ بِهِ قَوْمَهَا تَحْمِلُهُ ۖ
قَالُوا يَا مَرْيَمُ لَقَدْ جِئْتِ شَيْئًا فَرِيًّا ﴿٢٧﴾ يَا أُخْتَ
هَارُونَ مَا كَانَ أَبُوكِ امْرَأَ سَوْءٍ وَمَا كَانَتْ
أُمُّكِ بَغِيًّا ﴿٢٨﴾ فَأَشَارَتْ إِلَيْهِ ۖ قَالُوا كَيْفَ
نُكَلِّمُ مَن كَانَ فِي الْمَهْدِ صَبِيًّا ﴿٢٩﴾ قَالَ إِنِّي
عَبْدُ اللَّهِ آتَانِيَ الْكِتَابَ وَجَعَلَنِي نَبِيًّا ﴿٣٠﴾
وَجَعَلَنِي مُبَارَكًا أَيْنَ مَا كُنتُ وَأَوْصَانِي

may be, and He has enjoined upon me prayer and alms-giving so long as I live.
32. 'And (He has made me) dutiful to my mother, and He has not made me arrogant, graceless.
33. 'And peace was upon me the day I was born, and (peace will be upon me) the day I die, and the day I shall be raised up to life (again).'
34. Such was Jesus, son of Mary. (This is) a statement of true facts (about him), concerning which they so deeply disagree.
35. It does not behove (the Majesty of) Allâh to take to Himself a son. Holy is He. When He decrees a matter He only commands it 'Be' and it comes to be.
36. (Jesus said), 'Surely, Allâh is my Lord and your Lord. So worship Him (alone). This is the exact right path.'
37. Yet the various sects were divided among themselves. Woe shall befall those who deny the meeting of the great day.
38. How clear they will hear and how well they will see on the day they come to Us. But this day the unjust are steeped in manifest error.
39. Warn them of the day of intense regret when the matter is decided and it is all over, and they are (still) steeped in ignorance and negligence and they do not believe.
40. It is We Who will remain after the earth and (all) who are inhabiting it have perished. To Us shall they all be returned.

SECTION 3

41. **G**IVE an account of Abraham in this Book. Surely, he was a very truthful man, a Prophet.
42. Behold! he said to his sire, 'My dear sire, why do you worship that which can neither hear, nor see, nor can be of any avail to you?
43. 'My dear sire, indeed I have been given the sort of knowledge which has not been given to you, so follow me, I will guide you along the straight path.

بِالصَّلٰوةِ وَالزَّكٰوةِ مَا دُمْتُ حَيًّا ﴿٣١﴾ وَّبَرًّا
بِوَالِدَتِيْ وَلَمْ يَجْعَلْنِيْ جَبَّارًا شَقِيًّا ﴿٣٢﴾ وَالسَّلٰمُ
عَلَيَّ يَوْمَ وُلِدْتُّ وَيَوْمَ أَمُوْتُ وَيَوْمَ أُبْعَثُ
حَيًّا ﴿٣٣﴾ ذٰلِكَ عِيْسَى ابْنُ مَرْيَمَ قَوْلَ الْحَقِّ
الَّذِيْ فِيْهِ يَمْتَرُوْنَ ﴿٣٤﴾ مَا كَانَ لِلّٰهِ أَنْ يَّتَّخِذَ
مِنْ وَّلَدٍ سُبْحٰنَهٗ إِذَا قَضٰى أَمْرًا فَإِنَّمَا يَقُوْلُ
لَهٗ كُنْ فَيَكُوْنُ ﴿٣٥﴾ وَإِنَّ اللّٰهَ رَبِّيْ وَرَبُّكُمْ
فَاعْبُدُوْهُ هٰذَا صِرٰطٌ مُّسْتَقِيْمٌ ﴿٣٦﴾ فَاخْتَلَفَ
الْأَحْزَابُ مِنْ بَيْنِهِمْ فَوَيْلٌ لِّلَّذِيْنَ كَفَرُوْا
مِنْ مَّشْهَدِ يَوْمٍ عَظِيْمٍ ﴿٣٧﴾ أَسْمِعْ بِهِمْ وَأَبْصِرْ
يَوْمَ يَأْتُوْنَنَا لٰكِنِ الظّٰلِمُوْنَ الْيَوْمَ فِيْ ضَلٰلٍ
مُّبِيْنٍ ﴿٣٨﴾ وَأَنْذِرْهُمْ يَوْمَ الْحَسْرَةِ إِذْ قُضِيَ
الْأَمْرُ وَهُمْ فِيْ غَفْلَةٍ وَّهُمْ لَا يُؤْمِنُوْنَ ﴿٣٩﴾
إِنَّا نَحْنُ نَرِثُ الْأَرْضَ وَمَنْ عَلَيْهَا وَإِلَيْنَا
يُرْجَعُوْنَ ﴿٤٠﴾ وَاذْكُرْ فِي الْكِتٰبِ إِبْرٰهِيْمَ إِنَّهٗ
كَانَ صِدِّيْقًا نَّبِيًّا ﴿٤١﴾ إِذْ قَالَ لِأَبِيْهِ يٰٓأَبَتِ
لِمَ تَعْبُدُ مَا لَا يَسْمَعُ وَلَا يُبْصِرُ وَلَا يُغْنِيْ
عَنْكَ شَيْئًا ﴿٤٢﴾ يٰٓأَبَتِ إِنِّيْ قَدْ جَآءَنِيْ مِنَ الْعِلْمِ
مَا لَمْ يَأْتِكَ فَاتَّبِعْنِيْ أَهْدِكَ صِرٰطًا سَوِيًّا ﴿٤٣﴾

44. 'My dear sire, do not serve satan, surely satan is disobedient to the Most Gracious (God).

45. 'My dear sire, if you went on serving satan, I fear lest some punishment from the Most Gracious (God) should seize you so that you should become an associate of satan.'

46. (Thereupon Abraham's uncle) replied, 'Do you dare to be averse to my gods, O Abraham? If you do not give up, I shall certainly cut off all relations with you. You had better leave me alone for a time.'

47. (Abraham) said (leaving him), 'Peace be upon you. I will ask protection for you from my Lord. He is indeed gracious to me.

48. 'I shall keep away from you and from that which you call upon besides Allâh. I will pray to my Lord. I hope that in praying to my Lord I shall not be disappointed.'

49. So he (- Abraham) kept away from them and from that which they worshipped besides Allâh. We bestowed on him Isaac and Jacob. We made each one (of them) a Prophet.

50. And We bestowed Our blessings upon them, and We granted them a sublime and lasting good name, and made the people remember and mention them.

SECTION 4

51. **G**IVE an account of Moses in this Book. He was indeed a purified and chosen one and he was a Messenger, a Prophet.

52. And We called out to him from the blessed side of the Mount (Sinai) and We made him draw near (to Us) for close and special communion.

53. And out of Our mercy We bestowed upon him (as his helper) his brother Aaron, (also) a Prophet.

54. Give an account of Ismâ'îl in this Book. He (too) was strictly true to his promise. And he was a Messenger, a Prophet.

55. He enjoined his people to observe Prayer and

يٰٓأَبَتِ لَا تَعْبُدِ الشَّيْطٰنَ إِنَّ الشَّيْطٰنَ كَانَ
لِلرَّحْمٰنِ عَصِيًّا ﴿٤٤﴾ يٰٓأَبَتِ إِنِّيٓ أَخَافُ أَنْ يَّمَسَّكَ
عَذَابٌ مِّنَ الرَّحْمٰنِ فَتَكُونَ لِلشَّيْطٰنِ وَلِيًّا ﴿٤٥﴾
قَالَ أَرَاغِبٌ أَنْتَ عَنْ اٰلِهَتِي يٰٓإِبْرٰهِيمُ لَئِنْ
لَّمْ تَنْتَهِ لَأَرْجُمَنَّكَ وَاهْجُرْنِي مَلِيًّا ﴿٤٦﴾ قَالَ
سَلٰمٌ عَلَيْكَ سَأَسْتَغْفِرُ لَكَ رَبِّي إِنَّهُ كَانَ
بِي حَفِيًّا ﴿٤٧﴾ وَأَعْتَزِلُكُمْ وَمَا تَدْعُونَ مِنْ
دُونِ اللهِ وَأَدْعُوا رَبِّي عَسٰٓى أَلَّآ أَكُونَ
بِدُعَآءِ رَبِّي شَقِيًّا ﴿٤٨﴾ فَلَمَّا اعْتَزَلَهُمْ وَمَا
يَعْبُدُونَ مِنْ دُونِ اللهِ وَهَبْنَا لَهُ إِسْحٰقَ
وَيَعْقُوبَ وَكُلًّا جَعَلْنَا نَبِيًّا ﴿٤٩﴾ وَوَهَبْنَا لَهُمْ
مِّنْ رَّحْمَتِنَا وَجَعَلْنَا لَهُمْ لِسَانَ صِدْقٍ عَلِيًّا ﴿٥٠﴾ ركوع
وَاذْكُرْ فِي الْكِتٰبِ مُوسٰىٓ إِنَّهُ كَانَ مُخْلَصًا
وَكَانَ رَسُولًا نَّبِيًّا ﴿٥١﴾ وَنٰدَيْنٰهُ مِنْ جَانِبِ
الطُّورِ الْأَيْمَنِ وَقَرَّبْنٰهُ نَجِيًّا ﴿٥٢﴾ وَوَهَبْنَا لَهُ
مِنْ رَّحْمَتِنَآ أَخَاهُ هٰرُونَ نَبِيًّا ﴿٥٣﴾ وَاذْكُرْ فِي
الْكِتٰبِ إِسْمٰعِيلَ إِنَّهُ كَانَ صَادِقَ الْوَعْدِ
وَكَانَ رَسُولًا نَّبِيًّا ﴿٥٤﴾ وَكَانَ يَأْمُرُ أَهْلَهُ

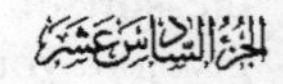

present alms. He was well pleasing to his Lord.
56. And give an account of Idrîs (- Enoch) in this Book. He was a very truthful man, a Prophet.
57. And We raised him to an exalted position.
58. It is these people on whom Allâh did bestow His blessings. They were all Prophets. They were of the posterity of Adam and of those whom We carried (in the Ark) with Noah. Some of them were of the posterity of Abraham and Israel, and of those whom We guided and chose. They would fall prostrating (glorifying God) and weeping when the Messages of the Most Gracious (Lord) were recited to them.

[PROSTRATION]

59. But after them evil descendants came, who neglected Prayer and pursued (their) evil passions. They are doomed to meet perdition.
60. Different, however, will be the case of those who turn (to God in repentance) and believe and do righteous deeds. It is these to whom no injustice shall be done in the least (and will get their due rewards). They shall enter Paradise,
61. Gardens of Eternity which the Most Gracious (God) has promised to his servants while (these Gardens are) yet hidden (from the sight). His promise is sure to come to pass.
62. There they will hear no idle talk, but all that they hear will be only (greetings of) peace. There they shall remain, provided with their sustenance, morning and evening (regularly and eternally).
63. Such is the Paradise which We give for a free gift and for an inheritance to those of Our servants who guard against evil.
64. And (the angels will say to them), 'We (the angels) do not descend without the command of your Lord. To Him belongs all that is before us (- the future) and all that is behind us (-the past) and all that is in between that (-the present). Your Lord is never forgetful (and will not

بِالصَّلٰوةِ وَالزَّكٰوةِ ۖ وَكَانَ عِنْدَ رَبِّهٖ مَرْضِيًّا ﴿٥٥﴾
وَاذْكُرْ فِي الْكِتٰبِ إِدْرِيسَ ۚ إِنَّهٗ كَانَ صِدِّيقًا
نَّبِيًّا ﴿٥٦﴾ وَّرَفَعْنٰهُ مَكَانًا عَلِيًّا ﴿٥٧﴾ أُولٰٓئِكَ الَّذِينَ
أَنْعَمَ اللّٰهُ عَلَيْهِمْ مِّنَ النَّبِيّٖنَ مِنْ ذُرِّيَّةِ اٰدَمَ
وَمِمَّنْ حَمَلْنَا مَعَ نُوحٍ ۡ وَّمِنْ ذُرِّيَّةِ إِبْرٰهِيمَ
وَإِسْرٰٓءِيلَ ۡ وَمِمَّنْ هَدَيْنَا وَاجْتَبَيْنَا ۚ إِذَا
تُتْلٰى عَلَيْهِمْ اٰيٰتُ الرَّحْمٰنِ خَرُّوا سُجَّدًا
وَّبُكِيًّا ﴿٥٨﴾ فَخَلَفَ مِنْ بَعْدِهِمْ خَلْفٌ أَضَاعُوا
الصَّلٰوةَ وَاتَّبَعُوا الشَّهَوٰتِ فَسَوْفَ يَلْقَوْنَ
غَيًّا ﴿٥٩﴾ إِلَّا مَنْ تَابَ وَاٰمَنَ وَعَمِلَ صٰلِحًا
فَأُولٰٓئِكَ يَدْخُلُونَ الْجَنَّةَ وَلَا يُظْلَمُونَ
شَيْـًٔا ﴿٦٠﴾ جَنّٰتِ عَدْنِ الَّتِي وَعَدَ الرَّحْمٰنُ
عِبَادَهٗ بِالْغَيْبِ ۚ إِنَّهٗ كَانَ وَعْدُهٗ مَأْتِيًّا ﴿٦١﴾
لَا يَسْمَعُونَ فِيهَا لَغْوًا إِلَّا سَلٰمًا ۖ وَلَهُمْ
رِزْقُهُمْ فِيهَا بُكْرَةً وَّعَشِيًّا ﴿٦٢﴾ تِلْكَ الْجَنَّةُ
الَّتِي نُورِثُ مِنْ عِبَادِنَا مَنْ كَانَ تَقِيًّا ﴿٦٣﴾
وَمَا نَتَنَزَّلُ إِلَّا بِأَمْرِ رَبِّكَ ۚ لَهٗ مَا بَيْنَ
أَيْدِينَا وَمَا خَلْفَنَا وَمَا بَيْنَ ذٰلِكَ ۚ وَمَا

سجدة

neglect you).
65. '(He is the) Lord of the heavens and the earth and all that is between the two. Worship Him, therefore, and remain constant and steadfast in His worship. Do you not know that no one is His peer?'

SECTION 5

66. **A** HUMAN being (disbelieving in the Day of Resurrection) says, 'What! shall I be really raised to life (again) when I am dead?'
67. Does not such a human being remember that We created him before, when he was nothing at all?
68. By your Lord! We will most certainly gather them together and (their) satans as well, then We shall bring them, in every case, crouching on their knees to the environs of Gehenna.
69. Then shall We pick out from every group the vilest of them in disobedience to the Most Gracious (God).
70. Behold! We surely know best those who are the most deserving of being cast and burnt therein (- the Hell).
71. There is none among you, (O those condemned to Hell!), but he shall reach there (- the Hell). This is (a promise) binding on your Lord, an absolute decree.
72. And (let Us tell you another thing,) We shall save those who guard against evil and are righteous. We shall leave only the wrong doing people therein (the Hell) fallen on their knees.
73. When Our clear Messages are recited to them the disbelievers say to those who believe, 'Which of the two parties of us is better in respect of position and (makes) more impressive society?'
74. And how many a generation have We destroyed before them, who were better off in assets and better in outward show and splendour (than these).
75. Say, 'The Most Gracious (God) gives

كَانَ رَبُّكَ نَسِيًّا ﴿٦٤﴾ رَبُّ السَّمٰوٰتِ وَالْأَرْضِ
وَمَا بَيْنَهُمَا فَاعْبُدْهُ وَاصْطَبِرْ لِعِبٰدَتِهٖ
هَلْ تَعْلَمُ لَهٗ سَمِيًّا ﴿٦٥﴾ وَيَقُوْلُ الْإِنْسٰنُ ءَإِذَا
مَا مِتُّ لَسَوْفَ أُخْرَجُ حَيًّا ﴿٦٦﴾ أَوَلَا يَذْكُرُ
الْإِنْسٰنُ أَنَّا خَلَقْنٰهُ مِنْ قَبْلُ وَلَمْ يَكُ
شَيْـًٔا ﴿٦٧﴾ فَوَرَبِّكَ لَنَحْشُرَنَّهُمْ وَالشَّيٰطِيْنَ ثُمَّ
لَنُحْضِرَنَّهُمْ حَوْلَ جَهَنَّمَ جِثِيًّا ﴿٦٨﴾ ثُمَّ لَنَنْزِعَنَّ
مِنْ كُلِّ شِيْعَةٍ أَيُّهُمْ أَشَدُّ عَلَى الرَّحْمٰنِ
عِتِيًّا ﴿٦٩﴾ ثُمَّ لَنَحْنُ أَعْلَمُ بِالَّذِيْنَ هُمْ أَوْلٰى
بِهَا صِلِيًّا ﴿٧٠﴾ وَإِنْ مِّنْكُمْ إِلَّا وَارِدُهَا كَانَ
عَلٰى رَبِّكَ حَتْمًا مَّقْضِيًّا ﴿٧١﴾ ثُمَّ نُنَجِّي الَّذِيْنَ
اتَّقَوْا وَّنَذَرُ الظّٰلِمِيْنَ فِيْهَا جِثِيًّا ﴿٧٢﴾ وَإِذَا
تُتْلٰى عَلَيْهِمْ اٰيٰتُنَا بَيِّنٰتٍ قَالَ الَّذِيْنَ كَفَرُوْا
لِلَّذِيْنَ اٰمَنُوْا أَيُّ الْفَرِيْقَيْنِ خَيْرٌ مَّقَامًا
وَّأَحْسَنُ نَدِيًّا ﴿٧٣﴾ وَكَمْ أَهْلَكْنَا قَبْلَهُمْ مِّنْ
قَرْنٍ هُمْ أَحْسَنُ أَثَاثًا وَّرِءْيًا ﴿٧٤﴾ قُلْ مَنْ
كَانَ فِي الضَّلٰلَةِ فَلْيَمْدُدْ لَهُ الرَّحْمٰنُ مَدًّا

those, who are steeped in error, long respite.' But when such people see that with which they are threatened, be it some (worldly) punishment or the Hour (of complete and final destruction), they shall realize who is worse placed and weaker in forces.

76. To those who follow guidance Allâh gives increased guidance. And from the point of view of reward and ultimate return, (you should bear in mind that) the righteous deeds that last and endure are best in the sight of your Lord.

77. Have you considered the case of one who denies Our Messages and says 'I shall indeed be given great wealth and a number of children.'

78. Has he looked into and gained knowledge of the unseen or has he taken a promise from the Most Gracious (God)?

79. Indeed not. We shall certainly record what he goes on saying and We shall continue prolonging for him the punishment to a great extent.

80. And We shall remain after his leaving behind all that of which he talks (so boastfully), and he shall come to Us all alone.

81. And they have chosen other gods besides Allâh that they may be a source of strength and honour to them.

82. Not at all! (they are utterly mistaken.) They (-their gods) will deny (one day) their worshipping them; they will turn hostile to them.

SECTION 6

83. **H**AVE you not considered that We do not keep away satans from the disbelievers (by force). These (satans) incite them greatly (in their acts of disobedience).

84. So do not be impatient with regard to (punishment against) them. We are counting their time out (and We are also keeping full account of their deeds).

85. (Look forward to) the day when the Most Gracious (God) shall gather those who guard against evil before Him as honoured delegates (to bestow honours on them).

86. And We shall drive those who cut off their

حَتّٰٓى إِذَا رَأَوْا مَا يُوعَدُونَ إِمَّا الْعَذَابَ وَإِمَّا
السَّاعَةَ فَسَيَعْلَمُونَ مَنْ هُوَ شَرٌّ مَّكَانًا
وَّأَضْعَفُ جُنْدًا ﴿٧٥﴾ وَيَزِيدُ اللّٰهُ الَّذِينَ اهْتَدَوْا
هُدًى ۗ وَالْبٰقِيٰتُ الصّٰلِحٰتُ خَيْرٌ عِنْدَ رَبِّكَ
ثَوَابًا وَّخَيْرٌ مَّرَدًّا ﴿٧٦﴾ أَفَرَءَيْتَ الَّذِي كَفَرَ بِأٰيٰتِنَا
وَقَالَ لَأُوتَيَنَّ مَالًا وَّوَلَدًا ﴿٧٧﴾ أَطَّلَعَ الْغَيْبَ
أَمِ اتَّخَذَ عِنْدَ الرَّحْمٰنِ عَهْدًا ﴿٧٨﴾ كَلَّا ۚ سَنَكْتُبُ
مَا يَقُولُ وَنَمُدُّ لَهُ مِنَ الْعَذَابِ مَدًّا ﴿٧٩﴾
وَّنَرِثُهُ مَا يَقُولُ وَيَأْتِينَا فَرْدًا ﴿٨٠﴾ وَاتَّخَذُوا مِنْ
دُونِ اللّٰهِ أٰلِهَةً لِّيَكُونُوا لَهُمْ عِزًّا ﴿٨١﴾ كَلَّا ۚ
سَيَكْفُرُونَ بِعِبَادَتِهِمْ وَيَكُونُونَ عَلَيْهِمْ
ضِدًّا ﴿٨٢﴾ أَلَمْ تَرَ أَنَّآ أَرْسَلْنَا الشَّيٰطِينَ عَلَى ع ١٧ ٨
الْكٰفِرِينَ تَؤُزُّهُمْ أَزًّا ﴿٨٣﴾ فَلَا تَعْجَلْ عَلَيْهِمْ ۖ
إِنَّمَا نَعُدُّ لَهُمْ عَدًّا ﴿٨٤﴾ يَوْمَ نَحْشُرُ الْمُتَّقِينَ
إِلَى الرَّحْمٰنِ وَفْدًا ﴿٨٥﴾ وَّنَسُوقُ الْمُجْرِمِينَ

ties (with Allâh) to Gehenna (like) a herd of thirsty animals (to quench their thirst).
87. (On that day,) intercession shall be denied to all, save him who holds a promise from the Most Gracious (God).
88. Some say, 'The Most Gracious (God) has taken to Himself a son (who will be our intercessor).'
89. (Say,) 'You have indeed uttered something exceedingly abominable and hideous.
90. 'The heavens are about to burst on account of that, and the earth about to split asunder, and the mountains to fall down in pieces.
91. 'Because they have ascribed a son to the Most Gracious (God).
92. 'Whereas it does not behove the Most Gracious (God) that He should take to Himself a son.'
93. Whoever is in the heavens and the earth shall come before the Most Gracious (God) in complete submission as a bondsman (would).
94. He indeed comprehends them (by His infinite knowledge) and having full power over them. He has numbered them (all) exactly.
95. And they shall all come to Him on the Day of Resurrection, all by themselves.
96. Those who believe and do deeds of righteousness, the Most Gracious (God) will surely bring about (in the hearts of the people) fondest love for them.
97. (Prophet!) We have made this (Qur'ân) easy (by revealing it) in your own tongue, that you may give glad tidings thereby to those who guard against evil and warn thereby a people stubbornly given to contention.
98. Many a generation have We destroyed before them! Can you find (so much as) a single one of them or can you hear (even) a whisper of them?

إِلَى جَهَنَّمَ وِرْدًا ﴿٨٦﴾ لَا يَمْلِكُونَ الشَّفَاعَةَ إِلَّا
مَنِ اتَّخَذَ عِنْدَ الرَّحْمٰنِ عَهْدًا ﴿٨٧﴾ وَقَالُوا
اتَّخَذَ الرَّحْمٰنُ وَلَدًا ﴿٨٨﴾ لَقَدْ جِئْتُمْ شَيْئًا إِدًّا ﴿٨٩﴾
تَكَادُ السَّمٰوٰتُ يَتَفَطَّرْنَ مِنْهُ وَتَنْشَقُّ الْأَرْضُ
وَتَخِرُّ الْجِبَالُ هَدًّا ﴿٩٠﴾ أَنْ دَعَوْا لِلرَّحْمٰنِ وَلَدًا ﴿٩١﴾
وَمَا يَنْبَغِي لِلرَّحْمٰنِ أَنْ يَتَّخِذَ وَلَدًا ﴿٩٢﴾ إِنْ
كُلُّ مَنْ فِي السَّمٰوٰتِ وَالْأَرْضِ إِلَّا آتِي
الرَّحْمٰنِ عَبْدًا ﴿٩٣﴾ لَقَدْ أَحْصٰهُمْ وَعَدَّهُمْ
عَدًّا ﴿٩٤﴾ وَكُلُّهُمْ آتِيهِ يَوْمَ الْقِيٰمَةِ فَرْدًا ﴿٩٥﴾ إِنَّ
الَّذِينَ آمَنُوا وَعَمِلُوا الصّٰلِحٰتِ سَيَجْعَلُ
لَهُمُ الرَّحْمٰنُ وُدًّا ﴿٩٦﴾ فَإِنَّمَا يَسَّرْنٰهُ بِلِسَانِكَ
لِتُبَشِّرَ بِهِ الْمُتَّقِينَ وَتُنْذِرَ بِهِ قَوْمًا لُدًّا ﴿٩٧﴾
وَكَمْ أَهْلَكْنَا قَبْلَهُمْ مِنْ قَرْنٍ هَلْ تُحِسُّ
مِنْهُمْ مِنْ أَحَدٍ أَوْ تَسْمَعُ لَهُمْ رِكْزًا ﴿٩٨﴾

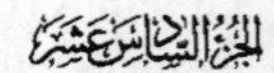

CHAPTER
20

سُورَةُ طٰهٰ ٢٠

TÂ HÂ

(Perfect Man! be at Rest)
(Revealed before Hijrah)

سُوْرَةُ طٰهٰ مَكِّيَّةٌ

With the name of Allâh,
the Most Gracious, the Ever Merciful
(I commence to read Sûrah Tâ Hâ).

بِسْمِ اللّٰهِ الرَّحْمٰنِ الرَّحِيْمِ

1. TÂ HÂ - O perfect man! be at rest.
2. We have not revealed this Qur'ân to you that you should fail in your mission.
3. But it is a reminder (of things inherent in human nature) to him who stands in awe (to God),
4. (And) a revelation from Him Who created the earth and the high heavens.
5. (He is) the Most Gracious (God, Who) is firmly and flawlessly established on (His) Throne (of Power).
6. All that is in the heavens and all that is on the earth and all that lies between them, and all that lies deep under the moist subsoil, belongs to Him.
7. If you speak aloud, (He does not stand in need of it), He knows the secret (thought) as well that which is yet deeper hidden.
8. He is Allâh. There is no other, cannot be and will never be One worthy of worship but He. All the most beautiful attributes belong to Him.
9. You must have surely received the narrative about Moses.
10. When he saw a fire, he said to his companions, 'Stay here for I perceive a fire (creating feelings of love and affection). I hope, I may bring you a fire brand from there. Rather I feel that I would find some guidance at the fire.'
11. And when he came close to this (fire) he

طٰهٰ ① مَآ أَنْزَلْنَا عَلَيْكَ الْقُرْاٰنَ لِتَشْقٰٓى ②
إِلَّا تَذْكِرَةً لِّمَنْ يَّخْشٰى ③ تَنْزِيْلًا مِّمَّنْ خَلَقَ
الْأَرْضَ وَالسَّمٰوٰتِ الْعُلٰى ④ اَلرَّحْمٰنُ عَلَى
الْعَرْشِ اسْتَوٰى ⑤ لَهٗ مَا فِي السَّمٰوٰتِ وَمَا فِي
الْأَرْضِ وَمَا بَيْنَهُمَا وَمَا تَحْتَ الثَّرٰى ⑥
وَإِنْ تَجْهَرْ بِالْقَوْلِ فَإِنَّهٗ يَعْلَمُ السِّرَّ وَأَخْفٰى ⑦
اَللّٰهُ لَآ إِلٰهَ إِلَّا هُوَ لَهُ الْأَسْمَآءُ الْحُسْنٰى ⑧
وَهَلْ أَتٰىكَ حَدِيْثُ مُوْسٰى ⑨ إِذْ رَاٰ نَارًا
فَقَالَ لِأَهْلِهِ امْكُثُوْٓا إِنِّيْٓ اٰنَسْتُ نَارًا لَّعَلِّيْٓ
اٰتِيْكُمْ مِّنْهَا بِقَبَسٍ أَوْ أَجِدُ عَلَى النَّارِ هُدًى ⑩

was hailed, 'O Moses!

12. 'Verily, I alone am your Lord. So take off your shoes (and stay, and make your heart free from every care), for you are in the sacred Valley of Tuwâ.

13. 'And I have chosen you, therefore listen to what is revealed to you.

14. 'I, and I alone am Allâh. There cannot be, is no other and will never be One worthy of worship but I, therefore worship Me alone. And observe Prayer so that you may keep Me in mind.

15. 'Surely, the Hour (of Resurrection) is bound to come. I am about to unveil it, so that every soul may be rewarded in accordance with its endeavour.

16. 'So do not allow the person who does not believe in it but pursues his (own) low desires, turn you away from (believing) it, lest you perish.

17. 'Moses, What is that you have in your right hand?'

18. (Moses) replied, 'This is my staff. I lean on it, and beat down leaves for my sheep with it, and it serves (also) my many other needs.'

19. (The Lord) said, 'Moses! cast it down.'

20. So he cast it down and lo! it was (like) a serpent; running about.

21. (The Lord) said, 'Get hold of it and do not fear. We shall restore it to its former state.

22. 'And put your hand close under your armpit, it shall come forth (shining) white, without any disease, (providing you with) another sign.

23. '(We have given you these signs) so that we may show you some of Our greater signs.

24. 'Go to Pharaoh, he has indeed exceeded (all) limits.'

SECTION 2

25. (MOSES) said, 'My Lord! (if you have chosen me for this mission) enlighten my mind,

سُورَةُ طٰهٰ ٢٠

فَلَمَّآ أَتٰىهَا نُودِيَ يٰمُوسٰى ١١ إِنِّيٓ أَنَا۠ رَبُّكَ
فَاخْلَعْ نَعْلَيْكَ إِنَّكَ بِالْوَادِ الْمُقَدَّسِ طُوًى ١٢
وَأَنَا اخْتَرْتُكَ فَاسْتَمِعْ لِمَا يُوحٰى ١٣ إِنَّنِيٓ أَنَا
اللّٰهُ لَآ إِلٰهَ إِلَّآ أَنَا۠ فَاعْبُدْنِي وَأَقِمِ الصَّلٰوةَ
لِذِكْرِي ١٤ إِنَّ السَّاعَةَ ءَاتِيَةٌ أَكَادُ أُخْفِيهَا لِتُجْزٰى
كُلُّ نَفْسٍۭ بِمَا تَسْعٰى ١٥ فَلَا يَصُدَّنَّكَ عَنْهَا مَنْ
لَّا يُؤْمِنُ بِهَا وَاتَّبَعَ هَوٰىهُ فَتَرْدٰى ١٦ وَمَا
تِلْكَ بِيَمِينِكَ يٰمُوسٰى ١٧ قَالَ هِيَ عَصَايَ أَتَوَكَّؤُا۟
عَلَيْهَا وَأَهُشُّ بِهَا عَلٰى غَنَمِي وَلِيَ فِيهَا مَـَٔارِبُ
أُخْرٰى ١٨ قَالَ أَلْقِهَا يٰمُوسٰى ١٩ فَأَلْقٰىهَا فَإِذَا هِيَ
حَيَّةٌ تَسْعٰى ٢٠ قَالَ خُذْهَا وَلَا تَخَفْ سَنُعِيدُهَا
سِيرَتَهَا الْأُولٰى ٢١ وَاضْمُمْ يَدَكَ إِلٰى جَنَاحِكَ
تَخْرُجْ بَيْضَآءَ مِنْ غَيْرِ سُوٓءٍ ءَايَةً أُخْرٰى ٢٢
لِنُرِيَكَ مِنْ ءَايٰتِنَا الْكُبْرٰى ٢٣ اذْهَبْ إِلٰى
فِرْعَوْنَ إِنَّهُۥ طَغٰى ٢٤ قَالَ رَبِّ اشْرَحْ لِي صَدْرِي ٢٥

26. 'And make my task easy for me.
27. 'And remove the impediments from my tongue,
28. 'So that they may understand my speech,
29. 'And grant me a helper from my family,
30. 'Aaron, my brother,
31. 'Raise my strength through him,
32. 'And associate him in my task;
33. 'That we may glorify You over and over;
34. 'And spread Your name far and wide,
35. 'Surely, You are indeed Ever-Watchful over us.'
36. (The Lord) said, 'Moses! you are granted what you have prayed for.
37. 'And We did confer on you a favour once before;
38. 'When We revealed to your mother that, which was an important revelation (saying),
39. "Place him (- Moses) in the chest and put it into the river. The river will cast it on to the bank and the person who is My enemy as well as his will pick him up." And I endowed you with My love with the result that you were brought up before My eyes and under My protection.
40. '(We bestowed another favour on you) when your sister walked along (the bank by the floating chest) and said (to those who picked up the chest from the bank of the river), "Shall I guide you to one (- a nurse) who will take charge of him?" In this way We restored you to your mother that she might be consoled and should not grieve. And (it came to pass that) you killed a person, but We delivered you from anguish. Then We purified you with various trials and you stayed for a number of years among the people of Midian. It was only then when you were properly groomed and came up to the standard (set by Us).
41. 'And I, (having made you perfect,) have chosen you for Myself.

وَيَسِّرۡ لِيٓ أَمۡرِي ﴿٢٦﴾ وَٱحۡلُلۡ عُقۡدَةً مِّن لِّسَانِي ﴿٢٧﴾
يَفۡقَهُواْ قَوۡلِي ﴿٢٨﴾ وَٱجۡعَل لِّي وَزِيرًا مِّنۡ أَهۡلِي ﴿٢٩﴾
هَٰرُونَ أَخِي ﴿٣٠﴾ ٱشۡدُدۡ بِهِۦٓ أَزۡرِي ﴿٣١﴾ وَأَشۡرِكۡهُ
فِيٓ أَمۡرِي ﴿٣٢﴾ كَيۡ نُسَبِّحَكَ كَثِيرًا ﴿٣٣﴾ وَنَذۡكُرَكَ
كَثِيرًا ﴿٣٤﴾ إِنَّكَ كُنتَ بِنَا بَصِيرًا ﴿٣٥﴾ قَالَ قَدۡ أُوتِيتَ
سُؤۡلَكَ يَٰمُوسَىٰ ﴿٣٦﴾ وَلَقَدۡ مَنَنَّا عَلَيۡكَ مَرَّةً أُخۡرَىٰٓ ﴿٣٧﴾
إِذۡ أَوۡحَيۡنَآ إِلَىٰٓ أُمِّكَ مَا يُوحَىٰٓ ﴿٣٨﴾ أَنِ ٱقۡذِفِيهِ فِي
ٱلتَّابُوتِ فَٱقۡذِفِيهِ فِي ٱلۡيَمِّ فَلۡيُلۡقِهِ ٱلۡيَمُّ بِٱلسَّاحِلِ
يَأۡخُذۡهُ عَدُوّٞ لِّي وَعَدُوّٞ لَّهُۥۚ وَأَلۡقَيۡتُ عَلَيۡكَ
مَحَبَّةٗ مِّنِّي وَلِتُصۡنَعَ عَلَىٰ عَيۡنِيٓ ﴿٣٩﴾ إِذۡ تَمۡشِيٓ
أُخۡتُكَ فَتَقُولُ هَلۡ أَدُلُّكُمۡ عَلَىٰ مَن يَكۡفُلُهُۥۖ
فَرَجَعۡنَٰكَ إِلَىٰٓ أُمِّكَ كَيۡ تَقَرَّ عَيۡنُهَا وَلَا تَحۡزَنَۚ
وَقَتَلۡتَ نَفۡسٗا فَنَجَّيۡنَٰكَ مِنَ ٱلۡغَمِّ وَفَتَنَّٰكَ
فُتُونٗاۚ فَلَبِثۡتَ سِنِينَ فِيٓ أَهۡلِ مَدۡيَنَ ثُمَّ
جِئۡتَ عَلَىٰ قَدَرٖ يَٰمُوسَىٰ ﴿٤٠﴾ وَٱصۡطَنَعۡتُكَ لِنَفۡسِي ﴿٤١﴾

42. 'Go you and your brother (Aaron) with My Messages and do not be remiss in remembering Me.
43. 'Go to Pharaoh, both of you, for he has transgressed all limits.
44. 'But speak to him a gentle speech, may be he pays heed and fears (the consequences).'
45. Both (Moses and Aaron) said, 'Our Lord! we fear lest he (- Pharaoh) should hasten to do us some harm or exceed all limits in transgression (against You).'
46. (The Lord) said, 'Have no fear. I am with you both. I hear (prayers) and I see (your condition).
47. 'So go to him (- Pharaoh), both of you, and say, "We are the Messengers of your Lord, so let the Children of Israel go with us and do not torture them. We have come to you with a Message from your Lord. Peace will be upon him who follows the guidance.
48. "It has been revealed to us that the punishment comes upon him who cries lies to (His Messages) and turns away".'
49. (When they had delivered the Message of God, Pharaoh) said, 'Moses! who, then, is the Lord of you two, (in whose kingdom you want to settle down)?'
50. (Moses) said, 'Our Lord is He Who gives every creation its (proper) form and character and then guides them along the path (of evolution in order to attain perfection and to do proper functions).'
51. (Pharaoh) said, 'What will be the fate of the former generations (who did not believe in these things)?'
52. (Moses) said, 'The knowledge of that is with my Lord (recorded) in a book. My Lord neither errs nor forgets.
53. 'It is He Who made the earth a bed for you and has threaded it with pathways for you. He sends down rain from the clouds. We bring forth by means of this (water) pairs of vegeta-

إِذْهَبْ أَنْتَ وَ أَخُوكَ بِاٰيٰتِي وَ لَا تَنِيَا فِي
ذِكْرِي ﴿٤٢﴾ إِذْهَبَآ إِلٰى فِرْعَوْنَ إِنَّهٗ طَغٰى ﴿٤٣﴾ فَقُوْلَا
لَهٗ قَوْلًا لَّيِّنًا لَّعَلَّهٗ يَتَذَكَّرُ أَوْ يَخْشٰى ﴿٤٤﴾ قَالَا
رَبَّنَآ إِنَّنَا نَخَافُ أَنْ يَّفْرُطَ عَلَيْنَآ أَوْ أَنْ يَّطْغٰى ﴿٤٥﴾
قَالَ لَا تَخَافَآ إِنَّنِي مَعَكُمَآ أَسْمَعُ وَ أَرٰى ﴿٤٦﴾
فَأْتِيٰهُ فَقُوْلَآ إِنَّا رَسُوْلَا رَبِّكَ فَأَرْسِلْ مَعَنَا
بَنِيٓ إِسْرَآءِيْلَ ۥ وَ لَا تُعَذِّبْهُمْ قَدْ جِئْنٰكَ
بِاٰيَةٍ مِّنْ رَّبِّكَ وَ السَّلٰمُ عَلٰى مَنِ اتَّبَعَ
الْهُدٰى ﴿٤٧﴾ إِنَّا قَدْ أُوْحِيَ إِلَيْنَآ أَنَّ الْعَذَابَ عَلٰى
مَنْ كَذَّبَ وَ تَوَلّٰى ﴿٤٨﴾ قَالَ فَمَنْ رَّبُّكُمَا يٰمُوْسٰى ﴿٤٩﴾
قَالَ رَبُّنَا الَّذِيٓ أَعْطٰى كُلَّ شَيْءٍ خَلْقَهٗ ثُمَّ
هَدٰى ﴿٥٠﴾ قَالَ فَمَا بَالُ الْقُرُوْنِ الْأُوْلٰى ﴿٥١﴾ قَالَ
عِلْمُهَا عِنْدَ رَبِّي فِي كِتٰبٍ لَا يَضِلُّ رَبِّي وَ لَا
يَنْسَى ﴿٥٢﴾ الَّذِي جَعَلَ لَكُمُ الْأَرْضَ مَهْدًا

tion of diverse kinds.
54. '(So that you may) eat it and pasture your cattle (upon it). Verily, in all this there are signs for the people possessing sound reason.'

SECTION 3

55. **W**E have created you from this (universe) and into this We will make you return and from this We will raise you to life a second time.
56. And We showed him (- Pharaoh) all sorts of Our signs, but (even then) he went on denying (them) and refused (to believe).
57. He said, 'Moses! have you come to us to turn us out of our country on the basis of your sorcery?
58. 'But we (too) shall certainly meet you with a matching sorcery. Make an appointment of time and place between us, which (appointment) neither we nor you shall fail to keep, (let the meeting be) at a place fair (for us both).'
59. (Moses) said, 'The day of the festival will be the day of your appointment, and let the people be assembled when the sun is risen high.'
60. Pharaoh then withdrew and concerted his plan then came (at the appointed time and place for the contest).
61. Moses said to them, 'Woe to you, forge no lies in the name of Allâh or He shall destroy you utterly by some calamity and surely he who forges a lie in the name of Allâh has ever been unsuccessful.'
62. Upon this they (- Pharaoh and his courtiers) began arguing their affair among themselves, and kept (their) discourse secret.
63. They said, 'Surely, these two (brothers, Moses and Aaron) are sorcerers who seek to drive you out of your country by dint of their

وَسَلَكَ لَكُمْ فِيهَا سُبُلًا وَأَنْزَلَ مِنَ السَّمَاءِ
مَاءً فَأَخْرَجْنَا بِهِ أَزْوَاجًا مِنْ نَبَاتٍ شَتَّىٰ ﴿٥٣﴾
كُلُوا وَارْعَوْا أَنْعَامَكُمْ إِنَّ فِي ذَٰلِكَ لَآيَاتٍ
لِأُولِي النُّهَىٰ ﴿٥٤﴾ مِنْهَا خَلَقْنَاكُمْ وَفِيهَا نُعِيدُكُمْ
وَمِنْهَا نُخْرِجُكُمْ تَارَةً أُخْرَىٰ ﴿٥٥﴾ وَلَقَدْ أَرَيْنَاهُ
آيَاتِنَا كُلَّهَا فَكَذَّبَ وَأَبَىٰ ﴿٥٦﴾ قَالَ أَجِئْتَنَا لِتُخْرِجَنَا
مِنْ أَرْضِنَا بِسِحْرِكَ يَا مُوسَىٰ ﴿٥٧﴾ فَلَنَأْتِيَنَّكَ بِسِحْرٍ
مِثْلِهِ فَاجْعَلْ بَيْنَنَا وَبَيْنَكَ مَوْعِدًا لَا
نُخْلِفُهُ نَحْنُ وَلَا أَنْتَ مَكَانًا سُوًى ﴿٥٨﴾ قَالَ
مَوْعِدُكُمْ يَوْمُ الزِّينَةِ وَأَنْ يُحْشَرَ النَّاسُ
ضُحًى ﴿٥٩﴾ فَتَوَلَّىٰ فِرْعَوْنُ فَجَمَعَ كَيْدَهُ ثُمَّ أَتَىٰ ﴿٦٠﴾
قَالَ لَهُمْ مُوسَىٰ وَيْلَكُمْ لَا تَفْتَرُوا عَلَى اللَّهِ
كَذِبًا فَيُسْحِتَكُمْ بِعَذَابٍ وَقَدْ خَابَ مَنِ
افْتَرَىٰ ﴿٦١﴾ فَتَنَازَعُوا أَمْرَهُمْ بَيْنَهُمْ وَأَسَرُّوا
النَّجْوَىٰ ﴿٦٢﴾ قَالُوا إِنْ هَٰذَانِ لَسَاحِرَانِ يُرِيدَانِ
أَنْ يُخْرِجَاكُمْ مِنْ أَرْضِكُمْ بِسِحْرِهِمَا وَيَذْهَبَا

sorcery and to do away with your ideal religious traditions.

64. 'Therefore you had better consolidate your resources, then come forward arrayed in a body and indeed he alone who gains the upper hand (and wins) shall be successful today.'

65. (The sorcerers) said, 'Moses! either you present (first what you have) or we shall be the first to present (what we have).'

66. (Moses) said, 'Nay, you present first what you have.' (Accordingly they were the first to present. No sooner did they present them) lo! their cords and their staves, appeared to him (- Moses) by their trickstery only as though they ran about.

67. So Moses felt afraid in his mind (lest the people be misled by their glittering tricks).

68. We said (to him), 'Have no fear. Surely, it is you who shall be the uppermost.

69. 'Now, cast down (on the ground) that (staff) which you have in your right hand. It will destroy all their artifices, for all they have wrought is nothing more than a device of a sorcerer, and the beguiler shall never succeed whichever way he may choose (to beguile).'

70. Then (it so happened that) the sorcerers were instantly made to fall down prostrate. They said, 'We believe in the Lord of Aaron and Moses.'

71. Pharaoh said, 'Dared you believe in him (- Moses) before I gave you permission? He (- Moses) must be your chief who has taught you sorcery. I will certainly cut off your hands and feet on alternate sides (by way of punishment) because of (your) disobedience. I will surely crucify you to death on the trunks of palm-trees and you shall, of a certainty, come to know which of us can inflict a more severe and more abiding punishment.'

72. They (- the sorcerers) said, 'We will certainly never prefer you to the clear proofs and

بِطَرِيقَتِكُمُ الْمُثْلَىٰ ﴿٦٣﴾ فَأَجْمِعُوا كَيْدَكُمْ ثُمَّ
ائْتُوا صَفًّا ۚ وَقَدْ أَفْلَحَ الْيَوْمَ مَنِ اسْتَعْلَىٰ ﴿٦٤﴾
قَالُوا يَا مُوسَىٰ إِمَّا أَنْ تُلْقِيَ وَإِمَّا أَنْ نَكُونَ
أَوَّلَ مَنْ أَلْقَىٰ ﴿٦٥﴾ قَالَ بَلْ أَلْقُوا ۖ فَإِذَا حِبَالُهُمْ
وَعِصِيُّهُمْ يُخَيَّلُ إِلَيْهِ مِنْ سِحْرِهِمْ أَنَّهَا
تَسْعَىٰ ﴿٦٦﴾ فَأَوْجَسَ فِي نَفْسِهِ خِيفَةً مُوسَىٰ ﴿٦٧﴾
قُلْنَا لَا تَخَفْ إِنَّكَ أَنْتَ الْأَعْلَىٰ ﴿٦٨﴾ وَأَلْقِ مَا
فِي يَمِينِكَ تَلْقَفْ مَا صَنَعُوا ۖ إِنَّمَا صَنَعُوا
كَيْدُ سَاحِرٍ ۖ وَلَا يُفْلِحُ السَّاحِرُ حَيْثُ أَتَىٰ ﴿٦٩﴾
فَأُلْقِيَ السَّحَرَةُ سُجَّدًا قَالُوا آمَنَّا بِرَبِّ هَارُونَ
وَمُوسَىٰ ﴿٧٠﴾ قَالَ آمَنْتُمْ لَهُ قَبْلَ أَنْ آذَنَ
لَكُمْ ۖ إِنَّهُ لَكَبِيرُكُمُ الَّذِي عَلَّمَكُمُ السِّحْرَ ۖ
فَلَأُقَطِّعَنَّ أَيْدِيَكُمْ وَأَرْجُلَكُمْ مِنْ خِلَافٍ
وَلَأُصَلِّبَنَّكُمْ فِي جُذُوعِ النَّخْلِ وَلَتَعْلَمُنَّ
أَيُّنَا أَشَدُّ عَذَابًا وَأَبْقَىٰ ﴿٧١﴾ قَالُوا لَنْ نُؤْثِرَكَ
عَلَىٰ مَا جَاءَنَا مِنَ الْبَيِّنَاتِ وَالَّذِي فَطَرَنَا

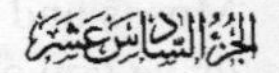

signs that have come to us, nor to Him Who originated us. You may decide what you like to decide. You can only decree concerning this present life and put an end to it (this our life).
73. 'We have surely believed in our Lord that He may protect us against our faults and (particularly forgive us) the sorcery which you did constrain us (to practise). Allâh is the Best and Ever Abiding.'
74. Verily, he who comes to his Lord in a state of sin, he will surely be consigned to Gehenna, where he shall neither die nor live.
75. But those who come to Him as believers, having done deeds of righteousness, there await them, indeed, exalted ranks,
76. Gardens of Eternity served with running streams; there they will abide. Such is the reward of those who keep themselves ever pure.

SECTION 4

77. **A**ND We directed Moses by revelation, 'Take away My servants by night and take them along a dry path through the wide plane. You will not be afraid of being overtaken nor will you have any cause of fear (of being drowned).'
78. Now Pharaoh pursued them with his armies. But there covered them (- Pharaoh and his host) that (tide of the) sea which engulfed them completely.
79. Indeed, Pharaoh caused his people to perish, and did not lead them in the right way.
80. O Children of Israel! We delivered you from your enemy and made a covenant with you on the right and blessed side of the Mount (Sinai), and We got Manna and quail to be sent down to you.
81. (And it was also said,) 'Eat of the good and pure things We have provided you, and do not exceed the limits in this respect or My displeasure shall descend upon you. Indeed, lost are those on whom My displeasure de-

فَاقْضِ مَآ أَنْتَ قَاضٍ إِنَّمَا تَقْضِي هٰذِهِ
الْحَيٰوةَ الدُّنْيَا ﴿٧٢﴾ إِنَّآ أٰمَنَّا بِرَبِّنَا لِيَغْفِرَ لَنَا
خَطٰيٰنَا وَمَآ أَكْرَهْتَنَا عَلَيْهِ مِنَ السِّحْرِ
وَاللّٰهُ خَيْرٌ وَّأَبْقٰى ﴿٧٣﴾ إِنَّهُ مَنْ يَّأْتِ رَبَّهُ
مُجْرِمًا فَإِنَّ لَهُ جَهَنَّمَ لَا يَمُوتُ فِيهَا وَلَا يَحْيٰى ﴿٧٤﴾
وَمَنْ يَّأْتِهِ مُؤْمِنًا قَدْ عَمِلَ الصّٰلِحٰتِ فَأُولٰٓئِكَ
لَهُمُ الدَّرَجٰتُ الْعُلٰى ﴿٧٥﴾ جَنّٰتُ عَدْنٍ تَجْرِي
مِنْ تَحْتِهَا الْأَنْهٰرُ خٰلِدِينَ فِيهَا وَذٰلِكَ
جَزَآءُ مَنْ تَزَكّٰى ﴿٧٦﴾ وَلَقَدْ أَوْحَيْنَآ إِلٰى مُوسٰٓى
أَنْ أَسْرِ بِعِبَادِي فَاضْرِبْ لَهُمْ طَرِيقًا فِي
الْبَحْرِ يَبَسًا لَّا تَخٰفُ دَرَكًا وَّلَا تَخْشٰى ﴿٧٧﴾
فَأَتْبَعَهُمْ فِرْعَوْنُ بِجُنُودِهِ فَغَشِيَهُمْ مِّنَ الْيَمِّ
مَا غَشِيَهُمْ ﴿٧٨﴾ وَأَضَلَّ فِرْعَوْنُ قَوْمَهُ وَمَا
هَدٰى ﴿٧٩﴾ يٰبَنِيٓ إِسْرٰٓءِيلَ قَدْ أَنْجَيْنٰكُمْ مِّنْ
عَدُوِّكُمْ وَوٰعَدْنٰكُمْ جَانِبَ الطُّورِ الْأَيْمَنَ
وَنَزَّلْنَا عَلَيْكُمُ الْمَنَّ وَالسَّلْوٰى ﴿٨٠﴾ كُلُوا مِنْ
طَيِّبٰتِ مَا رَزَقْنٰكُمْ وَلَا تَطْغَوْا فِيهِ فَيَحِلَّ
عَلَيْكُمْ غَضَبِي وَمَنْ يَّحْلِلْ عَلَيْهِ غَضَبِي

scends.'
82. But surely I am greatly protecting to him who turns (to Me) in repentance and believes and does righteous deeds and then sticks to guidance.
83. (When Moses went to the Mount, God said,) 'Moses! what has made you depart from your people in such haste?'
84. Moses said, 'They are close on my heels and I have hastened to You, my Lord, that You might be pleased.'
85. (The Lord) said, 'We have distinguished your people, the good from the bad in your absence and the Sâmirî has led them astray?'
86. So Moses returned to his people indignant and sorrowful. (Reaching there) he said, 'My people! did your Lord not make you a gracious promise? Did then the promised time (of forty nights and days) seem too long to you. Rather you desired that displeasure from your Lord should descend upon you that is why you failed in (your) promise with me.'
87. They said, 'We have not willfully failed to keep (our) promise with you but (the thing is that) we were laden with loads of the jewelry of the (Egyptian) people and we threw them away (into the fire). That was what the Sâmiri suggested.'
88. Then (it came to pass that) he (- Sâmirî) produced (an effigy of) a calf for the people (to worship), a mere body (without a soul) which emitted a lowing sound. And then they (- Sâmirî and his followers) said, 'This is your god as well as that of Moses,' so he (- Sâmirî) gave up (the religion of Moses).
89. Could they not see that this (calf) made them no answer and could neither avoid harm to them nor do good (to any).

SECTION 5

90. **A**ARON had, indeed, said to them before (the return of Moses from the Mount), 'My

فَقَدْ هَوٰى ﴿٨١﴾ وَ إِنِّي لَغَفَّارٌ لِّمَنْ تَابَ وَ أٰمَنَ
وَعَمِلَ صٰلِحًا ثُمَّ اهْتَدٰى ﴿٨٢﴾ وَمَآ أَعْجَلَكَ
عَنْ قَوْمِكَ يٰمُوسٰى ﴿٨٣﴾ قَالَ هُمْ أُولَآءِ عَلٰٓى
أَثَرِي وَعَجِلْتُ إِلَيْكَ رَبِّ لِتَرْضٰى ﴿٨٤﴾ قَالَ
فَإِنَّا قَدْ فَتَنَّا قَوْمَكَ مِنْۢ بَعْدِكَ وَ أَضَلَّهُمُ
السَّامِرِيُّ ﴿٨٥﴾ فَرَجَعَ مُوسٰٓى إِلٰى قَوْمِهٖ غَضْبٰنَ
أَسِفًا ۚ قَالَ يٰقَوْمِ أَلَمْ يَعِدْكُمْ رَبُّكُمْ وَعْدًا
حَسَنًا ۚ أَفَطَالَ عَلَيْكُمُ الْعَهْدُ أَمْ أَرَدْتُّمْ أَنْ
يَّحِلَّ عَلَيْكُمْ غَضَبٌ مِّنْ رَّبِّكُمْ فَأَخْلَفْتُمْ
مَّوْعِدِي ﴿٨٦﴾ قَالُوا مَآ أَخْلَفْنَا مَوْعِدَكَ بِمَلْكِنَا
وَلٰكِنَّا حُمِّلْنَآ أَوْزَارًا مِّنْ زِينَةِ الْقَوْمِ
فَقَذَفْنٰهَا فَكَذٰلِكَ أَلْقَى السَّامِرِيُّ ﴿٨٧﴾ فَأَخْرَجَ
لَهُمْ عِجْلًا جَسَدًا لَّهٗ خُوَارٌ فَقَالُوا هٰذَآ
إِلٰهُكُمْ وَ إِلٰهُ مُوسٰى ۚ فَنَسِيَ ﴿٨٨﴾ أَفَلَا يَرَوْنَ
أَلَّا يَرْجِعُ إِلَيْهِمْ قَوْلًا ۚ وَّلَا يَمْلِكُ لَهُمْ ضَرًّا
وَّلَا نَفْعًا ﴿٨٩﴾ وَ لَقَدْ قَالَ لَهُمْ هٰرُونُ مِنْ قَبْلُ

ع ١٣

people! you have only been tried by this (calf). Surely, the Most Gracious (God) is your Lord, so follow me and carry out my biddings.'

91. They said, 'We will never give up to cleave to the worship of this (calf) until Moses returns to us.'

92. (Moses turning to Aaron) said, 'Aaron! when you saw them going astray what prevented you

93. 'From following me (and punishing them)? Dared you then disobey my biddings?'

94. (Aaron) said, 'O son of my mother! do not hold me by my beard nor (pull me) by my head. (If I was not strict to them it was because) I was afraid lest you should say, "You have caused a disruption among the Children of Israel and did not preserve my word".'

95. (Moses now called upon Sâmirî to account for it and) said, 'What were you after (by acting as you did) O Sâmirî?'

96. He said, 'I perceived that which they did not perceive. (My perception and insight being stronger than theirs.) I had adopted only some of the traditions (and the teachings) of the Messenger (- Moses), but that (too) I cast away. That is what my mind made fair-seeming to me.'

97. (Moses) said, 'Begone then (if it is so). It shall be your punishment to proclaim (yourself) an untouchable throughout (your) life. Not only that there awaits yet another threat (of punishment of the Hereafter) for you from which you will have no escape. Now, look at the god to which you remained so ardently devoted (as a worshipper). We will destroy it utterly and then we will scatter it away into the sea.'

98. (Moses then addressing his people said,) 'Your God is only Allâh, there is no other,

يٰقَوْمِ إِنَّمَا فُتِنْتُم بِهِۦ ۖ وَإِنَّ رَبَّكُمُ الرَّحْمٰنُ
فَاتَّبِعُونِي وَأَطِيعُوٓا أَمْرِي ﴿٩٠﴾ قَالُوا لَن نَّبْرَحَ
عَلَيْهِ عٰكِفِينَ حَتّٰى يَرْجِعَ إِلَيْنَا مُوسٰى ﴿٩١﴾
قَالَ يٰهٰرُونُ مَا مَنَعَكَ إِذْ رَأَيْتَهُمْ ضَلُّوٓا ﴿٩٢﴾
أَلَّا تَتَّبِعَنِ ۖ أَفَعَصَيْتَ أَمْرِي ﴿٩٣﴾ قَالَ يَبْنَؤُمَّ
لَا تَأْخُذْ بِلِحْيَتِي وَلَا بِرَأْسِي ۖ إِنِّي خَشِيتُ
أَن تَقُولَ فَرَّقْتَ بَيْنَ بَنِي إِسْرٰٓءِيلَ وَلَمْ
تَرْقُبْ قَوْلِي ﴿٩٤﴾ قَالَ فَمَا خَطْبُكَ يٰسٰمِرِيُّ ﴿٩٥﴾
قَالَ بَصُرْتُ بِمَا لَمْ يَبْصُرُوا بِهِۦ فَقَبَضْتُ
قَبْضَةً مِّنْ أَثَرِ الرَّسُولِ فَنَبَذْتُهَا وَكَذٰلِكَ
سَوَّلَتْ لِي نَفْسِي ﴿٩٦﴾ قَالَ فَاذْهَبْ فَإِنَّ لَكَ
فِي الْحَيٰوةِ أَن تَقُولَ لَا مِسَاسَ ۖ وَإِنَّ لَكَ
مَوْعِدًا لَّن تُخْلَفَهُۥ ۖ وَانظُرْ إِلٰىٓ إِلٰهِكَ الَّذِي
ظَلْتَ عَلَيْهِ عَاكِفًا ۖ لَّنُحَرِّقَنَّهُۥ ثُمَّ لَنَنسِفَنَّهُۥ
فِي الْيَمِّ نَسْفًا ﴿٩٧﴾ إِنَّمَا إِلٰهُكُمُ اللّٰهُ الَّذِي لَا إِلٰهَ

cannot be and will never be one worthy of worship but He. He comprehends all things in (His) knowledge.'

99. In this way do We relate to you some of the important news of the days gone by. And We have indeed granted you from Us a (sublime) Reminder (- the Qur'ân).

100. Those who turn away from this shall bear a (heavy) burden on the Day of Resurrection,

101. Abiding thereunder, and grievous will the encumbrance be to them on the Day of Resurrection;

102. The Day when the trumpet shall be blown, and on that Day We shall gather the sinners together, blue-eyed (- the spiritually blind ones).

103. They will talk one to another in a hushed voice (consulting together and planning in secret and saying,) 'You have lived only for ten (centuries).'

104. We know best what they will say, when the one of the most upright conduct among them will say, 'You have lived (here) only for a day.'

SECTION 6

105. **T**hey ask you about mountains. Say, 'My Lord will (blow them up completely and) scatter them as dust.

106. 'And He will render them a desolate and a level plane.

107. 'Where you will find no curve, no depression and no elevation.'

108. On that day they will follow the call of him (-the Holy Prophet) in (the teachings of) whom is no crookedness. (All) voices shall be hushed up before the Most Gracious (God), so you will hear nothing but a faint murmur.

109. On that day no intercession shall help (anybody) except that of him whom the Most Gracious (God) grants permission and with whose sayings (and doings) He is pleased.

110. (God) knows all that is before them (- the people - their future) and all that is behind them

إِلَّا هُوَ وَسِعَ كُلَّ شَيْءٍ عِلْمًا ﴿٩٨﴾ كَذٰلِكَ نَقُصُّ
عَلَيْكَ مِنْ أَنْبَاءِ مَا قَدْ سَبَقَ وَقَدْ آتَيْنٰكَ
مِنْ لَدُنَّا ذِكْرًا ﴿٩٩﴾ مَنْ أَعْرَضَ عَنْهُ فَإِنَّهُ
يَحْمِلُ يَوْمَ الْقِيٰمَةِ وِزْرًا ﴿١٠٠﴾ خٰلِدِينَ فِيهِ
وَسَاءَ لَهُمْ يَوْمَ الْقِيٰمَةِ حِمْلًا ﴿١٠١﴾ يَوْمَ يُنْفَخُ
فِي الصُّورِ وَنَحْشُرُ الْمُجْرِمِينَ يَوْمَئِذٍ زُرْقًا ﴿١٠٢﴾
يَتَخٰفَتُونَ بَيْنَهُمْ إِنْ لَبِثْتُمْ إِلَّا عَشْرًا ﴿١٠٣﴾ نَحْنُ
أَعْلَمُ بِمَا يَقُولُونَ إِذْ يَقُولُ أَمْثَلُهُمْ طَرِيقَةً
إِنْ لَبِثْتُمْ إِلَّا يَوْمًا ﴿١٠٤﴾ وَيَسْئَلُونَكَ عَنِ الْجِبَالِ
فَقُلْ يَنْسِفُهَا رَبِّي نَسْفًا ﴿١٠٥﴾ فَيَذَرُهَا قَاعًا
صَفْصَفًا ﴿١٠٦﴾ لَا تَرٰى فِيهَا عِوَجًا وَلَا أَمْتًا ﴿١٠٧﴾
يَوْمَئِذٍ يَتَّبِعُونَ الدَّاعِيَ لَا عِوَجَ لَهُ
وَخَشَعَتِ الْأَصْوَاتُ لِلرَّحْمٰنِ فَلَا تَسْمَعُ إِلَّا
هَمْسًا ﴿١٠٨﴾ يَوْمَئِذٍ لَا تَنْفَعُ الشَّفٰعَةُ إِلَّا مَنْ
أَذِنَ لَهُ الرَّحْمٰنُ وَرَضِيَ لَهُ قَوْلًا ﴿١٠٩﴾ يَعْلَمُ مَا

(-their past); they cannot encompass Him with (their) knowledge.

111. And all persons shall humble themselves before the Living, the Self-Subsisting and All-Sustaining (God). And he who bears (the burden of) iniquity shall indeed fail (in his objective).

112. But he who does deeds of righteousness and is a believer, will have no fear that he will be deprived of his reward or suffer any withholding of his dues.

113. Just as (We have revealed these verses) We have revealed the entire Qur'ân in Arabic. We have explained in it in various ways Our warnings (against refusal and evil doings), so that the people may guard against evil and become righteous; or rather this (Qur'ân) will bring forth for them a great glory and eminence.

114. Highly Exalted is therefore Allâh, the true King. And make no haste to recite the Qur'ân (and anticipate the early fulfillment of its prophecies) before its revelation is completed to you. But say (in prayer), 'My Lord, increase my knowledge.'

115. We had given a stern command to Adam before this but he forgot; and We found no resolve on his part (to disobey Us).

SECTION 7

116. **A**ND (recall the time) when We said to the angels, 'Make obeisance to Adam (and his sons).' They (all) made obeisance, but *Iblîs* (did not), he refused (to submit).

117. At this We said, 'Adam! surely this fellow is an enemy to you and to your wife. Take care that he does not turn you both out of the garden (of earthly bliss) lest you fall into trouble.

118. 'It is (provided) for you that here you shall not feel hunger, nor shall you go naked,

119. 'And that here you shall feel no thirst nor

بين أيديهم وما خلفهم ولا يحيطون به
علما ﴿١١٠﴾ وعنت الوجوه للحي القيوم وقد
خاب من حمل ظلما ﴿١١١﴾ ومن يعمل من
الصلحت وهو مؤمن فلا يخاف ظلما ولا
هضما ﴿١١٢﴾ وكذلك أنزلنه قرءانا عربيا وصرفنا
فيه من الوعيد لعلهم يتقون أو يحدث لهم
ذكرا ﴿١١٣﴾ فتعلى الله الملك الحق ولا تعجل
بالقرءان من قبل أن يقضى إليك وحيه
وقل رب زدني علما ﴿١١٤﴾ ولقد عهدنا إلى ءادم
من قبل فنسي ولم نجد له عزما ﴿١١٥﴾ وإذ
قلنا للملئكة اسجدوا لءادم فسجدوا إلا
إبليس أبى ﴿١١٦﴾ فقلنا يءادم إن هذا عدو لك
ولزوجك فلا يخرجنكما من الجنة فتشقى ﴿١١٧﴾
إن لك ألا تجوع فيها ولا تعرى ﴿١١٨﴾ وأنك لا

ع

will you be exposed to the sun.'

120. But satan made an evil suggestion to him. He said, 'Adam! shall I direct you to the tree which leads to eternal life and a kingdom which never decays.

121. So they (Adam and his wife) ate from that (tree), so that their shortcomings became unveiled to them and they began to cover themselves with the leaves of the garden. Adam did not observe the commandment of his Lord, so he became miserable.

122. Then (it came to pass that) his Lord chose him (for His benedictions) and turned to him with mercy and guided (him) to the right path.

123. (The Lord) said, 'Go hence! both parties one and all, you being enemies one to another. There shall most certainly come to you guidance from Me, (bear in mind the law that) he who follows My guidance shall not be lost, nor shall he be unhappy.

124. 'But he who turns away from My remembrance, he shall surely lead a straitened life. And (what is more,) We shall raise him up blind on the Day of Resurrection.'

125. He will say, 'My Lord! what for have You raised me up in a state of blindness, while I possessed good sight before?'

126. He (the Lord) will say, 'That is how (you acted). Our signs came to you but you disregarded them. This day you will be disregarded in the like manner.'

127. That is how We recompense him who transgresses and does not believe in the Messages of his Lord. Indeed, the punishment of the Hereafter is extremely terrible and even more enduring.

128. Does it afford them no guidance that We destroyed before them many a generation in whose dwellings they now go about. Indeed, in this there are signs for those who possess

تَظْمَؤُا فِيهَا وَلَا تَضْحٰى ﴿١١٩﴾ فَوَسْوَسَ إِلَيْهِ
الشَّيْطٰنُ قَالَ يٰٓـَٔادَمُ هَلْ أَدُلُّكَ عَلٰى شَجَرَةِ
الْخُلْدِ وَمُلْكٍ لَّا يَبْلٰى ﴿١٢٠﴾ فَأَكَلَا مِنْهَا فَبَدَتْ
لَهُمَا سَوْءٰتُهُمَا وَطَفِقَا يَخْصِفٰنِ عَلَيْهِمَا مِنْ وَّرَقِ
الْجَنَّةِ وَعَصٰٓى ءَادَمُ رَبَّهٗ فَغَوٰى ﴿١٢١﴾ ثُمَّ اجْتَبٰهُ رَبُّهٗ
فَتَابَ عَلَيْهِ وَهَدٰى ﴿١٢٢﴾ قَالَ اهْبِطَا مِنْهَا جَمِيعًا
بَعْضُكُمْ لِبَعْضٍ عَدُوٌّ فَإِمَّا يَأْتِيَنَّكُمْ مِّنِّي هُدًى
فَمَنِ اتَّبَعَ هُدَايَ فَلَا يَضِلُّ وَلَا يَشْقٰى ﴿١٢٣﴾ وَمَنْ
أَعْرَضَ عَنْ ذِكْرِي فَإِنَّ لَهٗ مَعِيشَةً ضَنْكًا
وَّنَحْشُرُهٗ يَوْمَ الْقِيٰمَةِ أَعْمٰى ﴿١٢٤﴾ قَالَ رَبِّ لِمَ
حَشَرْتَنِيٓ أَعْمٰى وَقَدْ كُنْتُ بَصِيرًا ﴿١٢٥﴾ قَالَ
كَذٰلِكَ أَتَتْكَ ءَايٰتُنَا فَنَسِيتَهَا وَكَذٰلِكَ الْيَوْمَ
تُنْسٰى ﴿١٢٦﴾ وَكَذٰلِكَ نَجْزِي مَنْ أَسْرَفَ وَلَمْ يُؤْمِنْۢ
بِـَٔايٰتِ رَبِّهٖ وَلَعَذَابُ الْاٰخِرَةِ أَشَدُّ وَأَبْقٰى ﴿١٢٧﴾
أَفَلَمْ يَهْدِ لَهُمْ كَمْ أَهْلَكْنَا قَبْلَهُمْ مِّنَ الْقُرُونِ
يَمْشُونَ فِي مَسٰكِنِهِمْ إِنَّ فِي ذٰلِكَ لَأٰيٰتٍ لِّأُولِي

understanding.

SECTION 8

129. **B**UT for a word (of promise) already made by your Lord and the term (already) fixed (for them), the inevitable would surely have befallen them by now.

130. Hence put up patiently with what they say and glorify your Lord with (His) praise before the rising of the sun and before its setting. And glorify (Him) during the hours of the night and at the ends of the day (in Prayers), that you may attain (real) happiness (and true bliss).

131. Do not strain your eyes towards (and hanker after) the glamours of this life which some groups of these (disbelievers) have been provided by Us, that We may distinguish the good from the bad through that. The provisions of your Lord (and His gifts) are far better and more lasting (than all this).

132. And bid your people to Pray and be constant and steadfast therein. We do not ask you to provide sustenance (for Us). It is We who provide sustenance for you. The good future lies in guarding against evil.

133. And these (opponents) say, 'Why does he bring us no sign from his Lord?' Has there not come to them a clear evidence (about the advent of this Prophet) from what is (contained) in the former scriptures?

134. Had We punished and destroyed them with a calamity before (the advent of) this (Prophet), they would have certainly said, 'Our Lord! why did you not send a Messenger to us so that we might have followed your commandments before we were humiliated and disgraced?'

135. Say, 'Each one (of us) awaits (the end), therefore wait you (also). You will soon come to know who are the people of the right path and who followed right guidance (and who do not)?'

النُّهٰى ﴿١٢٨﴾ وَلَوْلَا كَلِمَةٌ سَبَقَتْ مِنْ رَّبِّكَ لَكَانَ
لِزَامًا وَّأَجَلٌ مُّسَمًّى ﴿١٢٩﴾ فَاصْبِرْ عَلٰى مَا يَقُوْلُوْنَ
وَسَبِّحْ بِحَمْدِ رَبِّكَ قَبْلَ طُلُوْعِ الشَّمْسِ وَقَبْلَ
غُرُوْبِهَا وَمِنْ اٰنَآئِ الَّيْلِ فَسَبِّحْ وَأَطْرَافَ
النَّهَارِ لَعَلَّكَ تَرْضٰى ﴿١٣٠﴾ وَلَا تَمُدَّنَّ عَيْنَيْكَ
إِلٰى مَا مَتَّعْنَا بِهٖٓ أَزْوَاجًا مِّنْهُمْ زَهْرَةَ الْحَيٰوةِ
الدُّنْيَا لِنَفْتِنَهُمْ فِيْهِ وَرِزْقُ رَبِّكَ خَيْرٌ
وَّأَبْقٰى ﴿١٣١﴾ وَأْمُرْ أَهْلَكَ بِالصَّلٰوةِ وَاصْطَبِرْ عَلَيْهَا
لَا نَسْئَلُكَ رِزْقًا نَحْنُ نَرْزُقُكَ وَالْعَاقِبَةُ
لِلتَّقْوٰى ﴿١٣٢﴾ وَقَالُوْا لَوْلَا يَأْتِيْنَا بِاٰيَةٍ مِّنْ رَّبِّهٖ
أَوَلَمْ تَأْتِهِمْ بَيِّنَةُ مَا فِي الصُّحُفِ الْأُوْلٰى ﴿١٣٣﴾
وَلَوْ أَنَّآ أَهْلَكْنٰهُمْ بِعَذَابٍ مِّنْ قَبْلِهٖ لَقَالُوْا
رَبَّنَا لَوْلَآ أَرْسَلْتَ إِلَيْنَا رَسُوْلًا فَنَتَّبِعَ اٰيٰتِكَ
مِنْ قَبْلِ أَنْ نَّذِلَّ وَنَخْزٰى ﴿١٣٤﴾ قُلْ كُلٌّ
مُّتَرَبِّصٌ فَتَرَبَّصُوْا فَسَتَعْلَمُوْنَ مَنْ أَصْحٰبُ
الصِّرَاطِ السَّوِيِّ وَمَنِ اهْتَدٰى ﴿١٣٥﴾

CHAPTER
21

سُوْرَةُ الْأَنْبِيَاءِ ٢١

AL-ANBIYÂ'

(The Prophets)

(Revealed before Hijrah)

With the name of Allâh,
the Most Gracious, the Ever Merciful
(I commence to read Sûrah Al-Anbiyâ').

PART الْجُزْءُ السَّابِعَ عَشَرَ XVII

1. **T**HERE has drawn nigh for the people (the Day of) their reckoning, yet they turn away in heedlessness.
2. No new Reminder comes to them from their Lord but they listen to it in a playful mood,
3. While their minds are inattentive. (Those of them who have transgressed the limits,) keep their counsels (against the Prophet of their time) secret (and say), 'He is only a human being like yourselves. Will you be seduced by his skillful eloquence while you see and know?'
4. (On the contrary the Prophet's way is different.) He replied, 'My Lord knows what is conceived in the heaven and the earth. And He is the All-Hearing, the All-Knowing.'
5. Nay, they say, 'This (Qur'ân) is (no revelation), but a jumble of confused dreams, rather he (- the Prophet) has forged it himself; he is a poet. (If it is not) so let him then bring us some sign (of destruction) just as the former (Prophets) were sent with.'
6. (Whereas) before them no people of a township whom We destroyed had ever believed. Would they then believe (to escape destruction).
7. (Prophet!) We sent none (as Messengers) before you but (they were) men to whom We made Our revelations. Therefore (O disbelievers!) ask the followers of the Reminder if you do not know (this).

سُوْرَةُ الْأَنْبِيَاءِ مَكِّيَّةٌ

بِسْمِ اللّٰهِ الرَّحْمٰنِ الرَّحِيْمِ

اِقْتَرَبَ لِلنَّاسِ حِسَابُهُمْ وَهُمْ فِيْ
غَفْلَةٍ مُّعْرِضُوْنَ ١ مَا يَأْتِيْهِمْ مِّنْ ذِكْرٍ
مِّنْ رَّبِّهِمْ مُّحْدَثٍ إِلَّا اسْتَمَعُوْهُ وَهُمْ
يَلْعَبُوْنَ ٢ لَاهِيَةً قُلُوْبُهُمْ وَأَسَرُّوا النَّجْوَى
الَّذِيْنَ ظَلَمُوْا هَلْ هٰذَآ إِلَّا بَشَرٌ مِّثْلُكُمْ
أَفَتَأْتُوْنَ السِّحْرَ وَأَنْتُمْ تُبْصِرُوْنَ ٣ قٰلَ
رَبِّيْ يَعْلَمُ الْقَوْلَ فِي السَّمَآءِ وَالْأَرْضِ
وَهُوَ السَّمِيْعُ الْعَلِيْمُ ٤ بَلْ قَالُوْٓا أَضْغٰثُ
أَحْلٰمٍ بَلِ افْتَرٰىهُ بَلْ هُوَ شَاعِرٌ فَلْيَأْتِنَا
بِأٰيَةٍ كَمَآ أُرْسِلَ الْأَوَّلُوْنَ ٥ مَآ أٰمَنَتْ
قَبْلَهُمْ مِّنْ قَرْيَةٍ أَهْلَكْنٰهَا أَفَهُمْ يُؤْمِنُوْنَ ٦
وَمَآ أَرْسَلْنَا قَبْلَكَ إِلَّا رِجَالًا نُّوْحِيْٓ إِلَيْهِمْ
فَسْئَلُوْٓا أَهْلَ الذِّكْرِ إِنْ كُنْتُمْ لَا تَعْلَمُوْنَ ٧

8. Nor did We give them such bodies as could go without food, neither were they people given unusually long lives (to enjoy).
9. (We sent Our revelations to them) then We fulfilled the promise We made to them so that We delivered them, and those whom We pleased (beside them), and We destroyed the transgressors.
10. (People!) Now We have revealed to you a (highly perfect) Book wherein there is a provision for your eminence. Why do you not then make use of your understanding?

SECTION 2

11. **A**ND We have utterly destroyed many a wrongdoing people of townships, and We raised up another people after them.
12. No sooner did they perceive Our punishment than they began to flee from it.
13. (Thereupon We called out to them,) 'Flee not but return to that (state of luxury) in which you were provided comforts and to your dwellings so that you might be called to account for (your conduct).'
14. They said, 'Woe to us! We were indeed wrongdoers.'
15. Then they continued repeating this cry of theirs, till We made them (like) mown down field (and extinguished their spark of life leaving them like) smouldering ashes.
16. We did not create the heaven and the earth and all that is between the two in idle sport.
17. If We had meant to make something vain and idle We would surely have made it so on Our part. (But) We were by no means to do (such a thing).
18. Nay, We hurl the truth at falsehood so that it knocks out its brains (and defeats it); and behold, it (- the falsehood) vanishes. And you deserve to be punished (with Gehenna) for what you ascribe (to God).
19. And whosoever is in the heavens and the earth belongs to Him. And those who are

سُوْرَةُ الْاَنْبِيَآءِ ٢١

وَمَا جَعَلْنٰهُمْ جَسَدًا لَّا يَأْكُلُوْنَ الطَّعَامَ
وَمَا كَانُوْا خٰلِدِيْنَ ﴿٨﴾ ثُمَّ صَدَقْنٰهُمُ الْوَعْدَ
فَاَنْجَيْنٰهُمْ وَمَنْ نَّشَآءُ وَاَهْلَكْنَا الْمُسْرِفِيْنَ ﴿٩﴾
لَقَدْ اَنْزَلْنَآ اِلَيْكُمْ كِتٰبًا فِيْهِ ذِكْرُكُمْ
اَفَلَا تَعْقِلُوْنَ ﴿١٠﴾ وَكَمْ قَصَمْنَا مِنْ قَرْيَةٍ ع
كَانَتْ ظَالِمَةً وَّاَنْشَاْنَا بَعْدَهَا قَوْمًا
اٰخَرِيْنَ ﴿١١﴾ فَلَمَّآ اَحَسُّوْا بَاْسَنَآ اِذَا هُمْ
مِّنْهَا يَرْكُضُوْنَ ﴿١٢﴾ لَا تَرْكُضُوْا وَارْجِعُوْٓا اِلٰى
مَآ اُتْرِفْتُمْ فِيْهِ وَمَسٰكِنِكُمْ لَعَلَّكُمْ
تُسْـَٔلُوْنَ ﴿١٣﴾ قَالُوْا يٰوَيْلَنَآ اِنَّا كُنَّا ظٰلِمِيْنَ ﴿١٤﴾
فَمَا زَالَتْ تِّلْكَ دَعْوٰىهُمْ حَتّٰى جَعَلْنٰهُمْ
حَصِيْدًا خٰمِدِيْنَ ﴿١٥﴾ وَمَا خَلَقْنَا السَّمَآءَ
وَالْاَرْضَ وَمَا بَيْنَهُمَا لٰعِبِيْنَ ﴿١٦﴾ لَوْ اَرَدْنَآ
اَنْ نَّتَّخِذَ لَهْوًا لَّاتَّخَذْنٰهُ مِنْ لَّدُنَّآ ۖ اِنْ
كُنَّا فٰعِلِيْنَ ﴿١٧﴾ بَلْ نَقْذِفُ بِالْحَقِّ عَلَى
الْبٰطِلِ فَيَدْمَغُهٗ فَاِذَا هُوَ زَاهِقٌ ۗ وَلَكُمُ
الْوَيْلُ مِمَّا تَصِفُوْنَ ﴿١٨﴾ وَلَهٗ مَنْ فِى السَّمٰوٰتِ

الْجُزْءُ السَّابِعَ عَشَرَ

close to Him do not disdain to worship Him, nor do they (ever) grow weary (to serve Him).
20. They glorify (Him) night and day (and) they flag not.
21. And yet some people have chosen (false) gods from the earth who (are supposed to) raise (the dead) to life.
22. Had there been in them (- the heaven and the earth) other gods beside Allâh, then surely both would have gone to ruin (because of chaos, disorder and confusion). Glorified then be Allâh the Lord of the Throne of power, far above what they attribute (to Him).
23. He cannot be questioned for what He does, (because the cause for an objection does not exist,) whereas all (others) will be questioned (for what they do).
24. Or have they chosen (other) gods beside Him? Say, 'Bring forth your clear proof (if there are other gods).' This (Unity of God) is the message of those who are with Me and the message of those (who have gone) before Me. The only thing is that most of them have no knowledge of the truth and that is why they have turned away (from it).
25. And We sent no Messenger before you but We revealed to him, (saying), 'The truth is that there is no other, cannot be and will never be one worthy of worship but Me, therefore worship Me (alone).'
26. And they say, 'The Most Gracious (God) has taken to Himself a son.' Holy is He. Rather they (whom they so designate) are (only His) honoured servants.
27. They do not precede Him in speech and they only carry out His biddings.
28. He knows all that is before them (- their future) and all that is behind them (- their past). And they do not intercede except for the person for whom He is pleased to accord permission. And they are full of awe and reverence out of His Majesty.

وَ الْأَرْضِ وَمَنْ عِنْدَهُ لَا يَسْتَكْبِرُوْنَ عَنْ
عِبَادَتِهِ وَ لَا يَسْتَحْسِرُوْنَ ﴿١٩﴾ يُسَبِّحُوْنَ
الَّيْلَ وَ النَّهَارَ لَا يَفْتُرُوْنَ ﴿٢٠﴾ أَمِ اتَّخَذُوْا
أٰلِهَةً مِّنَ الْأَرْضِ هُمْ يُنْشِرُوْنَ ﴿٢١﴾ لَوْ كَانَ
فِيهِمَا أٰلِهَةٌ إِلَّا اللّٰهُ لَفَسَدَتَا فَسُبْحٰنَ
اللّٰهِ رَبِّ الْعَرْشِ عَمَّا يَصِفُوْنَ ﴿٢٢﴾ لَا يُسْـَٔلُ
عَمَّا يَفْعَلُ وَ هُمْ يُسْـَٔلُوْنَ ﴿٢٣﴾ أَمِ اتَّخَذُوْا
مِنْ دُوْنِهِ أٰلِهَةً قُلْ هَاتُوْا بُرْهٰنَكُمْ
هٰذَا ذِكْرُ مَنْ مَّعِيَ وَ ذِكْرُ مَنْ قَبْلِي بَلْ
أَكْثَرُهُمْ لَا يَعْلَمُوْنَ الْحَقَّ فَهُمْ مُّعْرِضُوْنَ ﴿٢٤﴾
وَ مَا أَرْسَلْنَا مِنْ قَبْلِكَ مِنْ رَّسُوْلٍ إِلَّا
نُوْحِيْ إِلَيْهِ أَنَّهُ لَا إِلٰهَ إِلَّا أَنَا فَاعْبُدُوْنِ ﴿٢٥﴾
وَ قَالُوا اتَّخَذَ الرَّحْمٰنُ وَلَدًا سُبْحٰنَهُ بَلْ
عِبَادٌ مُّكْرَمُوْنَ ﴿٢٦﴾ لَا يَسْبِقُوْنَهُ بِالْقَوْلِ
وَ هُمْ بِأَمْرِهِ يَعْمَلُوْنَ ﴿٢٧﴾ يَعْلَمُ مَا بَيْنَ
أَيْدِيهِمْ وَ مَا خَلْفَهُمْ وَ لَا يَشْفَعُوْنَ إِلَّا
لِمَنِ ارْتَضٰى وَ هُمْ مِّنْ خَشْيَتِهِ مُشْفِقُوْنَ ﴿٢٨﴾

29. Should anyone of them say, 'I am a deity apart from Him;' him We will recompense with Gehenna for that is how We recompense the unjust.

SECTION 3

30. Do those who disbelieve not see that the heavens and the earth were (once) one mass all closed up, then We rent them apart. And it is from water that We created all life. Will they not believe (in the face of all this).
31. And We have made firm mountains on the earth so that they may be a source of benefit and provision for the people and lest it should quake with them. And We made on it wide pathways that people may find right guidance to reach the goal.
32. And We have made the heaven a roof, well protected, still they turn away paying no heed to its (heavenly) signs.
33. And it is He Who created the night and the day, the sun and the moon. They are all gliding along smoothly in (their respective) orbits.
34. And We have not assigned to any human being before you an unusually prolonged life. If you should die then shall they live unusually long while (here).
35. Every soul is bound to taste of death; and We prove (worth of) you now with evil, now with good, by way of trial. And you shall be made to return to Us.
36. And when those who disbelieve see you, they hold you for a mere trifle (and say), 'Is this the fellow who speaks (ill) of your gods?' While it is they themselves who deny (disdainfully) the great Eminence of the Most Gracious (God).
37. A human being is hasty by nature. I will certainly show you (O people!) My signs, but do not ask Me to hasten (them) before their (appointed) time.
38. And they say, 'When will this promise of punishment be fulfilled, (let us know) if you

وَمَنْ يَّقُلْ مِنْهُمْ إِنِّيٓ إِلٰهٌ مِّنْ دُونِهٖ
فَذٰلِكَ نَجْزِيهِ جَهَنَّمَ ۚ كَذٰلِكَ نَجْزِي
ع ١٩ الظّٰلِمِينَ ﴿٢٩﴾ أَوَلَمْ يَرَ الَّذِينَ كَفَرُوٓا أَنَّ
السَّمٰوٰتِ وَالْأَرْضَ كَانَتَا رَتْقًا فَفَتَقْنٰهُمَا ۖ
وَجَعَلْنَا مِنَ الْمَآءِ كُلَّ شَيْءٍ حَيٍّ ۖ أَفَلَا
يُؤْمِنُونَ ﴿٣٠﴾ وَجَعَلْنَا فِي الْأَرْضِ رَوٰسِيَ أَنْ
تَمِيدَ بِهِمْ وَجَعَلْنَا فِيهَا فِجَاجًا سُبُلًا لَّعَلَّهُمْ
يَهْتَدُونَ ﴿٣١﴾ وَجَعَلْنَا السَّمَآءَ سَقْفًا مَّحْفُوظًا ۚ
وَّهُمْ عَنْ اٰيٰتِهَا مُعْرِضُونَ ﴿٣٢﴾ وَهُوَ الَّذِي
خَلَقَ الَّيْلَ وَالنَّهَارَ وَالشَّمْسَ وَالْقَمَرَ ۖ
كُلٌّ فِي فَلَكٍ يَّسْبَحُونَ ﴿٣٣﴾ وَمَا جَعَلْنَا لِبَشَرٍ
مِّنْ قَبْلِكَ الْخُلْدَ ۖ أَفَإِي۟ن مِّتَّ فَهُمُ
الْخٰلِدُونَ ﴿٣٤﴾ كُلُّ نَفْسٍ ذَآئِقَةُ الْمَوْتِ ۗ
وَنَبْلُوكُمْ بِالشَّرِّ وَالْخَيْرِ فِتْنَةً ۖ وَإِلَيْنَا
تُرْجَعُونَ ﴿٣٥﴾ وَإِذَا رَاٰكَ الَّذِينَ كَفَرُوٓا إِنْ
يَّتَّخِذُونَكَ إِلَّا هُزُوًا ۖ أَهٰذَا الَّذِي يَذْكُرُ
اٰلِهَتَكُمْ ۚ وَهُمْ بِذِكْرِ الرَّحْمٰنِ هُمْ كٰفِرُونَ ﴿٣٦﴾
خُلِقَ الْإِنْسٰنُ مِنْ عَجَلٍ ۚ سَاُورِيكُمْ اٰيٰتِي
فَلَا تَسْتَعْجِلُونِ ﴿٣٧﴾ وَيَقُولُونَ مَتٰى هٰذَا الْوَعْدُ

are truthful?'

39. How good it would be if those who disbelieve could know the time when they will not be able to ward off (the flames of) the fire from their faces nor from their backs and they shall not be helped!

40. Nay it (- the punishment) shall come upon them unawares, so that it will confound them completely, and they will not be able to avert it and no respite shall be given them.

41. And certainly Messengers have (also) been treated as mere trifles even before you with the result that those who made light of them (- the Messengers) were caught by the very thing they held as vain and unimportant.

SECTION 4

42. **S**AY, 'Who can protect you by night and in the daytime from (the punishment of) the Most Gracious (God)?' But rather (thank Him) they are (truly) averse to proclaiming the greatness of their Lord.

43. Or do they have gods that can defend them against Us? They are not able to help (even) themselves, nor shall they receive any help from Us.

44. The thing is that We provided those and their fathers with the good things (of this world), until a long period (of enjoyment) passed over them (and now they are steeped in negligence). But do they not see that We are invading the land (of disbelief) and are gradually reducing it from its outlying borders? Can they even then be the victors?

45. Say, 'It is on the basis of (divine) revelation that I warn you.' But the (spiritually) deaf do not hear the call when they are warned.

46. And if the slightest punishment of your Lord befalls them they would surely cry out, 'Ah, Woe to Us! We were indeed unjust.'

47. And We shall set up scales of justice (to weigh their deeds) on the Day of Resurrec-

إِن كُنتُمْ صَٰدِقِينَ ﴿٣٨﴾ لَوْ يَعْلَمُ الَّذِينَ
كَفَرُوا حِينَ لَا يَكُفُّونَ عَن وُجُوهِهِمُ النَّارَ
وَلَا عَن ظُهُورِهِمْ وَلَا هُمْ يُنصَرُونَ ﴿٣٩﴾ بَلْ
تَأْتِيهِم بَغْتَةً فَتَبْهَتُهُمْ فَلَا يَسْتَطِيعُونَ
رَدَّهَا وَلَا هُمْ يُنظَرُونَ ﴿٤٠﴾ وَلَقَدِ اسْتُهْزِئَ
بِرُسُلٍ مِّن قَبْلِكَ فَحَاقَ بِالَّذِينَ سَخِرُوا
مِنْهُم مَّا كَانُوا بِهِ يَسْتَهْزِءُونَ ﴿٤١﴾ قُلْ مَن
يَكْلَؤُكُم بِاللَّيْلِ وَالنَّهَارِ مِنَ الرَّحْمَٰنِ
بَلْ هُمْ عَن ذِكْرِ رَبِّهِم مُّعْرِضُونَ ﴿٤٢﴾ أَمْ
لَهُمْ آلِهَةٌ تَمْنَعُهُم مِّن دُونِنَا لَا يَسْتَطِيعُونَ
نَصْرَ أَنفُسِهِمْ وَلَا هُم مِّنَّا يُصْحَبُونَ ﴿٤٣﴾ بَلْ
مَتَّعْنَا هَٰؤُلَاءِ وَآبَاءَهُمْ حَتَّىٰ طَالَ عَلَيْهِمُ
الْعُمُرُ أَفَلَا يَرَوْنَ أَنَّا نَأْتِي الْأَرْضَ نَنقُصُهَا
مِنْ أَطْرَافِهَا أَفَهُمُ الْغَٰلِبُونَ ﴿٤٤﴾ قُلْ إِنَّمَا
أُنذِرُكُم بِالْوَحْيِ وَلَا يَسْمَعُ الصُّمُّ الدُّعَاءَ
إِذَا مَا يُنذَرُونَ ﴿٤٥﴾ وَلَئِن مَّسَّتْهُمْ نَفْحَةٌ
مِّنْ عَذَابِ رَبِّكَ لَيَقُولُنَّ يَٰوَيْلَنَا إِنَّا كُنَّا
ظَٰلِمِينَ ﴿٤٦﴾ وَنَضَعُ الْمَوَٰزِينَ الْقِسْطَ لِيَوْمِ

tion so that no soul shall be done the least injustice. And even if it (the deeds of a person) were (as little as) the weight of a grain of mustard seed, We would bring it forth (for accurate account). And sufficient are We as Reckoners.

48. And We gave Moses and Aaron the arguments (telling the right from the wrong) and a light and a Reminder for those who guard against evil;

49. Those who stand in awe of their Lord even in their heart of hearts and who dread the Hour (of Judgment).

50. And (like those earlier Scriptures) We have revealed this (Qur'ân) as a Reminder, full of bliss. Will you then be the rejecters of this (Perfect Book)?

SECTION 5

51. AND We gave Abraham his rectitude (befitting his station as a Prophet of God) before (this). We knew him fully well (for his personal qualities).

52. (Recall the time) when he said to his sire and his people, 'What (good) are these images to which you sit down to worship with so much devotion?'

53. They said, 'We found our fathers worshipping them.'

54. He said, 'Surely, you yourselves and your fathers have been plainly mistaken.'

55. They said, 'Is it (really) the truth that you have brought us or are you of those playing a joke (on us)?'

56. (Abraham) said, '(I am playing no jokes on you.) Your (true) Lord is the (only) Lord of the heavens and the earth, Who originated them; and I am of those who bear witness to (the truth of) this before you.

57. 'And, by Allâh, I will indeed plan a stern plan against your idols after you have left turning your backs.'

58. So he smashed them all into pieces, except

الْقِيٰمَةِ فَلَا تُظْلَمُ نَفْسٌ شَيْـًٔا ۖ وَإِنْ كَانَ
مِثْقَالَ حَبَّةٍ مِّنْ خَرْدَلٍ أَتَيْنَا بِهَا ۖ وَكَفٰى
بِنَا حٰسِبِيْنَ ﴿٤٧﴾ وَلَقَدْ اٰتَيْنَا مُوسٰى وَهٰرُونَ
الْفُرْقَانَ وَضِيَآءً وَّذِكْرًا لِّلْمُتَّقِيْنَ ﴿٤٨﴾ الَّذِيْنَ
يَخْشَوْنَ رَبَّهُمْ بِالْغَيْبِ وَهُمْ مِّنَ السَّاعَةِ
مُشْفِقُوْنَ ﴿٤٩﴾ وَهٰذَا ذِكْرٌ مُّبٰرَكٌ أَنْزَلْنٰهُ ۚ
أَفَأَنْتُمْ لَهٗ مُنْكِرُوْنَ ﴿٥٠﴾ وَلَقَدْ اٰتَيْنَآ إِبْرٰهِيْمَ
رُشْدَهٗ مِنْ قَبْلُ وَكُنَّا بِهٖ عٰلِمِيْنَ ﴿٥١﴾
إِذْ قَالَ لِأَبِيْهِ وَقَوْمِهٖ مَا هٰذِهِ التَّمَاثِيْلُ
الَّتِيْٓ أَنْتُمْ لَهَا عٰكِفُوْنَ ﴿٥٢﴾ قَالُوْا وَجَدْنَآ
اٰبَآءَنَا لَهَا عٰبِدِيْنَ ﴿٥٣﴾ قَالَ لَقَدْ كُنْتُمْ
أَنْتُمْ وَاٰبَآؤُكُمْ فِيْ ضَلٰلٍ مُّبِيْنٍ ﴿٥٤﴾ قَالُوْٓا
أَجِئْتَنَا بِالْحَقِّ أَمْ أَنْتَ مِنَ اللّٰعِبِيْنَ ﴿٥٥﴾
قَالَ بَلْ رَّبُّكُمْ رَبُّ السَّمٰوٰتِ وَالْأَرْضِ
الَّذِيْ فَطَرَهُنَّ ۖ وَأَنَا عَلٰى ذٰلِكُمْ مِّنَ
الشّٰهِدِيْنَ ﴿٥٦﴾ وَتَاللّٰهِ لَأَكِيْدَنَّ أَصْنٰمَكُمْ
بَعْدَ أَنْ تُوَلُّوْا مُدْبِرِيْنَ ﴿٥٧﴾ فَجَعَلَهُمْ
جُذٰذًا إِلَّا كَبِيْرًا لَّهُمْ لَعَلَّهُمْ إِلَيْهِ

their chief (idol), that they might return to it (for inquiry as he planned).

59. (When they saw their idols broken,) they said, 'Who has done this to our gods? He (who has done this) must be of the wrongdoers indeed.'

60. Some (of the people) said, 'We heard a young man speaking (ill) of them, he is called Abraham.'

61. They said, 'Then bring him before the eyes of the people so that they may bear witness (against him).'

62. (When he was brought) they said, 'O Abraham! Is it you who did this to our gods?'

63. (Abraham) said, 'Well, of course, someone has done it. Here is their chief (idol which witnessed all this). So better ask (him and) them, if they can speak.'

64. Then they turned to their leaders and to one another and said, 'You, yourselves are surely in the wrong.'

65. Then they were made to hang down their heads (in shame and said to Abraham), 'Indeed, you know very well that these (idols) do not speak.'

66. (Abraham) said, 'Do you then worship, apart from Allâh, the things which can do no good to you, (who are their worshippers), nor can do harm to (those of) you (who are their destroyers).

67. 'Shame on you and on the things you worship apart from Allâh! Will you not then make use of (your) understanding?'

68. They said, (among themselves,) 'Burn him and help your gods if (at all) you would do (anything against Abraham).'

69. We said, 'O fire, be you a means of coolness and safety for Abraham.'

70. They intended a mistreatment of him, but We made them the worst losers (and they could not carry out their evil design of burning him).

71. And We delivered him and Lot (as well and

يَرۡجِعُونَ ﴿٥٨﴾ قَالُواْ مَن فَعَلَ هَٰذَا بِـَٔالِهَتِنَآ
إِنَّهُۥ لَمِنَ ٱلظَّٰلِمِينَ ﴿٥٩﴾ قَالُواْ سَمِعۡنَا فَتٗى
يَذۡكُرُهُمۡ يُقَالُ لَهُۥٓ إِبۡرَٰهِيمُ ﴿٦٠﴾ قَالُواْ
فَأۡتُواْ بِهِۦ عَلَىٰٓ أَعۡيُنِ ٱلنَّاسِ لَعَلَّهُمۡ
يَشۡهَدُونَ ﴿٦١﴾ قَالُوٓاْ ءَأَنتَ فَعَلۡتَ هَٰذَا
بِـَٔالِهَتِنَا يَٰٓإِبۡرَٰهِيمُ ﴿٦٢﴾ قَالَ بَلۡ فَعَلَهُۥ
كَبِيرُهُمۡ هَٰذَا فَسۡـَٔلُوهُمۡ إِن كَانُواْ
يَنطِقُونَ ﴿٦٣﴾ فَرَجَعُوٓاْ إِلَىٰٓ أَنفُسِهِمۡ فَقَالُوٓاْ
إِنَّكُمۡ أَنتُمُ ٱلظَّٰلِمُونَ ﴿٦٤﴾ ثُمَّ نُكِسُواْ
عَلَىٰ رُءُوسِهِمۡ لَقَدۡ عَلِمۡتَ مَا هَٰٓؤُلَآءِ
يَنطِقُونَ ﴿٦٥﴾ قَالَ أَفَتَعۡبُدُونَ مِن دُونِ
ٱللَّهِ مَا لَا يَنفَعُكُمۡ شَيۡـٔٗا وَلَا يَضُرُّكُمۡ ﴿٦٦﴾
أُفّٖ لَّكُمۡ وَلِمَا تَعۡبُدُونَ مِن دُونِ ٱللَّهِۚ
أَفَلَا تَعۡقِلُونَ ﴿٦٧﴾ قَالُواْ حَرِّقُوهُ وَٱنصُرُوٓاْ
ءَالِهَتَكُمۡ إِن كُنتُمۡ فَٰعِلِينَ ﴿٦٨﴾ قُلۡنَا يَٰنَارُ كُونِي
بَرۡدٗا وَسَلَٰمًا عَلَىٰٓ إِبۡرَٰهِيمَ ﴿٦٩﴾ وَأَرَادُواْ
بِهِۦ كَيۡدٗا فَجَعَلۡنَٰهُمُ ٱلۡأَخۡسَرِينَ ﴿٧٠﴾
وَنَجَّيۡنَٰهُ وَلُوطًا إِلَى ٱلۡأَرۡضِ ٱلَّتِي بَٰرَكۡنَا

brought them) towards the land (of Can'ân) which We had blessed for the peoples.

72. And We gave him Isaac out of Our bounty and Jacob, (an additional bounty), as a grandson. We made all (of them) righteous.

73. And We appointed them leaders, who guide (people) by Our command, and We revealed to them the doing of good deeds and the observing of Prayer and the giving of alms. And they were all worshippers of Us (alone).

74. And (We showed Our favours to) Lot, We gave him wisdom and knowledge and delivered him from the people of the town who indulged in abominable practices. They were indeed wicked and lawless people.

75. And We admitted him (- Lot) to Our mercy, for he was surely of the righteous.

SECTION 6

76. **A**ND (We showed Our favours to) Noah. Behold! He called (to Us) in the days bygone. So We heard his prayer and delivered him and his companions from the great distressful calamity.

77. And We helped him against the people who cried lies to Our Messages. They were surely people given to evil, so We drowned them all.

78. And (We bestowed Our favours on) David and Solomon. Behold! They gave their (respective) judgment in the disputed matter about a certain crop when the sheep of a certain people strayed into it at night, and We were bearers of witness to the judgment they gave (them).

79. So We gave Solomon the true appreciation of it (- the matter); to each one of them We gave wisdom and knowledge. And We had subjected the mountains and the birds who celebrated (Our) glory along with David. That is what We always do.

80. And We taught him (the art of) making coats of mail for you (people), that they designed to

فِيهَا لِلْعٰلَمِينَ ﴿٧١﴾ وَوَهَبْنَا لَهُۥٓ إِسْحٰقَ
وَيَعْقُوبَ نَافِلَةً ۖ وَكُلًّا جَعَلْنَا صٰلِحِينَ ﴿٧٢﴾
وَجَعَلْنٰهُمْ أَئِمَّةً يَهْدُونَ بِأَمْرِنَا
وَأَوْحَيْنَآ إِلَيْهِمْ فِعْلَ الْخَيْرٰتِ وَإِقَامَ
الصَّلٰوةِ وَإِيتَآءَ الزَّكٰوةِ ۖ وَكَانُوا لَنَا
عٰبِدِينَ ﴿٧٣﴾ وَلُوطًا ءَاتَيْنٰهُ حُكْمًا وَعِلْمًا
وَنَجَّيْنٰهُ مِنَ الْقَرْيَةِ الَّتِى كَانَت
تَّعْمَلُ الْخَبٰٓئِثَ ۗ إِنَّهُمْ كَانُوا قَوْمَ سَوْءٍ
فٰسِقِينَ ﴿٧٤﴾ وَأَدْخَلْنٰهُ فِى رَحْمَتِنَآ ۖ إِنَّهُۥ
مِنَ الصّٰلِحِينَ ﴿٧٥﴾ وَنُوحًا إِذْ نَادٰى مِنْ
قَبْلُ فَاسْتَجَبْنَا لَهُۥ فَنَجَّيْنٰهُ وَأَهْلَهُۥ
مِنَ الْكَرْبِ الْعَظِيمِ ﴿٧٦﴾ وَنَصَرْنٰهُ مِنَ
الْقَوْمِ الَّذِينَ كَذَّبُوا بِـَٔايٰتِنَآ ۚ إِنَّهُمْ
كَانُوا قَوْمَ سَوْءٍ فَأَغْرَقْنٰهُمْ أَجْمَعِينَ ﴿٧٧﴾
وَدَاوُۥدَ وَسُلَيْمٰنَ إِذْ يَحْكُمَانِ فِى
الْحَرْثِ إِذْ نَفَشَتْ فِيهِ غَنَمُ الْقَوْمِ ۚ
وَكُنَّا لِحُكْمِهِمْ شٰهِدِينَ ﴿٧٨﴾ فَفَهَّمْنٰهَا
سُلَيْمٰنَ ۚ وَكُلًّا ءَاتَيْنَا حُكْمًا وَعِلْمًا ۚ
وَسَخَّرْنَا مَعَ دَاوُۥدَ الْجِبَالَ يُسَبِّحْنَ
وَالطَّيْرَ ۚ وَكُنَّا فٰعِلِينَ ﴿٧٩﴾ وَعَلَّمْنٰهُ صَنْعَةَ
لَبُوسٍ لَّكُمْ لِتُحْصِنَكُم مِّنۢ بَأْسِكُمْ ۖ فَهَلْ

fortify you against (one another's) violence (in your wars). Will you then be grateful?
81. And (We subjected) to Solomon the violent wind; it blew according to his commandments towards the land (of Can'ân) which We had blessed and We have knowledge of all things.
82. And (We subjected to him) some of the expert deep divers who dived for him and did other (sundry) works besides that; and it was We Who kept watch over them.
83. And (We showed Our favours to) Job. Behold! He called out to his Lord, 'I am afflicted with some distress, and You are the Most Merciful of all who show mercy.'
84. So We heard his prayer and removed the affliction which he had and We restored his family to him and as many more (followers) with them by way of mercy from Ourself. This (event) serves as a reminder for (Our) devotees.
85. And (We showed Our favours to) Ismâîl, Idrîs (- Enoch), Dhul-Kifl (- Ezekiel, possessed of abundant portion), all of them were of the patiently persevering people.
86. And We admitted them to Our mercy. They were of the righteous indeed.
87. And (We showed Our favours to) Dhul-Nûn (Jonah). Behold! He left in anger (his people for the sake of God). He was sure in his mind that We would not cause him any distress. (But when We did,) he cried out in the midst of afflictions, 'There is no other God but you. Holy are You. I have indeed been of those hard pressed with difficulties and distress.'
88. So We heard his prayer and We delivered him from grief, and in this way do We deliver the (true) believers.
89. And (We showed Our favours to) Zachariah. Behold! He called out to his Lord and prayed to Him, 'My Lord, do not leave me solitary, alone (and heirless), You are Best of those who remain after (-You alone are the

أَنْتُمْ شٰكِرُونَ ﴿٨٠﴾ وَلِسُلَيْمٰنَ الرِّيحَ
عَاصِفَةً تَجْرِي بِأَمْرِهِ إِلَى الْأَرْضِ
الَّتِي بٰرَكْنَا فِيهَا وَكُنَّا بِكُلِّ شَيْءٍ
عٰلِمِينَ ﴿٨١﴾ وَمِنَ الشَّيٰطِينِ مَنْ يَغُوصُونَ
لَهُ وَيَعْمَلُونَ عَمَلًا دُونَ ذٰلِكَ وَكُنَّا
لَهُمْ حٰفِظِينَ ﴿٨٢﴾ وَأَيُّوبَ إِذْ نَادٰى رَبَّهُ
أَنِّي مَسَّنِيَ الضُّرُّ وَأَنْتَ أَرْحَمُ الرّٰحِمِينَ ﴿٨٣﴾
فَاسْتَجَبْنَا لَهُ فَكَشَفْنَا مَا بِهِ مِنْ ضُرٍّ
وَّءَاتَيْنٰهُ أَهْلَهُ وَمِثْلَهُمْ مَّعَهُمْ رَحْمَةً
مِّنْ عِنْدِنَا وَذِكْرٰى لِلْعٰبِدِينَ ﴿٨٤﴾
وَإِسْمٰعِيلَ وَإِدْرِيسَ وَذَا الْكِفْلِ كُلٌّ
مِّنَ الصّٰبِرِينَ ﴿٨٥﴾ وَأَدْخَلْنٰهُمْ فِي رَحْمَتِنَا
إِنَّهُمْ مِّنَ الصّٰلِحِينَ ﴿٨٦﴾ وَذَا النُّونِ إِذْ ذَّهَبَ
مُغٰضِبًا فَظَنَّ أَنْ لَّنْ نَّقْدِرَ عَلَيْهِ فَنَادٰى
فِي الظُّلُمٰتِ أَنْ لَّآ إِلٰهَ إِلَّآ أَنْتَ سُبْحٰنَكَ
إِنِّي كُنْتُ مِنَ الظّٰلِمِينَ ﴿٨٧﴾ فَاسْتَجَبْنَا لَهُ
وَنَجَّيْنٰهُ مِنَ الْغَمِّ وَكَذٰلِكَ نُـۨجِي
الْمُؤْمِنِينَ ﴿٨٨﴾ وَزَكَرِيَّآ إِذْ نَادٰى رَبَّهُ
رَبِّ لَا تَذَرْنِي فَرْدًا وَأَنْتَ خَيْرُ

Everlasting God).'
90. So We heard his prayer and granted him (a son) John, and cured his wife (of sterility) making her fit (for bearing children) for him. They used to vie one with another in (doing) good deeds and call upon Us with (mixed feelings of) hope and fear, and they were humble before Us.
91. And (We showed Our favours to) the woman (- Mary) who preserved her chastity, so We revealed to her some of Our words and We made her and her son (- Jesus) a sign (of eminence) for the nations.
92. (People!) Surely, this your religion is the one single religion (of all the Prophets), and I am your Lord, so worship Me.
93. But they (- the latter generations) split up their affair (of religion) among themselves (and became divided into factions), and all will return to Us.

SECTION 7

94. **S**o whoever does deeds of righteousness and is a believer (will find) there is no disapproval of his endeavours (and his strivings are not lost); and surely We are recorders (of his virtues) for him.
95. And it is not permissible to (the people of) a township whom We have destroyed to come back (to life of this world).
96. (This inviolable law will remain in force) even when (the great powers like) Gog and Magog are let loose and come crashing down from every height and from the crest of every wave, and when they occupy every point of vantage (dominating the whole world and when they excel all other nations).
97. And when the time (of the fulfillment) of the true promise (about the destruction of the forces of falsehood and materialism as represented by Gog and Magog) draws near, behold! The eyes of those who do not believe (in the triumph of truth), will be transfixed (and they

الْوٰرِثِينَ ﴿٨٩﴾ فَاسْتَجَبْنَا لَهُ وَوَهَبْنَا لَهُ
يَحْيٰى وَأَصْلَحْنَا لَهُ زَوْجَهُ إِنَّهُمْ كَانُوا
يُسٰرِعُونَ فِي الْخَيْرٰتِ وَيَدْعُونَنَا رَغَبًا
وَرَهَبًا وَكَانُوا لَنَا خٰشِعِينَ ﴿٩٠﴾ وَالَّتِي
أَحْصَنَتْ فَرْجَهَا فَنَفَخْنَا فِيهَا مِن
رُّوحِنَا وَجَعَلْنٰهَا وَابْنَهَا ءَايَةً لِّلْعٰلَمِينَ ﴿٩١﴾
إِنَّ هٰذِهِ أُمَّتُكُمْ أُمَّةً وٰحِدَةً وَأَنَا
رَبُّكُمْ فَاعْبُدُونِ ﴿٩٢﴾ وَتَقَطَّعُوا أَمْرَهُم
بَيْنَهُمْ كُلٌّ إِلَيْنَا رٰجِعُونَ ﴿٩٣﴾ فَمَن
يَعْمَلْ مِنَ الصّٰلِحٰتِ وَهُوَ مُؤْمِنٌ فَلَا
كُفْرَانَ لِسَعْيِهِ وَإِنَّا لَهُ كٰتِبُونَ ﴿٩٤﴾
وَحَرٰمٌ عَلٰى قَرْيَةٍ أَهْلَكْنٰهَا أَنَّهُمْ لَا
يَرْجِعُونَ ﴿٩٥﴾ حَتّٰى إِذَا فُتِحَتْ يَأْجُوجُ
وَمَأْجُوجُ وَهُم مِّن كُلِّ حَدَبٍ يَنسِلُونَ ﴿٩٦﴾
وَاقْتَرَبَ الْوَعْدُ الْحَقُّ فَإِذَا هِيَ شٰخِصَةٌ

will exclaim), 'Ah, woe to us! We were really forgetful of this (day), nay, we were of course unjust.'
98. (It will be said to them,) 'Surely, you and the things which you worship apart from Allâh are, of course, fuel of Gehenna, where you shall enter.'
99. Had these things been true gods (as you claim to be) they would not have come to it. But (as it is) they shall all enter it and abide in it for long.
100. Groaning shall be their lot therein and they will not hear in it (anything else).
101. But those to whom We have already promised a most fair treatment from Us, shall be kept far removed from it (-the Hell).
102. (Not to speak of entering it;) they will not hear the faintest sound of it and they shall be abiding in (the midst of all the blessings) which their souls desire.
103. The great terror (of the Judgment Day) will cause them no grief and the angels will receive them (with the greetings), 'This is your day which you were promised.'
104. This is the day when We shall roll up the heavens like the rolling up of the written scrolls by a scribe. Just as We started the process of the first creation so shall We reproduce it. This is a promise binding on Us; We shall certainly bring it about.
105. We have already stated in the *Zabûr* (Psalms - the Book of David) after (stating it in) the Reminder (-Torah) that My servants with right capacity (to rule) shall inherit the land.
106. Verily, in this (Qur'ân) is an important Message for a people who worship (Us).
107. And We did not send you (O Muhammad!) but as a blessing and mercy for all beings.
108. Say, 'Indeed it has been revealed to me that your God is but One God. Will you then, be the ones who submit (to Him)?'

أَبْصَٰرُ الَّذِينَ كَفَرُوا يَٰوَيْلَنَا قَدْ كُنَّا
فِي غَفْلَةٍ مِّنْ هَٰذَا بَلْ كُنَّا ظَٰلِمِينَ ﴿٩٧﴾
إِنَّكُمْ وَمَا تَعْبُدُونَ مِن دُونِ اللَّهِ حَصَبُ
جَهَنَّمَ أَنتُمْ لَهَا وَٰرِدُونَ ﴿٩٨﴾ لَوْ كَانَ
هَٰٓؤُلَآءِ ءَالِهَةً مَّا وَرَدُوهَا وَكُلٌّ فِيهَا
خَٰلِدُونَ ﴿٩٩﴾ لَهُمْ فِيهَا زَفِيرٌ وَهُمْ فِيهَا
لَا يَسْمَعُونَ ﴿١٠٠﴾ إِنَّ الَّذِينَ سَبَقَتْ لَهُم
مِّنَّا الْحُسْنَىٰٓ أُولَٰٓئِكَ عَنْهَا مُبْعَدُونَ ﴿١٠١﴾ لَا
يَسْمَعُونَ حَسِيسَهَا وَهُمْ فِي مَا اشْتَهَتْ
أَنفُسُهُمْ خَٰلِدُونَ ﴿١٠٢﴾ لَا يَحْزُنُهُمُ الْفَزَعُ
الْأَكْبَرُ وَتَتَلَقَّىٰهُمُ الْمَلَٰٓئِكَةُ هَٰذَا
يَوْمُكُمُ الَّذِي كُنتُمْ تُوعَدُونَ ﴿١٠٣﴾ يَوْمَ
نَطْوِي السَّمَآءَ كَطَيِّ السِّجِلِّ لِلْكُتُبِ كَمَا
بَدَأْنَآ أَوَّلَ خَلْقٍ نُّعِيدُهُۥ وَعْدًا عَلَيْنَآ
إِنَّا كُنَّا فَٰعِلِينَ ﴿١٠٤﴾ وَلَقَدْ كَتَبْنَا فِي الزَّبُورِ
مِنۢ بَعْدِ الذِّكْرِ أَنَّ الْأَرْضَ يَرِثُهَا
عِبَادِيَ الصَّٰلِحُونَ ﴿١٠٥﴾ إِنَّ فِي هَٰذَا لَبَلَٰغًا لِّقَوْمٍ
عَٰبِدِينَ ﴿١٠٦﴾ وَمَآ أَرْسَلْنَٰكَ إِلَّا رَحْمَةً
لِّلْعَٰلَمِينَ ﴿١٠٧﴾ قُلْ إِنَّمَا يُوحَىٰٓ إِلَيَّ أَنَّمَآ
إِلَٰهُكُمْ إِلَٰهٌ وَٰحِدٌ فَهَلْ أَنتُم مُّسْلِمُونَ ﴿١٠٨﴾

109. But if they still turn back say, 'I have given you clear warning in all fairness. I do not know, however, whether that threat held out to you will be (fulfilled in the) near or distant (future).
110. 'Verily, He knows the words you speak openly and He knows (the thoughts) which you hide.
111. 'And I do not know whether it (- the respite referred to above) is meant to put you on trial or it may be affording you a (worldly) provision for a short while.'
112. (The Prophet praying to his Lord) said, 'My Lord! Judge with truth,' Our Lord is the Most Gracious whose help is ever to be sought against what you (O disbelievers!) ascribe (to Him).'

فَإِن تَوَلَّوْا فَقُلْ ءَاذَنتُكُمْ عَلَىٰ سَوَآءٍ ۚ وَإِنْ
أَدْرِيٓ أَقَرِيبٌ أَم بَعِيدٌ مَّا تُوعَدُونَ ﴿١٠٩﴾
إِنَّهُۥ يَعْلَمُ الْجَهْرَ مِنَ الْقَوْلِ وَيَعْلَمُ مَا
تَكْتُمُونَ ﴿١١٠﴾ وَإِنْ أَدْرِي لَعَلَّهُۥ فِتْنَةٌ لَّكُمْ
وَمَتَٰعٌ إِلَىٰ حِينٍ ﴿١١١﴾ قَٰلَ رَبِّ احْكُم بِالْحَقِّ ۗ
وَرَبُّنَا الرَّحْمَٰنُ الْمُسْتَعَانُ عَلَىٰ مَا تَصِفُونَ ﴿١١٢﴾

CHAPTER
22

AL-HAJJ
(The Pilgrimage)
(Revealed after Hijrah)

سُورَةُ الْحَجِّ مَدَنِيَّةٌ

With the name of Allâh,
the Most Gracious, the Ever Merciful
(I commence to read Sûrah Al-Hajj).

بِسْمِ اللَّهِ الرَّحْمَٰنِ الرَّحِيمِ

1. **O** PEOPLE! Take your Lord as a shield (for) as a matter of fact the shock of the Hour is a tremendously dreadful thing;
2. On the day you behold it, you will find every woman giving suck abandoning (even) her suckling (in the confusion), and every pregnant one miscarrying, and people will appear to you to be drunk while they are not actually drunk; the punishment of Allâh will be (so) severe (that it will leave people in a terrible state of

يَٰٓأَيُّهَا النَّاسُ اتَّقُوا رَبَّكُمْ ۚ إِنَّ زَلْزَلَةَ
السَّاعَةِ شَيْءٌ عَظِيمٌ ﴿١﴾ يَوْمَ تَرَوْنَهَا تَذْهَلُ
كُلُّ مُرْضِعَةٍ عَمَّآ أَرْضَعَتْ وَتَضَعُ كُلُّ

horror and dread).
3. And there are some people who argue about Allâh without any knowledge and follow every satan (who is) devoid of all good.
4. About whom it is decreed that whoever makes friends with him, he will invariably lead him astray and conduct him to the sufferings of the flaming fire.
5. O people! If you doubt the Resurrection (then consider Our scheme of unformed things); We have indeed created you from dust, then, from a sperm-drop, then from a blood clot, and then from a lump of flesh (partly) formed and (partly) unformed that We make (Our power and the real state of things) clear to you. And We cause to stay in the wombs (that drop of fluid) when We please (to make a perfectly formed being) for a given period of time, then We bring you forth (formed) as infants, then (We bring you up) with the result that you reach your prime. And there are some of you who are called to death (early) and there are others of you who are made to live to the worst part of life; a miserable very old age, with the result that they know nothing after (having had) knowledge. While the earth appears to you lifeless and barren, it throbs (with life) and swells (with growth) and puts forth every kind of beautiful herbage, when We send down water upon it.
6. Such is (the cycle of life and nature) to prove that Allâh alone is the Truth and it is He Who brings the dead to life and He indeed is Possessor of power to do all that He will,
7. And that the Hour is bound to come, there is no doubt about it, and that Allâh will raise up those who are in the graves.
8. And among the people there is he who argues about Allâh though he has neither knowledge nor guidance and nor an illuminating Book;
9. Turning his side (out of pride) with the result that he leads (some) astray from the path of

ذَاتِ حَمْلٍ حَمْلَهَا وَتَرَى النَّاسَ سُكَٰرَىٰ
وَمَا هُم بِسُكَٰرَىٰ وَلَٰكِنَّ عَذَابَ اللَّهِ
شَدِيدٌ ۝٢ وَمِنَ النَّاسِ مَن يُجَٰدِلُ فِي
اللَّهِ بِغَيْرِ عِلْمٍ وَيَتَّبِعُ كُلَّ شَيْطَٰنٍ مَّرِيدٍ ۝٣
كُتِبَ عَلَيْهِ أَنَّهُ مَن تَوَلَّاهُ فَأَنَّهُ يُضِلُّهُ
وَيَهْدِيهِ إِلَىٰ عَذَابِ السَّعِيرِ ۝٤ يَٰأَيُّهَا النَّاسُ
إِن كُنتُمْ فِي رَيْبٍ مِّنَ الْبَعْثِ فَإِنَّا خَلَقْنَٰكُم
مِّن تُرَابٍ ثُمَّ مِن نُّطْفَةٍ ثُمَّ مِنْ عَلَقَةٍ
ثُمَّ مِن مُّضْغَةٍ مُّخَلَّقَةٍ وَغَيْرِ مُخَلَّقَةٍ
لِّنُبَيِّنَ لَكُمْ وَنُقِرُّ فِي الْأَرْحَامِ مَا نَشَاءُ
إِلَىٰ أَجَلٍ مُّسَمًّى ثُمَّ نُخْرِجُكُمْ طِفْلًا ثُمَّ
لِتَبْلُغُوا أَشُدَّكُمْ وَمِنكُم مَّن يُتَوَفَّىٰ
وَمِنكُم مَّن يُرَدُّ إِلَىٰ أَرْذَلِ الْعُمُرِ لِكَيْلَا
يَعْلَمَ مِن بَعْدِ عِلْمٍ شَيْـًٔا وَتَرَى الْأَرْضَ
هَامِدَةً فَإِذَا أَنزَلْنَا عَلَيْهَا الْمَاءَ اهْتَزَّتْ
وَرَبَتْ وَأَنۢبَتَتْ مِن كُلِّ زَوْجٍ بَهِيجٍ ۝٥
ذَٰلِكَ بِأَنَّ اللَّهَ هُوَ الْحَقُّ وَأَنَّهُ يُحْيِ
الْمَوْتَىٰ وَأَنَّهُ عَلَىٰ كُلِّ شَيْءٍ قَدِيرٌ ۝٦
وَأَنَّ السَّاعَةَ ءَاتِيَةٌ لَّا رَيْبَ فِيهَا وَأَنَّ اللَّهَ
يَبْعَثُ مَن فِي الْقُبُورِ ۝٧ وَمِنَ النَّاسِ
مَن يُجَٰدِلُ فِي اللَّهِ بِغَيْرِ عِلْمٍ وَلَا هُدًى
وَلَا كِتَٰبٍ مُّنِيرٍ ۝٨ ثَانِيَ عِطْفِهِ لِيُضِلَّ

Allâh. There is for him disgrace in this world and on the Day of Resurrection, We will make him suffer the punishment of burning.
10. And (to such it will be said,) 'This is the result of what your own hands have sent on before (- your deeds); and Allâh is not the least unjust to (His) servants.'

SECTION 2

11. **A**ND among people there is such a one who worships Allâh (as it were) on the very verge (in a wavering state of mind). If any good befalls him he is satisfied with it, but if there befalls a trial he returns to his (former) ways. He has lost both this world as well as the next. That indeed is the obvious loss.
12. He calls, apart from Allâh, upon the things which can do him neither harm nor good. That, indeed, is straying far away.
13. He calls upon him whose harm is much more likely than his good. How evil is this false god to be his patron and how evil is (he to be) his associate!
14. Allâh will surely cause those who believe and do righteous deeds to enter Gardens served with running streams (to keep them green and flourishing). Surely, Allâh does what He has a mind to.
15. Whoso thinks that Allâh will not help him (- the Prophet) in this present life nor in the next, let him help himself to go into the heaven by some means and cut (the divine help) off and then see if his device can take away that (God's help to the Prophet) which enrages (him).
16. That is how it is. We have revealed this (Qur'ân) comprising clear arguments. Yet the truth is that Allâh guides him (to the right way) who wishes (to be guided).
17. (Let) those who believe and those who judaised and the Sabians and the Christians and the Magians and those who associate other gods with God know that Allâh will decide between them on the Day of Resurrection.

عَنْ سَبِيلِ اللهِ لَهُ فِي الدُّنْيَا خِزْيٌ
وَنُذِيقُهُ يَوْمَ الْقِيٰمَةِ عَذَابَ الْحَرِيقِ ﴿٩﴾
ذٰلِكَ بِمَا قَدَّمَتْ يَدٰكَ وَأَنَّ اللهَ لَيْسَ
بِظَلَّامٍ لِّلْعَبِيدِ ﴿١٠﴾ وَمِنَ النَّاسِ مَنْ
يَعْبُدُ اللهَ عَلٰى حَرْفٍ فَإِنْ أَصَابَهُ خَيْرٌ
اطْمَأَنَّ بِهِ وَإِنْ أَصَابَتْهُ فِتْنَةٌ انْقَلَبَ
عَلٰى وَجْهِهِ خَسِرَ الدُّنْيَا وَالْأٰخِرَةَ
ذٰلِكَ هُوَ الْخُسْرَانُ الْمُبِينُ ﴿١١﴾ يَدْعُوا
مِنْ دُونِ اللهِ مَا لَا يَضُرُّهُ وَمَا لَا
يَنْفَعُهُ ذٰلِكَ هُوَ الضَّلٰلُ الْبَعِيدُ ﴿١٢﴾ يَدْعُوا
لَمَنْ ضَرُّهُ أَقْرَبُ مِنْ نَّفْعِهِ لَبِئْسَ
الْمَوْلٰى وَلَبِئْسَ الْعَشِيرُ ﴿١٣﴾ إِنَّ اللهَ يُدْخِلُ
الَّذِينَ أٰمَنُوا وَعَمِلُوا الصّٰلِحٰتِ جَنّٰتٍ
تَجْرِي مِنْ تَحْتِهَا الْأَنْهٰرُ إِنَّ اللهَ
يَفْعَلُ مَا يُرِيدُ ﴿١٤﴾ مَنْ كَانَ يَظُنُّ
أَنْ لَّنْ يَنْصُرَهُ اللهُ فِي الدُّنْيَا وَالْأٰخِرَةِ
فَلْيَمْدُدْ بِسَبَبٍ إِلَى السَّمَاءِ ثُمَّ لْيَقْطَعْ
فَلْيَنْظُرْ هَلْ يُذْهِبَنَّ كَيْدُهُ مَا يَغِيظُ ﴿١٥﴾
وَكَذٰلِكَ أَنْزَلْنٰهُ أٰيٰتٍ بَيِّنٰتٍ وَأَنَّ اللهَ
يَهْدِي مَنْ يُرِيدُ ﴿١٦﴾ إِنَّ الَّذِينَ أٰمَنُوا
وَالَّذِينَ هَادُوا وَالصّٰبِـِٔينَ وَالنَّصٰرٰى
وَالْمَجُوسَ وَالَّذِينَ أَشْرَكُوا إِنَّ اللهَ

ع ٢ ٨

Surely, Allâh is Witness over all things.

18. Have you not considered that whoever is in the heavens and whoever is on the earth, and (also) the sun, the moon and the stars, the mountains, the trees, the moving creatures and many of people make obeisance to Allâh? Yet many of (people) are those who become deserving of punishment (because of their disobedience). None can honour the person whom Allâh disgraces. Verily, Allâh does what He pleases.

[PROSTRATION]

19. These two (- the believers and the disbelievers) are two adversaries who dispute about their Lord. As for those who disbelieve, garments of fire have been tailored for them and boiling water shall be poured down over their heads,

20. Whereby whatever is in their bellies will be melted, and (their) skins as well (will come off their bones).

21. And (further more) there will be whips of iron for (punishing) them.

22. Every time they seek to escape from there in (their) anguish (and from its sorrows) they will be hurled back into it (and it will be said to them), 'Keep on suffering the torment of burning.'

SECTION 3

23. **A**s for those who believe and do righteous deeds, Allâh will admit them to Gardens served with running streams (to keep them green and flourishing). Therein they shall be given ornaments, bracelets of gold and pearls, and therein their raiments shall be of silk,

24. Because they were inspired to speak noble words and do noble deeds and were guided to the path of the Highly Praiseworthy (God).

25. (As to) those who disbelieve and hinder (people) from (following) the path of Allâh and (from going to) the Holy Mosque which We have made (a source of goodness and benefit) for all people, and where the inhabitants thereof

يَفْصِلُ بَيْنَهُمْ يَوْمَ الْقِيٰمَةِ ۚ إِنَّ اللّٰهَ عَلٰى
كُلِّ شَيْءٍ شَهِيدٌ ﴿١٧﴾ أَلَمْ تَرَ أَنَّ اللّٰهَ
يَسْجُدُ لَهُ مَنْ فِي السَّمٰوٰتِ وَمَنْ فِي
الْأَرْضِ وَالشَّمْسُ وَالْقَمَرُ وَالنُّجُومُ
وَالْجِبَالُ وَالشَّجَرُ وَالدَّوَابُّ وَكَثِيرٌ
مِّنَ النَّاسِ ۖ وَكَثِيرٌ حَقَّ عَلَيْهِ الْعَذَابُ ۗ
وَمَنْ يُّهِنِ اللّٰهُ فَمَا لَهُ مِنْ مُّكْرِمٍ ۚ
إِنَّ اللّٰهَ يَفْعَلُ مَا يَشَاءُ ﴿١٨﴾ هٰذٰنِ خَصْمٰنِ
اخْتَصَمُوا فِي رَبِّهِمْ ۖ فَالَّذِينَ كَفَرُوا
قُطِّعَتْ لَهُمْ ثِيَابٌ مِّنْ نَّارٍ ۚ يُصَبُّ مِنْ
فَوْقِ رُءُوسِهِمُ الْحَمِيمُ ﴿١٩﴾ يُصْهَرُ بِهِ مَا فِي
بُطُونِهِمْ وَالْجُلُودُ ﴿٢٠﴾ وَلَهُمْ مَّقٰمِعُ مِنْ
حَدِيدٍ ﴿٢١﴾ كُلَّمَا أَرَادُوا أَنْ يَّخْرُجُوا مِنْهَا
مِنْ غَمٍّ أُعِيدُوا فِيهَا وَذُوقُوا عَذَابَ
الْحَرِيقِ ﴿٢٢﴾ إِنَّ اللّٰهَ يُدْخِلُ الَّذِينَ اٰمَنُوا
وَعَمِلُوا الصّٰلِحٰتِ جَنّٰتٍ تَجْرِي مِنْ
تَحْتِهَا الْأَنْهٰرُ يُحَلَّوْنَ فِيهَا مِنْ أَسَاوِرَ مِنْ
ذَهَبٍ وَّلُؤْلُؤًا ۖ وَلِبَاسُهُمْ فِيهَا حَرِيرٌ ﴿٢٣﴾
وَهُدُوا إِلَى الطَّيِّبِ مِنَ الْقَوْلِ ۖ وَهُدُوا
إِلٰى صِرٰطِ الْحَمِيدِ ﴿٢٤﴾ إِنَّ الَّذِينَ كَفَرُوا
وَيَصُدُّونَ عَنْ سَبِيلِ اللّٰهِ وَالْمَسْجِدِ

(- of Makkah) and the visitors from outside are equal; and whoever seeks wrongfully to promote crookedness in it, We shall make him suffer woeful punishment.

SECTION 4

26. AND (recall the time) when We assigned to Abraham the site of the (Holy) House (bidding him), 'Associate none with Me and keep My House clean and pure for those who (go round it to) perform the circuits and for those who stay in it (for worshipping Me) devotedly, and for those who bow down, (and) fall prostrate (in Prayer before Me).'

27. (Prophet!) Call on people to make the Pilgrimage, they will come to you on foot and riding on all sorts of lean and fast (means of transport), coming from every distant deep highway (and mount track).

28. So that they (- the Pilgrims) may witness benefits (that lay therein) for them, and that (at the time of making a sacrifice) on days prescribed they may mention the name of Allâh over the beasts of the family of cattle He has given them. (When you have sacrificed the animal) then eat from this, (flesh of the animal thus sacrificed), yourselves and (also) feed the poor distressed one and the needy (on that).

29. Then let the people perform their needful rituals regarding the cleansing (of their bodies and shaving) and fulfill their voluntary promises made to Allâh and perform the (last) circuit of the Ancient, Free, Invulnerable House.

30. That is (the purpose behind the construction of the House), so he who honours the things declared sacred by Allâh (will find that) it is good for him in the sight of his Lord. And (remember that) all the cattle are made lawful to you except those already mentioned to you

الْحَرَامِ الَّذِي جَعَلْنٰهُ لِلنَّاسِ سَوَآءً الْعٰكِفُ
فِيهِ وَالْبَادِ ۚ وَمَنْ يُرِدْ فِيهِ بِإِلْحَادٍ
بِظُلْمٍ نُذِقْهُ مِنْ عَذَابٍ أَلِيمٍ ﴿٢٥﴾ وَإِذْ
بَوَّأْنَا لِإِبْرٰهِيمَ مَكَانَ الْبَيْتِ أَنْ لَّا
تُشْرِكْ بِي شَيْئًا وَطَهِّرْ بَيْتِيَ لِلطَّآئِفِينَ
وَالْقَآئِمِينَ وَالرُّكَّعِ السُّجُودِ ﴿٢٦﴾ وَأَذِّنْ فِي
النَّاسِ بِالْحَجِّ يَأْتُوكَ رِجَالًا وَعَلٰى كُلِّ
ضَامِرٍ يَأْتِينَ مِنْ كُلِّ فَجٍّ عَمِيقٍ ﴿٢٧﴾
لِيَشْهَدُوا مَنٰفِعَ لَهُمْ وَيَذْكُرُوا اسْمَ
اللّٰهِ فِي أَيَّامٍ مَّعْلُومٰتٍ عَلٰى مَا رَزَقَهُمْ
مِّنْ بَهِيمَةِ الْأَنْعٰمِ ۚ فَكُلُوا مِنْهَا
وَأَطْعِمُوا الْبَآئِسَ الْفَقِيرَ ﴿٢٨﴾ ثُمَّ لْيَقْضُوا
تَفَثَهُمْ وَلْيُوفُوا نُذُورَهُمْ وَلْيَطَّوَّفُوا بِالْبَيْتِ
الْعَتِيقِ ﴿٢٩﴾ ذٰلِكَ وَمَنْ يُعَظِّمْ حُرُمٰتِ اللّٰهِ
فَهُوَ خَيْرٌ لَّهُ عِنْدَ رَبِّهِ ۗ وَأُحِلَّتْ لَكُمُ
الْأَنْعٰمُ إِلَّا مَا يُتْلٰى عَلَيْكُمْ فَاجْتَنِبُوا الرِّجْسَ

(as unlawful in the Qur'ân). And abstain from unclean practice of idolatry and shun false speech.

31. Remaining upright (devoting yourselves in worship and obedience entirely) to Allâh, not associating anything with Him. Indeed, he who associates anything with Allâh falls, as it were, from on high, and either the birds snatch him away or the wind blows him off to some deep place very far away.

32. That is (the law which you should bear in mind). He who respects Symbols appointed by Allâh, will find that this (respect) proceeds from and leads to the piety of hearts.

33. It is lawful for you to take benefits from these (cattle to be offered for sacrifice) for an appointed term (- they can be used for riding, carrying burdens, for milk etc.), then the lawful place of their sacrifice is by the Ancient, Free and Invulnerable House.

SECTION 5

34. AND We have prescribed certain rites of sacrifice for every people that they may mention the name of Allâh over the beasts of the family of cattle He has provided for them. So (O people!) your God is One God, therefore you should all submit to Him alone. And give glad tidings (of success) to the humble and the submissive ones (to Him);

35. Whose hearts are filled with awe when the name of Allâh is mentioned and who are patiently persevering in whatever (of the afflictions) befalls them, and who observe Prayer and spend from that which We have provided them.

36. We have made the sacrificial animals among the Symbols appointed by Allâh for you. They are of immense good to you. So (whenever you offer them for sacrifice do it) in the name of Allâh (while they) stand (drawn up) in lines. When their flanks collapse, (on being slaughtered), eat from (the meat of) them and feed

مِنَ الْأَوْثَٰنِ وَ اجْتَنِبُوا قَوْلَ الزُّوْرِ ﴿٣٠﴾ حُنَفَاءَ
لِلّٰهِ غَيْرَ مُشْرِكِيْنَ بِهٖ ۚ وَ مَنْ يُّشْرِكْ بِاللّٰهِ
فَكَأَنَّمَا خَرَّ مِنَ السَّمَآءِ فَتَخْطَفُهُ الطَّيْرُ
أَوْ تَهْوِيْ بِهِ الرِّيْحُ فِيْ مَكَانٍ سَحِيْقٍ ﴿٣١﴾
ذٰلِكَ ۚ وَ مَنْ يُّعَظِّمْ شَعَٰٓئِرَ اللّٰهِ فَإِنَّهَا مِنْ
تَقْوَى الْقُلُوْبِ ﴿٣٢﴾ لَكُمْ فِيْهَا مَنَافِعُ إِلٰٓى
أَجَلٍ مُّسَمًّى ثُمَّ مَحِلُّهَآ إِلَى الْبَيْتِ
الْعَتِيْقِ ﴿٣٣﴾ وَ لِكُلِّ أُمَّةٍ جَعَلْنَا مَنْسَكًا
لِّيَذْكُرُوا اسْمَ اللّٰهِ عَلٰى مَا رَزَقَهُمْ مِّنْۢ
بَهِيْمَةِ الْأَنْعَٰمِ ۗ فَإِلٰهُكُمْ إِلٰهٌ وَّاحِدٌ فَلَهٗٓ
أَسْلِمُوْا ۗ وَ بَشِّرِ الْمُخْبِتِيْنَ ﴿٣٤﴾ الَّذِيْنَ إِذَا
ذُكِرَ اللّٰهُ وَجِلَتْ قُلُوْبُهُمْ وَ الصّٰبِرِيْنَ
عَلٰى مَآ أَصَابَهُمْ وَ الْمُقِيْمِي الصَّلٰوةِ ۙ وَ مِمَّا
رَزَقْنٰهُمْ يُنْفِقُوْنَ ﴿٣٥﴾ وَ الْبُدْنَ جَعَلْنٰهَا لَكُمْ
مِّنْ شَعَٰٓئِرِ اللّٰهِ لَكُمْ فِيْهَا خَيْرٌ ۖ فَاذْكُرُوا
اسْمَ اللّٰهِ عَلَيْهَا صَوَآفَّ ۚ فَإِذَا وَجَبَتْ
جُنُوْبُهَا فَكُلُوْا مِنْهَا وَ أَطْعِمُوا الْقَانِعَ
وَ الْمُعْتَرَّ ۚ كَذٰلِكَ سَخَّرْنٰهَا لَكُمْ لَعَلَّكُمْ

him who is (in need but) contented and him who begs. In this way We have made these (animals) subservient to you so that you may render thanks.
37. It is neither their flesh nor their blood (of these sacrifices) which matters to Allâh but it is guarding against evil and devotion to duty on your part that matters to Him. Thus He has made them subservient to you that you may proclaim the greatness of Allâh for His guiding you. And give glad tidings to the doers of good to others.
38. Allâh will certainly defend those who believe because Allâh loves no perfidious, ungrateful person.

SECTION 6

39. **P**ERMISSION (to fight in self-defense) is (now) given to those (Muslims) against whom war is waged (for no reason), because they have been done injustice to, and Allâh has indeed might and power to help them;
40. Those who have been driven out of their homes without any just cause. Their only fault was that they said, 'Our Lord is Allâh.' If Allâh had not repelled some peoples by means of others, cloisters and churches and synagogues and mosques wherein the name of Allâh is mentioned very frequently, would have been razed to the ground in large numbers. And Allâh will surely help one who helps His cause. Allâh is, indeed, All-Powerful, All-Mighty.
41. They are (the persecuted people) who, if We establish them in the land (giving them power) will observe Prayer and keep on presenting the *Zakât*, and enjoin (people) to do good and forbid evil. And Allâh will finally settle all issues.
42. And (Prophet!) if they cry lies to you (there is nothing new in it) even so before them, the people of Noah and (the tribes of) 'Âd and Thamûd also cried lies (to their Apostles of God).
43. (So did) the people of Abraham and the people of Lot;
44. And the inhabitants of Midian. And Moses

تَشْكُرُونَ ﴿٣٦﴾ لَنْ يَنَالَ اللَّهَ لُحُومُهَا وَلَا
دِمَاؤُهَا وَلَٰكِنْ يَنَالُهُ التَّقْوَىٰ مِنْكُمْ ۚ
كَذَٰلِكَ سَخَّرَهَا لَكُمْ لِتُكَبِّرُوا اللَّهَ عَلَىٰ مَا
هَدَاكُمْ ۗ وَبَشِّرِ الْمُحْسِنِينَ ﴿٣٧﴾ إِنَّ اللَّهَ
يُدَافِعُ عَنِ الَّذِينَ آمَنُوا ۗ إِنَّ اللَّهَ لَا يُحِبُّ
كُلَّ خَوَّانٍ كَفُورٍ ﴿٣٨﴾ أُذِنَ لِلَّذِينَ يُقَاتَلُونَ
بِأَنَّهُمْ ظُلِمُوا ۚ وَإِنَّ اللَّهَ عَلَىٰ نَصْرِهِمْ
لَقَدِيرٌ ﴿٣٩﴾ الَّذِينَ أُخْرِجُوا مِنْ دِيَارِهِمْ
بِغَيْرِ حَقٍّ إِلَّا أَنْ يَقُولُوا رَبُّنَا اللَّهُ ۗ
وَلَوْلَا دَفْعُ اللَّهِ النَّاسَ بَعْضَهُمْ بِبَعْضٍ
لَهُدِّمَتْ صَوَامِعُ وَبِيَعٌ وَصَلَوَاتٌ
وَمَسَاجِدُ يُذْكَرُ فِيهَا اسْمُ اللَّهِ كَثِيرًا ۗ
وَلَيَنْصُرَنَّ اللَّهُ مَنْ يَنْصُرُهُ ۗ إِنَّ اللَّهَ
لَقَوِيٌّ عَزِيزٌ ﴿٤٠﴾ الَّذِينَ إِنْ مَكَّنَّاهُمْ
فِي الْأَرْضِ أَقَامُوا الصَّلَاةَ وَآتَوُا الزَّكَاةَ
وَأَمَرُوا بِالْمَعْرُوفِ وَنَهَوْا عَنِ الْمُنْكَرِ ۗ
وَلِلَّهِ عَاقِبَةُ الْأُمُورِ ﴿٤١﴾ وَإِنْ يُكَذِّبُوكَ فَقَدْ
كَذَّبَتْ قَبْلَهُمْ قَوْمُ نُوحٍ وَعَادٌ وَثَمُودُ ﴿٤٢﴾
وَقَوْمُ إِبْرَاهِيمَ وَقَوْمُ لُوطٍ ﴿٤٣﴾ وَأَصْحَابُ
مَدْيَنَ ۖ وَكُذِّبَ مُوسَىٰ فَأَمْلَيْتُ لِلْكَافِرِينَ

(also) was cried lies to. But I granted respite the disbelievers for long, then I took them to task. (Imagine) how (terrible) was (the result of their) denial of Me! And how (awful) the change I effected (in them).

45. And how many a township have we destroyed, because (the people thereof) were given to wicked ways so that they have fallen down on their roofs, and (how many) a well is completely deserted, and (how many) a strongly built lofty castles (met the same doom because We destroyed their occupants).

46. Why do they not travel in the land so that they should have hearts that help them to understand and ears which can help them hear? As a matter of fact (when going astray) it is not the (physical) eyes that are blind but blind are the hearts which lie in the bosoms.

47. And they (- the disbelievers) demand of you to expedite (their) punishment. Allâh will not fail His promise. (Remember however that) one day with your Lord is (sometimes) equal to one thousand years by your counting.

48. And how many (people of) a township were given to wicked ways but I respited them long. Then I took them to task and to Me alone shall be the return (of all of them).

SECTION 7

49. **S**AY, 'O people! I am but a plain Warner to you all (against the evil consequences of refusal and misdeeds).'

50. There awaits protection and a generous and honourable provision for those who believe and do deeds of righteousness.

51. But those who strive hard against Our Messages seeking to frustrate (Us in Our aims and ends), it is they who will be the inmates of the flaming Fire.

52. And We have sent no Messenger, nor a Prophet before you but when he longed (to attain what he sought), satan (interfered and)

ثُمَّ أَخَذْتُهُمْ فَكَيْفَ كَانَ نَكِيرِ ﴿٤٤﴾ فَكَأَيِّن
مِّن قَرْيَةٍ أَهْلَكْنَٰهَا وَهِيَ ظَالِمَةٌ فَهِيَ
خَاوِيَةٌ عَلَىٰ عُرُوشِهَا وَبِئْرٍ مُّعَطَّلَةٍ
وَقَصْرٍ مَّشِيدٍ ﴿٤٥﴾ أَفَلَمْ يَسِيرُوا فِي الْأَرْضِ
فَتَكُونَ لَهُمْ قُلُوبٌ يَعْقِلُونَ بِهَا أَوْ ءَاذَانٌ
يَسْمَعُونَ بِهَا فَإِنَّهَا لَا تَعْمَى الْأَبْصَٰرُ
وَلَٰكِن تَعْمَى الْقُلُوبُ الَّتِي فِي الصُّدُورِ ﴿٤٦﴾
وَيَسْتَعْجِلُونَكَ بِالْعَذَابِ وَلَن يُخْلِفَ
اللَّهُ وَعْدَهُۥ وَإِنَّ يَوْمًا عِندَ رَبِّكَ كَأَلْفِ
سَنَةٍ مِّمَّا تَعُدُّونَ ﴿٤٧﴾ وَكَأَيِّن مِّن قَرْيَةٍ
أَمْلَيْتُ لَهَا وَهِيَ ظَالِمَةٌ ثُمَّ أَخَذْتُهَا
وَإِلَيَّ الْمَصِيرُ ﴿٤٨﴾ قُلْ يَٰٓأَيُّهَا النَّاسُ إِنَّمَا أَنَا۠
لَكُمْ نَذِيرٌ مُّبِينٌ ﴿٤٩﴾ فَالَّذِينَ ءَامَنُوا وَعَمِلُوا
الصَّٰلِحَٰتِ لَهُم مَّغْفِرَةٌ وَرِزْقٌ كَرِيمٌ ﴿٥٠﴾
وَالَّذِينَ سَعَوْا فِي ءَايَٰتِنَا مُعَٰجِزِينَ أُولَٰٓئِكَ
أَصْحَٰبُ الْجَحِيمِ ﴿٥١﴾ وَمَا أَرْسَلْنَا مِن قَبْلِكَ
مِن رَّسُولٍ وَلَا نَبِيٍّ إِلَّا إِذَا تَمَنَّىٰٓ أَلْقَى
الشَّيْطَٰنُ فِي أُمْنِيَّتِهِۦ فَيَنسَخُ اللَّهُ مَا يُلْقِي

ع ١٣

put hindrances in the way of what he sought after. But Allâh removes (the hindrances) that are placed by satan, then Allâh firmly establishes His Messages. And Allâh is All-Knowing, All-Wise.

53. (Allâh permits the interference of satan) so that He may make (the hindrance which satan puts in the way of the Messengers) serve as a trial for those whose hearts carry disease (of hypocrisy) and for those whose hearts are hardened (because of disbelief). In fact the wrongdoers have gone far (in their antagonism).

54. And (He permits this) so that those who have been given knowledge may know that this (Qur'ân) is the truth from your Lord and may believe in it and humble themselves before Him from their very hearts. And Allâh will indeed be the Guide of those who believe, to the straight and right path.

55. And those who have disbelieved will continue to have doubt about this (Qur'ân) until the Hour overtakes them suddenly, or the scourge of a destructive day befalls them.

56. On that day the kingdom shall belong to Allâh alone, He will judge between people so that those who believe and do deeds of righteousness will be (admitted) into blissful Gardens.

57. But those who disbelieve and cried lies to Our Messages, shall suffer a humiliating punishment.

SECTION 8

58. **A**ND Allâh will certainly provide for ever a goodly provision to those who leave their homes for the cause of Allâh and are then slain or die a natural death. Surely, Allâh, He is indeed the Best of constant Providers.

59. He will make them enter a place which they will like. Verily, Allâh is All-Knowing, Forbearing (in the matter of punishment).

60. That is (how it will be); and whoso retaliates in proportion to that (injury) which is inflicted on him, and again is transgressed against, Allâh will

الشَّيْطٰنُ ثُمَّ يُحْكِمُ اللّٰهُ اٰيٰتِهٖ ؕ وَاللّٰهُ عَلِيْمٌ
حَكِيْمٌ ﴿٥٢﴾ لِّيَجْعَلَ مَا يُلْقِي الشَّيْطٰنُ فِتْنَةً
لِّلَّذِيْنَ فِيْ قُلُوْبِهِمْ مَّرَضٌ وَّ الْقَاسِيَةِ قُلُوْبُهُمْ ؕ
وَ اِنَّ الظّٰلِمِيْنَ لَفِيْ شِقَاقٍۭ بَعِيْدٍ ﴿٥٣﴾ وَّ لِيَعْلَمَ
الَّذِيْنَ اُوْتُوا الْعِلْمَ اَنَّهُ الْحَقُّ مِنْ رَّبِّكَ
فَيُؤْمِنُوْا بِهٖ فَتُخْبِتَ لَهٗ قُلُوْبُهُمْ ؕ وَ اِنَّ اللّٰهَ
لَهَادِ الَّذِيْنَ اٰمَنُوْۤا اِلٰى صِرَاطٍ مُّسْتَقِيْمٍ ﴿٥٤﴾
وَ لَا يَزَالُ الَّذِيْنَ كَفَرُوْا فِيْ مِرْيَةٍ مِّنْهُ
حَتّٰى تَاْتِيَهُمُ السَّاعَةُ بَغْتَةً اَوْ يَاْتِيَهُمْ
عَذَابُ يَوْمٍ عَقِيْمٍ ﴿٥٥﴾ اَلْمُلْكُ يَوْمَئِذٍ لِّلّٰهِ ؕ
يَحْكُمُ بَيْنَهُمْ ؕ فَالَّذِيْنَ اٰمَنُوْا وَ عَمِلُوا
الصّٰلِحٰتِ فِيْ جَنّٰتِ النَّعِيْمِ ﴿٥٦﴾ وَ الَّذِيْنَ كَفَرُوْا
وَ كَذَّبُوْا بِاٰيٰتِنَا فَاُولٰٓئِكَ لَهُمْ عَذَابٌ مُّهِيْنٌ ﴿٥٧﴾ ع ١٤
وَ الَّذِيْنَ هَاجَرُوْا فِيْ سَبِيْلِ اللّٰهِ ثُمَّ قُتِلُوْۤا
اَوْ مَاتُوْا لَيَرْزُقَنَّهُمُ اللّٰهُ رِزْقًا حَسَنًا ؕ وَ اِنَّ
اللّٰهَ لَهُوَ خَيْرُ الرّٰزِقِيْنَ ﴿٥٨﴾ لَيُدْخِلَنَّهُمْ
مُّدْخَلًا يَّرْضَوْنَهٗ ؕ وَ اِنَّ اللّٰهَ لَعَلِيْمٌ حَلِيْمٌ ﴿٥٩﴾
ذٰلِكَ ۚ وَ مَنْ عَاقَبَ بِمِثْلِ مَا عُوْقِبَ بِهٖ
ثُمَّ بُغِيَ عَلَيْهِ لَيَنْصُرَنَّهُ اللّٰهُ ؕ اِنَّ اللّٰهَ لَعَفُوٌّ

certainly help him. Verily, Allâh is All-Pardoning (absolving people of their sins), All-Protecting.

61. That (system of requital) is to prove that it is Allâh Who makes the night gain on the day and makes the day gain on the night and that Allâh is All-Hearing, All-Seeing.

62. That is also (to show) that it is Allâh Who is the Ultimate Truth (- Self-Subsisting, All-Sustaining) and that which they call upon apart from Him is falsehood and perishable, and because Allâh is the High, the Great.

63. Do you not see that Allâh sends down water from the clouds and the (dry) earth becomes green? Verily, Allâh is the Knower of subtleties, the All-Aware.

64. All that is in the heavens and all that is on the earth belongs to Him and Allâh is Self-Sufficient (having no needs) and Worthy of all praise (in His Own right).

SECTION 9

65. **D**o you not consider that Allâh has made subservient to you all that is on the earth? (Do you not see that) the ships sail through the sea by His command? And He holds the rain back from falling upon the earth save by His permission. Verily, Allâh is Most Compassionate to people (and) Ever Merciful (to them).

66. And it is He Who gave you life, then He will call you to death, then will He bring you back to life (again). The thing is, a human being is most ungrateful.

67. We have prescribed for every people modes of worship which they should observe. Let them not, therefore, dispute with you in the matter (of Islamic mode of worship). And call (the people) to your Lord for you are indeed on the exact and right guidance.

68. And if they still contend with you, say, 'Allâh knows best all that you do.

69. 'Allâh will judge between you (and us) on the Day of Resurrection concerning all that in which you differ (from us).

غَفُورٌ ﴿٦٠﴾ ذٰلِكَ بِأَنَّ اللّٰهَ يُولِجُ الَّيْلَ فِي
النَّهَارِ وَيُولِجُ النَّهَارَ فِي الَّيْلِ وَأَنَّ اللّٰهَ
سَمِيعٌ بَصِيرٌ ﴿٦١﴾ ذٰلِكَ بِأَنَّ اللّٰهَ هُوَ الْحَقُّ
وَأَنَّ مَا يَدْعُونَ مِنْ دُونِهِ هُوَ الْبٰطِلُ
وَأَنَّ اللّٰهَ هُوَ الْعَلِيُّ الْكَبِيرُ ﴿٦٢﴾ أَلَمْ تَرَ أَنَّ
اللّٰهَ أَنْزَلَ مِنَ السَّمَآءِ مَآءً فَتُصْبِحُ الْأَرْضُ
مُخْضَرَّةً إِنَّ اللّٰهَ لَطِيفٌ خَبِيرٌ ﴿٦٣﴾ لَهُ مَا فِي
السَّمٰوٰتِ وَمَا فِي الْأَرْضِ وَإِنَّ اللّٰهَ لَهُوَ
الْغَنِيُّ الْحَمِيدُ ﴿٦٤﴾ أَلَمْ تَرَ أَنَّ اللّٰهَ سَخَّرَ لَكُمْ
مَا فِي الْأَرْضِ وَالْفُلْكَ تَجْرِي فِي الْبَحْرِ
بِأَمْرِهِ وَيُمْسِكُ السَّمَآءَ أَنْ تَقَعَ عَلَى
الْأَرْضِ إِلَّا بِإِذْنِهِ إِنَّ اللّٰهَ بِالنَّاسِ لَرَءُوفٌ
رَّحِيمٌ ﴿٦٥﴾ وَهُوَ الَّذِي أَحْيَاكُمْ ثُمَّ يُمِيتُكُمْ
ثُمَّ يُحْيِيكُمْ إِنَّ الْإِنْسٰنَ لَكَفُورٌ ﴿٦٦﴾ لِكُلِّ
أُمَّةٍ جَعَلْنَا مَنْسَكًا هُمْ نَاسِكُوهُ فَلَا
يُنٰزِعُنَّكَ فِي الْأَمْرِ وَادْعُ إِلَىٰ رَبِّكَ إِنَّكَ
لَعَلَىٰ هُدًى مُّسْتَقِيمٍ ﴿٦٧﴾ وَإِنْ جٰدَلُوكَ
فَقُلِ اللّٰهُ أَعْلَمُ بِمَا تَعْمَلُونَ ﴿٦٨﴾ اللّٰهُ يَحْكُمُ
بَيْنَكُمْ يَوْمَ الْقِيٰمَةِ فِيمَا كُنْتُمْ فِيهِ

70. 'Do you not know that Allâh knows whatsoever is in the heavens and the earth? Surely, this is (all recorded) in a Book (of laws) and, indeed, it is easy for Allâh (to bind them to a law).'
71. And they worship apart from Allâh the things for which He has revealed no authority and about which they themselves have no knowledge. And the wrong doers will find no helper.
72. And when Our clear Messages are recited to them you will notice an expression of disapproval on the faces of those who disbelieve. They would almost assault those who recite Our Messages to them. Say, 'Shall I then inform you of something even worse than this (which hurts you). (It is) the Fire! Allâh has promised it to those who disbelieve. And what a vile resort it is!'

SECTION 10

73. **O** PEOPLE! Here is a parable, so listen to it. Those whom you call upon apart from Allâh cannot create even a fly, though they may all join hands for it. And if the fly should snatch away something from them, they cannot recover it from it. Feeble indeed is the seeker (- the worshippers) and (feeble) the sought after (- the worshipped one).
74. They do not appreciate Allâh as He should be appreciated (and no true concept of His attribute they have formed to pay Him the respect He deserves). Surely, Allâh is All-Powerful, All-Mighty.
75. Allâh chooses His messengers from among angels and from among men. Verily, Allâh is All-Hearing, All-Seeing.
76. He knows the future of the people and their past; and to Allâh do all matters stand referred (for judgment).
77. O you who believe! Bow down and prostrate yourself, and worship your Lord and do good deeds so that you may attain your goal.

[PROSTRATION]

78. And strive your hardest to win the pleasure

تَخْتَلِفُونَ ﴿٦٩﴾ أَلَمْ تَعْلَمْ أَنَّ اللَّهَ يَعْلَمُ
مَا فِي السَّمَاءِ وَالْأَرْضِ ۗ إِنَّ ذَٰلِكَ فِي
كِتَابٍ ۚ إِنَّ ذَٰلِكَ عَلَى اللَّهِ يَسِيرٌ ﴿٧٠﴾
وَيَعْبُدُونَ مِنْ دُونِ اللَّهِ مَا لَمْ يُنَزِّلْ
بِهِ سُلْطَانًا وَمَا لَيْسَ لَهُمْ بِهِ عِلْمٌ ۗ
وَمَا لِلظَّالِمِينَ مِنْ نَصِيرٍ ﴿٧١﴾ وَإِذَا تُتْلَىٰ
عَلَيْهِمْ آيَاتُنَا بَيِّنَاتٍ تَعْرِفُ فِي وُجُوهِ
الَّذِينَ كَفَرُوا الْمُنْكَرَ ۖ يَكَادُونَ
يَسْطُونَ بِالَّذِينَ يَتْلُونَ عَلَيْهِمْ آيَاتِنَا ۗ
قُلْ أَفَأُنَبِّئُكُمْ بِشَرٍّ مِنْ ذَٰلِكُمُ ۗ النَّارُ
وَعَدَهَا اللَّهُ الَّذِينَ كَفَرُوا ۖ وَبِئْسَ
الْمَصِيرُ ﴿٧٢﴾ يَا أَيُّهَا النَّاسُ ضُرِبَ مَثَلٌ
فَاسْتَمِعُوا لَهُ ۚ إِنَّ الَّذِينَ تَدْعُونَ
مِنْ دُونِ اللَّهِ لَنْ يَخْلُقُوا ذُبَابًا
وَلَوِ اجْتَمَعُوا لَهُ ۖ وَإِنْ يَسْلُبْهُمُ الذُّبَابُ
شَيْئًا لَا يَسْتَنْقِذُوهُ مِنْهُ ۚ ضَعُفَ الطَّالِبُ
وَالْمَطْلُوبُ ﴿٧٣﴾ مَا قَدَرُوا اللَّهَ حَقَّ قَدْرِهِ ۗ
إِنَّ اللَّهَ لَقَوِيٌّ عَزِيزٌ ﴿٧٤﴾ اللَّهُ يَصْطَفِي
مِنَ الْمَلَائِكَةِ رُسُلًا وَمِنَ النَّاسِ ۚ
إِنَّ اللَّهَ سَمِيعٌ بَصِيرٌ ﴿٧٥﴾ يَعْلَمُ مَا بَيْنَ
أَيْدِيهِمْ وَمَا خَلْفَهُمْ ۗ وَإِلَى اللَّهِ تُرْجَعُ
الْأُمُورُ ﴿٧٦﴾ يَا أَيُّهَا الَّذِينَ آمَنُوا ارْكَعُوا
وَاسْجُدُوا وَاعْبُدُوا رَبَّكُمْ وَافْعَلُوا
الْخَيْرَ لَعَلَّكُمْ تُفْلِحُونَ ﴿٧٧﴾ وَجَاهِدُوا فِي

الجزء السابع عشر

of Allâh, as hard a striving as is possible and as it behoves you. He has chosen you and has imposed no hardship upon you in the matter of your faith, (so follow) the creed of your father Abraham. He named you Muslims (both) before this and (again) in this (Book the Qur'ân), so that the Messenger may be a guardian over you and that you may be guardians over people. Therefore, observe Prayer, keep on presenting the *Zakât* and hold fast to Allâh. He is your Patron, what a gracious Patron, and what a gracious Helper.

اللَّهِ حَقَّ جِهَادِهِ ۚ هُوَ اجْتَبَٰكُمْ وَمَا جَعَلَ عَلَيْكُمْ فِي الدِّينِ مِنْ حَرَجٍ ۚ مِلَّةَ أَبِيكُمْ إِبْرَٰهِيمَ ۚ هُوَ سَمَّٰكُمُ الْمُسْلِمِينَ ۥ مِنْ قَبْلُ وَفِي هَٰذَا لِيَكُونَ الرَّسُولُ شَهِيدًا عَلَيْكُمْ وَتَكُونُوا شُهَدَاءَ عَلَى النَّاسِ ۚ فَأَقِيمُوا الصَّلَوٰةَ وَأْتُوا الزَّكَوٰةَ وَاعْتَصِمُوا بِاللَّهِ ۚ هُوَ مَوْلَٰكُمْ ۚ فَنِعْمَ الْمَوْلَىٰ وَنِعْمَ النَّصِيرُ ٧٨

CHAPTER
23

AL-MU'MINÛN
(The Believers)
(Revealed before Hijrah)

سُورَةُ الْمُؤْمِنُونَ مَكِّيَّةٌ

With the name of Allâh,
the Most Gracious, the Ever Merciful
(I commence to read Sûrah Al-Mu'minûn).

بِسْمِ اللَّهِ الرَّحْمَٰنِ الرَّحِيمِ

PART الْجُزْءُ الثَّامِنَ عَشَرَ XVIII

1. TRULY, success in this life and in the Hereafter does come to the believers,
2. Who turn (to God) in all humility in their Prayer,
3. And who keep aloof from all that is vain and idle,
4. And who act conscientiously for the sake of purity (and regularly present the *Zakât*),
5. And who guard their private parts,

قَدْ أَفْلَحَ الْمُؤْمِنُونَ ١ الَّذِينَ هُمْ فِي صَلَاتِهِمْ خَٰشِعُونَ ٢ وَالَّذِينَ هُمْ عَنِ اللَّغْوِ مُعْرِضُونَ ٣ وَالَّذِينَ هُمْ لِلزَّكَوٰةِ فَٰعِلُونَ ٤ وَالَّذِينَ هُمْ لِفُرُوجِهِمْ حَٰفِظُونَ ٥

6. Except from their spouses, that is those whom they justly and rightfully own in proper wedlock, in that case they are not to be blamed,
7. But those who seek anything else (to satisfy their sexual desire) beyond this, it is they who are the transgressors,
8. And who look after their trusts and their covenants,
9. And who are strict in the observance of their Prayers.
10. It is they who are the real heirs;
11. Who will own Paradise where they shall abide forever.
12. We create a human being from an extract of clay;
13. Then We reduce him to a drop of sperm (and place him) in a safe depository;
14. Then We form the sperm into a clot; then We develop the clot into a lump of flesh; then We fashion bones out of this lump of flesh, then We clothe the bones with flesh, thereafter We evolve him into another being. Therefore blessed be Allâh the Best of Creators.
15. Then as you have passed (these seven stages of physical creation parallel to the above seven spiritual stages) you are heading towards death.
16. Then (after death), you will certainly be raised up to life on the Day of Resurrection.
17. And We have created above you seven ways, and We have never been neglectful of (the needs of) the creation.
18. And We send down water out of the cloud according to (a certain) measure and We lodge it in the earth (as long as it is required), and remember, surely it is We who determine its taking away (through the process of evaporation and many other processes),
19. And then with it (- the water) We grow for you gardens of date-palms and vines and you have plenty of fruit in these (gardens) and of these (fruit) you eat.
20. And (with the water We produce) a tree which grows on Mount Sinai (- olive tree)

إِلَّا عَلَىٰٓ أَزْوَٰجِهِمْ أَوْ مَا مَلَكَتْ أَيْمَٰنُهُمْ
فَإِنَّهُمْ غَيْرُ مَلُومِينَ ﴿٦﴾ فَمَنِ ٱبْتَغَىٰ وَرَآءَ
ذَٰلِكَ فَأُو۟لَٰٓئِكَ هُمُ ٱلْعَادُونَ ﴿٧﴾ وَٱلَّذِينَ هُمْ
لِأَمَٰنَٰتِهِمْ وَعَهْدِهِمْ رَٰعُونَ ﴿٨﴾ وَٱلَّذِينَ هُمْ
عَلَىٰ صَلَوَٰتِهِمْ يُحَافِظُونَ ﴿٩﴾ أُو۟لَٰٓئِكَ هُمُ ٱلْوَٰرِثُونَ ﴿١٠﴾
ٱلَّذِينَ يَرِثُونَ ٱلْفِرْدَوْسَ هُمْ فِيهَا خَٰلِدُونَ ﴿١١﴾
وَلَقَدْ خَلَقْنَا ٱلْإِنسَٰنَ مِن سُلَٰلَةٍ مِّن طِينٍ ﴿١٢﴾
ثُمَّ جَعَلْنَٰهُ نُطْفَةً فِى قَرَارٍ مَّكِينٍ ﴿١٣﴾
ثُمَّ خَلَقْنَا ٱلنُّطْفَةَ عَلَقَةً فَخَلَقْنَا ٱلْعَلَقَةَ
مُضْغَةً فَخَلَقْنَا ٱلْمُضْغَةَ عِظَٰمًا فَكَسَوْنَا
ٱلْعِظَٰمَ لَحْمًا ثُمَّ أَنشَأْنَٰهُ خَلْقًا ءَاخَرَ
فَتَبَارَكَ ٱللَّهُ أَحْسَنُ ٱلْخَٰلِقِينَ ﴿١٤﴾ ثُمَّ إِنَّكُم
بَعْدَ ذَٰلِكَ لَمَيِّتُونَ ﴿١٥﴾ ثُمَّ إِنَّكُمْ يَوْمَ
ٱلْقِيَٰمَةِ تُبْعَثُونَ ﴿١٦﴾ وَلَقَدْ خَلَقْنَا فَوْقَكُمْ
سَبْعَ طَرَآئِقَ وَمَا كُنَّا عَنِ ٱلْخَلْقِ
غَٰفِلِينَ ﴿١٧﴾ وَأَنزَلْنَا مِنَ ٱلسَّمَآءِ مَآءًۢ بِقَدَرٍ
فَأَسْكَنَّٰهُ فِى ٱلْأَرْضِ وَإِنَّا عَلَىٰ ذَهَابٍۭ
بِهِۦ لَقَٰدِرُونَ ﴿١٨﴾ فَأَنشَأْنَا لَكُم بِهِۦ جَنَّٰتٍ
مِّن نَّخِيلٍ وَأَعْنَٰبٍ لَّكُمْ فِيهَا فَوَٰكِهُ
كَثِيرَةٌ وَمِنْهَا تَأْكُلُونَ ﴿١٩﴾ وَشَجَرَةً تَخْرُجُ

which bears (in it) oil and (supplies) a condiment (also) for those who use it for food.

21. And you have an evidence in (the creation of) the cattle (too), which should lead you from ignorance to knowledge, We give you to drink of that (milk) which is in their bellies. You derive many other benefits from them and you (also) get food from some of them.

22. You are borne on them as well as on the ships.

SECTION 2

23. AND We sent Noah to his people and he said, 'O my people! Worship Allâh alone. You have no God other than He. Will you not then guard against evil and seek (His) protection?'

24. But the chiefs of those who disbelieved from among his people said, 'He is nothing but a human being like yourselves, (only) he seeks to assert (his) superiority over you. And if Allâh had so willed He could have certainly sent down angels (with him). We have never heard of this (sort of a thing) happen in the times of our fathers of old.

25. 'He is but a man gone mad, you had better bear with him for a while (and see the consequences).'

26. (Noah) said (praying), 'My Lord! Help me for they treat me as a liar.'

27. Then We sent Our revelation to him (directing him), 'Make the Ark under Our eyes and (according to the dictates of) Our revelation. And when (the time of) Our judgment comes and the waters of the valley gush forth, then embark there in (the Ark) two of every species, a pair (of every thing that you may need), and your companions, except those of them against whom (Our) word (of condemnation for their misdeeds) has already gone forth. But do not plead with Me in favour of those who have acted unjustly for they are (doomed) to be drowned.

28. 'Then when you and your companions are seated perfectly well in the Ark say (praying),

مِنْ طُورِ سَيْنَاءَ تَنْبُتُ بِالدُّهْنِ وَصِبْغٍ
لِلْأٰكِلِينَ ﴿٢٠﴾ وَإِنَّ لَكُمْ فِي الْأَنْعَامِ لَعِبْرَةً
نُسْقِيكُمْ مِمَّا فِي بُطُونِهَا وَلَكُمْ فِيهَا مَنَافِعُ
كَثِيرَةٌ وَمِنْهَا تَأْكُلُونَ ﴿٢١﴾ وَعَلَيْهَا وَعَلَى
الْفُلْكِ تُحْمَلُونَ ﴿٢٢﴾ وَلَقَدْ أَرْسَلْنَا نُوحًا إِلَىٰ
قَوْمِهِ فَقَالَ يَٰقَوْمِ اعْبُدُوا اللَّهَ مَا لَكُمْ
مِنْ إِلَٰهٍ غَيْرُهُ أَفَلَا تَتَّقُونَ ﴿٢٣﴾ فَقَالَ
الْمَلَؤُا الَّذِينَ كَفَرُوا مِنْ قَوْمِهِ مَا هَٰذَا
إِلَّا بَشَرٌ مِثْلُكُمْ يُرِيدُ أَنْ يَتَفَضَّلَ عَلَيْكُمْ
وَلَوْ شَاءَ اللَّهُ لَأَنْزَلَ مَلَٰئِكَةً مَا سَمِعْنَا
بِهَٰذَا فِي آبَائِنَا الْأَوَّلِينَ ﴿٢٤﴾ إِنْ هُوَ إِلَّا
رَجُلٌ بِهِ جِنَّةٌ فَتَرَبَّصُوا بِهِ حَتَّىٰ حِينٍ ﴿٢٥﴾
قَالَ رَبِّ انْصُرْنِي بِمَا كَذَّبُونِ ﴿٢٦﴾ فَأَوْحَيْنَا
إِلَيْهِ أَنِ اصْنَعِ الْفُلْكَ بِأَعْيُنِنَا وَوَحْيِنَا فَإِذَا
جَاءَ أَمْرُنَا وَفَارَ التَّنُّورُ فَاسْلُكْ فِيهَا مِنْ
كُلٍّ زَوْجَيْنِ اثْنَيْنِ وَأَهْلَكَ إِلَّا مَنْ سَبَقَ
عَلَيْهِ الْقَوْلُ مِنْهُمْ وَلَا تُخَٰطِبْنِي فِي الَّذِينَ
ظَلَمُوا إِنَّهُمْ مُغْرَقُونَ ﴿٢٧﴾ فَإِذَا اسْتَوَيْتَ أَنْتَ
وَمَنْ مَعَكَ عَلَى الْفُلْكِ فَقُلِ الْحَمْدُ لِلَّهِ

"All true and perfect praise belongs to Allâh Who has delivered us from the wicked people."

29. 'And say (while praying), "My Lord! Enable me to make a blessed landing, for You are the Best of those who provide (people) with the fairest landing place".'

30. Verily, this (account of Noah) is full of (many) signs. Surely, thus do We reveal the hidden truth (about the people and We did try the people of Noah).

31. Then We raised another generation after them.

32. And We sent to them a Messenger from among themselves, (who said,) 'Worship Allâh. You have no god other than He. Will you not then guard against evil (deeds)?'

SECTION 3

33. **A**ND the chiefs of his people who disbelieved and cried lies to the meeting (with the Lord) in the Hereafter, and whom We had given ease and comfort in the present life, said, 'He is but a human being like yourselves. He eats of (the food) which you eat and drinks of (the drinks) which you drink.

34. 'And, surely, if you obey a human being like yourselves you will then be the losers indeed.

35. 'Does he promise you that when you are dead and reduced to dust and bones you shall be brought forth (alive again from the graves)?

36. 'How very far and away (from truth and understanding) is that which you are promised!

37. 'There is no life beyond our present life. (It is here) we die and (here) we live, and we shall not at all be raised up (to life again, so that there awaits us no Resurrection).

38. 'He is only an ordinary man who has forged a lie in the name of Allâh and we are not at all going to believe in him.'

39. He said (praying), 'My Lord! Help me for they treat me as a liar.'

40. (The Lord) said, 'They shall be remorseful

الَّذِي نَجَّـٰنَا مِنَ الْقَوْمِ الظَّـٰلِمِينَ ﴿٢٨﴾ وَقُل
رَّبِّ أَنزِلْنِي مُنزَلًا مُّبَارَكًا وَأَنتَ خَيْرُ
الْمُنزِلِينَ ﴿٢٩﴾ إِنَّ فِي ذَٰلِكَ لَأَيَـٰتٍ وَإِن كُنَّا
لَمُبْتَلِينَ ﴿٣٠﴾ ثُمَّ أَنشَأْنَا مِنۢ بَعْدِهِمْ قَرْنًا
ءَاخَرِينَ ﴿٣١﴾ فَأَرْسَلْنَا فِيهِمْ رَسُولًا مِّنْهُمْ أَنِ
اعْبُدُوا اللَّهَ مَا لَكُم مِّنْ إِلَـٰهٍ غَيْرُهُۥٓ أَفَلَا
ع ٢ تَتَّقُونَ ﴿٣٢﴾ وَقَالَ الْمَلَأُ مِن قَوْمِهِ الَّذِينَ
كَفَرُوا وَكَذَّبُوا بِلِقَاءِ الْـَٔاخِرَةِ وَأَتْرَفْنَـٰهُمْ
فِي الْحَيَوٰةِ الدُّنْيَا مَا هَـٰذَآ إِلَّا بَشَرٌ مِّثْلُكُمْ
يَأْكُلُ مِمَّا تَأْكُلُونَ مِنْهُ وَيَشْرَبُ مِمَّا
تَشْرَبُونَ ﴿٣٣﴾ وَلَئِنْ أَطَعْتُم بَشَرًا مِّثْلَكُمْ
إِنَّكُمْ إِذًا لَّخَـٰسِرُونَ ﴿٣٤﴾ أَيَعِدُكُمْ أَنَّكُمْ إِذَا
مِتُّمْ وَكُنتُمْ تُرَابًا وَعِظَـٰمًا أَنَّكُم مُّخْرَجُونَ ﴿٣٥﴾
هَيْهَاتَ هَيْهَاتَ لِمَا تُوعَدُونَ ﴿٣٦﴾ إِنْ هِيَ إِلَّا
حَيَاتُنَا الدُّنْيَا نَمُوتُ وَنَحْيَا وَمَا نَحْنُ
بِمَبْعُوثِينَ ﴿٣٧﴾ إِنْ هُوَ إِلَّا رَجُلٌ افْتَرَىٰ عَلَى اللَّهِ
كَذِبًا وَمَا نَحْنُ لَهُۥ بِمُؤْمِنِينَ ﴿٣٨﴾ قَالَ رَبِّ
انصُرْنِي بِمَا كَذَّبُونِ ﴿٣٩﴾ قَالَ عَمَّا قَلِيلٍ

before long (when caught by some punishment).'

41. Then the punishment overtook them justly and rightfully and We made them as scum (of the flood), so the people who do wrong are far removed (from the mercy of God).

42. Then We raised other generations after them.

43. No community can go ahead of its appointed time (and thus manage to escape their doom) nor can they remain behind (it, or delay it).

44. Then We sent Our Messengers successively (one after the other). Whenever there came to a community its Messenger (of God), they treated him as a liar. So We made some of them follow others (to destruction) and We reduced them to mere legendary tales. Therefore the people who do not believe are far removed (from the mercy of their Lord).

45. Then We sent Moses and his brother Aaron with Our Messages and a clear authority,

46. To Pharaoh and his courtiers but they waxed proud for they were a haughty (type of) people.

47. And they said, 'Shall we believe in two human beings like ourselves while their people (- the Israelites) are our bondsmen?'

48. So they cried lies to both of them with the result they became of those who were destroyed.

49. And (after this event) We gave Moses the Book (-the Torah) so that they (- his people) might receive guidance (through it).

50. And We made the son of Mary and his mother a sign, (and a model of virtue), and We gave them both refuge upon a worth-living lofty plateau abounding in (green and fruitful) valleys and springs of running water.

SECTION 4

51. **O** YOU Messengers! Eat of the things which are clean, good and pure and (thus) do good works. Verily, I am Well-Aware of what you do.

52. Surely, (know that) this community of

لَيُصْبِحُنَّ نٰدِمِينَ ﴿٤٠﴾ فَأَخَذَتْهُمُ الصَّيْحَةُ
بِالْحَقِّ فَجَعَلْنٰهُمْ غُثَآءً فَبُعْدًا لِّلْقَوْمِ
الظّٰلِمِينَ ﴿٤١﴾ ثُمَّ أَنْشَأْنَا مِنْ بَعْدِهِمْ قُرُونًا
أٰخَرِينَ ﴿٤٢﴾ مَا تَسْبِقُ مِنْ أُمَّةٍ أَجَلَهَا وَمَا
يَسْتَـْٔخِرُونَ ﴿٤٣﴾ ثُمَّ أَرْسَلْنَا رُسُلَنَا تَتْرَا كُلَّ
مَا جَآءَ أُمَّةً رَّسُولُهَا كَذَّبُوهُ فَأَتْبَعْنَا
بَعْضَهُمْ بَعْضًا وَجَعَلْنٰهُمْ أَحَادِيثَ فَبُعْدًا
لِّقَوْمٍ لَّا يُؤْمِنُونَ ﴿٤٤﴾ ثُمَّ أَرْسَلْنَا مُوسٰى
وَأَخَاهُ هٰرُونَ بِـَٔايٰتِنَا وَسُلْطٰنٍ مُّبِينٍ ﴿٤٥﴾
إِلٰى فِرْعَوْنَ وَمَلَإِيْهِ فَاسْتَكْبَرُوا وَكَانُوا
قَوْمًا عَالِينَ ﴿٤٦﴾ فَقَالُوٓا أَنُؤْمِنُ لِبَشَرَيْنِ مِثْلِنَا
وَقَوْمُهُمَا لَنَا عٰبِدُونَ ﴿٤٧﴾ فَكَذَّبُوهُمَا فَكَانُوا
مِنَ الْمُهْلَكِينَ ﴿٤٨﴾ وَلَقَدْ ءَاتَيْنَا مُوسَى الْكِتٰبَ
لَعَلَّهُمْ يَهْتَدُونَ ﴿٤٩﴾ وَجَعَلْنَا ابْنَ مَرْيَمَ
وَأُمَّهُ ءَايَةً وَءَاوَيْنٰهُمَا إِلٰى رَبْوَةٍ ذَاتِ قَرَارٍ
وَمَعِينٍ ﴿٥٠﴾ يٰٓأَيُّهَا الرُّسُلُ كُلُوا مِنَ الطَّيِّبٰتِ
وَاعْمَلُوا صٰلِحًا إِنِّي بِمَا تَعْمَلُونَ عَلِيمٌ ﴿٥١﴾
وَإِنَّ هٰذِهِ أُمَّتُكُمْ أُمَّةً وٰحِدَةً وَأَنَا

yours is (in fact) one community (and your religion one religion), and I am your Lord, so take Me as (your) shield.

53. But the people, (rather than preserve their unity) split up their affair among themselves (forming themselves into factions) considering (each portion thus split up) as (the real) Scripture, every faction rejoicing in that which was with them.

54. So leave them in their utter confusion (due to their ignorance) for a time.

55. Do they think that because of what We go on adding to their (worldly) wealth and children,

56. We are in a hurry to do them good? Nay, but they do not realise (the true state of things).

57. As for those who out of the Majesty of their Lord are full of awe and reverence to Him,

58. And those who believe in the revelations of their Lord,

59. And those who associate not partners with their Lord,

60. And those who give whatever they can afford to give (as alms in the way of their Lord), while their hearts tremble (at the thought) that they are returning to their Lord (and whether their deeds will find His approval or not).

61. It is they who are quick and eager to do good works to outdo others and it is they who are (the) foremost for these (virtues, and shall win the race).

62. And We do not lay down responsibility upon any soul beyond its capacity and We have a book (of law) which speaks and acts justly and no injustice is done to anyone.

63. Nay, their (- the disbelievers') minds are in utter confusion (due to ignorance) about this (Qur'ân), and they are (engrossed) in deeds different from the (bindings of) revelations and they go on doing them.

64. Yet as soon as We take those of them given to a life of luxury to task, behold! They start appealing for succour.

رَبُّكُمْ فَاتَّقُوْنِ ﴿٥٢﴾ فَتَقَطَّعُوْٓا أَمْرَهُمْ بَيْنَهُمْ
زُبُرًا كُلُّ حِزْبٍ بِمَا لَدَيْهِمْ فَرِحُوْنَ ﴿٥٣﴾
فَذَرْهُمْ فِيْ غَمْرَتِهِمْ حَتّٰى حِيْنٍ ﴿٥٤﴾ أَيَحْسَبُوْنَ
أَنَّمَا نُمِدُّهُمْ بِهٖ مِنْ مَّالٍ وَّبَنِيْنَ ﴿٥٥﴾
نُسَارِعُ لَهُمْ فِي الْخَيْرٰتِ بَلْ لَّا يَشْعُرُوْنَ ﴿٥٦﴾
إِنَّ الَّذِيْنَ هُمْ مِّنْ خَشْيَةِ رَبِّهِمْ مُّشْفِقُوْنَ ﴿٥٧﴾
وَالَّذِيْنَ هُمْ بِاٰيٰتِ رَبِّهِمْ يُؤْمِنُوْنَ ﴿٥٨﴾
وَالَّذِيْنَ هُمْ بِرَبِّهِمْ لَا يُشْرِكُوْنَ ﴿٥٩﴾ وَالَّذِيْنَ
يُؤْتُوْنَ مَآ اٰتَوْا وَّقُلُوْبُهُمْ وَجِلَةٌ أَنَّهُمْ إِلٰى
رَبِّهِمْ رٰجِعُوْنَ ﴿٦٠﴾ أُولٰٓئِكَ يُسٰرِعُوْنَ فِي الْخَيْرٰتِ
وَهُمْ لَهَا سٰبِقُوْنَ ﴿٦١﴾ وَلَا نُكَلِّفُ نَفْسًا
إِلَّا وُسْعَهَا وَلَدَيْنَا كِتٰبٌ يَّنْطِقُ بِالْحَقِّ
وَهُمْ لَا يُظْلَمُوْنَ ﴿٦٢﴾ بَلْ قُلُوْبُهُمْ فِيْ
غَمْرَةٍ مِّنْ هٰذَا وَلَهُمْ أَعْمٰلٌ مِّنْ دُوْنِ
ذٰلِكَ هُمْ لَهَا عٰمِلُوْنَ ﴿٦٣﴾ حَتّٰىٓ إِذَآ أَخَذْنَا
مُتْرَفِيْهِمْ بِالْعَذَابِ إِذَا هُمْ يَجْـَٔرُوْنَ ﴿٦٤﴾

65. (Whereupon it will be said to them,) 'Do not appeal for succour this day, you shall receive no help from Us.
66. 'My Messages were recited to you but you used to turn back on your heels,
67. 'Treating them with disdain and arrogance, talking nonsense about this (Qur'ân) by night (in your meetings), you gave (it) up.'
68. Have they not then pondered over the (Divine) word? As a matter of fact there has come to them that which had not come to their fathers of old.
69. Or do they deny their Messenger because they do not recognise him?
70. Or do they say, 'He is possessed?' Nay, but the fact is that he has brought them the truth while most of them are averse to the truth.
71. And had the Eternal Truth (true God) followed their vain and low desires, the heavens and the earth and all those who are (living) in them would have surely gone to ruin. But We have brought them that which will raise them to eminence, yet they are turning aside from their own means of (raising them to) eminence.
72. Or do you ask of them a tribute? (There is no such thing) as the tribute of your Lord is the best, for He is the Best of Providers.
73. And most surely you are calling them to a straight and right path.
74. But those who do not believe in the Here after, are indeed deviating from that path.
75. And even if We had shown them mercy and relieved them of their distress they would still persist in their transgression, wandering on blindly.
76. And We did seize them with punishment (in the past) but they did not humble themselves before their Lord, nor would they supplicate (to Him for mercy).
77. Behold! No sooner did We let loose on them a severe punishment than they are utterly

لا تجئروا اليوم إنكم منا لا
تنصرون ﴿٦٥﴾ قد كانت ءايتي تتلى
عليكم فكنتم على أعقابكم تنكصون ﴿٦٦﴾
مستكبرين به سمرا تهجرون ﴿٦٧﴾ أفلم
يدبروا القول أم جاءهم ما لم يأت
ءاباءهم الأولين ﴿٦٨﴾ أم لم يعرفوا رسولهم
فهم له منكرون ﴿٦٩﴾ أم يقولون
به جنة بل جاءهم بالحق وأكثرهم
للحق كرهون ﴿٧٠﴾ ولو اتبع الحق أهواءهم
لفسدت السموت والأرض ومن فيهن
بل أتينهم بذكرهم فهم عن ذكرهم
معرضون ﴿٧١﴾ أم تسئلهم خرجا فخراج ربك
خير وهو خير الرزقين ﴿٧٢﴾ وإنك لتدعوهم
إلى صرط مستقيم ﴿٧٣﴾ وإن الذين لا يؤمنون
بالأخرة عن الصرط لنكبون ﴿٧٤﴾ ولو رحمنهم
وكشفنا ما بهم من ضر للجوا في طغينهم
يعمهون ﴿٧٥﴾ ولقد أخذنهم بالعذاب فما
استكانوا لربهم وما يتضرعون ﴿٧٦﴾ حتى إذا
فتحنا عليهم بابا ذا عذاب شديد إذا هم

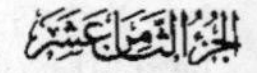

despaired (of God's mercy) thereat.

SECTION 5

78. **A**ND (disbelievers!) it is He Who has given you ears, eyes and hearts (yet) little is the gratitude you express.
79. And it is He Who has multiplied you in the earth and to Him you shall be gathered.
80. It is He Who gives life and causes death and He alone controls the alternation of night and day. Will you not then make use of your understanding?
81. But (rather than trying to understand) they repeated what the former people had said.
82. They had said, 'What! Shall we be certainly raised up to life when we are dead and reduced to mere dust and bones?
83. 'Surely, we and our forefathers have already been given such promises before. These are nothing but only fables of the former people.'
84. Ask, '(Tell me) if you know Whom the earth and all the creatures therein belong to.'
85. They will certainly say, 'To Allâh.' (Thereupon) say, 'Will you still pay no heed?'
86. Say, 'Who is the Lord of the seven heavens and the Lord of the Great Throne (of power)?'
87. They will surely say, '(They all belong) to Allâh.' Say, 'Will you not then guard against (refusal and evil deeds).'
88. Ask, '(Tell me) if you know Who is it in Whose hands lies the dominating control of everything and Who protects (all) while against Whom no protection can be had?'
89. They will indeed say, 'All these (attributes) belong to Allâh.' Say, 'How and whither are you then being led away?'
90. The thing is that We have brought them the truth (about the unity of God) but they are sticking to lies (by refusing it repeatedly).
91. Allâh has taken to Himself no son, nor is there any other god along with Him. (Had there been any) each god would have left with what he had created, and some of them would surely

ع

فِيهِ مُبْلِسُونَ ﴿٧٧﴾ وَهُوَ الَّذِي أَنْشَأَ لَكُمُ
السَّمْعَ وَالْأَبْصَارَ وَالْأَفْئِدَةَ قَلِيلًا مَا
تَشْكُرُونَ ﴿٧٨﴾ وَهُوَ الَّذِي ذَرَأَكُمْ فِي الْأَرْضِ
وَإِلَيْهِ تُحْشَرُونَ ﴿٧٩﴾ وَهُوَ الَّذِي يُحْيِي وَيُمِيتُ
وَلَهُ اخْتِلَافُ اللَّيْلِ وَالنَّهَارِ أَفَلَا تَعْقِلُونَ ﴿٨٠﴾
بَلْ قَالُوا مِثْلَ مَا قَالَ الْأَوَّلُونَ ﴿٨١﴾ قَالُوا أَإِذَا
مِتْنَا وَكُنَّا تُرَابًا وَعِظَامًا أَإِنَّا لَمَبْعُوثُونَ ﴿٨٢﴾ لَقَدْ
وُعِدْنَا نَحْنُ وَآبَاؤُنَا هَٰذَا مِنْ قَبْلُ إِنْ
هَٰذَا إِلَّا أَسَاطِيرُ الْأَوَّلِينَ ﴿٨٣﴾ قُلْ لِمَنِ الْأَرْضُ
وَمَنْ فِيهَا إِنْ كُنْتُمْ تَعْلَمُونَ ﴿٨٤﴾ سَيَقُولُونَ
لِلَّهِ قُلْ أَفَلَا تَذَكَّرُونَ ﴿٨٥﴾ قُلْ مَنْ رَبُّ
السَّمَاوَاتِ السَّبْعِ وَرَبُّ الْعَرْشِ الْعَظِيمِ ﴿٨٦﴾
سَيَقُولُونَ لِلَّهِ قُلْ أَفَلَا تَتَّقُونَ ﴿٨٧﴾ قُلْ مَنْ
بِيَدِهِ مَلَكُوتُ كُلِّ شَيْءٍ وَهُوَ يُجِيرُ وَلَا
يُجَارُ عَلَيْهِ إِنْ كُنْتُمْ تَعْلَمُونَ ﴿٨٨﴾ سَيَقُولُونَ
لِلَّهِ قُلْ فَأَنَّىٰ تُسْحَرُونَ ﴿٨٩﴾ بَلْ أَتَيْنَاهُمْ بِالْحَقِّ
وَإِنَّهُمْ لَكَاذِبُونَ ﴿٩٠﴾ مَا اتَّخَذَ اللَّهُ مِنْ وَلَدٍ
وَمَا كَانَ مَعَهُ مِنْ إِلَٰهٍ إِذًا لَذَهَبَ كُلُّ
إِلَٰهٍ بِمَا خَلَقَ وَلَعَلَا بَعْضُهُمْ عَلَىٰ بَعْضٍ

have dominated over others. Holy is Allâh, far above all they attribute (to Him).

92. He has knowledge of (both) the hidden and the manifest realities. He is Highly-Exalted above (all the things) they associate (with Him).

SECTION 6

93. SAY (in prayer), 'My Lord! If you should show me (in my lifetime) that (punishment) they are threatened with,

94. 'My Lord! Then do not leave me among the wrongdoing people.'

95. As a matter of fact, We have every power of showing you (in your lifetime) that (punishment) We threaten them with.

96. Repel (their) evil (by repaying it) with that which is the fairest. We know very well (the things) they allege (about you).

97. And say (in prayer), 'My Lord! I seek refuge in You from the mischief-mongerings of the rebellious (people);

98. 'Rather, I (also) seek refuge in You, my Lord! Lest they should even come near me.'

99. Behold! When death approaches one of them (- the rebellious ones) he says (making entreaties repeatedly), 'Send me back, My Lord! Send me back,

100. 'So that I may do righteous (deeds) which I failed to do (in the worldly life).' 'Never, that can never be,' (is the answer he receives). It is but a word (of excuse) which he utters. And there is a barrier behind them which shall remain till the day when they shall be raised to life (again).

101. So when the trumpet is blown, ties of kinship will cease to exist between them (- the people to render assistance) that day, nor will they ask after one another.

102. Then (on that day there shall be a true weighing so that) whose scales are heavy (and their deeds of righteousness preponderant and manifold) it is they who are the triumphant.

103. But whose scales are light (and their deeds

سُبْحٰنَ اللّٰهِ عَمَّا يَصِفُونَ ﴿٩١﴾ عٰلِمِ الْغَيْبِ
وَالشَّهٰدَةِ فَتَعٰلٰى عَمَّا يُشْرِكُونَ ﴿٩٢﴾ قُلْ رَّبِّ إِمَّا
تُرِيَنِّي مَا يُوعَدُونَ ﴿٩٣﴾ رَبِّ فَلَا تَجْعَلْنِي فِي
الْقَوْمِ الظّٰلِمِينَ ﴿٩٤﴾ وَإِنَّا عَلٰى أَنْ نُّرِيَكَ مَا
نَعِدُهُمْ لَقٰدِرُونَ ﴿٩٥﴾ إِدْفَعْ بِالَّتِي هِيَ أَحْسَنُ
السَّيِّئَةَ نَحْنُ أَعْلَمُ بِمَا يَصِفُونَ ﴿٩٦﴾ وَقُلْ
رَّبِّ أَعُوذُ بِكَ مِنْ هَمَزٰتِ الشَّيٰطِينِ ﴿٩٧﴾
وَأَعُوذُ بِكَ رَبِّ أَنْ يَّحْضُرُونِ ﴿٩٨﴾ حَتّٰى إِذَا جَاءَ
أَحَدَهُمُ الْمَوْتُ قَالَ رَبِّ ارْجِعُونِ ﴿٩٩﴾ لَعَلِّي
أَعْمَلُ صٰلِحًا فِيمَا تَرَكْتُ كَلَّا إِنَّهَا كَلِمَةٌ هُوَ
قَائِلُهَا وَمِنْ وَّرَائِهِمْ بَرْزَخٌ إِلٰى يَوْمِ يُبْعَثُونَ ﴿١٠٠﴾
فَإِذَا نُفِخَ فِي الصُّورِ فَلَا أَنْسَابَ بَيْنَهُمْ يَوْمَئِذٍ
وَّلَا يَتَسَاءَلُونَ ﴿١٠١﴾ فَمَنْ ثَقُلَتْ مَوٰزِينُهُ فَأُولٰئِكَ
هُمُ الْمُفْلِحُونَ ﴿١٠٢﴾ وَمَنْ خَفَّتْ مَوٰزِينُهُ فَأُولٰئِكَ

ع ٥

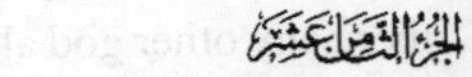

of righteousness of no account), it is they who have ruined their souls and who shall abide in Gehenna for long.

104 The Fire shall scorch their faces (so they will lie there disfigured with burning) and they will wear a grin (of pain and anguish).

105. (It will be said to them), 'Is it not true that My Messages were recited to you but you went on crying them lies?'

106. They will say, 'Our Lord! Our misfortune got the better of us (when we gave ourselves up to evil doings) and we were actually an erring people;

107. 'Our Lord! Deliver us from this (Hell), we shall indeed be unjust if we return (to our evil ways of disobedience).'

108. (God) will say, 'Begone with you, despised therein (the Hell), and do not speak to Me.

109. 'There was a section from among My servants who said, "Our Lord! We believe, so protect us (against our sins) and have mercy on us, for You are the Best of those who show mercy."

110. 'But you treated them as a laughingstock and (you continued to laugh at them) until that, (ridicule) made you give up (even) My remembrance while you ever went on laughing at them.

111. 'This day I have rewarded them for their patient endurance so that they are the ones who have attained their goals and achieved bliss.'

112. (God) will (then) say, 'What number of years have you tarried on the earth?'

113. They will say, 'We tarried only for a day or part of a day (we have no exact idea), but ask those who keep the count.'

114. (God) will say, 'You tarried but a little while, if only you knew (what loss you have incurred by missing doing good).

115. 'Did you then think that We had created you without purpose and that you would not be brought back to Us?'

116. Whereas Highly Exalted is Allâh, the Monarch, the Truly Existing One. There is no

الَّذِينَ خَسِرُوا أَنفُسَهُمْ فِي جَهَنَّمَ خَلِدُونَ ﴿١٠٣﴾ تَلْفَحُ
وُجُوهَهُمُ النَّارُ وَهُمْ فِيهَا كَلِحُونَ ﴿١٠٤﴾ أَلَمْ تَكُنْ
ءَايَتِي تُتْلَى عَلَيْكُمْ فَكُنتُم بِهَا تُكَذِّبُونَ ﴿١٠٥﴾ قَالُوا
رَبَّنَا غَلَبَتْ عَلَيْنَا شِقْوَتُنَا وَكُنَّا قَوْمًا ضَالِّينَ ﴿١٠٦﴾
رَبَّنَا أَخْرِجْنَا مِنْهَا فَإِنْ عُدْنَا فَإِنَّا ظَلِمُونَ ﴿١٠٧﴾
قَالَ اخْسَـُٔوا فِيهَا وَلَا تُكَلِّمُونِ ﴿١٠٨﴾ إِنَّهُ كَانَ
فَرِيقٌ مِّنْ عِبَادِي يَقُولُونَ رَبَّنَا ءَامَنَّا فَاغْفِرْ لَنَا
وَارْحَمْنَا وَأَنتَ خَيْرُ الرَّحِمِينَ ﴿١٠٩﴾ فَاتَّخَذْتُمُوهُمْ
سِخْرِيًّا حَتَّى أَنسَوْكُمْ ذِكْرِي وَكُنتُم مِّنْهُمْ
تَضْحَكُونَ ﴿١١٠﴾ إِنِّي جَزَيْتُهُمُ الْيَوْمَ بِمَا صَبَرُوا
أَنَّهُمْ هُمُ الْفَائِزُونَ ﴿١١١﴾ قَلَ كَمْ لَبِثْتُمْ فِي
الْأَرْضِ عَدَدَ سِنِينَ ﴿١١٢﴾ قَالُوا لَبِثْنَا يَوْمًا أَوْ
بَعْضَ يَوْمٍ فَسْـَٔلِ الْعَادِّينَ ﴿١١٣﴾ قَلَ إِن لَّبِثْتُمْ
إِلَّا قَلِيلًا لَّوْ أَنَّكُمْ كُنتُمْ تَعْلَمُونَ ﴿١١٤﴾ أَفَحَسِبْتُمْ
أَنَّمَا خَلَقْنَكُمْ عَبَثًا وَأَنَّكُمْ إِلَيْنَا لَا تُرْجَعُونَ ﴿١١٥﴾
فَتَعَلَى اللَّهُ الْمَلِكُ الْحَقُّ لَا إِلَهَ إِلَّا هُوَ رَبُّ

other, cannot be and will never be one worthy of worship but He, the Lord of the Glorious Throne!

117. And he who calls upon another god along with Allâh for (the god-head of) which he has no proof, shall have to render an account to his Lord. Certainly, such disbelievers will never gain their object.

118. And say (in your prayer), 'My Lord! Protect and have mercy, and you are the Best of those who show mercy.'

الْعَرْشِ الْكَرِيمِ ﴿١١٦﴾ وَمَنْ يَدْعُ مَعَ اللهِ
إِلٰهًا أٰخَرَ لَا بُرْهٰنَ لَهُ بِهِ فَإِنَّمَا حِسَابُهُ
عِنْدَ رَبِّهِ إِنَّهُ لَا يُفْلِحُ الْكٰفِرُونَ ﴿١١٧﴾ وَقُلْ
رَّبِّ اغْفِرْ وَارْحَمْ وَأَنْتَ خَيْرُ الرّٰحِمِينَ ﴿١١٨﴾ ع ٦

CHAPTER
24

AL-NÛR
(The Light)
(Revealed after Hijrah)

سُورَةُ النُّورِ مَدَنِيَّةٌ

With the name of Allâh,
the Most Gracious, the Ever Merciful
(I commence to read Sûrah Al-Nûr).

بِسْمِ اللهِ الرَّحْمٰنِ الرَّحِيمِ

1. (THIS is) a (highly dignified) Sûrah which We have revealed and (the ordinances of) which We have made obligatory and We have revealed in it clear commandments so that you may rise to great eminence.

2. Strike the fornicatress and adulteress and the fornicator and adulterer on the body of each one of them a hundred times. (This is the extreme limit,) and let no feelings of pity for the two hold you from obedience to Allâh (in executing His judgment), if you believe in Allâh and the Last Day. And let a section of the believers be present (there at the time of the execution of) their punishment.

3. The fornicator and adulterer cannot have sexual relations (without lawful marriage)

سُورَةٌ أَنْزَلْنٰهَا وَفَرَضْنٰهَا وَأَنْزَلْنَا فِيهَا أٰيٰتٍ
بَيِّنٰتٍ لَعَلَّكُمْ تَذَكَّرُونَ ﴿١﴾ اَلزَّانِيَةُ وَالزَّانِي
فَاجْلِدُوا كُلَّ وٰحِدٍ مِّنْهُمَا مِائَةَ جَلْدَةٍ
وَلَا تَأْخُذْكُمْ بِهِمَا رَأْفَةٌ فِي دِينِ اللهِ إِنْ
كُنْتُمْ تُؤْمِنُونَ بِاللهِ وَالْيَوْمِ الْأٰخِرِ وَلْيَشْهَدْ
عَذَابَهُمَا طَآئِفَةٌ مِّنَ الْمُؤْمِنِينَ ﴿٢﴾ اَلزَّانِي لَا

except with a fornicatress and adulteress or polytheistic woman (of low morality), and the fornicatress and adulteress, none can have sexual relations with her except a fornicator and adulterer or a polytheistic man (of low morality). And this (adultery and fornication) is forbidden to the believers.

4. Strike eighty times on the bodies of those who calumniate chaste women and who do not support (their accusation) with four witnesses, and never accept their testimony (because) it is they who are the disobedient (and break the law);

5. Except those who repent after this and make amends, they will find Allâh the Great Protector, Ever Merciful.

6. And those who charge their wives of adultery and have no witnesses (to support their charge) except their own selves, let each (husband) bear testimony (repeating it) four times over calling Allâh to witness that he is surely of those who speak the truth in (the matter of) charging his wife (of adultery).

7. And the fifth (time he should say on oath) that Allâh's wrath be upon him if he be of the liars.

8. But it shall avert the punishment from her (- the wife) if she calling Allâh to witness testifies four times over that he is of the liars (in bringing this charge against her).

9. And the fifth (time she should say on oath) that the wrath of Allâh be upon her if he (- her husband) has spoken the truth (about her).

10. But for Allâh's grace and His mercy (which rests) upon you and (but for the fact) that Allâh is Oft-Returning (with compassion), All-Wise (you would have come to grief).

SECTION 2

11. **V**ERILY, those (- hypocrites) who brought the false accusation (against *Âishah*, the wife of the Prophet), are a section of your own people. Do not think this (- incident) to be bad for you,

يَنكِحُ إِلَّا زَانِيَةً أَوْ مُشْرِكَةً وَّ الزَّانِيَةُ لَا
يَنكِحُهَآ إِلَّا زَانٍ أَوْ مُشْرِكٌ وَحُرِّمَ ذٰلِكَ
عَلَى الْمُؤْمِنِينَ ٣ وَالَّذِينَ يَرْمُونَ الْمُحْصَنٰتِ
ثُمَّ لَمْ يَأْتُوا بِأَرْبَعَةِ شُهَدَآءَ فَاجْلِدُوهُمْ
ثَمٰنِينَ جَلْدَةً وَّلَا تَقْبَلُوا لَهُمْ شَهٰدَةً أَبَدًا
وَأُولٰٓئِكَ هُمُ الْفٰسِقُونَ ٤ إِلَّا الَّذِينَ تَابُوا
مِنْ بَعْدِ ذٰلِكَ وَأَصْلَحُوا فَإِنَّ اللّٰهَ غَفُورٌ
رَّحِيمٌ ٥ وَالَّذِينَ يَرْمُونَ أَزْوٰجَهُمْ وَلَمْ يَكُن
لَّهُمْ شُهَدَآءُ إِلَّآ أَنفُسُهُمْ فَشَهٰدَةُ أَحَدِهِمْ
أَرْبَعُ شَهٰدٰتٍ بِاللّٰهِ إِنَّهُ لَمِنَ الصّٰدِقِينَ ٦
وَالْخٰمِسَةُ أَنَّ لَعْنَتَ اللّٰهِ عَلَيْهِ إِن كَانَ مِنَ
الْكٰذِبِينَ ٧ وَيَدْرَؤُا عَنْهَا الْعَذَابَ أَن تَشْهَدَ
أَرْبَعَ شَهٰدٰتٍ بِاللّٰهِ إِنَّهُ لَمِنَ الْكٰذِبِينَ ٨
وَالْخٰمِسَةَ أَنَّ غَضَبَ اللّٰهِ عَلَيْهَآ إِن كَانَ مِنَ
الصّٰدِقِينَ ٩ وَلَوْلَا فَضْلُ اللّٰهِ عَلَيْكُمْ
وَرَحْمَتُهُ وَأَنَّ اللّٰهَ تَوَّابٌ حَكِيمٌ ١٠ إِنَّ الَّذِينَ
جَآءُو بِالْإِفْكِ عُصْبَةٌ مِّنكُمْ لَا تَحْسَبُوهُ
شَرًّا لَّكُمْ بَلْ هُوَ خَيْرٌ لَّكُمْ لِكُلِّ امْرِئٍ

rather it is good for you. (As for the accusers,) everyone of them shall receive (his due punishment according to) that which he has accomplished in the form) of sin. As for him (- *Abdullâh bin Ubayy bin Salûl*) who among them took the principal part thereof (in fabricating and spreading malicious scandal against her) there awaits him a grievous punishment.
12. When you heard of this (accusation) why did not the believing men and believing women have a better opinion in respect of their own people and say, 'This (charge) is an obvious lie?'
13. Why did they (- the fabricators of this charge) not bring four witnesses in support of this (accusation of theirs)? Since they failed to produce the (required) witnesses, it is they who are the very liars in the sight of Allâh.
14. But for the fact that Allâh has shown His grace and mercy to you in the present world, and in the next a great punishment would have certainly befallen you on account of that (slander) which you spread.
15. When (some of) you began to learn this (slander) from each others tongues, you gave tongue to that (rumour and made statements) of which you had no knowledge; and you considered it a trivial thing while it was grave in the sight of Allâh.
16. And why did you not say as soon as you heard of it, 'It does not behove us to talk like this. Holy are You (O Gracious God). This is a monstrous calumny,'
17. If you are (true) believers (you should bear in mind that) Allâh admonishes you never to repeat such a thing again.
18. And Allâh explains to you (His) commandments and Allâh is All-Knowing, All-Wise.
19. Those who love to spread immorality among the believers, will have a woeful punishment in this world and the next. And Allâh knows while you do not know (the consequences of this evil).

مِنْهُم مَّا اكْتَسَبَ مِنَ الْإِثْمِ وَالَّذِي تَوَلَّى
كِبْرَهُ مِنْهُمْ لَهُ عَذَابٌ عَظِيمٌ ﴿١١﴾ لَوْلَا إِذْ سَمِعْتُمُوهُ
ظَنَّ الْمُؤْمِنُونَ وَالْمُؤْمِنَاتُ بِأَنفُسِهِمْ خَيْرًا
وَقَالُوا هَٰذَا إِفْكٌ مُّبِينٌ ﴿١٢﴾ لَوْلَا جَاءُو عَلَيْهِ
بِأَرْبَعَةِ شُهَدَاءَ فَإِذْ لَمْ يَأْتُوا بِالشُّهَدَاءِ فَأُولَٰئِكَ
عِندَ اللَّهِ هُمُ الْكَاذِبُونَ ﴿١٣﴾ وَلَوْلَا فَضْلُ اللَّهِ
عَلَيْكُمْ وَرَحْمَتُهُ فِي الدُّنْيَا وَالْآخِرَةِ لَمَسَّكُمْ
فِي مَا أَفَضْتُمْ فِيهِ عَذَابٌ عَظِيمٌ ﴿١٤﴾ إِذْ تَلَقَّوْنَهُ
بِأَلْسِنَتِكُمْ وَتَقُولُونَ بِأَفْوَاهِكُم مَّا لَيْسَ لَكُم
بِهِ عِلْمٌ وَتَحْسَبُونَهُ هَيِّنًا وَهُوَ عِندَ اللَّهِ
عَظِيمٌ ﴿١٥﴾ وَلَوْلَا إِذْ سَمِعْتُمُوهُ قُلْتُم مَّا يَكُونُ
لَنَا أَن نَّتَكَلَّمَ بِهَٰذَا سُبْحَانَكَ هَٰذَا بُهْتَانٌ
عَظِيمٌ ﴿١٦﴾ يَعِظُكُمُ اللَّهُ أَن تَعُودُوا لِمِثْلِهِ أَبَدًا إِن
كُنتُم مُّؤْمِنِينَ ﴿١٧﴾ وَيُبَيِّنُ اللَّهُ لَكُمُ الْآيَاتِ
وَاللَّهُ عَلِيمٌ حَكِيمٌ ﴿١٨﴾ إِنَّ الَّذِينَ يُحِبُّونَ أَن
تَشِيعَ الْفَاحِشَةُ فِي الَّذِينَ آمَنُوا لَهُمْ عَذَابٌ
أَلِيمٌ فِي الدُّنْيَا وَالْآخِرَةِ وَاللَّهُ يَعْلَمُ وَأَنتُمْ

20. But for the grace of Allâh and His mercy (that rests) upon you and (but for the fact) that Allâh is most Compassionate, Ever Merciful (none of you would have ever been so chaste and pure).

SECTION 3

21. **O** YOU who believe! Do not follow the footsteps of satan. He that follows the footsteps of satan (should remember that) he (- satan) surely enjoins immorality and indecency. But for the grace of Allâh and His mercy (that rests) upon you, not one of you would ever have been pure, but Allâh purifies him who wishes (to be purified). And Allâh is All-Hearing, All-Knowing.

22. And let not those of you who are possessed of grace (with moral virtue) and of plenty (of riches like *Abû Bakr*) swear that they will give nothing to the kindred, the needy and those who have left their homes for the cause of Allâh, but let them forgive and forbear (the offence). Do you not desire that Allâh should protect you (against your faults)? And Allâh is Great Protector, Ever Merciful.

23. Those who calumniate chaste, unwary, innocent believing women stand cursed in the present life and the Hereafter, and there awaits them a grievous punishment.

24. On the Day (of Requital) when their tongues and their hands and their feet shall bear witness against them for the (evil) deeds they used to do.

25. On that Day Allâh will pay them in full their just dues and they shall know that Allâh alone is the Absolute Truth, (and as well makes the Truth) manifest.

26. The evil and impure deeds are (a characteristic) of impure people and the bad and impure people are (inclined) towards the bad and impure deeds. Similarly good and pure deeds are (a characteristic) of good and pure people and

لَا تَعْلَمُوْنَ ﴿١٩﴾ وَلَوْلَا فَضْلُ اللّٰهِ عَلَيْكُمْ وَرَحْمَتُهٗ
وَأَنَّ اللّٰهَ رَءُوْفٌ رَّحِيْمٌ ﴿٢٠﴾ يٰٓأَيُّهَا الَّذِيْنَ اٰمَنُوْا
لَا تَتَّبِعُوْا خُطُوٰتِ الشَّيْطٰنِ ۚ وَمَنْ يَّتَّبِعْ
خُطُوٰتِ الشَّيْطٰنِ فَإِنَّهٗ يَأْمُرُ بِالْفَحْشَآءِ
وَالْمُنْكَرِ ۚ وَلَوْلَا فَضْلُ اللّٰهِ عَلَيْكُمْ وَرَحْمَتُهٗ
مَا زَكٰى مِنْكُمْ مِّنْ أَحَدٍ أَبَدًا ۙ وَّلٰكِنَّ اللّٰهَ
يُزَكِّيْ مَنْ يَّشَآءُ ۚ وَاللّٰهُ سَمِيْعٌ عَلِيْمٌ ﴿٢١﴾ وَلَا
يَأْتَلِ أُولُوا الْفَضْلِ مِنْكُمْ وَالسَّعَةِ أَنْ يُّؤْتُوْٓا
أُولِي الْقُرْبٰى وَالْمَسٰكِيْنَ وَالْمُهٰجِرِيْنَ فِيْ
سَبِيْلِ اللّٰهِ ۖ وَلْيَعْفُوْا وَلْيَصْفَحُوْا ۗ أَلَا تُحِبُّوْنَ
أَنْ يَّغْفِرَ اللّٰهُ لَكُمْ ۗ وَاللّٰهُ غَفُوْرٌ رَّحِيْمٌ ﴿٢٢﴾
إِنَّ الَّذِيْنَ يَرْمُوْنَ الْمُحْصَنٰتِ الْغٰفِلٰتِ الْمُؤْمِنٰتِ
لُعِنُوْا فِي الدُّنْيَا وَالْاٰخِرَةِ ۪ وَلَهُمْ عَذَابٌ عَظِيْمٌ ﴿٢٣﴾
يَّوْمَ تَشْهَدُ عَلَيْهِمْ أَلْسِنَتُهُمْ وَأَيْدِيْهِمْ وَأَرْجُلُهُمْ
بِمَا كَانُوْا يَعْمَلُوْنَ ﴿٢٤﴾ يَوْمَئِذٍ يُّوَفِّيْهِمُ اللّٰهُ
دِيْنَهُمُ الْحَقَّ وَيَعْلَمُوْنَ أَنَّ اللّٰهَ هُوَ الْحَقُّ
الْمُبِيْنُ ﴿٢٥﴾ أَلْخَبِيْثٰتُ لِلْخَبِيْثِيْنَ وَالْخَبِيْثُوْنَ
لِلْخَبِيْثٰتِ ۚ وَالطَّيِّبٰتُ لِلطَّيِّبِيْنَ وَالطَّيِّبُوْنَ

the good and pure people are (inclined) towards good and pure deeds. It is they (- the good and pure) who are innocent of all that they (- the accusers) may allege (about them). There awaits them protection and an honourable and generous provision.

SECTION 4

27. **O** YOU who believe! Do not enter houses other than your own unless you have obtained willing permission and (mind!) you should greet the inmates of these (houses). That is better for you. You have been given this commandment that you may be heedful.
28. But if you find nobody in them do not enter therein, unless you have got (from the owners or the rightful caretaker previous) permission. And go back if you are told to go back, that would be pure and best for you. Indeed, Allâh is Well-Aware of all that you do.
29. It is no sin on your part to enter (freely) non-residential houses wherein your goods are lying. And Allâh knows all that you profess and all that you conceal.
30. Tell the believers to restrain their looks (in the presence of women not closely related to them and so lawful for marriage) and guard their chastity. That is purer and best for them. Surely, Allâh is Well-Aware of what they do.
31. And tell the believing women to restrain their looks (also in the presence of men who are not near of kin and so lawful for marriage) and guard their chastity and not to disclose their (natural and makeup) beauty except such as cannot be helped (and is apparent) and draw their head coverings over their bosoms, and they should not display their beauty save to their husbands or to their fathers or to their fathers- in-law or to their own sons or to the sons of their husbands or to their own brothers, or to the sons of their brothers or to the sons of their sisters or their women (who are their decent companions) or to their bondsmen or to such of their male attendants as have no sexual

لِلطَّيِّبٰتِ ۚ أُولٰٓئِكَ مُبَرَّءُوْنَ مِمَّا يَقُوْلُوْنَ ۖ
لَهُمْ مَّغْفِرَةٌ وَّرِزْقٌ كَرِيْمٌ ﴿٢٦﴾ يٰٓأَيُّهَا الَّذِيْنَ اٰمَنُوْا
لَا تَدْخُلُوْا بُيُوْتًا غَيْرَ بُيُوْتِكُمْ حَتّٰى تَسْتَأْنِسُوْا
وَتُسَلِّمُوْا عَلٰٓى أَهْلِهَا ۚ ذٰلِكُمْ خَيْرٌ لَّكُمْ لَعَلَّكُمْ
تَذَكَّرُوْنَ ﴿٢٧﴾ فَإِنْ لَّمْ تَجِدُوْا فِيْهَآ أَحَدًا فَلَا
تَدْخُلُوْهَا حَتّٰى يُؤْذَنَ لَكُمْ ۚ وَإِنْ قِيْلَ لَكُمُ
ارْجِعُوْا فَارْجِعُوْا هُوَ أَزْكٰى لَكُمْ ۚ وَاللّٰهُ بِمَا
تَعْمَلُوْنَ عَلِيْمٌ ﴿٢٨﴾ لَيْسَ عَلَيْكُمْ جُنَاحٌ أَنْ
تَدْخُلُوْا بُيُوْتًا غَيْرَ مَسْكُوْنَةٍ فِيْهَا مَتٰعٌ لَّكُمْ ۚ
وَاللّٰهُ يَعْلَمُ مَا تُبْدُوْنَ وَمَا تَكْتُمُوْنَ ﴿٢٩﴾ قُلْ
لِّلْمُؤْمِنِيْنَ يَغُضُّوْا مِنْ أَبْصٰرِهِمْ وَيَحْفَظُوْا
فُرُوْجَهُمْ ۚ ذٰلِكَ أَزْكٰى لَهُمْ ۚ إِنَّ اللّٰهَ خَبِيْرٌۢ
بِمَا يَصْنَعُوْنَ ﴿٣٠﴾ وَقُلْ لِّلْمُؤْمِنٰتِ يَغْضُضْنَ مِنْ
أَبْصٰرِهِنَّ وَيَحْفَظْنَ فُرُوْجَهُنَّ وَلَا يُبْدِيْنَ
زِيْنَتَهُنَّ إِلَّا مَا ظَهَرَ مِنْهَا وَلْيَضْرِبْنَ بِخُمُرِهِنَّ
عَلٰى جُيُوْبِهِنَّ ۖ وَلَا يُبْدِيْنَ زِيْنَتَهُنَّ إِلَّا
لِبُعُوْلَتِهِنَّ أَوْ اٰبَآئِهِنَّ أَوْ اٰبَآءِ بُعُوْلَتِهِنَّ أَوْ
أَبْنَآئِهِنَّ أَوْ أَبْنَآءِ بُعُوْلَتِهِنَّ أَوْ إِخْوٰنِهِنَّ أَوْ
بَنِيْٓ إِخْوٰنِهِنَّ أَوْ بَنِيْٓ أَخَوٰتِهِنَّ أَوْ نِسَآئِهِنَّ أَوْ
مَا مَلَكَتْ أَيْمٰنُهُنَّ أَوِ التّٰبِعِيْنَ غَيْرِ أُولِي

appetite or to such young children as have yet no knowledge of the hidden parts of women. And let them not strike (the ground with) their feet so that which they (must) hide of their beauty or adornment may become known. And (O believers!) turn to Allâh; one and all, that you may attain (true happiness and) your ultimate goal.

32. Arrange marriages for those who are single, and for the males and females who serve you and are deserving and fit (to lead a married life). If they are poor Allâh will grant them means out of His bounty; Bountiful is Allâh, All-Knowing.

33. And those who find no (means of) marriage should (exercise restraint and) keep themselves chaste until Allâh grants them means (to marry) out of His grace and bounty. (There is another commandment,) as for those of your bondsmen (or women) as ask for a written contract (of freedom for themselves on payment of ransom), write this (deed of manumission for them) provided you find good capabilities in them and give them out of Allâh's wealth which He has given you. (Another commandment for you is that,) with a mind to gain (by this unrighteous means) the benefits of the present life do not constrain your slave-girls to unchaste life (by keeping them unmarried) when they desire (to marry) to preserve their virtue. But if anybody forces them (to abstain from marrying and to become unchaste) they will find, after they are forced, that God is Most Forgiving, Ever Merciful.

34. And We have sent down to you revelations which explain (to you the truth) and (have also revealed) some accounts of those who have passed away before you, and (we have sent in addition) an exhortation for those who guard against evil.

SECTION 5

35. **A**LLÂH is the Extensive Light of the heavens and the earth. His light can be compared to a (lustrous) pillar on which is a lamp. The lamp

الْإِرْبَةِ مِنَ الرِّجَالِ أَوِ الطِّفْلِ الَّذِينَ لَمْ
يَظْهَرُوا عَلَىٰ عَوْرَٰتِ النِّسَاءِ ۖ وَلَا يَضْرِبْنَ
بِأَرْجُلِهِنَّ لِيُعْلَمَ مَا يُخْفِينَ مِنْ زِينَتِهِنَّ ۚ
وَتُوبُوا إِلَى اللَّهِ جَمِيعًا أَيُّهَ الْمُؤْمِنُونَ لَعَلَّكُمْ
تُفْلِحُونَ ﴿٣١﴾ وَأَنْكِحُوا الْأَيَٰمَىٰ مِنْكُمْ وَالصَّٰلِحِينَ
مِنْ عِبَادِكُمْ وَإِمَائِكُمْ ۚ إِنْ يَكُونُوا فُقَرَاءَ
يُغْنِهِمُ اللَّهُ مِنْ فَضْلِهِ ۗ وَاللَّهُ وَٰسِعٌ عَلِيمٌ ﴿٣٢﴾
وَلْيَسْتَعْفِفِ الَّذِينَ لَا يَجِدُونَ نِكَاحًا
حَتَّىٰ يُغْنِيَهُمُ اللَّهُ مِنْ فَضْلِهِ ۗ وَالَّذِينَ
يَبْتَغُونَ الْكِتَٰبَ مِمَّا مَلَكَتْ أَيْمَٰنُكُمْ
فَكَاتِبُوهُمْ إِنْ عَلِمْتُمْ فِيهِمْ خَيْرًا ۖ وَآتُوهُمْ
مِنْ مَالِ اللَّهِ الَّذِي آتَٰكُمْ ۚ وَلَا تُكْرِهُوا
فَتَيَٰتِكُمْ عَلَى الْبِغَاءِ إِنْ أَرَدْنَ تَحَصُّنًا لِتَبْتَغُوا
عَرَضَ الْحَيَوٰةِ الدُّنْيَا ۚ وَمَنْ يُكْرِهْهُنَّ فَإِنَّ
اللَّهَ مِنْ بَعْدِ إِكْرَٰهِهِنَّ غَفُورٌ رَحِيمٌ ﴿٣٣﴾ وَلَقَدْ
أَنْزَلْنَا إِلَيْكُمْ آيَٰتٍ مُبَيِّنَٰتٍ وَمَثَلًا مِنَ الَّذِينَ
خَلَوْا مِنْ قَبْلِكُمْ وَمَوْعِظَةً لِلْمُتَّقِينَ ﴿٣٤﴾ اللَّهُ
نُورُ السَّمَٰوَٰتِ وَالْأَرْضِ ۚ مَثَلُ نُورِهِ كَمِشْكَوٰةٍ

is inside a crystal globe. The globe of glass is as if it were a glittering star. It (- the lamp) is lit by (the oil of) a blessed olive tree which belongs neither to the east nor to the west (rather welds the whole world in its fold). Its oil is likely to glow forth of itself even if no fire touch it. This (lamp) is a combination of many lights over and over. Allâh guides towards His light whoever desires (to be enlightened). And Allâh sets forth excellent parables for the people, and Allâh alone has full knowledge of every thing.

36. (This light is now lit) in houses (of the Companions) which Allâh has ordained to be exalted and His name be commemorated in them. Therein (are such as) glorify Him in the mornings and the evenings,

37. Men whom neither trade nor sale distracts from exalting (the name of) Allâh and from the observance of Prayer and from presenting *Zakât* (- purifying dues) regularly. They dread the day when the hearts and the eyes will be in a state of agitation and anguish;

38. With the result that Allâh will give them the reward according to their fairest deeds and will (even) give them much more by His grace and bounty. And Allâh does provide without measure to whom He will.

39. And (as to) those who disbelieve, their deeds are like a mirage in a desert, the thirsty man assumes it to be water until he comes up to it and finds it is nothing at all. And (instead of water by his side) he finds (that) Allâh (has always been present) with him, and He then pays him his account in full, and Allâh is Swift at reckoning.

40. Or (the deeds of the disbelievers are) like thick utter darkness of the fathomless deep sea, waves on top of which there are higher waves covering its surface which is overcast by clouds. These are (layers of) darkness (piled) one upon the other (as opposed to light upon light for the believers) so that a person, however much he may try, can hardly see his hand when he holds

فِيهَا مِصۡبَاحٌ ۖ ٱلۡمِصۡبَاحُ فِي زُجَاجَةٍ ۖ ٱلزُّجَاجَةُ
كَأَنَّهَا كَوۡكَبٌ دُرِّيٌّ يُوقَدُ مِن شَجَرَةٍ مُّبَٰرَكَةٍ
زَيۡتُونَةٍ لَّا شَرۡقِيَّةٍ وَلَا غَرۡبِيَّةٍ يَكَادُ
زَيۡتُهَا يُضِيٓءُ وَلَوۡ لَمۡ تَمۡسَسۡهُ نَارٌ ۚ نُّورٌ عَلَىٰ
نُورٍ ۚ يَهۡدِي ٱللَّهُ لِنُورِهِۦ مَن يَشَآءُ ۚ وَيَضۡرِبُ
ٱللَّهُ ٱلۡأَمۡثَٰلَ لِلنَّاسِ ۗ وَٱللَّهُ بِكُلِّ شَيۡءٍ عَلِيمٌ ﴿٣٥﴾
فِي بُيُوتٍ أَذِنَ ٱللَّهُ أَن تُرۡفَعَ وَيُذۡكَرَ
فِيهَا ٱسۡمُهُۥ يُسَبِّحُ لَهُۥ فِيهَا بِٱلۡغُدُوِّ وَٱلۡأٓصَالِ ﴿٣٦﴾
رِجَالٌ لَّا تُلۡهِيهِمۡ تِجَٰرَةٌ وَلَا بَيۡعٌ عَن ذِكۡرِ
ٱللَّهِ وَإِقَامِ ٱلصَّلَوٰةِ وَإِيتَآءِ ٱلزَّكَوٰةِ ۙ
يَخَافُونَ يَوۡمًا تَتَقَلَّبُ فِيهِ ٱلۡقُلُوبُ وَٱلۡأَبۡصَٰرُ ﴿٣٧﴾
لِيَجۡزِيَهُمُ ٱللَّهُ أَحۡسَنَ مَا عَمِلُواْ وَيَزِيدَهُم
مِّن فَضۡلِهِۦ ۗ وَٱللَّهُ يَرۡزُقُ مَن يَشَآءُ بِغَيۡرِ
حِسَابٍ ﴿٣٨﴾ وَٱلَّذِينَ كَفَرُوٓاْ أَعۡمَٰلُهُمۡ كَسَرَابٍۭ
بِقِيعَةٍ يَحۡسَبُهُ ٱلظَّمۡـَٔانُ مَآءً حَتَّىٰٓ إِذَا جَآءَهُۥ
لَمۡ يَجِدۡهُ شَيۡـًٔا وَوَجَدَ ٱللَّهَ عِندَهُۥ فَوَفَّىٰهُ
حِسَابَهُۥ ۗ وَٱللَّهُ سَرِيعُ ٱلۡحِسَابِ ﴿٣٩﴾ أَوۡ كَظُلُمَٰتٍ
فِي بَحۡرٍ لُّجِّيٍّ يَغۡشَىٰهُ مَوۡجٌ مِّن فَوۡقِهِۦ مَوۡجٌ

it out. Indeed, there is no light at all for the person whom Allâh gives no light.

SECTION 6

41. **H**AVE you not pondered that it is Allâh Whose praises celebrate those who are in the heavens and on the earth, and (so do) the birds on the wings. Each one of them knows his own (way of) prayer and glorification (according to his or its own faculties). And Allâh knows well what they do.
42. And to Allâh belongs the sovereignty of the heavens and the earth and to Allâh shall all (human beings) eventually return.
43. Have you not seen that Allâh drives the clouds steadily then He draws them together and then He makes them piled up so that you can see the rain pouring forth from their midst? And He sends down clouds (looking) like mountain, wherein is hail and He smites with them whom He pleases and averts them from whom He pleases. The (brilliant) flash of its lightening almost snatches away the sight (rendering the eyes sometimes blind).
44. Allâh sets the cycle of the night and the day. Surely, in this (law of retardation and acceleration working in this phenomenon of nature) is indeed a lesson (about the spiritual evolution of a human being) for those possessed of understanding.
45. And Allâh has created every animal from water. Some of them move upon their bellies and some move upon two feet and some among them move upon four. Allâh creates what He pleases. Verily, Allâh is Possessor of every power to do what He will.
46. We have certainly sent down revelations which explain the truth. And Allâh guides him who desires (to be guided) to the exact straight path.
47. And (some of the) people say, 'We believe in Allâh and the Messenger and obey (them).

مِّنْ فَوْقِهٖ سَحَابٌ ظُلُمٰتٌ بَعْضُهَا فَوْقَ
بَعْضٍ إِذَآ أَخْرَجَ يَدَهٗ لَمْ يَكَدْ يَرٰىهَا وَمَنْ
لَّمْ يَجْعَلِ اللهُ لَهٗ نُورًا فَمَا لَهٗ مِنْ نُّورٍ ﴿٤٠﴾
أَلَمْ تَرَ أَنَّ اللهَ يُسَبِّحُ لَهٗ مَنْ فِي السَّمٰوٰتِ
وَالْأَرْضِ وَالطَّيْرُ صٰٓفّٰتٍ كُلٌّ قَدْ عَلِمَ
صَلَاتَهٗ وَتَسْبِيحَهٗ وَاللهُ عَلِيمٌۢ بِمَا يَفْعَلُونَ ﴿٤١﴾
وَلِلّٰهِ مُلْكُ السَّمٰوٰتِ وَالْأَرْضِ وَإِلَى اللهِ
الْمَصِيرُ ﴿٤٢﴾ أَلَمْ تَرَ أَنَّ اللهَ يُزْجِي سَحَابًا ثُمَّ
يُؤَلِّفُ بَيْنَهٗ ثُمَّ يَجْعَلُهٗ رُكَامًا فَتَرَى الْوَدْقَ
يَخْرُجُ مِنْ خِلٰلِهٖ وَيُنَزِّلُ مِنَ السَّمَآءِ مِنْ
جِبَالٍ فِيهَا مِنْۢ بَرَدٍ فَيُصِيبُ بِهٖ مَنْ يَّشَآءُ
وَيَصْرِفُهٗ عَنْ مَّنْ يَّشَآءُ يَكَادُ سَنَا بَرْقِهٖ
يَذْهَبُ بِالْأَبْصٰرِ ﴿٤٣﴾ يُقَلِّبُ اللهُ الَّيْلَ وَالنَّهَارَ
إِنَّ فِي ذٰلِكَ لَعِبْرَةً لِّأُولِي الْأَبْصٰرِ ﴿٤٤﴾ وَاللهُ
خَلَقَ كُلَّ دَآبَّةٍ مِّنْ مَّآءٍ فَمِنْهُمْ مَّنْ يَّمْشِي
عَلٰى بَطْنِهٖ وَمِنْهُمْ مَّنْ يَّمْشِي عَلٰى رِجْلَيْنِ
وَمِنْهُمْ مَّنْ يَّمْشِي عَلٰٓى أَرْبَعٍ يَخْلُقُ اللهُ مَا يَشَآءُ
إِنَّ اللهَ عَلٰى كُلِّ شَيْءٍ قَدِيرٌ ﴿٤٥﴾ لَقَدْ أَنْزَلْنَآ
أٰيٰتٍ مُّبَيِّنٰتٍ وَاللهُ يَهْدِي مَنْ يَّشَآءُ إِلٰى
صِرٰطٍ مُّسْتَقِيمٍ ﴿٤٦﴾ وَيَقُولُونَ أٰمَنَّا بِاللهِ

But even after (professing) this a section of them (- the hypocrites) turn away. Such are no believers at all.

48. When they are summoned before Allâh and His Messenger, that he may judge between them, lo! A party of them turn away.

49. But if (they consider that) the right is on their side they come to him running showing submission.

50. Is it that their minds are diseased? Or do they suffer from doubts? Or do they fear that Allâh and His Messenger will deal with them unjustly? Nay, (wrong are their misgivings,) it is they themselves who are the unjust.

SECTION 7

51. THE only response of the believers, when they are summoned before Allâh and His Messenger so that he may judge between them, is that they say, 'We hear and we obey.' It is they who will attain their goal.

52. And those who obey Allâh and His Messenger and hold Allâh in awe and take Him as a shield (for protection) it is they who shall be triumphant.

53. They (- the hypocrites) swear to Allâh by their most earnest oaths that if you only command them (for defensive fight) they will certainly march forth (from their homes). Say, 'Do not swear, only reasonable obedience in what is right and lawful (is all that is required from you).' Surely, Allâh is Aware of what you do.

54. Say, 'Obey Allâh and obey the Messenger.' But if you turn your back (remember that) he (- the Messenger) is responsible for what he is charged with (- the responsibility of conveying the Message) and you are responsible for what you are charged with (- the responsibility of following him). Indeed if you obey him you will be following the right path. (But if you do not, bear in mind,)

وَ بِالرَّسُوۡلِ وَ اَطَعۡنَا ثُمَّ يَتَوَلّٰى فَرِيۡقٌ مِّنۡهُمۡ
مِّنۡۢ بَعۡدِ ذٰلِكَ ؕ وَ مَاۤ اُولٰٓئِكَ بِالۡمُؤۡمِنِيۡنَ ﴿٤٧﴾
وَ اِذَا دُعُوۡۤا اِلَى اللّٰهِ وَ رَسُوۡلِهٖ لِيَحۡكُمَ بَيۡنَهُمۡ
اِذَا فَرِيۡقٌ مِّنۡهُمۡ مُّعۡرِضُوۡنَ ﴿٤٨﴾ وَ اِنۡ يَّكُنۡ
لَّهُمُ الۡحَقُّ يَاۡتُوۡۤا اِلَيۡهِ مُذۡعِنِيۡنَ ﴿٤٩﴾ اَفِيۡ
قُلُوۡبِهِمۡ مَّرَضٌ اَمِ ارۡتَابُوۡۤا اَمۡ يَخَافُوۡنَ اَنۡ
يَّحِيۡفَ اللّٰهُ عَلَيۡهِمۡ وَ رَسُوۡلُهٗ ؕ بَلۡ اُولٰٓئِكَ هُمُ
الظّٰلِمُوۡنَ ﴿٥٠﴾ اِنَّمَا كَانَ قَوۡلَ الۡمُؤۡمِنِيۡنَ اِذَا دُعُوۡۤا
اِلَى اللّٰهِ وَ رَسُوۡلِهٖ لِيَحۡكُمَ بَيۡنَهُمۡ اَنۡ يَّقُوۡلُوۡا
سَمِعۡنَا وَ اَطَعۡنَا ؕ وَ اُولٰٓئِكَ هُمُ الۡمُفۡلِحُوۡنَ ﴿٥١﴾
وَ مَنۡ يُّطِعِ اللّٰهَ وَ رَسُوۡلَهٗ وَ يَخۡشَ اللّٰهَ وَ يَتَّقۡهِ
فَاُولٰٓئِكَ هُمُ الۡفَآئِزُوۡنَ ﴿٥٢﴾ وَ اَقۡسَمُوۡا بِاللّٰهِ جَهۡدَ
اَيۡمَانِهِمۡ لَئِنۡ اَمَرۡتَهُمۡ لَيَخۡرُجُنَّ ؕ قُلۡ لَّا تُقۡسِمُوۡا ۚ
طَاعَةٌ مَّعۡرُوۡفَةٌ ؕ اِنَّ اللّٰهَ خَبِيۡرٌۢ بِمَا تَعۡمَلُوۡنَ ﴿٥٣﴾
قُلۡ اَطِيۡعُوا اللّٰهَ وَ اَطِيۡعُوا الرَّسُوۡلَ ۚ فَاِنۡ تَوَلَّوۡا
فَاِنَّمَا عَلَيۡهِ مَا حُمِّلَ وَ عَلَيۡكُمۡ مَّا حُمِّلۡتُمۡ ؕ
وَ اِنۡ تُطِيۡعُوۡهُ تَهۡتَدُوۡا ؕ وَ مَا عَلَى الرَّسُوۡلِ اِلَّا الۡبَلٰغُ

ع ٧ ١٢

the Messenger is not responsible but for the delivery (of the message to all) in clear terms.

55. Allâh has promised those of you who believe and do deeds of righteousness that surely, He will make them successors (vouchsafed with both spiritual and temporal leadership) on the earth as He made successors (from among) their predecessors, and that He will surely establish for them their Faith which He has approved for them, and that He will surely replace their state of fear with a state of security and peace. They will worship Me (alone) and they will not associate anything with Me. And those who show ingratitude for all the favours done to them after that (His promise is fulfilled), it is they who will be reckoned as the worst disobedient.

56. And (believers!) observe the Prayer, keep on presenting the *Zakât* (purifying dues) and obey the Messenger that you may be shown mercy.

57. Think not (O reader!) that those who disbelieve can ever be able to frustrate (Our plan on the earth) and escape Us. Their abode is Fire; what an evil resort!

SECTION 8

58. **O** YOU who believe! It is binding on those whom your right hands possess (domestic servants) and those (of your children) who have not reached the age of puberty to ask your permission (before coming into your private rooms) in three instances, before the morning Prayer, and when you lay aside your clothes due to the heat (in summer) at noon and after the night Prayer. These are three times when your privacy should be respected. At other times no blame shall lie on you or on them (if they come to you without permission), for they have to move about (waiting upon you) some of you (attending) upon

الْمُبِيْنُ ﴿٥٤﴾ وَعَدَ اللّٰهُ الَّذِيْنَ أٰمَنُوْا مِنْكُمْ وَعَمِلُوا
الصّٰلِحٰتِ لَيَسْتَخْلِفَنَّهُمْ فِي الْأَرْضِ كَمَا اسْتَخْلَفَ
الَّذِيْنَ مِنْ قَبْلِهِمْ وَلَيُمَكِّنَنَّ لَهُمْ دِيْنَهُمُ
الَّذِي ارْتَضٰى لَهُمْ وَلَيُبَدِّلَنَّهُمْ مِّنْ بَعْدِ خَوْفِهِمْ
أَمْنًا ؕ يَعْبُدُوْنَنِيْ لَا يُشْرِكُوْنَ بِيْ شَيْـًٔا ؕ وَمَنْ
كَفَرَ بَعْدَ ذٰلِكَ فَأُولٰٓئِكَ هُمُ الْفٰسِقُوْنَ ﴿٥٥﴾ وَأَقِيْمُوا
الصَّلٰوةَ وَأٰتُوا الزَّكٰوةَ وَأَطِيْعُوا الرَّسُوْلَ لَعَلَّكُمْ
تُرْحَمُوْنَ ﴿٥٦﴾ لَا تَحْسَبَنَّ الَّذِيْنَ كَفَرُوْا مُعْجِزِيْنَ
فِي الْأَرْضِ ۚ وَمَأْوٰىهُمُ النَّارُ ؕ وَلَبِئْسَ الْمَصِيْرُ ﴿٥٧﴾ ع ٧ ١٣
يٰٓأَيُّهَا الَّذِيْنَ أٰمَنُوْا لِيَسْتَأْذِنْكُمُ الَّذِيْنَ مَلَكَتْ
أَيْمٰنُكُمْ وَالَّذِيْنَ لَمْ يَبْلُغُوا الْحُلُمَ مِنْكُمْ ثَلٰثَ
مَرّٰتٍ ؕ مِنْ قَبْلِ صَلٰوةِ الْفَجْرِ وَحِيْنَ تَضَعُوْنَ
ثِيَابَكُمْ مِّنَ الظَّهِيْرَةِ وَمِنْ بَعْدِ صَلٰوةِ الْعِشَآءِ ۚ
ثَلٰثُ عَوْرٰتٍ لَّكُمْ ؕ لَيْسَ عَلَيْكُمْ وَلَا عَلَيْهِمْ
جُنَاحٌ بَعْدَهُنَّ ؕ طَوّٰفُوْنَ عَلَيْكُمْ بَعْضُكُمْ عَلٰى
بَعْضٍ ؕ كَذٰلِكَ يُبَيِّنُ اللّٰهُ لَكُمُ الْأٰيٰتِ ؕ وَاللّٰهُ

others (according to need). That is how Allâh explains to you His commandments, for Allâh is All-Knowing, All-Wise.

59. When the children among you reach the age of puberty they (too) should seek permission (to come to your rooms) just as those (elderly people mentioned) before them do. That is how Allâh explains to you His commandments and Allâh is All-Knowing, All-Wise.

60. And (as to the elderly spinsters who are past child-bearing age and) who do not hope for sexual intercourse, it is no offence for them to lay aside their outer garments provided they do not do it to display their beauty. But if they abstain (even from that) it is much better for them. Indeed Allâh is All-Hearing, All- Knowing.

61. There is no bar on (and not improper for) the blind, nor is there any bar on (nor improper for) the lame, nor is any bar on (nor improper for) the sick, nor on your people that you eat from your own houses, or the houses of your fathers (and children) or the houses of your mothers, or the houses of your brothers, or the houses of your sisters, or the houses of your paternal uncles, or the houses of your paternal aunts, or the houses of your maternal uncles, or the houses of your maternal aunts, or (from) that of which the keys are in your possessions (- which is under your charge), or (from the house of) a friend of yours. No blame lies on you whether you eat together or separately. And when you enter houses greet your people (present therein) with the salutation prescribed by Allâh (a salutation) full of blessings and purity. That is how Allâh explains to you (His) commandments that you may abstain (from evils).

SECTION 9

62. **T**RUE believers are only those who believe in Allâh and His Messenger, and who when they are with him (- the Messenger to confer) upon

عَلِيمٌ حَكِيمٌ ﴿٥٨﴾ وَإِذَا بَلَغَ الْأَطْفَالُ مِنكُمُ الْحُلُمَ
فَلْيَسْتَأْذِنُوا كَمَا اسْتَأْذَنَ الَّذِينَ مِن
قَبْلِهِمْ ۚ كَذَٰلِكَ يُبَيِّنُ اللَّهُ لَكُمْ آيَاتِهِ ۗ وَاللَّهُ
عَلِيمٌ حَكِيمٌ ﴿٥٩﴾ وَالْقَوَاعِدُ مِنَ النِّسَاءِ اللَّاتِي لَا
يَرْجُونَ نِكَاحًا فَلَيْسَ عَلَيْهِنَّ جُنَاحٌ أَن
يَضَعْنَ ثِيَابَهُنَّ غَيْرَ مُتَبَرِّجَاتٍ بِزِينَةٍ ۖ وَأَن
يَسْتَعْفِفْنَ خَيْرٌ لَّهُنَّ ۗ وَاللَّهُ سَمِيعٌ عَلِيمٌ ﴿٦٠﴾
لَّيْسَ عَلَى الْأَعْمَىٰ حَرَجٌ وَلَا عَلَى الْأَعْرَجِ حَرَجٌ
وَلَا عَلَى الْمَرِيضِ حَرَجٌ وَلَا عَلَىٰ أَنفُسِكُمْ أَن
تَأْكُلُوا مِن بُيُوتِكُمْ أَوْ بُيُوتِ آبَائِكُمْ أَوْ بُيُوتِ
أُمَّهَاتِكُمْ أَوْ بُيُوتِ إِخْوَانِكُمْ أَوْ بُيُوتِ أَخَوَاتِكُمْ
أَوْ بُيُوتِ أَعْمَامِكُمْ أَوْ بُيُوتِ عَمَّاتِكُمْ أَوْ بُيُوتِ
أَخْوَالِكُمْ أَوْ بُيُوتِ خَالَاتِكُمْ أَوْ مَا مَلَكْتُم
مَّفَاتِحَهُ أَوْ صَدِيقِكُمْ ۚ لَيْسَ عَلَيْكُمْ جُنَاحٌ
أَن تَأْكُلُوا جَمِيعًا أَوْ أَشْتَاتًا ۚ فَإِذَا دَخَلْتُم
بُيُوتًا فَسَلِّمُوا عَلَىٰ أَنفُسِكُمْ تَحِيَّةً مِّنْ عِندِ
اللَّهِ مُبَارَكَةً طَيِّبَةً ۚ كَذَٰلِكَ يُبَيِّنُ اللَّهُ لَكُمُ
الْآيَاتِ لَعَلَّكُمْ تَعْقِلُونَ ﴿٦١﴾ إِنَّمَا الْمُؤْمِنُونَ الَّذِينَ
آمَنُوا بِاللَّهِ وَرَسُولِهِ وَإِذَا كَانُوا مَعَهُ عَلَىٰ أَمْرٍ
جَامِعٍ لَّمْ يَذْهَبُوا حَتَّىٰ يَسْتَأْذِنُوهُ ۚ إِنَّ الَّذِينَ

ع ٨ ١٤

any matter of common importance which has brought (them) together, do not leave (the Messenger) until they have asked permission of him. Surely, it is those who ask your permission who (truly) believe in Allâh and His Messenger. So when they ask your permission for some (urgent and important) affair of their own, give your permission to whom you will of them and ask Allâh's protection for them. Verily, Allâh is Great Protector, Ever Merciful.

63. (Believers!) Do not treat the call of the Messenger among yourselves like the call of one of you to another. Allâh indeed knows those of you who sneak away stealthily (from the conference). So let those who go against His command beware, lest some calamity should befall them or they receive some painful punishment.

64. Beware! Whatever is in the heavens and on the earth belongs to Allâh. He ever knows in what state you are (and He knows what you are holding to). The day when all people shall be made to return to Him, He will tell them all they had been doing, for Allâh is the Possessor of full knowledge of everything.

يَسْتَـْٔذِنُونَكَ أُولَٰٓئِكَ الَّذِينَ يُؤْمِنُونَ بِاللهِ
وَرَسُولِهِۦ ۚ فَإِذَا اسْتَـْٔذَنُوكَ لِبَعْضِ شَأْنِهِمْ
فَأْذَن لِّمَن شِئْتَ مِنْهُمْ وَاسْتَغْفِرْ لَهُمُ اللهَ ۚ
إِنَّ اللهَ غَفُورٌ رَّحِيمٌ ﴿٦٢﴾ لَا تَجْعَلُوا دُعَآءَ الرَّسُولِ
بَيْنَكُمْ كَدُعَآءِ بَعْضِكُم بَعْضًا ۚ قَدْ يَعْلَمُ اللهُ
الَّذِينَ يَتَسَلَّلُونَ مِنكُمْ لِوَاذًا ۚ فَلْيَحْذَرِ
الَّذِينَ يُخَالِفُونَ عَنْ أَمْرِهِۦٓ أَن تُصِيبَهُمْ
فِتْنَةٌ أَوْ يُصِيبَهُمْ عَذَابٌ أَلِيمٌ ﴿٦٣﴾ أَلَآ إِنَّ
لِلّٰهِ مَا فِي السَّمٰوٰتِ وَالْأَرْضِ ۖ قَدْ يَعْلَمُ مَآ
أَنتُمْ عَلَيْهِ وَيَوْمَ يُرْجَعُونَ إِلَيْهِ فَيُنَبِّئُهُم
بِمَا عَمِلُوا ۗ وَاللهُ بِكُلِّ شَيْءٍ عَلِيمٌ ﴿٦٤﴾ ع ٩ ٣ ١٥

CHAPTER 25

AL-FURQÂN
(The Standard of Truth and Falsehood)
(Revealed before Hijrah)

سُورَةُ الفُرقَانِ مَكِّيَّةٌ

With the name of Allâh,
the Most Gracious, the Ever Merciful
(I commence to read Sûrah Al-Furqân).

بِسْمِ اللهِ الرَّحْمٰنِ الرَّحِيمِ

1. **B**LESSED is He Who revealed *Al-Furqân* (- this Qur'ân) to His servant that he may be a Warner to all the peoples.

2. It is He to Whom the Sovereignty of the

تَبَارَكَ الَّذِي نَزَّلَ الْفُرْقَانَ عَلَىٰ عَبْدِهِۦ
لِيَكُونَ لِلْعٰلَمِينَ نَذِيرًا ﴿١﴾ الَّذِي لَهُۥ مُلْكُ
السَّمٰوٰتِ وَالْأَرْضِ وَلَمْ يَتَّخِذْ وَلَدًا وَّلَمْ

heavens and the earth belongs. And He has begotten nor taken to Himself a son, nor is there any associate with Him in the sovereignty. He has created everything and has determined its proper measure.

3. Yet people worship apart from Him gods who, rather than create anything, are themselves created and who have no power of (averting) harm or (doing) good to themselves, nor have they any control over death or life or Resurrection.

4. But those who disbelieve say, 'This (Qur'ân) is nothing but a big lie which he (- the false claimant to Prophethood) has forged and other people have helped him in this,' (by) so (saying) they have perpetrated a great injustice and a big falsehood.

5. They (also) say, '(This Qur'ân consists of) fables of the ancients that he has got written down and now they are read out to him morning and evening.'

6. Say, 'He Who knows every secret of the heavens and the earth has revealed this (Qur'ân). Verily, He is Great Protector, Ever Merciful.'

7. They say, 'What sort of a Messenger is this that he even eats food and (also) goes about in the marketplaces? Why has no angel been sent down to him that he may (help him and) be a warner along with him?

8. 'Or a treasure should have been sent to him or there should have been a garden from which he might eat.' Not only that, these unjust people say, 'You follow none but a (mere) man who is given food.'

9. Look, what fantastic stories they concoct with regard to you! It is therefore that they have gone astray and are unable to find a way.

SECTION 2

10. **B**LESSED is He Who is pleased to assign to you (at the time of the Final victory of the Muslims) better than that (garden they devise for you) gardens (of Mesopotamia) served with

يَكُن لَّهُۥ شَرِيكٌ فِي ٱلۡمُلۡكِ وَخَلَقَ كُلَّ
شَيۡءٖ فَقَدَّرَهُۥ تَقۡدِيرٗا ۝٢ وَٱتَّخَذُواْ مِن دُونِهِۦٓ
ءَالِهَةٗ لَّا يَخۡلُقُونَ شَيۡـٔٗا وَهُمۡ يُخۡلَقُونَ وَلَا
يَمۡلِكُونَ لِأَنفُسِهِمۡ ضَرّٗا وَلَا نَفۡعٗا وَلَا
يَمۡلِكُونَ مَوۡتٗا وَلَا حَيَوٰةٗ وَلَا نُشُورٗا ۝٣
وَقَالَ ٱلَّذِينَ كَفَرُوٓاْ إِنۡ هَٰذَآ إِلَّآ إِفۡكٌ ٱفۡتَرَىٰهُ
وَأَعَانَهُۥ عَلَيۡهِ قَوۡمٌ ءَاخَرُونَۖ فَقَدۡ جَآءُو ظُلۡمٗا
وَزُورٗا ۝٤ وَقَالُوٓاْ أَسَٰطِيرُ ٱلۡأَوَّلِينَ ٱكۡتَتَبَهَا
فَهِيَ تُمۡلَىٰ عَلَيۡهِ بُكۡرَةٗ وَأَصِيلٗا ۝٥ قُلۡ أَنزَلَهُ
ٱلَّذِي يَعۡلَمُ ٱلسِّرَّ فِي ٱلسَّمَٰوَٰتِ وَٱلۡأَرۡضِۚ
إِنَّهُۥ كَانَ غَفُورٗا رَّحِيمٗا ۝٦ وَقَالُواْ مَالِ هَٰذَا
ٱلرَّسُولِ يَأۡكُلُ ٱلطَّعَامَ وَيَمۡشِي فِي ٱلۡأَسۡوَاقِ
لَوۡلَآ أُنزِلَ إِلَيۡهِ مَلَكٞ فَيَكُونَ مَعَهُۥ نَذِيرًا ۝٧
أَوۡ يُلۡقَىٰٓ إِلَيۡهِ كَنزٌ أَوۡ تَكُونُ لَهُۥ جَنَّةٞ يَأۡكُلُ
مِنۡهَاۚ وَقَالَ ٱلظَّٰلِمُونَ إِن تَتَّبِعُونَ إِلَّا رَجُلٗا
مَّسۡحُورًا ۝٨ ٱنظُرۡ كَيۡفَ ضَرَبُواْ لَكَ ٱلۡأَمۡثَٰلَ
فَضَلُّواْ فَلَا يَسۡتَطِيعُونَ سَبِيلٗا ۝٩ تَبَارَكَ ٱلَّذِيٓ
إِن شَآءَ جَعَلَ لَكَ خَيۡرٗا مِّن ذَٰلِكَ جَنَّٰتٖ

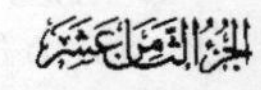

running streams (rivers like Euphrate, Tigris and *Jihûn* and *Sihûn*), and will also assign to you palaces (of the Persian and Byzantine Emperors, and also the treasures of Chosroes and Caesars would be placed at your feet).
11. Nay, (the real fact is) they (- the disbelievers) cry lies to the Hour (of the evil doom of the disbelievers and final victory of the Muslims) and We have in store a blazing hell for him who cries lies to the Hour.
12. When it (- the blazing Fire) sees them from afar, they will hear its raging and roaring.
13. And when they are thrown into some narrow place of it, chained in fetters, they will call out for (total) destruction, there and then.
14. (It will be said to them,) 'This is no time to call out for a single death, you had better call out for a series of deaths.'
15. Say, 'Is this (end) better or the everlasting Paradise which is promised to those who guard against evil and which is their due reward and (ultimate) resort.
16. They shall have there all that they desire and they will abide (in this state of bliss forever). It is a promise binding on your Lord (and) to be always earnestly prayed for (from Him).
17. Beware of the day when He will gather them together, and the things they worship, apart from Allâh. He will ask, 'Was it you who led these servants of mine astray or did they themselves stray away from the right path?'
18. They will say, 'Holy is Your name! It did not behove us to take patrons apart from You. But You bestowed on them and their fathers the good things of life to such an extent that they gave up remembrance of You and became a ruined people.'
19. (Then We shall say to the idol-worshipers), 'Now these (deities) have given you the lie (and contradict you) with regard to what you said, so (today) you have no power to avert (the penalty) or get help (of any sort for yourselves); (remember) whosoever of you acts unjustly and

تَجْرِي مِنْ تَحْتِهَا الْأَنْهٰرُ وَيَجْعَلْ لَّكَ
قُصُورًا ﴿١٠﴾ بَلْ كَذَّبُوا بِالسَّاعَةِ وَأَعْتَدْنَا
لِمَنْ كَذَّبَ بِالسَّاعَةِ سَعِيرًا ﴿١١﴾ إِذَا رَأَتْهُم
مِّنْ مَّكَانٍ بَعِيدٍ سَمِعُوا لَهَا تَغَيُّظًا
وَّزَفِيرًا ﴿١٢﴾ وَإِذَا أُلْقُوا مِنْهَا مَكَانًا ضَيِّقًا
مُّقَرَّنِينَ دَعَوْا هُنَالِكَ ثُبُورًا ﴿١٣﴾ لَا تَدْعُوا
الْيَوْمَ ثُبُورًا وَّاحِدًا وَّادْعُوا ثُبُورًا كَثِيرًا ﴿١٤﴾
قُلْ أَذٰلِكَ خَيْرٌ أَمْ جَنَّةُ الْخُلْدِ الَّتِي
وُعِدَ الْمُتَّقُونَ كَانَتْ لَهُمْ جَزَاءً وَّمَصِيرًا ﴿١٥﴾
لَهُمْ فِيهَا مَا يَشَاءُونَ خٰلِدِينَ كَانَ
عَلٰى رَبِّكَ وَعْدًا مَّسْئُولًا ﴿١٦﴾ وَيَوْمَ يَحْشُرُهُمْ
وَمَا يَعْبُدُونَ مِنْ دُونِ اللّٰهِ فَيَقُولُ ءَأَنْتُمْ
أَضْلَلْتُمْ عِبَادِي هٰؤُلَاءِ أَمْ هُمْ ضَلُّوا
السَّبِيلَ ﴿١٧﴾ قَالُوا سُبْحٰنَكَ مَا كَانَ يَنْبَغِي
لَنَا أَنْ نَّتَّخِذَ مِنْ دُونِكَ مِنْ أَوْلِيَاءَ
وَلٰكِنْ مَّتَّعْتَهُمْ وَآبَاءَهُمْ حَتّٰى نَسُوا
الذِّكْرَ وَكَانُوا قَوْمًا بُورًا ﴿١٨﴾ فَقَدْ كَذَّبُوكُمْ
بِمَا تَقُولُونَ فَمَا تَسْتَطِيعُونَ صَرْفًا وَّلَا
نَصْرًا وَمَنْ يَظْلِمْ مِّنْكُمْ نُذِقْهُ عَذَابًا

goes wrong we shall make him suffer a great punishment.'

20. And We sent no Messengers before you but they surely ate food and walked in the market-places (and were human models for you to follow in every walk of life). And We try you one with another (to show) if you will (then) patiently persevere. And your Lord is ever All-Seeing.

كَبِيرًا ۝١٩ وَمَآ أَرْسَلْنَا قَبْلَكَ مِنَ الْمُرْسَلِينَ إِلَّآ إِنَّهُمْ لَيَأْكُلُونَ الطَّعَامَ وَيَمْشُونَ فِي الْأَسْوَاقِ ۗ وَجَعَلْنَا بَعْضَكُمْ لِبَعْضٍ فِتْنَةً أَتَصْبِرُونَ ۚ وَكَانَ رَبُّكَ بَصِيرًا ۝٢٠

ع ١١/١٧

PART الجزء التاسع عشر XIX

SECTION 3

21. THOSE who entertain no fear about being present before Us, nor do they expect it, say, 'Why should not the angels be sent down to us? Or we see our Lord?' They have indeed thought very highly of themselves and have exceeded all limits of transgression.

22. (Do they not realize that) the day when they will see the angels there will be no good tidings that day for those who cut off their ties (with God), and they will say (in distress), 'Would that there were some strong barrier (between us and this punishment).'

23. And We have turned (Our attention) to whatsoever attempt they have made (against Islam) and so We will render this (attempt) like thin dust particles scattered about (as it was in the battle of *Badr*).

24. (Only) the owners of Paradise will be better off with regard to (their) abode and happier still in respect of (their) place of repose.

25. (Call to mind) the day when the heaven shall burst and melt into raining clouds and the angels shall be made to descend in large numbers;

26. The true sovereignty that day shall belong only to the Most Gracious (God) and it shall be really a (very) hard day for the disbelievers.

27. On that day the unjust shall bite his hands (in

وَقَالَ الَّذِينَ لَا يَرْجُونَ لِقَآءَنَا لَوْلَآ أُنْزِلَ عَلَيْنَا الْمَلَٰٓئِكَةُ أَوْ نَرَىٰ رَبَّنَا ۗ لَقَدِ اسْتَكْبَرُوا فِيٓ أَنْفُسِهِمْ وَعَتَوْ عُتُوًّا كَبِيرًا ۝٢١ يَوْمَ يَرَوْنَ الْمَلَٰٓئِكَةَ لَا بُشْرَىٰ يَوْمَئِذٍ لِلْمُجْرِمِينَ وَيَقُولُونَ حِجْرًا مَحْجُورًا ۝٢٢ وَقَدِمْنَآ إِلَىٰ مَا عَمِلُوا مِنْ عَمَلٍ فَجَعَلْنَٰهُ هَبَآءً مَنْثُورًا ۝٢٣ أَصْحَٰبُ الْجَنَّةِ يَوْمَئِذٍ خَيْرٌ مُسْتَقَرًّا وَأَحْسَنُ مَقِيلًا ۝٢٤ وَيَوْمَ تَشَقَّقُ السَّمَآءُ بِالْغَمَٰمِ وَنُزِّلَ الْمَلَٰٓئِكَةُ تَنْزِيلًا ۝٢٥ الْمُلْكُ يَوْمَئِذٍ الْحَقُّ لِلرَّحْمَٰنِ ۚ وَكَانَ يَوْمًا عَلَى الْكَٰفِرِينَ عَسِيرًا ۝٢٦ وَيَوْمَ

regret); he will say, 'If only I had followed the (same) path along with the Messenger!

28. 'Ah, woe is me! Would that I had not made friends with so and so.

29. 'He indeed led me astray from this source of rising to eminence (- the Qur'ân) after it had come to me. And satan is ever a deserter of human being (in the hour of need).

30. And (on that Day) the Messenger will say, 'My Lord! My people treated even this Qur'ân (full of blessings) as (a thing) abandoned.

31. (Just as We have turned them into your enemies) so do We make those who cut off their ties (with Allâh) as the enemies of each and every Prophet. Yet your Lord is sufficient to guide and (enough) in respect of rendering help.

32. And those who disbelieve say, 'Why has not (the whole of) the Qur'ân been revealed to him all at once? (But We have revealed it) in this manner (- piece by piece out of necessity). And (inspite of the fact that it has not been revealed all at once,) We have arranged it in an excellent (form and order of) arrangement (and free of all contradictions) so that We may thereby lend strength to your heart.

33. And they bring you no parable (by way of an objection) but We have provided you with the true fact and perfect interpretation (of it, in answer to the objection beforehand).

34. And those who shall be brought to Gehenna dragged on their faces (and along with their leaders) are the worst placed and they have completely lost the straight path.

SECTION 4

35. **A**ND We gave Moses the Scripture and made with him his brother Aaron a sharer of (his) burden.

36. We said, 'Go both of you to the people who have cried lies to Our commandments. Then

يَعَضُّ الظَّالِمُ عَلَىٰ يَدَيْهِ يَقُولُ يَٰلَيْتَنِي
اتَّخَذْتُ مَعَ الرَّسُولِ سَبِيلًا ﴿٢٧﴾ يَٰوَيْلَتَىٰ لَيْتَنِي
لَمْ أَتَّخِذْ فُلَانًا خَلِيلًا ﴿٢٨﴾ لَّقَدْ أَضَلَّنِي عَنِ
الذِّكْرِ بَعْدَ إِذْ جَاءَنِي ۗ وَكَانَ الشَّيْطَٰنُ
لِلْإِنسَٰنِ خَذُولًا ﴿٢٩﴾ وَقَالَ الرَّسُولُ يَٰرَبِّ إِنَّ
قَوْمِي اتَّخَذُوا هَٰذَا الْقُرْءَانَ مَهْجُورًا ﴿٣٠﴾ وَكَذَٰلِكَ
جَعَلْنَا لِكُلِّ نَبِيٍّ عَدُوًّا مِّنَ الْمُجْرِمِينَ ۗ وَكَفَىٰ
بِرَبِّكَ هَادِيًا وَنَصِيرًا ﴿٣١﴾ وَقَالَ الَّذِينَ كَفَرُوا
لَوْلَا نُزِّلَ عَلَيْهِ الْقُرْءَانُ جُمْلَةً وَٰحِدَةً ۚ كَذَٰلِكَ
لِنُثَبِّتَ بِهِۦ فُؤَادَكَ ۖ وَرَتَّلْنَٰهُ تَرْتِيلًا ﴿٣٢﴾ وَلَا
يَأْتُونَكَ بِمَثَلٍ إِلَّا جِئْنَٰكَ بِالْحَقِّ وَأَحْسَنَ
تَفْسِيرًا ﴿٣٣﴾ الَّذِينَ يُحْشَرُونَ عَلَىٰ وُجُوهِهِمْ
إِلَىٰ جَهَنَّمَ أُولَٰٓئِكَ شَرٌّ مَّكَانًا وَأَضَلُّ سَبِيلًا ﴿٣٤﴾
وَلَقَدْ ءَاتَيْنَا مُوسَى الْكِتَٰبَ وَجَعَلْنَا مَعَهُۥٓ
أَخَاهُ هَٰرُونَ وَزِيرًا ﴿٣٥﴾ فَقُلْنَا اذْهَبَآ إِلَى الْقَوْمِ

(when they had accomplished their mission of conveying the Message and were again rejected) We destroyed these disbelievers with an utter destruction.

37. And (We destroyed) the people of Noah (too), when they treated (Our) Messengers as liars, We drowned them and made them a sign (to learn a lesson from) for people. Indeed We have in store a woeful punishment for (such of) the wrongdoers.

38. And (tribes of) 'Âd and Thamûd and the People of the Rass and many a generation in between them (were all destroyed).

39. And for (the guidance of) each one (of them) We quoted excellent pieces of advice and (when they still persisted in refusal) We ruined each one of them, a complete ruination.

40. And certainly these (Makkan disbelievers) pass by the (ruined) township (of Sodom situated on the highway between Arabia and Syria) which suffered a painful rain (of stones). Have they not been seeing the ruins of this (township of the people of Lot). Of course they have, (seen it, but the reason behind their refusal is) they do not (believe and) expect not to be resurrected (after death and to be called to account for their deeds).

41. And Whenever they see you they treat you disdainfully (saying), 'What! Is this the man whom Allâh has raised for a Messenger?

42. 'He indeed had well-nigh led us astray from our gods if we had not adhered to them steadfastly.' And they shall soon know for certain, when they see the punishment who had completely lost the straight path.

43. Have you considered (over the plight of) one who has taken his own low desires for his deity? Can you then be a guardian over such a one?

44. Do you think that most of these (opponents) can hear and understand (what you say)? They are only like cattle, rather they are even worse in their ways and behaviour.

سُورَةُ الفُرْقَانِ ٢٥

الَّذِينَ كَذَّبُوا بِآيَاتِنَا فَدَمَّرْنَاهُمْ تَدْمِيرًا ﴿٣٦﴾
وَقَوْمَ نُوحٍ لَّمَّا كَذَّبُوا الرُّسُلَ أَغْرَقْنَاهُمْ
وَجَعَلْنَاهُمْ لِلنَّاسِ آيَةً ۖ وَأَعْتَدْنَا لِلظَّالِمِينَ
عَذَابًا أَلِيمًا ﴿٣٧﴾ وَعَادًا وَثَمُودَا وَأَصْحَابَ الرَّسِّ
وَقُرُونًا بَيْنَ ذَٰلِكَ كَثِيرًا ﴿٣٨﴾ وَكُلًّا ضَرَبْنَا لَهُ
الْأَمْثَالَ ۖ وَكُلًّا تَبَّرْنَا تَتْبِيرًا ﴿٣٩﴾ وَلَقَدْ أَتَوْا
عَلَى الْقَرْيَةِ الَّتِي أُمْطِرَتْ مَطَرَ السَّوْءِ ۚ أَفَلَمْ
يَكُونُوا يَرَوْنَهَا ۚ بَلْ كَانُوا لَا يَرْجُونَ نُشُورًا ﴿٤٠﴾
وَإِذَا رَأَوْكَ إِن يَتَّخِذُونَكَ إِلَّا هُزُوًا أَهَٰذَا
الَّذِي بَعَثَ اللَّهُ رَسُولًا ﴿٤١﴾ إِن كَادَ لَيُضِلُّنَا
عَنْ آلِهَتِنَا لَوْلَا أَن صَبَرْنَا عَلَيْهَا ۚ وَسَوْفَ
يَعْلَمُونَ حِينَ يَرَوْنَ الْعَذَابَ مَنْ أَضَلُّ
سَبِيلًا ﴿٤٢﴾ أَرَأَيْتَ مَنِ اتَّخَذَ إِلَٰهَهُ هَوَاهُ
أَفَأَنتَ تَكُونُ عَلَيْهِ وَكِيلًا ﴿٤٣﴾ أَمْ تَحْسَبُ أَنَّ
أَكْثَرَهُمْ يَسْمَعُونَ أَوْ يَعْقِلُونَ ۚ إِنْ هُمْ إِلَّا
كَالْأَنْعَامِ ۖ بَلْ هُمْ أَضَلُّ سَبِيلًا ﴿٤٤﴾ أَلَمْ تَرَ

الجزء التاسع عشر

SECTION 5

45. **D**o you not see (the wonderful doing of) your Lord how He stretches the shadow? If He had pleased He could have made it still. Not only that (We stretch the shadow) We make (the position of) the sun its indicator.

46. Then (as the sun rises higher in the sky), We withdraw it (- the shadow) to Ourselves; a gradual withdrawing.

47. It is He Who has made the night as a covering mantle for you and (Who has made) sleep for (a short) rest (as well as a sign of eternal rest - the death), and (has made) the day for rising up and going about (to seek livelihood and also a sign of Resurrection).

48. And it is He Who sends the winds as happy heralds of His mercy, and We send down from above water (also representing Divine revelation) for the purification (of the souls as well).

49. That We may thereby bring the dead land to life and give it as a drink to (most of the things) whom We have created, beasts and people in large numbers.

50. And We have explained this (topic) to them in diverse ways so that they may take heed, but most of the people would refuse (to adopt any other attitude) except (that of) disbelief.

51. If We had so willed We would surely have raised (in place of universal Prophethood) a Warner in every town.

52. So do not follow the disbelievers, and strive hard against them with the help of this (Qur'ân), a mighty striving.

53. It is He Who has let the two spans of water loose to flow, one of them (- a river) sweet and thirst-quenching while the other (a sea) saltish (and) bitter, and He has set a barrier and an insurmountable partition between them; (still both exist side by side in the world and would continue).

54. And it is He Who created human being from water and has given him relations by descent

إِلَىٰ رَبِّكَ كَيْفَ مَدَّ الظِّلَّ وَلَوْ شَاءَ لَجَعَلَهُ
سَاكِنًا ثُمَّ جَعَلْنَا الشَّمْسَ عَلَيْهِ دَلِيلًا ﴿٤٥﴾ ثُمَّ
قَبَضْنَاهُ إِلَيْنَا قَبْضًا يَسِيرًا ﴿٤٦﴾ وَهُوَ الَّذِي
جَعَلَ لَكُمُ الَّيْلَ لِبَاسًا وَالنَّوْمَ سُبَاتًا وَجَعَلَ
النَّهَارَ نُشُورًا ﴿٤٧﴾ وَهُوَ الَّذِي أَرْسَلَ الرِّيحَ بُشْرًا
بَيْنَ يَدَيْ رَحْمَتِهِ وَأَنْزَلْنَا مِنَ السَّمَاءِ مَاءً
طَهُورًا ﴿٤٨﴾ لِنُحْيِيَ بِهِ بَلْدَةً مَيْتًا وَنُسْقِيَهُ مِمَّا
خَلَقْنَا أَنْعَامًا وَأَنَاسِيَّ كَثِيرًا ﴿٤٩﴾ وَلَقَدْ صَرَّفْنَاهُ
بَيْنَهُمْ لِيَذَّكَّرُوا فَأَبَىٰ أَكْثَرُ النَّاسِ إِلَّا كُفُورًا ﴿٥٠﴾
وَلَوْ شِئْنَا لَبَعَثْنَا فِي كُلِّ قَرْيَةٍ نَذِيرًا ﴿٥١﴾ فَلَا
تُطِعِ الْكَافِرِينَ وَجَاهِدْهُمْ بِهِ جِهَادًا كَبِيرًا ﴿٥٢﴾
وَهُوَ الَّذِي مَرَجَ الْبَحْرَيْنِ هَٰذَا عَذْبٌ فُرَاتٌ
وَهَٰذَا مِلْحٌ أُجَاجٌ وَجَعَلَ بَيْنَهُمَا بَرْزَخًا
وَحِجْرًا مَحْجُورًا ﴿٥٣﴾ وَهُوَ الَّذِي خَلَقَ مِنَ الْمَاءِ

and (kinship) by marriage (and thus sought to establish a civilization and social life based on oneness of humanity under oneness of God). And your Lord is All-Powerful.

55. Yet they (- the disbelievers) worship apart from Allâh the things which can neither do them good nor avert harm from them. And the disbeliever is ever a helper (of the upholders of the cause of untruth) against his Lord.

56. But We have sent you only as a Bearer of happy tidings (to the doers of good) and as a Warner (to the wicked and the unjust).

57. Say, 'I ask of you no recompense for it (- the services I render). All that I ask is that whosoever chooses may follow the path (that leads) to his Lord.'

58. Hence put your trust in the Ever-Living (God) Who is free from death, and glorify His holiness along with (celebrating) His praise and (also tell,) 'Sufficient is He as being Well-Aware of the shortcomings of His servants.'

59. It is He Who created the heavens and the earth and all that lies between them in six aeons. Besides He is firmly established on the Throne (of Power). He is the Most Gracious (God). And ask concerning Him one who knows (- the Prophet Muhammad).

60. And when it is said to them, 'Prostrate (to show submission) to the Most Gracious (God).' They say, 'What (thing) is this the Most Gracious (God)? Shall we prostrate to whatever you bid us to show submission?' So this (bidding of the Prophet to submit to the Lord) increased them in aversion (to the truth).

[PROSTRATION]

SECTION 6

61. **B**LESSED is He Who has placed stars in the heaven and has set in it the glowing sun (that produces light) and the glittering moon (that reflects light).

62. And it is He Who has made the night and the day, one following the other; (He has done it)

سُورَةُ الْفُرْقَانِ ٢٥

بَشَرًا فَجَعَلَهُ نَسَبًا وَصِهْرًا ۗ وَكَانَ رَبُّكَ قَدِيرًا ﴿٥٤﴾
وَيَعْبُدُونَ مِنْ دُونِ اللَّهِ مَا لَا يَنْفَعُهُمْ وَلَا
يَضُرُّهُمْ ۗ وَكَانَ الْكَافِرُ عَلَىٰ رَبِّهِ ظَهِيرًا ﴿٥٥﴾ وَمَا
أَرْسَلْنَاكَ إِلَّا مُبَشِّرًا وَنَذِيرًا ﴿٥٦﴾ قُلْ مَا أَسْأَلُكُمْ
عَلَيْهِ مِنْ أَجْرٍ إِلَّا مَنْ شَاءَ أَنْ يَتَّخِذَ إِلَىٰ
رَبِّهِ سَبِيلًا ﴿٥٧﴾ وَتَوَكَّلْ عَلَى الْحَيِّ الَّذِي لَا يَمُوتُ
وَسَبِّحْ بِحَمْدِهِ ۚ وَكَفَىٰ بِهِ بِذُنُوبِ عِبَادِهِ
خَبِيرًا ﴿٥٨﴾ الَّذِي خَلَقَ السَّمَاوَاتِ وَالْأَرْضَ وَمَا
بَيْنَهُمَا فِي سِتَّةِ أَيَّامٍ ثُمَّ اسْتَوَىٰ عَلَى الْعَرْشِ ۚ
الرَّحْمَٰنُ فَاسْأَلْ بِهِ خَبِيرًا ﴿٥٩﴾ وَإِذَا قِيلَ لَهُمُ
اسْجُدُوا لِلرَّحْمَٰنِ قَالُوا وَمَا الرَّحْمَٰنُ أَنَسْجُدُ
لِمَا تَأْمُرُنَا وَزَادَهُمْ نُفُورًا ﴿٦٠﴾ تَبَارَكَ الَّذِي جَعَلَ
فِي السَّمَاءِ بُرُوجًا وَجَعَلَ فِيهَا سِرَاجًا وَقَمَرًا
مُنِيرًا ﴿٦١﴾ وَهُوَ الَّذِي جَعَلَ اللَّيْلَ وَالنَّهَارَ خِلْفَةً

for (the benefit of) the person who would care to receive exhortation and who would care to be grateful.

63. Those alone are the true servants of the Most Gracious (God) who walk upon the earth in all humility, (but in a dignified manner), and when the ignorant address them, they (do not wrangle but) observe a peaceful attitude.

64. And who pass the nights for the sake of their Lord prostrating and standing up (before Him in Prayer).

65. And who say (while praying), 'Our Lord, avert from us the punishment of Gehenna, for its punishment is indeed most vehement and unshakable.

66. 'It is of course, an evil place to lodge temporarily and an evil abode to remain therein permanently.'

67. And (the true servants of God are those) who, when spending, are neither extravagant nor niggardly, (but their spending follow) a middle course, ever moderate;

68. And who invoke none as god along with Allâh and who do not kill anyone whom Allâh has forbidden (to be killed), except for a just and lawful cause, and who do not commit fornication and adultery; and he who does (these things) shall meet the punishment of (his) sin.

69. His punishment shall be doubled on the Day of Resurrection. Humiliated and disgraced he shall suffer the punishment for long.

70. Different however shall be the case of him who turns (to God in repentance) and believes and does righteous deeds. For such people only Allâh will replace their evil deeds with good ones. And Allâh is Great Protector, Ever Merciful.

71. And he who turns (to God in sincere repentance) and accordingly does righteous deeds, no doubt he turns to Allâh in proper and true repentance.

72. And those who do not give false evidence and when they pass by something vain they (do

لِمَنْ أَرَادَ أَن يَذَّكَّرَ أَوْ أَرَادَ شُكُورًا ﴿٦٢﴾ وَعِبَادُ
الرَّحْمٰنِ الَّذِينَ يَمْشُونَ عَلَى الْأَرْضِ هَوْنًا
وَإِذَا خَاطَبَهُمُ الْجٰهِلُونَ قَالُوا سَلٰمًا ﴿٦٣﴾ وَالَّذِينَ
يَبِيتُونَ لِرَبِّهِمْ سُجَّدًا وَقِيٰمًا ﴿٦٤﴾ وَالَّذِينَ
يَقُولُونَ رَبَّنَا اصْرِفْ عَنَّا عَذَابَ جَهَنَّمَ إِنَّ
عَذَابَهَا كَانَ غَرَامًا ﴿٦٥﴾ إِنَّهَا سَاءَتْ مُسْتَقَرًّا
وَمُقَامًا ﴿٦٦﴾ وَالَّذِينَ إِذَا أَنفَقُوا لَمْ يُسْرِفُوا وَلَمْ
يَقْتُرُوا وَكَانَ بَيْنَ ذٰلِكَ قَوَامًا ﴿٦٧﴾ وَالَّذِينَ
لَا يَدْعُونَ مَعَ اللّٰهِ إِلٰهًا أٰخَرَ وَلَا يَقْتُلُونَ
النَّفْسَ الَّتِي حَرَّمَ اللّٰهُ إِلَّا بِالْحَقِّ وَلَا يَزْنُونَ
وَمَن يَفْعَلْ ذٰلِكَ يَلْقَ أَثَامًا ﴿٦٨﴾ يُضٰعَفْ لَهُ
الْعَذَابُ يَوْمَ الْقِيٰمَةِ وَيَخْلُدْ فِيهِ مُهَانًا ﴿٦٩﴾
إِلَّا مَن تَابَ وَأٰمَنَ وَعَمِلَ عَمَلًا صٰلِحًا
فَأُولٰٓئِكَ يُبَدِّلُ اللّٰهُ سَيِّاٰتِهِمْ حَسَنٰتٍ وَكَانَ
اللّٰهُ غَفُورًا رَّحِيمًا ﴿٧٠﴾ وَمَن تَابَ وَعَمِلَ صٰلِحًا
فَإِنَّهُ يَتُوبُ إِلَى اللّٰهِ مَتَابًا ﴿٧١﴾ وَالَّذِينَ لَا يَشْهَدُونَ

not indulge in it, but) pass on with dignity.
73. And who do not shut their ears and eyes to the commandments of their Lord (but listen to them attentively and with their eyes open) when they are reminded of them (so that their belief is based on conviction and not on mere hear-say).
74. And who (in their prayers) say, 'O our Lord! Grant that our wives and our children be (a source of) comfort for (our) eyes and make us a model for those who guard against evil.'
75. It is such of those who will be rewarded the highest place (in Paradise) for their fortitude and they will be received therein with greeting and salutation of peace.
76. They will abide therein (forever). How excellent it is as a lodging place (to rest) and how noble as an abode for permanent stay.
77. Say (to the disbelievers), 'My Lord will not hold you to be of any worth if you do not call on Him (in your prayers seeking His protection). Since you cried lies (to the word of God), so you must now encounter a lasting punishment.'

الزُّورَ وَإِذَا مَرُّوا بِاللَّغْوِ مَرُّوا كِرَامًا ﴿٧٢﴾ وَالَّذِينَ
إِذَا ذُكِّرُوا بِآيٰتِ رَبِّهِمْ لَمْ يَخِرُّوا عَلَيْهَا صُمًّا
وَّعُمْيَانًا ﴿٧٣﴾ وَالَّذِينَ يَقُولُونَ رَبَّنَا هَبْ لَنَا مِنْ
أَزْوٰجِنَا وَذُرِّيّٰتِنَا قُرَّةَ أَعْيُنٍ وَّاجْعَلْنَا لِلْمُتَّقِينَ
إِمَامًا ﴿٧٤﴾ أُولٰٓئِكَ يُجْزَوْنَ الْغُرْفَةَ بِمَا صَبَرُوا
وَيُلَقَّوْنَ فِيهَا تَحِيَّةً وَّسَلٰمًا ﴿٧٥﴾ خٰلِدِينَ فِيهَا
حَسُنَتْ مُسْتَقَرًّا وَّمُقَامًا ﴿٧٦﴾ قُلْ مَا يَعْبَؤُا
بِكُمْ رَبِّي لَوْلَا دُعَآؤُكُمْ فَقَدْ كَذَّبْتُمْ
فَسَوْفَ يَكُونُ لِزَامًا ﴿٧٧﴾

CHAPTER
26

AL-SHU'ARÂ'
(The Poets)
(Revealed before Hijrah)

سُورَةُ الشُّعَرَاءِ مَكِّيَّةٌ

With the name of Allâh,
the Most Gracious, the Ever Merciful
(I commence to read Sûrah Al-Shu'arâ').

بِسْمِ اللّٰهِ الرَّحْمٰنِ الرَّحِيمِ

1. Tâ Sîn Mîm - Allâh is Benign, All-Hearing and All-Knowing.
2. These are the verses of the perfect Book which tells the right from the wrong (and which also makes the meaning and significance of the verses clear).
3. Perhaps you will consume yourself away (with anxiety) because they do not become believers.
4. If We so please We can send down upon

طٰسٓمٓ ﴿١﴾ تِلْكَ آيٰتُ الْكِتٰبِ الْمُبِينِ ﴿٢﴾ لَعَلَّكَ
بٰخِعٌ نَّفْسَكَ أَلَّا يَكُونُوا مُؤْمِنِينَ ﴿٣﴾ إِنْ نَّشَأْ

them such a sign from above that their necks would bend (and heads bow down) in submission to it.
5. There never comes to them a fresh Reminder (in a new form and with new details) from the Most Gracious (God) but they turn away from it.
6. Now, when they have cried lies (to the Messages of their Lord and denied the Qur'ân), there will soon come to them the great tidings (about their own doom and predominance of Islam) which they used to take lightly.
7. Do they not see the earth, how many excellent and useful things of all species We have caused to grow on it?
8. Indeed, there is a sign in this, yet most of them would not believe.
9. And your Lord, of course, He is the All-Mighty, the Ever Merciful.

SECTION 2

10. **A**ND (recall the time) when your Lord called to Moses (directing him), 'Go to the wrongdoing people,
11. 'The people of Pharaoh (and say to them), "Will they not guard against evil?'"
12. (Moses) said, 'My Lord! I am afraid they will cry me lies.
13. 'And my bosom straitens (and my heart fails me), and my tongue is not fluent (for feeling inadequate to deliver the message I am entrusted with), therefore send to Aaron (to help me).
14. 'Moreover, they have a charge (of the murder of an Egyptian) against me, so I fear they will kill me (before I am able to deliver Your Message to them).'
15. (The Lord) said, 'That shall not be, go then both of you, with Our Messages and We are assuredly with you listening (to your prayers).
16. 'Go to Pharaoh both of you and say, "We are bearers of a Message from the Lord of the worlds.
17. "(Who commands you) to send the Children of Israel with us".'

نُنَزِّلْ عَلَيْهِم مِّنَ السَّمَاءِ آيَةً فَظَلَّتْ
أَعْنَاقُهُمْ لَهَا خَاضِعِينَ ﴿٤﴾ وَمَا يَأْتِيهِم مِّنْ
ذِكْرٍ مِّنَ الرَّحْمَٰنِ مُحْدَثٍ إِلَّا كَانُوا عَنْهُ
مُعْرِضِينَ ﴿٥﴾ فَقَدْ كَذَّبُوا فَسَيَأْتِيهِمْ أَنبَاءُ مَا
كَانُوا بِهِ يَسْتَهْزِئُونَ ﴿٦﴾ أَوَلَمْ يَرَوْا إِلَى الْأَرْضِ
كَمْ أَنبَتْنَا فِيهَا مِن كُلِّ زَوْجٍ كَرِيمٍ ﴿٧﴾ إِنَّ فِي
ذَٰلِكَ لَآيَةً ۖ وَمَا كَانَ أَكْثَرُهُم مُّؤْمِنِينَ ﴿٨﴾
ع ٩ ٥ وَإِنَّ رَبَّكَ لَهُوَ الْعَزِيزُ الرَّحِيمُ ﴿٩﴾ وَإِذْ نَادَىٰ رَبُّكَ
مُوسَىٰ أَنِ ائْتِ الْقَوْمَ الظَّالِمِينَ ﴿١٠﴾ قَوْمَ فِرْعَوْنَ
أَلَا يَتَّقُونَ ﴿١١﴾ قَالَ رَبِّ إِنِّي أَخَافُ أَن يُكَذِّبُونِ ﴿١٢﴾
وَيَضِيقُ صَدْرِي وَلَا يَنطَلِقُ لِسَانِي فَأَرْسِلْ
إِلَىٰ هَارُونَ ﴿١٣﴾ وَلَهُمْ عَلَيَّ ذَنبٌ فَأَخَافُ أَن
يَقْتُلُونِ ﴿١٤﴾ قَالَ كَلَّا ۖ فَاذْهَبَا بِآيَاتِنَا ۖ إِنَّا مَعَكُم
مُّسْتَمِعُونَ ﴿١٥﴾ فَأْتِيَا فِرْعَوْنَ فَقُولَا إِنَّا رَسُولُ
رَبِّ الْعَالَمِينَ ﴿١٦﴾ أَنْ أَرْسِلْ مَعَنَا بَنِي إِسْرَائِيلَ ﴿١٧﴾

18. (So when Moses and Aaron went to Pharaoh) he said (to Moses), 'Did we not bring you up among us when you were a mere babe? And you stayed with us many years of your life.
19. 'And you have surely committed an act (of homicide), and you are of the ungrateful.'
20. (Moses) said, 'Indeed I did it (then inadvertently and) as I was lost (for the love of my people and was in a perplexed state of mind).
21. 'So I fled from you when I apprehended (injustice from) you; then (it came to pass that) my Lord granted me knowledge and (right) judgment and made me (one) of the Messengers.
22. 'And this insignificant favour (of your bringing me up) that you (so tauntingly) remind me of (can be no reasonable excuse) for you have enslaved (the whole community of) the Children of Israel (for no fault of theirs).'
23. Pharaoh (was confounded and turning the topic of the conversation) said, 'What is (this) Lord of the world (by Whom you claim to be sent?)'
24. (Moses) said, '(In respect of apace) He is the Lord of the heavens and the earth and of all that lies between the two; if you (and your companions) be convinced (of this true knowledge and have faith in Him).'
25. (Thereupon Pharaoh) said to those around him, 'Do you not hear (what is being said)?'
26. (Moses continued, 'He is the same Who is) your Lord and the Lord of your fathers of yore.'
27. (Pharaoh) said, 'Most surely, this Messenger of yours who has been sent to you is a mad man indeed.'
28. (Moses) said (continuing his speech), '(In respect of time the Lord of the worlds is the same as) the Lord of the east and of the west and of all that lies between the two. (You can be rightly guided) if you could only use your senses.'
29. (Pharaoh) said, 'If you worship any god

سورة الشعراء ٢٦

قال ألم نربك فينا وليدا ولبثت فينا من عمرك سنين (١٨) وفعلت فعلتك التي فعلت وأنت من الكفرين (١٩) قال فعلتها إذا وأنا من الضالين (٢٠) ففررت منكم لما خفتكم فوهب لي ربي حكما وجعلني من المرسلين (٢١) وتلك نعمة تمنها علي أن عبدت بني إسراءيل (٢٢) قال فرعون وما رب العلمين (٢٣) قال رب السموت والأرض وما بينهما إن كنتم موقنين (٢٤) قال لمن حوله ألا تستمعون (٢٥) قال ربكم ورب ءابائكم الأولين (٢٦) قال إن رسولكم الذي أرسل إليكم لمجنون (٢٧) قال رب المشرق والمغرب وما بينهما إن كنتم تعقلون (٢٨) قال لئن

other than me, I will certainly make you one of the imprisoned.'

30. (Moses) said, '(Will you do this,) even though I bring to you something that makes (the truth of my statement) clear to you?'

31. (Pharaoh) said, 'Bring it then, if you are of the truthful.'

32. So he put his staff (on the ground) and behold, it was a serpent plainly visible.

33. And he stuck his hand out and lo! It was (shining) white to the beholders.

SECTION 3

34. (**P**HARAOH) said to the courtiers around him, 'This (man) is surely a skilled sorcerer,

35. 'Who seeks to turn you out of your country by dint of his sorcery. Now, what do you advise?'

36. They said, 'Detain him and his brother for a while and send heralds into the cities to collect;

37. 'And bring to you all skilled and very expert sorcerers.'

38. So the sorcerers were gathered together at the appointed time and place on a fixed day.

39. And it was said to the people, 'Will you (also) assemble together (in the field of contest);

40. 'So that we may follow the sorcerers if they win clear supremacy.'

41. So when all the sorcerers came they said to Pharaoh, 'Shall we be really and richly rewarded if we gain clear supremacy?'

42. He said, 'Yes, and surely you will in that case be among my close companions.'

43. Moses said to them, '(Now) put forward (of your things of sorcery), what you have to put forward.'

44. So they put down (on the ground) their ropes and their staffs and said, 'By Pharaoh's honour and might it is we who will certainly

اتَّخَذْتَ إِلٰهًا غَيْرِي لَأَجْعَلَنَّكَ مِنَ الْمَسْجُونِينَ ﴿٢٩﴾
قَالَ أَوَلَوْ جِئْتُكَ بِشَيْءٍ مُّبِينٍ ﴿٣٠﴾ قَالَ فَأْتِ
بِهِ إِنْ كُنْتَ مِنَ الصّٰدِقِينَ ﴿٣١﴾ فَأَلْقٰى عَصَاهُ
فَإِذَا هِيَ ثُعْبَانٌ مُّبِينٌ ﴿٣٢﴾ وَّنَزَعَ يَدَهُ فَإِذَا هِيَ
بَيْضَآءُ لِلنّٰظِرِينَ ﴿٣٣﴾ قَالَ لِلْمَلَإِ حَوْلَهُ إِنَّ هٰذَا
لَسٰحِرٌ عَلِيمٌ ﴿٣٤﴾ يُّرِيدُ أَنْ يُّخْرِجَكُمْ مِّنْ أَرْضِكُمْ
بِسِحْرِهِ فَمَاذَا تَأْمُرُونَ ﴿٣٥﴾ قَالُوٓا أَرْجِهْ وَأَخَاهُ
وَابْعَثْ فِي الْمَدَآئِنِ حٰشِرِينَ ﴿٣٦﴾ يَأْتُوكَ بِكُلِّ
سَحَّارٍ عَلِيمٍ ﴿٣٧﴾ فَجُمِعَ السَّحَرَةُ لِمِيقٰتِ يَوْمٍ
مَّعْلُومٍ ﴿٣٨﴾ وَّقِيلَ لِلنَّاسِ هَلْ أَنْتُمْ
مُّجْتَمِعُونَ ﴿٣٩﴾ لَعَلَّنَا نَتَّبِعُ السَّحَرَةَ إِنْ كَانُوا هُمُ
الْغٰلِبِينَ ﴿٤٠﴾ فَلَمَّا جَآءَ السَّحَرَةُ قَالُوا لِفِرْعَوْنَ
أَئِنَّ لَنَا لَأَجْرًا إِنْ كُنَّا نَحْنُ الْغٰلِبِينَ ﴿٤١﴾ قَالَ
نَعَمْ وَإِنَّكُمْ إِذًا لَّمِنَ الْمُقَرَّبِينَ ﴿٤٢﴾ قَالَ لَهُمْ
مُّوسٰى أَلْقُوا مَآ أَنْتُمْ مُّلْقُونَ ﴿٤٣﴾ فَأَلْقَوْا حِبَالَهُمْ
وَعِصِيَّهُمْ وَقَالُوا بِعِزَّةِ فِرْعَوْنَ إِنَّا لَنَحْنُ

be the winners.'
45. Then Moses put down (on the ground) his staff; lo! It instantly destroyed all that they had fabricated.
46. Thereupon the sorcerers were impelled to fall down prostrating;
47. And they said, 'We believe in the Lord of the worlds;
48. 'The Lord of Moses and Aaron.'
49. (Pharaoh) said, 'Have you believed in him before I gave you leave? Indeed he is your chief, the same who taught you sorcery. So you will soon know (your horrible end). I will most surely cut off your hands and your feet on alternate sides for (your this) opposition (to me); and I will crucify you to death one and all.'
50. They said, 'It does not matter at all. We have, after all, to return to our Lord.
51. 'We do hope that our Lord will forgive us our offences, since we are the first to believe.'

SECTION 4

52. **A**ND We revealed to Moses (directing him), 'Take away My servants by night for you shall certainly be pursued.'
53. Pharaoh (when he came to know of the exodus) sent heralds to the towns to collect (troops and announce saying),
54. 'These (Israelites) are indeed a despicable party, a few in number,
55. 'Yet they have offended us (by defying us and making good their escape),
56. 'And we are, (as compared with them,) a united multitude, fully equipped and vigilant.'
57. So We made them (- Pharaoh and his troops) leave the land of gardens and springs,
58. As well as (every place with) treasures and every abode of honour (and grandeur).
59. That is what We did (for their wrong- doings). And We gave (the like of) these (- gardens and springs) as a free gift to the Children of Israel.
60. And they (- the hosts of Pharaoh) pursued them at sunrise.

الْغٰلِبُونَ ﴿٤٤﴾ فَأَلْقٰى مُوسٰى عَصَاهُ فَإِذَا هِيَ تَلْقَفُ
مَا يَأْفِكُونَ ﴿٤٥﴾ فَأُلْقِيَ السَّحَرَةُ سٰجِدِينَ ﴿٤٦﴾ قَالُوٓا
اٰمَنَّا بِرَبِّ الْعٰلَمِينَ ﴿٤٧﴾ رَبِّ مُوسٰى وَهٰرُونَ ﴿٤٨﴾
قَالَ اٰمَنْتُمْ لَهُ قَبْلَ أَنْ اٰذَنَ لَكُمْ إِنَّهُ
لَكَبِيرُكُمُ الَّذِي عَلَّمَكُمُ السِّحْرَ فَلَسَوْفَ تَعْلَمُونَ
لَأُقَطِّعَنَّ أَيْدِيَكُمْ وَأَرْجُلَكُمْ مِّنْ خِلٰفٍ
وَّلَأُصَلِّبَنَّكُمْ أَجْمَعِينَ ﴿٤٩﴾ قَالُوا لَا ضَيْرَ إِنَّآ إِلٰى
رَبِّنَا مُنْقَلِبُونَ ﴿٥٠﴾ إِنَّا نَطْمَعُ أَنْ يَّغْفِرَ لَنَا رَبُّنَا
خَطٰيٰنَآ أَنْ كُنَّآ أَوَّلَ الْمُؤْمِنِينَ ﴿٥١﴾ وَأَوْحَيْنَآ
إِلٰى مُوسٰىٓ أَنْ أَسْرِ بِعِبَادِيٓ إِنَّكُمْ مُّتَّبَعُونَ ﴿٥٢﴾
فَأَرْسَلَ فِرْعَوْنُ فِي الْمَدَآئِنِ حٰشِرِينَ ﴿٥٣﴾ إِنَّ
هٰٓؤُلَآءِ لَشِرْذِمَةٌ قَلِيلُونَ ﴿٥٤﴾ وَإِنَّهُمْ لَنَا لَغَآئِظُونَ ﴿٥٥﴾
وَإِنَّا لَجَمِيعٌ حٰذِرُونَ ﴿٥٦﴾ فَأَخْرَجْنٰهُمْ مِّنْ جَنّٰتٍ
وَّعُيُونٍ ﴿٥٧﴾ وَّكُنُوزٍ وَّمَقَامٍ كَرِيمٍ ﴿٥٨﴾ كَذٰلِكَ
وَأَوْرَثْنٰهَا بَنِيٓ إِسْرَآءِيلَ ﴿٥٩﴾ فَأَتْبَعُوهُمْ مُّشْرِقِينَ ﴿٦٠﴾

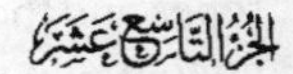

61. And when the two hosts sighted each other the companions of Moses said, 'We are surely overtaken.'
62. (Moses) said, 'No, not at all, my Lord is with me, He will lead me out of the impasse (and to safety).'
63. Then We revealed to Moses (saying), 'Strike the sea with your staff. (And as he did) so it parted, and each part (of the two hosts) looked like a huge mound.
64. And We caused the others (the pursuers, the people of Pharaoh,) draw near the same place.
65. And We saved Moses and those who were with him all together.
66. Then We drowned the others.
67. Behold! There is a (marvelous) sign in this (episode), yet most of them would not be believers.
68. And indeed your Lord, He is the All-Mighty (to crush His enemies), the Ever Merciful (towards His servants).

SECTION 5

69. **A**ND narrate to them the important event (of the life) of Abraham.
70. When he said to his sire and his people, 'What things are those which you worship?'
71. 'We worship idols and will remain constantly devoted to them,' said they.
72. Abraham said, 'Can they listen to you when you call (on them)?
73. 'Or can they do you good or avert harm from you?'
74. They said, 'Nay, it is not so, but we found our fathers doing likewise.'
75. (Abraham) said, 'But have you (ever) considered what you have been worshipping,
76. 'You and your fathers before you,
77. 'They are (all) enemies to me. Different however is the case of the Lord of the world (Who is kind to me).
78. 'He has created me and it is He Who will

فَلَمَّا تَرَاءَا الْجَمْعَانِ قَالَ أَصْحٰبُ مُوسٰى إِنَّا
لَمُدْرَكُونَ ﴿٦١﴾ قَالَ كَلَّا إِنَّ مَعِيَ رَبِّي سَيَهْدِينِ ﴿٦٢﴾
فَأَوْحَيْنَا إِلٰى مُوسٰى أَنِ اضْرِب بِّعَصَاكَ الْبَحْرَ
فَانْفَلَقَ فَكَانَ كُلُّ فِرْقٍ كَالطَّوْدِ الْعَظِيمِ ﴿٦٣﴾
وَأَزْلَفْنَا ثَمَّ الْأٰخَرِينَ ﴿٦٤﴾ وَأَنْجَيْنَا مُوسٰى وَمَن
مَّعَهُ أَجْمَعِينَ ﴿٦٥﴾ ثُمَّ أَغْرَقْنَا الْأٰخَرِينَ ﴿٦٦﴾ إِنَّ
فِي ذٰلِكَ لَأٰيَةً وَمَا كَانَ أَكْثَرُهُم مُّؤْمِنِينَ ﴿٦٧﴾
وَإِنَّ رَبَّكَ لَهُوَ الْعَزِيزُ الرَّحِيمُ ﴿٦٨﴾ وَاتْلُ
عَلَيْهِمْ نَبَأَ إِبْرٰهِيمَ ﴿٦٩﴾ إِذْ قَالَ لِأَبِيهِ وَقَوْمِهِ
مَا تَعْبُدُونَ ﴿٧٠﴾ قَالُوا نَعْبُدُ أَصْنَامًا فَنَظَلُّ
لَهَا عٰكِفِينَ ﴿٧١﴾ قَالَ هَلْ يَسْمَعُونَكُمْ إِذْ
تَدْعُونَ ﴿٧٢﴾ أَوْ يَنْفَعُونَكُمْ أَوْ يَضُرُّونَ ﴿٧٣﴾ قَالُوا بَلْ
وَجَدْنَا أٰبَاءَنَا كَذٰلِكَ يَفْعَلُونَ ﴿٧٤﴾ قَالَ أَفَرَءَيْتُم
مَّا كُنْتُمْ تَعْبُدُونَ ﴿٧٥﴾ أَنْتُمْ وَأٰبَاؤُكُمُ الْأَقْدَمُونَ ﴿٧٦﴾
فَإِنَّهُمْ عَدُوٌّ لِّي إِلَّا رَبَّ الْعٰلَمِينَ ﴿٧٧﴾ الَّذِي

ع ١٧ / ٨

guide me to reach the goal.
79. 'And Who gives me food and drink,
80. 'And Who restores me to health, (through His grace and mercy), whenever I am taken ill (due to some fault of mine),
81. 'And Who will call me to death and then will raise me to life (again).
82. 'And Who, I eagerly hope, will protect me from (the undesirable consequences of) my faults on the Day of Requital.'
83. (Abraham then turned to his Lord and said,) 'My Lord! Grant me strong and right judgment and make me follow and join the righteous.
84. 'And ordain for me a noble, true and lasting reputation among posterity;
85. 'And make me one of the heirs of the Garden of Great Bliss.
86. 'And protect my sire (- Âzar against his faults), he is of course of the erring ones.
87. 'And do not put me to shame and disgrace on the day when people will be resurrected,
88. 'The day when wealth will not avail, nor sons (be of any good),
89. 'But (he alone will be saved) who comes to Allâh with a sound and pure heart.'
90. (The day when) Paradise will be brought near to those who guard against evil,
91. And Gehenna shall be unveiled and placed in full view to those (wretched ones) who had deviated from the right path;
92. And who shall be asked, 'Where are (your deities) that you worshipped,
93. 'Apart from Allâh? Can they come to your help or inflict punishment?'
94. Then they (- the false deities) shall all be hurled headlong into the depths of it (- the Hell), again and again, and along with them all those (wretched fellows) who had deviated from the right path.
95. And the supporters of *Iblîs* all together.
96. They will say disputing therein (- in the Hell) among themselves,
97. 'By Allâh! We were certainly in manifest

خَلَقَنِي فَهُوَ يَهْدِينِ ﴿٧٨﴾ وَالَّذِي هُوَ يُطْعِمُنِي
وَيَسْقِينِ ﴿٧٩﴾ وَإِذَا مَرِضْتُ فَهُوَ يَشْفِينِ ﴿٨٠﴾
وَالَّذِي يُمِيتُنِي ثُمَّ يُحْيِينِ ﴿٨١﴾ وَالَّذِي أَطْمَعُ
أَنْ يَغْفِرَ لِي خَطِيئَتِي يَوْمَ الدِّينِ ﴿٨٢﴾ رَبِّ
هَبْ لِي حُكْمًا وَأَلْحِقْنِي بِالصَّالِحِينَ ﴿٨٣﴾ وَاجْعَلْ
لِي لِسَانَ صِدْقٍ فِي الْآخِرِينَ ﴿٨٤﴾ وَاجْعَلْنِي مِنْ
وَرَثَةِ جَنَّةِ النَّعِيمِ ﴿٨٥﴾ وَاغْفِرْ لِأَبِي إِنَّهُ كَانَ
مِنَ الضَّالِّينَ ﴿٨٦﴾ وَلَا تُخْزِنِي يَوْمَ يُبْعَثُونَ ﴿٨٧﴾
يَوْمَ لَا يَنْفَعُ مَالٌ وَلَا بَنُونَ ﴿٨٨﴾ إِلَّا مَنْ أَتَى
اللَّهَ بِقَلْبٍ سَلِيمٍ ﴿٨٩﴾ وَأُزْلِفَتِ الْجَنَّةُ لِلْمُتَّقِينَ ﴿٩٠﴾
وَبُرِّزَتِ الْجَحِيمُ لِلْغَاوِينَ ﴿٩١﴾ وَقِيلَ لَهُمْ أَيْنَ
مَا كُنْتُمْ تَعْبُدُونَ ﴿٩٢﴾ مِنْ دُونِ اللَّهِ هَلْ
يَنْصُرُونَكُمْ أَوْ يَنْتَصِرُونَ ﴿٩٣﴾ فَكُبْكِبُوا فِيهَا
هُمْ وَالْغَاوُونَ ﴿٩٤﴾ وَجُنُودُ إِبْلِيسَ أَجْمَعُونَ ﴿٩٥﴾
قَالُوا وَهُمْ فِيهَا يَخْتَصِمُونَ ﴿٩٦﴾ تَاللَّهِ إِنْ

(and deep) error,
98. 'In holding you (- deities) as equal with the Lord of the worlds,
99. 'And none but those who cut off their ties with Allâh led us astray,
100. 'So that (now) we have none of the intercessors,
101. 'Nor any warmhearted true friend.
102. 'Could we have but another (chance to) return (to the world) then we would surely become of the (true) believers.'
103. Verily, there is a remarkable sign in this (episode of Abraham's life), yet most of the people would not be believers.
104. And of course your Lord, He is the All-Mighty (to crush and obliterate His enemies and), the Ever Merciful (to the supporters of true faith).

SECTION 6

105. **T**HE people of Noah cried lies to the Messengers.
106. (Recall the time) when their kinsman Noah said to them, 'Will you not guard against evil?
107. 'Surely, I am to you a Messenger, faithful to (my) trust.
108. 'So take Allâh as a shield and obey me.
109. 'And I ask no reward from you for it (- the delivery of the Message of God). My reward lies with the Lord of the worlds alone.
110. 'So take Allâh as a shield and obey me.'
111. They (- the disbelievers) said, 'Shall we believe in you whereas (we see that) only the people of a very low status follow you?'
112. He said, 'I have no knowledge what (good) deeds they did (in the past that now they have the honour to accept the truth).
113. 'It is only up to my Lord to call them to account; if you could but perceive.
114. 'I cannot drive away the believers (thinking them to be of low status).

كُنَّا لَفِي ضَلٰلٍ مُّبِينٍ ﴿٩٧﴾ إِذْ نُسَوِّيكُمْ بِرَبِّ
الْعٰلَمِينَ ﴿٩٨﴾ وَ مَآ أَضَلَّنَآ إِلَّا الْمُجْرِمُونَ ﴿٩٩﴾ فَمَا
لَنَا مِنْ شٰفِعِينَ ﴿١٠٠﴾ وَلَا صَدِيقٍ حَمِيمٍ ﴿١٠١﴾ فَلَوْ
أَنَّ لَنَا كَرَّةً فَنَكُونَ مِنَ الْمُؤْمِنِينَ ﴿١٠٢﴾ إِنَّ فِي
ذٰلِكَ لَأٰيَةً وَ مَا كَانَ أَكْثَرُهُمْ مُّؤْمِنِينَ ﴿١٠٣﴾
وَ إِنَّ رَبَّكَ لَهُوَ الْعَزِيزُ الرَّحِيمُ ﴿١٠٤﴾ كَذَّبَتْ
قَوْمُ نُوحٍ الْمُرْسَلِينَ ﴿١٠٥﴾ إِذْ قَالَ لَهُمْ أَخُوهُمْ
نُوحٌ أَلَا تَتَّقُونَ ﴿١٠٦﴾ إِنِّي لَكُمْ رَسُولٌ أَمِينٌ ﴿١٠٧﴾
فَاتَّقُوا اللّٰهَ وَ أَطِيعُونِ ﴿١٠٨﴾ وَ مَآ أَسْئَلُكُمْ عَلَيْهِ
مِنْ أَجْرٍ إِنْ أَجْرِيَ إِلَّا عَلٰى رَبِّ الْعٰلَمِينَ ﴿١٠٩﴾
فَاتَّقُوا اللّٰهَ وَ أَطِيعُونِ ﴿١١٠﴾ قَالُوٓا أَنُؤْمِنُ لَكَ
وَ اتَّبَعَكَ الْأَرْذَلُونَ ﴿١١١﴾ قَالَ وَ مَا عِلْمِي بِمَا كَانُوا
يَعْمَلُونَ ﴿١١٢﴾ إِنْ حِسَابُهُمْ إِلَّا عَلٰى رَبِّي لَوْ
تَشْعُرُونَ ﴿١١٣﴾ وَ مَآ أَنَا بِطَارِدِ الْمُؤْمِنِينَ ﴿١١٤﴾ إِنْ

115. ‘I am but a plain Warner.’

116. ‘Noah!’ They said, ‘If you do not desist, you shall be excommunicated or done away with.’

117. (Noah) said (praying), ‘My Lord! My people have treated me as a liar,

118. ‘So judge between me and them, a decisive judgment, and deliver me and the believers who are with me.’

119. So We delivered him and all those who were with him by means of the fully-laden Ark.

120. Then after that We drowned the remaining ones.

121. Behold! There is a great sign in this (episode), yet most of them would not be believers.

122. And indeed your Lord, He is the All-Mighty, the Ever Merciful.

SECTION 7

123. (THE tribe of) ‘Âd (too) cried lies to the Messengers (sent to them).

124. (Recall the time) when their kinsman Hûd said to them, ‘Will you not guard against evil?

125. ‘Surely, I am to you a Messenger; faithful to (my) trust.

126. ‘Therefore take Allâh as a shield and obey me.

127. ‘I ask no reward from you for this (service I render). My reward lies only with the Lord of the worlds.

128. ‘What is (wrong with you)? You build a monument on every prominent place, in vain you do it.

129. ‘And you raise fortresses in the hope that you will abide till long.

130. ‘And when you lay hold (on anyone), you do it like tyrants.

131. ‘You should take Allâh as a shield and obey me.

132. ‘And take Him as a shield Who has helped you with all (the favours and blessings) that you

أَنَا إِلَّا نَذِيرٌ مُّبِينٌ ﴿١١٥﴾ قَالُوا لَئِن لَّمْ تَنتَهِ
يٰنُوحُ لَتَكُونَنَّ مِنَ الْمَرْجُومِينَ ﴿١١٦﴾ قَالَ رَبِّ
إِنَّ قَوْمِي كَذَّبُونِ ﴿١١٧﴾ فَافْتَحْ بَيْنِي وَبَيْنَهُمْ
فَتْحًا وَنَجِّنِي وَمَن مَّعِيَ مِنَ الْمُؤْمِنِينَ ﴿١١٨﴾
فَأَنجَيْنٰهُ وَمَن مَّعَهُ فِي الْفُلْكِ الْمَشْحُونِ ﴿١١٩﴾
ثُمَّ أَغْرَقْنَا بَعْدُ الْبَاقِينَ ﴿١٢٠﴾ إِنَّ فِي ذٰلِكَ لَآيَةً
وَمَا كَانَ أَكْثَرُهُم مُّؤْمِنِينَ ﴿١٢١﴾ وَإِنَّ رَبَّكَ
لَهُوَ الْعَزِيزُ الرَّحِيمُ ﴿١٢٢﴾ كَذَّبَتْ عَادٌ الْمُرْسَلِينَ ﴿١٢٣﴾
إِذْ قَالَ لَهُمْ أَخُوهُمْ هُودٌ أَلَا تَتَّقُونَ ﴿١٢٤﴾ إِنِّي
لَكُمْ رَسُولٌ أَمِينٌ ﴿١٢٥﴾ فَاتَّقُوا اللهَ وَأَطِيعُونِ ﴿١٢٦﴾
وَمَا أَسْئَلُكُمْ عَلَيْهِ مِنْ أَجْرٍ إِنْ أَجْرِيَ
إِلَّا عَلَىٰ رَبِّ الْعٰلَمِينَ ﴿١٢٧﴾ أَتَبْنُونَ بِكُلِّ رِيعٍ
آيَةً تَعْبَثُونَ ﴿١٢٨﴾ وَتَتَّخِذُونَ مَصَانِعَ لَعَلَّكُمْ
تَخْلُدُونَ ﴿١٢٩﴾ وَإِذَا بَطَشْتُم بَطَشْتُمْ جَبَّارِينَ ﴿١٣٠﴾
فَاتَّقُوا اللهَ وَأَطِيعُونِ ﴿١٣١﴾ وَاتَّقُوا الَّذِي أَمَدَّكُم

know of.
133. ‘He has helped you with cattle and sons,
134. ‘And gardens and springs.
135. ‘Indeed, I fear lest the punishment of an awful day should befall you.’
136. They said, ‘It makes no difference with us whether you admonish us or be not of the admonishers.
137. ‘This way (of admonition) is merely the manner of the ancients.
138. ‘And we are not at all going to be punished.’
139. Thus they cried him lies and We destroyed them. There is indeed, a remarkable sign in this (episode), yet most of them would not be believers.
140. And in fact your Lord, He is the All-Mighty (to crush and obliterate His enemies), and the Ever Merciful (towards His obedient servants).

SECTION 8

141. (THE tribe of) Thamûd (too) cried lies to the Messengers.
142. (Recall the time) when their kinsman Sâlih said to them, ‘Will you not guard against evil?
143. ‘Surely, I am to you a Messenger, faithful to (my) trust.
144. ‘So take Allâh as a shield and obey me.
145. ‘I ask no reward from you for this (service I render). My reward lies with the Lord of the worlds alone.
146. ‘(Do you think that) you will be left in peace amidst all (enjoyable things) which you have here,
147. ‘Amidst gardens and springs,
148. ‘And cornfields and date-palms having (fine and heavy) spathes near breaking.
149. ‘And you hew out houses in the mountains with great skill and elated with your greatness.
150. ‘Take Allâh as a shield and obey me.
151. ‘And do not obey the biddings of those who exceed the bounds.
152. ‘Who create disorder in the country and set not (things) in order (to promote security

بِمَا تَعْلَمُونَ ١٣٢ أَمَدَّكُم بِأَنْعَامٍ وَبَنِينَ ١٣٣
وَجَنَّاتٍ وَعُيُونٍ ١٣٤ إِنِّي أَخَافُ عَلَيْكُمْ عَذَابَ
يَوْمٍ عَظِيمٍ ١٣٥ قَالُوا سَوَاءٌ عَلَيْنَا أَوَعَظْتَ أَمْ
لَمْ تَكُن مِّنَ الْوَاعِظِينَ ١٣٦ إِنْ هَٰذَا إِلَّا خُلُقُ
الْأَوَّلِينَ ١٣٧ وَمَا نَحْنُ بِمُعَذَّبِينَ ١٣٨ فَكَذَّبُوهُ
فَأَهْلَكْنَاهُمْ إِنَّ فِي ذَٰلِكَ لَآيَةً وَمَا كَانَ
أَكْثَرُهُم مُّؤْمِنِينَ ١٣٩ وَإِنَّ رَبَّكَ لَهُوَ الْعَزِيزُ
الرَّحِيمُ ١٤٠ كَذَّبَتْ ثَمُودُ الْمُرْسَلِينَ ١٤١ إِذْ قَالَ ع ٨ ١١
لَهُمْ أَخُوهُمْ صَالِحٌ أَلَا تَتَّقُونَ ١٤٢ إِنِّي لَكُمْ
رَسُولٌ أَمِينٌ ١٤٣ فَاتَّقُوا اللَّهَ وَأَطِيعُونِ ١٤٤ وَمَا
أَسْأَلُكُمْ عَلَيْهِ مِنْ أَجْرٍ إِنْ أَجْرِيَ إِلَّا عَلَىٰ
رَبِّ الْعَالَمِينَ ١٤٥ أَتُتْرَكُونَ فِي مَا هَاهُنَا آمِنِينَ ١٤٦
فِي جَنَّاتٍ وَعُيُونٍ ١٤٧ وَزُرُوعٍ وَنَخْلٍ طَلْعُهَا
هَضِيمٌ ١٤٨ وَتَنْحِتُونَ مِنَ الْجِبَالِ بُيُوتًا
فَارِهِينَ ١٤٩ فَاتَّقُوا اللَّهَ وَأَطِيعُونِ ١٥٠ وَلَا تُطِيعُوا
أَمْرَ الْمُسْرِفِينَ ١٥١ الَّذِينَ يُفْسِدُونَ فِي
الْأَرْضِ وَلَا يُصْلِحُونَ ١٥٢ قَالُوا إِنَّمَا أَنتَ

and peace).'
153. They said, 'You are merely one of those (mortals) who are (dependent on being) given food.
154. 'You are nothing but a human being like ourselves. So bring (us) a sign if you are of the truthful.'
155. (Sâli<u>h</u>) said, 'Here is a she-camel. She will have her share of water (at the watercourse), while you will have your share of water at a time appointed (for you).
156. 'And you shall do her no harm otherwise the punishment of an awful day shall befall you.'
157. Notwithstanding (all this warning) they hamstrung her and then they became regretful.
158. Consequently (the threatened) punishment overtook them. Behold! There is a remarkably great sign in this (episode); yet most of them would not be believers.
159. And indeed your Lord, He is the All-Mighty, the Ever Merciful.

SECTION 9

160. AND the people of Lot cried lies to the Messengers.
161. (Recall the time) when their kinsman Lot said to them, 'Will you not guard against evil?
162. 'Verily, I am to you a Messenger, faithful to (my) trust.
163. 'So take Allâh as a shield and obey me.
164. 'And I ask no reward from you for this (service I render). My reward lies with the Lord of the worlds alone.
165. '(Is it not true that) of all people you alone approach males (for sexual satisfaction),
166. 'And leave that (abode of love) which your Lord has created for you in your wives. 'Nay, (the real fact is) you are a people who know no limits.'
167. They said, 'If you desist not (of admonishing us for sodomy) O Lot! You shall indeed be of the banished ones.'

مِنَ الْمُسَحَّرِينَ ﴿١٥٣﴾ مَا أَنْتَ إِلَّا بَشَرٌ مِّثْلُنَا
فَأْتِ بِآيَةٍ إِنْ كُنْتَ مِنَ الصّٰدِقِينَ ﴿١٥٤﴾ قَالَ
هٰذِهِ نَاقَةٌ لَّهَا شِرْبٌ وَّلَكُمْ شِرْبُ يَوْمٍ
مَّعْلُومٍ ﴿١٥٥﴾ وَلَا تَمَسُّوهَا بِسُوٓءٍ فَيَأْخُذَكُمْ
عَذَابُ يَوْمٍ عَظِيمٍ ﴿١٥٦﴾ فَعَقَرُوهَا فَأَصْبَحُوا نٰدِمِينَ ﴿١٥٧﴾
فَأَخَذَهُمُ الْعَذَابُ إِنَّ فِي ذٰلِكَ لَأٰيَةً وَمَا
كَانَ أَكْثَرُهُم مُّؤْمِنِينَ ﴿١٥٨﴾ وَإِنَّ رَبَّكَ لَهُوَ
الْعَزِيزُ الرَّحِيمُ ﴿١٥٩﴾ كَذَّبَتْ قَوْمُ لُوطٍ الْمُرْسَلِينَ ﴿١٦٠﴾
إِذْ قَالَ لَهُمْ أَخُوهُمْ لُوطٌ أَلَا تَتَّقُونَ ﴿١٦١﴾ إِنِّي
لَكُمْ رَسُولٌ أَمِينٌ ﴿١٦٢﴾ فَاتَّقُوا اللّٰهَ وَأَطِيعُونِ ﴿١٦٣﴾
وَمَا أَسْـَٔلُكُمْ عَلَيْهِ مِنْ أَجْرٍ إِنْ أَجْرِيَ
إِلَّا عَلٰى رَبِّ الْعٰلَمِينَ ﴿١٦٤﴾ أَتَأْتُونَ الذُّكْرَانَ
مِنَ الْعٰلَمِينَ ﴿١٦٥﴾ وَتَذَرُونَ مَا خَلَقَ لَكُمْ رَبُّكُم
مِّنْ أَزْوٰجِكُم بَلْ أَنْتُمْ قَوْمٌ عَادُونَ ﴿١٦٦﴾ قَالُوا
لَئِن لَّمْ تَنْتَهِ يٰلُوطُ لَتَكُونَنَّ مِنَ الْمُخْرَجِينَ ﴿١٦٧﴾

168. He said, ‘I surely abhor your practice (of going to males),
169. ‘My Lord! Save me and my followers from (the evil consequences) of their deeds.’
170. So We saved him and his followers, all of them,
171. Except an old woman (- wife of Lot), who was among those who stayed behind,
172. Then We destroyed the others.
173. And We pelted them with a terrible rain (of stones). Look! How terrible was the rain (that descended) upon those who were warned.
174. There is a great sign in this (episode), yet most of them would not be believers.
175. And indeed your Lord, He is the All-Mighty, the Ever Merciful.

SECTION 10

176. THE dwellers of the Wood (in Midian) cried lies to the Messengers.
177. (Recall) when Shu‘aib said to them, ‘Will you not guard against evil?
178. ‘Indeed, I am to you a Messenger, faithful to (my) trust.
179. ‘Therefore take Allâh for (your) shield and obey me.
180. ‘And I ask no reward from you for it (- the services I render). Surely, my reward lies with the Lord of the worlds alone.
181. ‘Give full measure and be not of those who give short;
182. ‘And weigh with even and balanced scales.
183. ‘And do not defraud people of their things. Do not go about acting corruptly, creating disorder in the country.
184. ‘Take Him Who has created you and former generations as a shield.’
185. They said, ‘You are simply of those who stand in need of being given food.
186. ‘And you are but a human being like ourselves; as a matter of fact we believe you to be of the liars.
187. ‘So let a fragment of the cloud fall upon

قَالَ إِنِّي لِعَمَلِكُم مِّنَ الْقَالِينَ ﴿١٦٨﴾ رَبِّ نَجِّنِي
وَأَهْلِي مِمَّا يَعْمَلُونَ ﴿١٦٩﴾ فَنَجَّيْنَٰهُ وَأَهْلَهُۥٓ أَجْمَعِينَ ﴿١٧٠﴾
إِلَّا عَجُوزًا فِي الْغَٰبِرِينَ ﴿١٧١﴾ ثُمَّ دَمَّرْنَا الْأٓخَرِينَ ﴿١٧٢﴾
وَأَمْطَرْنَا عَلَيْهِم مَّطَرًا فَسَآءَ مَطَرُ الْمُنذَرِينَ ﴿١٧٣﴾
إِنَّ فِي ذَٰلِكَ لَأٓيَةً وَمَا كَانَ أَكْثَرُهُم
مُّؤْمِنِينَ ﴿١٧٤﴾ وَإِنَّ رَبَّكَ لَهُوَ الْعَزِيزُ الرَّحِيمُ ﴿١٧٥﴾
كَذَّبَ أَصْحَٰبُ لْـَٔيْكَةِ الْمُرْسَلِينَ ﴿١٧٦﴾ إِذْ قَالَ
لَهُمْ شُعَيْبٌ أَلَا تَتَّقُونَ ﴿١٧٧﴾ إِنِّي لَكُمْ رَسُولٌ
أَمِينٌ ﴿١٧٨﴾ فَاتَّقُوا اللَّهَ وَأَطِيعُونِ ﴿١٧٩﴾ وَمَآ أَسْـَٔلُكُمْ
عَلَيْهِ مِنْ أَجْرٍ إِنْ أَجْرِيَ إِلَّا عَلَىٰ رَبِّ
الْعَٰلَمِينَ ﴿١٨٠﴾ أَوْفُوا الْكَيْلَ وَلَا تَكُونُوا مِنَ
الْمُخْسِرِينَ ﴿١٨١﴾ وَزِنُوا بِالْقِسْطَاسِ الْمُسْتَقِيمِ ﴿١٨٢﴾
وَلَا تَبْخَسُوا النَّاسَ أَشْيَآءَهُمْ وَلَا تَعْثَوْا فِي
الْأَرْضِ مُفْسِدِينَ ﴿١٨٣﴾ وَاتَّقُوا الَّذِي خَلَقَكُمْ
وَالْجِبِلَّةَ الْأَوَّلِينَ ﴿١٨٤﴾ قَالُوٓا إِنَّمَآ أَنتَ مِنَ
الْمُسَحَّرِينَ ﴿١٨٥﴾ وَمَآ أَنتَ إِلَّا بَشَرٌ مِّثْلُنَا
وَإِن نَّظُنُّكَ لَمِنَ الْكَٰذِبِينَ ﴿١٨٦﴾ فَأَسْقِطْ عَلَيْنَا

us (by way of punishment) if you are of the truthful.’

188. (Shu‘aib thereupon) said, ‘My Lord knows best all that you do.’

189. Yet they cried him lies, so the punishment of the gloomy day with dark overshadowing clouds overtook them; it was indeed the punishment of an awful day.

190. Behold! There is a great sign in this (episode), yet most of them would not be believers.

191. Though in fact your Lord, He is the All-Mighty, the Ever Merciful.

SECTION 11

192. **A**ND verily this (Qur’ân) is a revelation from the Lord of the worlds.

193. The Spirit, Faithful to the Trust (- Gabriel) has descended with it.

194. (Revealing it) to your heart with the result that you became of the Warners (- a Prophet of God);

195. (The Qur’ân has been revealed) in plain and clear Arabic language.

196. Verily, it (is the Book which) finds mention in the Scriptures of the earlier peoples.

197. Is it not a sufficient proof for them that the learned among the Children of Israel recognize it (- the Qur’ân)?

198. And if We had revealed it to one of the non-Arabs,

199. And he had recited this (eloquent word of God in Arabic) to them, (even then) they would never have believed in it.

200. That is how We cause it (- the disbelief) take root in the hearts of those who cut off their ties (with God),

201. (That) they will not believe in it until they see the grievous punishment.

202. So this (punishment) will come upon them all of a sudden (taking them unaware), while they do not perceive (and calculate it).

203. They will say then, ‘Shall we be given

كِسَفًا مِّنَ السَّمَآءِ إِن كُنتَ مِنَ الصّٰدِقِينَ ﴿١٨٧﴾
قَالَ رَبِّيٓ أَعْلَمُ بِمَا تَعْمَلُونَ ﴿١٨٨﴾ فَكَذَّبُوهُ
فَأَخَذَهُمْ عَذَابُ يَوْمِ الظُّلَّةِ إِنَّهُۥ كَانَ
عَذَابَ يَوْمٍ عَظِيمٍ ﴿١٨٩﴾ إِنَّ فِي ذٰلِكَ لَأٰيَةً
وَمَا كَانَ أَكْثَرُهُم مُّؤْمِنِينَ ﴿١٩٠﴾ وَإِنَّ رَبَّكَ
لَهُوَ الْعَزِيزُ الرَّحِيمُ ﴿١٩١﴾ وَإِنَّهُۥ لَتَنزِيلُ رَبِّ
الْعٰلَمِينَ ﴿١٩٢﴾ نَزَلَ بِهِ الرُّوحُ الْأَمِينُ ﴿١٩٣﴾ عَلٰى
قَلْبِكَ لِتَكُونَ مِنَ الْمُنذِرِينَ ﴿١٩٤﴾ بِلِسَانٍ عَرَبِيٍّ
مُّبِينٍ ﴿١٩٥﴾ وَإِنَّهُۥ لَفِي زُبُرِ الْأَوَّلِينَ ﴿١٩٦﴾ أَوَلَمْ
يَكُن لَّهُمْ ءَايَةً أَن يَعْلَمَهُۥ عُلَمٰٓؤُا بَنِيٓ
إِسْرٰٓءِيلَ ﴿١٩٧﴾ وَلَوْ نَزَّلْنٰهُ عَلٰى بَعْضِ الْأَعْجَمِينَ ﴿١٩٨﴾
فَقَرَأَهُۥ عَلَيْهِم مَّا كَانُوا بِهِ مُؤْمِنِينَ ﴿١٩٩﴾ كَذٰلِكَ
سَلَكْنٰهُ فِي قُلُوبِ الْمُجْرِمِينَ ﴿٢٠٠﴾ لَا يُؤْمِنُونَ
بِهِ حَتّٰى يَرَوُا الْعَذَابَ الْأَلِيمَ ﴿٢٠١﴾ فَيَأْتِيَهُم
بَغْتَةً وَهُمْ لَا يَشْعُرُونَ ﴿٢٠٢﴾ فَيَقُولُوا هَلْ نَحْنُ

some respite?'
204. Is that why they seek to expedite Our punishment?
205. Do you not see that even if We let them enjoy (worldly bounties) for some more years,
206. And then that (punishment) with which they are threatened befalls them;
207. That (respite) which they were allowed to enjoy will be of no avail to them?
208. And never did We destroy (any people of) a township but it had (its) Warners;
209. So that they may be admonished and We are never unjust.
210. It was not the evil ones who have brought this (Qur'ân) down.
211. It does neither suit them nor have they the power (to reveal it).
212. In fact, they (- the evil ones) are precluded from listening (to the Divine revelation).
213. Therefore call on no god beside Allâh, for (if you do) you will become of those who are (severely) punished.
214. And (Prophet!) warn your nearest kinsmen,
215. And be gentle and affectionate to the believers who follow you.
216. But if they (- your kinsmen) disobey you, say (to them), 'Surely, I am not responsible for what you do.'
217. And put your trust in the All-Mighty, the Ever Merciful (God),
218. Who sees you (at the time) when you stand up (in Prayer, and also for calling the people to the right path).
219. And (Who sees) your moving about among those (Companions) who prostrate themselves (before the All-Mighty Lord).
220. Verily, He is the All-Hearing, the All-Knowing
221. Shall I tell you to whom the evil ones appear?
222. They appear to every habitual and hardened liar (and) great sinner;
223. Who listen eagerly (to what the evil ones

سُورَةُ الشُّعَرَاءِ ٢٦

مُنظَرُونَ ۝٢٠٣ أَفَبِعَذَابِنَا يَسْتَعْجِلُونَ ۝٢٠٤ أَفَرَءَيْتَ
إِن مَّتَّعْنَٰهُمْ سِنِينَ ۝٢٠٥ ثُمَّ جَآءَهُم مَّا كَانُوا
يُوعَدُونَ ۝٢٠٦ مَآ أَغْنَىٰ عَنْهُم مَّا كَانُوا يُمَتَّعُونَ ۝٢٠٧
وَمَآ أَهْلَكْنَا مِن قَرْيَةٍ إِلَّا لَهَا مُنذِرُونَ ۝٢٠٨
ذِكْرَىٰ وَمَا كُنَّا ظَٰلِمِينَ ۝٢٠٩ وَمَا تَنَزَّلَتْ بِهِ
الشَّيَٰطِينُ ۝٢١٠ وَمَا يَنۢبَغِي لَهُمْ وَمَا يَسْتَطِيعُونَ ۝٢١١
إِنَّهُمْ عَنِ السَّمْعِ لَمَعْزُولُونَ ۝٢١٢ فَلَا تَدْعُ مَعَ
اللَّهِ إِلَٰهًا ءَاخَرَ فَتَكُونَ مِنَ الْمُعَذَّبِينَ ۝٢١٣
وَأَنذِرْ عَشِيرَتَكَ الْأَقْرَبِينَ ۝٢١٤ وَاخْفِضْ جَنَاحَكَ
لِمَنِ اتَّبَعَكَ مِنَ الْمُؤْمِنِينَ ۝٢١٥ فَإِنْ عَصَوْكَ
فَقُلْ إِنِّي بَرِيٓءٌ مِّمَّا تَعْمَلُونَ ۝٢١٦ وَتَوَكَّلْ عَلَى
الْعَزِيزِ الرَّحِيمِ ۝٢١٧ الَّذِي يَرَىٰكَ حِينَ تَقُومُ ۝٢١٨
وَتَقَلُّبَكَ فِي السَّٰجِدِينَ ۝٢١٩ إِنَّهُۥ هُوَ السَّمِيعُ
الْعَلِيمُ ۝٢٢٠ هَلْ أُنَبِّئُكُمْ عَلَىٰ مَن تَنَزَّلُ
الشَّيَٰطِينُ ۝٢٢١ تَنَزَّلُ عَلَىٰ كُلِّ أَفَّاكٍ أَثِيمٍ ۝٢٢٢ يُلْقُونَ

say), yet mostly they tell them lies.
224. And (as for) the poets, it is the erring ones who follow them.
225. Do you not see how they wander distracted in every valley,
226. And they say (such things) which they do not practice (themselves),
227. Except those (poets) who believe and do deeds of righteousness and who mention the greatness of Allâh over and over again and who retaliate (and defend themselves) only after they are done injustice to. Behold! Those who acted unjustly will soon know to what (a wretched) end they are heading for.

السَّمْعَ وَ أَكْثَرُهُمْ كٰذِبُونَ ﴿٢٢٣﴾ وَ الشُّعَرَاءُ يَتَّبِعُهُمُ
الْغَاوٗنَ ﴿٢٢٤﴾ أَلَمْ تَرَ أَنَّهُمْ فِي كُلِّ وَادٍ يَهِيمُونَ ﴿٢٢٥﴾
وَ أَنَّهُمْ يَقُولُونَ مَا لَا يَفْعَلُونَ ﴿٢٢٦﴾ إِلَّا الَّذِينَ
أٰمَنُوا وَ عَمِلُوا الصّٰلِحٰتِ وَ ذَكَرُوا اللّٰهَ كَثِيرًا
وَّ انْتَصَرُوا مِنْ بَعْدِ مَا ظُلِمُوا وَ سَيَعْلَمُ
الَّذِينَ ظَلَمُوا أَيَّ مُنْقَلَبٍ يَنْقَلِبُونَ ﴿٢٢٧﴾

CHAPTER
27

AL-NAML
(The Tribe of Naml)
(Revealed before Hijrah)

سُورَةُ النَّمْلِ مَكِّيَّةٌ

With the name of Allâh,
the Most Gracious, the Ever Merciful
(I commence to read Sûrah Al-Naml).

بِسْمِ اللّٰهِ الرَّحْمٰنِ الرَّحِيمِ

1. TÂ SÎN - I am the Benign, the All-Hearing (God). These are the verses of the Qur'ân, of the Book that tells the right from the wrong and makes (the truth) manifest.
2. (It is) a guidance and good tidings to the believers;
3. Who observe Prayer and (regularly) spend in charity and who are such people as have firm faith in the Hereafter.
4. (As to those) who do not believe in the

طسٓ تِلْكَ أٰيٰتُ الْقُرْأٰنِ وَ كِتَابٍ مُّبِينٍ ﴿١﴾
هُدًى وَّ بُشْرٰى لِلْمُؤْمِنِينَ ﴿٢﴾ الَّذِينَ
يُقِيمُونَ الصَّلٰوةَ وَ يُؤْتُونَ الزَّكٰوةَ وَ هُمْ
بِالْأٰخِرَةِ هُمْ يُوقِنُونَ ﴿٣﴾ إِنَّ الَّذِينَ لَا يُؤْمِنُونَ

Hereafter We had made their deeds (they ought to do) fair-seeming to them, but they wander on aimlessly (making all sorts of blunders).
5. It is they for whom there awaits a grievous punishment. It is these alone who shall be the greatest losers in the Hereafter.
6. And as a matter of fact you are being made to learn the Qur'ân from the presence of the All-Wise, the All-Knowing (God).
7. (Recall) when Moses said to his companions, 'Surely I see with feelings of warmth, of love, something like a fire. I will soon bring you some important information from there or at least bring you a flaming brand so that you may warm yourselves.'
8. So when he came (close) to it (- the fire) he was called by a voice, 'Blessed be he who is in quest of the fire (of Divine light) and blessed are those around this (place of the fire), Holy is Allâh, the Lord of the worlds.
9. 'O Moses! The fact is that I am Allâh, the All-Mighty, the All-Wise.
10. 'And put down your staff (on the ground).' When (Moses put down his staff) he saw it shifting about as if it were a tiny serpent with quick movements, he turned his back retreating and did not look behind. (Whereupon We said,) 'O Moses! Do not fear. Verily, I am the One in Whose presence the Messengers need have no fear.
11. 'Nor (does he fear) who acts unjustly and commits some evil deed and then changes over to good after giving up evil. I am to such a person a Great Protector, Ever Merciful, indeed.
12. 'And put your hand into your bosom, it will come forth (sparkling) white without any disease. (These are two signs) from among the nine signs (which you shall show) to Pharaoh and his people. They are truly a rebellious people.'
13. But when Our eye-opening signs were shown to them (- Pharaoh and his people) they said, 'This is plain witchcraft (to cause

بِالْأٰخِرَةِ زَيَّنَّا لَهُمْ أَعْمَٰلَهُمْ فَهُمْ يَعْمَهُونَ ٤
أُولَٰٓئِكَ الَّذِينَ لَهُمْ سُوٓءُ الْعَذَابِ وَهُمْ فِي
الْأٰخِرَةِ هُمُ الْأَخْسَرُونَ ٥ وَإِنَّكَ لَتُلَقَّى
الْقُرْءَانَ مِن لَّدُنْ حَكِيمٍ عَلِيمٍ ٦ إِذْ قَالَ
مُوسَىٰ لِأَهْلِهِۦٓ إِنِّيٓ ءَانَسْتُ نَارًا سَـَٔاتِيكُم
مِّنْهَا بِخَبَرٍ أَوْ ءَاتِيكُم بِشِهَابٍ قَبَسٍ لَّعَلَّكُمْ
تَصْطَلُونَ ٧ فَلَمَّا جَآءَهَا نُودِيَ أَن بُورِكَ مَن
فِي النَّارِ وَمَنْ حَوْلَهَا وَسُبْحَٰنَ اللَّهِ رَبِّ
الْعَٰلَمِينَ ٨ يَٰمُوسَىٰٓ إِنَّهُۥٓ أَنَا اللَّهُ الْعَزِيزُ الْحَكِيمُ ٩
وَأَلْقِ عَصَاكَ فَلَمَّا رَءَاهَا تَهْتَزُّ كَأَنَّهَا جَآنٌّ وَلَّىٰ
مُدْبِرًا وَلَمْ يُعَقِّبْ يَٰمُوسَىٰ لَا تَخَفْ إِنِّي لَا
يَخَافُ لَدَيَّ الْمُرْسَلُونَ ١٠ إِلَّا مَن ظَلَمَ ثُمَّ بَدَّلَ
حُسْنًا بَعْدَ سُوٓءٍ فَإِنِّي غَفُورٌ رَّحِيمٌ ١١ وَأَدْخِلْ
يَدَكَ فِي جَيْبِكَ تَخْرُجْ بَيْضَآءَ مِنْ غَيْرِ
سُوٓءٍ فِي تِسْعِ ءَايَٰتٍ إِلَىٰ فِرْعَوْنَ وَقَوْمِهِۦٓ إِنَّهُمْ
كَانُوا قَوْمًا فَٰسِقِينَ ١٢ فَلَمَّا جَآءَتْهُمْ ءَايَٰتُنَا

disruption among the people).'

14. And they strongly rejected them (- the signs) out of spite and arrogance, although their minds were convinced of (the truth in) them. Look, then how (evil) was the end of those who acted corruptly.

سورة النمل ٢٧

SECTION 2

15. **A**ND We granted knowledge to David and Solomon, and they said, 'All true and perfect praise belongs to Allâh alone Who has exalted us over many of His believing servants.'

16. And Solomon succeeded David and he said, 'O you people! We have been taught the language of the birds (and also the technique of horsemanship), and bestowed with everything (essential for us). This indeed is a distinct favour (of God and His grace).'

17. And there were gathered together before Solomon his hosts comprising of *jinn* (- haughty) and (ordinary) men and birds and swift footed horses, and they were then arranged in separate well-disciplined columns.

18. (Once he was marching with them) until when they (his armies) reached the valley of (the tribe named) al-Naml, a distinguished Namlite said, 'O al-Naml! Get into your habitations lest Solomon and his hosts should crush you unknowingly.'

19. Thereupon he (- Solomon) wondered and was pleased with (the good opinion the Namlite expressed about his own and his army's power and piety) and said (praying), 'My Lord! Rouse me up that I may offer thanks for the favours You have shown me and my forefathers and that I should do such deeds as are righteous and may please You, and count me through Your mercy with Your righteous servants.'

20. And (once) he reviewed the birds and the (cavalry of) swift running horses and said, 'How is it that I do not see (my officer named) Hudhud? Is he deliberately absent?

21. 'I will certainly punish him very severely,

مُبْصِرَةً قَالُوا هَٰذَا سِحْرٌ مُّبِينٌ ﴿١٣﴾ وَجَحَدُوا
بِهَا وَاسْتَيْقَنَتْهَا أَنفُسُهُمْ ظُلْمًا وَعُلُوًّا فَانظُرْ
كَيْفَ كَانَ عَاقِبَةُ الْمُفْسِدِينَ ﴿١٤﴾ وَلَقَدْ آتَيْنَا
دَاوُدَ وَسُلَيْمَٰنَ عِلْمًا وَقَالَا الْحَمْدُ لِلَّهِ
الَّذِي فَضَّلَنَا عَلَىٰ كَثِيرٍ مِّنْ عِبَادِهِ الْمُؤْمِنِينَ ﴿١٥﴾
وَوَرِثَ سُلَيْمَٰنُ دَاوُدَ وَقَالَ يَٰأَيُّهَا النَّاسُ
عُلِّمْنَا مَنطِقَ الطَّيْرِ وَأُوتِينَا مِن كُلِّ شَيْءٍ
إِنَّ هَٰذَا لَهُوَ الْفَضْلُ الْمُبِينُ ﴿١٦﴾ وَحُشِرَ
لِسُلَيْمَٰنَ جُنُودُهُ مِنَ الْجِنِّ وَالْإِنسِ
وَالطَّيْرِ فَهُمْ يُوزَعُونَ ﴿١٧﴾ حَتَّىٰ إِذَا أَتَوْا عَلَىٰ وَادِ
النَّمْلِ قَالَتْ نَمْلَةٌ يَٰأَيُّهَا النَّمْلُ ادْخُلُوا
مَسَٰكِنَكُمْ لَا يَحْطِمَنَّكُمْ سُلَيْمَٰنُ وَجُنُودُهُ
وَهُمْ لَا يَشْعُرُونَ ﴿١٨﴾ فَتَبَسَّمَ ضَاحِكًا مِّن
قَوْلِهَا وَقَالَ رَبِّ أَوْزِعْنِي أَنْ أَشْكُرَ نِعْمَتَكَ
الَّتِي أَنْعَمْتَ عَلَيَّ وَعَلَىٰ وَٰلِدَيَّ وَأَنْ أَعْمَلَ
صَٰلِحًا تَرْضَىٰهُ وَأَدْخِلْنِي بِرَحْمَتِكَ فِي عِبَادِكَ
الصَّٰلِحِينَ ﴿١٩﴾ وَتَفَقَّدَ الطَّيْرَ فَقَالَ مَا لِيَ لَا أَرَى

ع ٤
١٦

الجزء التاسع عشر

rather I will execute him or else he must give me some valid excuse (for remaining absent).

22. But he (- Solomon) had not to wait long (before Hudhud came) and said, 'I have acquired that information which you do not possess. I have come to you from (the territory of a Yemanite tribe) Saba' with sure and important news (to tell).

23. 'I found (there) a (wonderful) woman ruling over them (- the Sabaeans) and she has been given everything (she requires) and owns a magnificent throne.

24. 'I (also) found her and her people worshipping the sun instead of Allâh. And satan has made their deeds fair-seeming to them (so that they take pride in their practices), and has thus hindered them from the right way, so that they do not follow true guidance.

25. 'And (satan has done this) so that they do not worship Allâh while Allâh is He Who brings to light all that lies hidden in the heavens and the earth and knows all that you (O people!) conceal (in your minds) and all that you make known (of your designs).

26. 'Allâh! There is no other, cannot be and will never be one worthy of worship but He, the Lord of the Mighty Throne.'

[PROSTRATION]

27. (Thereupon Solomon) said, 'We will now look into it and see whether you have spoken the truth or whether you are of the liars.

28. 'Take this letter of mine, deliver it to them (-the people of Saba') then withdraw from them and wait what (answer) they make in return,

29. (When the Queen saw the letter) she said, 'Chieftains! There has been delivered to me a noble letter.

30. 'It is from Solomon and it says, "With the name of Allâh, the Most Gracious, the Ever Merciful (I commence to write to you).

31. "Do not rise up against me but come to me

الْهُدْهُدَ أَمْ كَانَ مِنَ الْغَائِبِينَ ﴿٢٠﴾ لَأُعَذِّبَنَّهُ
عَذَابًا شَدِيدًا أَوْ لَأَذْبَحَنَّهُ أَوْ لَيَأْتِيَنِّي
بِسُلْطَانٍ مُبِينٍ ﴿٢١﴾ فَمَكَثَ غَيْرَ بَعِيدٍ فَقَالَ
أَحَطتُ بِمَا لَمْ تُحِطْ بِهِ وَجِئْتُكَ مِنْ سَبَإٍ
بِنَبَإٍ يَقِينٍ ﴿٢٢﴾ إِنِّي وَجَدتُّ امْرَأَةً تَمْلِكُهُمْ
وَأُوتِيَتْ مِنْ كُلِّ شَيْءٍ وَلَهَا عَرْشٌ عَظِيمٌ ﴿٢٣﴾
وَجَدتُّهَا وَقَوْمَهَا يَسْجُدُونَ لِلشَّمْسِ مِنْ
دُونِ اللَّهِ وَزَيَّنَ لَهُمُ الشَّيْطَانُ أَعْمَالَهُمْ
فَصَدَّهُمْ عَنِ السَّبِيلِ فَهُمْ لَا يَهْتَدُونَ ﴿٢٤﴾
أَلَّا يَسْجُدُوا لِلَّهِ الَّذِي يُخْرِجُ الْخَبْءَ فِي
السَّمَاوَاتِ وَالْأَرْضِ وَيَعْلَمُ مَا تُخْفُونَ وَمَا
تُعْلِنُونَ ﴿٢٥﴾ اللَّهُ لَا إِلَٰهَ إِلَّا هُوَ رَبُّ الْعَرْشِ
الْعَظِيمِ ۩ ﴿٢٦﴾ قَالَ سَنَنظُرُ أَصَدَقْتَ أَمْ كُنتَ
مِنَ الْكَاذِبِينَ ﴿٢٧﴾ اذْهَب بِّكِتَابِي هَٰذَا فَأَلْقِهْ
إِلَيْهِمْ ثُمَّ تَوَلَّ عَنْهُمْ فَانظُرْ مَاذَا يَرْجِعُونَ ﴿٢٨﴾
قَالَتْ يَا أَيُّهَا الْمَلَأُ إِنِّي أُلْقِيَ إِلَيَّ كِتَابٌ كَرِيمٌ ﴿٢٩﴾
إِنَّهُ مِن سُلَيْمَانَ وَإِنَّهُ بِسْمِ اللَّهِ الرَّحْمَٰنِ

(surrendering yourselves) in submission".'

SECTION 3

32. **S**HE said, 'Chieftains! Give me your sound and mature advice in the matter which confronts me, (for) I decide no important matter except when you are present with me (to advise).'

33. They said, 'We are a people possessing (extraordinary) power and are gallant fighters; but as for the decision it rests with you, therefore you may thoroughly consider what order you want to give.'

34. She said, 'Surely, when the kings enter a township (as invaders) they ruin it and reduce its most honourable residents to the most degraded positions. And such indeed will be their (- of Solomon and his men's) ways.

35. 'I am going to send them a (significant) gift and shall wait to see what (answer) the envoys bring back.'

36. So when he (- the Queen's envoy) came (with the present) to Solomon he (- Solomon) said, 'Do you mean to help me with (your) wealth? Well, what Allâh has given me is far better than what He has given you. You seem to be rather proud of your gift.

37. 'Go back to them (and tell your people that), we shall certainly come down upon them with hosts they have no power to withstand and we shall, surely, drive them out from there (- their country) disgraced, while they are subjugated?'

38. (Later on addressing his courtiers Solomon) said, 'Nobles! Which one of you will bring me a throne befitting her (- the Queen) before they come to me surrendering in submission.'

39. A stalwart from among the *jinn* said, 'I will bring it to you (prepared as you desire), before you rise and depart from your place of encampment. Surely, I am strong and expert enough (to accomplish this task and can be) trusted (with it).'

سُورَةُ النَّمْلِ ٢٧

الرَّحِيمِ ﴿٣٠﴾ أَلَّا تَعْلُوا عَلَيَّ وَأْتُونِي مُسْلِمِينَ ﴿٣١﴾
قَالَتْ يَأَيُّهَا الْمَلَؤُا أَفْتُونِي فِي أَمْرِي مَا كُنتُ
قَاطِعَةً أَمْرًا حَتَّى تَشْهَدُونِ ﴿٣٢﴾ قَالُوا نَحْنُ
أُولُوا قُوَّةٍ وَأُولُوا بَأْسٍ شَدِيدٍ وَالْأَمْرُ
إِلَيْكِ فَانظُرِي مَاذَا تَأْمُرِينَ ﴿٣٣﴾ قَالَتْ إِنَّ
الْمُلُوكَ إِذَا دَخَلُوا قَرْيَةً أَفْسَدُوهَا وَجَعَلُوا
أَعِزَّةَ أَهْلِهَا أَذِلَّةً وَكَذَٰلِكَ يَفْعَلُونَ ﴿٣٤﴾ وَإِنِّي
مُرْسِلَةٌ إِلَيْهِم بِهَدِيَّةٍ فَنَاظِرَةٌ بِمَ يَرْجِعُ
الْمُرْسَلُونَ ﴿٣٥﴾ فَلَمَّا جَاءَ سُلَيْمَٰنَ قَالَ أَتُمِدُّونَنِ
بِمَالٍ فَمَا آتَانِيَ اللَّهُ خَيْرٌ مِّمَّا آتَاكُم
بَلْ أَنتُم بِهَدِيَّتِكُمْ تَفْرَحُونَ ﴿٣٦﴾ ارْجِعْ إِلَيْهِمْ
فَلَنَأْتِيَنَّهُم بِجُنُودٍ لَّا قِبَلَ لَهُم بِهَا وَلَنُخْرِجَنَّهُم
مِّنْهَا أَذِلَّةً وَهُمْ صَاغِرُونَ ﴿٣٧﴾ قَالَ يَأَيُّهَا
الْمَلَؤُا أَيُّكُمْ يَأْتِينِي بِعَرْشِهَا قَبْلَ أَن يَأْتُونِي
مُسْلِمِينَ ﴿٣٨﴾ قَالَ عِفْرِيتٌ مِّنَ الْجِنِّ أَنَا
آتِيكَ بِهِ قَبْلَ أَن تَقُومَ مِن مَّقَامِكَ
وَإِنِّي عَلَيْهِ لَقَوِيٌّ أَمِينٌ ﴿٣٩﴾ قَالَ الَّذِي عِندَهُ

الْجُزْءُ التَّاسِعَ عَشَرَ

40. One (Israelite) who had knowledge of the Scripture said, 'I will bring it to you before your Yemanite (noble guests) come to you.' And when he (- Solomon) saw it (- the throne) set before him he said, 'This is due to the grace of my Lord; so that He may reveal my inner self to show whether I am grateful (for all His favours) or ungrateful. Indeed, he who thanks, his thanksgiving is for his own good, and he who shows ingratitude (let him remember that) My Lord is truly Self-Sufficient (and is in need of no praise), Oft-Generous (and Noble in His own right).'

41. He (further) said, 'Make her own (old) throne seem discredited to her (in her own estimation by making this new throne of a very excellent standard). We shall see (thereby) whether she follows the right way (by discarding her old idolatrous throne) or whether she is (one) of those who do not follow the right way.'

42. When she came (to Solomon) it was said to her, 'Is your throne like this?' She said, 'It is as though it were much the same. We had been given the knowledge (about your excellence and perfection) before this and we have already surrendered in submission (to you).'

43. And (Solomon) held her back from the things she used to worship apart from Allâh, for she belonged to an unbelieving people.

44. It was said to her, 'Enter the palace.' And when she saw it she took it for a great expanse of water. She was greatly perturbed. (Solomon) said, 'It is a palace paved smooth with slabs of glass.' She (realizing the truth that she worshipped outward objects like the sun in place of Reality, the true God,) said, 'My Lord! I have done injustice to myself and (now) I submit myself through Solomon to Allâh, the Lord of the worlds.'

SECTION 4

45. **A**ND (likewise) We sent to Thamûd their

عِلْمٌ مِّنَ الْكِتٰبِ أَنَا اٰتِيكَ بِهٖ قَبْلَ أَنْ
يَّرْتَدَّ إِلَيْكَ طَرْفُكَ ۚ فَلَمَّا رَاٰهُ مُسْتَقِرًّا عِنْدَهٗ
قَالَ هٰذَا مِنْ فَضْلِ رَبِّيْ ۗ لِيَبْلُوَنِيْٓ ءَأَشْكُرُ
أَمْ أَكْفُرُ ۗ وَمَنْ شَكَرَ فَإِنَّمَا يَشْكُرُ
لِنَفْسِهٖ ۚ وَمَنْ كَفَرَ فَإِنَّ رَبِّيْ غَنِيٌّ كَرِيْمٌ ﴿٤٠﴾
قَالَ نَكِّرُوْا لَهَا عَرْشَهَا نَنْظُرْ أَتَهْتَدِيْٓ أَمْ
تَكُوْنُ مِنَ الَّذِيْنَ لَا يَهْتَدُوْنَ ﴿٤١﴾ فَلَمَّا جَآءَتْ
قِيْلَ أَهٰكَذَا عَرْشُكِ ۗ قَالَتْ كَأَنَّهٗ هُوَ ۚ
وَأُوْتِيْنَا الْعِلْمَ مِنْ قَبْلِهَا وَكُنَّا مُسْلِمِيْنَ ﴿٤٢﴾
وَصَدَّهَا مَا كَانَتْ تَّعْبُدُ مِنْ دُوْنِ اللّٰهِ ۗ
إِنَّهَا كَانَتْ مِنْ قَوْمٍ كٰفِرِيْنَ ﴿٤٣﴾ قِيْلَ لَهَا
ادْخُلِي الصَّرْحَ ۚ فَلَمَّا رَأَتْهُ حَسِبَتْهُ لُجَّةً
وَّكَشَفَتْ عَنْ سَاقَيْهَا ۗ قَالَ إِنَّهٗ صَرْحٌ
مُّمَرَّدٌ مِّنْ قَوَارِيْرَ ۗ قَالَتْ رَبِّ إِنِّيْ ظَلَمْتُ
نَفْسِيْ وَأَسْلَمْتُ مَعَ سُلَيْمٰنَ لِلّٰهِ رَبِّ
الْعٰلَمِيْنَ ﴿٤٤﴾ وَلَقَدْ أَرْسَلْنَآ إِلٰى ثَمُوْدَ أَخَاهُمْ
صٰلِحًا أَنِ اعْبُدُوا اللّٰهَ فَإِذَا هُمْ فَرِيْقٰنِ

ع ٣ ١٨

kinsman Sâlih, (who said), 'Worship Allâh.' But (as soon as they heard this preaching) they broke up into two factions who contended with each another.

46. He said, 'O my people! Why do you seek to hasten on evil, rather than good, (and you ask for a sign of destruction instead of that of bliss for you)? Why do you not ask for Allâh's protection so that you may be shown mercy?'

47. They said, 'We have suffered due to you and your companions.' (Sâlih) said, 'Your deeds and true cause of your sufferings is with Allâh (Who is punishing you for your evil deeds). Nay, you are a people who are being tried (to distinguish the good of you from the bad).

48. And there were in the city a gang of nine (persons) who had upset the order and peace in the country and would not reform (themselves).

49. They said one to another, 'Let us swear by Allâh that we will surely make a raid on him (-Sâlih) and his family by night and then we will say to his claimant (- the next of kin, if he seeks vengeance) that we were not present at the time and place of the destruction of his family and most surely we speak the truth.'

50. And they hatched a plot and We likewise brought forth a counter plan of which they were not aware (that their plotting would go in vain).

51. Look, then how (evil) was the end their planning met; We utterly destroyed them and their people one and all.

52. So their houses are lying deserted over there because of their acting unjustly. Indeed, in this (episode) there is a great sign for a people who would know.

53. (Whereas We destroyed them,) We saved those who had believed and used to guard against evil.

54. And (We also sent) Lot (as a Messenger). (Recall) when he said to his people, 'Do you commit obscenity while you see (the evil thereof).

55. 'What! (is it true) you approach men instead of (your) women to satisfy (your) lust?

يَخۡتَصِمُونَ ﴿٤٥﴾ قَالَ يَٰقَوۡمِ لِمَ تَسۡتَعۡجِلُونَ
بِالسَّيِّئَةِ قَبۡلَ الۡحَسَنَةِۚ لَوۡلَا تَسۡتَغۡفِرُونَ
اللّٰهَ لَعَلَّكُمۡ تُرۡحَمُونَ ﴿٤٦﴾ قَالُوا اطَّيَّرۡنَا بِكَ
وَبِمَنۡ مَّعَكَۚ قَالَ طَٰٓئِرُكُمۡ عِنۡدَ اللّٰهِ بَلۡ
أَنۡتُمۡ قَوۡمٌ تُفۡتَنُونَ ﴿٤٧﴾ وَكَانَ فِي الۡمَدِينَةِ
تِسۡعَةُ رَهۡطٍ يُفۡسِدُونَ فِي الۡأَرۡضِ وَلَا
يُصۡلِحُونَ ﴿٤٨﴾ قَالُوا تَقَاسَمُوا بِاللّٰهِ لَنُبَيِّتَنَّهُ
وَأَهۡلَهُ ثُمَّ لَنَقُولَنَّ لِوَلِيِّهِ مَا شَهِدۡنَا
مَهۡلِكَ أَهۡلِهِ وَإِنَّا لَصَٰدِقُونَ ﴿٤٩﴾ وَمَكَرُوا
مَكۡرًا وَّمَكَرۡنَا مَكۡرًا وَّهُمۡ لَا يَشۡعُرُونَ ﴿٥٠﴾
فَانۡظُرۡ كَيۡفَ كَانَ عَٰقِبَةُ مَكۡرِهِمۡ أَنَّا
دَمَّرۡنَٰهُمۡ وَقَوۡمَهُمۡ أَجۡمَعِينَ ﴿٥١﴾ فَتِلۡكَ بُيُوتُهُمۡ
خَاوِيَةًۢ بِمَا ظَلَمُواۚ إِنَّ فِي ذَٰلِكَ لَأٓيَةً لِّقَوۡمٍ
يَعۡلَمُونَ ﴿٥٢﴾ وَأَنۡجَيۡنَا الَّذِينَ ءَامَنُوا وَكَانُوا
يَتَّقُونَ ﴿٥٣﴾ وَلُوطًا إِذۡ قَالَ لِقَوۡمِهِۦٓ أَتَأۡتُونَ
الۡفَٰحِشَةَ وَأَنۡتُمۡ تُبۡصِرُونَ ﴿٥٤﴾ أَئِنَّكُمۡ لَتَأۡتُونَ
الرِّجَالَ شَهۡوَةً مِّنۡ دُونِ النِّسَآءِۚ بَلۡ أَنۡتُمۡ

Nay, you are indeed a people who act senselessly.'

56. But his people had no reply except that they said, 'Drive the followers of Lot out of your township. They are a people who would pose (and parade) to be extra pure and righteous (internally and externally).'

57. So the result was that We saved him and his followers except his wife. We had ordained about her (for her foul deeds) to be with those who stayed behind (and thus would not be saved).

58. And We pelted them with a terrible rain (of stones). So (look,) how evil was the rain which descended upon those who had been warned!

SECTION 5

59. SAY, 'All kind of true and perfect praise belongs to Allâh. And peace be upon those of His servants whom He has chosen.' Who is to be preferred, Allâh or the things they associate (with Him)?

سُوْرَةُ النَّمْلِ ٢٧

قَوْمٌ تَجْهَلُوْنَ ۝٥٥ فَمَا كَانَ جَوَابَ قَوْمِهٖٓ
إِلَّآ أَنْ قَالُوْٓا أَخْرِجُوْٓا اٰلَ لُوْطٍ مِّنْ قَرْيَتِكُمْ
إِنَّهُمْ أُنَاسٌ يَّتَطَهَّرُوْنَ ۝٥٦ فَأَنْجَيْنٰهُ وَأَهْلَهٗٓ
إِلَّا امْرَأَتَهٗ قَدَّرْنٰهَا مِنَ الْغٰبِرِيْنَ ۝٥٧
وَأَمْطَرْنَا عَلَيْهِمْ مَّطَرًا فَسَآءَ مَطَرُ
الْمُنْذَرِيْنَ ۝٥٨ قُلِ الْحَمْدُ لِلّٰهِ وَسَلٰمٌ عَلٰى عِبَادِهِ
الَّذِيْنَ اصْطَفٰى ءَآللّٰهُ خَيْرٌ أَمَّا يُشْرِكُوْنَ ۝٥٩

ع ١٤ ١٩

PART الجزء العشرون XX

60. OR Who is it that created the heavens and the earth, and sends down water for you from the clouds? (It is We.) Then We cause to grow with it orchards full of bloom and loveliness. You had no power to cause their trees to grow. Is there any god with Allâh? (There is none;) yet there are a people who ascribe (to Him) equals (in all these works, and deviate from the right path).

61. Or Who is it that made the earth a resting place; and made the rivers flow in it; and raised (on the earth) firm mountains for its advantage; and put a barrier between the two waters? Is there a god with Allâh (as an associate with Him in His works)? Nay, not so, yet most of them do

أَمَّنْ خَلَقَ السَّمٰوٰتِ وَالْأَرْضَ وَأَنْزَلَ
لَكُمْ مِّنَ السَّمَآءِ مَآءً فَأَنْۢبَتْنَا بِهٖ حَدَآئِقَ
ذَاتَ بَهْجَةٍ مَا كَانَ لَكُمْ أَنْ تُنْۢبِتُوْا
شَجَرَهَا ءَإِلٰهٌ مَّعَ اللّٰهِ بَلْ هُمْ قَوْمٌ
يَّعْدِلُوْنَ ۝٦٠ أَمَّنْ جَعَلَ الْأَرْضَ قَرَارًا
وَّجَعَلَ خِلٰلَهَآ أَنْهٰرًا وَّجَعَلَ لَهَا رَوَاسِيَ
وَجَعَلَ بَيْنَ الْبَحْرَيْنِ حَاجِزًا ءَإِلٰهٌ مَّعَ اللّٰهِ

الجزء العشرون

not know (the truth).

62. Or Who is it that answers the distressed person when he calls on Him, and removes (his) distress? And Who is it that makes you (the) rulers in the land? Is there any other god with Allâh? Little is the heed you take!

63. Or Who is it that guides you (to the path of salvation) in all kinds of darkness (and vicissitudes) on the land and the sea; and Who is it that sends the winds as heralds of His mercy. Is there any god with Allâh (to do such things)? Highly-Exalted is Allâh above all the things they associate (with Him).

64. Or Who is it that originates the creation then keeps on repeating and reproducing it, and Who is it that provides for your sustenance (both physical and spiritual) from the heaven and the earth? Is there any other god with Allâh (capable of being a partner with Him in all these works)? Say, 'Bring forward your proof (in support of your polytheistic beliefs) if you are truthful (in what you claim).'

65. Say, 'There is no one in the heavens and the earth who knows the hidden realities save Allâh. And they (- the disbelievers) do not perceive when they will be raised up (to life again after death).'

66. Nay, (the fact is) their knowledge about the Hereafter has found its limit. Rather they are in doubt about it (- the life after death). Rather they are totally blind to it (- the existence of God Himself).

SECTION 6

67. **A**ND those who disbelieve say, 'Is it that when we and our forefathers have been reduced to dust we shall really be brought forth (alive again)?

68. 'We have been surely given this promise once before (this) and also our forefathers. But such a thing is nothing but tales of the ancients.'

69. Say, 'Travel through the land and behold how (evil) has been the end of those who cut off

سورة النمل ٢٧

بل أكثرهم لا يعلمون ﴿٦١﴾ أمن يجيب
المضطر إذا دعاه ويكشف السوء
ويجعلكم خلفاء الأرض ۗ أإله مع الله ۚ
قليلا ما تذكرون ﴿٦٢﴾ أمن يهديكم في
ظلمت البر والبحر ومن يرسل الريح
بشرا بين يدي رحمته ۗ أإله مع الله ۚ
تعلى الله عما يشركون ﴿٦٣﴾ أمن يبدؤا الخلق
ثم يعيده ومن يرزقكم من السماء
والأرض ۗ أإله مع الله ۚ قل هاتوا برهنكم
إن كنتم صدقين ﴿٦٤﴾ قل لا يعلم من في
السموت والأرض الغيب إلا الله ۚ وما
يشعرون أيان يبعثون ﴿٦٥﴾ بل ادرك علمهم
في الأخرة ۚ بل هم في شك منها ۖ بل هم
منها عمون ﴿٦٦﴾ وقال الذين كفروا أإذا كنا
ترابا وآباؤنا أئنا لمخرجون ﴿٦٧﴾ لقد وعدنا
هذا نحن وآباؤنا من قبل إن هذا
إلا أسطير الأولين ﴿٦٨﴾ قل سيروا في الأرض

ع ٨

their ties (with God).'

70. (Prophet!) Do not grieve for them, nor feel distressed on account of their (hostile) intrigues (against you).

71. They say, 'When will this promise (of your victory) come to pass if you are truthful?'

72. Say, 'It is possible that a part of that (victory) which you are keen to precipitate may be close on your heels.'

73. And in fact your Lord is full of grace to humankind, yet most of them render (Him) no thanks.

74. And surely your Lord knows the things which they hide in their hearts and those which they profess.

75. There is nothing hidden in the heavens and the earth but it is recorded in a Book revealing (the Divine decree).

76. Verily, this Qur'ân explains to the Children of Israel (both the Jews and the Christians) most of the things concerning which they are at variance.

77. And surely, this is a (source of) guidance and mercy for the believers.

78. (Prophet!) Your Lord will rightly judge between them (- the believing and the disbelieving people) with His command (- the Qur'ân). He is the All-Mighty, the All-Knowing.

79. So put your trust in Allâh, for surely you stand on manifest truth.

80. Of course you cannot make the dead hear nor can you make the deaf hear (your) call when they retreat turning their backs (on you).

81. And you cannot guide the blind (as well) out of their error. You can make only those to hear who believe in Our Messages and so have surrendered themselves in submission (to Our will).

82. And when the judgment becomes due against them (-the unjust) We shall bring forth for them a (grossly) materialistic person which will rule over them (and also an insect which

فَانظُرُوا كَيْفَ كَانَ عَٰقِبَةُ الْمُجْرِمِينَ ﴿٦٩﴾
وَلَا تَحْزَنْ عَلَيْهِمْ وَلَا تَكُن فِي ضَيْقٍ مِّمَّا
يَمْكُرُونَ ﴿٧٠﴾ وَيَقُولُونَ مَتَىٰ هَٰذَا الْوَعْدُ إِن
كُنتُمْ صَٰدِقِينَ ﴿٧١﴾ قُلْ عَسَىٰ أَن يَكُونَ
رَدِفَ لَكُم بَعْضُ الَّذِي تَسْتَعْجِلُونَ ﴿٧٢﴾ وَإِنَّ
رَبَّكَ لَذُو فَضْلٍ عَلَى النَّاسِ وَلَٰكِنَّ أَكْثَرَهُمْ
لَا يَشْكُرُونَ ﴿٧٣﴾ وَإِنَّ رَبَّكَ لَيَعْلَمُ مَا تُكِنُّ
صُدُورُهُمْ وَمَا يُعْلِنُونَ ﴿٧٤﴾ وَمَا مِنْ غَائِبَةٍ
فِي السَّمَاءِ وَالْأَرْضِ إِلَّا فِي كِتَٰبٍ مُّبِينٍ ﴿٧٥﴾
إِنَّ هَٰذَا الْقُرْآنَ يَقُصُّ عَلَىٰ بَنِي إِسْرَاءِيلَ
أَكْثَرَ الَّذِي هُمْ فِيهِ يَخْتَلِفُونَ ﴿٧٦﴾ وَإِنَّهُ
لَهُدًى وَرَحْمَةٌ لِّلْمُؤْمِنِينَ ﴿٧٧﴾ إِنَّ رَبَّكَ
يَقْضِي بَيْنَهُم بِحُكْمِهِ ۚ وَهُوَ الْعَزِيزُ
الْعَلِيمُ ﴿٧٨﴾ فَتَوَكَّلْ عَلَى اللَّهِ ۖ إِنَّكَ عَلَى
الْحَقِّ الْمُبِينِ ﴿٧٩﴾ إِنَّكَ لَا تُسْمِعُ الْمَوْتَىٰ
وَلَا تُسْمِعُ الصُّمَّ الدُّعَاءَ إِذَا وَلَّوْا مُدْبِرِينَ ﴿٨٠﴾
وَمَا أَنتَ بِهَٰدِي الْعُمْيِ عَن ضَلَٰلَتِهِمْ ۖ إِن
تُسْمِعُ إِلَّا مَن يُؤْمِنُ بِآيَٰتِنَا فَهُم مُّسْلِمُونَ ﴿٨١﴾
وَإِذَا وَقَعَ الْقَوْلُ عَلَيْهِمْ أَخْرَجْنَا لَهُمْ
دَابَّةً مِّنَ الْأَرْضِ تُكَلِّمُهُمْ أَنَّ النَّاسَ

shall wound them to cause plague). That is because the people did not have firm faith in Our Messages.

SECTION 7

83. **A**ND (remind them of) the day when We shall gather together from every people a large group of those who cried lies to Our Messages; then they shall be arranged in separate columns.
84. Until when they arrive (before their Lord) He will say, 'Did you not cry lies to My Messages before you had gained full knowledge about them? Or what (else) was it that you had been doing (about them)?'
85. And the judgment becomes due against them because they acted wrongly and they will not be able to speak (in their defence).
86. Do they not consider that We have made the night for them to rest and (have made) the day for giving light. Surely, in this there are signs for a people who would believe.
87. And (remind them of) the day when the trumpet will be blown, then, excepting those whom Allâh will (to keep them safe from terror), all those who are in the heavens and all those who are on the earth will be stricken with fear. And everyone shall come in submission to Him.
88. You see the mountains and think them to be firmly fixed while in fact they are passing away like clouds. (Such are) the works of Allâh Who has made everything perfect (in every way). Verily, He is fully Aware of your deeds.
89. Those who come with good deeds (before their Lord) shall have (even) better reward than they actually deserve. Such people will be secure from fear that day.
90. Those who come with (something) evil shall be hurled headlong into the Fire (and it will be said to them,) 'You are certainly reaping the fruit of what you have been doing.'
91. Say, 'In fact I am commanded to worship only the Lord of this city (- Makkah) which He

كَانُوا بِآيٰتِنَا لَا يُوقِنُونَ ﴿٨٢﴾ وَيَوْمَ نَحْشُرُ
مِنْ كُلِّ أُمَّةٍ فَوْجًا مِّمَّنْ يُكَذِّبُ بِآيٰتِنَا
فَهُمْ يُوزَعُونَ ﴿٨٣﴾ حَتّٰى إِذَا جَاءُو قَالَ أَكَذَّبْتُمْ
بِآيٰتِي وَلَمْ تُحِيطُوا بِهَا عِلْمًا أَمَّا ذَا كُنْتُمْ
تَعْمَلُونَ ﴿٨٤﴾ وَوَقَعَ الْقَوْلُ عَلَيْهِمْ بِمَا ظَلَمُوا
فَهُمْ لَا يَنْطِقُونَ ﴿٨٥﴾ أَلَمْ يَرَوْا أَنَّا جَعَلْنَا
الَّيْلَ لِيَسْكُنُوا فِيهِ وَالنَّهَارَ مُبْصِرًا ۚ إِنَّ
فِي ذٰلِكَ لَآيٰتٍ لِّقَوْمٍ يُؤْمِنُونَ ﴿٨٦﴾ وَيَوْمَ
يُنْفَخُ فِي الصُّورِ فَفَزِعَ مَنْ فِي السَّمٰوٰتِ
وَمَنْ فِي الْأَرْضِ إِلَّا مَنْ شَاءَ اللّٰهُ ۚ وَكُلٌّ
أَتَوْهُ دٰخِرِينَ ﴿٨٧﴾ وَتَرَى الْجِبَالَ تَحْسَبُهَا
جَامِدَةً وَّهِيَ تَمُرُّ مَرَّ السَّحَابِ ۚ صُنْعَ اللّٰهِ
الَّذِي أَتْقَنَ كُلَّ شَيْءٍ ۚ إِنَّهُ خَبِيرٌ بِمَا
تَفْعَلُونَ ﴿٨٨﴾ مَنْ جَاءَ بِالْحَسَنَةِ فَلَهُ خَيْرٌ
مِّنْهَا وَهُمْ مِّنْ فَزَعٍ يَّوْمَئِذٍ أٰمِنُونَ ﴿٨٩﴾
وَمَنْ جَاءَ بِالسَّيِّئَةِ فَكُبَّتْ وُجُوهُهُمْ
فِي النَّارِ ۚ هَلْ تُجْزَوْنَ إِلَّا مَا كُنْتُمْ
تَعْمَلُونَ ﴿٩٠﴾ إِنَّمَا أُمِرْتُ أَنْ أَعْبُدَ رَبَّ

has declared sacred. Everything belongs to Him. And I have also been commanded to be (one) of those who submit (to His will),
92. 'And to recite (to the people), and follow the Qur'ân; so one who (on listening to it) follows guidance, does it for his own good. And (tell him) who goes astray (from the straight path) that my mission is only to give warning.'
93. And also say, 'All true praise belongs to Allâh He will soon show you His signs and you shall recognise them. And your Lord is not at all unaware of what you do.

هٰذِهِ الْبَلْدَةِ الَّذِي حَرَّمَهَا وَلَهُ كُلُّ
شَيْءٍ وَأُمِرْتُ أَنْ أَكُونَ مِنَ الْمُسْلِمِينَ ﴿٩١﴾
وَأَنْ أَتْلُوَا الْقُرْآنَ فَمَنِ اهْتَدَى فَإِنَّمَا
يَهْتَدِي لِنَفْسِهِ وَمَنْ ضَلَّ فَقُلْ إِنَّمَا
أَنَا مِنَ الْمُنْذِرِينَ ﴿٩٢﴾ وَقُلِ الْحَمْدُ
لِلّٰهِ سَيُرِيكُمْ آيَاتِهِ فَتَعْرِفُونَهَا وَمَا
رَبُّكَ بِغَافِلٍ عَمَّا تَعْمَلُونَ ﴿٩٣﴾

CHAPTER
28

AL-QASAS
(The Narrative)
(Revealed before Hijrah)

سُورَةُ الْقَصَصِ مَكِّيَّةٌ

With the name of Allâh,
the Most Gracious, the Ever Merciful
(I commence to read Sûrah Al-Qasas).

بِسْمِ اللّٰهِ الرَّحْمٰنِ الرَّحِيمِ

1. TÂ SÎN MÎM - the Benign, the All-Hearing, the All-Knowing.
2. These are the verses of the perfect Book which explains everything vividly.
3. We recount to you (a portion) of the true account of Moses and Pharaoh with all accuracy for the benefit of the people who would believe.
4. (The facts are,) Pharaoh behaved arrogantly in (his) land. He divided its inhabitants into parties. He (oppressed them and thus) sought to weaken a section of them (- the Israelites). He killed their sons and sought to make their women immodest by sparing them. In fact he was of the evil doers.

طسم ﴿١﴾ تِلْكَ آيَاتُ الْكِتَابِ الْمُبِينِ ﴿٢﴾
نَتْلُوا عَلَيْكَ مِنْ نَبَإِ مُوسَى وَفِرْعَوْنَ
بِالْحَقِّ لِقَوْمٍ يُؤْمِنُونَ ﴿٣﴾ إِنَّ فِرْعَوْنَ عَلَا
فِي الْأَرْضِ وَجَعَلَ أَهْلَهَا شِيَعًا يَسْتَضْعِفُ
طَائِفَةً مِنْهُمْ يُذَبِّحُ أَبْنَاءَهُمْ وَيَسْتَحْيِي
نِسَاءَهُمْ إِنَّهُ كَانَ مِنَ الْمُفْسِدِينَ ﴿٤﴾

5. And We chose to confer favour upon those who had been rendered weak in the land and to make them leaders and to bestow a kingdom upon them, thus make them inheritors (of Our blessings).
6. And (We chose) to establish them with all powers in the country and to visit Pharaoh and Hâmân and their hordes with that (power and supremacy) which they dreaded from those (Israelites rendered weak by them).
7. And We revealed to the mother of Moses (saying), 'Give him (- Moses) suck. But when you have fear about him (- his life) cast him (placing him in a chest) into the river and entertain no fear, nor grief (about his welfare). Verily, We shall restore him to you and shall make him (one) of the Messengers.'
8. (Moses' mother cast him into the river according to the revelation,) then one of the family of Pharaoh picked him up with the result that he (one day) became an enemy to and (a source of) grief for them. Verily, Pharaoh, Hâmân and the hordes of them both were all wrongdoers.
9. And a woman of (the family of) Pharaoh said, '(This child will be) a (source of) joy and comfort to my and your eyes. Do not kill him, he may (prove to) be useful to us, or we may adopt him as a son.' And they did not perceive (Our purpose).
10. And the heart of the mother of Moses became free (from anxiety). She would have nearly disclosed his identity (out of joy, how Allâh had become guardian of her child) had We not strengthened her heart to help her remain of the (firm minded) believers.
11. She said to his (- Moses') sister, 'Follow him.' So she (followed and) watched him from a distance while they (- Pharaoh's people) took no notice (that she was keeping a watch over him).
12. And We had already (ordained and) made him refuse the wet nurses (to be suckled). So

سُورَةُ القَصَصِ ٢٨

وَنُرِيدُ أَن نَّمُنَّ عَلَى الَّذِينَ اسْتُضْعِفُوا
فِي الْأَرْضِ وَنَجْعَلَهُمْ أَئِمَّةً وَنَجْعَلَهُمُ
الْوَارِثِينَ ۝٥ وَنُمَكِّنَ لَهُمْ فِي الْأَرْضِ
وَنُرِيَ فِرْعَوْنَ وَهَامَانَ وَجُنُودَهُمَا مِنْهُم
مَّا كَانُوا يَحْذَرُونَ ۝٦ وَأَوْحَيْنَا إِلَىٰ أُمِّ مُوسَىٰ
أَنْ أَرْضِعِيهِ ۖ فَإِذَا خِفْتِ عَلَيْهِ فَأَلْقِيهِ
فِي الْيَمِّ وَلَا تَخَافِي وَلَا تَحْزَنِي ۖ إِنَّا رَادُّوهُ
إِلَيْكِ وَجَاعِلُوهُ مِنَ الْمُرْسَلِينَ ۝٧ فَالْتَقَطَهُ
آلُ فِرْعَوْنَ لِيَكُونَ لَهُمْ عَدُوًّا وَحَزَنًا ۗ إِنَّ
فِرْعَوْنَ وَهَامَانَ وَجُنُودَهُمَا كَانُوا خَاطِئِينَ ۝٨
وَقَالَتِ امْرَأَتُ فِرْعَوْنَ قُرَّتُ عَيْنٍ لِّي
وَلَكَ ۖ لَا تَقْتُلُوهُ عَسَىٰ أَن يَنفَعَنَا أَوْ نَتَّخِذَهُ
وَلَدًا وَهُمْ لَا يَشْعُرُونَ ۝٩ وَأَصْبَحَ فُؤَادُ أُمِّ
مُوسَىٰ فَارِغًا ۖ إِن كَادَتْ لَتُبْدِي بِهِ لَوْلَا
أَن رَّبَطْنَا عَلَىٰ قَلْبِهَا لِتَكُونَ مِنَ الْمُؤْمِنِينَ ۝١٠
وَقَالَتْ لِأُخْتِهِ قُصِّيهِ ۖ فَبَصُرَتْ بِهِ عَن
جُنُبٍ وَهُمْ لَا يَشْعُرُونَ ۝١١ وَحَرَّمْنَا عَلَيْهِ

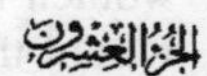

(when the question of his suckling arose after Moses was picked up from the river,) she (- Moses sister) said, 'Shall I point out to you the people of a household who will bring him up for you and will be his sincere well-wishers?'
13. This was how We restored him to his mother so that she might be consoled (to see her child) and should no longer grieve and that she might know that the promise of Allâh was true; (a fact which) most of these (disbelievers of the Holy Prophet) do not know.

SECTION 2

14. **A**ND when he (- Moses) reached his (age of) full growth (and maturity) and attained perfection, We granted him wisdom and knowledge. That is how We reward the doers of good.
15. And (one day Moses) entered the city at a time when its inhabitants were idling (in a state of heedlessness), and found therein two men fighting with one another; one of his own party (- an Israelite), while the other (belonged to that) of his enemies. The one who belonged to his own people sought his (- Moses') help against the other who belonged to those of his enemies. Thereat Moses struck him (the latter) with his fist and this brought about his death. He (- Moses) said, 'This (death of his) has occurred owing to (his) satanic action; he (- satan) is of course an enemy (of yours) misleading (and) cutting your ties (with God).'
16. (Moses) said (praying), 'My Lord! I have involved myself into trouble, so protect me.' Thereupon He protected him (from the evil consequences of his act). Verily, He is the Great Protector, the Ever Merciful.
17. He (also) added, 'My Lord! Since You have always been kind and gracious to me, I can never be a helper and a supporter of the guilty.'
18. (The next day) early in the morning he entered the city apprehensive (of the enemy and) observing (the situation). And lo! The man who had sought his help the day before

الْمَرَاضِعَ مِنْ قَبْلُ فَقَالَتْ هَلْ أَدُلُّكُمْ
عَلَىٰ أَهْلِ بَيْتٍ يَكْفُلُونَهُ لَكُمْ وَهُمْ
لَهُ نَاصِحُونَ ﴿١٢﴾ فَرَدَدْنَاهُ إِلَىٰ أُمِّهِ كَيْ تَقَرَّ
عَيْنُهَا وَلَا تَحْزَنَ وَلِتَعْلَمَ أَنَّ وَعْدَ اللَّهِ
حَقٌّ وَلَٰكِنَّ أَكْثَرَهُمْ لَا يَعْلَمُونَ ﴿١٣﴾ وَلَمَّا
بَلَغَ أَشُدَّهُ وَاسْتَوَىٰ آتَيْنَاهُ حُكْمًا
وَعِلْمًا ۚ وَكَذَٰلِكَ نَجْزِي الْمُحْسِنِينَ ﴿١٤﴾
وَدَخَلَ الْمَدِينَةَ عَلَىٰ حِينِ غَفْلَةٍ مِنْ
أَهْلِهَا فَوَجَدَ فِيهَا رَجُلَيْنِ يَقْتَتِلَانِ هَٰذَا
مِنْ شِيعَتِهِ وَهَٰذَا مِنْ عَدُوِّهِ ۖ فَاسْتَغَاثَهُ
الَّذِي مِنْ شِيعَتِهِ عَلَى الَّذِي مِنْ عَدُوِّهِ
فَوَكَزَهُ مُوسَىٰ فَقَضَىٰ عَلَيْهِ ۖ قَالَ هَٰذَا مِنْ
عَمَلِ الشَّيْطَانِ ۖ إِنَّهُ عَدُوٌّ مُضِلٌّ مُبِينٌ ﴿١٥﴾
قَالَ رَبِّ إِنِّي ظَلَمْتُ نَفْسِي فَاغْفِرْ لِي
فَغَفَرَ لَهُ ۚ إِنَّهُ هُوَ الْغَفُورُ الرَّحِيمُ ﴿١٦﴾ قَالَ
رَبِّ بِمَا أَنْعَمْتَ عَلَيَّ فَلَنْ أَكُونَ ظَهِيرًا
لِلْمُجْرِمِينَ ﴿١٧﴾ فَأَصْبَحَ فِي الْمَدِينَةِ خَائِفًا

(again that day) cried out to him for help. Moses said to him, 'You are a misguided fellow, away from the path of peace and piety.'
19. And when Moses intended to lay hold of the man (of the day before) who was (now) an enemy to both of them, the man said, 'Moses! Do you intend to kill me (today) as you killed a person yesterday? You are only trying to figure as a tyrant in the country. You have no mind to be of the promoters of peace.'
20. (Then it came to pass that) a man came running from the far end of the city (and) said, 'Moses the chiefs are consulting together to kill you. Therefore leave (this place at once), I am, of course, your sincere well-wisher.'
21. So (Moses) left that (city) in fear and he kept watching (around) carefully. He said (praying at that time), 'My Lord! Deliver me from the unjust people.'

SECTION 3

22. **W**HEN (Moses) set out turning his face towards Midian he said, 'I hope my Lord will put me on the right course till I reach the goal.'
23. And when he arrived at the water of Midian, he found there a party of men watering (their flocks) and he found two ladies (standing) apart from them, holding (their flock) back. He said, 'What is your problem?' They replied, 'We cannot water (our flock) until the shepherds depart (having driven their flocks away), and our father is a very old man.'
24. So (Moses) watered (their flock) for them. Then he retired to (a place with) the shade and said, 'My Lord! I stand in need of whatever good You may bestow on me.'
25. Now one of the two ladies came to him walking bashfully. She said, 'My father calls you so that he may reward you for your having watered our flock (for us).' So when he (Moses) came to him and told him all that had taken place (with him), he (the father of the two ladies) said, 'Have no fear, you have escaped

يَتَرَقَّبُ فَإِذَا الَّذِي اسْتَنْصَرَهُ بِالْأَمْسِ
يَسْتَصْرِخُهُ قَالَ لَهُ مُوسَىٰ إِنَّكَ لَغَوِيٌّ
مُبِينٌ ﴿١٨﴾ فَلَمَّا أَنْ أَرَادَ أَنْ يَبْطِشَ بِالَّذِي
هُوَ عَدُوٌّ لَهُمَا قَالَ يَا مُوسَىٰ أَتُرِيدُ أَنْ
تَقْتُلَنِي كَمَا قَتَلْتَ نَفْسًا بِالْأَمْسِ إِنْ
تُرِيدُ إِلَّا أَنْ تَكُونَ جَبَّارًا فِي الْأَرْضِ
وَمَا تُرِيدُ أَنْ تَكُونَ مِنَ الْمُصْلِحِينَ ﴿١٩﴾
وَجَاءَ رَجُلٌ مِنْ أَقْصَا الْمَدِينَةِ يَسْعَىٰ
قَالَ يَا مُوسَىٰ إِنَّ الْمَلَأَ يَأْتَمِرُونَ بِكَ
لِيَقْتُلُوكَ فَاخْرُجْ إِنِّي لَكَ مِنَ النَّاصِحِينَ ﴿٢٠﴾
فَخَرَجَ مِنْهَا خَائِفًا يَتَرَقَّبُ قَالَ رَبِّ
نَجِّنِي مِنَ الْقَوْمِ الظَّالِمِينَ ﴿٢١﴾ وَلَمَّا تَوَجَّهَ
تِلْقَاءَ مَدْيَنَ قَالَ عَسَىٰ رَبِّي أَنْ يَهْدِيَنِي
سَوَاءَ السَّبِيلِ ﴿٢٢﴾ وَلَمَّا وَرَدَ مَاءَ مَدْيَنَ
وَجَدَ عَلَيْهِ أُمَّةً مِنَ النَّاسِ يَسْقُونَ
وَوَجَدَ مِنْ دُونِهِمُ امْرَأَتَيْنِ تَذُودَانِ
قَالَ مَا خَطْبُكُمَا قَالَتَا لَا نَسْقِي حَتَّىٰ
يُصْدِرَ الرِّعَاءُ وَأَبُونَا شَيْخٌ كَبِيرٌ ﴿٢٣﴾
فَسَقَىٰ لَهُمَا ثُمَّ تَوَلَّىٰ إِلَى الظِّلِّ فَقَالَ رَبِّ
إِنِّي لِمَا أَنْزَلْتَ إِلَيَّ مِنْ خَيْرٍ فَقِيرٌ ﴿٢٤﴾
فَجَاءَتْهُ إِحْدَاهُمَا تَمْشِي عَلَى اسْتِحْيَاءٍ
قَالَتْ إِنَّ أَبِي يَدْعُوكَ لِيَجْزِيَكَ أَجْرَ مَا
سَقَيْتَ لَنَا فَلَمَّا جَاءَهُ وَقَصَّ عَلَيْهِ الْقَصَصَ

ع ٢ ٨ ٥

from the unjust people.'

26. One of the two ladies said, 'My dear father! Take him into your service. You cannot do better than employ a man who is strong and trustworthy.'

27. He (their father) said (to Moses), 'I intend to marry one of these two daughters of mine to you, provided you stay in my service for eight years. But if you extend (your stay) making it complete ten (years) it will be an act of grace on your part. I have no desire to be hard on you by laying any more burden (of responsibility) on you. Allâh willing, you will find me an upright person.'

28. (Moses) said, (accepting the proposal), 'This is (a covenant) between us; whichever of the two terms I complete, I will be free from obligation and there shall be no injustice to me, and Allâh is witness over what we have agreed.'

SECTION 4

29. **A**ND when Moses had completed the agreed term and set forth with his family, he saw with feelings of warmth of affection and love, a sort of fire (on the way at a place) in the direction of the mount. He said to his family, 'You stay (here) I have seen with feelings of warmth of love and affection a fire. I hope to bring you some useful and important information from there or (at least) a burning brand from the fire that you may warm yourselves.'

30. And when he came close to it (- the fire) a voice called out to him from a blessed spot on the right side of the valley, from the direction of a tree, 'Moses! Surely I am, Allâh, the Lord of the worlds.

31. 'And put down your staff on the ground.' Then, no sooner did he see it (- the staff) shifting like a tiny quickly moving serpent, than he turned his back and retreated and would not even look back. (God said,) 'Moses! Come forward, and have no fear. Surely, you are of

قَالَ لَا تَخَفْ نَجَوْتَ مِنَ الْقَوْمِ الظّٰلِمِيْنَ ﴿٢٥﴾
قَالَتْ إِحْدٰىهُمَا يٰٓأَبَتِ اسْتَـْٔجِرْهُ إِنَّ خَيْرَ
مَنِ اسْتَـْٔجَرْتَ الْقَوِيُّ الْأَمِيْنُ ﴿٢٦﴾ قَالَ إِنِّيْٓ
أُرِيْدُ أَنْ أُنْكِحَكَ إِحْدَى ابْنَتَيَّ هٰتَيْنِ
عَلٰٓى أَنْ تَأْجُرَنِيْ ثَمٰنِيَ حِجَجٍ فَإِنْ أَتْمَمْتَ
عَشْرًا فَمِنْ عِنْدِكَ وَمَآ أُرِيْدُ أَنْ أَشُقَّ
عَلَيْكَ سَتَجِدُنِيْٓ إِنْ شَآءَ اللّٰهُ مِنَ الصّٰلِحِيْنَ ﴿٢٧﴾
قَالَ ذٰلِكَ بَيْنِيْ وَبَيْنَكَ أَيَّمَا الْأَجَلَيْنِ
قَضَيْتُ فَلَا عُدْوٰنَ عَلَيَّ وَاللّٰهُ عَلٰى مَا نَقُوْلُ
وَكِيْلٌ ﴿٢٨﴾ فَلَمَّا قَضٰى مُوْسَى الْأَجَلَ وَسَارَ
بِأَهْلِهِٓ اٰنَسَ مِنْ جَانِبِ الطُّوْرِ نَارًا قَالَ
لِأَهْلِهِ امْكُثُوْٓا إِنِّيْٓ اٰنَسْتُ نَارًا لَّعَلِّيْٓ
اٰتِيْكُمْ مِّنْهَا بِخَبَرٍ أَوْ جَذْوَةٍ مِّنَ النَّارِ
لَعَلَّكُمْ تَصْطَلُوْنَ ﴿٢٩﴾ فَلَمَّآ أَتٰىهَا نُوْدِيَ مِنْ
شَاطِئِ الْوَادِ الْأَيْمَنِ فِي الْبُقْعَةِ الْمُبٰرَكَةِ
مِنَ الشَّجَرَةِ أَنْ يّٰمُوْسٰٓى إِنِّيْٓ أَنَا اللّٰهُ رَبُّ
الْعٰلَمِيْنَ ﴿٣٠﴾ وَأَنْ أَلْقِ عَصَاكَ فَلَمَّا رَاٰهَا
تَهْتَزُّ كَأَنَّهَا جَآنٌّ وَّلّٰى مُدْبِرًا وَّلَمْ يُعَقِّبْ
يٰمُوْسٰٓى أَقْبِلْ وَلَا تَخَفْ إِنَّكَ مِنَ

those who are safe.

32. 'Insert your hand into your bosom, it will come forth flawless (sparkling) white and draw back your arm towards yourself (to compose yourself) when you encounter fear. So these (two signs) are two proofs from your Lord to (be presented before) Pharaoh and his courtiers. For surely they are lawless and disobedient people.

33. (Moses) said, 'My Lord! I killed a person from among them (accidentally) and I fear that they will kill me (before I am able to fulfill my mission).

34. 'And my brother Aaron is more fluent and eloquent in speech than I, so send him with me as a helper to bear me out (for) I fear that they will treat me as a liar.'

35. (God) said, 'We will surely strengthen your arm with your brother and We will give both of you so much power that they shall not reach you (to do you harm). So (go armed) with Our signs; you two and your followers will come out victorious.'

36. So when Moses came to them (- the people of Pharaoh) with Our clear signs they said, 'This is but a forged and unprecedented fraud. We never heard such a thing in the time of our forefathers.'

37. And Moses said, 'My Lord knows best who it is that has brought true guidance from Him, and who shall meet a good end in this world (and will have the reward of final abode in the Hereafter). The truth is that these wrongdoers shall never prosper.'

38. And Pharaoh said, 'O chiefs of my court! I know for you no god other than myself. And O Hâmân! Light a fire for me on (the bricks of) clay and get a high building, (high like a tower) be built for me that I may (by climbing over it) have a look at the God of Moses, for I take him to be certainly of those who tell lies.'

39. And he (- Pharaoh) and his hosts behaved arrogantly in the land without any justification

الْأٰمِنِينَ ﴿٣١﴾ أُسْلُكْ يَدَكَ فِي جَيْبِكَ تَخْرُجْ
بَيْضَآءَ مِنْ غَيْرِ سُوْٓءٍ وَّ اضْمُمْ إِلَيْكَ
جَنَاحَكَ مِنَ الرَّهْبِ فَذٰنِكَ بُرْهٰنٰنِ مِنْ
رَّبِّكَ إِلٰى فِرْعَوْنَ وَ مَلَا۟ئِهٖ ۭ إِنَّهُمْ كَانُوْا
قَوْمًا فٰسِقِينَ ﴿٣٢﴾ قَالَ رَبِّ إِنِّي قَتَلْتُ
مِنْهُمْ نَفْسًا فَأَخَافُ أَنْ يَّقْتُلُوْنِ ﴿٣٣﴾ وَأَخِي
هٰرُوْنُ هُوَ أَفْصَحُ مِنِّي لِسَانًا فَأَرْسِلْهُ مَعِيَ
رِدْءًا يُّصَدِّقُنِيٓ إِنِّيٓ أَخَافُ أَنْ يُّكَذِّبُوْنِ ﴿٣٤﴾
قَالَ سَنَشُدُّ عَضُدَكَ بِأَخِيكَ وَ نَجْعَلُ
لَكُمَا سُلْطٰنًا فَلَا يَصِلُوْنَ إِلَيْكُمَا ۚ بِأٰيٰتِنَآ ۚ
أَنْتُمَا وَ مَنِ اتَّبَعَكُمَا الْغٰلِبُوْنَ ﴿٣٥﴾ فَلَمَّا جَآءَهُمْ
مُّوْسٰى بِأٰيٰتِنَا بَيِّنٰتٍ قَالُوْا مَا هٰذَآ إِلَّا
سِحْرٌ مُّفْتَرًى وَّ مَا سَمِعْنَا بِهٰذَا فِيٓ
أٰبَآئِنَا الْأَوَّلِينَ ﴿٣٦﴾ وَ قَالَ مُوْسٰى رَبِّيٓ أَعْلَمُ
بِمَنْ جَآءَ بِالْهُدٰى مِنْ عِنْدِهٖ وَ مَنْ
تَكُوْنُ لَهٗ عٰقِبَةُ الدَّارِ ۭ إِنَّهٗ لَا يُفْلِحُ
الظّٰلِمُوْنَ ﴿٣٧﴾ وَ قَالَ فِرْعَوْنُ يٰٓأَيُّهَا الْمَلَأُ مَا
عَلِمْتُ لَكُمْ مِّنْ إِلٰهٍ غَيْرِيْ ۚ فَأَوْقِدْ لِيْ
يٰهٰمٰنُ عَلَى الطِّينِ فَاجْعَلْ لِّيْ صَرْحًا لَّعَلِّيٓ
أَطَّلِعُ إِلٰٓى إِلٰهِ مُوْسٰى ۙ وَ إِنِّي لَأَظُنُّهٗ مِنَ
الْكٰذِبِينَ ﴿٣٨﴾ وَ اسْتَكْبَرَ هُوَ وَ جُنُوْدُهٗ فِي

and as if they thought that they would never be brought back to Us.
40. So We seized him and his hosts and We cast them into the Sea. Behold, how (evil) was the end of these wrongdoers!
41. And We made them archetypes (of evil) who invited (people) to the Fire, and on the Day of Resurrection they will find no help.
42. And We have made them to be followed by a curse in this world and on the Day of Resurrection they will be among those deprived of all good.

SECTION 5

43. **A**FTER We had destroyed the earlier generations We gave Moses the Scripture (which contained) enlightening arguments for the people (of Israel) and (served as) a guidance and (promised them) mercy so that they might take heed.
44. (Prophet!) You were not on the western side (of the Mount of Sinai) when We granted Moses the commission (of prophethood), nor were you (personally) present with the witnesses (there when they were making the prophecy about your advent).
45. But We have raised many a generation since then (after Moses) and a long period of time has passed over them. Nor have you been living among the people of Midian reciting Our Messages to them. Indeed it is We Who have sent you as a Messenger and have revealed all this information (to you).
46. And you were not (present) at the foot of the Mount (with Moses) when We called (to you); but all these (revelation) are from the mercy of your Lord, so that you may warn the people to whom no Warner had come (for a long time) before you, that they may attain eminence.
47. And (We have sent you to them) lest when some evil befalls them because of that their hands have sent forward, they should say, 'Our Lord, why did You not send a Messenger to us?

الْأَرْضِ بِغَيْرِ الْحَقِّ وَظَنُّوٓا أَنَّهُمْ إِلَيْنَا
لَا يُرْجَعُونَ ﴿٣٩﴾ فَأَخَذْنٰهُ وَجُنُودَهُ فَنَبَذْنٰهُمْ
فِي الْيَمِّ فَانْظُرْ كَيْفَ كَانَ عٰقِبَةُ الظّٰلِمِينَ ﴿٤٠﴾
وَجَعَلْنٰهُمْ أَئِمَّةً يَدْعُونَ إِلَى النَّارِ
وَيَوْمَ الْقِيٰمَةِ لَا يُنْصَرُونَ ﴿٤١﴾ وَأَتْبَعْنٰهُمْ
فِي هٰذِهِ الدُّنْيَا لَعْنَةً وَيَوْمَ الْقِيٰمَةِ
هُمْ مِّنَ الْمَقْبُوحِينَ ﴿٤٢﴾ وَلَقَدْ ءَاتَيْنَا مُوسَى
الْكِتٰبَ مِنْ بَعْدِ مَآ أَهْلَكْنَا الْقُرُونَ الْأُولٰى
بَصَآئِرَ لِلنَّاسِ وَهُدًى وَّرَحْمَةً لَّعَلَّهُمْ
يَتَذَكَّرُونَ ﴿٤٣﴾ وَمَا كُنْتَ بِجَانِبِ الْغَرْبِيِّ
إِذْ قَضَيْنَآ إِلٰى مُوسَى الْأَمْرَ وَمَا كُنْتَ
مِنَ الشّٰهِدِينَ ﴿٤٤﴾ وَلٰكِنَّآ أَنْشَأْنَا قُرُونًا
فَتَطَاوَلَ عَلَيْهِمُ الْعُمُرُ وَمَا كُنْتَ ثَاوِيًا
فِيٓ أَهْلِ مَدْيَنَ تَتْلُوا عَلَيْهِمْ ءَايٰتِنَا وَلٰكِنَّا
كُنَّا مُرْسِلِينَ ﴿٤٥﴾ وَمَا كُنْتَ بِجَانِبِ الطُّورِ
إِذْ نَادَيْنَا وَلٰكِنْ رَّحْمَةً مِّنْ رَّبِّكَ لِتُنْذِرَ
قَوْمًا مَّآ أَتٰهُمْ مِّنْ نَّذِيرٍ مِّنْ قَبْلِكَ
لَعَلَّهُمْ يَتَذَكَّرُونَ ﴿٤٦﴾ وَلَوْلَآ أَنْ تُصِيبَهُمْ

(If You had sent one) we would have followed Your commandments and would have been of the believers.'

48. But now that the truth has come to them from Us they say, 'Why has he (- this Messenger) not been given the like of that which was given to Moses?' Did the people (- the disbelievers) not reject before this that which was given to Moses? They say, 'They (- Moses and Muhammad) are both frauds who support each other.' They also say, 'We reject (the claim of) each one of them.'

49. Say, 'If (Moses and Muhammad are both fraudulent and) you speak the truth, then bring a Book from Allâh which is a better guide than these two (- the Torah and the Qur'ân), that I may follow it.'

50. If they (do not accept the challenge and) do not answer you, know that they are just following their own low and evil desires. And who should be more erring than one who leaving aside the guidance from Allâh only follows his own low and evil desires. Verily, Allâh does not guide the wrongdoing people to success.

SECTION 6

51. **W**E have been sending uninterrupted revelations to them so that they may rise to eminence.

52. (Many of) the people to whom We gave the Scripture before this (- the Qur'ân) believe in it (too).

53. And when this (Qur'ân) is recited to them, they say, 'We believe in it. It is (a revelation) from our Lord, full of truth and wisdom. Indeed, we had submitted (to Him) even before it.'

54. They are the people who will be given their reward twice over for they have been suffering patiently (for the cause of the truth). They meet evil by repaying it with good and spend (in the cause of Allâh) out of that which We have

مُّصِيبَةٌۢ بِمَا قَدَّمَتْ أَيْدِيهِمْ فَيَقُولُوا
رَبَّنَا لَوْلَآ أَرْسَلْتَ إِلَيْنَا رَسُولًا فَنَتَّبِعَ
ءَايَٰتِكَ وَنَكُونَ مِنَ الْمُؤْمِنِينَ ﴿٤٧﴾ فَلَمَّا
جَآءَهُمُ الْحَقُّ مِنْ عِندِنَا قَالُوا لَوْلَآ
أُوتِيَ مِثْلَ مَآ أُوتِيَ مُوسَىٰٓ أَوَلَمْ يَكْفُرُوا
بِمَآ أُوتِيَ مُوسَىٰ مِن قَبْلُ قَالُوا سِحْرَانِ
تَظَٰهَرَا وَقَالُوٓا إِنَّا بِكُلٍّ كَٰفِرُونَ ﴿٤٨﴾ قُلْ
فَأْتُوا بِكِتَٰبٍ مِّنْ عِندِ اللَّهِ هُوَ أَهْدَىٰ
مِنْهُمَآ أَتَّبِعْهُ إِن كُنتُمْ صَٰدِقِينَ ﴿٤٩﴾ فَإِن
لَّمْ يَسْتَجِيبُوا لَكَ فَاعْلَمْ أَنَّمَا يَتَّبِعُونَ
أَهْوَآءَهُمْ وَمَنْ أَضَلُّ مِمَّنِ اتَّبَعَ هَوَىٰهُ
بِغَيْرِ هُدًى مِّنَ اللَّهِ إِنَّ اللَّهَ لَا يَهْدِي
الْقَوْمَ الظَّٰلِمِينَ ﴿٥٠﴾ وَلَقَدْ وَصَّلْنَا لَهُمُ الْقَوْلَ
لَعَلَّهُمْ يَتَذَكَّرُونَ ﴿٥١﴾ الَّذِينَ ءَاتَيْنَٰهُمُ الْكِتَٰبَ
مِن قَبْلِهِۦ هُم بِهِۦ يُؤْمِنُونَ ﴿٥٢﴾ وَإِذَا يُتْلَىٰ
عَلَيْهِمْ قَالُوٓا ءَامَنَّا بِهِۦٓ إِنَّهُ الْحَقُّ مِن رَّبِّنَآ
إِنَّا كُنَّا مِن قَبْلِهِۦ مُسْلِمِينَ ﴿٥٣﴾ أُولَٰٓئِكَ
يُؤْتَوْنَ أَجْرَهُم مَّرَّتَيْنِ بِمَا صَبَرُوا
وَيَدْرَءُونَ بِالْحَسَنَةِ السَّيِّئَةَ وَمِمَّا

provided them with.
55. And when they hear something vain they turn away from it and say (to those who indulge in vain talk), 'We shall reap the fruit of our deeds and you shall reap the fruit of yours.' (Bidding them goodbye then say,) 'Peace be upon you. We have no desire to have any concern with the ignorant.'
56. (Prophet!) It is not possible for you to guide whomsoever you wish, but Allâh guides whomsoever He will. He knows fully well those who would accept guidance.
57. (Some of the) people say, 'If we join you and follow (this Qur'ânic) guidance we shall be snatched away from our country.' (Tell them on Our behalf,) 'Have We not settled them in a safe (and) secure place to which all kinds of fruit are brought? It is a goodly provision made by Us.' Yet most of them do not know (this true fact).
58. We destroyed (so many people of) many a township, who were proud of their civilization and their (easy and plentiful) means of livelihood. There lie their dwellings (all in ruin). They have been but little occupied since. It is We alone Who are Everlasting.
59. Your Lord would never destroy the towns until He has raised a Messenger in their central place to recite to the people thereof Our Messages, nor would We destroy the towns unless their citizens be unjust.
60. And (O people!) whatever of anything you have been given is only the passing enjoyment of the present life and its (mere) pomp and show. But that (reward) which Allâh has (for you) is much better and more lasting than this. Will you not then make use of your understanding?

SECTION 7

61. **C**AN the person to whom We have made a fair promise, which will be also made good to him, be compared to the one whom We have provided with good things (of passing nature)

رَزَقْنٰهُمْ يُنْفِقُوْنَ ﴿٥٤﴾ وَ إِذَا سَمِعُوا اللَّغْوَ
أَعْرَضُوْا عَنْهُ وَ قَالُوْا لَنَا أَعْمٰلُنَا وَ لَكُمْ
أَعْمٰلُكُمْ سَلٰمٌ عَلَيْكُمْ لَا نَبْتَغِي الْجٰهِلِيْنَ ﴿٥٥﴾
إِنَّكَ لَا تَهْدِيْ مَنْ أَحْبَبْتَ وَ لٰكِنَّ اللّٰهَ
يَهْدِيْ مَنْ يَّشَآءُ وَ هُوَ أَعْلَمُ بِالْمُهْتَدِيْنَ ﴿٥٦﴾
وَ قَالُوْا إِنْ نَّتَّبِعِ الْهُدٰى مَعَكَ نُتَخَطَّفْ
مِنْ أَرْضِنَا أَوَ لَمْ نُمَكِّنْ لَّهُمْ حَرَمًا أٰمِنًا
يُّجْبٰى إِلَيْهِ ثَمَرٰتُ كُلِّ شَيْءٍ رِّزْقًا مِّنْ
لَّدُنَّا وَ لٰكِنَّ أَكْثَرَهُمْ لَا يَعْلَمُوْنَ ﴿٥٧﴾ وَ كَمْ
أَهْلَكْنَا مِنْ قَرْيَةٍ بَطِرَتْ مَعِيْشَتَهَا فَتِلْكَ
مَسٰكِنُهُمْ لَمْ تُسْكَنْ مِّنْ بَعْدِهِمْ إِلَّا قَلِيْلًا
وَ كُنَّا نَحْنُ الْوٰرِثِيْنَ ﴿٥٨﴾ وَ مَا كَانَ رَبُّكَ
مُهْلِكَ الْقُرٰى حَتّٰى يَبْعَثَ فِيْ أُمِّهَا رَسُوْلًا
يَّتْلُوْا عَلَيْهِمْ أٰيٰتِنَا وَ مَا كُنَّا مُهْلِكِي الْقُرٰى
إِلَّا وَ أَهْلُهَا ظٰلِمُوْنَ ﴿٥٩﴾ وَ مَا أُوْتِيْتُمْ مِّنْ
شَيْءٍ فَمَتٰعُ الْحَيٰوةِ الدُّنْيَا وَ زِيْنَتُهَا
وَ مَا عِنْدَ اللّٰهِ خَيْرٌ وَّ أَبْقٰى أَفَلَا تَعْقِلُوْنَ ﴿٦٠﴾ ع ٦/ ٩
أَفَمَنْ وَّعَدْنٰهُ وَعْدًا حَسَنًا فَهُوَ لَاقِيْهِ كَمَنْ

of this life and who will be among those brought (before Us to render an account of his deeds).

62. (Let these people not forget) the day when He will call to them and say, 'Where are My (so called) associated partners about whom you had made (such) pretensions?'

63. (Thus) those who have been doomed to condemnation will say, 'Our Lord! These are the people whom we led astray, we led them astray even as we had gone astray ourselves. (Now we declare before You that) we have nothing to do with them and we turn to You. It was not us that they worshipped.'

64. It will be said (to them), 'Call on your (so called) associated partners (with God).' So they will call on them but they will give them no answer. And they will (actually) see the punishment. (How good it would have been) if they had followed the right path!

65. (Let these disbelievers not forget) the day when He will call on them and say, 'What response did you make to (the call of) the Messengers?'

66. But on that day they will become confused and forget all their excuses and they will not even (be in a position to) consult one another.

67. Yet he who repents and believes and does deeds of righteousness, is likely to be of those who attain the goal.

68. And your Lord creates what He will, and chooses (for humankind) whatever is best for them. People have no (such power and) choice. Holy is Allâh and far above all that they associate with Him.

69. Your Lord knows what they keep secret in their hearts, and (He knows) all that they profess.

70. And He is Allâh, there is no other, cannot be and will never be one worthy of worship but He. All kind of true and perfect praise belongs to Him in the beginning and the Hereafter. The sovereignty and the judgment belongs to Him

مَتَّعْنٰهُ مَتٰعَ الْحَيٰوةِ الدُّنْيَا ثُمَّ هُوَ يَوْمَ الْقِيٰمَةِ مِنَ الْمُحْضَرِينَ ﴿٦١﴾ وَيَوْمَ يُنَادِيهِمْ فَيَقُولُ أَيْنَ شُرَكَاءِيَ الَّذِينَ كُنْتُمْ تَزْعُمُونَ ﴿٦٢﴾ قَالَ الَّذِينَ حَقَّ عَلَيْهِمُ الْقَوْلُ رَبَّنَا هٰؤُلَاءِ الَّذِينَ أَغْوَيْنَا أَغْوَيْنٰهُمْ كَمَا غَوَيْنَا تَبَرَّأْنَا إِلَيْكَ مَا كَانُوا إِيَّانَا يَعْبُدُونَ ﴿٦٣﴾ وَقِيلَ ادْعُوا شُرَكَاءَكُمْ فَدَعَوْهُمْ فَلَمْ يَسْتَجِيبُوا لَهُمْ وَرَأَوُا الْعَذَابَ لَوْ أَنَّهُمْ كَانُوا يَهْتَدُونَ ﴿٦٤﴾ وَيَوْمَ يُنَادِيهِمْ فَيَقُولُ مَاذَا أَجَبْتُمُ الْمُرْسَلِينَ ﴿٦٥﴾ فَعَمِيَتْ عَلَيْهِمُ الْأَنْبَاءُ يَوْمَئِذٍ فَهُمْ لَا يَتَسَاءَلُونَ ﴿٦٦﴾ فَأَمَّا مَنْ تَابَ وَأٰمَنَ وَعَمِلَ صٰلِحًا فَعَسٰى أَنْ يَكُونَ مِنَ الْمُفْلِحِينَ ﴿٦٧﴾ وَرَبُّكَ يَخْلُقُ مَا يَشَاءُ وَيَخْتَارُ مَا كَانَ لَهُمُ الْخِيَرَةُ سُبْحٰنَ اللّٰهِ وَتَعٰلٰى عَمَّا يُشْرِكُونَ ﴿٦٨﴾ وَرَبُّكَ يَعْلَمُ مَا تُكِنُّ صُدُورُهُمْ وَمَا يُعْلِنُونَ ﴿٦٩﴾ وَهُوَ اللّٰهُ لَا إِلٰهَ إِلَّا هُوَ لَهُ الْحَمْدُ فِي الْأُولٰى وَالْأٰخِرَةِ وَلَهُ الْحُكْمُ وَإِلَيْهِ

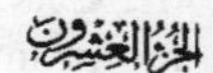

and to Him shall you be brought back.

71. Say, 'Have you (ever) considered that if Allâh should make the night continue over you perpetually till the Day of Resurrection there is no god other than Allâh Who could bring you light? Will you not (then) give ear (to the Message of God)?'

72. Say, 'Have you (ever) considered that if Allâh should make the day to continue over you perpetually till the Day of Resurrection, there is no god other than Allâh Who could bring you night wherein you might take rest? Will you not (then) use your eyes (to witness the signs of Allâh)?'

73. Behold! It is through His mercy that He has made the night and the day for you so that you may take rest therein and seek of His bounty and so that you may render (Him) thanks.

74. And (let these disbelievers not forget) the day when He will call to them and say, 'Where are My (so called) associated partners about whom you had many pretensions?'

75. And We shall (on that day) bring out a witness from every people and then say (to the polytheist), 'Bring a clear proof of your claim.' Then they will know that the true right (to Godhood) only belongs to Allâh and all (their false deities) that they used to forge will be lost to them.

SECTION 8

76. **V**ERILY, Korah belonged to the tribe of Moses (- the Israelites) but he rose against them (- his own people). We had given him so much riches that his hoarded wealth would have weighed down a party of strong men. (Recall the time) when his people said to him, 'Do not exult too much for Allâh surely does not love those who exult beyond measure.

77. 'And seek the home of the Hereafter by means of that which Allâh has given you. And do not neglect (to acquire) your portion (of righteous deeds) in the present life. And do

تُرْجَعُونَ ﴿٧٠﴾ قُلْ أَرَءَيْتُمْ إِنْ جَعَلَ اللَّهُ
عَلَيْكُمُ الَّيْلَ سَرْمَدًا إِلَىٰ يَوْمِ الْقِيَٰمَةِ
مَنْ إِلَٰهٌ غَيْرُ اللَّهِ يَأْتِيكُمْ بِضِيَاءٍ أَفَلَا
تَسْمَعُونَ ﴿٧١﴾ قُلْ أَرَءَيْتُمْ إِنْ جَعَلَ اللَّهُ
عَلَيْكُمُ النَّهَارَ سَرْمَدًا إِلَىٰ يَوْمِ الْقِيَٰمَةِ مَنْ
إِلَٰهٌ غَيْرُ اللَّهِ يَأْتِيكُمْ بِلَيْلٍ تَسْكُنُونَ
فِيهِ أَفَلَا تُبْصِرُونَ ﴿٧٢﴾ وَمِنْ رَّحْمَتِهِ جَعَلَ
لَكُمُ الَّيْلَ وَالنَّهَارَ لِتَسْكُنُوا فِيهِ وَلِتَبْتَغُوا
مِنْ فَضْلِهِ وَلَعَلَّكُمْ تَشْكُرُونَ ﴿٧٣﴾ وَيَوْمَ
يُنَادِيهِمْ فَيَقُولُ أَيْنَ شُرَكَاءِيَ الَّذِينَ
كُنْتُمْ تَزْعُمُونَ ﴿٧٤﴾ وَنَزَعْنَا مِنْ كُلِّ أُمَّةٍ
شَهِيدًا فَقُلْنَا هَاتُوا بُرْهَٰنَكُمْ فَعَلِمُوا أَنَّ
الْحَقَّ لِلَّهِ وَضَلَّ عَنْهُمْ مَّا كَانُوا يَفْتَرُونَ ﴿٧٥﴾ ع ٧/١٠
إِنَّ قَٰرُونَ كَانَ مِنْ قَوْمِ مُوسَىٰ فَبَغَىٰ
عَلَيْهِمْ وَءَاتَيْنَٰهُ مِنَ الْكُنُوزِ مَا إِنَّ
مَفَاتِحَهُ لَتَنُوأُ بِالْعُصْبَةِ أُولِي الْقُوَّةِ إِذْ
قَالَ لَهُ قَوْمُهُ لَا تَفْرَحْ إِنَّ اللَّهَ لَا يُحِبُّ
الْفَرِحِينَ ﴿٧٦﴾ وَابْتَغِ فِيمَا ءَاتَىٰكَ اللَّهُ الدَّارَ
الْآخِرَةَ وَلَا تَنْسَ نَصِيبَكَ مِنَ الدُّنْيَا

good to others as Allâh has done good to you. And do not seek to promote evil in the land, for Allâh does not love the evil doers who create mischief.'

78. (Korah) said, '(All) this (wealth) that I have been given is because of the knowledge I possess.' But did he not know that Allâh had destroyed before him generations of people who were mightier than he and greater in riches and number? And the guilty shall not be questioned about their sins (their sins being self evident).

79. Then (it came to pass one day that) he (- Korah) appeared before his people in all his pomp and show. (Thereupon) those who were desirous of (the provisions and enjoyment of) the life of this world said, 'If only we could have the like of all that Korah has been given. He is, truly speaking, the master of a great fortune.'

80. But the men of knowledge said, 'Woe to you! The reward which Allâh has for those who believe and do good deeds is much better (than all this), but it shall be granted only to those who are patiently persevering.'

81. Then (it came about that) We made him and his household extinct into the bowels of the earth so that he had no party who could help him against Allâh, nor was he of those who could defend themselves and could ask for help.

82. Now the very people who had coveted his (lot and) position the day before began to say, 'Ruin seize you! It is indeed Allâh Who multiplies the means of livelihood for such of His servants as He will and makes them scant (for such of His people as He will). Had not Allâh been gracious to us He would have sunk us (also into the bowels of the earth). Ruin seize you! (the fact is that) those who are ungrateful never prosper.'

SECTION 9

83. **T**HIS is the Abode of the Hereafter, We

وَأَحْسِنْ كَمَآ أَحْسَنَ اللّٰهُ إِلَيْكَ وَلَا
تَبْغِ الْفَسَادَ فِي الْأَرْضِ إِنَّ اللّٰهَ لَا يُحِبُّ
الْمُفْسِدِينَ ﴿٧٧﴾ قَالَ إِنَّمَآ أُوتِيتُهُ عَلَىٰ عِلْمٍ
عِنْدِيْ أَوَلَمْ يَعْلَمْ أَنَّ اللّٰهَ قَدْ أَهْلَكَ
مِنْ قَبْلِهِ مِنَ الْقُرُونِ مَنْ هُوَ أَشَدُّ مِنْهُ
قُوَّةً وَّأَكْثَرُ جَمْعًا وَلَا يُسْئَلُ عَنْ
ذُنُوبِهِمُ الْمُجْرِمُونَ ﴿٧٨﴾ فَخَرَجَ عَلَىٰ قَوْمِهِ
فِيْ زِينَتِهِ قَالَ الَّذِينَ يُرِيدُونَ الْحَيٰوةَ
الدُّنْيَا يٰلَيْتَ لَنَا مِثْلَ مَآ أُوتِيَ قٰرُونُ
إِنَّهُ لَذُوْ حَظٍّ عَظِيمٍ ﴿٧٩﴾ وَقَالَ الَّذِينَ
أُوتُوا الْعِلْمَ وَيْلَكُمْ ثَوَابُ اللّٰهِ خَيْرٌ
لِّمَنْ أٰمَنَ وَعَمِلَ صٰلِحًا وَلَا يُلَقّٰهَآ إِلَّا
الصّٰبِرُونَ ﴿٨٠﴾ فَخَسَفْنَا بِهِ وَبِدَارِهِ الْأَرْضَ
فَمَا كَانَ لَهُ مِنْ فِئَةٍ يَّنْصُرُونَهُ مِنْ
دُونِ اللّٰهِ وَمَا كَانَ مِنَ الْمُنْتَصِرِينَ ﴿٨١﴾
وَأَصْبَحَ الَّذِينَ تَمَنَّوْا مَكَانَهُ بِالْأَمْسِ
يَقُولُونَ وَيْكَأَنَّ اللّٰهَ يَبْسُطُ الرِّزْقَ لِمَنْ
يَّشَآءُ مِنْ عِبَادِهِ وَيَقْدِرُ لَوْلَآ أَنْ مَّنَّ
اللّٰهُ عَلَيْنَا لَخَسَفَ بِنَا وَيْكَأَنَّهُ لَا يُفْلِحُ
الْكٰفِرُونَ ﴿٨٢﴾ تِلْكَ الدَّارُ الْأٰخِرَةُ نَجْعَلُهَا

assign it to those only who do not seek self-exaltation in the earth, nor corruption. Indeed, those who guard against evil shall meet a happy end.

84. He who brings good deeds (into the presence of his Lord on the Day of judgment) shall have a reward (at His hand) better than he merits. But he who brings evil (let him bear in mind that) those who do evil shall only reap the fruit according to what they did.

85. (Prophet!) He Who has made (the teaching of) the Qur'ân binding on you shall most surely bring you back to your ordained place of return, (the place of Pilgrimage - Makkah). Say, 'My Lord knows him best who has brought guidance as well as those who are steeped in clear error.'

86. (Prophet!) You had never expected that the Book would be revealed to you. It is only the mercy of your Lord (that it has been revealed to you). So do not be a supporter of the disbelievers.

87. And do not let them (the disbelievers) turn you away from the commandments of Allâh when once they have been revealed to you. And call (humankind) to your Lord and be not of those who associate partners (with Him).

88. Call on no other god beside Allâh. There is no other, cannot be and will never be one worthy of worship but He. Everything is liable to perish but those (righteous deeds) by means of which you seek His attention. The sovereignty as well as judgment belongs to Him and to Him you shall all be brought back.

لِلَّذِينَ لَا يُرِيدُونَ عُلُوًّا فِي الْأَرْضِ وَلَا
فَسَادًا ۚ وَالْعَٰقِبَةُ لِلْمُتَّقِينَ ﴿٨٣﴾ مَنْ جَآءَ
بِالْحَسَنَةِ فَلَهُۥ خَيْرٌ مِّنْهَا ۖ وَمَنْ جَآءَ
بِالسَّيِّئَةِ فَلَا يُجْزَى الَّذِينَ عَمِلُوا السَّيِّـَٔاتِ
إِلَّا مَا كَانُوا يَعْمَلُونَ ﴿٨٤﴾ إِنَّ الَّذِي فَرَضَ
عَلَيْكَ الْقُرْءَانَ لَرَآدُّكَ إِلَىٰ مَعَادٍ ۚ قُل رَّبِّيٓ
أَعْلَمُ مَنْ جَآءَ بِالْهُدَىٰ وَمَنْ هُوَ فِي
ضَلَٰلٍ مُّبِينٍ ﴿٨٥﴾ وَمَا كُنتَ تَرْجُوٓا أَن
يُلْقَىٰٓ إِلَيْكَ الْكِتَٰبُ إِلَّا رَحْمَةً مِّن رَّبِّكَ
فَلَا تَكُونَنَّ ظَهِيرًا لِّلْكَٰفِرِينَ ﴿٨٦﴾ وَلَا يَصُدُّنَّكَ
عَنْ ءَايَٰتِ اللَّهِ بَعْدَ إِذْ أُنزِلَتْ إِلَيْكَ
وَادْعُ إِلَىٰ رَبِّكَ وَلَا تَكُونَنَّ مِنَ
الْمُشْرِكِينَ ﴿٨٧﴾ وَلَا تَدْعُ مَعَ اللَّهِ إِلَٰهًا
ءَاخَرَ لَآ إِلَٰهَ إِلَّا هُوَ ۚ كُلُّ شَيْءٍ هَالِكٌ إِلَّا
وَجْهَهُۥ ۚ لَهُ الْحُكْمُ وَإِلَيْهِ تُرْجَعُونَ ﴿٨٨﴾

سُوْرَةُ الْعَنْكَبُوْتِ ٢٩

CHAPTER
29

AL-'ANKABÛT
(The Spider)
(Revealed before Hijrah)

سُوْرَةُ الْعَنْكَبُوْتِ مَكِّيَّةٌ

With the name of Allâh,
the Most Gracious, the Ever Merciful
(I commence to read Sûrah Al-'Ankabût).

بِسْمِ اللّٰهِ الرَّحْمٰنِ الرَّحِيْمِ

1. **A**LIF LÂM MÎM - I am Allâh, the All-Knowing.
2. Do the people think that they will be left alone and not tried with hardships for the mere fact that they profess belief.
3. Whereas We did already try those who were before them with hardships. Allâh will surely bring to light those who are true in their faith as He will bring to light also the liars (by putting them into troubles).
4. Or do those who do evil deeds think that they will escape Our punishment? How ill they judge!
5. He that looks forward to meet Allâh (let him be prepared for it) for the time appointed by Allâh is bound to come. He is the All-Hearing, the All-Knowing.
6. And he who strives hard (in the way of Allâh) does it, in fact, for his own good. Verily, Allâh is Independent of the worlds.
7. And those who believe and do deeds of righteousness We shall invariably rid them of their evils and We shall, of course, reward them according to the best of their deeds.
8. We have enjoined on a human being to be kind to his parents, but should they stress upon you to associate with Me things which you know to be nothing at all you shall not obey them. You shall all have to return to Me (after all). I shall tell you all that you have been doing (in your life).
9. And as to those who believe and do deeds of

الٓمّٓ ① أَحَسِبَ النَّاسُ أَنْ يُّتْرَكُوْٓا أَنْ
يَّقُوْلُوْٓا اٰمَنَّا وَهُمْ لَا يُفْتَنُوْنَ ② وَلَقَدْ فَتَنَّا
الَّذِيْنَ مِنْ قَبْلِهِمْ فَلَيَعْلَمَنَّ اللّٰهُ الَّذِيْنَ
صَدَقُوْا وَلَيَعْلَمَنَّ الْكٰذِبِيْنَ ③ أَمْ حَسِبَ
الَّذِيْنَ يَعْمَلُوْنَ السَّيِّاٰتِ أَنْ يَّسْبِقُوْنَا
سَآءَ مَا يَحْكُمُوْنَ ④ مَنْ كَانَ يَرْجُوْا لِقَآءَ
اللّٰهِ فَإِنَّ أَجَلَ اللّٰهِ لَاٰتٍ وَهُوَ السَّمِيْعُ
الْعَلِيْمُ ⑤ وَمَنْ جٰهَدَ فَإِنَّمَا يُجٰهِدُ لِنَفْسِهٖ
إِنَّ اللّٰهَ لَغَنِيٌّ عَنِ الْعٰلَمِيْنَ ⑥ وَالَّذِيْنَ
اٰمَنُوْا وَعَمِلُوا الصّٰلِحٰتِ لَنُكَفِّرَنَّ
عَنْهُمْ سَيِّاٰتِهِمْ وَلَنَجْزِيَنَّهُمْ أَحْسَنَ
الَّذِيْ كَانُوْا يَعْمَلُوْنَ ⑦ وَوَصَّيْنَا
الْإِنْسٰنَ بِوٰلِدَيْهِ حُسْنًا وَإِنْ جٰهَدٰكَ
لِتُشْرِكَ بِيْ مَا لَيْسَ لَكَ بِهٖ عِلْمٌ فَلَا
تُطِعْهُمَا إِلَيَّ مَرْجِعُكُمْ فَأُنَبِّئُكُمْ بِمَا
كُنْتُمْ تَعْمَلُوْنَ ⑧ وَالَّذِيْنَ اٰمَنُوْا وَعَمِلُوا

righteousness We will certainly admit them to (the fold of) the righteous.

10. There are some (hypocrites) among the people who say, 'We believe in Allâh.' But when they are made to suffer in the cause of Allâh they regard the persecution by people as it were the punishment from Allâh. Yet if help comes from your Lord (and He gives you victory) they are sure to say, 'Of course, we were with you, (we should also have a share in it).' Why! Does not Allâh know well enough what lies hidden in the hearts of all beings?

11. Indeed, Allâh will bring to light those who believe, and He will also reveal the hypocrites.

12. And those who disbelieve say to those who believe, 'Follow our way and we will bear (the consequences of) your sins (at the time of judgment), whereas they can bear nothing whatsoever of their sins. They are as a matter of fact liars.

13. (On the other hand) they will certainly have to bear the burdens of their own sins as well as (some) burdens (of leading others astray) over and above their own burdens. And they will be questioned on the Day of Resurrection about (the lies) that they used to fabricate.

SECTION 2

14. **A**ND we indeed sent Noah to his people and he (- his teachings) stayed among them for (as long as) a thousand years short of fifty years (- nine hundred and fifty years). While his people were steeped in wrongdoings they were caught in the Deluge.

15. However, We delivered him and (along with him all) those who were in the Ark, and We made this (event) a sign for the peoples.

16. And (We sent) Abraham. (Recall the time) when he said to his people, 'Worship Allâh and take Him as a shield. That is best for you if you but knew.

17. '(The things) you worship apart from Allâh are only false gods. And (in calling them gods) you forge lies. Those (gods) whom you wor-

الصّٰلِحٰتِ لَنُدْخِلَنَّهُمْ فِي الصّٰلِحِيْنَ ﴿٩﴾
وَ مِنَ النَّاسِ مَنْ يَّقُوْلُ اٰمَنَّا بِاللّٰهِ
فَإِذَآ أُوْذِيَ فِي اللّٰهِ جَعَلَ فِتْنَةَ النَّاسِ
كَعَذَابِ اللّٰهِ ؕ وَ لَئِنْ جَآءَ نَصْرٌ مِّنْ
رَّبِّكَ لَيَقُوْلُنَّ إِنَّا كُنَّا مَعَكُمْ ؕ أَوَ لَيْسَ
اللّٰهُ بِأَعْلَمَ بِمَا فِيْ صُدُوْرِ الْعٰلَمِيْنَ ﴿١٠﴾
وَ لَيَعْلَمَنَّ اللّٰهُ الَّذِيْنَ اٰمَنُوْا وَ لَيَعْلَمَنَّ
الْمُنٰفِقِيْنَ ﴿١١﴾ وَ قَالَ الَّذِيْنَ كَفَرُوْا
لِلَّذِيْنَ اٰمَنُوا اتَّبِعُوْا سَبِيْلَنَا وَ لْنَحْمِلْ
خَطٰيٰكُمْ ؕ وَ مَا هُمْ بِحٰمِلِيْنَ مِنْ خَطٰيٰهُمْ
مِّنْ شَيْءٍ ؕ إِنَّهُمْ لَكٰذِبُوْنَ ﴿١٢﴾ وَ لَيَحْمِلُنَّ
أَثْقَالَهُمْ وَ أَثْقَالًا مَّعَ أَثْقَالِهِمْ ؗ وَ لَيُسْـَٔلُنَّ
يَوْمَ الْقِيٰمَةِ عَمَّا كَانُوْا يَفْتَرُوْنَ ﴿١٣﴾ ع ١٣
وَ لَقَدْ أَرْسَلْنَا نُوْحًا إِلٰى قَوْمِهٖ فَلَبِثَ
فِيْهِمْ أَلْفَ سَنَةٍ إِلَّا خَمْسِيْنَ عَامًا ؕ
فَأَخَذَهُمُ الطُّوْفَانُ وَ هُمْ ظٰلِمُوْنَ ﴿١٤﴾
فَأَنْجَيْنٰهُ وَ أَصْحٰبَ السَّفِيْنَةِ وَ جَعَلْنٰهَآ
اٰيَةً لِّلْعٰلَمِيْنَ ﴿١٥﴾ وَ إِبْرٰهِيْمَ إِذْ قَالَ
لِقَوْمِهِ اعْبُدُوا اللّٰهَ وَ اتَّقُوْهُ ؕ ذٰلِكُمْ
خَيْرٌ لَّكُمْ إِنْ كُنْتُمْ تَعْلَمُوْنَ ﴿١٦﴾ إِنَّمَا
تَعْبُدُوْنَ مِنْ دُوْنِ اللّٰهِ أَوْثٰنًا وَّ تَخْلُقُوْنَ
إِفْكًا ؕ إِنَّ الَّذِيْنَ تَعْبُدُوْنَ مِنْ دُوْنِ

ship beside Allâh do not have the means to provide sustenance for you. Therefore seek sustenance and provision for yourselves from Allâh and worship Him and give Him thanks for you will be brought back to Him (one day).
18. 'And if you deny (me) then (you should not forget that) people before you have also cried lies (to their respective Messengers), and the Messenger is responsible only for conveying (the Divine Message to the people) in clear terms.
19. 'Do the people not (ever) consider how Allâh originates the creation, then continues repeating and reproducing it. This (work of creation and reproduction) is indeed easy for Allâh.'
20. Say, 'Travel through the earth and observe how He brought about the first creation. Allâh will as well bring about the second creation in the Hereafter. Verily, Allâh is Possessor of (prudential) powers over all (His) desired things.
21. 'He punishes whom He will (of the guilty) and shows mercy to whom He will and to Him you shall have to be turned back.
22. 'You cannot escape (Him) on the earth or in the heaven and you have no patron nor (even) a helper apart from Allâh.'

SECTION 3

23. **A**ND those who deny the signs of Allâh and (deny) that they will meet Him are actually despaired of My mercy. It is they for whom awaits a grievous punishment.
24. His people had no response to make (to Abraham) but they said, 'Kill him (- Abraham) or rather burn him.' (At last they decided upon burning him) but Allâh delivered him from the fire. There are sure signs in this (episode) for the people who would believe.
25. (Abraham) said, 'You have certainly taken for yourselves idols (for worship) apart from Allâh as a mark of mutual love between you (all polytheist brethren) in the present life. But on

سُوْرَةُ الْعَنْكَبُوتِ ٢٩

اللّٰهِ لَا يَمْلِكُوْنَ لَكُمْ رِزْقًا فَابْتَغُوْا
عِنْدَ اللّٰهِ الرِّزْقَ وَ اعْبُدُوْهُ وَ اشْكُرُوْا
لَهٗ إِلَيْهِ تُرْجَعُوْنَ ١٧ وَ إِنْ تُكَذِّبُوْا فَقَدْ
كَذَّبَ أُمَمٌ مِّنْ قَبْلِكُمْ وَ مَا عَلَى
الرَّسُوْلِ إِلَّا الْبَلٰغُ الْمُبِيْنُ ١٨ أَوَ لَمْ يَرَوْا
كَيْفَ يُبْدِئُ اللّٰهُ الْخَلْقَ ثُمَّ يُعِيْدُهٗ
إِنَّ ذٰلِكَ عَلَى اللّٰهِ يَسِيْرٌ ١٩ قُلْ سِيْرُوْا
فِي الْأَرْضِ فَانْظُرُوْا كَيْفَ بَدَأَ الْخَلْقَ
ثُمَّ اللّٰهُ يُنْشِئُ النَّشْأَةَ الْأٰخِرَةَ إِنَّ اللّٰهَ
عَلٰى كُلِّ شَيْءٍ قَدِيْرٌ ٢٠ يُعَذِّبُ مَنْ يَّشَاءُ
وَ يَرْحَمُ مَنْ يَّشَاءُ وَ إِلَيْهِ تُقْلَبُوْنَ ٢١
وَ مَا أَنْتُمْ بِمُعْجِزِيْنَ فِي الْأَرْضِ وَ لَا
فِي السَّمَاءِ وَ مَا لَكُمْ مِّنْ دُوْنِ اللّٰهِ
مِنْ وَّلِيٍّ وَّ لَا نَصِيْرٍ ٢٢ وَ الَّذِيْنَ كَفَرُوْا
بِأٰيٰتِ اللّٰهِ وَ لِقَائِهٖ أُولٰٓئِكَ يَئِسُوْا مِنْ
رَّحْمَتِيْ وَ أُولٰٓئِكَ لَهُمْ عَذَابٌ أَلِيْمٌ ٢٣
فَمَا كَانَ جَوَابَ قَوْمِهٖ إِلَّا أَنْ قَالُوا
اقْتُلُوْهُ أَوْ حَرِّقُوْهُ فَأَنْجٰهُ اللّٰهُ مِنَ
النَّارِ إِنَّ فِيْ ذٰلِكَ لَأٰيٰتٍ لِّقَوْمٍ يُّؤْمِنُوْنَ ٢٤
وَ قَالَ إِنَّمَا اتَّخَذْتُمْ مِّنْ دُوْنِ اللّٰهِ
أَوْثَانًا مَّوَدَّةَ بَيْنِكُمْ فِي الْحَيٰوةِ الدُّنْيَا

the Day of Resurrection you will disown one another and curse one another and your resort will be the Fire and you will have none to help you.'

26. And Lot became a believer because of him, and (Abraham) said, 'I shall migrate (where I have been commanded to) by my Lord. He is the All-Mighty, the All-Wise.'

27. And We bestowed on him (righteous offsprings,) Isaac (a son) and Jacob (a grandson), and We perpetuated (the gift of) prophethood and the Scripture in his descendants. And We gave him his reward in this life and he will most surely (occupy an eminent place) among the righteous in the Hereafter.

28. And (We sent) Lot. Behold, he said to his people, 'You indulge in such an obscenity as is unprecedented and unsurpassed in the whole world.

29. 'Is it not true you approach men (lustfully) and commit highway robbery? (Is it not true also) you commit indecent action in your gatherings?' But his people had no response to make, (yet) they said, 'Bring upon us the punishment of Allâh if you are of those who speak the truth.'

30. (Thereupon Lot) said, 'Help me, my Lord! Against these people who work corruption.'

SECTION 4

31. **A**ND when Our messengers came to Abraham with important news, they said, 'We are going to destroy people of this township for its inhabitants are certainly wrongdoers.'

32. (Abraham) said, 'But Lot is (living) there (in that township).' They said, 'We know very well who are (living) in it. We will surely save him and his family except his wife, who is among those who stay behind.'

33. And when Our messengers came to Lot he felt distressed on account of their (coming) for he felt helpless to give them protection. But they (- the messenger) said, 'Have no fear and do not grieve, (Allâh promises you protection

ثُمَّ يَوْمَ الْقِيٰمَةِ يَكْفُرُ بَعْضُكُمْ بِبَعْضٍ
وَّ يَلْعَنُ بَعْضُكُمْ بَعْضًا وَّ مَأْوٰىكُمُ النَّارُ
وَ مَا لَكُمْ مِّنْ نّٰصِرِيْنَ ﴿٢٥﴾ فَاٰمَنَ لَهٗ
لُوْطٌ وَ قَالَ إِنِّيْ مُهَاجِرٌ إِلٰى رَبِّيْ إِنَّهٗ
هُوَ الْعَزِيْزُ الْحَكِيْمُ ﴿٢٦﴾ وَ وَهَبْنَا لَهٗٓ
إِسْحٰقَ وَ يَعْقُوْبَ وَ جَعَلْنَا فِيْ ذُرِّيَّتِهِ
النُّبُوَّةَ وَ الْكِتٰبَ وَ اٰتَيْنٰهُ أَجْرَهٗ فِي
الدُّنْيَا وَ إِنَّهٗ فِي الْاٰخِرَةِ لَمِنَ الصّٰلِحِيْنَ ﴿٢٧﴾
وَ لُوْطًا إِذْ قَالَ لِقَوْمِهٖٓ إِنَّكُمْ لَتَأْتُوْنَ
الْفٰحِشَةَ مَا سَبَقَكُمْ بِهَا مِنْ أَحَدٍ
مِّنَ الْعٰلَمِيْنَ ﴿٢٨﴾ أَئِنَّكُمْ لَتَأْتُوْنَ الرِّجَالَ
وَ تَقْطَعُوْنَ السَّبِيْلَ ۵ وَ تَأْتُوْنَ فِيْ نَادِيْكُمُ
الْمُنْكَرَ فَمَا كَانَ جَوَابَ قَوْمِهٖٓ إِلَّآ
أَنْ قَالُوا ائْتِنَا بِعَذَابِ اللهِ إِنْ كُنْتَ
مِنَ الصّٰدِقِيْنَ ﴿٢٩﴾ قَالَ رَبِّ انْصُرْنِيْ عَلَى
الْقَوْمِ الْمُفْسِدِيْنَ ﴿٣٠﴾ وَ لَمَّا جَآءَتْ رُسُلُنَآ
إِبْرٰهِيْمَ بِالْبُشْرٰى قَالُوْٓا إِنَّا مُهْلِكُوْٓا
أَهْلِ هٰذِهِ الْقَرْيَةِ إِنَّ أَهْلَهَا كَانُوْا
ظٰلِمِيْنَ ﴿٣١﴾ قَالَ إِنَّ فِيْهَا لُوْطًا قَالُوْا
نَحْنُ أَعْلَمُ بِمَنْ فِيْهَا لَنُنَجِّيَنَّهٗ وَ أَهْلَهٗٓ
إِلَّا امْرَأَتَهٗ كَانَتْ مِنَ الْغٰبِرِيْنَ ﴿٣٢﴾
وَ لَمَّآ أَنْ جَآءَتْ رُسُلُنَا لُوْطًا سِيْٓءَ بِهِمْ
وَ ضَاقَ بِهِمْ ذَرْعًا وَّ قَالُوْا لَا تَخَفْ وَ لَا

ع ٣ ٨ ١٥

saying,) "We will deliver you and all your household except your wife (who will not leave the place stricken with calamity and) who is among those staying behind.
34. '(As for) the inhabitants of this township; We are going to bring down upon them an unavoidable calamity, for they have been behaving disobediently.'''
35. Behold! We have left there (- in the ruins of this township) a clear sign for a people who would care to understand.
36. And to Midianites (We sent) their kinsman Shu'aib. He said, 'My people worship Allâh and hope (putting your faithful confidence in it) for the Last Day and do not act corruptly, behaving lawlessly in the country.'
37. But (instead of obeying him) they cried him (-Shu'aib) lies. So they were caught in a violent earthquake and they became (corpses) laid down on their chests on the ground in their dwellings.
38. And (We destroyed the tribes of) 'Âd and Thamûd; and (this) must have become clear to you from their dwellings. Satan made their (evil) deeds fair-seeming to them and (by making them take pride in their doings) turned them away from the right way, though they were enlightened and sagacious people.
39. And (similar was the fate met by) Korah, Pharaoh and Hâmân. Moses had come to them with manifest signs but they behaved arrogantly on the earth yet they could not outstrip (Us and thus escape Our punishment).
40. In short We took each one of them to task for his sins. Against some of them We sent a violent storm of sand and stones while others were overtaken by a roaring blast and some others We made extinct in (the bowels of) the earth, and yet others We drowned. It was far from Allâh to have done injustice to them. Rather they were doing wrong to themselves.
41. The case of those who take helping friends

تَحْزَنْ إِنَّا مُنَجُّوكَ وَأَهْلَكَ إِلَّا امْرَأَتَكَ
كَانَتْ مِنَ الْغٰبِرِينَ ﴿٣٣﴾ إِنَّا مُنْزِلُونَ عَلٰى
أَهْلِ هٰذِهِ الْقَرْيَةِ رِجْزًا مِّنَ السَّمَآءِ
بِمَا كَانُوا يَفْسُقُونَ ﴿٣٤﴾ وَلَقَدْ تَّرَكْنَا
مِنْهَآ اٰيَةً بَيِّنَةً لِّقَوْمٍ يَّعْقِلُونَ ﴿٣٥﴾ وَإِلٰى
مَدْيَنَ أَخَاهُمْ شُعَيْبًا فَقَالَ يٰقَوْمِ
اعْبُدُوا اللّٰهَ وَارْجُوا الْيَوْمَ الْاٰخِرَ وَلَا
تَعْثَوْا فِي الْأَرْضِ مُفْسِدِينَ ﴿٣٦﴾ فَكَذَّبُوهُ
فَأَخَذَتْهُمُ الرَّجْفَةُ فَأَصْبَحُوا فِي دَارِهِمْ
جٰثِمِينَ ﴿٣٧﴾ وَعَادًا وَّثَمُودَاْ وَقَدْ تَّبَيَّنَ
لَكُمْ مِّنْ مَّسٰكِنِهِمْ وَزَيَّنَ لَهُمُ
الشَّيْطٰنُ أَعْمٰلَهُمْ فَصَدَّهُمْ عَنِ
السَّبِيلِ وَكَانُوا مُسْتَبْصِرِينَ ﴿٣٨﴾
وَقٰرُونَ وَفِرْعَوْنَ وَهٰمٰنَ وَلَقَدْ
جَآءَهُمْ مُّوسٰى بِالْبَيِّنٰتِ فَاسْتَكْبَرُوا
فِي الْأَرْضِ وَمَا كَانُوا سٰبِقِينَ ﴿٣٩﴾
فَكُلًّا أَخَذْنَا بِذَنْبِهِ فَمِنْهُمْ مَّنْ
أَرْسَلْنَا عَلَيْهِ حَاصِبًا وَمِنْهُمْ مَّنْ
أَخَذَتْهُ الصَّيْحَةُ وَمِنْهُمْ مَّنْ خَسَفْنَا
بِهِ الْأَرْضَ وَمِنْهُمْ مَّنْ أَغْرَقْنَا
وَمَا كَانَ اللّٰهُ لِيَظْلِمَهُمْ وَلٰكِنْ كَانُوا
أَنْفُسَهُمْ يَظْلِمُونَ ﴿٤٠﴾ مَثَلُ الَّذِينَ

apart from Allâh is like the case of the spider that takes (to itself) a house, yet of (all) houses the house of the spider is the frailest. If they but knew (the flimsiness and fragility of their idols they would not have sought their protection).
42. Verily, Allâh knows whatever they call upon apart from Him. He is the All-Mighty, the All-Wise.
43 These are the (various) situations which We set forth for the (benefit of) humankind, yet, except for the learned, nobody tries to grasp them.
44. Allâh has created the heavens and the earth to suit the requirements of truth and wisdom (and for a significant end). In this there is, in fact, a great sign for the believers.

سورة العنكبوت ٢٩

اتخذوا من دون الله أولياء كمثل
العنكبوت اتخذت بيتا وإن أوهن
البيوت لبيت العنكبوت لو كانوا
يعلمون ﴿٤١﴾ إن الله يعلم ما يدعون
من دونه من شيء وهو العزيز
الحكيم ﴿٤٢﴾ وتلك الأمثال نضربها
للناس وما يعقلها إلا العلمون ﴿٤٣﴾
خلق الله السموت والأرض بالحق
إن في ذلك لأية للمؤمنين ﴿٤٤﴾

PART الجزء الحادي والعشرون XXI

SECTION 5

45. **R**ECITE (preach, follow and meditate on) that which has been revealed to you of the Book (-the Qur'ân) and observe Prayer. Verily, Prayer restrains (the observer) from indecency and abominable things and loathsome deeds and from all that runs counter to reason and moral sense. Yet of all, the greatest thing is that Allâh will remember you and help you rise to eminence. And Allâh knows all that you do.
46. (Believers!) observe all the propriety when you argue with the people of the Scripture; but those who are bent upon behaving unjustly among them do not agree to these principles (so deal with them accordingly). And say (to them), 'We believe in all that is revealed to us and in that which has been revealed to you, and our God and your God is One, and to Him we stand resigned.'
47. And for a similar purpose (of confirming and testifying to the truth of all previous Scriptures) have We sent down to you this perfect

اتل ما أوحي إليك من الكتب وأقم
الصلوة إن الصلوة تنهى عن الفحشاء
والمنكر ولذكر الله أكبر والله يعلم
ما تصنعون ﴿٤٥﴾ ولا تجدلوا أهل الكتب
إلا بالتي هي أحسن إلا الذين ظلموا
منهم وقولوا أمنا بالذي أنزل إلينا
وأنزل إليكم وإلهنا وإلهكم وحد
ونحن له مسلمون ﴿٤٦﴾ وكذلك أنزلنا

Book. And those whom We have given (the true knowledge of) the Book (Torah) believe in it and of these (Makkans who possessed no sacred Scriptures before) there are some who believe in it (- the Qur'ân). And it is only the ungrateful (disbelievers) who deny Our revelations deliberately and persistently.

48. (Prophet!) you read no book, nor did you write one with your own hand before this (Qur'ân was revealed). (Had it been so,) those who declare (it) as false could then (have the cause to) entertain some doubts.

49. Nay, (far from being an invention) this (Qur'ân) is full of clear signs in the minds of those who have been given true knowledge. It is only the unjust indeed who deny Our signs deliberately.

50. And they say, 'Why have no signs (of punishment) been revealed to him from his Lord?' Say (to them), 'The signs are many with Allâh, accordingly I am about to give you plain warning (concerning some of the signs of punishment).'

51. Well, is this (sign of mercy) not enough for them that We have revealed to you this perfect Book which is recited to them. As a matter of fact it comprises mercy (and blessings) and is a means to rise to eminence for the people who would believe.

SECTION 6

52. **S**AY, 'Sufficient is Allâh as a Witness between me and you. He knows all that lies in the heavens and on the earth. And lost are those who believe in falsehood and disbelieve in Allâh.

53. They demand you to precipitate the (sign of their) punishment. Had not their term been stated (as a respite to mend their evil ways), the punishment would surely have come upon them. It shall come and will befall them unexpectedly and take them unawares.

54. They still demand you to precipitate (their) punishment, while Gehenna will most

إِلَيْكَ الْكِتٰبَ فَالَّذِينَ ءَاتَيْنٰهُمُ الْكِتٰبَ
يُؤْمِنُونَ بِهِ وَمِنْ هٰٓؤُلَآءِ مَنْ يُؤْمِنُ
بِهِ وَمَا يَجْحَدُ بِـَٔايٰتِنَآ إِلَّا الْكٰفِرُونَ ﴿٤٧﴾
وَمَا كُنْتَ تَتْلُوا مِنْ قَبْلِهِ مِنْ كِتٰبٍ وَلَا
تَخُطُّهُ بِيَمِينِكَ إِذًا لَّارْتَابَ الْمُبْطِلُونَ ﴿٤٨﴾
بَلْ هُوَ ءَايٰتٌۢ بَيِّنٰتٌ فِي صُدُورِ الَّذِينَ أُوتُوا
الْعِلْمَ وَمَا يَجْحَدُ بِـَٔايٰتِنَآ إِلَّا الظّٰلِمُونَ ﴿٤٩﴾
وَقَالُوا لَوْلَآ أُنْزِلَ عَلَيْهِ ءَايٰتٌ مِّنْ رَّبِّهِ قُلْ
إِنَّمَا الْءَايٰتُ عِنْدَ اللهِ وَإِنَّمَآ أَنَا۠ نَذِيرٌ
مُّبِينٌ ﴿٥٠﴾ أَوَلَمْ يَكْفِهِمْ أَنَّآ أَنْزَلْنَا عَلَيْكَ
الْكِتٰبَ يُتْلٰى عَلَيْهِمْ إِنَّ فِي ذٰلِكَ لَرَحْمَةً
وَذِكْرٰى لِقَوْمٍ يُؤْمِنُونَ ﴿٥١﴾ قُلْ كَفٰى بِاللهِ
بَيْنِي وَبَيْنَكُمْ شَهِيدًا يَعْلَمُ مَا فِي السَّمٰوٰتِ
وَالْأَرْضِ وَالَّذِينَ ءَامَنُوا بِالْبٰطِلِ وَكَفَرُوا
بِاللهِ أُولٰٓئِكَ هُمُ الْخٰسِرُونَ ﴿٥٢﴾ وَيَسْتَعْجِلُونَكَ
بِالْعَذَابِ وَلَوْلَآ أَجَلٌ مُّسَمًّى لَّجَآءَهُمُ الْعَذَابُ
وَلَيَأْتِيَنَّهُمْ بَغْتَةً وَهُمْ لَا يَشْعُرُونَ ﴿٥٣﴾
يَسْتَعْجِلُونَكَ بِالْعَذَابِ وَإِنَّ جَهَنَّمَ

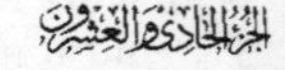

surely spell the end of these disbelievers.
55. (It shall be) the day when the punishment will overwhelm them from above their heads and (will come upon them) from below their feet. And He will say, 'Suffer the consequences of your (evil) deeds.'
56. My believing servants! My earth is indeed vast. You should worship Me and Me alone.
57. Every living being shall encounter death, then you shall be made to return to Us.
58. And those who believe and do deeds of righteousness We shall certainly lodge them in lofty chambers of Paradise. (The Gardens of which are) served with running streams. There they shall abide for ever. The reward of those who take pains (for doing good) is always excellent,
59. Those who patiently persevere and put their trust in their Lord.
60. How many moving creatures there are that do not carry their own sustenance (but do not go without food). It is Allâh Who provides for them and for you. And He is the All-Hearing, the All-Knowing.
61. In case you ask them, 'Who has created the heavens and the earth and harnessed the sun and the moon (into the service of humankind)?' They will answer, 'Allâh.' Then whither are they being turned away (from accepting the truth).
62. Allâh multiplies (the means of) sustenance for such of His servants as He will and makes those (means) scant for whom He will. Verily, Allâh is fully Aware of each and everything.
63. And if you question them, 'Who rains water from the clouds and thereby breathes life into the earth after its death (making it fertile and green)?' They will certainly say, 'Allâh.' Say, 'All sorts of perfect and true praise belongs to Allâh.' Yet most of them do not make use of their understanding.

لَمُحِيطَةٌ بِالْكٰفِرِينَ ﴿٥٤﴾ يَوْمَ يَغْشٰهُمُ الْعَذَابُ
مِنْ فَوْقِهِمْ وَ مِنْ تَحْتِ أَرْجُلِهِمْ وَ يَقُولُ
ذُوقُوا مَا كُنْتُمْ تَعْمَلُونَ ﴿٥٥﴾ يٰعِبَادِيَ الَّذِينَ
اٰمَنُوا إِنَّ أَرْضِي وٰسِعَةٌ فَإِيّٰيَ فَاعْبُدُونِ ﴿٥٦﴾
كُلُّ نَفْسٍ ذَآئِقَةُ الْمَوْتِ ثُمَّ إِلَيْنَا تُرْجَعُونَ ﴿٥٧﴾
وَ الَّذِينَ اٰمَنُوا وَ عَمِلُوا الصّٰلِحٰتِ لَنُبَوِّئَنَّهُمْ
مِّنَ الْجَنَّةِ غُرَفًا تَجْرِي مِنْ تَحْتِهَا الْأَنْهٰرُ
خٰلِدِينَ فِيهَا نِعْمَ أَجْرُ الْعٰمِلِينَ ﴿٥٨﴾ الَّذِينَ
صَبَرُوا وَ عَلٰى رَبِّهِمْ يَتَوَكَّلُونَ ﴿٥٩﴾ وَ كَأَيِّنْ
مِّنْ دَآبَّةٍ لَّا تَحْمِلُ رِزْقَهَا اللّٰهُ يَرْزُقُهَا
وَ إِيَّاكُمْ وَ هُوَ السَّمِيعُ الْعَلِيمُ ﴿٦٠﴾ وَ لَئِنْ
سَأَلْتَهُمْ مَّنْ خَلَقَ السَّمٰوٰتِ وَ الْأَرْضَ
وَ سَخَّرَ الشَّمْسَ وَ الْقَمَرَ لَيَقُولُنَّ اللّٰهُ فَأَنّٰى
يُؤْفَكُونَ ﴿٦١﴾ اللّٰهُ يَبْسُطُ الرِّزْقَ لِمَنْ يَشَآءُ
مِنْ عِبَادِهِ وَ يَقْدِرُ لَهُ إِنَّ اللّٰهَ بِكُلِّ شَيْءٍ
عَلِيمٌ ﴿٦٢﴾ وَ لَئِنْ سَأَلْتَهُمْ مَّنْ نَّزَّلَ مِنَ السَّمَآءِ
مَآءً فَأَحْيَا بِهِ الْأَرْضَ مِنْ بَعْدِ مَوْتِهَا لَيَقُولُنَّ
اللّٰهُ قُلِ الْحَمْدُ لِلّٰهِ بَلْ أَكْثَرُهُمْ لَا

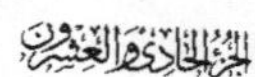

SECTION 7

64. **T**HE life of this world is nothing but futile and frivolous and the abode of the Hereafter is the real life (being eternal). If they but knew (they would have paid heed).

65. And when they board a ship (and find themselves in danger they pray to Allâh with sincere and single-minded faith in Him; but as soon as He lands them safe they begin to associate partners (with Him again),

66. With the result that they show ingratitude for what We have given them and also with the result that they indulge in worldly enjoyment (though only for a short time). But they will soon come to know (the consequences of their conduct).

67. Have the people not seen that We have made the Sanctuary (of Makkah) a place of peace and security while people are carried off (by force) all around them? Do they continue to believe in falsehood and (thus) deny the favour of Allâh?

68. And who is more unjust than he who forges a lie in the name of Allâh or cries lies to the truth when it comes to him. Is not Gehenna a (befitting) resort for such disbelievers.

69. And those who strive hard in Our cause We will certainly guide them in the ways that lead to Us. Verily, Allâh is always with the doers of good.

سُورَةُ الْعَنْكَبُوتِ ٢٩

يَعْقِلُونَ ﴿٦٣﴾ وَمَا هٰذِهِ الْحَيٰوةُ الدُّنْيَآ إِلَّا لَهْوٌ
وَلَعِبٌ ۚ وَإِنَّ الدَّارَ الْأٰخِرَةَ لَهِيَ الْحَيَوَانُ ۘ
لَوْ كَانُوا يَعْلَمُونَ ﴿٦٤﴾ فَإِذَا رَكِبُوا فِي الْفُلْكِ
دَعَوُا اللّٰهَ مُخْلِصِينَ لَهُ الدِّينَ ۚ فَلَمَّا نَجّٰهُمْ
إِلَى الْبَرِّ إِذَا هُمْ يُشْرِكُونَ ﴿٦٥﴾ لِيَكْفُرُوا بِمَآ
أٰتَيْنٰهُمْ ۚ وَلِيَتَمَتَّعُوا ۚ فَسَوْفَ يَعْلَمُونَ ﴿٦٦﴾
أَوَلَمْ يَرَوْا أَنَّا جَعَلْنَا حَرَمًا أٰمِنًا وَيُتَخَطَّفُ
النَّاسُ مِنْ حَوْلِهِمْ ۚ أَفَبِالْبٰطِلِ يُؤْمِنُونَ
وَبِنِعْمَةِ اللّٰهِ يَكْفُرُونَ ﴿٦٧﴾ وَمَنْ أَظْلَمُ مِمَّنِ
افْتَرٰى عَلَى اللّٰهِ كَذِبًا أَوْ كَذَّبَ بِالْحَقِّ لَمَّا
جَآءَهُ ۚ أَلَيْسَ فِي جَهَنَّمَ مَثْوًى لِّلْكٰفِرِينَ ﴿٦٨﴾
وَالَّذِينَ جٰهَدُوا فِينَا لَنَهْدِيَنَّهُمْ سُبُلَنَا ۚ
وَإِنَّ اللّٰهَ لَمَعَ الْمُحْسِنِينَ ﴿٦٩﴾

CHAPTER
30

AL-RÛM
(The Byzantines)
(Revealed before Hijrah)

With the name of Allâh,
the Most Gracious, the Ever Merciful
(I commence to read Sûrah Al-Rûm).

1. **A**LIF LÂM MÎM - I am Allâh, the All- Knowing.
2. The Byzantines have been defeated,
3. In the land nearby (- Syria and Palestine); and they after their defeat shall overpower (their enemies, the Persians)
4. Within three to nine years. The power belongs to Allâh after (their defeat) as (it belonged to Him) before it. And on that day the believers (too) will rejoice
5. Over the victory (given to them) by Allâh. He gives victory to whom He will, and He is the All-Mighty, the Ever Merciful.
6. (This is) Allâh's promise. It is far from Allâh to break His promise. Yet most of the people do not know (this).
7. They know only the apparent side of the present life, and they are completely unmindful of the next.
8. Do they never think over in their own minds that Allâh has created the heavens and the earth and all that lies between the two only to suit the requirements of truth and wisdom (and with a definite end in view), but for a stated term (after which the doom must come)? Yet many among the people do not believe in the meeting with their Lord ever.
9. Have they not travelled through the land and seen how (evil) was the end of those who were before them? They (- their predecessors) were superior to them in prowess and strength. They tilled the land (built structures and dug up

سُوْرَةُ الرُّوْمِ ٣٠

سُوْرَةُ الرُّوْمِ مَكِّيَّةٌ

بِسْمِ اللّٰهِ الرَّحْمٰنِ الرَّحِيْمِ

الٓمٓ ﴿١﴾ غُلِبَتِ الرُّوْمُ ﴿٢﴾ فِيْٓ أَدْنَى الْأَرْضِ
وَهُمْ مِّنْۢ بَعْدِ غَلَبِهِمْ سَيَغْلِبُوْنَ ﴿٣﴾ فِيْ بِضْعِ
سِنِيْنَ ۬ لِلّٰهِ الْأَمْرُ مِنْ قَبْلُ وَمِنْۢ بَعْدُ
وَيَوْمَئِذٍ يَّفْرَحُ الْمُؤْمِنُوْنَ ﴿٤﴾ بِنَصْرِ اللّٰهِ
يَنْصُرُ مَنْ يَّشَآءُ وَهُوَ الْعَزِيْزُ الرَّحِيْمُ ﴿٥﴾
وَعْدَ اللّٰهِ لَا يُخْلِفُ اللّٰهُ وَعْدَهٗ وَلٰكِنَّ
أَكْثَرَ النَّاسِ لَا يَعْلَمُوْنَ ﴿٦﴾ يَعْلَمُوْنَ ظٰهِرًا
مِّنَ الْحَيٰوةِ الدُّنْيَا وَهُمْ عَنِ الْآخِرَةِ
هُمْ غٰفِلُوْنَ ﴿٧﴾ أَوَلَمْ يَتَفَكَّرُوْا فِيْٓ أَنْفُسِهِمْ
مَا خَلَقَ اللّٰهُ السَّمٰوٰتِ وَالْأَرْضَ وَمَا بَيْنَهُمَآ
إِلَّا بِالْحَقِّ وَأَجَلٍ مُّسَمًّى وَإِنَّ كَثِيْرًا مِّنَ
النَّاسِ بِلِقَآئِ رَبِّهِمْ لَكٰفِرُوْنَ ﴿٨﴾ أَوَلَمْ
يَسِيْرُوْا فِي الْأَرْضِ فَيَنْظُرُوْا كَيْفَ كَانَ
عٰقِبَةُ الَّذِيْنَ مِنْ قَبْلِهِمْ كَانُوْٓا أَشَدَّ

minerals from it), and populated it more and better than these have populated it. And their Messengers (of God) had come to them with manifest signs (but they denied them and were destroyed). It was indeed far from Allâh to have done injustice to them but they themselves wronged their own souls.

10. Then evil was the end of those who did evil, because they cried lies to the Messages of Allâh and they treated them as something of least importance

SECTION 2

11. **A**LLÂH originates creation then He keeps on repeating and reproducing it, then to Him shall you be brought back.

12. And on the day when the (promised) Hour (of Reckoning) will arrive those who have cut their ties (with Allâh and were lost in sin) will be confronted with despair.

13. None from among their associate-gods will intercede for them, though they had renounced their faith (in Allâh) because of these gods whom they associated (with Him).

14. And day when the Hour (of Reckoning) will arrive on that day they (the virtuous and the sinful) will be sorted out (into different groups).

15. Then as for those who had believed and done deeds of righteousness, they will be welcomed with all honours and entertained in a stately and delightful Garden.

16. But as for those who had disbelieved and cried lies to Our Messages and the meeting of the Hereafter, it is they who shall be given over to punishment (lasting long).

17. So glorify Allâh when you enter the evening and when you enter the morning,

18. For to Him belongs all type of perfect and true praise in the heavens and the earth, and (glorify Him) in the afternoon and when you enter upon the hour of noon.

19. Out of the dead He brings forth the living and out of the living He brings forth the dead.

مِنْهُمْ قُوَّةً وَّ أَثَارُوا الْأَرْضَ وَعَمَرُوهَا أَكْثَرَ
مِمَّا عَمَرُوهَا وَجَآءَتْهُمْ رُسُلُهُمْ بِالْبَيِّنٰتِ
فَمَا كَانَ اللّٰهُ لِيَظْلِمَهُمْ وَلٰكِنْ كَانُوٓا أَنْفُسَهُمْ
يَظْلِمُونَ ٩ ثُمَّ كَانَ عٰقِبَةَ الَّذِينَ أَسَآءُوا
السُّوٓأٰى أَنْ كَذَّبُوا بِأٰيٰتِ اللّٰهِ وَكَانُوا
بِهَا يَسْتَهْزِءُونَ ١٠ اَللّٰهُ يَبْدَؤُا الْخَلْقَ ثُمَّ
يُعِيدُهُ ثُمَّ إِلَيْهِ تُرْجَعُونَ ١١ وَيَوْمَ تَقُومُ
السَّاعَةُ يُبْلِسُ الْمُجْرِمُونَ ١٢ وَلَمْ يَكُنْ لَّهُمْ
مِّنْ شُرَكَآئِهِمْ شُفَعٰٓؤُا وَكَانُوا بِشُرَكَآئِهِمْ
كٰفِرِينَ ١٣ وَيَوْمَ تَقُومُ السَّاعَةُ يَوْمَئِذٍ
يَتَفَرَّقُونَ ١٤ فَأَمَّا الَّذِينَ أٰمَنُوا وَعَمِلُوا
الصّٰلِحٰتِ فَهُمْ فِي رَوْضَةٍ يُّحْبَرُونَ ١٥ وَأَمَّا
الَّذِينَ كَفَرُوا وَكَذَّبُوا بِأٰيٰتِنَا وَلِقَآئِ
الْأٰخِرَةِ فَأُولٰٓئِكَ فِي الْعَذَابِ مُحْضَرُونَ ١٦
فَسُبْحٰنَ اللّٰهِ حِينَ تُمْسُونَ وَحِينَ تُصْبِحُونَ ١٧
وَلَهُ الْحَمْدُ فِي السَّمٰوٰتِ وَالْأَرْضِ وَعَشِيًّا
وَّحِينَ تُظْهِرُونَ ١٨ يُخْرِجُ الْحَيَّ مِنَ الْمَيِّتِ
وَيُخْرِجُ الْمَيِّتَ مِنَ الْحَيِّ وَيُحْيِ الْأَرْضَ

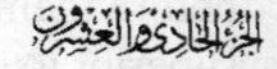

And He gives life to the earth (making it look green and flourishing) after its death. That is how you shall be raised (to life from the state of death).

SECTION 3

20. **A**nd (it is one) of His signs that He created you of dust; and then lo, you are human beings who are spreading (far and wide over the earth).

21. And (it is one) of His signs that He has created spouses for you from your own species that you may find comfort in them. And He has induced mutual love and tenderness between you. Behold! there are signs in this for a people who would reflect.

22. The creation of the heavens and the earth and the diversity of your tongues and colours are (also some) of His signs. Behold there are sure signs for the learned people in this (unity of humankind and Oneness of the Creator).

23. And among His signs is your sleeping and your seeking of His bounty by night and day. Behold, there are sure signs in this for a people who would listen.

24. And (one) of His signs is that He shows you (the flash of) lightning to create fear (of thunder and storm) and hope (for fruitful rain), and sends down water from the clouds and revives therewith the earth after its death (like barrenness). Behold there are (many) signs in this for a people who make use of their understanding.

25. And (it is one) of His signs that the heavens and the earth stand firm by His command. Then as soon as He calls you forth from the earth by a single call, behold you will come forth all at once and suddenly

26. All those who are in the heavens and the earth belong to Him (and serve Him); all are obedient to Him.

27. It is He Who originates the creation then keeps on repeating and reproducing it. This (work of creation and reproduction) is most

ع ٥

بَعْدَ مَوْتِهَا ۚ وَكَذَٰلِكَ تُخْرَجُونَ ﴿١٩﴾ وَمِنْ
آيَاتِهِ أَنْ خَلَقَكُم مِّن تُرَابٍ ثُمَّ إِذَا أَنتُم
بَشَرٌ تَنتَشِرُونَ ﴿٢٠﴾ وَمِنْ آيَاتِهِ أَنْ خَلَقَ
لَكُم مِّنْ أَنفُسِكُمْ أَزْوَاجًا لِّتَسْكُنُوا إِلَيْهَا
وَجَعَلَ بَيْنَكُم مَّوَدَّةً وَرَحْمَةً ۚ إِنَّ فِي
ذَٰلِكَ لَآيَاتٍ لِّقَوْمٍ يَتَفَكَّرُونَ ﴿٢١﴾ وَمِنْ آيَاتِهِ
خَلْقُ السَّمَاوَاتِ وَالْأَرْضِ وَاخْتِلَافُ أَلْسِنَتِكُمْ
وَأَلْوَانِكُمْ ۚ إِنَّ فِي ذَٰلِكَ لَآيَاتٍ لِّلْعَالِمِينَ ﴿٢٢﴾
وَمِنْ آيَاتِهِ مَنَامُكُم بِاللَّيْلِ وَالنَّهَارِ
وَابْتِغَاؤُكُم مِّن فَضْلِهِ ۚ إِنَّ فِي ذَٰلِكَ لَآيَاتٍ
لِّقَوْمٍ يَسْمَعُونَ ﴿٢٣﴾ وَمِنْ آيَاتِهِ يُرِيكُمُ
الْبَرْقَ خَوْفًا وَطَمَعًا وَيُنَزِّلُ مِنَ السَّمَاءِ
مَاءً فَيُحْيِي بِهِ الْأَرْضَ بَعْدَ مَوْتِهَا ۚ إِنَّ
فِي ذَٰلِكَ لَآيَاتٍ لِّقَوْمٍ يَعْقِلُونَ ﴿٢٤﴾ وَمِنْ
آيَاتِهِ أَن تَقُومَ السَّمَاءُ وَالْأَرْضُ بِأَمْرِهِ ۚ
ثُمَّ إِذَا دَعَاكُمْ دَعْوَةً مِّنَ الْأَرْضِ إِذَا
أَنتُمْ تَخْرُجُونَ ﴿٢٥﴾ وَلَهُ مَن فِي السَّمَاوَاتِ
وَالْأَرْضِ ۖ كُلٌّ لَّهُ قَانِتُونَ ﴿٢٦﴾ وَهُوَ الَّذِي
يَبْدَأُ الْخَلْقَ ثُمَّ يُعِيدُهُ وَهُوَ أَهْوَنُ عَلَيْهِ

easy, for Him. His is the most exalted state (and the noblest attributes) in the heavens and the earth; and He is the All-Mighty, the All-Wise.

SECTION 4

28. **H**E sets forth for you an illustration drawn from your own lives. Do any of those whom your right hands own equally share with you that which We have provided you with. It is, however, a fact that you all (the owner and the owned) are equal (partners) in it, so that you take care of them as you take care of your own selves. That is how We explain many of Our Messages to a people who make use of their understanding.

29. Nay, but those who behave unjustly, they pursue their own low desires without (any) knowledge (whatsoever). So who can guide one whom Allâh has adjudged as lost? There will be none to help them.

30. So pay your whole-hearted attention to (the cause of) faith as one devoted (to pure faith), turning away from all that is false. (And follow) the Faith of Allâh (-Islam) to suit the requirements of which He has made the nature of humankind. There can be no change in the nature (of creation) which Allâh has made. That is the right and most perfect Faith, yet most people do not know (it).

31. (Believers! you should all be attentive to Him) turning to Him (in repentance), and take Him as (your) shield (for protection) and observe Prayer and be not of those who associate partners (with Him) -

32. Of those who have split up their faith and have divided themselves into sects so that every party is happy with what they have.

33. When some evil befalls the people they call on their Lord, turning sincerely to Him (in repentance). But no sooner He lets them enjoy mercy from Him than a section of them associate partners with Him (and starts wor-

وَلَهُ الْمَثَلُ الْأَعْلٰى فِي السَّمٰوٰتِ وَالْأَرْضِ
وَهُوَ الْعَزِيزُ الْحَكِيمُ ﴿٢٧﴾ ضَرَبَ لَكُمْ مَّثَلًا
مِّنْ أَنْفُسِكُمْ هَلْ لَّكُمْ مِّنْ مَّا مَلَكَتْ
أَيْمٰنُكُمْ مِّنْ شُرَكَاءَ فِي مَا رَزَقْنٰكُمْ فَأَنْتُمْ
فِيهِ سَوَاءٌ تَخَافُونَهُمْ كَخِيفَتِكُمْ أَنْفُسَكُمْ
كَذٰلِكَ نُفَصِّلُ الْأٰيٰتِ لِقَوْمٍ يَعْقِلُونَ ﴿٢٨﴾
بَلِ اتَّبَعَ الَّذِينَ ظَلَمُوا أَهْوَاءَهُمْ بِغَيْرِ عِلْمٍ
فَمَنْ يَهْدِي مَنْ أَضَلَّ اللّٰهُ وَمَا لَهُمْ
مِّنْ نّٰصِرِينَ ﴿٢٩﴾ فَأَقِمْ وَجْهَكَ لِلدِّينِ حَنِيفًا
فِطْرَتَ اللّٰهِ الَّتِي فَطَرَ النَّاسَ عَلَيْهَا لَا
تَبْدِيلَ لِخَلْقِ اللّٰهِ ذٰلِكَ الدِّينُ الْقَيِّمُ
وَلٰكِنَّ أَكْثَرَ النَّاسِ لَا يَعْلَمُونَ ﴿٣٠﴾ مُنِيبِينَ
إِلَيْهِ وَاتَّقُوهُ وَأَقِيمُوا الصَّلٰوةَ وَلَا تَكُونُوا
مِنَ الْمُشْرِكِينَ ﴿٣١﴾ مِنَ الَّذِينَ فَرَّقُوا
دِينَهُمْ وَكَانُوا شِيَعًا كُلُّ حِزْبٍ بِمَا
لَدَيْهِمْ فَرِحُونَ ﴿٣٢﴾ وَإِذَا مَسَّ النَّاسَ ضُرٌّ
دَعَوْا رَبَّهُمْ مُّنِيبِينَ إِلَيْهِ ثُمَّ إِذَا أَذَاقَهُمْ
مِّنْهُ رَحْمَةً إِذَا فَرِيقٌ مِّنْهُمْ بِرَبِّهِمْ

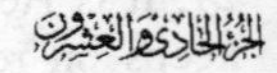

shipping gods besides Allâh),
34. With the result that they show ingratitude for what We have given them. So (you ungrateful people,) enjoy yourselves (for a while) but shortly you will come to know (the consequences).
35. Have We revealed to them some authoritative proof which speaks (highly in favour) of what they associate with Him?
36. And when We let people enjoy Our mercy they rejoice over it. But no sooner does an evil befall them, because of their own evil deeds, then they grow despondent.
37. Do they not see that Allâh multiplies the means of livelihood for whomsoever He will and makes them scant (for whomsoever He will). Behold there are signs in this for a people who would believe.
38. So present to the near of kin his due, and to the needy and the wayfarer. This is best for those who seek the pleasure of Allâh, it is they alone who will attain their goal.
39. And that which you lay out as interest and usuary with a view to increase the wealth of the people does not help increase it in the sight of Allâh. But that which you present as the *Zakât* (purifying dues) with a view to seek (thereby) the pleasure of Allâh, it is they (- the regular payers of the *Zakât*) then who will increase (their wealth) many times over.
40. It is Allâh Who has created you, then He provides for you, then He will call you to death, (and) then He will bring you to life. Is there any of your (so-called) associate-gods who can do the least of these things? Holy is He and Highly-Exalted and far above the things they associate (with Him).

SECTION 5

41. **D**ISORDER and corruption has prevailed on land and sea owing to the evil (deeds) which people have wrought. The result will be that He will make them taste (in this world) the fruit of

يُشْرِكُوْنَ ﴿٣٣﴾ لِيَكْفُرُوْا بِمَآ اٰتَيْنٰهُمْ فَتَمَتَّعُوْا
فَسَوْفَ تَعْلَمُوْنَ ﴿٣٤﴾ اَمْ اَنْزَلْنَا عَلَيْهِمْ سُلْطٰنًا
فَهُوَ يَتَكَلَّمُ بِمَا كَانُوْا بِهٖ يُشْرِكُوْنَ ﴿٣٥﴾ وَاِذَآ
اَذَقْنَا النَّاسَ رَحْمَةً فَرِحُوْا بِهَا ؕ وَاِنْ
تُصِبْهُمْ سَيِّئَةٌۢ بِمَا قَدَّمَتْ اَيْدِيْهِمْ اِذَا
هُمْ يَقْنَطُوْنَ ﴿٣٦﴾ اَوَلَمْ يَرَوْا اَنَّ اللّٰهَ يَبْسُطُ
الرِّزْقَ لِمَنْ يَّشَآءُ وَيَقْدِرُ ؕ اِنَّ فِيْ ذٰلِكَ
لَاٰيٰتٍ لِّقَوْمٍ يُّؤْمِنُوْنَ ﴿٣٧﴾ فَاٰتِ ذَا الْقُرْبٰى
حَقَّهٗ وَالْمِسْكِيْنَ وَابْنَ السَّبِيْلِ ؕ ذٰلِكَ
خَيْرٌ لِّلَّذِيْنَ يُرِيْدُوْنَ وَجْهَ اللّٰهِ ۫ وَاُولٰٓئِكَ
هُمُ الْمُفْلِحُوْنَ ﴿٣٨﴾ وَمَآ اٰتَيْتُمْ مِّنْ رِّبًا
لِّيَرْبُوَا۠ فِيْۤ اَمْوَالِ النَّاسِ فَلَا يَرْبُوْا عِنْدَ اللّٰهِ ۚ
وَمَآ اٰتَيْتُمْ مِّنْ زَكٰوةٍ تُرِيْدُوْنَ وَجْهَ
اللّٰهِ فَاُولٰٓئِكَ هُمُ الْمُضْعِفُوْنَ ﴿٣٩﴾ اَللّٰهُ الَّذِيْ
خَلَقَكُمْ ثُمَّ رَزَقَكُمْ ثُمَّ يُمِيْتُكُمْ ثُمَّ يُحْيِيْكُمْ ؕ
هَلْ مِنْ شُرَكَآئِكُمْ مَّنْ يَّفْعَلُ مِنْ ذٰلِكُمْ
مِّنْ شَيْءٍ ؕ سُبْحٰنَهٗ وَتَعٰلٰى عَمَّا يُشْرِكُوْنَ ﴿٤٠﴾
ظَهَرَ الْفَسَادُ فِي الْبَرِّ وَالْبَحْرِ بِمَا كَسَبَتْ
اَيْدِي النَّاسِ لِيُذِيْقَهُمْ بَعْضَ الَّذِيْ عَمِلُوْا

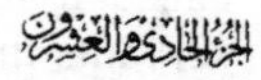

(some of) their misdeeds so that they may return (to the right path, giving up their evil ways).
42. Say, 'Travel all over the earth and behold how (evil) the end of your predecessors was. Most of them were those who assigned associates (with God).'
43. So pay your whole-hearted attention to (the cause of) the right and perfect faith before there comes from Allâh the day for which there will be no averting. On that day they (- the believers and disbelievers) shall split up (into different groups).
44. So that those who disbelieve will pay for their disbelief while those who do righteous deeds will find that they have made provisions for their own good.
45. And so that He will reward those who believe and do deeds of righteousness through His bounty and grace. And He does not love the disbelievers, of course.
46. And (it is one) of His signs that He sends the winds as heralds of glad-tidings. He does it that He may let you enjoy (the blessings of) His mercy and that the ships may sail at His command and that you may seek His bounty and grace and so that you may render (Him) thanks.
47. Indeed, We have already sent Messengers to their (respective) people before you, and they came to them with clear proofs. Then We punished those who had (denied their Apostles and) cut their ties (with God). And it is of course ever incumbent upon Us to help the believers.
48. It is Allâh alone who sends forth the winds and they raise (the vapours to form) a cloud which He spreads out in the sky as He will and sets it layer upon layer, and you see the rain falling from its midst. And no sooner does He cause it to fall on whom He will of His servants than they are filled with joy,
49. Though shortly before it was sent down upon them they were in a state of despondency.

لَعَلَّهُمْ يَرْجِعُونَ ﴿٤١﴾ قُلْ سِيرُوا فِي الْأَرْضِ
فَانْظُرُوا كَيْفَ كَانَ عَاقِبَةُ الَّذِينَ مِنْ قَبْلُ
كَانَ أَكْثَرُهُمْ مُشْرِكِينَ ﴿٤٢﴾ فَأَقِمْ وَجْهَكَ
لِلدِّينِ الْقَيِّمِ مِنْ قَبْلِ أَنْ يَأْتِيَ يَوْمٌ لَا
مَرَدَّ لَهُ مِنَ اللَّهِ يَوْمَئِذٍ يَصَّدَّعُونَ ﴿٤٣﴾ مَنْ
كَفَرَ فَعَلَيْهِ كُفْرُهُ وَمَنْ عَمِلَ صَالِحًا
فَلِأَنْفُسِهِمْ يَمْهَدُونَ ﴿٤٤﴾ لِيَجْزِيَ الَّذِينَ آمَنُوا
وَعَمِلُوا الصَّالِحَاتِ مِنْ فَضْلِهِ إِنَّهُ لَا يُحِبُّ
الْكَافِرِينَ ﴿٤٥﴾ وَمِنْ آيَاتِهِ أَنْ يُرْسِلَ الرِّيَاحَ
مُبَشِّرَاتٍ وَلِيُذِيقَكُمْ مِنْ رَحْمَتِهِ وَلِتَجْرِيَ
الْفُلْكُ بِأَمْرِهِ وَلِتَبْتَغُوا مِنْ فَضْلِهِ وَلَعَلَّكُمْ
تَشْكُرُونَ ﴿٤٦﴾ وَلَقَدْ أَرْسَلْنَا مِنْ قَبْلِكَ رُسُلًا
إِلَىٰ قَوْمِهِمْ فَجَاءُوهُمْ بِالْبَيِّنَاتِ فَانْتَقَمْنَا
مِنَ الَّذِينَ أَجْرَمُوا وَكَانَ حَقًّا عَلَيْنَا
نَصْرُ الْمُؤْمِنِينَ ﴿٤٧﴾ اللَّهُ الَّذِي يُرْسِلُ الرِّيَاحَ
فَتُثِيرُ سَحَابًا فَيَبْسُطُهُ فِي السَّمَاءِ كَيْفَ
يَشَاءُ وَيَجْعَلُهُ كِسَفًا فَتَرَى الْوَدْقَ يَخْرُجُ
مِنْ خِلَالِهِ فَإِذَا أَصَابَ بِهِ مَنْ يَشَاءُ مِنْ
عِبَادِهِ إِذَا هُمْ يَسْتَبْشِرُونَ ﴿٤٨﴾ وَإِنْ كَانُوا
مِنْ قَبْلِ أَنْ يُنَزَّلَ عَلَيْهِمْ مِنْ قَبْلِهِ
لَمُبْلِسِينَ ﴿٤٩﴾ فَانْظُرْ إِلَىٰ آثَارِ رَحْمَتِ اللَّهِ كَيْفَ

50. Look, therefore, at the evidences of Allâh's mercy! how He breathes life into the earth (making it green and flourishing) after its (state of) death. Surely, He (it is), the same (God), Who will raise the dead to life (in the Hereafter), for He is the Possessor of power over every desired thing.
51. And if We send (another kind of blasting) wind and they see it turn yellow (for its having taken the form of punishment) they will even after that continue to disbelieve (for their being engrossed in evil doings).
52. And you cannot make the dead hear, nor can you make the deaf hear the call when they retreat turning their backs (on you),
53. Nor can you guide the blind out of their error. You can make only those hear who would believe in Our Messages and submit (to Us).

SECTION 6

54. (**I**T IS) Allâh alone Who creates you in (a state of) weakness, He then replaces your weakness with strength (of youth) and again (replaces your) strength with weakness and gray hair (of old age). He creates what He will. He is the All-Knowing, the All-Powerful.
55. And on the day when the Hour shall arrive (and the Resurrection takes place) the guilty will swear that they stayed (in the world) for not more than a very brief period. Just as they had been turned away (from the right way so they will be turned away from Allâh's protection on that day).
56. And those who (in their present life) have been given (true) knowledge and the faith will say, 'You have indeed stayed (behind) according to the Record of Allâh till the Day of being raised up (to life of the Hereafter). This then is the Day of being raised up (to life) but you did not (care to) know.
57. So on that Day no excuses (in their defence) will avail those who had acted unjustly, nor will they be allowed to approach the threshold (to be

يحي الأرض بعد موتها إن ذلك لمحي الموتى وهو على كل شيء قدير ﴿٥٠﴾ ولئن أرسلنا ريحا فرأوه مصفرا لظلوا من بعده يكفرون ﴿٥١﴾ فإنك لا تسمع الموتى ولا تسمع الصم الدعاء إذا ولوا مدبرين ﴿٥٢﴾ وما أنت بهد العمي عن ضللتهم إن تسمع إلا من يؤمن بآيتنا فهم مسلمون ﴿٥٣﴾

ع ٦ ٨

الله الذي خلقكم من ضعف ثم جعل من بعد ضعف قوة ثم جعل من بعد قوة ضعفا وشيبة يخلق ما يشاء وهو العليم القدير ﴿٥٤﴾ ويوم تقوم الساعة يقسم المجرمون ما لبثوا غير ساعة كذلك كانوا يؤفكون ﴿٥٥﴾ وقال الذين أوتوا العلم والإيمن لقد لبثتم في كتب الله إلى يوم البعث فهذا يوم البعث ولكنكم كنتم لا تعلمون ﴿٥٦﴾ فيومئذ لا ينفع الذين ظلموا

admitted into the fold of the near ones of God).

58. We have indeed described for humankind every excellent thing in this Qur'ân; and even if you bring them a sign those who disbelieve would certainly say, 'You and your followers are all devotees of falsehood.'

59. That is how Allâh seals the hearts of those who do not (bother to) know (and be guided).

60. Therefore, (Prophet!) have patience and perseverance. Surely, the promise of Allâh (about your victory and the defeat of the disbelievers) is (bound to be) true; so let not those who are not convinced of the truth hold you in light estimation (so as to move you from your stand).

مَعْذِرَتُهُمْ وَلَا هُمْ يُسْتَعْتَبُونَ ﴿٥٧﴾ وَلَقَدْ
ضَرَبْنَا لِلنَّاسِ فِي هَٰذَا الْقُرْآنِ مِنْ كُلِّ
مَثَلٍ ۚ وَلَئِنْ جِئْتَهُمْ بِآيَةٍ لَيَقُولَنَّ الَّذِينَ
كَفَرُوا إِنْ أَنْتُمْ إِلَّا مُبْطِلُونَ ﴿٥٨﴾ كَذَٰلِكَ
يَطْبَعُ اللَّهُ عَلَىٰ قُلُوبِ الَّذِينَ لَا يَعْلَمُونَ ﴿٥٩﴾
فَاصْبِرْ إِنَّ وَعْدَ اللَّهِ حَقٌّ ۖ وَلَا يَسْتَخِفَّنَّكَ
الَّذِينَ لَا يُوقِنُونَ ﴿٦٠﴾

CHAPTER
31

LUQMÂN

(Revealed before Hijrah)

سُورَةُ لُقْمَانَ مَكِّيَّةٌ

With the name of Allâh,
the Most Gracious, the Ever Merciful
(I commence to read Sûrah Luqmân).

بِسْمِ اللَّهِ الرَّحْمَٰنِ الرَّحِيمِ

1. ALIF LÂM MÎM - I am Allâh the All-Knowing.

2. These are the verses of the perfect Book (which is) full of wisdom.

3. (Promising) a thorough guidance and mercy for the doers of good to others,

4. Those who observe Prayer and present the *Zakât* (- purifying dues) and who have firm faith in (the requital of) the Hereafter,

5. It is they who follow guidance from their Lord and it is they who shall prosper (in the Hereafter as well as in this world).

6. (On the other hand) there are some people

الٓمٓ ﴿١﴾ تِلْكَ آيَاتُ الْكِتَابِ الْحَكِيمِ ﴿٢﴾ هُدًى
وَرَحْمَةً لِلْمُحْسِنِينَ ﴿٣﴾ الَّذِينَ يُقِيمُونَ
الصَّلَاةَ وَيُؤْتُونَ الزَّكَاةَ وَهُمْ بِالْآخِرَةِ هُمْ
يُوقِنُونَ ﴿٤﴾ أُولَٰئِكَ عَلَىٰ هُدًى مِنْ رَبِّهِمْ ۖ
وَأُولَٰئِكَ هُمُ الْمُفْلِحُونَ ﴿٥﴾ وَمِنَ النَّاسِ مَنْ

يشتري لهو الحديث ليضل عن سبيل الله
بغير علم ۖ ويتخذها هزوا ۚ أولئك لهم عذاب
مهين ﴿٦﴾ وإذا تتلى عليه آياتنا ولى مستكبرا
كأن لم يسمعها كأن في أذنيه وقرا ۖ فبشره
بعذاب أليم ﴿٧﴾ إن الذين آمنوا وعملوا
الصلحت لهم جنت النعيم ﴿٨﴾ خلدين فيها ۖ
وعد الله حقا ۚ وهو العزيز الحكيم ﴿٩﴾ خلق
السموت بغير عمد ترونها ۖ وألقى في الأرض
رواسي أن تميد بكم وبث فيها من كل
دابة ۚ وأنزلنا من السماء ماء فأنبتنا
فيها من كل زوج كريم ﴿١٠﴾ هذا خلق الله
فأروني ماذا خلق الذين من دونه ۚ بل
الظلمون في ضلل مبين ﴿١١﴾ ولقد آتينا
لقمن الحكمة أن اشكر لله ۚ ومن يشكر
فإنما يشكر لنفسه ۖ ومن كفر فإن الله
غني حميد ﴿١٢﴾ وإذ قال لقمن لابنه وهو
يعظه يبني لا تشرك بالله ۖ إن الشرك

ع ١٠

who follow ways of causing diversion (from guidance), with the result that they, in their ignorance, lead (people) astray from Allâh's path and treat it (- Allâh's path) as something of least importance. A humiliating punishment awaits such people.

7. And when Our Messages are recited to such a person he turns his back (upon them) in disdain as though he never heard them (and) as if he were deaf in both ears. So give him the important tiding of a grievous punishment.

8. As for those who believe and do deeds of righteousness they will have Gardens full of delight and bliss (in Paradise).

9. There in they shall live for ever. (This is) a true promise of Allâh. And He is the All-Mighty, the All-Wise.

10. He has created the heavens without any such pillars as you can see. And He has placed firm mountains in the earth that it may not quake with you and to provide you food. And He has scattered in it all kinds of creatures and has rained water from the clouds and caused to grow in it (animals and vegetation) of different fine species.

11. So this is Allâh's creation! Now, you show me the things that those (whom you worship as gods) other than Allâh, have created. Nay, but the unjust (who do not believe in One God) are (engrossed) in obvious error.

SECTION 2

12. **B**EHOLD! We bestowed wisdom on Luqmân and said, 'Give thanks to Allâh, for he who gives thanks does it only for his own good; and he who shows ingratitude (should know that) Allâh (needs no gratitude, He) is Self-Sufficient, Praiseworthy (in His own right).

13. And (recall the time) when Luqmân admonished his son and said, 'My dear son! associate no partners with Allâh, surely this (act of) associating partners (with Him) is a

grievous wrong.

14. 'And (Allâh says), "We have enjoined on every human being concerning his parents (to be good to them). His mother is worn and wasted in bearing him and it takes her two years to wean him. And give thanks to Me and to your parents. To Me shall be the (ultimate) return (of you all).

15. "But if they (-the parents) impose upon you to set up equals with Me, the things that you know to be nothing at all, do not obey them (so far as this wish of theirs is concerned). Yet keep company with them showing uniform courtesy, love and kindness to them in (all) worldly affairs. But (in spiritual matters) follow the way of one who turns to Me (in obedience and repentance). Then to Me will be the ultimate return of you all and I shall inform you all about your deeds".'

16. (Luqmân continued,) 'My dear son! even if it (-the deed, good or bad) be as little as the weight of a grain of a mustard seed and even though it be hidden in (the hard layers of) a rock or in (the lofty heights of) the heavens or in (the dark womb of) the earth, Allâh is sure to bring it (to light and take an account of it). Verily, Allâh is the Knower of all subtleties (and all hidden secrets) and is All-Aware.

17. 'My dear son! observe the Prayer and enjoin what is good and just and forbid what is evil and wrong and endure with fortitude what befalls you. Verily, all these are matters (which stand in need) of strong resolve.

18. 'And do not turn your face away from people in scorn and pride, nor walk about on the earth haughtily. Surely, Allâh does not love any self-conceited boaster.

19. 'Rather walk with modest pace and talk in soft gentle tone. Surely, the most repugnant of voices is the braying of the donkey.'

SECTION 3

20. Do you not see how Allâh has made subservient to you all that is in the heavens and

سُوۡرَةُ لُقۡمَانَ ٣١

لَظُلۡمٌ عَظِيۡمٌ ﴿١٣﴾ وَوَصَّيۡنَا الۡاِنۡسٰنَ بِوٰلِدَيۡهِ ۚ
حَمَلَتۡهُ اُمُّهٗ وَهۡنًا عَلٰى وَهۡنٍ وَّفِصٰلُهٗ فِىۡ
عَامَيۡنِ اَنِ اشۡكُرۡ لِىۡ وَ لِوٰلِدَيۡكَ ؕ اِلَىَّ
الۡمَصِيۡرُ ﴿١٤﴾ وَاِنۡ جٰهَدٰكَ عَلٰۤى اَنۡ تُشۡرِكَ
بِىۡ مَا لَيۡسَ لَكَ بِهٖ عِلۡمٌ فَلَا تُطِعۡهُمَا
وَصَاحِبۡهُمَا فِى الدُّنۡيَا مَعۡرُوۡفًا وَّاتَّبِعۡ سَبِيۡلَ
مَنۡ اَنَابَ اِلَىَّ ۚ ثُمَّ اِلَىَّ مَرۡجِعُكُمۡ فَاُنَبِّئُكُمۡ
بِمَا كُنۡتُمۡ تَعۡمَلُوۡنَ ﴿١٥﴾ يٰبُنَىَّ اِنَّهَاۤ اِنۡ تَكُ
مِثۡقَالَ حَبَّةٍ مِّنۡ خَرۡدَلٍ فَتَكُنۡ فِىۡ صَخۡرَةٍ
اَوۡ فِى السَّمٰوٰتِ اَوۡ فِى الۡاَرۡضِ يَاۡتِ بِهَا اللّٰهُ ؕ
اِنَّ اللّٰهَ لَطِيۡفٌ خَبِيۡرٌ ﴿١٦﴾ يٰبُنَىَّ اَقِمِ الصَّلٰوةَ
وَاۡمُرۡ بِالۡمَعۡرُوۡفِ وَانۡهَ عَنِ الۡمُنۡكَرِ
وَاصۡبِرۡ عَلٰى مَاۤ اَصَابَكَ ؕ اِنَّ ذٰلِكَ مِنۡ عَزۡمِ
الۡاُمُوۡرِ ﴿١٧﴾ وَلَا تُصَعِّرۡ خَدَّكَ لِلنَّاسِ وَلَا
تَمۡشِ فِى الۡاَرۡضِ مَرَحًا ؕ اِنَّ اللّٰهَ لَا يُحِبُّ
كُلَّ مُخۡتَالٍ فَخُوۡرٍ ﴿١٨﴾ وَاقۡصِدۡ فِىۡ مَشۡيِكَ
وَاغۡضُضۡ مِنۡ صَوۡتِكَ ؕ اِنَّ اَنۡكَرَ الۡاَصۡوَاتِ
لَصَوۡتُ الۡحَمِيۡرِ ﴿١٩﴾ اَلَمۡ تَرَوۡا اَنَّ اللّٰهَ سَخَّرَ لَكُمۡ
مَّا فِى السَّمٰوٰتِ وَمَا فِى الۡاَرۡضِ وَاَسۡبَغَ

all that is on the earth and lavished upon you His blessings (both) visible and invisible? Still there are some among humankind who argue about Allâh though they have no knowledge, no guidance and no illuminating Book.

21. And when it is said to them, 'Follow that which Allâh has revealed.' They say, 'We would rather follow that which we found our forefathers (following).' (Would they do so) even though satan was inviting them (by that means) to the punishment of the flaming Fire?

22. And he who resigns himself wholly and solely to the will of Allâh and is a doer of good to others has indeed a hold on a support, firm and strong. And the end of all matters rests with Allâh (Who causes their results).

23. And as for him who disbelieves, let not his disbelief grieve you. To Us is their return (in the long run); We shall inform them all that they did. Verily, Allâh knows full well the innermost (thoughts) of their minds.

24. We shall let them enjoy (the worldly provisions) for a short while, then We shall drive them helplessly to a severe punishment.

25. And if you ask them, 'Who has created the heavens and the earth?' They will certainly answer, 'Allâh.' Say, 'All type of perfect and true praise belongs to Allâh!' But most of them do not know (the meanings implied in it).

26. All that lies in the heavens and the earth belongs to Allâh. Verily, Allâh is Self-Sufficient, and is Praiseworthy (in His own right).

27. And if all the trees on the earth were to be pens and the vast ocean (be full of ink) and besides that many (more) such oceans to replenish it (and were to supply ink to write the words of God) even then the words of Allâh would not be finished. Verily, Allâh is All-Mighty, All-Wise.

28. The creation of you all and your resurrection (for Him) are only like (the creation and resurrection of) one single soul; (all human

عَلَيْكُمْ نِعَمَهُ ظَٰهِرَةً وَّبَاطِنَةً ۚ وَمِنَ النَّاسِ
مَنْ يُّجَٰدِلُ فِي اللّٰهِ بِغَيْرِ عِلْمٍ وَّلَا هُدًى
وَّلَا كِتٰبٍ مُّنِيرٍ ﴿٢٠﴾ وَإِذَا قِيلَ لَهُمُ اتَّبِعُوا
مَا أَنْزَلَ اللّٰهُ قَالُوا بَلْ نَتَّبِعُ مَا وَجَدْنَا
عَلَيْهِ أٰبَآءَنَا ۚ أَوَلَوْ كَانَ الشَّيْطٰنُ يَدْعُوهُمْ
إِلٰى عَذَابِ السَّعِيرِ ﴿٢١﴾ وَمَنْ يُّسْلِمْ وَجْهَهُۥٓ إِلَى
اللّٰهِ وَهُوَ مُحْسِنٌ فَقَدِ اسْتَمْسَكَ بِالْعُرْوَةِ
الْوُثْقٰى ۗ وَإِلَى اللّٰهِ عٰقِبَةُ الْأُمُورِ ﴿٢٢﴾ وَمَنْ
كَفَرَ فَلَا يَحْزُنْكَ كُفْرُهُۥ ۚ إِلَيْنَا مَرْجِعُهُمْ
فَنُنَبِّئُهُمْ بِمَا عَمِلُوا ۚ إِنَّ اللّٰهَ عَلِيمٌۢ بِذَاتِ
الصُّدُورِ ﴿٢٣﴾ نُمَتِّعُهُمْ قَلِيلًا ثُمَّ نَضْطَرُّهُمْ إِلٰى
عَذَابٍ غَلِيظٍ ﴿٢٤﴾ وَلَئِنْ سَأَلْتَهُمْ مَّنْ خَلَقَ
السَّمٰوٰتِ وَالْأَرْضَ لَيَقُولُنَّ اللّٰهُ ۚ قُلِ الْحَمْدُ
لِلّٰهِ ۚ بَلْ أَكْثَرُهُمْ لَا يَعْلَمُونَ ﴿٢٥﴾ لِلّٰهِ مَا فِي
السَّمٰوٰتِ وَالْأَرْضِ ۚ إِنَّ اللّٰهَ هُوَ الْغَنِيُّ
الْحَمِيدُ ﴿٢٦﴾ وَلَوْ أَنَّمَا فِي الْأَرْضِ مِنْ شَجَرَةٍ
أَقْلٰمٌ وَّالْبَحْرُ يَمُدُّهُۥ مِنْۢ بَعْدِهِۦ سَبْعَةُ
أَبْحُرٍ مَّا نَفِدَتْ كَلِمٰتُ اللّٰهِ ۚ إِنَّ اللّٰهَ عَزِيزٌ
حَكِيمٌ ﴿٢٧﴾ مَا خَلْقُكُمْ وَلَا بَعْثُكُمْ إِلَّا كَنَفْسٍ

beings are subject to the same laws of God). Verily, Allâh is All-Hearing, All-Seeing.

29. Do you not see that Allâh makes the night gain on the day and makes the day gain on the night and He has harnessed the sun and the moon (into the service of humankind) each one of them pursuing its course for a stated term? And (do you not see) that Allâh is Well-Aware of your deeds?

30. All this is (going on) because Allâh alone is the Ultimate Truth and because all that they call upon beside Him are false (gods) and because Allâh alone is the Most Exalted, the Incomparably Great.

SECTION 4

31. Do you not see that the ships sail through the sea carrying bounty by the favour of Allâh. (He has ordained it so) that He may show some of His signs to you. Surely, in this are important signs for every patiently persevering and grateful person.

32. And when a huge wave covers (the sailors) like (so many) canopies, they call upon Allâh bearing sincere faith in Him. But when He brings them safe to land then (only) some of them keep to the right course (and some of them become indifferent). Yet none denies Our signs except every perfidious ungrateful person.

33. O People! take your Lord as a shield and guard against the day when a father will be of no avail to his son, nor will (any of) the offspring be availing his father. Allâh's promise (about the coming of that day) is true indeed. Therefore,do not let the present life beguile you, nor let an arch-deceiver entice you away from Allâh.

34. Verily, Allâh alone has the knowledge of the Hour (of Resurrection). He sends down the rain. And He knows what the wombs contain. And nobody knows what he will accomplish on the morrow. And nobody knows the land where he will die. Verily, Allâh (alone) is the All-Knowing, All-Aware.

وَّاحِدَةٍ إِنَّ اللّٰهَ سَمِيعٌ بَصِيرٌ ﴿٢٨﴾ أَلَمْ تَرَ
أَنَّ اللّٰهَ يُولِجُ الَّيْلَ فِي النَّهَارِ وَيُولِجُ النَّهَارَ
فِي الَّيْلِ وَسَخَّرَ الشَّمْسَ وَالْقَمَرَ كُلٌّ
يَجْرِي إِلَى أَجَلٍ مُّسَمًّى وَأَنَّ اللّٰهَ بِمَا
تَعْمَلُونَ خَبِيرٌ ﴿٢٩﴾ ذٰلِكَ بِأَنَّ اللّٰهَ هُوَ الْحَقُّ
وَأَنَّ مَا يَدْعُونَ مِنْ دُونِهِ الْبٰطِلُ وَأَنَّ
اللّٰهَ هُوَ الْعَلِيُّ الْكَبِيرُ ﴿٣٠﴾ أَلَمْ تَرَ أَنَّ الْفُلْكَ
تَجْرِي فِي الْبَحْرِ بِنِعْمَتِ اللّٰهِ لِيُرِيَكُمْ مِّنْ
اٰيٰتِهِ إِنَّ فِي ذٰلِكَ لَاٰيٰتٍ لِّكُلِّ صَبَّارٍ
شَكُورٍ ﴿٣١﴾ وَإِذَا غَشِيَهُمْ مَّوْجٌ كَالظُّلَلِ دَعَوُا
اللّٰهَ مُخْلِصِينَ لَهُ الدِّينَ فَلَمَّا نَجّٰهُمْ
إِلَى الْبَرِّ فَمِنْهُمْ مُّقْتَصِدٌ وَمَا يَجْحَدُ
بِاٰيٰتِنَا إِلَّا كُلُّ خَتَّارٍ كَفُورٍ ﴿٣٢﴾ يٰأَيُّهَا النَّاسُ
اتَّقُوا رَبَّكُمْ وَاخْشَوْا يَوْمًا لَّا يَجْزِي وَالِدٌ
عَنْ وَّلَدِهِ وَلَا مَوْلُودٌ هُوَ جَازٍ عَنْ وَّالِدِهِ
شَيْئًا إِنَّ وَعْدَ اللّٰهِ حَقٌّ فَلَا تَغُرَّنَّكُمُ
الْحَيٰوةُ الدُّنْيَا وَلَا يَغُرَّنَّكُمْ بِاللّٰهِ الْغَرُورُ ﴿٣٣﴾
إِنَّ اللّٰهَ عِنْدَهُ عِلْمُ السَّاعَةِ وَيُنَزِّلُ
الْغَيْثَ وَيَعْلَمُ مَا فِي الْأَرْحَامِ وَمَا تَدْرِي
نَفْسٌ مَّاذَا تَكْسِبُ غَدًا وَمَا تَدْرِي نَفْسٌ
بِأَيِّ أَرْضٍ تَمُوتُ إِنَّ اللّٰهَ عَلِيمٌ خَبِيرٌ ﴿٣٤﴾

CHAPTER
32

سُورَةُ السَّجْدَةِ ٣٢

AL-SAJDAH
(The Prostration)
(Revealed before Hijrah)

With the name of Allâh,
the Most Gracious, the Ever Merciful
(I commence to read Sûrah Al-Sajdah).

1. ALIF LÂM MÎM - I am Allâh, the All-Knowing.
2. This Book (-the Qur'ân) which is wanting in naught, containing nothing doubtful, disturbing and there is no false charge in it, has been revealed by the Lord of the worlds.
3. Do the people say, 'He has invented it?' It is not so; it is the truth from your Lord. It has been revealed that you may warn the people to whom no Warner before you (for a long long time) has come so that they may receive guidance.
4. Allâh is He Who created the heavens and the earth and all that lies between the two in six aeons. Again (listen to another great truth,) He is firmly settled on the Throne (of sovereignty). You have no real patron nor an intercessor beside Him; will you take no heed then?
5. He plans the scheme from the heaven (and sends it) to the earth, then it shall ascend to Him in (the course of) a day the duration of which is a thousand years according to your computation (in this world).
6. Such is He Who knows the hidden reality and the obvious, the All-Mighty, the Ever Merciful,
7. Who made perfectly well all that He created. And He originated the creation of a human being from clay.
8. Then He created his seed from an extract

سُورَةُ السَّجْدَةِ مَكِّيَّةٌ

بِسْمِ اللهِ الرَّحْمٰنِ الرَّحِيْمِ

الٓمّٓ ① تَنْزِيْلُ الْكِتٰبِ لَا رَيْبَ فِيْهِ مِنْ
رَّبِّ الْعٰلَمِيْنَ ② أَمْ يَقُوْلُوْنَ افْتَرٰىهُ ۚ بَلْ
هُوَ الْحَقُّ مِنْ رَّبِّكَ لِتُنْذِرَ قَوْمًا مَّآ أَتٰىهُمْ
مِّنْ نَّذِيْرٍ مِّنْ قَبْلِكَ لَعَلَّهُمْ يَهْتَدُوْنَ ③ اَللهُ
الَّذِيْ خَلَقَ السَّمٰوٰتِ وَالْأَرْضَ وَمَا بَيْنَهُمَا
فِيْ سِتَّةِ أَيَّامٍ ثُمَّ اسْتَوٰى عَلَى الْعَرْشِ ۗ مَا
لَكُمْ مِّنْ دُوْنِهٖ مِنْ وَّلِيٍّ وَّلَا شَفِيْعٍ ۗ أَفَلَا
تَتَذَكَّرُوْنَ ④ يُدَبِّرُ الْأَمْرَ مِنَ السَّمَآءِ إِلَى
الْأَرْضِ ثُمَّ يَعْرُجُ إِلَيْهِ فِيْ يَوْمٍ كَانَ
مِقْدَارُهٗٓ أَلْفَ سَنَةٍ مِّمَّا تَعُدُّوْنَ ⑤ ذٰلِكَ
عٰلِمُ الْغَيْبِ وَالشَّهٰدَةِ الْعَزِيْزُ الرَّحِيْمُ ⑥ الَّذِيْٓ
أَحْسَنَ كُلَّ شَيْءٍ خَلَقَهٗ وَبَدَأَ خَلْقَ الْإِنْسٰنِ
مِنْ طِيْنٍ ⑦ ثُمَّ جَعَلَ نَسْلَهٗ مِنْ سُلٰلَةٍ مِّنْ

الجزء الحادي والعشرون

of an insignificant fluid (derived by his consuming food produced from clay or soil).
9. Then He endowed him with perfect faculties (of head and heart in accordance with what he is meant to be) and breathed into him of His spirit (thus made him the recipient of the Divine word). And He has given you hearing, eyes and hearts. Yet little are the thanks you give.
10. And they say, 'Shall we really be (raised to life as) a new creation when we are lost in the earth (after being buried in it)?' The truth is that they are disbelievers in the meeting with their Lord (that is why they are talking like this).
11. Say, 'The angel of death who has been put in charge of you will carry your soul off, then to your Lord you will be made to return.'

SECTION 2

12. **C**OULD you but see (their state) when the guilty will be (standing) before their Lord with their heads hanging down (and saying), 'Our Lord! we have seen and we have heard. So send us back (to worldly life), we will act righteously, for (now) we are convinced (of the truth about the Hereafter).'
13. Had We (enforced) Our will We would have (already) given every soul its (appropriate) guidance. But (as it is) the word from Me has come true (that) I will surely fill Gehenna with some of the *jinn* (- haughty) and (ordinary) people, all (the erring ones) together.
14. So suffer (the punishment for your evil deeds). Since you had given up (the idea of) the meeting of this day of yours so We too have forsaken you (now). Suffer therefore the long-lasting punishment because of the misdeeds you used to do.
15. Only those believe in Our revelations who, when they are reminded by means of them, fall down prostrate and proclaim the (divine) glory with the praises of their Lord and they are not proud.

[PROSTRATION]

16. (While getting up for late-night, *Tahajjud*

مَآءٍ مَّهِينٍ ۝٨ ثُمَّ سَوّٰىهُ وَنَفَخَ فِيهِ مِنْ
رُّوحِهِ وَجَعَلَ لَكُمُ السَّمْعَ وَالْأَبْصٰرَ
وَالْأَفْـِٔدَةَ قَلِيلًا مَّا تَشْكُرُونَ ۝٩ وَقَالُوٓا
ءَإِذَا ضَلَلْنَا فِي الْأَرْضِ ءَإِنَّا لَفِي خَلْقٍ
جَدِيدٍ بَلْ هُمْ بِلِقَآءِ رَبِّهِمْ كٰفِرُونَ ۝١٠
قُلْ يَتَوَفّٰكُمْ مَّلَكُ الْمَوْتِ الَّذِي وُكِّلَ
بِكُمْ ثُمَّ إِلٰى رَبِّكُمْ تُرْجَعُونَ ۝١١ وَلَوْ تَرٰٓى إِذِ
الْمُجْرِمُونَ نَاكِسُوا رُءُوسِهِمْ عِنْدَ رَبِّهِمْ
رَبَّنَآ أَبْصَرْنَا وَسَمِعْنَا فَارْجِعْنَا نَعْمَلْ صٰلِحًا
إِنَّا مُوقِنُونَ ۝١٢ وَلَوْ شِئْنَا لَأٰتَيْنَا كُلَّ نَفْسٍ
هُدٰىهَا وَلٰكِنْ حَقَّ الْقَوْلُ مِنِّي لَأَمْلَـَٔنَّ
جَهَنَّمَ مِنَ الْجِنَّةِ وَالنَّاسِ أَجْمَعِينَ ۝١٣ فَذُوقُوا
بِمَا نَسِيتُمْ لِقَآءَ يَوْمِكُمْ هٰذَا إِنَّا نَسِينٰكُمْ
وَذُوقُوا عَذَابَ الْخُلْدِ بِمَا كُنْتُمْ تَعْمَلُونَ ۝١٤
إِنَّمَا يُؤْمِنُ بِـَٔايٰتِنَا الَّذِينَ إِذَا ذُكِّرُوا بِهَا
خَرُّوا سُجَّدًا وَسَبَّحُوا بِحَمْدِ رَبِّهِمْ وَهُمْ
لَا يَسْتَكْبِرُونَ ۝١٥ تَتَجَافٰى جُنُوبُهُمْ عَنِ

ع ١١/١٤

Prayer) they forsake (their comfortable) beds calling upon their Lord with an awe-inspired and hopeful state of mind. And they spend out of that which We have provided them.
17. And no soul knows what (comforts) lie hidden for them (-the believers in the form) of a joy to the eyes as a reward for their righteous deeds.
18. What! can one who has been a believer (be treated) like one who has been a disobedient sinner. They cannot be alike.
19. There awaits those who believe and do deeds of righteousness Gardens of Eternal Abode in hospitality in return for their good deeds.
20. But as for them who show disobedience their abode will be the Fire. Every time they try to get out of it they shall be hurled back into it and it shall be said to them, 'Suffer the torment of the Fire which you used to cry lies to.'
21. And of course We will let them suffer the minor and nearer punishment before the greater punishment befalls them so that they may turn to Us (in repentance).
22. And who is more unjust than the person who is reminded through the Messages of his Lord; yet he turns away from them? We will surely punish such of those who have severed their ties (with God).

SECTION 3

23. **A**ND We gave Moses the Scripture, therefore (Prophet!) have no doubt about receiving a similar perfect Book (yourself). And We made that (Torah a source of) guidance for the Children of Israel.
24. So long as they remained steadfast We raised leaders from among them. They guided (the people) by Our command; and the people had firm faith in Our signs.
25. And your Lord is One Who on the Day of Resurrection will judge between them concerning every issue over which they used to disagree;
26. Does this (fact) provide them no guidance that We destroyed many a generation in whose

الْمَضَاجِعِ يَدْعُونَ رَبَّهُمْ خَوْفًا وَطَمَعًا
وَمِمَّا رَزَقْنَاهُمْ يُنْفِقُونَ ﴿١٦﴾ فَلَا تَعْلَمُ نَفْسٌ مَا
أُخْفِيَ لَهُمْ مِنْ قُرَّةِ أَعْيُنٍ جَزَاءً بِمَا كَانُوا
يَعْمَلُونَ ﴿١٧﴾ أَفَمَنْ كَانَ مُؤْمِنًا كَمَنْ كَانَ
فَاسِقًا لَا يَسْتَوُونَ ﴿١٨﴾ أَمَّا الَّذِينَ آمَنُوا
وَعَمِلُوا الصَّالِحَاتِ فَلَهُمْ جَنَّاتُ الْمَأْوَىٰ نُزُلًا
بِمَا كَانُوا يَعْمَلُونَ ﴿١٩﴾ وَأَمَّا الَّذِينَ فَسَقُوا
فَمَأْوَاهُمُ النَّارُ كُلَّمَا أَرَادُوا أَنْ يَخْرُجُوا مِنْهَا
أُعِيدُوا فِيهَا وَقِيلَ لَهُمْ ذُوقُوا عَذَابَ النَّارِ
الَّذِي كُنْتُمْ بِهِ تُكَذِّبُونَ ﴿٢٠﴾ وَلَنُذِيقَنَّهُمْ مِنَ
الْعَذَابِ الْأَدْنَىٰ دُونَ الْعَذَابِ الْأَكْبَرِ لَعَلَّهُمْ
يَرْجِعُونَ ﴿٢١﴾ وَمَنْ أَظْلَمُ مِمَّنْ ذُكِّرَ بِآيَاتِ
رَبِّهِ ثُمَّ أَعْرَضَ عَنْهَا إِنَّا مِنَ الْمُجْرِمِينَ
ع مُنْتَقِمُونَ ﴿٢٢﴾ وَلَقَدْ آتَيْنَا مُوسَى الْكِتَابَ فَلَا
تَكُنْ فِي مِرْيَةٍ مِنْ لِقَائِهِ وَجَعَلْنَاهُ هُدًى
لِبَنِي إِسْرَائِيلَ ﴿٢٣﴾ وَجَعَلْنَا مِنْهُمْ أَئِمَّةً يَهْدُونَ
بِأَمْرِنَا لَمَّا صَبَرُوا وَكَانُوا بِآيَاتِنَا يُوقِنُونَ ﴿٢٤﴾
إِنَّ رَبَّكَ هُوَ يَفْصِلُ بَيْنَهُمْ يَوْمَ الْقِيَامَةِ فِيمَا
كَانُوا فِيهِ يَخْتَلِفُونَ ﴿٢٥﴾ أَوَلَمْ يَهْدِ لَهُمْ كَمْ أَهْلَكْنَا

(ruined) dwelling places they (now) walk about? There are sure signs in all this. Will they not then listen (and pay heed).
27. Have they never seen (the sight) how We convey water to the barren land and produce thereby the crop of which they and their cattle eat? Will they not then see (and understand)?
28. And they say, 'If you speak the truth tell us when this victory (of yours) will come.'
29. Say, 'Those who have denied (the truth), their believing on the day of victory will not help them, nor shall they be given respite (to accept the true faith).'
30. So turn aside from them and wait. They are also waiting.

مِنْ قَبْلِهِمْ مِّنَ الْقُرُونِ يَمْشُونَ فِي مَسَٰكِنِهِمْ
إِنَّ فِي ذَٰلِكَ لَأٰيَٰتٍ أَفَلَا يَسْمَعُونَ ﴿٢٦﴾ أَوَ لَمْ
يَرَوْا أَنَّا نَسُوقُ الْمَآءَ إِلَى الْأَرْضِ الْجُرُزِ
فَنُخْرِجُ بِهِۦ زَرْعًا تَأْكُلُ مِنْهُ أَنْعَٰمُهُمْ وَأَنفُسُهُمْ
أَفَلَا يُبْصِرُونَ ﴿٢٧﴾ وَيَقُولُونَ مَتَىٰ هَٰذَا الْفَتْحُ
إِن كُنتُمْ صَٰدِقِينَ ﴿٢٨﴾ قُلْ يَوْمَ الْفَتْحِ لَا يَنفَعُ
الَّذِينَ كَفَرُوٓا إِيمَٰنُهُمْ وَلَا هُمْ يُنظَرُونَ ﴿٢٩﴾
فَأَعْرِضْ عَنْهُمْ وَانتَظِرْ إِنَّهُم مُّنتَظِرُونَ ﴿٣٠﴾

CHAPTER
33

AL-AHZÂB
(The Confederates)
(*Revealed after Hijrah)*

سُورَةُ الْأَحْزَابِ مَدَنِيَّةٌ

With the name of Allâh,
the Most Gracious the Ever Merciful
(I commence to read Sûrah Al-Ahzâb).

بِسْمِ اللَّهِ الرَّحْمَٰنِ الرَّحِيمِ

1. **O** YOU Prophet!, take Allâh as a shield (seeking protection in Him) and do not follow (the wishes of) the disbelievers and the hypocrites. Verily, Allâh is All-Knowing, All-Wise.
2. And follow that which is revealed to you from your Lord. Verily, Allâh is Well Aware of what you people do.
3. And put your trust in Allâh. Allâh is sufficient as a Disposer of affairs.
4. Allâh has not placed two hearts in the bosom of any man, nor does He regard as your mothers those of your wives whom you desert by *(Zihâr)*

يَٰٓأَيُّهَا النَّبِيُّ اتَّقِ اللَّهَ وَلَا تُطِعِ الْكَٰفِرِينَ
وَالْمُنَٰفِقِينَ إِنَّ اللَّهَ كَانَ عَلِيمًا حَكِيمًا ﴿١﴾ وَاتَّبِعْ مَا
يُوحَىٰٓ إِلَيْكَ مِن رَّبِّكَ إِنَّ اللَّهَ كَانَ بِمَا تَعْمَلُونَ
خَبِيرًا ﴿٢﴾ وَتَوَكَّلْ عَلَى اللَّهِ وَكَفَىٰ بِاللَّهِ وَكِيلًا ﴿٣﴾
مَّا جَعَلَ اللَّهُ لِرَجُلٍ مِّن قَلْبَيْنِ فِي جَوْفِهِۦ

calling them as such, nor does He regard those whom you adopt as your children as your own (real) children. These are mere words that you speak; but Allâh declares the truth and He guides to the (straight) path.

5. Call them (- the adopted ones) after (the names of) their (real) fathers. This is more just and equitable in the sight of Allâh. But if you do not know (the names of) their fathers then (they are) your brothers-in-faith and your friends or wards. And no blame shall lie on you with regard to any mistake you may have unintentionally made (before) in such a case. But (you are accountable for) that which you wilfully and premeditatingly do. And Allâh is Great Protector, Ever Merciful.

6. The Prophet has a better claim on the believers than (that) they even have on themselves. (Not only that) his wives are (as) mothers to them. (But in the matters of inheritance) the blood relations are nearer one to another (and more deserving to get the heritage) in (accordance with) the Law of Allâh than the other believers (from among the *Ansâr*) as well as the immigrants (-*Muhâjirs* whom the *Ansâr* took as brothers and united with themselves). Yet you can do an act of kindness (to do honourable favour) to your friends. This is also laid down in the Book of Law.

7. And (recall the time) when We made a covenant with the Prophets and We made it with you, and with Noah, Abraham, Moses and Jesus, son of Mary; and We made a solemn covenant with them.

8. (The Lord did it) so that He may let the truthful give expression to their truthfulness (- whether they were true to their covenant). And (whereas He will reward the true believers); He has in store a woeful punishment for the disbelievers.

وَمَا جَعَلَ أَزْوَٰجَكُمُ الَّٰٓـِٔي تُظَٰهِرُونَ مِنْهُنَّ
أُمَّهَٰتِكُمْ وَمَا جَعَلَ أَدْعِيَآءَكُمْ أَبْنَآءَكُمْ ذَٰلِكُمْ
قَوْلُكُم بِأَفْوَٰهِكُمْ وَاللَّهُ يَقُولُ الْحَقَّ وَهُوَ يَهْدِي
السَّبِيلَ ④ ادْعُوهُمْ لِآبَآئِهِمْ هُوَ أَقْسَطُ عِندَ
اللَّهِ فَإِن لَّمْ تَعْلَمُوٓا ءَابَآءَهُمْ فَإِخْوَٰنُكُمْ فِي الدِّينِ
وَمَوَٰلِيكُمْ وَلَيْسَ عَلَيْكُمْ جُنَاحٌ فِيمَآ أَخْطَأْتُم
بِهِ وَلَٰكِن مَّا تَعَمَّدَتْ قُلُوبُكُمْ وَكَانَ اللَّهُ
غَفُورًا رَّحِيمًا ⑤ النَّبِيُّ أَوْلَىٰ بِالْمُؤْمِنِينَ مِنْ
أَنفُسِهِمْ وَأَزْوَٰجُهُ أُمَّهَٰتُهُمْ وَأُولُوا الْأَرْحَامِ
بَعْضُهُمْ أَوْلَىٰ بِبَعْضٍ فِي كِتَٰبِ اللَّهِ مِنَ
الْمُؤْمِنِينَ وَالْمُهَٰجِرِينَ إِلَّآ أَن تَفْعَلُوٓا إِلَىٰٓ
أَوْلِيَآئِكُم مَّعْرُوفًا كَانَ ذَٰلِكَ فِي الْكِتَٰبِ
مَسْطُورًا ⑥ وَإِذْ أَخَذْنَا مِنَ النَّبِيِّۦنَ مِيثَٰقَهُمْ
وَمِنكَ وَمِن نُّوحٍ وَإِبْرَٰهِيمَ وَمُوسَىٰ وَعِيسَى
ابْنِ مَرْيَمَ وَأَخَذْنَا مِنْهُم مِّيثَٰقًا غَلِيظًا ⑦
لِّيَسْـَٔلَ الصَّٰدِقِينَ عَن صِدْقِهِمْ وَأَعَدَّ لِلْكَٰفِرِينَ

SECTION 2

9. **B**ELIEVERS! remember how Allâh favoured you when (the combined) forces (of the *Quraish* and their allies) came against you (in the Battle of *Ahzâb*) and We sent against them (the forces of nature) a strong wind and hosts (of angels) that you could not see. And Allâh is ever a close observer of your (painstaking efforts and toilsome) deeds.

10. (Recall how He favoured you) when they (-your enemies) invaded you (at Madînah) from above you (from the highlands on the east) and from below you (-from the valley to the west) and when (your) eyes were dazed (in terror) and your hearts rose up to (your) throats while (some of) you entertained diverse thoughts about Allâh.

11. That was the time when the believers were put to hard trial and were violently shaken.

12. (Recall the time,) when the hypocrites and those who carried a (spiritual) disease in their hearts said, 'Allâh and His Messenger only made us a false and delusive promise (of victory).

13. And (recall) when a party of them (also) said, 'O people of Yathrib (- Madînah)! you can put up no stand (in the face of the enemy); you had better go back (to your homes or your old faith to save your lives). And a section of them asked the Prophet for leave saying, 'Surely, our homes are lying exposed (to danger) whereas they were not actually lying exposed, but they only sought to flee (from the battlefield).

14. And if entry (of the enemy-forces) were effected (in the town of Madînah) against them from its diverse quarters and then they were incited to (treachery and) join in the disturbance (against the Companions) they would have readily gone for it. But (afterwards as it happened) they could not stay there (in their so called undefended houses) but a little while.

15. And previous to that they had made a covenant with Allâh that they would not turn (their) backs. And a covenant (made) with

عَذَابًا أَلِيمًا ﴿٨﴾ يَا أَيُّهَا الَّذِينَ آمَنُوا اذْكُرُوا
نِعْمَةَ اللَّهِ عَلَيْكُمْ إِذْ جَاءَتْكُمْ جُنُودٌ فَأَرْسَلْنَا
عَلَيْهِمْ رِيحًا وَجُنُودًا لَمْ تَرَوْهَا ۚ وَكَانَ اللَّهُ
بِمَا تَعْمَلُونَ بَصِيرًا ﴿٩﴾ إِذْ جَاءُوكُمْ مِنْ فَوْقِكُمْ
وَمِنْ أَسْفَلَ مِنْكُمْ وَإِذْ زَاغَتِ الْأَبْصَارُ
وَبَلَغَتِ الْقُلُوبُ الْحَنَاجِرَ وَتَظُنُّونَ بِاللَّهِ الظُّنُونَا ﴿١٠﴾
هُنَالِكَ ابْتُلِيَ الْمُؤْمِنُونَ وَزُلْزِلُوا زِلْزَالًا شَدِيدًا ﴿١١﴾
وَإِذْ يَقُولُ الْمُنَافِقُونَ وَالَّذِينَ فِي قُلُوبِهِمْ مَرَضٌ
مَا وَعَدَنَا اللَّهُ وَرَسُولُهُ إِلَّا غُرُورًا ﴿١٢﴾ وَإِذْ قَالَتْ
طَائِفَةٌ مِنْهُمْ يَا أَهْلَ يَثْرِبَ لَا مُقَامَ لَكُمْ
فَارْجِعُوا ۚ وَيَسْتَأْذِنُ فَرِيقٌ مِنْهُمُ النَّبِيَّ يَقُولُونَ
إِنَّ بُيُوتَنَا عَوْرَةٌ وَمَا هِيَ بِعَوْرَةٍ ۖ إِنْ يُرِيدُونَ
إِلَّا فِرَارًا ﴿١٣﴾ وَلَوْ دُخِلَتْ عَلَيْهِمْ مِنْ أَقْطَارِهَا
ثُمَّ سُئِلُوا الْفِتْنَةَ لَآتَوْهَا وَمَا تَلَبَّثُوا بِهَا إِلَّا
يَسِيرًا ﴿١٤﴾ وَلَقَدْ كَانُوا عَاهَدُوا اللَّهَ مِنْ قَبْلُ لَا

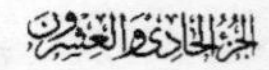

Allâh will have to be answered for.

16. Say, 'It would be of no avail to you if you flee from death or the battlefield and in case you do, you will not (be allowed to) enjoy yourselves but for a short while.

17. Who will save you from (the punishment of) Allâh if it be His will to do you some harm or (who will withhold His favour from you) if it be His will to show you mercy? And they will not find apart from Allâh a patron or a helper for them.

18. Verily, Allâh knows those of you who turn others away (from fighting in the cause of Allâh), and (He knows) also those (of you) who say to their brethren, 'Come to us (to follow the right course).' But they themselves seldom join the fight (in the cause of Allâh),

19. They are niggardly (having no desire) to help you. But when danger is in sight you can see them looking towards you, their eyes rolling like (the eyes of) one who swoons due to (the agony of) death. But when (the time of) danger passes away they lash you (tauntingly) with the sharp (edges of their) tongues being niggardly of any good (coming to your way). These people have never, infact, believed (sincerely), so Allâh has rendered void all their activities (against Islam). And (doing) that is always an easy thing for Allâh.

20. They (still) think that the (invading) confederates have not yet withdrawn. Should the confederates come (again) they would wish to be (desert dwellers) among the bedouins in the desert asking for news about you (whether you were safe or destroyed). And had they been among you they would not have fought (along with you), save a few.

SECTION 3

21. **C**ERTAINLY, you have an excellent model in the Messenger of Allâh for one who hopes (to meet) Allâh and the Last Day and who remem-

يُوَلُّونَ الْأَدْبٰرَ ۚ وَكَانَ عَهْدُ اللهِ مَسْـُٔولًا ﴿١٥﴾ قُل
لَّن يَنفَعَكُمُ الْفِرَارُ إِن فَرَرْتُم مِّنَ الْمَوْتِ أَوِ
الْقَتْلِ وَإِذًا لَّا تُمَتَّعُونَ إِلَّا قَلِيلًا ﴿١٦﴾ قُلْ مَنْ
ذَا الَّذِي يَعْصِمُكُم مِّنَ اللهِ إِنْ أَرَادَ بِكُمْ
سُوٓءًا أَوْ أَرَادَ بِكُمْ رَحْمَةً ۚ وَلَا يَجِدُونَ لَهُم
مِّن دُونِ اللهِ وَلِيًّا وَلَا نَصِيرًا ﴿١٧﴾ قَدْ يَعْلَمُ اللهُ
الْمُعَوِّقِينَ مِنكُمْ وَالْقَآئِلِينَ لِإِخْوٰنِهِمْ هَلُمَّ
إِلَيْنَا ۖ وَلَا يَأْتُونَ الْبَأْسَ إِلَّا قَلِيلًا ﴿١٨﴾ أَشِحَّةً
عَلَيْكُمْ ۖ فَإِذَا جَآءَ الْخَوْفُ رَأَيْتَهُمْ يَنظُرُونَ
إِلَيْكَ تَدُورُ أَعْيُنُهُمْ كَالَّذِي يُغْشٰى عَلَيْهِ مِنَ
الْمَوْتِ ۖ فَإِذَا ذَهَبَ الْخَوْفُ سَلَقُوكُم بِأَلْسِنَةٍ
حِدَادٍ أَشِحَّةً عَلَى الْخَيْرِ ۚ أُولٰٓئِكَ لَمْ يُؤْمِنُوا
فَأَحْبَطَ اللهُ أَعْمٰلَهُمْ ۚ وَكَانَ ذٰلِكَ عَلَى اللهِ
يَسِيرًا ﴿١٩﴾ يَحْسَبُونَ الْأَحْزَابَ لَمْ يَذْهَبُوا ۖ
وَإِن يَأْتِ الْأَحْزَابُ يَوَدُّوا لَوْ أَنَّهُم بَادُونَ
فِي الْأَعْرَابِ يَسْـَٔلُونَ عَنْ أَنۢبَآئِكُمْ ۖ وَلَوْ
كَانُوا فِيكُم مَّا قٰتَلُوٓا إِلَّا قَلِيلًا ﴿٢٠﴾ لَقَدْ كَانَ
لَكُمْ فِي رَسُولِ اللهِ أُسْوَةٌ حَسَنَةٌ لِّمَن
كَانَ يَرْجُوا اللهَ وَالْيَوْمَ الْأٰخِرَ وَذَكَرَ اللهَ

ع ٢/١٢ ١٨

bers Allâh again and again.

22. And as soon as the believers saw (the troops of) the confederates they said, 'This is what Allâh and His Messenger promised us (about the defeat and discomfiture of the hosts of disbelievers and eventual victory of Islam); and Allâh and His Messenger spoke the truth. Look! this (entire episode) made them all the more faithful and obedient (to God).

23. There are some remarkable men among the believers who have been true to the covenant they made with Allâh. There are some among them who fulfilled their vow (and fell martyrs). And there are others among them who are (still) waiting to fulfill. They have never changed (their minds, their conduct or stand they had taken) in the least.

24. (The Muslims were granted victory in this battle) so that Allâh may reward the truthful for their having been true (to their covenant) and that He may punish the hypocrites or turn to them in mercy whichever pleases Him. Allâh is Great Protector (against faults), Ever Merciful.

25. And Allâh repulsed the disbelievers back (from Madînah and they turned back) afire with rage (and full of spite for the Muslims); they gained no good. And Allâh sufficed the believers in (their) fighting. Allâh is Ever Powerful, All-Mighty.

26. And He brought down from their strongholds those of the people of the Scripture (- the Jews of Madînah, the perfidious *Banû Quraizâh*) who had backed them (-the invading enemies). He inspired awful terror into their hearts (so much so that) some of them you were able to slay and others you could take as captives.

27. And He allowed you to inherit their land, their homes and their belongings. And He shall give you yet more lands (the land of *Khaibar*; and the land of the Persian and Roman Empires) on which you have not so far set your foot. And Allâh is Possessor of power over all that He will.

كَثِيرًا ﴿٢١﴾ وَلَمَّا رَءَا الْمُؤْمِنُونَ الْأَحْزَابَ قَالُوا
هَٰذَا مَا وَعَدَنَا اللهُ وَرَسُولُهُ وَصَدَقَ
اللهُ وَرَسُولُهُ وَمَا زَادَهُمْ إِلَّا إِيمَٰنًا
وَتَسْلِيمًا ﴿٢٢﴾ مِنَ الْمُؤْمِنِينَ رِجَالٌ صَدَقُوا
مَا عَٰهَدُوا اللهَ عَلَيْهِ فَمِنْهُم مَّن قَضَىٰ
نَحْبَهُ وَمِنْهُم مَّن يَنتَظِرُ وَمَا بَدَّلُوا
تَبْدِيلًا ﴿٢٣﴾ لِيَجْزِيَ اللهُ الصَّٰدِقِينَ بِصِدْقِهِمْ
وَيُعَذِّبَ الْمُنَٰفِقِينَ إِن شَاءَ أَوْ يَتُوبَ
عَلَيْهِمْ إِنَّ اللهَ كَانَ غَفُورًا رَّحِيمًا ﴿٢٤﴾
وَرَدَّ اللهُ الَّذِينَ كَفَرُوا بِغَيْظِهِمْ لَمْ
يَنَالُوا خَيْرًا وَكَفَى اللهُ الْمُؤْمِنِينَ الْقِتَالَ
وَكَانَ اللهُ قَوِيًّا عَزِيزًا ﴿٢٥﴾ وَأَنزَلَ الَّذِينَ
ظَٰهَرُوهُم مِّنْ أَهْلِ الْكِتَٰبِ مِن صَيَاصِيهِمْ
وَقَذَفَ فِي قُلُوبِهِمُ الرُّعْبَ فَرِيقًا تَقْتُلُونَ
وَتَأْسِرُونَ فَرِيقًا ﴿٢٦﴾ وَأَوْرَثَكُمْ أَرْضَهُمْ
وَدِيَٰرَهُمْ وَأَمْوَٰلَهُمْ وَأَرْضًا لَّمْ تَطَـُٔوهَا
وَكَانَ اللهُ عَلَىٰ كُلِّ شَيْءٍ قَدِيرًا ﴿٢٧﴾

SECTION 4

سُوْرَةُ الْأَحْزَاب ٣٣

28. **O** PROPHET! Say to your wives, 'If you desire the present life and its beautiful things of adornment, come then, I will provide for you worldly provisions and allow you to depart in a handsome manner, a kindly departing.

29. 'But if you choose (the good will of) Allâh and (of) this Messenger and (in this way prefer) the Abode of the Hereafter, then truly Allâh has prepared a great reward for the doers of good among you.'

30. O wives of the Prophet! If any of you be guilty of manifest improper conduct (-a conduct falling short of the highest standard of faith, as you are made an excellent model for others) you will receive punishment twice over. It is indeed easy for Allâh (to double your punishment).

يَٰأَيُّهَا النَّبِيُّ قُل لِّأَزْوٰجِكَ إِن كُنْتُنَّ
تُرِدْنَ الْحَيٰوةَ الدُّنْيَا وَزِينَتَهَا
فَتَعَالَيْنَ أُمَتِّعْكُنَّ وَأُسَرِّحْكُنَّ سَرَاحًا
جَمِيلًا ﴿٢٨﴾ وَإِن كُنْتُنَّ تُرِدْنَ اللهَ
وَرَسُولَهُ وَالدَّارَ الْأٰخِرَةَ فَإِنَّ اللهَ أَعَدَّ
لِلْمُحْسِنٰتِ مِنْكُنَّ أَجْرًا عَظِيمًا ﴿٢٩﴾ يٰنِسَآءَ
النَّبِيِّ مَن يَأْتِ مِنْكُنَّ بِفٰحِشَةٍ
مُّبَيِّنَةٍ يُضٰعَفْ لَهَا الْعَذَابُ ضِعْفَيْنِ
وَكَانَ ذٰلِكَ عَلَى اللهِ يَسِيرًا ﴿٣٠﴾

PART الْجُزْءُ الثَّانِي وَالْعِشْرُونَ XXII

31. **B**UT whoever of you is obedient to Allâh and His Messenger and does righteous deeds, We shall give her reward twice over and We have prepared for her an honourable provision.

32. O wives of the Prophet! You are like no other women, if you would guard against evil, so be not soft in speech lest he who carries a disease in his heart should feel tempted, and you should speak decent words in a dignified tone.

33. And remain in your houses with grace and dignity (you being the mothers of the believers will not be allowed to marry) and do not show yourselves off as (did the women) in the bygone days of ignorance (who displayed their finery), and observe Prayer, present the *Zakât* (- the purifying dues) regularly and obey Allâh and His Messenger. Members of the house (of the Prophet of God)! verily,

وَمَن يَقْنُتْ مِنْكُنَّ لِلّٰهِ وَرَسُولِهِ وَتَعْمَلْ
صٰلِحًا نُّؤْتِهَآ أَجْرَهَا مَرَّتَيْنِ وَأَعْتَدْنَا لَهَا
رِزْقًا كَرِيمًا ﴿٣١﴾ يٰنِسَآءَ النَّبِيِّ لَسْتُنَّ كَأَحَدٍ
مِّنَ النِّسَآءِ إِنِ اتَّقَيْتُنَّ فَلَا تَخْضَعْنَ بِالْقَوْلِ
فَيَطْمَعَ الَّذِي فِي قَلْبِهِ مَرَضٌ وَقُلْنَ قَوْلًا
مَّعْرُوفًا ﴿٣٢﴾ وَقَرْنَ فِي بُيُوتِكُنَّ وَلَا تَبَرَّجْنَ
تَبَرُّجَ الْجٰهِلِيَّةِ الْأُولٰى وَأَقِمْنَ الصَّلٰوةَ
وَأٰتِينَ الزَّكٰوةَ وَأَطِعْنَ اللهَ وَرَسُولَهُ إِنَّمَا

Allâh desires to rid you of (all) uncleanliness and to purify you completely.
34. And keep in mind the Messages of Allâh and the (words of) wisdom which are recited in your homes. Verily, Benign is Allâh, All-Aware.

SECTION 5

35. **V**ERILY, Allâh has in store protection (from faults) and a great reward for the men and the women who submit themselves (to the will of God), and for the men and the women who believe, and for the men and the women who are obedient to Allâh, and for the men and the women who are true (to Allâh), and for the men and the women who are patiently persevering (in their faith and righteousness), and for the men and the women who are humble (before God), and for the men and the women who give alms, and for the men and the women who are true to Allâh, and for the men and the women who fast, and for the men and the women who guard their chastity, and for the men and the women who remember and glorify Allâh (with all His praises) again and again.
36. It does not behove a believing man or a believing woman to exercise an option in their affair after Allâh and His Messenger have decided the matter. Indeed, he who disobeys Allâh and His Messenger surely strays far away in clear error.
37. And (recall the time) when you said to the man (- *Zaid* son of *Hârithah,* a slave freed by the Prophet) on whom Allâh had bestowed His favour and whom you also had favoured, 'Keep your wife (- *Zainab*) to yourself (and do not divorce her) and take Allâh as a shield. And you (O *Zaid*!) conceal (the cause of the failure of the marriage) in your mind, what Allâh is going to bring to light (that the responsibility of the failure rests more upon *Zaid* than upon *Zainab*); and you are (also) afraid of the people whereas Allâh has a better right that you should stand in awe of Him.' However when *Zaid* had done

يُرِيدُ اللَّهُ لِيُذْهِبَ عَنكُمُ الرِّجْسَ أَهْلَ
الْبَيْتِ وَيُطَهِّرَكُمْ تَطْهِيرًا ﴿٣٣﴾ وَاذْكُرْنَ
مَا يُتْلَىٰ فِي بُيُوتِكُنَّ مِنْ آيَاتِ اللَّهِ وَالْحِكْمَةِ
إِنَّ اللَّهَ كَانَ لَطِيفًا خَبِيرًا ﴿٣٤﴾ إِنَّ الْمُسْلِمِينَ
وَالْمُسْلِمَاتِ وَالْمُؤْمِنِينَ وَالْمُؤْمِنَاتِ
وَالْقَانِتِينَ وَالْقَانِتَاتِ وَالصَّادِقِينَ وَالصَّادِقَاتِ
وَالصَّابِرِينَ وَالصَّابِرَاتِ وَالْخَاشِعِينَ
وَالْخَاشِعَاتِ وَالْمُتَصَدِّقِينَ وَالْمُتَصَدِّقَاتِ
وَالصَّائِمِينَ وَالصَّائِمَاتِ وَالْحَافِظِينَ
فُرُوجَهُمْ وَالْحَافِظَاتِ وَالذَّاكِرِينَ اللَّهَ كَثِيرًا
وَالذَّاكِرَاتِ أَعَدَّ اللَّهُ لَهُم مَّغْفِرَةً وَأَجْرًا
عَظِيمًا ﴿٣٥﴾ وَمَا كَانَ لِمُؤْمِنٍ وَلَا مُؤْمِنَةٍ
إِذَا قَضَى اللَّهُ وَرَسُولُهُ أَمْرًا أَن يَكُونَ
لَهُمُ الْخِيَرَةُ مِنْ أَمْرِهِمْ وَمَن يَعْصِ
اللَّهَ وَرَسُولَهُ فَقَدْ ضَلَّ ضَلَالًا مُّبِينًا ﴿٣٦﴾
وَإِذْ تَقُولُ لِلَّذِي أَنْعَمَ اللَّهُ عَلَيْهِ
وَأَنْعَمْتَ عَلَيْهِ أَمْسِكْ عَلَيْكَ زَوْجَكَ
وَاتَّقِ اللَّهَ وَتُخْفِي فِي نَفْسِكَ مَا اللَّهُ مُبْدِيهِ
وَتَخْشَى النَّاسَ وَاللَّهُ أَحَقُّ أَن تَخْشَاهُ
فَلَمَّا قَضَىٰ زَيْدٌ مِّنْهَا وَطَرًا زَوَّجْنَاكَهَا لِكَيْ

what he intended to do with her (- his wife and dissolved the marriage tie with her), We gave her (- the divorced lady) in marriage to you, so that the believers might incur no blame in (getting married to) the wives of their adopted sons after they had dissolved the marriage tie with them. Indeed, the decree of Allâh is ever executed.

38. No blame shall lie on the Prophet for (doing) that which Allâh has made incumbent upon him. (Such indeed has been) the law of Allâh with regard to those (Prophets) who have passed away. Indeed, the command of Allâh is a decree that is made absolute;

39. Those who deliver the Messages of Allâh and who stand in awe of Him and stand in awe of none except Allâh. And Sufficient is Allâh to take account.

40. Muhammad is no father to any man among you but (he is rather) the Messenger of Allâh and the Seal of the Prophets. Indeed Allâh has full knowledge of all things.

SECTION 6

41. **B**ELIEVERS! Remember Allâh with much remembrance.

42. And glorify Him morning and evening.

43. It is He Who sends (His) blessings on you (and) His angels (pray for you) with the result that He brings you out of (all kinds) of utter darkness and leads you to light. And He is Ever Merciful to the believers.

44. They will be greeted with peace the day they meet Him. And He has an honorous reward in store for them.

45. Prophet! We have sent you to be a Witness, a Bearer of glad tidings and a Warner.

46. And (We have sent you) to be a Summoner to Allâh by His command and to serve as a bright sun which spreads light.

47. And (Prophet!) give the believers glad tidings that there awaits them great grace from Allâh.

لَا يَكُونَ عَلَى الْمُؤْمِنِينَ حَرَجٌ فِيٓ أَزْوَاجِ
أَدْعِيَآئِهِمْ إِذَا قَضَوْا مِنْهُنَّ وَطَرًا ۚ وَكَانَ
أَمْرُ اللّٰهِ مَفْعُولًا ﴿٣٧﴾ مَا كَانَ عَلَى النَّبِيِّ مِنْ
حَرَجٍ فِيمَا فَرَضَ اللّٰهُ لَهُ ۖ سُنَّةَ اللّٰهِ فِي
الَّذِينَ خَلَوْا مِنْ قَبْلُ ۚ وَكَانَ أَمْرُ اللّٰهِ
قَدَرًا مَّقْدُورًا ﴿٣٨﴾ الَّذِينَ يُبَلِّغُونَ رِسٰلٰتِ
اللّٰهِ وَيَخْشَوْنَهُ وَلَا يَخْشَوْنَ أَحَدًا إِلَّا
اللّٰهَ ۗ وَكَفٰى بِاللّٰهِ حَسِيبًا ﴿٣٩﴾ مَا كَانَ مُحَمَّدٌ
أَبَآ أَحَدٍ مِّنْ رِّجَالِكُمْ وَلٰكِنْ رَّسُولَ اللّٰهِ
وَخَاتَمَ النَّبِيّٖنَ ۗ وَكَانَ اللّٰهُ بِكُلِّ شَيْءٍ
عَلِيمًا ﴿٤٠﴾ ع ٢ يٰٓأَيُّهَا الَّذِينَ ءَامَنُوا اذْكُرُوا اللّٰهَ ذِكْرًا
كَثِيرًا ﴿٤١﴾ وَسَبِّحُوهُ بُكْرَةً وَأَصِيلًا ﴿٤٢﴾ هُوَ
الَّذِي يُصَلِّي عَلَيْكُمْ وَمَلٰٓئِكَتُهُ لِيُخْرِجَكُمْ
مِّنَ الظُّلُمٰتِ إِلَى النُّورِ ۚ وَكَانَ بِالْمُؤْمِنِينَ
رَحِيمًا ﴿٤٣﴾ تَحِيَّتُهُمْ يَوْمَ يَلْقَوْنَهُ سَلٰمٌ ۚ وَأَعَدَّ
لَهُمْ أَجْرًا كَرِيمًا ﴿٤٤﴾ يٰٓأَيُّهَا النَّبِيُّ إِنَّآ أَرْسَلْنٰكَ
شٰهِدًا وَمُبَشِّرًا وَنَذِيرًا ﴿٤٥﴾ وَدَاعِيًا إِلَى
اللّٰهِ بِإِذْنِهِ وَسِرَاجًا مُّنِيرًا ﴿٤٦﴾ وَبَشِّرِ
الْمُؤْمِنِينَ بِأَنَّ لَهُم مِّنَ اللّٰهِ فَضْلًا كَبِيرًا ﴿٤٧﴾
وَلَا تُطِعِ الْكٰفِرِينَ وَالْمُنٰفِقِينَ وَدَعْ

48. And do not follow the disbelievers and the hypocrites and overlook their insulting remarks and annoying ways, and put your trust in Allâh, for Sufficient is Allâh as a Disposer of affairs.
49. Believers! When you marry believing women and then divorce them before you have had access to them they are under no obligation to wait for *'Iddat* (- the prescribed period of waiting) that you count with regard to them (before they can marry). You had better give them some provision and send them away in a handsome manner.
50. Prophet! We have made lawful to you, your wives whom you have paid their dowers and (similarly) those (wives) whom your right hand owns (after granting them freedom in lieu of their dower in marriage) from among those whom Allâh has given you as gains of war. (And also lawful for the marriage are) the daughters of your paternal uncles and of your paternal aunts, and the daughters of your maternal uncles and of your maternal aunts as have emigrated with you. And (also has been made lawful to the Prophet) any other believing woman who offers herself to the Prophet (for marriage without claiming dower), provided the Prophet (too) desires to wed her. (This is a special permission of marrying more than four wives at a time) only for you to the exclusion of (other) believers in order that there may be no difficulty for you (in explaining the law to the believers). We know what We have enjoined on them (in the Qur'ân) regarding their wives (from among the free women) and also about (their marrying of) those whom their right hands own, in order that there may be no difficulty for you (in explaining the law to them). And Allâh is Great Protector, Ever Merciful.
51. (Prophet!) You may put aside such of them (- your wives) as you like and you may keep with yourself such of them as you like. (Simi-

أَذٰىهُمْ وَ تَوَكَّلْ عَلَى اللّٰهِ وَ كَفٰى بِاللّٰهِ وَكِيلًا ﴿٤٨﴾
يٰٓأَيُّهَا الَّذِينَ ءَامَنُوٓا إِذَا نَكَحْتُمُ الْمُؤْمِنٰتِ
ثُمَّ طَلَّقْتُمُوهُنَّ مِنْ قَبْلِ أَنْ تَمَسُّوهُنَّ
فَمَا لَكُمْ عَلَيْهِنَّ مِنْ عِدَّةٍ تَعْتَدُّونَهَا
فَمَتِّعُوهُنَّ وَ سَرِّحُوهُنَّ سَرَاحًا جَمِيلًا ﴿٤٩﴾
يٰٓأَيُّهَا النَّبِيُّ إِنَّآ أَحْلَلْنَا لَكَ أَزْوٰجَكَ الّٰتِيٓ
ءَاتَيْتَ أُجُورَهُنَّ وَ مَا مَلَكَتْ يَمِينُكَ مِمَّآ
أَفَآءَ اللّٰهُ عَلَيْكَ وَ بَنَاتِ عَمِّكَ وَ بَنَاتِ
عَمّٰتِكَ وَ بَنَاتِ خَالِكَ وَ بَنَاتِ خٰلٰتِكَ الّٰتِي
هَاجَرْنَ مَعَكَ وَ امْرَأَةً مُّؤْمِنَةً إِنْ وَّهَبَتْ
نَفْسَهَا لِلنَّبِيِّ إِنْ أَرَادَ النَّبِيُّ أَنْ يَّسْتَنْكِحَهَا
خَالِصَةً لَّكَ مِنْ دُونِ الْمُؤْمِنِينَ قَدْ
عَلِمْنَا مَا فَرَضْنَا عَلَيْهِمْ فِيٓ أَزْوٰجِهِمْ وَ مَا
مَلَكَتْ أَيْمٰنُهُمْ لِكَيْلَا يَكُونَ عَلَيْكَ حَرَجٌ
وَ كَانَ اللّٰهُ غَفُورًا رَّحِيمًا ﴿٥٠﴾ تُرْجِي مَنْ تَشَآءُ
مِنْهُنَّ وَ تُـٔوِيٓ إِلَيْكَ مَنْ تَشَآءُ وَ مَنِ
ابْتَغَيْتَ مِمَّنْ عَزَلْتَ فَلَا جُنَاحَ عَلَيْكَ

larly) no blame shall lie on you if you take back such of them as you desire of those (wives) whom you have had put aside (in the matter) provisionally. It is more likely this should console them and relieve them of their grief; and make everyone of them well-pleased with what you have given them. And Allâh knows best what lies hidden in your hearts. And Allâh is All-Knowing, All-Clement.

52. (Prophet!) You are not allowed (to marry) other woman after this, nor to change them (-your present wives)for other wives however much you may admire their good qualities. Only those (will remain with you) whom your right hand owns (after your having properly and lawfully wedded them). Remember that Allâh is Ever Watchful over everything.

SECTION 7

53. **B**ELIEVERS! Do not enter the houses of the Prophet unless permission (to enter) has been given you for a meal (with him). Moreover do not wait (there) for the meal time. Rather you should come when you are invited, and disperse when you have had your meal, (nor should you stay over) seeking to listen to (idle) conversation. Surely, this behaviour of yours causes inconvenience to the Prophet, and he (being considerate of your feelings) forbears from (saying anything to) you. But Allâh forbears not from (saying) what is true. And when you ask the women for any commodity, ask them from behind a curtain. Such (a conduct) will better ensure the purity of your minds as well as theirs. And it is never proper for you to cause inconvenience to the Messenger of Allâh, nor (is it proper for you) that you should ever marry his wives after him. Indeed (if you do so) it would be a grievous thing in the sight of Allâh.

54. (It makes little difference) whether you do a thing openly or conceal it. Allâh has full knowledge of everything.

55. No blame shall lie on the women (if they

ذٰلِكَ أَدْنٰى أَنْ تَقَرَّ أَعْيُنُهُنَّ وَلَا يَحْزَنَّ
وَيَرْضَيْنَ بِمَآ أٰتَيْتَهُنَّ كُلُّهُنَّ وَاللّٰهُ يَعْلَمُ مَا
فِي قُلُوبِكُمْ وَكَانَ اللّٰهُ عَلِيمًا حَلِيمًا ﴿٥١﴾ لَا
يَحِلُّ لَكَ النِّسَآءُ مِنْ بَعْدُ وَلَآ أَنْ تَبَدَّلَ
بِهِنَّ مِنْ أَزْوٰجٍ وَلَوْ أَعْجَبَكَ حُسْنُهُنَّ إِلَّا
مَا مَلَكَتْ يَمِينُكَ وَكَانَ اللّٰهُ عَلٰى كُلِّ شَيْءٍ
رَقِيبًا ﴿٥٢﴾ يٰٓأَيُّهَا الَّذِينَ أٰمَنُوا لَا تَدْخُلُوا بُيُوتَ
النَّبِيِّ إِلَّآ أَنْ يُؤْذَنَ لَكُمْ إِلٰى طَعَامٍ غَيْرَ
نٰظِرِينَ إِنٰىهُ وَلٰكِنْ إِذَا دُعِيتُمْ فَادْخُلُوا
فَإِذَا طَعِمْتُمْ فَانْتَشِرُوا وَلَا مُسْتَـْٔنِسِينَ
لِحَدِيثٍ إِنَّ ذٰلِكُمْ كَانَ يُؤْذِي النَّبِيَّ
فَيَسْتَحْيِي مِنْكُمْ وَاللّٰهُ لَا يَسْتَحْيِي مِنَ
الْحَقِّ وَإِذَا سَأَلْتُمُوهُنَّ مَتٰعًا فَسْـَٔلُوهُنَّ
مِنْ وَّرَآءِ حِجَابٍ ذٰلِكُمْ أَطْهَرُ لِقُلُوبِكُمْ
وَقُلُوبِهِنَّ وَمَا كَانَ لَكُمْ أَنْ تُؤْذُوا رَسُولَ اللّٰهِ
وَلَآ أَنْ تَنْكِحُوٓا أَزْوٰجَهُ مِنْ بَعْدِهِ أَبَدًا
إِنَّ ذٰلِكُمْ كَانَ عِنْدَ اللّٰهِ عَظِيمًا ﴿٥٣﴾ إِنْ تُبْدُوا
شَيْـًٔا أَوْ تُخْفُوهُ فَإِنَّ اللّٰهَ كَانَ بِكُلِّ شَيْءٍ
عَلِيمًا ﴿٥٤﴾ لَا جُنَاحَ عَلَيْهِنَّ فِيٓ أٰبَآئِهِنَّ وَلَآ
أَبْنَآئِهِنَّ وَلَآ إِخْوٰنِهِنَّ وَلَآ أَبْنَآءِ إِخْوٰنِهِنَّ

appear) before their fathers or their sons or their brothers or their brothers' sons or the sons of their sisters or the womenfolk of their own (category) or those whom their right hands own. And you (all womenfolk) take (each of you) Allâh as a shield. Verily, Allâh is Ever Witness over all things.

56. Verily, Allâh and His angels bless this Prophet. Believers! You (also) invoke Allâh's blessings upon him and salute (him) with the salutation of peace.

57. Verily, those who malign Allâh and His Messenger (and are guilty of false accusation), Allâh has condemned them in this world and in the next and He has prepared a humiliating punishment for them.

58. And those who malign believing men and believing women for no fault of theirs, are guilty of false accusation and bear the burden of flagrant sin.

SECTION 8

59. **P**ROPHET! Tell your wives, your daughters and women of the believers that (while going out of their houses) they should draw lower upon themselves the portions of their (loose) outer coverings from over their heads on to their bosoms (so as to veil therewith the arms, the neck, the hair and ornaments worn over them). This practice is more likely to help them to be distinguished (from other women who make a display of their beauty and ornamentation) and so saves them from trouble. Allâh is Great Protector, Ever Merciful.

60. If the hypocrites, those who carry a disease in their hearts and the scandalmongers (who circulate false rumours to cause agitation) in the city, do not give up (their evil designs and stop their activities), We shall (one day) make you exercise authority over them, then they will not dwell long in this (city) with you (as your neighbours).

61. (They are) bereft of Allâh's grace, and will

وَلَآ أَبْنَآءِ أَخَوٰتِهِنَّ وَلَا نِسَآئِهِنَّ وَلَا مَا
مَلَكَتْ أَيْمَٰنُهُنَّ ۚ وَاتَّقِينَ اللَّهَ ۚ إِنَّ اللَّهَ
كَانَ عَلَىٰ كُلِّ شَيْءٍ شَهِيدًا ﴿٥٥﴾ إِنَّ اللَّهَ
وَمَلَٰٓئِكَتَهُۥ يُصَلُّونَ عَلَى النَّبِيِّ ۚ يَٰٓأَيُّهَا الَّذِينَ
ءَامَنُوا صَلُّوا عَلَيْهِ وَسَلِّمُوا تَسْلِيمًا ﴿٥٦﴾ إِنَّ
الَّذِينَ يُؤْذُونَ اللَّهَ وَرَسُولَهُۥ لَعَنَهُمُ اللَّهُ
فِي الدُّنْيَا وَالْأٓخِرَةِ وَأَعَدَّ لَهُمْ عَذَابًا مُّهِينًا ﴿٥٧﴾
وَالَّذِينَ يُؤْذُونَ الْمُؤْمِنِينَ وَالْمُؤْمِنَٰتِ
بِغَيْرِ مَا اكْتَسَبُوا فَقَدِ احْتَمَلُوا بُهْتَٰنًا
وَإِثْمًا مُّبِينًا ﴿٥٨﴾ يَٰٓأَيُّهَا النَّبِيُّ قُل لِّأَزْوَٰجِكَ
وَبَنَاتِكَ وَنِسَآءِ الْمُؤْمِنِينَ يُدْنِينَ عَلَيْهِنَّ
مِن جَلَٰبِيبِهِنَّ ۚ ذَٰلِكَ أَدْنَىٰٓ أَن يُعْرَفْنَ فَلَا
يُؤْذَيْنَ ۗ وَكَانَ اللَّهُ غَفُورًا رَّحِيمًا ﴿٥٩﴾ لَّئِن لَّمْ
يَنتَهِ الْمُنَٰفِقُونَ وَالَّذِينَ فِي قُلُوبِهِم مَّرَضٌ
وَالْمُرْجِفُونَ فِي الْمَدِينَةِ لَنُغْرِيَنَّكَ بِهِمْ
ثُمَّ لَا يُجَاوِرُونَكَ فِيهَآ إِلَّا قَلِيلًا ﴿٦٠﴾ مَّلْعُونِينَ ۖ
أَيْنَمَا ثُقِفُوٓا أُخِذُوا وَقُتِّلُوا تَقْتِيلًا ﴿٦١﴾ سُنَّةَ

be held wherever they are found and put to death.
62. Such has been the way of Allâh in the case of those who have gone before and you will find no change in the way of Allâh.
63. People ask you about this (promised) Hour (When the such people will be treated like that). Say, 'Allâh alone has the knowledge of it. And what shall make you know that the Hour may be near at hand.
64. Allâh has surely condemned the disbelievers and has a blazing Fire in store for them.
65. They will live long in it. And they will find (therein) no patron nor helper.
66. The day when their leaders are turned over and over into the Fire, they will say, 'O would that we had obeyed Allâh! Would that we had obeyed the Messenger!'
67. The people (in general) will say, 'Our Lord! We obeyed our leaders and our great ones but they led us astray from (Your) path.
68. 'Our Lord! Give them (their) punishment twice over (for their own evil deeds and for their misleading us), and deprive them totally of your grace.

SECTION 9

69. **B**ELIEVERS! Be not as those who maligned Moses. Indeed Allâh absolved him of their allegations. And he (- Moses) is ever highly honored in the sight of Allâh.
70. Believers! Take Allâh as a shield and say the right thing in a straight forward words that hits the mark (and is devoid of hidden meanings).
71. He will set right your actions for you, and protect you against (the consequences of) your sins. And one who obeys Allâh and His Messenger, has of course achieved a great achievement.
72. Verily, We presented the trust (- Our injunctions and laws) to the heavens and the earth and the mountains and they refused to prove false to it, and they were struck with awe of it. On the other hand a human-being has

اللهِ فِي الَّذِينَ خَلَوْا مِنْ قَبْلُ وَلَنْ تَجِدَ
لِسُنَّةِ اللهِ تَبْدِيلًا ﴿٦٢﴾ يَسْـَٔلُكَ النَّاسُ عَنِ
السَّاعَةِ قُلْ إِنَّمَا عِلْمُهَا عِنْدَ اللهِ وَمَا
يُدْرِيكَ لَعَلَّ السَّاعَةَ تَكُونُ قَرِيبًا ﴿٦٣﴾ إِنَّ
اللهَ لَعَنَ الْكٰفِرِينَ وَأَعَدَّ لَهُمْ سَعِيرًا ﴿٦٤﴾ خٰلِدِينَ
فِيهَا أَبَدًا لَا يَجِدُونَ وَلِيًّا وَلَا نَصِيرًا ﴿٦٥﴾
يَوْمَ تُقَلَّبُ وُجُوهُهُمْ فِي النَّارِ يَقُولُونَ يٰلَيْتَنَا
أَطَعْنَا اللهَ وَأَطَعْنَا الرَّسُولَا ﴿٦٦﴾ وَقَالُوا رَبَّنَا
إِنَّا أَطَعْنَا سَادَتَنَا وَكُبَرَاءَنَا فَأَضَلُّونَا السَّبِيلَا ﴿٦٧﴾
رَبَّنَا آتِهِمْ ضِعْفَيْنِ مِنَ الْعَذَابِ وَالْعَنْهُمْ
لَعْنًا كَبِيرًا ﴿٦٨﴾ يٰأَيُّهَا الَّذِينَ آمَنُوا لَا تَكُونُوا
كَالَّذِينَ آذَوْا مُوسٰى فَبَرَّأَهُ اللهُ مِمَّا قَالُوا
وَكَانَ عِنْدَ اللهِ وَجِيهًا ﴿٦٩﴾ يٰأَيُّهَا الَّذِينَ
آمَنُوا اتَّقُوا اللهَ وَقُولُوا قَوْلًا سَدِيدًا ﴿٧٠﴾
يُصْلِحْ لَكُمْ أَعْمٰلَكُمْ وَيَغْفِرْ لَكُمْ ذُنُوبَكُمْ
وَمَنْ يُطِعِ اللهَ وَرَسُولَهُ فَقَدْ فَازَ فَوْزًا
عَظِيمًا ﴿٧١﴾ إِنَّا عَرَضْنَا الْأَمَانَةَ عَلَى السَّمٰوٰتِ
وَالْأَرْضِ وَالْجِبَالِ فَأَبَيْنَ أَنْ يَحْمِلْنَهَا
وَأَشْفَقْنَ مِنْهَا وَحَمَلَهَا الْإِنْسٰنُ إِنَّهُ كَانَ

ظَلُوۡمًا جَهُوۡلًا ﴿٧٢﴾ لِّيُعَذِّبَ اللّٰهُ الۡمُنٰفِقِيۡنَ
وَالۡمُنٰفِقٰتِ وَالۡمُشۡرِكِيۡنَ وَالۡمُشۡرِكٰتِ
وَيَتُوۡبَ اللّٰهُ عَلَى الۡمُؤۡمِنِيۡنَ وَالۡمُؤۡمِنٰتِ ؕ
وَكَانَ اللّٰهُ غَفُوۡرًا رَّحِيۡمًا ﴿٧٣﴾

proved false to it (by betraying the trust and violating the Divine commandments), for he could be unjust and is forgetful.

73. With the result that Allâh will punish the hypocritical men and hypocritical women and the polytheistic men and the polytheistic women (who proved false to the trust). Whereas He turns with grace and mercy to the believing men and the believing women. Indeed, Allâh is Great Protector, Ever Merciful.

CHAPTER
34

SABA'
(Sheba)
(Revealed before Hijrah)

سُوۡرَةُ سَبَاٍ مَكِّيَّةٌ

بِسۡمِ اللّٰهِ الرَّحۡمٰنِ الرَّحِيۡمِ

With the name of Allâh,
the Most Gracious, the Ever Merciful
(I commence to read Sûrah Saba').

اَلۡحَمۡدُ لِلّٰهِ الَّذِيۡ لَهٗ مَا فِي السَّمٰوٰتِ وَمَا
فِي الۡاَرۡضِ وَلَهُ الۡحَمۡدُ فِي الۡاٰخِرَةِ ؕ وَهُوَ
الۡحَكِيۡمُ الۡخَبِيۡرُ ﴿١﴾ يَعۡلَمُ مَا يَلِجُ فِي الۡاَرۡضِ
وَمَا يَخۡرُجُ مِنۡهَا وَمَا يَنۡزِلُ مِنَ السَّمَآءِ وَمَا
يَعۡرُجُ فِيۡهَا ؕ وَهُوَ الرَّحِيۡمُ الۡغَفُوۡرُ ﴿٢﴾ وَقَالَ
الَّذِيۡنَ كَفَرُوۡا لَا تَاۡتِيۡنَا السَّاعَةُ ؕ قُلۡ بَلٰى
وَرَبِّيۡ لَتَاۡتِيَنَّكُمۡ عٰلِمِ الۡغَيۡبِ ۚ لَا يَعۡزُبُ عَنۡهُ
مِثۡقَالُ ذَرَّةٍ فِي السَّمٰوٰتِ وَلَا فِي الۡاَرۡضِ
وَلَاۤ اَصۡغَرُ مِنۡ ذٰلِكَ وَلَاۤ اَكۡبَرُ اِلَّا فِيۡ

1. ALL kind of true and perfect praise is due to Allâh, to Whom belongs whatsoever lies in the heavens and whatsoever lies in the earth. To Him alone shall all praise belong in the Hereafter. And He is the All-Wise, the All-Aware.

2. He (- God the Almighty) knows all that goes into the earth and all that comes forth from it, and all that comes down from the heaven and all that goes up to it. And He is the Ever Merciful, the Great Protector.

3. And those who disbelieve say, 'The Hour will never come upon us.' Say, 'Why not, by my Lord, who knows the unseen, it is bound to come upon you. Nothing escapes Him (unobserved), not even so much as an atom's weight in the heavens or in the earth, nor is anything there smaller or greater than that (but is recorded) in a book revealing (the truth, and is

governed by a plain law).

4. (The Hour shall come) so that He may reward those who believe and do deeds of righteousness. It is they for whom there awaits protection (from the consequences of sin), and honourable and generous provision.

5. But (as to) those who strive hard against Our revelations seeking to frustrate (Our plan), it is they who will suffer a harrowing punishment of the worst sort.

6. Those who have been given knowledge know that whatever has been revealed to you from your Lord is the very lasting truth, and that it guides to the path of (One Who is) the All-Mighty, the Highly Praiseworthy (in His own right).

7. And those who disbelieve say (one to another), 'Shall we show you a man who gives you the important news (that) when you are (dead and) broken up into a complete disintegration, you shall then be raised to a new life.

8. 'Has he forged a lie in the name of Allâh? Or is he afflicted with madness?' Neither of the two, of course, (is true,) the thing is that those who do not believe in the Hereafter are courting a sure agony and are steeped in a dismal error.

9. Do they not see (how they are surrounded on all sides by) the heaven and the earth that lie before and behind them? If We (so) please, We can make them low (and abased) in the land (and thus show some signs of the earth), or let some portion of the clouds fall down upon them (showing some heavenly signs). Behold! There is a sign in this for every penitent servant (of God).

SECTION 2

10. **A**ND certainly We bestowed Our (gracious) favours on David. (We said,) 'O (you dwellers of the) mountains, obey him.' And (We assigned) the birds and the swift footed horses (their duty); and We made the iron soft and pliant for him.

سُورَةُ سَبَإٍ ٣٤

كِتَٰبٍ مُّبِينٍ ٣ لِّيَجْزِيَ الَّذِينَ ءَامَنُوا وَعَمِلُوا
الصَّٰلِحَٰتِ أُولَٰٓئِكَ لَهُم مَّغْفِرَةٌ وَرِزْقٌ كَرِيمٌ ٤
وَالَّذِينَ سَعَوْ فِيٓ ءَايَٰتِنَا مُعَٰجِزِينَ أُولَٰٓئِكَ
لَهُمْ عَذَابٌ مِّن رِّجْزٍ أَلِيمٌ ٥ وَيَرَى الَّذِينَ
أُوتُوا الْعِلْمَ الَّذِيٓ أُنْزِلَ إِلَيْكَ مِن رَّبِّكَ
هُوَ الْحَقَّ وَيَهْدِيٓ إِلَىٰ صِرَٰطِ الْعَزِيزِ
الْحَمِيدِ ٦ وَقَالَ الَّذِينَ كَفَرُوا هَلْ نَدُلُّكُمْ
عَلَىٰ رَجُلٍ يُنَبِّئُكُمْ إِذَا مُزِّقْتُمْ كُلَّ مُمَزَّقٍ
إِنَّكُمْ لَفِي خَلْقٍ جَدِيدٍ ٧ أَفْتَرَىٰ عَلَى اللَّهِ
كَذِبًا أَم بِهِۦ جِنَّةٌ بَلِ الَّذِينَ لَا يُؤْمِنُونَ
بِالْأٓخِرَةِ فِي الْعَذَابِ وَالضَّلَٰلِ الْبَعِيدِ ٨
أَفَلَمْ يَرَوْا إِلَىٰ مَا بَيْنَ أَيْدِيهِمْ وَمَا
خَلْفَهُم مِّنَ السَّمَآءِ وَالْأَرْضِ إِن نَّشَأْ
نَخْسِفْ بِهِمُ الْأَرْضَ أَوْ نُسْقِطْ عَلَيْهِمْ
كِسَفًا مِّنَ السَّمَآءِ إِنَّ فِي ذَٰلِكَ لَأٓيَةً لِّكُلِّ
عَبْدٍ مُّنِيبٍ ٩ وَلَقَدْ ءَاتَيْنَا دَاوُۥدَ مِنَّا فَضْلًا ع ٩ ٧
يَٰجِبَالُ أَوِّبِي مَعَهُۥ وَالطَّيْرَ وَأَلَنَّا لَهُ

11. (We said to him,) 'Make full length coats of mail (to cover the whole body) forging links of proper measure (for their smooth working).' (And We also said to him and his followers,) 'Do righteous deeds. I am a keen Observer of what you do.'

12. And We made such winds serve Solomon the blowing of which in the forenoon (and thus help sailing of his ships) was equal to (a voyage of) a month (by the other ships); similarly its blowing in the afternoon was (also) equal to (a voyage of) a month (by them). And We made a spring of molten copper to flow for him. Also (given into his service were) some of the *jinns* (- wild and rebellious mountain tribes known as *Amalaqites*), who worked under him as trained craftsmen) by the command of his Lord. And (We also told them) whoever of them deviated from and disobeyed Our command (- that they should obey Solomon) We shall make him suffer the agony of burning.

13. Those (*jinns* -handy craftsmen) made for him (- Solomon) whatever he desired, places for worship and plans and basins (as large) as the tanks and large and heavy cooking pots well-set (on their trivets due to their large size). (And We said,) 'Act gratefully, O people of David.' Yet few are My people who are (really) grateful.

14. And when We ordained death for him (- Solomon) the people only came to know of it (- his death) through a (worthless) creature of earth (- Solomon's son) that was eating away his (father's) staff (- ruling power and glory). So when it fell down the *jinn* realized then plainly that had they known the secret (of the hollowness of the kingdom) they would have never remained in (a state of) humiliating torment.

15. There was indeed a great sign for Sheba in their homeland. (They had) two gardens (one) on the right and (one) on the left, (and We had said to them,) 'Eat of the provisions (and enjoy

الْحَدِيدَ ﴿١٠﴾ أَنِ اعْمَلْ سَٰبِغَٰتٍ وَقَدِّرْ فِي السَّرْدِ وَاعْمَلُوا صَٰلِحًا إِنِّي بِمَا تَعْمَلُونَ بَصِيرٌ ﴿١١﴾ وَلِسُلَيْمَٰنَ الرِّيحَ غُدُوُّهَا شَهْرٌ وَرَوَاحُهَا شَهْرٌ وَأَسَلْنَا لَهُ عَيْنَ الْقِطْرِ وَمِنَ الْجِنِّ مَنْ يَعْمَلُ بَيْنَ يَدَيْهِ بِإِذْنِ رَبِّهِ وَمَنْ يَزِغْ مِنْهُمْ عَنْ أَمْرِنَا نُذِقْهُ مِنْ عَذَابِ السَّعِيرِ ﴿١٢﴾ يَعْمَلُونَ لَهُ مَا يَشَاءُ مِنْ مَحَٰرِيبَ وَتَمَٰثِيلَ وَجِفَانٍ كَالْجَوَابِ وَقُدُورٍ رَّاسِيَٰتٍ اعْمَلُوا آلَ دَاوُدَ شُكْرًا وَقَلِيلٌ مِنْ عِبَادِيَ الشَّكُورُ ﴿١٣﴾ فَلَمَّا قَضَيْنَا عَلَيْهِ الْمَوْتَ مَا دَلَّهُمْ عَلَىٰ مَوْتِهِ إِلَّا دَابَّةُ الْأَرْضِ تَأْكُلُ مِنْسَأَتَهُ فَلَمَّا خَرَّ تَبَيَّنَتِ الْجِنُّ أَنْ لَوْ كَانُوا يَعْلَمُونَ الْغَيْبَ مَا لَبِثُوا فِي الْعَذَابِ الْمُهِينِ ﴿١٤﴾ لَقَدْ كَانَ لِسَبَإٍ فِي مَسْكَنِهِمْ آيَةٌ جَنَّتَانِ عَنْ يَمِينٍ وَشِمَالٍ كُلُوا مِنْ رِزْقِ رَبِّكُمْ وَاشْكُرُوا لَهُ بَلْدَةٌ

the gifts) of your Lord and render Him thanks. (Yours is) a happy and beautiful land and Lord a Great Protector.'

16. But they turned away. Thereupon We sent against them a devastating flood. And We replaced their two (excellent) gardens by two (other) gardens bearing bitter fruit and (containing) Tamarisk and a few nettle shrubs (here and there).

17. That is how We recompensed them because of their ingratitude. It is only the ungrateful whom We recompense (in the like manner).

18. And We had placed between them (- the Shebians) and the towns (of Syria) which We had blessed, (other) towns facing each other and prominently visible, and We had fixed easy (journeying) stages between them. (We said to the people of Sheba), 'Journey through them by night and day, safe and secure.'

19. But (due to their ingratitude) they wanted (as if) to say, 'Our Lord! Make longer the distance between (the stages of) our journeys.' And they did injustice to themselves. So We reduced them to mere legends and We broke them into complete disintegration (and scattered them far and wide). Behold! There are signs in this for all those who are patiently-persevering and highly grateful persons.

20. And *Iblîs* found that he judged regarding them correctly, (that he would be successful in leading the progeny of Adam astray,) excepting (only) a party of true believers, so (all) the rest of the people followed him;

21. Though he (- *Iblîs*) had no authority over them (for it is by their own wrong beliefs and evil deeds that mankind brings about their spiritual ruin). (It happened thus) so that We might distinguish those who believed in the Hereafter from those who were suffering from doubts about it. Indeed, your Lord is Watchful over and Preserver of everything.

SECTION 3

22. SAY, 'Call on those whom you take (for

طَيِّبَةٌ وَّرَبٌّ غَفُوْرٌ ﴿١٥﴾ فَأَعْرَضُوْا فَأَرْسَلْنَا
عَلَيْهِمْ سَيْلَ الْعَرِمِ وَ بَدَّلْنٰهُمْ بِجَنَّتَيْهِمْ
جَنَّتَيْنِ ذَوَاتَيْ أُكُلٍ خَمْطٍ وَّ أَثْلٍ وَّ شَيْءٍ مِّنْ
سِدْرٍ قَلِيْلٍ ﴿١٦﴾ ذٰلِكَ جَزَيْنٰهُمْ بِمَا كَفَرُوْا وَ هَلْ
نُجْزِيْٓ إِلَّا الْكَفُوْرَ ﴿١٧﴾ وَ جَعَلْنَا بَيْنَهُمْ وَ بَيْنَ
الْقُرَى الَّتِيْ بٰرَكْنَا فِيْهَا قُرًى ظٰهِرَةً وَّ قَدَّرْنَا
فِيْهَا السَّيْرَ سِيْرُوْا فِيْهَا لَيَالِيَ وَ أَيَّامًا أٰمِنِيْنَ ﴿١٨﴾
فَقَالُوْا رَبَّنَا بٰعِدْ بَيْنَ أَسْفَارِنَا وَ ظَلَمُوْٓا
أَنْفُسَهُمْ فَجَعَلْنٰهُمْ أَحَادِيْثَ وَ مَزَّقْنٰهُمْ كُلَّ
مُمَزَّقٍ إِنَّ فِيْ ذٰلِكَ لَأٰيٰتٍ لِّكُلِّ صَبَّارٍ شَكُوْرٍ ﴿١٩﴾
وَ لَقَدْ صَدَّقَ عَلَيْهِمْ إِبْلِيْسُ ظَنَّهٗ فَاتَّبَعُوْهُ
إِلَّا فَرِيْقًا مِّنَ الْمُؤْمِنِيْنَ ﴿٢٠﴾ وَ مَا كَانَ لَهٗ عَلَيْهِمْ
مِّنْ سُلْطٰنٍ إِلَّا لِنَعْلَمَ مَنْ يُّؤْمِنُ بِالْأٰخِرَةِ
مِمَّنْ هُوَ مِنْهَا فِيْ شَكٍّ وَ رَبُّكَ عَلٰى كُلِّ
شَيْءٍ حَفِيْظٌ ﴿٢١﴾ قُلِ ادْعُوا الَّذِيْنَ زَعَمْتُمْ مِّنْ
دُوْنِ اللّٰهِ لَا يَمْلِكُوْنَ مِثْقَالَ ذَرَّةٍ فِي السَّمٰوٰتِ

gods) besides Allâh. They possess no power not even so much as the weight of an atom in the heavens or in the earth, nor do they share any control over either of them, nor does He receive any support from these (false gods).'

23. No intercession will avail with Him except (for him about) whom He permits (it). (Those for whom the intercession is permitted will keep waiting) until when their hearts are relieved of awe they would ask (one another), 'What is it that your Lord said?' Some of them will reply, '(He said) the truth.' And He is the Highest, the Greatest.

24. Say, 'Who provides you sustenance from the heavens and the earth?' (Then) tell, '(None other than) Allâh.' Surely, we (- the believers) are on the right guidance, nonetheless you (the disbelievers) are engrossed in evident error.

25. Say, 'You will not be called upon to account for our sins, nor shall we be called upon to account for your doings.'

26. Say, 'Our Lord will bring us together (in a battlefield as opponents) and then He will judge between us with truth for He alone is the Supreme Judge, the All-Knowing.

27. Say, 'Show me those beings whom you number with Him as (His) associates. By no means (should you associate partners with Him) for it is Allâh (alone) Who is the All-Mighty, the All-Wise.

28. (Prophet!) We have sent you not but towards entire humankind (till the end of time) as a Bearer of glad-tidings and as a Warner but most people do not know (that the Message of Islam is universal and the Qur'ân the last revealed Book).

29. And they say, 'Tell us, if you speak the truth when this promise will be (fulfilled).'

30. Say, 'For you is the appointment of a day which you cannot delay by a single moment (and thus avoid it), nor shall you be able to go ahead (of it to find an escape from it for a

وَلَا فِي الْأَرْضِ وَمَا لَهُمْ فِيهِمَا مِنْ شِرْكٍ
وَمَا لَهُ مِنْهُمْ مِنْ ظَهِيرٍ ﴿٢٢﴾ وَلَا تَنْفَعُ الشَّفَاعَةُ
عِنْدَهُ إِلَّا لِمَنْ أَذِنَ لَهُ حَتَّى إِذَا فُزِّعَ عَنْ
قُلُوبِهِمْ قَالُوا مَاذَا قَالَ رَبُّكُمْ قَالُوا الْحَقَّ
وَهُوَ الْعَلِيُّ الْكَبِيرُ ﴿٢٣﴾ قُلْ مَنْ يَرْزُقُكُمْ مِنَ
السَّمٰوٰتِ وَالْأَرْضِ قُلِ اللّٰهُ وَإِنَّا أَوْ إِيَّاكُمْ
لَعَلَىٰ هُدًى أَوْ فِي ضَلٰلٍ مُبِينٍ ﴿٢٤﴾ قُلْ لَا
تُسْـَٔلُونَ عَمَّا أَجْرَمْنَا وَلَا نُسْـَٔلُ عَمَّا
تَعْمَلُونَ ﴿٢٥﴾ قُلْ يَجْمَعُ بَيْنَنَا رَبُّنَا ثُمَّ يَفْتَحُ
بَيْنَنَا بِالْحَقِّ وَهُوَ الْفَتَّاحُ الْعَلِيمُ ﴿٢٦﴾ قُلْ
أَرُونِيَ الَّذِينَ أَلْحَقْتُمْ بِهِ شُرَكَاءَ كَلَّا بَلْ
هُوَ اللّٰهُ الْعَزِيزُ الْحَكِيمُ ﴿٢٧﴾ وَمَا أَرْسَلْنٰكَ إِلَّا
كَافَّةً لِلنَّاسِ بَشِيرًا وَنَذِيرًا وَلٰكِنَّ أَكْثَرَ
النَّاسِ لَا يَعْلَمُونَ ﴿٢٨﴾ وَيَقُولُونَ مَتَىٰ هٰذَا
الْوَعْدُ إِنْ كُنْتُمْ صٰدِقِينَ ﴿٢٩﴾ قُلْ لَكُمْ
مِيعَادُ يَوْمٍ لَا تَسْتَـْٔخِرُونَ عَنْهُ سَاعَةً

single moment).'

SECTION 4

31. **A**ND those who disbelieve say, 'We will never believe in this Qur'ân nor in (the Books) that preceded it.' Could you but see their condition when the wrongdoers will be made to stand before their Lord, they will be bandying words (and so throwing back the blame) on one another. Those who had been suppressed and made weak will say to those who considered themselves superior, 'Had it not been for you we would surely have been believers.'

32. (Thereupon) those who considered themselves superior will say to those who had been suppressed and made weak (in the world), 'Was it we who kept you away from (following) the guidance after it had come to you? No, this was not the case. Rather you were guilty in your own right.'

33. And those who were suppressed and made weak (in the world) will say to those who considered themselves superior, 'Nay, (We did not become guilty in our own right) rather it was due to your schemes (which you hatched) by day and night (that kept us away from guidance); for then you urged us to disbelieve in Allâh and set up equals with Him (to be worshipped).' And they will not be able to conceal their remorse when they see the punishment; We shall put shackles round the necks of these disbelievers. They will be recompensed only according to their (actual) deeds.

34. We sent no Warner to any town but its corrupted well-to-do people said, 'Surely we disbelieve in the Messages that you have been sent with.'

35. And they (also) say, 'We are better off in respect of wealth and children (as compared with others) and we are not at all going to be made to suffer.'

36. Say, 'Verily, my Lord multiplies the means of livelihood for whom He will and makes them scant (for whom He pleases), but most people

وَلَا تَسْتَقْدِمُونَ ﴿٣٠﴾ وَقَالَ الَّذِينَ كَفَرُوا لَن
نُّؤْمِنَ بِهَٰذَا الْقُرْآنِ وَلَا بِالَّذِي بَيْنَ يَدَيْهِ
وَلَوْ تَرَىٰ إِذِ الظَّٰلِمُونَ مَوْقُوفُونَ عِندَ رَبِّهِمْ
يَرْجِعُ بَعْضُهُمْ إِلَىٰ بَعْضٍ الْقَوْلَ يَقُولُ الَّذِينَ
اسْتُضْعِفُوا لِلَّذِينَ اسْتَكْبَرُوا لَوْلَا أَنتُمْ
لَكُنَّا مُؤْمِنِينَ ﴿٣١﴾ قَالَ الَّذِينَ اسْتَكْبَرُوا لِلَّذِينَ
اسْتُضْعِفُوا أَنَحْنُ صَدَدْنَٰكُمْ عَنِ الْهُدَىٰ
بَعْدَ إِذْ جَاءَكُم بَلْ كُنتُم مُّجْرِمِينَ ﴿٣٢﴾
وَقَالَ الَّذِينَ اسْتُضْعِفُوا لِلَّذِينَ اسْتَكْبَرُوا
بَلْ مَكْرُ الَّيْلِ وَالنَّهَارِ إِذْ تَأْمُرُونَنَا أَن
نَّكْفُرَ بِاللَّهِ وَنَجْعَلَ لَهُ أَندَادًا وَأَسَرُّوا
النَّدَامَةَ لَمَّا رَأَوُا الْعَذَابَ وَجَعَلْنَا الْأَغْلَٰلَ
فِي أَعْنَاقِ الَّذِينَ كَفَرُوا هَلْ يُجْزَوْنَ إِلَّا
مَا كَانُوا يَعْمَلُونَ ﴿٣٣﴾ وَمَا أَرْسَلْنَا فِي قَرْيَةٍ
مِّن نَّذِيرٍ إِلَّا قَالَ مُتْرَفُوهَا إِنَّا بِمَا أُرْسِلْتُم
بِهِ كَٰفِرُونَ ﴿٣٤﴾ وَقَالُوا نَحْنُ أَكْثَرُ أَمْوَٰلًا وَأَوْلَٰدًا
وَمَا نَحْنُ بِمُعَذَّبِينَ ﴿٣٥﴾ قُلْ إِنَّ رَبِّي يَبْسُطُ
الرِّزْقَ لِمَن يَشَاءُ وَيَقْدِرُ وَلَٰكِنَّ أَكْثَرَ

do not know (the reason behind).

SECTION 5

37. NEITHER your wealth nor your children are a means that can bring you near to Us in rank. But it is only those who believe and do righteous deeds (whose faith and virtue will be the means to bring them near to Us). They shall have the reward for their (virtuous) deeds many times over and shall be occupying the lofty places with peace and security.

38. But those who strive hard in their opposition to Our Messages seeking to render (Our plan) null and void (and thinking they will escape Us), it is they who will be brought to face punishment.

39. Say, 'Surely, my Lord multiplies the means of livelihood for such of His servants as He will and makes them scant for him (whom He pleases). And whatever you spend (in some noble cause) He exceeds it (in giving reward) so as to leave it (- your own contribution) behind; He is the Best of Providers.

40. (Never be oblivious of) the day when He will gather them all together, then He will say to the angels, 'Are these the ones who used to worship you?'

41. They will say, 'Holy is Your name. It is You Who are our Protector against them, not they. It was not us but the *jinns* that they worshipped. It was in them that most of them believed (and not in Us).

42. So (it will be said to the false gods and their worshippers,) 'This day you have no power to help or harm one another.' And We shall say to the wrongdoers, 'Suffer the agony of the Fire which you used to cry lies to.'

43. And when Our clear Messages are recited to them they say, 'This fellow is but a man who wishes to keep you away from (worshipping the gods) that your fathers used to worship.' And they say (of the Qur'ân), 'This is nothing but a forged lie unprecedented.' And those who disbelieve say regarding this (perfect) truth when

ع ١٠

النَّاسِ لَا يَعْلَمُونَ ﴿٣٦﴾ وَمَا أَمْوَٰلُكُمْ وَلَا
أَوْلَٰدُكُم بِالَّتِي تُقَرِّبُكُمْ عِندَنَا زُلْفَىٰٓ إِلَّا مَنْ
ءَامَنَ وَعَمِلَ صَٰلِحًا فَأُوْلَٰٓئِكَ لَهُمْ جَزَآءُ
الضِّعْفِ بِمَا عَمِلُوا وَهُمْ فِي الْغُرُفَٰتِ
ءَامِنُونَ ﴿٣٧﴾ وَالَّذِينَ يَسْعَوْنَ فِيٓ ءَايَٰتِنَا
مُعَٰجِزِينَ أُوْلَٰٓئِكَ فِي الْعَذَابِ مُحْضَرُونَ ﴿٣٨﴾
قُلْ إِنَّ رَبِّي يَبْسُطُ الرِّزْقَ لِمَن يَشَآءُ مِنْ
عِبَادِهِۦ وَيَقْدِرُ لَهُۥ وَمَآ أَنفَقْتُم مِّن شَيْءٍ
فَهُوَ يُخْلِفُهُۥ وَهُوَ خَيْرُ الرَّٰزِقِينَ ﴿٣٩﴾ وَيَوْمَ
يَحْشُرُهُمْ جَمِيعًا ثُمَّ يَقُولُ لِلْمَلَٰٓئِكَةِ أَهَٰٓؤُلَآءِ
إِيَّاكُمْ كَانُوا يَعْبُدُونَ ﴿٤٠﴾ قَالُوا سُبْحَٰنَكَ أَنتَ
وَلِيُّنَا مِن دُونِهِم بَلْ كَانُوا يَعْبُدُونَ
الْجِنَّ أَكْثَرُهُم بِهِم مُّؤْمِنُونَ ﴿٤١﴾ فَالْيَوْمَ
لَا يَمْلِكُ بَعْضُكُمْ لِبَعْضٍ نَّفْعًا وَلَا ضَرًّا
وَنَقُولُ لِلَّذِينَ ظَلَمُوا ذُوقُوا عَذَابَ النَّارِ
الَّتِي كُنتُم بِهَا تُكَذِّبُونَ ﴿٤٢﴾ وَإِذَا تُتْلَىٰ عَلَيْهِمْ
ءَايَٰتُنَا بَيِّنَٰتٍ قَالُوا مَا هَٰذَآ إِلَّا رَجُلٌ يُرِيدُ
أَن يَصُدَّكُمْ عَمَّا كَانَ يَعْبُدُ ءَابَآؤُكُمْ وَقَالُوا
مَا هَٰذَآ إِلَّآ إِفْكٌ مُّفْتَرًى وَقَالَ الَّذِينَ

it has come to them, 'This is nothing but a hoax causing a split (among the people).'
44. Whereas We had given them none of (Our) Books which they studied, nor did We send to them any Warner (in the recent past) before you (that they should have known the abuses involved in forging lies).
45. Their predecessors had also cried lies (to the Prophets of their time). And these (Makkans) have not attained (even) a tenth of that (resources of wealth and strength) which We had given their predecessors, yet they cried lies to My Messages so (let these see) how (terrible) was the change I brought about and how (tremendous) was (the result of) My disapproval.

SECTION 6

46. **S**AY, 'I advise you (to do) one thing, (it is) that you keep Allâh (before) you, stand up in twos (- collectively) and ones (- singly) and then ponder (over the teachings of this Prophet). (You will come to the conclusion) that there is no vestige of insanity in (this) companion of yours (- Muhammad). He is only a Warner to you of a great calamity which is impending (over you).
47. Say, 'Whatever reward I might have asked of you (for my this exhortation) you can keep it with you. (I claim) my reward only from Allâh for He is the Witness over all things.'
48. Say, 'My Lord will do away (with falsehood) by means of the truth. (He is) thoroughly Aware of the hidden realities.'
49. Say, 'The perfect truth has come (in Makkah) and (as a prophecy keep it in mind that) falsehood (and idol-worship has gone) never to sprout (again from this soil) and never to return (to it).
50. Say, 'If I am lost, it is I who suffer the loss (for my own faults), but if I am rightly guided, it is entirely due to (the truth) that my Lord has revealed to me. Verily, He is All-

كَفَرُوا لِلْحَقِّ لَمَّا جَآءَهُمْ إِنْ هَٰذَآ إِلَّا سِحْرٌ
مُّبِينٌ ﴿٤٣﴾ وَمَآ ءَاتَيْنَٰهُم مِّنْ كُتُبٍ يَدْرُسُونَهَا
وَمَآ أَرْسَلْنَآ إِلَيْهِمْ قَبْلَكَ مِن نَّذِيرٍ ﴿٤٤﴾
وَكَذَّبَ الَّذِينَ مِن قَبْلِهِمْ وَمَا بَلَغُوا مِعْشَارَ
مَآ ءَاتَيْنَٰهُمْ فَكَذَّبُوا رُسُلِي فَكَيْفَ كَانَ
نَكِيرِ ﴿٤٥﴾ قُلْ إِنَّمَآ أَعِظُكُم بِوَٰحِدَةٍ أَن تَقُومُوا
لِلَّهِ مَثْنَىٰ وَفُرَٰدَىٰ ثُمَّ تَتَفَكَّرُوا مَا
بِصَاحِبِكُم مِّن جِنَّةٍ إِنْ هُوَ إِلَّا نَذِيرٌ لَّكُم
بَيْنَ يَدَيْ عَذَابٍ شَدِيدٍ ﴿٤٦﴾ قُلْ مَا سَأَلْتُكُم
مِّنْ أَجْرٍ فَهُوَ لَكُمْ إِنْ أَجْرِيَ إِلَّا عَلَى اللَّهِ
وَهُوَ عَلَىٰ كُلِّ شَيْءٍ شَهِيدٌ ﴿٤٧﴾ قُلْ إِنَّ رَبِّي
يَقْذِفُ بِالْحَقِّ عَلَّٰمُ الْغُيُوبِ ﴿٤٨﴾ قُلْ جَآءَ
الْحَقُّ وَمَا يُبْدِئُ الْبَٰطِلُ وَمَا يُعِيدُ ﴿٤٩﴾ قُلْ
إِن ضَلَلْتُ فَإِنَّمَآ أَضِلُّ عَلَىٰ نَفْسِي وَإِنِ
اهْتَدَيْتُ فَبِمَا يُوحِيٓ إِلَيَّ رَبِّيٓ إِنَّهُۥ سَمِيعٌ

Hearing, Ever Nigh.

51. And (you will be simply astonished) if you could only see when these (disbelievers) will be in the grip of fear; but then there will be no escape and they will be seized (with punishment) at a place nearby (- at *Badr*).

52. Then they will say, 'We (now) believe in this (- Qur'ân). But how can the attainment (of faith) be possible from a position (of disbelief) so far off,

53. While they had indeed disbelieved in it before this, and they were shooting at the unknown (and making far fetched and useless conjectures about the failure of the Prophet and their own triumph) from a place far off.

54. A barrier has been placed between them and their longings (and they will fail to see the realisation of their hearts desire, the failure of the Prophet in his mission), as was done with the people similar to them before (this). They (too) suffered from disquieting doubts.

قَرِيبٌ ﴿٥٠﴾ وَلَوْ تَرَىٰٓ إِذْ فَزِعُوا فَلَا فَوْتَ
وَأُخِذُوا مِن مَّكَانٍ قَرِيبٍ ﴿٥١﴾ وَقَالُوٓا ءَامَنَّا
بِهِۦ وَأَنَّىٰ لَهُمُ التَّنَاوُشُ مِن مَّكَانٍۭ بَعِيدٍ ﴿٥٢﴾
وَقَدْ كَفَرُوا بِهِۦ مِن قَبْلُ وَيَقْذِفُونَ بِالْغَيْبِ
مِن مَّكَانٍۭ بَعِيدٍ ﴿٥٣﴾ وَحِيلَ بَيْنَهُمْ وَبَيْنَ
مَا يَشْتَهُونَ كَمَا فُعِلَ بِأَشْيَاعِهِم مِّن
قَبْلُ إِنَّهُمْ كَانُوا فِي شَكٍّ مُّرِيبٍ ﴿٥٤﴾ ع ١٢

CHAPTER
35

FÂṮIR
(Originator)
(Revealed before Hijrah)

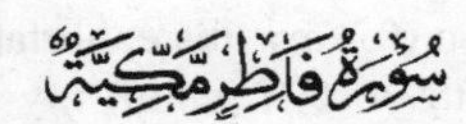

With the name of Allâh,
the Most Gracious, the Ever Merciful
(I commence to read Sûrah Fâṯir).

بِسْمِ اللَّهِ الرَّحْمَٰنِ الرَّحِيمِ

1. **A**LL kind of true and perfect praise belongs to Allâh, the Originator of the heavens and the earth, Who employs as (His) messengers the angels, having two or three or four pairs of wings (and so possessed of powers, speed and qualities in varying degrees). He adds to the creation (of these wings and thus to the powers and abilities of the angels) as much as He will

اَلْحَمْدُ لِلَّهِ فَاطِرِ السَّمٰوٰتِ وَالْأَرْضِ جَاعِلِ
الْمَلٰٓئِكَةِ رُسُلًا أُولِيٓ أَجْنِحَةٍ مَّثْنٰى وَثُلٰثَ
وَرُبٰعَ يَزِيدُ فِي الْخَلْقِ مَا يَشَآءُ إِنَّ اللَّهَ

(in accordance with the importance of the work entrusted to each one of them), for Allâh is Possessor of power over (His) every desired thing.

2. Whatever (blessings of) mercy Allâh showers upon people there is none to withhold them. And none can grant that which He withholds after it (has once been withheld by Him). He is the All-Mighty, the All-Wise.

3. O People! Remember the favour of Allâh that rests upon you. Is there any Creator other than Allâh who provides (all sorts of provisions) for you from the heaven and the earth? There is no other, cannot be and will never be One worthy of worship but He. Whither are you then being led astray?

4. If they cry lies to you (you need not bother because) other Messengers (of God) have already been cried lies to before you. Yet all matters stand referred to Allâh (for His final judgment).

5. O People! The promise of Allâh is undoubtedly true, so do not let the present life deceive you, and do not let the avowed seducer seduce you away from Allâh.

6. Surely, satan is an enemy to you, so treat him as an enemy. He calls his party only (to follow him) with the result that they become of the inmates of the blazing Fire.

7. There awaits a severe punishment for those who disbelieve. But there awaits His protection and a great reward for those who believe and (also) do deeds of righteousness.

SECTION 2

8. **C**AN the person, the evil of whose conduct is made to appear pleasing and regards it as good, (be in a position to discern the truth and so be rightly guided). Allâh forsakes him who wishes to go astray (as it is His law). And He guides (him) aright who wishes (to get right guidance). So do not fret yourself to death because of them. Surely, Allâh knows what they do.

سُوْرَةُ فَاطِرٍ ٣٥

عَلَى كُلِّ شَيْءٍ قَدِيرٌ ① مَا يَفْتَحِ اللَّهُ لِلنَّاسِ
مِنْ رَحْمَةٍ فَلَا مُمْسِكَ لَهَا وَمَا يُمْسِكْ
فَلَا مُرْسِلَ لَهُ مِنْ بَعْدِهِ وَهُوَ الْعَزِيزُ
الْحَكِيمُ ② يَا أَيُّهَا النَّاسُ اذْكُرُوا نِعْمَتَ اللَّهِ
عَلَيْكُمْ هَلْ مِنْ خَالِقٍ غَيْرُ اللَّهِ يَرْزُقُكُمْ
مِنَ السَّمَاءِ وَالْأَرْضِ لَا إِلَهَ إِلَّا هُوَ فَأَنَّى
تُؤْفَكُونَ ③ وَإِنْ يُكَذِّبُوكَ فَقَدْ كُذِّبَتْ
رُسُلٌ مِنْ قَبْلِكَ وَإِلَى اللَّهِ تُرْجَعُ الْأُمُورُ ④
يَا أَيُّهَا النَّاسُ إِنَّ وَعْدَ اللَّهِ حَقٌّ فَلَا تَغُرَّنَّكُمُ
الْحَيَاةُ الدُّنْيَا وَلَا يَغُرَّنَّكُمْ بِاللَّهِ الْغَرُورُ ⑤
إِنَّ الشَّيْطَانَ لَكُمْ عَدُوٌّ فَاتَّخِذُوهُ عَدُوًّا
إِنَّمَا يَدْعُو حِزْبَهُ لِيَكُونُوا مِنْ أَصْحَابِ
السَّعِيرِ ⑥ الَّذِينَ كَفَرُوا لَهُمْ عَذَابٌ شَدِيدٌ
وَالَّذِينَ آمَنُوا وَعَمِلُوا الصَّالِحَاتِ لَهُمْ مَغْفِرَةٌ
وَأَجْرٌ كَبِيرٌ ⑦ أَفَمَنْ زُيِّنَ لَهُ سُوءُ عَمَلِهِ
فَرَآهُ حَسَنًا فَإِنَّ اللَّهَ يُضِلُّ مَنْ يَشَاءُ
وَيَهْدِي مَنْ يَشَاءُ فَلَا تَذْهَبْ نَفْسُكَ
عَلَيْهِمْ حَسَرَاتٍ إِنَّ اللَّهَ عَلِيمٌ بِمَا يَصْنَعُونَ ⑧

ع ١٣

9. And Allâh is He Who sends the winds which raise (vapours in the form of) clouds. (When the clouds rise) We drive them towards a tract of land which has no sign of life and make thereby the barren land fertile, green and flourishing. That is how the quickening (of the dead shall come to pass).

10. Whoever seeks glory (let him turn to God as) all glory belongs to Allâh. All good and pure words (of faith) go up to Him and all the righteous deeds exalt that (faith). As for those who plan evil plots, there awaits them an agony of a severe nature; the evil planning of such is doomed to fail.

11. And Allâh created you out of dust and then from a drop of fluid and then made you pairs (- male and female). And no female conceives (a child) nor does she give birth (to it) but it is in accordance with His (- the Creator's) knowledge. And no one who is granted long life gets his life prolonged or gets it reduced but (all this) is in (conformity with) some law. Verily, it is easy for Allâh (to impose such laws).

12. The two great bodies of water are not alike; this one is palatable, sweet and pleasant to drink while the other is saltish and bitter. Yet (inspite of all this) you take for food fresh and wholesome meat (of fish) from them both; and bring out from them (pearl-like things used in) ornaments for your wear. And you can see the ships cleaving (their way) through it so that you may seek of His bounty (by means of commercial navigation), and so that you may give (Him) thanks.

13. He causes the night to gain on the day and He causes the day to gain on the night and He has harnessed the sun and the moon into service. Each one (of them) will go on moving for a specified term. Such is (the majesty of) Allâh, your Lord! All power belongs to Him. But those whom you call upon apart from Him have no power at all, not even equal to the husk of a date stone.

وَاللّٰهُ الَّذِيْٓ اَرْسَلَ الرِّيٰحَ فَتُثِيْرُ سَحَابًا
فَسُقْنٰهُ اِلٰى بَلَدٍ مَّيِّتٍ فَاَحْيَيْنَا بِهِ الْاَرْضَ
بَعْدَ مَوْتِهَا ۭ كَذٰلِكَ النُّشُوْرُ ٩ مَنْ كَانَ
يُرِيْدُ الْعِزَّةَ فَلِلّٰهِ الْعِزَّةُ جَمِيْعًا ۭ اِلَيْهِ يَصْعَدُ
الْكَلِمُ الطَّيِّبُ وَالْعَمَلُ الصّٰلِحُ يَرْفَعُهٗ ۭ
وَالَّذِيْنَ يَمْكُرُوْنَ السَّيِّاٰتِ لَهُمْ عَذَابٌ شَدِيْدٌ ۭ
وَمَكْرُ اُولٰۗىِٕكَ هُوَ يَبُوْرُ ١٠ وَاللّٰهُ خَلَقَكُمْ مِّنْ
تُرَابٍ ثُمَّ مِنْ نُّطْفَةٍ ثُمَّ جَعَلَكُمْ اَزْوَاجًا ۭ وَمَا
تَحْمِلُ مِنْ اُنْثٰى وَلَا تَضَعُ اِلَّا بِعِلْمِهٖ ۭ وَمَا
يُعَمَّرُ مِنْ مُّعَمَّرٍ وَّلَا يُنْقَصُ مِنْ عُمُرِهٖٓ
اِلَّا فِيْ كِتٰبٍ ۭ اِنَّ ذٰلِكَ عَلَى اللّٰهِ يَسِيْرٌ ١١ وَمَا
يَسْتَوِي الْبَحْرٰنِ ڰ هٰذَا عَذْبٌ فُرَاتٌ سَاۗىِٕغٌ
شَرَابُهٗ وَهٰذَا مِلْحٌ اُجَاجٌ ۭ وَمِنْ كُلٍّ
تَاْكُلُوْنَ لَحْمًا طَرِيًّا وَّتَسْتَخْرِجُوْنَ حِلْيَةً
تَلْبَسُوْنَهَا ۚ وَتَرَى الْفُلْكَ فِيْهِ مَوَاخِرَ لِتَبْتَغُوْا
مِنْ فَضْلِهٖ وَلَعَلَّكُمْ تَشْكُرُوْنَ ١٢ يُوْلِجُ الَّيْلَ
فِي النَّهَارِ وَيُوْلِجُ النَّهَارَ فِي الَّيْلِ ۙ وَسَخَّرَ
الشَّمْسَ وَالْقَمَرَ ڮ كُلٌّ يَّجْرِيْ لِاَجَلٍ مُّسَمًّى ۭ
ذٰلِكُمُ اللّٰهُ رَبُّكُمْ لَهُ الْمُلْكُ ۭ وَالَّذِيْنَ
تَدْعُوْنَ مِنْ دُوْنِهٖ مَا يَمْلِكُوْنَ مِنْ

14. If you pray to them they do not hear your call; and even if they could hear it at all they could make you no response (so as to be of any use to you). And on the Day of Resurrection they will deny that you associated (them as partners with God). And none can inform you (about the all important truth) like (Allâh) Who is All-Aware.

SECTION 3

15. O People! It is you who are dependent upon Allâh (for your physical and spiritual needs), but Allâh, He is Self-Sufficient (- independent of all needs), the Praiseworthy (in His Own right).
16. If He please, He may destroy you and replace you with another people;
17. And that is not at all difficult for Allâh (to do so).
18. And no soul that bears (its own) burden (of responsibility) can bear the burden of another. And if a soul heavily laden (with the weight of sins) calls to (be relieved of) its burden, not the least of its burden shall be borne (by the other) even though (it calls its) near kinsman. You can warn only those who hold their Lord in awe in the heart of their hearts and observe Prayer. And one who purifies oneself shall do it only for the good of one's own soul, for to Allâh shall be the eternal return.
19. The blind person and the person who sees are not alike;
20. Nor the thick darkness (of ignorance) and the light (of Islam);
21. Nor the shades (of the Heaven) and the horrid heat (of the Hell-fire).
22. The (spiritually) living and the (spiritually) dead are not alike. Allâh causes to hear whom He will. But you cannot make those hear who are (lying buried) in the graves (of ignorance and prejudice).
23. You are only a Warner.
24. Verily, We have sent you with the lasting truth (as) a Bearer of glad-tidings and (as) a

قِطْمِيرٍ ﴿١٣﴾ إِنْ تَدْعُوهُمْ لَا يَسْمَعُوا دُعَاءَكُمْ
وَلَوْ سَمِعُوا مَا اسْتَجَابُوا لَكُمْ ۖ وَيَوْمَ الْقِيٰمَةِ
يَكْفُرُونَ بِشِرْكِكُمْ ۚ وَلَا يُنَبِّئُكَ مِثْلُ خَبِيرٍ ﴿١٤﴾
يٰأَيُّهَا النَّاسُ أَنْتُمُ الْفُقَرَاءُ إِلَى اللَّهِ ۖ وَاللَّهُ
هُوَ الْغَنِيُّ الْحَمِيدُ ﴿١٥﴾ إِنْ يَشَأْ يُذْهِبْكُمْ
وَيَأْتِ بِخَلْقٍ جَدِيدٍ ﴿١٦﴾ وَمَا ذٰلِكَ عَلَى اللَّهِ
بِعَزِيزٍ ﴿١٧﴾ وَلَا تَزِرُ وَازِرَةٌ وِزْرَ أُخْرٰى ۚ وَإِنْ
تَدْعُ مُثْقَلَةٌ إِلٰى حِمْلِهَا لَا يُحْمَلْ مِنْهُ
شَيْءٌ وَلَوْ كَانَ ذَا قُرْبٰى ۗ إِنَّمَا تُنْذِرُ الَّذِينَ
يَخْشَوْنَ رَبَّهُمْ بِالْغَيْبِ وَأَقَامُوا الصَّلٰوةَ ۚ
وَمَنْ تَزَكّٰى فَإِنَّمَا يَتَزَكّٰى لِنَفْسِهِ ۚ وَإِلَى اللَّهِ
الْمَصِيرُ ﴿١٨﴾ وَمَا يَسْتَوِي الْأَعْمٰى وَالْبَصِيرُ ﴿١٩﴾
وَلَا الظُّلُمٰتُ وَلَا النُّورُ ﴿٢٠﴾ وَلَا الظِّلُّ وَلَا
الْحَرُورُ ﴿٢١﴾ وَمَا يَسْتَوِي الْأَحْيَاءُ وَلَا الْأَمْوَاتُ ۚ
إِنَّ اللَّهَ يُسْمِعُ مَنْ يَشَاءُ ۖ وَمَا أَنْتَ بِمُسْمِعٍ
مَنْ فِي الْقُبُورِ ﴿٢٢﴾ إِنْ أَنْتَ إِلَّا نَذِيرٌ ﴿٢٣﴾
إِنَّا أَرْسَلْنٰكَ بِالْحَقِّ بَشِيرًا وَنَذِيرًا ۚ

Warner (to them), for there has been no people but have (been warned by) a Warner (from God).
25. And if they cry you lies, (remember) their predecessors (also) cried lies (to their Messengers of God) though their Messengers had brought to them clear proofs, the Scriptures and the illuminating Book.
26. Then I took those who disbelieved to task, then (you saw) how (terrible) was the result of My disapproval (of them, and how tremendous was the change I brought)!

SECTION 4

27. **D**o you not see that Allâh sends down water from above and brings forth therewith fruits of diverse varieties? And there are white and red strata in the mountains. They have various other colours (also) and (some are) jet-black.
28. Likewise there are some (species of) human beings, beasts and cattle of colours varying from one another. Only those of His servants who are endowed with right knowledge (and who can visualize the unity of the Creator by pondering over the diversity of the Creation) hold Allâh in reverential awe. Mighty is Allâh, Great Protector.
29. Surely, (only) those who follow the Book of Allâh and observe Prayer and spend (for the cause of Allâh) privately and in public out of that which We have provided for them (thereby) hope (to do) a bargain which will never fail.
30. The result of it is that He will give them their full reward (for their righteous deeds) and (even) increase them out of His grace and bounty. Verily, He is Great Protector, Most Appreciating (of their right endeavours and Multiplier of reward).
31. And the perfect Book which We have revealed to you is the lasting truth (itself and contains all that is required). It confirms the truth (of the prophecies about the advent of Islam contained in the revelations) that preceded it. Verily, Allâh is All-Aware of His servants and a keen Observer (of them).
32. We (always) made only those whom We

وَإِنْ مِّنْ أُمَّةٍ إِلَّا خَلَا فِيهَا نَذِيرٌ ﴿٢٤﴾ وَإِنْ
يُكَذِّبُوكَ فَقَدْ كَذَّبَ الَّذِينَ مِنْ قَبْلِهِمْ
جَاءَتْهُمْ رُسُلُهُمْ بِالْبَيِّنٰتِ وَبِالزُّبُرِ
وَبِالْكِتٰبِ الْمُنِيرِ ﴿٢٥﴾ ثُمَّ أَخَذْتُ الَّذِينَ
كَفَرُوا فَكَيْفَ كَانَ نَكِيرِ ﴿٢٦﴾ أَلَمْ تَرَ أَنَّ اللهَ
أَنْزَلَ مِنَ السَّمَاءِ مَاءً فَأَخْرَجْنَا بِهِ
ثَمَرٰتٍ مُّخْتَلِفًا أَلْوٰنُهَا وَمِنَ الْجِبَالِ
جُدَدٌ بِيضٌ وَّحُمْرٌ مُّخْتَلِفٌ أَلْوٰنُهَا
وَغَرَابِيبُ سُودٌ ﴿٢٧﴾ وَمِنَ النَّاسِ وَالدَّوَابِّ
وَالْأَنْعٰمِ مُخْتَلِفٌ أَلْوٰنُهُ كَذٰلِكَ إِنَّمَا
يَخْشَى اللهَ مِنْ عِبَادِهِ الْعُلَمٰٓؤُا إِنَّ اللهَ
عَزِيزٌ غَفُورٌ ﴿٢٨﴾ إِنَّ الَّذِينَ يَتْلُونَ كِتٰبَ
اللهِ وَأَقَامُوا الصَّلٰوةَ وَأَنْفَقُوا مِمَّا رَزَقْنٰهُمْ
سِرًّا وَّعَلَانِيَةً يَّرْجُونَ تِجٰرَةً لَّنْ تَبُورَ ﴿٢٩﴾
لِيُوَفِّيَهُمْ أُجُورَهُمْ وَيَزِيدَهُمْ مِّنْ فَضْلِهِ
إِنَّهُ غَفُورٌ شَكُورٌ ﴿٣٠﴾ وَالَّذِي أَوْحَيْنَا إِلَيْكَ
مِنَ الْكِتٰبِ هُوَ الْحَقُّ مُصَدِّقًا لِّمَا بَيْنَ يَدَيْهِ
إِنَّ اللهَ بِعِبَادِهِ لَخَبِيرٌ بَصِيرٌ ﴿٣١﴾ ثُمَّ أَوْرَثْنَا

ع ٣ ١٢ ١٥

had chosen from among Our servants, the inheritors of (Our) Book. Some of them are (hard upon themselves and so) unjust to their souls (for suppressing their egos sternly). There are others among them who are moderate and are following the middle course. There are yet others among them who, by the leave of Allâh, are foremost in acts of goodness. That indeed is the great distinction.

33. (Their reward will be) Gardens of Eternity; they shall enter them. And there they shall be adorned with bracelets of gold and pearls and their robes therein will be (made of) silk.

34. And (there) they will say, 'All true and perfect praise belongs to Allâh Who has rid us of all (our) sorrows. Surely, our Lord is Great Protector, Most Appreciating.

35. It is He Who has lodged us in the Lasting Abode by His grace. Herein we know no toil, herein we know no weariness.

36. But as to those who disbelieve, there awaits them the fire of Gehenna. It will not be the end of them so that they might die, (for decree of death would end all their agony) nor shall (some part of) its agony be reduced for them. That is how We requite every ungrateful person.

37. And therein they will clamour for help (saying), 'Our Lord, take us out (of Hell) we will do righteous deeds different from those we used to do (in our previous life).' (We shall say to them,) 'Did We not give you life long enough so that he who might have liked to take heed could take heed during its course? There came a Warner to you as well. So suffer now (the agony of Hell). There is none to help the wrong doers (here).

SECTION 5

38. **V**erily, Allâh knows the hidden realities of the heavens and the earth. He knows full well the innermost secret of the minds (of the people).

الْكِتٰبَ الَّذِيْنَ اصْطَفَيْنَا مِنْ عِبَادِنَا ۚ
فَمِنْهُمْ ظَالِمٌ لِّنَفْسِهٖ ۚ وَمِنْهُمْ مُّقْتَصِدٌ ۚ
وَمِنْهُمْ سَابِقٌ بِالْخَيْرٰتِ بِإِذْنِ اللّٰهِ ؕ
ذٰلِكَ هُوَ الْفَضْلُ الْكَبِيْرُ ﴿٣٣﴾ جَنّٰتُ عَدْنٍ
يَّدْخُلُوْنَهَا يُحَلَّوْنَ فِيْهَا مِنْ أَسَاوِرَ مِنْ
ذَهَبٍ وَّ لُؤْلُؤًا ۚ وَ لِبَاسُهُمْ فِيْهَا حَرِيْرٌ ﴿٣٤﴾
وَ قَالُوا الْحَمْدُ لِلّٰهِ الَّذِيْٓ أَذْهَبَ عَنَّا
الْحَزَنَ ؕ إِنَّ رَبَّنَا لَغَفُوْرٌ شَكُوْرٌ ﴿٣٥﴾ الَّذِيْٓ
أَحَلَّنَا دَارَ الْمُقَامَةِ مِنْ فَضْلِهٖ ۚ لَا
يَمَسُّنَا فِيْهَا نَصَبٌ وَّ لَا يَمَسُّنَا فِيْهَا
لُغُوْبٌ ﴿٣٦﴾ وَ الَّذِيْنَ كَفَرُوْا لَهُمْ نَارُ جَهَنَّمَ ۚ
لَا يُقْضٰى عَلَيْهِمْ فَيَمُوْتُوْا وَ لَا يُخَفَّفُ
عَنْهُمْ مِّنْ عَذَابِهَا ؕ كَذٰلِكَ نَجْزِيْ كُلَّ
كَفُوْرٍ ﴿٣٧﴾ وَهُمْ يَصْطَرِخُوْنَ فِيْهَا ۚ رَبَّنَآ
أَخْرِجْنَا نَعْمَلْ صٰلِحًا غَيْرَ الَّذِيْ كُنَّا
نَعْمَلُ ؕ أَوَلَمْ نُعَمِّرْكُمْ مَّا يَتَذَكَّرُ فِيْهِ
مَنْ تَذَكَّرَ وَجَآءَكُمُ النَّذِيْرُ ؕ فَذُوْقُوْا فَمَا
لِلظّٰلِمِيْنَ مِنْ نَّصِيْرٍ ﴿٣٨﴾ إِنَّ اللّٰهَ عٰلِمُ غَيْبِ
السَّمٰوٰتِ وَ الْأَرْضِ ؕ إِنَّهٗ عَلِيْمٌ بِذَاتِ

ع ١١/١٦

39. It is He Who made you rulers on the earth. So one who chooses to disbelieve now will suffer the consequences of his disbelief. Their faithlessness will win for the disbelievers nothing but increased displeasure of their Lord. Indeed, their faithlessness will only make worse the loss of the disbelievers.

40. Say, 'Have you considered regarding your associate-gods whom you call upon apart from Allâh? Show Me then what they have created of the earth. Or have they any partnership in (the creation of) the heavens? Or have We given these (worshippers of false deities) a Book so that they are supported by some clear proofs (mentioned) therein? Nay, not so at all, but (the truth is that) the wrongdoers hold out vain promises one to another only to deceive.

41. Verily, Allâh sustains the heavens and the earth lest they should swerve away from their course. Should they swerve away there is none to uphold them (and save them from destruction) but He. Verily, He is Ever-Forbearing, Great Protector.

42. These people used to swear by Allâh by their most ardent oaths that if ever a Warner should come to them from Allâh they would be more rightly guided than anyone of the nations. But when a Warner did come to them this (coming of his) only increased them in aversion,

43. And made them behave arrogantly on the earth and devise evil schemes; yet evil scheming recoils on none but its authors. They are, then, only waiting that We should follow (the same) practice which We did (in dealing) with the peoples of old. And you will find no change in that law of Allâh, nor will you ever find the law of Allâh shifting from its course.

44. Have they not travelled in the land and seen how (evil) was the end of their predecessors, while those were (a people) superior to and stronger than these in might? There is nothing

الصُّدُورِ ﴿٣٨﴾ هُوَ الَّذِي جَعَلَكُمْ خَلَٰٓئِفَ
فِي الْأَرْضِ ۚ فَمَنْ كَفَرَ فَعَلَيْهِ كُفْرُهُ ۖ
وَلَا يَزِيدُ الْكٰفِرِينَ كُفْرُهُمْ عِنْدَ رَبِّهِمْ
إِلَّا مَقْتًا ۖ وَلَا يَزِيدُ الْكٰفِرِينَ كُفْرُهُمْ إِلَّا
خَسَارًا ﴿٣٩﴾ قُلْ أَرَءَيْتُمْ شُرَكَآءَكُمُ الَّذِينَ
تَدْعُونَ مِنْ دُونِ اللّٰهِ ۖ أَرُونِي مَاذَا خَلَقُوا
مِنَ الْأَرْضِ أَمْ لَهُمْ شِرْكٌ فِي السَّمٰوٰتِ ۚ
أَمْ ءَاتَيْنٰهُمْ كِتٰبًا فَهُمْ عَلٰى بَيِّنَتٍ مِنْهُ ۚ
بَلْ إِنْ يَعِدُ الظّٰلِمُونَ بَعْضُهُمْ بَعْضًا إِلَّا
غُرُورًا ﴿٤٠﴾ إِنَّ اللّٰهَ يُمْسِكُ السَّمٰوٰتِ
وَالْأَرْضَ أَنْ تَزُولَا ۚ وَلَئِنْ زَالَتَآ إِنْ
أَمْسَكَهُمَا مِنْ أَحَدٍ مِنْ بَعْدِهِ ۚ إِنَّهُ كَانَ
حَلِيمًا غَفُورًا ﴿٤١﴾ وَأَقْسَمُوا بِاللّٰهِ جَهْدَ
أَيْمٰنِهِمْ لَئِنْ جَآءَهُمْ نَذِيرٌ لَيَكُونُنَّ
أَهْدٰى مِنْ إِحْدَى الْأُمَمِ ۖ فَلَمَّا جَآءَهُمْ
نَذِيرٌ مَا زَادَهُمْ إِلَّا نُفُورًا ﴿٤٢﴾ اسْتِكْبَارًا
فِي الْأَرْضِ وَمَكْرَ السَّيِّئِ ۚ وَلَا يَحِيقُ
الْمَكْرُ السَّيِّئُ إِلَّا بِأَهْلِهِ ۚ فَهَلْ يَنْظُرُونَ
إِلَّا سُنَّتَ الْأَوَّلِينَ ۚ فَلَنْ تَجِدَ لِسُنَّتِ
اللّٰهِ تَبْدِيلًا ۚ وَلَنْ تَجِدَ لِسُنَّتِ اللّٰهِ
تَحْوِيلًا ﴿٤٣﴾ أَوَلَمْ يَسِيرُوا فِي الْأَرْضِ فَيَنْظُرُوا
كَيْفَ كَانَ عٰقِبَةُ الَّذِينَ مِنْ قَبْلِهِمْ وَكَانُوا
أَشَدَّ مِنْهُمْ قُوَّةً ۚ وَمَا كَانَ اللّٰهُ لِيُعْجِزَهُ مِنْ
شَيْءٍ فِي السَّمٰوٰتِ وَلَا فِي الْأَرْضِ ۚ إِنَّهُ كَانَ

in the heavens or on the earth that can render void (the plans) of Allâh. Verily, He is Possessor of perfect knowledge, All-Powerful.

45. If Allâh were to take people to task for (every little of) their evil doings He would not leave on the surface of this (earth) a single living creature. But He (out of His all embracing mercy) grants them respite till a stated term. And when their appointed time comes (they come to realise that) Allâh has His servants well under (His) eyes (He deals with them according to the nature of their deeds).

عَلِيمًا قَدِيرًا ﴿٤٤﴾ وَلَوْ يُؤَاخِذُ اللّٰهُ النَّاسَ بِمَا
كَسَبُوا مَا تَرَكَ عَلَىٰ ظَهْرِهَا مِنْ دَآبَّةٍ
وَلٰكِنْ يُؤَخِّرُهُمْ إِلَىٰٓ أَجَلٍ مُّسَمًّى فَإِذَا جَآءَ
أَجَلُهُمْ فَإِنَّ اللّٰهَ كَانَ بِعِبَادِهِ بَصِيرًا ﴿٤٥﴾

CHAPTER
36

YÂ SÎN
(O Perfect Man!)
(Revealed before Hijrah)

سُورَةُ يٰسٓ مَكِّيَّةٌ

With the name of Allâh,
the Most Gracious, the Ever Merciful
(I commence to read Sûrah Yâ Sîn).

بِسْمِ اللّٰهِ الرَّحْمٰنِ الرَّحِيمِ

1. **Y**Â SÎN - O perfect man (Muhammad)!
2. I call to witness the perfect Qur'ân full of (convincing proofs and) wisdom.
3. (That) you are indeed one of the Messengers,
4. (Standing) on the right and straight path.
5. (This Qur'ân is) a great revelation sent by the All-Mighty (and) the Ever Merciful (God),
6. So that you may warn the people who are ignorant because their forefathers have not been warned (for a long time).
7. Surely, most of them merit the sentence of Our punishment for they would not believe.
8. Surely, We have put shackles (of customs and prejudices) round their necks and they are

يٰسٓ ﴿١﴾ وَالْقُرْءَانِ الْحَكِيمِ ﴿٢﴾ إِنَّكَ لَمِنَ
الْمُرْسَلِينَ ﴿٣﴾ عَلَىٰ صِرٰطٍ مُّسْتَقِيمٍ ﴿٤﴾ تَنْزِيلَ
الْعَزِيزِ الرَّحِيمِ ﴿٥﴾ لِتُنْذِرَ قَوْمًا مَّآ أُنْذِرَ
ءَابَآؤُهُمْ فَهُمْ غٰفِلُونَ ﴿٦﴾ لَقَدْ حَقَّ الْقَوْلُ
عَلَىٰٓ أَكْثَرِهِمْ فَهُمْ لَا يُؤْمِنُونَ ﴿٧﴾ إِنَّا
جَعَلْنَا فِيٓ أَعْنٰقِهِمْ أَغْلٰلًا فَهِيَ إِلَى

(reaching right) up to their chins, so that they have become stiff-necked (due to their pride and false notions of superiority).

9. And We have placed barriers (of their stubbornness rendering them unable to look forward to the bright future of Islam and rise to eminence by accepting it) in front of them, and barriers (of their prejudices) behind them (thus rendering them unable to look back at the doom of those who rejected the truth in the past). Thus We have kept them behind the veil so that they cannot see (so have become totally devoid of spiritual light).

10. And it is all the same to them whether you warn them or do not warn them, they will not believe (for they have deliberately shut their eyes and ears to the truth).

11. You can warn only those who would follow the Reminder (- the Qur'ân) and are full of reverential awe of the Most Gracious (God) in the heart of their hearts. Therefore proclaim to them the glad tidings of protection (from the evil consequences of sins) and an honorable provision (from Us).

12. Surely, it is We alone Who raise the dead to life. And We shall preserve (their noble deeds) which they send forward and their prints (of virtue and knowledge which they leave behind for others to emulate). Every thing We have comprehensively preserved in a clear record.

SECTION 2

13. **A**ND set forth to them for their good a parable of a people of the town when the Messengers (of God) came to them.

14. (At first) We sent to them two (Messengers, Moses and Jesus) but they cried lies to them. Then We strengthened (Our Apostles) with a third (- the Prophet Muhammad by fulfilling in his person their prophecies about his advent). So they said, (as a general Message to the people), 'We have been sent to

الْأَذْقَانِ فَهُمْ مُّقْمَحُوْنَ ⑧ وَجَعَلْنَا مِنْۢ
بَيْنِ أَيْدِيْهِمْ سَدًّا وَّ مِنْ خَلْفِهِمْ سَدًّا
فَأَغْشَيْنٰهُمْ فَهُمْ لَا يُبْصِرُوْنَ ⑨ وَسَوَآءٌ
عَلَيْهِمْ ءَأَنْذَرْتَهُمْ أَمْ لَمْ تُنْذِرْهُمْ لَا
يُؤْمِنُوْنَ ⑩ إِنَّمَا تُنْذِرُ مَنِ اتَّبَعَ الذِّكْرَ
وَخَشِيَ الرَّحْمٰنَ بِالْغَيْبِ فَبَشِّرْهُ بِمَغْفِرَةٍ
وَّأَجْرٍ كَرِيْمٍ ⑪ إِنَّا نَحْنُ نُحْيِ الْمَوْتٰى
وَنَكْتُبُ مَا قَدَّمُوْا وَأٰثٰرَهُمْ وَكُلَّ
شَيْءٍ أَحْصَيْنٰهُ فِيْٓ إِمَامٍ مُّبِيْنٍ ⑫ وَاضْرِبْ
لَهُمْ مَّثَلًا أَصْحٰبَ الْقَرْيَةِ إِذْ جَآءَهَا
الْمُرْسَلُوْنَ ⑬ إِذْ أَرْسَلْنَآ إِلَيْهِمُ اثْنَيْنِ
فَكَذَّبُوْهُمَا فَعَزَّزْنَا بِثَالِثٍ فَقَالُوْٓا إِنَّآ

you (as Messengers by God).'
15. They (- the contemporaries of the Messengers) gave (a general) reply, 'You are only human beings like ourselves. The Most Gracious (God) has revealed nothing (to you). You are simply telling lies.'
16. They said, 'Our Lord knows that we have been, of course, sent to you,
17. 'And our duty is only to convey (the Message) in clear terms.'
18. They (- the people of the town) said, 'We augur ill from you (for we were seized with one calamity or the other after your advent). If you do not give it (- your preaching) over we will certainly excommunicate you and a painful punishment shall befall you at our hands.'
19. They said, 'Your ills are of your own making. (Do you say all this) because you have been admonished? Nay, but the real thing is you are a pack of transgressors.'
20. Now, there came a man running from the farthest end of the town. He said, 'O my people! Follow the Messengers.
21. 'Follow those who ask no reward from you and who are following the right path.

إِلَيْكُمْ مُرْسَلُونَ ﴿١٤﴾ قَالُوا مَا أَنْتُمْ إِلَّا
بَشَرٌ مِثْلُنَا وَمَا أَنْزَلَ الرَّحْمٰنُ مِنْ شَيْءٍ
إِنْ أَنْتُمْ إِلَّا تَكْذِبُونَ ﴿١٥﴾ قَالُوا رَبُّنَا يَعْلَمُ
إِنَّا إِلَيْكُمْ لَمُرْسَلُونَ ﴿١٦﴾ وَمَا عَلَيْنَا إِلَّا
الْبَلٰغُ الْمُبِينُ ﴿١٧﴾ قَالُوا إِنَّا تَطَيَّرْنَا بِكُمْ
لَئِنْ لَمْ تَنْتَهُوا لَنَرْجُمَنَّكُمْ وَلَيَمَسَّنَّكُمْ
مِنَّا عَذَابٌ أَلِيمٌ ﴿١٨﴾ قَالُوا طٰٓئِرُكُمْ مَعَكُمْ
أَئِنْ ذُكِّرْتُمْ بَلْ أَنْتُمْ قَوْمٌ مُسْرِفُونَ ﴿١٩﴾
وَجَاءَ مِنْ أَقْصَا الْمَدِينَةِ رَجُلٌ يَسْعٰى
قَالَ يٰقَوْمِ اتَّبِعُوا الْمُرْسَلِينَ ﴿٢٠﴾ اتَّبِعُوا
مَنْ لَا يَسْئَلُكُمْ أَجْرًا وَهُمْ مُهْتَدُونَ ﴿٢١﴾

PART الْجُزْءُ الثَّالِثُ وَالْعِشْرُونَ XXIII

22. 'WHAT reason have I not to worship Him Who has created me, and to Whom you all shall be brought back?
23. 'Shall I take apart from Him others as gods whose intercession, if the Most Gracious (God) should decide to do me some harm, will be of no avail to me, nor will they be able (even) to rescue me (from that harm)?
24. 'Surely, in case (I do anything of the kind) I should be (falling) in (to) a clear error.
25. 'I have believed in your (true) Lord, therefore listen to me.'
26. It was said (to him by God), 'Enter Paradise

وَمَا لِيَ لَا أَعْبُدُ الَّذِي فَطَرَنِي وَإِلَيْهِ
تُرْجَعُونَ ﴿٢٢﴾ ءَأَتَّخِذُ مِنْ دُونِهِ آلِهَةً إِنْ
يُرِدْنِ الرَّحْمٰنُ بِضُرٍّ لَا تُغْنِ عَنِّي شَفٰعَتُهُمْ
شَيْئًا وَلَا يُنْقِذُونِ ﴿٢٣﴾ إِنِّي إِذًا لَفِي ضَلٰلٍ
مُبِينٍ ﴿٢٤﴾ إِنِّي آمَنْتُ بِرَبِّكُمْ فَاسْمَعُونِ ﴿٢٥﴾
قِيلَ ادْخُلِ الْجَنَّةَ قَالَ يٰلَيْتَ قَوْمِي

(while you are still living).' He said, 'O, would that my people knew,

27. 'For what reason has my Lord granted me protection (from pitfalls in this life) and included me among the honoured (servants of His)!'

28. We sent no contingent (of force) from heaven, against his people (to destroy them), after that (he has believed) nor do We ever command (any of such things).

29. It was just a single blast and behold! They were all (extinct) like a (spark of) fire extinguished.

30. Alas for (My) servants! Not a single Messenger comes to (reform) them but they treat him lightly.

31. Have they not seen how many generations We have ruined before them, and that those (generations) never come back to them (after their ruination)?

32. Indeed, they, one and all, shall most certainly, be brought before Us.

SECTION 3

33. THE dead earth which We bring to life and from which We bring forth (a large variety of) grains, of which they eat, is an important sign for them.

34. And We have made to grow there on (the earth) gardens of date-palms and vine, and We have caused springs to gush forth from it;

35. So that they may enjoy its fruit and (enjoy) that which their hands have worked for. Will they then render (Us) no thanks (and follow Our guidance)?

36. Glory be to Him Who has created pairs of all type of the thing that the earth grows and of their own species and of the things yet unknown to them.

37. The night from which We strip off (the last vestige) of the day, so that (afterwards) they are left in pitch darkness, is a (great) sign for them.

38. And the sun is moving (on its ordained

يَعْلَمُوْنَ ﴿٢٦﴾ بِمَا غَفَرَ لِيْ رَبِّيْ وَ جَعَلَنِيْ مِنَ
الْمُكْرَمِيْنَ ﴿٢٧﴾ وَ مَآ أَنْزَلْنَا عَلٰى قَوْمِهٖ مِنْۢ
بَعْدِهٖ مِنْ جُنْدٍ مِّنَ السَّمَآءِ وَ مَا كُنَّا
مُنْزِلِيْنَ ﴿٢٨﴾ إِنْ كَانَتْ إِلَّا صَيْحَةً وَّاحِدَةً
فَإِذَا هُمْ خٰمِدُوْنَ ﴿٢٩﴾ يٰحَسْرَةً عَلَى الْعِبَادِ
مَا يَأْتِيْهِمْ مِّنْ رَّسُوْلٍ إِلَّا كَانُوْا بِهٖ
يَسْتَهْزِءُوْنَ ﴿٣٠﴾ أَلَمْ يَرَوْا كَمْ أَهْلَكْنَا قَبْلَهُمْ
مِّنَ الْقُرُوْنِ أَنَّهُمْ إِلَيْهِمْ لَا يَرْجِعُوْنَ ﴿٣١﴾
وَ إِنْ كُلٌّ لَّمَّا جَمِيْعٌ لَّدَيْنَا مُحْضَرُوْنَ ﴿٣٢﴾
وَ اٰيَةٌ لَّهُمُ الْأَرْضُ الْمَيْتَةُ أَحْيَيْنٰهَا
وَ أَخْرَجْنَا مِنْهَا حَبًّا فَمِنْهُ يَأْكُلُوْنَ ﴿٣٣﴾
وَ جَعَلْنَا فِيْهَا جَنّٰتٍ مِّنْ نَّخِيْلٍ وَّ أَعْنَابٍ
وَّ فَجَّرْنَا فِيْهَا مِنَ الْعُيُوْنِ ﴿٣٤﴾ لِيَأْكُلُوْا مِنْ
ثَمَرِهٖ وَ مَا عَمِلَتْهُ أَيْدِيْهِمْ أَفَلَا يَشْكُرُوْنَ ﴿٣٥﴾
سُبْحٰنَ الَّذِيْ خَلَقَ الْأَزْوَاجَ كُلَّهَا مِمَّا
تُنْۢبِتُ الْأَرْضُ وَ مِنْ أَنْفُسِهِمْ وَ مِمَّا لَا
يَعْلَمُوْنَ ﴿٣٦﴾ وَ اٰيَةٌ لَّهُمُ الَّيْلُ نَسْلَخُ مِنْهُ
النَّهَارَ فَإِذَا هُمْ مُّظْلِمُوْنَ ﴿٣٧﴾ وَ الشَّمْسُ

course) towards the goal determined for it. That is the determining of the All-Mighty, the Possessor of perfect knowledge.

39. And (think over the phases of) the moon, We have determined its various mansions, so that (after traversing these mansions) it returns (to the stage when it appears) like an old dry twig of a palm-tree.

40. It is not given to the sun to attain to (the purpose ordained for) the moon, nor is it given to the night to outstrip the day. All of these (luminaries) go on floating smoothly in an orbit (of their own).

41. And it is a sign for these people that We carry their children in the fully laden ships.

42. And We will make for them other (means of transport) such things as they will board.

43. If We (so) willed, We would drown them, then they would have no (one to) succour (them), nor would they be rescued.

44. It is only through mercy from Us (that We save them) and (let them have) an enjoyment of worldly gains for a while.

45. And when it is said to them, 'Guard yourself against that (punishment) which is (impending) before you and that which is behind you (and may befall you as a consequence of your evil past) so that you may be shown mercy (they turn away).'

46. There never comes to them a Message from the Messages of their Lord but they always turn away from it.

47. And when it is said to them, 'Spend out of that which Allâh has provided for you,' those who disbelieve say to those who believe, 'Shall we feed those whom, if Allâh so will, He could feed? You are only steeped in obvious error.'

48. They (also) say, '(Tell us) if indeed you are truthful when this warning (about punishment) shall come to pass.'

49. They are (thus) only waiting for one sudden onslaught of calamity which will overtake them while they are yet disputing (about it) among

تَجۡرِي لِمُسۡتَقَرٍّ لَّهَاۚ ذٰلِكَ تَقۡدِيرُ الۡعَزِيزِ
الۡعَلِيمِ ﴿٣٨﴾ وَ الۡقَمَرَ قَدَّرۡنٰهُ مَنَازِلَ حَتّٰى عَادَ
كَالۡعُرۡجُونِ الۡقَدِيمِ ﴿٣٩﴾ لَا الشَّمۡسُ يَنۢبَغِي لَهَآ
أَنۡ تُدۡرِكَ الۡقَمَرَ وَ لَا الَّيۡلُ سَابِقُ النَّهَارِ ؕ
وَ كُلٌّ فِي فَلَكٍ يَّسۡبَحُونَ ﴿٤٠﴾ وَ اٰيَةٌ لَّهُمۡ أَنَّا
حَمَلۡنَا ذُرِّيَّتَهُمۡ فِي الۡفُلۡكِ الۡمَشۡحُونِ ﴿٤١﴾
وَ خَلَقۡنَا لَهُمۡ مِّنۡ مِّثۡلِهٖ مَا يَرۡكَبُونَ ﴿٤٢﴾
وَ إِنۡ نَّشَأۡ نُغۡرِقۡهُمۡ فَلَا صَرِيخَ لَهُمۡ وَ لَا هُمۡ
يُنۡقَذُونَ ﴿٤٣﴾ إِلَّا رَحۡمَةً مِّنَّا وَ مَتَاعًا إِلٰى حِينٍ ﴿٤٤﴾
وَ إِذَا قِيلَ لَهُمُ اتَّقُوا مَا بَيۡنَ أَيۡدِيكُمۡ وَ مَا
خَلۡفَكُمۡ لَعَلَّكُمۡ تُرۡحَمُونَ ﴿٤٥﴾ وَ مَا تَأۡتِيهِمۡ
مِّنۡ اٰيَةٍ مِّنۡ اٰيٰتِ رَبِّهِمۡ إِلَّا كَانُوا عَنۡهَا
مُعۡرِضِينَ ﴿٤٦﴾ وَ إِذَا قِيلَ لَهُمۡ أَنۡفِقُوا مِمَّا
رَزَقَكُمُ اللّٰهُ قَالَ الَّذِينَ كَفَرُوا لِلَّذِينَ اٰمَنُوٓا
أَنُطۡعِمُ مَنۡ لَّوۡ يَشَآءُ اللّٰهُ أَطۡعَمَهٗٓ ۖ إِنۡ أَنۡتُمۡ
إِلَّا فِي ضَلٰلٍ مُّبِينٍ ﴿٤٧﴾ وَ يَقُولُونَ مَتٰى هٰذَا
الۡوَعۡدُ إِنۡ كُنۡتُمۡ صٰدِقِينَ ﴿٤٨﴾ مَا يَنۡظُرُونَ

themselves.

50. And so (sudden will be their end) that they will not be able to leave instructions about their affairs nor to their own people will they return.

SECTION 4

51. AND the trumpet shall be blown, and behold! (rising) from their graves they will hasten on to their Lord.

52. They will say (to one an other), 'O woe be on us! Who has aroused us from our sleeping place?' 'This is the same thing as the Most Gracious (God) had promised and the Messengers (of God) did indeed speak the truth' (will be the reply they receive).

53. It will only be a single blast, and behold! They shall all be brought before Us.

54. So on this Day no injustice whatsoever shall be done to any soul. You shall reap the fruit of your deeds.

55. On this Day, the owners of Paradise will be occupied (in their pursuits), rejoicing.

56. They and their companions will be in (pleasant) shades, reclining on raised couches.

57. Therein they shall have fruits, and they will have all that they ask for.

58. 'Peace (be upon you)' (shall be) the word (of greeting to them) from the Ever Merciful Lord.

59. And (it will be said to the sinners), 'O guilty ones! Remain apart (as distinguished from the righteous) this day.

60. 'O Children of Adam! Did I not enjoin on you never to worship satan, for he is to you an enemy severing (your) ties (with Me).

61. 'And (did I not charge you) to worship Me, (for) this is the straight and right path?

62. 'Yet he (- satan) has certainly led astray a number of people from among you. Why do you not even then make use of your understanding (so

إِلَّا صَيْحَةً وَٰحِدَةً تَأْخُذُهُمْ وَهُمْ يَخِصِّمُونَ ﴿٤٩﴾
فَلَا يَسْتَطِيعُونَ تَوْصِيَةً وَلَآ إِلَىٰٓ أَهْلِهِمْ
يَرْجِعُونَ ﴿٥٠﴾ وَنُفِخَ فِي ٱلصُّورِ فَإِذَا هُم مِّنَ
ٱلْأَجْدَاثِ إِلَىٰ رَبِّهِمْ يَنسِلُونَ ﴿٥١﴾ قَالُوا۟ يَٰوَيْلَنَا
مَنۢ بَعَثَنَا مِن مَّرْقَدِنَا ۜ هَٰذَا مَا وَعَدَ
ٱلرَّحْمَٰنُ وَصَدَقَ ٱلْمُرْسَلُونَ ﴿٥٢﴾ إِن كَانَتْ
إِلَّا صَيْحَةً وَٰحِدَةً فَإِذَا هُمْ جَمِيعٌ لَّدَيْنَا
مُحْضَرُونَ ﴿٥٣﴾ فَٱلْيَوْمَ لَا تُظْلَمُ نَفْسٌ شَيْـًٔا
وَلَا تُجْزَوْنَ إِلَّا مَا كُنتُمْ تَعْمَلُونَ ﴿٥٤﴾ إِنَّ أَصْحَٰبَ
ٱلْجَنَّةِ ٱلْيَوْمَ فِي شُغُلٍ فَٰكِهُونَ ﴿٥٥﴾ هُمْ
وَأَزْوَٰجُهُمْ فِي ظِلَٰلٍ عَلَى ٱلْأَرَآئِكِ مُتَّكِـُٔونَ ﴿٥٦﴾
لَهُمْ فِيهَا فَٰكِهَةٌ وَلَهُم مَّا يَدَّعُونَ ﴿٥٧﴾ سَلَٰمٌ
قَوْلًا مِّن رَّبٍّ رَّحِيمٍ ﴿٥٨﴾ وَٱمْتَٰزُوا۟ ٱلْيَوْمَ أَيُّهَا
ٱلْمُجْرِمُونَ ﴿٥٩﴾ أَلَمْ أَعْهَدْ إِلَيْكُمْ يَٰبَنِىٓ ءَادَمَ أَن
لَّا تَعْبُدُوا۟ ٱلشَّيْطَٰنَ ۖ إِنَّهُۥ لَكُمْ عَدُوٌّ مُّبِينٌ ﴿٦٠﴾
وَأَنِ ٱعْبُدُونِى ۚ هَٰذَا صِرَٰطٌ مُّسْتَقِيمٌ ﴿٦١﴾
وَلَقَدْ أَضَلَّ مِنكُمْ جِبِلًّا كَثِيرًا ۖ أَفَلَمْ تَكُونُوا۟

ع ٣ ١٨

as to rectify your error)?
63. 'This is the Gehenna you were warned against.
64. 'Enter it this day, because of your disbelief.'
65. On that day We shall seal the mouths of these (disbelievers). Their hands will speak to Us (about the actions they wrought), and their feet shall bear witness to all their (sinful) doings.
66. If We had (so) willed, We could certainly have deprived these (disbelievers) of their eyesight so that they would have gone ahead on their path (unseeing). But, how should they find (the path) now (in this state of their blindness).
67. If We had (so) willed, We could have surely destroyed them where they were, so that they would not be able to move forward nor turn back.

SECTION 5

68. **W**E reverse the mechanism of the person to whom We grant (extraordinary) long life by making the state of his constitution weak. Do they not (even then) make use of their understanding?
69. We have not taught him (- the Prophet Muhammad the art of composing) verses, nor does it become him (to be a poet). This (Qur'ân) is but a means to attain to eminence; a (Book) that is widely read, and tells the right from the wrong.
70. (It has been revealed) so that he (- the Prophet) may warn those who are still (somewhat spiritually) alive (and so capable of receiving and responding to the call of truth), and (that) the verdict (of condemnation) be justified against the disbelievers.
71. Do they not see that among the things that We have made with Our power are the cattle which We have created for them, and of which they are masters (now).
72. And We have subdued these (cattle) for

تَعْقِلُونَ ﴿٦٢﴾ هٰذِهٖ جَهَنَّمُ الَّتِي كُنْتُمْ تُوعَدُونَ ﴿٦٣﴾
اِصْلَوْهَا الْيَوْمَ بِمَا كُنْتُمْ تَكْفُرُونَ ﴿٦٤﴾ اَلْيَوْمَ
نَخْتِمُ عَلٰٓى اَفْوَاهِهِمْ وَ تُكَلِّمُنَآ اَيْدِيهِمْ
وَتَشْهَدُ اَرْجُلُهُمْ بِمَا كَانُوْا يَكْسِبُوْنَ ﴿٦٥﴾ وَلَوْ
نَشَآءُ لَطَمَسْنَا عَلٰٓى اَعْيُنِهِمْ فَاسْتَبَقُوا الصِّرَاطَ
فَاَنّٰى يُبْصِرُوْنَ ﴿٦٦﴾ وَلَوْ نَشَآءُ لَمَسَخْنٰهُمْ عَلٰى
مَكَانَتِهِمْ فَمَا اسْتَطٰعُوْا مُضِيًّا وَّلَا يَرْجِعُوْنَ ﴿٦٧﴾
وَمَنْ نُّعَمِّرْهُ نُنَكِّسْهُ فِي الْخَلْقِ ۚ اَفَلَا
يَعْقِلُوْنَ ﴿٦٨﴾ وَمَا عَلَّمْنٰهُ الشِّعْرَ وَمَا يَنْۢبَغِي
لَهٗ ۚ اِنْ هُوَ اِلَّا ذِكْرٌ وَّقُرْاٰنٌ مُّبِيْنٌ ﴿٦٩﴾
لِّيُنْذِرَ مَنْ كَانَ حَيًّا وَّيَحِقَّ الْقَوْلُ عَلَى
الْكٰفِرِيْنَ ﴿٧٠﴾ اَوَلَمْ يَرَوْا اَنَّا خَلَقْنَا لَهُمْ
مِّمَّا عَمِلَتْ اَيْدِيْنَآ اَنْعَامًا فَهُمْ لَهَا مٰلِكُوْنَ ﴿٧١﴾
وَذَلَّلْنٰهَا لَهُمْ فَمِنْهَا رَكُوْبُهُمْ وَمِنْهَا

their use and benefit. So that some of them serve as their riding (beasts) and through others they obtain their food.

73. They have many other uses in them. They provide them with drinks (of various kinds). Will they still give (Us) no thanks?

74. (Inspite of all this) they worship other gods apart from Allâh (falsely) that they may find some help through them.

75. These (false gods) are not capable of helping them. On the contrary these (gods) will (turn out for them to) be a host (of rebels) brought (before the Almighty to receive their due punishment).

76. And do not let their words cause you grief. Verily, We know what they conceal and what they profess (and they will be paid back in their own coins).

77. Has not a human being seen how We have created him out of a (very insignificant) sperm drop? Yet behold! He is an open adversary (to Us).

78. And he coins strange things about Us and forgets his own creation. He says, 'Who will quicken the dead bones to life when they are decayed?'

79. Say, 'He Who evolved them the first time will again raise them to life. He is fully conversant with all (types and methods of) creation.

80. 'It is He Who produces fire for you out of the green tree, that you kindle (another fire) from it (even so new faith is kindled when the spiritually weak come in contact with the Divine Reformer).'

81. Has He, Who has created the heavens and the earth, not the power of creating (other people) like them? Why not! He is the Supreme Creator (and) Possessor of all knowledge.

82. Verily, His command, when He intends (to evolve) a thing, is (only) that He says to it, 'Be' and it comes into being (at proper time).

83. Therefore, glory be to Him in Whose hand lies the perfect control of every thing, and towards Whom you shall all be made to return.

يَأْكُلُونَ ﴿٧٢﴾ وَ لَهُمْ فِيهَا مَنَٰفِعُ وَ مَشَارِبُ
أَفَلَا يَشْكُرُونَ ﴿٧٣﴾ وَ اتَّخَذُوا مِنْ دُونِ اللهِ
ءَالِهَةً لَّعَلَّهُمْ يُنْصَرُونَ ﴿٧٤﴾ لَا يَسْتَطِيعُونَ
نَصْرَهُمْ وَ هُمْ لَهُمْ جُنْدٌ مُّحْضَرُونَ ﴿٧٥﴾ فَلَا
يَحْزُنْكَ قَوْلُهُمْ إِنَّا نَعْلَمُ مَا يُسِرُّونَ
وَ مَا يُعْلِنُونَ ﴿٧٦﴾ أَوَ لَمْ يَرَ الْإِنْسَٰنُ أَنَّا خَلَقْنَٰهُ
مِنْ نُّطْفَةٍ فَإِذَا هُوَ خَصِيمٌ مُّبِينٌ ﴿٧٧﴾
وَ ضَرَبَ لَنَا مَثَلًا وَّ نَسِيَ خَلْقَهُ
قَالَ مَنْ يُّحْيِ الْعِظَٰمَ وَ هِيَ رَمِيمٌ ﴿٧٨﴾
قُلْ يُحْيِيهَا الَّذِيٓ أَنْشَأَهَآ أَوَّلَ مَرَّةٍ
وَ هُوَ بِكُلِّ خَلْقٍ عَلِيمٌ ﴿٧٩﴾ الَّذِي
جَعَلَ لَكُمْ مِّنَ الشَّجَرِ الْأَخْضَرِ نَارًا
فَإِذَآ أَنْتُمْ مِّنْهُ تُوقِدُونَ ﴿٨٠﴾ أَوَ لَيْسَ الَّذِي
خَلَقَ السَّمَٰوَٰتِ وَ الْأَرْضَ بِقَٰدِرٍ عَلَىٰٓ
أَنْ يَّخْلُقَ مِثْلَهُمْ بَلَىٰ وَ هُوَ الْخَلَّٰقُ
الْعَلِيمُ ﴿٨١﴾ إِنَّمَآ أَمْرُهُۥٓ إِذَآ أَرَادَ شَيْئًا
أَنْ يَّقُولَ لَهُۥ كُنْ فَيَكُونُ ﴿٨٢﴾ فَسُبْحَٰنَ
الَّذِي بِيَدِهِۦ مَلَكُوتُ كُلِّ شَيْءٍ
وَّ إِلَيْهِ تُرْجَعُونَ ﴿٨٣﴾ ع ٤

CHAPTER
37

سُوْرَةُ الصَّافَّاتِ ٣٧

AL-SÂFFÂT

(Those Ranging in Ranks)
(Revealed before Hijrah)

With the name of Allâh,
the Most Gracious, the Ever Merciful
(I commence to read Sûrah Al-Sâffât).

1. CITED as witness are those who range themselves in close ranks (in various fields of life),
2. And those who drive away (the forces of evil) vigorously,
3. And those who recite and follow the Reminder (- the Qur'ân),
4. Verily, your God is One,
5. Lord of the heavens and the earth and all that lies between them and Lord of the places of the rising and spreading of light.
6. Verily, We have beautified and embellished the nearer space (- the heaven visible to you) with an excellent embellishment, the stars and planets.
7. And (We have placed therein) an effective safeguard against every insolently disobedient satan.
8. They (having no access to the source of prophecy) cannot listen to (what goes on in) the exalted assembly (of the arch angels). They are reproached (for their false conjectures) from every side,
9. They are repulsed. A perpetual punishment awaits them.
10. Yet if anyone of them snatches away but once (to find out something), he is pursued by a bright shining flame.
11. Therefore, ask them (- your opponents) whether it is they (- the worldly people) who are harder in creation or those (spiritual beings)

سُوْرَةُ الصّٰفّٰتِ مَكِّيَّةٌ

بِسْمِ اللّٰهِ الرَّحْمٰنِ الرَّحِيْمِ

وَ الصّٰٓفّٰتِ صَفًّا ﴿١﴾ فَالزّٰجِرٰتِ زَجْرًا ﴿٢﴾
فَالتّٰلِيٰتِ ذِكْرًا ﴿٣﴾ إِنَّ إِلٰهَكُمْ لَوٰحِدٌ ﴿٤﴾
رَبُّ السَّمٰوٰتِ وَ الْأَرْضِ وَ مَا بَيْنَهُمَا
وَ رَبُّ الْمَشٰرِقِ ﴿٥﴾ إِنَّا زَيَّنَّا السَّمَآءَ الدُّنْيَا
بِزِيْنَةِ الْكَوَاكِبِ ﴿٦﴾ وَ حِفْظًا مِّنْ كُلِّ
شَيْطٰنٍ مَّارِدٍ ﴿٧﴾ لَا يَسَّمَّعُوْنَ إِلَى الْمَلَإِ
الْأَعْلٰى وَ يُقْذَفُوْنَ مِنْ كُلِّ جَانِبٍ ﴿٨﴾
دُحُوْرًا وَّ لَهُمْ عَذَابٌ وَّاصِبٌ ﴿٩﴾ إِلَّا مَنْ
خَطِفَ الْخَطْفَةَ فَأَتْبَعَهُ شِهَابٌ ثَاقِبٌ ﴿١٠﴾
فَاسْتَفْتِهِمْ أَهُمْ أَشَدُّ خَلْقًا أَمْ مَّنْ

whom We have created. Them We have created out of adhesive sticking clay (so of firm and strong character).
12. Whereas you marvel (at this mighty spiritual revelation) they hold you in low estimation.
13. When they are admonished they pay no heed;
14. And when they see a sign they seek to scoff (at it),
15. And they say, 'This is nothing but an enchantment; (a device) causing a split (among the people).
16. 'Well (can it be possible that) when we are dead and reduced to dust and bones we shall be raised to life (again)?
17. 'And shall our forefathers of earlier times be (also)?'
18. Say, 'Yes, and you shall then be disgraced.'
19. Then there shall be but a single driving shout and behold! They will be (up and) looking on.
20. And they will say, 'O woe be on us! This is the Day of Requital.'
21. (They will be told,) 'This is the Day of the (last) judgment, (yes) the very day you used to cry lies to.'

SECTION 2

22. (ANGELS will be commanded,) 'Round up those who acted unjustly and their companions and the things they used to worship
23. 'Beside Allâh, then lead them towards the way of Hell.
24. 'And hold them up for a while for they have to be questioned.'
25. (They will be asked,) 'What is the matter with you that you do not help one another (this day)?'
26. Rather they will on that day (being ashamed) be completely submissive (bending their heads low).
27. Some of them will turn to the others, questioning to one another (reproachingly).
28. They (the seduced ones) will say (to the

خَلَقْنَا ۗ إِنَّا خَلَقْنَٰهُم مِّن طِينٍ لَّازِبٍ ﴿١١﴾
بَلْ عَجِبْتَ وَيَسْخَرُونَ ﴿١٢﴾ وَإِذَا ذُكِّرُوا
لَا يَذْكُرُونَ ﴿١٣﴾ وَإِذَا رَأَوْا آيَةً يَسْتَسْخِرُونَ ﴿١٤﴾
وَقَالُوا إِنْ هَٰذَا إِلَّا سِحْرٌ مُّبِينٌ ﴿١٥﴾ أَإِذَا
مِتْنَا وَكُنَّا تُرَابًا وَعِظَامًا أَإِنَّا لَمَبْعُوثُونَ ﴿١٦﴾
أَوَآبَاؤُنَا الْأَوَّلُونَ ﴿١٧﴾ قُلْ نَعَمْ وَأَنتُمْ
دَاخِرُونَ ﴿١٨﴾ فَإِنَّمَا هِيَ زَجْرَةٌ وَاحِدَةٌ فَإِذَا هُمْ
يَنظُرُونَ ﴿١٩﴾ وَقَالُوا يَا وَيْلَنَا هَٰذَا يَوْمُ الدِّينِ ﴿٢٠﴾
هَٰذَا يَوْمُ الْفَصْلِ الَّذِي كُنتُم بِهِ تُكَذِّبُونَ ﴿٢١﴾ ع ١/٥
احْشُرُوا الَّذِينَ ظَلَمُوا وَأَزْوَاجَهُمْ وَمَا
كَانُوا يَعْبُدُونَ ﴿٢٢﴾ مِن دُونِ اللَّهِ فَاهْدُوهُمْ
إِلَىٰ صِرَاطِ الْجَحِيمِ ﴿٢٣﴾ وَقِفُوهُمْ ۖ إِنَّهُم
مَّسْئُولُونَ ﴿٢٤﴾ مَا لَكُمْ لَا تَنَاصَرُونَ ﴿٢٥﴾ بَلْ
هُمُ الْيَوْمَ مُسْتَسْلِمُونَ ﴿٢٦﴾ وَأَقْبَلَ بَعْضُهُمْ
عَلَىٰ بَعْضٍ يَتَسَاءَلُونَ ﴿٢٧﴾ قَالُوا إِنَّكُمْ كُنتُمْ

seducers), 'Surely, you used to approach us with great force swearing (your sincerity to guide us aright).'
29. They (- seducers) will reply, 'It was not so. Rather you yourselves were not (inclined to be) the believers.
30. 'And we had no authority over you (to seduce you). The truth is that you yourselves were an unrestrained people (and given to excesses).
31. 'So (today) we all deserve the judgment of our Lord. We are the sufferers (of the punishment for our own evil deeds).
32. 'So (it is) we (who) led you astray, for we ourselves had indeed gone astray.'
33. On that day all of them shall surely share the punishment.
34. Surely, that is how We deal with the guilty.
35. For when it was said to them, 'There is no other, cannot be and will never be one worthy of worship but Allâh,' they ever turned away in disdain.
36. And they used to say, 'Are we to forsake our gods for the sake of a mad poet?'
37. Nay, (this Prophet is neither insane nor a poet,) the fact is that he brought the everlasting truth and has testified to the truth of (all) the Messengers (gone before him).
38. (Disbelievers!) You will suffer the woeful punishment, most certainly.
39. You shall be made to reap the fruit of your own deeds.
40. Different however is the case of the (chosen) servants of Allâh, the true and purified ones.
41. It is they for whom there awaits a provision (especially) earmarked,
42. Fruits, moreover they shall be the honored ones (and generously treated)
43. In the Gardens of Bliss.
44. (They shall be seated) on thrones (of happiness and dignity), face to face.
45. They will be served in a round with a bowl

تَأْتُونَنَا عَنِ الْيَمِينِ ﴿٢٨﴾ قَالُوا بَلْ لَمْ تَكُونُوا
مُؤْمِنِينَ ﴿٢٩﴾ وَمَا كَانَ لَنَا عَلَيْكُمْ مِنْ
سُلْطَانٍ ۚ بَلْ كُنْتُمْ قَوْمًا طَاغِينَ ﴿٣٠﴾ فَحَقَّ عَلَيْنَا
قَوْلُ رَبِّنَا ۖ إِنَّا لَذَائِقُونَ ﴿٣١﴾ فَأَغْوَيْنَاكُمْ إِنَّا
كُنَّا غَاوِينَ ﴿٣٢﴾ فَإِنَّهُمْ يَوْمَئِذٍ فِي الْعَذَابِ
مُشْتَرِكُونَ ﴿٣٣﴾ إِنَّا كَذَٰلِكَ نَفْعَلُ بِالْمُجْرِمِينَ ﴿٣٤﴾
إِنَّهُمْ كَانُوا إِذَا قِيلَ لَهُمْ لَا إِلَٰهَ إِلَّا اللَّهُ
يَسْتَكْبِرُونَ ﴿٣٥﴾ وَيَقُولُونَ أَئِنَّا لَتَارِكُوا
آلِهَتِنَا لِشَاعِرٍ مَجْنُونٍ ﴿٣٦﴾ بَلْ جَاءَ بِالْحَقِّ
وَصَدَّقَ الْمُرْسَلِينَ ﴿٣٧﴾ إِنَّكُمْ لَذَائِقُوا
الْعَذَابِ الْأَلِيمِ ﴿٣٨﴾ وَمَا تُجْزَوْنَ إِلَّا مَا
كُنْتُمْ تَعْمَلُونَ ﴿٣٩﴾ إِلَّا عِبَادَ اللَّهِ الْمُخْلَصِينَ ﴿٤٠﴾
أُولَٰئِكَ لَهُمْ رِزْقٌ مَعْلُومٌ ﴿٤١﴾ فَوَاكِهُ ۖ وَهُمْ
مُكْرَمُونَ ﴿٤٢﴾ فِي جَنَّاتِ النَّعِيمِ ﴿٤٣﴾ عَلَىٰ سُرُرٍ
مُتَقَابِلِينَ ﴿٤٤﴾ يُطَافُ عَلَيْهِمْ بِكَأْسٍ مِنْ

containing pure drink filled at a limpid flowing fountain,
46 (Sparkling) white, delicious to the drinkers, (as a reward for their leading pure sweet and flawless lives).
47. Neither these (drinks) will cause any ruinous effect, nor they will be deprived of intellectual faculties thereby.
48. And they will have (chaste wives) by their sides, damsels, with restrained and modest looks (and) with large beautiful eyes.
49. Just as though they were eggs carefully guarded (- of pure and unspoiled character).
50. Then (sipping their cups) they will turn one to another asking questions;
51. One of them will say, 'Surely I had an intimate companion (in the world),
52. 'Who used to say, "Are you indeed one of those who confirm (and really believe in the Resurrection)?
53. "Is it true that we shall be reunited when we are dead and reduced to dust and bones?"'
54. He (- the confirmer of the Resurrection) will then add (saying), 'Have a look (at that companion of mine to find how he fares!)?'
55. Then as he will have a look (at his companion) he will find him right in the midst of Hell.
56. He will then say (to that companion), 'By Allâh, you had almost caused me to perish;
57. 'But for the favour and grace of my Lord, I would have also been one of those who are facing (the punishment today).'
58. The owners of Paradise will then ask one another, 'Is it not true that we are not going to suffer death (again)?
59. 'Ours was only the death we have already met (in the world), and we are going to suffer no punishment.
60. 'This indeed, is the mighty achievement (on our part).
61. 'Let those who would strive, then strive for the like of this (supreme triumph)!'
62. Does all this (state of bliss) make a better

مَّعِينٍ (٤٥) بَيْضَاءَ لَذَّةٍ لِّلشَّرِبِينَ (٤٦) لَا فِيهَا
غَوْلٌ وَلَا هُمْ عَنْهَا يُنزَفُونَ (٤٧) وَعِندَهُمْ
قَٰصِرَٰتُ الطَّرْفِ عِينٌ (٤٨) كَأَنَّهُنَّ بَيْضٌ
مَّكْنُونٌ (٤٩) فَأَقْبَلَ بَعْضُهُمْ عَلَىٰ بَعْضٍ
يَتَسَاءَلُونَ (٥٠) قَالَ قَائِلٌ مِّنْهُمْ إِنِّي كَانَ
لِي قَرِينٌ (٥١) يَقُولُ ءَإِنَّكَ لَمِنَ الْمُصَدِّقِينَ (٥٢)
ءَإِذَا مِتْنَا وَكُنَّا تُرَابًا وَعِظَٰمًا ءَإِنَّا
لَمَدِينُونَ (٥٣) قَالَ هَلْ أَنتُم مُّطَّلِعُونَ (٥٤)
فَاطَّلَعَ فَرَءَاهُ فِي سَوَاءِ الْجَحِيمِ (٥٥) قَالَ
تَاللَّهِ إِن كِدتَّ لَتُرْدِينِ (٥٦) وَلَوْلَا نِعْمَةُ
رَبِّي لَكُنتُ مِنَ الْمُحْضَرِينَ (٥٧) أَفَمَا نَحْنُ
بِمَيِّتِينَ (٥٨) إِلَّا مَوْتَتَنَا الْأُولَىٰ وَمَا نَحْنُ
بِمُعَذَّبِينَ (٥٩) إِنَّ هَٰذَا لَهُوَ الْفَوْزُ الْعَظِيمُ (٦٠)
لِمِثْلِ هَٰذَا فَلْيَعْمَلِ الْعَٰمِلُونَ (٦١) أَذَٰلِكَ خَيْرٌ

welcome than the tree of *Zaqqûm* (which will serve as food for the people of Gehenna)?
63. For We have made this (tree) a scourge for the wrongdoers.
64. It is a tree which springs forth from the bottom of Hell.
65. Its produce is as though it were the heads of serpents.
66. And most surely they, (the inmates of Hell,) shall eat of it and fill (their) bellies with it.
67. In addition to (all) this, they will have (therein) a mixture of boiling water (to drink).
68. Then most surely they shall finally go to Hell.
69. The thing is, they found their forefathers erring,
70. And they are rushing on in their footsteps (as if driven by some inward urge).
71. And most of the ancient people had erred before them.
72. Though We had already sent Warners among them.
73. Behold! Then, how (evil) was the end of those who were warned.
74. Different, however, was the case of the chosen servants of Allâh, the true and purified ones.

SECTION 3

75. **A**ND Noah did call upon Us (in his hour of trial); how Gracious We are in answering prayers! (and how excellent a response did We make!)
76. We delivered him and his people from the great distress.
77. And We let his progeny alone to survive.
78. And We left behind him (a blessed salutation) for the later generations (to remember him by).
79. 'Peace be upon Noah,' (the prayer being invoked upon him) among all the peoples.
80. That is how We reward the performers of excellent deeds.
81. He was surely (one) of Our believing servants.

نُزُلًا أَمْ شَجَرَةُ الزَّقُّومِ ﴿٦٢﴾ إِنَّا جَعَلْنَاهَا فِتْنَةً
لِّلظَّالِمِينَ ﴿٦٣﴾ إِنَّهَا شَجَرَةٌ تَخْرُجُ فِي أَصْلِ الْجَحِيمِ ﴿٦٤﴾
طَلْعُهَا كَأَنَّهُ رُءُوسُ الشَّيَاطِينِ ﴿٦٥﴾ فَإِنَّهُمْ
لَآكِلُونَ مِنْهَا فَمَالِئُونَ مِنْهَا الْبُطُونَ ﴿٦٦﴾
ثُمَّ إِنَّ لَهُمْ عَلَيْهَا لَشَوْبًا مِّنْ حَمِيمٍ ﴿٦٧﴾ ثُمَّ
إِنَّ مَرْجِعَهُمْ لَإِلَى الْجَحِيمِ ﴿٦٨﴾ إِنَّهُمْ أَلْفَوْا
آبَاءَهُمْ ضَالِّينَ ﴿٦٩﴾ فَهُمْ عَلَىٰ آثَارِهِمْ يُهْرَعُونَ ﴿٧٠﴾
وَلَقَدْ ضَلَّ قَبْلَهُمْ أَكْثَرُ الْأَوَّلِينَ ﴿٧١﴾ وَلَقَدْ
أَرْسَلْنَا فِيهِم مُّنذِرِينَ ﴿٧٢﴾ فَانظُرْ كَيْفَ كَانَ
عَاقِبَةُ الْمُنذَرِينَ ﴿٧٣﴾ إِلَّا عِبَادَ اللَّهِ الْمُخْلَصِينَ ﴿٧٤﴾ ع
وَلَقَدْ نَادَانَا نُوحٌ فَلَنِعْمَ الْمُجِيبُونَ ﴿٧٥﴾
وَنَجَّيْنَاهُ وَأَهْلَهُ مِنَ الْكَرْبِ الْعَظِيمِ ﴿٧٦﴾
وَجَعَلْنَا ذُرِّيَّتَهُ هُمُ الْبَاقِينَ ﴿٧٧﴾ وَتَرَكْنَا عَلَيْهِ
فِي الْآخِرِينَ ﴿٧٨﴾ سَلَامٌ عَلَىٰ نُوحٍ فِي الْعَالَمِينَ ﴿٧٩﴾
إِنَّا كَذَٰلِكَ نَجْزِي الْمُحْسِنِينَ ﴿٨٠﴾ إِنَّهُ مِنْ

82. And (whereas We saved him and his people) We drowned the rest.
83. And Abraham also belonged to his (Noah's) school of thought.
84. (Recall the time) when he came to his Lord with a pure heart,
85. (And) when he asked his sire and his people, 'What is it that you worship?
86. 'Do you choose (to worship) gods made falsely leaving Allâh aside,
87. 'So what do you take the Lord of the worlds to be (as you people worship false gods)?'
88. Then he cast a glance at the stars (intimating that their discussion has dragged far into the night);
89. And said, 'I am indeed sick (of your worshipping false gods).'
90. So those people turned their backs upon him and left him.
91. Then he turned (his attention) towards their gods and (with a mind to make their worshippers realise their folly) said (addressing the gods), 'Do you not eat (any of the things that lie before you)?
92. 'What is wrong with you that you do not even speak?'
93. He then came upon them hitting them hard with the right hand.
94. (Hearing this news) the people came running to him.
95. He said (to them), 'You worship the things you have chiselled yourselves;
96. 'Whereas (it is) Allâh (Who) has created you, but what is it that you are doing?'
97. (His opponents) said, 'Build up a pyre for him and throw him into the blazing fire.'
98. Thus they designed a plan against him, but We made them to be the most humiliated.
99. (Abraham) said, 'I shall go where my Lord bids me. He will surely guide me right

عبادنا المؤمنين ﴿٨١﴾ ثم أغرقنا الآخرين ﴿٨٢﴾
وإن من شيعته لإبرهيم ﴿٨٣﴾ إذ جاء ربه
بقلب سليم ﴿٨٤﴾ إذ قال لأبيه وقومه ما
ذا تعبدون ﴿٨٥﴾ أئفكا آلهة دون الله
تريدون ﴿٨٦﴾ فما ظنكم برب العلمين ﴿٨٧﴾ فنظر
نظرة في النجوم ﴿٨٨﴾ فقال إني سقيم ﴿٨٩﴾ فتولوا
عنه مدبرين ﴿٩٠﴾ فراغ إلى آلهتهم فقال
ألا تأكلون ﴿٩١﴾ ما لكم لا تنطقون ﴿٩٢﴾ فراغ
عليهم ضربا باليمين ﴿٩٣﴾ فأقبلوا إليه
يزفون ﴿٩٤﴾ قال أتعبدون ما تنحتون ﴿٩٥﴾
والله خلقكم وما تعملون ﴿٩٦﴾ قالوا ابنوا له
بنينا فألقوه في الجحيم ﴿٩٧﴾ فأرادوا به
كيدا فجعلنهم الأسفلين ﴿٩٨﴾ وقال إني

(to the path leading to success in my mission).'
100. (And he prayed,) 'My Lord! Grant me (an issue who is) of the righteous.'
101. So We gave him the good tidings of (the birth of) a wise and forbearing son.
102. Now, when that (son, Ismâîl) was (old enough) to work along with him, (his father, Abraham) said, 'My dear son! I have seen in a dream that I sacrifice you. So consider (it and tell me) what you think (of it).' (The son) said, 'My dear father! Do as you are commanded. If Allâh will you will find me of the calm and steadfast.'
103. Now, (it so happened) when both of them submitted themselves (to the will of God) and he (- Abraham) had laid him (- Ismâîl) down on his forehead,
104. We called out to him (saying), 'O Abraham!
105. 'You have already fulfilled the vision.' That is how We reward those who perform excellent deeds.
106. That was obviously a disciplinary test (crowned with a mighty reward,)
107. And a great sacrifice was the ransom with which We redeemed him (- Ismâîl).
108. And We left behind him (- Abraham) among the succeeding generations (the noble salutation to invoke blessings upon him).
109. 'Peace be upon Abraham!'
110. That is how We reward the performers of excellent deeds.
111. Surely, he was (one) of Our believing servants.
112. And We gave him (also) the good tidings of (the birth of) Isaac, a Prophet (and who is) one of the righteous.
113. And We bestowed (Our) blessings on him (- Ismâîl) and on Isaac. And among the progeny of both there are (some persons) who perform excellent deeds and (also some) who are clearly unjust to themselves.

ذَاهِبٌ إِلَىٰ رَبِّي سَيَهْدِينِ ﴿٩٩﴾ رَبِّ هَبْ لِي
مِنَ الصَّٰلِحِينَ ﴿١٠٠﴾ فَبَشَّرْنَٰهُ بِغُلَٰمٍ حَلِيمٍ ﴿١٠١﴾
فَلَمَّا بَلَغَ مَعَهُ السَّعْيَ قَالَ يَٰبُنَيَّ إِنِّي أَرَىٰ
فِي الْمَنَامِ أَنِّي أَذْبَحُكَ فَانْظُرْ مَاذَا تَرَىٰ
قَالَ يَٰأَبَتِ افْعَلْ مَا تُؤْمَرُ سَتَجِدُنِي إِنْ
شَاءَ اللَّهُ مِنَ الصَّٰبِرِينَ ﴿١٠٢﴾ فَلَمَّا أَسْلَمَا
وَتَلَّهُ لِلْجَبِينِ ﴿١٠٣﴾ وَنَٰدَيْنَٰهُ أَنْ يَٰإِبْرَٰهِيمُ ﴿١٠٤﴾
قَدْ صَدَّقْتَ الرُّءْيَا إِنَّا كَذَٰلِكَ نَجْزِي
الْمُحْسِنِينَ ﴿١٠٥﴾ إِنَّ هَٰذَا لَهُوَ الْبَلَٰٓؤُا الْمُبِينُ ﴿١٠٦﴾
وَفَدَيْنَٰهُ بِذِبْحٍ عَظِيمٍ ﴿١٠٧﴾ وَتَرَكْنَا عَلَيْهِ
فِي الْأٰخِرِينَ ﴿١٠٨﴾ سَلَٰمٌ عَلَىٰ إِبْرَٰهِيمَ ﴿١٠٩﴾ كَذَٰلِكَ
نَجْزِي الْمُحْسِنِينَ ﴿١١٠﴾ إِنَّهُ مِنْ عِبَادِنَا
الْمُؤْمِنِينَ ﴿١١١﴾ وَبَشَّرْنَٰهُ بِإِسْحَٰقَ نَبِيًّا مِّنَ
الصَّٰلِحِينَ ﴿١١٢﴾ وَبَٰرَكْنَا عَلَيْهِ وَعَلَىٰ إِسْحَٰقَ
وَمِنْ ذُرِّيَّتِهِمَا مُحْسِنٌ وَظَالِمٌ لِّنَفْسِهِۦ

SECTION 4

114. **W**E did bestow (Our) favours on Moses and Aaron.
115. We delivered them both and their people from the great distress.
116. And We came to their help (against the people of Pharaoh). So it was they who gained clear supremacy.
117. And We gave them both the Manifesting Book.
118. And We guided them both to the right and straight path.
119. And We left behind both of them (a blessed salutation) among the generations to come.
120. 'Peace be upon Moses and Aaron!'
121. That is how We reward the performers of excellent deeds.
122. Surely, they were both among Our believing servants.
123. Verily, Elias was (also) one of the Messengers.
124. (Recall the time) when he said to his people, 'Will you not guard against evil (deeds)?
125. 'Do you call upon *Ba'l* (- the sun-god), and forsake the Best Creator,
126 'Allâh, your Lord and the Lord of your forefathers of old.'
127. But they cried lies to him and they will surely be brought (before God to account for their deeds).
128. Different, however, shall be the case of the chosen servants of Allâh, the purified ones.
129. And We left behind him (- Elias) among the succeeding generations (the blessed salutation to be invoked upon him),
130. 'Peace be upon Elias and his people!'
131. That is how We reward the performers of excellent deeds.
132. Surely, he was (one) of Our believing servants.
133. And verily, Lot was (also) one of the

مُبِينٌ ﴿١١٣﴾ وَلَقَدْ مَنَنَّا عَلَى مُوسَى وَهٰرُونَ ﴿١١٤﴾
وَنَجَّيْنٰهُمَا وَقَوْمَهُمَا مِنَ الْكَرْبِ الْعَظِيمِ ﴿١١٥﴾
وَنَصَرْنٰهُمْ فَكَانُوا هُمُ الْغٰلِبِينَ ﴿١١٦﴾ وَاٰتَيْنٰهُمَا
الْكِتٰبَ الْمُسْتَبِينَ ﴿١١٧﴾ وَهَدَيْنٰهُمَا الصِّرٰطَ
الْمُسْتَقِيمَ ﴿١١٨﴾ وَتَرَكْنَا عَلَيْهِمَا فِي الْاٰخِرِينَ ﴿١١٩﴾
سَلٰمٌ عَلَى مُوسَى وَهٰرُونَ ﴿١٢٠﴾ إِنَّا كَذٰلِكَ
نَجْزِي الْمُحْسِنِينَ ﴿١٢١﴾ إِنَّهُمَا مِنْ عِبَادِنَا
الْمُؤْمِنِينَ ﴿١٢٢﴾ وَإِنَّ إِلْيَاسَ لَمِنَ الْمُرْسَلِينَ ﴿١٢٣﴾
إِذْ قَالَ لِقَوْمِهِ أَلَا تَتَّقُونَ ﴿١٢٤﴾ أَتَدْعُونَ
بَعْلًا وَّتَذَرُونَ أَحْسَنَ الْخٰلِقِينَ ﴿١٢٥﴾ اللّٰهَ
رَبَّكُمْ وَرَبَّ اٰبَائِكُمُ الْأَوَّلِينَ ﴿١٢٦﴾ فَكَذَّبُوهُ
فَإِنَّهُمْ لَمُحْضَرُونَ ﴿١٢٧﴾ إِلَّا عِبَادَ اللّٰهِ الْمُخْلَصِينَ ﴿١٢٨﴾
وَتَرَكْنَا عَلَيْهِ فِي الْاٰخِرِينَ ﴿١٢٩﴾ سَلٰمٌ عَلَى
إِلْ يَاسِينَ ﴿١٣٠﴾ إِنَّا كَذٰلِكَ نَجْزِي الْمُحْسِنِينَ ﴿١٣١﴾
إِنَّهُ مِنْ عِبَادِنَا الْمُؤْمِنِينَ ﴿١٣٢﴾ وَإِنَّ لُوطًا

Messengers.
134. (Recall the time) when We delivered him and his followers all together,
135. Except an old woman (who) was among those who stayed behind (and did not go with those delivered).
136. And We utterly destroyed the rest.
137. And you surely pass by them, (their ruins sometimes), in the morning,
138. And (sometimes) by night. Do you not still make use of (your) understanding (and take heed)?

SECTION 5

139. **A**ND surely, Jonah (also) was (one) of the Messengers.
140. (Recall the time) when he fled (from his people) towards the fully laden ship.
141. So he was with those (crew) who cast lots (on board of the ill-fated ship, and his name was among those who were to be thrown overboard in order to keep the ship light and well-balanced on account of the storm) and so he was (also) of those who were cast off (in the sea).
142. Then (it came about that) a big fish took him in its mouth while he was reproaching (himself).
143. Had he not been of those who glorify (God)
144. He would have surely remained in its belly till the time people are raised up (after their death).
145. Then (it came to pass) that We cast him on a bare and wide tract of land and he was completely worn out and sick.
146. And We caused a plant (of the gourd type) bearing large-size fruit but the creeper of slender stem to grow near him.
147. And We sent him (back as a Messenger at Nineveh) to a people hundred thousand strong, rather they were even more.
148. They all believed (in him) so We provided them gains till the end of their lives.
149. Now ask these (disbelievers) whether

لَمِنَ الْمُرْسَلِينَ ﴿١٣٣﴾ إِذْ نَجَّيْنَٰهُ وَأَهْلَهُۥٓ
أَجْمَعِينَ ﴿١٣٤﴾ إِلَّا عَجُوزًا فِي الْغَٰبِرِينَ ﴿١٣٥﴾ ثُمَّ
دَمَّرْنَا الْأَخَرِينَ ﴿١٣٦﴾ وَإِنَّكُمْ لَتَمُرُّونَ عَلَيْهِم
مُّصْبِحِينَ ﴿١٣٧﴾ وَبِالَّيْلِ أَفَلَا تَعْقِلُونَ ﴿١٣٨﴾ وَإِنَّ
يُونُسَ لَمِنَ الْمُرْسَلِينَ ﴿١٣٩﴾ إِذْ أَبَقَ إِلَى الْفُلْكِ
الْمَشْحُونِ ﴿١٤٠﴾ فَسَاهَمَ فَكَانَ مِنَ الْمُدْحَضِينَ ﴿١٤١﴾
فَالْتَقَمَهُ الْحُوتُ وَهُوَ مُلِيمٌ ﴿١٤٢﴾ فَلَوْلَآ أَنَّهُۥ
كَانَ مِنَ الْمُسَبِّحِينَ ﴿١٤٣﴾ لَلَبِثَ فِي بَطْنِهِۦٓ إِلَىٰ
يَوْمِ يُبْعَثُونَ ﴿١٤٤﴾ فَنَبَذْنَٰهُ بِالْعَرَآءِ وَهُوَ
سَقِيمٌ ﴿١٤٥﴾ وَأَنۢبَتْنَا عَلَيْهِ شَجَرَةً مِّن يَقْطِينٍ ﴿١٤٦﴾
وَأَرْسَلْنَٰهُ إِلَىٰ مِائَةِ أَلْفٍ أَوْ يَزِيدُونَ ﴿١٤٧﴾
فَـَٔامَنُوا فَمَتَّعْنَٰهُمْ إِلَىٰ حِينٍ ﴿١٤٨﴾ فَاسْتَفْتِهِمْ

daughters are for your Lord (as they assert), and sons for themselves.
150. Or did We create the angels as females (in their presence) while they were witnesses (of their birth).
151. Beware! It is (one) of their fabrications that they say,
152. 'Allâh has begotten (those as His children).' They are liars, of course.
153. Has He chosen daughters in preference to sons?
154. What is the matter with you? How (wrongly) you judge!
155. Will you take no heed?
156. Or have you a clear authority (in your defence for your false beliefs)?
157. If so then come out with your (authoritative) scripture if you are truthful.
158. And they have set up a kinship between Him and the *jinn* (- strong and mighty men), whereas the *jinn* know fully well that they themselves shall be called to account for their deeds.
159. Holy is Allâh, far beyond the things they attribute (to Him).
160. But the chosen servants of Allâh, the purified ones (attribute nothing derogatory to Him).
161. (Disbelievers!) Neither you of course, nor the things you worship;
162. None of you can mislead anyone against Him,
163. Excepting (only) the person who is (himself) going to enter Hell.
164. (The righteous say,) 'Each one of us has his assigned place.
165. 'And most surely we are the ones who stand ranged in rows (attending to the command of God).
166. 'Verily, we are the ones who glorify Him (and sing His praise).
167. And surely, these (infidels) used to say,

أَلِرَبِّكَ الْبَنَاتُ وَلَهُمُ الْبَنُونَ ﴿١٤٩﴾ أَمْ خَلَقْنَا
الْمَلَٰٓئِكَةَ إِنَاثًا وَهُمْ شَٰهِدُونَ ﴿١٥٠﴾ أَلَآ إِنَّهُم
مِّنْ إِفْكِهِمْ لَيَقُولُونَ ﴿١٥١﴾ وَلَدَ اللَّهُ وَإِنَّهُمْ
لَكَٰذِبُونَ ﴿١٥٢﴾ أَصْطَفَى الْبَنَاتِ عَلَى الْبَنِينَ ﴿١٥٣﴾
مَا لَكُمْ كَيْفَ تَحْكُمُونَ ﴿١٥٤﴾ أَفَلَا تَذَكَّرُونَ ﴿١٥٥﴾
أَمْ لَكُمْ سُلْطَٰنٌ مُّبِينٌ ﴿١٥٦﴾ فَأْتُوا بِكِتَٰبِكُمْ إِن
كُنتُمْ صَٰدِقِينَ ﴿١٥٧﴾ وَجَعَلُوا بَيْنَهُ وَبَيْنَ
الْجِنَّةِ نَسَبًا وَلَقَدْ عَلِمَتِ الْجِنَّةُ إِنَّهُمْ
لَمُحْضَرُونَ ﴿١٥٨﴾ سُبْحَٰنَ اللَّهِ عَمَّا يَصِفُونَ ﴿١٥٩﴾
إِلَّا عِبَادَ اللَّهِ الْمُخْلَصِينَ ﴿١٦٠﴾ فَإِنَّكُمْ وَمَا
تَعْبُدُونَ ﴿١٦١﴾ مَآ أَنتُمْ عَلَيْهِ بِفَٰتِنِينَ ﴿١٦٢﴾ إِلَّا
مَنْ هُوَ صَالِ الْجَحِيمِ ﴿١٦٣﴾ وَمَا مِنَّآ إِلَّا لَهُۥ
مَقَامٌ مَّعْلُومٌ ﴿١٦٤﴾ وَإِنَّا لَنَحْنُ الصَّآفُّونَ ﴿١٦٥﴾
وَإِنَّا لَنَحْنُ الْمُسَبِّحُونَ ﴿١٦٦﴾ وَإِن كَانُوا

168. 'Had there been with us an exhortation from the people of old.
169. 'We would surely have been the chosen servants of Allâh, the purified ones.'
170. But (now) they have disbelieved in this (Book, the Qur'ân when it has come to them). So they will soon come to know (the consequences of their disbelief).
171. And We have already given Our word (of promise) to Our servants, the Apostles,
172. That it is they alone who shall receive Our help (against the infidels).
173. And (that) it is Our armies that shall gain clear supremacy.
174. So turn away from them until a time (of your success),
175. And watch (what happens to) them, and they (too) will soon see (their own doom).
176. Do they seek to hasten on Our punishment?
177. But evil shall be the morning of those who were warned when this punishment shall descend in their precincts.
178. So turn away from them until a time (-that of your supremacy);
179. And watch (what happens to) them and they (too) will soon see (their end).
180. Holy is your Lord, the Lord of all honour and power. He is far above the (polytheistic) things they attribute (to Him).
181. And peace be ever upon all the Messengers.
182. And all type of perfect and true praise belongs to Allâh, the Lord of the worlds.

لَيَقُولُونَ ١٦٧ لَوْ أَنَّ عِنْدَنَا ذِكْرًا مِّنَ
الْأَوَّلِينَ ١٦٨ لَكُنَّا عِبَادَ اللَّهِ الْمُخْلَصِينَ ١٦٩
فَكَفَرُوا بِهِ فَسَوْفَ يَعْلَمُونَ ١٧٠ وَلَقَدْ سَبَقَتْ
كَلِمَتُنَا لِعِبَادِنَا الْمُرْسَلِينَ ١٧١ إِنَّهُمْ لَهُمُ
الْمَنصُورُونَ ١٧٢ وَإِنَّ جُندَنَا لَهُمُ الْغَالِبُونَ ١٧٣
فَتَوَلَّ عَنْهُمْ حَتَّىٰ حِينٍ ١٧٤ وَأَبْصِرْهُمْ فَسَوْفَ
يُبْصِرُونَ ١٧٥ أَفَبِعَذَابِنَا يَسْتَعْجِلُونَ ١٧٦ فَإِذَا
نَزَلَ بِسَاحَتِهِمْ فَسَاءَ صَبَاحُ الْمُنذَرِينَ ١٧٧
وَتَوَلَّ عَنْهُمْ حَتَّىٰ حِينٍ ١٧٨ وَأَبْصِرْ فَسَوْفَ
يُبْصِرُونَ ١٧٩ سُبْحَانَ رَبِّكَ رَبِّ الْعِزَّةِ
عَمَّا يَصِفُونَ ١٨٠ وَسَلَامٌ عَلَى الْمُرْسَلِينَ ١٨١
وَالْحَمْدُ لِلَّهِ رَبِّ الْعَالَمِينَ ١٨٢

CHAPTER
38

سُوۡرَةُ صٓ ٣٨

SÂD
(The Truthful God)
(Revealed before Hijrah)

With the name of Allâh,
the Most Gracious, the Ever Merciful
(I commence to read Sûrah Sâd).

1. **S**ÂD - Allâh is the Truthful, (as proof of this fact) the Qur'ân which exalts (humankind) to eminence bears witness.

2. (There is nothing wrong with the Prophet,) the only thing is that the disbelievers are suffering from a sense of (false) pride and are hostile (to him).

3. (Do they not see that) We have destroyed so many generations before them? (They did not care to listen to the warning at first) then (later) they cried (for help) but the time for escape had passed.

4. They wonder that there should come to them a Warner from among themselves, and the disbelievers say, 'He is a sorcerer, a great liar (in his claim).

5. 'Has he turned (the whole lot of) gods (we worshipped) into One God? Very strange indeed is this thing.'

6. And the leaders among them go about saying, 'Go (from here) and adhere constantly to (the worship of) your gods. This (claim of the Qur'ân about the unity of God) is a thing designed (with some purpose behind it).

7. 'We heard nothing of its kind about any of the previous creeds. This is nothing but a forgery.

8. 'Is it that this Reminder (- the Qur'ân) has been revealed only to him (the chosen Warner) in (preference to) all of us?' The thing is they

سُوۡرَةُ صٓ مَكِّيَّةٌ

بِسۡمِ اللّٰهِ الرَّحۡمٰنِ الرَّحِيۡمِ

صٓ وَ الۡقُرۡاٰنِ ذِي الذِّكۡرِ ۝١ بَلِ الَّذِيۡنَ كَفَرُوۡا
فِيۡ عِزَّةٍ وَّ شِقَاقٍ ۝٢ كَمۡ اَهۡلَكۡنَا مِنۡ قَبۡلِهِمۡ
مِّنۡ قَرۡنٍ فَنَادَوۡا وَّ لَاتَ حِيۡنَ مَنَاصٍ ۝٣
وَعَجِبُوۡۤا اَنۡ جَآءَهُمۡ مُّنۡذِرٌ مِّنۡهُمۡ وَقَالَ
الۡكٰفِرُوۡنَ هٰذَا سٰحِرٌ كَذَّابٌ ۝٤ اَجَعَلَ الۡاٰلِهَةَ
اِلٰهًا وَّاحِدًا ۚ اِنَّ هٰذَا لَشَيۡءٌ عُجَابٌ ۝٥
وَانۡطَلَقَ الۡمَلَاُ مِنۡهُمۡ اَنِ امۡشُوۡا وَاصۡبِرُوۡا عَلٰٓى
اٰلِهَتِكُمۡ ۚ اِنَّ هٰذَا لَشَيۡءٌ يُّرَادُ ۝٦ مَا سَمِعۡنَا
بِهٰذَا فِي الۡمِلَّةِ الۡاٰخِرَةِ ۚ اِنۡ هٰذَاۤ اِلَّا
اخۡتِلَاقٌ ۝٧ ءَاُنۡزِلَ عَلَيۡهِ الذِّكۡرُ مِنۡ بَيۡنِنَا ؕ

have doubts about My Reminder (itself). As a matter of fact they have not (yet) suffered (the agony of) My punishment.

9. Do they possess the treasures of the mercy of your Lord, the All-Mighty, the Great Bestower?

10. Or does the kingdom of the heavens and the earth and all that lies between them belong to them? (If so) then let them rise higher with the means (at their disposal and stop the onward march of Islam).

11. (But bear in mind the prophecy:) there will be several hosts of the confederates which shall be completely routed here (at Madînah).

12. The people of Noah, (the tribe of) 'Âd and Pharaoh, lord of mighty hosts, treated (their Apostles) before them as liars.

13. So did (the tribe of) Th̲amûd and the people of Lot, and the dwellers of the Thicket. These were (all routed) groups of people.

14. Each one had cried lies to the Messengers. So My punishment rightly became due (on them).

SECTION 2

15. **A**ND also for these (people of your time) awaits a sudden punishment which shall know no pause.

16. They say, 'Our Lord! Hurry up with our portion (of punishment in this very life) before the Day of Reckoning.'

17. Bear with patience what they say. And remember (the event of the life of) Our servant David, the possessor of might. Verily, he was ever turning (to God).

18. Indeed, We made (the people of) the mountains subservient to him (and) they celebrated (Our) praises at nightfall and at sunrise,

19. And (We made) the birds and the people (who were) full of dislike for habitations to flock together (to him). All of them were

بَلْ هُمْ فِي شَكٍّ مِّنْ ذِكْرِيْ ۚ بَل لَّمَّا يَذُوقُوا عَذَابِ ۝٨ أَمْ عِنْدَهُمْ خَزَآئِنُ رَحْمَةِ رَبِّكَ الْعَزِيزِ الْوَهَّابِ ۝٩ أَمْ لَهُم مُّلْكُ السَّمٰوٰتِ وَالْأَرْضِ وَمَا بَيْنَهُمَا ۫ فَلْيَرْتَقُوا فِي الْأَسْبٰبِ ۝١٠ جُنْدٌ مَّا هُنَالِكَ مَهْزُومٌ مِّنَ الْأَحْزَابِ ۝١١ كَذَّبَتْ قَبْلَهُمْ قَوْمُ نُوحٍ وَّعَادٌ وَّفِرْعَوْنُ ذُو الْأَوْتَادِ ۝١٢ وَثَمُودُ وَقَوْمُ لُوطٍ وَّأَصْحٰبُ لْـَٔيْكَةِ ۚ أُولٰٓئِكَ الْأَحْزَابُ ۝١٣ إِنْ كُلٌّ إِلَّا كَذَّبَ الرُّسُلَ فَحَقَّ عِقَابِ ۝١٤ وَمَا يَنْظُرُ هٰٓؤُلَآءِ إِلَّا صَيْحَةً وّٰحِدَةً مَّا لَهَا مِنْ فَوَاقٍ ۝١٥ وَقَالُوا رَبَّنَا عَجِّلْ لَّنَا قِطَّنَا قَبْلَ يَوْمِ الْحِسَابِ ۝١٦ إِصْبِرْ عَلٰى مَا يَقُولُونَ وَاذْكُرْ عَبْدَنَا دَاوٗدَ ذَا الْأَيْدِ ۚ إِنَّهٗٓ أَوَّابٌ ۝١٧ إِنَّا سَخَّرْنَا الْجِبَالَ مَعَهٗ يُسَبِّحْنَ بِالْعَشِيِّ وَالْإِشْرَاقِ ۝١٨ وَالطَّيْرَ مَحْشُورَةً ۚ كُلٌّ لَّهٗٓ

always turning in obedience (to God) on his account.

20. And We strengthened his kingdom, and We granted him wisdom and decisive judgment.

21. Have you heard the news of the adversaries (of David) who scaled the rampart of the fortress (to take David unawares in his chamber)?

22. When they intruded upon David and (found that) he had become alert (on account of) them, they said, (by way of an excuse,) 'Have no fear. We are two parties litigants. One of us has transgressed against the other, therefore judge between us as justice demands, and delay not (by giving the date of decision,) and guide us (in our litigation) to the fair way.

23. '(The case of the litigation is that,) this is my brother. He has ninety nine ewes while I have one ewe; still he says, "Make it over to me," and he has been prevailing by his arguments upon me.'

24. (David) said, 'He has certainly been unjust to you in demanding your ewe (to be added) to his own ewes. And surely many partners transgress against one another except those who believe (in God) and do deeds of righteousness. Yet how few are these!' (While saying this) David realised that We had tried him, therefore he sought protection of his Lord and fell down bowing in worship and turned (to his Lord) in repentance.

PROSTRATION

25. So We gave him that protection (sought for by him from that danger he felt). And verily he enjoyed Our close proximity and an excellent status.

26. (We said,) 'O David! Verily We have made you the ruler in this land. So rule among the people according to (the tenants of) justice, and do not follow their vain desires, (for if you do) it will lead you astray from the path leading to Allâh. Behold! A severe punishment awaits those who go astray from Allâh's way, because

أَوَّابٌ ﴿١٩﴾ وَشَدَدْنَا مُلْكَهُۥ وَءَاتَيْنَٰهُ ٱلْحِكْمَةَ
وَفَصْلَ ٱلْخِطَابِ ﴿٢٠﴾ وَهَلْ أَتَىٰكَ نَبَؤُا۟ ٱلْخَصْمِ
إِذْ تَسَوَّرُوا۟ ٱلْمِحْرَابَ ﴿٢١﴾ إِذْ دَخَلُوا۟ عَلَىٰ دَاوُۥدَ
فَفَزِعَ مِنْهُمْ قَالُوا۟ لَا تَخَفْ خَصْمَانِ بَغَىٰ
بَعْضُنَا عَلَىٰ بَعْضٍ فَٱحْكُم بَيْنَنَا بِٱلْحَقِّ وَلَا
تُشْطِطْ وَٱهْدِنَآ إِلَىٰ سَوَآءِ ٱلصِّرَٰطِ ﴿٢٢﴾ إِنَّ هَٰذَآ
أَخِى لَهُۥ تِسْعٌ وَتِسْعُونَ نَعْجَةً وَلِىَ نَعْجَةٌ
وَٰحِدَةٌ فَقَالَ أَكْفِلْنِيهَا وَعَزَّنِى فِى ٱلْخِطَابِ ﴿٢٣﴾
قَالَ لَقَدْ ظَلَمَكَ بِسُؤَالِ نَعْجَتِكَ إِلَىٰ نِعَاجِهِۦ
وَإِنَّ كَثِيرًا مِّنَ ٱلْخُلَطَآءِ لَيَبْغِى بَعْضُهُمْ عَلَىٰ
بَعْضٍ إِلَّا ٱلَّذِينَ ءَامَنُوا۟ وَعَمِلُوا۟ ٱلصَّٰلِحَٰتِ
وَقَلِيلٌ مَّا هُمْ وَظَنَّ دَاوُۥدُ أَنَّمَا فَتَنَّٰهُ
فَٱسْتَغْفَرَ رَبَّهُۥ وَخَرَّ رَاكِعًا وَأَنَابَ ۩ ﴿٢٤﴾ فَغَفَرْنَا
لَهُۥ ذَٰلِكَ وَإِنَّ لَهُۥ عِندَنَا لَزُلْفَىٰ وَحُسْنَ مَـَٔابٍ ﴿٢٥﴾
يَٰدَاوُۥدُ إِنَّا جَعَلْنَٰكَ خَلِيفَةً فِى ٱلْأَرْضِ فَٱحْكُم
بَيْنَ ٱلنَّاسِ بِٱلْحَقِّ وَلَا تَتَّبِعِ ٱلْهَوَىٰ فَيُضِلَّكَ
عَن سَبِيلِ ٱللَّهِ إِنَّ ٱلَّذِينَ يَضِلُّونَ عَن
سَبِيلِ ٱللَّهِ لَهُمْ عَذَابٌ شَدِيدٌۢ بِمَا نَسُوا۟

they have forgotten the Day of Reckoning.

SECTION 3

27. AND We have not created the heavens and the earth and all that lies between them in vain. That is the view of the disbelievers only. Therefore woe to those who disbelieve because of (the punishment by means of) the Fire (that awaits them).
28. Are We to treat those who believe and do deeds of righteousness in the same way as the creators of disorder in the land? Or are We to treat those who guard against evil in the same way as the wicked and impious?
29. (Behold! This Qur'ân is) a great Book which We have revealed to you; full of excellencies, so that these (people) may ponder over its verses and so that those gifted with pure understanding may take heed.
30. And We gave (a pious son like) Solomon to David. How excellent a servant (of Ours) he was! For he turned to Us in obedience and repentance again and again.
31. (Think of the time) when towards the close of the day, steeds of the noblest breed and swift of foot were brought before him.
32. He said, 'I prefer the love of good things because they make (me) remember (God), my Lord.' And (he remained busy in his devotion and prayer), when these (horses) disappeared (while passing by) behind the veil (of distance),
33. (He said,) 'Bring them back to me.' Then (as they were brought) he began to stroke their hind legs and necks (with kindness).
34. Behold! We tried Solomon (too) and We placed on his throne (of kingdom) a (mere) body (without any spirit or faith). Then he turned (to God seeking His mercy).
35. He said (praying), 'My Lord! Grant me protection and bestow on me a kingdom that belongs to none (by inheritance) after me. You indeed are the Great Bestower.'
36. So (We accepted his prayer and) We sub-

يَوْمَ الْحِسَابِ ﴿٢٦﴾ وَمَا خَلَقْنَا السَّمَاءَ وَالْأَرْضَ
وَمَا بَيْنَهُمَا بَاطِلًا ذَٰلِكَ ظَنُّ الَّذِينَ كَفَرُوا
فَوَيْلٌ لِّلَّذِينَ كَفَرُوا مِنَ النَّارِ ﴿٢٧﴾ أَمْ نَجْعَلُ
الَّذِينَ آمَنُوا وَعَمِلُوا الصَّالِحَاتِ كَالْمُفْسِدِينَ
فِي الْأَرْضِ أَمْ نَجْعَلُ الْمُتَّقِينَ كَالْفُجَّارِ ﴿٢٨﴾
كِتَابٌ أَنزَلْنَاهُ إِلَيْكَ مُبَارَكٌ لِّيَدَّبَّرُوا آيَاتِهِ
وَلِيَتَذَكَّرَ أُولُو الْأَلْبَابِ ﴿٢٩﴾ وَوَهَبْنَا لِدَاوُودَ
سُلَيْمَانَ نِعْمَ الْعَبْدُ إِنَّهُ أَوَّابٌ ﴿٣٠﴾ إِذْ عُرِضَ
عَلَيْهِ بِالْعَشِيِّ الصَّافِنَاتُ الْجِيَادُ ﴿٣١﴾ فَقَالَ
إِنِّي أَحْبَبْتُ حُبَّ الْخَيْرِ عَن ذِكْرِ رَبِّي حَتَّىٰ
تَوَارَتْ بِالْحِجَابِ ﴿٣٢﴾ رُدُّوهَا عَلَيَّ فَطَفِقَ
مَسْحًا بِالسُّوقِ وَالْأَعْنَاقِ ﴿٣٣﴾ وَلَقَدْ فَتَنَّا
سُلَيْمَانَ وَأَلْقَيْنَا عَلَىٰ كُرْسِيِّهِ جَسَدًا ثُمَّ
أَنَابَ ﴿٣٤﴾ قَالَ رَبِّ اغْفِرْ لِي وَهَبْ لِي مُلْكًا
لَّا يَنبَغِي لِأَحَدٍ مِّنْ بَعْدِي إِنَّكَ أَنتَ
الْوَهَّابُ ﴿٣٥﴾ فَسَخَّرْنَا لَهُ الرِّيحَ تَجْرِي بِأَمْرِهِ

jected to him a gentle wind. It blew gently according to his requirements in the direction he desired to go.
37. And (We also subjugated to him) the rebellious people (- the unruly *Amâliqah* people of far off lands), all (their) builders and divers;
38. And others (among them, who were) bound in chains.
39. (We said to him,) 'This is Our gift that knows no measure. So give it freely or withhold it (from whomsoever you deem fit) without reckoning.
40. Behold! There is for him (- Solomon) Our close proximity and an excellent resort.

SECTION 4

41. **A**ND recall Our servant Job when he called to his Lord (saying), 'The devil (of the desert - thirst) has afflicted me with weariness and torment.'
42. (We directed him,) 'Urge (your riding beast) with your foot (and depart swiftly). There lies (yonder) a cool bathing place and a (refreshing) drink.'
43. (Not only that rather) We gave him his own family (and the followers he had before) and as many more with them (in the form of new adherents) by way of mercy from Ourselves (the lesson thus taught will serve) as a means to attain eminence for those gifted with pure and clear understanding.
44. And (We commanded him,) 'Take in your hand a handful of twigs and strike (the riding beast) therewith. And do not ever incline towards falsehood. Indeed, We found him steadfast. An excellent servant was he. He was always turning (towards God) in obedience.
45. Recall Our servants Abraham, Isaac and Jacob (all) endowed with power for action, and insight.
46. We had indeed chosen them for one special purpose; for reminding (people) of the abode (of the Hereafter).

رُخَآءً حَيْثُ أَصَابَ ﴿٣٦﴾ وَالشَّيٰطِينَ كُلَّ بَنَّآءٍ وَغَوَّاصٍ ﴿٣٧﴾ وَآخَرِينَ مُقَرَّنِينَ فِي الْأَصْفَادِ ﴿٣٨﴾ هٰذَا عَطَآؤُنَا فَامْنُنْ أَوْ أَمْسِكْ بِغَيْرِ حِسَابٍ ﴿٣٩﴾ وَإِنَّ لَهُ عِنْدَنَا لَزُلْفٰى وَحُسْنَ مَآبٍ ﴿٤٠﴾ وَاذْكُرْ عَبْدَنَآ أَيُّوبَ إِذْ نَادٰى رَبَّهُ أَنِّي مَسَّنِيَ الشَّيْطٰنُ بِنُصْبٍ وَعَذَابٍ ﴿٤١﴾ اُرْكُضْ بِرِجْلِكَ هٰذَا مُغْتَسَلٌ بَارِدٌ وَشَرَابٌ ﴿٤٢﴾ وَوَهَبْنَا لَهُ أَهْلَهُ وَمِثْلَهُمْ مَعَهُمْ رَحْمَةً مِنَّا وَذِكْرٰى لِأُولِي الْأَلْبَابِ ﴿٤٣﴾ وَخُذْ بِيَدِكَ ضِغْثًا فَاضْرِبْ بِهِ وَلَا تَحْنَثْ إِنَّا وَجَدْنٰهُ صَابِرًا نِعْمَ الْعَبْدُ إِنَّهُ أَوَّابٌ ﴿٤٤﴾ وَاذْكُرْ عِبٰدَنَآ إِبْرٰهِيمَ وَإِسْحٰقَ وَيَعْقُوبَ أُولِي الْأَيْدِي وَالْأَبْصَارِ ﴿٤٥﴾ إِنَّآ أَخْلَصْنٰهُمْ بِخَالِصَةٍ ذِكْرَى الدَّارِ ﴿٤٦﴾ وَإِنَّهُمْ

47. And of course they are in Our sight among the elect and the select.
48. And recall Ismâîl, Elisha and D̲h̲ul Kifl (- Ezekiel); they were all of (Our) chosen ones.
49. This (narrative) is the way to eminence. Behold! There awaits the righteous a beautiful and excellent resort;
50. Gardens of Eternity with their gates thrown open to receive them.
51. There they will be reclining (comfortably) on couches and there they will order (at pleasure) for many (sorts of) fruits and drinks.
52. And they will have by their sides chaste mates with downcast and restrained looks, and of suitable age (and matching in every aspect).
53. This is what you are promised for the Day of Reckoning.
54. Verily, this is Our provision which knows no end.
55. This is (the reward for the righteous only). As for the rebellious, surely evil is their end,
56. Gehenna, wherein they will enter. And (it shall be) an evil cradling (for nursing them to spiritual growth).
57. This is (what the disbelievers will have), so let them suffer from it a burning despair and intensely cold and stinking drink.
58. And other various (torments) of similar nature.
59. (It will be said to their leaders of mischief,) 'This is a whole army (of yours) which is rushing headlong with you (into Hell). There is no welcome for them. They are bound to enter the Fire.'
60. They (- their followers) will say (to their leaders), 'Nay, it is rather you (who deserve Hell)! There is no welcome for you (either). In truth it was you that brought about this (evil punishment) for us (by leading us astray), what an evil resting place it is!'
61. They will (then) say, 'Our Lord! Whoso brought about this (evil end) for us, increase for

عِنْدَنَا لَمِنَ الْمُصْطَفَيْنَ الْأَخْيَارِ ﴿٤٧﴾ وَاذْكُرْ إِسْمٰعِيلَ وَالْيَسَعَ وَذَا الْكِفْلِ ۖ وَكُلٌّ مِّنَ الْأَخْيَارِ ﴿٤٨﴾ هٰذَا ذِكْرٌ ۚ وَإِنَّ لِلْمُتَّقِينَ لَحُسْنَ مَاٰبٍ ﴿٤٩﴾ جَنّٰتِ عَدْنٍ مُّفَتَّحَةً لَّهُمُ الْأَبْوَابُ ﴿٥٠﴾ مُتَّكِـِٔينَ فِيهَا يَدْعُونَ فِيهَا بِفٰكِهَةٍ كَثِيرَةٍ وَّشَرَابٍ ﴿٥١﴾ وَعِنْدَهُمْ قٰصِرٰتُ الطَّرْفِ أَتْرَابٌ ﴿٥٢﴾ هٰذَا مَا تُوعَدُونَ لِيَوْمِ الْحِسَابِ ﴿٥٣﴾ إِنَّ هٰذَا لَرِزْقُنَا مَا لَهُۥ مِنْ نَّفَادٍ ﴿٥٤﴾ هٰذَا ۚ وَإِنَّ لِلطّٰغِينَ لَشَرَّ مَاٰبٍ ﴿٥٥﴾ جَهَنَّمَ ۚ يَصْلَوْنَهَا ۚ فَبِئْسَ الْمِهَادُ ﴿٥٦﴾ هٰذَا فَلْيَذُوقُوهُ حَمِيمٌ وَّغَسَّاقٌ ﴿٥٧﴾ وَّاٰخَرُ مِنْ شَكْلِهِۦٓ أَزْوٰجٌ ﴿٥٨﴾ هٰذَا فَوْجٌ مُّقْتَحِمٌ مَّعَكُمْ ۚ لَا مَرْحَبًۢا بِهِمْ ۚ إِنَّهُمْ صَالُوا النَّارِ ﴿٥٩﴾ قَالُوا بَلْ أَنْتُمْ ۖ لَا مَرْحَبًۢا بِكُمْ ۖ أَنْتُمْ قَدَّمْتُمُوهُ لَنَا ۖ فَبِئْسَ الْقَرَارُ ﴿٦٠﴾ قَالُوا رَبَّنَا

him more and more agony in the Fire.'
62. And these (inmates of Hell) will say, 'What is the matter with us that we do not see (here) the men whom we used to count among the wicked.
63. 'Is it because we (unjustly) held them in scorn or (is it) that (our) eyes have missed them?'
64. Behold! This is an invariable fact that the inmates of the Fire will be disputing together.

SECTION 5

65. **S**ay, 'I am only a Warner. There is no other, cannot be and will never be one worthy of worship but Allâh, the One, the Subduer of all.
66. 'The Lord of the heavens, and the earth and all that lies between the two, the All-Mighty, the Great Protector.'
67. Say, 'This (universal call of Islam) is a very important announcement.
68. 'Yet you are turning away from this.
69. 'I had no knowledge of the Exalted assembly (comprising of the angels in the upper zones) when they discussed (the matter) among themselves.
70. 'But all that has been revealed to me is that I am a Warner telling the right from the wrong.'
71. (Call to mind) when your Lord said to the angels, 'I am about to create a human being from clay,
72. 'And when I have fashioned him in perfection and I have inspired into him of My revelation then fall down submitting to him.'
73. So (when He inspired into him His revelation) the angels submitted one and all.
74. But *Iblîs* did not, he behaved arrogantly for he was of the disbelievers.
75. (God) said, 'O *Iblîs!* What prevented you from submitting to him whom I have created

مَنْ قَدَّمَ لَنَا هٰذَا فَزِدْهُ عَذَابًا ضِعْفًا
فِي النَّارِ ﴿٦١﴾ وَقَالُوا مَا لَنَا لَا نَرٰى رِجَالًا كُنَّا
نَعُدُّهُمْ مِنَ الْأَشْرَارِ ﴿٦٢﴾ أَتَّخَذْنٰهُمْ سِخْرِيًّا
أَمْ زَاغَتْ عَنْهُمُ الْأَبْصٰرُ ﴿٦٣﴾ إِنَّ ذٰلِكَ لَحَقٌّ
تَخَاصُمُ أَهْلِ النَّارِ ﴿٦٤﴾ قُلْ إِنَّمَا أَنَا مُنْذِرٌ
وَمَا مِنْ إِلٰهٍ إِلَّا اللّٰهُ الْوٰحِدُ الْقَهَّارُ ﴿٦٥﴾ رَبُّ
السَّمٰوٰتِ وَالْأَرْضِ وَمَا بَيْنَهُمَا الْعَزِيزُ الْغَفّٰرُ ﴿٦٦﴾
قُلْ هُوَ نَبَؤٌا عَظِيمٌ ﴿٦٧﴾ أَنْتُمْ عَنْهُ مُعْرِضُونَ ﴿٦٨﴾
مَا كَانَ لِيَ مِنْ عِلْمٍ بِالْمَلَإِ الْأَعْلٰى إِذْ
يَخْتَصِمُونَ ﴿٦٩﴾ إِنْ يُوحٰى إِلَيَّ إِلَّا أَنَّمَا أَنَا
نَذِيرٌ مُبِينٌ ﴿٧٠﴾ إِذْ قَالَ رَبُّكَ لِلْمَلٰئِكَةِ إِنِّي
خٰلِقٌ بَشَرًا مِنْ طِينٍ ﴿٧١﴾ فَإِذَا سَوَّيْتُهُ وَنَفَخْتُ
فِيهِ مِنْ رُوحِي فَقَعُوا لَهُ سٰجِدِينَ ﴿٧٢﴾ فَسَجَدَ
الْمَلٰئِكَةُ كُلُّهُمْ أَجْمَعُونَ ﴿٧٣﴾ إِلَّا إِبْلِيسَ
اسْتَكْبَرَ وَكَانَ مِنَ الْكٰفِرِينَ ﴿٧٤﴾ قَالَ يٰإِبْلِيسُ
مَا مَنَعَكَ أَنْ تَسْجُدَ لِمَا خَلَقْتُ بِيَدَيَّ

with My own special powers (bestowing him with the maximum attributes). Is it that you seek to be great or is it that you are (really) of the highly proud ones (above obeying My command)?'
76. (*Iblîs*) said, 'I am better than he. You created me from fire while him You created from clay.'
77. (God) said, 'Then get out of this (state); you are surely driven away (from My mercy).
78. 'And surely upon you shall be My disapproval till the Day of Judgment.'
79. (*Iblîs*) said, 'My Lord! Reprieve me till the day when the people are raised to life (spiritually whether here or in the Hereafter).'
80. (God) said, 'You are of course of the reprieved ones
81. 'Till the Day of which the time is known and fixed.'
82. (*Iblîs*) said, '(I swear) by Your might, I will surely seduce them all,
83. 'Except your servants from among them, the true and purified ones (who are out of my powers).'
84. (God) said, 'Truth has dawned and I speak the truth,
85. 'That I will fill Gehenna with the like of you and with all those from among them who follow you.'
86. Say (O Prophet!), 'I ask no reward from you for it (for preaching the Message of truth, and for warning the people,) nor am I of those who are given to affectation (and are impostors).
87. 'This (Qur'ân) is nothing but a means to rise to eminence for the peoples,
88. And you shall surely know (the truth of) the news thereof before long.'

أَسْتَكْبَرْتَ أَمْ كُنْتَ مِنَ الْعَالِينَ ﴿٧٥﴾ قَالَ أَنَا
خَيْرٌ مِّنْهُ خَلَقْتَنِي مِنْ نَّارٍ وَّ خَلَقْتَهُ مِنْ
طِينٍ ﴿٧٦﴾ قَالَ فَاخْرُجْ مِنْهَا فَإِنَّكَ رَجِيمٌ ﴿٧٧﴾
وَّإِنَّ عَلَيْكَ لَعْنَتِيَ إِلَىٰ يَوْمِ الدِّينِ ﴿٧٨﴾ قَالَ رَبِّ
فَأَنْظِرْنِيَ إِلَىٰ يَوْمِ يُبْعَثُونَ ﴿٧٩﴾ قَالَ فَإِنَّكَ مِنَ
الْمُنْظَرِينَ ﴿٨٠﴾ إِلَىٰ يَوْمِ الْوَقْتِ الْمَعْلُومِ ﴿٨١﴾ قَالَ
فَبِعِزَّتِكَ لَأُغْوِيَنَّهُمْ أَجْمَعِينَ ﴿٨٢﴾ إِلَّا عِبَادَكَ
مِنْهُمُ الْمُخْلَصِينَ ﴿٨٣﴾ قَالَ فَالْحَقُّ وَ الْحَقَّ
أَقُولُ ﴿٨٤﴾ لَأَمْلَأَنَّ جَهَنَّمَ مِنْكَ وَمِمَّنْ تَبِعَكَ
مِنْهُمْ أَجْمَعِينَ ﴿٨٥﴾ قُلْ مَا أَسْئَلُكُمْ عَلَيْهِ مِنْ أَجْرٍ
وَّمَا أَنَا مِنَ الْمُتَكَلِّفِينَ ﴿٨٦﴾ إِنْ هُوَ إِلَّا ذِكْرٌ
لِّلْعٰلَمِينَ ﴿٨٧﴾ وَلَتَعْلَمُنَّ نَبَأَهُ بَعْدَ حِينٍ ﴿٨٨﴾

CHAPTER
39

سُورَةُ الزُّمَرِ ٣٩

AL-ZUMAR
(The Multitudes)
(Revealed before Hijrah)

سُورَةُ الزُّمَرِ مَكِّيَّةٌ

With the name of Allâh,
the Most Gracious, the Ever Merciful
(I commence to read Sûrah Al-Zumar).

بِسْمِ اللّٰهِ الرَّحْمٰنِ الرَّحِيمِ

1. THE orderly arrangement and authentic compilation of this wonderfully perfect Book is from Allâh, the All-Mighty, the All-Wise.
2. Surely, it is We Who have revealed the Book to you with the established truth to suit the requirements of truth and wisdom. So worship Allâh, being truly sincere to Him in obedience.
3. Beware! Sincere and true obedience is due to Allâh alone. Those who choose others as a patron beside Him (say), 'We serve them only that they may bring us near to Allâh in station.' (It is absolutely wrong.) Allâh will judge the differences between these (believers and disbelievers). Indeed, Allâh does not guide him to success who is a liar, highly ungrateful.
4. If Allâh had intended to take to Himself a son He could have chosen from His creation the one He pleased (and would not have left it to you). Holy is He! He is Allâh, the One, the All-Dominant.
5. He created the heavens and the earth to suit the requirements of truth and wisdom. He causes the night to revolve upon the day and causes the day to revolve upon the night and He has pressed the sun and the moon into service; each pursues its course for an appointed term. Behold! He is the All-Mighty, the Great Protector.
6. He created you from a single soul, then from that (same stock that He created a human being) He created his spouse. And He has given you

تَنْزِيلُ الْكِتٰبِ مِنَ اللّٰهِ الْعَزِيزِ الْحَكِيمِ (١)
إِنَّآ أَنْزَلْنَآ إِلَيْكَ الْكِتٰبَ بِالْحَقِّ فَاعْبُدِ
اللّٰهَ مُخْلِصًا لَّهُ الدِّينَ (٢) أَلَا لِلّٰهِ الدِّينُ
الْخَالِصُ ۚ وَالَّذِينَ اتَّخَذُوا مِنْ دُونِهِ أَوْلِيَآءَ
مَا نَعْبُدُهُمْ إِلَّا لِيُقَرِّبُونَآ إِلَى اللّٰهِ زُلْفَىٰ ۖ
إِنَّ اللّٰهَ يَحْكُمُ بَيْنَهُمْ فِي مَا هُمْ فِيهِ يَخْتَلِفُونَ ۗ
إِنَّ اللّٰهَ لَا يَهْدِي مَنْ هُوَ كٰذِبٌ كَفَّارٌ (٣)
لَّوْ أَرَادَ اللّٰهُ أَنْ يَتَّخِذَ وَلَدًا لَّاصْطَفٰى مِمَّا
يَخْلُقُ مَا يَشَآءُ ۚ سُبْحٰنَهُ ۖ هُوَ اللّٰهُ الْوٰحِدُ
الْقَهَّارُ (٤) خَلَقَ السَّمٰوٰتِ وَالْأَرْضَ بِالْحَقِّ ۚ
يُكَوِّرُ الَّيْلَ عَلَى النَّهَارِ وَيُكَوِّرُ النَّهَارَ عَلَى
الَّيْلِ وَسَخَّرَ الشَّمْسَ وَالْقَمَرَ ۖ كُلٌّ يَجْرِي
لِأَجَلٍ مُّسَمًّى ۗ أَلَا هُوَ الْعَزِيزُ الْغَفّٰرُ (٥)
خَلَقَكُمْ مِّنْ نَّفْسٍ وّٰحِدَةٍ ثُمَّ جَعَلَ مِنْهَا
زَوْجَهَا وَأَنْزَلَ لَكُمْ مِّنَ الْأَنْعٰمِ ثَمٰنِيَةَ
أَزْوٰجٍ ۚ يَخْلُقُكُمْ فِي بُطُونِ أُمَّهٰتِكُمْ خَلْقًا

eight (varieties of) cattle in pairs. He creates you in the wombs of your mothers, a creation, stage by stage, (making you pass) through three periods of darkness. Such is Allâh your Lord. The sovereignty and power belongs to Him alone. There is no other, cannot be and will never be one worthy of worship but He. Where are you, then, being turned away?

7. If you show ingratitude, surely, Allâh is Independent of you (He does not require your thanks). Yet He does not approve of His people to be ungrateful. (Indeed it is for your own sake that) He approves of you being grateful. And no soul that bears a burden can bear the burden (of the sins) of another. Behold! To your Lord shall you all return so that He will inform you of all that you have been doing. He knows full well (even) the innermost secrets of the hearts.

8. And when an affliction befalls a person he prays to his Lord turning (penitently) to Him. But when He confers a favour upon him from Himself, he forgets (the affliction) for (the removal of) which he used to pray (to Him) and starts assigning peers with Allâh, with the result that he causes the people to go astray from His path (the path leading to One God). Say, 'Enjoy your ingratitude for a little while, you are sure to be of the inmates of the Fire.'

9. Can he who is obedient and prays (to Allâh) devoutly in the hours of the night, (now) falling prostrate, (now) standing upright (in Prayer) taking precaution against (the grave sequel of) the Hereafter and hopes for the mercy of His Lord, (be treated like him who is disobedient)? Say, 'Are those who know (their obligations) equal to those who know (them) not? Only those (endowed) with pure understanding do take heed.'

مِّنْۢ بَعْدِ خَلْقٍ فِيْ ظُلُمٰتٍ ثَلٰثٍ ذٰلِكُمُ اللّٰهُ
رَبُّكُمْ لَهُ الْمُلْكُ لَآ إِلٰهَ إِلَّا هُوَ فَأَنّٰى تُصْرَفُوْنَ ﴿٦﴾
إِنْ تَكْفُرُوْا فَإِنَّ اللّٰهَ غَنِيٌّ عَنْكُمْ وَلَا يَرْضٰى
لِعِبَادِهِ الْكُفْرَ وَإِنْ تَشْكُرُوْا يَرْضَهُ لَكُمْ
وَلَا تَزِرُ وَازِرَةٌ وِّزْرَ أُخْرٰى ثُمَّ إِلٰى رَبِّكُمْ
مَّرْجِعُكُمْ فَيُنَبِّئُكُمْ بِمَا كُنْتُمْ تَعْمَلُوْنَ إِنَّهُ عَلِيْمٌۢ
بِذَاتِ الصُّدُوْرِ ﴿٧﴾ وَإِذَا مَسَّ الْإِنْسٰنَ ضُرٌّ
دَعَا رَبَّهُ مُنِيْبًا إِلَيْهِ ثُمَّ إِذَا خَوَّلَهُ نِعْمَةً
مِّنْهُ نَسِيَ مَا كَانَ يَدْعُوْٓا إِلَيْهِ مِنْ قَبْلُ
وَجَعَلَ لِلّٰهِ أَنْدَادًا لِّيُضِلَّ عَنْ سَبِيْلِهِ قُلْ
تَمَتَّعْ بِكُفْرِكَ قَلِيْلًا إِنَّكَ مِنْ أَصْحٰبِ النَّارِ ﴿٨﴾
أَمَّنْ هُوَ قٰنِتٌ أٰنَآءَ الَّيْلِ سَاجِدًا وَّقَآئِمًا
يَّحْذَرُ الْأٰخِرَةَ وَيَرْجُوْا رَحْمَةَ رَبِّهِ قُلْ هَلْ
يَسْتَوِي الَّذِيْنَ يَعْلَمُوْنَ وَالَّذِيْنَ لَا يَعْلَمُوْنَ
إِنَّمَا يَتَذَكَّرُ أُولُوا الْأَلْبٰبِ ﴿٩﴾ قُلْ يٰعِبَادِ ع ١٥

SECTION 2

10. **S**AY, 'O My servants who believe! Take your Lord as a shield. There is a good reward for those who do good in (the life of) this

world. And (if you are persecuted for your faith know that) the earth of Allâh is vast and spacious (enough to provide you shelter). Certainly the patiently, persevering and steadfast will be given their reward beyond measure.'

11. Say, 'Verily, I have orders to worship Allâh, being truly sincere to Him alone in obedience.

12. 'And I have orders to be the foremost among those who surrender themselves (to His will).'

13. Say, 'If I disobey my Lord I have to fear the torment of a dreadful day.'

14. Say, 'It is Allâh I worship, being purely sincere to Him in my obedience.

15. 'Again, (as for you) you may go and worship whomsoever you please apart from Him.' Say, 'The true losers are those who ruin their own souls and their families on the Day of Resurrection.' Beware! Surely that is the manifest loss!

16. They shall have coverings of the fire over them and (sheets of similar) coverings below them (allowing them no escape). That is (the sort of punishment) against which Allâh warns His servants, 'My servants! (Do not invite My punishment, rather) take Me as (your) shield.'

17. But there await good tidings for those who restrain themselves from worshipping the transgressor (of the limit as defined by God) and turn to Allâh. So give glad tidings to My servants,

18. Who listen to the word (of advice) and follow the best (injunction productive of the best results) thereof. It is they whom Allâh has guided and it is they who are endowed with pure and clear understanding.

19. Can he then, against whom the verdict of punishment becomes due (and who therefore merits punishment, be saved?) Can you rescue him who is consigned to the Fire?

20. But for those who take their Lord as a

الَّذِينَ اٰمَنُوا اتَّقُوا رَبَّكُمْ ۭ لِلَّذِينَ أَحْسَنُوا
فِي هٰذِهِ الدُّنْيَا حَسَنَةٌ ۭ وَ أَرْضُ اللّٰهِ
وٰسِعَةٌ ۭ إِنَّمَا يُوَفَّى الصّٰبِرُونَ أَجْرَهُمْ
بِغَيْرِ حِسَابٍ ﴿١٠﴾ قُلْ إِنِّيٓ أُمِرْتُ أَنْ أَعْبُدَ
اللّٰهَ مُخْلِصًا لَّهُ الدِّينَ ﴿١١﴾ وَ أُمِرْتُ لِأَنْ
أَكُونَ أَوَّلَ الْمُسْلِمِينَ ﴿١٢﴾ قُلْ إِنِّيٓ أَخَافُ
إِنْ عَصَيْتُ رَبِّي عَذَابَ يَوْمٍ عَظِيمٍ ﴿١٣﴾
قُلِ اللّٰهَ أَعْبُدُ مُخْلِصًا لَّهُ دِينِي ﴿١٤﴾ فَاعْبُدُوا
مَا شِئْتُمْ مِّنْ دُونِهِ ۭ قُلْ إِنَّ الْخٰسِرِينَ
الَّذِينَ خَسِرُوٓا أَنْفُسَهُمْ وَ أَهْلِيهِمْ يَوْمَ
الْقِيٰمَةِ ۭ أَلَا ذٰلِكَ هُوَ الْخُسْرَانُ الْمُبِينُ ﴿١٥﴾
لَهُمْ مِّنْ فَوْقِهِمْ ظُلَلٌ مِّنَ النَّارِ وَ مِنْ
تَحْتِهِمْ ظُلَلٌ ۭ ذٰلِكَ يُخَوِّفُ اللّٰهُ بِهٖ عِبَادَهُ ۭ
يٰعِبَادِ فَاتَّقُونِ ﴿١٦﴾ وَ الَّذِينَ اجْتَنَبُوا الطّٰغُوتَ
أَنْ يَعْبُدُوهَا وَ أَنَابُوٓا إِلَى اللّٰهِ لَهُمُ الْبُشْرٰى ۚ
فَبَشِّرْ عِبَادِ ﴿١٧﴾ الَّذِينَ يَسْتَمِعُونَ الْقَوْلَ
فَيَتَّبِعُونَ أَحْسَنَهُ ۭ أُولٰٓئِكَ الَّذِينَ هَدٰىهُمُ
اللّٰهُ وَ أُولٰٓئِكَ هُمْ أُولُوا الْأَلْبٰبِ ﴿١٨﴾ أَفَمَنْ
حَقَّ عَلَيْهِ كَلِمَةُ الْعَذَابِ ۭ أَفَأَنْتَ تُنْقِذُ
مَنْ فِي النَّارِ ﴿١٩﴾ لٰكِنِ الَّذِينَ اتَّقَوْا

shield, there awaits them lofty mansions, storey upon storey with streams running beneath them. (This is) the promise of Allâh; (and) Allâh will never fail in (His) promise.

21. Have you not seen (the sight) that Allâh sends down water from the clouds and causes it to flow (in the form of) streamlets on the earth and then brings forth herbage of various kinds and of diverse hues with it, then it dries up (after ripening) so that you see it turn yellow; then He turns it into chaff. Behold! In this (similitude) is a reminder for people endowed with pure and clear understanding.

SECTION 3

22. **I**s he whose mind Allâh has opened for (the acceptance of) Islam, so that he follows the light from his Lord, (like one who gropes in the darkness of disbelief)? Woe to those whose hearts are hardened against the remembrance of Allâh. Such indeed are (steeped) in clear error.

23. Allâh has revealed the best Message (the fairest discourse), this wonderfully coherent Book (the verses of which are mutually supplementing and) repeated, (narrating both sides of the case in various ways to drive home the divine injunctions to human minds). It makes the (very) skins of those who stand in awe of their Lord creep and their hearts tremble (at its recital). Yet their hearts and skins soften towards the remembrance of Allâh. This is Allâh's guidance, He guides him thereby who wishes (to be guided). Yet none can guide him whom Allâh forsakes and adjudges to be astray.

24. Is he, then, who has only his own person to shield him from the evil punishment on the Day of Resurrection (like him who is secure). And it will be said to the unjust (on that Day), 'Suffer the punishment of what you used to commit deliberately.'

25. Their predecessors also cried lies (to their Messengers of God,) so that (Our) punishment

رَبَّهُمْ لَهُمْ غُرَفٌ مِّنْ فَوْقِهَا غُرَفٌ
مَّبْنِيَّةٌ تَجْرِي مِنْ تَحْتِهَا الْأَنْهٰرُ ۥ وَعْدَ
اللّٰهِ لَا يُخْلِفُ اللّٰهُ الْمِيعَادَ ﴿٢٠﴾ أَلَمْ تَرَ أَنَّ
اللّٰهَ أَنْزَلَ مِنَ السَّمَآءِ مَآءً فَسَلَكَهُ
يَنٰبِيعَ فِي الْأَرْضِ ثُمَّ يُخْرِجُ بِهِ زَرْعًا
مُّخْتَلِفًا أَلْوٰنُهُ ثُمَّ يَهِيجُ فَتَرٰىهُ مُصْفَرًّا
ثُمَّ يَجْعَلُهُ حُطٰمًا إِنَّ فِي ذٰلِكَ لَذِكْرٰى
لِأُولِي الْأَلْبٰبِ ﴿٢١﴾ أَفَمَنْ شَرَحَ اللّٰهُ صَدْرَهُ ع ٢ ١٦
لِلْإِسْلٰمِ فَهُوَ عَلٰى نُورٍ مِّنْ رَّبِّهِ فَوَيْلٌ
لِّلْقٰسِيَةِ قُلُوبُهُمْ مِّنْ ذِكْرِ اللّٰهِ أُولٰٓئِكَ
فِي ضَلٰلٍ مُّبِينٍ ﴿٢٢﴾ اللّٰهُ نَزَّلَ أَحْسَنَ
الْحَدِيثِ كِتٰبًا مُّتَشٰبِهًا مَّثَانِيَ تَقْشَعِرُّ
مِنْهُ جُلُودُ الَّذِينَ يَخْشَوْنَ رَبَّهُمْ ثُمَّ
تَلِينُ جُلُودُهُمْ وَقُلُوبُهُمْ إِلٰى ذِكْرِ اللّٰهِ
ذٰلِكَ هُدَى اللّٰهِ يَهْدِي بِهِ مَنْ يَشَآءُ
وَمَنْ يُضْلِلِ اللّٰهُ فَمَا لَهُ مِنْ هَادٍ ﴿٢٣﴾ أَفَمَنْ
يَتَّقِي بِوَجْهِهِ سُوٓءَ الْعَذَابِ يَوْمَ الْقِيٰمَةِ
وَقِيلَ لِلظّٰلِمِينَ ذُوقُوا مَا كُنْتُمْ تَكْسِبُونَ ﴿٢٤﴾
كَذَّبَ الَّذِينَ مِنْ قَبْلِهِمْ فَأَتٰهُمُ الْعَذَابُ

came upon them from quarters they little perceived.

26. So Allâh made them suffer humiliation in the present life, and the punishment (in store for them) in the Hereafter will be greater still, if they but realise (it).

27. And We have set forth for the people all sorts of excellent and useful proofs in this Qur'ân that they may take heed,

28. (We have revealed the) Qur'ân in Arabic, there is no deviation from rectitude (in it and is free from all flaws), that they may guard against sufferings.

29. Allâh describes the condition of a man belonging to several partners contending with one another; and (there is) another man devoted wholly to one person. Are the two alike in condition? (No how can they be?) All true and perfect praise belongs to Allâh. But most of them do not know (this truth).

30. (One day), you will surely die and so shall they (after a brief span of life).

31. Then, on the Day of Resurrection, you will all dispute one with another before your Lord.

مِنْ حَيْثُ لَا يَشْعُرُونَ ﴿٢٥﴾ فَأَذَاقَهُمُ اللَّهُ
الْخِزْيَ فِي الْحَيَوٰةِ الدُّنْيَا وَلَعَذَابُ الْآخِرَةِ
أَكْبَرُ لَوْ كَانُوا يَعْلَمُونَ ﴿٢٦﴾ وَلَقَدْ ضَرَبْنَا
لِلنَّاسِ فِي هَٰذَا الْقُرْآنِ مِنْ كُلِّ مَثَلٍ
لَعَلَّهُمْ يَتَذَكَّرُونَ ﴿٢٧﴾ قُرْآنًا عَرَبِيًّا غَيْرَ ذِي
عِوَجٍ لَعَلَّهُمْ يَتَّقُونَ ﴿٢٨﴾ ضَرَبَ اللَّهُ مَثَلًا
رَجُلًا فِيهِ شُرَكَاءُ مُتَشَاكِسُونَ وَرَجُلًا
سَلَمًا لِرَجُلٍ هَلْ يَسْتَوِيَانِ مَثَلًا
الْحَمْدُ لِلَّهِ بَلْ أَكْثَرُهُمْ لَا يَعْلَمُونَ ﴿٢٩﴾
إِنَّكَ مَيِّتٌ وَإِنَّهُمْ مَيِّتُونَ ﴿٣٠﴾ ثُمَّ إِنَّكُمْ
يَوْمَ الْقِيَامَةِ عِنْدَ رَبِّكُمْ تَخْتَصِمُونَ ﴿٣١﴾ ع ٣ ١٧

PART الجزء الرابع والعشرون XXIV

SECTION 4

32. **W**HO then is more unjust than the one who invents lies about Allâh and cries lies to the very truth when it comes to him? Is there not in Gehenna an abode for (such) disbelievers?

33. But he who brings the truth and testifies wholeheartedly to it (by accepting it as true) these it is who become secure against evil.

34. They will have all that they desire with their Lord. Such is the reward of those who do excellent deeds.

35. It is they who best deserve that Allâh should rid them of the worst (of evils) which they committed (before accepting Islam) and reward

فَمَنْ أَظْلَمُ مِمَّنْ كَذَبَ عَلَى اللَّهِ وَكَذَّبَ
بِالصِّدْقِ إِذْ جَاءَهُ أَلَيْسَ فِي جَهَنَّمَ مَثْوًى
لِلْكَافِرِينَ ﴿٣٢﴾ وَالَّذِي جَاءَ بِالصِّدْقِ وَصَدَّقَ
بِهِ أُولَٰئِكَ هُمُ الْمُتَّقُونَ ﴿٣٣﴾ لَهُمْ مَا يَشَاءُونَ
عِنْدَ رَبِّهِمْ ذَٰلِكَ جَزَاءُ الْمُحْسِنِينَ ﴿٣٤﴾ لِيُكَفِّرَ
اللَّهُ عَنْهُمْ أَسْوَأَ الَّذِي عَمِلُوا وَيَجْزِيَهُمْ

them according to the best and the noblest of their deeds.

36. Is not Allâh sufficient for His servant? And yet they would try to frighten you with those (false gods they worship) other than Him (they cannot succeed). None can guide the person to success whom Allâh forsakes and adjudges to be astray.

37. And none can mislead the person whom Allâh guides. Is not Allâh All-Mighty, the Lord of retribution?

38. If you ask them who created the heavens and the earth, they will certainly say, 'Allâh.' Say, 'Have you ever judged (the worth of) that you call upon apart from Allâh? If Allâh ever intended to do me some harm, will these (whom you worship) be able to avert His harm (from me)? Or can they withhold His mercy if He is pleased to treat me with mercy?' Say, 'Allâh is sufficient for me. (In Him do I put my trust.)' Those who have learnt to trust place their trust in Him alone.'

39. Say, 'O my people, do your worst, I shall go on doing (my best). You shall soon know,

40. 'Who receives a punishment that will disgrace him (in this life), and who suffers from a lasting torment (in the Hereafter)?'

41. Behold! We have revealed to you the perfect Book, it comprises the truth and wisdom. (It is) for the good of humankind. So he who follows (this) guidance will do so for the good of his own soul, and he who goes astray will do so to its own detriment (and so will himself suffer the loss). You are not responsible for them.

SECTION 5

42. **ALLÂH** takes away the souls (of human being) at the time of their death and (also) of those who are not (yet) dead during their sleep. He detains (the souls of) those against whom He passes the verdict of death and sends (back those of) others till a fixed period of time.

أجرهم بأحسن الذي كانوا يعملون ﴿٣٥﴾
أليس الله بكاف عبده ويخوفونك
بالذين من دونه ومن يضلل الله
فما له من هاد ﴿٣٦﴾ ومن يهد الله فما
له من مضل أليس الله بعزيز ذي
انتقام ﴿٣٧﴾ ولئن سألتهم من خلق السموت
والأرض ليقولن الله قل أفرءيتم
ما تدعون من دون الله إن أرادني الله
بضر هل هن كشفت ضره أو أرادني
برحمة هل هن ممسكت رحمته قل
حسبي الله عليه يتوكل المتوكلون ﴿٣٨﴾
قل يقوم اعملوا على مكانتكم إني عمل
فسوف تعلمون ﴿٣٩﴾ من يأتيه عذاب يخزيه
ويحل عليه عذاب مقيم ﴿٤٠﴾ إنا أنزلنا
عليك الكتب للناس بالحق فمن اهتدى
فلنفسه ومن ضل فإنما يضل عليها
وما أنت عليهم بوكيل ﴿٤١﴾ الله يتوفى
الأنفس حين موتها والتي لم تمت
في منامها فيمسك التي قضى عليها
الموت ويرسل الأخرى إلى أجل مسمى

ع

There are signs in this for a people who would reflect.

43. Have these (polytheists) chosen (certain other) intercessors apart from Allâh? Say, 'What! (will they intercede for you?) Though they have no authority at all and understand nothing.'

44. Say, 'All intercession belongs to Allâh entirely. To Him belongs the sovereignty of the heavens and the earth, then towards Him you shall (all) be brought back.'

45. When (the name of) Allâh alone is mentioned, the hearts of those who do not believe in the Hereafter shrink with aversion but when (the names of) those who are below His high station are mentioned, behold they are at once filled with joy.

46. Say, 'O Allâh! Originator of the heavens and the earth, Possessor of the knowledge of the unseen and the seen, You alone judge between Your servants concerning that wherein they differ.'

47. And had the wrongdoers owned all that the earth contains and as much in addition to it, they would certainly offer it on the Day of Resurrection to redeem themselves from the woeful punishment; yet there would appear to them from Allâh that which they had never even thought of.

48. And the evil (consequences) of the deeds they had deliberately done will become clear to them. And they will be caught by the very punishment they took no account of.

49. And when harm afflicts a human being he calls upon Us. But when We confer Our favour on him he says, 'I have been given this only on account of (my own) knowledge. It is not right, it is only a trial, yet most people do not know.

50. Their predecessors had said the same thing, yet all their acquisitions were of no avail to them,

51. And the evil (consequences) of their deeds did overtake them. As for the wrongdoers from

إِنَّ فِي ذٰلِكَ لَاٰيٰتٍ لِّقَوْمٍ يَّتَفَكَّرُوْنَ ﴿٤٢﴾ أَمِ
اتَّخَذُوْا مِنْ دُوْنِ اللّٰهِ شُفَعَآءَ ۚ قُلْ أَوَ لَوْ
كَانُوْا لَا يَمْلِكُوْنَ شَيْـًٔا وَّ لَا يَعْقِلُوْنَ ﴿٤٣﴾
قُلْ لِّلّٰهِ الشَّفَاعَةُ جَمِيْعًا ۚ لَهٗ مُلْكُ السَّمٰوٰتِ
وَ الْأَرْضِ ۚ ثُمَّ إِلَيْهِ تُرْجَعُوْنَ ﴿٤٤﴾ وَ إِذَا ذُكِرَ
اللّٰهُ وَحْدَهُ اشْمَأَزَّتْ قُلُوْبُ الَّذِيْنَ لَا
يُؤْمِنُوْنَ بِالْاٰخِرَةِ ۚ وَ إِذَا ذُكِرَ الَّذِيْنَ
مِنْ دُوْنِهٖٓ إِذَا هُمْ يَسْتَبْشِرُوْنَ ﴿٤٥﴾ قُلِ
اللّٰهُمَّ فَاطِرَ السَّمٰوٰتِ وَ الْأَرْضِ عٰلِمَ
الْغَيْبِ وَ الشَّهٰدَةِ أَنْتَ تَحْكُمُ بَيْنَ عِبَادِكَ
فِيْ مَا كَانُوْا فِيْهِ يَخْتَلِفُوْنَ ﴿٤٦﴾ وَ لَوْ أَنَّ لِلَّذِيْنَ
ظَلَمُوْا مَا فِي الْأَرْضِ جَمِيْعًا وَّ مِثْلَهٗ مَعَهٗ
لَافْتَدَوْا بِهٖ مِنْ سُوْٓءِ الْعَذَابِ يَوْمَ الْقِيٰمَةِ ۚ
وَ بَدَا لَهُمْ مِّنَ اللّٰهِ مَا لَمْ يَكُوْنُوْا
يَحْتَسِبُوْنَ ﴿٤٧﴾ وَ بَدَا لَهُمْ سَيِّاٰتُ مَا كَسَبُوْا
وَ حَاقَ بِهِمْ مَّا كَانُوْا بِهٖ يَسْتَهْزِءُوْنَ ﴿٤٨﴾
فَإِذَا مَسَّ الْإِنْسٰنَ ضُرٌّ دَعَانَا ۫ ثُمَّ إِذَا
خَوَّلْنٰهُ نِعْمَةً مِّنَّا ۙ قَالَ إِنَّمَآ أُوْتِيْتُهٗ عَلٰى
عِلْمٍ ۚ بَلْ هِيَ فِتْنَةٌ وَّ لٰكِنَّ أَكْثَرَهُمْ لَا
يَعْلَمُوْنَ ﴿٤٩﴾ قَدْ قَالَهَا الَّذِيْنَ مِنْ قَبْلِهِمْ
فَمَآ أَغْنٰى عَنْهُمْ مَّا كَانُوْا يَكْسِبُوْنَ ﴿٥٠﴾
فَأَصَابَهُمْ سَيِّاٰتُ مَا كَسَبُوْا ۚ وَ الَّذِيْنَ

among these (rejecters of the truth), the evil (consequences) of their deeds shall surely overtake them also. They will never be able to frustrate (God's plan).

52. Do they not know that Allâh multiplies the means of livelihood (for such of His people) as He will, and makes them scant (for such of them as He pleases.) Behold! There are signs in all this for the people who would believe.

SECTION 6

53. **S**AY, 'O My servants who have committed excesses against their own souls, do not despair of the mercy of Allâh. Surely, Allâh forgives all sins. Verily, He is the Great Protector, the Ever Merciful.'

54. And turn to your Lord (penitently), and submit yourselves to Him before the punishment befalls you; for (once it does) you shall not be helped.

55. And follow the best (teaching suiting your condition) that has been revealed to you from your Lord before you receive the punishment which will come upon you all of a sudden and take you unawares.

56. Lest (when it comes,) anyone (of you) should say, 'Woe to me for failing in my duty towards Allâh! For I made fun of (His revelations.)'

57. Or lest anyone (of you) should say, 'If Allâh had only guided me (by force) I would of course, have been of those who became secure against evil (by fully carrying out my duties).'

58. Or lest anyone of you should say when he sees the punishment, 'If I could only have the chance to return (to the world), I (too) would then be of those who do good.'

59. (God will say,) 'No! This cannot be. There did come to you My Messages but you cried them lies and you behaved arrogantly and were of the disbelievers.'

60. And on the Day of Resurrection you will find the faces of those who invented lies in the name of Allâh, overcast with gloom and sor-

ظَلَمُوا مِنْ هٰٓؤُلَآءِ سَيُصِيبُهُمْ سَيِّاٰتُ مَا
كَسَبُوا وَمَا هُمْ بِمُعْجِزِينَ ﴿٥١﴾ أَوَلَمْ يَعْلَمُوٓا
أَنَّ اللّٰهَ يَبْسُطُ الرِّزْقَ لِمَنْ يَّشَآءُ وَيَقْدِرُ
إِنَّ فِي ذٰلِكَ لَاٰيٰتٍ لِّقَوْمٍ يُّؤْمِنُونَ ﴿٥٢﴾ قُلْ
يٰعِبَادِيَ الَّذِينَ أَسْرَفُوا عَلٰٓى أَنْفُسِهِمْ لَا
تَقْنَطُوا مِنْ رَّحْمَةِ اللّٰهِ إِنَّ اللّٰهَ يَغْفِرُ
الذُّنُوبَ جَمِيعًا إِنَّهُ هُوَ الْغَفُورُ الرَّحِيمُ ﴿٥٣﴾
وَأَنِيبُوٓا إِلٰى رَبِّكُمْ وَأَسْلِمُوا لَهُ مِنْ قَبْلِ
أَنْ يَّأْتِيَكُمُ الْعَذَابُ ثُمَّ لَا تُنْصَرُونَ ﴿٥٤﴾
وَاتَّبِعُوٓا أَحْسَنَ مَآ أُنْزِلَ إِلَيْكُمْ مِّنْ
رَّبِّكُمْ مِّنْ قَبْلِ أَنْ يَّأْتِيَكُمُ الْعَذَابُ بَغْتَةً
وَّأَنْتُمْ لَا تَشْعُرُونَ ﴿٥٥﴾ أَنْ تَقُولَ نَفْسٌ
يّٰحَسْرَتٰى عَلٰى مَا فَرَّطْتُّ فِي جَنْبِ اللّٰهِ
وَإِنْ كُنْتُ لَمِنَ السّٰخِرِينَ ﴿٥٦﴾ أَوْ تَقُولَ لَوْ أَنَّ
اللّٰهَ هَدٰىنِي لَكُنْتُ مِنَ الْمُتَّقِينَ ﴿٥٧﴾ أَوْ
تَقُولَ حِينَ تَرَى الْعَذَابَ لَوْ أَنَّ لِي كَرَّةً
فَأَكُونَ مِنَ الْمُحْسِنِينَ ﴿٥٨﴾ بَلٰى قَدْ جَآءَتْكَ
اٰيٰتِي فَكَذَّبْتَ بِهَا وَاسْتَكْبَرْتَ وَكُنْتَ
مِنَ الْكٰفِرِينَ ﴿٥٩﴾ وَيَوْمَ الْقِيٰمَةِ تَرَى الَّذِينَ
كَذَبُوا عَلَى اللّٰهِ وُجُوهُهُمْ مُّسْوَدَّةٌ أَلَيْسَ

ع ١١ ٢

row. (It will be said to them,) 'Is there not a resort in Gehenna for such arrogant people?'

61. (On the contrary) Allâh will deliver and grant salvation to those who guarded against evil and will lead them to a place of security and success befitting their dignity. No evil shall touch them (there), nor shall they ever grieve.

62. Allâh is the Creator of all things and He is an Authority over every thing to control.

63. To Him belong all that encircle the heavens and the earth. Those who deny the Messages of Allâh these it is who are the very losers.

SECTION 7

64. **S**AY, 'Do you bid me to worship other (beings) than Allâh, O you ignorant ones!'

65. Mind! It has already been revealed to you and your predecessors, 'In case you associate partners (with Allâh in your worship) all your (such) works shall go in vain entirely, and you shall certainly be of the losers.

66. 'Rather you should worship Allâh alone and be of the thankful (to Him).'

67. They have not yet appreciated (the attributes of) Allâh with the importance and appreciation that He deserves. The earth altogether shall be in His grip of power on the Day of Resurrection, and the heavens shall be rolled up in His All-Powerful hand (and will so lie at His absolute disposal). Holy is He. (He is) far above and beyond the things these (polytheists) associate (with Him).

68. (That Day) there shall be a blast on the trumpet and all who are in the heavens and all who are on the earth will fall into a swoon except whom Allâh will like (to spare). Then there will be a blast another time and behold! These people shall stand up awaiting (judgment before their Lord).

69. And the earth shall radiate with the light of her Lord. And the record (of their deeds) will be produced (before them), and the Prophets and the (other) witnesses shall be brought

فِي جَهَنَّمَ مَثْوًى لِّلْمُتَكَبِّرِينَ ﴿٦٠﴾ وَيُنَجِّي اللّٰهُ
الَّذِينَ اتَّقَوْا بِمَفَازَتِهِمْ لَا يَمَسُّهُمُ السُّوٓءُ
وَلَا هُمْ يَحْزَنُونَ ﴿٦١﴾ اَللّٰهُ خَالِقُ كُلِّ شَيْءٍ
وَّهُوَ عَلٰى كُلِّ شَيْءٍ وَّكِيلٌ ﴿٦٢﴾ لَهٗ مَقَالِيدُ
السَّمٰوٰتِ وَالْاَرْضِ وَالَّذِينَ كَفَرُوا
بِاٰيٰتِ اللّٰهِ اُولٰٓئِكَ هُمُ الْخٰسِرُونَ ﴿٦٣﴾ قُلْ
اَفَغَيْرَ اللّٰهِ تَاْمُرُوٓنِّيٓ اَعْبُدُ اَيُّهَا الْجٰهِلُونَ ﴿٦٤﴾
وَلَقَدْ اُوْحِيَ اِلَيْكَ وَاِلَى الَّذِينَ مِنْ قَبْلِكَ
لَئِنْ اَشْرَكْتَ لَيَحْبَطَنَّ عَمَلُكَ وَلَتَكُونَنَّ
مِنَ الْخٰسِرِينَ ﴿٦٥﴾ بَلِ اللّٰهَ فَاعْبُدْ وَكُنْ
مِّنَ الشّٰكِرِينَ ﴿٦٦﴾ وَمَا قَدَرُوا اللّٰهَ حَقَّ قَدْرِهٖ
وَالْاَرْضُ جَمِيعًا قَبْضَتُهٗ يَوْمَ الْقِيٰمَةِ
وَالسَّمٰوٰتُ مَطْوِيّٰتٌ بِيَمِينِهٖ سُبْحٰنَهٗ وَتَعٰلٰى
عَمَّا يُشْرِكُونَ ﴿٦٧﴾ وَنُفِخَ فِي الصُّورِ فَصَعِقَ مَنْ
فِي السَّمٰوٰتِ وَمَنْ فِي الْاَرْضِ اِلَّا مَنْ شَآءَ
اللّٰهُ ثُمَّ نُفِخَ فِيهِ اُخْرٰى فَاِذَا هُمْ قِيَامٌ
يَّنْظُرُونَ ﴿٦٨﴾ وَاَشْرَقَتِ الْاَرْضُ بِنُورِ رَبِّهَا
وَوُضِعَ الْكِتٰبُ وَجِايْٓءَ بِالنَّبِيّٖنَ وَالشُّهَدَآءِ

forward; people shall be judged in all fairness and no injustice shall be done to anyone of them.

70. And every soul shall be repaid in full for its deeds; for He (the Almighty Lord) is well-aware of all that they do.

SECTION 8

71. **A**ND those who disbelieve will be driven to Gehenna in multitudes, until when they reach it, its gates will be opened and its keepers will say to them, 'Did there not come to you Messengers from among yourselves to proclaim to you the Messages of your Lord and to warn you about the meeting of this Day of yours?' They will say, 'They did come, yet Allâh's verdict of the punishment was justly due to have proved true against the disbelievers.'

72. It will be said (to them), 'Enter the gates of Gehenna, (you will be) abiding therein for long.' How evil is the abode of the arrogant people!

73. And those who took their Lord as a shield will be conducted to Paradise in multitudes until when they reach it and its gates are opened (to welcome them) and its keepers say to them, 'Peace be upon you! Be you happy and prosperous! Enter it, (you will be) abiding (therein) for ever and ever.'

74. They will say, 'All true and perfect praise belongs to Allâh alone Who has fulfilled His promise made to us; and has allowed us to inherit the land enabling us to dwell in Paradise wherever we please.' How excellent is the reward of the doers of (righteous) deeds!

75. And you will see the angels thronging around the Throne (of Power), glorifying their Lord with (His) praise. And judgment will be given between the people with justice, and it will be said, 'All type of true and perfect praise belongs to Allâh, the Lord of the worlds.'

وَقُضِيَ بَيْنَهُمْ بِالْحَقِّ وَهُمْ لَا يُظْلَمُونَ ﴿٦٩﴾
وَوُفِّيَتْ كُلُّ نَفْسٍ مَّا عَمِلَتْ وَهُوَ أَعْلَمُ
بِمَا يَفْعَلُونَ ﴿٧٠﴾ وَسِيقَ الَّذِينَ كَفَرُوا إِلَى
جَهَنَّمَ زُمَرًا حَتَّى إِذَا جَاءُوهَا فُتِحَتْ
أَبْوَابُهَا وَقَالَ لَهُمْ خَزَنَتُهَا أَلَمْ يَأْتِكُمْ
رُسُلٌ مِّنْكُمْ يَتْلُونَ عَلَيْكُمْ آيَاتِ رَبِّكُمْ
وَيُنْذِرُونَكُمْ لِقَاءَ يَوْمِكُمْ هَٰذَا قَالُوا بَلَىٰ
وَلَٰكِنْ حَقَّتْ كَلِمَةُ الْعَذَابِ عَلَى الْكَافِرِينَ ﴿٧١﴾
قِيلَ ادْخُلُوا أَبْوَابَ جَهَنَّمَ خَالِدِينَ فِيهَا
فَبِئْسَ مَثْوَى الْمُتَكَبِّرِينَ ﴿٧٢﴾ وَسِيقَ الَّذِينَ
اتَّقَوْا رَبَّهُمْ إِلَى الْجَنَّةِ زُمَرًا حَتَّىٰ إِذَا جَاءُوهَا
وَفُتِحَتْ أَبْوَابُهَا وَقَالَ لَهُمْ خَزَنَتُهَا سَلَامٌ
عَلَيْكُمْ طِبْتُمْ فَادْخُلُوهَا خَالِدِينَ ﴿٧٣﴾ وَقَالُوا
الْحَمْدُ لِلَّهِ الَّذِي صَدَقَنَا وَعْدَهُ وَأَوْرَثَنَا
الْأَرْضَ نَتَبَوَّأُ مِنَ الْجَنَّةِ حَيْثُ نَشَاءُ فَنِعْمَ
أَجْرُ الْعَامِلِينَ ﴿٧٤﴾ وَتَرَى الْمَلَائِكَةَ حَافِّينَ مِنْ
حَوْلِ الْعَرْشِ يُسَبِّحُونَ بِحَمْدِ رَبِّهِمْ وَقُضِيَ
بَيْنَهُمْ بِالْحَقِّ وَقِيلَ الْحَمْدُ لِلَّهِ رَبِّ الْعَالَمِينَ ﴿٧٥﴾

CHAPTER
40

سُورَةُ غَافِرٍ ٤٠

GHÂFIR

(Granter of Protection)
(Revealed before Hijrah)

With the name of Allâh,
the Most Gracious, the Ever Merciful
(I commence to read Sûrah Ghâfir).

1. HÂ MÎM - Allâh is Praiseworthy and Lord of Honour.
2. The gradual revelation of this perfect Book is from Allâh, the All-Mighty, the All-Knowing.
3. Granter of protection against all sins and Acceptor of repentance, Severe in respect of punishment and the Lord of beneficence. There is no other, cannot be and will never be One worthy of worship but He. Towards Him is the eventual return.
4. None disputes with regard to the commandments of Allâh except those who choose disbelief. Therefore do not let their moving about and control in the land create misgivings in you.
5. The people of Noah cried lies (to Our Messages) before these (disbelievers) and (so did) various other groups after them (- the people of Noah). And every community strove to seize their Messenger (of God) with a mind to destroy his mission. And they had begun arguing (with him) by means of false reasoning that they might thereby refute the truth. At this I seized them (with punishment). Behold! How (terrible) was My retribution (as a sequel to their evil deeds).
6. And it was in this way that the verdict of your Lord, that they shall be the inmates of the Fire, was confirmed against those who persisted in disbelief.
7. Those who bear the Throne (of Power, the

سُورَةُ غَافِرٍ مَكِّيَّةٌ

بِسْمِ اللّٰهِ الرَّحْمٰنِ الرَّحِيْمِ

حٰمٓ ﴿١﴾ تَنْزِيْلُ الْكِتٰبِ مِنَ اللّٰهِ الْعَزِيْزِ
الْعَلِيْمِ ﴿٢﴾ غَافِرِ الذَّنْبِ وَ قَابِلِ التَّوْبِ شَدِيْدِ
الْعِقَابِ ذِي الطَّوْلِ لَآ إِلٰهَ إِلَّا هُوَ إِلَيْهِ
الْمَصِيْرُ ﴿٣﴾ مَا يُجٰدِلُ فِيْٓ اٰيٰتِ اللّٰهِ إِلَّا الَّذِيْنَ
كَفَرُوْا فَلَا يَغْرُرْكَ تَقَلُّبُهُمْ فِي الْبِلٰدِ ﴿٤﴾
كَذَّبَتْ قَبْلَهُمْ قَوْمُ نُوْحٍ وَّ الْأَحْزَابُ مِنْ
بَعْدِهِمْ وَ هَمَّتْ كُلُّ أُمَّةٍ بِرَسُوْلِهِمْ
لِيَأْخُذُوْهُ وَ جٰدَلُوْا بِالْبٰطِلِ لِيُدْحِضُوْا بِهِ
الْحَقَّ فَأَخَذْتُهُمْ فَكَيْفَ كَانَ عِقَابِ ﴿٥﴾
وَ كَذٰلِكَ حَقَّتْ كَلِمَتُ رَبِّكَ عَلَى الَّذِيْنَ
كَفَرُوْٓا أَنَّهُمْ أَصْحٰبُ النَّارِ ﴿٦﴾ اَلَّذِيْنَ

angels and the Prophets) and those who are around it declare the glory of their Lord along with extolling (His name and) praises. They believe in Him and seek protection for those who believe (saying,) 'Our Lord, You embrace each and everything in Your mercy and knowledge, so grant protection to those who repent and follow the way shown by You and protect them from the torment of Hell.

8. 'Our Lord! Admit them together with such of their fathers, their spouses, and their children as are righteous and so worthy, to the Gardens of Eternity which You have promised them. You, indeed, are the All-Mighty, the All-Wise.

9. 'And save them from all types of evils. Indeed, You will have shown mercy to the person whom, on that Day, you save from evils. And that (to be saved) is indeed the great achievement.'

SECTION 2

10. **T**HOSE who disbelieve will be called and told (on the Day of Requital), 'Of course, Allâh's abhorrence (of you because of your persisting in disbelief) is greater than your own abhorrence of yourselves (this day). (Recall) when you were called to the faith but you refused (to come to it).'

11. They will say, 'Our Lord! Twice You have caused us to die (as the state without life before birth is a sort of death and the end of this life is the second) and twice You have given us life. We confess our sins (now). Is then, there, a way out (of the torment)?'

12. (They will be answered,) 'This is because when Allâh alone was called upon (as One worthy to be worshipped) you rejected, but when partners were associated with Him, you accepted. So (the fact is established beyond doubt that) this day sovereignty belongs only to Allâh, the Most Sublime, the Incomparably Great.

13. It is He Who shows you His signs and sends

سورة غافر ٤٠

يحملون العرش ومن حوله يسبحون
بحمد ربهم ويؤمنون به ويستغفرون
للذين ءامنوا ربنا وسعت كل شيء رحمة
وعلما فاغفر للذين تابوا واتبعوا سبيلك
وقهم عذاب الجحيم ⑦ ربنا وأدخلهم
جنت عدن التي وعدتهم ومن صلح
من ءابائهم وأزوجهم وذريتهم إنك
أنت العزيز الحكيم ⑧ وقهم السيئات
ومن تق السيئات يومئذ فقد رحمته
وذلك هو الفوز العظيم ⑨ إن الذين
كفروا ينادون لمقت الله أكبر من
مقتكم أنفسكم إذ تدعون إلى الإيمن
فتكفرون ⑩ قالوا ربنا أمتنا اثنتين
وأحييتنا اثنتين فاعترفنا بذنوبنا فهل
إلى خروج من سبيل ⑪ ذلكم بأنه إذا
دعي الله وحده كفرتم وإن يشرك به
تؤمنوا فالحكم لله العلي الكبير ⑫ هو
الذي يريكم ءايته وينزل لكم من

ع

الجزء الرابع والعشرون

down for you provision from above (for your physical and spiritual well-being), yet none heed (His revelations) except one who turns (to Him) again and again.

14. Therefore call upon Allâh being sincere to Him in obedience, though the disbelievers (and polytheists) may be averse (to it).

15. He it is Who exalts (the people) in ranks, Lord of the Throne (of Power); He sends His revelation by His own command to such of His servants as He will (and judges as deserving), that He may warn (humankind) of the Day of Meeting (with the Lord).

16. The day when they will (all) appear (in their true light) and nothing about them is ever hidden from Allâh. (On that Day they will be asked,) 'To whom belongs the sovereignty this day?' They will reply, '(It belongs) only to Allâh, the One, the All-Dominant.'

17. This day every soul shall be requited for deeds it has accomplished. No injustice (will be done) this day. Allâh's reckoning will be swift indeed.

18. And warn these people of the day drawing nigh, (day by day,) when the hearts will leap to their throats due to suppressed grief. The unjust will have no warm (hearted) friend, nor any intercessor who will be listened to (and could prevail for them on that day).

19. He knows the treachery of the eyes even (when they commit sinful acts secretly) and what the hearts conceal.

20. And Allâh judges in all fairness, but those (idols) whom they call upon apart from Allâh can judge nothing at all. It is Allâh Who is the All-Hearing, the All-Seeing.

SECTION 3

21. **H**AVE they never travelled in the land that they could see how (evil) was the end of their predecessors? They were mightier than these in power and in respect of leaving stronger marks (- monuments etc.) in the land. But Allâh took

سورة غافر ٤٠

السَّمَاءِ رِزْقًا ۚ وَمَا يَتَذَكَّرُ إِلَّا مَنْ يُنِيبُ ﴿١٣﴾
فَادْعُوا اللَّهَ مُخْلِصِينَ لَهُ الدِّينَ وَلَوْ
كَرِهَ الْكَافِرُونَ ﴿١٤﴾ رَفِيعُ الدَّرَجَاتِ ذُو الْعَرْشِ
يُلْقِي الرُّوحَ مِنْ أَمْرِهِ عَلَىٰ مَنْ يَشَاءُ مِنْ
عِبَادِهِ لِيُنْذِرَ يَوْمَ التَّلَاقِ ﴿١٥﴾ يَوْمَ هُمْ
بَارِزُونَ ۖ لَا يَخْفَىٰ عَلَى اللَّهِ مِنْهُمْ شَيْءٌ ۚ
لِمَنِ الْمُلْكُ الْيَوْمَ ۖ لِلَّهِ الْوَاحِدِ الْقَهَّارِ ﴿١٦﴾
الْيَوْمَ تُجْزَىٰ كُلُّ نَفْسٍ بِمَا كَسَبَتْ ۚ لَا
ظُلْمَ الْيَوْمَ ۚ إِنَّ اللَّهَ سَرِيعُ الْحِسَابِ ﴿١٧﴾
وَأَنْذِرْهُمْ يَوْمَ الْآزِفَةِ إِذِ الْقُلُوبُ لَدَى
الْحَنَاجِرِ كَاظِمِينَ ۚ مَا لِلظَّالِمِينَ مِنْ حَمِيمٍ
وَلَا شَفِيعٍ يُطَاعُ ﴿١٨﴾ يَعْلَمُ خَائِنَةَ الْأَعْيُنِ
وَمَا تُخْفِي الصُّدُورُ ﴿١٩﴾ وَاللَّهُ يَقْضِي بِالْحَقِّ ۖ
وَالَّذِينَ يَدْعُونَ مِنْ دُونِهِ لَا يَقْضُونَ
بِشَيْءٍ ۗ إِنَّ اللَّهَ هُوَ السَّمِيعُ الْبَصِيرُ ﴿٢٠﴾ أَوَلَمْ
يَسِيرُوا فِي الْأَرْضِ فَيَنْظُرُوا كَيْفَ كَانَ
عَاقِبَةُ الَّذِينَ كَانُوا مِنْ قَبْلِهِمْ ۚ كَانُوا هُمْ
أَشَدَّ مِنْهُمْ قُوَّةً وَآثَارًا فِي الْأَرْضِ فَأَخَذَهُمُ

الجزء الرابع والعشرون

them to task (and destroyed them) for their sins and they had no saviour from (the punishment of) Allâh.

22. That was because their Messengers (of God) came to them with evident proofs but they refused to believe (in them). So Allâh seized them (with destruction). Powerful is He and Stern His retribution.

23. And indeed We had already sent Moses with Our Messages and a clear authority,

24. Towards Pharaoh, Hâmân and Korah, yet they said, '(This man is) a sorcerer, a great liar.'

25. So when he brought them the truth from Us they said, 'Go on slaying the sons of those who have believed and joined with him, and go on sparing their womenfolk to make them immodest.' But futile are the schemes of the disbelievers (and ever bound to fail).

26. And Pharaoh said, 'Leave me alone; I will kill Moses. Let him call on his Lord. I fear lest he should change your faith or cause disorder to spread in the land.'

27. (On the other hand) Moses said, (to his people,) 'I seek refuge in (Him Who is) my Lord and your Lord from every arrogant (person) who does not believe in the Day of Reckoning.'

SECTION 4

28. **A**ND a man who was a believer and belonged to the people of Pharaoh (and) kept his faith hidden said, 'Are you bent upon killing a man simply because he says, "Allâh alone is my Lord," while he has already brought you clear proofs from your Lord? If he is a liar he will suffer (the sad consequences of) his lie, and if he is truthful then some of the things he threatens you with are sure to befall you. Indeed, Allâh does not guide (to success) the person who exceeds the bounds and is a great liar.

29. 'O my people! Yours is the sovereignty today and you dominate over the country. But

اللّٰهُ بِذُنُوبِهِمْ ۚ وَمَا كَانَ لَهُمْ مِّنَ اللّٰهِ
مِنْ وَّاقٍ ﴿٢١﴾ ذٰلِكَ بِأَنَّهُمْ كَانَتْ تَّأْتِيهِمْ
رُسُلُهُمْ بِالْبَيِّنٰتِ فَكَفَرُوا فَأَخَذَهُمُ اللّٰهُ ۚ
إِنَّهُ قَوِيٌّ شَدِيدُ الْعِقَابِ ﴿٢٢﴾ وَلَقَدْ أَرْسَلْنَا
مُوسٰى بِاٰيٰتِنَا وَسُلْطٰنٍ مُّبِينٍ ﴿٢٣﴾ إِلٰى فِرْعَوْنَ
وَهٰمٰنَ وَقٰرُونَ فَقَالُوا سٰحِرٌ كَذَّابٌ ﴿٢٤﴾
فَلَمَّا جَاءَهُمْ بِالْحَقِّ مِنْ عِنْدِنَا قَالُوا اقْتُلُوا
أَبْنَاءَ الَّذِينَ اٰمَنُوا مَعَهُ وَاسْتَحْيُوا نِسَاءَهُمْ ۚ
وَمَا كَيْدُ الْكٰفِرِينَ إِلَّا فِي ضَلٰلٍ ﴿٢٥﴾ وَقَالَ
فِرْعَوْنُ ذَرُونِي أَقْتُلْ مُوسٰى وَلْيَدْعُ رَبَّهُ ۚ
إِنِّي أَخَافُ أَنْ يُبَدِّلَ دِينَكُمْ أَوْ أَنْ يُظْهِرَ
فِي الْأَرْضِ الْفَسَادَ ﴿٢٦﴾ وَقَالَ مُوسٰى إِنِّي عُذْتُ
بِرَبِّي وَرَبِّكُمْ مِّنْ كُلِّ مُتَكَبِّرٍ لَّا يُؤْمِنُ
بِيَوْمِ الْحِسَابِ ﴿٢٧﴾ وَقَالَ رَجُلٌ مُّؤْمِنٌ ۖ مِّنْ
اٰلِ فِرْعَوْنَ يَكْتُمُ إِيمٰنَهُ أَتَقْتُلُونَ رَجُلًا
أَنْ يَقُولَ رَبِّيَ اللّٰهُ وَقَدْ جَاءَكُمْ بِالْبَيِّنٰتِ
مِنْ رَّبِّكُمْ ۚ وَإِنْ يَكُ كٰذِبًا فَعَلَيْهِ كَذِبُهُ ۚ
وَإِنْ يَكُ صَادِقًا يُصِبْكُمْ بَعْضُ الَّذِي
يَعِدُكُمْ ۚ إِنَّ اللّٰهَ لَا يَهْدِي مَنْ هُوَ مُسْرِفٌ
كَذَّابٌ ﴿٢٨﴾ يٰقَوْمِ لَكُمُ الْمُلْكُ الْيَوْمَ ظٰهِرِينَ

ع ٣ / ٨

who will help us and save us from the punishment of Allâh if it visits us?' Pharaoh said, 'I only point out to you that which I see and understand myself, and I guide you only to the path of rectitude.'

30. And he who had infect believed (in the faith brought by Moses) said, 'O my people! I fear lest you should encounter the like of the day (of disaster) which befell (other) parties of people (of the past);

31. '(And I fear lest you should meet) the like of fate which followed the ways of the people of Noah and 'Âd and (the people of) Thamûd and those who came after them. And Allâh does not want His servants to go wrong.

32. 'My people! I fear lest you should have to suffer on the day of calling one another (for help in frightful distress);

33. 'A day when you will retreat turning your backs. No defender shall you have against (the punishment of) Allâh. Yet none can guide him (to success) whom Allâh forsakes and adjudges to be astray.

34. 'And Joseph did come to you before (this) with clear proofs but you continued to be in doubt about that which he brought to you, till when he died, you said, "Allâh will never raise a Messenger after him". That is how Allâh forsakes and adjudges him as having gone astray who is a transgressor and doubter.

35. 'Those who dispute concerning the Messages of Allâh without any proof and authority having come to them (from Allâh to support them). This (attitude of theirs) is extremely abhorring to Allâh and to those who believe. That is how it is! Allâh sets a seal upon the heart of every arrogant (and) haughty person.'

36. And Pharaoh said, 'O Hâmân! Build for me a lofty tower that I may find access to the means -

37. 'The means (of access) to the heavens, so that I may have a look at the God of Moses.

فِي الْأَرْضِ فَمَنْ يَنْصُرُنَا مِنْ بَأْسِ اللَّهِ
إِنْ جَاءَنَا قَالَ فِرْعَوْنُ مَا أُرِيكُمْ إِلَّا
مَا أَرَى وَمَا أَهْدِيكُمْ إِلَّا سَبِيلَ الرَّشَادِ ﴿٢٩﴾
وَقَالَ الَّذِي آمَنَ يَقَوْمِ إِنِّي أَخَافُ عَلَيْكُمْ
مِثْلَ يَوْمِ الْأَحْزَابِ ﴿٣٠﴾ مِثْلَ دَأْبِ قَوْمِ نُوحٍ
وَعَادٍ وَثَمُودَ وَالَّذِينَ مِنْ بَعْدِهِمْ وَمَا
اللَّهُ يُرِيدُ ظُلْمًا لِلْعِبَادِ ﴿٣١﴾ وَيَقَوْمِ إِنِّي
أَخَافُ عَلَيْكُمْ يَوْمَ التَّنَادِ ﴿٣٢﴾ يَوْمَ تُوَلُّونَ
مُدْبِرِينَ مَا لَكُمْ مِنَ اللَّهِ مِنْ عَاصِمٍ
وَمَنْ يُضْلِلِ اللَّهُ فَمَا لَهُ مِنْ هَادٍ ﴿٣٣﴾ وَلَقَدْ
جَاءَكُمْ يُوسُفُ مِنْ قَبْلُ بِالْبَيِّنَتِ فَمَا
زِلْتُمْ فِي شَكٍّ مِمَّا جَاءَكُمْ بِهِ حَتَّى إِذَا
هَلَكَ قُلْتُمْ لَنْ يَبْعَثَ اللَّهُ مِنْ بَعْدِهِ رَسُولًا
كَذَٰلِكَ يُضِلُّ اللَّهُ مَنْ هُوَ مُسْرِفٌ مُرْتَابٌ ﴿٣٤﴾
الَّذِينَ يُجَدِلُونَ فِي آيَتِ اللَّهِ بِغَيْرِ سُلْطَنٍ
أَتَهُمْ كَبُرَ مَقْتًا عِنْدَ اللَّهِ وَعِنْدَ الَّذِينَ
آمَنُوا كَذَٰلِكَ يَطْبَعُ اللَّهُ عَلَى كُلِّ قَلْبِ
مُتَكَبِّرٍ جَبَّارٍ ﴿٣٥﴾ وَقَالَ فِرْعَوْنُ يَهَمَنُ ابْنِ
لِي صَرْحًا لَعَلِّي أَبْلُغُ الْأَسْبَبَ ﴿٣٦﴾ أَسْبَبَ
السَّمَوَتِ فَأَطَّلِعَ إِلَى إِلَهِ مُوسَى وَإِنِّي

Indeed, I consider him to be a liar.' And in this way his own evil conduct was made fairseeming to Pharaoh and so he was prevented from following the (right) path. Yet all the schemes of Pharaoh resulted only in ruin.

SECTION 5

38. **A**ND he who had believed (in Moses from the people of Pharaoh) said, 'O my people! Follow me and I will guide you in the way of rectitude.

39. 'O my people! The life of this world is but a provision (of a passing nature), and the Hereafter alone is the permanent home.

40. 'Those who do evil will be recompensed in proportion thereto (- to their evil deeds). But the men and women who believe and (at the same time) do righteous deeds, it is they who will enter Paradise where they will be provided for without measure.

41. 'O my people! How (strange) it is with me that I call you to salvation whereas you call me to the Fire.

42. 'You call me to renounce Allâh and to associate with Him that of which I have no knowledge (of being His associate at all), while I call you to the All-Mighty, the Great Protector.

43. 'No doubt that what you call me to, has no title to be called upon in this world nor in the Hereafter. There is no doubt that we shall all return to Allâh and that the transgressors will be the inmates of the Fire.

44. 'So you will soon remember what I say to you (by way of advice). I entrust my cause to Allâh. Indeed, Allâh keeps a keen watch over His servants.'

45. Thereupon Allâh saved him (- the believer) from the evil of their plans (against him) and the severest of punishment befell the people of Pharaoh.

46. (Their abode is) the Fire. They are pre-

لَأَظُنُّهُ كَٰذِبًا ۚ وَكَذَٰلِكَ زُيِّنَ لِفِرْعَوْنَ
سُوٓءُ عَمَلِهِۦ وَصُدَّ عَنِ ٱلسَّبِيلِ ۚ وَمَا
كَيْدُ فِرْعَوْنَ إِلَّا فِى تَبَابٍ ﴿٣٧﴾ وَقَالَ ٱلَّذِىٓ
ءَامَنَ يَٰقَوْمِ ٱتَّبِعُونِ أَهْدِكُمْ سَبِيلَ ٱلرَّشَادِ ﴿٣٨﴾
يَٰقَوْمِ إِنَّمَا هَٰذِهِ ٱلْحَيَوٰةُ ٱلدُّنْيَا مَتَٰعٌ
وَإِنَّ ٱلْءَاخِرَةَ هِىَ دَارُ ٱلْقَرَارِ ﴿٣٩﴾ مَنْ عَمِلَ
سَيِّئَةً فَلَا يُجْزَىٰٓ إِلَّا مِثْلَهَا ۖ وَمَنْ عَمِلَ
صَٰلِحًا مِّن ذَكَرٍ أَوْ أُنثَىٰ وَهُوَ مُؤْمِنٌ
فَأُو۟لَٰٓئِكَ يَدْخُلُونَ ٱلْجَنَّةَ يُرْزَقُونَ فِيهَا
بِغَيْرِ حِسَابٍ ﴿٤٠﴾ وَيَٰقَوْمِ مَا لِىٓ أَدْعُوكُمْ
إِلَى ٱلنَّجَوٰةِ وَتَدْعُونَنِىٓ إِلَى ٱلنَّارِ ﴿٤١﴾ تَدْعُونَنِى
لِأَكْفُرَ بِٱللَّهِ وَأُشْرِكَ بِهِۦ مَا لَيْسَ لِى
بِهِۦ عِلْمٌ وَأَنَا۠ أَدْعُوكُمْ إِلَى ٱلْعَزِيزِ ٱلْغَفَّٰرِ ﴿٤٢﴾
لَا جَرَمَ أَنَّمَا تَدْعُونَنِىٓ إِلَيْهِ لَيْسَ لَهُۥ
دَعْوَةٌ فِى ٱلدُّنْيَا وَلَا فِى ٱلْءَاخِرَةِ وَأَنَّ
مَرَدَّنَآ إِلَى ٱللَّهِ وَأَنَّ ٱلْمُسْرِفِينَ هُمْ
أَصْحَٰبُ ٱلنَّارِ ﴿٤٣﴾ فَسَتَذْكُرُونَ مَآ أَقُولُ
لَكُمْ ۚ وَأُفَوِّضُ أَمْرِىٓ إِلَى ٱللَّهِ ۚ إِنَّ ٱللَّهَ
بَصِيرٌۢ بِٱلْعِبَادِ ﴿٤٤﴾ فَوَقَىٰهُ ٱللَّهُ سَيِّـَٔاتِ مَا
مَكَرُوا۟ ۖ وَحَاقَ بِـَٔالِ فِرْعَوْنَ سُوٓءُ ٱلْعَذَابِ ﴿٤٥﴾
ٱلنَّارُ يُعْرَضُونَ عَلَيْهَا غُدُوًّا وَعَشِيًّا ۖ

sented to it morning and evening. And on the day when the (appointed) Hour comes to pass, (the angels will be commanded,) 'Put Pharaoh's people into the severest torment.'

47. And (think of the time) when these (disbelievers) will argue one with another in the Fire and the humble will say to those who sought to be great, 'Verily, we were your followers, will you not then relieve us of a portion (of the punishment) of the Fire.'

48. Those who sought to be great will say, 'Now we are all (adjudged to suffer) in it. Verily, Allâh has already passed (His) true judgment between (His) servants.'

49. And those in the Fire will say to the Keepers of Gehenna, 'Call to your Lord that He may relieve us of our agony for a while.'

50. These (Keepers) will say, 'Did not your Messengers (of God) come to you with clear signs?' They will answer, 'Yes indeed!' They (the Keepers of Gehenna) will say, 'Then call (yourselves and your false deities).' But the call of the disbelievers will be of no avail.

SECTION 6

51. **B**E assured that We do help Our Messengers and those who believe (in them) in the present life and (shall help them) on the day when witnesses will stand forth (to give evidence).

52. The day when their apologies will not avail the wrongdoers and they shall have the disapproval of Allâh, and the evil abode will be their lot.

53. And indeed We gave Moses (Our) guidance and made the Children of Israel inherit the Scripture.

54. (It was a source of) guidance and (served as) a reminder for the possessors of pure and clear understanding.

55. So patiently persevere. The promise of Allâh is true. Ask His protection for (those who committed) offence against you and declare the holiness of your Lord along with His praise at

ويوم تقوم الساعة أدخلوا آل فرعون
أشد العذاب ﴿٤٦﴾ وإذ يتحاجون في النار
فيقول الضعفؤا للذين استكبروا إنا كنا
لكم تبعا فهل أنتم مغنون عنا نصيبا
من النار ﴿٤٧﴾ قال الذين استكبروا إنا
كل فيها إن الله قد حكم بين العباد ﴿٤٨﴾
وقال الذين في النار لخزنة جهنم ادعوا
ربكم يخفف عنا يوما من العذاب ﴿٤٩﴾
قالوا أو لم تك تأتيكم رسلكم بالبينت
قالوا بلى قالوا فادعوا وما دعؤا الكفرين
إلا في ضلل ﴿٥٠﴾ إنا لننصر رسلنا والذين
امنوا في الحيوة الدنيا ويوم يقوم
الأشهد ﴿٥١﴾ يوم لا ينفع الظلمين معذرتهم
ولهم اللعنة ولهم سوء الدار ﴿٥٢﴾ ولقد
اتينا موسى الهدى وأورثنا بني إسراءيل
الكتب ﴿٥٣﴾ هدى وذكرى لأولي الألبب ﴿٥٤﴾
فاصبر إن وعد الله حق واستغفر
لذنبك وسبح بحمد ربك بالعشي

nightfall and in the early hours of the morning.
56. Those who dispute regarding the Messages of Allâh without any authoritative proof having come to them (from God in their support), there is nothing in their minds but (an ambition for) greatness to which (goal) they can never attain. So (do not bother about them rather) go on seeking refuge in Allâh (against their mischiefs). Surely, He alone is the All-Hearing, the All-Seeing.
57. Of course, the creation of the heavens and the earth is (a) greater (performance) than the creation of humankind but most people do not know (it).
58. The blind and the seeing are not alike, nor are those who believe and do deeds of righteousness (like) the evil doers; yet little is the heed you give.
59. (O disbelievers!) The Hour (of your destruction) is about to come. There is no doubt about it. Yet most people do not believe.
60. And your Lord says, 'Call on Me, I will answer your prayer. But those who wax too proud to worship Me will surely enter Gehenna, humbled and despised.'

وَالْإِبْكَٰرِ ﴿٥٥﴾ إِنَّ الَّذِينَ يُجَٰدِلُونَ فِي ءَايَٰتِ
اللَّهِ بِغَيْرِ سُلْطَٰنٍ أَتَٰهُمْ إِنْ فِي صُدُورِهِمْ
إِلَّا كِبْرٌ مَّا هُم بِبَٰلِغِيهِ فَاسْتَعِذْ بِاللَّهِ
إِنَّهُ هُوَ السَّمِيعُ الْبَصِيرُ ﴿٥٦﴾ لَخَلْقُ السَّمَٰوَٰتِ
وَالْأَرْضِ أَكْبَرُ مِنْ خَلْقِ النَّاسِ وَلَٰكِنَّ
أَكْثَرَ النَّاسِ لَا يَعْلَمُونَ ﴿٥٧﴾ وَمَا يَسْتَوِي
الْأَعْمَىٰ وَالْبَصِيرُ وَالَّذِينَ ءَامَنُوا وَعَمِلُوا
الصَّٰلِحَٰتِ وَلَا الْمُسِيٓءُ قَلِيلًا مَّا تَتَذَكَّرُونَ ﴿٥٨﴾
إِنَّ السَّاعَةَ لَأٓتِيَةٌ لَّا رَيْبَ فِيهَا وَلَٰكِنَّ أَكْثَرَ
النَّاسِ لَا يُؤْمِنُونَ ﴿٥٩﴾ وَقَالَ رَبُّكُمُ ادْعُونِي
أَسْتَجِبْ لَكُمْ إِنَّ الَّذِينَ يَسْتَكْبِرُونَ عَنْ
عِبَادَتِي سَيَدْخُلُونَ جَهَنَّمَ دَٰخِرِينَ ﴿٦٠﴾
اللَّهُ الَّذِي جَعَلَ لَكُمُ الَّيْلَ لِتَسْكُنُوا فِيهِ
وَالنَّهَارَ مُبْصِرًا إِنَّ اللَّهَ لَذُو فَضْلٍ عَلَى
النَّاسِ وَلَٰكِنَّ أَكْثَرَ النَّاسِ لَا يَشْكُرُونَ ﴿٦١﴾
ذَٰلِكُمُ اللَّهُ رَبُّكُمْ خَٰلِقُ كُلِّ شَيْءٍ لَّا إِلَٰهَ
إِلَّا هُوَ فَأَنَّىٰ تُؤْفَكُونَ ﴿٦٢﴾ كَذَٰلِكَ يُؤْفَكُ
الَّذِينَ كَانُوا بِـَٔايَٰتِ اللَّهِ يَجْحَدُونَ ﴿٦٣﴾ اللَّهُ
الَّذِي جَعَلَ لَكُمُ الْأَرْضَ قَرَارًا وَالسَّمَآءَ
بِنَآءً وَصَوَّرَكُمْ فَأَحْسَنَ صُوَرَكُمْ

SECTION 7

61. IT is Allâh who made for your benefit the night so that you may repose in it, and the day giving light (enabling you to see). Verily, Allâh is full of Grace to humankind, but most people do not give thanks.
62. Such (Gracious Being) is Allâh, your Lord, the Creator of everything. There is no other, cannot be and will never be One worthy of worship but He. Whither, then, are you being turned away?
63. Thus indeed were turned away those who persistently denied the Messages of Allâh.
64. It is Allâh Who made for you the earth a resting place, and the heaven a means of protection; and physically shaped you (endowing you with special faculties of reasoning and wisdom)

and perfected your shapes and faculties (making them excellent in every respect), and provided you with good and pure things. Such is Allâh, your Lord. So blessed be Allâh, Lord of the worlds.

65. He alone is the Ever Living and the Fountain head of all life. There is no other, cannot be and will never be One worthy of worship but He. So pray to Him; being sincere to Him in obedience (saying), 'All true and perfect praise belongs to Allâh, the Lord of the worlds.'

66. Say, 'I have, of course, been forbidden to worship those whom you call upon apart from Allâh; (how can I,) since there have come to me clear proofs (of their worthlessness) from my Lord. And I have been justly commanded to submit myself solely to the will of the Lord of the worlds.'

67. It is He Who created you from dust then from a sperm drop, then from a blood clot, then He brings you forth as an infant, (then He lets you live and grow,) with the result, that you attain to your young age of full strength. Afterwards it so happens that you become old. Though there are some of you who are called to death earlier. Indeed, He lets you live that you may reach (and complete your) appointed term and that you may refrain (from evil).

68. He it is Who gives life and causes death. And when He decides a thing to be, He says to it only, 'Be' and it comes to be (in due course).

SECTION 8

69. **H**AVE you not considered the case of those who dispute about the teachings of Allâh? How they are being turned away (from the right course).

70. Those who cried lies to the Book and to that (Message) with which We sent Our Messengers, shall soon come to know (the consequences of their denial);

71. When the shackles and the chains are (put) round their necks (and) they shall be dragged;

وَرَزَقَكُم مِّنَ الطَّيِّبَٰتِ ذَٰلِكُمُ اللَّهُ رَبُّكُمْ
فَتَبَارَكَ اللَّهُ رَبُّ الْعَٰلَمِينَ ﴿٦٤﴾ هُوَ الْحَيُّ
لَآ إِلَٰهَ إِلَّا هُوَ فَادْعُوهُ مُخْلِصِينَ لَهُ
الدِّينَ الْحَمْدُ لِلَّهِ رَبِّ الْعَٰلَمِينَ ﴿٦٥﴾ قُلْ
إِنِّي نُهِيتُ أَنْ أَعْبُدَ الَّذِينَ تَدْعُونَ
مِن دُونِ اللَّهِ لَمَّا جَآءَنِيَ الْبَيِّنَٰتُ مِن
رَّبِّي وَأُمِرْتُ أَنْ أُسْلِمَ لِرَبِّ الْعَٰلَمِينَ ﴿٦٦﴾
هُوَ الَّذِي خَلَقَكُم مِّن تُرَابٍ ثُمَّ مِن
نُّطْفَةٍ ثُمَّ مِنْ عَلَقَةٍ ثُمَّ يُخْرِجُكُمْ طِفْلًا
ثُمَّ لِتَبْلُغُوٓا أَشُدَّكُمْ ثُمَّ لِتَكُونُوا شُيُوخًا
وَمِنكُم مَّن يُتَوَفَّىٰ مِن قَبْلُ وَلِتَبْلُغُوٓا
أَجَلًا مُّسَمًّى وَلَعَلَّكُمْ تَعْقِلُونَ ﴿٦٧﴾ هُوَ الَّذِي
يُحْيِۦ وَيُمِيتُ فَإِذَا قَضَىٰٓ أَمْرًا فَإِنَّمَا يَقُولُ
لَهُ كُن فَيَكُونُ ﴿٦٨﴾ أَلَمْ تَرَ إِلَى الَّذِينَ
يُجَٰدِلُونَ فِيٓ ءَايَٰتِ اللَّهِ أَنَّىٰ يُصْرَفُونَ ﴿٦٩﴾
الَّذِينَ كَذَّبُوا بِالْكِتَٰبِ وَبِمَآ أَرْسَلْنَا بِهِۦ
رُسُلَنَا فَسَوْفَ يَعْلَمُونَ ﴿٧٠﴾ إِذِ الْأَغْلَٰلُ فِيٓ

72. Into boiling water, then they shall be burnt in the Fire.
73. It will be said to them then, 'Where are those (false deities) whom you associated (with Him),
74. '(And worshipped them) apart from Allâh?' They will say, 'They are lost to us. In fact, we never prayed to anything (beside Allâh) before this.' Thus does Allâh adjudge the disbelievers to be lost.
75. (It will be said to them,) 'That is because you exulted in the land without any justification and because you behaved with vanity.
76. '(Now) enter the gates of Gehenna to abide therein for long. So (you see) how evil will be the resort of the arrogant!'
77. Patiently persevere then. Verily, the promise of Allâh is bound to be fulfilled, whether We let you see (descend on them in your lifetime) a part of that punishment We have promised them, and whether We cause you to die before (you see it, it matters little), to Us they will be brought back.
78. And indeed We have already sent (Our) Messengers before you. There are some of them whom We have mentioned to you and of them there are some whom We have not mentioned to you. And it is not given to a Messenger to bring a Message by himself except by the leave of Allâh. But when the judgment of Allâh comes to pass the issues are settled in all fairness, and it is then that who endeavour to nullify the truth suffer the loss.

SECTION 9

79. **I**T is Allâh Who made for you the cattle so that you may ride on some of them and you obtain your food through some of them.
80. And indeed these (cattle) are of much use to you and through them you (satisfy other) desire which rests in your hearts. You are borne on them (by land) and on the ships (by sea).
81. And He is showing you His signs. Which of

أَعْنٰقِهِمْ وَ السَّلٰسِلُ يُسْحَبُوْنَ ﴿٧١﴾ فِي الْحَمِيْمِ
ثُمَّ فِي النَّارِ يُسْجَرُوْنَ ﴿٧٢﴾ ثُمَّ قِيْلَ لَهُمْ
أَيْنَ مَا كُنْتُمْ تُشْرِكُوْنَ ﴿٧٣﴾ مِنْ دُوْنِ اللّٰهِ
قَالُوْا ضَلُّوْا عَنَّا بَلْ لَّمْ نَكُنْ نَّدْعُوْا مِنْ
قَبْلُ شَيْـًٔا كَذٰلِكَ يُضِلُّ اللّٰهُ الْكٰفِرِيْنَ ﴿٧٤﴾
ذٰلِكُمْ بِمَا كُنْتُمْ تَفْرَحُوْنَ فِي الْأَرْضِ بِغَيْرِ
الْحَقِّ وَ بِمَا كُنْتُمْ تَمْرَحُوْنَ ﴿٧٥﴾ أُدْخُلُوْا أَبْوٰبَ
جَهَنَّمَ خٰلِدِيْنَ فِيْهَا فَبِئْسَ مَثْوَى
الْمُتَكَبِّرِيْنَ ﴿٧٦﴾ فَاصْبِرْ إِنَّ وَعْدَ اللّٰهِ حَقٌّ
فَإِمَّا نُرِيَنَّكَ بَعْضَ الَّذِيْ نَعِدُهُمْ أَوْ
نَتَوَفَّيَنَّكَ فَإِلَيْنَا يُرْجَعُوْنَ ﴿٧٧﴾ وَلَقَدْ أَرْسَلْنَا
رُسُلًا مِّنْ قَبْلِكَ مِنْهُمْ مَّنْ قَصَصْنَا
عَلَيْكَ وَ مِنْهُمْ مَّنْ لَّمْ نَقْصُصْ عَلَيْكَ
وَ مَا كَانَ لِرَسُوْلٍ أَنْ يَّأْتِيَ بِاٰيَةٍ إِلَّا بِإِذْنِ
اللّٰهِ فَإِذَا جَآءَ أَمْرُ اللّٰهِ قُضِيَ بِالْحَقِّ
وَ خَسِرَ هُنَالِكَ الْمُبْطِلُوْنَ ﴿٧٨﴾ اَللّٰهُ الَّذِيْ جَعَلَ
لَكُمُ الْأَنْعٰمَ لِتَرْكَبُوْا مِنْهَا وَ مِنْهَا تَأْكُلُوْنَ ﴿٧٩﴾
وَ لَكُمْ فِيْهَا مَنَافِعُ وَ لِتَبْلُغُوْا عَلَيْهَا حَاجَةً
فِيْ صُدُوْرِكُمْ وَ عَلَيْهَا وَ عَلَى الْفُلْكِ
تُحْمَلُوْنَ ﴿٨٠﴾ وَ يُرِيْكُمْ اٰيٰتِهٖ فَأَيَّ اٰيٰتِ اللّٰهِ

ع ١٣

the signs of Allâh will you then deny?
82. Have they never travelled in the land so that they could see how (miserable) the end of their predecessors was? They were superior to them in numbers, mightier in force and stronger in respect of the (firm) marks, (fortification and monumental buildings) in the land; yet all their acquisitions were of no avail to them.
83. And when their Messengers (of God) came to them with clear proofs they (vainly) boasted of their own partial knowledge. But they were caught by the very thing (- the calamity) which they used to treat very lightly.
84. So when they saw Our punishment they said, 'We believe in Allâh alone, and We reject (all) that we used to associate with Him.'
85. But their belief was of little use to them when they have (actually) seen Our calamity. Such is the law of Allâh that has ever been in vogue in respect of His servants. It is at such times that the disbelievers suffer a loss (and are reminded).

تُنكِرُونَ ﴿٨١﴾ أَفَلَمْ يَسِيرُوا فِي الْأَرْضِ فَيَنظُرُوا كَيْفَ كَانَ عَاقِبَةُ الَّذِينَ مِن قَبْلِهِمْ كَانُوا أَكْثَرَ مِنْهُمْ وَأَشَدَّ قُوَّةً وَآثَارًا فِي الْأَرْضِ فَمَا أَغْنَىٰ عَنْهُم مَّا كَانُوا يَكْسِبُونَ ﴿٨٢﴾ فَلَمَّا جَاءَتْهُمْ رُسُلُهُم بِالْبَيِّنَاتِ فَرِحُوا بِمَا عِندَهُم مِّنَ الْعِلْمِ وَحَاقَ بِهِم مَّا كَانُوا بِهِ يَسْتَهْزِئُونَ ﴿٨٣﴾ فَلَمَّا رَأَوْا بَأْسَنَا قَالُوا آمَنَّا بِاللَّهِ وَحْدَهُ وَكَفَرْنَا بِمَا كُنَّا بِهِ مُشْرِكِينَ ﴿٨٤﴾ فَلَمْ يَكُ يَنفَعُهُمْ إِيمَانُهُمْ لَمَّا رَأَوْا بَأْسَنَا سُنَّتَ اللَّهِ الَّتِي قَدْ خَلَتْ فِي عِبَادِهِ وَخَسِرَ هُنَالِكَ الْكَافِرُونَ ﴿٨٥﴾

CHAPTER
41

FUSSILAT
(Detailed and Clear in Exposition)
(Revealed before Hijrah)

سُورَةُ فُصِّلَتْ مَكِّيَّةٌ

With the name of Allâh,
the Most Gracious, the Ever Merciful
(I commence to read Sûrah Fussilat).

بِسْمِ اللَّهِ الرَّحْمَٰنِ الرَّحِيمِ

1. **H**Â MÎM - Allâh is Praiseworthy, Lord of Honour.
2. The compilation and orderly arrangement (of this Qur'ân) proceeds from the Most Gracious, the Ever Merciful (God).

حم ﴿١﴾ تَنزِيلٌ مِّنَ الرَّحْمَٰنِ الرَّحِيمِ ﴿٢﴾

3. (It is) a Book, the verses of which are detailed and clear in exposition. It is beautifully interlinked, (and it is in a language that) makes the meanings eloquently clear. It is very useful for a people who have knowledge.
4. It is a bearer of good tidings and a warner, yet most of these (people) turn away (from it) because they do not (even) give (it) ear.
5. And they say, 'Our hearts are (fortified) within a covering against that (Book) towards which you call us. We are deaf in the ear and there exists a barrier between us and you. So carry on your work (according to your creed) and surely we are the workers (in accordance with our own doctrines).'
6. Say, 'I am but a human being like yourselves (with the only difference that) it is revealed to me that your God is One God, so stick to the straight path (leading) to Him and ask for His protection.' And woe be to the polytheists;
7. Those who do not present the *Zakât* (- purifying dues) and who are disbelievers in the Hereafter also.
8. (On the contrary) those who believe and do deeds of righteousness, there awaits them a reward never to be cut off.

SECTION 2

9. **S**AY, 'Would you really disbelieve in Him Who created the earth in two aeons? And do you set up compeers with Him?' He alone is the Lord of the worlds.
10. He placed therein (- in the earth) firm mountains rising above (its surface) and showered it with His blessings and placed in it various provisions according to a set measure, (provisions to which) all those who require them have equal rights, (and all this He created) in four aeons.
11. Again, He directed Himself towards the space. Behold! It was (like) a mass of gas. (The Almighty God) said to it (- the space) and to the earth, 'Come both of you (in obedience to Me)

سورة فصلت ٤١

كِتٰبٌ فُصِّلَتْ اٰيٰتُهٗ قُرْاٰنًا عَرَبِيًّا لِّقَوْمٍ
يَّعْلَمُوْنَ ﴿٣﴾ بَشِيْرًا وَّ نَذِيْرًا فَاَعْرَضَ اَكْثَرُهُمْ
فَهُمْ لَا يَسْمَعُوْنَ ﴿٤﴾ وَ قَالُوْا قُلُوْبُنَا فِيْٓ اَكِنَّةٍ
مِّمَّا تَدْعُوْنَآ اِلَيْهِ وَ فِيْٓ اٰذَانِنَا وَقْرٌ وَّ مِنْۢ
بَيْنِنَا وَ بَيْنِكَ حِجَابٌ فَاعْمَلْ اِنَّنَا
عٰمِلُوْنَ ﴿٥﴾ قُلْ اِنَّمَآ اَنَا بَشَرٌ مِّثْلُكُمْ يُوْحٰٓى
اِلَيَّ اَنَّمَآ اِلٰهُكُمْ اِلٰهٌ وَّاحِدٌ فَاسْتَقِيْمُوْٓا
اِلَيْهِ وَ اسْتَغْفِرُوْهُ وَ وَيْلٌ لِّلْمُشْرِكِيْنَ ﴿٦﴾
الَّذِيْنَ لَا يُؤْتُوْنَ الزَّكٰوةَ وَ هُمْ بِالْاٰخِرَةِ
هُمْ كٰفِرُوْنَ ﴿٧﴾ اِنَّ الَّذِيْنَ اٰمَنُوْا وَ عَمِلُوا
الصّٰلِحٰتِ لَهُمْ اَجْرٌ غَيْرُ مَمْنُوْنٍ ﴿٨﴾ قُلْ
اَئِنَّكُمْ لَتَكْفُرُوْنَ بِالَّذِيْ خَلَقَ الْاَرْضَ
فِيْ يَوْمَيْنِ وَ تَجْعَلُوْنَ لَهٗٓ اَنْدَادًا ذٰلِكَ
رَبُّ الْعٰلَمِيْنَ ﴿٩﴾ وَ جَعَلَ فِيْهَا رَوَاسِيَ مِنْ
فَوْقِهَا وَ بٰرَكَ فِيْهَا وَ قَدَّرَ فِيْهَآ اَقْوَاتَهَا
فِيْٓ اَرْبَعَةِ اَيَّامٍ سَوَآءً لِّلسَّآئِلِيْنَ ﴿١٠﴾ ثُمَّ
اسْتَوٰٓى اِلَى السَّمَآءِ وَ هِيَ دُخَانٌ فَقَالَ

willingly or unwillingly.' They said, 'We obey you with all our will.'

12. So He ordained them seven heavens in two aeons and assigned to each (heaven) its (relevant) function. And We decked the nearest heaven with lamps (- shining stars for light) and made it to guard. Such is the decree of the All-Mighty, the All-Knowing.

13. But if even now they turn away then say, 'I have warned you of a scourge which will be like the scourge (that befell the people) of 'Âd and Thamûd.'

14. When the Messengers (of God) came to them (successively) from before them and from behind them (- from all directions with the teaching) 'Worship none but Allâh.' They said, 'If Allâh had willed (to send Messengers), He would certainly have sent angels. So we are indeed disbelievers in that (teaching) with which you have been sent.'

15. As for (the people of) 'Âd, they behaved arrogantly in the land without any justification and said, 'Who is mightier than we?' Do they not see that Allâh, Who had created them, is Mightier than they? And (not only that they behaved arrogantly) they went on denying Our Messages persistently.

16. So We sent upon them a furious wind for several (of their) ominous days in order to make them suffer a punishment of humiliation in this life, and the punishment which awaits them in the Hereafter will surely be more humiliating, and against which they will not be helped.

17. As for (the tribe of) Thamûd, We gave them guidance, but they preferred misguidance to guidance so the scourge of a humiliating punishment seized them on account of the (bad) deeds they had done.

18. Yet We delivered those who believed and guarded against evil.

لَهَا وَلِلْأَرْضِ ائْتِيَا طَوْعًا أَوْ كَرْهًا
قَالَتَا أَتَيْنَا طَائِعِينَ ﴿١١﴾ فَقَضَاهُنَّ سَبْعَ
سَمَاوَاتٍ فِي يَوْمَيْنِ وَأَوْحَىٰ فِي كُلِّ
سَمَاءٍ أَمْرَهَا ۚ وَزَيَّنَّا السَّمَاءَ الدُّنْيَا
بِمَصَابِيحَ وَحِفْظًا ۚ ذَٰلِكَ تَقْدِيرُ الْعَزِيزِ
الْعَلِيمِ ﴿١٢﴾ فَإِنْ أَعْرَضُوا فَقُلْ أَنذَرْتُكُمْ
صَاعِقَةً مِّثْلَ صَاعِقَةِ عَادٍ وَثَمُودَ ﴿١٣﴾ إِذْ
جَاءَتْهُمُ الرُّسُلُ مِن بَيْنِ أَيْدِيهِمْ
وَمِنْ خَلْفِهِمْ أَلَّا تَعْبُدُوا إِلَّا اللَّهَ ۖ قَالُوا
لَوْ شَاءَ رَبُّنَا لَأَنزَلَ مَلَائِكَةً فَإِنَّا بِمَا
أُرْسِلْتُم بِهِ كَافِرُونَ ﴿١٤﴾ فَأَمَّا عَادٌ فَاسْتَكْبَرُوا
فِي الْأَرْضِ بِغَيْرِ الْحَقِّ وَقَالُوا مَنْ أَشَدُّ
مِنَّا قُوَّةً ۖ أَوَلَمْ يَرَوْا أَنَّ اللَّهَ الَّذِي
خَلَقَهُمْ هُوَ أَشَدُّ مِنْهُمْ قُوَّةً ۖ وَكَانُوا بِآيَاتِنَا
يَجْحَدُونَ ﴿١٥﴾ فَأَرْسَلْنَا عَلَيْهِمْ رِيحًا صَرْصَرًا
فِي أَيَّامٍ نَّحِسَاتٍ لِّنُذِيقَهُمْ عَذَابَ الْخِزْيِ
فِي الْحَيَاةِ الدُّنْيَا ۖ وَلَعَذَابُ الْآخِرَةِ أَخْزَىٰ
وَهُمْ لَا يُنصَرُونَ ﴿١٦﴾ وَأَمَّا ثَمُودُ فَهَدَيْنَاهُمْ
فَاسْتَحَبُّوا الْعَمَىٰ عَلَى الْهُدَىٰ فَأَخَذَتْهُمْ
صَاعِقَةُ الْعَذَابِ الْهُونِ بِمَا كَانُوا
يَكْسِبُونَ ﴿١٧﴾ وَنَجَّيْنَا الَّذِينَ آمَنُوا وَكَانُوا

SECTION 3

19. **A**ND (beware of) the day when the enemies of Allâh will be resurrected (and) driven towards the Fire; while they will be formed into different groups.
20. Till, when they all reach it (- the Hell) their hearing and their eyes and their skins will be (testifying to and) bearing witness against them as to their (mis)deeds.
21. And they will say to their skins, 'Why did you bear witness against us?' They will reply, 'Allâh made us speak as He had given speech to everything else. And (disbelievers!) it is He Who created you the first time and to Him you have been brought back.
22. 'And (while committing sinful acts) you could not hide yourselves from the fact that neither your (own) hearing, nor your own eyes, nor your own skins should bear witness against you. As a matter of fact you had assumed that (even) Allâh did not know much of what you used to do,
23. 'And it was this (very wrong) belief of yours which you hold about your Lord that has ruined you, so that you have now become of the losers.'
24. Now, if (in this state of theirs) they show patience (even then) the Fire is their resort. And if they ask to be allowed to approach the threshold (of God's Throne) they will not be of those who are allowed to approach the threshold (to seek His forgiveness and mercy).
25. And We had assigned to them certain companions who made (the sinful acts) which were being committed in their presence, and those which had been done behind them (in their past), seem fair and attractive to them. The verdict (of punishment) stands confirmed against them as it did in the case of the sinful communities of *jinn* (- fiery and haughty natured) and (ordinary) people who had passed away before them. As a matter of fact they all were losers.

ع ٢ / ١٢
يَتَّقُونَ ﴿١٨﴾ وَيَوْمَ يُحْشَرُ أَعْدَاءُ اللهِ إِلَى
النَّارِ فَهُمْ يُوزَعُونَ ﴿١٩﴾ حَتَّى إِذَا مَا
جَاءُوهَا شَهِدَ عَلَيْهِمْ سَمْعُهُمْ وَأَبْصَارُهُمْ
وَجُلُودُهُمْ بِمَا كَانُوا يَعْمَلُونَ ﴿٢٠﴾
وَقَالُوا لِجُلُودِهِمْ لِمَ شَهِدْتُّمْ عَلَيْنَا
قَالُوا أَنْطَقَنَا اللهُ الَّذِي أَنْطَقَ كُلَّ
شَيْءٍ وَهُوَ خَلَقَكُمْ أَوَّلَ مَرَّةٍ وَإِلَيْهِ
تُرْجَعُونَ ﴿٢١﴾ وَمَا كُنْتُمْ تَسْتَتِرُونَ أَنْ
يَشْهَدَ عَلَيْكُمْ سَمْعُكُمْ وَلَا أَبْصَارُكُمْ
وَلَا جُلُودُكُمْ وَلَكِنْ ظَنَنْتُمْ أَنَّ اللهَ
لَا يَعْلَمُ كَثِيرًا مِّمَّا تَعْمَلُونَ ﴿٢٢﴾ وَذَلِكُمْ
ظَنُّكُمُ الَّذِي ظَنَنْتُمْ بِرَبِّكُمْ أَرْدَاكُمْ
فَأَصْبَحْتُمْ مِّنَ الْخَاسِرِينَ ﴿٢٣﴾ فَإِنْ يَصْبِرُوا
فَالنَّارُ مَثْوًى لَّهُمْ وَإِنْ يَسْتَعْتِبُوا فَمَا
هُمْ مِّنَ الْمُعْتَبِينَ ﴿٢٤﴾ وَقَيَّضْنَا لَهُمْ قُرَنَاءَ
فَزَيَّنُوا لَهُمْ مَّا بَيْنَ أَيْدِيهِمْ وَمَا خَلْفَهُمْ
وَحَقَّ عَلَيْهِمُ الْقَوْلُ فِي أُمَمٍ قَدْ خَلَتْ
مِنْ قَبْلِهِمْ مِّنَ الْجِنِّ وَالْإِنْسِ إِنَّهُمْ

SECTION 4

26. AND those who took to disbelief say, 'Do not listen to this Qur'ân, but (when it is recited) interrupt it by making noise so that you may gain the upper hand.'
27. We shall most surely make those who disbelieve meet with severe punishment and we shall certainly recompense them for the worst what they did.
28. Such is the punishment of the enemies of Allâh. It is the Fire. They shall find in it a long-lasting home. (The punishment is) a recompense of their persistently denying of Our Messages.
29. (There) the disbelievers will say, 'Our Lord! Show us those (two sets of people) who led us astray from among both the *jinn* (-haughty) and (ordinary) people that we may trample them under our feet with the result that they become of the most abased and humiliated ones.'
30. Verily, those who say, 'Allâh is our Lord,' and then remain steadfast (and follow the straight path), the angels will descend upon them (saying), 'Have no fear nor grieve rather rejoice at the glad tidings of receiving the Gardens (of Paradise) which you have been promised.
31. 'We are your Patron in the present life and in the Hereafter and you shall find in that (Paradise) all that you desire and you shall have therein all that you ask for,
32. 'By way of hospitality and reward from the Great Protector, Ever Merciful (God).'

SECTION 5

33. AND who speaks more fair than the person who calls people towards Allâh and (accordingly) does what is right and says, 'I am invariably of those who submit (before God).'
34. And good and evil are not alike. Repel (evil) with that (benign and graceful way) which is best, and lo, the person between whom and you there is enmity will behave as if he

سُورَةُ فُصِّلَتْ ٤١

كَانُوا خٰسِرِينَ ﴿٢٥﴾ وَقَالَ الَّذِينَ كَفَرُوا
لَا تَسْمَعُوا لِهٰذَا الْقُرْاٰنِ وَالْغَوْا فِيهِ
لَعَلَّكُمْ تَغْلِبُونَ ﴿٢٦﴾ فَلَنُذِيقَنَّ الَّذِينَ كَفَرُوا
عَذَابًا شَدِيدًا وَّلَنَجْزِيَنَّهُمْ أَسْوَأَ الَّذِي
كَانُوا يَعْمَلُونَ ﴿٢٧﴾ ذٰلِكَ جَزَآءُ أَعْدَآءِ اللهِ
النَّارُ لَهُمْ فِيهَا دَارُ الْخُلْدِ جَزَآءًۢ بِمَا
كَانُوا بِاٰيٰتِنَا يَجْحَدُونَ ﴿٢٨﴾ وَقَالَ الَّذِينَ
كَفَرُوا رَبَّنَآ أَرِنَا الَّذَيْنِ أَضَلّٰنَا مِنَ
الْجِنِّ وَالْإِنْسِ نَجْعَلْهُمَا تَحْتَ أَقْدَامِنَا
لِيَكُونَا مِنَ الْأَسْفَلِينَ ﴿٢٩﴾ إِنَّ الَّذِينَ قَالُوا
رَبُّنَا اللهُ ثُمَّ اسْتَقٰمُوا تَتَنَزَّلُ عَلَيْهِمُ
الْمَلٰٓئِكَةُ أَلَّا تَخَافُوا وَلَا تَحْزَنُوا وَأَبْشِرُوا
بِالْجَنَّةِ الَّتِي كُنْتُمْ تُوعَدُونَ ﴿٣٠﴾ نَحْنُ
أَوْلِيَآؤُكُمْ فِي الْحَيٰوةِ الدُّنْيَا وَفِي الْاٰخِرَةِ
وَلَكُمْ فِيهَا مَا تَشْتَهِيٓ أَنْفُسُكُمْ وَلَكُمْ
فِيهَا مَا تَدَّعُونَ ﴿٣١﴾ نُزُلًا مِّنْ غَفُورٍ رَّحِيمٍ ﴿٣٢﴾
وَمَنْ أَحْسَنُ قَوْلًا مِّمَّنْ دَعَآ إِلَى اللهِ
وَعَمِلَ صٰلِحًا وَّقَالَ إِنَّنِي مِنَ الْمُسْلِمِينَ ﴿٣٣﴾
وَلَا تَسْتَوِي الْحَسَنَةُ وَلَا السَّيِّئَةُ
اِدْفَعْ بِالَّتِي هِيَ أَحْسَنُ فَإِذَا الَّذِي بَيْنَكَ

were your warmhearted friend.
35. Yet it is only the steadfast and patiently persevering who are allowed this (grace) and it is only those who possess a large share of good who are allowed this (moral standard).
36. Should some sort of trouble from satan vex you, seek refuge in Allâh. For surely He, only He is the All-Hearing, All-Knowing.
37. And the night and the day, and the sun and the moon are some of His signs. Pay no homage to the sun or the moon, rather pay homage to Allâh Who created them, if it is Him Whom you really worship.
38. If they wax too proud (to prostrate before Him let them know that) those who are the near ones of your Lord glorify Him night and day and they never grow weary (of it).

(PROSTRATION)

39. And it is (one) of His signs that the earth that looks to you desolate stirs up (with life) and swells (producing herbage) when We shower rainwater on it. Verily, He (the Almighty Lord) Who gives it life will surely raise the dead to life (as well). Verily, He is the Possessor of power over every desired thing.
40. Surely, those who follow crooked ways regarding Our teachings, are not hidden from Us. (You can judge for yourselves) whether he who is cast into the Fire better or he who comes on the Day of Resurrection in peaceful security. (Now after this clarification you are free to) do what you will but (remember) He keeps a keen watch over all that you do.
41. Those who disbelieve in the Reminder (- the Qur'ân) when it comes to them, while it is truly an invincible Book (they will meet the fate of the lost ones).
42. Falsehood cannot approach it (- the Qur'ân) neither from the front nor from behind. (It is) a revelation that proceeds portion by portion from One All-Wise, the Most Praiseworthy (God).
43. Nothing is said (in the form of objection) to

وَبَيْنَهُ عَدَاوَةٌ كَأَنَّهُ وَلِيٌّ حَمِيمٌ ﴿٣٤﴾
وَمَا يُلَقَّاهَا إِلَّا الَّذِينَ صَبَرُوا وَمَا
يُلَقَّاهَا إِلَّا ذُو حَظٍّ عَظِيمٍ ﴿٣٥﴾ وَإِمَّا
يَنْزَغَنَّكَ مِنَ الشَّيْطَانِ نَزْغٌ فَاسْتَعِذْ
بِاللَّهِ إِنَّهُ هُوَ السَّمِيعُ الْعَلِيمُ ﴿٣٦﴾ وَمِنْ
آيَاتِهِ اللَّيْلُ وَالنَّهَارُ وَالشَّمْسُ
وَالْقَمَرُ لَا تَسْجُدُوا لِلشَّمْسِ وَلَا لِلْقَمَرِ
وَاسْجُدُوا لِلَّهِ الَّذِي خَلَقَهُنَّ إِنْ
كُنْتُمْ إِيَّاهُ تَعْبُدُونَ ﴿٣٧﴾ فَإِنِ اسْتَكْبَرُوا
فَالَّذِينَ عِنْدَ رَبِّكَ يُسَبِّحُونَ لَهُ بِاللَّيْلِ
وَالنَّهَارِ وَهُمْ لَا يَسْأَمُونَ ﴿٣٨﴾ وَمِنْ
آيَاتِهِ أَنَّكَ تَرَى الْأَرْضَ خَاشِعَةً فَإِذَا
أَنْزَلْنَا عَلَيْهَا الْمَاءَ اهْتَزَّتْ وَرَبَتْ إِنَّ
الَّذِي أَحْيَاهَا لَمُحْيِي الْمَوْتَىٰ إِنَّهُ عَلَىٰ
كُلِّ شَيْءٍ قَدِيرٌ ﴿٣٩﴾ إِنَّ الَّذِينَ يُلْحِدُونَ
فِي آيَاتِنَا لَا يَخْفَوْنَ عَلَيْنَا أَفَمَنْ يُلْقَىٰ
فِي النَّارِ خَيْرٌ أَمْ مَنْ يَأْتِي آمِنًا يَوْمَ
الْقِيَامَةِ اعْمَلُوا مَا شِئْتُمْ إِنَّهُ بِمَا
تَعْمَلُونَ بَصِيرٌ ﴿٤٠﴾ إِنَّ الَّذِينَ كَفَرُوا
بِالذِّكْرِ لَمَّا جَاءَهُمْ وَإِنَّهُ لَكِتَابٌ
عَزِيزٌ ﴿٤١﴾ لَا يَأْتِيهِ الْبَاطِلُ مِنْ بَيْنِ
يَدَيْهِ وَلَا مِنْ خَلْفِهِ تَنْزِيلٌ مِنْ
حَكِيمٍ حَمِيدٍ ﴿٤٢﴾ مَا يُقَالُ لَكَ إِلَّا مَا

you what was not already said to the Messengers before you. Verily, your Lord is Master of Protection (for the believers) and (also) Master of woeful retribution (for the disbelievers).

44. Had We made it a Qur'ân in indistinct and inexpressive language, these (faultfinders) would have surely said, 'Why has not (the subject matter of) its verses been made clear in exposition?' What! Can indistinct and inexpressive language and an eloquently clear language (be one and the same thing). Say, 'It is a wonderful guidance and healing to those who believe.' But (as to those) who do not believe there is deafness in their ears and this (Qur'ân) is obscure to them (with regard to its factual truth). And they are (as if to say) being called to from a place afar.

SECTION 6

45. **A**ND indeed We gave Moses the Scripture but (when the followers of the Scripture began tampering with it) differences arose about it. Had it not been a word (of promise) already made by your Lord the judgment (between them the disbelievers) would have been passed long ago (by the destruction of those who dispute about the prophecy). And they are in disquieting and grave doubt concerning this (-the fulfillment of the prophecy).

46. He that does right, does it for the good of his own soul, and he that does evil, it shall recoil on him. And your Lord is the least unjust to (His) servants.

سُوْرَةُ فُصِّلَتْ ٤١

قَدْ قِيلَ لِلرُّسُلِ مِنْ قَبْلِكَ إِنَّ رَبَّكَ
لَذُو مَغْفِرَةٍ وَّ ذُو عِقَابٍ أَلِيمٍ ﴿٤٣﴾
وَلَوْ جَعَلْنٰهُ قُرْءَانًا أَعْجَمِيًّا لَّقَالُوا لَوْلَا
فُصِّلَتْ ءَايٰتُهُ ءَأَعْجَمِيٌّ وَّعَرَبِيٌّ قُلْ هُوَ
لِلَّذِينَ ءَامَنُوا هُدًى وَّ شِفَآءٌ وَالَّذِينَ
لَا يُؤْمِنُونَ فِيٓ ءَاذَانِهِمْ وَقْرٌ وَّ هُوَ
عَلَيْهِمْ عَمًى أُولٰٓئِكَ يُنَادَوْنَ مِنْ
مَّكَانٍ بَعِيدٍ ﴿٤٤﴾ وَلَقَدْ ءَاتَيْنَا مُوسَى
الْكِتٰبَ فَاخْتُلِفَ فِيهِ وَلَوْلَا كَلِمَةٌ
سَبَقَتْ مِنْ رَّبِّكَ لَقُضِيَ بَيْنَهُمْ
وَإِنَّهُمْ لَفِي شَكٍّ مِّنْهُ مُرِيبٍ ﴿٤٥﴾ مَنْ
عَمِلَ صٰلِحًا فَلِنَفْسِهِۦ وَمَنْ أَسَآءَ
فَعَلَيْهَا وَمَا رَبُّكَ بِظَلّٰمٍ لِّلْعَبِيدِ ﴿٤٦﴾

ع ١٢ ١٩

PART الْجُزْءُ الْخَامِسُ وَالْعِشْرُونَ XXV

47. **H**E alone is accredited to have knowledge of the (promised) Hour. And no fruit come forth from their sheaths, nor does any female conceive nor does she give birth (to a being), but (everything takes place) according to His knowledge. The day when He will call out to

إِلَيْهِ يُرَدُّ عِلْمُ السَّاعَةِ وَمَا تَخْرُجُ مِنْ
ثَمَرٰتٍ مِّنْ أَكْمَامِهَا وَمَا تَحْمِلُ مِنْ أُنْثَى
وَلَا تَضَعُ إِلَّا بِعِلْمِهِۦ وَيَوْمَ يُنَادِيهِمْ أَيْنَ

الْجُزْءُ الْخَامِسُ وَالْعِشْرُونَ

them (the polytheists, saying), 'Where are My partners (you associated with Me)?' They will say, 'We declare before You, none of us is a confessor (now that they are Your partners).'

48. (Not only that) those (false gods) whom they called upon (in their worship) before that, will be lost to them, they will know for certain that they have no place of escape.

49. A person does not grow weary of praying for good but if evil befalls him, he becomes despondent, despaired of all hope.

50. Yet if We show him mercy from Ourselves after he has suffered affliction, he will surely say, 'This is my due. I do not believe that the (promised) Hour will (ever) come (to be established). And if I am (at all) brought back to my Lord, I shall of course, have with Him the very best (of all the goodly things). Yet (on the Day of Requital) We will surely tell those who disbelieve plainly all that they did, and accordingly We will make them suffer a terrible punishment.

51. And when We bestow a favour on a person he turns aside (ungratefully) and behaves with pride. But when evil befalls him, he is full of lengthy supplications and prayers.

52. Say, 'Have you ever considered that if it (- the Qur'ân) be from Allâh and yet you disbelieve in it, who is steeped in greater error than the one who has gone far in opposition (to Him and His Qur'ân)?'

53. We shall soon show these (disbelievers for their guidance) Our signs even in the remotest regions (of the earth) and in their own persons until it becomes quite manifest to them that this (Qur'ân) is the lasting truth in fact. Is it not enough (for them) that your Lord indeed keeps watch over everything?

54. Look! They are in disquieting and grave doubt about the meeting with their Lord. Beware! He certainly encompasses every thing (in His Knowledge and power).

سُورَةُ فُصِّلَتْ ٤١

شُرَكَآءِي قَالُوٓا ءَاذَنّٰكَ مَا مِنَّا مِنْ شَهِيدٍ ﴿٤٧﴾
وَضَلَّ عَنْهُم مَّا كَانُوا يَدْعُونَ مِنْ قَبْلُ
وَظَنُّوا مَا لَهُم مِّن مَّحِيصٍ ﴿٤٨﴾ لَا يَسْـَٔمُ الْإِنْسٰنُ
مِنْ دُعَآءِ الْخَيْرِ وَإِن مَّسَّهُ الشَّرُّ فَيَـُٔوسٌ
قَنُوطٌ ﴿٤٩﴾ وَلَئِنْ أَذَقْنٰهُ رَحْمَةً مِّنَّا مِنْ بَعْدِ
ضَرَّآءَ مَسَّتْهُ لَيَقُولَنَّ هٰذَا لِي وَمَآ أَظُنُّ
السَّاعَةَ قَآئِمَةً وَلَئِن رُّجِعْتُ إِلٰى رَبِّيٓ إِنَّ
لِي عِنْدَهُ لَلْحُسْنٰى فَلَنُنَبِّئَنَّ الَّذِينَ كَفَرُوا
بِمَا عَمِلُوا وَلَنُذِيقَنَّهُم مِّنْ عَذَابٍ غَلِيظٍ ﴿٥٠﴾
وَإِذَآ أَنْعَمْنَا عَلَى الْإِنْسٰنِ أَعْرَضَ وَنَا بِجَانِبِهِ
وَإِذَا مَسَّهُ الشَّرُّ فَذُو دُعَآءٍ عَرِيضٍ ﴿٥١﴾ قُلْ
أَرَءَيْتُمْ إِن كَانَ مِنْ عِنْدِ اللهِ ثُمَّ كَفَرْتُم
بِهِ مَنْ أَضَلُّ مِمَّنْ هُوَ فِي شِقَاقٍ بَعِيدٍ ﴿٥٢﴾
سَنُرِيهِمْ ءَايٰتِنَا فِي الْأٰفَاقِ وَفِيٓ أَنْفُسِهِمْ حَتّٰى
يَتَبَيَّنَ لَهُمْ أَنَّهُ الْحَقُّ أَوَلَمْ يَكْفِ بِرَبِّكَ
أَنَّهُ عَلٰى كُلِّ شَيْءٍ شَهِيدٌ ﴿٥٣﴾ أَلَآ إِنَّهُمْ فِي مِرْيَةٍ
مِّن لِّقَآءِ رَبِّهِمْ أَلَآ إِنَّهُ بِكُلِّ شَيْءٍ مُّحِيطٌ ﴿٥٤﴾

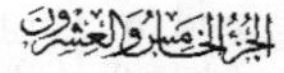

CHAPTER
42

سُورَةُ الشُّورٰى ٤٢

AL-SHÛRÂ
(The Counsel)
(Revealed before Hijrah)

سُورَةُ الشُّورٰى مَكِّيَّةٌ

With the name of Allâh,
the Most Gracious, the Ever Merciful
(I commence to read Sûrah Al-Shûrâ).

بِسْمِ اللّٰهِ الرَّحْمٰنِ الرَّحِيمِ

1. HÂ MÎM - Allâh is Praiseworthy, Lord of all honour;
2. 'Ain Sîn Qâf - All-Knowing, All-Hearing, All-Powerful.
3. (Just as He has sent this revelation) so does Allâh, the All-Mighty, the All-Wise reveals to you, and so has He also revealed to those (Messengers) who preceded you.
4. All that lies in the heavens and all that lies in the earth belongs to Him. And He is the Most Sublime, the All-Great.
5. The heavens may well-nigh rend asunder from above these (disbelievers due to His displeasure of them). But the angels are declaring the Holiness of their Lord along with His praise and they ask His protection for those on the earth. Behold! It is Allâh alone Who is All-Protecting, the Ever Merciful.
6. As for those who have taken to themselves patrons apart from Him, Allâh is Watchful over them and goes on keeping the record of the deeds (which serve as a proof) against them. And you are in no way responsible of their affairs.
7. (Just as We have sent this revelation,) so We have sent (as another favour) to you the Qur'ân in Arabic through revelation so that you may warn the (people of) Metropolis (- the Makkans) and (all) those around it and that you may warn (them) of the Day of (general) Gathering, (the Day) about the advent of which there is no

حٰمٓ ① عٓسٓقٓ ② كَذٰلِكَ يُوحِيٓ إِلَيْكَ وَ إِلَى
الَّذِينَ مِنْ قَبْلِكَ اللّٰهُ الْعَزِيزُ الْحَكِيمُ ③ لَهُ
مَا فِي السَّمٰوٰتِ وَ مَا فِي الْأَرْضِ وَ هُوَ الْعَلِيُّ
الْعَظِيمُ ④ تَكَادُ السَّمٰوٰتُ يَتَفَطَّرْنَ مِنْ فَوْقِهِنَّ
وَ الْمَلٰٓئِكَةُ يُسَبِّحُونَ بِحَمْدِ رَبِّهِمْ وَ يَسْتَغْفِرُونَ
لِمَنْ فِي الْأَرْضِ أَلَآ إِنَّ اللّٰهَ هُوَ الْغَفُورُ
الرَّحِيمُ ⑤ وَ الَّذِينَ اتَّخَذُوا مِنْ دُونِهِٓ أَوْلِيَآءَ
اللّٰهُ حَفِيظٌ عَلَيْهِمْ وَ مَآ أَنْتَ عَلَيْهِمْ بِوَكِيلٍ ⑥
وَ كَذٰلِكَ أَوْحَيْنَآ إِلَيْكَ قُرْءَانًا عَرَبِيًّا لِّتُنْذِرَ
أُمَّ الْقُرٰى وَ مَنْ حَوْلَهَا وَ تُنْذِرَ يَوْمَ الْجَمْعِ

doubt; (the Day) there will be a party (of those going) in to Paradise and another party (of those going) in the blazing Fire.

8. And if Allâh had wanted (to enforce His will) He would have made all these people one nation (of believers). But He admits (him) to His Mercy who wishes (so). As for the wrongdoers they will have neither a patron nor a helper (in the Hereafter).

9. Have they taken to themselves (other) patrons apart from Him (the only God)? But the (real) Patron is Allâh alone. He alone raises the dead to life and He is the Possessor of every power over every desired thing.

SECTION 2

10. **A**ND whatever may your differences be in a thing, the (ultimate) decision of it rests with Allâh. Such is Allâh, my Lord! On Him alone have I (always) put my trust, and towards Him do I turn (seeking His mercy).

11. He is the Originator of the heavens and the earth. He has made your mates from your own species and has made mates of the cattle (also from their own species). That is the way (of mating together) whereby He multiplies you. Naught is as His exegesis, (He is beyond all comparison,) and He is the All-Hearing, the All-Seeing.

12. The things encircling the heavens and the earth belong to Him. He multiplies the means of livelihood for such of them as He will, and makes them scant (for such of them as He will). He has indeed full-knowledge of each and everything.

13. He has ordained for you the same course of faith as He enjoined on Noah (to adopt), and which We have revealed to you, and it is that (same faith) which We enjoined on Abraham, Moses, Jesus, so keep the faith and do not differ in it. (He ordains you) to establish obedience (to Allâh) and not to be divided (in sects) therein. Hard upon the polytheists is that (teach-

لَا رَيْبَ فِيهِ ۚ فَرِيقٌ فِي الْجَنَّةِ وَفَرِيقٌ فِي
السَّعِيرِ ﴿٧﴾ وَلَوْ شَاءَ اللَّهُ لَجَعَلَهُمْ أُمَّةً وَاحِدَةً
وَلَٰكِن يُدْخِلُ مَن يَشَاءُ فِي رَحْمَتِهِ ۚ
وَالظَّالِمُونَ مَا لَهُم مِّن وَلِيٍّ وَلَا نَصِيرٍ ﴿٨﴾ أَمِ
اتَّخَذُوا مِن دُونِهِ أَوْلِيَاءَ ۖ فَاللَّهُ هُوَ الْوَلِيُّ
وَهُوَ يُحْيِي الْمَوْتَىٰ وَهُوَ عَلَىٰ كُلِّ شَيْءٍ قَدِيرٌ ﴿٩﴾ ع ٢
وَمَا اخْتَلَفْتُمْ فِيهِ مِن شَيْءٍ فَحُكْمُهُ إِلَى اللَّهِ ۚ
ذَٰلِكُمُ اللَّهُ رَبِّي عَلَيْهِ تَوَكَّلْتُ وَإِلَيْهِ أُنِيبُ ﴿١٠﴾
فَاطِرُ السَّمَاوَاتِ وَالْأَرْضِ ۚ جَعَلَ لَكُم مِّنْ
أَنفُسِكُمْ أَزْوَاجًا وَمِنَ الْأَنْعَامِ أَزْوَاجًا ۖ يَذْرَؤُكُمْ
فِيهِ ۚ لَيْسَ كَمِثْلِهِ شَيْءٌ ۖ وَهُوَ السَّمِيعُ الْبَصِيرُ ﴿١١﴾
لَهُ مَقَالِيدُ السَّمَاوَاتِ وَالْأَرْضِ ۖ يَبْسُطُ
الرِّزْقَ لِمَن يَشَاءُ وَيَقْدِرُ ۚ إِنَّهُ بِكُلِّ شَيْءٍ
عَلِيمٌ ﴿١٢﴾ شَرَعَ لَكُم مِّنَ الدِّينِ مَا وَصَّىٰ بِهِ
نُوحًا وَالَّذِي أَوْحَيْنَا إِلَيْكَ وَمَا وَصَّيْنَا
بِهِ إِبْرَاهِيمَ وَمُوسَىٰ وَعِيسَىٰ أَنْ أَقِيمُوا
الدِّينَ وَلَا تَتَفَرَّقُوا فِيهِ ۚ كَبُرَ عَلَى الْمُشْرِكِينَ

ing) which you call them to. Allâh draws (him) towards Himself who wishes (to be drawn to Him), and guides him to Himself who turns (towards Him with a sincere heart).

14. And these (rejecters of the faith) split themselves into factions only after (true) knowledge (of the fundamental principles of faith) had come to them (and that too) out of jealousy among themselves and to spite one another. But for the word (of promise) already gone forth from your Lord, (that they would be given respite) for a fixed term, the judgment upon these (disbelievers) would surely have long been passed (by their complete annihilation). As for those who have been made to inherit the Scripture after these (Prophets) they are in a disquieting and grave doubt about this (Qur'ân).

15. (Since they are split up and divided,) call (them) to this (true faith), and go on following the straight path as you have been bidden. Do not follow their vain desires but say, 'I believe in what Allâh has revealed of the Book, and I have orders to do justice between you. Allâh is Our Lord as well as your Lord. We shall reap (the fruit of) our deeds and you shall reap (the fruit of) yours. There exists no cause of dispute between us and you. Allâh will gather us together (to judge between us with justice) and towards Him is the (eventual) return (of us all).'

16. And as for those who dispute about Allâh after His call has generally been responded, futile and void will be their argument in the sight of their Lord and (His) displeasure will come down upon them and there awaits them a severe punishment.

17. Allâh is He Who has sent down the perfect Book, suiting your requirements, with the lasting truth, and an Equitable law. How should you know that the (promised) Hour may be near at hand?

مَا تَدْعُوهُمْ إِلَيْهِ ۚ اللَّهُ يَجْتَبِي إِلَيْهِ مَنْ
يَشَاءُ وَيَهْدِي إِلَيْهِ مَنْ يُنِيبُ ﴿١٣﴾ وَمَا
تَفَرَّقُوا إِلَّا مِنْ بَعْدِ مَا جَاءَهُمُ الْعِلْمُ بَغْيًا
بَيْنَهُمْ ۚ وَلَوْلَا كَلِمَةٌ سَبَقَتْ مِنْ رَبِّكَ إِلَىٰ
أَجَلٍ مُسَمًّى لَقُضِيَ بَيْنَهُمْ ۚ وَإِنَّ الَّذِينَ
أُورِثُوا الْكِتَابَ مِنْ بَعْدِهِمْ لَفِي شَكٍّ مِنْهُ
مُرِيبٍ ﴿١٤﴾ فَلِذَٰلِكَ فَادْعُ ۖ وَاسْتَقِمْ كَمَا أُمِرْتَ
وَلَا تَتَّبِعْ أَهْوَاءَهُمْ ۖ وَقُلْ آمَنْتُ بِمَا أَنْزَلَ
اللَّهُ مِنْ كِتَابٍ ۖ وَأُمِرْتُ لِأَعْدِلَ بَيْنَكُمُ ۖ
اللَّهُ رَبُّنَا وَرَبُّكُمْ ۖ لَنَا أَعْمَالُنَا وَلَكُمْ أَعْمَالُكُمْ ۖ
لَا حُجَّةَ بَيْنَنَا وَبَيْنَكُمُ ۖ اللَّهُ يَجْمَعُ بَيْنَنَا ۖ
وَإِلَيْهِ الْمَصِيرُ ﴿١٥﴾ وَالَّذِينَ يُحَاجُّونَ فِي اللَّهِ
مِنْ بَعْدِ مَا اسْتُجِيبَ لَهُ حُجَّتُهُمْ دَاحِضَةٌ
عِنْدَ رَبِّهِمْ وَعَلَيْهِمْ غَضَبٌ وَلَهُمْ عَذَابٌ
شَدِيدٌ ﴿١٦﴾ اللَّهُ الَّذِي أَنْزَلَ الْكِتَابَ بِالْحَقِّ
وَالْمِيزَانَ ۗ وَمَا يُدْرِيكَ لَعَلَّ السَّاعَةَ

18. Only those who do not believe in it, seek to hasten it. But those who believe (in the truth about the Hour) dread it and are full of awe regarding it. And they know that it is in fact, a certainty. Beware! Those who dispute about the Hour are (steeped) in far-gone error.
19. Allâh is Benignant to His servants. He bestows (His gifts) on whomsoever He pleases. He is All-Powerful, All-Mighty.

SECTION 3

20. **F**OR he who seeks the harvest (- the reward) of the Hereafter We shall add to his harvest. But he who seeks the harvest of this world We shall give him a portion of it and he shall have no share whatsoever in the Hereafter.
21. Do these (disbelievers) have such associate partners (with Allâh) who have decreed a law which is contrary to (the law) Allâh has sanctioned? Had We not given (Our) verdict (about the respited time) of (the final) judgment, the orders (of destruction) would have long been passed between them. Indeed, there awaits the wrongdoers a woeful punishment.
22. (On the Day of Judgment) you shall see these wrongdoers full of dread and awe on account of the evil deeds they have committed. Yet this (punishment as a consequence to their evil deeds) is sure to befall them. But those who believe and (accordingly) do deeds of righteousness will be in (flowering and delightful) meadows of the Gardens. There is (present) with their Lord whatever they desire. That indeed is the bounteous favour (of Allâh).
23. That is (the same bounteous favour) of which Allâh gives the glad tidings to His servants who believe and (accordingly) do deeds of righteousness. Say, 'I ask no reward from you for it (- my preaching). All that I ask you is to cherish the strongest love to be near (to Him).' He that does a good deed, We make this (good deed) look all the more beautiful to him. Verily, Allâh is All-Protecting, Most Appreciating (of our service to Him).

قَرِيبٌ ﴿١٧﴾ يَسْتَعْجِلُ بِهَا الَّذِينَ لَا يُؤْمِنُونَ
بِهَا ۚ وَالَّذِينَ آمَنُوا مُشْفِقُونَ مِنْهَا وَيَعْلَمُونَ
أَنَّهَا الْحَقُّ ۗ أَلَا إِنَّ الَّذِينَ يُمَارُونَ فِي
السَّاعَةِ لَفِي ضَلَالٍ بَعِيدٍ ﴿١٨﴾ اللَّهُ لَطِيفٌ بِعِبَادِهِ
يَرْزُقُ مَنْ يَشَاءُ ۖ وَهُوَ الْقَوِيُّ الْعَزِيزُ ﴿١٩﴾ مَنْ ع ٣
كَانَ يُرِيدُ حَرْثَ الْآخِرَةِ نَزِدْ لَهُ فِي حَرْثِهِ
وَمَنْ كَانَ يُرِيدُ حَرْثَ الدُّنْيَا نُؤْتِهِ مِنْهَا
وَمَا لَهُ فِي الْآخِرَةِ مِنْ نَصِيبٍ ﴿٢٠﴾ أَمْ لَهُمْ
شُرَكَاءُ شَرَعُوا لَهُمْ مِنَ الدِّينِ مَا لَمْ
يَأْذَنْ بِهِ اللَّهُ ۚ وَلَوْلَا كَلِمَةُ الْفَصْلِ لَقُضِيَ
بَيْنَهُمْ ۗ وَإِنَّ الظَّالِمِينَ لَهُمْ عَذَابٌ أَلِيمٌ ﴿٢١﴾
تَرَى الظَّالِمِينَ مُشْفِقِينَ مِمَّا كَسَبُوا وَهُوَ
وَاقِعٌ بِهِمْ ۗ وَالَّذِينَ آمَنُوا وَعَمِلُوا الصَّالِحَاتِ
فِي رَوْضَاتِ الْجَنَّاتِ ۖ لَهُمْ مَا يَشَاءُونَ عِنْدَ
رَبِّهِمْ ۚ ذَٰلِكَ هُوَ الْفَضْلُ الْكَبِيرُ ﴿٢٢﴾ ذَٰلِكَ الَّذِي
يُبَشِّرُ اللَّهُ عِبَادَهُ الَّذِينَ آمَنُوا وَعَمِلُوا
الصَّالِحَاتِ ۗ قُلْ لَا أَسْأَلُكُمْ عَلَيْهِ أَجْرًا إِلَّا
الْمَوَدَّةَ فِي الْقُرْبَىٰ ۗ وَمَنْ يَقْتَرِفْ حَسَنَةً نَزِدْ
لَهُ فِيهَا حُسْنًا ۚ إِنَّ اللَّهَ غَفُورٌ شَكُورٌ ﴿٢٣﴾ أَمْ

24. Rather they say, 'He has forged a lie against Allâh (by presenting this Qur'ân).' If Allâh so willed He would set a seal (against them) upon your heart. But Allâh eradicates falsehood (through you) and establishes the truth by (dint of) His words (-prophecies and revelation). He is indeed, One knowing full well (even) the innermost thoughts of the hearts.
25. It is He Who accepts penitence of His servants and pardons (them their) evil deeds, and He knows all that you do.
26. And He responds to the prayers of those who believe and (accordingly) do deeds of righteousness and gives them (even) more (than they pray for) through His grace and bounty. As for the disbelievers there awaits them a severe punishment
27. And if Allâh were to grant abundant provision for all His people, they would certainly commit rebellious transgression in the land. But as it is He sends it down according to a set and proper measure as He deems fit. He is indeed Well-Aware of His people (and) All-Seeing (of their condition).
28. And He it is Who sends down rain after the people have lost all hope and unfolds His mercy. And He alone is the Patron, the Praise-worthy.
29. The creation of the heavens and the earth and (the creation of) each living thing He has spread forth in them both are some of His Signs. Indeed He is Possessor of every power over gathering them together whenever He will.

SECTION 4

30. **A**ND whatever calamity befalls you is of your own making. And (yet) He goes on forgiving a great many of your sins (out of His mercy).
31. And you cannot frustrate (Allâh's) purpose in the earth, nor have you, apart from Allâh, any real protecting friend or helper.
32. And the towering ships sailing in the sea like mountain-tops are some of His signs (as well).

سُوْرَةُ الشُّوْرٰى ٤٢

يَقُولُونَ افْتَرٰى عَلَى اللّٰهِ كَذِبًا فَإِنْ يَّشَإِ اللّٰهُ
يَخْتِمْ عَلٰى قَلْبِكَ وَيَمْحُ اللّٰهُ الْبٰطِلَ وَيُحِقُّ
الْحَقَّ بِكَلِمٰتِهِ إِنَّهُ عَلِيمٌ بِذَاتِ الصُّدُورِ ﴿٢٤﴾
وَهُوَ الَّذِي يَقْبَلُ التَّوْبَةَ عَنْ عِبَادِهِ
وَيَعْفُوا عَنِ السَّيِّاٰتِ وَيَعْلَمُ مَا تَفْعَلُونَ ﴿٢٥﴾
وَيَسْتَجِيبُ الَّذِينَ اٰمَنُوا وَعَمِلُوا الصّٰلِحٰتِ
وَيَزِيدُهُمْ مِّنْ فَضْلِهِ وَالْكٰفِرُونَ لَهُمْ عَذَابٌ
شَدِيدٌ ﴿٢٦﴾ وَلَوْ بَسَطَ اللّٰهُ الرِّزْقَ لِعِبَادِهِ لَبَغَوْا
فِي الْأَرْضِ وَلٰكِنْ يُّنَزِّلُ بِقَدَرٍ مَّا يَشَآءُ إِنَّهُ
بِعِبَادِهِ خَبِيرٌ بَصِيرٌ ﴿٢٧﴾ وَهُوَ الَّذِي يُنَزِّلُ
الْغَيْثَ مِنْ بَعْدِ مَا قَنَطُوا وَيَنْشُرُ رَحْمَتَهُ
وَهُوَ الْوَلِيُّ الْحَمِيدُ ﴿٢٨﴾ وَمِنْ اٰيٰتِهِ خَلْقُ السَّمٰوٰتِ
وَالْأَرْضِ وَمَا بَثَّ فِيهِمَا مِنْ دَآبَّةٍ وَهُوَ
عَلٰى جَمْعِهِمْ إِذَا يَشَآءُ قَدِيرٌ ﴿٢٩﴾ وَمَآ أَصٰبَكُمْ
مِّنْ مُّصِيبَةٍ فَبِمَا كَسَبَتْ أَيْدِيكُمْ وَيَعْفُوا
عَنْ كَثِيرٍ ﴿٣٠﴾ وَمَآ أَنْتُمْ بِمُعْجِزِينَ فِي الْأَرْضِ
وَمَا لَكُمْ مِّنْ دُونِ اللّٰهِ مِنْ وَّلِيٍّ وَّلَا نَصِيرٍ ﴿٣١﴾
وَمِنْ اٰيٰتِهِ الْجَوَارِ فِي الْبَحْرِ كَالْأَعْلٰمِ ﴿٣٢﴾ إِنْ يَّشَأْ

33. And if He so will He can cause the wind to become still so that they stand motionless on its surface. Surely, there are signs in this for every patiently persevering (and) grateful person.
34. Or He (if He so will) can also destroy (the occupants of) these ships making them too heavy because of the (sinful) deeds they have committed; while He has pardoned a great many (of their sins and could save them).
35. (Yet He destroys them) so that those who dispute concerning Our teachings may know that there is no escape for them.
36. (People!) Whatever you have been given is only the passing enjoyment of the present life. But much better and more lasting is that (reward) which Allâh has for those who believe and put there trust in their Lord;
37. Those who avoid the more grievous sins and acts of indecency and who forgive when their anger is aroused,
38. And those who respond to their Lord and observe Prayer and whose affairs are (decided by) mutual consultation, and who go on spending (in Our cause) out of what We have provided for them,
39. And those who, when they meet wrongful aggression, defend themselves.
40. And (they keep in mind that) the recompense of an evil done is a punishment equal to it (for an evil merits an equal evil). But he who pardons (an offender) and (thereby) improves the matter (and effects thereby a reform in the offender) shall have his reward from Allâh. Behold! He does not love the wrong doers.
41. No blame shall lie on those who defend themselves after a wrong is done to them.
42. The blame only lies on those who wrong people and commit aggression in the land without justification. It is they for whom there awaits a grievous punishment.
43. But the one who bears (the wrong done to him) and forgives, (let it be remembered that) surely to do so is a matter of great fortitude and high resolve.

يُسْكِنِ الرِّيحَ فَيَظْلَلْنَ رَوَاكِدَ عَلَى ظَهْرِهِ ۚ إِنَّ
فِي ذَٰلِكَ لَآيَٰتٍ لِّكُلِّ صَبَّارٍ شَكُورٍ ﴿٣٣﴾ أَوْ
يُوبِقْهُنَّ بِمَا كَسَبُوا وَيَعْفُ عَنْ كَثِيرٍ ﴿٣٤﴾
وَيَعْلَمَ الَّذِينَ يُجَٰدِلُونَ فِي آيَٰتِنَا ۖ مَا لَهُم مِّن
مَّحِيصٍ ﴿٣٥﴾ فَمَا أُوتِيتُم مِّن شَيْءٍ فَمَتَٰعُ الْحَيَوٰةِ
الدُّنْيَا ۚ وَمَا عِندَ اللَّهِ خَيْرٌ وَأَبْقَى لِلَّذِينَ
آمَنُوا وَعَلَى رَبِّهِمْ يَتَوَكَّلُونَ ﴿٣٦﴾ وَالَّذِينَ
يَجْتَنِبُونَ كَبَٰٓئِرَ الْإِثْمِ وَالْفَوَٰحِشَ وَإِذَا مَا
غَضِبُوا هُمْ يَغْفِرُونَ ﴿٣٧﴾ وَالَّذِينَ اسْتَجَابُوا
لِرَبِّهِمْ وَأَقَامُوا الصَّلَوٰةَ وَأَمْرُهُمْ شُورَى
بَيْنَهُمْ وَمِمَّا رَزَقْنَٰهُمْ يُنفِقُونَ ﴿٣٨﴾ وَالَّذِينَ
إِذَا أَصَابَهُمُ الْبَغْيُ هُمْ يَنتَصِرُونَ ﴿٣٩﴾ وَجَزَٰٓؤُا
سَيِّئَةٍ سَيِّئَةٌ مِّثْلُهَا ۚ فَمَنْ عَفَا وَأَصْلَحَ
فَأَجْرُهُ عَلَى اللَّهِ ۚ إِنَّهُ لَا يُحِبُّ الظَّٰلِمِينَ ﴿٤٠﴾
وَلَمَنِ انتَصَرَ بَعْدَ ظُلْمِهِ فَأُولَٰٓئِكَ مَا عَلَيْهِم
مِّن سَبِيلٍ ﴿٤١﴾ إِنَّمَا السَّبِيلُ عَلَى الَّذِينَ
يَظْلِمُونَ النَّاسَ وَيَبْغُونَ فِي الْأَرْضِ بِغَيْرِ
الْحَقِّ ۚ أُولَٰٓئِكَ لَهُمْ عَذَابٌ أَلِيمٌ ﴿٤٢﴾ وَلَمَن

SECTION 5

44. **A**s for the person whom Allâh forsakes and adjudges as lost there is no protecting-friend for him except He. And you will find that when the wrongdoers see the punishment (about to overtake them) they will say, 'Is there any way back?'

45. And you shall see them being presented to it (the agony) humiliating themselves because of disgrace, looking with a furtive glance. And those who believe will say, 'As a matter of fact, the losers are those who have lost themselves and their families on the Day of Resurrection.' Beware! The wrongdoers will be, in fact, suffering from constant agony.

46. They will have no protecting-friends to help them apart from Allâh. And there is no way (of escape left) for him whom Allâh forsakes and adjudges as lost.

47. (Humankind!) Respond to your Lord before there comes a day from Allâh for which there is no averting (contrary to the decree of God). There shall be no refuge for you on that day, nor will there be for you any (possibility of) denial (of your sins).

48. But if they turn away (inspite of all your exhortation) then (it is their own responsibility). We have not sent you as a custodian over them. Your duty is only to deliver (Our Message) well. Look! When We let a person to have a taste of Our mercy he rejoices over it. But if some evil befalls them on account of what they have themselves done (they are displeased thereat); as a matter of fact such a person is (really) ungrateful.

49. The kingdom of the heavens and the earth belongs to Allâh. He creates what He will. He grants daughters to whom He will (according to His wise plan) and He grants sons to whom He will.

50. Or (to some) He grants mixed - sons and

سُوۡرَةُ الشُّوۡرٰى ٤٢

صَبَرَ وَغَفَرَ اِنَّ ذٰلِكَ لَمِنۡ عَزۡمِ الۡاُمُوۡرِ ﴿٤٣﴾
وَمَنۡ يُّضۡلِلِ اللّٰهُ فَمَا لَهٗ مِنۡ وَّلِيٍّ مِّنۡۢ
بَعۡدِهٖ ؕ وَتَرَى الظّٰلِمِيۡنَ لَمَّا رَاَوُا الۡعَذَابَ
يَقُوۡلُوۡنَ هَلۡ اِلٰى مَرَدٍّ مِّنۡ سَبِيۡلٍ ﴿٤٤﴾ وَتَرٰىهُمۡ
يُعۡرَضُوۡنَ عَلَيۡهَا خٰشِعِيۡنَ مِنَ الذُّلِّ يَنۡظُرُوۡنَ
مِنۡ طَرۡفٍ خَفِيٍّ ؕ وَقَالَ الَّذِيۡنَ اٰمَنُوۡۤا اِنَّ
الۡخٰسِرِيۡنَ الَّذِيۡنَ خَسِرُوۡۤا اَنۡفُسَهُمۡ وَاَهۡلِيۡهِمۡ
يَوۡمَ الۡقِيٰمَةِ ؕ اَلَاۤ اِنَّ الظّٰلِمِيۡنَ فِيۡ عَذَابٍ
مُّقِيۡمٍ ﴿٤٥﴾ وَمَا كَانَ لَهُمۡ مِّنۡ اَوۡلِيَآءَ يَنۡصُرُوۡنَهُمۡ
مِّنۡ دُوۡنِ اللّٰهِ ؕ وَمَنۡ يُّضۡلِلِ اللّٰهُ فَمَا لَهٗ
مِنۡ سَبِيۡلٍ ﴿٤٦﴾ اِسۡتَجِيۡبُوۡا لِرَبِّكُمۡ مِّنۡ قَبۡلِ
اَنۡ يَّاۡتِيَ يَوۡمٌ لَّا مَرَدَّ لَهٗ مِنَ اللّٰهِ ؕ مَا لَكُمۡ
مِّنۡ مَّلۡجَاٍ يَّوۡمَئِذٍ وَّمَا لَكُمۡ مِّنۡ نَّكِيۡرٍ ﴿٤٧﴾ فَاِنۡ
اَعۡرَضُوۡا فَمَاۤ اَرۡسَلۡنٰكَ عَلَيۡهِمۡ حَفِيۡظًا ؕ اِنۡ
عَلَيۡكَ اِلَّا الۡبَلٰغُ ؕ وَاِنَّاۤ اِذَاۤ اَذَقۡنَا الۡاِنۡسٰنَ
مِنَّا رَحۡمَةً فَرِحَ بِهَا ۚ وَاِنۡ تُصِبۡهُمۡ سَيِّئَةٌۢ
بِمَا قَدَّمَتۡ اَيۡدِيۡهِمۡ فَاِنَّ الۡاِنۡسٰنَ كَفُوۡرٌ ﴿٤٨﴾
لِلّٰهِ مُلۡكُ السَّمٰوٰتِ وَالۡاَرۡضِ ؕ يَخۡلُقُ مَا
يَشَآءُ ؕ يَهَبُ لِمَنۡ يَّشَآءُ اِنَاثًا وَّيَهَبُ لِمَنۡ
يَّشَآءُ الذُّكُوۡرَ ﴿٤٩﴾ اَوۡ يُزَوِّجُهُمۡ ذُكۡرَانًا وَّاِنَاثًا

daughters, and He makes whom He will barren (of having a child). Indeed, He is All-Knowing, All-Powerful.

51. It is not given to a human being that Allâh should speak to him except by direct revelation or from behind a veil or by sending a messenger (- an angel) who should reveal (to him) by His command what He pleases. Indeed, He is the Most Sublime, the All-Wise.

52. (Prophet!) Just so (as We sent revelations to other Prophets), We revealed to you the Word by Our command. (Before this revelation) you did not know what the Divine Book was nor (which of) the faith (it teaches), but We made it (- Our revelation to you) a light, whereby We guide such of Our servants as We will. And truly you are guiding (humankind) on to the straight and right path,

53. The path of Allâh to Whom belongs all that lies in the heavens and all that lies in the earth. Behold! To Allâh do all things eventually return.

وَيَجْعَلُ مَنْ يَشَآءُ عَقِيمًا إِنَّهُ عَلِيمٌ قَدِيرٌ ﴿٥٠﴾
وَمَا كَانَ لِبَشَرٍ أَنْ يُكَلِّمَهُ اللهُ إِلَّا وَحْيًا
أَوْ مِنْ وَرَآئِ حِجَابٍ أَوْ يُرْسِلَ رَسُولًا فَيُوحِيَ
بِإِذْنِهِ مَا يَشَآءُ إِنَّهُ عَلِيٌّ حَكِيمٌ ﴿٥١﴾ وَكَذٰلِكَ
أَوْحَيْنَآ إِلَيْكَ رُوحًا مِنْ أَمْرِنَا مَا كُنْتَ
تَدْرِي مَا الْكِتٰبُ وَلَا الْإِيْمٰنُ وَلٰكِنْ جَعَلْنٰهُ
نُورًا نَهْدِي بِهِ مَنْ نَشَآءُ مِنْ عِبَادِنَا
وَإِنَّكَ لَتَهْدِيٓ إِلٰى صِرٰطٍ مُسْتَقِيمٍ ﴿٥٢﴾ صِرٰطِ
اللهِ الَّذِي لَهُ مَا فِي السَّمٰوٰتِ وَمَا فِي
الْأَرْضِ أَلَآ إِلَى اللهِ تَصِيرُ الْأُمُورُ ﴿٥٣﴾ ع

CHAPTER
43

AL-ZUKHRUF
(The Ornaments)
(Revealed before Hijrah)

سُورَةُ الزُّخْرُفِ مَكِّيَّةٌ

With the name of Allâh,
the Most Gracious, the Ever Merciful
(I commence to read Sûrah Al-Zukhruf).

بِسْمِ اللهِ الرَّحْمٰنِ الرَّحِيمِ

1. HÂ MÎM - Allâh is Praiseworthy, the Lord of all Honour.

2. This perfect Book that makes (the truth) perspicuously clear bears witness (to the above truth).

3. Verily, We have made it a Qur'ân, such (a Scripture) that brings (the nations) together, and (a Scripture) eloquently expressive so that

حٰمٓ ﴿١﴾ وَالْكِتٰبِ الْمُبِينِ ﴿٢﴾ إِنَّا جَعَلْنٰهُ قُرْءٰنًا

you may make use of your understanding.
4. And it (- the Qur'ân) lies (safe) with Us in the Mother of the Book (which is the source of all knowledge), and (it is) indeed eminently sublime and full of wisdom.
5. Should We then leave you altogether, and turn away from (giving) you the Reminder, the source of eminence (for you) just because you are a people exceeding all limits (and wasting your ownselves)?
6. And so many a Prophet did We send among the earlier peoples,
7. Yet there never came to them a Prophet but they treated him as of no importance.
8. Look! We destroyed those who were stronger than these (Makkans) in valour, and the example of the former peoples has already gone before. (So how can they escape meeting the same fate?)
9. And if you ask them who created the heavens and the earth, they will certainly say, '(It is) the All-Mighty, (and) the All-Knowing (God) Who has created them.'
10. (It is He) Who made the earth a resting place for you and Who has, for your benefit, forged in it pathways so that you may follow the right path.
11. And (it is He) Who sends down again and again water from the clouds according to a set decree and in proper measure and by this means We revive the dead territory. That is how you (too) shall be brought forth (alive).
12. (It is He) Who has created pairs of all things, He has also made for you the ships and created the cattle whereon you ride;
13. So that you may sit firmly on their backs (and) then you may remember the favour of your Lord when you are firmly seated (and settled) on them and say, 'Glory be to Him Who has made these things subservient to us, while we (if left to) ourselves were not capable of (the task of) subduing them.
14. 'Certainly, we are the ones bound to return to our Lord.'

عَرَبِيًّا لَّعَلَّكُمْ تَعْقِلُونَ ۝٣ وَإِنَّهُ فِي أُمِّ الْكِتٰبِ
لَدَيْنَا لَعَلِيٌّ حَكِيمٌ ۝٤ أَفَنَضْرِبُ عَنْكُمُ الذِّكْرَ
صَفْحًا أَنْ كُنْتُمْ قَوْمًا مُّسْرِفِينَ ۝٥ وَكَمْ أَرْسَلْنَا
مِنْ نَّبِيٍّ فِي الْأَوَّلِينَ ۝٦ وَمَا يَأْتِيهِمْ مِّنْ نَّبِيٍّ
إِلَّا كَانُوا بِهِ يَسْتَهْزِءُونَ ۝٧ فَأَهْلَكْنَا أَشَدَّ مِنْهُمْ
بَطْشًا وَمَضٰى مَثَلُ الْأَوَّلِينَ ۝٨ وَلَئِنْ سَأَلْتَهُمْ
مَّنْ خَلَقَ السَّمٰوٰتِ وَالْأَرْضَ لَيَقُولُنَّ خَلَقَهُنَّ
الْعَزِيزُ الْعَلِيمُ ۝٩ الَّذِي جَعَلَ لَكُمُ الْأَرْضَ
مَهْدًا وَجَعَلَ لَكُمْ فِيهَا سُبُلًا لَّعَلَّكُمْ تَهْتَدُونَ ۝١٠
وَالَّذِي نَزَّلَ مِنَ السَّمَاءِ مَاءً بِقَدَرٍ فَأَنْشَرْنَا
بِهِ بَلْدَةً مَّيْتًا كَذٰلِكَ تُخْرَجُونَ ۝١١ وَالَّذِي
خَلَقَ الْأَزْوٰجَ كُلَّهَا وَجَعَلَ لَكُمْ مِّنَ الْفُلْكِ
وَالْأَنْعٰمِ مَا تَرْكَبُونَ ۝١٢ لِتَسْتَوُوا عَلٰى ظُهُورِهِ
ثُمَّ تَذْكُرُوا نِعْمَةَ رَبِّكُمْ إِذَا اسْتَوَيْتُمْ عَلَيْهِ
وَتَقُولُوا سُبْحٰنَ الَّذِي سَخَّرَ لَنَا هٰذَا وَمَا كُنَّا
لَهُ مُقْرِنِينَ ۝١٣ وَإِنَّآ إِلٰى رَبِّنَا لَمُنْقَلِبُونَ ۝١٤

15. (Though they say that Allâh alone is the Creator of the heavens and the earth) yet they have made some of His servants His part (- His son), such a human being is evidently ungrateful.

SECTION 2

16. **O**R has He taken to Himself daughters from the things He Himself has created (as the pagans describe the angels to be God's daughters) and has chosen you for (honouring with) the sons.
17. Yet (as to themselves) when one of them is given the news (of the birth of a female child), the like of which (sex) he ascribes to the Most Gracious (God), his face becomes gloomy and he is choked with inward grief.
18. (Is he your god) who is brought up in the midst of ornaments and who is unable to make a clear expression (to an argument) and a plain speech in disputation (and discussions).
19. And they regard the angels who are the servants of the Most Gracious (God) as females. Did they witness their creation? In that case their testimony will be recorded and they will be questioned (about it).
20. And they say, 'If the Most Gracious (God) had (so) willed, we should never have worshipped them.' They have no real knowledge whatsoever in that matter. They do nothing but make conjectures.
21. Have We given them a Scripture before this (Qur'ân) so that they are thereby adducing an argument (in support of their conjectures)?
22. Nay, but they go on saying, 'We have found our forefathers on a certain course, and we (while walking) in their footsteps, are following the right course (of true guidance).
23. It has always been the case, We never sent any Warner to any township before you but its insolent leaders and well-to-do persons said, 'We have found our forefathers on a certain course and we are the followers in their footsteps (to the right direction).'
24. (Thereupon the Warner to them) said,

وَجَعَلُوا لَهُ مِنْ عِبَادِهِ جُزْءًا إِنَّ الْإِنسَـٰنَ
لَكَفُورٌ مُّبِينٌ ﴿١٥﴾ أَمِ اتَّخَذَ مِمَّا يَخْلُقُ بَنَاتٍ
وَأَصْفَـٰكُم بِالْبَنِينَ ﴿١٦﴾ وَإِذَا بُشِّرَ أَحَدُهُم
بِمَا ضَرَبَ لِلرَّحْمَـٰنِ مَثَلًا ظَلَّ وَجْهُهُ مُسْوَدًّا
وَهُوَ كَظِيمٌ ﴿١٧﴾ أَوَمَن يُنَشَّؤُا فِي الْحِلْيَةِ وَهُوَ
فِي الْخِصَامِ غَيْرُ مُبِينٍ ﴿١٨﴾ وَجَعَلُوا الْمَلَـٰٓئِكَةَ
الَّذِينَ هُمْ عِبَـٰدُ الرَّحْمَـٰنِ إِنَـٰثًا أَشَهِدُوا
خَلْقَهُمْ سَتُكْتَبُ شَهَـٰدَتُهُمْ وَيُسْـَٔلُونَ ﴿١٩﴾
وَقَالُوا لَوْ شَاءَ الرَّحْمَـٰنُ مَا عَبَدْنَـٰهُم مَّا لَهُم
بِذَٰلِكَ مِنْ عِلْمٍ إِنْ هُمْ إِلَّا يَخْرُصُونَ ﴿٢٠﴾
أَمْ ءَاتَيْنَـٰهُمْ كِتَـٰبًا مِّن قَبْلِهِ فَهُم بِهِ
مُسْتَمْسِكُونَ ﴿٢١﴾ بَلْ قَالُوا إِنَّا وَجَدْنَا ءَابَاءَنَا
عَلَىٰ أُمَّةٍ وَإِنَّا عَلَىٰ ءَاثَـٰرِهِم مُّهْتَدُونَ ﴿٢٢﴾ وَكَذَٰلِكَ
مَا أَرْسَلْنَا مِن قَبْلِكَ فِي قَرْيَةٍ مِّن نَّذِيرٍ
إِلَّا قَالَ مُتْرَفُوهَا إِنَّا وَجَدْنَا ءَابَاءَنَا عَلَىٰ أُمَّةٍ
وَإِنَّا عَلَىٰ ءَاثَـٰرِهِم مُّقْتَدُونَ ﴿٢٣﴾ قَـٰلَ أَوَلَوْ جِئْتُكُم

'(Would you still follow the wrong course in their footsteps) even though I bring a (teaching giving) better guidance than that on which you found your fathers.' They said, 'We are disbelievers altogether (in the teaching) with which you are sent.'

25. So We were displeased with them. Behold! How miserable was the end of those who cried lies (to Our Prophets).

SECTION 3

26. AND (recall the time) when Abraham said to his sire and his people, 'I definitely disown what you worship;

27. 'But not Him (the true God) Who created me, and He will surely guide me to the right way.'

28. And he (- Abraham) made it (- the Divine Unity) a word to abide (as a permanent legacy) among his posterity, so that they might turn (to One God).

29. (Yet when these disbelievers took to idol-worship I did not obliterate them) rather I allowed them and their fathers to enjoy worldly provisions until there came to them this lasting truth and a great Messenger who tells the right from the wrong.

30. Yet no sooner did the lasting truth come to them than they said, 'This is enchanting, but we are disbelievers in it altogether.'

31. Moreover they said, 'Why has not this Qur'ân been revealed to some man of importance from (either of) the two townships (- Makkah or Tâ'if, the two centres of social and political life).'

32. What! Is it they who distribute the grace of your Lord? Nay, but it is We Who distribute among them their livelihood pertaining to the present life. We exalt them (in rank) one over another so that some of them may take others in service. And the grace of your Lord is much better than what they amass (of the worldly provisions).

33. And were it not (for the fact) that all humankind would become (followers) of one course (of disbelief) We would have given to

سُورَةُ الزُّخْرُفِ ٤٣

بِأَهْدَىٰ مِمَّا وَجَدتُّمْ عَلَيْهِ آبَاءَكُمْ قَالُوا
إِنَّا بِمَا أُرْسِلْتُم بِهِ كَافِرُونَ ﴿٢٤﴾ فَانتَقَمْنَا مِنْهُمْ
فَانظُرْ كَيْفَ كَانَ عَاقِبَةُ الْمُكَذِّبِينَ ﴿٢٥﴾ وَإِذْ
قَالَ إِبْرَاهِيمُ لِأَبِيهِ وَقَوْمِهِ إِنَّنِي بَرَاءٌ مِّمَّا
تَعْبُدُونَ ﴿٢٦﴾ إِلَّا الَّذِي فَطَرَنِي فَإِنَّهُ سَيَهْدِينِ ﴿٢٧﴾
وَجَعَلَهَا كَلِمَةً بَاقِيَةً فِي عَقِبِهِ لَعَلَّهُمْ يَرْجِعُونَ ﴿٢٨﴾
بَلْ مَتَّعْتُ هَٰؤُلَاءِ وَآبَاءَهُمْ حَتَّىٰ جَاءَهُمُ
الْحَقُّ وَرَسُولٌ مُّبِينٌ ﴿٢٩﴾ وَلَمَّا جَاءَهُمُ الْحَقُّ
قَالُوا هَٰذَا سِحْرٌ وَإِنَّا بِهِ كَافِرُونَ ﴿٣٠﴾ وَقَالُوا
لَوْلَا نُزِّلَ هَٰذَا الْقُرْآنُ عَلَىٰ رَجُلٍ مِّنَ الْقَرْيَتَيْنِ
عَظِيمٍ ﴿٣١﴾ أَهُمْ يَقْسِمُونَ رَحْمَتَ رَبِّكَ نَحْنُ
قَسَمْنَا بَيْنَهُم مَّعِيشَتَهُمْ فِي الْحَيَاةِ الدُّنْيَا
وَرَفَعْنَا بَعْضَهُمْ فَوْقَ بَعْضٍ دَرَجَاتٍ لِّيَتَّخِذَ
بَعْضُهُم بَعْضًا سُخْرِيًّا وَرَحْمَتُ رَبِّكَ خَيْرٌ
مِّمَّا يَجْمَعُونَ ﴿٣٢﴾ وَلَوْلَا أَن يَكُونَ النَّاسُ

those who disbelieve in the Most Gracious (God) roofs of silver for their houses and (silver) stairways whereby they could ascend;
34. And for their houses (We would have given similar) doors and couches (of silver) whereon they could recline.
35. And many more ornamental things (of silver and gold). Yet all this (pomp and show) is nothing but an enjoyment (of fleeting nature) pertaining only to the present life. And (the comfort of) the Hereafter with your Lord belongs exclusively to those who become secure against evil.

SECTION 4

36. As for him who forsakes the admonition of the Most Gracious (God), We appoint for him a satan who then becomes an intimate companion for him.
37. These (satans) turn the people away from the right path and the people think (about themselves) that they are following the right course of guidance;
38. Till when such a person comes before Us (on the Day of Judgment) he will say (to his respective satan), 'Would that there had been the distance of the east and the west between you and me. What an evil companion is he!
39. (It will be said to the satanic people that Day,) 'Now, when (it has been once proved) that you have acted unjustly, (the fact) that you are sharers in the punishment (with those who misled you) will be of no use to you at all this Day.
40. (In this state of theirs, Prophet!) Would you make the deaf to hear, or guide the blind and him who is (engrossed) in glaring error.
41. And even if We take you away (from this world) We shall punish them (in all events);
42. Or We shall show you (in your lifetime) that (punishment) which We have promised them, for, evidently, We have absolute power over them.
43. Therefore hold fast to that which has been

أُمَّةً وَاحِدَةً لَجَعَلْنَا لِمَنْ يَكْفُرُ بِالرَّحْمَٰنِ
لِبُيُوتِهِمْ سُقُفًا مِنْ فِضَّةٍ وَمَعَارِجَ عَلَيْهَا
يَظْهَرُونَ ﴿٣٣﴾ وَلِبُيُوتِهِمْ أَبْوَابًا وَسُرُرًا عَلَيْهَا
يَتَّكِئُونَ ﴿٣٤﴾ وَزُخْرُفًا ۚ وَإِنْ كُلُّ ذَٰلِكَ لَمَّا
مَتَاعُ الْحَيَاةِ الدُّنْيَا ۚ وَالْآخِرَةُ عِنْدَ رَبِّكَ
لِلْمُتَّقِينَ ﴿٣٥﴾ وَمَنْ يَعْشُ عَنْ ذِكْرِ الرَّحْمَٰنِ
نُقَيِّضْ لَهُ شَيْطَانًا فَهُوَ لَهُ قَرِينٌ ﴿٣٦﴾ وَإِنَّهُمْ
لَيَصُدُّونَهُمْ عَنِ السَّبِيلِ وَيَحْسَبُونَ أَنَّهُمْ
مُهْتَدُونَ ﴿٣٧﴾ حَتَّىٰ إِذَا جَاءَنَا قَالَ يَا لَيْتَ بَيْنِي
وَبَيْنَكَ بُعْدَ الْمَشْرِقَيْنِ فَبِئْسَ الْقَرِينُ ﴿٣٨﴾
وَلَنْ يَنْفَعَكُمُ الْيَوْمَ إِذْ ظَلَمْتُمْ أَنَّكُمْ فِي
الْعَذَابِ مُشْتَرِكُونَ ﴿٣٩﴾ أَفَأَنْتَ تُسْمِعُ الصُّمَّ
أَوْ تَهْدِي الْعُمْيَ وَمَنْ كَانَ فِي ضَلَالٍ مُبِينٍ ﴿٤٠﴾
فَإِمَّا نَذْهَبَنَّ بِكَ فَإِنَّا مِنْهُمْ مُنْتَقِمُونَ ﴿٤١﴾
أَوْ نُرِيَنَّكَ الَّذِي وَعَدْنَاهُمْ فَإِنَّا عَلَيْهِمْ
مُقْتَدِرُونَ ﴿٤٢﴾ فَاسْتَمْسِكْ بِالَّذِي أُوحِيَ

revealed to you, for you are surely on the exact right and straight path.
44. And truly this (Qur'ân) is a source of rising to eminence for you and for your people. And you shall all be asked about (whether you did the duty you owed to it).
45. And ask those of Our Messenger whom We sent before you whether We (ever) appointed any deities to be worshipped apart from the Most Gracious (God).

SECTION 5

46. **A**ND We sent Moses with Our Messages towards Pharaoh and his courtiers, accordingly he said (to them), 'I am, truly, a Messenger from the Lord of the worlds.'
47. But no sooner did he bring them Our signs than they laughed at them.
48. We showed them no sign but it was greater than its kind (preceding it). And We seized them with the calamity so that they might return (to the ways of righteousness).
49. (Every time the calamity visited them) they said, 'O man of vast learning, pray for us to your Lord, invoking Him in view of the promises He has made with you. (If He removes this affliction from us) we will surely follow the right course (of true guidance).'
50. But no sooner did We relieve them of their affliction than they broke their word.
51. Now, Pharaoh proclaimed among his people (wherein) he said, 'O my people! Does not the kingdom of Egypt belong to me? And these streams are flowing at my command. Do you not even see?
52. Nay, I am better than this (- Moses) who is a miserable wretch and can hardly express (himself) distinctly.
53. '(If he be a specially favoured one of God) why have not then bracelets of gold been bestowed on him (and thus a chiefdom conferred on him), or (rather why have no) angels accompanied him following him in procession formed in serried ranks?'
54. Thus did he (- Pharaoh) instigate his people

إِلَيْكَ إِنَّكَ عَلَى صِرَاطٍ مُّسْتَقِيمٍ ﴿٤٣﴾ وَإِنَّهُ
لَذِكْرٌ لَّكَ وَلِقَوْمِكَ وَسَوْفَ تُسْئَلُونَ ﴿٤٤﴾
وَسْئَلْ مَنْ أَرْسَلْنَا مِنْ قَبْلِكَ مِنْ رُّسُلِنَا
أَجَعَلْنَا مِنْ دُونِ الرَّحْمٰنِ آلِهَةً يُعْبَدُونَ ﴿٤٥﴾
وَلَقَدْ أَرْسَلْنَا مُوسٰى بِآيٰتِنَا إِلٰى فِرْعَوْنَ
وَمَلَإِيْهِ فَقَالَ إِنِّي رَسُولُ رَبِّ الْعٰلَمِينَ ﴿٤٦﴾
فَلَمَّا جَاءَهُمْ بِآيٰتِنَا إِذَا هُمْ مِّنْهَا يَضْحَكُونَ ﴿٤٧﴾
وَمَا نُرِيهِمْ مِّنْ آيَةٍ إِلَّا هِيَ أَكْبَرُ مِنْ
أُخْتِهَا وَأَخَذْنٰهُمْ بِالْعَذَابِ لَعَلَّهُمْ
يَرْجِعُونَ ﴿٤٨﴾ وَقَالُوا يٰأَيُّهَ السَّاحِرُ ادْعُ لَنَا
رَبَّكَ بِمَا عَهِدَ عِنْدَكَ إِنَّنَا لَمُهْتَدُونَ ﴿٤٩﴾
فَلَمَّا كَشَفْنَا عَنْهُمُ الْعَذَابَ إِذَا هُمْ يَنْكُثُونَ ﴿٥٠﴾
وَنَادٰى فِرْعَوْنُ فِي قَوْمِهِ قَالَ يٰقَوْمِ أَلَيْسَ
لِي مُلْكُ مِصْرَ وَهٰذِهِ الْأَنْهٰرُ تَجْرِي مِنْ
تَحْتِي أَفَلَا تُبْصِرُونَ ﴿٥١﴾ أَمْ أَنَا خَيْرٌ مِّنْ هٰذَا
الَّذِي هُوَ مَهِينٌ وَلَا يَكَادُ يُبِينُ ﴿٥٢﴾ فَلَوْلَا
أُلْقِيَ عَلَيْهِ أَسْوِرَةٌ مِّنْ ذَهَبٍ أَوْ جَاءَ مَعَهُ
الْمَلٰئِكَةُ مُقْتَرِنِينَ ﴿٥٣﴾ فَاسْتَخَفَّ قَوْمَهُ

(against Moses and demanded prompt obedience from them); and they obeyed him. They were indeed a wicked people.

55. And no sooner did they displease Us (with their wicked ways) than We punished them and drowned them all together.

56. And We made them a thing of the past and an example (to take warning from) for the coming generations.

سُورَةُ الزُّخْرُفِ ٤٣

SECTION 6

57. **W**HEN (the case of Jesus,) the son of Mary is cited as an example, lo, your people start raising a clamour at it,

58. And they said, 'What! Are our gods better or he (- the Christ)?' They have mentioned his case to you only by way of disputation. Nay, but (the thing is that) they are a contentious people.

59. He was no more than a servant (of Ours) whom We graced with Our blessings and favours and We made him (to be) an example (of virtue and piety) for the Children of Israel.

60. And if We so willed We could make some from among you (like) angels who could be Our vicegerents in the land.

61. And indeed this (Qur'ân) gives the knowledge of the (promised) Hour. So have no doubt about it, rather you should follow Me. This is the straight and right path.

62. Do not let the satan turn you away from following it, for he is your enemy cutting off (your) ties (with God).

63. And when Jesus came (to his people) with clear proofs he said, 'I have indeed brought to you wisdom, and (I have come) to explain to you clearly some of the things over which you differ. So take Allâh as a shield and obey me.

64. 'The truth of the matter is that Allâh alone is my Lord and your Lord, so worship Him, this is the straight path.'

65. But (hearing this) various groups (of the people addressed) fell into variance among themselves, therefore woe to those who act

فَأَطَاعُوهُ ۚ إِنَّهُمْ كَانُوا قَوْمًا فَاسِقِينَ ﴿٥٤﴾ فَلَمَّا
آسَفُونَا انْتَقَمْنَا مِنْهُمْ فَأَغْرَقْنَاهُمْ أَجْمَعِينَ ﴿٥٥﴾
فَجَعَلْنَاهُمْ سَلَفًا وَمَثَلًا لِلْآخِرِينَ ﴿٥٦﴾ وَلَمَّا
ضُرِبَ ابْنُ مَرْيَمَ مَثَلًا إِذَا قَوْمُكَ مِنْهُ
يَصِدُّونَ ﴿٥٧﴾ وَقَالُوا أَآلِهَتُنَا خَيْرٌ أَمْ هُوَ ۚ مَا
ضَرَبُوهُ لَكَ إِلَّا جَدَلًا ۚ بَلْ هُمْ قَوْمٌ خَصِمُونَ ﴿٥٨﴾
إِنْ هُوَ إِلَّا عَبْدٌ أَنْعَمْنَا عَلَيْهِ وَجَعَلْنَاهُ
مَثَلًا لِبَنِي إِسْرَائِيلَ ﴿٥٩﴾ وَلَوْ نَشَاءُ لَجَعَلْنَا
مِنْكُمْ مَلَائِكَةً فِي الْأَرْضِ يَخْلُفُونَ ﴿٦٠﴾ وَإِنَّهُ
لَعِلْمٌ لِلسَّاعَةِ فَلَا تَمْتَرُنَّ بِهَا وَاتَّبِعُونِ ۚ
هَٰذَا صِرَاطٌ مُسْتَقِيمٌ ﴿٦١﴾ وَلَا يَصُدَّنَّكُمُ الشَّيْطَانُ ۖ
إِنَّهُ لَكُمْ عَدُوٌّ مُبِينٌ ﴿٦٢﴾ وَلَمَّا جَاءَ عِيسَىٰ
بِالْبَيِّنَاتِ قَالَ قَدْ جِئْتُكُمْ بِالْحِكْمَةِ وَلِأُبَيِّنَ
لَكُمْ بَعْضَ الَّذِي تَخْتَلِفُونَ فِيهِ ۖ فَاتَّقُوا اللَّهَ
وَأَطِيعُونِ ﴿٦٣﴾ إِنَّ اللَّهَ هُوَ رَبِّي وَرَبُّكُمْ فَاعْبُدُوهُ ۚ
هَٰذَا صِرَاطٌ مُسْتَقِيمٌ ﴿٦٤﴾ فَاخْتَلَفَ الْأَحْزَابُ
مِنْ بَيْنِهِمْ ۖ فَوَيْلٌ لِلَّذِينَ ظَلَمُوا مِنْ عَذَابِ

ع ١١

unjustly because of the torments of a woeful Day.

66. These (opponents of the truth) await only the (promised) Hour so that it may befall them suddenly and take them unawares.

67. On that Day friends will turn into foes one against another. Such, however, will not be the case with those who have become secure against evil.

SECTION 7

68. (GOD will say to the righteous,) 'O My servants! This Day you have nothing to fear, nor shall you ever grieve;

69. '(You) who believed in Our teachings and submitted (to Our will);

70. 'Enter Paradise, you and your spouses, you will be honoured and cheered (here).'

71. (Then it will so happen that) there they will be served in a round with bowls of gold and drinking cups and there, (in Paradise) will be (present) all that (their) souls desire and (their) eyes find delight in. And you will be abiding therein for ever.

72. And such is the Paradise which you shall have as your own, because of your (righteous) deeds.

73. Therein you shall have fruit in abundance, enough for you to eat (and spare).

74. (On the other side) the guilty will, of course, be abiding (long) in the torment of Gehenna.

75. That (torment) will not be allowed to abate for them, and once caught in it they shall completely despair.

76. (By punishing them so) We did them no injustice, rather, it was they themselves who were the unjust and wrongdoers indeed.

77. And they will cry, 'O Mâlik (- the angel in charge of the Hell), let your Lord finish with us (and thus rid us of the torment once for all).' He will reply, 'You have to remain (here) in this very state.'

78. (God will say,) 'We really brought you the Truth, yet most of you were those who found

يَوْمٍ أَلِيمٍ ﴿٦٥﴾ هَلْ يَنظُرُونَ إِلَّا السَّاعَةَ أَن
تَأْتِيَهُم بَغْتَةً وَهُمْ لَا يَشْعُرُونَ ﴿٦٦﴾ الْأَخِلَّاءُ
يَوْمَئِذٍ بَعْضُهُمْ لِبَعْضٍ عَدُوٌّ إِلَّا الْمُتَّقِينَ ﴿٦٧﴾
يَا عِبَادِ لَا خَوْفٌ عَلَيْكُمُ الْيَوْمَ وَلَا أَنتُمْ
تَحْزَنُونَ ﴿٦٨﴾ الَّذِينَ آمَنُوا بِآيَاتِنَا وَكَانُوا
مُسْلِمِينَ ﴿٦٩﴾ ادْخُلُوا الْجَنَّةَ أَنتُمْ وَأَزْوَاجُكُمْ
تُحْبَرُونَ ﴿٧٠﴾ يُطَافُ عَلَيْهِم بِصِحَافٍ مِّن ذَهَبٍ
وَأَكْوَابٍ وَفِيهَا مَا تَشْتَهِيهِ الْأَنفُسُ وَتَلَذُّ
الْأَعْيُنُ وَأَنتُمْ فِيهَا خَالِدُونَ ﴿٧١﴾ وَتِلْكَ
الْجَنَّةُ الَّتِي أُورِثْتُمُوهَا بِمَا كُنتُمْ تَعْمَلُونَ ﴿٧٢﴾
لَكُمْ فِيهَا فَاكِهَةٌ كَثِيرَةٌ مِّنْهَا تَأْكُلُونَ ﴿٧٣﴾ إِنَّ
الْمُجْرِمِينَ فِي عَذَابِ جَهَنَّمَ خَالِدُونَ ﴿٧٤﴾ لَا يُفَتَّرُ
عَنْهُمْ وَهُمْ فِيهِ مُبْلِسُونَ ﴿٧٥﴾ وَمَا ظَلَمْنَاهُمْ
وَلَٰكِن كَانُوا هُمُ الظَّالِمِينَ ﴿٧٦﴾ وَنَادَوْا يَا مَالِكُ
لِيَقْضِ عَلَيْنَا رَبُّكَ قَالَ إِنَّكُم مَّاكِثُونَ ﴿٧٧﴾ لَقَدْ

the truth hard (to follow).'

79. (Now) these (opponents of truth) have taken a decision (to kill the Prophet), so We have also taken Our decision (of the case of his saving).

80. Nay, but they think that We do not hear their secret (talks) and their private consultation (against Our Prophet). Indeed, We do (hear)! Not only that (private talk) but Our envoys (who remain) by their side are noting down (everything).

81. Say, 'The Most Gracious (God) has no son and I am the foremost to bear witness to this fact.

82. 'Holy is the Lord of the heavens and the earth, and the Lord of the Throne (of Power far) above and free from that (polytheistic things) they ascribe (to Him).'

83. So leave them alone to indulge in vain talk and to keep themselves occupied with unreal things until they meet their time (of punishment) which they have been promised.

84. He it is Who is (the Only) God in all the heavens and (the only) God in the whole of the earth and He alone is the All-Wise, the All-Knowing.

85. And blessed be He to Whom belongs the sovereignty of the heavens and the earth and all that lies between them and He alone has the knowledge of the promised Hour and to Him you shall all be made to return.

86. And all those whom they call upon, apart from Him, have no authority to intercede (with their Lord), but (this right is given to him) who bears witness to the truth and they know him (the Prophet) and his good conduct well.

87. If you were to ask them, 'Who created them.' They will no doubt say, 'Allâh.' Then whither are they being led astray?

88. And (He has the knowledge of) his (- the Prophet's repeated) cry (and appeal), 'O my Lord! These are a people who do not believe.'

89. So (Prophet!) Leave them alone and (bid-

جِئْنٰكُم بِالْحَقِّ وَ لٰكِنَّ أَكْثَرَكُمْ لِلْحَقِّ كٰرِهُونَ ﴿٧٨﴾
أَمْ أَبْرَمُوٓا أَمْرًا فَإِنَّا مُبْرِمُونَ ﴿٧٩﴾ أَمْ يَحْسَبُونَ
أَنَّا لَا نَسْمَعُ سِرَّهُمْ وَ نَجْوٰىهُم بَلٰى
وَ رُسُلُنَا لَدَيْهِمْ يَكْتُبُونَ ﴿٨٠﴾ قُلْ إِنْ كَانَ
لِلرَّحْمٰنِ وَلَدٌ فَأَنَا أَوَّلُ الْعٰبِدِينَ ﴿٨١﴾ سُبْحٰنَ
رَبِّ السَّمٰوٰتِ وَ الْأَرْضِ رَبِّ الْعَرْشِ عَمَّا
يَصِفُونَ ﴿٨٢﴾ فَذَرْهُمْ يَخُوضُوا وَ يَلْعَبُوا حَتّٰى
يُلٰقُوا يَوْمَهُمُ الَّذِي يُوعَدُونَ ﴿٨٣﴾ وَ هُوَ الَّذِي
فِي السَّمَآءِ إِلٰهٌ وَ فِي الْأَرْضِ إِلٰهٌ وَ هُوَ
الْحَكِيمُ الْعَلِيمُ ﴿٨٤﴾ وَ تَبٰرَكَ الَّذِي لَهُ مُلْكُ
السَّمٰوٰتِ وَ الْأَرْضِ وَ مَا بَيْنَهُمَا وَ عِنْدَهُ
عِلْمُ السَّاعَةِ وَ إِلَيْهِ تُرْجَعُونَ ﴿٨٥﴾ وَ لَا يَمْلِكُ
الَّذِينَ يَدْعُونَ مِنْ دُونِهِ الشَّفٰعَةَ إِلَّا مَنْ
شَهِدَ بِالْحَقِّ وَ هُمْ يَعْلَمُونَ ﴿٨٦﴾ وَ لَئِنْ سَأَلْتَهُم
مَّنْ خَلَقَهُمْ لَيَقُولُنَّ اللّٰهُ فَأَنّٰى يُؤْفَكُونَ ﴿٨٧﴾ وَ قِيلِهِ
يٰرَبِّ إِنَّ هٰٓؤُلَآءِ قَوْمٌ لَّا يُؤْمِنُونَ ﴿٨٨﴾ فَاصْفَحْ

ding them good-bye) say, 'Peace!' They shall soon know (the truth and the folly they are committing).

عَنْهُمْ وَقُلْ سَلٰمٌ فَسَوْفَ يَعْلَمُونَ ٨٩

CHAPTER
44

AL-DUKHÂN
(The Drought)
(Revealed before Hijrah)

سُورَةُ الدُّخَانِ مَكِّيَّةٌ

With the name of Allâh,
the Most Gracious, the Ever Merciful
(I commence to read Sûrah Al-Dukhân).

بِسْمِ اللّٰهِ الرَّحْمٰنِ الرَّحِيمِ

1. HÂ MÎM - Allâh is Praiseworthy, the Lord of all Honour.
2. This perfect Book that makes (the truth) perspicuously clear bears testimony (to the above statement).
3. Truly, We revealed this (Book) in a Night full of blessings (*Lailatul Qadr*, as) it has been Our wont to warn (people against evil).
4. During this (night) every matter full of wisdom (and substance) is explained distinctly;
5. (Every matter to be decided and done) by Our own command. Verily, We have ever been sending (Messengers),
6. As a mercy from your Lord. Behold! He is the All-Hearing, the All-Knowing,
7. The Lord of the heavens and the earth and all that lies between them, if you would (only) be convinced (to have faith in something) have faith in Him.
8. There is no other, cannot be and will never be one worthy of worship but He. He alone gives life and causes to die. (He is) your Lord as well as the Lord of your forefathers.
9. Yet (they have no faith,) they are steeped in doubt (and) occupied with unreal things.

حمٓ ١ وَالْكِتٰبِ الْمُبِينِ ٢ إِنَّآ أَنْزَلْنٰهُ فِي لَيْلَةٍ مُّبٰرَكَةٍ إِنَّا كُنَّا مُنْذِرِينَ ٣ فِيهَا يُفْرَقُ كُلُّ أَمْرٍ حَكِيمٍ ٤ أَمْرًا مِّنْ عِنْدِنَا إِنَّا كُنَّا مُرْسِلِينَ ٥ رَحْمَةً مِّنْ رَّبِّكَ إِنَّهُ هُوَ السَّمِيعُ الْعَلِيمُ ٦ رَبِّ السَّمٰوٰتِ وَالْأَرْضِ وَمَا بَيْنَهُمَآ إِنْ كُنْتُمْ مُّوقِنِينَ ٧ لَآ إِلٰهَ إِلَّا هُوَ يُحْيِ وَيُمِيتُ رَبُّكُمْ وَرَبُّ أٰبَآئِكُمُ الْأَوَّلِينَ ٨ بَلْ هُمْ

10. So (Prophet!) watch for the day when the sky will bring about a clear drought;
11. That will envelop these people. This is that woeful calamity (which is foretold).
12. (Seeing this the people will cry out,) 'Our Lord! Rid us of this calamity, truly we will be believers.'
13. How shall they take heed (now in this condition) for there has already come to them a Great Messenger telling the right from the wrong.
14. Yet they turned away from him and said, 'He is a man tutored (by others), a man bereft of his senses.'
15. Look! We shall relax your punishment for a short while (but) you are sure to revert (to your former evil ways).
16. (After this respite) We shall again seize (you) with the mighty onslaught one day, then We shall inflict a sure and stern punishment.
17. And We afflicted the people of Pharaoh with a torment before them for there had come to them (too) a noble and respectable Messenger,
18. (Saying,) 'Deliver to me the servants of Allâh (- the Children of Israel). In fact I am to you a Messenger, faithful to (my) trust,
19. 'And do not rise up in defiance of Allâh. Surely, I bring to you a clear authoritative proof.
20. 'And I have taken refuge with my Lord and your Lord lest you should stone me (to death).
21. 'You had better leave me alone if you do not believe in me.'
22. Thereupon (when they denied him) he (- Moses) called to his Lord (saying), 'These are a people guilty indeed.'
23. Then (the order was), 'Set forth with My servants in a watch of the night, (for) you are going to be chased.
24. 'And leave (when) the sea (is calm and not in tide) by its depressed portion (crossing on the dunes). Surely, these (pursuers, Pharaoh and

سُورَةُ الدُّخَانِ ٤٤

فِي شَكٍّ يَلْعَبُونَ ﴿٩﴾ فَارْتَقِبْ يَوْمَ تَأْتِي السَّمَاءُ بِدُخَانٍ مُّبِينٍ ﴿١٠﴾ يَغْشَى النَّاسَ هَٰذَا عَذَابٌ أَلِيمٌ ﴿١١﴾ رَبَّنَا اكْشِفْ عَنَّا الْعَذَابَ إِنَّا مُؤْمِنُونَ ﴿١٢﴾ أَنَّىٰ لَهُمُ الذِّكْرَىٰ وَقَدْ جَاءَهُمْ رَسُولٌ مُّبِينٌ ﴿١٣﴾ ثُمَّ تَوَلَّوْا عَنْهُ وَقَالُوا مُعَلَّمٌ مَّجْنُونٌ ﴿١٤﴾ إِنَّا كَاشِفُو الْعَذَابِ قَلِيلًا إِنَّكُمْ عَائِدُونَ ﴿١٥﴾ يَوْمَ نَبْطِشُ الْبَطْشَةَ الْكُبْرَىٰ إِنَّا مُنتَقِمُونَ ﴿١٦﴾ وَلَقَدْ فَتَنَّا قَبْلَهُمْ قَوْمَ فِرْعَوْنَ وَجَاءَهُمْ رَسُولٌ كَرِيمٌ ﴿١٧﴾ أَنْ أَدُّوا إِلَيَّ عِبَادَ اللَّهِ إِنِّي لَكُمْ رَسُولٌ أَمِينٌ ﴿١٨﴾ وَأَن لَّا تَعْلُوا عَلَى اللَّهِ إِنِّي آتِيكُم بِسُلْطَانٍ مُّبِينٍ ﴿١٩﴾ وَإِنِّي عُذْتُ بِرَبِّي وَرَبِّكُمْ أَن تَرْجُمُونِ ﴿٢٠﴾ وَإِن لَّمْ تُؤْمِنُوا لِي فَاعْتَزِلُونِ ﴿٢١﴾ فَدَعَا رَبَّهُ أَنَّ هَٰؤُلَاءِ قَوْمٌ مُّجْرِمُونَ ﴿٢٢﴾ فَأَسْرِ بِعِبَادِي لَيْلًا إِنَّكُم مُّتَّبَعُونَ ﴿٢٣﴾ وَاتْرُكِ

his people) are a host (of people) doomed to be drowned.'
25. (So they were drowned;) and many a garden and springs they left behind,
26. And the cornfields, and how beautiful a place of high status;
27. And the prosperity and comfort that they enjoyed and took delight in.
28. That is how it shall happen (now with the rejecters of the prophet). And We gave all such things to another people.
29. And neither (the residents of) the heaven nor (those of) the earth mourned over them, nor were they reprieved.

SECTION 2

30. LOOK! We delivered the Children of Israel from the disgraceful torment.
31. From (the torment of) Pharaoh. He was surely haughty (and one) of the transgressors.
32. And We chose them (- the Children of Israel) on the basis of Our knowledge, over all their contemporary people.
33. And We gave them some of the signs wherein were (placed) unmixed blessings.
34. These people (of this time) do say,
35. 'It is but our first death (- the only one we will encounter) and (after that) we shall never be the revived ones.
36. 'So bring our forefathers (back to life) if you (O Muslims!) are truthful (in what you say about Resurrection).'
37. Are they superior to the people of (Yemanite King) *Tubba'*, and to those (who flourished) even before them? We destroyed them (all) because they were certainly guilty.
38. And we did not create the heavens and the earth and all that lies between them just because We were doers of some purposeless work.
39. (That) We created them, (it was) only (for an eternal purpose) to establish the truth, yet most of them do not know this.
40. Verily, the Day of Decision is the promised time appointed for all of them,

الْبَحْرَ رَهْوًا ۖ إِنَّهُمْ جُندٌ مُّغْرَقُونَ ﴿٢٤﴾ كَمْ تَرَكُوا
مِن جَنَّاتٍ وَعُيُونٍ ﴿٢٥﴾ وَزُرُوعٍ وَمَقَامٍ كَرِيمٍ ﴿٢٦﴾
وَنَعْمَةٍ كَانُوا فِيهَا فَاكِهِينَ ﴿٢٧﴾ كَذَٰلِكَ ۖ وَأَوْرَثْنَاهَا
قَوْمًا آخَرِينَ ﴿٢٨﴾ فَمَا بَكَتْ عَلَيْهِمُ السَّمَاءُ
وَالْأَرْضُ وَمَا كَانُوا مُنظَرِينَ ﴿٢٩﴾ وَلَقَدْ نَجَّيْنَا
بَنِي إِسْرَائِيلَ مِنَ الْعَذَابِ الْمُهِينِ ﴿٣٠﴾ مِن
فِرْعَوْنَ ۚ إِنَّهُ كَانَ عَالِيًا مِّنَ الْمُسْرِفِينَ ﴿٣١﴾
وَلَقَدِ اخْتَرْنَاهُمْ عَلَىٰ عِلْمٍ عَلَى الْعَالَمِينَ ﴿٣٢﴾
وَآتَيْنَاهُم مِّنَ الْآيَاتِ مَا فِيهِ بَلَاءٌ مُّبِينٌ ﴿٣٣﴾
إِنَّ هَٰؤُلَاءِ لَيَقُولُونَ ﴿٣٤﴾ إِنْ هِيَ إِلَّا مَوْتَتُنَا
الْأُولَىٰ وَمَا نَحْنُ بِمُنشَرِينَ ﴿٣٥﴾ فَأْتُوا بِآبَائِنَا
إِن كُنتُمْ صَادِقِينَ ﴿٣٦﴾ أَهُمْ خَيْرٌ أَمْ قَوْمُ تُبَّعٍ
وَالَّذِينَ مِن قَبْلِهِمْ ۚ أَهْلَكْنَاهُمْ ۖ إِنَّهُمْ كَانُوا
مُجْرِمِينَ ﴿٣٧﴾ وَمَا خَلَقْنَا السَّمَاوَاتِ وَالْأَرْضَ
وَمَا بَيْنَهُمَا لَاعِبِينَ ﴿٣٨﴾ مَا خَلَقْنَاهُمَا إِلَّا بِالْحَقِّ
وَلَٰكِنَّ أَكْثَرَهُمْ لَا يَعْلَمُونَ ﴿٣٩﴾ إِنَّ يَوْمَ الْفَصْلِ
مِيقَاتُهُمْ أَجْمَعِينَ ﴿٤٠﴾ يَوْمَ لَا يُغْنِي مَوْلًى عَن

41. The Day when no friend shall avail a friend in the least nor shall they be helped.
42. Different however shall be the case of those to whom Allâh will show mercy. Verily, He alone is the Mighty, the Ever Merciful.

SECTION 3

43. **V**ERILY, the (despicable) tree of *Zaqqûm*
44. Shall be the food of the arch-sinners.
45. (It will act) like molten copper. It will boil in (their) bellies;
46. As the boiling of scalding water.
47. (The word shall then pass about the guilty,) 'Take hold of him then drag him into the midst of Hell.
48. 'Again pour boiling water upon his head, by way of torment (to him).'
49. (It will be said to him,) 'Suffer this (punishment of yours which you doubted). You (deemed yourself) as if you were the mighty, the honourable one.
50. 'This of course is (the very punishment) about which you used to wrangle.'
51. As for the righteous, they shall be (lodged) in havens of peace and security;
52. In the midst of (a land of) gardens and springs.
53. They shall wear fine silk and heavy brocade (and will be sitting) face to face.
54. Thus (shall it actually happen). And We shall pair them with pure maidens having beautiful large eyes.
55. They will order therein every (kind of) fruit, and will be safe and secure.
56. They will meet therein no death after the first death (met by them in the world). And Allâh saved them from the torment of the Hell.
57. (All this will take place by way of) grace from your Lord. That is the very great achievement indeed.
58. And We have made this (Qur'ân) easy (by revealing it) in your (Arabic) tongue, so that the people may take heed.
59. Now await (their end), for they are (also) awaiting (yours).

مَوْلًى شَيْئًا وَلَا هُمْ يُنْصَرُونَ ﴿٤١﴾ إِلَّا مَنْ رَّحِمَ
اللّٰهُ ۚ إِنَّهُ هُوَ الْعَزِيزُ الرَّحِيمُ ﴿٤٢﴾ إِنَّ شَجَرَتَ
الزَّقُّومِ ﴿٤٣﴾ طَعَامُ الْأَثِيمِ ﴿٤٤﴾ كَالْمُهْلِ ۚ يَغْلِي فِي
الْبُطُونِ ﴿٤٥﴾ كَغَلْيِ الْحَمِيمِ ﴿٤٦﴾ خُذُوهُ فَاعْتِلُوهُ
إِلَىٰ سَوَاءِ الْجَحِيمِ ﴿٤٧﴾ ثُمَّ صُبُّوا فَوْقَ رَأْسِهِ
مِنْ عَذَابِ الْحَمِيمِ ﴿٤٨﴾ ذُقْ إِنَّكَ أَنْتَ الْعَزِيزُ
الْكَرِيمُ ﴿٤٩﴾ إِنَّ هٰذَا مَا كُنْتُمْ بِهِ تَمْتَرُونَ ﴿٥٠﴾
إِنَّ الْمُتَّقِينَ فِي مَقَامٍ أَمِينٍ ﴿٥١﴾ فِي جَنّٰتٍ
وَعُيُونٍ ﴿٥٢﴾ يَلْبَسُونَ مِنْ سُنْدُسٍ وَإِسْتَبْرَقٍ
مُتَقٰبِلِينَ ﴿٥٣﴾ كَذٰلِكَ وَزَوَّجْنٰهُمْ بِحُورٍ عِينٍ ﴿٥٤﴾
يَدْعُونَ فِيهَا بِكُلِّ فٰكِهَةٍ أٰمِنِينَ ﴿٥٥﴾ لَا
يَذُوقُونَ فِيهَا الْمَوْتَ إِلَّا الْمَوْتَةَ الْأُولَىٰ
وَوَقٰهُمْ عَذَابَ الْجَحِيمِ ﴿٥٦﴾ فَضْلًا مِّنْ
رَّبِّكَ ۚ ذٰلِكَ هُوَ الْفَوْزُ الْعَظِيمُ ﴿٥٧﴾ فَإِنَّمَا
يَسَّرْنٰهُ بِلِسَانِكَ لَعَلَّهُمْ يَتَذَكَّرُونَ ﴿٥٨﴾
فَارْتَقِبْ إِنَّهُمْ مُّرْتَقِبُونَ ﴿٥٩﴾

CHAPTER
45

سُورَةُ الْجَاثِيَةِ ٤٥

AL-JÂTHIYAH
(The Fallen on the Knees)
(Revealed before Hijrah)

With the name of Allâh,
the Most Gracious, the Ever Merciful
(I commence to read Sûrah Al-Jâthiyah).

1. HÂ MÎM - Allâh is Praiseworthy, the Lord of all Honour.
2. The gradual revelation of this perfect Book proceeds from Allâh, the All-Mighty, the All-Wise.
3. The fact is that there are signs for believers in the heavens and in the earth,
4. And for the people who have firm faith, there are signs in your own creation and (in) that of all (living) creatures which He spreads abroad.
5. And in the alternation of night and day and the sustenance that Allâh sends down through clouds, whereby He revives the earth after its desolation, and (in) the veering of the winds, there are signs for a people who make use of their understanding.
6. These are the signs of Allâh which We describe to you with precision. In what other announcement will they believe after (they have rejected the word of) Allâh and His signs?
7. Woeful agony awaits every sinful habitual liar,
8. Who hears the Messages of Allâh which are recited to him and then he very proudly persists (in his disbelief) as though he has not heard these (Messages). So give him the tidings of a woeful punishment.
9. And when he comes to know something of Our messages he holds them as of little importance. It is such people for whom there awaits

سُورَةُ الْجَاثِيَةِ مَكِّيَّةٌ

بِسْمِ اللّٰهِ الرَّحْمٰنِ الرَّحِيمِ

حمٓ ۝١ تَنْزِيلُ الْكِتٰبِ مِنَ اللّٰهِ الْعَزِيزِ
الْحَكِيمِ ۝٢ إِنَّ فِي السَّمٰوٰتِ وَ الْأَرْضِ لَأٰيٰتٍ
لِّلْمُؤْمِنِينَ ۝٣ وَ فِي خَلْقِكُمْ وَ مَا يَبُثُّ مِنْ
دَآبَّةٍ أٰيٰتٌ لِّقَوْمٍ يُوقِنُونَ ۝٤ وَ اخْتِلٰفِ
الَّيْلِ وَ النَّهَارِ وَ مَآ أَنْزَلَ اللّٰهُ مِنَ السَّمَآءِ
مِنْ رِّزْقٍ فَأَحْيَا بِهِ الْأَرْضَ بَعْدَ مَوْتِهَا
وَ تَصْرِيفِ الرِّيٰحِ أٰيٰتٌ لِّقَوْمٍ يَعْقِلُونَ ۝٥
تِلْكَ أٰيٰتُ اللّٰهِ نَتْلُوهَا عَلَيْكَ بِالْحَقِّ فَبِأَيِّ
حَدِيثٍ بَعْدَ اللّٰهِ وَ أٰيٰتِهِ يُؤْمِنُونَ ۝٦ وَيْلٌ
لِّكُلِّ أَفَّاكٍ أَثِيمٍ ۝٧ يَسْمَعُ أٰيٰتِ اللّٰهِ تُتْلٰى
عَلَيْهِ ثُمَّ يُصِرُّ مُسْتَكْبِرًا كَأَنْ لَّمْ يَسْمَعْهَا
فَبَشِّرْهُ بِعَذَابٍ أَلِيمٍ ۝٨ وَ إِذَا عَلِمَ مِنْ
أٰيٰتِنَا شَيْـًٔا اتَّخَذَهَا هُزُوًا أُولٰٓئِكَ لَهُمْ عَذَابٌ

a disgraceful punishment.

10. (In addition to this worldly punishment) they have Gehenna before them. The wealth they have acquired shall not avail them, nor shall these (guardians of theirs) whom they have taken for (their) helping friends apart from Allâh (be of any help to them). And there awaits them a dreadful punishment.

11. This (Qur'ân) is (true and) a complete guidance. But those who deny the commandment of their Lord shall suffer the scourge of a woeful punishment.

SECTION 2

12. **I**T is Allâh Who has made the sea subservient to you so that the ships may sail upon it by His command and so that by means of these ships you may seek His bounty and give (Him) thanks.

13. And He has made subservient to you all that lies in the heavens and all that lies in the earth. All these (benedictions) are from Him. In all this there are signs for a people who would reflect.

14. Tell those who believe to let alone those who do not accept the (contesting) days of Allâh on which the righteous will be successful in the land and the wicked will suffer disaster in order that He may Himself recompense every people according to their deeds.

15. He who does good, does it for (the good of) his own soul and he who does evil (the sad consequences of it) shall befall him, (for, after all) you will be brought back to your Lord.

16. And indeed We gave the Children of Israel the Scripture (of mosaic law) and power of judgment and prophethood, and provided them with good and pure things and exalted them over the contemporary peoples.

17. And We gave them clear signs regarding this affair (of the advent of this Prophet). And they did not differ (about it) but after true knowledge (in the form of the Qur'ân) had come to them, (and this difference was) to spite

مُّهِينٌ ۝٩ مِّن وَرَآئِهِمْ جَهَنَّمُ ۖ وَلَا يُغْنِي عَنْهُم
مَّا كَسَبُوا شَيْئًا وَلَا مَا اتَّخَذُوا مِن دُونِ
اللَّهِ أَوْلِيَاءَ ۖ وَلَهُمْ عَذَابٌ عَظِيمٌ ۝١٠ هَٰذَا
هُدًى ۖ وَالَّذِينَ كَفَرُوا بِآيَاتِ رَبِّهِمْ لَهُمْ
عَذَابٌ مِّن رِّجْزٍ أَلِيمٌ ۝١١ اللَّهُ الَّذِي سَخَّرَ
لَكُمُ الْبَحْرَ لِتَجْرِيَ الْفُلْكُ فِيهِ بِأَمْرِهِ
وَلِتَبْتَغُوا مِن فَضْلِهِ وَلَعَلَّكُمْ تَشْكُرُونَ ۝١٢
وَسَخَّرَ لَكُم مَّا فِي السَّمَاوَاتِ وَمَا فِي الْأَرْضِ
جَمِيعًا مِّنْهُ ۚ إِنَّ فِي ذَٰلِكَ لَآيَاتٍ لِّقَوْمٍ يَتَفَكَّرُونَ ۝١٣
قُل لِّلَّذِينَ آمَنُوا يَغْفِرُوا لِلَّذِينَ لَا يَرْجُونَ
أَيَّامَ اللَّهِ لِيَجْزِيَ قَوْمًا بِمَا كَانُوا يَكْسِبُونَ ۝١٤
مَنْ عَمِلَ صَالِحًا فَلِنَفْسِهِ ۖ وَمَنْ أَسَاءَ
فَعَلَيْهَا ۖ ثُمَّ إِلَىٰ رَبِّكُمْ تُرْجَعُونَ ۝١٥ وَلَقَدْ آتَيْنَا
بَنِي إِسْرَائِيلَ الْكِتَابَ وَالْحُكْمَ وَالنُّبُوَّةَ
وَرَزَقْنَاهُم مِّنَ الطَّيِّبَاتِ وَفَضَّلْنَاهُمْ عَلَى الْعَالَمِينَ ۝١٦
وَآتَيْنَاهُم بَيِّنَاتٍ مِّنَ الْأَمْرِ ۖ فَمَا اخْتَلَفُوا
إِلَّا مِن بَعْدِ مَا جَاءَهُمُ الْعِلْمُ بَغْيًا بَيْنَهُمْ

ع ١١/٢ ١٧

one another. Behold! Your Lord will judge between them on the Day of Resurrection concerning all their differences.

18. Then We (gave you a system of law and) set you on a clear highway regarding this affair. Follow it and do not follow the caprices of those who have no knowledge.

19. Verily, they can be of no avail to you against (the displeasure of) Allâh. Surely, the wrongdoers are helping-friends one of the other, but Allâh is the helping-friend of those who have become secure against evil.

20. Those (teachings of the Qur'ân) are a means to grant insight to humankind and a source of complete guidance and a mercy for a people who have firm faith.

21. Do those who commit evil deeds think that We will treat them like those who believe and (accordingly) do deeds of righteousness so that their lives and deaths be alike? How ill they judge!

SECTION 3

22. **A**LLÂH has created the heavens and the earth with an eternal purpose to ensure that every soul be recompensed according to his deeds and no one be done injustice to.

23. Have you considered the case of him who has taken his own low desires for his god and whom Allâh has forsaken and adjudged as lost on the basis of (His infinite) knowledge, and whose ears and heart He has sealed and whose eyes He has covered with a veil? Who then will guide him after Allâh (has condemned him for his being given to evil ways)? Will you then pay no heed?

24. They say, 'We have only this our present life (to live). We (people of one generation) die and we (people of a new generation from among us) come to life again (here in this very world). It is (the passage of) time alone that deals us death. But they have no real knowledge whatsoever about the matter (- the Hereafter).

إِنَّ رَبَّكَ يَقْضِي بَيْنَهُمْ يَوْمَ الْقِيٰمَةِ فِيمَا
كَانُوا فِيهِ يَخْتَلِفُونَ ﴿١٧﴾ ثُمَّ جَعَلْنٰكَ عَلٰى
شَرِيعَةٍ مِّنَ الْأَمْرِ فَاتَّبِعْهَا وَلَا تَتَّبِعْ
أَهْوَآءَ الَّذِينَ لَا يَعْلَمُونَ ﴿١٨﴾ إِنَّهُمْ لَنْ يُّغْنُوا
عَنْكَ مِنَ اللّٰهِ شَيْـًٔا ۚ وَإِنَّ الظّٰلِمِينَ بَعْضُهُمْ
أَوْلِيَآءُ بَعْضٍ ۚ وَاللّٰهُ وَلِيُّ الْمُتَّقِينَ ﴿١٩﴾ هٰذَا
بَصٰٓئِرُ لِلنَّاسِ وَهُدًى وَّرَحْمَةٌ لِّقَوْمٍ
يُّوقِنُونَ ﴿٢٠﴾ أَمْ حَسِبَ الَّذِينَ اجْتَرَحُوا
السَّيِّاٰتِ أَنْ نَّجْعَلَهُمْ كَالَّذِينَ اٰمَنُوا
وَعَمِلُوا الصّٰلِحٰتِ سَوَآءً مَّحْيَاهُمْ وَمَمَاتُهُمْ
سَآءَ مَا يَحْكُمُونَ ﴿٢١﴾ وَخَلَقَ اللّٰهُ السَّمٰوٰتِ
وَالْأَرْضَ بِالْحَقِّ وَلِتُجْزٰى كُلُّ نَفْسٍ بِمَا
كَسَبَتْ وَهُمْ لَا يُظْلَمُونَ ﴿٢٢﴾ أَفَرَءَيْتَ مَنِ
اتَّخَذَ إِلٰهَهُ هَوٰىهُ وَأَضَلَّهُ اللّٰهُ عَلٰى عِلْمٍ
وَّخَتَمَ عَلٰى سَمْعِهِ وَقَلْبِهِ وَجَعَلَ عَلٰى
بَصَرِهِ غِشٰوَةً ۗ فَمَنْ يَّهْدِيهِ مِنْ بَعْدِ اللّٰهِ ۗ
أَفَلَا تَذَكَّرُونَ ﴿٢٣﴾ وَقَالُوا مَا هِيَ إِلَّا حَيَاتُنَا
الدُّنْيَا نَمُوتُ وَنَحْيَا وَمَا يُهْلِكُنَآ إِلَّا الدَّهْرُ
وَمَا لَهُمْ بِذٰلِكَ مِنْ عِلْمٍ ۚ إِنْ هُمْ إِلَّا

ع ٢ ١٨

They merely make conjectures.
25. And when Our clear messages are recited to them their only contention is that they say, 'Bring back our forefathers (alive) if you are true (in your belief in the life after death).'
26. Say, '(It is) Allâh alone Who gives you life then He causes you to die, then He will gather you together on the Day of Resurrection, (the day) about the advent of which there is no doubt. Yet most of the people do not know (this truth).'

SECTION 4

27. **T**HE kingdom of the heavens and the earth belongs to Allâh. At the time when the (promised) Hour shall come to pass the falsifiers (of the truth with vanity) shall be in the loss on that day.
28. And (at that promised time) you shall see every community fallen on (their) knees. Every community will be summoned to (face) their records (of deeds). (And it shall be said to them,) 'This day you shall be recompensed according to your deeds.
29. 'Here is Our (prepared) record. It speaks the truth about you. Indeed, We have been getting all your deeds fully registered and preserved.'
30. Now as for those who believed and did deeds of righteousness, their Lord will admit them into His mercy. This indeed is a manifest achievement.
31. But as for those who disbelieved (God will say,) 'Is it not that My Messages were recited to you yet you behaved arrogantly and you became those who cut off their ties (with us)?
32. 'And when it was said (to you), "The promise of Allâh is of course true and the Hour (of Resurrection) there is no doubt about it," you said, "We do not know what the Hour may be, we have only a faint notion about it and we are, by no means, convinced (of its certainty)".'
33. And (on that day) the evils (inherent) in their deeds will become apparent to them. They

يَظُنُّونَ ﴿٢٤﴾ وَإِذَا تُتْلَىٰ عَلَيْهِمْ ءَايَٰتُنَا بَيِّنَٰتٍ
مَّا كَانَ حُجَّتَهُمْ إِلَّآ أَن قَالُوا ائْتُوا بِـَٔابَآئِنَآ
إِن كُنتُمْ صَٰدِقِينَ ﴿٢٥﴾ قُلِ اللَّهُ يُحْيِيكُمْ ثُمَّ
يُمِيتُكُمْ ثُمَّ يَجْمَعُكُمْ إِلَىٰ يَوْمِ الْقِيَٰمَةِ لَا رَيْبَ
فِيهِ وَلَٰكِنَّ أَكْثَرَ النَّاسِ لَا يَعْلَمُونَ ﴿٢٦﴾ وَلِلَّهِ
مُلْكُ السَّمَٰوَٰتِ وَالْأَرْضِ وَيَوْمَ تَقُومُ
السَّاعَةُ يَوْمَئِذٍ يَخْسَرُ الْمُبْطِلُونَ ﴿٢٧﴾ وَتَرَىٰ
كُلَّ أُمَّةٍ جَاثِيَةً كُلُّ أُمَّةٍ تُدْعَىٰ إِلَىٰ
كِتَٰبِهَا الْيَوْمَ تُجْزَوْنَ مَا كُنتُمْ تَعْمَلُونَ ﴿٢٨﴾
هَٰذَا كِتَٰبُنَا يَنطِقُ عَلَيْكُم بِالْحَقِّ إِنَّا كُنَّا
نَسْتَنسِخُ مَا كُنتُمْ تَعْمَلُونَ ﴿٢٩﴾ فَأَمَّا الَّذِينَ
ءَامَنُوا وَعَمِلُوا الصَّٰلِحَٰتِ فَيُدْخِلُهُمْ رَبُّهُمْ
فِي رَحْمَتِهِ ذَٰلِكَ هُوَ الْفَوْزُ الْمُبِينُ ﴿٣٠﴾ وَأَمَّا
الَّذِينَ كَفَرُوا أَفَلَمْ تَكُنْ ءَايَٰتِي تُتْلَىٰ عَلَيْكُمْ
فَاسْتَكْبَرْتُمْ وَكُنتُمْ قَوْمًا مُّجْرِمِينَ ﴿٣١﴾ وَإِذَا قِيلَ
إِنَّ وَعْدَ اللَّهِ حَقٌّ وَالسَّاعَةُ لَا رَيْبَ فِيهَا
قُلْتُم مَّا نَدْرِي مَا السَّاعَةُ إِن نَّظُنُّ إِلَّا ظَنًّا
وَمَا نَحْنُ بِمُسْتَيْقِنِينَ ﴿٣٢﴾ وَبَدَا لَهُمْ سَيِّـَٔاتُ مَا

will be caught by that (very destruction) they used to hold in very low estimation.
34. And it will be said (to them), 'This Day We have given you up just as you gave up (the idea) that you will meet this Day of yours. Now, your resort is the Fire and you have no one for a helper.
35. 'This (end of yours) is because you took no account of the commandments of Allâh, and the life of this world seduced you.' So that Day they will not be taken out of it nor will they be able to reach even the threshold (of the Divine Presence seeking to make amends and to win His favour).
36. All type of perfect and true praise, therefore, belongs to Allâh, Lord of the heavens, Lord of the earth and Lord of the worlds.
37. And all the majesty in the heavens and the earth belongs to Him alone. And He alone is the All-Mighty, the All-Wise.

عَمِلُوا وَحَاقَ بِهِم مَّا كَانُوا بِهِ يَسْتَهْزِءُونَ ٣٣
وَقِيلَ الْيَوْمَ نَنسَاكُمْ كَمَا نَسِيتُمْ لِقَاءَ يَوْمِكُمْ
هَٰذَا وَمَأْوَاكُمُ النَّارُ وَمَا لَكُم مِّن نَّاصِرِينَ ٣٤
ذَٰلِكُم بِأَنَّكُمُ اتَّخَذْتُمْ آيَاتِ اللَّهِ هُزُوًا وَغَرَّتْكُمُ
الْحَيَاةُ الدُّنْيَا فَالْيَوْمَ لَا يُخْرَجُونَ مِنْهَا وَلَا
هُمْ يُسْتَعْتَبُونَ ٣٥ فَلِلَّهِ الْحَمْدُ رَبِّ السَّمَاوَاتِ
وَرَبِّ الْأَرْضِ رَبِّ الْعَالَمِينَ ٣٦ وَلَهُ الْكِبْرِيَاءُ
فِي السَّمَاوَاتِ وَالْأَرْضِ وَهُوَ الْعَزِيزُ الْحَكِيمُ ٣٧

CHAPTER
46

AL-AHQÂF
(The Sand Dunes)
(Revealed before Hijrah)

سُورَةُ الأَحْقَافِ مَكِّيَّةٌ

With the name of Allâh,
the Most Gracious, the Ever Merciful
(I commence to read Sûrah Al-Ahqâf).

بِسْمِ اللَّهِ الرَّحْمَٰنِ الرَّحِيمِ

PART الجُزْءُ السَّادِسُ وَالعِشْرُونَ XXVI

1. HÂ MÎM - Allâh is Praiseworthy, the Lord of All Honour.
2. The gradual revelation of this perfect Book proceeds from Allâh the All-Mighty, the All-Wise.
3. We have not created the heavens and the earth and what lies between them both but with an eternal purpose and for a term appointed. Yet those who have disbelieved in what they

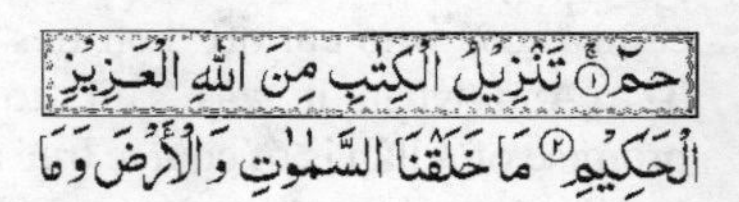

have been warned of are the ones who turn away (from this Qur'ân).

4. Say, 'Do you realize what it is you call on, apart from Allâh? Show me what portion of the earth they have created. Or have they (played) a part in (the planning and creation of) the heavens? Bring me any Book (revealed) before this or some vestige of knowledge (to confirm your practices) if you are truthful (in your claim).'

5. And who is more misguided than the person who instead of (praying to) Allâh prays to those who will not answer him till the Day of Resurrection and these (deities they worship) are even unaware of their prayers (to them).

6. And when the people shall be gathered together (on the Day of Judgment and Justice) these (false gods) will become enemies to them (- their worshippers) and will (even) disown their worship.

7. When Our clear Messages are recited to them, these disbelievers say with regard to the Truth when it comes to them, 'This is an obvious sorcery.'

8. Do they say, 'He himself has forged this (Qur'ân)?' Say, 'If I have forged it, you have no power to help me in anyway against Allâh, He knows what nonsensical talk you are indulging in. Sufficient is He for a witness between me and you. And He is the Great Protector, the Ever Merciful.'

9. Say, 'I am no novel (Apostle) among the Messengers nor do I know what will be done to me (on your behalf) or to you. I simply follow what is revealed to me and I am nought but a plain Warner.'

10. Say, 'Have you considered (that) if this (Qur'ân) is from Allâh and you do not believe in it (there will be no way of escape for you); (more so because) a witness (in the person of Moses) from among the Children of Israel has borne witness to (the advent of) his like. So, whereas he has believed (in those prophecies)

بَيْنَهُمَآ إِلَّا بِالْحَقِّ وَ أَجَلٍ مُّسَمًّى ۚ وَ الَّذِيْنَ
كَفَرُوْا عَمَّآ أُنْذِرُوْا مُعْرِضُوْنَ ﴿٣﴾ قُلْ أَرَءَيْتُمْ مَّا
تَدْعُوْنَ مِنْ دُوْنِ اللهِ أَرُوْنِيْ مَاذَا خَلَقُوْا
مِنَ الْأَرْضِ أَمْ لَهُمْ شِرْكٌ فِي السَّمٰوٰتِ ۭ
إِيْتُوْنِيْ بِكِتٰبٍ مِّنْ قَبْلِ هٰذَآ أَوْ أَثٰرَةٍ
مِّنْ عِلْمٍ إِنْ كُنْتُمْ صٰدِقِيْنَ ﴿٤﴾ وَ مَنْ
أَضَلُّ مِمَّنْ يَّدْعُوْا مِنْ دُوْنِ اللهِ مَنْ
لَّا يَسْتَجِيْبُ لَهٗٓ إِلٰى يَوْمِ الْقِيٰمَةِ وَ هُمْ
عَنْ دُعَآئِهِمْ غٰفِلُوْنَ ﴿٥﴾ وَ إِذَا حُشِرَ النَّاسُ
كَانُوْا لَهُمْ أَعْدَآءً وَّ كَانُوْا بِعِبَادَتِهِمْ كٰفِرِيْنَ ﴿٦﴾
وَ إِذَا تُتْلٰى عَلَيْهِمْ أٰيٰتُنَا بَيِّنٰتٍ قَالَ الَّذِيْنَ
كَفَرُوْا لِلْحَقِّ لَمَّا جَآءَهُمْ هٰذَا سِحْرٌ مُّبِيْنٌ ﴿٧﴾
أَمْ يَقُوْلُوْنَ افْتَرٰىهُ ۭ قُلْ إِنِ افْتَرَيْتُهٗ فَلَا
تَمْلِكُوْنَ لِيْ مِنَ اللهِ شَيْـًٔا ۭ هُوَ أَعْلَمُ بِمَا
تُفِيْضُوْنَ فِيْهِ ۭ كَفٰى بِهٖ شَهِيْدًۢا بَيْنِيْ
وَ بَيْنَكُمْ ۭ وَ هُوَ الْغَفُوْرُ الرَّحِيْمُ ﴿٨﴾ قُلْ مَا
كُنْتُ بِدْعًا مِّنَ الرُّسُلِ وَ مَآ أَدْرِيْ مَا
يُفْعَلُ بِيْ وَ لَا بِكُمْ ۭ إِنْ أَتَّبِعُ إِلَّا مَا
يُوْحٰٓى إِلَيَّ وَ مَآ أَنَا۠ إِلَّا نَذِيْرٌ مُّبِيْنٌ ﴿٩﴾ قُلْ
أَرَءَيْتُمْ إِنْ كَانَ مِنْ عِنْدِ اللهِ وَ كَفَرْتُمْ
بِهٖ وَ شَهِدَ شَاهِدٌ مِّنْ بَنِيْٓ إِسْرَآءِيْلَ
عَلٰى مِثْلِهٖ فَأٰمَنَ وَ اسْتَكْبَرْتُمْ ۭ إِنَّ اللهَ

but you turn away in disdain, (how should you fare then? Bear in mind) Allâh guides no unjust people (to success).

SECTION 2

11. AND those who disbelieve say of those who believe, 'If these (- the Qur'ânic doctrines) were any good they would not have taken precedence over us in believing in it.' Since they themselves have received no guidance from it they say (out of malice), 'It is an old lie.'

12. Whereas the Scripture of Moses (which was) a guide and a mercy preceded it, this (Qur'ân) is a Book which fulfills (the prophecies contained in the previous Scriptures) making its meanings and significance eloquently clear. (It has been revealed) so that it may warn those who do wrong and give glad tidings to the doers of righteous deeds.

13. Verily, those who say, 'Allâh is our Lord,' then remain steadfast (in their belief) shall have nothing to fear nor shall they grieve.

14. It is they who are the owners of the Paradise. They shall be abiding therein for ever as a reward for their deeds.

15. And We have enjoined on a human being to do good to his parents. His mother bears him with trouble and pain and brings him forth with trouble and pain. The bearing of him and his weaning (takes) thirty months, till when he attains his full maturity and reaches (the age of) forty years he says to his Lord, 'My Lord! Rouse me up that I may give thanks for the favours You have bestowed on me and on my parents and that I may do such righteous deeds as may please You. And (my Lord!) establish righteousness among my progeny for me. To You indeed I turn penitently and I am surely of those who submit themselves (to You).'

16. Such are the people the best of whose deeds We accept and reward, and whose evil deeds We pass over. (They shall be) among the owners of Paradise, (in fulfillment of) the true

لَا يَهْدِي الْقَوْمَ الظَّٰلِمِينَ ﴿١٠﴾ وَقَالَ الَّذِينَ
كَفَرُوا لِلَّذِينَ ءَامَنُوا لَوْ كَانَ خَيْرًا مَّا سَبَقُونَا
إِلَيْهِ وَإِذْ لَمْ يَهْتَدُوا بِهِ فَسَيَقُولُونَ
هَٰذَا إِفْكٌ قَدِيمٌ ﴿١١﴾ وَمِن قَبْلِهِ كِتَٰبُ
مُوسَىٰ إِمَامًا وَرَحْمَةً وَهَٰذَا كِتَٰبٌ مُّصَدِّقٌ
لِّسَانًا عَرَبِيًّا لِّيُنذِرَ الَّذِينَ ظَلَمُوا وَبُشْرَىٰ
لِلْمُحْسِنِينَ ﴿١٢﴾ إِنَّ الَّذِينَ قَالُوا رَبُّنَا اللَّهُ
ثُمَّ اسْتَقَٰمُوا فَلَا خَوْفٌ عَلَيْهِمْ وَلَا هُمْ
يَحْزَنُونَ ﴿١٣﴾ أُولَٰئِكَ أَصْحَٰبُ الْجَنَّةِ خَٰلِدِينَ
فِيهَا جَزَاءً بِمَا كَانُوا يَعْمَلُونَ ﴿١٤﴾ وَوَصَّيْنَا
الْإِنسَٰنَ بِوَٰلِدَيْهِ إِحْسَٰنًا حَمَلَتْهُ أُمُّهُ
كُرْهًا وَوَضَعَتْهُ كُرْهًا وَحَمْلُهُ وَفِصَٰلُهُ
ثَلَٰثُونَ شَهْرًا حَتَّىٰ إِذَا بَلَغَ أَشُدَّهُ وَبَلَغَ
أَرْبَعِينَ سَنَةً قَالَ رَبِّ أَوْزِعْنِي أَنْ أَشْكُرَ
نِعْمَتَكَ الَّتِي أَنْعَمْتَ عَلَيَّ وَعَلَىٰ وَٰلِدَيَّ
وَأَنْ أَعْمَلَ صَٰلِحًا تَرْضَىٰهُ وَأَصْلِحْ لِي فِي
ذُرِّيَّتِي إِنِّي تُبْتُ إِلَيْكَ وَإِنِّي مِنَ الْمُسْلِمِينَ ﴿١٥﴾
أُولَٰئِكَ الَّذِينَ نَتَقَبَّلُ عَنْهُمْ أَحْسَنَ مَا
عَمِلُوا وَنَتَجَاوَزُ عَن سَيِّـَٔاتِهِمْ فِي أَصْحَٰبِ

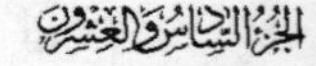

promise which was made to them.
17. Yet there is another (hard-hearted) one who says to his parents, 'Fie upon you both! Do you threaten me that I shall be resurrected (to live again after death), when so many generations have already passed away before me (without any one of them having been raised to life).' While both (- the believing parents) ask Allâh's help (and say to their child), 'Alas for you. Have faith, surely the promise of Allâh is true.' But he says, 'This is nothing but mere fables of the ancients.'
18. Such are the people against whom the sentence of punishment becomes due along with the communities of the *jinn* (- haughty) and (ordinary) people that preceded them. Of course, they were the losers.
19. And all shall have positions and grades (with their Lord) according to the worth of their deeds; and (it shall be so) that He may repay them fully for their deeds and that they may not be treated unjustly.
20. And on that day those who disbelieve will be exposed to the (Hell) Fire. (It will be said to them,) 'You consumed your good things during your life of the world and you enjoyed them. So this day you shall be recompensed with disgraceful punishment, because you waxed proud on the earth without justification and because you committed transgression.'

SECTION 3

21. AND make mention of the kinsman of 'Âd (- Hûd, a Messenger of God to them), when he warned his people (living) in wind-curved sand-dunes (in *Hadzramût*, south of Arabia) to whom Warners had already come before him and after him (saying), 'Worship none but Allâh. I, indeed, fear lest the agony of a dreadful day should befall you.'
22. They said, 'Have you come to us to seduce us and turn us away from our gods. Bring down on us (the punishment) you threaten us with, if indeed you are of the truthful.'

الْجَنَّةِ ۖ وَعْدَ الصِّدْقِ الَّذِي كَانُوا يُوعَدُونَ ﴿١٦﴾
وَالَّذِي قَالَ لِوَالِدَيْهِ أُفٍّ لَّكُمَا أَتَعِدَانِنِي
أَنْ أُخْرَجَ وَقَدْ خَلَتِ الْقُرُونُ مِن قَبْلِي
وَهُمَا يَسْتَغِيثَانِ اللَّهَ وَيْلَكَ آمِنْ إِنَّ
وَعْدَ اللَّهِ حَقٌّ فَيَقُولُ مَا هَٰذَا إِلَّا أَسَاطِيرُ
الْأَوَّلِينَ ﴿١٧﴾ أُولَٰئِكَ الَّذِينَ حَقَّ عَلَيْهِمُ
الْقَوْلُ فِي أُمَمٍ قَدْ خَلَتْ مِن قَبْلِهِم
مِّنَ الْجِنِّ وَالْإِنسِ ۖ إِنَّهُمْ كَانُوا خَاسِرِينَ ﴿١٨﴾
وَلِكُلٍّ دَرَجَاتٌ مِّمَّا عَمِلُوا ۖ وَلِيُوَفِّيَهُمْ
أَعْمَالَهُمْ وَهُمْ لَا يُظْلَمُونَ ﴿١٩﴾ وَيَوْمَ يُعْرَضُ
الَّذِينَ كَفَرُوا عَلَى النَّارِ أَذْهَبْتُمْ طَيِّبَاتِكُمْ
فِي حَيَاتِكُمُ الدُّنْيَا وَاسْتَمْتَعْتُم بِهَا فَالْيَوْمَ
تُجْزَوْنَ عَذَابَ الْهُونِ بِمَا كُنتُمْ تَسْتَكْبِرُونَ
فِي الْأَرْضِ بِغَيْرِ الْحَقِّ وَبِمَا كُنتُمْ تَفْسُقُونَ ﴿٢٠﴾
وَاذْكُرْ أَخَا عَادٍ إِذْ أَنذَرَ قَوْمَهُ بِالْأَحْقَافِ
وَقَدْ خَلَتِ النُّذُرُ مِن بَيْنِ يَدَيْهِ وَمِنْ
خَلْفِهِ أَلَّا تَعْبُدُوا إِلَّا اللَّهَ إِنِّي أَخَافُ عَلَيْكُمْ
عَذَابَ يَوْمٍ عَظِيمٍ ﴿٢١﴾ قَالُوا أَجِئْتَنَا لِتَأْفِكَنَا
عَنْ آلِهَتِنَا فَأْتِنَا بِمَا تَعِدُنَا إِن كُنتَ

23. He said, 'Allâh alone has the true knowledge (of the time of the punishment). I am only conveying to you that (Message) I have been sent with. But I see that you are a people behaving obstinately (for no reason).'
24. Then, when they saw this (punishment they were threatened with) in the form of a cloud (spreading in the sky) heading towards their valleys, they said, 'This is a cloud which will rain over us.' (They were told,) 'It is no such thing, rather it is that (punishment) which you sought to hasten. (It is) a hurricane carrying a woeful punishment.
25. 'This (hurricane) will go on destroying everything by the command of its Lord.' Accordingly (the hurricane struck them and) they became such that nothing could be seen (of them) except their dwellings. That is how do We recompense the guilty people.
26. (Makkans!) We had given them power to do such things as We have not given you. We gave them hearing, eyes and hearts. But their hearing, their eyes and their hearts availed them not, since they persistently denied the signs of Allâh. And they were caught by that (punishment) which they held in very low estimation.

SECTION 4

27. **A**ND We have destroyed several of the townships (which were situated) around you. We have repeatedly explained the Messages in diverse ways so that the people might turn (to Us giving up their atrocities).
28. Why then, did not those beings whom they had taken up for gods apart from Allâh to bring (them) close (to Him) help them? Instead (of being any help to them) they were lost to them. Such was (the outcome of) their lie and (of) what they fabricated (that their gods were a means to bring them close to God).
29. And (Prophet! Recall the time) when We brought some people from among the *jinns* to you. They wished to listen to the Qur'ân. When they attended it (- its recitation) they said (one

مِنَ الصّٰدِقِيْنَ ﴿٢٢﴾ قَالَ إِنَّمَا الْعِلْمُ عِنْدَ اللّٰهِ ۖ
وَأُبَلِّغُكُمْ مَّا أُرْسِلْتُ بِهٖ وَلٰكِنِّيْ أَرٰىكُمْ
قَوْمًا تَجْهَلُوْنَ ﴿٢٣﴾ فَلَمَّا رَأَوْهُ عَارِضًا مُّسْتَقْبِلَ
أَوْدِيَتِهِمْ قَالُوْا هٰذَا عَارِضٌ مُّمْطِرُنَا ۚ بَلْ
هُوَ مَا اسْتَعْجَلْتُمْ بِهٖ ۖ رِيْحٌ فِيْهَا عَذَابٌ
أَلِيْمٌ ﴿٢٤﴾ تُدَمِّرُ كُلَّ شَيْءٍ بِأَمْرِ رَبِّهَا فَأَصْبَحُوْا
لَا يُرٰى إِلَّا مَسٰكِنُهُمْ ۚ كَذٰلِكَ نَجْزِي الْقَوْمَ
الْمُجْرِمِيْنَ ﴿٢٥﴾ وَلَقَدْ مَكَّنّٰهُمْ فِيْمَا إِنْ مَّكَّنّٰكُمْ
فِيْهِ وَجَعَلْنَا لَهُمْ سَمْعًا وَّأَبْصٰرًا وَّأَفْئِدَةً ۖ
فَمَا أَغْنٰى عَنْهُمْ سَمْعُهُمْ وَلَا أَبْصٰرُهُمْ وَلَا
أَفْئِدَتُهُمْ مِّنْ شَيْءٍ إِذْ كَانُوْا يَجْحَدُوْنَ
بِاٰيٰتِ اللّٰهِ وَحَاقَ بِهِمْ مَّا كَانُوْا بِهٖ
يَسْتَهْزِءُوْنَ ﴿٢٦﴾ وَلَقَدْ أَهْلَكْنَا مَا حَوْلَكُمْ
مِّنَ الْقُرٰى وَصَرَّفْنَا الْاٰيٰتِ لَعَلَّهُمْ يَرْجِعُوْنَ ﴿٢٧﴾
فَلَوْلَا نَصَرَهُمُ الَّذِيْنَ اتَّخَذُوْا مِنْ دُوْنِ
اللّٰهِ قُرْبَانًا اٰلِهَةً ۖ بَلْ ضَلُّوْا عَنْهُمْ ۚ وَذٰلِكَ
إِفْكُهُمْ وَمَا كَانُوْا يَفْتَرُوْنَ ﴿٢٨﴾ وَإِذْ صَرَفْنَا
إِلَيْكَ نَفَرًا مِّنَ الْجِنِّ يَسْتَمِعُوْنَ الْقُرْاٰنَ ۚ

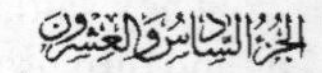

to another), 'Be silent (and listen).' When this (recitation) was over they went back to their people as warners.

30. They (having gone there) said, 'O our people! We have listened to a Book which has been revealed after (the time of) Moses confirming that (divine Scripture) which is before it. It guides to the truth and to the right and straight path.

31. 'O our people! Accept the call of one calling to Allâh and believe in Him. (If you do so) He will keep you safe from (the woeful consequences of) your sins and will screen you from the woeful punishment.

32. 'But one who does not accept (the call of) one calling to Allâh, cannot be the frustrator (of God's purpose) in the earth (and will not escape His punishment), nor can he have protecting friends apart from Him. Such people are steeped in clear error'.

33. Have they not considered that Allâh Who has created the heavens and the earth and was not wearied by their creation, is (in every way) Possessor of power to give life to the dead? Yes, verily He is Possessor of sovereign power to do every desired thing.

34. And the day those who disbelieve will be exposed to the Fire, (they will be asked,) 'Has this (punishment) not actually come to pass?' They will say, 'Yes, it has, by our Lord.' He will then say, '(Now) suffer the punishment because of your disbelief.'

35. Patiently persevere then (O Prophet!) as did all the Messengers possessed of high-resolve did, and do not seek to hasten on for them (- the disbelievers, the doom which they are being promised). On the day when they will witness that they have been threatened with (they will feel) as if they have not tarried (in this world) but for an hour of a day. (It is) enough as delivery (of fair-warning from God). Who shall be destroyed now, if not the disobedient sinful people?

فَلَمَّا حَضَرُوهُ قَالُوٓا أَنْصِتُوا ۚ فَلَمَّا قُضِيَ وَلَّوْا
إِلَىٰ قَوْمِهِمْ مُّنْذِرِينَ ﴿٢٩﴾ قَالُوا يٰقَوْمَنَآ إِنَّا
سَمِعْنَا كِتٰبًا أُنْزِلَ مِنْ بَعْدِ مُوسٰى مُصَدِّقًا
لِّمَا بَيْنَ يَدَيْهِ يَهْدِيٓ إِلَى الْحَقِّ وَإِلٰى
طَرِيقٍ مُّسْتَقِيمٍ ﴿٣٠﴾ يٰقَوْمَنَآ أَجِيبُوا دَاعِيَ
اللّٰهِ وَأٰمِنُوا بِهٖ يَغْفِرْ لَكُمْ مِّنْ ذُنُوبِكُمْ
وَيُجِرْكُمْ مِّنْ عَذَابٍ أَلِيمٍ ﴿٣١﴾ وَمَنْ لَّا
يُجِبْ دَاعِيَ اللّٰهِ فَلَيْسَ بِمُعْجِزٍ فِي الْأَرْضِ
وَلَيْسَ لَهٗ مِنْ دُونِهٖٓ أَوْلِيَآءُ ۚ أُولٰٓئِكَ فِي
ضَلٰلٍ مُّبِينٍ ﴿٣٢﴾ أَوَلَمْ يَرَوْا أَنَّ اللّٰهَ الَّذِي
خَلَقَ السَّمٰوٰتِ وَالْأَرْضَ وَلَمْ يَعْيَ بِخَلْقِهِنَّ
بِقٰدِرٍ عَلٰٓى أَنْ يُّحْيِيَ الْمَوْتٰى ۚ بَلٰٓى إِنَّهٗ عَلٰى
كُلِّ شَيْءٍ قَدِيرٌ ﴿٣٣﴾ وَيَوْمَ يُعْرَضُ الَّذِينَ
كَفَرُوا عَلَى النَّارِ ۚ أَلَيْسَ هٰذَا بِالْحَقِّ ۚ قَالُوا
بَلٰى وَرَبِّنَا ۚ قَالَ فَذُوقُوا الْعَذَابَ بِمَا كُنْتُمْ
تَكْفُرُونَ ﴿٣٤﴾ فَاصْبِرْ كَمَا صَبَرَ أُولُوا الْعَزْمِ
مِنَ الرُّسُلِ وَلَا تَسْتَعْجِلْ لَّهُمْ ۚ كَأَنَّهُمْ
يَوْمَ يَرَوْنَ مَا يُوعَدُونَ لَمْ يَلْبَثُوٓا إِلَّا سَاعَةً
مِّنْ نَّهَارٍ ۚ بَلٰغٌ ۚ فَهَلْ يُهْلَكُ إِلَّا الْقَوْمُ الْفٰسِقُونَ ﴿٣٥﴾ ع

CHAPTER
47

سُورَةُ مُحَمَّدٍ ٤٧

MUHAMMAD
(Revealed after Hijrah)

سُورَةُ مُحَمَّدٍ مَّدَنِيَّةٌ

With the name of Allâh,
the Most Gracious, the Ever Merciful
(I commence to read Sûrah Muhammad).

بِسۡمِ اللّٰهِ الرَّحۡمٰنِ الرَّحِيۡمِ

1. **T**HOSE who disbelieve and bar people from the path of Allâh, He renders their works vain,
2. But as for those who bear faith and do deeds of righteousness and believe in that which is revealed to Muhammad, for it is the very Truth revealed by their Lord, He has purged them of their sins and has improved their (spiritual and temporal) condition.
3. That is because those who disbelieve follow falsehood while those who believe follow the Truth (revealed) by their Lord. That is how Allâh explains their conditions to people (to make them understand).
4. So (believers! Now that you know the will of your Lord), when you meet in (regular) battle those who disbelieve strike off their heads. After you have bound them fast in fetters (as prisoners of war), then, afterwards, (release them, a must), either by way of grace or by (accepting) ransom. (That is the law,) until war lays down its weapons (and it is over). Such is (the ordinance of Allâh). Indeed if Allâh pleased He could have punished them (in other ways). But (the ways of warfare have been resorted to) so that He may reveal your worth at the hands of one another. As of those who are slain in the cause of Allâh He will never let their works go vain.
5. He will guide them (to success) and will improve their condition.
6. Rather He will admit them into the Garden which He has made known to them (in the

اَلَّذِيۡنَ كَفَرُوۡا وَصَدُّوۡا عَنۡ سَبِيۡلِ اللّٰهِ
اَضَلَّ اَعۡمَالَهُمۡ ﴿۱﴾ وَالَّذِيۡنَ اٰمَنُوۡا وَعَمِلُوا
الصّٰلِحٰتِ وَاٰمَنُوۡا بِمَا نُزِّلَ عَلٰى مُحَمَّدٍ
وَّهُوَ الۡحَقُّ مِنۡ رَّبِّهِمۡ كَفَّرَ عَنۡهُمۡ سَيِّاٰتِهِمۡ
وَاَصۡلَحَ بَالَهُمۡ ﴿۲﴾ ذٰلِكَ بِاَنَّ الَّذِيۡنَ كَفَرُوا اتَّبَعُوا
الۡبَاطِلَ وَاَنَّ الَّذِيۡنَ اٰمَنُوا اتَّبَعُوا الۡحَقَّ مِنۡ
رَّبِّهِمۡ كَذٰلِكَ يَضۡرِبُ اللّٰهُ لِلنَّاسِ اَمۡثَالَهُمۡ ﴿۳﴾
فَاِذَا لَقِيۡتُمُ الَّذِيۡنَ كَفَرُوۡا فَضَرۡبَ الرِّقَابِ
حَتّٰٓى اِذَاۤ اَثۡخَنۡتُمُوۡهُمۡ فَشُدُّوا الۡوَثَاقَ فَاِمَّا
مَنًّا بَعۡدُ وَاِمَّا فِدَآءً حَتّٰى تَضَعَ الۡحَرۡبُ
اَوۡزَارَهَا ذٰلِكَ وَلَوۡ يَشَآءُ اللّٰهُ لَانۡتَصَرَ مِنۡهُمۡ
وَلٰكِنۡ لِّيَبۡلُوَا بَعۡضَكُمۡ بِبَعۡضٍ وَالَّذِيۡنَ قُتِلُوۡا
فِيۡ سَبِيۡلِ اللّٰهِ فَلَنۡ يُّضِلَّ اَعۡمَالَهُمۡ ﴿۴﴾ سَيَهۡدِيۡهِمۡ
وَيُصۡلِحُ بَالَهُمۡ ﴿۵﴾ وَيُدۡخِلُهُمُ الۡجَنَّةَ عَرَّفَهَا

Qur'ân).

7. O You who believe! If you help (the cause of) Allâh He will help you and make your steps firm.

8. As for those who disbelieve there awaits them perdition. He will make their works (to see Islam fail and come to nought) bear no fruit.

9. That is because they consider the revelations of Allâh a burden. That is why He has made their works all go waste.

10. Have they not travelled in the land and seen how (miserable) was the end to which their predecessors (who had disbelieved in the former Prophets) had come? Allâh utterly destroyed them. The same fate awaits these disbelievers.

11. That is because, (whereas) Allâh is a protecting friend of those who believe, the disbelievers have no protecting-friend.

SECTION 2

12. **ALLÂH** will make those who believe and do deeds of righteousness enter the Gardens served with running streams (to keep them green and flourishing). As for the disbelievers they will enjoy themselves (a little in this life) and eat even as the cattle eat and the Fire will be the last resort for them.

13. (Prophet!) So many townships were more powerful than this your town (of Makkah) which has driven you out, but We destroyed them, and they had no helper.

14. Can those people who take their stand upon a clear proof from their Lord, be compared to those to whom the evils of their deeds are made to seem attractive and who follow their low desires?

15. (Here is) a description of the Garden promised to those who guard against evil. Therein are streams of water (which is) unstaling, and streams of milk the taste and flavour of which does not change, and streams of juice extracted from grapes, a delight to the drinkers, and

لَهُمْ ⑥ يٰٓأَيُّهَا الَّذِيْنَ اٰمَنُوْٓا إِنْ تَنْصُرُوا اللّٰهَ
يَنْصُرْكُمْ وَ يُثَبِّتْ أَقْدَامَكُمْ ⑦ وَ الَّذِيْنَ كَفَرُوْا
فَتَعْسًا لَّهُمْ وَ أَضَلَّ أَعْمٰلَهُمْ ⑧ ذٰلِكَ بِأَنَّهُمْ
كَرِهُوْا مَآ أَنْزَلَ اللّٰهُ فَأَحْبَطَ أَعْمٰلَهُمْ ⑨ أَفَلَمْ
يَسِيْرُوْا فِي الْأَرْضِ فَيَنْظُرُوْا كَيْفَ كَانَ
عٰقِبَةُ الَّذِيْنَ مِنْ قَبْلِهِمْ دَمَّرَ اللّٰهُ عَلَيْهِمْ
وَ لِلْكٰفِرِيْنَ أَمْثٰلُهَا ⑩ ذٰلِكَ بِأَنَّ اللّٰهَ مَوْلَى
الَّذِيْنَ اٰمَنُوْا وَ أَنَّ الْكٰفِرِيْنَ لَا مَوْلٰى لَهُمْ ⑪
إِنَّ اللّٰهَ يُدْخِلُ الَّذِيْنَ اٰمَنُوْا وَ عَمِلُوا
الصّٰلِحٰتِ جَنّٰتٍ تَجْرِيْ مِنْ تَحْتِهَا الْأَنْهٰرُ
وَ الَّذِيْنَ كَفَرُوْا يَتَمَتَّعُوْنَ وَ يَأْكُلُوْنَ كَمَا
تَأْكُلُ الْأَنْعٰمُ وَ النَّارُ مَثْوًى لَّهُمْ ⑫ وَ كَأَيِّنْ
مِّنْ قَرْيَةٍ هِيَ أَشَدُّ قُوَّةً مِّنْ قَرْيَتِكَ الَّتِيْٓ
أَخْرَجَتْكَ أَهْلَكْنٰهُمْ فَلَا نَاصِرَ لَهُمْ ⑬ أَفَمَنْ
كَانَ عَلٰى بَيِّنَةٍ مِّنْ رَّبِّهِ كَمَنْ زُيِّنَ لَهُ سُوْٓءُ
عَمَلِهِ وَ اتَّبَعُوْٓا أَهْوَآءَهُمْ ⑭ مَثَلُ الْجَنَّةِ الَّتِيْ
وُعِدَ الْمُتَّقُوْنَ فِيْهَآ أَنْهٰرٌ مِّنْ مَّآءٍ غَيْرِ اٰسِنٍ
وَ أَنْهٰرٌ مِّنْ لَّبَنٍ لَّمْ يَتَغَيَّرْ طَعْمُهُ وَ أَنْهٰرٌ مِّنْ
خَمْرٍ لَّذَّةٍ لِّلشّٰرِبِيْنَ وَ أَنْهٰرٌ مِّنْ عَسَلٍ
مُّصَفًّى وَ لَهُمْ فِيْهَا مِنْ كُلِّ الثَّمَرٰتِ وَ مَغْفِرَةٌ

streams (too) of clarified honey, and they will have in it all kinds of fruit, and (a provision of) protection from their Lord. Can (those who enjoy such blessings of this Garden) be like those who shall abide in the Fire for long and who will be given boiling water to drink so that it tears their bowels into pieces.

16. And there are some (hypocrites) among them who (pretend to) listen to you. Yet when they go out from your presence they say to those who have been given knowledge, 'What was it he said just now?' These are the people whose hearts Allâh has sealed and who follow their low desires.

17. As for those who follow true guidance He leads them far ahead in their right ways (in the light of His guidance) and grants them piety and restraints from evil suited to their condition.

18. These (disbelievers) only wait for the (promised) Hour (of doom) to take them unaware. Its signs have already appeared. But of what (avail) will their admonition be to them (and how will they be able to repent) when it actually comes upon them (all of a sudden).

19. (Believer!) Know, therefore, that there is no other, cannot be and will never be one worthy of worship other than Allâh and seek His protection and forgiveness for your (human) shortcomings and (also) for the believing men and the believing women. Allâh knows your haunt (where you move about), and your resting-place.

SECTION 3

20. **T**HOSE who believe say, 'Why is no Sûrah (- Qur'ânic chapter permitting us to go to war) revealed?' But when a (definite) Sûrah of basic and categorical meaning and speaking of war was revealed you find those in whose hearts is a disease (of hypocrisy) looking at you like the looking of a person whose understanding is clouded for (fear of approaching) death. There-

مِّنْ رَّبِّهِمْ كَمَنْ هُوَ خٰلِدٌ فِي النَّارِ وَ سُقُوْا مَآءً
حَمِيْمًا فَقَطَّعَ أَمْعَآءَهُمْ ⑮ وَ مِنْهُمْ مَّنْ يَّسْتَمِعُ
إِلَيْكَ حَتّٰى إِذَا خَرَجُوْا مِنْ عِنْدِكَ قَالُوْا لِلَّذِيْنَ
أُوْتُوا الْعِلْمَ مَاذَا قَالَ أٰنِفًا أُولٰٓئِكَ الَّذِيْنَ
طَبَعَ اللهُ عَلٰى قُلُوْبِهِمْ وَ اتَّبَعُوْٓا أَهْوَآءَهُمْ ⑯
وَ الَّذِيْنَ اهْتَدَوْا زَادَهُمْ هُدًى وَّ أٰتٰهُمْ
تَقْوٰهُمْ ⑰ فَهَلْ يَنْظُرُوْنَ إِلَّا السَّاعَةَ أَنْ تَأْتِيَهُمْ
بَغْتَةً فَقَدْ جَآءَ أَشْرَاطُهَا فَأَنّٰى لَهُمْ إِذَا جَآءَتْهُمْ
ذِكْرٰىهُمْ ⑱ فَاعْلَمْ أَنَّهُ لَآ إِلٰهَ إِلَّا اللهُ وَ اسْتَغْفِرْ
لِذَنْبِكَ وَ لِلْمُؤْمِنِيْنَ وَ الْمُؤْمِنٰتِ وَ اللهُ يَعْلَمُ
مُتَقَلَّبَكُمْ وَ مَثْوٰىكُمْ ⑲ وَ يَقُوْلُ الَّذِيْنَ أٰمَنُوْا
لَوْلَا نُزِّلَتْ سُوْرَةٌ فَإِذَآ أُنْزِلَتْ سُوْرَةٌ مُّحْكَمَةٌ
وَّ ذُكِرَ فِيْهَا الْقِتَالُ رَأَيْتَ الَّذِيْنَ فِيْ قُلُوْبِهِمْ
مَّرَضٌ يَّنْظُرُوْنَ إِلَيْكَ نَظَرَ الْمَغْشِيِّ عَلَيْهِ مِنَ

fore woe to them!

21. (More fitting and proper for them was) to obey and to say what is just and good. And when the matter (of fighting) is (once) resolved upon (and war breaks out) it is better for them if they remain true to Allâh (and fulfill the covenant they made with Him).

22. (Hypocrites!) It is more likely that if you are given authority and power, you will create disorder in the land and violate your ties of kinship.

23. Such are the people whom Allâh has deprived of His mercy, so that He has made them deaf (to hear the truth) and has made their eyes blind (so they cannot see the right way).

24. Is it that they do not earnestly seek to understand the Qur'ân? Rather (their) hearts are securely locked up by their own locks.

25. Surely, those who turned back (to apostasy) after true guidance had dawned upon them, satan has made fair-seeming to them (this action of theirs) and has held out false hopes to them.

26. That is because they (- the hypocrites) said (in secret) to these (Jews) who consider the revelations of Allâh as a burden, 'We will obey you in some matters.' But Allâh knows their secrets.

27. But how (will they fare), when the angels cause them to die, smiting them on their faces and their backs?

28. (They will be treated) thus, because they followed that which called forth the displeasure of Allâh and were averse to (seeking) His good pleasure. That is why He will make their deeds fruitless.

SECTION 4

29. **D**o the people with diseased minds suppose that Allâh will never bring their malice to light?

30. Indeed, if We so will We could show them to you so that you would know them by their appearance, yet you shall of course recognise them from the tenor of (their) speech. (Allâh knows their empty words as) He knows your

الْمَوْتِ فَأَوْلَىٰ لَهُمْ ﴿٢٠﴾ طَاعَةٌ وَقَوْلٌ مَّعْرُوفٌ
فَإِذَا عَزَمَ الْأَمْرُ فَلَوْ صَدَقُوا اللَّهَ لَكَانَ خَيْرًا
لَّهُمْ ﴿٢١﴾ فَهَلْ عَسَيْتُمْ إِن تَوَلَّيْتُمْ أَن تُفْسِدُوا
فِي الْأَرْضِ وَتُقَطِّعُوا أَرْحَامَكُمْ ﴿٢٢﴾ أُولَٰئِكَ الَّذِينَ
لَعَنَهُمُ اللَّهُ فَأَصَمَّهُمْ وَأَعْمَىٰ أَبْصَارَهُمْ ﴿٢٣﴾ أَفَلَا
يَتَدَبَّرُونَ الْقُرْآنَ أَمْ عَلَىٰ قُلُوبٍ أَقْفَالُهَا ﴿٢٤﴾ إِنَّ
الَّذِينَ ارْتَدُّوا عَلَىٰ أَدْبَارِهِم مِّن بَعْدِ مَا تَبَيَّنَ
لَهُمُ الْهُدَى ۙ الشَّيْطَانُ سَوَّلَ لَهُمْ وَأَمْلَىٰ لَهُمْ ﴿٢٥﴾
ذَٰلِكَ بِأَنَّهُمْ قَالُوا لِلَّذِينَ كَرِهُوا مَا نَزَّلَ اللَّهُ
سَنُطِيعُكُمْ فِي بَعْضِ الْأَمْرِ ۖ وَاللَّهُ يَعْلَمُ
إِسْرَارَهُمْ ﴿٢٦﴾ فَكَيْفَ إِذَا تَوَفَّتْهُمُ الْمَلَائِكَةُ
يَضْرِبُونَ وُجُوهَهُمْ وَأَدْبَارَهُمْ ﴿٢٧﴾ ذَٰلِكَ بِأَنَّهُمُ
اتَّبَعُوا مَا أَسْخَطَ اللَّهَ وَكَرِهُوا رِضْوَانَهُ فَأَحْبَطَ
أَعْمَالَهُمْ ﴿٢٨﴾ أَمْ حَسِبَ الَّذِينَ فِي قُلُوبِهِم مَّرَضٌ
أَن لَّن يُخْرِجَ اللَّهُ أَضْغَانَهُمْ ﴿٢٩﴾ وَلَوْ نَشَاءُ
لَأَرَيْنَاكَهُمْ فَلَعَرَفْتَهُم بِسِيمَاهُمْ ۚ وَلَتَعْرِفَنَّهُمْ

ع ٤ ٧

(solid) deeds.

31. (Muslims!) We will put you to trial until We make manifest those among you who strive their utmost (in the cause of Allâh), and those who persevere in patience, and We will (entrust you with such tasks as may) bring to light your reported mettle (and inner merits).

32. Those who disbelieve and hinder (people) from following the path of Allâh and oppose the Messenger after true guidance has become clear to them, can do no harm to Allâh. But He will let (such) deeds of theirs bear no fruit.

33. O you who believe! Obey Allâh and obey the Messengers and do not let your deeds go in vain.

34. Allâh will never grant protection (from their sins) to those who disbelieved and hindered (people) from (following) the path of Allâh and then died while they were (still) disbelievers.

35. (Believers! When fighting once starts) do not slack so as to sue for peace. You will certainly have the upper hand. Allâh is with you. He will never let you suffer a loss in (the reward) of your (good) deeds.

36. (Hypocrites!) The present life is only idle sport and makes you ignore and forgetful (of your duties towards God). If you believe and guard against evil He will give you your reward and will not ask of you your wealth (to confiscate it from you but He wishes to repay the efforts you make with your wealth).

37. Should He ask you for it (- your wealth) and press you (for it), you would show stinginess and this (niggardliness) will bring to surface your malice (and hatred towards the divine Faith).

38. Behold! You are those who are called upon to spend in the cause of Allâh. Yet some of you are niggardly. (Remember that) whoever is niggardly is niggardly only against his own self. Otherwise Allâh is Self-Sufficient (having no needs) and it is you who are the needy ones. And if you turn back (from the truth), He will replace you with another people and they will not (behave) like you.

سُوْرَةُ مُحَمَّدٍ ٤٧

فِي لَحْنِ الْقَوْلِ ۚ وَاللّٰهُ يَعْلَمُ أَعْمٰلَكُمْ ﴿٣٠﴾ وَلَنَبْلُوَنَّكُمْ
حَتّٰى نَعْلَمَ الْمُجٰهِدِينَ مِنْكُمْ وَالصّٰبِرِينَ
وَنَبْلُوَا۟ أَخْبَارَكُمْ ﴿٣١﴾ إِنَّ الَّذِينَ كَفَرُوا وَصَدُّوا
عَنْ سَبِيلِ اللّٰهِ وَشَآقُّوا الرَّسُولَ مِنْ بَعْدِ
مَا تَبَيَّنَ لَهُمُ الْهُدٰى لَنْ يَضُرُّوا اللّٰهَ شَيْـًٔا ۖ
وَسَيُحْبِطُ أَعْمٰلَهُمْ ﴿٣٢﴾ يٰٓأَيُّهَا الَّذِينَ ءَامَنُوٓا أَطِيعُوا
اللّٰهَ وَأَطِيعُوا الرَّسُولَ وَلَا تُبْطِلُوٓا أَعْمٰلَكُمْ ﴿٣٣﴾
إِنَّ الَّذِينَ كَفَرُوا وَصَدُّوا عَنْ سَبِيلِ اللّٰهِ
ثُمَّ مَاتُوا وَهُمْ كُفَّارٌ فَلَنْ يَغْفِرَ اللّٰهُ لَهُمْ ﴿٣٤﴾
فَلَا تَهِنُوا وَتَدْعُوٓا إِلَى السَّلْمِ ۖ وَأَنْتُمُ
الْأَعْلَوْنَ ۖ وَاللّٰهُ مَعَكُمْ وَلَنْ يَتِرَكُمْ أَعْمٰلَكُمْ ﴿٣٥﴾
إِنَّمَا الْحَيٰوةُ الدُّنْيَا لَعِبٌ وَلَهْوٌ ۚ وَإِنْ تُؤْمِنُوا
وَتَتَّقُوا يُؤْتِكُمْ أُجُورَكُمْ وَلَا يَسْـَٔلْكُمْ أَمْوٰلَكُمْ ﴿٣٦﴾
إِنْ يَسْـَٔلْكُمُوهَا فَيُحْفِكُمْ تَبْخَلُوا وَيُخْرِجْ
أَضْغٰنَكُمْ ﴿٣٧﴾ هٰٓأَنْتُمْ هٰٓؤُلَآءِ تُدْعَوْنَ لِتُنْفِقُوا
فِي سَبِيلِ اللّٰهِ فَمِنْكُمْ مَنْ يَبْخَلُ ۚ وَمَنْ
يَبْخَلْ فَإِنَّمَا يَبْخَلُ عَنْ نَفْسِهِ ۚ وَاللّٰهُ الْغَنِيُّ
وَأَنْتُمُ الْفُقَرَآءُ ۚ وَإِنْ تَتَوَلَّوْا يَسْتَبْدِلْ
قَوْمًا غَيْرَكُمْ ثُمَّ لَا يَكُونُوٓا أَمْثٰلَكُمْ ﴿٣٨﴾

CHAPTER 48

AL-FATH
(The Victory)
(Revealed after Hijrah)

سورة الفتح مدنية

With the name of Allâh,
the Most Gracious, the Ever Merciful
(I commence to read Sûrah Al-Fath).

بسم الله الرحمن الرحيم

1. (**P**ROPHET! The treaty of *Hudaibiyah* is a great victory in that) We opened for you the way to (another) clear victory (which led to the preaching and expansion of Islam).

2. The result of this is that Allâh will protect you from (the ill consequences of) the fault attributed to you in the past and those to follow, and that He will make His favour perfect upon you and will lead you to the goal of the exact right path;

3. And that Allâh will grant you His mighty help.

4. It is He Who gave to the believers *Shechinah* (tranquillity and peace of mind) so that they might grow all the more in faith over and above the faith they (already) possessed. Indeed all the hosts of the heavens and of the earth belong to Allâh. And Allâh is All-Knowing, All-Wise.

5. (Allâh has decreed the war against the aggressor) so that He may admit the believers both men and women to Gardens served with running streams (to keep them green and flourishing), (the Gardens) where they will abide for ever, and so that He might absolve them of their evils. This indeed is a supreme achievement (for you) in the sight of Allâh.

6. And (He has decreed it so that) He may punish the hypocrites both men and women and the polytheists both men and women who entertain evil thoughts about Allâh. There awaits

إِنَّا فَتَحْنَا لَكَ فَتْحًا مُّبِينًا ① لِّيَغْفِرَ لَكَ اللَّهُ مَا
تَقَدَّمَ مِن ذَنْبِكَ وَمَا تَأَخَّرَ وَيُتِمَّ نِعْمَتَهُ
عَلَيْكَ وَيَهْدِيَكَ صِرَاطًا مُّسْتَقِيمًا ② وَيَنصُرَكَ
اللَّهُ نَصْرًا عَزِيزًا ③ هُوَ الَّذِي أَنزَلَ السَّكِينَةَ
فِي قُلُوبِ الْمُؤْمِنِينَ لِيَزْدَادُوا إِيمَانًا مَّعَ
إِيمَانِهِمْ وَلِلَّهِ جُنُودُ السَّمَاوَاتِ وَالْأَرْضِ
وَكَانَ اللَّهُ عَلِيمًا حَكِيمًا ④ لِّيُدْخِلَ الْمُؤْمِنِينَ
وَالْمُؤْمِنَاتِ جَنَّاتٍ تَجْرِي مِن تَحْتِهَا الْأَنْهَارُ
خَالِدِينَ فِيهَا وَيُكَفِّرَ عَنْهُمْ سَيِّئَاتِهِمْ
وَكَانَ ذَٰلِكَ عِندَ اللَّهِ فَوْزًا عَظِيمًا ⑤ وَيُعَذِّبَ
الْمُنَافِقِينَ وَالْمُنَافِقَاتِ وَالْمُشْرِكِينَ

them an evil term (of calamity). Allâh is angry with them and has deprived them of His mercy and has Gehenna in store for them, and evil it is for destination.

7. And all the hosts of the heavens and of the earth belong to Allâh. And Allâh is All-Mighty, All-Wise.

8. (Prophet!) We have sent you as a Witness (to Our existence and attributes), and a Bearer of glad tidings and a Warner.

9. (O people! We have done it) so that you may have faith in Allâh and His Messenger and so that you may help him in a respectful manner and honour him, and so that you may glorify Him morning and evening.

10. (Prophet!) Those who swear allegiance to you as a matter of fact swear allegiance to Allâh. Allâh's (helpful and benign) hand is above their hands. So he who breaks (his oath of allegiance) breaks (it) to his own loss. And as for the person who fulfills the great covenant he made with Allâh (- at *Bai't al-Ridzwân*, by *Hudaibiyah*), He will surely give such a person a great reward.

SECTION 2

11. **T**HOSE of the desert Arabs (who contrived to be) left behind will say to you (by way of apology), 'We were occupied in looking after our belongings and families, so ask for protection for us (from God).' They say with their tongues that which is not in their hearts. Say, 'Who has any power to help you against (the decree of) Allâh if He intends to do you some harm? Or (who can avert His grace) if He intends to do you some good. Indeed, Allâh is Well Aware of all that you do (and He will treat you accordingly).

12. '(Hypocrites!) Nay, the fact is that you thought that the Messenger and the believers would never return to their families. (This was a thought) that was made to appear pleasing to your minds. You entertained an evil thought.

وَ الْمُشْرِكٰتِ الظَّآنِّيْنَ بِاللّٰهِ ظَنَّ السَّوْءِ عَلَيْهِمْ
دَآئِرَةُ السَّوْءِ وَ غَضِبَ اللّٰهُ عَلَيْهِمْ وَ لَعَنَهُمْ
وَ أَعَدَّ لَهُمْ جَهَنَّمَ وَ سَآءَتْ مَصِيْرًا ﴿٦﴾ وَ لِلّٰهِ
جُنُوْدُ السَّمٰوٰتِ وَ الْأَرْضِ وَ كَانَ اللّٰهُ
عَزِيْزًا حَكِيْمًا ﴿٧﴾ إِنَّآ أَرْسَلْنٰكَ شٰهِدًا وَّ مُبَشِّرًا
وَّ نَذِيْرًا ﴿٨﴾ لِّتُؤْمِنُوْا بِاللّٰهِ وَ رَسُوْلِهٖ وَ تُعَزِّرُوْهُ
وَ تُوَقِّرُوْهُ وَ تُسَبِّحُوْهُ بُكْرَةً وَّ أَصِيْلًا ﴿٩﴾ إِنَّ
الَّذِيْنَ يُبَايِعُوْنَكَ إِنَّمَا يُبَايِعُوْنَ اللّٰهَ يَدُ
اللّٰهِ فَوْقَ أَيْدِيْهِمْ فَمَنْ نَّكَثَ فَإِنَّمَا يَنْكُثُ
عَلٰى نَفْسِهٖ وَ مَنْ أَوْفٰى بِمَا عٰهَدَ عَلَيْهُ اللّٰهَ
ع ٩ فَسَيُؤْتِيْهِ أَجْرًا عَظِيْمًا ﴿١٠﴾ سَيَقُوْلُ لَكَ الْمُخَلَّفُوْنَ
مِنَ الْأَعْرَابِ شَغَلَتْنَآ أَمْوٰلُنَا وَ أَهْلُوْنَا فَاسْتَغْفِرْ
لَنَا يَقُوْلُوْنَ بِأَلْسِنَتِهِمْ مَّا لَيْسَ فِيْ قُلُوْبِهِمْ
قُلْ فَمَنْ يَّمْلِكُ لَكُمْ مِّنَ اللّٰهِ شَيْـًٔا إِنْ أَرَادَ
بِكُمْ ضَرًّا أَوْ أَرَادَ بِكُمْ نَفْعًا بَلْ كَانَ اللّٰهُ
بِمَا تَعْمَلُوْنَ خَبِيْرًا ﴿١١﴾ بَلْ ظَنَنْتُمْ أَنْ لَّنْ
يَّنْقَلِبَ الرَّسُوْلُ وَ الْمُؤْمِنُوْنَ إِلٰى أَهْلِيْهِمْ

And you were a people doomed to perish.'
13. Let such a person who does not believe in Allâh and His Messenger (bear in mind that) We have surely prepared a blazing Fire for the disbelievers.
14. The sovereignty of the heavens and the earth belongs to Allâh. He grants protection to the person who wishes (to come under His protection) and punishes whom He will. Yet the fact is that Allâh is Great Protector, Ever Merciful.
15. When you are free to set out to take the spoils (of the war of *Khaibar*), those who (contrived to be) left behind (from joining you at *Hudaibiyah*) will say, 'Permit us to follow you.' They would like to change the word of Allâh (and His decree). Say, 'You shall not follow us. This is what Allâh has declared beforehand.' They will thereupon say, '(There is no such foreword,) you are in fact jealous of us.' (What they say is in fact wrong.) Little do they understand (that this is the punishment for their not being present at *Hudaibiyah*).
16. (Prophet!) Say to those of the desert Arabs who (contrived to be) left behind, 'You shall soon be called upon (to take up arms) against a people (- the Byzantine and the Persians) who are fighters of mighty valour. Then you shall fight until they submit. Allâh will grant you a goodly reward if you obey. But if you turn your backs, as you did before, He will punish you, a woeful punishment.'
17. No blame shall lie on the blind, no blame shall lie on the lame, and no blame shall lie on the sick (if they do not join the fight). Yet he that obeys Allâh and His Messenger He will make him enter Gardens served with running streams (to keep them green and flourishing), but he that turns his back He will inflict upon him a woeful punishment.

أَبَدًا وَزُيِّنَ ذَٰلِكَ فِي قُلُوبِكُمْ وَظَنَنتُمْ ظَنَّ
السَّوْءِ وَكُنتُمْ قَوْمًا بُورًا ﴿١٢﴾ وَمَن لَّمْ يُؤْمِن
بِاللَّهِ وَرَسُولِهِ فَإِنَّا أَعْتَدْنَا لِلْكَٰفِرِينَ سَعِيرًا ﴿١٣﴾
وَلِلَّهِ مُلْكُ السَّمَٰوَٰتِ وَالْأَرْضِ يَغْفِرُ لِمَن
يَشَاءُ وَيُعَذِّبُ مَن يَشَاءُ وَكَانَ اللَّهُ
غَفُورًا رَّحِيمًا ﴿١٤﴾ سَيَقُولُ الْمُخَلَّفُونَ إِذَا
انطَلَقْتُمْ إِلَىٰ مَغَانِمَ لِتَأْخُذُوهَا ذَرُونَا نَتَّبِعْكُمْ
يُرِيدُونَ أَن يُبَدِّلُوا كَلَٰمَ اللَّهِ قُل لَّن تَتَّبِعُونَا
كَذَٰلِكُمْ قَالَ اللَّهُ مِن قَبْلُ فَسَيَقُولُونَ بَلْ
تَحْسُدُونَنَا بَلْ كَانُوا لَا يَفْقَهُونَ إِلَّا قَلِيلًا ﴿١٥﴾
قُل لِّلْمُخَلَّفِينَ مِنَ الْأَعْرَابِ سَتُدْعَوْنَ إِلَىٰ
قَوْمٍ أُولِي بَأْسٍ شَدِيدٍ تُقَٰتِلُونَهُمْ أَوْ يُسْلِمُونَ
فَإِن تُطِيعُوا يُؤْتِكُمُ اللَّهُ أَجْرًا حَسَنًا وَإِن تَتَوَلَّوْا
كَمَا تَوَلَّيْتُم مِّن قَبْلُ يُعَذِّبْكُمْ عَذَابًا أَلِيمًا ﴿١٦﴾
لَّيْسَ عَلَى الْأَعْمَىٰ حَرَجٌ وَلَا عَلَى الْأَعْرَجِ حَرَجٌ
وَلَا عَلَى الْمَرِيضِ حَرَجٌ وَمَن يُطِعِ اللَّهَ
وَرَسُولَهُ يُدْخِلْهُ جَنَّٰتٍ تَجْرِي مِن تَحْتِهَا الْأَنْهَٰرُ
وَمَن يَتَوَلَّ يُعَذِّبْهُ عَذَابًا أَلِيمًا ﴿١٧﴾ لَقَدْ رَضِيَ

SECTION 3

18. (PROPHET!) Allâh was well-pleased with the (fourteen hundred) believers when they swore allegiance to you (known as *Bai'at al-Ridzwân*) under the (acacia) tree (at *Hudaibiyah*) He revealed (the high standard of faith) that they had in their hearts and sent down *Shechinah* (- peace and tranquillity) upon them and He rewarded them with an early victory (at *Khaibar*).
19. And a great many gains (await them) that they will take. Allâh is All-Mighty, All-Wise.
20. (Muslims!) Allâh has promised you many gains that you will take, and He has given you this (victory at *Khaibar*) in advance. And (as a result of the Treaty of *Hudaibiyah*) He restrained the hands of the people from (committing aggression against) you that it may serve the believers as a sign and that He may lead you on the straight and right path leading to the goal.
21. There are (in addition to this) other (victories) which you have not been able to achieve, yet Allâh has surely encompassed them (with His power and kept them safe for you). And Allâh has every power over every desired thing.
22. And if those who disbelieved had fought you (at *Hudaibiyah*), they would have certainly turned their backs and then would find neither a protecting friend nor helper.
23. (Allâh has explained to you) His wont which has been in practice since the very past. You will find no change at all in Allâh's wont.
24. It is He Who restrained their hands from you and your hands from them in the Valley of Makkah (on the occasion of the Treaty of *Hudaibiyah*) after He had given you victory over them. Allâh observes all that you do.
25. These (your Makkan enemies) were the people who disbelieved and prevented you

اللّٰهُ عَنِ الْمُؤْمِنِينَ إِذْ يُبَايِعُونَكَ تَحْتَ الشَّجَرَةِ
فَعَلِمَ مَا فِي قُلُوبِهِمْ فَأَنْزَلَ السَّكِينَةَ عَلَيْهِمْ
وَأَثَابَهُمْ فَتْحًا قَرِيبًا ﴿١٨﴾ وَمَغَانِمَ كَثِيرَةً يَأْخُذُونَهَا
وَكَانَ اللّٰهُ عَزِيزًا حَكِيمًا ﴿١٩﴾ وَعَدَكُمُ اللّٰهُ مَغَانِمَ
كَثِيرَةً تَأْخُذُونَهَا فَعَجَّلَ لَكُمْ هٰذِهِ وَكَفَّ
أَيْدِيَ النَّاسِ عَنْكُمْ وَلِتَكُونَ آيَةً لِلْمُؤْمِنِينَ
وَيَهْدِيَكُمْ صِرَاطًا مُسْتَقِيمًا ﴿٢٠﴾ وَأُخْرَىٰ لَمْ
تَقْدِرُوا عَلَيْهَا قَدْ أَحَاطَ اللّٰهُ بِهَا وَكَانَ اللّٰهُ
عَلَىٰ كُلِّ شَيْءٍ قَدِيرًا ﴿٢١﴾ وَلَوْ قَاتَلَكُمُ الَّذِينَ
كَفَرُوا لَوَلَّوُا الْأَدْبَارَ ثُمَّ لَا يَجِدُونَ وَلِيًّا وَلَا
نَصِيرًا ﴿٢٢﴾ سُنَّةَ اللّٰهِ الَّتِي قَدْ خَلَتْ مِنْ قَبْلُ
وَلَنْ تَجِدَ لِسُنَّةِ اللّٰهِ تَبْدِيلًا ﴿٢٣﴾ وَهُوَ الَّذِي
كَفَّ أَيْدِيَهُمْ عَنْكُمْ وَأَيْدِيَكُمْ عَنْهُمْ بِبَطْنِ
مَكَّةَ مِنْ بَعْدِ أَنْ أَظْفَرَكُمْ عَلَيْهِمْ وَكَانَ
اللّٰهُ بِمَا تَعْمَلُونَ بَصِيرًا ﴿٢٤﴾ هُمُ الَّذِينَ كَفَرُوا

from the Holy Mosque while even the sacrificial animals were stopped from reaching their destination (- the place of sacrifice). Had not there been (at Makkah) some believing men and believing women as were unknown to you, and had there been no danger that (in case of war) you might have trodden them down and thus you might have incurred some harm unknowingly on their account, (We would have allowed you to invade Makkah but We did not allow this) so that Allâh might show His mercy to him who wishes (to be shown mercy). Had these (believers living in Makkah) left from there (and had been separated from them), We would have surely punished those of them (-the Makkans) who disbelieved, with a woeful punishment.

26. (These events belong to the time) when those who disbelieved nurtured in their hearts prideful indignation and cant, the indignation and cant (of the days) of Ignorance, and Allâh granted *Shechinah* (peace and tranquillity) from Himself to His Messenger and the believers and made them observe closely and firmly the code of self-restraint, (the code) they were best entitled to receive and were also really worthy of it. Allâh has full knowledge of everything.

SECTION 4

27. **ALLÂH** had surely fulfilled for His Messenger the vision, that conformed to the rules of wisdom. '(My faithful Companions!) You shall enter the Holy Mosque if Allâh will, safe and secure, some of you with your heads shaved and (others) with (their) hair only cut short (as is a prescribed rite for a Pilgrim), you will have nothing to fear.' (As for the time involved in its fulfillment) He knows what you do not know. He has, in fact, ordained for you a victory (near at hand, at *Khaibar*) to be gained before (the fulfillment of) that (vision).

وَصَدُّوكُمْ عَنِ الْمَسْجِدِ الْحَرَامِ وَالْهَدْيَ
مَعْكُوفًا أَنْ يَبْلُغَ مَحِلَّهُ وَلَوْلَا رِجَالٌ مُّؤْمِنُونَ
وَنِسَاءٌ مُّؤْمِنَٰتٌ لَّمْ تَعْلَمُوهُمْ أَنْ تَطَـُٔوهُمْ
فَتُصِيبَكُم مِّنْهُم مَّعَرَّةٌۢ بِغَيْرِ عِلْمٍ لِّيُدْخِلَ
اللَّهُ فِي رَحْمَتِهِ مَنْ يَشَاءُ لَوْ تَزَيَّلُوا لَعَذَّبْنَا
الَّذِينَ كَفَرُوا مِنْهُمْ عَذَابًا أَلِيمًا ﴿٢٥﴾ إِذْ جَعَلَ
الَّذِينَ كَفَرُوا فِي قُلُوبِهِمُ الْحَمِيَّةَ حَمِيَّةَ الْجَٰهِلِيَّةِ
فَأَنْزَلَ اللَّهُ سَكِينَتَهُ عَلَىٰ رَسُولِهِ وَعَلَى الْمُؤْمِنِينَ
وَأَلْزَمَهُمْ كَلِمَةَ التَّقْوَىٰ وَكَانُوا أَحَقَّ بِهَا
وَأَهْلَهَا وَكَانَ اللَّهُ بِكُلِّ شَيْءٍ عَلِيمًا ﴿٢٦﴾ لَقَدْ
صَدَقَ اللَّهُ رَسُولَهُ الرُّءْيَا بِالْحَقِّ لَتَدْخُلُنَّ
الْمَسْجِدَ الْحَرَامَ إِنْ شَاءَ اللَّهُ ءَامِنِينَ مُحَلِّقِينَ
رُءُوسَكُمْ وَمُقَصِّرِينَ لَا تَخَافُونَ فَعَلِمَ مَا لَمْ
تَعْلَمُوا فَجَعَلَ مِنْ دُونِ ذَٰلِكَ فَتْحًا قَرِيبًا ﴿٢٧﴾

28. It is He Who has sent His Messenger with guidance and true Faith so that He may help it prevail over all other faiths. Indeed, Allâh is Sufficient to bear witness (to the truth of Islam).

29. Muhammad is the Messenger of Allâh, and those who are with him are (also) firm and strict against the disbelievers (to accept their influence), but soft-hearted and compassionate towards one another. (Reader!) You will find them kneeling and prostrating themselves (in Prayer). They seek grace from Allâh and His good pleasure. Their distinctive indication is (apparent) on their faces from the illuminous traces of (their) prostration. Such is the description (of these attributes of theirs) in the Torah, and their description in the Evangel is that they (will be) like a seed-produce that sends forth its sprout, then makes it strong. It then becomes stout and stands firm on its stem giving delight to the sowers; (Allâh will in a similar way raise the believers from strength to strength) with the result that He may make the disbelievers suffer an impotent rage because of them. Allâh has promised His protection and a great reward to those who believe and do deeds of righteousness.

هُوَ الَّذِيٓ أَرْسَلَ رَسُولَهُ بِالْهُدٰى وَدِينِ
الْحَقِّ لِيُظْهِرَهُ عَلَى الدِّينِ كُلِّهِ ۚ وَكَفٰى بِاللهِ
شَهِيدًا ﴿٢٨﴾ مُحَمَّدٌ رَّسُولُ اللهِ ۚ وَالَّذِينَ مَعَهُ
أَشِدَّآءُ عَلَى الْكُفَّارِ رُحَمَآءُ بَيْنَهُمْ تَرٰىهُمْ
رُكَّعًا سُجَّدًا يَبْتَغُونَ فَضْلًا مِّنَ اللهِ وَرِضْوَانًا
سِيمَاهُمْ فِي وُجُوهِهِم مِّنْ أَثَرِ السُّجُودِ ۚ ذٰلِكَ
مَثَلُهُمْ فِي التَّوْرٰىةِ ۚ وَمَثَلُهُمْ فِي الْإِنْجِيلِ ۚ
كَزَرْعٍ أَخْرَجَ شَطْـَٔهُ فَـَٔازَرَهُ فَاسْتَغْلَظَ فَاسْتَوٰى
عَلٰى سُوقِهِ يُعْجِبُ الزُّرَّاعَ لِيَغِيظَ بِهِمُ الْكُفَّارَ ۗ
وَعَدَ اللهُ الَّذِينَ أٰمَنُوا وَعَمِلُوا الصّٰلِحٰتِ
مِنْهُم مَّغْفِرَةً وَّأَجْرًا عَظِيمًا ﴿٢٩﴾

ع ١٢

CHAPTER 49

سُورَةُ الحُجُرٰتِ مَدَنِيَّةٌ

AL-HUJURÂT

(The Chambers)

(Revealed after Hijrah)

With the name of Allâh,
the Most Gracious, the Ever Merciful
(I commence to read Sûrah Al-Hujurât).

بِسْمِ اللهِ الرَّحْمٰنِ الرَّحِيمِ

1. **O** YOU who believe! Do not anticipate Allâh and His Messenger, (putting yourselves forward before their cause and) be full of reverence to

يٰٓأَيُّهَا الَّذِينَ أٰمَنُوا لَا تُقَدِّمُوا بَيْنَ يَدَيِ اللهِ

Allâh and take Him as a shield. Behold, Allâh is All-Hearing, All-Knowing.

2. O you who believe! Raise not your voices above the voice of the Prophet, nor address him in loud tones, the way you speak loudly to one another, lest your deeds should come to naught while you do not realise.

3. Those who keep their voices subdued in the presence of Allâh's Messenger are those whose hearts Allâh has purified for piety and restraint. There awaits such of them provision for protection and a great reward.

4. The people who call out to you (O Prophet of God!) from outside your (private) chambers (most of them) lack understanding.

5. If they only had patience to wait until you could come out to them it would be better for them, yet Allâh is Great Protector (against faults), Ever Merciful.

6. O you who believe! If a wicked person brings you any important news, examine it carefully, lest you should harm some people in ignorance and afterwards you may have to repent for what you did.

7. Keep in mind that Allâh's Messenger is among you (at the time). If he were to follow your wishes in many matters, you would certainly land yourself in trouble. But (as it is) Allâh has inspired you with the love of the Faith, and has made it look beautiful to your minds and has made disbelief, transgression and disobedience hateful to you. Such indeed are those who follow the right course (of guidance).

8. This is sheer Allâh's grace and His favour. And Allâh is All-Knowing, All-Wise.

9. (O you who believe!) If two parties of the believers fall out and fight each other, make peace between them. And should one of them commit aggression against the other, then fight (you all) against the party that transgresses till it complies with the command of Allâh (and returns to peace and reconciliation). Then if it returns make peace between them with equity

وَرَسُولِهِۦ وَاتَّقُوا اللَّهَ إِنَّ اللَّهَ سَمِيعٌ عَلِيمٌ ١
يَٰٓأَيُّهَا الَّذِينَ ءَامَنُوا لَا تَرْفَعُوٓا أَصْوَٰتَكُمْ فَوْقَ
صَوْتِ النَّبِيِّ وَلَا تَجْهَرُوا لَهُۥ بِالْقَوْلِ كَجَهْرِ
بَعْضِكُمْ لِبَعْضٍ أَن تَحْبَطَ أَعْمَٰلُكُمْ وَأَنتُمْ لَا
تَشْعُرُونَ ٢ إِنَّ الَّذِينَ يَغُضُّونَ أَصْوَٰتَهُمْ عِندَ
رَسُولِ اللَّهِ أُولَٰٓئِكَ الَّذِينَ امْتَحَنَ اللَّهُ قُلُوبَهُمْ
لِلتَّقْوَىٰ لَهُم مَّغْفِرَةٌ وَأَجْرٌ عَظِيمٌ ٣ إِنَّ الَّذِينَ
يُنَادُونَكَ مِن وَرَآءِ الْحُجُرَٰتِ أَكْثَرُهُمْ لَا
يَعْقِلُونَ ٤ وَلَوْ أَنَّهُمْ صَبَرُوا حَتَّىٰ تَخْرُجَ إِلَيْهِمْ
لَكَانَ خَيْرًا لَّهُمْ وَاللَّهُ غَفُورٌ رَّحِيمٌ ٥ يَٰٓأَيُّهَا
الَّذِينَ ءَامَنُوٓا إِن جَآءَكُمْ فَاسِقٌ بِنَبَإٍ فَتَبَيَّنُوٓا
أَن تُصِيبُوا قَوْمًا بِجَهَٰلَةٍ فَتُصْبِحُوا عَلَىٰ مَا
فَعَلْتُمْ نَٰدِمِينَ ٦ وَاعْلَمُوٓا أَنَّ فِيكُمْ رَسُولَ
اللَّهِ لَوْ يُطِيعُكُمْ فِي كَثِيرٍ مِّنَ الْأَمْرِ لَعَنِتُّمْ
وَلَٰكِنَّ اللَّهَ حَبَّبَ إِلَيْكُمُ الْإِيمَٰنَ وَزَيَّنَهُۥ فِي
قُلُوبِكُمْ وَكَرَّهَ إِلَيْكُمُ الْكُفْرَ وَالْفُسُوقَ
وَالْعِصْيَانَ أُولَٰٓئِكَ هُمُ الرَّٰشِدُونَ ٧ فَضْلًا
مِّنَ اللَّهِ وَنِعْمَةً وَاللَّهُ عَلِيمٌ حَكِيمٌ ٨ وَإِن
طَآئِفَتَانِ مِنَ الْمُؤْمِنِينَ اقْتَتَلُوا فَأَصْلِحُوا
بَيْنَهُمَا فَإِنۢ بَغَتْ إِحْدَىٰهُمَا عَلَى الْأُخْرَىٰ
فَقَٰتِلُوا الَّتِي تَبْغِي حَتَّىٰ تَفِيٓءَ إِلَىٰٓ أَمْرِ اللَّهِ
فَإِن فَآءَتْ فَأَصْلِحُوا بَيْنَهُمَا بِالْعَدْلِ وَأَقْسِطُوٓا

and act justly, for Allâh loves those who do justice.
10. Believers are but a single brotherhood, so make peace and effect reconciliation between the two (contending) brethren and take Allâh as (your) shield so that you may be shown mercy.

SECTION 2

11. **O** YOU who believe! Let no people look down upon another people for the (latter) people may be better than they, nor let women (look down) upon other women, who (- the women who are treated lightly) may be better than the other ones. And find not fault in one another (in order to defame your own people), nor call one another by nicknames. Bad is the reputation of wickedness after the (profession of) belief. Highly unjust are the people who would not abstain from what they are forbidden.
12. O you who believe! Eschew much suspicion, for suspicion in some cases is a sin. And do not spy into the secrets of one another, nor backbite one another, would anyone of you like to eat the flesh of his dead brother? Why, you would loath it. Take Allâh as (your) shield. Surely, Allâh is Oft-Returning (with compassion and is) Ever Merciful.
13. O people! We have created you out of a male and a female, and We have made you tribes and sub-tribes that you may recognise (and do good to) one another. Surely the most honourable of you in the sight of Allâh is he Who guards against evil the most. Verily, Allâh is All-Knowing, All-Aware.
14. The Arabs of the desert say, 'We believe.' Say, 'You have not yet truly believed, (you should) rather say, "We obey and have submitted," for true faith has not yet entered your hearts. But if you obey Allâh and His Messenger He will not diminish aught of your deeds.' Surely, Allâh is Great Protector, Ever Merciful.
15. The believers are only those who (truly)

إِنَّ اللّٰهَ يُحِبُّ الْمُقْسِطِيْنَ ۝٩ إِنَّمَا الْمُؤْمِنُوْنَ
إِخْوَةٌ فَأَصْلِحُوْا بَيْنَ أَخَوَيْكُمْ وَاتَّقُوا اللّٰهَ
لَعَلَّكُمْ تُرْحَمُوْنَ ۝١٠ يٰٓأَيُّهَا الَّذِيْنَ اٰمَنُوْا لَا يَسْخَرْ
قَوْمٌ مِّنْ قَوْمٍ عَسٰٓى أَنْ يَّكُوْنُوْا خَيْرًا مِّنْهُمْ
وَلَا نِسَآءٌ مِّنْ نِّسَآءٍ عَسٰٓى أَنْ يَّكُنَّ خَيْرًا
مِّنْهُنَّ وَلَا تَلْمِزُوْٓا أَنْفُسَكُمْ وَلَا تَنَابَزُوْا
بِالْأَلْقَابِ بِئْسَ الِاسْمُ الْفُسُوْقُ بَعْدَ
الْإِيْمٰنِ وَمَنْ لَّمْ يَتُبْ فَأُولٰٓئِكَ هُمُ الظّٰلِمُوْنَ ۝١١
يٰٓأَيُّهَا الَّذِيْنَ اٰمَنُوا اجْتَنِبُوْا كَثِيْرًا مِّنَ الظَّنِّ
إِنَّ بَعْضَ الظَّنِّ إِثْمٌ وَّلَا تَجَسَّسُوْا وَلَا يَغْتَبْ
بَّعْضُكُمْ بَعْضًا أَيُحِبُّ أَحَدُكُمْ أَنْ يَّأْكُلَ
لَحْمَ أَخِيْهِ مَيْتًا فَكَرِهْتُمُوْهُ وَاتَّقُوا اللّٰهَ إِنَّ
اللّٰهَ تَوَّابٌ رَّحِيْمٌ ۝١٢ يٰٓأَيُّهَا النَّاسُ إِنَّا خَلَقْنٰكُمْ
مِّنْ ذَكَرٍ وَّأُنْثٰى وَجَعَلْنٰكُمْ شُعُوْبًا وَّقَبَآئِلَ
لِتَعَارَفُوْا إِنَّ أَكْرَمَكُمْ عِنْدَ اللّٰهِ أَتْقٰىكُمْ إِنَّ
اللّٰهَ عَلِيْمٌ خَبِيْرٌ ۝١٣ قَالَتِ الْأَعْرَابُ اٰمَنَّا قُلْ
لَّمْ تُؤْمِنُوْا وَلٰكِنْ قُوْلُوْٓا أَسْلَمْنَا وَلَمَّا يَدْخُلِ
الْإِيْمٰنُ فِيْ قُلُوْبِكُمْ وَإِنْ تُطِيْعُوا اللّٰهَ وَرَسُوْلَهٗ
لَا يَلِتْكُمْ مِّنْ أَعْمٰلِكُمْ شَيْـًٔا إِنَّ اللّٰهَ غَفُوْرٌ
رَّحِيْمٌ ۝١٤ إِنَّمَا الْمُؤْمِنُوْنَ الَّذِيْنَ اٰمَنُوْا بِاللّٰهِ

believe in Allâh and His Messenger, and then doubt not, and who strive hard with their possessions and their lives in the cause of Allâh. It is they who are the true to their words (and Muslims of a high standard).'

16. Say, 'Would you make known your faith to Allâh, while Allâh knows whatsoever is in the heavens and whatsoever is in the earth? And Allâh knows all things full well.'

17. They lay you under obligation because they have embraced Islam. Say, 'Lay me not under any obligation on account of your (embracing) Islam. On the contrary Allâh has bestowed a favour on you, because He has guided you to the true Faith, if you are truthful.'

18. Verily, Allâh knows the hidden realities of the heavens and the earth. And Allâh sees all your deeds.

وَرَسُولِهِ ثُمَّ لَمْ يَرْتَابُوا وَجٰهَدُوا بِأَمْوٰلِهِمْ وَأَنْفُسِهِمْ فِي سَبِيلِ اللهِ أُولٰٓئِكَ هُمُ الصّٰدِقُونَ ﴿١٥﴾ قُلْ أَتُعَلِّمُونَ اللهَ بِدِينِكُمْ وَاللهُ يَعْلَمُ مَا فِي السَّمٰوٰتِ وَمَا فِي الْأَرْضِ وَاللهُ بِكُلِّ شَيْءٍ عَلِيمٌ ﴿١٦﴾ يَمُنُّونَ عَلَيْكَ أَنْ أَسْلَمُوا قُلْ لَا تَمُنُّوا عَلَيَّ إِسْلٰمَكُمْ بَلِ اللهُ يَمُنُّ عَلَيْكُمْ أَنْ هَدٰكُمْ لِلْإِيمٰنِ إِنْ كُنْتُمْ صٰدِقِينَ ﴿١٧﴾ إِنَّ اللهَ يَعْلَمُ غَيْبَ السَّمٰوٰتِ وَالْأَرْضِ وَاللهُ بَصِيرٌ بِمَا تَعْمَلُونَ ﴿١٨﴾

ع ٢ ٨ ١٤

CHAPTER
50

QÂF

(Allâh is Almighty)

(Revealed before Hijrah)

سُورَةُ قٓ مَكِّيَّةٌ

With the name of Allâh,
the Most Gracious, the Ever Merciful
(I commence to read Sûrah Qâf).

بِسْمِ اللهِ الرَّحْمٰنِ الرَّحِيمِ

1. QÂF - Allâh is Almighty. The glorious Qur'ân bears witness (to it).

2. Behold! These (disbelievers) wonder that there has come to them a Warner who hails from among themselves. And the disbelievers say, 'This is a strange thing,

3. 'What! When we are dead and reduced to dust, (shall we be raised to life again)? This (sort of) return is highly impossible.'

4. We know how much of them the earth consumes (and how much it adds to them). We have with Us a book that preserves (everything

قٓ وَالْقُرْاٰنِ الْمَجِيدِ ﴿١﴾ بَلْ عَجِبُوٓا أَنْ جَآءَهُمْ مُنْذِرٌ مِنْهُمْ فَقَالَ الْكٰفِرُونَ هٰذَا شَيْءٌ عَجِيبٌ ﴿٢﴾ ءَإِذَا مِتْنَا وَكُنَّا تُرَابًا ذٰلِكَ رَجْعٌ بَعِيدٌ ﴿٣﴾ قَدْ عَلِمْنَا مَا تَنْقُصُ

- the Law of conservation).

5. Nay, (the truth of the matter is that) they denied the truth when it came to them, and so they are in a state of confusion.

6. Do they not look at the sky above them, how We have made it and decked it out fair, so that it has no flaws?

7. (Do they not look at) the earth how We have spread it out and stretched it forth, and set firm mountains in it, and caused to grow in it every beautiful species (of growth).

8. (We have done all this so that it may serve as) a source of enlightenment and a means of admonition to every servant (of Ours) who turns to Us.

9. And We send down from the clouds water which is of great utility and blessings, and We cause to produce with it gardens and grains of the crop that is reaped,

10. And tall (and stately) palm-trees laden with spathes, cluster over cluster,

11. To serve Our servants for sustenance. And by means of this (water) We raise the dead land to life. That is how the Resurrection shall come to be.

12. The people of Noah denied (the Hereafter) before them and so did the people of the Rass, and (the tribe of) Thamûd,

13. And (the tribe of) ʻÂd and Pharaoh and the kinsmen of Lot,

14. And the dwellers of the Thicket and the people of *Tubba'*. All of them cried lies to the Messengers (of God) so that My threatened punishment duly befell them.

15. Are We wearied with the first creation (that We will not be able to create them the second time on the Day of Resurrection)? The fact is that they are in confusing doubt about a new creation.

SECTION 2

16. **W**E created a human being and We know what (dark) suggestions his mind makes to him.

سُورَةُ قٓ ٥٠

الْأَرْضُ مِنْهُمْ وَعِنْدَنَا كِتٰبٌ حَفِيظٌ ﴿٤﴾
بَلْ كَذَّبُوا بِالْحَقِّ لَمَّا جَآءَهُمْ فَهُمْ فِيٓ أَمْرٍ
مَّرِيجٍ ﴿٥﴾ أَفَلَمْ يَنْظُرُوٓا إِلَى السَّمَآءِ فَوْقَهُمْ
كَيْفَ بَنَيْنٰهَا وَزَيَّنّٰهَا وَمَا لَهَا مِنْ فُرُوجٍ ﴿٦﴾
وَالْأَرْضَ مَدَدْنٰهَا وَأَلْقَيْنَا فِيهَا رَوٰسِيَ
وَأَنْبَتْنَا فِيهَا مِنْ كُلِّ زَوْجٍ بَهِيجٍ ﴿٧﴾ تَبْصِرَةً
وَّذِكْرٰى لِكُلِّ عَبْدٍ مُّنِيبٍ ﴿٨﴾ وَنَزَّلْنَا
مِنَ السَّمَآءِ مَآءً مُّبٰرَكًا فَأَنْبَتْنَا بِهِ جَنّٰتٍ
وَّحَبَّ الْحَصِيدِ ﴿٩﴾ وَالنَّخْلَ بَاسِقٰتٍ لَّهَا
طَلْعٌ نَّضِيدٌ ﴿١٠﴾ رِّزْقًا لِّلْعِبَادِ وَأَحْيَيْنَا بِهِ
بَلْدَةً مَّيْتًا كَذٰلِكَ الْخُرُوجُ ﴿١١﴾ كَذَّبَتْ
قَبْلَهُمْ قَوْمُ نُوحٍ وَّأَصْحٰبُ الرَّسِّ وَثَمُودُ ﴿١٢﴾
وَعَادٌ وَّفِرْعَوْنُ وَإِخْوٰنُ لُوطٍ ﴿١٣﴾ وَّأَصْحٰبُ
الْأَيْكَةِ وَقَوْمُ تُبَّعٍ كُلٌّ كَذَّبَ الرُّسُلَ
فَحَقَّ وَعِيدِ ﴿١٤﴾ أَفَعَيِينَا بِالْخَلْقِ الْأَوَّلِ بَلْ
هُمْ فِي لَبْسٍ مِّنْ خَلْقٍ جَدِيدٍ ﴿١٥﴾ وَلَقَدْ
خَلَقْنَا الْإِنْسٰنَ وَنَعْلَمُ مَا تُوَسْوِسُ بِهِ

ع ١٥

We are nearer to him than even (his) jugular vein.
17. Behold, the two recording (angels) sitting one on (his) right and one on (his) left go on preparing the record (of his deeds).
18. He utters not a word but (it is noted down by) a guardian (angel of his who) stands ready by his side (to record his words).
19. (O people!) The stupor of death has truly to come. This is the thing which you were trying to avoid.
20. And the trumpet shall be sounded. That will be the Day, the warning of which has (already) been given.
21. And every soul shall come forth (to account for his deeds). He will be accompanied by (an angel) who shall drive it and (an angel) who shall bear witness.
22. (Then We shall say,) 'Certainly, you were heedless of this day. But (now) We have removed from you your veil and your sight is very sharp this day.'
23. And his (other angel) companion (who will come to bear witness) shall say, 'Here is (the record of his deeds) ready with me.'
24. (The sentence will be,) 'Cast you two (angels), yes, cast in to Gehenna every hardened disbelieving enemy (of truth),
25. 'Forbidder of good, transgressor, entertainer of doubts,
26. 'Who sets up (for worship) another deity beside Allâh. So cast you two, yes, cast him in to the severe punishment.'
27. (The disbeliever will blame) his (evil) associate (who) will say, 'O our Lord! It was not I that seduced him to transgress but he himself was deeply sunk in error.'
28. He (- God) will say, 'Dispute not (with each other) in My presence. I had already given you the warning (of this punishment) beforehand.
29. 'The judgment given by Me cannot be

نَفْسُهُۥ ۖ وَنَحْنُ أَقْرَبُ إِلَيْهِ مِنْ حَبْلِ الْوَرِيدِ ﴿١٦﴾
إِذْ يَتَلَقَّى الْمُتَلَقِّيَانِ عَنِ الْيَمِينِ وَعَنِ
الشِّمَالِ قَعِيدٌ ﴿١٧﴾ مَا يَلْفِظُ مِنْ قَوْلٍ إِلَّا
لَدَيْهِ رَقِيبٌ عَتِيدٌ ﴿١٨﴾ وَجَاءَتْ سَكْرَةُ
الْمَوْتِ بِالْحَقِّ ۖ ذَٰلِكَ مَا كُنتَ مِنْهُ تَحِيدُ ﴿١٩﴾
وَنُفِخَ فِي الصُّورِ ۚ ذَٰلِكَ يَوْمُ الْوَعِيدِ ﴿٢٠﴾
وَجَاءَتْ كُلُّ نَفْسٍ مَّعَهَا سَائِقٌ وَشَهِيدٌ ﴿٢١﴾
لَقَدْ كُنتَ فِي غَفْلَةٍ مِّنْ هَٰذَا فَكَشَفْنَا
عَنكَ غِطَاءَكَ فَبَصَرُكَ الْيَوْمَ حَدِيدٌ ﴿٢٢﴾
وَقَالَ قَرِينُهُ هَٰذَا مَا لَدَيَّ عَتِيدٌ ﴿٢٣﴾ أَلْقِيَا
فِي جَهَنَّمَ كُلَّ كَفَّارٍ عَنِيدٍ ﴿٢٤﴾ مَّنَّاعٍ لِّلْخَيْرِ
مُعْتَدٍ مُّرِيبٍ ﴿٢٥﴾ الَّذِي جَعَلَ مَعَ اللَّهِ إِلَٰهًا
آخَرَ فَأَلْقِيَاهُ فِي الْعَذَابِ الشَّدِيدِ ﴿٢٦﴾ قَالَ
قَرِينُهُ رَبَّنَا مَا أَطْغَيْتُهُ وَلَٰكِن كَانَ فِي
ضَلَالٍ بَعِيدٍ ﴿٢٧﴾ قَالَ لَا تَخْتَصِمُوا لَدَيَّ وَقَدْ
قَدَّمْتُ إِلَيْكُم بِالْوَعِيدِ ﴿٢٨﴾ مَا يُبَدَّلُ الْقَوْلُ

changed and I am not at all unjust to (My) servants.'

SECTION 3

30. **O**N that Day We will ask Gehenna, 'Are you filled up (with the inmates of the hell)?' It will go on saying (expressing its state), 'Are there anymore (that I can take)?'
31. (On that Day) Paradise will be brought near to those who had become secure against evil, (it will be) no more a thing distant (from them).
32. (It will be said,) 'Here is that (Paradise) you were promised. (It is) for those who turned (to their Lord) again and again (seeking His mercy) and observed (His laws) with care,
33. 'Those who stood in awe of the Gracious (God) in the heart of their hearts, even unseen and came to Him with a heart turned in sincere devotion (to Him).
34. 'Enter this (Paradise) in peace. This is a period lasting for ever.'
35. They will have there all that they desire and We have in store much more (than this to give them).
36. So many (a guilty) generation, who were mightier than these people in powers, have We destroyed (for their wrongs) before them. They journeyed from land to land (to escape). (But We seized them with Our punishment.) Was there any asylum (for them) to take refuge?
37. All this contains a lesson for every such person as has (an understanding) heart, or gives ear (while) his mind is attentive.
38. And verily, We created the heavens and the earth and all that lies between them in six aeons, and no weariness (even) touched Us.
39. So bear with patience what they say, and glorify your Lord with His praises and extol His Holiness before sunrise and sunset,
40. And celebrate His praises during parts of the night and after (prescribed) prostrations (in your Prayers).
41. (Reader) hearken! On the day when one that

سُوْرَةُ قٓ ٥٠

ع ١٦

لَدَيَّ وَمَآ أَنَا۠ بِظَلَّٰمٍ لِّلْعَبِيدِ ﴿٢٩﴾ يَوْمَ نَقُولُ
لِجَهَنَّمَ هَلِ امْتَلَأْتِ وَتَقُولُ هَلْ مِن
مَّزِيدٍ ﴿٣٠﴾ وَأُزْلِفَتِ الْجَنَّةُ لِلْمُتَّقِينَ غَيْرَ
بَعِيدٍ ﴿٣١﴾ هَٰذَا مَا تُوعَدُونَ لِكُلِّ أَوَّابٍ حَفِيظٍ ﴿٣٢﴾
مَّنْ خَشِيَ الرَّحْمَٰنَ بِالْغَيْبِ وَجَآءَ بِقَلْبٍ
مُّنِيبٍ ﴿٣٣﴾ ادْخُلُوهَا بِسَلَٰمٍ ذَٰلِكَ يَوْمُ الْخُلُودِ ﴿٣٤﴾
لَهُم مَّا يَشَآءُونَ فِيهَا وَلَدَيْنَا مَزِيدٌ ﴿٣٥﴾ وَكَمْ
أَهْلَكْنَا قَبْلَهُم مِّن قَرْنٍ هُمْ أَشَدُّ مِنْهُم
بَطْشًا فَنَقَّبُوا فِي الْبِلَٰدِ هَلْ مِن مَّحِيصٍ ﴿٣٦﴾
إِنَّ فِي ذَٰلِكَ لَذِكْرَىٰ لِمَن كَانَ لَهُۥ قَلْبٌ
أَوْ أَلْقَى السَّمْعَ وَهُوَ شَهِيدٌ ﴿٣٧﴾ وَلَقَدْ خَلَقْنَا
السَّمَٰوَٰتِ وَالْأَرْضَ وَمَا بَيْنَهُمَا فِي سِتَّةِ
أَيَّامٍ وَمَا مَسَّنَا مِن لُّغُوبٍ ﴿٣٨﴾ فَاصْبِرْ عَلَىٰ
مَا يَقُولُونَ وَسَبِّحْ بِحَمْدِ رَبِّكَ قَبْلَ طُلُوعِ
الشَّمْسِ وَقَبْلَ الْغُرُوبِ ﴿٣٩﴾ وَمِنَ الَّيْلِ
فَسَبِّحْهُ وَأَدْبَٰرَ السُّجُودِ ﴿٤٠﴾ وَاسْتَمِعْ يَوْمَ

calls will call from a place quite near,
42. The day they hear the inevitable mighty blast, that will be the day of coming forth (from the graves).
43. It is We Who give life and cause death and to Us is the (final) return (of all).
44. The day when the earth shall cleave asunder from above the people and they be revealed. They will come rushing forth. It will be easy for Us to raise them to life and gather them together.
45. We are well-aware of what they say. You are not one to overawe them and cannot reform them by means of force. (Therefore pay no heed to what they say,) rather admonish with the Qur'ân such of them as shall fear My warning.

يُنَادِ الْمُنَادِ مِنْ مَّكَانٍ قَرِيْبٍ ﴿٤١﴾ يَّوْمَ
يَسْمَعُوْنَ الصَّيْحَةَ بِالْحَقِّ ذٰلِكَ يَوْمُ
الْخُرُوْجِ ﴿٤٢﴾ إِنَّا نَحْنُ نُحْيٖ وَنُمِيْتُ وَإِلَيْنَا
الْمَصِيْرُ ﴿٤٣﴾ يَوْمَ تَشَقَّقُ الْأَرْضُ عَنْهُمْ سِرَاعًا
ذٰلِكَ حَشْرٌ عَلَيْنَا يَسِيْرٌ ﴿٤٤﴾ نَحْنُ أَعْلَمُ بِمَا
يَقُوْلُوْنَ وَمَآ أَنْتَ عَلَيْهِمْ بِجَبَّارٍ فَذَكِّرْ
بِالْقُرْاٰنِ مَنْ يَّخَافُ وَعِيْدِ ﴿٤٥﴾ ع ٣ ١٧

CHAPTER
51

AL-DHÂRIYÂT
(The Scatterers)
(Revealed before Hijrah)

سُوْرَةُ الذّٰرِيٰتِ مَكِّيَّةٌ

With the name of Allâh,
the Most Gracious, the Ever Merciful
(I commence to read Sûrah Al-Dhâriyât).

بِسْمِ اللّٰهِ الرَّحْمٰنِ الرَّحِيْمِ

1. I CALL to witness those (beings) who went forth to scatter (the Qur'ânic teachings) far and wide with a true scattering,
2. They carry (their blessed) load (of truth),
3. Then speed along (exposing the wrong belief and evil practices) with love and peace,
4. And then distribute and apportion the work by (Our) command,
5. Verily, the promise you are made (about the spread of Islam) is true,

وَالذّٰرِيٰتِ ذَرْوًا ﴿١﴾ فَالْحٰمِلٰتِ وِقْرًا ﴿٢﴾ فَالْجٰرِيٰتِ
يُسْرًا ﴿٣﴾ فَالْمُقَسِّمٰتِ أَمْرًا ﴿٤﴾ إِنَّمَا تُوْعَدُوْنَ

6. And the Requital must indeed come to pass.
7. And I call to witness the sky with (its) numerous orbits (of celestial bodies),
8. That contradictory are the things you say (for your not believing in God's word and in His Prophet),
9. Through which are deluded away (from the truth) such as would be deluded (to falsehood).
10. Woe to the falsehood-mongers,
11. Who are in the depths of obstinacy and confusion (due to false-beliefs) and give no heed (to the truth).
12. They ask, 'When will the Day of Requital be?'
13. (Say), 'It shall be a day when they will be tormented at the Fire.'
14. (It will be said to them), 'Taste your torment. This is what you used to ask to be hastened.'
15. But surely those who have become secure against evil will indeed be in (the land of) Gardens and Springs,
16. Receiving the gifts that their Lord will give them for they used to do excellent deeds before that.
17. They were in the habit of sleeping but a little by night (for their being occupied in God's worship).
18. Also in the hours of the early dawn as well they were (found) praying for His protection.
19. And in their wealth and belongings was a rightful share for those who asked (for help) and for those who could not.
20. There are signs on the earth for the people of knowledge and assured faith.
21. And (you have signs) in your own persons. Have you no eyes to perceive
22. Your sustenance is in the heavens, besides you shall have all that you are promised (-triumph and prosperity to the believers and warnings to disbelievers).
23. By the Lord of the heavens and the earth

سُوْرَةُ الذّٰرِيٰتِ ٥١

لَصَادِقٌ ﴿٥﴾ وَّإِنَّ الدِّيْنَ لَوٰقِعٌ ﴿٦﴾ وَ السَّمَآءِ
ذَاتِ الْحُبُكِ ﴿٧﴾ إِنَّكُمْ لَفِيْ قَوْلٍ مُّخْتَلِفٍ ﴿٨﴾
يُّؤْفَكُ عَنْهُ مَنْ أُفِكَ ﴿٩﴾ قُتِلَ الْخَرّٰصُوْنَ ﴿١٠﴾
الَّذِيْنَ هُمْ فِيْ غَمْرَةٍ سَاهُوْنَ ﴿١١﴾ يَسْـَٔلُوْنَ
أَيَّانَ يَوْمُ الدِّيْنِ ﴿١٢﴾ يَوْمَ هُمْ عَلَى النَّارِ
يُفْتَنُوْنَ ﴿١٣﴾ ذُوْقُوْا فِتْنَتَكُمْ هٰذَا الَّذِيْ كُنْتُمْ بِهٖ
تَسْتَعْجِلُوْنَ ﴿١٤﴾ إِنَّ الْمُتَّقِيْنَ فِيْ جَنّٰتٍ وَّعُيُوْنٍ ﴿١٥﴾
أٰخِذِيْنَ مَآ أٰتٰهُمْ رَبُّهُمْ إِنَّهُمْ كَانُوْا قَبْلَ
ذٰلِكَ مُحْسِنِيْنَ ﴿١٦﴾ كَانُوْا قَلِيْلًا مِّنَ الَّيْلِ مَا
يَهْجَعُوْنَ ﴿١٧﴾ وَ بِالْأَسْحَارِ هُمْ يَسْتَغْفِرُوْنَ ﴿١٨﴾ وَ فِيْٓ
أَمْوٰلِهِمْ حَقٌّ لِّلسَّآئِلِ وَالْمَحْرُوْمِ ﴿١٩﴾ وَفِي الْأَرْضِ
أٰيٰتٌ لِّلْمُوْقِنِيْنَ ﴿٢٠﴾ وَفِيْٓ أَنْفُسِكُمْ أَفَلَا تُبْصِرُوْنَ ﴿٢١﴾
وَفِي السَّمَآءِ رِزْقُكُمْ وَ مَا تُوْعَدُوْنَ ﴿٢٢﴾ فَوَرَبِّ

الجزء السادس والعشرون

that which you are promised is true. It is as true as the fact that you can speak to one another.

سُوۡرَةُ الذّٰرِيٰتِ ٥١

SECTION 2

24. **H**AVE you heard the news of the honoured guests of Abraham?
25. Behold! They came to him and greeted him with peace, he said (in reply), '(On you be) peace.' (He thought) they were all strangers.
26. And he went (quietly but) quickly to his household and brought a fatted calf (after getting it roasted for the guests).
27. And he placed it before them. (Seeing their hesitation) he said, 'Will you not eat?'
28. (When they did not eat) he felt afraid of them. They said, 'Have no fear.' And they proclaimed to him the good news of (the birth of) a son who would be blessed with knowledge.
29. Then his wife came to him extremely embarrassed. She smote her forehead and said, '(I am but) an old woman then barren, (how can I ever be able to give birth to a child?)
30. They said, 'Even so has your Lord said.' Surely, He is the All-Wise, the All-Knowing.

السَّمَآءِ وَ الۡاَرۡضِ اِنَّهٗ لَحَقٌّ مِّثۡلَ مَاۤ اَنَّكُمۡ
تَنۡطِقُوۡنَ ﴿٢٣﴾ هَلۡ اَتٰىكَ حَدِيۡثُ ضَيۡفِ اِبۡرٰهِيۡمَ
الۡمُكۡرَمِيۡنَ ﴿٢٤﴾ اِذۡ دَخَلُوۡا عَلَيۡهِ فَقَالُوۡا سَلٰمًا ؕ قَالَ
سَلٰمٌ ۚ قَوۡمٌ مُّنۡكَرُوۡنَ ﴿٢٥﴾ فَرَاغَ اِلٰۤى اَهۡلِهٖ فَجَآءَ
بِعِجۡلٍ سَمِيۡنٍ ﴿٢٦﴾ فَقَرَّبَهٗۤ اِلَيۡهِمۡ قَالَ اَلَا
تَاۡكُلُوۡنَ ﴿٢٧﴾ فَاَوۡجَسَ مِنۡهُمۡ خِيۡفَةً ؕ قَالُوۡا لَا تَخَفۡ ؕ
وَبَشَّرُوۡهُ بِغُلٰمٍ عَلِيۡمٍ ﴿٢٨﴾ فَاَقۡبَلَتِ امۡرَاَتُهٗ فِىۡ صَرَّةٍ
فَصَكَّتۡ وَجۡهَهَا وَ قَالَتۡ عَجُوۡزٌ عَقِيۡمٌ ﴿٢٩﴾ قَالُوۡا
كَذٰلِكِ ۙ قَالَ رَبُّكِ ؕ اِنَّهٗ هُوَ الۡحَكِيۡمُ الۡعَلِيۡمُ ﴿٣٠﴾

ع ٢ ١٨

PART الجزء السابع والعشرون XXVII

31. (ABRAHAM) said (to them), 'Now what is your errand, O you who have been sent (by God)!
32. They said, 'We have been sent towards a guilty people who have severed their ties (with God).
33. 'That we may rain stones of wet clay upon them,
34. '(Which are) earmarked from your Lord for (inflicting punishment on) those guilty of excesses.'
35. (God says,) 'Then (it came to pass) We brought forth all the believers who were there

قَالَ فَمَا خَطۡبُكُمۡ اَيُّهَا الۡمُرۡسَلُوۡنَ ﴿٣١﴾ قَالُوۡۤا
اِنَّاۤ اُرۡسِلۡنَاۤ اِلٰى قَوۡمٍ مُّجۡرِمِيۡنَ ﴿٣٢﴾ لِنُرۡسِلَ
عَلَيۡهِمۡ حِجَارَةً مِّنۡ طِيۡنٍ ﴿٣٣﴾ مُّسَوَّمَةً عِنۡدَ
رَبِّكَ لِلۡمُسۡرِفِيۡنَ ﴿٣٤﴾ فَاَخۡرَجۡنَا مَنۡ كَانَ

(in that township to keep them safe and secure).
36. But in fact We found there only a single house of those who had submitted (to Us, and that was the house of Lot).
37. And (after destroying the townships) We left in them a sign (to serve as a lesson) to those who fear the woeful punishment.
38. And in (the case of) Moses (there is also a sign). (Remember the time) when We sent him to Pharaoh with a clear authoritative proof.
39. But he turned away (from Moses) in the pride of his power and said, '(He is) a sorcerer, or rather a madman.'
40. So We took him and his forces to task and threw them into the sea. Indeed, he (- Pharaoh) was himself blameworthy.
41. And (there is a sign) in (the destruction of the Tribe of) 'Âd, when We let loose on them the destructive wild-blowing wind.
42. It spared nothing whatever it came upon but reduced it to (dust-like stuff of) rotten bones.
43. And (there is a sign) in (the case of the tribe of) Thamûd. Behold! They were told, 'Enjoy yourselves for a while.'
44. But they disdainfully disobeyed the commandment of their Lord, so a thunderbolt struck them while they looked on (utterly confused).
45. And they were not able (even) to get up on their feet nor could they get anybody's help to defend themselves.
46. And (We destroyed) the people of Noah before (them). They too were disobedient people.

SECTION 3

47. **A**s for the heaven, We have built it with (Our) Mighty power, and verily We are Makers of the vast extent.
48. And the earth, We have spread it out and how excellently We lay things out.
49. And We have created all things in pairs so that you may give heed (to the wonderful creation of God).

فِيهَا مِنَ الْمُؤْمِنِينَ ﴿٣٥﴾ فَمَا وَجَدْنَا فِيهَا
غَيْرَ بَيْتٍ مِّنَ الْمُسْلِمِينَ ﴿٣٦﴾ وَتَرَكْنَا
فِيهَا آيَةً لِّلَّذِينَ يَخَافُونَ الْعَذَابَ الْأَلِيمَ ﴿٣٧﴾
وَفِي مُوسَىٰ إِذْ أَرْسَلْنَاهُ إِلَىٰ فِرْعَوْنَ بِسُلْطَانٍ
مُّبِينٍ ﴿٣٨﴾ فَتَوَلَّىٰ بِرُكْنِهِ وَقَالَ سَاحِرٌ أَوْ
مَجْنُونٌ ﴿٣٩﴾ فَأَخَذْنَاهُ وَجُنُودَهُ فَنَبَذْنَاهُمْ
فِي الْيَمِّ وَهُوَ مُلِيمٌ ﴿٤٠﴾ وَفِي عَادٍ إِذْ أَرْسَلْنَا
عَلَيْهِمُ الرِّيحَ الْعَقِيمَ ﴿٤١﴾ مَا تَذَرُ مِن شَيْءٍ
أَتَتْ عَلَيْهِ إِلَّا جَعَلَتْهُ كَالرَّمِيمِ ﴿٤٢﴾ وَفِي
ثَمُودَ إِذْ قِيلَ لَهُمْ تَمَتَّعُوا حَتَّىٰ حِينٍ ﴿٤٣﴾
فَعَتَوْا عَنْ أَمْرِ رَبِّهِمْ فَأَخَذَتْهُمُ الصَّاعِقَةُ
وَهُمْ يَنظُرُونَ ﴿٤٤﴾ فَمَا اسْتَطَاعُوا مِن قِيَامٍ
وَمَا كَانُوا مُنتَصِرِينَ ﴿٤٥﴾ وَقَوْمَ نُوحٍ مِّن
قَبْلُ إِنَّهُمْ كَانُوا قَوْمًا فَاسِقِينَ ﴿٤٦﴾ وَالسَّمَاءَ
بَنَيْنَاهَا بِأَيْدٍ وَإِنَّا لَمُوسِعُونَ ﴿٤٧﴾ وَالْأَرْضَ
فَرَشْنَاهَا فَنِعْمَ الْمَاهِدُونَ ﴿٤٨﴾ وَمِن كُلِّ شَيْءٍ
خَلَقْنَا زَوْجَيْنِ لَعَلَّكُمْ تَذَكَّرُونَ ﴿٤٩﴾ فَفِرُّوا

50. Therefore (say to them), 'Wing your way to Allâh. Verily, I am a plain Warner to you from Him.

51. 'Never set up another god (to be worshipped) along with Allâh. Surely, I am a plain Warner to you from Him.'

52. Even so, no Messenger came to their predecessors but they said, '(He is) a sorcerer, or (rather) a madman,

53. Have they bequeathed this (way of saying things) to one another. The fact is they themselves are a people who transgress limits.

54. So turn away from them (and their foul way of talk). There lies no blame on you (for what they do).

55. Yet keep on exhorting (the people), for, verily, exhortation proves useful to the believers.

56. And I have created the *jinn* (fiery natured and houghty) and the (ordinary) people only that they may worship Me.

57. (Prophet! Tell them that) no provision do I require from them, nor do I require that they should feed Me.

58. Surely, it is Allâh alone Who is the Great Sustainer, the Lord of immense power, the Almighty.

59. Those who do injustice (to Our Messengers) should meet the fate (of miseries) like the fate of their fellows (of old). Therefore do not let them ask Me to hasten on (the punishment which awaits them).

60. (Yet they should not forget that) destruction is in store for those who disbelieve, on account of that day of theirs the punishment of which they have been promised.

إِلَى اللَّهِ إِنِّي لَكُم مِّنْهُ نَذِيرٌ مُّبِينٌ ۝٥٠ وَلَا
تَجْعَلُوا مَعَ اللَّهِ إِلَٰهًا آخَرَ إِنِّي لَكُم مِّنْهُ
نَذِيرٌ مُّبِينٌ ۝٥١ كَذَٰلِكَ مَا أَتَى الَّذِينَ مِن
قَبْلِهِم مِّن رَّسُولٍ إِلَّا قَالُوا سَاحِرٌ أَوْ
مَجْنُونٌ ۝٥٢ أَتَوَاصَوْا بِهِ بَلْ هُمْ قَوْمٌ
طَاغُونَ ۝٥٣ فَتَوَلَّ عَنْهُمْ فَمَا أَنتَ بِمَلُومٍ ۝٥٤
وَذَكِّرْ فَإِنَّ الذِّكْرَىٰ تَنفَعُ الْمُؤْمِنِينَ ۝٥٥
وَمَا خَلَقْتُ الْجِنَّ وَالْإِنسَ إِلَّا لِيَعْبُدُونِ ۝٥٦
مَا أُرِيدُ مِنْهُم مِّن رِّزْقٍ وَمَا أُرِيدُ أَن
يُطْعِمُونِ ۝٥٧ إِنَّ اللَّهَ هُوَ الرَّزَّاقُ ذُو الْقُوَّةِ
الْمَتِينُ ۝٥٨ فَإِنَّ لِلَّذِينَ ظَلَمُوا ذَنُوبًا مِّثْلَ
ذَنُوبِ أَصْحَابِهِمْ فَلَا يَسْتَعْجِلُونِ ۝٥٩ فَوَيْلٌ
لِّلَّذِينَ كَفَرُوا مِن يَوْمِهِمُ الَّذِي يُوعَدُونَ ۝٦٠

CHAPTER
52

AL-TÛR
(The Mount)
(Revealed before Hijrah)

With the name of Allâh,
the Most Gracious, the Ever Merciful
(I commence to read Sûrah Al-Tûr).

1. I CALL to witness the Mount (of revelation),
2. And a Book inscribed
3. On open unrolled parchments,
4. And the ever so much-frequented House (-Ka'abah),
5. And (its) Elevated Roof,
6. And the dry and empty sea,
7. That the punishment of your Lord is bound to descend.
8. None can avert it.
9. The day the sky shall reel and rock (in a state of terrific commotion),
10. And the mountains shall move fast,
11. On that day destruction awaits those who cry lies (to the Messengers of God),
12. Who indulge in idle talk and who are busy in vain pursuits.
13. On that day they shall be urged to and thrust into the Fire of Gehenna with a violent and irresistible urging.
14. (They will be told,) 'This is the Fire you used to cry lies to.
15. 'Is this an illusion or is it you who are still unable to see?
16. 'Burn you in it, and whether you show patience or you show (it) not, will be the same to you, (for) you will be requited only for your deeds.'
17. Verily, those who guarded against evil will be in Gardens and in (a state of) bliss,
18. Rejoicing at those (gifts) which their Lord will have granted them, and (they will render

سُورَةُ الطُّورِ ٥٢

سُورَةُ الطُّورِ مَكِّيَّةٌ

بِسْمِ اللّٰهِ الرَّحْمٰنِ الرَّحِيمِ

وَالطُّورِ ① وَكِتٰبٍ مَّسْطُورٍ ② فِي رَقٍّ مَّنْشُورٍ ③
وَّالْبَيْتِ الْمَعْمُورِ ④ وَالسَّقْفِ الْمَرْفُوعِ ⑤
وَالْبَحْرِ الْمَسْجُورِ ⑥ إِنَّ عَذَابَ رَبِّكَ لَوٰقِعٌ ⑦
مَّا لَهُ مِنْ دَافِعٍ ⑧ يَّوْمَ تَمُورُ السَّمَآءُ مَوْرًا ⑨
وَّتَسِيرُ الْجِبَالُ سَيْرًا ⑩ فَوَيْلٌ يَّوْمَئِذٍ
لِّلْمُكَذِّبِينَ ⑪ الَّذِينَ هُمْ فِي خَوْضٍ يَّلْعَبُونَ ⑫
يَوْمَ يُدَعُّونَ إِلٰى نَارِ جَهَنَّمَ دَعًّا ⑬ هٰذِهِ
النَّارُ الَّتِي كُنْتُمْ بِهَا تُكَذِّبُونَ ⑭ أَفَسِحْرٌ هٰذَآ
أَمْ أَنْتُمْ لَا تُبْصِرُونَ ⑮ إِصْلَوْهَا فَاصْبِرُوٓا
أَوْ لَا تَصْبِرُوا سَوَآءٌ عَلَيْكُمْ إِنَّمَا تُجْزَوْنَ
مَا كُنْتُمْ تَعْمَلُونَ ⑯ إِنَّ الْمُتَّقِينَ فِي جَنّٰتٍ
وَّنَعِيمٍ ⑰ فٰكِهِينَ بِمَآ أٰتٰهُمْ رَبُّهُمْ وَوَقٰهُمْ

Him thanks that) their Lord has guarded them against the torments of Hell.

19. (It will be said to them,) 'Eat and drink and enjoy yourselves as a reward of your (good) deeds.'

20. They will (on that day) be reclining on couches ranged in parallel rows. And We shall pair them with fair and pure houris.

21. We shall unite with those who believe such of their children who follow them in Faith even (though they do not attain the high standard of their forefathers' righteousness) yet We will not deprive them the least of the reward of their deeds. Every soul stands pledged for his own deeds (and is neither deprived of the reward nor can escape the punishment of his bad deeds).

22. We shall provide these (owners of Paradise) with such fruit and meat in abundance as they desire.

23. Therein they will pass one to another a cup (of refreshing drink) which shall induce neither foul talk nor sin.

24. Their own young sons as pure as though they were (virgin) pearls embedded in their shells, shall go round them.

25. And they will accost one another asking mutual questions.

26. They will say, 'Before (this) we were very much haunted by fear, in the midst of our family (about the consequences of our deeds).

27. 'But Allâh has been gracious to us and has saved us from the torment of the burning blast;

28. 'We used to call upon Him before (in prayer). Surely, He alone is the Most Beneficent, the Ever Merciful.'

SECTION 2

29. **S**o (Prophet!) Keep on exhorting, as by the grace of your Lord, you are neither a soothsayer, nor a madman.

30. Yet they say (about you), '(He is only) a poet, (and) we await the vicissitudes, which

سورة الطور ٥٢

ربهم عذاب الجحيم ﴿١٨﴾ كلوا واشربوا هنيئا
بما كنتم تعملون ﴿١٩﴾ متكئين على سرر
مصفوفة وزوجناهم بحور عين ﴿٢٠﴾ والذين
آمنوا واتبعتهم ذريتهم بإيمان ألحقنا بهم
ذريتهم وما ألتناهم من عملهم من شيء
كل امرئ بما كسب رهين ﴿٢١﴾ وأمددناهم
بفاكهة ولحم مما يشتهون ﴿٢٢﴾ يتنازعون فيها
كأسا لا لغو فيها ولا تأثيم ﴿٢٣﴾ ويطوف عليهم
غلمان لهم كأنهم لؤلؤ مكنون ﴿٢٤﴾ وأقبل
بعضهم على بعض يتساءلون ﴿٢٥﴾ قالوا إنا كنا
قبل في أهلنا مشفقين ﴿٢٦﴾ فمن الله علينا
ووقانا عذاب السموم ﴿٢٧﴾ إنا كنا من
قبل ندعوه إنه هو البر الرحيم ﴿٢٨﴾ فذكر
فما أنت بنعمت ربك بكاهن ولا مجنون ﴿٢٩﴾
أم يقولون شاعر نتربص به ريب المنون ﴿٣٠﴾

time will bring upon him.'

31. Say, 'Await you (the calamities), I too am with you among those who are awaiting.'

32. As a matter of fact their reason prompts them to (think of the Prophet in) these (terms). They are, rather, a people transgressing limits.

33. They say, 'He has fabricated it (- the Qur'ân).' The fact is that they have no belief (in God).

34. Let them, then bring forth a discourse like this (Qur'ân) if they are truthful (in their objection).

35. Have they been created without a (creative) agency (or purpose)? Or are they their own creators?

36. Have they created the heavens and the earth? The thing is only that they have no faith (in God).

37. Do they hold the treasures of your Lord or are they the Lord Supreme?

38. Have they the means through which they can overhear (the Lord)? If so, let their listener bring forth a clear authoritative proof (just as the Prophet of God does).

39. (O disbelievers, as you believe,) does He have daughters while you have sons?

40. Do you ask a reward from them (for your conveying the Message) so that they are weighed down with a load of undue debts (and so are finding it hard to pay).

41. Do they have (the knowledge of) the unseen so that they write down (and judge things in its light).

42. Do they intend to wage a war (against you)? But (remember) it is those who disbelieve that will be the victims of (their own) strategy of war.

43. Have they a god other than Allâh? Indeed, Highly Exalted is Allâh far above all the things they associate with Him.

44. And (even) if they see a fragment of the sky falling down (in the form of punishment) they would say, '(It is only) piled up clouds (and not

قُلْ تَرَبَّصُوا فَإِنِّي مَعَكُم مِّنَ الْمُتَرَبِّصِينَ ﴿٣١﴾
أَمْ تَأْمُرُهُمْ أَحْلَامُهُم بِهَٰذَا ۚ أَمْ هُمْ قَوْمٌ
طَاغُونَ ﴿٣٢﴾ أَمْ يَقُولُونَ تَقَوَّلَهُ ۚ بَل لَّا يُؤْمِنُونَ ﴿٣٣﴾
فَلْيَأْتُوا بِحَدِيثٍ مِّثْلِهِ إِن كَانُوا صَادِقِينَ ﴿٣٤﴾
أَمْ خُلِقُوا مِنْ غَيْرِ شَيْءٍ أَمْ هُمُ الْخَالِقُونَ ﴿٣٥﴾
أَمْ خَلَقُوا السَّمَاوَاتِ وَالْأَرْضَ ۚ بَل لَّا يُوقِنُونَ ﴿٣٦﴾
أَمْ عِندَهُمْ خَزَائِنُ رَبِّكَ أَمْ هُمُ الْمُصَيْطِرُونَ ﴿٣٧﴾
أَمْ لَهُمْ سُلَّمٌ يَسْتَمِعُونَ فِيهِ ۖ فَلْيَأْتِ مُسْتَمِعُهُم
بِسُلْطَانٍ مُّبِينٍ ﴿٣٨﴾ أَمْ لَهُ الْبَنَاتُ وَلَكُمُ الْبَنُونَ ﴿٣٩﴾
أَمْ تَسْأَلُهُمْ أَجْرًا فَهُم مِّن مَّغْرَمٍ مُّثْقَلُونَ ﴿٤٠﴾
أَمْ عِندَهُمُ الْغَيْبُ فَهُمْ يَكْتُبُونَ ﴿٤١﴾ أَمْ
يُرِيدُونَ كَيْدًا ۖ فَالَّذِينَ كَفَرُوا هُمُ الْمَكِيدُونَ ﴿٤٢﴾
أَمْ لَهُمْ إِلَٰهٌ غَيْرُ اللَّهِ ۚ سُبْحَانَ اللَّهِ عَمَّا
يُشْرِكُونَ ﴿٤٣﴾ وَإِن يَرَوْا كِسْفًا مِّنَ السَّمَاءِ
سَاقِطًا يَقُولُوا سَحَابٌ مَّرْكُومٌ ﴿٤٤﴾ فَذَرْهُمْ

a sign of punishment whatsoever).
45. So leave them alone till they meet that day of theirs (- the day of the battle of *Badr*) when they will be driven into the fire (of warfare).
46. The day when their stratagem of warfare will be of no avail to them and no help will be rendered to them (from any quarter).
47. There awaits the wrongdoers yet another punishment even prior to that (punishment of war). But most of them do not know.
48. (Prophet!) Await with patience and perseverance (the implementation of) the judgment of your Lord. You are under Our (loving care and) protection. And extol the Holiness of your Lord along with His praises when you rise (from sleep for Prayer).
49. And proclaim His glory for part of the night and also at the declining of the stars (when the night is about to end).

حَتّٰى يُلٰقُوا يَوْمَهُمُ الَّذِي فِيهِ يُصْعَقُونَ (٤٥)
يَوْمَ لَا يُغْنِي عَنْهُمْ كَيْدُهُمْ شَيْـًٔا وَّ لَا هُمْ
يُنْصَرُونَ (٤٦) وَ إِنَّ لِلَّذِينَ ظَلَمُوا عَذَابًا دُونَ
ذٰلِكَ وَلٰكِنَّ أَكْثَرَهُمْ لَا يَعْلَمُونَ (٤٧) وَاصْبِرْ لِحُكْمِ
رَبِّكَ فَإِنَّكَ بِأَعْيُنِنَا وَسَبِّحْ بِحَمْدِ رَبِّكَ حِينَ
تَقُومُ (٤٨) وَمِنَ الَّيْلِ فَسَبِّحْهُ وَإِدْبَارَ النُّجُومِ (٤٩)

CHAPTER
53

AL-NAJM
(Parts of the Qur'ân)
(Revealed before Hijrah)

سُورَةُ النَّجْمِ مَكِّيَّةٌ

With the name of Allâh,
the Most Gracious, the Ever Merciful
(I commence to read Sûrah Al-Najm).

بِسْمِ اللّٰهِ الرَّحْمٰنِ الرَّحِيمِ

1. **I** CALL to witness every part of the Qur'ân when it is revealed,
2. That your comrade (Mu<u>h</u>ammad) has neither deviated (from true guidance in his practices) nor has he erred (in his beliefs).
3. He does not say anything out of (his own) fanciful desire.
4. This (Qur'ân) is nothing but (pure) revelation, revealed (to him by God).
5. The Lord of Mighty Powers has taught him

وَالنَّجْمِ إِذَا هَوٰى (١) مَا ضَلَّ صَاحِبُكُمْ وَمَا
غَوٰى (٢) وَمَا يَنْطِقُ عَنِ الْهَوٰى (٣) إِنْ هُوَ إِلَّا
وَحْيٌ يُّوحٰى (٤) عَلَّمَهُ شَدِيدُ الْقُوٰى (٥) ذُو مِرَّةٍ

(this discourse).
6. (The Lord) Whose powers become manifest in manifold and frequent ways, with the result that he (- this Messenger of God) attained perfection and fullest vigour (both intellectually and physically).
7. And he attained to the zenith of heights (in his spiritual ascension).
8. Then he drew near to Him and afterwards he descended (to humankind, for their guidance).
9. So that he became (as it were) one chord to two bows or closer still.
10. Then He revealed that excellent and mighty (Qur'ânic) revelation which He had to send to His servant (Muhammad),
11. Whose mind made no mistake in (the interpretation of) that which he saw (during the ascension).
12. Will you doubt and dispute with him concerning that (sight) which he saw with his own eyes (it being no figment of imagination)?
13. And, of course, he saw Him (in His another manifestation to him) yet another time.
14. It was near the *Sidrah* which stands at the farthest end (of knowledge),
15. Near where also is the Garden which is the real eternal abode.
16. (This was) when the sublime thing (- the Divine Manifestation) which was to cover *Sidrah* had covered it.
17. (When he saw the Divine Manifestation) his eye deviated not (from the certainty of the Truth) nor did it wander away (from the invincible faith on which he stood).
18. (It was the moment when) he saw the greatly important signs of his Lord.
19. Have you had a look at *Lât* and *'Uzzâ* (the gods of idolaters),
20. And another, the third (goddess of no account) *Manât*?
21. What (an ignoble idea you have)! Are you to have the sons and He the daughters?

سُوْرَةُ النَّجْمِ ٥٣

فَاسْتَوَىٰ ۝٦ وَهُوَ بِالْأُفُقِ الْأَعْلَىٰ ۝٧ ثُمَّ دَنَا
فَتَدَلَّىٰ ۝٨ فَكَانَ قَابَ قَوْسَيْنِ أَوْ أَدْنَىٰ ۝٩
فَأَوْحَىٰ إِلَىٰ عَبْدِهِ مَا أَوْحَىٰ ۝١٠ مَا كَذَبَ
الْفُؤَادُ مَا رَأَىٰ ۝١١ أَفَتُمَارُونَهُ عَلَىٰ مَا يَرَىٰ ۝١٢
وَلَقَدْ رَآهُ نَزْلَةً أُخْرَىٰ ۝١٣ عِنْدَ سِدْرَةِ
الْمُنْتَهَىٰ ۝١٤ عِنْدَهَا جَنَّةُ الْمَأْوَىٰ ۝١٥ إِذْ يَغْشَى
السِّدْرَةَ مَا يَغْشَىٰ ۝١٦ مَا زَاغَ الْبَصَرُ وَمَا طَغَىٰ ۝١٧
لَقَدْ رَأَىٰ مِنْ آيَاتِ رَبِّهِ الْكُبْرَىٰ ۝١٨ أَفَرَأَيْتُمُ
اللَّاتَ وَالْعُزَّىٰ ۝١٩ وَمَنَاةَ الثَّالِثَةَ الْأُخْرَىٰ ۝٢٠
أَلَكُمُ الذَّكَرُ وَلَهُ الْأُنْثَىٰ ۝٢١ تِلْكَ إِذًا قِسْمَةٌ

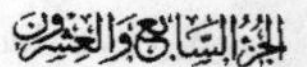

22. That indeed is an unjust division (and unbecoming from your own point of view which looks upon the birth of a daughter with condemnation).
23. (The fact is that) these are mere names (bearing no significance) which you have coined, you and your forefathers, for which Allâh has revealed no authority (for their being worshipped as gods and goddesses). These (idol-worshippers) follow nothing but mere conjectures and the fancies of (their own) minds. (They do this) even though true guidance has already come to them from their Lord.
24. Can a person always have whatever he desires?
25. Rather (all the blessings of) the Hereafter as well as (those of) this present life belong to Allâh.

SECTION 2

26. **B**EHOLD! So many an angel is there in the heavens but their intercession can be of no avail except after Allâh has given (them) permission regarding him whom He wills and with whom He is pleased.
27. (Verily, it is only) those who do not believe in the Hereafter and (who) give feminine names to the angels (because they ascribe them to Allâh as His daughters);
28. But they have no knowledge of the matter. They follow nothing but conjecture, yet by no means can a conjecture be a substitute for the established Truth.
29. So turn aside from him who turns away from Our remembrance, and seeks nothing but the present life.
30. That is the highest attainment of their knowledge. Verily, your Lord knows very well those who go astray from His path, as He knows very well those who follow the right guidance.
31. And all that lies in the heavens and all that lies in the earth belongs to Allâh alone. The result of this is that He recompenses the evil

سُورَةُ النَّجْمِ ٥٣

ضِيزَىٰ ﴿٢٢﴾ إِنْ هِيَ إِلَّآ أَسْمَآءٌ سَمَّيْتُمُوهَآ
أَنْتُمْ وَ ءَابَآؤُكُم مَّآ أَنْزَلَ اللهُ بِهَا مِنْ
سُلْطٰنٍ ۚ إِنْ يَتَّبِعُونَ إِلَّا الظَّنَّ وَ مَا تَهْوَى
الْأَنْفُسُ ۚ وَ لَقَدْ جَآءَهُم مِّن رَّبِّهِمُ الْهُدَىٰ ﴿٢٣﴾
أَمْ لِلْإِنْسٰنِ مَا تَمَنَّىٰ ﴿٢٤﴾ فَلِلّٰهِ الْأٰخِرَةُ وَالْأُولَىٰ ﴿٢٥﴾ ع ٥
وَ كَم مِّن مَّلَكٍ فِي السَّمٰوٰتِ لَا تُغْنِي شَفٰعَتُهُمْ
شَيْـًٔا إِلَّا مِنْ بَعْدِ أَنْ يَأْذَنَ اللهُ لِمَن يَشَآءُ
وَ يَرْضَىٰ ﴿٢٦﴾ إِنَّ الَّذِينَ لَا يُؤْمِنُونَ بِالْأٰخِرَةِ
لَيُسَمُّونَ الْمَلٰٓئِكَةَ تَسْمِيَةَ الْأُنْثَىٰ ﴿٢٧﴾ وَ مَا لَهُم
بِهِ مِنْ عِلْمٍ ۖ إِنْ يَتَّبِعُونَ إِلَّا الظَّنَّ ۖ وَ إِنَّ
الظَّنَّ لَا يُغْنِي مِنَ الْحَقِّ شَيْـًٔا ﴿٢٨﴾ فَأَعْرِضْ عَن
مَّن تَوَلَّىٰ عَن ذِكْرِنَا وَ لَمْ يُرِدْ إِلَّا الْحَيٰوةَ
الدُّنْيَا ﴿٢٩﴾ ذٰلِكَ مَبْلَغُهُم مِّنَ الْعِلْمِ ۚ إِنَّ رَبَّكَ
هُوَ أَعْلَمُ بِمَن ضَلَّ عَن سَبِيلِهِ وَ هُوَ أَعْلَمُ
بِمَنِ اهْتَدَىٰ ﴿٣٠﴾ وَ لِلّٰهِ مَا فِي السَّمٰوٰتِ وَ مَا
فِي الْأَرْضِ لِيَجْزِيَ الَّذِينَ أَسٰٓـُٔوا بِمَا عَمِلُوا

الجزء السابع والعشرون

doers according to (the evil of) their deeds and rewards those who do good deeds with the fairest reward.
32. Those who avoid grave sins and open shameful deeds but (who are sometimes guilty) only (of) minor offences (will find) your Lord is Lord of immense protection (and resorts to His mercy in such cases). He knows you full well (since) when He created you from the earth and when you were embryos in the wombs of your mothers. So make no pretensions to the purity of your souls. It is He Who knows best who (truly and fully) guards against evil.

SECTION 3

33. **H**AVE you taken notice of the one who turns away (from guidance),
34. And gives but a little (in the cause of Allâh) and does it grudgingly.
35. Has he the knowledge of the unseen so that he can see (his own future)?
36. Has he not been informed of the contents of the Scriptures of Moses,
37. And (those of) Abraham who thoroughly and faithfully fulfilled (the commandments of his Lord).
38. (The Scriptures say that) no soul that bears a burden shall bear the burden of another (soul).
39. And that a human being will have (to his account) what he strives for.
40. And that his strivings shall necessarily be seen (and evaluated),
41. Then will he be recompensed fully and fairly.
42. And that to your Lord is the eventual return.
43. And that it is He alone Who makes people laugh and weep.
44. And that it is He alone Who causes death and brings to life.
45. And that He Himself created the two species - male and female;
46. From a sperm-drop when it is emitted.
47. That it is He upon whom rests the raising (of

وَيَجْزِيَ الَّذِينَ أَحْسَنُوا بِالْحُسْنَى ۝٣١ الَّذِينَ
يَجْتَنِبُونَ كَبَٰٓئِرَ الْإِثْمِ وَالْفَوَٰحِشَ إِلَّا اللَّمَمَ
إِنَّ رَبَّكَ وَٰسِعُ الْمَغْفِرَةِ هُوَ أَعْلَمُ بِكُمْ إِذْ
أَنْشَأَكُمْ مِّنَ الْأَرْضِ وَإِذْ أَنْتُمْ أَجِنَّةٌ فِي
بُطُونِ أُمَّهَٰتِكُمْ فَلَا تُزَكُّوٓا أَنْفُسَكُمْ هُوَ أَعْلَمُ
بِمَنِ اتَّقَىٰ ۝٣٢ أَفَرَءَيْتَ الَّذِي تَوَلَّىٰ ۝٣٣ وَأَعْطَىٰ
قَلِيلًا وَّأَكْدَىٰ ۝٣٤ أَعِنْدَهُ عِلْمُ الْغَيْبِ فَهُوَ
يَرَىٰ ۝٣٥ أَمْ لَمْ يُنَبَّأْ بِمَا فِي صُحُفِ مُوسَىٰ ۝٣٦
وَإِبْرَٰهِيمَ الَّذِي وَفَّىٰٓ ۝٣٧ أَلَّا تَزِرُ وَازِرَةٌ وِزْرَ
أُخْرَىٰ ۝٣٨ وَأَنْ لَّيْسَ لِلْإِنْسَٰنِ إِلَّا مَا سَعَىٰ ۝٣٩
وَأَنَّ سَعْيَهُ سَوْفَ يُرَىٰ ۝٤٠ ثُمَّ يُجْزَىٰهُ الْجَزَآءَ
الْأَوْفَىٰ ۝٤١ وَأَنَّ إِلَىٰ رَبِّكَ الْمُنْتَهَىٰ ۝٤٢ وَأَنَّهُ هُوَ
أَضْحَكَ وَأَبْكَىٰ ۝٤٣ وَأَنَّهُ هُوَ أَمَاتَ وَأَحْيَا ۝٤٤
وَأَنَّهُ خَلَقَ الزَّوْجَيْنِ الذَّكَرَ وَالْأُنْثَىٰ ۝٤٥ مِنْ
نُّطْفَةٍ إِذَا تُمْنَىٰ ۝٤٦ وَأَنَّ عَلَيْهِ النَّشْأَةَ الْأُخْرَىٰ ۝٤٧

the dead) again to life.

48. And that it is He Who fulfills the needs and endows (the gift of) capital contentment, and grants wealth.

49. And that it is He Who is the Lord of *Sirius* (- a star worshipped by some polytheists).

50. And that He destroyed the ancient (tribe of) ʻÂd;

51. And (the tribe of) Thamûd, so that He spared not a single soul of them.

52. And (He destroyed) the people of Noah before (them). They were extremely wicked and most rebellious.

53. And (that it is He) Who totally pulled down the subverted cities (- Sodom and Gomorrah of the people of Lot),

54. So they were completely covered with that which overwhelms (when the punishment befalls).

55. (O human being!) Which of the bounties of your Lord will you then doubt and dispute?

56. This (Prophet) is a Warner (towards all the peoples of the worlds) from among the (series of) Warners (to one particular people) of old.

57. (The Hour of punishment) that was (promised) to come has drawn nigh.

58. None can avert this (doom) besides Allâh.

59. Do you then wonder at this announcement (and yet pay no heed to it),

60. (For on hearing the mention of the Hour of punishment) you laugh rather than weep.

61. And you remain proudly heedless and haughty.

62. You should better prostrate yourselves before Allâh and worship (Him).

[PROSTRATION]

وَأَنَّهُۥ هُوَ أَغْنَىٰ وَأَقْنَىٰ ﴿٤٨﴾ وَأَنَّهُۥ هُوَ رَبُّ
الشِّعْرَىٰ ﴿٤٩﴾ وَأَنَّهُۥٓ أَهْلَكَ عَادًا الْأُولَىٰ ﴿٥٠﴾
وَثَمُودَاْ فَمَآ أَبْقَىٰ ﴿٥١﴾ وَقَوْمَ نُوحٍ مِّن قَبْلُ إِنَّهُمْ
كَانُواْ هُمْ أَظْلَمَ وَأَطْغَىٰ ﴿٥٢﴾ وَالْمُؤْتَفِكَةَ أَهْوَىٰ ﴿٥٣﴾
فَغَشَّىٰهَا مَا غَشَّىٰ ﴿٥٤﴾ فَبِأَيِّ ءَالَآءِ رَبِّكَ تَتَمَارَىٰ ﴿٥٥﴾
هَٰذَا نَذِيرٌ مِّنَ النُّذُرِ الْأُولَىٰ ﴿٥٦﴾ أَزِفَتِ الْأَزِفَةُ ﴿٥٧﴾
لَيْسَ لَهَا مِن دُونِ اللَّهِ كَاشِفَةٌ ﴿٥٨﴾ أَفَمِنْ هَٰذَا
الْحَدِيثِ تَعْجَبُونَ ﴿٥٩﴾ وَتَضْحَكُونَ وَلَا تَبْكُونَ ﴿٦٠﴾
وَأَنتُمْ سَٰمِدُونَ ﴿٦١﴾ فَاسْجُدُواْ لِلَّهِ وَاعْبُدُواْ ﴿٦٢﴾

سُورَةُ الْقَمَرِ ٥٤

CHAPTER
54

AL-QAMAR
(The Moon)
(Revealed before Hijrah)

سُوْرَةُ الْقَمَرِ مَكِّيَّةٌ

With the name of Allâh,
the Most Gracious, the Ever Merciful
(I commence to read Sûrah Al-Qamar).

بِسْمِ اللّٰهِ الرَّحْمٰنِ الرَّحِيْمِ

1. THE Hour (of doom of the enemies of the Prophet) has drawn nigh and (to indicate it) the moon is rent asunder.
2. Yet, whenever these (disbelievers) see a sign they turn away (paying it no heed) and say, '(It is) an oft-repeated and tremendous illusion.'
3. They have cried lies (even to this sign) and have followed their low desires. Yet every decree (of God) shall certainly come to pass.
4. And certainly there has already come to them the important accounts (concerning the fate of the ancients) in which there is provision of abstaining (from obstinately following the wrong course).
5. (And wherein is) profound and perfect wisdom but the warnings were of no avail (to them).
6. Therefore turn away from them, (and await) the day when the summoner will summon them to a most disagreeable thing,
7. While (with the sense of remorse) their eyes will be downcast, they will come forth from (their) graves as though they were (swarms of) locusts being scattered about,
8. Rushing headlong towards the summoner. The disbelievers will say, 'This is a hard day.'
9. The people of Noah cried lies (to Our Prophets) before them. Accordingly they rejected Our servant and said (about him), 'A

اِقْتَرَبَتِ السَّاعَةُ وَانْشَقَّ الْقَمَرُ ١ وَإِنْ يَّرَوْا
اٰيَةً يُّعْرِضُوْا وَيَقُوْلُوْا سِحْرٌ مُّسْتَمِرٌّ ٢ وَكَذَّبُوْا
وَاتَّبَعُوْا أَهْوَاءَهُمْ وَكُلُّ أَمْرٍ مُّسْتَقِرٌّ ٣ وَلَقَدْ
جَاءَهُمْ مِّنَ الْأَنْبَاءِ مَا فِيْهِ مُزْدَجَرٌ ٤ حِكْمَةٌ
بٰلِغَةٌ فَمَا تُغْنِ النُّذُرُ ٥ فَتَوَلَّ عَنْهُمْ يَوْمَ يَدْعُ
الدَّاعِ إِلٰى شَيْءٍ نُّكُرٍ ٦ خُشَّعًا أَبْصَارُهُمْ يَخْرُجُوْنَ
مِنَ الْأَجْدَاثِ كَأَنَّهُمْ جَرَادٌ مُّنْتَشِرٌ ٧ مُّهْطِعِيْنَ
إِلَى الدَّاعِ يَقُوْلُ الْكٰفِرُوْنَ هٰذَا يَوْمٌ عَسِرٌ ٨
كَذَّبَتْ قَبْلَهُمْ قَوْمُ نُوْحٍ فَكَذَّبُوْا عَبْدَنَا وَقَالُوْا

madman and one who is spurned and chided (by our idols).'

10. At last he prayed to his Lord (saying), 'I am overcome so come to (my) help to defend me.'

11. Thereupon We opened the gates of the clouds and allowed water to pour down in torrents.

12. And We caused the land to burst with gushing springs so that the (two) waters gathered together for a great purpose (of divine punishment) that was decreed.

13. And We bore him (- Noah) on that (Ark which was made) of planks and nails.

14. It floated on (the waters of the deluge) under Our supervision and care. This (punishment) was for the sake of him (- Noah) who had been denied.

15. And We left this (incident of deluge for the succeeding generations to serve them) as a sign. But is there anyone who would take heed?

16. Then (behold!) how terrible was My punishment and (how true) My warning!

17. Indeed, We have made the Qur'ân easy for admonition and to understand, follow and remember. But is there anyone who would take heed?

18. (The tribe of) 'Âd (too) cried lies (to the warning of the Prophet, Hûd) and behold, how (terrible) was My punishment and (how true) My warning!

19. We let loose upon them a clamorous and alarmingly furious wind on a day (when) the sky remained red like copper till long.

20. It (- the howling wind) tore the people away as though they were the hollowed stumps of uprooted palm-trees.

21. Behold how (terrible) was My punishment and (how true) My warning!

22. And We have indeed made the Qur'ân easy for admonition and to understand, follow and remember. But is there anyone who would take heed?

SECTION 2

23. (**T**HE tribe of) Thamûd (too in rejecting Sâlih) cried lies to all the (Divine) Warners.

24. And they said, 'Shall we follow a man who

مَجْنُونٌ وَّازْدُجِرَ ٩ فَدَعَا رَبَّهُۥٓ أَنِّي مَغْلُوبٌ
فَانْتَصِرْ ١٠ فَفَتَحْنَآ أَبْوَابَ السَّمَآءِ بِمَآءٍ مُّنْهَمِرٍ ١١
وَّفَجَّرْنَا الْأَرْضَ عُيُونًا فَالْتَقَى الْمَآءُ عَلَىٰٓ أَمْرٍ
قَدْ قُدِرَ ١٢ وَحَمَلْنٰهُ عَلَىٰ ذَاتِ أَلْوٰحٍ وَّدُسُرٍ ١٣
تَجْرِي بِأَعْيُنِنَا جَزَآءً لِّمَنْ كَانَ كُفِرَ ١٤ وَلَقَدْ
تَّرَكْنٰهَآ ءَايَةً فَهَلْ مِنْ مُّدَّكِرٍ ١٥ فَكَيْفَ كَانَ
عَذَابِي وَنُذُرِ ١٦ وَلَقَدْ يَسَّرْنَا الْقُرْءَانَ لِلذِّكْرِ فَهَلْ
مِنْ مُّدَّكِرٍ ١٧ كَذَّبَتْ عَادٌ فَكَيْفَ كَانَ عَذَابِي
وَنُذُرِ ١٨ إِنَّآ أَرْسَلْنَا عَلَيْهِمْ رِيحًا صَرْصَرًا فِي
يَوْمِ نَحْسٍ مُّسْتَمِرٍّ ١٩ تَنْزِعُ النَّاسَ كَأَنَّهُمْ أَعْجَازُ
نَخْلٍ مُّنْقَعِرٍ ٢٠ فَكَيْفَ كَانَ عَذَابِي وَنُذُرِ ٢١
وَلَقَدْ يَسَّرْنَا الْقُرْءَانَ لِلذِّكْرِ فَهَلْ مِنْ مُّدَّكِرٍ ٢٢
كَذَّبَتْ ثَمُودُ بِالنُّذُرِ ٢٣ فَقَالُوٓا أَبَشَرًا مِّنَّا

hails from ourselves and is all alone? (If we do) indeed we, in that case, would be (involved) in a great error and (suffering from) insanity.
25. 'Is it that, from amongst all of us, the Reminder has been revealed to him (alone)? Nay (what he says is wrong), he is an impudent liar and self conceited.'
26. (God said to S̲âlih̲,) 'Very shortly shall they know who is the impudent liar and self-conceited.
27. 'We, in order to distinguish the good from the bad of them, are going to send a she-camel (in a state that she is not to be interfered with, in anyway). Therefore, wait (till their end comes), and patiently persevere (against their insults).
28. 'And inform them that their water is to be shared by them (and the she-camel), each time of drinking to be attended (by everyone) in turns.'
29. Thereupon they called their comrade who seized her (- the she-camel) quite unlawfully with the help of others and hamstrung (her, and they were then overtaken by a calamity).
30. And (behold!) how (terrible) then was My punishment and (how true) My warning!
31. And We let loose a single and sudden blast against them and they became crushed like dry twigs whittled down by an enclosure-maker.
32. And We have made the Qur'ân easy for admonition, and to understand, follow and remember. But is there anyone who would take heed?
33. Lot's people (also in rejecting Lot) cried lies to all (the Divine) Warners.
34. We let loose a (destructive) storm upon all of them except the family of Lot whom We delivered (through Our mercy from the punishment) by early dawn.
35. (It was) a favour from Us. That is how We reward those who give thanks.
36. While he (- Lot) had warned them of Our

سُوْرَةُ الْقَمَرِ ٥٤

وَٰحِدًا نَّتَّبِعُهُۥٓ إِنَّآ إِذًا لَّفِي ضَلَٰلٍ وَسُعُرٍ ﴿٢٤﴾
ءَأُلْقِيَ الذِّكْرُ عَلَيْهِ مِنۢ بَيْنِنَا بَلْ هُوَ كَذَّابٌ
أَشِرٌ ﴿٢٥﴾ سَيَعْلَمُونَ غَدًا مَّنِ الْكَذَّابُ الْأَشِرُ ﴿٢٦﴾
إِنَّا مُرْسِلُوا النَّاقَةِ فِتْنَةً لَّهُمْ فَارْتَقِبْهُمْ
وَاصْطَبِرْ ﴿٢٧﴾ وَنَبِّئْهُمْ أَنَّ الْمَآءَ قِسْمَةٌۢ بَيْنَهُمْ
كُلُّ شِرْبٍ مُّحْتَضَرٌ ﴿٢٨﴾ فَنَادَوْا صَاحِبَهُمْ فَتَعَاطَىٰ
فَعَقَرَ ﴿٢٩﴾ فَكَيْفَ كَانَ عَذَابِي وَنُذُرِ ﴿٣٠﴾ إِنَّآ أَرْسَلْنَا
عَلَيْهِمْ صَيْحَةً وَٰحِدَةً فَكَانُوا كَهَشِيمِ الْمُحْتَظِرِ ﴿٣١﴾
وَلَقَدْ يَسَّرْنَا الْقُرْءَانَ لِلذِّكْرِ فَهَلْ مِن مُّدَّكِرٍ ﴿٣٢﴾
كَذَّبَتْ قَوْمُ لُوطٍۭ بِالنُّذُرِ ﴿٣٣﴾ إِنَّآ أَرْسَلْنَا عَلَيْهِمْ
حَاصِبًا إِلَّآ ءَالَ لُوطٍ نَّجَّيْنَٰهُم بِسَحَرٍ ﴿٣٤﴾ نِّعْمَةً مِّنْ
عِندِنَا كَذَٰلِكَ نَجْزِي مَن شَكَرَ ﴿٣٥﴾ وَلَقَدْ أَنذَرَهُم

seizure (with punishment) but they doubted this warning and disputed over it.
37. And they (deceitfully) sought to turn him away from his guests. So We put a covering on their eyes. (And We said to them,) 'Now taste My punishment and (suffer the consequences of ignoring) My warning.'
38. And certainly there overtook them early in the morning a lasting punishment.
39. Now taste My punishment and (suffer the consequences of ignoring) My warning.
40. And indeed We have made the Qur'ân easy for admonition and to understand, follow and remember. But is there anyone who would take heed?

SECTION 3

41. **A**ND surely the Warners came to the people of Pharaoh (also);
42. But they cried lies to all Our signs. So We took them to task such as befitted the Mighty, the Powerful.
43. Are those of you who are disbelievers better than these? Or have you been promised amnesty (from punishment) in the (previous) Scriptures.
44. Or do (Makkan disbelievers) say, 'We are a united force, capable of defending one another (against any calamity)?
45. Soon that united force shall surely be routed. They will turn (their) backs (and flee before the Muslims).
46. The (promised) Hour (of their complete discomfiture) is their appointed time. The fact is that the Hour will be grievously calamitous and most bitter.
47. Surely, the guilty are (involved) in clear error and (suffering from) insanity.
48. On that day they shall be dragged on their faces into the fire (of the battle, it will be said to them), 'Suffer the smite of fire.'
49. Verily, all things have We created in correct proportion and measure.
50. Our command is (at once carried out

بَطْشَتَنَا فَتَمَارَوْا بِالنُّذُرِ ﴿٣٦﴾ وَلَقَدْ رَاوَدُوهُ عَنْ
ضَيْفِهِ فَطَمَسْنَا أَعْيُنَهُمْ فَذُوقُوا عَذَابِي
وَنُذُرِ ﴿٣٧﴾ وَلَقَدْ صَبَّحَهُم بُكْرَةً عَذَابٌ مُّسْتَقِرٌّ ﴿٣٨﴾
فَذُوقُوا عَذَابِي وَنُذُرِ ﴿٣٩﴾ وَلَقَدْ يَسَّرْنَا الْقُرْآنَ
لِلذِّكْرِ فَهَلْ مِن مُّدَّكِرٍ ﴿٤٠﴾ وَلَقَدْ جَاءَ آلَ فِرْعَوْنَ
النُّذُرُ ﴿٤١﴾ كَذَّبُوا بِآيَاتِنَا كُلِّهَا فَأَخَذْنَاهُمْ أَخْذَ
عَزِيزٍ مُّقْتَدِرٍ ﴿٤٢﴾ أَكُفَّارُكُمْ خَيْرٌ مِّنْ أُولَٰئِكُمْ
أَمْ لَكُم بَرَاءَةٌ فِي الزُّبُرِ ﴿٤٣﴾ أَمْ يَقُولُونَ نَحْنُ جَمِيعٌ
مُّنتَصِرٌ ﴿٤٤﴾ سَيُهْزَمُ الْجَمْعُ وَيُوَلُّونَ الدُّبُرَ ﴿٤٥﴾ بَلِ
السَّاعَةُ مَوْعِدُهُمْ وَالسَّاعَةُ أَدْهَىٰ وَأَمَرُّ ﴿٤٦﴾ إِنَّ
الْمُجْرِمِينَ فِي ضَلَالٍ وَسُعُرٍ ﴿٤٧﴾ يَوْمَ يُسْحَبُونَ فِي
النَّارِ عَلَىٰ وُجُوهِهِمْ ذُوقُوا مَسَّ سَقَرَ ﴿٤٨﴾ إِنَّا كُلَّ
شَيْءٍ خَلَقْنَاهُ بِقَدَرٍ ﴿٤٩﴾ وَمَا أَمْرُنَا إِلَّا وَاحِدَةٌ كَلَمْحٍ

by) only one (word) as quickly as the twinkling of an eye.
51. We have surely destroyed (gangs of) people like you (O disbelievers! before). But is there anyone who would take heed?
52. Everything they did is (recorded) in scrolls (of deeds).
53. And everything, small and big, has been noted down.
54. (That is why) those who became secure against evil and were dutiful (to God) shall be amidst gardens and bounties;
55. Occupying positions of honour and excellence with the Omnipotent Sovereign.

بِالْبَصَرِ ﴿٥٠﴾ وَلَقَدْ أَهْلَكْنَآ أَشْيَاعَكُمْ فَهَلْ مِن مُّدَّكِرٍ ﴿٥١﴾ وَكُلُّ شَيْءٍ فَعَلُوهُ فِي الزُّبُرِ ﴿٥٢﴾ وَكُلُّ صَغِيرٍ وَّكَبِيرٍ مُّسْتَطَرٌ ﴿٥٣﴾ إِنَّ الْمُتَّقِينَ فِي جَنّٰتٍ وَّنَهَرٍ ﴿٥٤﴾ فِي مَقْعَدِ صِدْقٍ عِنْدَ مَلِيكٍ مُّقْتَدِرٍ ﴿٥٥﴾ ع

CHAPTER
55

AL-RAHMÂN
(The Most Gracious)
(Revealed after Hijrah)

سُوْرَةُ الرَّحْمٰنِ مَدَنِيَّةٌ

With the name of Allâh,
the Most Gracious, the Ever Merciful
(I commence to read Sûrah Al-Rahmân).

بِسْمِ اللّٰهِ الرَّحْمٰنِ الرَّحِيْمِ

1. The Most Gracious (God)
2. Has taught this Qur'ân.
3. He created human being;
4. And taught him (the art of) intelligent and distinct speech.
5. The sun and the moon pursue their scheduled courses on their axis according to a fixed reckoning
6. And the stemless plants and the trees humbly submit (to His will);
7. And He raised the heaven high and set up the (law of) harmony and balance
8. (He explains this to you) that you should not violate the (law of) harmony and balance.

اَلرَّحْمٰنُ ﴿١﴾ عَلَّمَ الْقُرْاٰنَ ﴿٢﴾ خَلَقَ الْإِنْسٰنَ ﴿٣﴾ عَلَّمَهُ الْبَيَانَ ﴿٤﴾ اَلشَّمْسُ وَالْقَمَرُ بِحُسْبَانٍ ﴿٥﴾ وَّالنَّجْمُ وَالشَّجَرُ يَسْجُدٰنِ ﴿٦﴾ وَالسَّمَآءَ رَفَعَهَا وَوَضَعَ الْمِيزَانَ ﴿٧﴾ أَلَّا تَطْغَوْا فِي الْمِيزَانِ ﴿٨﴾

9. Hold balance with justice (giving every one his due avoiding extremes) and do not disturb the (law of) harmony in the least.
10. And He has set the earth for (the common good of) all (His) creatures.
11. In it there are all kinds of fruit and palm-trees (laden) with sheathed clusters,
12. And the grains with the husk-coverings and fragrant flowery plants.
13. Which of the benefactions of your Lord will you twain (believers and disbelievers), then, deny?
14. He created human being from the essence extracted from dry ringing clay like a piece of baked pottery (-with the faculty of speech and possessing pliant and submissive nature).
15. And He created the *jinn* from a flame of fire (- possessing fiery nature).
16. Which of the benefactions of your Lord will you twain, then, deny?
17. (He is) the Lord of the two easts and Lord of the two wests.
18. Which of the benefactions of your Lord will you twain, then, deny?
19. He has let the two bodies of water flow freely they will (one day) join together.
20. (At present) a barrier stands between them. They cannot encroach one upon the other.
21. Which of the benefactions of your Lord will you twain, then, deny?
22. Pearls and corals come out of both (these seas).
23. Which of the benefactions of your Lord will you twain, then, deny?
24. And to Him belong the ships raised aloft in the sea like mountain peaks.
25. Which of the benefactions of your Lord will you twain, then, deny?

SECTION 2

26. **A**LL that is on it (- the earth) is subject to decay and doomed to pass away.
27. But (only) the Majesty of your Lord and

وَأَقِيمُوا الْوَزْنَ بِالْقِسْطِ وَلَا تُخْسِرُوا الْمِيزَانَ ﴿٩﴾
وَالْأَرْضَ وَضَعَهَا لِلْأَنَامِ ﴿١٠﴾ فِيهَا فَاكِهَةٌ
وَالنَّخْلُ ذَاتُ الْأَكْمَامِ ﴿١١﴾ وَالْحَبُّ ذُو الْعَصْفِ
وَالرَّيْحَانُ ﴿١٢﴾ فَبِأَيِّ آلَاءِ رَبِّكُمَا تُكَذِّبَانِ ﴿١٣﴾
خَلَقَ الْإِنْسَانَ مِنْ صَلْصَالٍ كَالْفَخَّارِ ﴿١٤﴾ وَخَلَقَ
الْجَانَّ مِنْ مَارِجٍ مِنْ نَارٍ ﴿١٥﴾ فَبِأَيِّ آلَاءِ رَبِّكُمَا
تُكَذِّبَانِ ﴿١٦﴾ رَبُّ الْمَشْرِقَيْنِ وَرَبُّ الْمَغْرِبَيْنِ ﴿١٧﴾
فَبِأَيِّ آلَاءِ رَبِّكُمَا تُكَذِّبَانِ ﴿١٨﴾ مَرَجَ الْبَحْرَيْنِ
يَلْتَقِيَانِ ﴿١٩﴾ بَيْنَهُمَا بَرْزَخٌ لَا يَبْغِيَانِ ﴿٢٠﴾ فَبِأَيِّ
آلَاءِ رَبِّكُمَا تُكَذِّبَانِ ﴿٢١﴾ يَخْرُجُ مِنْهُمَا اللُّؤْلُؤُ
وَالْمَرْجَانُ ﴿٢٢﴾ فَبِأَيِّ آلَاءِ رَبِّكُمَا تُكَذِّبَانِ ﴿٢٣﴾
وَلَهُ الْجَوَارِ الْمُنْشَآتُ فِي الْبَحْرِ كَالْأَعْلَامِ ﴿٢٤﴾
فَبِأَيِّ آلَاءِ رَبِّكُمَا تُكَذِّبَانِ ﴿٢٥﴾ كُلُّ مَنْ عَلَيْهَا ع

that which is under the care of your Lord, the Lord of Glory and Honour endures for ever.
28. Which of the benefactions of your Lord will you twain, then, deny?
29. All of the rational beings that are in the heavens and on the earth do beg of Him. Every moment He manifests Himself in a new state (of glory).
30. Which of the benefactions of your Lord will you twain, then, deny?
31. We shall reckon with you O you two big groups (of the righteous and the rebellious).
32. Which of the benefactions of your Lord will you twain, then, deny?
33. O body of *the jinn* (- fiery natured) and the (ordinary) people! If you have the power and capacity to go beyond the confines of the heavens and the earth, then do go. But you will not be able to go unless you have the necessary and unusual power.
34. Which of the benefactions of your Lord will you twain, then, deny?
35. Flames of fire, smoke and molten copper will be let loose upon you and you will not be able to defend yourselves.
36. Which of the benefactions of your Lord will you twain, then, deny?
37. And when the heaven splits up and turns crimson like red hide (how will you fare then)?
38. Which of the benefactions of your Lord will you twain, then, deny?
39. On that day none of people nor of *jinn* will be questioned about his sin.
40. Which of the benefactions of your Lord will you twain, then, deny?
41. The guilty will be known by their appearance (and the expression of their faces), then they will be seized by (their) forelocks and the feet.
42. Which of the benefactions of your Lord will you twain, then, deny?
43. (They will be told) 'This is the Gehenna that the guilty have cried lies to.

فَانٍ ﴿٢٦﴾ وَّ يَبْقٰى وَجْهُ رَبِّكَ ذُو الْجَلٰلِ وَالْإِكْرَامِ ﴿٢٧﴾
فَبِأَيِّ اٰلَآءِ رَبِّكُمَا تُكَذِّبٰنِ ﴿٢٨﴾ يَسْئَلُهُ مَنْ فِي
السَّمٰوٰتِ وَ الْأَرْضِ كُلَّ يَوْمٍ هُوَ فِي شَأْنٍ ﴿٢٩﴾
فَبِأَيِّ اٰلَآءِ رَبِّكُمَا تُكَذِّبٰنِ ﴿٣٠﴾ سَنَفْرُغُ لَكُمْ
أَيُّهَ الثَّقَلٰنِ ﴿٣١﴾ فَبِأَيِّ اٰلَآءِ رَبِّكُمَا تُكَذِّبٰنِ ﴿٣٢﴾
يٰمَعْشَرَ الْجِنِّ وَ الْإِنْسِ إِنِ اسْتَطَعْتُمْ أَنْ
تَنْفُذُوا مِنْ أَقْطَارِ السَّمٰوٰتِ وَ الْأَرْضِ
فَانْفُذُوا لَا تَنْفُذُونَ إِلَّا بِسُلْطٰنٍ ﴿٣٣﴾ فَبِأَيِّ
اٰلَآءِ رَبِّكُمَا تُكَذِّبٰنِ ﴿٣٤﴾ يُرْسَلُ عَلَيْكُمَا شُوَاظٌ
مِّنْ نَّارٍ وَّ نُحَاسٌ فَلَا تَنْتَصِرٰنِ ﴿٣٥﴾ فَبِأَيِّ
اٰلَآءِ رَبِّكُمَا تُكَذِّبٰنِ ﴿٣٦﴾ فَإِذَا انْشَقَّتِ السَّمَآءُ
فَكَانَتْ وَرْدَةً كَالدِّهَانِ ﴿٣٧﴾ فَبِأَيِّ اٰلَآءِ رَبِّكُمَا
تُكَذِّبٰنِ ﴿٣٨﴾ فَيَوْمَئِذٍ لَّا يُسْئَلُ عَنْ ذَنْبِهٖٓ
إِنْسٌ وَّ لَا جَآنٌّ ﴿٣٩﴾ فَبِأَيِّ اٰلَآءِ رَبِّكُمَا تُكَذِّبٰنِ ﴿٤٠﴾
يُعْرَفُ الْمُجْرِمُونَ بِسِيْمٰهُمْ فَيُؤْخَذُ بِالنَّوَاصِي
وَ الْأَقْدَامِ ﴿٤١﴾ فَبِأَيِّ اٰلَآءِ رَبِّكُمَا تُكَذِّبٰنِ ﴿٤٢﴾
هٰذِهٖ جَهَنَّمُ الَّتِي يُكَذِّبُ بِهَا الْمُجْرِمُونَ ﴿٤٣﴾

44. 'They will take turns (restlessly) between it (- the hell-fire) and boiling hot liquid.'
45. Which of the benefactions of your Lord will you twain, then, deny?

SECTION 3

46. **T**HERE are two Gardens (of bliss here and the Hereafter) for such as fear (the time) when they will stand before (the judgment seat of) your Lord (to account for their deeds).
47. Which of the benefactions of your Lord will you twain, then, deny?
48. Both (the Gardens of Paradise) are abounding in varieties (of trees and rich greenery accompanied with delightful comforts).
49. Which of the benefactions of your Lord will you twain, then, deny?
50. There are two springs flowing (free) in each of them.
51. Which of the benefactions of your Lord will you twain, then, deny?
52. In both of these (Gardens) there are fruit of all kinds in two varieties.
53. Which of the benefactions of your Lord, will you twain, then, deny?
54. They (- the owners of Paradise) will be reclining (on couches) over carpets, the linings of which will be of thick brocade. And the ripe fruit of both the Gardens will be bending (so) low (as to be within their easy reach to pluck).
55. Which of the benefactions of your Lord will you twain, then, deny?
56. There they shall have (chaste and modest) maidens restraining their glances (to look at them only), whom (in this state) neither man nor *jinn* has ever touched before them.
57. Which of the benefactions of your Lord will you twain, then, deny?
58. (These maidens will look) as if they were (made of) rubies and small pearls.
59. Which of the benefactions of your Lord will you twain, then, deny?
60. Goodness alone is the reward of goodness .

يَطُوفُونَ بَيْنَهَا وَبَيْنَ حَمِيمٍ ءَانٍ ﴿٤٤﴾ فَبِأَيِّ
ءَالَآءِ رَبِّكُمَا تُكَذِّبَانِ ﴿٤٥﴾ وَلِمَنْ خَافَ مَقَامَ
رَبِّهِۦ جَنَّتَانِ ﴿٤٦﴾ فَبِأَيِّ ءَالَآءِ رَبِّكُمَا تُكَذِّبَانِ ﴿٤٧﴾
ذَوَاتَآ أَفْنَانٍ ﴿٤٨﴾ فَبِأَيِّ ءَالَآءِ رَبِّكُمَا تُكَذِّبَانِ ﴿٤٩﴾
فِيهِمَا عَيْنَانِ تَجْرِيَانِ ﴿٥٠﴾ فَبِأَيِّ ءَالَآءِ رَبِّكُمَا
تُكَذِّبَانِ ﴿٥١﴾ فِيهِمَا مِن كُلِّ فَٰكِهَةٍ زَوْجَانِ ﴿٥٢﴾
فَبِأَيِّ ءَالَآءِ رَبِّكُمَا تُكَذِّبَانِ ﴿٥٣﴾ مُتَّكِـِٔينَ عَلَىٰ
فُرُشٍۭ بَطَآئِنُهَا مِنْ إِسْتَبْرَقٍ وَجَنَى ٱلْجَنَّتَيْنِ
دَانٍ ﴿٥٤﴾ فَبِأَيِّ ءَالَآءِ رَبِّكُمَا تُكَذِّبَانِ ﴿٥٥﴾ فِيهِنَّ
قَٰصِرَٰتُ ٱلطَّرْفِ لَمْ يَطْمِثْهُنَّ إِنسٌ قَبْلَهُمْ
وَلَا جَآنٌّ ﴿٥٦﴾ فَبِأَيِّ ءَالَآءِ رَبِّكُمَا تُكَذِّبَانِ ﴿٥٧﴾
كَأَنَّهُنَّ ٱلْيَاقُوتُ وَٱلْمَرْجَانُ ﴿٥٨﴾ فَبِأَيِّ ءَالَآءِ
رَبِّكُمَا تُكَذِّبَانِ ﴿٥٩﴾ هَلْ جَزَآءُ ٱلْإِحْسَٰنِ إِلَّا

ع ٢ ١٢

61. Which of the benefactions of your Lord will you twain, then, deny?
62. And besides these two (Paradises) there are two other Gardens,
63. Which of the benefactions of your Lord will you twain, then, deny?
64. Both of them are dark green with thick foliage.
65. Which of the benefactions of your Lord will you twain, then, deny?
66. Both of these two have two springs gushing forth.
67. Which of the benefactions of your Lord will you twain, then, deny?
68. Both of these two have all kinds of fruit and dates and pomegranates
69. Which of the benefactions of your Lord will you twain, then, deny?
70. Therein will be (maidens) pious (and) beautiful.
71. Which of the benefactions of your Lord will you twain, then, deny?
72. Pure and chaste houris confined to (their goodly) pavilions (enjoying the shade of God's mercy).
73. Which of the benefactions of your Lord will you twain, then, deny?
74. Whom neither man nor *jinn* has ever touched before them (in this state).
75. Which of the benefactions of your Lord will you twain, then, deny?
76. (The owners of Paradise will be) reclining on green cushions and rich carpets of lovely beauty.
77. Which of the benefactions of your Lord will you twain, then, deny?
78. Blessed be the name of your Lord, the Master of Glory and Honour.

الْإِحْسٰنُ ۝٦٠ فَبِأَيِّ اٰلَآءِ رَبِّكُمَا تُكَذِّبٰنِ ۝٦١
وَ مِنْ دُوْنِهِمَا جَنَّتٰنِ ۝٦٢ فَبِأَيِّ اٰلَآءِ رَبِّكُمَا
تُكَذِّبٰنِ ۝٦٣ مُدْهَآمَّتٰنِ ۝٦٤ فَبِأَيِّ اٰلَآءِ رَبِّكُمَا
تُكَذِّبٰنِ ۝٦٥ فِيْهِمَا عَيْنٰنِ نَضَّاخَتٰنِ ۝٦٦ فَبِأَيِّ
اٰلَآءِ رَبِّكُمَا تُكَذِّبٰنِ ۝٦٧ فِيْهِمَا فٰكِهَةٌ وَّ نَخْلٌ
وَّ رُمَّانٌ ۝٦٨ فَبِأَيِّ اٰلَآءِ رَبِّكُمَا تُكَذِّبٰنِ ۝٦٩ فِيْهِنَّ
خَيْرٰتٌ حِسَانٌ ۝٧٠ فَبِأَيِّ اٰلَآءِ رَبِّكُمَا تُكَذِّبٰنِ ۝٧١
حُوْرٌ مَّقْصُوْرٰتٌ فِي الْخِيَامِ ۝٧٢ فَبِأَيِّ اٰلَآءِ رَبِّكُمَا
تُكَذِّبٰنِ ۝٧٣ لَمْ يَطْمِثْهُنَّ إِنْسٌ قَبْلَهُمْ وَ لَا
جَآنٌّ ۝٧٤ فَبِأَيِّ اٰلَآءِ رَبِّكُمَا تُكَذِّبٰنِ ۝٧٥ مُتَّكِـِٔيْنَ
عَلٰى رَفْرَفٍ خُضْرٍ وَّ عَبْقَرِيٍّ حِسَانٍ ۝٧٦ فَبِأَيِّ
اٰلَآءِ رَبِّكُمَا تُكَذِّبٰنِ ۝٧٧ تَبٰرَكَ اسْمُ رَبِّكَ
ذِي الْجَلٰلِ وَ الْإِكْرَامِ ۝٧٨

ع ٣

CHAPTER 56

AL-WÂQI'AH
(The Great Event)
(Revealed before Hijrah)

سُورَةُ الوَاقِعَةِ مَكِّيَّةٌ

With the name of Allâh,
the Most Gracious, the Ever Merciful
(I commence to read Sûrah Al-Wâqi'ah).

بِسْمِ اللَّهِ الرَّحْمَٰنِ الرَّحِيمِ

1. (**B**EWARE of the time) when the inevitable (and the promised) Event shall come to pass.
2. There is no denying its coming to pass.
3. (This event shall be) lowering (the status of some and) exalting (that of others).
4. (This will take place) when the earth shall be shaken with a violent shaking
5. And the mountains shall be completely shattered,
6. So that they shall all be reduced to particles of dust scattered about.
7. And (at that time) you shall be (sorted out into) three distinct categories,
8. (First) those that are blessed. How (lucky) the blessed will be!
9. And (then) those that are wretched, how (miserable) the condition of the wretched will be!
10. And (third) those that are foremost (in faith). They are by all means the foremost (in the Hereafter).
11. It is they who have (really) achieved nearness (to their Lord).
12. (They shall abide) in Gardens of bliss.
13. A large party of them (will hail) from the early (believers);
14. While a few (of them will hail) from the later ones.
15. (They will be in the Garden seated) on couches inlaid (with gold and precious jewels).
16. (They will be) reclining thereupon (and sitting) face to face.

إِذَا وَقَعَتِ الْوَاقِعَةُ ۝١ لَيْسَ لِوَقْعَتِهَا كَاذِبَةٌ ۝٢
خَافِضَةٌ رَّافِعَةٌ ۝٣ إِذَا رُجَّتِ الْأَرْضُ رَجًّا ۝٤
وَبُسَّتِ الْجِبَالُ بَسًّا ۝٥ فَكَانَتْ هَبَاءً مُّنْبَثًّا ۝٦
وَكُنْتُمْ أَزْوَاجًا ثَلَاثَةً ۝٧ فَأَصْحَابُ الْمَيْمَنَةِ
مَا أَصْحَابُ الْمَيْمَنَةِ ۝٨ وَأَصْحَابُ الْمَشْأَمَةِ
مَا أَصْحَابُ الْمَشْأَمَةِ ۝٩ وَالسَّابِقُونَ السَّابِقُونَ ۝١٠
أُولَٰئِكَ الْمُقَرَّبُونَ ۝١١ فِي جَنَّاتِ النَّعِيمِ ۝١٢ ثُلَّةٌ مِّنَ
الْأَوَّلِينَ ۝١٣ وَقَلِيلٌ مِّنَ الْآخِرِينَ ۝١٤ عَلَىٰ سُرُرٍ

17. (Their) young sons will go round about them, who will remain as young as ever,
18. Carrying goblets and (shining) beakers and cups (full) of pure and clean drink
19. They will get no headache (or giddiness) from their (drinks), nor will they be inebriated and talk nonsense.
20. And (carrying) such fruits as they choose,
21. And (with) flesh of birds exactly to their taste.
22. And (there will be present) fair houris with lovely large eyes.
23. (Chaste) like pearls, well-guarded and well preserved.
24. (Such shall be) the reward of their (good) deeds.
25. There they shall hear no idle-talk, no sinful speech.
26. But (all that they hear on all sides will be) good and pure words (of salutation) - ‘Peace be, peace be.’
27. Those that are blessed - how (lucky) the blessed will be!
28. They shall abide amidst (the land of thornless) *Sidrah* (- Lote tree, a symbol of bliss);
29. And (in the Garden of) clustered bananas;
30. And (in) extended shades;
31. And (near) water falling from heights;
32. And (amidst) abundant fruit;
33. (The season of) which is not limited, and (they are) never forbidden.
34. And (they will have) noble spouses.
35. Verily, We have made them (women) excellent and have raised them into a special new creation;
36. And have made them virgins, pure and undefiled.
37. They are the loving ones (of their husbands), suiting to their ages and matching them in every respect.
38. (They are meant) for the blessed ones.

سُورَةُ الْوَاقِعَةِ ٥٦

مَوْضُونَةٍ ﴿١٥﴾ مُتَّكِئِينَ عَلَيْهَا مُتَقَابِلِينَ ﴿١٦﴾ يَطُوفُ
عَلَيْهِمْ وِلْدَانٌ مُخَلَّدُونَ ﴿١٧﴾ بِأَكْوَابٍ
وَأَبَارِيقَ وَكَأْسٍ مِنْ مَعِينٍ ﴿١٨﴾ لَا يُصَدَّعُونَ
عَنْهَا وَلَا يُنْزِفُونَ ﴿١٩﴾ وَفَاكِهَةٍ مِمَّا يَتَخَيَّرُونَ ﴿٢٠﴾
وَلَحْمِ طَيْرٍ مِمَّا يَشْتَهُونَ ﴿٢١﴾ وَحُورٌ عِينٌ ﴿٢٢﴾
كَأَمْثَالِ اللُّؤْلُؤِ الْمَكْنُونِ ﴿٢٣﴾ جَزَاءً بِمَا كَانُوا
يَعْمَلُونَ ﴿٢٤﴾ لَا يَسْمَعُونَ فِيهَا لَغْوًا وَلَا تَأْثِيمًا ﴿٢٥﴾
إِلَّا قِيلًا سَلَامًا سَلَامًا ﴿٢٦﴾ وَأَصْحَابُ الْيَمِينِ
مَا أَصْحَابُ الْيَمِينِ ﴿٢٧﴾ فِي سِدْرٍ مَخْضُودٍ ﴿٢٨﴾
وَطَلْحٍ مَنْضُودٍ ﴿٢٩﴾ وَظِلٍّ مَمْدُودٍ ﴿٣٠﴾ وَمَاءٍ
مَسْكُوبٍ ﴿٣١﴾ وَفَاكِهَةٍ كَثِيرَةٍ ﴿٣٢﴾ لَا مَقْطُوعَةٍ
وَلَا مَمْنُوعَةٍ ﴿٣٣﴾ وَفُرُشٍ مَرْفُوعَةٍ ﴿٣٤﴾ إِنَّا
أَنْشَأْنَاهُنَّ إِنْشَاءً ﴿٣٥﴾ فَجَعَلْنَاهُنَّ أَبْكَارًا ﴿٣٦﴾
عُرُبًا أَتْرَابًا ﴿٣٧﴾ لِأَصْحَابِ الْيَمِينِ ﴿٣٨﴾ ثُلَّةٌ مِنَ

SECTION 2

39. (THIS group will consist of) a large party

from the earlier people (of Islam);
40. And a large party from the later ones.
41. But as for those that are wretched, how (sad) will be the plight of those that are wretched!
42. (They shall dwell) in the midst of (painfully) scorching winds and scalding water;
43. And (under) the shadow of black smoke,
44. (Which is) neither cool (to refresh) nor honourable nor of any good to please at all.
45. They, of course, lived a life of ease and abundance before this (in the present world).
46. But (they) persisted in extreme sinfulness.
47. And they were wont to say, ‘Is it that when we are dead and reduced to dust and bones we shall then be raised to life (again)?
48. ‘And is it that our fathers of yore (shall also be raised to a new life with us)?’
49. Say, ‘Most surely, the earlier people and the later ones
50. ‘Shall all be gathered together at the fixed time of an appointed day.
51. ‘Then, O you that have gone astray and cried lies (to the truth)!
52. ‘You will certainly eat of *Zaqqûm*-tree (a symbol of agony),
53. ‘And will fill your bellies with it.
54. ‘Then you shall drink over it boiling water;
55. Lapping it down like the lapping of the camels that suffer from insatiable thirst.
56. This will be their (of the wretched ones) entertainment on the Day of Requital.
57. It is We Who have created you (the first time), why do you not then realise the reality (of the Resurrection).
58. Have you given thought to (the sperm drop, your life-germ) that you emit?
59. Is it you that create it yourselves, or are We the Creator (of it)?
60. It is We that have ordained death for all of you. And We cannot be stopped from (it),

الْأَوَّلِينَ ﴿٣٩﴾ وَثُلَّةٌ مِّنَ الْآخِرِينَ ﴿٤٠﴾ وَأَصْحَابُ
الشِّمَالِ مَا أَصْحَابُ الشِّمَالِ ﴿٤١﴾ فِي سَمُومٍ
وَحَمِيمٍ ﴿٤٢﴾ وَظِلٍّ مِّن يَحْمُومٍ ﴿٤٣﴾ لَّا بَارِدٍ
وَلَا كَرِيمٍ ﴿٤٤﴾ إِنَّهُمْ كَانُوا قَبْلَ ذَٰلِكَ مُتْرَفِينَ ﴿٤٥﴾
وَكَانُوا يُصِرُّونَ عَلَى الْحِنثِ الْعَظِيمِ ﴿٤٦﴾ وَكَانُوا
يَقُولُونَ أَئِذَا مِتْنَا وَكُنَّا تُرَابًا وَعِظَامًا أَإِنَّا
لَمَبْعُوثُونَ ﴿٤٧﴾ أَوَآبَاؤُنَا الْأَوَّلُونَ ﴿٤٨﴾ قُلْ إِنَّ
الْأَوَّلِينَ وَالْآخِرِينَ ﴿٤٩﴾ لَمَجْمُوعُونَ إِلَىٰ
مِيقَاتِ يَوْمٍ مَّعْلُومٍ ﴿٥٠﴾ ثُمَّ إِنَّكُمْ أَيُّهَا
الضَّالُّونَ الْمُكَذِّبُونَ ﴿٥١﴾ لَآكِلُونَ مِن شَجَرٍ
مِّن زَقُّومٍ ﴿٥٢﴾ فَمَالِئُونَ مِنْهَا الْبُطُونَ ﴿٥٣﴾
فَشَارِبُونَ عَلَيْهِ مِنَ الْحَمِيمِ ﴿٥٤﴾ فَشَارِبُونَ
شُرْبَ الْهِيمِ ﴿٥٥﴾ هَٰذَا نُزُلُهُمْ يَوْمَ الدِّينِ ﴿٥٦﴾
نَحْنُ خَلَقْنَاكُمْ فَلَوْلَا تُصَدِّقُونَ ﴿٥٧﴾ أَفَرَأَيْتُم
مَّا تُمْنُونَ ﴿٥٨﴾ أَأَنتُمْ تَخْلُقُونَهُ أَمْ نَحْنُ
الْخَالِقُونَ ﴿٥٩﴾ نَحْنُ قَدَّرْنَا بَيْنَكُمُ الْمَوْتَ وَمَا

سُورَةُ الْوَاقِعَةِ ٥٦

61. From replacing you with beings similar to you, (or from) evolving you into a form which is unknown to you (at present).
62. And you certainly know of the first evolution. Then, why do you not reflect?
63. Have you ever given thought to that which you sow?
64. Is it you that cause it grow or is it We Who are the Growers?
65. If We (so) pleased We could reduce it to chaff (before it is ripe and ready to be harvested). And then you would remain lamenting and talking bitterly;
66. (And saying,) ‘Surely, we have been left indebted,
67. ‘Rather we have been left with nothing (indeed we are finished).’
68. Have you ever given thought to the water that you drink?
69. Is it you who bring it down from the clouds, or is it We Who rain it?
70. If We (so) pleased We could make it brackish. Then why do you not give thanks?
71. Have you given thought to the fire which you kindle?
72. Is it you who produce the tree for (kindling) it (into fire) or is it We the producer (of it)?
73. We have made it a source of admonition (for the people) and a means to live upon for the needy and the wayfarer.
74. Glorify, therefore, the name of your Lord, the Incomparably Great.

SECTION 3

75. **A**s to me, I swear by the places and times of the revelation of the portions of the Qur'ân;
76. And behold! It is a mighty oath, if you only care to know;
77. That this is most surely a Holy Qur'ân (bestowing bounteous blessings of God),
78. In a Book well preserved (in all its purity).
79. No one can achieve true insight into it

نَحْنُ بِمَسْبُوقِينَ ٦٠ عَلَىٰ أَن نُّبَدِّلَ أَمْثَٰلَكُمْ
وَنُنشِئَكُمْ فِي مَا لَا تَعْلَمُونَ ٦١ وَلَقَدْ عَلِمْتُمُ
النَّشْأَةَ الْأُولَىٰ فَلَوْلَا تَذَكَّرُونَ ٦٢ أَفَرَءَيْتُم
مَّا تَحْرُثُونَ ٦٣ ءَأَنتُمْ تَزْرَعُونَهُ أَمْ نَحْنُ
الزَّٰرِعُونَ ٦٤ لَوْ نَشَاءُ لَجَعَلْنَٰهُ حُطَٰمًا فَظَلْتُمْ
تَفَكَّهُونَ ٦٥ إِنَّا لَمُغْرَمُونَ ٦٦ بَلْ نَحْنُ مَحْرُومُونَ ٦٧
أَفَرَءَيْتُمُ الْمَاءَ الَّذِي تَشْرَبُونَ ٦٨ ءَأَنتُمْ
أَنزَلْتُمُوهُ مِنَ الْمُزْنِ أَمْ نَحْنُ الْمُنزِلُونَ ٦٩
لَوْ نَشَاءُ جَعَلْنَٰهُ أُجَاجًا فَلَوْلَا تَشْكُرُونَ ٧٠
أَفَرَءَيْتُمُ النَّارَ الَّتِي تُورُونَ ٧١ ءَأَنتُمْ أَنشَأْتُمْ
شَجَرَتَهَا أَمْ نَحْنُ الْمُنشِـُٔونَ ٧٢ نَحْنُ جَعَلْنَٰهَا
تَذْكِرَةً وَمَتَٰعًا لِّلْمُقْوِينَ ٧٣ فَسَبِّحْ بِاسْمِ رَبِّكَ
الْعَظِيمِ ٧٤ فَلَا أُقْسِمُ بِمَوَٰقِعِ النُّجُومِ ٧٥ ع ٢ ١٥
وَإِنَّهُ لَقَسَمٌ لَّوْ تَعْلَمُونَ عَظِيمٌ ٧٦ إِنَّهُ لَقُرْءَانٌ
كَرِيمٌ ٧٧ فِي كِتَٰبٍ مَّكْنُونٍ ٧٨ لَّا يَمَسُّهُ إِلَّا

except those who are purified (by leading righteous lives).
80. (It is) a revelation from the Lord of the worlds.
81. Is it this (Divine) discourse that you are the deniers of?
82. And do you make the denial of it your lot?
83. Why, then, when the soul (of the dying person) reaches the throat,
84. And you are at that time looking on (helplessly),
85. And (when) We are nearer to him than you, though you do not see.
86. Why, then, if you are not governed by any authority and are not to be requited,
87. You do not bring it (- the soul) back (to the body of the dying person), if you are truthful (in your claim of being independent of the supreme authority)?
88. And if he (the departed person) belongs to those who have attained nearness (to God and are His chosen ones),
89. Then (he will have) happiness, comfort and plenty and Garden of Bliss.
90. And if he (- the departed person) belongs to the blessed people,
91. Then (it will be said to him,) 'Peace be upon you ever, (O you) of the blessed people!'
92. But if he belongs to those who deny the truth and are steeped in error,
93. Then (he will be offered) boiling water for an entertainment,
94. And burning in Hell.
95. Verily, this (fact) is a perfect certainty (not merely a certainty by inference or sight),
96. Therefore glorify the name of your Lord, the Incomparably Great.

الْمُطَهَّرُونَ ٧٩ تَنزِيلٌ مِّن رَّبِّ الْعٰلَمِينَ ٨٠
أَفَبِهٰذَا الْحَدِيثِ أَنتُم مُّدْهِنُونَ ٨١ وَتَجْعَلُونَ
رِزْقَكُمْ أَنَّكُمْ تُكَذِّبُونَ ٨٢ فَلَوْلَآ إِذَا بَلَغَتِ
الْحُلْقُومَ ٨٣ وَأَنتُمْ حِينَئِذٍ تَنظُرُونَ ٨٤ وَنَحْنُ
أَقْرَبُ إِلَيْهِ مِنكُمْ وَلٰكِن لَّا تُبْصِرُونَ ٨٥
فَلَوْلَآ إِن كُنتُمْ غَيْرَ مَدِينِينَ ٨٦ تَرْجِعُونَهَآ
إِن كُنتُمْ صٰدِقِينَ ٨٧ فَأَمَّآ إِن كَانَ مِنَ
الْمُقَرَّبِينَ ٨٨ فَرَوْحٌ وَّرَيْحَانٌ ۥ وَّجَنَّتُ نَعِيمٍ ٨٩
وَأَمَّآ إِن كَانَ مِنْ أَصْحٰبِ الْيَمِينِ ٩٠ فَسَلٰمٌ
لَّكَ مِنْ أَصْحٰبِ الْيَمِينِ ٩١ وَأَمَّآ إِن كَانَ
مِنَ الْمُكَذِّبِينَ الضَّآلِّينَ ٩٢ فَنُزُلٌ مِّنْ حَمِيمٍ ٩٣
وَتَصْلِيَةُ جَحِيمٍ ٩٤ إِنَّ هٰذَا لَهُوَ حَقُّ الْيَقِينِ ٩٥
ع ٣ ١٦ فَسَبِّحْ بِاسْمِ رَبِّكَ الْعَظِيمِ ٩٦

CHAPTER
57

سُوْرَةُ الْحَدِيْدِ ٥٧

AL-HADÎD
(The Iron)
(Revealed after Hijrah)

With the name of Allâh,
the Most Gracious, the Ever Merciful
(I commence to read Sûrah Al-Hadîd).

1. **W**HATEVER is in the heavens and the earth declares the glory of Allâh. And He is the All-Mighty the All-Wise.
2. The kingdom of the heavens and the earth belongs to Him. He gives life and causes death and He is the Possessor of power to do all that He will.
3. He is (from) the very First (there was nothing before Him), and (He will exist to) the Last (there will be nothing after Him), and when nothing remains He will remain (He being an eternal Being). He is the Supreme Being (subordinate to no one). And (whereas He comprehends everything) He is Incomprehensible. He has full knowledge of every thing.
4. It is He Who created the heavens and the earth in six aeons. And He is established on the Throne (of Power). He knows what goes down into the earth and what comes out of it, and what descends from above and what ascends to it. He is with you wherever you may be. Allâh is watchful of all that you do.
5. The kingdom of the heavens and the earth belongs to Him. All matters are referred to Allâh (for His judgment).
6. He causes the night to gain on the day (in one season) and He causes the day to gain on the night (in the other season). He has full knowledge of the inmost secrets of hearts.
7. (O people!) Believe in Allâh and His Messenger and spend (in the cause of Allâh) out of the possessions He has entrusted you with as His

سُوْرَةُ الْحَدِيْدِ مَدَنِيَّةٌ

بِسْمِ اللّٰهِ الرَّحْمٰنِ الرَّحِيْمِ

سَبَّحَ لِلّٰهِ مَا فِي السَّمٰوٰتِ وَ الْأَرْضِ وَهُوَ
الْعَزِيزُ الْحَكِيمُ ۝١ لَهُ مُلْكُ السَّمٰوٰتِ وَالْأَرْضِ
يُحْيِ وَيُمِيتُ وَهُوَ عَلٰى كُلِّ شَيْءٍ قَدِيرٌ ۝٢
هُوَ الْأَوَّلُ وَالْآخِرُ وَالظّٰهِرُ وَالْبَاطِنُ وَهُوَ
بِكُلِّ شَيْءٍ عَلِيمٌ ۝٣ هُوَ الَّذِي خَلَقَ السَّمٰوٰتِ
وَالْأَرْضَ فِي سِتَّةِ أَيَّامٍ ثُمَّ اسْتَوٰى عَلَى
الْعَرْشِ يَعْلَمُ مَا يَلِجُ فِي الْأَرْضِ وَمَا يَخْرُجُ
مِنْهَا وَمَا يَنْزِلُ مِنَ السَّمَاءِ وَمَا يَعْرُجُ
فِيهَا وَهُوَ مَعَكُمْ أَيْنَ مَا كُنْتُمْ وَاللّٰهُ بِمَا
تَعْمَلُونَ بَصِيرٌ ۝٤ لَهُ مُلْكُ السَّمٰوٰتِ
وَالْأَرْضِ وَإِلَى اللّٰهِ تُرْجَعُ الْأُمُورُ ۝٥ يُولِجُ
الَّيْلَ فِي النَّهَارِ وَيُولِجُ النَّهَارَ فِي الَّيْلِ
وَهُوَ عَلِيمٌ بِذَاتِ الصُّدُورِ ۝٦ آمِنُوا بِاللّٰهِ
وَرَسُولِهِ وَأَنْفِقُوا مِمَّا جَعَلَكُمْ مُسْتَخْلَفِينَ

vicegerent. Indeed, there awaits a great reward for such of you as believe and spend (in His cause).

8. What is wrong with you that you do not believe in Allâh, though the Messenger invites you to believe in your Lord, and though He has already bound you to a covenant. (Now is the time) if you care to believe.

9. It is He Who sends down clear signs to His servant that He may lead you from all kinds of darkness into the light (of faith). And behold, Allâh is Compassionate and Ever Merciful to you.

10. What is wrong with you that you do not spend in the way of Allâh, for all that the heavens and the earth contain shall finally revert to Allâh. Those of you who spent and fought (in the cause of Allâh) before the Victory (of *Hudaibiyah*) cannot be equal (to those who joined the ranks later). They are higher in rank than those who spent and fought afterwards (after the truth had gained ground). Yet Allâh has promised a good reward to them all. Allâh is Well-Aware of what you do.

SECTION 2

11. **W**HO is he that will separate a handsome portion (of his possessions) to give (in the cause of) Allâh? (Let him remember) He will increase it manifold (to repay it to him many times over). Indeed, there awaits such a one a generous and honourable reward.

12. (Think of) the day when you will see the believing men and the believing women that their (faith having become a torch of) light is advancing rapidly in front of them and on their right sides. (It will be said to them,) 'Glad tidings to you this day. (There await you) Gardens (of Paradise) served with running streams.' (The recipients of glad tidings) will abide therein (for ever). This indeed is a mighty achievement!

فِيهِ ۖ فَالَّذِينَ آمَنُوا مِنْكُمْ وَأَنْفَقُوا لَهُمْ
أَجْرٌ كَبِيرٌ ⑦ وَمَا لَكُمْ لَا تُؤْمِنُونَ بِاللَّهِ ۙ
وَالرَّسُولُ يَدْعُوكُمْ لِتُؤْمِنُوا بِرَبِّكُمْ وَقَدْ أَخَذَ
مِيثَاقَكُمْ إِنْ كُنْتُمْ مُؤْمِنِينَ ⑧ هُوَ الَّذِي
يُنَزِّلُ عَلَىٰ عَبْدِهِ آيَاتٍ بَيِّنَاتٍ لِيُخْرِجَكُمْ
مِنَ الظُّلُمَاتِ إِلَى النُّورِ ۚ وَإِنَّ اللَّهَ بِكُمْ
لَرَءُوفٌ رَحِيمٌ ⑨ وَمَا لَكُمْ أَلَّا تُنْفِقُوا فِي
سَبِيلِ اللَّهِ وَلِلَّهِ مِيرَاثُ السَّمَاوَاتِ وَالْأَرْضِ ۚ
لَا يَسْتَوِي مِنْكُمْ مَنْ أَنْفَقَ مِنْ قَبْلِ الْفَتْحِ
وَقَاتَلَ ۚ أُولَٰئِكَ أَعْظَمُ دَرَجَةً مِنَ الَّذِينَ
أَنْفَقُوا مِنْ بَعْدُ وَقَاتَلُوا ۚ وَكُلًّا وَعَدَ اللَّهُ
الْحُسْنَىٰ ۚ وَاللَّهُ بِمَا تَعْمَلُونَ خَبِيرٌ ⑩ مَنْ ع ١٠ ١٧
ذَا الَّذِي يُقْرِضُ اللَّهَ قَرْضًا حَسَنًا فَيُضَاعِفَهُ
لَهُ وَلَهُ أَجْرٌ كَرِيمٌ ⑪ يَوْمَ تَرَى الْمُؤْمِنِينَ
وَالْمُؤْمِنَاتِ يَسْعَىٰ نُورُهُمْ بَيْنَ أَيْدِيهِمْ
وَبِأَيْمَانِهِمْ بُشْرَاكُمُ الْيَوْمَ جَنَّاتٌ تَجْرِي مِنْ
تَحْتِهَا الْأَنْهَارُ خَالِدِينَ فِيهَا ۚ ذَٰلِكَ هُوَ الْفَوْزُ

13. That day the hypocritical men and hypocritical women will say to those who believe, 'Wait for us so that we might obtain some illumination from your (this) light.' It will be said to them, 'Go back (if you can) and seek for light.' Then a wall with a gateway will be set up separating them (and the believers). The inside of it will be all mercy (where the righteous have to go) and the outside of it shall be facing torment (where the hypocrites have to stay).

14. These (hypocrites) will call out to these (believers), 'Were we not with you (in the worldly life)?' They will reply, 'Yes, but you let yourselves fall into temptations and you waited (uselessly for our destruction), and you doubted (about the truth). In fact, your vain desires deceived you till the decree of Allâh (about your punishment) came to be implemented. And the arch-deceiver deceived you in respect of Allâh.

15. 'So this day, no ransom shall be accepted from you, nor from those who disbelieved. Hell-Fire is the final abode of you all. That is your friendly-protector. And very evil is that resort.'

16. Is it not yet time for those who believe that their hearts should feel humbled at the mention (of the name) of Allâh and at the truth that has been revealed to them (in the form of the Qur'ân), and that they do not become like those who were given the Scripture before (them). But their hearts hardened because a long period of time passed over them (enjoying the favours of Allâh. (As for their present state) they are mostly transgressors.

17. Know that Allâh brings (the inhabitants of) the earth to life after their death. We have indeed explained Our Messages to you that you may abstain (from evil deeds).

18. Verily, (as to) the men who give alms and the women who give alms and those who perform excellent deeds for the sake of Allâh, their recompense shall be increased manifold

الْعَظِيمُ ﴿١٢﴾ يَوْمَ يَقُولُ الْمُنٰفِقُونَ وَالْمُنٰفِقٰتُ
لِلَّذِينَ اٰمَنُوا انْظُرُونَا نَقْتَبِسْ مِنْ نُّورِكُمْ ج
قِيلَ ارْجِعُوا وَرَآءَكُمْ فَالْتَمِسُوا نُورًا ط فَضُرِبَ
بَيْنَهُمْ بِسُورٍ لَّهٗ بَابٌ ط بَاطِنُهٗ فِيهِ الرَّحْمَةُ
وَظٰهِرُهٗ مِنْ قِبَلِهِ الْعَذَابُ ﴿١٣﴾ يُنَادُونَهُمْ أَلَمْ
نَكُنْ مَّعَكُمْ ط قَالُوا بَلٰى وَلٰكِنَّكُمْ فَتَنْتُمْ أَنْفُسَكُمْ
وَتَرَبَّصْتُمْ وَارْتَبْتُمْ وَغَرَّتْكُمُ الْأَمَانِيُّ حَتّٰى
جَآءَ أَمْرُ اللّٰهِ وَغَرَّكُمْ بِاللّٰهِ الْغَرُورُ ﴿١٤﴾ فَالْيَوْمَ
لَا يُؤْخَذُ مِنْكُمْ فِدْيَةٌ وَّلَا مِنَ الَّذِينَ كَفَرُوا ط
مَأْوٰىكُمُ النَّارُ ط هِيَ مَوْلٰىكُمْ ط وَبِئْسَ الْمَصِيرُ ﴿١٥﴾
أَلَمْ يَأْنِ لِلَّذِينَ اٰمَنُوا أَنْ تَخْشَعَ قُلُوبُهُمْ
لِذِكْرِ اللّٰهِ وَمَا نَزَلَ مِنَ الْحَقِّ وَلَا يَكُونُوا
كَالَّذِينَ أُوتُوا الْكِتٰبَ مِنْ قَبْلُ فَطَالَ عَلَيْهِمُ
الْأَمَدُ فَقَسَتْ قُلُوبُهُمْ ط وَكَثِيرٌ مِّنْهُمْ
فٰسِقُونَ ﴿١٦﴾ إِعْلَمُوا أَنَّ اللّٰهَ يُحْيِ الْأَرْضَ بَعْدَ
مَوْتِهَا ط قَدْ بَيَّنَّا لَكُمُ الْاٰيٰتِ لَعَلَّكُمْ تَعْقِلُونَ ﴿١٧﴾
إِنَّ الْمُصَّدِّقِينَ وَالْمُصَّدِّقٰتِ وَأَقْرَضُوا اللّٰهَ

for them and (there awaits them) a generous and honourable reward.

19. And for those who believe in Allâh and His Messengers they alone are the truthful people and faithful witnesses in the sight of their Lord, they will have their full reward and their light. But those who disbelieve and cry lies to Our commandments are the very inmates of Hell.

SECTION 3

20. **K**NOW that the life of this world is but a sport, wanton, an empty show, (a source of) boasting among yourselves and an emulous quest for more riches and children. It is like the rain, the vegetation produced whereby pleases the cultivators. Then it (- the vegetation) blooms and flourishes so that you can see it turn yellow (on ripening). Then (there comes a time when) it becomes (worthless) chaff. But the Hereafter promises both, a severe punishment (for the wicked) and (for the righteous there is) protection from Allâh and (His) pleasure. The life of this world is nothing but a (temporary) enjoyment of delusive things.

21. (O people!) Advance quickly, outstripping one another, towards the protection from your Lord and (towards) a Garden the extensiveness of which is (beyond measure) as the extensiveness of the heaven and the earth. It has been prepared for those who believe in Allâh and His Messengers; that (protection) is Allâh's grace and bounty. He grants it to such of those who wish to attain it (and strive for it). Allâh is the Lord of immense grace and bounty.

22. No disaster befalls either on the earth or in your ownselves but it forms part of the divine Law before We bring it into being. Indeed, it is easy for Allâh (to make such a law).

23. (Allâh has apprised you of this) that you may neither grieve over that (good) which is lost to you, nor exult because of that which He has granted you. Allâh has no love for all those

سُوْرَةُ الْحَدِيدِ ٥٧

قَرْضًا حَسَنًا يُضٰعَفُ لَهُمْ وَلَهُمْ أَجْرٌ كَرِيمٌ ﴿١٨﴾
وَالَّذِينَ ءَامَنُوا بِاللّٰهِ وَرُسُلِهِۦٓ أُولٰٓئِكَ هُمُ
الصِّدِّيقُونَ ۖ وَالشُّهَدَآءُ عِنْدَ رَبِّهِمْ ۖ لَهُمْ
أَجْرُهُمْ وَنُورُهُمْ ۖ وَالَّذِينَ كَفَرُوا وَكَذَّبُوا
بِـَٔايٰتِنَآ أُولٰٓئِكَ أَصْحٰبُ الْجَحِيمِ ﴿١٩﴾ اِعْلَمُوٓا
أَنَّمَا الْحَيٰوةُ الدُّنْيَا لَعِبٌ وَلَهْوٌ وَزِينَةٌ
وَتَفَاخُرٌۢ بَيْنَكُمْ وَتَكَاثُرٌ فِي الْأَمْوٰلِ وَالْأَوْلٰدِ ۖ
كَمَثَلِ غَيْثٍ أَعْجَبَ الْكُفَّارَ نَبَاتُهُۥ ثُمَّ
يَهِيجُ فَتَرٰىهُ مُصْفَرًّا ثُمَّ يَكُونُ حُطٰمًا ۖ
وَفِي الْأٰخِرَةِ عَذَابٌ شَدِيدٌ ۙ وَمَغْفِرَةٌ مِّنَ اللّٰهِ
وَرِضْوٰنٌ ۚ وَمَا الْحَيٰوةُ الدُّنْيَآ إِلَّا مَتٰعُ
الْغُرُورِ ﴿٢٠﴾ سَابِقُوٓا إِلٰى مَغْفِرَةٍ مِّنْ رَّبِّكُمْ
وَجَنَّةٍ عَرْضُهَا كَعَرْضِ السَّمَآءِ وَالْأَرْضِ ۙ
أُعِدَّتْ لِلَّذِينَ ءَامَنُوا بِاللّٰهِ وَرُسُلِهِۦ ۚ ذٰلِكَ
فَضْلُ اللّٰهِ يُؤْتِيهِ مَنْ يَشَآءُ ۚ وَاللّٰهُ ذُو
الْفَضْلِ الْعَظِيمِ ﴿٢١﴾ مَآ أَصَابَ مِنْ مُّصِيبَةٍ
فِي الْأَرْضِ وَلَا فِيٓ أَنْفُسِكُمْ إِلَّا فِي كِتٰبٍ
مِّنْ قَبْلِ أَنْ نَّبْرَأَهَا ۚ إِنَّ ذٰلِكَ عَلَى اللّٰهِ
يَسِيرٌ ﴿٢٢﴾ لِّكَيْلَا تَأْسَوْا عَلٰى مَا فَاتَكُمْ وَلَا
تَفْرَحُوا بِمَآ ءَاتٰىكُمْ ۗ وَاللّٰهُ لَا يُحِبُّ كُلَّ مُخْتَالٍ

ع ٢ / ٩ / ١٨

who are haughty and boastful.

24. (Neither has He love for) those who practice niggardliness themselves and (also) enjoin others to be niggardly. He who turns his back (upon His commandments should beware). Verily, Allâh is Self-Sufficient (free from all needs and) Worthy of all praise (in His own right).

25. Certainly, We sent Our Messengers with clear proofs and We (also) sent down with them the Code (of *Sharî'at* - law and justice) and the Balance (- the practice of the Prophet and right use of the Book of God) so that people might conduct themselves with equity and justice. And We have given (to them) iron (which has great strength and) wherein is (material for) violent warfare and for many (other) uses for people. (All this has been done) that Allâh may distinguish those who help Him and His Messengers without having seen Him. Indeed Allâh is All-Powerful, All- Mighty.

SECTION 4

26. INDEED, We sent Noah and Abraham and We set up among their children (a system of) Prophethood and the Book. So some of them followed true guidance but many of them became transgressors.

27. Then We caused a series of Our Messengers one after the other to follow them closely in their footsteps, and We caused Jesus, son of Mary, to follow them, and We gave him (- Jesus) the Evangel. And We placed compassion and mercy in the hearts of those who followed him, but as for monasticism they invented it themselves, We did not enjoin it upon them. (They started monastic life) to seek Allâh's pleasure, but they did not observe it (as faithfully) as it should have been observed. Yet We duly rewarded such of them as (truly) believed but many of them were transgressors.

28. O you who believe! Take Allâh as a shield and believe in His Messenger. (If you do so)

سورة الحديد ٥٧

فخور ﴿٢٣﴾ الذين يبخلون ويأمرون الناس
بالبخل ومن يتول فإن الله هو الغني
الحميد ﴿٢٤﴾ لقد أرسلنا رسلنا بالبينت
وأنزلنا معهم الكتب والميزان ليقوم الناس
بالقسط وأنزلنا الحديد فيه بأس شديد
ومنفع للناس وليعلم الله من ينصره
ورسله بالغيب إن الله قوي عزيز ﴿٢٥﴾
ولقد أرسلنا نوحا وإبرهيم وجعلنا في
ذريتهما النبوة والكتب فمنهم مهتد
وكثير منهم فسقون ﴿٢٦﴾ ثم قفينا على
أثرهم برسلنا وقفينا بعيسى ابن مريم
وأتينه الإنجيل وجعلنا في قلوب
الذين اتبعوه رأفة ورحمة ورهبانية
ابتدعوها ما كتبنها عليهم إلا ابتغاء
رضون الله فما رعوها حق رعايتها فأتينا
الذين أمنوا منهم أجرهم وكثير
منهم فسقون ﴿٢٧﴾ يأيها الذين أمنوا
اتقوا الله وأمنوا برسوله يؤتكم

ع ٣ ١٩

الجزء السابع والعشرون

Allâh will grant you double the share of His mercy (in this world and the Hereafter) and will provide for you a light with the help of which you will advance forward and will grant you protection (against pitfalls). And Allâh is Great Protector, Ever Merciful.
29. (You will be so treated) lest the people of the Scripture should think that they (- the Muslims) have no control over the attainment of the grace and bounty of Allâh and (so that they should know) that grace and bounty is entirely in the hands of Allâh; He bestows it upon such as wishes to be granted (and strives for it). And Allâh is the Lord of immense grace and bounty.

كِفْلَيْنِ مِن رَّحْمَتِهِ وَيَجْعَل لَّكُمْ نُورًا
تَمْشُونَ بِهِ وَيَغْفِرْ لَكُمْ وَاللَّهُ غَفُورٌ
رَّحِيمٌ ﴿٢٨﴾ لِّئَلَّا يَعْلَمَ أَهْلُ الْكِتَٰبِ أَلَّا
يَقْدِرُونَ عَلَىٰ شَيْءٍ مِّن فَضْلِ اللَّهِ وَأَنَّ
الْفَضْلَ بِيَدِ اللَّهِ يُؤْتِيهِ مَن يَشَاءُ
وَاللَّهُ ذُو الْفَضْلِ الْعَظِيمِ ﴿٢٩﴾

CHAPTER
58

AL-MUJÂDILAH
(The Pleading Woman)
(Revealed after Hijrah)

سُورَةُ الْمُجَادِلَةِ مَدَنِيَّةٌ

With the name of Allâh,
the Most Gracious, the Ever Merciful
(I commence to read Sûrah Al-Mujâdilah).

بِسْمِ اللَّهِ الرَّحْمَٰنِ الرَّحِيمِ

PART الْجُزْءُ الثَّامِنُ وَالْعِشْرُونَ XXVIII

1. **A**LLÂH has indeed heard the plea of her (- *Khoulah* wife of *Aus bin Sâmit*) who pleads with you (O Muhammad!) with regard to her husband and makes her complaint to Allâh (seeking His help). Allâh has heard both of you conversing together. Verily, Allâh is All-Hearing, All-Seeing.
2. Such of you who give up (conjugal relationship with) their wives by calling them mothers (should realise that) they do not thereby become their mothers. Their mothers are only those who have given them birth. And they (by

قَدْ سَمِعَ اللَّهُ قَوْلَ الَّتِي تُجَٰدِلُكَ فِي
زَوْجِهَا وَتَشْتَكِي إِلَى اللَّهِ وَاللَّهُ يَسْمَعُ
تَحَاوُرَكُمَا إِنَّ اللَّهَ سَمِيعٌ بَصِيرٌ ﴿١﴾ الَّذِينَ
يُظَٰهِرُونَ مِنكُم مِّن نِّسَائِهِم مَّا هُنَّ
أُمَّهَٰتِهِمْ إِنْ أُمَّهَٰتُهُمْ إِلَّا الَّٰئِي وَلَدْنَهُمْ

calling their wives mothers by Zihâr) utter words that are most unseeming and false. And of course Allâh is All-Pardoning, Great Protector (against faults).

3. Such of those who thus happen to call their wives their mothers and then retract what they have said, must free a slave before they two touch each other (for reestablishing conjugal relationship). This is what you are enjoined (to do in case you commit such a hateful thing). And Allâh is Well-Aware of what you do.

4. He that cannot afford (a slave to be set free) shall then (observe) fasts for two consecutive months before he and his wife touch each other (for conjugal relationship). But he who has not even the strength (to fast for that time) shall feed sixty poor people. This has been so (ordained) that you may have faith in Allâh and really submit before Him and His Messenger. These are the limits (enjoining you to give up foul practices and injustice to women) prescribed by Allâh. And the deniers of these shall receive grievous punishment.

5. Surely, those who oppose Allâh and His Messenger shall be laid low and humbled as those (opponents of the truth) who before them were laid low and humble. And We have already revealed clear ordinances (as to how to uplift the status of women). And the deniers of (these ordinances) shall receive a humiliating punishment.

6. (This punishment will also take place on) the day when Allâh will raise them up all together, then He will inform them of all they have been doing. Allâh has kept a recorded account of it (- their deeds), while they have forgotten it. Allâh is Witness over every thing.

SECTION 2

7. **D**o you not see that Allâh knows whatever lies in the heavens and whatever lies in the earth? There are no three holding a secret counsel but He is their fourth. There are no such

سُوْرَةُ الْمُجَادَلَةِ ٥٨

وَإِنَّهُمْ لَيَقُولُونَ مُنْكَرًا مِّنَ الْقَوْلِ وَزُورًا ۚ
وَإِنَّ اللهَ لَعَفُوٌّ غَفُورٌ ﴿٢﴾ وَالَّذِينَ يُظٰهِرُونَ
مِنْ نِّسَآئِهِمْ ثُمَّ يَعُودُونَ لِمَا قَالُوا فَتَحْرِيرُ
رَقَبَةٍ مِّنْ قَبْلِ أَنْ يَّتَمَآسَّا ۚ ذٰلِكُمْ تُوعَظُونَ
بِهٖ ۚ وَاللهُ بِمَا تَعْمَلُونَ خَبِيرٌ ﴿٣﴾ فَمَنْ لَّمْ
يَجِدْ فَصِيَامُ شَهْرَيْنِ مُتَتَابِعَيْنِ مِنْ قَبْلِ
أَنْ يَّتَمَآسَّا ۖ فَمَنْ لَّمْ يَسْتَطِعْ فَإِطْعَامُ سِتِّينَ
مِسْكِينًا ۚ ذٰلِكَ لِتُؤْمِنُوا بِاللهِ وَرَسُولِهٖ ۚ
وَتِلْكَ حُدُودُ اللهِ ۚ وَلِلْكٰفِرِينَ عَذَابٌ أَلِيمٌ ﴿٤﴾
إِنَّ الَّذِينَ يُحَآدُّونَ اللهَ وَرَسُولَهٗ كُبِتُوا
كَمَا كُبِتَ الَّذِينَ مِنْ قَبْلِهِمْ وَقَدْ أَنْزَلْنَآ
أٰيٰتٍۭ بَيِّنٰتٍ ۚ وَلِلْكٰفِرِينَ عَذَابٌ مُّهِينٌ ﴿٥﴾
يَوْمَ يَبْعَثُهُمُ اللهُ جَمِيعًا فَيُنَبِّئُهُمْ بِمَا عَمِلُوا ۚ
أَحْصٰهُ اللهُ وَنَسُوهُ ۚ وَاللهُ عَلٰى كُلِّ شَيْءٍ
ع شَهِيدٌ ﴿٦﴾ أَلَمْ تَرَ أَنَّ اللهَ يَعْلَمُ مَا فِي
السَّمٰوٰتِ وَمَا فِي الْأَرْضِ ۖ مَا يَكُونُ مِنْ

five but He is their sixth. Whether they are fewer than that or more, He is with them, no matter where they are. Then on the Day of Resurrection He will tell them (in the form of requital) all that they have been doing. Surely, Allâh is Possessor of full-knowledge of all things.

8. Have you not seen those who were forbidden (to hold) secret counsels and yet repeatedly returned to what they were forbidden to do, and they conferred together secretly (encouraging) sin, transgression and disobedience to the Messenger? When they come to you they greet you (with words) with which Allâh has not greeted you, but they say one to another, 'Why does Allâh not cause us to suffer for what we say (hypocritically).' Sufficient for them is Gehenna (to reckon with them satisfactorily). They shall enter it. What an evil resort!

9. O you who believe! When you hold secret counsels do not confer to promote sin, transgression and disobedience to the Messenger. Rather confer (to promote) piety, and righteousness and restraint from evil. And take Allâh as a shield, (Allâh) before Whom you shall be gathered together.

10. Holding secret counsels (with evil intentions) is (the work) of satan (who does it) to cause unrest and distress to those who believe. Yet he can do them no harm at all except by the leave of Allâh. Therefore let the believers repose their trust in Allâh.

11. O you who believe! When you are asked to extend the circle of a sitting (leaving reasonable space between one another when sitting together) in your assemblies, then do extend it. Allâh will make ample room for you. And disperse when you are told to disperse. Allâh will exalt such of you as believe and such of you as have been given knowledge, to high degrees (of rank). And Allâh is Well-Aware of what you do.

12. O you who believe! When you want to

نَجْوٰى ثَلٰثَةٍ إِلَّا هُوَ رَابِعُهُمْ وَلَا خَمْسَةٍ
إِلَّا هُوَ سَادِسُهُمْ وَلَا أَدْنٰى مِنْ ذٰلِكَ وَلَا
أَكْثَرَ إِلَّا هُوَ مَعَهُمْ أَيْنَ مَا كَانُوا ثُمَّ
يُنَبِّئُهُمْ بِمَا عَمِلُوا يَوْمَ الْقِيٰمَةِ إِنَّ اللّٰهَ
بِكُلِّ شَيْءٍ عَلِيمٌ ﴿٧﴾ أَلَمْ تَرَ إِلَى الَّذِينَ نُهُوا
عَنِ النَّجْوٰى ثُمَّ يَعُودُونَ لِمَا نُهُوا عَنْهُ
وَيَتَنٰجَوْنَ بِالْإِثْمِ وَالْعُدْوٰنِ وَمَعْصِيَتِ
الرَّسُولِ وَإِذَا جَاءُوكَ حَيَّوْكَ بِمَا لَمْ يُحَيِّكَ
بِهِ اللّٰهُ وَيَقُولُونَ فِي أَنْفُسِهِمْ لَوْلَا يُعَذِّبُنَا
اللّٰهُ بِمَا نَقُولُ حَسْبُهُمْ جَهَنَّمُ يَصْلَوْنَهَا
فَبِئْسَ الْمَصِيرُ ﴿٨﴾ يٰأَيُّهَا الَّذِينَ آمَنُوا إِذَا
تَنٰجَيْتُمْ فَلَا تَتَنٰجَوْا بِالْإِثْمِ وَالْعُدْوٰنِ
وَمَعْصِيَتِ الرَّسُولِ وَتَنٰجَوْا بِالْبِرِّ وَالتَّقْوٰى
وَاتَّقُوا اللّٰهَ الَّذِي إِلَيْهِ تُحْشَرُونَ ﴿٩﴾ إِنَّمَا
النَّجْوٰى مِنَ الشَّيْطٰنِ لِيَحْزُنَ الَّذِينَ آمَنُوا
وَلَيْسَ بِضَارِّهِمْ شَيْئًا إِلَّا بِإِذْنِ اللّٰهِ
وَعَلَى اللّٰهِ فَلْيَتَوَكَّلِ الْمُؤْمِنُونَ ﴿١٠﴾ يٰأَيُّهَا الَّذِينَ
آمَنُوا إِذَا قِيلَ لَكُمْ تَفَسَّحُوا فِي الْمَجٰلِسِ
فَافْسَحُوا يَفْسَحِ اللّٰهُ لَكُمْ وَإِذَا قِيلَ
انْشُزُوا فَانْشُزُوا يَرْفَعِ اللّٰهُ الَّذِينَ آمَنُوا
مِنْكُمْ وَالَّذِينَ أُوتُوا الْعِلْمَ دَرَجٰتٍ
وَاللّٰهُ بِمَا تَعْمَلُونَ خَبِيرٌ ﴿١١﴾ يٰأَيُّهَا الَّذِينَ

consult the Messenger in private then advance a charity (for the needy) before your (such) consultations. This is best for you and will help you to better standards of purity. But if you cannot afford it then (never mind) remember that Allâh is Great Protector, Ever Merciful.
13. Do you fear that you will not (be able to) give charity before your consultation? So when you do it not and Allâh has turned to you (mercifully), observe Prayer and present the *Zakât* and obey Allâh and His Messenger, and Allâh is Well-Aware of what you do.

SECTION 3

14. **H**AVE you not seen those (hypocrites) who befriend a people who have incurred the displeasure of Allâh? Such people belong neither to you nor to them and they swear to falsehood, and that (they do it) knowingly.
15. Allâh has in store for them a severe punishment. Evil indeed are the deeds they used to do.
16. They have taken shelter behind their oaths (for their falsehood) so that they turn (people) away from Allâh's way. So there awaits them a humiliating punishment.
17. Neither their belongings nor their children will be of any avail to them against (the punishment of) Allâh. They are the inmates of the Fire wherein they will be abiding long.
18. The day when Allâh shall raise them (to life) all together, they will swear to Him as they swear to you and they will think that they have something (reasonable to serve them as a good plea). Beware! It is they who are in fact the liars.
19. Satan has gained mastery over them and has made them give up the remembrance of Allâh. They are the gang of satan. Now, as a matter of fact the gangsters of satan are the losers.
20. Certainly, those who oppose Allâh and His Messenger will rank with the lowest of the low.
21. Allâh has decreed, 'Most certainly, I will prevail, I and My Messengers.' Verily, Allâh is

أٰمَنُوْٓا إِذَا نٰجَيْتُمُ الرَّسُوْلَ فَقَدِّمُوْا بَيْنَ
يَدَيْ نَجْوٰىكُمْ صَدَقَةً ۚ ذٰلِكَ خَيْرٌ لَّكُمْ
وَأَطْهَرُ ۚ فَإِنْ لَّمْ تَجِدُوْا فَإِنَّ اللّٰهَ غَفُوْرٌ
رَّحِيْمٌ ﴿١٢﴾ ءَأَشْفَقْتُمْ أَنْ تُقَدِّمُوْا بَيْنَ يَدَيْ
نَجْوٰىكُمْ صَدَقٰتٍ ۚ فَإِذْ لَمْ تَفْعَلُوْا وَتَابَ
اللّٰهُ عَلَيْكُمْ فَأَقِيْمُوا الصَّلٰوةَ وَأٰتُوا الزَّكٰوةَ
وَأَطِيْعُوا اللّٰهَ وَرَسُوْلَهٗ ۚ وَاللّٰهُ خَبِيْرٌۢ بِمَا
تَعْمَلُوْنَ ﴿١٣﴾ أَلَمْ تَرَ إِلَى الَّذِيْنَ تَوَلَّوْا قَوْمًا
غَضِبَ اللّٰهُ عَلَيْهِمْ ۚ مَا هُمْ مِّنْكُمْ وَلَا مِنْهُمْ
وَيَحْلِفُوْنَ عَلَى الْكَذِبِ وَهُمْ يَعْلَمُوْنَ ﴿١٤﴾
أَعَدَّ اللّٰهُ لَهُمْ عَذَابًا شَدِيْدًا ۚ إِنَّهُمْ سَآءَ
مَا كَانُوْا يَعْمَلُوْنَ ﴿١٥﴾ اِتَّخَذُوْٓا أَيْمٰنَهُمْ جُنَّةً
فَصَدُّوْا عَنْ سَبِيْلِ اللّٰهِ فَلَهُمْ عَذَابٌ مُّهِيْنٌ ﴿١٦﴾
لَنْ تُغْنِيَ عَنْهُمْ أَمْوٰلُهُمْ وَلَآ أَوْلٰدُهُمْ مِّنَ
اللّٰهِ شَيْـًٔا ۚ أُولٰٓئِكَ أَصْحٰبُ النَّارِ ۚ هُمْ فِيْهَا
خٰلِدُوْنَ ﴿١٧﴾ يَوْمَ يَبْعَثُهُمُ اللّٰهُ جَمِيْعًا فَيَحْلِفُوْنَ
لَهٗ كَمَا يَحْلِفُوْنَ لَكُمْ وَيَحْسَبُوْنَ أَنَّهُمْ عَلٰى
شَيْءٍ ۚ أَلَآ إِنَّهُمْ هُمُ الْكٰذِبُوْنَ ﴿١٨﴾ اِسْتَحْوَذَ
عَلَيْهِمُ الشَّيْطٰنُ فَأَنْسٰهُمْ ذِكْرَ اللّٰهِ ۚ أُولٰٓئِكَ
حِزْبُ الشَّيْطٰنِ ۚ أَلَآ إِنَّ حِزْبَ الشَّيْطٰنِ
هُمُ الْخٰسِرُوْنَ ﴿١٩﴾ إِنَّ الَّذِيْنَ يُحَآدُّوْنَ
اللّٰهَ وَرَسُوْلَهٗ أُولٰٓئِكَ فِي الْأَذَلِّيْنَ ﴿٢٠﴾
كَتَبَ اللّٰهُ لَأَغْلِبَنَّ أَنَا وَرُسُلِيْ ۚ إِنَّ اللّٰهَ

All-Powerful, All-Mighty.
22. You will find no such people who (truly) believe in Allâh and the Last Day, loving those who oppose Allâh and His Messenger, even though they (the opponents of Allâh) be their fathers, or their sons or their brethren or their kindred. It is they in whose hearts Allâh has inscribed (true) faith and has strengthened them with His own revelation. He will admit them to Gardens served with running streams. They shall abide there for ever. Allâh is well pleased with them and they are well pleased with Him. They are Allâh's party. Behold! It is Allâh's party alone that are the winners of the goal.

قَوِيٌّ عَزِيزٌ ﴿٢١﴾ لَا تَجِدُ قَوْمًا يُؤْمِنُونَ بِاللَّهِ
وَالْيَوْمِ الْآخِرِ يُوَادُّونَ مَنْ حَادَّ اللَّهَ
وَرَسُولَهُ وَلَوْ كَانُوا آبَاءَهُمْ أَوْ أَبْنَاءَهُمْ
أَوْ إِخْوَانَهُمْ أَوْ عَشِيرَتَهُمْ ۚ أُولَٰئِكَ كَتَبَ
فِي قُلُوبِهِمُ الْإِيمَانَ وَأَيَّدَهُمْ بِرُوحٍ
مِنْهُ ۖ وَيُدْخِلُهُمْ جَنَّاتٍ تَجْرِي مِنْ
تَحْتِهَا الْأَنْهَارُ خَالِدِينَ فِيهَا ۚ رَضِيَ
اللَّهُ عَنْهُمْ وَرَضُوا عَنْهُ ۚ أُولَٰئِكَ
حِزْبُ اللَّهِ ۚ أَلَا إِنَّ حِزْبَ اللَّهِ هُمُ
الْمُفْلِحُونَ ﴿٢٢﴾

ع ٣

CHAPTER
59

AL-HASHR
(The Banishment)
(Revealed after Hijrah)

With the name of Allâh,
the most Gracious, the Ever Merciful
(I commence to read Sûrah Al-Hashr).

1. **W**HATEVER lies in the heavens and whatever lies in the earth declares the glory of Allâh. He is the All-Mighty, the All-Wise.
2. It is He Who turned out from their homes those who had disbelieved *(- Banû Nadzîr)* from among the People of the Scripture on (the occasion of) the first banishment. You never thought that they would quit, while they (themselves) thought that their strongholds would defend them against (the judgment of) Allâh. But (the punishment from) Allâh came upon them from quarters they little expected. He struck their hearts with terror so that they demolished their houses (partly) with their own

سُورَةُ الْحَشْرِ مَدَنِيَّةٌ

بِسْمِ اللَّهِ الرَّحْمَٰنِ الرَّحِيمِ

سَبَّحَ لِلَّهِ مَا فِي السَّمَاوَاتِ وَمَا فِي الْأَرْضِ ۖ
وَهُوَ الْعَزِيزُ الْحَكِيمُ ﴿١﴾ هُوَ الَّذِي أَخْرَجَ
الَّذِينَ كَفَرُوا مِنْ أَهْلِ الْكِتَابِ مِنْ دِيَارِهِمْ
لِأَوَّلِ الْحَشْرِ ۚ مَا ظَنَنْتُمْ أَنْ يَخْرُجُوا ۖ
وَظَنُّوا أَنَّهُمْ مَانِعَتُهُمْ حُصُونُهُمْ مِنَ اللَّهِ

hands and (what remained of them was being destroyed) at the hands of the believers. So take warning from them O you who have insight!

3. And had not Allâh decreed exile for them, He would have punished them (in some other way) in this world, and in the Hereafter they shall certainly have the punishment of the Fire,

4. Because they cut themselves off from Allâh and His Messenger and he who cuts himself from Allâh (should bear in mind) that Allâh is severe in retribution.

5. You cut down no palm-tree (of theirs, bearing small dates of inferior quality) or left it standing on its roots but it was by Allâh's leave. (Allâh gave you this leave) so that He might disgrace the transgressors.

6. Whatever (property and goods) Allâh has given as spoils to His Messenger (and taken away) from these (enemies after they had made preparation for war against the Muslims, is of God's grace). You made no expedition with either cavalry or camelry for (the attainment of) this. Rather the fact is that Allâh gives His Messengers authority over whom He will. Allâh is Possessor of every power to do all things desired (by Him).

7. Whatever (property and wealth) Allâh has given to His Messenger without warfare as spoils, (taking it) from the dwellers of the towns, it is for Allâh, His Messenger and for the near of kin and the orphans and the needy and the wayfarer. (It has been) so (ordained) that the (wealth) should not circulate (only) among your rich people. And take whatever the Messenger gives you and forbear from what he forbids you. Take Allâh as a shield. Surely, Allâh is Severe in retribution.

8. (The wealth so obtained is also meant) for the poor (indigent) Refugees (*- Muhâjirîn*) who have been turned out of their houses and (made to part with) their possessions (while they were) seeking the grace and bounty from Allâh

فَأَتٰهُمُ اللّٰهُ مِنْ حَيْثُ لَمْ يَحْتَسِبُوا وَقَذَفَ
فِي قُلُوبِهِمُ الرُّعْبَ يُخْرِبُونَ بُيُوتَهُمْ بِأَيْدِيهِمْ
وَأَيْدِي الْمُؤْمِنِينَ فَاعْتَبِرُوا يٰأُولِي الْأَبْصٰرِ ﴿٢﴾
وَلَوْلَا أَنْ كَتَبَ اللّٰهُ عَلَيْهِمُ الْجَلَاءَ لَعَذَّبَهُمْ
فِي الدُّنْيَا وَلَهُمْ فِي الْاٰخِرَةِ عَذَابُ النَّارِ ﴿٣﴾
ذٰلِكَ بِأَنَّهُمْ شَاقُّوا اللّٰهَ وَرَسُولَهُ وَمَنْ
يُشَاقِّ اللّٰهَ فَإِنَّ اللّٰهَ شَدِيدُ الْعِقَابِ ﴿٤﴾
مَا قَطَعْتُمْ مِنْ لِينَةٍ أَوْ تَرَكْتُمُوهَا قَائِمَةً
عَلٰى أُصُولِهَا فَبِإِذْنِ اللّٰهِ وَلِيُخْزِيَ الْفٰسِقِينَ ﴿٥﴾
وَمَا أَفَاءَ اللّٰهُ عَلٰى رَسُولِهِ مِنْهُمْ فَمَا أَوْجَفْتُمْ
عَلَيْهِ مِنْ خَيْلٍ وَلَا رِكَابٍ وَلٰكِنَّ اللّٰهَ
يُسَلِّطُ رُسُلَهُ عَلٰى مَنْ يَشَاءُ وَاللّٰهُ عَلٰى كُلِّ
شَيْءٍ قَدِيرٌ ﴿٦﴾ مَا أَفَاءَ اللّٰهُ عَلٰى رَسُولِهِ مِنْ
أَهْلِ الْقُرٰى فَلِلّٰهِ وَلِلرَّسُولِ وَلِذِي الْقُرْبٰى
وَالْيَتٰمٰى وَالْمَسٰكِينِ وَابْنِ السَّبِيلِ كَيْ لَا
يَكُونَ دُولَةً بَيْنَ الْأَغْنِيَاءِ مِنْكُمْ وَمَا
اٰتٰكُمُ الرَّسُولُ فَخُذُوهُ وَمَا نَهٰكُمْ عَنْهُ
فَانْتَهُوا وَاتَّقُوا اللّٰهَ إِنَّ اللّٰهَ شَدِيدُ
الْعِقَابِ ﴿٧﴾ لِلْفُقَرَاءِ الْمُهٰجِرِينَ الَّذِينَ أُخْرِجُوا

and (His) good pleasure, and who helped (the cause of) Allâh and His Messenger. They are the people who prove their claim (of being sincere in their faith and) to be true.

9. And (in this wealth there is also a share) for those (*Ansâr*, the Helpers) who had settled in the city (of Madînah) and had embraced the Faith before these (Refugees arrived there). They love those who migrated to them for refuge and (who) even though poverty be their own lot, found no desire in their hearts for that which is given to them (- Refugees) but they gave them (- Refugees) preference over themselves. And (bear in mind that) those saved from the covetousness of their souls are the ones to achieve the goal.

10. And (this is also meant for) those who came (into the fold of Islam) after them. They say, 'Our Lord! Protect us and our brethren who took precedence over us in (accepting) the faith and let no rancour or spite occupy our hearts against those who believe. Our Lord! You are surely Compassionate, Ever Merciful.'

SECTION 2

11. **H**AVE you not given thought to (the case of) those who practice hypocrisy. They say to their (friendly Jewish) brethren, those from the People of the Scripture who have committed breach of faith, 'If you are turned out (of Madînah) we will certainly leave with you and we will never obey anyone where you are concerned. And if you are fought against, we will certainly help you.' But Allâh bears witness that they are surely liars.

12. If they are turned out they will never leave with them and if they are fought against, they will never help them. And if ever they come out to their help then they will surely run away showing (their) backs, and then they themselves will have none to help them.

13. (Muslims!) The truth is that you are (held)

مِنْ دِيَٰرِهِمْ وَأَمْوَٰلِهِمْ يَبْتَغُونَ فَضْلًا مِّنَ
اللَّهِ وَرِضْوَٰنًا وَيَنصُرُونَ اللَّهَ وَرَسُولَهُۥ ۚ
أُولَٰٓئِكَ هُمُ الصَّٰدِقُونَ ﴿٨﴾ وَالَّذِينَ تَبَوَّءُو
الدَّارَ وَالْإِيمَٰنَ مِن قَبْلِهِمْ يُحِبُّونَ مَنْ
هَاجَرَ إِلَيْهِمْ وَلَا يَجِدُونَ فِي صُدُورِهِمْ
حَاجَةً مِّمَّآ أُوتُوا وَيُؤْثِرُونَ عَلَىٰٓ أَنفُسِهِمْ
وَلَوْ كَانَ بِهِمْ خَصَاصَةٌ ۚ وَمَن يُوقَ شُحَّ
نَفْسِهِۦ فَأُولَٰٓئِكَ هُمُ الْمُفْلِحُونَ ﴿٩﴾ وَالَّذِينَ
جَآءُو مِنۢ بَعْدِهِمْ يَقُولُونَ رَبَّنَا اغْفِرْ لَنَا
وَلِإِخْوَٰنِنَا الَّذِينَ سَبَقُونَا بِالْإِيمَٰنِ وَلَا
تَجْعَلْ فِي قُلُوبِنَا غِلًّا لِّلَّذِينَ ءَامَنُوا رَبَّنَآ
إِنَّكَ رَءُوفٌ رَّحِيمٌ ﴿١٠﴾ أَلَمْ تَرَ إِلَى الَّذِينَ
نَافَقُوا يَقُولُونَ لِإِخْوَٰنِهِمُ الَّذِينَ كَفَرُوا
مِنْ أَهْلِ الْكِتَٰبِ لَئِنْ أُخْرِجْتُمْ لَنَخْرُجَنَّ
مَعَكُمْ وَلَا نُطِيعُ فِيكُمْ أَحَدًا أَبَدًا وَإِن
قُوتِلْتُمْ لَنَنصُرَنَّكُمْ وَاللَّهُ يَشْهَدُ إِنَّهُمْ
لَكَٰذِبُونَ ﴿١١﴾ لَئِنْ أُخْرِجُوا لَا يَخْرُجُونَ مَعَهُمْ
وَلَئِن قُوتِلُوا لَا يَنصُرُونَهُمْ وَلَئِن نَّصَرُوهُمْ
لَيُوَلُّنَّ الْأَدْبَٰرَ ثُمَّ لَا يُنصَرُونَ ﴿١٢﴾ لَأَنتُمْ

in a greater fear than (these hypocrites hold) of Allâh. That is because they are a people who are devoid of (all) reason.

14. They (- the Jews) will not (even) fight against you offering a joint front. They will fight only (from) within fortified towns or from behind ramparts. Their fighting spirit among themselves is (desperately) severe. You think them to be united but their hearts are divided. That is because they are a people who do not refrain (from mischief).

15. (Their case is) like the case of (*Banû Qainuqa'*, a Jew tribe at Madînah) their immediate predecessors (who were defeated). They suffered the evil consequences of their (evil) doings, and they received a woeful punishment.

16. Again, (the case of the hypocrites is) like (that of) satan. Behold! He says to a human being, 'Disbelieve!' But when he disbelieves, he says, 'I have nothing to do with you. I fear Allâh, the Lord of the worlds.'

17. And the end of both of them is that they are both in the fire. There these two shall abide (for a long time). Such is the recompense of the wrongdoers.

SECTION 3

18. **O** YOU who believe! Be mindful of your duty to Allâh. Let every soul look to what it sends forward for the morrow (- the Day of Requital). And take Allâh as a shield (to guard against the consequences of evils and further commitment of them). Verily, Allâh is Well Aware of all that you do.

19. And do not be like those who gave Allâh up so that He too made them give their ownselves up. It is they who are downright sinners.

20. The inmates of the Fire and the owners of the Garden of (Paradise) are not alike. It is the owners of the Garden that have achieved

أَشَدُّ رَهْبَةً فِي صُدُورِهِم مِّنَ اللهِ ذٰلِكَ
بِأَنَّهُمْ قَوْمٌ لَّا يَفْقَهُونَ ﴿١٣﴾ لَا يُقٰتِلُونَكُمْ
جَمِيعًا إِلَّا فِي قُرًى مُّحَصَّنَةٍ أَوْ مِن وَرَاءِ
جُدُرٍ بَأْسُهُم بَيْنَهُمْ شَدِيدٌ تَحْسَبُهُمْ
جَمِيعًا وَقُلُوبُهُمْ شَتّٰى ذٰلِكَ بِأَنَّهُمْ قَوْمٌ
لَّا يَعْقِلُونَ ﴿١٤﴾ كَمَثَلِ الَّذِينَ مِن قَبْلِهِمْ
قَرِيبًا ذَاقُوا وَبَالَ أَمْرِهِمْ وَلَهُمْ عَذَابٌ
أَلِيمٌ ﴿١٥﴾ كَمَثَلِ الشَّيْطٰنِ إِذْ قَالَ لِلْإِنْسٰنِ
اكْفُرْ فَلَمَّا كَفَرَ قَالَ إِنِّي بَرِيءٌ مِّنكَ إِنِّي
أَخَافُ اللهَ رَبَّ الْعٰلَمِينَ ﴿١٦﴾ فَكَانَ عٰقِبَتَهُمَا
أَنَّهُمَا فِي النَّارِ خٰلِدَيْنِ فِيهَا وَذٰلِكَ جَزٰٓؤُا
الظّٰلِمِينَ ﴿١٧﴾ يٰٓأَيُّهَا الَّذِينَ اٰمَنُوا اتَّقُوا اللهَ
وَلْتَنظُرْ نَفْسٌ مَّا قَدَّمَتْ لِغَدٍ وَاتَّقُوا اللهَ
إِنَّ اللهَ خَبِيرٌ بِمَا تَعْمَلُونَ ﴿١٨﴾ وَلَا تَكُونُوا
كَالَّذِينَ نَسُوا اللهَ فَأَنسٰهُمْ أَنفُسَهُمْ أُولٰٓئِكَ
هُمُ الْفٰسِقُونَ ﴿١٩﴾ لَا يَسْتَوِي أَصْحٰبُ النَّارِ
وَأَصْحٰبُ الْجَنَّةِ أَصْحٰبُ الْجَنَّةِ هُمُ

their goal.

21. Had We revealed this Qur'ân on a mountain, you would have surely seen it falling down in all humility and splitting asunder for awe of Allâh. These are wonderful things which We narrate for people that they may give thought.

22. He is Allâh, He is the One beside whom there is no other, cannot be and will never be one worthy of worship but He. (He is) the Knower of the unseen and the seen. He is the Most Gracious, the Ever Merciful.

23. He is Allâh, beside Whom there is no other, cannot be and will never be one worthy of worship but He, (He is) the Supreme Sovereign, the Holy One, the Most Perfect, Bestower of peaceful Security, the Guardian, the All-Mighty, the Compensator of losses, the Possessor of all greatness. Holy is Allâh, far beyond and above the things they associate with Him.

24. He is Allâh, the Creator (of the matter and the spirit), the Maker, the Bestower of forms (and fashioner of everything suiting to its requirement). All fair attributes belong to Him. All that lies in the heavens and the earth declares His glory; He is the All-Mighty, the All-Wise.

الفَائِزُونَ ﴿٢٠﴾ لَوْ أَنزَلْنَا هَٰذَا الْقُرْآنَ عَلَىٰ جَبَلٍ لَّرَأَيْتَهُ خَاشِعًا مُّتَصَدِّعًا مِّنْ خَشْيَةِ اللَّهِ ۚ وَتِلْكَ الْأَمْثَالُ نَضْرِبُهَا لِلنَّاسِ لَعَلَّهُمْ يَتَفَكَّرُونَ ﴿٢١﴾ هُوَ اللَّهُ الَّذِي لَا إِلَٰهَ إِلَّا هُوَ ۖ عَالِمُ الْغَيْبِ وَالشَّهَادَةِ ۖ هُوَ الرَّحْمَٰنُ الرَّحِيمُ ﴿٢٢﴾ هُوَ اللَّهُ الَّذِي لَا إِلَٰهَ إِلَّا هُوَ الْمَلِكُ الْقُدُّوسُ السَّلَامُ الْمُؤْمِنُ الْمُهَيْمِنُ الْعَزِيزُ الْجَبَّارُ الْمُتَكَبِّرُ ۚ سُبْحَانَ اللَّهِ عَمَّا يُشْرِكُونَ ﴿٢٣﴾ هُوَ اللَّهُ الْخَالِقُ الْبَارِئُ الْمُصَوِّرُ ۖ لَهُ الْأَسْمَاءُ الْحُسْنَىٰ ۚ يُسَبِّحُ لَهُ مَا فِي السَّمَاوَاتِ وَالْأَرْضِ ۖ وَهُوَ الْعَزِيزُ الْحَكِيمُ ﴿٢٤﴾

CHAPTER
60

سُورَةُ المُمْتَحَنَة مَدَنِيَّة

AL-MUMTAHANAH

(She that is to be Examined)

(Revealed after Hijrah)

With the name of Allâh,
the Most Gracious, the Ever Merciful
(I commence to read Sûrah Al-Mumtahanah).

بِسْمِ اللَّهِ الرَّحْمَٰنِ الرَّحِيمِ

1. **O** YOU who believe! Do not take those who are enemies of Me and to you for friends. Would you send them messages of love and

يَا أَيُّهَا الَّذِينَ آمَنُوا لَا تَتَّخِذُوا عَدُوِّي وَعَدُوَّكُمْ أَوْلِيَاءَ تُلْقُونَ إِلَيْهِم بِالْمَوَدَّةِ

friendship while they have denied the Truth that has come to you (and) have driven out the Messenger and yourselves (from your homes merely) because you believe in Allâh, your Lord? (How can you do so) if you migrated indeed to strive in My cause and seek My pleasure? Would (some of) you make secret offers of friendship and love to them while I am fully aware of all that you conceal and all that you profess openly? And whoever of you does such a thing (let him realize that he) has indeed strayed away from the straight path.

2. If they (- your so-called friends from the disbelievers) somehow get the upper hand of you they will (turn out to) be active enemies to you and will lay their hand on you and (lash you with) their tongues to do (you) harm, and they ardently desire that you should disbelieve.

3. Neither your kinfolks, nor your children will be of any good to you on the Day of Resurrection. He, (your true Lord) will separate you, one from another (and decide between you). And Allâh is a keen observer of all you do.

4. There is indeed a noble example for you (to follow) in Abraham and his companions. Behold! They said to their people, 'We have nothing to do with you and We disown that you worship apart from Allâh. We disapprove of all that you say and do. A long lasting (type of) enmity and rancour has arisen and become apparent between you and us, no doubt. (It will last) till you believe in Allâh alone.' But (you have no example to emulate) in the words of Abraham to his sire (when he said), 'I will surely ask forgiveness for you from Allâh though I can do nothing against (the will of) Allâh.' (Abraham and his companions also prayed to their Lord), 'Our Lord! In You we put our trust, and to You alone do we turn (in repentance), and towards You alone is the (final) return.

5. 'Our Lord! Do not allow that we have to face ordeals at the hands of the disbelievers (thus

وقد كفروا بما جاءكم من الحق يخرجون
الرسول وإياكم أن تؤمنوا بالله ربكم
إن كنتم خرجتم جهدا في سبيلي
وابتغاء مرضاتي تسرون إليهم بالمودة
وأنا أعلم بما أخفيتم وما أعلنتم
ومن يفعله منكم فقد ضل سواء
السبيل ① إن يثقفوكم يكونوا لكم
أعداء ويبسطوا إليكم أيديهم وألسنتهم
بالسوء وودوا لو تكفرون ② لن تنفعكم
أرحامكم ولا أولدكم يوم القيمة
يفصل بينكم والله بما تعملون بصير ③
قد كانت لكم أسوة حسنة في إبرهيم
والذين معه إذ قالوا لقومهم إنا برءؤا
منكم ومما تعبدون من دون الله كفرنا
بكم وبدا بيننا وبينكم العدوة
والبغضاء أبدا حتى تؤمنوا بالله وحده
إلا قول إبرهيم لأبيه لأستغفرن لك
وما أملك لك من الله من شيء ربنا
عليك توكلنا وإليك أنبنا وإليك
المصير ④ ربنا لا تجعلنا فتنة للذين

providing them pleasure at our cost), and protect us (against the consequences of our faults). Our Lord! For You alone are the All-Mighty, the All-Wise.'

6. Surely, you have a noble example (to follow) in these people, and (also) for everyone who hopes (to see) Allâh (and also fears Him) and the Last Day. And he who turns away from (following) it (should know that) Allâh is truly Self-Sufficient (free from all needs) and Praiseworthy (in His own right).

SECTION 2

7. **I**t is well-nigh that (these disbelievers embrace the Faith and thus) Allâh may establish goodwill between you and those of them with whom you are at enmity (at present), for Allâh is All-Powerful, and Allâh is Great Protector, Ever-Merciful.

8. Allâh does not forbid you to be kind and good and to deal justly with those who have not fought you because of your faith and have not turned you out of your homes. In fact Allâh loves those who are equitable.

9. Allâh only forbids you to make friends with those who have fought you because of your faith and who have turned you out of your homes, and have abetted your expulsion. Indeed, those who make friends with them are really the unjust.

10. O you who believe! When the believing women come to you having fled their homes, examine them. Allâh knows best the state of their faith. If you ascertain them to be (true) believers do not send them back to the disbelievers. These (believing women) are not lawful (wives) to those (disbelievers); nor are they lawful (husbands) to these (women). You shall however give them (their former disbelieving husbands) what they have spent on them. And you will be doing nothing unlawful if you marry these women after you have given them their dowries. And do not hold matrimonial ties

كفروا واغفر لنا ربنا إنك أنت العزيز
الحكيم ﴿٥﴾ لقد كان لكم فيهم أسوة حسنة
لمن كان يرجوا الله واليوم الآخر ومن
يتول فإن الله هو الغني الحميد ﴿٦﴾ عسى
الله أن يجعل بينكم وبين الذين
عاديتم منهم مودة والله قدير والله
غفور رحيم ﴿٧﴾ لا ينهىكم الله عن الذين
لم يقتلوكم في الدين ولم يخرجوكم
من ديركم أن تبروهم وتقسطوا إليهم
إن الله يحب المقسطين ﴿٨﴾ إنما ينهىكم الله
عن الذين قتلوكم في الدين وأخرجوكم
من ديركم وظهروا على إخراجكم أن
تولوهم ومن يتولهم فأولئك هم الظلمون ﴿٩﴾
يأيها الذين آمنوا إذا جاءكم المؤمنت
مهجرت فامتحنوهن الله أعلم بإيمنهن
فإن علمتموهن مؤمنت فلا ترجعوهن
إلى الكفار لا هن حل لهم ولا هم يحلون
لهن وآتوهم ما أنفقوا ولا جناح عليكم
أن تنكحوهن إذا آتيتموهن أجورهن
ولا تمسكوا بعصم الكوافر وسئلوا ما

with the disbelieving women, (should they join the disbelievers) you can claim what you have spent on them. So can (the disbelieving husbands) claim that which they have spent (on these believing women). This is the judgment of Allâh. He implements this judgment between you. Allâh is All-Knowing, All-Wise.

11. If any part of (the dowries of) your wives has passed over to the disbelievers from you and then your turn comes (to pay to the disbelievers when a woman from the disbelievers' side comes over to you), give to those whose wives have come over an amount equal to that which they have spent. Keep your duty to Allâh in Whom you believe.

12. Prophet! When women come to you after having believed and they take the oath of allegiance that they will not associate anything with Allâh, and that they will not steal and will not commit fornication and adultery, nor kill their children, nor bring forth a scandalous charge which they themselves have deliberately forged, nor disobey your just and rightful orders, then accept their allegiance and seek Allâh's protection for them. Indeed, Allâh is Great Protector, Ever Merciful.

13. O you who believe! Do not make friends with a people who have incurred the displeasure of Allâh. They are indeed despaired of the Hereafter (since they have no faith in it), just as the disbelievers are despaired of those who are in the graves (as they do not believe that the dead will ever come to life again).

أَنفَقْتُمْ وَلْيَسْـَٔلُوا مَآ أَنفَقُوا ذَٰلِكُمْ حُكْمُ
اللَّهِ يَحْكُمُ بَيْنَكُمْ وَاللَّهُ عَلِيمٌ حَكِيمٌ ﴿١٠﴾
وَإِن فَاتَكُمْ شَيْءٌ مِّنْ أَزْوَٰجِكُمْ إِلَى الْكُفَّارِ
فَعَاقَبْتُمْ فَـَٔاتُوا الَّذِينَ ذَهَبَتْ أَزْوَٰجُهُم
مِّثْلَ مَآ أَنفَقُوا وَاتَّقُوا اللَّهَ الَّذِيٓ أَنتُم
بِهِۦ مُؤْمِنُونَ ﴿١١﴾ يَٰٓأَيُّهَا النَّبِيُّ إِذَا جَآءَكَ
الْمُؤْمِنَٰتُ يُبَايِعْنَكَ عَلَىٰٓ أَن لَّا يُشْرِكْنَ
بِاللَّهِ شَيْـًٔا وَلَا يَسْرِقْنَ وَلَا يَزْنِينَ وَلَا
يَقْتُلْنَ أَوْلَٰدَهُنَّ وَلَا يَأْتِينَ بِبُهْتَٰنٍ
يَفْتَرِينَهُۥ بَيْنَ أَيْدِيهِنَّ وَأَرْجُلِهِنَّ
وَلَا يَعْصِينَكَ فِي مَعْرُوفٍ فَبَايِعْهُنَّ
وَاسْتَغْفِرْ لَهُنَّ اللَّهَ إِنَّ اللَّهَ غَفُورٌ رَّحِيمٌ ﴿١٢﴾
يَٰٓأَيُّهَا الَّذِينَ ءَامَنُوا لَا تَتَوَلَّوْا قَوْمًا غَضِبَ اللَّهُ
عَلَيْهِمْ قَدْ يَئِسُوا مِنَ الْأٓخِرَةِ كَمَا يَئِسَ
الْكُفَّارُ مِنْ أَصْحَٰبِ الْقُبُورِ ﴿١٣﴾

CHAPTER
61

AL-SAFF
(The Ranks)
(Revealed after Hijrah)

With the name of Allâh,
the Most Gracious, the Ever Merciful
(I commence to read Sûrah Al-Saff).

1. **W**HATEVER lies in the heavens and whatever lies in the earth glorifies Allâh, for He is the All-Mighty, the All-Wise.
2. O you who believe! Why should you say what you do not do.
3. It is very hateful in the sight of Allâh that you should profess what you do not practise.
4. Indeed, Allâh loves those who fight in His cause in compact ranks (so arrayed) as if they were a solid structure cemented with (molten) lead.
5. (Recall the time) when Moses said to his people, 'My people! Why do you malign me when you know that I am certainly a Messenger from Allâh to you.' But when they deviated from the right course, Allâh let their hearts deviate (as they were), for Allâh guides no transgressing people to success.
6. And (recall the time) when Jesus, son of Mary, said, 'O Children of Israel! Surely I am a Messenger sent to you by Allâh fulfilling (the prophecies contained in) the Torah which preceded me and pronouncing the good news of (the advent of) a great Messenger named Ahmad, who will come after me.' But when he (- the Prophet Muhammad) came to them with clear proofs, they said, 'His are the enchanting ways separating (us from our people).'
7. But who is more unjust than he (who believes in the trinity of God), who forges a lie in the name of Allâh (by calling Jesus the son of God), while he is called (to join the fold of Islam). And

سُوْرَةُ الصَّفِّ ٦١

سُوْرَةُ الصَّفِّ مَدَنِيَّةٌ

بِسْمِ اللّٰهِ الرَّحْمٰنِ الرَّحِيْمِ

سَبَّحَ لِلّٰهِ مَا فِي السَّمٰوٰتِ وَ مَا فِي الْأَرْضِ
وَ هُوَ الْعَزِيْزُ الْحَكِيْمُ ① يٰٓأَيُّهَا الَّذِيْنَ أٰمَنُوْا
لِمَ تَقُوْلُوْنَ مَا لَا تَفْعَلُوْنَ ② كَبُرَ مَقْتًا
عِنْدَ اللّٰهِ أَنْ تَقُوْلُوْا مَا لَا تَفْعَلُوْنَ ③ إِنَّ
اللّٰهَ يُحِبُّ الَّذِيْنَ يُقٰتِلُوْنَ فِيْ سَبِيْلِهٖ
صَفًّا كَأَنَّهُمْ بُنْيٰنٌ مَّرْصُوْصٌ ④ وَ إِذْ قَالَ
مُوْسٰى لِقَوْمِهٖ يٰقَوْمِ لِمَ تُؤْذُوْنَنِيْ وَ قَدْ
تَّعْلَمُوْنَ أَنِّيْ رَسُوْلُ اللّٰهِ إِلَيْكُمْ فَلَمَّا زَاغُوْٓا
أَزَاغَ اللّٰهُ قُلُوْبَهُمْ وَ اللّٰهُ لَا يَهْدِي الْقَوْمَ
الْفٰسِقِيْنَ ⑤ وَ إِذْ قَالَ عِيْسَى ابْنُ مَرْيَمَ يٰبَنِيْٓ
إِسْرَآءِيْلَ إِنِّيْ رَسُوْلُ اللّٰهِ إِلَيْكُمْ مُّصَدِّقًا لِّمَا
بَيْنَ يَدَيَّ مِنَ التَّوْرٰىةِ وَ مُبَشِّرًا بِرَسُوْلٍ
يَّأْتِيْ مِنْ بَعْدِي اسْمُهٗٓ أَحْمَدُ فَلَمَّا جَآءَهُمْ
بِالْبَيِّنٰتِ قَالُوْا هٰذَا سِحْرٌ مُّبِيْنٌ ⑥ وَ مَنْ
أَظْلَمُ مِمَّنِ افْتَرٰى عَلَى اللّٰهِ الْكَذِبَ وَهُوَ
يُدْعٰٓى إِلَى الْإِسْلٰمِ وَ اللّٰهُ لَا يَهْدِي الْقَوْمَ

Allâh guides no unjust people to the ways of success.

8. They desire to extinguish the light of Allâh with (the breath of) their mouths. But Allâh will perfect His light even though the disbelievers consider it hard.

9. It is He Who sent His Messenger with (the source of) guidance and true lasting faith, that he may help it prevail over all other faith, even though the polytheists consider it difficult.

SECTION 2

10. **O** YOU who believe! Shall I direct you to a bargain that will save you from a woeful punishment?

11. (The bargain is that) keep your faith in Allâh and His Messenger and keep on striving hard in the cause of Allâh with your possessions and your persons. That would be best for you if only you realise.

12. He will protect you against the evil consequences of your sins and admit you into Gardens served with running streams and (into) delightful and pure dwelling places (lying) in the Gardens of Eternity. This is the (way to) supreme achievement.

13. And (He will confer upon you) yet another (favour) which you love. (It is the) help from Allâh and an early victory (that you will win in this very world). So give glad tidings (of it) to the believers.

14. O you who believe! Be helpers of (the cause of) Allâh (as did the disciples of Jesus), for when Jesus, son of Mary, said to the disciples, 'Who will join me as my helper towards (the cause of) Allâh?' The disciples replied, 'We are helpers of (the cause of) Allâh.' So a section of the Children of the Israel believed (firmly in Jesus), while another section rejected (him). Thereupon We helped those who believed, against their enemies and (at last) these (believers) gained predominant victory (over the nonbelievers).

سُورَةُ الصَّفِّ ٦١

الظّٰلِمِينَ ﴿٧﴾ يُرِيدُونَ لِيُطْفِـُٔوا نُورَ اللّٰهِ بِأَفْوٰهِهِمْ وَاللّٰهُ مُتِمُّ نُورِهِ وَلَوْ كَرِهَ الْكٰفِرُونَ ﴿٨﴾ هُوَ الَّذِيٓ أَرْسَلَ رَسُولَهُ بِالْهُدٰى وَدِينِ الْحَقِّ لِيُظْهِرَهُ عَلَى الدِّينِ كُلِّهِ وَلَوْ كَرِهَ الْمُشْرِكُونَ ﴿٩﴾ يٰٓأَيُّهَا الَّذِينَ أٰمَنُوا هَلْ أَدُلُّكُمْ عَلٰى تِجٰرَةٍ تُنْجِيكُمْ مِّنْ عَذَابٍ أَلِيمٍ ﴿١٠﴾ تُؤْمِنُونَ بِاللّٰهِ وَرَسُولِهِ وَتُجٰهِدُونَ فِي سَبِيلِ اللّٰهِ بِأَمْوٰلِكُمْ وَأَنْفُسِكُمْ ذٰلِكُمْ خَيْرٌ لَّكُمْ إِنْ كُنْتُمْ تَعْلَمُونَ ﴿١١﴾ يَغْفِرْ لَكُمْ ذُنُوبَكُمْ وَيُدْخِلْكُمْ جَنّٰتٍ تَجْرِي مِنْ تَحْتِهَا الْأَنْهٰرُ وَمَسٰكِنَ طَيِّبَةً فِي جَنّٰتِ عَدْنٍ ذٰلِكَ الْفَوْزُ الْعَظِيمُ ﴿١٢﴾ وَأُخْرٰى تُحِبُّونَهَا نَصْرٌ مِّنَ اللّٰهِ وَفَتْحٌ قَرِيبٌ وَبَشِّرِ الْمُؤْمِنِينَ ﴿١٣﴾ يٰٓأَيُّهَا الَّذِينَ أٰمَنُوا كُونُوٓا أَنْصَارَ اللّٰهِ كَمَا قَالَ عِيسَى ابْنُ مَرْيَمَ لِلْحَوَارِيِّنَ مَنْ أَنْصَارِيٓ إِلَى اللّٰهِ قَالَ الْحَوَارِيُّونَ نَحْنُ أَنْصَارُ اللّٰهِ فَأٰمَنَتْ طَّآئِفَةٌ مِّنْ بَنِيٓ إِسْرَآءِيلَ وَكَفَرَتْ طَّآئِفَةٌ فَأَيَّدْنَا الَّذِينَ أٰمَنُوا عَلٰى عَدُوِّهِمْ فَأَصْبَحُوا ظٰهِرِينَ ﴿١٤﴾

CHAPTER
62

AL-JUMU'AH
(The Congregation)
(Revealed after Hijrah)

With the name of Allâh,
the Most Gracious, the Ever Merciful
(I commence to read Sûrah Al-Jumu'ah).

1. **W**HATEVER lies in the heavens and whatever lies in the earth glorifies Allâh, the Supreme Sovereign, the Holy, the All-Mighty, the All-Wise.

2. He it is Who has raised among the Arabs a grand Messenger (who hails) from among themselves, who recites to them His revelations to rid them of their impurities and teaches them the Book and Wisdom, though before (the advent of the Prophet) they were steeped in error which disconnected them (from God).

3. And (He will raise this Prophet among) others of them (their brethren) who have not yet joined them. And He is the All-Mighty, the All-Wise.

4. This is Allâh's grace. He bestows it on whom He pleases. And Allâh is the Lord of immense Grace.

5. The case of those who were charged to observe (the law of) Torah but did not carry out (its commandments in its true spirit), is like the case of a donkey that carries (a load of) volumes (of Books; he neither understands them nor gathers any advantage from them). Wretched is the case of the people who cry lies to the Message of Allâh. And Allâh guides not unjust people (to success).

6. Say, 'O you who stand on Judaism! If you claim that you are the favourites of Allâh to the exclusion of all other peoples, then, if what you claim to be true, express your wish (in prayer-contest) for death (either invoking it on

سُوۡرَةُ الۡجُمُعَةِ ٦٢

سُوۡرَةُ الۡجُمُعَةِ مَدَنِيَّةٌ

بِسۡمِ اللّٰهِ الرَّحۡمٰنِ الرَّحِيۡمِ

يُسَبِّحُ لِلّٰهِ مَا فِي السَّمٰوٰتِ وَ مَا فِي الۡأَرۡضِ
الۡمَلِكِ الۡقُدُّوۡسِ الۡعَزِيۡزِ الۡحَكِيۡمِ ١ هُوَ الَّذِيۡ
بَعَثَ فِي الۡأُمِّيّٖنَ رَسُوۡلًا مِّنۡهُمۡ يَتۡلُوۡا عَلَيۡهِمۡ
اٰيٰتِهٖ وَ يُزَكِّيۡهِمۡ وَ يُعَلِّمُهُمُ الۡكِتٰبَ
وَ الۡحِكۡمَةَ ۚ وَ إِنۡ كَانُوۡا مِنۡ قَبۡلُ لَفِيۡ ضَلٰلٍ
مُّبِيۡنٍ ٢ وَّ اٰخَرِيۡنَ مِنۡهُمۡ لَمَّا يَلۡحَقُوۡا بِهِمۡ ؕ
وَ هُوَ الۡعَزِيۡزُ الۡحَكِيۡمُ ٣ ذٰلِكَ فَضۡلُ اللّٰهِ
يُؤۡتِيۡهِ مَنۡ يَّشَآءُ ؕ وَ اللّٰهُ ذُو الۡفَضۡلِ الۡعَظِيۡمِ ٤
مَثَلُ الَّذِيۡنَ حُمِّلُوا التَّوۡرٰىةَ ثُمَّ لَمۡ يَحۡمِلُوۡهَا
كَمَثَلِ الۡحِمَارِ يَحۡمِلُ أَسۡفَارًا ؕ بِئۡسَ مَثَلُ
الۡقَوۡمِ الَّذِيۡنَ كَذَّبُوۡا بِاٰيٰتِ اللّٰهِ ؕ وَ اللّٰهُ لَا
يَهۡدِي الۡقَوۡمَ الظّٰلِمِيۡنَ ٥ قُلۡ يٰۤأَيُّهَا الَّذِيۡنَ
هَادُوۡۤا إِنۡ زَعَمۡتُمۡ أَنَّكُمۡ أَوۡلِيَآءُ لِلّٰهِ مِنۡ
دُوۡنِ النَّاسِ فَتَمَنَّوُا الۡمَوۡتَ إِنۡ كُنۡتُمۡ

yourselves if you are on falsehood, or on me in case you think I am an impostor).'
7. But they will never wish for it (- the death) because of (the sinful deeds) their hands have sent forward. And Allâh is fully Aware of the wrongdoers.
8. Say, 'The death from which you flee is sure to overtake you. Then you will be brought before the Knower of the unseen and the seen, and He will inform you of the truth about all that you had been doing.'

SECTION 2

9. **O** YOU who believe! When the call is made for (the Congregational) Prayer on Friday then hasten to extol the name of Allâh and leave off all business. That is best for you if you only knew.
10. And when the Prayer is finished, disperse in the land and seek Allâh's grace and bounty (and restart your business), and go on remembering Allâh much that you may achieve an all-round success.
11. But (Prophet!) when some people see some merchandise or any form of amusement, they run for it and leave you standing (on the pulpit), say, 'That (reward of worshipping Allâh) which Allâh has (for you) is far better than any amusement or merchandise, and Allâh is the Best of Providers.

CHAPTER
63

AL-MUNÂFIQÛN
(The Hypocrites)
(Revealed after Hijrah)

With the name of Allâh,
the Most Gracious, the Ever Merciful
(I commence to read Sûrah Al-Munâfiqûn).
1. **W**HEN the hypocrites come to you, they say, 'We bear witness that you are in fact the Messenger of Allâh.' And Allâh knows that you

صٰدِقِينَ ۝٦ وَلَا يَتَمَنَّوْنَهٗٓ أَبَدًا بِمَا قَدَّمَتْ
أَيْدِيهِمْ وَاللّٰهُ عَلِيمٌ بِالظّٰلِمِينَ ۝٧ قُلْ إِنَّ
الْمَوْتَ الَّذِي تَفِرُّونَ مِنْهُ فَإِنَّهٗ مُلٰقِيكُمْ
ثُمَّ تُرَدُّونَ إِلٰى عٰلِمِ الْغَيْبِ وَالشَّهٰدَةِ
فَيُنَبِّئُكُمْ بِمَا كُنْتُمْ تَعْمَلُونَ ۝٨ يٰٓأَيُّهَا الَّذِينَ
أٰمَنُوٓا إِذَا نُودِيَ لِلصَّلٰوةِ مِنْ يَوْمِ الْجُمُعَةِ
فَاسْعَوْا إِلٰى ذِكْرِ اللّٰهِ وَذَرُوا الْبَيْعَ ذٰلِكُمْ
خَيْرٌ لَّكُمْ إِنْ كُنْتُمْ تَعْلَمُونَ ۝٩ فَإِذَا قُضِيَتِ
الصَّلٰوةُ فَانْتَشِرُوا فِي الْأَرْضِ وَابْتَغُوا مِنْ
فَضْلِ اللّٰهِ وَاذْكُرُوا اللّٰهَ كَثِيرًا لَّعَلَّكُمْ
تُفْلِحُونَ ۝١٠ وَإِذَا رَأَوْا تِجٰرَةً أَوْ لَهْوًا انْفَضُّوٓا
إِلَيْهَا وَتَرَكُوكَ قَآئِمًا قُلْ مَا عِنْدَ اللّٰهِ خَيْرٌ
مِّنَ اللَّهْوِ وَمِنَ التِّجٰرَةِ وَاللّٰهُ خَيْرُ الرّٰزِقِينَ ۝١١

سُورَةُ الْمُنٰفِقُونَ مَدَنِيَّةٌ

بِسْمِ اللّٰهِ الرَّحْمٰنِ الرَّحِيمِ

إِذَا جَآءَكَ الْمُنٰفِقُونَ قَالُوا نَشْهَدُ إِنَّكَ
لَرَسُولُ اللّٰهِ وَاللّٰهُ يَعْلَمُ إِنَّكَ لَرَسُولُهٗ

الْجُزْءُ الثَّامِنُ وَالْعِشْرُونَ

are indeed His Messenger. Yet Allâh (at the same time) bears witness that the hypocrites are truly liars.

2. They take shelter behind their oaths (to hide their evil designs). Thus they keep people back from the way of Allâh. Surely, evil is the practice they follow.

3. That (they follow this practice) is because (outwardly) they believed but (inwardly) they disbelieved, so that their hearts are sealed and (now) they do not even understand.

4. When you see them, their (handsome) figures please you, and if they speak (a masked and polished speech), you listen to their speech. (They look) as though they were wooden statues clad in garments. They think every loud cry is one (raised) against them. They themselves are (your) enemies (in reality), so beware of them. May Allâh ruin them! To what (perversities) are they being turned away (from the Truth)?

5. And when it is said to them, 'Come so that the Messenger of Allâh may ask forgiveness for you,' they turn their heads aside (by way of refusal and out of scorn and pride). And you see them keeping others (also) back, while they swell big with pride.

6. It makes no difference to them whether you ask forgiveness for them or do not ask, Allâh will not forgive them. Indeed, Allâh will guide no transgressing people to success.

7. They are a people who say, 'Do not spend on those who are with the Messenger of Allâh until they (are obliged to) disperse (and desert him). Yet the treasures of the heavens and the earth belong to Allâh, but the hypocrites do not understand (it).

8. They say, 'If we return to Madînah, the most honourable and mightier will drive out the most mean from there.' But (true) power and honour belongs to Allâh and His Messenger and to the believers. Yet the hypocrites do not know (it).

سُورَةُ المُنَافِقُونَ ٦٣

وَاللَّهُ يَشْهَدُ إِنَّ الْمُنَافِقِينَ لَكَاذِبُونَ ١
اتَّخَذُوا أَيْمَانَهُمْ جُنَّةً فَصَدُّوا عَنْ سَبِيلِ
اللَّهِ إِنَّهُمْ سَاءَ مَا كَانُوا يَعْمَلُونَ ٢ ذَٰلِكَ
بِأَنَّهُمْ آمَنُوا ثُمَّ كَفَرُوا فَطُبِعَ عَلَىٰ قُلُوبِهِمْ
فَهُمْ لَا يَفْقَهُونَ ٣ وَإِذَا رَأَيْتَهُمْ تُعْجِبُكَ
أَجْسَامُهُمْ وَإِنْ يَقُولُوا تَسْمَعْ لِقَوْلِهِمْ
كَأَنَّهُمْ خُشُبٌ مُسَنَّدَةٌ يَحْسَبُونَ كُلَّ
صَيْحَةٍ عَلَيْهِمْ هُمُ الْعَدُوُّ فَاحْذَرْهُمْ قَاتَلَهُمُ
اللَّهُ أَنَّىٰ يُؤْفَكُونَ ٤ وَإِذَا قِيلَ لَهُمْ تَعَالَوْا
يَسْتَغْفِرْ لَكُمْ رَسُولُ اللَّهِ لَوَّوْا رُءُوسَهُمْ
وَرَأَيْتَهُمْ يَصُدُّونَ وَهُمْ مُسْتَكْبِرُونَ ٥
سَوَاءٌ عَلَيْهِمْ أَسْتَغْفَرْتَ لَهُمْ أَمْ لَمْ
تَسْتَغْفِرْ لَهُمْ لَنْ يَغْفِرَ اللَّهُ لَهُمْ إِنَّ اللَّهَ
لَا يَهْدِي الْقَوْمَ الْفَاسِقِينَ ٦ هُمُ الَّذِينَ
يَقُولُونَ لَا تُنْفِقُوا عَلَىٰ مَنْ عِنْدَ رَسُولِ
اللَّهِ حَتَّىٰ يَنْفَضُّوا وَلِلَّهِ خَزَائِنُ السَّمَاوَاتِ
وَالْأَرْضِ وَلَٰكِنَّ الْمُنَافِقِينَ لَا يَفْقَهُونَ ٧
يَقُولُونَ لَئِنْ رَجَعْنَا إِلَى الْمَدِينَةِ لَيُخْرِجَنَّ
الْأَعَزُّ مِنْهَا الْأَذَلَّ وَلِلَّهِ الْعِزَّةُ وَلِرَسُولِهِ
وَلِلْمُؤْمِنِينَ وَلَٰكِنَّ الْمُنَافِقِينَ لَا يَعْلَمُونَ ٨

SECTION 2

9. **O** YOU who believe! Do not let your possessions and your children make you forget the remembrance of Allâh. And those who do so shall be the real losers.
10. And spend out of that with which We have provided you, before death visits one of you and he says, 'My Lord! Would that you had granted me reprieve for a short while, (for if you had,) I would have given alms and would have become of the righteous.'
11. And Allâh does not grant reprieve to a soul when its appointed time is come. And Allâh is Well-Aware of what you do.

يٰٓأَيُّهَا الَّذِيْنَ اٰمَنُوْا لَا تُلْهِكُمْ أَمْوٰلُكُمْ
وَ لَآ أَوْلٰدُكُمْ عَنْ ذِكْرِ اللّٰهِ ۚ وَ مَنْ يَّفْعَلْ
ذٰلِكَ فَأُولٰٓئِكَ هُمُ الْخٰسِرُوْنَ (٩) وَ أَنْفِقُوْا
مِنْ مَّا رَزَقْنٰكُمْ مِّنْ قَبْلِ أَنْ يَّأْتِيَ أَحَدَكُمُ
الْمَوْتُ فَيَقُوْلَ رَبِّ لَوْلَآ أَخَّرْتَنِيْٓ إِلٰٓى
أَجَلٍ قَرِيْبٍ ۙ فَأَصَّدَّقَ وَ أَكُنْ مِّنَ
الصّٰلِحِيْنَ (١٠) وَ لَنْ يُّؤَخِّرَ اللّٰهُ نَفْسًا إِذَا جَآءَ
أَجَلُهَا ۚ وَ اللّٰهُ خَبِيْرٌۢ بِمَا تَعْمَلُوْنَ (١١)

CHAPTER
64

AL-TAGHÂBUN

(Manifestation of Loss)
(Revealed after Hijrah)

سُوْرَةُ التَّغَابُنِ مَدَنِيَّةٌ

With the name of Allâh,
the Most Gracious, the Ever Merciful
(I commence to read Sûrah Al-Taghâbun).

بِسْمِ اللّٰهِ الرَّحْمٰنِ الرَّحِيْمِ

1. **W**HATEVER lies in the heavens and whatever lies in the earth glorifies Allâh. To Him belongs sovereignty and all true praises (as well). He is the Possessor of Power to do every desired thing.
2. It is He Who created you. Some of you become disbelievers while others become believers. Allâh sees what you do.
3. He created the heavens and the earth with an eternal purpose and to suit the requirements of truth and wisdom. And He shaped you and made your shapes beautiful, and to Him is the ultimate return.
4. He knows whatever lies in the heavens and

يُسَبِّحُ لِلّٰهِ مَا فِي السَّمٰوٰتِ وَ مَا فِي الْأَرْضِ ۚ
لَهُ الْمُلْكُ وَ لَهُ الْحَمْدُ ۫ وَ هُوَ عَلٰى كُلِّ
شَيْءٍ قَدِيْرٌ (١) هُوَ الَّذِيْ خَلَقَكُمْ فَمِنْكُمْ
كَافِرٌ وَّ مِنْكُمْ مُّؤْمِنٌ ۚ وَ اللّٰهُ بِمَا تَعْمَلُوْنَ
بَصِيْرٌ (٢) خَلَقَ السَّمٰوٰتِ وَ الْأَرْضَ بِالْحَقِّ
وَ صَوَّرَكُمْ فَأَحْسَنَ صُوَرَكُمْ ۚ وَ إِلَيْهِ
الْمَصِيْرُ (٣) يَعْلَمُ مَا فِي السَّمٰوٰتِ وَ الْأَرْضِ

the earth and He knows what you conceal and what you do publicly. Allâh knows the innermost thoughts of the hearts.

5. (Disbelievers!) Have you had no news of those who disbelieved in the past? They suffered the evil consequences of their conduct and for them is decreed a woeful punishment.

6. That was because their Messengers (of God) kept on coming to them with clear proofs but they said, 'Shall a mere human being guide us?' So they disbelieved and turned away (paying no heed). Thereupon Allâh showed them that He had no need of them. Indeed Allâh is Self-Sufficient (above all needs), Worthy of All-Praise (in His own right).

7. Those who disbelieve claim that they will not be raised (from the dead). Say, 'No doubt, by my Lord, you shall surely be raised and then you shall be told all that you have done (in life). And that is easy for Allâh.'

8. Therefore believe in Allâh and His Messenger and the Light (- the Qur'ân) which We have revealed. And Allâh is Well-Aware of all that you do.

9. Beware of the day when He shall gather you together for the Day of Gathering. That will be the Day of the Manifestation of losses. Those who believe in Allâh and act to suit the requirement of it (- the true Faith), will be acquitted of their evil deeds. He will admit them to the Gardens served with running streams. They will abide therein forever and ever. That is the grand achievement!

10. But those who disbelieved and cried lies to our Messages, these are the inmates of Fire. They will abide therein for a long time. What an evil resort it is!

SECTION 2

11. **N**o calamity befalls, but by the leave of Allâh. (When it happens) Allâh guides the mind of the person who believes in Him (into

وَيَعْلَمُ مَا تُسِرُّونَ وَمَا تُعْلِنُونَ ۚ وَاللَّهُ
عَلِيمٌ بِذَاتِ الصُّدُورِ ﴿٤﴾ أَلَمْ يَأْتِكُمْ
نَبَؤُا الَّذِينَ كَفَرُوا مِنْ قَبْلُ فَذَاقُوا
وَبَالَ أَمْرِهِمْ وَلَهُمْ عَذَابٌ أَلِيمٌ ﴿٥﴾ ذٰلِكَ
بِأَنَّهُ كَانَتْ تَأْتِيهِمْ رُسُلُهُمْ بِالْبَيِّنٰتِ
فَقَالُوا أَبَشَرٌ يَهْدُونَنَا فَكَفَرُوا وَتَوَلَّوا
وَّاسْتَغْنَى اللَّهُ ۚ وَاللَّهُ غَنِيٌّ حَمِيدٌ ﴿٦﴾ زَعَمَ
الَّذِينَ كَفَرُوا أَنْ لَّنْ يُبْعَثُوا ۚ قُلْ بَلٰى وَرَبِّي
لَتُبْعَثُنَّ ثُمَّ لَتُنَبَّؤُنَّ بِمَا عَمِلْتُمْ ۚ وَذٰلِكَ عَلَى
اللَّهِ يَسِيرٌ ﴿٧﴾ فَأٰمِنُوا بِاللَّهِ وَرَسُولِهِ وَالنُّورِ
الَّذِي أَنْزَلْنَا ۚ وَاللَّهُ بِمَا تَعْمَلُونَ خَبِيرٌ ﴿٨﴾
يَوْمَ يَجْمَعُكُمْ لِيَوْمِ الْجَمْعِ ذٰلِكَ يَوْمُ التَّغَابُنِ ۚ
وَمَنْ يُؤْمِنْ بِاللَّهِ وَيَعْمَلْ صٰلِحًا يُكَفِّرْ
عَنْهُ سَيِّاٰتِهِ وَيُدْخِلْهُ جَنّٰتٍ تَجْرِي مِنْ
تَحْتِهَا الْأَنْهٰرُ خٰلِدِينَ فِيهَا أَبَدًا ۚ ذٰلِكَ
الْفَوْزُ الْعَظِيمُ ﴿٩﴾ وَالَّذِينَ كَفَرُوا وَكَذَّبُوا
بِأٰيٰتِنَا أُولٰٓئِكَ أَصْحٰبُ النَّارِ خٰلِدِينَ فِيهَا ۚ
وَبِئْسَ الْمَصِيرُ ﴿١٠﴾ مَا أَصَابَ مِنْ مُّصِيبَةٍ
إِلَّا بِإِذْنِ اللَّهِ ۚ وَمَنْ يُؤْمِنْ بِاللَّهِ يَهْدِ

the ways of its purification and enlightenment). And Allâh knows all things very well.

12. Obey Allâh and obey the Messenger. But if you turn away (paying no heed) then (bear in mind that) Our Messenger is responsible only for the plain conveying (the Messages).

13. Allâh, there is no other, cannot be and will never be one worthy of worship but He. So let the believers put their trust in Allâh.

14. O you who believe! Some of your spouses and children are enemies to you, so beware of them. And (if you overlook their shortcomings) and forgive and pardon (them), you will find that surely Allâh is Great Protector, Ever Merciful.

15. Verily, your possessions and your children are a means to reveal your hidden attributes. As for Allâh there awaits an immense reward with Him.

16. Therefore do your duty towards Allâh to the best of your ability, and listen to Him and Obey Him, and go on spending in (His cause). (If you do so) it will be best for your ownselves. For only those who are rid of covetousness of their souls shall be really successful in every way.

17. If you set apart a handsome portion of your wealth for (the cause of) Allâh, He will multiply it for you and will protect you (against your lapses). And Allâh is Most-Appreciating, All-Forbearing.

18. He is the Omniscient of the unseen and the seen. (He is) the All-Mighty, the All-Wise.

قَلْبَهُ وَاللَّهُ بِكُلِّ شَيْءٍ عَلِيمٌ ﴿١١﴾ وَأَطِيعُوا
اللَّهَ وَأَطِيعُوا الرَّسُولَ فَإِن تَوَلَّيْتُمْ فَإِنَّمَا
عَلَىٰ رَسُولِنَا الْبَلَٰغُ الْمُبِينُ ﴿١٢﴾ اللَّهُ لَا إِلَٰهَ
إِلَّا هُوَ وَعَلَى اللَّهِ فَلْيَتَوَكَّلِ الْمُؤْمِنُونَ ﴿١٣﴾
يَٰأَيُّهَا الَّذِينَ ءَامَنُوا إِنَّ مِنْ أَزْوَٰجِكُمْ
وَأَوْلَٰدِكُمْ عَدُوًّا لَّكُمْ فَاحْذَرُوهُمْ وَإِن تَعْفُوا
وَتَصْفَحُوا وَتَغْفِرُوا فَإِنَّ اللَّهَ غَفُورٌ رَّحِيمٌ ﴿١٤﴾
إِنَّمَا أَمْوَٰلُكُمْ وَأَوْلَٰدُكُمْ فِتْنَةٌ وَاللَّهُ
عِندَهُ أَجْرٌ عَظِيمٌ ﴿١٥﴾ فَاتَّقُوا اللَّهَ مَا اسْتَطَعْتُمْ
وَاسْمَعُوا وَأَطِيعُوا وَأَنفِقُوا خَيْرًا لِّأَنفُسِكُمْ
وَمَن يُوقَ شُحَّ نَفْسِهِ فَأُولَٰئِكَ هُمُ
الْمُفْلِحُونَ ﴿١٦﴾ إِن تُقْرِضُوا اللَّهَ قَرْضًا
حَسَنًا يُضَٰعِفْهُ لَكُمْ وَيَغْفِرْ لَكُمْ وَاللَّهُ
شَكُورٌ حَلِيمٌ ﴿١٧﴾ عَٰلِمُ الْغَيْبِ وَالشَّهَٰدَةِ
الْعَزِيزُ الْحَكِيمُ ﴿١٨﴾

ع ٢ ١٦

CHAPTER
65

AL-TALÂQ
(The Divorce)
(Revealed after Hijrah)

With the name of Allâh,
the Most Gracious, the Ever Merciful
(I commence to read Sûrah Al-Talâq).

1. **P**ROPHET! (Tell the believers that) when you decide to divorce (your) women divorce them at a time when their *'Iddat* (- period of three monthly courses, for which they must wait before they can remarry) can be calculated; (the divorce should be given when she has cleansed herself after the menstrual discharge) and after divorce calculate the period (of *'Iddat* exactly). And keep your duty to Allâh, your Lord. You shall not turn them out (during this period of *'Iddat*) from their homes except they commit flagrant sin, nor shall they themselves go out (of them). And these are the limits imposed by Allâh and he that violates the limits imposed by Allâh, indeed does injustice to himself. You never know (Allâh's will), for it may be that after this (divorce) Allâh will bring about a new situation (of reconciliation between you).

2. And when they are about to reach their prescribed term (of *'Iddat*) either keep them (by revoking the divorce) in an honourable and fair manner or part with them in honourable and fair manner and two honest and just persons from among you witness (your decision). (Let the witnesses) bear true testimony for the sake of Allâh (regarding the situation that resulted in the pronouncement of divorce). Thus the person (who acts according to these guidelines and) who believes in Allâh and the Last Day is

سُوْرَةُ الطَّلَاقِ ٦٥

سُوْرَةُ الطَّلَاقِ مَدَنِيَّةٌ

بِسْمِ اللّٰهِ الرَّحْمٰنِ الرَّحِيْمِ

يٰۤاَيُّهَا النَّبِيُّ اِذَا طَلَّقْتُمُ النِّسَآءَ فَطَلِّقُوْهُنَّ لِعِدَّتِهِنَّ وَ اَحْصُوا الْعِدَّةَ ۚ وَ اتَّقُوا اللّٰهَ رَبَّكُمْ ۚ لَا تُخْرِجُوْهُنَّ مِنْۢ بُيُوْتِهِنَّ وَ لَا يَخْرُجْنَ اِلَّاۤ اَنْ يَّاْتِيْنَ بِفٰحِشَةٍ مُّبَيِّنَةٍ ؕ وَ تِلْكَ حُدُوْدُ اللّٰهِ ؕ وَ مَنْ يَّتَعَدَّ حُدُوْدَ اللّٰهِ فَقَدْ ظَلَمَ نَفْسَهٗ ؕ لَا تَدْرِيْ لَعَلَّ اللّٰهَ يُحْدِثُ بَعْدَ ذٰلِكَ اَمْرًا ① فَاِذَا بَلَغْنَ اَجَلَهُنَّ فَاَمْسِكُوْهُنَّ بِمَعْرُوْفٍ اَوْ فَارِقُوْهُنَّ بِمَعْرُوْفٍ وَّ اَشْهِدُوْا ذَوَيْ عَدْلٍ مِّنْكُمْ وَ اَقِيْمُوا الشَّهَادَةَ لِلّٰهِ ؕ ذٰلِكُمْ يُوْعَظُ بِهٖ مَنْ كَانَ يُؤْمِنُ بِاللّٰهِ وَ الْيَوْمِ الْاٰخِرِ ؕ

exhorted. And he who takes Allâh as (his) shield, He will always make a way out (of his ordeals) for him.

3. And He will provide him sustenance from where he least expects. And he who puts his trust in Allâh, He is sufficient for him (to fulfill his needs). Allâh is sure to accomplish His purpose. Allâh has set a measure for everything.

4. If you are in doubt (how to calculate the period) of such of your women as have despaired of monthly courses, then (know that) period for which they must wait is three months and (the same holds good) for such women as have not menstruated (for some other reasons). And (as to) pregnant women, their term (will end) when they are delivered of their burden (after giving birth to a child). And (bear in mind) for the one who keeps his duty to Allâh, He will provide facility in his affair for him.

5. That is the command of Allâh. He has revealed this to you. For the one who takes Allâh as a shield He will rid him of (the evil consequences of) his sins and will grant him a very great reward.

6. Lodge (the divorced) women (during the prescribed period in some part of the house) where you are lodging, according to (the best of) your means. Do not harass them so as to make (their stay) hard for them. If they be pregnant, bear their expanses until they are delivered of the child. And if they suckle (the child) for you (as the period of waiting is over with delivery) pay them their dues (for suckling), and (in order to settle it) consult together in all fairness (making only reasonable demands on one another). But if you find it mutually difficult (to come to a settled agreement) then let another woman suckle (the child) for him (- the father).

7. Let a man with (plentiful) means spend (for the maintenance of the suckling woman) according to his means. And let him whose

وَمَن يَتَّقِ اللَّهَ يَجْعَل لَّهُ مَخْرَجًا ﴿٢﴾ وَيَرْزُقْهُ
مِنْ حَيْثُ لَا يَحْتَسِبُ ۚ وَمَن يَتَوَكَّلْ
عَلَى اللَّهِ فَهُوَ حَسْبُهُ ۚ إِنَّ اللَّهَ بَالِغُ أَمْرِهِ ۚ
قَدْ جَعَلَ اللَّهُ لِكُلِّ شَيْءٍ قَدْرًا ﴿٣﴾ وَالَّٰٓئِي
يَئِسْنَ مِنَ الْمَحِيضِ مِن نِّسَآئِكُمْ إِنِ
ارْتَبْتُمْ فَعِدَّتُهُنَّ ثَلَٰثَةُ أَشْهُرٍ وَالَّٰٓئِي لَمْ
يَحِضْنَ ۚ وَأُولَٰتُ الْأَحْمَالِ أَجَلُهُنَّ أَن
يَضَعْنَ حَمْلَهُنَّ ۚ وَمَن يَتَّقِ اللَّهَ يَجْعَل لَّهُ
مِنْ أَمْرِهِ يُسْرًا ﴿٤﴾ ذَٰلِكَ أَمْرُ اللَّهِ أَنزَلَهُ
إِلَيْكُمْ ۚ وَمَن يَتَّقِ اللَّهَ يُكَفِّرْ عَنْهُ
سَيِّـَٔاتِهِ وَيُعْظِمْ لَهُ أَجْرًا ﴿٥﴾ أَسْكِنُوهُنَّ
مِنْ حَيْثُ سَكَنتُم مِّن وُجْدِكُمْ وَلَا
تُضَآرُّوهُنَّ لِتُضَيِّقُوا عَلَيْهِنَّ ۚ وَإِن كُنَّ
أُولَٰتِ حَمْلٍ فَأَنفِقُوا عَلَيْهِنَّ حَتَّىٰ يَضَعْنَ
حَمْلَهُنَّ ۚ فَإِنْ أَرْضَعْنَ لَكُمْ فَـَٔاتُوهُنَّ أُجُورَهُنَّ
وَأْتَمِرُوا بَيْنَكُم بِمَعْرُوفٍ ۖ وَإِن تَعَاسَرْتُمْ
فَسَتُرْضِعُ لَهُ أُخْرَىٰ ﴿٦﴾ لِيُنفِقْ ذُو سَعَةٍ مِّن

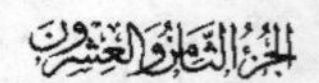

means of subsistence are limited spend according to what Allâh has given him. Allâh burdens no person (with responsibility) beyond what He has given him. Allâh will soon bring about easy times after hardships.

سُوْرَةُ الطَّلَاقِ ٦٥

SECTION 2

8. **S**o many (people of) townships rebelled against the command of their Lord and His Messengers so that We reckoned with them sternly and punished them with a dire punishment.

9. So they suffered the (evil) consequences of their deeds, and the subsequent end of their affairs was (in the form of) loss.

10. Allâh has in store for them a terrible punishment. So take Allâh as a shield O you persons of excellent and pure understanding who have believed! Allâh has indeed sent down to you means of (attaining) eminence -

11. (In the form of) an eminent Messenger who recites to you the clear revelations of Allâh, which tell the right from the wrong and thus He brings those who believe and (accordingly) do good deeds, out of all kinds of darkness into light. And he who believes in Allâh and does good deeds He will admit him to the Gardens served with running streams to abide therein for ever. Allâh has indeed made a (very) handsome provision for him.

12. It is Allâh Who has created seven heavens and (He has created) as many earths. The (divine) law permeates through them. (He tells this to you) so that you may know that Allâh is Possessor of all power to do every desired thing and Allâh encompasses everything in His knowledge.

سَعَتِهٖ ؕ وَ مَنْ قُدِرَ عَلَيْهِ رِزْقُهٗ فَلْيُنْفِقْ
مِمَّآ اٰتٰىهُ اللّٰهُ ؕ لَا يُكَلِّفُ اللّٰهُ نَفْسًا اِلَّا مَآ
اٰتٰىهَا ؕ سَيَجْعَلُ اللّٰهُ بَعْدَ عُسْرٍ يُّسْرًا ﴿٧﴾ ع ١٧
وَ كَاَيِّنْ مِّنْ قَرْيَةٍ عَتَتْ عَنْ اَمْرِ رَبِّهَا
وَ رُسُلِهٖ فَحَاسَبْنٰهَا حِسَابًا شَدِيْدًا ۙ وَّ عَذَّبْنٰهَا
عَذَابًا نُّكْرًا ﴿٨﴾ فَذَاقَتْ وَبَالَ اَمْرِهَا وَ كَانَ
عَاقِبَةُ اَمْرِهَا خُسْرًا ﴿٩﴾ اَعَدَّ اللّٰهُ لَهُمْ عَذَابًا
شَدِيْدًا ۙ فَاتَّقُوا اللّٰهَ يٰۤاُولِي الْاَلْبَابِ ۚ الَّذِيْنَ
اٰمَنُوْا ۚ قَدْ اَنْزَلَ اللّٰهُ اِلَيْكُمْ ذِكْرًا ﴿١٠﴾ رَّسُوْلًا
يَّتْلُوْا عَلَيْكُمْ اٰيٰتِ اللّٰهِ مُبَيِّنٰتٍ لِّيُخْرِجَ الَّذِيْنَ
اٰمَنُوْا وَ عَمِلُوا الصّٰلِحٰتِ مِنَ الظُّلُمٰتِ اِلَى
النُّوْرِ ؕ وَ مَنْ يُّؤْمِنْ بِاللّٰهِ وَ يَعْمَلْ صٰلِحًا
يُّدْخِلْهُ جَنّٰتٍ تَجْرِيْ مِنْ تَحْتِهَا الْاَنْهٰرُ
خٰلِدِيْنَ فِيْهَاۤ اَبَدًا ؕ قَدْ اَحْسَنَ اللّٰهُ لَهٗ
رِزْقًا ﴿١١﴾ اَللّٰهُ الَّذِيْ خَلَقَ سَبْعَ سَمٰوٰتٍ
وَّ مِنَ الْاَرْضِ مِثْلَهُنَّ ؕ يَتَنَزَّلُ الْاَمْرُ بَيْنَهُنَّ
لِتَعْلَمُوْۤا اَنَّ اللّٰهَ عَلٰى كُلِّ شَيْءٍ قَدِيْرٌ ۙ
وَّ اَنَّ اللّٰهَ قَدْ اَحَاطَ بِكُلِّ شَيْءٍ عِلْمًا ﴿١٢﴾ ع ١٨

CHAPTER
66

AL-TAHRÎM
(The Prohibition)
(Revealed after Hijrah)

سُورَةُ التَّحْرِيمِ مَدَنِيَّةٌ

With the name of Allâh,
the most Gracious, the Ever Merciful
(I commence to read Sûrah Al-Tahrîm).

بِسْمِ اللّٰهِ الرَّحْمٰنِ الرَّحِيمِ

1. PROPHET! Why do you forbid yourself the things which Allâh has made lawful to you? You seek the pleasure (of Allâh) for your wives. And Allâh is Great Protector, Ever Merciful.

2. Allâh has indeed sanctioned to you (- the Muslims) the expiation of your (expiable) oaths. And Allâh is your Patron and He is the All-Knowing, the All-Wise.

3. (Recall the time) when the Prophet confided to one of his wives *(-Hafsah)* a certain (secret) matter. When she divulged it (to another of his wives *Âishah*), and Allâh informed him (- the Prophet) of this, he then made known (to her) a part of it (to reprove her for what she had done) and avoided mentioning the other part. So when he told her about it she said, 'Who has informed you of this?' He (- the Prophet) said, 'The All-Knowing, the All-Aware (God) has informed me.'

4. If both of you women (*-Âishah* and *Hafsah)* turn to Allâh repentant, (He will accept your repentance) for your hearts are already inclined (to God). But if you abet (each other) against him (- the Prophet), (then bear in mind) Allâh is his helper as also Gabriel and the righteous among the believers and further more all the angels are also his helpers.

5. It may be that in case he divorces you, his Lord will give him instead wives better than yourselves; (wives who will be) submissive (to Allâh), faithful, obedient, penitent, devout

يٰٓأَيُّهَا النَّبِيُّ لِمَ تُحَرِّمُ مَآ أَحَلَّ اللّٰهُ لَكَ
تَبْتَغِي مَرْضَاتَ أَزْوٰجِكَ وَاللّٰهُ غَفُورٌ رَّحِيمٌ ①
قَدْ فَرَضَ اللّٰهُ لَكُمْ تَحِلَّةَ أَيْمٰنِكُمْ
وَاللّٰهُ مَوْلٰىكُمْ وَهُوَ الْعَلِيمُ الْحَكِيمُ ②
وَإِذْ أَسَرَّ النَّبِيُّ إِلٰى بَعْضِ أَزْوٰجِهِ حَدِيثًا
فَلَمَّا نَبَّأَتْ بِهِ وَأَظْهَرَهُ اللّٰهُ عَلَيْهِ عَرَّفَ
بَعْضَهُ وَأَعْرَضَ عَنْ بَعْضٍ فَلَمَّا نَبَّأَهَا بِهِ
قَالَتْ مَنْ أَنْبَأَكَ هٰذَا قَالَ نَبَّأَنِيَ الْعَلِيمُ
الْخَبِيرُ ③ إِنْ تَتُوبَآ إِلَى اللّٰهِ فَقَدْ صَغَتْ
قُلُوبُكُمَا وَإِنْ تَظٰهَرَا عَلَيْهِ فَإِنَّ اللّٰهَ
هُوَ مَوْلٰىهُ وَجِبْرِيلُ وَصٰلِحُ الْمُؤْمِنِينَ
وَالْمَلٰٓئِكَةُ بَعْدَ ذٰلِكَ ظَهِيرٌ ④ عَسٰى رَبُّهُ
إِنْ طَلَّقَكُنَّ أَنْ يُبْدِلَهُ أَزْوٰجًا خَيْرًا
مِّنْكُنَّ مُسْلِمٰتٍ مُّؤْمِنٰتٍ قٰنِتٰتٍ تٰٓئِبٰتٍ
عٰبِدٰتٍ سٰٓئِحٰتٍ ثَيِّبٰتٍ وَّأَبْكَارًا ⑤

(worshippers of God), given to fasting. (And they may consist of) divorcees, widows and virgins.

6. O you who believe! Save yourselves and your families from a Fire of which (ordinary) human beings and stone (- hearted people) are fuel and over which angels are appointed, fierce and ferocious, who never disobey the command of Allâh and who do as they are told.

7. O you who disbelieve! (Now when you are cast into the Fire) make no excuses this day. You are only requited for what you used to do.

SECTION 2

8. **O** YOU who believe! Turn to Allâh in sincere repentance, may be that your Lord will acquit you of your evil deeds and admit you to Gardens served with running streams. On that day Allâh will not disgrace the Prophet nor those who have believed with him. Their light will advance swiftly (radiating) in front of them and on their right hands while they will go on (praying and) saying, 'Our Lord! Perfect our light for us and protect us (against our lapses). Verily you are Possessor of prudential power to do every desired thing.'

9. Prophet! Strive hard against the disbelievers and the hypocrites and be stern with them; their resort is Gehenna. What an evil destination!

10. Allâh compares those who disbelieve to the wife of Noah and the wife of Lot. They were both under (the wedlock of) two of Our righteous servants but acted treacherously towards them both. So they (- Noah and Lot) could do nothing to save them from (the punishment of) Allâh. And it was said to them, 'Enter you both into the (Hell) Fire along with those (of your category) who enter therein.

11. And Allâh compares those who believe to the wife of Pharaoh. Behold! She said, 'My Lord! Make for me an abode in the Garden (of Paradise) close to You and deliver me from Pharaoh and his work and deliver me from the wrongdoing people.

12. And (Allâh next compares the believers to

سورة التحريم ٦٦

يَأَيُّهَا الَّذِينَ ءَامَنُوا قُوا أَنفُسَكُمْ وَأَهْلِيكُمْ
نَارًا وَقُودُهَا النَّاسُ وَالْحِجَارَةُ عَلَيْهَا مَلَٰٓئِكَةٌ
غِلَاظٌ شِدَادٌ لَّا يَعْصُونَ اللَّهَ مَا أَمَرَهُمْ
وَيَفْعَلُونَ مَا يُؤْمَرُونَ ٦ يَأَيُّهَا الَّذِينَ
كَفَرُوا لَا تَعْتَذِرُوا الْيَوْمَ إِنَّمَا تُجْزَوْنَ
مَا كُنتُمْ تَعْمَلُونَ ٧ يَأَيُّهَا الَّذِينَ ءَامَنُوا ع ٢ ١٩
تُوبُوا إِلَى اللَّهِ تَوْبَةً نَّصُوحًا عَسَىٰ رَبُّكُمْ
أَن يُكَفِّرَ عَنكُمْ سَيِّـَٔاتِكُمْ وَيُدْخِلَكُمْ
جَنَّٰتٍ تَجْرِي مِن تَحْتِهَا الْأَنْهَٰرُ يَوْمَ
لَا يُخْزِي اللَّهُ النَّبِيَّ وَالَّذِينَ ءَامَنُوا مَعَهُ
نُورُهُمْ يَسْعَىٰ بَيْنَ أَيْدِيهِمْ وَبِأَيْمَٰنِهِمْ
يَقُولُونَ رَبَّنَا أَتْمِمْ لَنَا نُورَنَا وَاغْفِرْ لَنَا
إِنَّكَ عَلَىٰ كُلِّ شَيْءٍ قَدِيرٌ ٨ يَأَيُّهَا النَّبِيُّ
جَٰهِدِ الْكُفَّارَ وَالْمُنَٰفِقِينَ وَاغْلُظْ عَلَيْهِمْ
وَمَأْوَىٰهُمْ جَهَنَّمُ وَبِئْسَ الْمَصِيرُ ٩ ضَرَبَ
اللَّهُ مَثَلًا لِّلَّذِينَ كَفَرُوا امْرَأَتَ نُوحٍ وَامْرَأَتَ
لُوطٍ كَانَتَا تَحْتَ عَبْدَيْنِ مِنْ عِبَادِنَا
صَٰلِحَيْنِ فَخَانَتَاهُمَا فَلَمْ يُغْنِيَا عَنْهُمَا مِنَ
اللَّهِ شَيْـًٔا وَقِيلَ ادْخُلَا النَّارَ مَعَ الدَّٰخِلِينَ ١٠
وَضَرَبَ اللَّهُ مَثَلًا لِّلَّذِينَ ءَامَنُوا امْرَأَتَ
فِرْعَوْنَ إِذْ قَالَتْ رَبِّ ابْنِ لِي عِندَكَ بَيْتًا
فِي الْجَنَّةِ وَنَجِّنِي مِن فِرْعَوْنَ وَعَمَلِهِ
وَنَجِّنِي مِنَ الْقَوْمِ الظَّٰلِمِينَ ١١ وَمَرْيَمَ ابْنَتَ

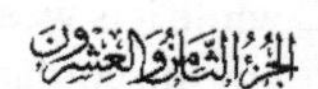

Mary, the daughter of Imrân, she who took care to guard her chastity, so we breathed into *him* (the believer who is exemplified here) Our inspiration while she declared her faith in the revelations of her Lord and His Scriptures and she became of the devoted ones to prayers and obedient to Him.

عِمْرٰنَ الَّتِيْٓ أَحْصَنَتْ فَرْجَهَا فَنَفَخْنَا فِيْهِ
مِنْ رُّوْحِنَا وَ صَدَّقَتْ بِكَلِمٰتِ رَبِّهَا
وَ كُتُبِهٖ وَ كَانَتْ مِنَ الْقٰنِتِيْنَ

ع ٥ ٢

CHAPTER
67

AL-MULK

(The Supreme Power)
(Revealed before Hijrah)

With the name of Allâh,
the Most Gracious, the Ever Merciful
(I commence to read Sûrah Al-Mulk).

PART الْجُزْءُ التَّاسِعُ وَ الْعِشْرُوْنَ XXIX

سُوْرَةُ الْمُلْكِ مَكِّيَّةٌ

بِسْمِ اللّٰهِ الرَّحْمٰنِ الرَّحِيْمِ

1. **B**LESSED is He Who holds complete Supreme power. He is the Possessor of prudential power to do every desired thing.
2. It is He Who has created death and life so that He may reward you (after trying you as to) which of you excels in doing good deeds. He is the All-Mighty, the Great Protector.
3. It is He Who has created seven heavens, one upon another in conformity (with each other). You can see no flaw, no incongruity and no imperfection in the creation of the Most Gracious (God). Then look up once more (to heaven). Do you see any flaw?
4. Look again and yet again (to find out any confusion in Divine law). (The result will only be that) your eye will return to you dazzled while it is weary (and you will be unable to find any discordance).
5. We have, certainly, adorned the lowest heaven with (stars-like) lamps and We have

تَبٰرَكَ الَّذِيْ بِيَدِهِ الْمُلْكُ وَ هُوَ عَلٰى كُلِّ
شَيْءٍ قَدِيْرٌ ﴿١﴾ الَّذِيْ خَلَقَ الْمَوْتَ وَ الْحَيٰوةَ
لِيَبْلُوَكُمْ أَيُّكُمْ أَحْسَنُ عَمَلًا وَ هُوَ الْعَزِيْزُ
الْغَفُوْرُ ﴿٢﴾ الَّذِيْ خَلَقَ سَبْعَ سَمٰوٰتٍ طِبَاقًا
مَا تَرٰى فِيْ خَلْقِ الرَّحْمٰنِ مِنْ تَفٰوُتٍ فَارْجِعِ
الْبَصَرَ هَلْ تَرٰى مِنْ فُطُوْرٍ ﴿٣﴾ ثُمَّ ارْجِعِ الْبَصَرَ
كَرَّتَيْنِ يَنْقَلِبْ إِلَيْكَ الْبَصَرُ خَاسِئًا
وَّ هُوَ حَسِيْرٌ ﴿٤﴾ وَ لَقَدْ زَيَّنَّا السَّمَآءَ الدُّنْيَا

made them as means of conjecture for the evil ones (and the astrologers who invent good or bad omens from the movement of the stars). (Remember) We have prepared for these (soothsayers) the punishment of the blazing Fire.
6. And there awaits the punishment of Gehenna for those who disbelieve in their Lord, what a horrid resort it is!
7. When they are cast therein they will hear its roaring and a loud moaning while it heaves up (boiling with them).
8. It almost bursts with the intense fury (of the fire). As often as a host (of wrongdoers) is cast into it, its wardens will ask them, 'Did no Warner come to you (from the Lord)?'
9. They will say, 'No doubt, a Warner did come to (warn) us but we cried lies (to him) and we said, "Allâh has revealed nothing, you are only in great error".'
10. And they will add, 'If we had only listened and tried to understand we would not have been among the inmates of the blazing Fire (this day).'
11. They will thus confess to their sins (when confession will be of no use). The inmates of the blazing Fire are far removed (from God's mercy).
12. Verily, as to those who hold their Lord in awe in their heart of hearts, there awaits them protection (against lapses) and a great reward.
13. (O people!) Whether you conceal your thoughts or speak them openly (it makes little difference to Him) for He knows well the innermost secrets of the hearts.
14. Does He Who has created (all things) not know (His own creation)? He knows all that is abstruse and subtle, and is All-Aware.

SECTION 2

15. **H**E it is Who has made the earth smooth and subservient to you (for your benefit), so traverse (far and deep) into its spacious paths (for your spiritual and material advancement), and (thus by active labour) eat of His sustenance

بِمَصَٰبِيحَ وَجَعَلْنَٰهَا رُجُومًا لِّلشَّيَٰطِينِ
وَأَعْتَدْنَا لَهُمْ عَذَابَ السَّعِيرِ ٥
وَلِلَّذِينَ كَفَرُوا بِرَبِّهِمْ عَذَابُ جَهَنَّمَ
وَبِئْسَ الْمَصِيرُ ٦ إِذَا أُلْقُوا فِيهَا سَمِعُوا
لَهَا شَهِيقًا وَهِيَ تَفُورُ ٧ تَكَادُ تَمَيَّزُ
مِنَ الْغَيْظِ كُلَّمَا أُلْقِيَ فِيهَا فَوْجٌ سَأَلَهُمْ
خَزَنَتُهَا أَلَمْ يَأْتِكُمْ نَذِيرٌ ٨ قَالُوا بَلَىٰ قَدْ
جَاءَنَا نَذِيرٌ فَكَذَّبْنَا وَقُلْنَا مَا نَزَّلَ اللَّهُ
مِن شَيْءٍ إِنْ أَنتُمْ إِلَّا فِي ضَلَٰلٍ كَبِيرٍ ٩
وَقَالُوا لَوْ كُنَّا نَسْمَعُ أَوْ نَعْقِلُ مَا كُنَّا فِي
أَصْحَٰبِ السَّعِيرِ ١٠ فَاعْتَرَفُوا بِذَنبِهِمْ فَسُحْقًا
لِّأَصْحَٰبِ السَّعِيرِ ١١ إِنَّ الَّذِينَ يَخْشَوْنَ
رَبَّهُم بِالْغَيْبِ لَهُم مَّغْفِرَةٌ وَأَجْرٌ كَبِيرٌ ١٢
وَأَسِرُّوا قَوْلَكُمْ أَوِ اجْهَرُوا بِهِ إِنَّهُ عَلِيمٌ
بِذَاتِ الصُّدُورِ ١٣ أَلَا يَعْلَمُ مَنْ خَلَقَ وَهُوَ
اللَّطِيفُ الْخَبِيرُ ١٤ هُوَ الَّذِي جَعَلَ لَكُمُ
الْأَرْضَ ذَلُولًا فَامْشُوا فِي مَنَاكِبِهَا وَكُلُوا

(and enjoy His gifts). To Him will you all return after your having been raised to life.

16. Do you feel secure from Him Who is overhead (to you all, thinking) that He may leave you downtrodden in the earth and may cause it to sink with you when all of a sudden it begins to shake?

17. Do you feel secure from Him who reigns in the heaven (above you seeing), that He may send a violent storm raising dust and pebbles on you. Look! You shall soon realize how (true) was My warning!

18. And certainly their predecessors treated (My Messengers to them) as liars, then, see how (destructive) was My disapproval (at their denial).

19. Have they not seen above them the birds with spread out wings (in flight) which they also draw in (to swoop down on the prey). None but the Most Gracious (God) holds them (there). Verily, He has knowledge of each and everything.

20. Or who is it that can serve as an army to help you against the Most Gracious (God if He intends to do you harm). The disbelievers are only labouring under a misconception (in thinking to baffle the cause of God).

21. Or who is it that will provide sustenance for you if He withholds His gifts? The fact is that they persist in transgression and are running away (from the truth).

22. Is he, who goes grovelling on his face, better guided or he who walks upright on a straight and right path?

23. Say, 'It is He Who has brought you into being and made for you ears (to hear), eyes (to see) and hearts (to understand). Yet little thanks do you give!'

24. Say, 'It is He Who has multiplied you in the earth and to Him you shall all be gathered.'

25. And they say (to the Muslims), 'When will this threat be executed if you are truthful (in

مِن رِّزْقِهِۦ ۖ وَإِلَيْهِ ٱلنُّشُورُ ﴿١٥﴾ ءَأَمِنتُم مَّن
فِى ٱلسَّمَآءِ أَن يَخْسِفَ بِكُمُ ٱلْأَرْضَ فَإِذَا
هِىَ تَمُورُ ﴿١٦﴾ أَمْ أَمِنتُم مَّن فِى ٱلسَّمَآءِ أَن
يُرْسِلَ عَلَيْكُمْ حَاصِبًا ۖ فَسَتَعْلَمُونَ كَيْفَ
نَذِيرِ ﴿١٧﴾ وَلَقَدْ كَذَّبَ ٱلَّذِينَ مِن قَبْلِهِمْ
فَكَيْفَ كَانَ نَكِيرِ ﴿١٨﴾ أَوَلَمْ يَرَوْا۟ إِلَى ٱلطَّيْرِ
فَوْقَهُمْ صَٰٓفَّٰتٍ وَيَقْبِضْنَ ۚ مَا يُمْسِكُهُنَّ
إِلَّا ٱلرَّحْمَٰنُ ۚ إِنَّهُۥ بِكُلِّ شَىْءٍۭ بَصِيرٌ ﴿١٩﴾ أَمَّنْ
هَٰذَا ٱلَّذِى هُوَ جُندٌ لَّكُمْ يَنصُرُكُم مِّن
دُونِ ٱلرَّحْمَٰنِ ۚ إِنِ ٱلْكَٰفِرُونَ إِلَّا فِى غُرُورٍ ﴿٢٠﴾
أَمَّنْ هَٰذَا ٱلَّذِى يَرْزُقُكُمْ إِنْ أَمْسَكَ رِزْقَهُۥ ۚ
بَل لَّجُّوا۟ فِى عُتُوٍّ وَنُفُورٍ ﴿٢١﴾ أَفَمَن يَمْشِى مُكِبًّا
عَلَىٰ وَجْهِهِۦٓ أَهْدَىٰٓ أَمَّن يَمْشِى سَوِيًّا عَلَىٰ
صِرَٰطٍ مُّسْتَقِيمٍ ﴿٢٢﴾ قُلْ هُوَ ٱلَّذِىٓ أَنشَأَكُمْ
وَجَعَلَ لَكُمُ ٱلسَّمْعَ وَٱلْأَبْصَٰرَ وَٱلْأَفْـِٔدَةَ ۖ
قَلِيلًا مَّا تَشْكُرُونَ ﴿٢٣﴾ قُلْ هُوَ ٱلَّذِى ذَرَأَكُمْ
فِى ٱلْأَرْضِ وَإِلَيْهِ تُحْشَرُونَ ﴿٢٤﴾ وَيَقُولُونَ
مَتَىٰ هَٰذَا ٱلْوَعْدُ إِن كُنتُمْ صَٰدِقِينَ ﴿٢٥﴾

your assertions)?'

26. Say, 'The knowledge (of the time of its occurrence) is with Allâh. I am only a plain Warner.'

27. But when they see it (- the threatened punishment) nigh, the faces of those who disbelieve will wear a grieved look. And it will be said (to them), 'This is what you used to ask for so persistently.'

28. Say, 'Have you considered if Allâh destroys me and those who are with me (my companions of faith)? Rather He will have mercy on us. Who is there to protect the disbelievers from a woeful punishment, (for the guilty will, all the same, reap the fruit of their evil deeds)?'

29. Say, 'He is the Most Gracious (God), in Him have we believed and in Him have we put our trust. And you will soon know which one of us is in manifest error.'

30. Say, 'Have you considered if (all) your water were to disappear (in the depths of the earth) who, then, will bring you pure flowing water?'

قُلْ إِنَّمَا الْعِلْمُ عِنْدَ اللّٰهِ وَإِنَّمَا أَنَا نَذِيرٌ
مُّبِينٌ ﴿٢٦﴾ فَلَمَّا رَأَوْهُ زُلْفَةً سِيْٓـَٔتْ وُجُوهُ
الَّذِينَ كَفَرُوا وَقِيلَ هٰذَا الَّذِي كُنْتُم
بِهِ تَدَّعُونَ ﴿٢٧﴾ قُلْ أَرَءَيْتُمْ إِنْ أَهْلَكَنِيَ اللّٰهُ
وَمَن مَّعِيَ أَوْ رَحِمَنَا فَمَن يُجِيرُ الْكٰفِرِينَ
مِنْ عَذَابٍ أَلِيمٍ ﴿٢٨﴾ قُلْ هُوَ الرَّحْمٰنُ ءَامَنَّا
بِهِ وَعَلَيْهِ تَوَكَّلْنَا فَسَتَعْلَمُونَ مَنْ هُوَ
فِي ضَلٰلٍ مُّبِينٍ ﴿٢٩﴾ قُلْ أَرَءَيْتُمْ إِنْ أَصْبَحَ
مَاؤُكُمْ غَوْرًا فَمَن يَأْتِيكُم بِمَآءٍ مَّعِينٍ ﴿٣٠﴾

CHAPTER

68

سُورَةُ القَلَمِ مَكِّيَّةٌ

AL-QALAM
(The Pen)
(Revealed before Hijrah)

With the name of Allâh,
the Most Gracious, the Ever Merciful
(I commence to read Sûrah Al-Qalam).

بِسْمِ اللّٰهِ الرَّحْمٰنِ الرَّحِيمِ

1. **T**HE ink - stand and the pen and all that they (the owners of the pen - the scholars) write, bear witness (to the fact that),

2. By the grace of your Lord you are not a mad man at all.

نٓ وَالْقَلَمِ وَمَا يَسْطُرُونَ ﴿١﴾ مَآ أَنْتَ
بِنِعْمَةِ رَبِّكَ بِمَجْنُونٍ ﴿٢﴾ وَإِنَّ لَكَ لَأَجْرًا

سُورَةُ الْقَلَمِ ٦٨

غَيْرَ مَمْنُونٍ ٣ وَإِنَّكَ لَعَلَىٰ خُلُقٍ عَظِيمٍ ٤
فَسَتُبْصِرُ وَيُبْصِرُونَ ٥ بِأَييِّكُمُ الْمَفْتُونُ ٦
إِنَّ رَبَّكَ هُوَ أَعْلَمُ بِمَنْ ضَلَّ عَنْ سَبِيلِهِ
وَهُوَ أَعْلَمُ بِالْمُهْتَدِينَ ٧ فَلَا تُطِعِ
الْمُكَذِّبِينَ ٨ وَدُّوا لَوْ تُدْهِنُ فَيُدْهِنُونَ ٩
وَلَا تُطِعْ كُلَّ حَلَّافٍ مَهِينٍ ١٠ هَمَّازٍ
مَشَّاءٍ بِنَمِيمٍ ١١ مَنَّاعٍ لِلْخَيْرِ مُعْتَدٍ أَثِيمٍ ١٢
عُتُلٍّ بَعْدَ ذَٰلِكَ زَنِيمٍ ١٣ أَنْ كَانَ ذَا
مَالٍ وَبَنِينَ ١٤ إِذَا تُتْلَىٰ عَلَيْهِ آيَاتُنَا قَالَ
أَسَاطِيرُ الْأَوَّلِينَ ١٥ سَنَسِمُهُ عَلَى الْخُرْطُومِ ١٦
إِنَّا بَلَوْنَاهُمْ كَمَا بَلَوْنَا أَصْحَابَ الْجَنَّةِ إِذْ
أَقْسَمُوا لَيَصْرِمُنَّهَا مُصْبِحِينَ ١٧ وَلَا
يَسْتَثْنُونَ ١٨ فَطَافَ عَلَيْهَا طَائِفٌ مِنْ رَبِّكَ

3. (And) most surely, there awaits you a reward never to be cut off.
4. And you possess outstandingly high standard of moral (excellence).
5. And you shall soon know and so will these (-the disbelievers),
6. As to which of you is afflicted with madness.
7. Surely, your Lord knows best those who go astray from His path and He (also) knows best those who follow the right guidance.
8. So do not listen to those who cry lies to (the Truth).
9. They wish you to be (dishonestly) pliant (and not condemn their evil deeds in strong language) so they (too) would (in return) adopt a conciliatory attitude.
10. Do not listen to any wretched swearer,
11. Who is a backbiter, one who goes about with slander and evil talk,
12. Any hinderer of people from doing good, a transgressor, a sinful (person).
13. (Nor listen to any) hard-hearted ruffian who is, above all this, utterly useless and known for mischief making,
14. Only because he owns wealth and (numerous) sons (and influence).
15. When Our Messages are recited to him he says, '(These are mere) stories of the ancients (so outdated rubbish).'
16. We will soon brand him on the snout (and stigmatize him with indelible disgrace).
17. (Thus) have We made these (opponents) undergo a trial just as We had made the owners of a garden undergo it when they swore (one to another) that they would pluck (all) its fruit the next morning.
18. And (they were so sure of it that) they made no reservation (for the poor and did not say, 'If it be Allâh's will').
19. So a sudden and awful visitation (a calamity) from your Lord visited it while they were

asleep.
20. So that this (garden) became as it were a dark desolate spot whose (all) fruit had been already plucked.
21. Meanwhile they called one to another at the break of dawn,
22. (Saying), 'Go forth early at dawn to your field if you would pluck and gather the fruit.'
23. So they set out talking together in low tones,
24. (Saying), 'Let not a single indigent person break through you to enter this (garden) today.'
25. And they repaired to the garden early with the dawn (thinking about themselves as) having the power to shut out (the poor from entry).
26. When they saw it (desolated) they said, 'We have surely mistaken the way.
27. 'Rather we have been deprived (of all the fruit of our labour), Indeed we have lost every thing.'
28. The most upright (man) among them said, 'Did I not say to you why do you not give glory (to God)?'
29. (Thereupon) they said, 'Glory be to our Lord. Certainly we have been wrongdoers.'
30. Then some of them turned their faces to the others, reproaching one another.
31. They said, 'O Woe to us! We have been, indeed, transgressors.
32. 'We hope our Lord will give us something better instead of this. To our Lord surely we turn humbly.'
33. Such is the punishment (for the disbelieving Makkans) in the very life and greater still is the punishment of the Hereafter, if they but understand.

SECTION 2

34. **T**HERE are indeed gardens of bliss with their Lord for those (dutiful) who (carefully) guard against evil.
35. Are We to treat those who submit (to Our will) as (We treat) those who sever their con-

وَهُمْ نَآئِمُونَ ﴿١٩﴾ فَأَصْبَحَتْ كَالصَّرِيمِ ﴿٢٠﴾
فَتَنَادَوْا مُصْبِحِينَ ﴿٢١﴾ أَنِ اغْدُوا عَلَىٰ حَرْثِكُمْ
إِنْ كُنْتُمْ صَارِمِينَ ﴿٢٢﴾ فَانْطَلَقُوا وَهُمْ
يَتَخَافَتُونَ ﴿٢٣﴾ أَنْ لَا يَدْخُلَنَّهَا الْيَوْمَ عَلَيْكُمْ
مِسْكِينٌ ﴿٢٤﴾ وَغَدَوْا عَلَىٰ حَرْدٍ قَادِرِينَ ﴿٢٥﴾ فَلَمَّا
رَأَوْهَا قَالُوا إِنَّا لَضَالُّونَ ﴿٢٦﴾ بَلْ نَحْنُ
مَحْرُومُونَ ﴿٢٧﴾ قَالَ أَوْسَطُهُمْ أَلَمْ أَقُلْ لَكُمْ
لَوْلَا تُسَبِّحُونَ ﴿٢٨﴾ قَالُوا سُبْحَانَ رَبِّنَا إِنَّا كُنَّا
ظَالِمِينَ ﴿٢٩﴾ فَأَقْبَلَ بَعْضُهُمْ عَلَىٰ بَعْضٍ يَتَلَاوَمُونَ ﴿٣٠﴾
قَالُوا يَا وَيْلَنَا إِنَّا كُنَّا طَاغِينَ ﴿٣١﴾ عَسَىٰ رَبُّنَا
أَنْ يُبْدِلَنَا خَيْرًا مِنْهَا إِنَّا إِلَىٰ رَبِّنَا رَاغِبُونَ ﴿٣٢﴾
كَذَٰلِكَ الْعَذَابُ ۖ وَلَعَذَابُ الْآخِرَةِ أَكْبَرُ ۚ
لَوْ كَانُوا يَعْلَمُونَ ﴿٣٣﴾ إِنَّ لِلْمُتَّقِينَ عِنْدَ رَبِّهِمْ
جَنَّاتِ النَّعِيمِ ﴿٣٤﴾ أَفَنَجْعَلُ الْمُسْلِمِينَ

nection (with Us)?
36. What is wrong with you? How (ill) you judge!
37. (O Makkans!) Have you a Book wherein you read;
38. That you will surely have in it (- in the Hereafter) whatever you choose?
39. Or have you taken a covenant (which is) binding on Us till the Day of Resurrection, that you shall have there all that you ask for?
40. Ask them, which of them will vouch for that?
41. Or have they any associate-gods (to vouch for it)? If so, (then) let them bring their associate-gods, if they are truthful.
42. On the day when there is severe affliction and the truth is laid bare and they will be called upon to prostrate (themselves), but they will not be able to do so.
43. Their looks will be downcast and they will be overwhelmed with disgrace. (Before this state of theirs) they had been called upon to prostrate themselves (before God) while they were (still) safe and sound (but they had refused).
44. Therefore leave Me alone to deal with those who deny this revelation. We shall overtake them (leading them to their ruin) step by step, in a manner they do not know.
45. Yet I shall give them respite (to mend their ways). Verily, My plan is invincible and firm.
46. (Prophet!) Do you ask from them a reward (for conveying to them the Message of prophethood) so that they are weighed down by (this undue) debt (which they find hard to pay)?
47. Or have they (the knowledge of) the unseen so that they write it down (to judge things in its light)?
48. So persevere patiently (in carrying out) the commandment of your Lord and do not behave like the Man of the big fish (- Jonah) when he called (to his Lord), and he was depressed with grief.
49. Had not a gracious favour from his Lord

سُورَةُ الْقَلَمِ ٦٨

كَالْمُجْرِمِينَ ﴿٣٥﴾ مَا لَكُمْ كَيْفَ تَحْكُمُونَ ﴿٣٦﴾
أَمْ لَكُمْ كِتَٰبٌ فِيهِ تَدْرُسُونَ ﴿٣٧﴾ إِنَّ لَكُمْ
فِيهِ لَمَا تَخَيَّرُونَ ﴿٣٨﴾ أَمْ لَكُمْ أَيْمَٰنٌ عَلَيْنَا
بَٰلِغَةٌ إِلَىٰ يَوْمِ الْقِيَٰمَةِ إِنَّ لَكُمْ لَمَا
تَحْكُمُونَ ﴿٣٩﴾ سَلْهُمْ أَيُّهُم بِذَٰلِكَ زَعِيمٌ ﴿٤٠﴾
أَمْ لَهُمْ شُرَكَاءُ فَلْيَأْتُوا بِشُرَكَائِهِمْ إِن كَانُوا
صَٰدِقِينَ ﴿٤١﴾ يَوْمَ يُكْشَفُ عَن سَاقٍ وَيُدْعَوْنَ
إِلَى السُّجُودِ فَلَا يَسْتَطِيعُونَ ﴿٤٢﴾ خَٰشِعَةً أَبْصَٰرُهُمْ
تَرْهَقُهُمْ ذِلَّةٌ وَقَدْ كَانُوا يُدْعَوْنَ إِلَى
السُّجُودِ وَهُمْ سَٰلِمُونَ ﴿٤٣﴾ فَذَرْنِي وَمَن
يُكَذِّبُ بِهَٰذَا الْحَدِيثِ سَنَسْتَدْرِجُهُم مِّنْ
حَيْثُ لَا يَعْلَمُونَ ﴿٤٤﴾ وَأُمْلِي لَهُمْ إِنَّ كَيْدِي
مَتِينٌ ﴿٤٥﴾ أَمْ تَسْأَلُهُمْ أَجْرًا فَهُم مِّن مَّغْرَمٍ
مُّثْقَلُونَ ﴿٤٦﴾ أَمْ عِندَهُمُ الْغَيْبُ فَهُمْ يَكْتُبُونَ ﴿٤٧﴾
فَاصْبِرْ لِحُكْمِ رَبِّكَ وَلَا تَكُن كَصَاحِبِ
الْحُوتِ إِذْ نَادَىٰ وَهُوَ مَكْظُومٌ ﴿٤٨﴾ لَّوْلَا أَن

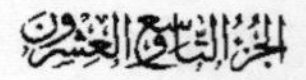

reached him (and) saved him he would surely have been cast off on a barren tract of land while he was in this miserable plight.
50. But his Lord chose him and made him (one) of the righteous.
51. Those who disbelieve would feign have dislodged you (from your God-given mission) with their (angry) looks when they heard the Reminder full of admonition (- the Qur'ân, but you were firm and steadfast). And they say, 'He is certainly a madman.'
52. And (they say so although) this (Qur'ân) is nothing less than a means to rise to eminence for all nations.

تَدٰرَكَهُ نِعْمَةٌ مِّن رَّبِّهِ لَنُبِذَ بِالْعَرَاءِ
وَهُوَ مَذْمُومٌ ﴿٤٩﴾ فَاجْتَبٰهُ رَبُّهُ فَجَعَلَهُ مِنَ
الصّٰلِحِينَ ﴿٥٠﴾ وَإِن يَكَادُ الَّذِينَ كَفَرُوا
لَيُزْلِقُونَكَ بِأَبْصٰرِهِمْ لَمَّا سَمِعُوا الذِّكْرَ
وَيَقُولُونَ إِنَّهُ لَمَجْنُونٌ ﴿٥١﴾ وَمَا هُوَ إِلَّا
ذِكْرٌ لِّلْعٰلَمِينَ ﴿٥٢﴾

CHAPTER
69

AL-HÂQQAH
(The Great Inevitable Reality)
(Revealed before Hijrah)

With the name of Allâh,
the Most Gracious, the Ever Merciful
(I commence to read sûrah Al-Hâqqah).

1. THE great inevitable reality!
2. What is that great inevitable reality?
3. (Before it actually takes place) you know little (what it is) and what should make you know what that great inevitable reality is?
4. (The tribe of) Thamûd and 'Âd treated (the news of) the calamity which strikes (peoples' hearts with terror to make them realize) as a lie.
5. As for Thamûd, they were destroyed by (the shock of) an exceedingly violent and thunderous blast.
6. As for 'Âd, they were destroyed by a furious wind blowing with extraordinary force,
7. Which He let loose on them for seven nights and eight days, with no break, so that (if you

سُورَةُ الحَاقَّةِ مَكِّيَّةٌ

بِسْمِ اللهِ الرَّحْمٰنِ الرَّحِيمِ

الْحَاقَّةُ ﴿١﴾ مَا الْحَاقَّةُ ﴿٢﴾ وَمَا أَدْرٰىكَ مَا
الْحَاقَّةُ ﴿٣﴾ كَذَّبَتْ ثَمُودُ وَعَادٌ بِالْقَارِعَةِ ﴿٤﴾
فَأَمَّا ثَمُودُ فَأُهْلِكُوا بِالطَّاغِيَةِ ﴿٥﴾ وَأَمَّا
عَادٌ فَأُهْلِكُوا بِرِيحٍ صَرْصَرٍ عَاتِيَةٍ ﴿٦﴾
سَخَّرَهَا عَلَيْهِمْ سَبْعَ لَيَالٍ وَثَمٰنِيَةَ أَيَّامٍ

had been there) you would have seen the people lying therein sprawled (looking) as though they were hollow trunks of palm-trees fallen down.
8. Now (when they are dead and gone) do you see any of their remnants?
9. Pharaoh and his predecessors and (the inhabitants of) the overthrown cities (of Sodom and Gomorrah) persistently indulged in evil ways.
10. They disobeyed (in their respective times) the Messenger of their Lord, so He seized them with an ever-increasing punishment.
11. (Similarly Noah was disobeyed) and no sooner did the water (begin to) rise high than We carried (people like) you in the floating Ark.
12. (We relate these events to you) so that We might make them an example for you (O people!), and so that the listening ear might listen (and bear in mind).
13. When the trumpet is blown with a single blast,
14. And the earth and the mountains are borne away and then crushed into fine dust with a single crash,
15. Then, on that day the great and sure Reality shall come to be.
16. And the heaven will cleave asunder for it will have become frail on that day.
17. And the angels will be (standing) on all sides (of the heaven) and eight (divine powers) will on that day be above them bearing the Throne of Power of your Lord.
18. On that day, you shall be brought (before God) and none of your secrets will remain hidden.
19. Now, he who is given his record (of deeds) in his right hand will say (joyfully to others), 'Here, take and read my record (of deeds).
20. 'Verily, I was sure that I would have to face my reckoning (one day)'.

حُسُومًا فَتَرَى الْقَوْمَ فِيهَا صَرْعَىٰ كَأَنَّهُمْ
أَعْجَازُ نَخْلٍ خَاوِيَةٍ ﴿٧﴾ فَهَلْ تَرَىٰ لَهُم مِّنْ
بَاقِيَةٍ ﴿٨﴾ وَجَاءَ فِرْعَوْنُ وَمَن قَبْلَهُ وَالْمُؤْتَفِكَٰتُ
بِالْخَاطِئَةِ ﴿٩﴾ فَعَصَوْا رَسُولَ رَبِّهِمْ فَأَخَذَهُمْ
أَخْذَةً رَّابِيَةً ﴿١٠﴾ إِنَّا لَمَّا طَغَا الْمَاءُ حَمَلْنَٰكُمْ
فِي الْجَارِيَةِ ﴿١١﴾ لِنَجْعَلَهَا لَكُمْ تَذْكِرَةً
وَتَعِيَهَا أُذُنٌ وَّاعِيَةٌ ﴿١٢﴾ فَإِذَا نُفِخَ فِي الصُّورِ
نَفْخَةٌ وَّٰحِدَةٌ ﴿١٣﴾ وَحُمِلَتِ الْأَرْضُ وَالْجِبَالُ
فَدُكَّتَا دَكَّةً وَّٰحِدَةً ﴿١٤﴾ فَيَوْمَئِذٍ وَقَعَتِ
الْوَاقِعَةُ ﴿١٥﴾ وَانشَقَّتِ السَّمَاءُ فَهِيَ يَوْمَئِذٍ
وَاهِيَةٌ ﴿١٦﴾ وَالْمَلَكُ عَلَىٰ أَرْجَائِهَا وَيَحْمِلُ
عَرْشَ رَبِّكَ فَوْقَهُمْ يَوْمَئِذٍ ثَمَٰنِيَةٌ ﴿١٧﴾ يَوْمَئِذٍ
تُعْرَضُونَ لَا تَخْفَىٰ مِنكُمْ خَافِيَةٌ ﴿١٨﴾ فَأَمَّا
مَنْ أُوتِيَ كِتَٰبَهُ بِيَمِينِهِ فَيَقُولُ هَاؤُمُ
اقْرَءُوا كِتَٰبِيَهْ ﴿١٩﴾ إِنِّي ظَنَنتُ أَنِّي مُلَٰقٍ
حِسَابِيَهْ ﴿٢٠﴾ فَهُوَ فِي عِيشَةٍ رَّاضِيَةٍ ﴿٢١﴾

21. So he shall lead an (everlasting) life of blissful happiness,
22. In a lofty Garden,
23. The clusters of fruit of which will be hanging low, within easy reach (to gather).
24. (It will be said to those therein,) 'Eat and drink delightfully (and to your hearts' content) on account of the good deeds you accomplished in the past days.'
25. But he who will be given the record (of his deeds) in his left hand, will say, 'O would that I had not been given my record!
26. 'And I had not known my reckoning.
27. 'Would that it (- the death) had made an end of me!
28. 'My wealth has been of no avail to me (this day).
29. 'My arguments have failed me, and my authority gone.'
30. (Orders shall be issued about such a one,) 'Lay hold of him and bind him down with fetters,
31. 'Then cast him into the burning Fire.
32. 'And string him with a chain the length of which is seventy cubits (according to the average length of human life in years).
33. 'Verily, he did not believe in Allâh, the Great.
34. 'And he did not urge (the people) to feed the poor,
35. 'He has, therefore, no warm friend here this day.
36. 'Nor (will he be served with) any food excepting something extremely hot,
37. 'Which none but the wrongdoers shall take.'

SECTION 2

38. **B**UT nay! I call to witness those (signs) which you see,
39. And that which you do not see,
40. That this (Qur'ân) is surely the word (brought) by an honourable Messenger.

سُورَةُ الحَاقَّة ٦٩

فِي جَنَّةٍ عَالِيَةٍ ﴿٢٢﴾ قُطُوفُهَا دَانِيَةٌ ﴿٢٣﴾ كُلُوا
وَاشْرَبُوا هَنِيئًا بِمَا أَسْلَفْتُمْ فِي الْأَيَّامِ
الْخَالِيَةِ ﴿٢٤﴾ وَأَمَّا مَنْ أُوتِيَ كِتَابَهُ بِشِمَالِهِ
فَيَقُولُ يَا لَيْتَنِي لَمْ أُوتَ كِتَابِيَهْ ﴿٢٥﴾ وَلَمْ
أَدْرِ مَا حِسَابِيَهْ ﴿٢٦﴾ يَا لَيْتَهَا كَانَتِ الْقَاضِيَةَ ﴿٢٧﴾
مَا أَغْنَىٰ عَنِّي مَالِيَهْ ﴿٢٨﴾ هَلَكَ عَنِّي سُلْطَانِيَهْ ﴿٢٩﴾
خُذُوهُ فَغُلُّوهُ ﴿٣٠﴾ ثُمَّ الْجَحِيمَ صَلُّوهُ ﴿٣١﴾
ثُمَّ فِي سِلْسِلَةٍ ذَرْعُهَا سَبْعُونَ ذِرَاعًا
فَاسْلُكُوهُ ﴿٣٢﴾ إِنَّهُ كَانَ لَا يُؤْمِنُ بِاللَّهِ
الْعَظِيمِ ﴿٣٣﴾ وَلَا يَحُضُّ عَلَىٰ طَعَامِ الْمِسْكِينِ ﴿٣٤﴾
فَلَيْسَ لَهُ الْيَوْمَ هَاهُنَا حَمِيمٌ ﴿٣٥﴾ وَلَا
طَعَامٌ إِلَّا مِنْ غِسْلِينٍ ﴿٣٦﴾ لَا يَأْكُلُهُ
إِلَّا الْخَاطِئُونَ ﴿٣٧﴾ فَلَا أُقْسِمُ بِمَا تُبْصِرُونَ ﴿٣٨﴾ ع ٥
وَمَا لَا تُبْصِرُونَ ﴿٣٩﴾ إِنَّهُ لَقَوْلُ رَسُولٍ كَرِيمٍ ﴿٤٠﴾
وَمَا هُوَ بِقَوْلِ شَاعِرٍ قَلِيلًا مَا تُؤْمِنُونَ ﴿٤١﴾
وَلَا بِقَوْلِ كَاهِنٍ قَلِيلًا مَا تَذَكَّرُونَ ﴿٤٢﴾

41. It is not at all the word of a poet. Little is the faith you have!
42. Neither it is the word of a soothsayer. Little is the heed you give!
43. (It is) a revelation from the Lord of the worlds.
44. Had he (- Muhammad) forged and attributed some saying to Us (and said, 'This is what Allâh has revealed to me').
45. We would have certainly seized him strongly by the right hand (and so deprived him of all his power),
46. And then surely We would have cut off his jugular vein;
47. Then none of you could have stopped (Us) from (punishing) him (and thus stood in Our way of dealing justly).
48. Behold! This (Qur'ân) is a means to rise to eminence for those who are dutiful and guard against evil.
49. We know, indeed, that there are some among you who reject it (- the Qur'ân).
50. Verily, this will be a (source of) regret for the disbelievers.
51. It is the absolute truth, a certainty.
52. So glorify the name of your Lord, the Great.

تَنْزِيلٌ مِّن رَّبِّ الْعٰلَمِينَ ﴿٤٣﴾ وَلَوْ تَقَوَّلَ عَلَيْنَا بَعْضَ الْأَقَاوِيلِ ﴿٤٤﴾ لَأَخَذْنَا مِنْهُ بِالْيَمِينِ ﴿٤٥﴾ ثُمَّ لَقَطَعْنَا مِنْهُ الْوَتِينَ ﴿٤٦﴾ فَمَا مِنكُم مِّنْ أَحَدٍ عَنْهُ حٰجِزِينَ ﴿٤٧﴾ وَإِنَّهُ لَتَذْكِرَةٌ لِّلْمُتَّقِينَ ﴿٤٨﴾ وَإِنَّا لَنَعْلَمُ أَنَّ مِنكُم مُّكَذِّبِينَ ﴿٤٩﴾ وَإِنَّهُ لَحَسْرَةٌ عَلَى الْكٰفِرِينَ ﴿٥٠﴾ وَإِنَّهُ لَحَقُّ الْيَقِينِ ﴿٥١﴾ فَسَبِّحْ بِاسْمِ رَبِّكَ الْعَظِيمِ ﴿٥٢﴾

CHAPTER
70

AL-MA'ÂRIJ
(The Ways Of Ascent)
(Revealed before Hijrah)

سُورَةُ الْمَعَارِجِ مَكِّيَّةٌ

With the name of Allâh,
the Most Gracious, the Ever Merciful,
(I commence to read Sûrah Al-Ma'ârij).

بِسْمِ اللّٰهِ الرَّحْمٰنِ الرَّحِيمِ

1. **A** SOLICITOR solicited the punishment which is bound to befall.
2. (Let him know) there will be none to ward it

سَأَلَ سَائِلٌ بِعَذَابٍ وَاقِعٍ ﴿١﴾ لِّلْكٰفِرِينَ

off from the disbelievers.

3. (It shall come) from Allâh the Master of the ways of ascent; (which even enable a person to rise higher and higher, so why not solicit His grace?)

4. The angels and the Spirit (of the faithful) ascend to Him in a day the measure of which is (equal to) fifty thousand years (a day of spiritual advancement of the faithful is equivalent to fifty thousand years of material advancement, thus the development and progress of the human soul knows no end).

5. So (while waiting) patiently persevere, an admirable and graceful persevering.

6. They think it (- the Day of Judgment) to be far off.

7. But We know it to be near (at hand).

8. The day (it befalls), the heaven shall become (red) like molten copper.

9. And the mountains shall become like flakes of multicoloured wool.

10. No warm friend will inquire after a warm friend.

11. (Though) they will be placed in sight of one another. The guilty person would wish to redeem himself from the punishment of that day (even) by (offering) his children (as ransom);

12. (The guilty will gladly sacrifice) his wife and his brother (to redeem himself);

13. And even his kinfolk who gave him shelter (in time of distress)

14. And (by offering) all that is on the earth put together, (thinking) if only thus he might deliver himself (from the punishment).

15. By no means! (He can never be redeemed). Surely, it (- the punishment you are warned against) is a blazing Fire,

16. Stripping off the skin even to the extremities (of the human body).

17. It will claim the person (for consumption) who drew back (from accepting the truth) and turned away (refusing to obey).

18. (It will claim) him who amassed (wealth)

سُورَةُ الْمَعَارِجِ ٧٠

لَيْسَ لَهُ دَافِعٌ ۝٢ مِّنَ اللّٰهِ ذِي الْمَعَارِجِ ۝٣
تَعْرُجُ الْمَلٰٓئِكَةُ وَ الرُّوحُ إِلَيْهِ فِي يَوْمٍ كَانَ
مِقْدَارُهُ خَمْسِينَ أَلْفَ سَنَةٍ ۝٤ فَاصْبِرْ
صَبْرًا جَمِيلًا ۝٥ إِنَّهُمْ يَرَوْنَهُ بَعِيدًا ۝٦
وَّ نَرٰىهُ قَرِيبًا ۝٧ يَوْمَ تَكُونُ السَّمَآءُ
كَالْمُهْلِ ۝٨ وَ تَكُونُ الْجِبَالُ كَالْعِهْنِ ۝٩ وَلَا
يَسْئَلُ حَمِيمٌ حَمِيمًا ۝١٠ يُبَصَّرُونَهُمْ يَوَدُّ
الْمُجْرِمُ لَوْ يَفْتَدِي مِنْ عَذَابِ يَوْمِئِذٍ
بِبَنِيهِ ۝١١ وَ صٰحِبَتِهِ وَ أَخِيهِ ۝١٢ وَ فَصِيلَتِهِ
الَّتِي تُـْٔوِيهِ ۝١٣ وَ مَنْ فِي الْأَرْضِ جَمِيعًا ثُمَّ
يُنْجِيهِ ۝١٤ كَلَّا إِنَّهَا لَظٰى ۝١٥ نَزَّاعَةً لِّلشَّوٰى ۝١٦
تَدْعُوا مَنْ أَدْبَرَ وَ تَوَلّٰى ۝١٧ وَ جَمَعَ فَأَوْعٰى ۝١٨

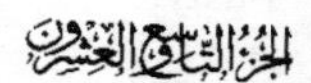

and withheld (it).

19. Verily, such a person is impatient and miserly by nature.

20. He loses heart and becomes fretful when evil afflicts him.

21. But is niggardly when good falls to his lot.

22. Different however is the case of those devoted to Prayers,

23. Those persons who remain constant and steadfast in their Prayers,

24. And those in whose wealth there is a recognised right (- a fixed share),

25. (Set apart) for one who asks (for help) and also (for one) who is prevented (even from asking for one reason or the other);

26. (Different also is the case of) those who accepted the truth of the Day of Requital;

27. And those who are fearful of the punishment from their Lord.

28. The fact is that the punishment of their Lord is not (a thing) to be felt secure from;

29. (Different as well is the case of) those who guard their private parts (by restraining their passions).

30. Except from their (free) wives or those (wives of theirs) whom their right hands own (- slave wives), for which they are not to blame.

31. But it is those who seek (to satisfy their lust) in any other way excepting that (of marriage) that are the transgressors.

32. And (different also is the case of) those persons who are watchful of their trusts and their covenants,

33. And those who are upright in their evidences (and bear true testimony),

34. And those persons who are strict in the observance of their Prayers.

35. All these (mentioned above) shall be dwelling in Gardens, honoured and treated generously.

سُورَةُ الْمَعَارِجِ ٧٠

إِنَّ الْإِنْسٰنَ خُلِقَ هَلُوعًا ۝١٩ إِذَا مَسَّهُ الشَّرُّ
جَزُوعًا ۝٢٠ وَإِذَا مَسَّهُ الْخَيْرُ مَنُوعًا ۝٢١ إِلَّا
الْمُصَلِّينَ ۝٢٢ الَّذِينَ هُمْ عَلٰى صَلَاتِهِمْ
دَآئِمُونَ ۝٢٣ وَالَّذِينَ فِيٓ أَمْوٰلِهِمْ حَقٌّ مَّعْلُومٌ ۝٢٤
لِّلسَّآئِلِ وَالْمَحْرُومِ ۝٢٥ وَالَّذِينَ يُصَدِّقُونَ
بِيَوْمِ الدِّينِ ۝٢٦ وَالَّذِينَ هُمْ مِّنْ عَذَابِ رَبِّهِمْ
مُّشْفِقُونَ ۝٢٧ إِنَّ عَذَابَ رَبِّهِمْ غَيْرُ مَأْمُونٍ ۝٢٨
وَالَّذِينَ هُمْ لِفُرُوجِهِمْ حٰفِظُونَ ۝٢٩ إِلَّا عَلٰىٓ
أَزْوٰجِهِمْ أَوْ مَا مَلَكَتْ أَيْمٰنُهُمْ فَإِنَّهُمْ
غَيْرُ مَلُومِينَ ۝٣٠ فَمَنِ ابْتَغٰى وَرَآءَ ذٰلِكَ
فَأُولٰٓئِكَ هُمُ الْعَادُونَ ۝٣١ وَالَّذِينَ هُمْ
لِأَمٰنٰتِهِمْ وَعَهْدِهِمْ رٰعُونَ ۝٣٢ وَالَّذِينَ
هُمْ بِشَهٰدٰتِهِمْ قَآئِمُونَ ۝٣٣ وَالَّذِينَ هُمْ
عَلٰى صَلَاتِهِمْ يُحَافِظُونَ ۝٣٤ أُولٰٓئِكَ فِي جَنّٰتٍ
مُّكْرَمُونَ ۝٣٥ فَمَالِ الَّذِينَ كَفَرُوا قِبَلَكَ

SECTION 2

36. **W**HAT is wrong with those who disbelieve

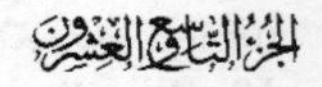

that they come running headlong towards you,
37. From the right hand and from the left (- from all directions) in various parties.
38. Does each and every one of them covet to be admitted to the Garden of Bliss.
39. No (never shall they enter it). We have created them for that substantial purpose (the worth of) which they know (- to discharge their obligations to God and people and to themselves).
40. But nay! I call to witness the Lord of the easts and the wests. We are certainly Powerful
41. To change (them into) better beings than they are and that We can never be frustrated (in Our purpose).
42. Therefore, leave them alone to indulge in unimportant conversation and to amuse themselves (in idle pursuits) until they meet that day of theirs that they are warned of,
43. The day when they (having risen to life) will come out hastily from their graves as though they were racing to a target (which they must meet).
44. Their eyes will be downcast and shameful; humiliation will be overwhelming them. Such shall be the punishment of the day with which they are being threatened.

مُهْطِعِينَ ﴿٣٦﴾ عَنِ الْيَمِينِ وَعَنِ الشِّمَالِ
عِزِينَ ﴿٣٧﴾ أَيَطْمَعُ كُلُّ امْرِئٍ مِّنْهُمْ أَن
يُدْخَلَ جَنَّةَ نَعِيمٍ ﴿٣٨﴾ كَلَّا إِنَّا خَلَقْنَهُم
مِّمَّا يَعْلَمُونَ ﴿٣٩﴾ فَلَآ أُقْسِمُ بِرَبِّ الْمَشْرِقِ
وَالْمَغْرِبِ إِنَّا لَقَدِرُونَ ﴿٤٠﴾ عَلَىٰٓ أَن
نُّبَدِّلَ خَيْرًا مِّنْهُمْ وَمَا نَحْنُ بِمَسْبُوقِينَ ﴿٤١﴾
فَذَرْهُمْ يَخُوضُوا وَيَلْعَبُوا حَتَّىٰ يُلَٰقُوا
يَوْمَهُمُ الَّذِي يُوعَدُونَ ﴿٤٢﴾ يَوْمَ يَخْرُجُونَ
مِنَ الْأَجْدَاثِ سِرَاعًا كَأَنَّهُمْ إِلَىٰ نُصُبٍ
يُوفِضُونَ ﴿٤٣﴾ خَٰشِعَةً أَبْصَٰرُهُمْ تَرْهَقُهُمْ
ذِلَّةٌ ذَٰلِكَ الْيَوْمُ الَّذِي كَانُوا
يُوعَدُونَ ﴿٤٤﴾

CHAPTER 71

NÛH
(Noah)
(Revealed before Hijrah)

سُورَةُ نُوحٍ مَكِّيَّةٌ

With the name of Allâh, the Most Gracious, the Ever Merciful (I commence to read Sûrah Nûh).

بِسْمِ اللهِ الرَّحْمٰنِ الرَّحِيمِ

1. **W**E sent Noah to his people (saying), 'Warn your people before a grievous punishment comes upon them.'

إِنَّآ أَرْسَلْنَا نُوحًا إِلَىٰ قَوْمِهِۦٓ أَنْ أَنذِرْ
قَوْمَكَ مِن قَبْلِ أَن يَأْتِيَهُمْ عَذَابٌ أَلِيمٌ ﴿١﴾

2. He said, 'O my people! I am a plain Warner to you.
3. '(I say to you,) that you should worship Allâh and take Him as a shield and obey me.
4. '(If you do so,) He will protect you from (the commitment of sins and also the punishment of) your sins. And (by prolonging your lives) He will grant you reprieve till an appointed term. Verily, the time (of the divine decree) appointed by Allâh cannot be held back once it falls due. If only you had been a possessor of true knowledge (you would have known this).'
5. (Then seeing his people's persistent denial) he (-Noah) said (at long last), 'My Lord! I have called my people (to You) day in and day out,
6. 'But the more I call them the more they flee (from me).
7. 'As often as I called them to You so that You might protect them (against the commitment of further sins and also against the evil consequences of their sins) they plugged their ears with their fingers, and drew their cloaks around them (and thus covered their hearts), and persisted (in their stubbornness and denial) and behaved in an extremely insolent manner.
8. 'Then I invited them (to You) openly.
9. 'Then I spoke to them in public as well as in private (to make them understand the truth somehow).
10. 'And I said, "Seek the protection of your Lord for He is Great Protector as ever.
11. "(If you listen to me) He will send upon you clouds raining over and over again, in abundance.
12. "He will add to you wealth and children. He will provide for you gardens and will place streams at your disposal (to make you prosperous)".'
13. (And so did Prophet Muhammad said,) 'People! What is wrong with you that you have no (faith in the Majesty of Allâh and no) hopes for (being granted) honour and greatness from Allâh.
14. 'Whereas He has created you by (passing

سُورَةُ نُوحٍ ٧١

قَالَ يٰقَوْمِ إِنِّي لَكُمْ نَذِيرٌ مُّبِينٌ ﴿٢﴾ أَنِ
اعْبُدُوا اللّٰهَ وَ اتَّقُوهُ وَ أَطِيعُونِ ﴿٣﴾ يَغْفِرْ
لَكُمْ مِّنْ ذُنُوبِكُمْ وَ يُؤَخِّرْكُمْ إِلَىٰ أَجَلٍ
مُّسَمًّى إِنَّ أَجَلَ اللّٰهِ إِذَا جَآءَ لَا يُؤَخَّرُ
لَوْ كُنْتُمْ تَعْلَمُونَ ﴿٤﴾ قَالَ رَبِّ إِنِّي دَعَوْتُ
قَوْمِي لَيْلًا وَّ نَهَارًا ﴿٥﴾ فَلَمْ يَزِدْهُمْ دُعَآءِي
إِلَّا فِرَارًا ﴿٦﴾ وَ إِنِّي كُلَّمَا دَعَوْتُهُمْ لِتَغْفِرَ لَهُمْ
جَعَلُوا أَصٰبِعَهُمْ فِي أٰذَانِهِمْ وَ اسْتَغْشَوْا
ثِيَابَهُمْ وَ أَصَرُّوا وَ اسْتَكْبَرُوا اسْتِكْبَارًا ﴿٧﴾
ثُمَّ إِنِّي دَعَوْتُهُمْ جِهَارًا ﴿٨﴾ ثُمَّ إِنِّي أَعْلَنْتُ لَهُمْ
وَ أَسْرَرْتُ لَهُمْ إِسْرَارًا ﴿٩﴾ فَقُلْتُ اسْتَغْفِرُوا
رَبَّكُمْ إِنَّهُ كَانَ غَفَّارًا ﴿١٠﴾ يُرْسِلِ السَّمَآءَ
عَلَيْكُمْ مِّدْرَارًا ﴿١١﴾ وَّ يُمْدِدْكُمْ بِأَمْوٰلٍ وَّ بَنِينَ
وَ يَجْعَلْ لَّكُمْ جَنّٰتٍ وَّ يَجْعَلْ لَّكُمْ أَنْهٰرًا ﴿١٢﴾
مَا لَكُمْ لَا تَرْجُونَ لِلّٰهِ وَقَارًا ﴿١٣﴾ وَ قَدْ خَلَقَكُمْ

you through) various stages (and endowed you with different qualities).
15. 'Do you not consider how Allâh created the seven heavens one upon another in (perfect) conformity with one another.
16. 'And He has set the moon in their midst for light and the sun He has made as a glorious lamp.
17. 'It is Allâh Who germinated you from the earth in a (wonderful) growth,
18. 'Then will He return you to it and then raise you to (a new) life (on the Day of Awakening).
19. 'Allâh has made the earth a vast expanse for you,
20. 'That you may traverse its spacious paths (for the development of civilization and also to attain spiritual perfection).'

SECTION 2

21. **N**OAH said, 'My Lord! They (- my people) have disobeyed me. They follow (such leaders) whose wealth and children only add to their loss.'
22. They have devised a mighty and heinous plan (against the Prophet),
23. And they say (one to another), 'Never abandon your gods; neither abandon *Wadd* (their idol in the form of man), nor *Suwâ'* (- in that of a woman), nor (should you abandon) *Yaghûth* (- in that of a lion), and *Ya'ûq* (- in that of a horse) and *Nasr* (- in that of an eagle).
24. (Thereupon the Prophet prayed, '(Lord!) And indeed they have led many people astray, and add to the disappointment of these wrong-doers.'
25. (Accordingly) these people were drowned and made to enter the Fire because of their wrong doings. They found none against Allâh who could help them.
26. And Noah had prayed (to his God), 'My Lord! Do not leave a single dweller from among the disbelievers on the land.
27. 'For if you leave them (thus) they will

أَطْوَارًا ﴿١٤﴾ أَلَمْ تَرَوْا كَيْفَ خَلَقَ اللَّهُ سَبْعَ
سَمَٰوَٰتٍ طِبَاقًا ﴿١٥﴾ وَجَعَلَ الْقَمَرَ فِيهِنَّ نُورًا
وَجَعَلَ الشَّمْسَ سِرَاجًا ﴿١٦﴾ وَاللَّهُ أَنْبَتَكُمْ
مِنَ الْأَرْضِ نَبَاتًا ﴿١٧﴾ ثُمَّ يُعِيدُكُمْ فِيهَا
وَيُخْرِجُكُمْ إِخْرَاجًا ﴿١٨﴾ وَاللَّهُ جَعَلَ لَكُمُ الْأَرْضَ
بِسَاطًا ﴿١٩﴾ لِتَسْلُكُوا مِنْهَا سُبُلًا فِجَاجًا ﴿٢٠﴾ قَالَ
نُوحٌ رَبِّ إِنَّهُمْ عَصَوْنِي وَاتَّبَعُوا مَنْ لَمْ
يَزِدْهُ مَالُهُ وَوَلَدُهُ إِلَّا خَسَارًا ﴿٢١﴾ وَمَكَرُوا
مَكْرًا كُبَّارًا ﴿٢٢﴾ وَقَالُوا لَا تَذَرُنَّ آلِهَتَكُمْ
وَلَا تَذَرُنَّ وَدًّا وَلَا سُوَاعًا وَلَا يَغُوثَ
وَيَعُوقَ وَنَسْرًا ﴿٢٣﴾ وَقَدْ أَضَلُّوا كَثِيرًا
وَلَا تَزِدِ الظَّالِمِينَ إِلَّا ضَلَالًا ﴿٢٤﴾ مِمَّا خَطِيئَاتِهِمْ
أُغْرِقُوا فَأُدْخِلُوا نَارًا فَلَمْ يَجِدُوا
لَهُمْ مِنْ دُونِ اللَّهِ أَنْصَارًا ﴿٢٥﴾ وَقَالَ نُوحٌ
رَبِّ لَا تَذَرْ عَلَى الْأَرْضِ مِنَ الْكَافِرِينَ
دَيَّارًا ﴿٢٦﴾ إِنَّكَ إِنْ تَذَرْهُمْ يُضِلُّوا عِبَادَكَ

(only) lead Your servants astray and will beget only immoral and ungrateful (children).
28. 'My Lord! Protect me and my parents and those who enter my house bearing true faith and all the believing men and believing women. (Lord!) as for the wrongdoers grant them no increase except in perdition.'

وَلَا يَلِدُوٓا إِلَّا فَاجِرًا كَفَّارًا ﴿٢٧﴾ رَّبِّ
اغْفِرْ لِي وَلِوَٰلِدَيَّ وَلِمَن دَخَلَ بَيْتِيَ
مُؤْمِنًا وَلِلْمُؤْمِنِينَ وَالْمُؤْمِنَٰتِ وَلَا
تَزِدِ الظَّٰلِمِينَ إِلَّا تَبَارًا ﴿٢٨﴾

CHAPTER
72

AL-JINN
(The Jinn)
(Revealed before Hijrah)

سُورَةُ الْجِنِّ مَكِّيَّةٌ

With the name of Allâh,
the Most Gracious, the Ever Merciful
(I commence to read Sûrah Al-Jinn).

بِسْمِ اللَّهِ الرَّحْمَٰنِ الرَّحِيمِ

1. **S**AY, 'It has been revealed to me that a party of the *jinn* (- the non-Arab Jews of *Nasîbîn,* called *Jinn* because of their being strong, sharp and effective in affairs) listened (to the Qur'ân), so they said (to their people on their return), "Surely, we have heard a wonderful Qur'ân,
2. "It guides towards righteousness, so we declare our faith in it. We shall no longer worship any god besides our Lord.
3. "And the truth is that the Majesty of our Lord is exalted. He has taken to Himself no consort nor (has He begotten) a son,
4. "And (we admit) that the foolish among us used to say many exaggerated and blasphemous things against Allâh.
5. "And (we acknowledge) that (we believed in them because) we never thought that men and *jinn* could ever possibly utter a lie about Allâh.
6. "The fact is that some humble and lowly men from among the common folk used to seek refuge with some (big and influential) men

قُلْ أُوحِيَ إِلَيَّ أَنَّهُ اسْتَمَعَ نَفَرٌ مِّنَ الْجِنِّ
فَقَالُوٓا إِنَّا سَمِعْنَا قُرْءَانًا عَجَبًا ﴿١﴾ يَهْدِيٓ
إِلَى الرُّشْدِ فَـَٔامَنَّا بِهِۦ وَلَن نُّشْرِكَ بِرَبِّنَآ
أَحَدًا ﴿٢﴾ وَأَنَّهُ تَعَٰلَىٰ جَدُّ رَبِّنَا مَا اتَّخَذَ
صَٰحِبَةً وَلَا وَلَدًا ﴿٣﴾ وَأَنَّهُ كَانَ يَقُولُ
سَفِيهُنَا عَلَى اللَّهِ شَطَطًا ﴿٤﴾ وَأَنَّا ظَنَنَّآ أَن
لَّن تَقُولَ الْإِنسُ وَالْجِنُّ عَلَى اللَّهِ كَذِبًا ﴿٥﴾
وَأَنَّهُ كَانَ رِجَالٌ مِّنَ الْإِنسِ يَعُوذُونَ

from among the *jinns* and (thus) they increased these *(jinns)* in arrogance (and conceit).
7. "These men (from the *jinn*) believed even as you believe that Allâh would raise no one (as Messenger).
8. "And we (- the non-Arab Jews, the *jinn* who had listened to the Qur'ân, as diviners and astrologers) had primarily sought to probe the secrets of space above but we found it teeming with strong guards and shooting stars (a phenomenon which generally occurs before the advent of a divine Reformer).
9. "And that we used to sit in some of the observatories to listen to something. But he that tries to listen (in order to forecast some event) now (with the advent of Islam) finds a shooting star in ambush for him.
10. "(We confess that) we do not know whether evil is (hereby) augured for those who are on the earth or whether their Lord (thereby) intends to bestow right guidance for them.
11. "And some of us are righteous and some of us are otherwise. We follow different ways.
12. "And we have come to know for certain that we can never frustrate the purpose of Allâh in the earth, nor can we escape Him by flight (in any direction).
13. "No sooner did we hear the guidance (contained in the Qur'ân) than we believed in it. And he who believes in His Lord does not have to fear that his reward will be reduced or injustice will be (done to him).
14. "And some of us submit (to the will of God) while some of us are deviators (from the right course)".' (It has also been revealed to the Prophet that) those who submit (to God's commandments) are actually those who earnestly aim at the right way and find it out;
15. And that the deviators from the right course are the fuel of Gehenna.
16. And that if these (Makkan disbelievers) keep to the right path (and accept the divine

سُورَةُ الْجِنِّ ٧٢

بِرِجَالٍ مِّنَ الْجِنِّ فَزَادُوهُمْ رَهَقًا ﴿٦﴾
وَأَنَّهُمْ ظَنُّوا كَمَا ظَنَنتُمْ أَن لَّن يَبْعَثَ
اللَّهُ أَحَدًا ﴿٧﴾ وَأَنَّا لَمَسْنَا السَّمَاءَ فَوَجَدْنَاهَا
مُلِئَتْ حَرَسًا شَدِيدًا وَشُهُبًا ﴿٨﴾ وَأَنَّا كُنَّا
نَقْعُدُ مِنْهَا مَقَاعِدَ لِلسَّمْعِ ۖ فَمَن يَسْتَمِعِ
الْآنَ يَجِدْ لَهُ شِهَابًا رَّصَدًا ﴿٩﴾ وَأَنَّا لَا
نَدْرِي أَشَرٌّ أُرِيدَ بِمَن فِي الْأَرْضِ أَمْ
أَرَادَ بِهِمْ رَبُّهُمْ رَشَدًا ﴿١٠﴾ وَأَنَّا مِنَّا
الصَّالِحُونَ وَمِنَّا دُونَ ذَٰلِكَ ۖ كُنَّا طَرَائِقَ
قِدَدًا ﴿١١﴾ وَأَنَّا ظَنَنَّا أَن لَّن نُّعْجِزَ اللَّهَ فِي
الْأَرْضِ وَلَن نُّعْجِزَهُ هَرَبًا ﴿١٢﴾ وَأَنَّا لَمَّا
سَمِعْنَا الْهُدَىٰ آمَنَّا بِهِ ۖ فَمَن يُؤْمِن بِرَبِّهِ
فَلَا يَخَافُ بَخْسًا وَلَا رَهَقًا ﴿١٣﴾ وَأَنَّا مِنَّا
الْمُسْلِمُونَ وَمِنَّا الْقَاسِطُونَ ۖ فَمَنْ أَسْلَمَ
فَأُولَٰئِكَ تَحَرَّوْا رَشَدًا ﴿١٤﴾ وَأَمَّا الْقَاسِطُونَ
فَكَانُوا لِجَهَنَّمَ حَطَبًا ﴿١٥﴾ وَأَن لَّوِ اسْتَقَامُوا

Message) We will certainly provide them with abundant water (-wealth and other material benefits in the present life) to avail from.

17. With the result that (in that case) We will thereby purify them thoroughly and well. And he who turns away from the remembrance of his Lord, He will drive him into an overwhelmingly stern punishment.

18. And that the mosques are meant for (the worship of) Allâh, so call on no one (therein) beside Allâh.

19. And when (- Muhammad) Allâh's servant stands up calling to Him, these (- disbelievers) crowd upon him, well nigh suffocating him (to stifle and smother his voice).

SECTION 2

20. **S**AY, 'I invoke only my Lord and I associate no one with Him (as His partner).'

21. Say, 'I have no power to avoid either harm from you or to do some good to you.'

22. Say, 'Surely, none can grant me shelter against Allâh if I disobey Him, nor can I find any refuge besides Him.

23. '(My responsibility is), only to convey what is revealed (to me) from Allâh and complete the mission of Prophethood.' And there awaits those who disobey Allâh and His Messenger the Fire of Gehenna wherein they shall abide for a long time.

24. (They will continue to oppose the Prophet) until they see that (punishment) they are threatened with. And soon they will know who is weaker in respect of helpers and less in numbers.

25. Say, 'I have no knowledge whether that (punishment) you are threatened with is near (at hand) or whether my Lord will fix a later term for it.'

26. He alone knows the hidden (future) and He does not grant predominance to any one over His secrets,

سُورَةُ الجِنِّ ٧٢

عَلَى الطَّرِيقَةِ لَأَسْقَيْنَٰهُم مَّآءً غَدَقًا ﴿١٦﴾
لِّنَفْتِنَهُمْ فِيهِ ۚ وَمَن يُعْرِضْ عَن ذِكْرِ
رَبِّهِۦ يَسْلُكْهُ عَذَابًا صَعَدًا ﴿١٧﴾ وَأَنَّ الْمَسَٰجِدَ
لِلَّهِ فَلَا تَدْعُوا مَعَ اللَّهِ أَحَدًا ﴿١٨﴾ وَأَنَّهُۥ لَمَّا
قَامَ عَبْدُ اللَّهِ يَدْعُوهُ كَادُوا يَكُونُونَ
عَلَيْهِ لِبَدًا ﴿١٩﴾ قُلْ إِنَّمَآ أَدْعُوا رَبِّي وَلَآ أُشْرِكُ
بِهِۦٓ أَحَدًا ﴿٢٠﴾ قُلْ إِنِّي لَآ أَمْلِكُ لَكُمْ ضَرًّا
وَلَا رَشَدًا ﴿٢١﴾ قُلْ إِنِّي لَن يُجِيرَنِي مِنَ اللَّهِ
أَحَدٌ وَلَنْ أَجِدَ مِن دُونِهِۦ مُلْتَحَدًا ﴿٢٢﴾
إِلَّا بَلَٰغًا مِّنَ اللَّهِ وَرِسَٰلَٰتِهِۦ ۚ وَمَن يَعْصِ
اللَّهَ وَرَسُولَهُۥ فَإِنَّ لَهُۥ نَارَ جَهَنَّمَ خَٰلِدِينَ
فِيهَآ أَبَدًا ﴿٢٣﴾ حَتَّىٰٓ إِذَا رَأَوْا مَا يُوعَدُونَ
فَسَيَعْلَمُونَ مَنْ أَضْعَفُ نَاصِرًا وَأَقَلُّ
عَدَدًا ﴿٢٤﴾ قُلْ إِنْ أَدْرِيٓ أَقَرِيبٌ مَّا تُوعَدُونَ
أَمْ يَجْعَلُ لَهُۥ رَبِّيٓ أَمَدًا ﴿٢٥﴾ عَٰلِمُ الْغَيْبِ فَلَا

27. Except to him whom He chooses to be a Messenger (of His, to whom He frequently tells many news about the hidden future). (And when He does this) He orders an escort of (guarding angels) to go before him and behind him;
28. That He may make it known (to the people) that they (- the Divine Messengers) have properly delivered the Messages of their Lord. He encompasses (in His knowledge) all that they have, and keeps count of all things.

يُظْهِرُ عَلَىٰ غَيْبِهِۦٓ أَحَدًا ﴿٢٦﴾ إِلَّا مَنِ ٱرْتَضَىٰ مِن
رَّسُولٍ فَإِنَّهُۥ يَسْلُكُ مِنۢ بَيْنِ يَدَيْهِ
وَمِنْ خَلْفِهِۦ رَصَدًا ﴿٢٧﴾ لِّيَعْلَمَ أَن قَدْ أَبْلَغُوا۟
رِسَٰلَٰتِ رَبِّهِمْ وَأَحَاطَ بِمَا لَدَيْهِمْ وَأَحْصَىٰ
كُلَّ شَيْءٍ عَدَدًۢا ﴿٢٨﴾

ع ٢ ١٢

CHAPTER
73

AL-MUZZAMMIL
(He That Has Wrapped Himself Up)
(Revealed before Hijrah)

With the name of Allâh,
the Most Gracious, the Ever Merciful
(I commence to read Sûrah Al-Muzzammil).

1. **O** YOU that have wrapped yourself up in robes (of Prophethood)!
2. Stand up (in Prayer) at night except for a small portion of it,
3. Half of it or you may however reduce it a little,
4. Or prolong it (a little more) and keep on reciting the Qur'ân distinctly and thoughtfully well.
5. Verily, We are soon going to charge you with the enormous and important responsibility of (conveying to people) the Message (of your Lord).
6. Verily, getting up at night (for Prayer) is the most effective means of subduing (one's self), and the most upright way to acquire firm

سُورَةُ المُزَّمِّلِ مَكِّيَّةٌ

بِسْمِ ٱللَّهِ ٱلرَّحْمَٰنِ ٱلرَّحِيمِ

يَٰٓأَيُّهَا ٱلْمُزَّمِّلُ ﴿١﴾ قُمِ ٱلَّيْلَ إِلَّا قَلِيلًا ﴿٢﴾
نِّصْفَهُۥٓ أَوِ ٱنقُصْ مِنْهُ قَلِيلًا ﴿٣﴾ أَوْ زِدْ عَلَيْهِ
وَرَتِّلِ ٱلْقُرْءَانَ تَرْتِيلًا ﴿٤﴾ إِنَّا سَنُلْقِى عَلَيْكَ
قَوْلًا ثَقِيلًا ﴿٥﴾ إِنَّ نَاشِئَةَ ٱلَّيْلِ هِىَ أَشَدُّ

control over one's actions and speech.
7. Indeed, you have a long (chain of) engagements during the day.
8. Therefore extol the name of your Lord and devote (yourself) to Him with exclusive and sincere devotion.
9. He is the Lord of the east and the west. There is no other, cannot be and will never be one worthy of worship but He, therefore take Him as Disposer of (your) affairs (putting your full trust in Him).
10. And patiently persevere in the face of all that these (enemies) say and withdraw from them in a graceful manner.
11. Leave Me to (deal with) those who belie (the truth) and who are possessors of ease and plenty. And give them a little respite.
12. We have (a variety of) fetters ready (to bind them with) and a raging Fire (to throw them into),
13. And food that chokes and a woeful punishment.
14. (That punishment will befall them) on the day when the earth and the mountains shall quake and the mountains shall crumble into heaps of sand dunes.
15. (O people!) We have indeed sent a (great) Messenger to you who is a Witness over you just as We sent (Moses as) a Messenger towards Pharaoh.
16. But Pharaoh disobeyed the Messenger so We seized him with a terrible punishment (so all of you be on your guard against such an attitude!)
17. But if you also disobey (the Messenger sent to you), how will you then guard yourselves from the (calamity of the) day which will turn (even) children (prematurely) gray-headed.
18. And because of which the heaven shall be rent asunder. (This is the promise of God,) (remember) His promise is bound to be fulfilled.
19. Verily, this (Qur'ân) is a Reminder, therefore, let him, who will, follow the way leading

وَطْـًٔا وَّ أَقْوَمُ قِيلًا ⑥ إِنَّ لَكَ فِي النَّهَارِ سَبْحًا
طَوِيلًا ⑦ وَاذْكُرِ اسْمَ رَبِّكَ وَتَبَتَّلْ إِلَيْهِ
تَبْتِيلًا ⑧ رَبُّ الْمَشْرِقِ وَالْمَغْرِبِ لَآ إِلٰهَ
إِلَّا هُوَ فَاتَّخِذْهُ وَكِيلًا ⑨ وَاصْبِرْ عَلٰى مَا
يَقُولُونَ وَاهْجُرْهُمْ هَجْرًا جَمِيلًا ⑩ وَذَرْنِي
وَالْمُكَذِّبِينَ أُولِي النَّعْمَةِ وَمَهِّلْهُمْ قَلِيلًا ⑪
إِنَّ لَدَيْنَآ أَنْكَالًا وَّجَحِيمًا ⑫ وَّطَعَامًا
ذَا غُصَّةٍ وَّعَذَابًا أَلِيمًا ⑬ يَوْمَ تَرْجُفُ الْأَرْضُ
وَالْجِبَالُ وَكَانَتِ الْجِبَالُ كَثِيبًا مَّهِيلًا ⑭
إِنَّآ أَرْسَلْنَآ إِلَيْكُمْ رَسُولًا شَاهِدًا عَلَيْكُمْ
كَمَآ أَرْسَلْنَآ إِلٰى فِرْعَوْنَ رَسُولًا ⑮ فَعَصٰى
فِرْعَوْنُ الرَّسُولَ فَأَخَذْنٰهُ أَخْذًا وَّبِيلًا ⑯
فَكَيْفَ تَتَّقُونَ إِنْ كَفَرْتُمْ يَوْمًا يَّجْعَلُ
الْوِلْدَانَ شِيبًا ⑰ السَّمَآءُ مُنْفَطِرٌ بِهٖ
كَانَ وَعْدُهُ مَفْعُولًا ⑱ إِنَّ هٰذِهٖ تَذْكِرَةٌ
فَمَنْ شَآءَ اتَّخَذَ إِلٰى رَبِّهٖ سَبِيلًا ⑲ إِنَّ رَبَّكَ

ع ١٣

towards his Lord.

سورة المزمل ٧٣

SECTION 2

20. **S**URELY, your Lord knows that you remain standing (to say Night Prayers) for nearly two thirds of the night and (sometimes) half or one third of it; and so does a party of those (of your believing Companions) who are with you. And Allâh determines the night and the day (- sometime the nights are long and sometime they are short and sometime the day and the night are equal). He knows that you (- the Muslims in general) will not be able to keep up so long a vigil (to say Night Prayer). He has, therefore, turned to you with mercy. Recite then, as much of the Qur'ân (in your Night Prayer) as is easily possible. He knows that some of you may be taken ill and others may be moving about in the land seeking Allâh's bounty, and still others who may be fighting for the cause of Allâh, so (O Muslims!) recite as much of it (- the Qur'ân) as is easily possible (for you). You shall, however, observe Prayer (regularly five times a day in all events). And go on presenting the *Zakât* and set apart a goodly portion (of your possessions to give for (the sake of) Allâh. And whatever good you send on before for yourselves, you will find it with Allâh as the best of things meriting the greatest reward. And seek protection of Allâh. Verily, Allâh is All-Protecting, Ever Merciful.

يَعْلَمُ أَنَّكَ تَقُومُ أَدْنٰى مِنْ ثُلُثَيِ الَّيْلِ
وَنِصْفَهُ وَثُلُثَهُ وَطَآئِفَةٌ مِّنَ الَّذِيْنَ مَعَكَ
وَاللّٰهُ يُقَدِّرُ الَّيْلَ وَالنَّهَارَ عَلِمَ أَنْ لَّنْ
تُحْصُوْهُ فَتَابَ عَلَيْكُمْ فَاقْرَءُوْا مَا تَيَسَّرَ
مِنَ الْقُرْاٰنِ عَلِمَ أَنْ سَيَكُوْنُ مِنْكُمْ
مَّرْضٰى وَاٰخَرُوْنَ يَضْرِبُوْنَ فِي الْأَرْضِ
يَبْتَغُوْنَ مِنْ فَضْلِ اللّٰهِ وَاٰخَرُوْنَ يُقٰتِلُوْنَ
فِيْ سَبِيْلِ اللّٰهِ فَاقْرَءُوْا مَا تَيَسَّرَ مِنْهُ
وَأَقِيْمُوا الصَّلٰوةَ وَاٰتُوا الزَّكٰوةَ وَأَقْرِضُوا اللّٰهَ
قَرْضًا حَسَنًا وَمَا تُقَدِّمُوْا لِأَنْفُسِكُمْ مِّنْ
خَيْرٍ تَجِدُوْهُ عِنْدَ اللّٰهِ هُوَ خَيْرًا وَّأَعْظَمَ
أَجْرًا وَاسْتَغْفِرُوا اللّٰهَ إِنَّ اللّٰهَ غَفُوْرٌ رَّحِيْمٌ ٢٠

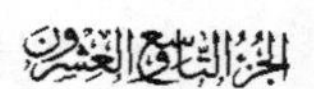

CHAPTER
74

AL-MUDDATHTHIR

(One Endowed with Excellent Capabilities)
(Revealed before Hijrah)

With the name of Allâh,
the Most Gracious, the Ever Merciful
(I commence to read Sûrah Al-Muddaththir).

1. **O** YOU who have been endowed with excellent capabilities!
2. Arise (with the Divine Message) and warn.
3. And your Lord, do announce His supremacy.
4. And purify your clothes and your heart.
5. And idol-worship, (spare no pains to) exterminate it and shun all uncleanliness.
6. And bestow no favour seeking to get more (in return).
7. And endure (your trials) with perseverance for the sake of your Lord.
8. And the day the trumpet (of the Prophet's call to the people) is sounded,
9. That will be a day full of woe and distress (for the opponents of Truth for this day will spell final defeat of disbelief).
10. For the disbelievers it will not be easy (to behold the complete triumph of Truth).
11. Leave Me alone to deal with him whom I created,
12. To whom I gave abundant wealth,
13. And sons that remain present (with him),
14. And I provided for him all necessary equipment;
15. Yet he covets that I should give (him) more.
16. Certainly not, for he has been a stubborn opponent to Our Messages.
17. Rather I will inflict on him an increasingly overwhelming torment.

سُورَةُ الْمُدَّثِّرِ ٧٤

سُورَةُ الْمُدَّثِّرِ مَكِّيَّةٌ

بِسْمِ اللَّهِ الرَّحْمَٰنِ الرَّحِيمِ

يَا أَيُّهَا الْمُدَّثِّرُ ﴿١﴾ قُمْ فَأَنذِرْ ﴿٢﴾ وَرَبَّكَ
فَكَبِّرْ ﴿٣﴾ وَثِيَابَكَ فَطَهِّرْ ﴿٤﴾ وَالرُّجْزَ فَاهْجُرْ ﴿٥﴾
وَلَا تَمْنُن تَسْتَكْثِرُ ﴿٦﴾ وَلِرَبِّكَ فَاصْبِرْ ﴿٧﴾
فَإِذَا نُقِرَ فِي النَّاقُورِ ﴿٨﴾ فَذَٰلِكَ يَوْمَئِذٍ يَوْمٌ
عَسِيرٌ ﴿٩﴾ عَلَى الْكَافِرِينَ غَيْرُ يَسِيرٍ ﴿١٠﴾ ذَرْنِي
وَمَنْ خَلَقْتُ وَحِيدًا ﴿١١﴾ وَجَعَلْتُ لَهُ مَالًا
مَّمْدُودًا ﴿١٢﴾ وَبَنِينَ شُهُودًا ﴿١٣﴾ وَمَهَّدتُّ لَهُ
تَمْهِيدًا ﴿١٤﴾ ثُمَّ يَطْمَعُ أَنْ أَزِيدَ ﴿١٥﴾ كَلَّا إِنَّهُ
كَانَ لِآيَاتِنَا عَنِيدًا ﴿١٦﴾ سَأُرْهِقُهُ صَعُودًا ﴿١٧﴾ إِنَّهُ

18. Lo! He pondered and planned,
19. Ruin seize him! How (maliciously) he planned,
20. Again ruin seize him! How (maliciously) he planned,
21. Then he looked about (to give his calculations and planning another thought),
22. Then he frowned and scowled (in disdain),
23. Then he turned back (in scorn) and waxed proud,
24. And said, 'This (Qur'ân) is nothing but an age long magic handed down (by tradition).
25. 'This is nothing but mere words of a human being.'
26. Soon I shall cast him into the Hell-Fire.
27. How should you realize what the Hell-fire is?
28. It spares none. It leaves nothing (unconsumed).
29. It scorches the face, the skin and the body.
30. Nineteen (wardens) are appointed over it (-the Hell-fire in consonance with the nineteen human faculties the misuse of which results in punishment for the sinners).
31. None but angels have We appointed as wardens of the Hell-Fire. We have fixed their number in order to purify (and purge) the sins of those who disbelieve. The result of this is that the people of the Scripture will be convinced, and those who believe will increase in faith (and act with righteousness). And those who have been given the Scriptures as well as the believers may (both) attain certainty (and will not be misguided). And the people with diseased hearts and the disbelievers will say, 'What does Allâh mean by such an illustration?' Thus does Allâh forsake him who wishes (to go astray), and guides him who wishes (to be guided). And none knows (the number) of the hosts of your Lord but He. And this (Qur'ân) is nothing but a means for human beings to rise to eminence.

فَكَّرَ وَقَدَّرَ ﴿١٨﴾ فَقُتِلَ كَيْفَ قَدَّرَ ﴿١٩﴾ ثُمَّ قُتِلَ
كَيْفَ قَدَّرَ ﴿٢٠﴾ ثُمَّ نَظَرَ ﴿٢١﴾ ثُمَّ عَبَسَ وَبَسَرَ ﴿٢٢﴾
ثُمَّ أَدْبَرَ وَاسْتَكْبَرَ ﴿٢٣﴾ فَقَالَ إِنْ هٰذَآ إِلَّا
سِحْرٌ يُؤْثَرُ ﴿٢٤﴾ إِنْ هٰذَآ إِلَّا قَوْلُ الْبَشَرِ ﴿٢٥﴾
سَأُصْلِيهِ سَقَرَ ﴿٢٦﴾ وَمَآ أَدْرٰىكَ مَا سَقَرُ ﴿٢٧﴾
لَا تُبْقِي وَلَا تَذَرُ ﴿٢٨﴾ لَوَّاحَةٌ لِّلْبَشَرِ ﴿٢٩﴾ عَلَيْهَا
تِسْعَةَ عَشَرَ ﴿٣٠﴾ وَمَا جَعَلْنَآ أَصْحٰبَ النَّارِ
إِلَّا مَلٰٓئِكَةً وَمَا جَعَلْنَا عِدَّتَهُمْ إِلَّا فِتْنَةً
لِّلَّذِينَ كَفَرُوا لِيَسْتَيْقِنَ الَّذِينَ أُوتُوا الْكِتٰبَ
وَيَزْدَادَ الَّذِينَ ءَامَنُوٓا إِيمٰنًا وَلَا يَرْتَابَ
الَّذِينَ أُوتُوا الْكِتٰبَ وَالْمُؤْمِنُونَ وَلِيَقُولَ
الَّذِينَ فِي قُلُوبِهِم مَّرَضٌ وَالْكٰفِرُونَ مَاذَآ
أَرَادَ اللّٰهُ بِهٰذَا مَثَلًا كَذٰلِكَ يُضِلُّ اللّٰهُ
مَن يَشَآءُ وَيَهْدِي مَن يَشَآءُ وَمَا يَعْلَمُ
جُنُودَ رَبِّكَ إِلَّا هُوَ وَمَا هِيَ إِلَّا ذِكْرٰى

سورة المدثر ٧٤

SECTION 2

32. **N**AY, I call the moon to witness,
33. And also the night when it departs,
34. And the dawn when it shines forth,
35. Verily, it (- the Fire of Hell) in itself is one of the great calamities,
36. A warning to humankind.
37. Yet whosoever of you wants to go ahead (may do so), or whoever of you wants to lag behind (may do so, for warning avails only those who are really keen to be guided aright).
38. Every soul is bound to pay for its deeds.
39. Different, however, is the case of the blessed ones.
40. (They will be) in Gardens inquiring
41. Of the guilty ones,
42. 'What has brought you into Hell?'
43. They will reply, 'We were not of those who offered Prayers;
44. 'Nor did we feed the poor.
45. 'And we indulged in vain talk along with those who indulged therein,
46. 'And we always cried lies to the Day of Requital,
47. 'Till death overtook us.'
48. That is why the intercession of the intercessors will be of no avail to them.
49. What is the wrong with them, then, that they are thus turning away from the exhortation (of the Qur'ân),
50. (They behave) as if they were frightened donkeys (making others frightful too),
51. Running away from a lion?
52. The fact is that everyone of them desires that he should (individually) be given open Scripture (direct from heaven).
53. This can never be so. The fact is that they have no fear of the Hereafter.
54. This should not be so. Verily, this (Qur'ân)

لِلْبَشَرِ ﴿٣١﴾ كَلَّا وَالْقَمَرِ ﴿٣٢﴾ وَالَّيْلِ إِذْ أَدْبَرَ ﴿٣٣﴾
وَالصُّبْحِ إِذَا أَسْفَرَ ﴿٣٤﴾ إِنَّهَا لَإِحْدَى الْكُبَرِ ﴿٣٥﴾
نَذِيرًا لِّلْبَشَرِ ﴿٣٦﴾ لِمَنْ شَاءَ مِنْكُمْ أَنْ
يَتَقَدَّمَ أَوْ يَتَأَخَّرَ ﴿٣٧﴾ كُلُّ نَفْسٍ بِمَا كَسَبَتْ
رَهِينَةٌ ﴿٣٨﴾ إِلَّا أَصْحٰبَ الْيَمِينِ ﴿٣٩﴾ فِي جَنّٰتٍ
يَتَسَاءَلُونَ ﴿٤٠﴾ عَنِ الْمُجْرِمِينَ ﴿٤١﴾ مَا سَلَكَكُمْ
فِي سَقَرَ ﴿٤٢﴾ قَالُوا لَمْ نَكُ مِنَ الْمُصَلِّينَ ﴿٤٣﴾
وَلَمْ نَكُ نُطْعِمُ الْمِسْكِينَ ﴿٤٤﴾ وَكُنَّا نَخُوضُ
مَعَ الْخَائِضِينَ ﴿٤٥﴾ وَكُنَّا نُكَذِّبُ بِيَوْمِ
الدِّينِ ﴿٤٦﴾ حَتّٰى أَتٰنَا الْيَقِينُ ﴿٤٧﴾ فَمَا تَنْفَعُهُمْ
شَفٰعَةُ الشّٰفِعِينَ ﴿٤٨﴾ فَمَا لَهُمْ عَنِ التَّذْكِرَةِ
مُعْرِضِينَ ﴿٤٩﴾ كَأَنَّهُمْ حُمُرٌ مُّسْتَنْفِرَةٌ ﴿٥٠﴾ فَرَّتْ
مِنْ قَسْوَرَةٍ ﴿٥١﴾ بَلْ يُرِيدُ كُلُّ امْرِئٍ مِّنْهُمْ
أَنْ يُؤْتٰى صُحُفًا مُّنَشَّرَةً ﴿٥٢﴾ كَلَّا بَلْ لَا
يَخَافُونَ الْآخِرَةَ ﴿٥٣﴾ كَلَّا إِنَّهُ تَذْكِرَةٌ ﴿٥٤﴾

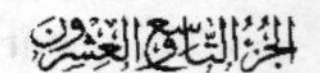

is a means to rise to eminence.
55. Let him then, who will, remember it (to win glory and honour for himself),
56. But these (deniers) will not remember it unless Allâh (so) will. He alone is worthy to be taken as a shield and He alone is most worthy of granting protection.

فَمَن شَآءَ ذَكَرَهُۥ ﴿٥٥﴾ وَمَا يَذْكُرُونَ إِلَّآ أَن يَشَآءَ اللَّهُ ۚ هُوَ أَهْلُ التَّقْوَىٰ وَأَهْلُ الْمَغْفِرَةِ ﴿٥٦﴾

CHAPTER
75

AL-QIYÂMAH
(The Resurrection)
(Revealed before Hijrah)

سُورَةُ الْقِيَـٰمَةِ مَكِّيَّةٌ

With the name of Allâh,
the Most Gracious, the Ever Merciful
(I commence to read Sûrah Al-Qiyâmah).

بِسْمِ اللَّهِ الرَّحْمَـٰنِ الرَّحِيمِ

1. **N**AY, (it is not like what you imagine,) I swear by the Day of Resurrection;
2. And I swear by the self-reproaching soul (at the doing of an evil deed as an evidence to the truth of Final Resurrection).
3. Does a human-being think that We will not assemble his bones? (We will indeed.)
4. No doubt, We have the power to reproduce him to a complete form even to the very tips of his fingers.
5. (His denial of Resurrection is because) a human being likes to continue in his evil ways in (the life) that is before him (without fearing the consequences of his deeds).
6. He asks (with contempt and doubt), 'When shall the Day of Resurrection come to be?'
7. (It shall be the day) when the sight (of a person) is confused (and he is confounded for being unable to find the right course).
8. And the moon will eclipse.
9. And the sun and the moon will be brought

لَآ أُقْسِمُ بِيَوْمِ الْقِيَـٰمَةِ ﴿١﴾ وَلَآ أُقْسِمُ بِالنَّفْسِ اللَّوَّامَةِ ﴿٢﴾ أَيَحْسَبُ الْإِنسَـٰنُ أَلَّن نَّجْمَعَ عِظَامَهُۥ ﴿٣﴾ بَلَىٰ قَـٰدِرِينَ عَلَىٰٓ أَن نُّسَوِّيَ بَنَانَهُۥ ﴿٤﴾ بَلْ يُرِيدُ الْإِنسَـٰنُ لِيَفْجُرَ أَمَامَهُۥ ﴿٥﴾ يَسْـَٔلُ أَيَّانَ يَوْمُ الْقِيَـٰمَةِ ﴿٦﴾ فَإِذَا بَرِقَ الْبَصَرُ ﴿٧﴾ وَخَسَفَ الْقَمَرُ ﴿٨﴾ وَجُمِعَ الشَّمْسُ وَالْقَمَرُ ﴿٩﴾

together.
10. The human being shall say on that day, 'Whither to flee?'
11. To nowhere at all, there is no refuge.
12. Upon that day the recourse shall be to your Lord.
13. Upon that day every soul shall be informed about all his commissions and omissions.
14. Rather a human being is himself well-aware of his own self (and so himself is a witness against his own soul).
15. (No excuse will be accepted from him) even though he puts forth his (all possible) excuses, (to prove his innocence).
16. (Prophet! When We reveal the Qur'ân) do not move your tongue (with a mind) to repeat (this revelation in order to commit it to your memory) hurriedly.
17. The responsibility of its collection and its arrangement lies on Us.
18. When We recite it, then follow its recitation.
19. The responsibility of explaining it lies again on Us.
20. Behold! You people love the present transient (life),
21. And neglect the Hereafter.
22. On that day some faces will be fresh, beaming and bright,
23. Looking (absorbed in the vision of) their Lord;
24. And also on that day some faces will look gloomy and dismal,
25. Because they will realise that a backbreaking calamity is about to befall them.
26. Behold! When it (- the soul of a dying person) reaches the throat (to leave his body in death)
27. And (when those around the dying person say), 'Who is the physician to cure and save him?'
28. And he himself realizes that it is the (time

سُورَةُ الْقِيٰمَةِ ٧٥

يَقُولُ الْإِنْسٰنُ يَوْمَئِذٍ أَيْنَ الْمَفَرُّ ۝١٠ كَلَّا
لَا وَزَرَ ۝١١ إِلٰى رَبِّكَ يَوْمَئِذٍ الْمُسْتَقَرُّ ۝١٢ يُنَبَّؤُا
الْإِنْسٰنُ يَوْمَئِذٍ بِمَا قَدَّمَ وَ أَخَّرَ ۝١٣ بَلِ
الْإِنْسٰنُ عَلٰى نَفْسِهِ بَصِيرَةٌ ۝١٤ وَلَوْ أَلْقٰى
مَعَاذِيرَهُ ۝١٥ لَا تُحَرِّكْ بِهِ لِسَانَكَ لِتَعْجَلَ
بِهِ ۝١٦ إِنَّ عَلَيْنَا جَمْعَهُ وَ قُرْاٰنَهُ ۝١٧ فَإِذَا
قَرَأْنٰهُ فَاتَّبِعْ قُرْاٰنَهُ ۝١٨ ثُمَّ إِنَّ عَلَيْنَا بَيَانَهُ ۝١٩
كَلَّا بَلْ تُحِبُّونَ الْعَاجِلَةَ ۝٢٠ وَتَذَرُونَ
الْاٰخِرَةَ ۝٢١ وُجُوهٌ يَوْمَئِذٍ نَاضِرَةٌ ۝٢٢ إِلٰى رَبِّهَا
نَاظِرَةٌ ۝٢٣ وَوُجُوهٌ يَوْمَئِذٍ بَاسِرَةٌ ۝٢٤ تَظُنُّ
أَنْ يُفْعَلَ بِهَا فَاقِرَةٌ ۝٢٥ كَلَّا إِذَا بَلَغَتِ
التَّرَاقِيَ ۝٢٦ وَقِيلَ مَنْ رَاقٍ ۝٢٧ وَظَنَّ أَنَّهُ

of) parting.
29. And one shank rubs against the other (in death agony) and one distress will be combined with another distress (for the departing soul).
30. On that day people will be driven towards your Lord (to reap the fruit of the deeds done in this life).

SECTION 2

31. **For** this person (being unmindful of the consequences) neither accepted the truth nor offered Prayer.
32. Rather he cried lies (to the truth and the Prophet) and turned away (refusing to obey His commandments).
33. Then he went to his kinfolk strutting along (in false pride).
34. Woe be to you! Then woe upon woe (in this very life).
35. Again (in the Hereafter) woe be to you, then woe upon woe!
36. Does a person think that he will be left alone without purpose.
37. Was he not a small drop of semen ejected (into a proper place).
38. (Which drop) then became a clot of blood, then He fashioned (him through various stages) and perfected (him in his make).
39. Then He made of him a pair, the male and the female.
40. Has not such a One (Who creates from an inanimate source) the power of raising the (physically and spiritually) dead to life.

الۡفِرَاقُ ﴿٢٨﴾ وَالۡتَفَّتِ السَّاقُ بِالسَّاقِ ﴿٢٩﴾ إِلَىٰ
رَبِّكَ يَوۡمَئِذٍ الۡمَسَاقُ ﴿٣٠﴾ فَلَا صَدَّقَ وَلَا
صَلَّىٰ ﴿٣١﴾ وَلَٰكِنۡ كَذَّبَ وَتَوَلَّىٰ ﴿٣٢﴾ ثُمَّ ذَهَبَ
إِلَىٰ أَهۡلِهِۦ يَتَمَطَّىٰ ﴿٣٣﴾ أَوۡلَىٰ لَكَ فَأَوۡلَىٰ ﴿٣٤﴾ ثُمَّ
أَوۡلَىٰ لَكَ فَأَوۡلَىٰ ﴿٣٥﴾ أَيَحۡسَبُ الۡإِنسَٰنُ أَن يُتۡرَكَ
سُدًى ﴿٣٦﴾ أَلَمۡ يَكُ نُطۡفَةً مِّن مَّنِيٍّ يُمۡنَىٰ ﴿٣٧﴾
ثُمَّ كَانَ عَلَقَةً فَخَلَقَ فَسَوَّىٰ ﴿٣٨﴾ فَجَعَلَ مِنۡهُ
الزَّوۡجَيۡنِ الذَّكَرَ وَالۡأُنثَىٰ ﴿٣٩﴾ أَلَيۡسَ ذَٰلِكَ
بِقَٰدِرٍ عَلَىٰ أَن يُحۡـِۧيَ الۡمَوۡتَىٰ ﴿٤٠﴾

ع ١٧
ع ١٨

CHAPTER
76

AL-INSÂN
(The Human Being)
(Revealed after Hijrah)

With the name of Allâh,
the Most Gracious, the Ever Merciful
(I commence to read Sûrah Al-Insân).

1. THERE did pass over a human being a period comprising of a long space of time when he was not a thing worth mentioning.
2. We have surely created a human being from a sperm drop uniting (it) with (an ovum); We wanted to bestow Our favour on him. That is why We made him hearing and seeing (- enjoying discretion and volition, and so responsible for his actions).
3. Verily, We have shown him the path clearly (giving him the full choice) whether he be grateful or ungrateful.
4. We have indeed prepared for the ungrateful chains and shackles and the blazing Fire.
5. The virtuous shall truly drink of a cup tempered with camphor (a symbol of purity and coolness).
6. (The drink is from) a spring from which the devotees of Allâh shall drink. They will strive hard in directing it to flow in abundance (enabling others to drink from it).
7. They fulfill (their) vows (by doing their duty to God and people) and fear a day the woes of which shall be widespread.
8. They give food for the love of Him to the indigent, the orphan and the captive.
9. (Assuring them by their gestures,) 'We feed you only to seek the pleasure of Allâh, we desire no recompense from you nor thanks.
10. 'We surely fear from our Lord (the punish-

سُوْرَةُ الْإِنْسَانِ مَدَنِيَّةٌ

بِسْمِ اللّٰهِ الرَّحْمٰنِ الرَّحِيْمِ

هَلْ أَتٰى عَلَى الْإِنْسٰنِ حِيْنٌ مِّنَ الدَّهْرِ
لَمْ يَكُنْ شَيْـًٔا مَّذْكُوْرًا ١ إِنَّا خَلَقْنَا
الْإِنْسٰنَ مِنْ نُّطْفَةٍ أَمْشَاجٍ ۖ نَّبْتَلِيْهِ فَجَعَلْنٰهُ
سَمِيْعًا بَصِيْرًا ٢ إِنَّا هَدَيْنٰهُ السَّبِيْلَ إِمَّا
شَاكِرًا وَّ إِمَّا كَفُوْرًا ٣ إِنَّا أَعْتَدْنَا لِلْكٰفِرِيْنَ
سَلٰسِلَا۟ وَ أَغْلٰلًا وَّ سَعِيْرًا ٤ إِنَّ الْأَبْرَارَ
يَشْرَبُوْنَ مِنْ كَأْسٍ كَانَ مِزَاجُهَا كَافُوْرًا ٥
عَيْنًا يَّشْرَبُ بِهَا عِبَادُ اللّٰهِ يُفَجِّرُوْنَهَا
تَفْجِيْرًا ٦ يُوْفُوْنَ بِالنَّذْرِ وَ يَخَافُوْنَ يَوْمًا
كَانَ شَرُّهٗ مُسْتَطِيْرًا ٧ وَ يُطْعِمُوْنَ الطَّعَامَ
عَلٰى حُبِّهٖ مِسْكِيْنًا وَّ يَتِيْمًا وَّ أَسِيْرًا ٨ إِنَّمَا
نُطْعِمُكُمْ لِوَجْهِ اللّٰهِ لَا نُرِيْدُ مِنْكُمْ جَزَآءً
وَّ لَا شُكُوْرًا ٩ إِنَّا نَخَافُ مِنْ رَّبِّنَا يَوْمًا

ment of) a day (on which the wrong doers will be) frowning and distressful.'

11. So Allâh will guard them from the evil of that day and will bestow on them cheerfulness (of face) and happiness (of mind).

12. And will reward them for their having persevered, with (a blissful) Garden (to live in) and silk (to wear).

13. (They shall be) reclining on raised couches. They shall experience therein neither excessive heat of the sun nor intense cold.

14. There shall be spreading close over them the shades of it (- the Garden full of trees), and their clustered fruit brought low within their easy reach.

15. They shall be served round in vessels of silver and goblets of glass,

16. (Looking) crystal clear (but made) of silver, made in special mould determined (by the agents of the Lord of judgment and measure).

17. And therein they shall be given to drink a cup which is tempered with ginger (a symbol of strength),

18. (Which flows from) a spring therein called *Salsabîl* (- inquire about the way).

19. Sons of perpetual bloom shall go round (waiting upon) them. When you see them you will take them to be pearls scattered about.

20. When you look (considering the Garden as a whole) you will find therein blessings abounding everywhere and (all the equipments of) a splendid kingdom.

21. Over them shall be robes of fine green silk and of thick brocade, and they shall be given bracelets of silver as ornaments. And their Lord shall give them to drink a purifying beverage.

22. (It will be said,) 'This is indeed a reward for you, and your striving has been fully appreciated.'

SECTION 2

23. **S**URELY, it is We Who have revealed to you

سُورَةُ الْإِنسَانِ ٧٦

عَبُوسًا قَمْطَرِيرًا ﴿١٠﴾ فَوَقَاهُمُ اللَّهُ شَرَّ ذَٰلِكَ
الْيَوْمِ وَلَقَّاهُمْ نَضْرَةً وَسُرُورًا ﴿١١﴾ وَجَزَاهُم
بِمَا صَبَرُوا جَنَّةً وَحَرِيرًا ﴿١٢﴾ مُتَّكِئِينَ فِيهَا
عَلَى الْأَرَائِكِ لَا يَرَوْنَ فِيهَا شَمْسًا وَلَا
زَمْهَرِيرًا ﴿١٣﴾ وَدَانِيَةً عَلَيْهِمْ ظِلَالُهَا
وَذُلِّلَتْ قُطُوفُهَا تَذْلِيلًا ﴿١٤﴾ وَيُطَافُ عَلَيْهِم
بِآنِيَةٍ مِّن فِضَّةٍ وَأَكْوَابٍ كَانَتْ قَوَارِيرَا ﴿١٥﴾
قَوَارِيرَا مِن فِضَّةٍ قَدَّرُوهَا تَقْدِيرًا ﴿١٦﴾
وَيُسْقَوْنَ فِيهَا كَأْسًا كَانَ مِزَاجُهَا
زَنجَبِيلًا ﴿١٧﴾ عَيْنًا فِيهَا تُسَمَّىٰ سَلْسَبِيلًا ﴿١٨﴾
وَيَطُوفُ عَلَيْهِمْ وِلْدَانٌ مُّخَلَّدُونَ إِذَا
رَأَيْتَهُمْ حَسِبْتَهُمْ لُؤْلُؤًا مَّنثُورًا ﴿١٩﴾ وَإِذَا
رَأَيْتَ ثَمَّ رَأَيْتَ نَعِيمًا وَمُلْكًا كَبِيرًا ﴿٢٠﴾
عَالِيَهُمْ ثِيَابُ سُندُسٍ خُضْرٌ وَإِسْتَبْرَقٌ
وَحُلُّوا أَسَاوِرَ مِن فِضَّةٍ وَسَقَاهُمْ رَبُّهُمْ
شَرَابًا طَهُورًا ﴿٢١﴾ إِنَّ هَٰذَا كَانَ لَكُمْ جَزَاءً
وَكَانَ سَعْيُكُم مَّشْكُورًا ﴿٢٢﴾ إِنَّا نَحْنُ ع ٢٢ ١٩
نَزَّلْنَا عَلَيْكَ الْقُرْآنَ تَنزِيلًا ﴿٢٣﴾ فَاصْبِرْ لِحُكْمِ

the Qur'ân by a gradual and piecemeal revelation.
24. Therefore abide perseveringly by the commandments of your Lord (and wait for the fulfillment of the prophecies) and yield to none of the sinful and ungrateful (disbelievers).
25. Extol the name of your Lord morning and evening,
26. And prostrate yourselves before Him for a part of the night and give Him glory for long hours of the night
27. Verily, these (disbelieving people) love the present transient life and neglect very hard day (which lies) ahead of them.
28 It is We Who have created them and strengthened their make, and We shall replace them with their like whenever We please.
29. Verily, this Qur'ân is a Reminder. So let him who wishes, take a way to his Lord.
30. And you (true believers) should wish no other way except as Allâh wishes (for you). Verily, Allâh is All-Knowing, All-Wise.
31. He admits to His mercy those who wish (and strive) for it. As to the wrongdoers, He has prepared a woeful punishment for them.

رَبِّكَ وَلَا تُطِعْ مِنْهُمْ اٰثِمًا اَوْ كَفُوْرًا ﴿٢٤﴾ وَاذْكُرِ اسْمَ رَبِّكَ بُكْرَةً وَّاَصِيْلًا ﴿٢٥﴾ وَمِنَ الَّيْلِ فَاسْجُدْ لَهٗ وَسَبِّحْهُ لَيْلًا طَوِيْلًا ﴿٢٦﴾ اِنَّ هٰٓؤُلَآءِ يُحِبُّوْنَ الْعَاجِلَةَ وَيَذَرُوْنَ وَرَآءَهُمْ يَوْمًا ثَقِيْلًا ﴿٢٧﴾ نَحْنُ خَلَقْنٰهُمْ وَشَدَدْنَآ اَسْرَهُمْ ۚ وَاِذَا شِئْنَا بَدَّلْنَآ اَمْثَالَهُمْ تَبْدِيْلًا ﴿٢٨﴾ اِنَّ هٰذِهٖ تَذْكِرَةٌ ۚ فَمَنْ شَآءَ اتَّخَذَ اِلٰى رَبِّهٖ سَبِيْلًا ﴿٢٩﴾ وَمَا تَشَآءُوْنَ اِلَّآ اَنْ يَّشَآءَ اللّٰهُ ؕ اِنَّ اللّٰهَ كَانَ عَلِيْمًا حَكِيْمًا ﴿٣٠﴾ يُّدْخِلُ مَنْ يَّشَآءُ فِيْ رَحْمَتِهٖ ؕ وَالظّٰلِمِيْنَ اَعَدَّ لَهُمْ عَذَابًا اَلِيْمًا ﴿٣١﴾

CHAPTER
77

سُوْرَةُ الْمُرْسَلٰتِ مَكِّيَّةٌ

AL-MURSALÂT
(Those Sent Forth)
(Revealed before Hijrah)

With the name of Allâh,
the Most Gracious, the Ever Merciful
(I commence to read Sûrah Al-Mursalât).

بِسْمِ اللّٰهِ الرَّحْمٰنِ الرَّحِيْمِ

1. **I** CALL to witness those (messengers of Truth) who are sent forth to spread goodness (in continual series),
2. Those that drive off forcefully (falsehood

وَالْمُرْسَلٰتِ عُرْفًا ﴿١﴾ فَالْعٰصِفٰتِ عَصْفًا ﴿٢﴾

and forces of evil as chaff is carried before the wind),
3. And those that spread (the truth) far and wide,
4. And those that fully distinguish (the right from the wrong),
5. And those carrying the Message of (rising to) eminence far and wide (- the Qur'ân),
6. (And those presenting this source of eminence) in an attempt to purify (some) from the abomination of sin and to warn (others),
7. Verily, that which you are promised must come to pass.
8. So when the small stars will be made to lose their light,
9. And when the heaven shall be opened,
10. And when the mountains shall be blown down to pieces,
11. And when the Messengers shall be made to appear (in the guise of one person) at the appointed time. (It is after that the Resurrection shall take place).
12. To what day have these (portents) been deferred;
13. To the Day of Judgment.
14. How shall you know what the Day of Judgment is?
15. On that day woe shall befall those who belie (the truth).
16. Did We not destroy the earlier peoples?
17. We will now cause the later generations to follow suit.
18. That is how We deal with the guilty.
19. On that day woe shall befall those who belie (the truth).
20. Did We not create you from an insignificant fluid,
21. Then We placed it in a secure and safe place,
22. Till an appointed term?
23. Thus did We determine, and how good We are at determining!
24. On that day woe shall befall those who belie (the truth).

وَّالنّٰشِرٰتِ نَشْرًا ﴿٣﴾ فَالْفٰرِقٰتِ فَرْقًا ﴿٤﴾
فَالْمُلْقِيٰتِ ذِكْرًا ﴿٥﴾ عُذْرًا اَوْ نُذْرًا ﴿٦﴾
اِنَّمَا تُوْعَدُوْنَ لَوَاقِعٌ ﴿٧﴾ فَاِذَا النُّجُوْمُ طُمِسَتْ ﴿٨﴾
وَ اِذَا السَّمَآءُ فُرِجَتْ ﴿٩﴾ وَ اِذَا الْجِبَالُ نُسِفَتْ ﴿١٠﴾
وَ اِذَا الرُّسُلُ اُقِّتَتْ ﴿١١﴾ لِاَيِّ يَوْمٍ اُجِّلَتْ ﴿١٢﴾
لِيَوْمِ الْفَصْلِ ﴿١٣﴾ وَ مَآ اَدْرٰىكَ مَا يَوْمُ الْفَصْلِ ﴿١٤﴾
وَيْلٌ يَّوْمَئِذٍ لِّلْمُكَذِّبِيْنَ ﴿١٥﴾ اَلَمْ نُهْلِكِ
الْاَوَّلِيْنَ ﴿١٦﴾ ثُمَّ نُتْبِعُهُمُ الْاٰخِرِيْنَ ﴿١٧﴾ كَذٰلِكَ
نَفْعَلُ بِالْمُجْرِمِيْنَ ﴿١٨﴾ وَيْلٌ يَّوْمَئِذٍ
لِّلْمُكَذِّبِيْنَ ﴿١٩﴾ اَلَمْ نَخْلُقْكُّمْ مِّنْ مَّآءٍ
مَّهِيْنٍ ﴿٢٠﴾ فَجَعَلْنٰهُ فِيْ قَرَارٍ مَّكِيْنٍ ﴿٢١﴾ اِلٰى
قَدَرٍ مَّعْلُوْمٍ ﴿٢٢﴾ فَقَدَرْنَا فَنِعْمَ الْقٰدِرُوْنَ ﴿٢٣﴾
وَيْلٌ يَّوْمَئِذٍ لِّلْمُكَذِّبِيْنَ ﴿٢٤﴾ اَلَمْ نَجْعَلِ

25. Have We not made the earth revolving and capable of drawing (other bodies) towards itself,
26. The living and the dead?
27. And (have We not) made therein lofty mountains and (by means of them) We provide you sweet and wholesome water to drink?
28. On that day woe shall befall those who belie (the truth).
29. (It will be said to the followers of Trinity,) 'Now, move on towards that (punishment) which you cried lies to,
30. 'Move on to the shadow that has three branches,
31. '(Which is) neither affording shade (to you) nor protects (you) from the flame.'
32. Rather it throws huge sparks as huge and high as towers,
33. (Sparks) that look like tawny camels.
34. On that day woe shall befall those who belie (the truth).
35. This is a day when they shall not be able to speak,
36. Nor shall they be allowed to offer excuses.
37. On that day woe shall befall those who belie (the truth).
38. (God will tell them,) 'This is the Day of Judgment (when) We have gathered you and all the earlier peoples together;
39. 'If you have any device try it against Me (to escape this punishment).'
40. On that day woe shall befall those who belie (the truth)

SECTION 2

41. (**A**s for) those who guarded against evil and were dutiful (to God and people) they shall, indeed, on that day live in the midst of comforts and (in places with) springs,
42. And fruits, such as they desire.
43. (It will be said to them,) 'Eat and drink delightfully as a reward for that which you used to do (in your lifetime).'

الْأَرْضَ كِفَاتًا ﴿٢٥﴾ أَحْيَاءً وَ أَمْوَاتًا ﴿٢٦﴾ وَ جَعَلْنَا
فِيهَا رَوَاسِيَ شٰمِخٰتٍ وَ أَسْقَيْنٰكُمْ مَّاءً
فُرَاتًا ﴿٢٧﴾ وَيْلٌ يَّوْمَئِذٍ لِّلْمُكَذِّبِينَ ﴿٢٨﴾
إِنْطَلِقُوْا إِلٰى مَا كُنْتُمْ بِهٖ تُكَذِّبُوْنَ ﴿٢٩﴾
إِنْطَلِقُوْا إِلٰى ظِلٍّ ذِي ثَلٰثِ شُعَبٍ ﴿٣٠﴾ لَا
ظَلِيلٍ وَّ لَا يُغْنِي مِنَ اللَّهَبِ ﴿٣١﴾ إِنَّهَا تَرْمِي
بِشَرَرٍ كَالْقَصْرِ ﴿٣٢﴾ كَأَنَّهٗ جِمٰلَتٌ صُفْرٌ ﴿٣٣﴾
وَيْلٌ يَّوْمَئِذٍ لِّلْمُكَذِّبِينَ ﴿٣٤﴾ هٰذَا يَوْمُ لَا
يَنْطِقُوْنَ ﴿٣٥﴾ وَ لَا يُؤْذَنُ لَهُمْ فَيَعْتَذِرُوْنَ ﴿٣٦﴾
وَيْلٌ يَّوْمَئِذٍ لِّلْمُكَذِّبِينَ ﴿٣٧﴾ هٰذَا يَوْمُ
الْفَصْلِ جَمَعْنٰكُمْ وَ الْأَوَّلِينَ ﴿٣٨﴾ فَإِنْ كَانَ
لَكُمْ كَيْدٌ فَكِيدُوْنِ ﴿٣٩﴾ وَيْلٌ يَّوْمَئِذٍ
لِّلْمُكَذِّبِينَ ﴿٤٠﴾ إِنَّ الْمُتَّقِينَ فِي ظِلٰلٍ ع ٢١
وَّ عُيُوْنٍ ﴿٤١﴾ وَّ فَوَاكِهَ مِمَّا يَشْتَهُوْنَ ﴿٤٢﴾ كُلُوْا
وَ اشْرَبُوْا هَنِيْٓـًٔا بِمَا كُنْتُمْ تَعْمَلُوْنَ ﴿٤٣﴾

44. Truly that is how We reward the doers of good.
45. On that day woe shall befall those who belie (the Truth).
46. (Disbelievers!) Eat and enjoy yourselves for a little while (in the world). Surely, you are the guilty (ones).
47. On that day woe shall befall those who belie (the Truth).
48. When it is said to them, 'Bow down (before your Lord)!' they bow not down.
49. On that day woe shall befall those who belie (the Truth).
50. Look! In what other revelation will they believe after this (when they have refused to accept such an infallible Book as this Qur'ân).

إِنَّا كَذَٰلِكَ نَجْزِي الْمُحْسِنِينَ ﴿٤٤﴾ وَيْلٌ يَوْمَئِذٍ لِّلْمُكَذِّبِينَ ﴿٤٥﴾ كُلُوا وَتَمَتَّعُوا قَلِيلًا إِنَّكُم مُّجْرِمُونَ ﴿٤٦﴾ وَيْلٌ يَوْمَئِذٍ لِّلْمُكَذِّبِينَ ﴿٤٧﴾ وَإِذَا قِيلَ لَهُمُ ارْكَعُوا لَا يَرْكَعُونَ ﴿٤٨﴾ وَيْلٌ يَوْمَئِذٍ لِّلْمُكَذِّبِينَ ﴿٤٩﴾ فَبِأَيِّ حَدِيثٍ بَعْدَهُ يُؤْمِنُونَ ﴿٥٠﴾

CHAPTER
78

AL-NABA'

(The Important Announcement)
(Revealed before Hijrah)

سُوْرَةُ النَّبَإِ مَكِّيَّةٌ

With the name of Allâh,
the Most Gracious, the Ever Merciful
(I commence to read Sûrah Al-Naba').

بِسْمِ اللَّهِ الرَّحْمَٰنِ الرَّحِيمِ

PART الجُزْءُ الثَّلَاثُونَ XXX

1. **W**HAT is that these (disbelievers) are asking one another about?
2. (Is it) about the greatly important and very useful announcement leading to knowledge;
3. About which they differ (from the Muslims and among themselves)?
4. It is not as they assume. They shall surely know (the truth thereof).

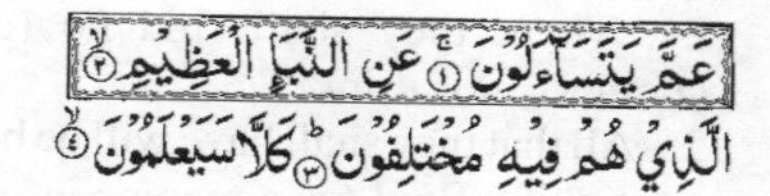
عَمَّ يَتَسَاءَلُونَ ﴿١﴾ عَنِ النَّبَإِ الْعَظِيمِ ﴿٢﴾
الَّذِي هُمْ فِيهِ مُخْتَلِفُونَ ﴿٣﴾ كَلَّا سَيَعْلَمُونَ ﴿٤﴾

5. (We say it) again, the real thing is not as they believe. They shall surely come to know (the truth thereof).
6. Have We not made the earth as a bed,
7. And the mountains as (a series of) pegs?
8. And We have created you in pairs (males and females);
9. And We have made your sleep a source of rest.
10. And We have made the night as a covering,
11. And We have made the day for (following) the (various) pursuits of life.
12. And We have built above you seven strong (heavenly bodies of the solar system),
13. And We have made (therein) the sun providing immense light and heat from a long distance,
14. And We pour down from the dripping clouds water in torrent,
15. That We may bring forth therewith (all kinds of) grain and vegetation,
16. And (grow with it) gardens thick and luxuriant.
17. Surely, the Day of Judgment is an appointed time.
18. The day when the trumpet will be blown, and you will come in large troops.
19. And the heaven shall be flung open and it shall become (all) doors.
20. And the mountains shall be wiped out and shall become (as if reduced to) plains of sand.
21. Surely, only Gehenna shall be in wait (for those who deny the truth).
22. A (nursing) home for the rebellious.
23. There they shall be staying for ages (till all their maladies are completely treated).
24. There they shall find no (comfort of) coolness, nor drink.
25. All that they shall have will be boiling water or stinking fluid (as a recompense),
26. A befitting recompense (for the evils done by them).
27. They did not fear any reckoning at all;
28. And they had belied Our Messages outright.
29. And everything (of their deeds) We have

ثُمَّ كَلَّا سَيَعْلَمُونَ ٥ أَلَمْ نَجْعَلِ الْأَرْضَ
مِهَادًا ٦ وَالْجِبَالَ أَوْتَادًا ٧ وَخَلَقْنَاكُمْ
أَزْوَاجًا ٨ وَجَعَلْنَا نَوْمَكُمْ سُبَاتًا ٩ وَجَعَلْنَا
اللَّيْلَ لِبَاسًا ١٠ وَجَعَلْنَا النَّهَارَ مَعَاشًا ١١
وَبَنَيْنَا فَوْقَكُمْ سَبْعًا شِدَادًا ١٢ وَجَعَلْنَا
سِرَاجًا وَهَّاجًا ١٣ وَأَنْزَلْنَا مِنَ الْمُعْصِرَاتِ
مَاءً ثَجَّاجًا ١٤ لِنُخْرِجَ بِهِ حَبًّا وَنَبَاتًا ١٥
وَجَنَّاتٍ أَلْفَافًا ١٦ إِنَّ يَوْمَ الْفَصْلِ كَانَ
مِيقَاتًا ١٧ يَوْمَ يُنْفَخُ فِي الصُّورِ فَتَأْتُونَ
أَفْوَاجًا ١٨ وَفُتِحَتِ السَّمَاءُ فَكَانَتْ أَبْوَابًا ١٩
وَسُيِّرَتِ الْجِبَالُ فَكَانَتْ سَرَابًا ٢٠ إِنَّ
جَهَنَّمَ كَانَتْ مِرْصَادًا ٢١ لِلطَّاغِينَ مَآبًا ٢٢
لَابِثِينَ فِيهَا أَحْقَابًا ٢٣ لَا يَذُوقُونَ فِيهَا
بَرْدًا وَلَا شَرَابًا ٢٤ إِلَّا حَمِيمًا وَغَسَّاقًا ٢٥
جَزَاءً وِفَاقًا ٢٦ إِنَّهُمْ كَانُوا لَا يَرْجُونَ حِسَابًا ٢٧
وَكَذَّبُوا بِآيَاتِنَا كِذَّابًا ٢٨ وَكُلَّ شَيْءٍ

fully recorded in a book (of deeds).
30. (It shall be said to them when they are about to be punished,) 'Suffer therefore (the consequences of your evil deeds), We will do no more than increase your torment.

SECTION 2

31. **A**s for those who guarded against evil there awaits them a triumph,
32. Orchards and vineyards;
33. And (blooming) young maidens suiting their age, and also matching in all other respects,
34. And overflowing cups of pure and clean drink.
35. Therein they will hear no vain discourse, no (topics based on) falsehood.
36. (It will be said to each, 'All this is) bestowed (on you) by your Lord, (both) by way of gift, (and) by reckoning.'
37. The Lord of the heavens and the earth and of all that lies between them, the Most Gracious (God), Whom they dare not address.
38. (All this will be) on the Day (of Resurrection) when the Perfect Spirit and the angels will stand in rows, none shall speak except he (- Muhammad) to whom the Most Gracious (God) will grant permission and who will speak (only) what is right.
39. That day is bound to come, so let him, who will, seek recourse to his Lord.
40. Verily, We have warned you of a punishment which is close at hand, a day when a person shall see what (good or evil deeds) he has sent on before (for the next life), and the disbeliever will say, 'Would that I were mere dust.'

سُوْرَةُ النَّبَاِ ٧٨

أَحْصَيْنٰهُ كِتٰبًا ﴿٢٩﴾ فَذُوقُوا فَلَنْ نَّزِيدَكُمْ
إِلَّا عَذَابًا ﴿٣٠﴾ إِنَّ لِلْمُتَّقِينَ مَفَازًا ﴿٣١﴾ حَدَآئِقَ
وَأَعْنٰبًا ﴿٣٢﴾ وَكَوَاعِبَ أَتْرَابًا ﴿٣٣﴾ وَكَأْسًا
دِهَاقًا ﴿٣٤﴾ لَا يَسْمَعُونَ فِيهَا لَغْوًا وَلَا كِذّٰبًا ﴿٣٥﴾
جَزَآءً مِّنْ رَّبِّكَ عَطَآءً حِسَابًا ﴿٣٦﴾ رَّبِّ
السَّمٰوٰتِ وَالْأَرْضِ وَمَا بَيْنَهُمَا الرَّحْمٰنِ
لَا يَمْلِكُونَ مِنْهُ خِطَابًا ﴿٣٧﴾ يَوْمَ يَقُومُ الرُّوحُ
وَالْمَلٰٓئِكَةُ صَفًّا لَّا يَتَكَلَّمُونَ إِلَّا مَنْ
أَذِنَ لَهُ الرَّحْمٰنُ وَقَالَ صَوَابًا ﴿٣٨﴾ ذٰلِكَ
الْيَوْمُ الْحَقُّ فَمَنْ شَآءَ اتَّخَذَ إِلٰى رَبِّهِ
مَاٰبًا ﴿٣٩﴾ إِنَّآ أَنْذَرْنٰكُمْ عَذَابًا قَرِيبًا يَوْمَ
يَنْظُرُ الْمَرْءُ مَا قَدَّمَتْ يَدَاهُ وَيَقُولُ
الْكَافِرُ يٰلَيْتَنِي كُنْتُ تُرٰبًا ﴿٤٠﴾

CHAPTER
79

سُورَةُ النَّازِعَاتِ ٧٩

AL-NÂZI'ÂT
(Those Who Perform Their Duties Vigorously)
(Revealed before Hijrah)

سُورَةُ النّٰزِعٰتِ مَكِّيَّةٌ

With the name of Allâh,
the Most Gracious, the Ever Merciful
(I commence to read Sûrah Al-Nâzi'ât).

بِسْمِ اللهِ الرَّحْمٰنِ الرَّحِيمِ

1. I CALL to witness those groups of beings, who perform their duties (towards their Lord and people and themselves) with intense zeal and to the best of their capacity,
2. And those who exert themselves vigorously,
3. And those who steer their course swiftly and skillfully,
4. Then those who going foremost greatly excel (all others and attain the topmost positions),
5. Then those who administer the affairs in an excellent manner (shall reap the fruit of their striving).
6. (It shall be) on the day when the quacking (earth) shall quake;
7. Quakes after quakes shall follow this.
8. On that day many hearts will be trembling with fear,
9. Their eyes will be downcast (in disgrace).
10. (These are the people) who say, 'Shall we (really) be restored to (our) former state (after we are dead)?
11. 'Shall it be (even) when we are (reduced to) hollow bones?'
12. (And) who say, 'Then such a resurrection shall indeed be fraught with loss.'
13. (Let them say what they think,) It will be no more than a single scary blast.
14. And behold! (After that) they will all be

وَالنّٰزِعٰتِ غَرْقًا ﴿١﴾ وَّالنّٰشِطٰتِ نَشْطًا ﴿٢﴾
وَّالسّٰبِحٰتِ سَبْحًا ﴿٣﴾ فَالسّٰبِقٰتِ سَبْقًا ﴿٤﴾
فَالْمُدَبِّرٰتِ أَمْرًا ﴿٥﴾ يَوْمَ تَرْجُفُ الرَّاجِفَةُ ﴿٦﴾
تَتْبَعُهَا الرَّادِفَةُ ﴿٧﴾ قُلُوبٌ يَّوْمَئِذٍ وَّاجِفَةٌ ﴿٨﴾
أَبْصٰرُهَا خٰشِعَةٌ ﴿٩﴾ يَقُولُونَ ءَإِنَّا لَمَرْدُودُونَ
فِي الْحَافِرَةِ ﴿١٠﴾ ءَإِذَا كُنَّا عِظٰمًا نَّخِرَةً ﴿١١﴾
قَالُوا تِلْكَ إِذًا كَرَّةٌ خَاسِرَةٌ ﴿١٢﴾ فَإِنَّمَا هِيَ
زَجْرَةٌ وّٰحِدَةٌ ﴿١٣﴾ فَإِذَا هُمْ بِالسَّاهِرَةِ ﴿١٤﴾ هَلْ

(awakened and come out) in the open.
15. The story of Moses has reached you.
16. When his Lord called out to him in the Sacred Valley of Tuwâ,
17. (And directed him,) 'Go to Pharaoh, he has transgressed all limits.
18. 'And say (to him), "Would you like to purify yourself;
19. "That I should guide you to your Lord so that you may stand in awe of Him?"'
20. So (Moses went to Pharaoh and) he showed him the great sign (of the staff).
21. But he belied (Moses) and disobeyed,
22. Then he turned back striving (and devising schemes against him).
23. And he gathered (his people) and proclaimed,
24. Saying, 'I (- Pharaoh) am your supreme lord.'
25. So Allâh seized him for the punishment of (both) the next and the present life.
26. Indeed, there is a lesson in this (event) for him who stands in awe (of his Lord).

SECTION 2

27. (**O** PEOPLE!) Are you harder to be created (again) or the heaven? He (the Almighty Lord) has made it.
28. He has raised the height thereof, and has made it flawlessly perfect and well-balanced.
29. And He gave darkness to its night, and brought forth the morn thereof.
30. And along with it He hurled the earth away (from a bigger mass) and spread it forth.
31. He produced from it its water and pasture.
32. He set the mountains firmly.
33. (He has done all this to serve as) a goodly provisions for you and your cattle.
34. Behold! When that great calamity comes to pass,
35. On that day every person will call to mind all that he strove for.

أَتٰكَ حَدِيثُ مُوسٰى (١٥) إِذْ نَادٰهُ رَبُّهُ
بِالْوَادِ الْمُقَدَّسِ طُوًى (١٦) إِذْهَبْ إِلٰى فِرْعَوْنَ
إِنَّهُ طَغٰى (١٧) فَقُلْ هَلْ لَّكَ إِلٰى أَنْ تَزَكّٰى (١٨)
وَ أَهْدِيَكَ إِلٰى رَبِّكَ فَتَخْشٰى (١٩) فَأَرٰىهُ الْأٰيَةَ
الْكُبْرٰى (٢٠) فَكَذَّبَ وَعَصٰى (٢١) ثُمَّ أَدْبَرَ يَسْعٰى (٢٢)
فَحَشَرَ فَنَادٰى (٢٣) فَقَالَ أَنَا رَبُّكُمُ الْأَعْلٰى (٢٤)
فَأَخَذَهُ اللّٰهُ نَكَالَ الْأٰخِرَةِ وَ الْأُولٰى (٢٥) إِنَّ
فِي ذٰلِكَ لَعِبْرَةً لِّمَنْ يَّخْشٰى (٢٦) ءَأَنْتُمْ أَشَدُّ
خَلْقًا أَمِ السَّمَاءُ بَنٰهَا (٢٧) رَفَعَ سَمْكَهَا
فَسَوّٰهَا (٢٨) وَ أَغْطَشَ لَيْلَهَا وَ أَخْرَجَ ضُحٰهَا (٢٩)
وَ الْأَرْضَ بَعْدَ ذٰلِكَ دَحٰهَا (٣٠) أَخْرَجَ مِنْهَا
مَاءَهَا وَ مَرْعٰهَا (٣١) وَ الْجِبَالَ أَرْسٰهَا (٣٢)
مَتٰعًا لَّكُمْ وَ لِأَنْعٰمِكُمْ (٣٣) فَإِذَا جَاءَتِ
الطَّامَّةُ الْكُبْرٰى (٣٤) يَوْمَ يَتَذَكَّرُ الْإِنْسٰنُ
مَا سَعٰى (٣٥) وَ بُرِّزَتِ الْجَحِيمُ لِمَنْ يَرٰى (٣٦)

36. And Hell shall be brought in view of him who sees.
37. Then as for the one who transgresses,
38. And prefers the present life (to the Hereafter),
39. (Let him remember that) the Hell shall surely be (his) abode.
40. But as for the one who fears to stand before his Lord and restrains himself from evil desires,
41. Then Garden (of bliss) shall surely be (his permanent) abode.
42. The people ask you concerning the Hour (saying), 'When shall it come to pass?'
43. Why (do they ask this question)? It is you who are its reminder (you being one of its signs).
44. The ultimate end of it is decreed by your Lord.
45. You are only a Warner to one who fears it.
46. The day they witness it (-the Hour, they will feel) as if they had stayed (in the world and the grave) for an afternoon or a (short) forenoon thereof.

فَأَمَّا مَنْ طَغٰى ﴿٣٧﴾ وَ ءَاثَرَ الْحَيٰوةَ الدُّنْيَا ﴿٣٨﴾ فَإِنَّ الْجَحِيمَ هِيَ الْمَأْوٰى ﴿٣٩﴾ وَ أَمَّا مَنْ خَافَ مَقَامَ رَبِّهِۦ وَ نَهَى النَّفْسَ عَنِ الْهَوٰى ﴿٤٠﴾ فَإِنَّ الْجَنَّةَ هِيَ الْمَأْوٰى ﴿٤١﴾ يَسْـَٔلُونَكَ عَنِ السَّاعَةِ أَيَّانَ مُرْسٰهَا ﴿٤٢﴾ فِيمَ أَنْتَ مِنْ ذِكْرٰىهَا ﴿٤٣﴾ إِلٰى رَبِّكَ مُنْتَهٰهَا ﴿٤٤﴾ إِنَّمَآ أَنْتَ مُنْذِرُ مَنْ يَخْشٰهَا ﴿٤٥﴾ كَأَنَّهُمْ يَوْمَ يَرَوْنَهَا لَمْ يَلْبَثُوٓا إِلَّا عَشِيَّةً أَوْ ضُحٰىهَا ﴿٤٦﴾

CHAPTER 80

سُورَةُ عَبَسَ مَكِّيَّةٌ

'ABASA
(He Frowned)
(Revealed before Hijrah)

With the name of Allâh,
the Most Gracious, the Ever Merciful
(I commence to read Sûrah 'Abasa).

بِسْمِ اللّٰهِ الرَّحْمٰنِ الرَّحِيمِ

1. **HE** (- the Prophet) frowned and turned aside,
2. Because the blind man (- *Ibn umme Maktûm*) came to him (interrupting him unknowingly).
3. And what could make you (O Prophet!)

عَبَسَ وَ تَوَلّٰىٓ ﴿١﴾ أَنْ جَآءَهُ الْأَعْمٰى ﴿٢﴾ وَمَا يُدْرِيكَ لَعَلَّهُۥ يَزَّكّٰىٓ ﴿٣﴾ أَوْ يَذَّكَّرُ فَتَنْفَعَهُ

know that he might purify himself.
4. Or that he might have paid heed to the admonition (that God has revealed to you) and this admonition would have done him good as well.
5. But as to him who considers himself self-sufficient and is indifferent (to the Truth);
6. To this one you were very attentive,
7. Though you are not to blame if he does not purify himself.
8. Whereas (the blind man) who came to you striving in right earnest (to learn the Qur'ân),
9. And all the while he stands in awe (of God);
10. But you neglect him and pay him no regard.
11. This should not have been so. Verily, this (Qur'ân) is a means to rise to eminence (for you all).
12. So let him who desires, pay heed to it and rise to eminence.
13. (This Qur'ân is preserved) in such written leaves (of the Book) as are greatly honoured,
14. (Which are) ranked high (and) are rid of all impurities,
15. Which are in the hands of scribes,
16. Noble and virtuous.
17. Ruin seize the person (- one too proud to accept the reminder)! How ungrateful he is!
18. (Let him consider) from what (an insignificant) material He has created him!
19. From a mere sperm-drop! He (at first) creates him, then endows him with infinite capacity (to make progress),
20. Then makes (his) passage (through all affairs of life) easy for him.
21. Then He calls him to death and He assigns to him (an interim state of) a grave.
22. And He will again raise him to life when He so wishes.
23. It cannot be (that there is no resurrection;) he has not yet carried out what He commanded him to do.
24. Therefore let such a person look at his food.

الذِّكْرَىٰ ﴿٤﴾ أَمَّا مَنِ اسْتَغْنَىٰ ﴿٥﴾ فَأَنتَ لَهُ
تَصَدَّىٰ ﴿٦﴾ وَمَا عَلَيْكَ أَلَّا يَزَّكَّىٰ ﴿٧﴾ وَأَمَّا
مَن جَاءَكَ يَسْعَىٰ ﴿٨﴾ وَهُوَ يَخْشَىٰ ﴿٩﴾ فَأَنتَ
عَنْهُ تَلَهَّىٰ ﴿١٠﴾ كَلَّا إِنَّهَا تَذْكِرَةٌ ﴿١١﴾ فَمَن
شَاءَ ذَكَرَهُ ﴿١٢﴾ فِي صُحُفٍ مُّكَرَّمَةٍ ﴿١٣﴾ مَّرْفُوعَةٍ
مُّطَهَّرَةٍ ﴿١٤﴾ بِأَيْدِي سَفَرَةٍ ﴿١٥﴾ كِرَامٍ بَرَرَةٍ ﴿١٦﴾
قُتِلَ الْإِنسَانُ مَا أَكْفَرَهُ ﴿١٧﴾ مِنْ أَيِّ
شَيْءٍ خَلَقَهُ ﴿١٨﴾ مِن نُّطْفَةٍ خَلَقَهُ فَقَدَّرَهُ ﴿١٩﴾
ثُمَّ السَّبِيلَ يَسَّرَهُ ﴿٢٠﴾ ثُمَّ أَمَاتَهُ فَأَقْبَرَهُ ﴿٢١﴾
ثُمَّ إِذَا شَاءَ أَنشَرَهُ ﴿٢٢﴾ كَلَّا لَمَّا يَقْضِ مَا
أَمَرَهُ ﴿٢٣﴾ فَلْيَنظُرِ الْإِنسَانُ إِلَىٰ طَعَامِهِ ﴿٢٤﴾
أَنَّا صَبَبْنَا الْمَاءَ صَبًّا ﴿٢٥﴾ ثُمَّ شَقَقْنَا الْأَرْضَ

25. How (at first) We pour down water in abundance,
26. Then We cleave the earth, a proper cleaving,
27. So that We cause grain to grow therein,
28. As well as grapes, vegetables,
29. The olive, the date-palm,
30. Orchards with dense trees,
31. Fruits and herbage;
32. A goodly provision for you and your cattle.
33. Again (you should also consider) when the deafening shout shall come,
34. The day when a person shall flee from his brother,
35. And (from) his mother and his father,
36. And (from) his spouse and his sons,
37. On that day every person among them shall be concerned enough (regarding his own affairs to occupy him and) to make him indifferent (to others).
38. Some faces, that day, will be beaming,
39. Smiling (and) joyous.
40. Some other faces, on that day, will have dust upon them,
41. Gloom covering them.
42. Those will be (the faces of) the disbelievers and (of) the doers of evil.

شَقًّا ﴿٢٦﴾ فَأَنۢبَتۡنَا فِيهَا حَبًّا ﴿٢٧﴾ وَعِنَبًا وَقَضۡبًا ﴿٢٨﴾
وَزَيۡتُونًا وَنَخۡلًا ﴿٢٩﴾ وَحَدَآئِقَ غُلۡبًا ﴿٣٠﴾
وَفَٰكِهَةً وَأَبًّا ﴿٣١﴾ مَّتَٰعًا لَّكُمۡ وَلِأَنۡعَٰمِكُمۡ ﴿٣٢﴾
فَإِذَا جَآءَتِ ٱلصَّآخَّةُ ﴿٣٣﴾ يَوۡمَ يَفِرُّ ٱلۡمَرۡءُ
مِنۡ أَخِيهِ ﴿٣٤﴾ وَأُمِّهِۦ وَأَبِيهِ ﴿٣٥﴾ وَصَٰحِبَتِهِۦ
وَبَنِيهِ ﴿٣٦﴾ لِكُلِّ ٱمۡرِيٍٕ مِّنۡهُمۡ يَوۡمَئِذٍ شَأۡنٌ
يُغۡنِيهِ ﴿٣٧﴾ وُجُوهٌ يَوۡمَئِذٍ مُّسۡفِرَةٌ ﴿٣٨﴾ ضَاحِكَةٌ
مُّسۡتَبۡشِرَةٌ ﴿٣٩﴾ وَوُجُوهٌ يَوۡمَئِذٍ عَلَيۡهَا
غَبَرَةٌ ﴿٤٠﴾ تَرۡهَقُهَا قَتَرَةٌ ﴿٤١﴾ أُوْلَٰٓئِكَ
هُمُ ٱلۡكَفَرَةُ ٱلۡفَجَرَةُ ﴿٤٢﴾ ع ٥

سُورَةُ التَّكۡوِيرِ مَكِّيَّةٌ

CHAPTER 81

AL-TAKWÎR

(Losing of the Light)

(Revealed before Hijrah)

With the name of Allâh,
the Most Gracious, the Ever Merciful
(I commence to read Sûrah Al-Takwîr).

بِسۡمِ ٱللَّهِ ٱلرَّحۡمَٰنِ ٱلرَّحِيمِ

إِذَا ٱلشَّمۡسُ كُوِّرَتۡ ﴿١﴾ وَإِذَا ٱلنُّجُومُ
ٱنكَدَرَتۡ ﴿٢﴾ وَإِذَا ٱلۡجِبَالُ سُيِّرَتۡ ﴿٣﴾

سُورَةُ التَّكْوِيرِ ٨١

1. **W**HEN the sun be folded up and darkened,
2. And when the stars are obscured,
3. And when the mountains are made to pass away,
4. And when the excellent she-camels will be discarded,
5. And when the wild beasts will be herded together,
6. And when the rivers will be drained away,
7. And when (various) people will be united together,
8. And when the baby girl who is buried alive will be questioned about;
9. For what offence was she killed?
10. And when books and papers will be spread abroad,
11. And when the heights will be discovered,
12. And when the Hell-Fire will be set ablaze,
13. And when the Paradise will be brought near,
14. Every soul will know then what (store of deeds) it has brought forward.
15. Nay, I call to witness those (planets) that recede while advancing in one direction,
16. Those (planets) that continue their forward course (along their orbits) and then disappear.
17. And (I call to witness) the night when its darkness begins to depart,
18. And the dawn as it begins to breathe (and brightens up),
19. That verily this (Qur'ân) is indeed the word (revealed to and) uttered by a noble (and illustrious) Messenger (- Muhammad),
20. Possessor of power, occupying a (glorious) secure position with the Lord of the Throne,
21. Who is entitled to be obeyed and who is trustworthy.
22. And that this companion of yours (- Muhammad) is not at all mad.
23. And he has most surely seen himself (shining in the resplendence of his own light) in the clear horizon (- in the remotest corners of

وَإِذَا الْعِشَارُ عُطِّلَتْ ﴿٤﴾ وَإِذَا الْوُحُوشُ
حُشِرَتْ ﴿٥﴾ وَإِذَا الْبِحَارُ سُجِّرَتْ ﴿٦﴾ وَإِذَا
النُّفُوسُ زُوِّجَتْ ﴿٧﴾ وَإِذَا الْمَوْءُدَةُ سُئِلَتْ ﴿٨﴾
بِأَيِّ ذَنْبٍ قُتِلَتْ ﴿٩﴾ وَإِذَا الصُّحُفُ نُشِرَتْ ﴿١٠﴾
وَإِذَا السَّمَاءُ كُشِطَتْ ﴿١١﴾ وَإِذَا الْجَحِيمُ
سُعِّرَتْ ﴿١٢﴾ وَإِذَا الْجَنَّةُ أُزْلِفَتْ ﴿١٣﴾ عَلِمَتْ
نَفْسٌ مَّا أَحْضَرَتْ ﴿١٤﴾ فَلَا أُقْسِمُ بِالْخُنَّسِ ﴿١٥﴾
الْجَوَارِ الْكُنَّسِ ﴿١٦﴾ وَالَّيْلِ إِذَا عَسْعَسَ ﴿١٧﴾
وَالصُّبْحِ إِذَا تَنَفَّسَ ﴿١٨﴾ إِنَّهُ لَقَوْلُ رَسُولٍ
كَرِيمٍ ﴿١٩﴾ ذِي قُوَّةٍ عِنْدَ ذِي الْعَرْشِ
مَكِينٍ ﴿٢٠﴾ مُّطَاعٍ ثَمَّ أَمِينٍ ﴿٢١﴾ وَمَا
صَاحِبُكُمْ بِمَجْنُونٍ ﴿٢٢﴾ وَلَقَدْ رَاٰهُ بِالْأُفُقِ
الْمُبِينِ ﴿٢٣﴾ وَمَا هُوَ عَلَى الْغَيْبِ بِضَنِينٍ ﴿٢٤﴾
وَمَا هُوَ بِقَوْلِ شَيْطٰنٍ رَّجِيمٍ ﴿٢٥﴾ فَأَيْنَ

the world).
24. And he is not at all niggardly, nor a forgerer in disclosing the hidden realties.
25. Nor is this (Qur'ân) the word of satan who is driven away (from divine presence).
26. Where do you wander to (leaving this Qur'ân and the Messenger aside)?
27. This is but a means to rise to eminence for all people,
28. For such of you who wish to walk straight (to attain eminence).
29. And you should not desire (otherwise) except that which Allâh, the Lord of the worlds, desires (for you).

تَذۡهَبُونَ ﴿٢٦﴾ إِنۡ هُوَ إِلَّا ذِكۡرٌ لِّلۡعٰلَمِينَ ﴿٢٧﴾
لِمَن شَآءَ مِنكُمۡ أَن يَسۡتَقِيمَ ﴿٢٨﴾
وَمَا تَشَآءُونَ إِلَّآ أَن يَشَآءَ اللّٰهُ
رَبُّ الۡعٰلَمِينَ ﴿٢٩﴾

CHAPTER
82

سُورَةُ الانفِطَارِ مَكِّيَّةٌ

AL-INFIT̲ÂR
(The Cleaving Asunder)
(Revealed before Hijrah)

بِسۡمِ اللّٰهِ الرَّحۡمٰنِ الرَّحِيمِ

With the name of Allâh, the Most Gracious, the Ever Merciful (I commence to read Sûrah Al-Infit̲âr).

1. WHEN the sky will be cleft asunder,
2. And when the planets will become dispersed,
3. And when the rivers are widely split up and made to flow forth (into canals),
4. And when the graves will be laid open,
5. Every person shall know (then) what (evil) actions (which he should not have done) he has committed, and what (good actions he should have done) he has omitted.
6. O (ungrateful) human being! What has enticed you away from your Lord, the Honoured One,

إِذَا السَّمَآءُ انفَطَرَتۡ ﴿١﴾ وَإِذَا الۡكَوَاكِبُ
انتَثَرَتۡ ﴿٢﴾ وَإِذَا الۡبِحَارُ فُجِّرَتۡ ﴿٣﴾ وَإِذَا
الۡقُبُورُ بُعۡثِرَتۡ ﴿٤﴾ عَلِمَتۡ نَفۡسٌ مَّا قَدَّمَتۡ
وَأَخَّرَتۡ ﴿٥﴾ يٰٓأَيُّهَا الۡإِنسٰنُ مَا غَرَّكَ بِرَبِّكَ
الۡكَرِيمِ ﴿٦﴾ الَّذِي خَلَقَكَ فَسَوّٰىكَ
فَعَدَلَكَ ﴿٧﴾ فِيٓ أَيِّ صُورَةٍ مَّا شَآءَ رَكَّبَكَ ﴿٨﴾

7. Who created you, then perfected you (with wisdom), then endowed you with great natural powers and faculties,
8. And He fashioned you in whatever form it pleased Him.
9. Surely, (it is) not at all (as you think), the truth is that you treat the Requital as a lie.
10. Verily, there are (appointed) guardians over you,
11. Noble (angel) recorders (of your commissions and omissions),
12. Who know (all) that you do.
13. The virtuous shall invariably be in (a state of) bliss.
14. But the wicked shall, of course, be in the flaming Fire.
15. They will enter therein on the Day of Requital,
16. And they shall not at all (be able to) keep themselves away (by escaping) from it.
17. What should make you know what the Day of Requital is!
18. Again (We repeat) how can you know what the Day of Requital is!
19. (It is) the day when no person shall be able to do anything for another! On that day the (absolute) Judgment of every sort shall entirely belong to Allâh.

كَلَّا بَلْ تُكَذِّبُونَ بِالدِّينِ ﴿٩﴾ وَإِنَّ عَلَيْكُمْ لَحَٰفِظِينَ ﴿١٠﴾ كِرَامًا كَٰتِبِينَ ﴿١١﴾ يَعْلَمُونَ مَا تَفْعَلُونَ ﴿١٢﴾ إِنَّ الْأَبْرَارَ لَفِي نَعِيمٍ ﴿١٣﴾ وَإِنَّ الْفُجَّارَ لَفِي جَحِيمٍ ﴿١٤﴾ يَصْلَوْنَهَا يَوْمَ الدِّينِ ﴿١٥﴾ وَمَا هُمْ عَنْهَا بِغَائِبِينَ ﴿١٦﴾ وَمَا أَدْرَىٰكَ مَا يَوْمُ الدِّينِ ﴿١٧﴾ ثُمَّ مَا أَدْرَىٰكَ مَا يَوْمُ الدِّينِ ﴿١٨﴾ يَوْمَ لَا تَمْلِكُ نَفْسٌ لِّنَفْسٍ شَيْـًٔا وَالْأَمْرُ يَوْمَئِذٍ لِّلَّهِ ﴿١٩﴾

CHAPTER
83

سُورَةُ الْمُطَفِّفِينَ مَكِّيَّةٌ

AL-MUṮAFFIFÎN

(The Defaulters In Duty)
(Revealed before Hijrah)

With the name of Allâh,
the Most Gracious, the Ever Merciful
(I commence to read Sûrah Al-Muṯaffifîn).

بِسْمِ اللَّهِ الرَّحْمَٰنِ الرَّحِيمِ

وَيْلٌ لِّلْمُطَفِّفِينَ ﴿١﴾ الَّذِينَ إِذَا اكْتَالُوا عَلَى النَّاسِ يَسْتَوْفُونَ ﴿٢﴾ وَإِذَا كَالُوهُمْ

1. WOE be to those who make a default in any of their duties and give short measure.
2. When they receive measure from other people they receive in full (not allowing the least shortage and loss),
3. But when they give by measure to others or weigh to them they give them less (than what is due).
4. Do not such people realize that they will be raised (to life again),
5. To face (and hear the Judgment of) that Great Day?
6. The Day when people shall stand before the Lord of the worlds?
7. Nay, (not at all as they believe) the record of (the deeds) of the wicked is in *Sijjîn* (- the register of a prison).
8. What should make you know what that Sijjîn is?
9. (It is) a book written (distinctly and comprehensively).
10. On that Day woe shall befall those who belie (the truth);
11. Those that belie the Day of Requital.
12. No one can treat it as a lie except every sinful transgressor,
13. (Who) when Our Messages are recited to him says, '(These are) mere fables of the ancients.'
14. Nay (not at all so), the truth is that their (evil) deeds have rusted their hearts.
15. Nay (We repeat, not at all so). Verily, they shall be debarred from (the sight and mercy of) their Lord that day.
16. Then they shall surely enter into the flaming Fire,
17. Then it shall be said (to them), 'This is that (very punishment) which you used to cry lies to.'
18. Behold! Verily the record (of the righteous deeds) of the virtuous will be in *'Illîyyîn* (- the register of those enjoying the most exalted ranks).

سُورَةُ الْمُطَفِّفِينَ ٨٣

أَوْ وَّزَنُوهُمْ يُخْسِرُونَ ﴿٣﴾ أَلَا يَظُنُّ أُولَٰٓئِكَ
أَنَّهُم مَّبْعُوثُونَ ﴿٤﴾ لِيَوْمٍ عَظِيمٍ ﴿٥﴾ يَّوْمَ
يَقُومُ النَّاسُ لِرَبِّ الْعٰلَمِينَ ﴿٦﴾ كَلَّآ
إِنَّ كِتٰبَ الْفُجَّارِ لَفِي سِجِّينٍ ﴿٧﴾ وَمَآ
أَدْرٰىكَ مَا سِجِّينٌ ﴿٨﴾ كِتٰبٌ مَّرْقُومٌ ﴿٩﴾
وَيْلٌ يَوْمَئِذٍ لِّلْمُكَذِّبِينَ ﴿١٠﴾ الَّذِينَ
يُكَذِّبُونَ بِيَوْمِ الدِّينِ ﴿١١﴾ وَمَا يُكَذِّبُ
بِهٖٓ إِلَّا كُلُّ مُعْتَدٍ أَثِيمٍ ﴿١٢﴾ إِذَا تُتْلٰى
عَلَيْهِ اٰيٰتُنَا قَالَ أَسٰطِيرُ الْأَوَّلِينَ ﴿١٣﴾
كَلَّا بَلْ رَانَ عَلٰى قُلُوبِهِم مَّا كَانُوا
يَكْسِبُونَ ﴿١٤﴾ كَلَّآ إِنَّهُمْ عَن رَّبِّهِمْ يَوْمَئِذٍ
لَّمَحْجُوبُونَ ﴿١٥﴾ ثُمَّ إِنَّهُمْ لَصَالُوا الْجَحِيمِ ﴿١٦﴾
ثُمَّ يُقَالُ هٰذَا الَّذِي كُنتُم بِهٖ تُكَذِّبُونَ ﴿١٧﴾
كَلَّآ إِنَّ كِتٰبَ الْأَبْرَارِ لَفِي عِلِّيِّينَ ﴿١٨﴾
وَمَآ أَدْرٰىكَ مَا عِلِّيُّونَ ﴿١٩﴾ كِتٰبٌ مَّرْقُومٌ ﴿٢٠﴾

19. And what should make you know what *'Illîyyûn* is?
20. It is a book (distinctly and comprehensively) written,
21. Which those drawn near (to their Lord) will find present.
22. The virtuous shall indeed be in (a state of) bliss (that Day).
23. (Reclining) upon raised couches they shall be looking (at every thing all around).
24. You shall find freshness and bloom of bliss in their faces.
25. They shall be given to drink a pure and delightfully refreshing beverage sealed (and secure from all contamination).
26. (Even) the sealing and dregs of which will have flavour of musk, so to this (noble end) let (all) the aspirants aspire.
27. And this (beverage) will be tempered with *Tasnîm* (flowing from on high).
28. (This *Tasnîm* is) a spring of which those drawn near (to God) shall drink.
29. Those who had severed their ties (with God) used to laugh at those who believed,
30. And when they passed by them (- the believers) they winked at one another (by way of ridiculously finding fault with them),
31. And when they returned to their companions they returned exulting with pride,
32. And when they saw these (Muslims) they said, 'These are surely the straying ones!'
33. Though they were not deputed as guardians (to guard) over them.
34. Now, on this day (of Judgment) it is the believers who will wonder at the disbelievers,
35. (Seated) on raised couches of (dignity). They (- the believers) will be looking (at the miserable state of the disbelievers in Gehenna).
36. (Then it shall be said,) 'The disbelievers have been duly requited for (the misdeeds) that they used to do.'

يَشْهَدُهُ الْمُقَرَّبُونَ ﴿٢١﴾ إِنَّ الْأَبْرَارَ لَفِي نَعِيمٍ ﴿٢٢﴾
عَلَى الْأَرَائِكِ يَنْظُرُونَ ﴿٢٣﴾ تَعْرِفُ فِي
وُجُوهِهِمْ نَضْرَةَ النَّعِيمِ ﴿٢٤﴾ يُسْقَوْنَ مِنْ
رَحِيقٍ مَخْتُومٍ ﴿٢٥﴾ خِتَامُهُ مِسْكٌ ۚ وَفِي
ذَٰلِكَ فَلْيَتَنَافَسِ الْمُتَنَافِسُونَ ﴿٢٦﴾ وَمِزَاجُهُ
مِنْ تَسْنِيمٍ ﴿٢٧﴾ عَيْنًا يَشْرَبُ بِهَا الْمُقَرَّبُونَ ﴿٢٨﴾
إِنَّ الَّذِينَ أَجْرَمُوا كَانُوا مِنَ الَّذِينَ آمَنُوا
يَضْحَكُونَ ﴿٢٩﴾ وَإِذَا مَرُّوا بِهِمْ يَتَغَامَزُونَ ﴿٣٠﴾
وَإِذَا انْقَلَبُوا إِلَىٰ أَهْلِهِمُ انْقَلَبُوا فَكِهِينَ ﴿٣١﴾
وَإِذَا رَأَوْهُمْ قَالُوا إِنَّ هَٰؤُلَاءِ لَضَالُّونَ ﴿٣٢﴾
وَمَا أُرْسِلُوا عَلَيْهِمْ حَافِظِينَ ﴿٣٣﴾ فَالْيَوْمَ
الَّذِينَ آمَنُوا مِنَ الْكُفَّارِ يَضْحَكُونَ ﴿٣٤﴾
عَلَى الْأَرَائِكِ يَنْظُرُونَ ﴿٣٥﴾ هَلْ ثُوِّبَ
الْكُفَّارُ مَا كَانُوا يَفْعَلُونَ ﴿٣٦﴾

CHAPTER
84

سُوۡرَةُ الانشقاق ٨٤

AL-INSHIQÂQ

(The Bursting Asunder)
(Revealed before Hijrah)

سُوۡرَةُ الۡاِنۡشِقَاقِ مَكِّيَّةٌ

With the name of Allâh,
the Most Gracious, the Ever Merciful
(I commence to read Sûrah Al-Inshiqâq).

بِسۡمِ اللّٰهِ الرَّحۡمٰنِ الرَّحِيۡمِ

1. **W**HEN the sky bursts asunder,
2. And gives ear to (the command of) its Lord to obey, and it is fittingly disposed (to do so),
3. And when the earth is stretched out and receives fresh manure (for the spiritual and physical progress of its dwellers),
4. And casts forth all that it has in it, and becomes (as if) empty,
5. And gives ear to (the command of) its Lord to obey, and it is fittingly disposed (to do so).
6. O People! Verily you are (by nature) toiling on towards your Lord a laborious toiling, then (through arduous service to Him) you shall surely meet Him.
7. Then as for the person who is given his record (of deeds) in his right hand,
8. He shall soon be reckoned an easy reckoning,
9. And he will return to his people joyfully.
10. But as for the one who will have his record (of deeds) given to him behind his back (as a sign that he had thrown the divine teachings behind his back),
11. He shall soon call (so to say) for complete destruction (to end his agonies).
12. And he will enter into a blazing Fire.
13. Verily, (before this) he used to be joyful among his companions (and neglected the Hereafter).

إِذَا السَّمَآءُ انۡشَقَّتۡ (١) وَ أَذِنَتۡ لِرَبِّهَا
وَحُقَّتۡ (٢) وَ إِذَا الۡأَرۡضُ مُدَّتۡ (٣)
وَأَلۡقَتۡ مَا فِيۡهَا وَ تَخَلَّتۡ (٤) وَأَذِنَتۡ لِرَبِّهَا
وَحُقَّتۡ (٥) يٰٓأَيُّهَا الۡإِنۡسٰنُ إِنَّكَ كَادِحٌ إِلٰى
رَبِّكَ كَدۡحًا فَمُلٰقِيۡهِ (٦) فَأَمَّا مَنۡ أُوۡتِيَ
كِتٰبَهٗ بِيَمِيۡنِهٖ (٧) فَسَوۡفَ يُحَاسَبُ حِسَابًا
يَّسِيۡرًا (٨) وَّ يَنۡقَلِبُ إِلٰٓى أَهۡلِهٖ مَسۡرُوۡرًا (٩)
وَ أَمَّا مَنۡ أُوۡتِيَ كِتٰبَهٗ وَرَآءَ ظَهۡرِهٖ (١٠)
فَسَوۡفَ يَدۡعُوۡا ثُبُوۡرًا (١١) وَّ يَصۡلٰى سَعِيۡرًا (١٢)
إِنَّهٗ كَانَ فِيۡۤ أَهۡلِهٖ مَسۡرُوۡرًا (١٣) إِنَّهٗ ظَنَّ

14. He deemed that he would never return (to God).
15. Yet he did (return to God to account for his deeds), surely his Lord was ever watchful of him.
16. Behold! I call to witness the twilight of sunset,
17. And the night and (all) that it envelopes,
18. And the moon when it become full,
19. That you shall invariably pass on from one stage to another.
20. So what is wrong with them that they do not believe?
21. And they do not prostrate in submission when the Qur'ân is recited to them?
[PROSTRATION]

22. On the contrary, these disbelievers cry lies (to the Qur'ân).
23. And Allâh knows best all that they keep hidden (in their hearts).
24. So (do not bother about them, rather) give them the news of a woeful punishment.
25. Different, however, is the case of those who believe and do deeds of righteousness. There awaits them an unending reward.

سُورَةُ الانشقاق ٨٤ سُورَةُ البروج ٨٥

أَن لَّن يَحُورَ ﴿١٤﴾ بَلَىٰٓ إِنَّ رَبَّهُۥ كَانَ بِهِۦ
بَصِيرًا ﴿١٥﴾ فَلَآ أُقْسِمُ بِالشَّفَقِ ﴿١٦﴾ وَالَّيْلِ
وَمَا وَسَقَ ﴿١٧﴾ وَالْقَمَرِ إِذَا اتَّسَقَ ﴿١٨﴾ لَتَرْكَبُنَّ
طَبَقًا عَن طَبَقٍ ﴿١٩﴾ فَمَا لَهُمْ لَا يُؤْمِنُونَ ﴿٢٠﴾
وَإِذَا قُرِئَ عَلَيْهِمُ الْقُرْءَانُ لَا يَسْجُدُونَ ﴿٢١﴾
بَلِ الَّذِينَ كَفَرُوا يُكَذِّبُونَ ﴿٢٢﴾ وَاللَّهُ
أَعْلَمُ بِمَا يُوعُونَ ﴿٢٣﴾ فَبَشِّرْهُم بِعَذَابٍ
أَلِيمٍ ﴿٢٤﴾ إِلَّا الَّذِينَ ءَامَنُوا وَعَمِلُوا الصَّٰلِحَٰتِ
لَهُمْ أَجْرٌ غَيْرُ مَمْنُونٍ ﴿٢٥﴾

CHAPTER 85

AL-BURÛJ
(The Starry Spangles)
(Revealed before Hijrah)

سُورَةُ البُرُوجِ مَكِّيَّةٌ

With the name of Allâh,
the Most Gracious, the Ever Merciful
(I commence to read Sûrah Al-Burûj).

بِسْمِ اللَّهِ الرَّحْمَٰنِ الرَّحِيمِ

1. **I** CALL to witness the starry spangles of the sky,
2. And the Promised Day,
3. And the Bearer of witness (- the Prophet), and that about whom the witness is borne (- the

وَالسَّمَاءِ ذَاتِ الْبُرُوجِ ﴿١﴾ وَالْيَوْمِ
الْمَوْعُودِ ﴿٢﴾ وَشَاهِدٍ وَمَشْهُودٍ ﴿٣﴾ قُتِلَ

Prophet's community),
4. (That these disbelievers will face destruction as were) destroyed the Fellows of the Trenches.
5. (These trenches had) the fire (fed) with fuel,
6. When they sat by them (- the trenches).
7. And they were the witnesses of those (wrongs) they were doing to the believers.
8. They hated and tortured these (believers) for no reason other than that they had believed in Allâh, the Almighty, the Praiseworthy,
9. To Whom belongs the sovereignty of the heavens and the earth; and Allâh is Witness over all things.
10. Those who (deliberately) persecute the believing men and women and then do not repent, shall suffer the punishment of Gehenna and they shall suffer the torment of (heart) burning (in the present life).
11. But those who believe and do deeds of righteousness shall have Gardens served with running streams (to keep them green and flourishing). This indeed is the great achievement.
12. Terrible indeed is the seizing of your Lord.
13. It is He Who originates and continues reproducing.
14. And He is the Protector, the Most Loving;
15. Lord of the Throne (of Power), the Lord of all Glory,
16. Absolute Performer of what He intends (to carry out).
17. There has reached you the account of the hosts
18. Of Pharaoh, and Thamûd.
19. The truth is that the disbelievers are persisting in belying (the Divine Messages),
20. And Allâh encompasses (them from all sides,) from behind (and from in front of) them (to punish them).
21. This is also the truth that it is a glorious Qur'ân,
22. (Inscribed) in a Tablet well-guarded (against corruption, distortion and destruction).

أَصْحٰبُ الْأُخْدُودِ (٤) النَّارِ ذَاتِ الْوَقُودِ (٥)
إِذْ هُمْ عَلَيْهَا قُعُودٌ (٦) وَهُمْ عَلٰى مَا يَفْعَلُونَ
بِالْمُؤْمِنِينَ شُهُودٌ (٧) وَمَا نَقَمُوا مِنْهُمْ
إِلَّا أَنْ يُؤْمِنُوا بِاللّٰهِ الْعَزِيزِ الْحَمِيدِ (٨)
الَّذِي لَهُ مُلْكُ السَّمٰوٰتِ وَالْأَرْضِ
وَاللّٰهُ عَلٰى كُلِّ شَيْءٍ شَهِيدٌ (٩) إِنَّ الَّذِينَ
فَتَنُوا الْمُؤْمِنِينَ وَالْمُؤْمِنٰتِ ثُمَّ لَمْ
يَتُوبُوا فَلَهُمْ عَذَابُ جَهَنَّمَ وَلَهُمْ عَذَابُ
الْحَرِيقِ (١٠) إِنَّ الَّذِينَ اٰمَنُوا وَعَمِلُوا الصّٰلِحٰتِ
لَهُمْ جَنّٰتٌ تَجْرِي مِنْ تَحْتِهَا الْأَنْهٰرُ
ذٰلِكَ الْفَوْزُ الْكَبِيرُ (١١) إِنَّ بَطْشَ رَبِّكَ
لَشَدِيدٌ (١٢) إِنَّهُ هُوَ يُبْدِئُ وَيُعِيدُ (١٣)
وَهُوَ الْغَفُورُ الْوَدُودُ (١٤) ذُو الْعَرْشِ الْمَجِيدُ (١٥)
فَعَّالٌ لِمَا يُرِيدُ (١٦) هَلْ أَتٰىكَ حَدِيثُ
الْجُنُودِ (١٧) فِرْعَوْنَ وَثَمُودَ (١٨) بَلِ الَّذِينَ كَفَرُوا
فِي تَكْذِيبٍ (١٩) وَاللّٰهُ مِنْ وَرَائِهِمْ مُحِيطٌ (٢٠)
بَلْ هُوَ قُرْاٰنٌ مَجِيدٌ (٢١) فِي لَوْحٍ مَحْفُوظٍ (٢٢) ع ٢٢/١٠

CHAPTER
86

سُوۡرَۃُ الطَّارِقِ ٨٦

AL-TÂRIQ
(The Night Visitant)
(Revealed before Hijrah)

With the name of Allâh,
the Most Gracious, the Ever Merciful
(I commence to read Sûrah Al-Târiq).

1. **I** CALL to witness the heaven and the visitant (in the darkness) of the night.
2. And what should make you know what the night-visitant is?
3. (It is) the star of piercing brightness.
4. Remember! A guardian is appointed (by God) over every soul.
5. Therefore let (every) human being consider from what material he is created.
6. He is created from a jetting fluid,
7. Which issues forth from between the loins and the breastbones.
8. Verily, He (Who created him the first time) has the power of bringing him back to life (in the Hereafter).
9. On the Day, when the hidden things shall be exposed,
10. Then the person (who has engrossed himself in worldly affairs) shall have neither power to defend himself nor will he have any (other) helper.
11. I call to witness the clouds that rain over and over again,
12. And the earth that bursts forth (with herbage and with springs),
13. (That) verily, this (Qur'ân) is a decisive word.
14. And it is not a vain (revelation).
15. And they (- the disbelievers) devise a device (against it).
16. And (in return) I (too) devise a (counter) device.
17. Therefore grant the disbelievers respite, yes grant them respite for a little while.

سُوۡرَۃُ الطَّارِقِ مَکِّیَّۃٌ

بِسۡمِ اللّٰہِ الرَّحۡمٰنِ الرَّحِیۡمِ

وَ السَّمَآءِ وَ الطَّارِقِ ۙ﴿۱﴾ وَ مَاۤ اَدۡرٰىکَ
مَا الطَّارِقُ ۙ﴿۲﴾ النَّجۡمُ الثَّاقِبُ ۙ﴿۳﴾ اِنۡ کُلُّ
نَفۡسٍ لَّمَّا عَلَیۡہَا حَافِظٌ ؕ﴿۴﴾ فَلۡیَنۡظُرِ الۡاِنۡسٰنُ
مِمَّ خُلِقَ ؕ﴿۵﴾ خُلِقَ مِنۡ مَّآءٍ دَافِقٍ ۙ﴿۶﴾ یَّخۡرُجُ
مِنۡۢ بَیۡنِ الصُّلۡبِ وَ التَّرَآئِبِ ؕ﴿۷﴾ اِنَّہٗ عَلٰی
رَجۡعِہٖ لَقَادِرٌ ؕ﴿۸﴾ یَوۡمَ تُبۡلَی السَّرَآئِرُ ۙ﴿۹﴾ فَمَا
لَہٗ مِنۡ قُوَّۃٍ وَّ لَا نَاصِرٍ ﴿ؕ۱۰﴾ وَ السَّمَآءِ ذَاتِ
الرَّجۡعِ ﴿ۙ۱۱﴾ وَ الۡاَرۡضِ ذَاتِ الصَّدۡعِ ﴿ۙ۱۲﴾ اِنَّہٗ
لَقَوۡلٌ فَصۡلٌ ﴿ۙ۱۳﴾ وَّ مَا ہُوَ بِالۡہَزۡلِ ﴿ؕ۱۴﴾ اِنَّہُمۡ
یَکِیۡدُوۡنَ کَیۡدًا ﴿ۙ۱۵﴾ وَّ اَکِیۡدُ کَیۡدًا ﴿ۚۖ۱۶﴾
فَمَہِّلِ الۡکٰفِرِیۡنَ اَمۡہِلۡہُمۡ رُوَیۡدًا ﴿۱۷﴾

CHAPTER
87

سُورَةُ الْأَعْلَى ٨٧

AL-A'LÂ
(The Most High)
(Revealed before Hijrah)

With the name of Allâh,
the Most Gracious, the Ever Merciful
(I commence to read Sûrah Al-A'lâ).

1. **E**XTOL the holiness of the name of your Lord, the Most High.
2. Who creates (all things) and gives (them) suitable and perfect shapes.
3. Who determines (the capacities and faculties) and furnishes them with (appropriate) guidance to achieve the final goal.
4. And Who brings forth the pasturage,
5. And then turns it into dried up rubbish, gray coloured.
6. We will soon teach (you and) make you recite (the Qur'ân) so that you shall not forget (any part of it).
7. Except whatever (other things which) Allâh will (and which things you are apt to forget as a human being). Indeed He knows all that is manifest and all that is hidden.
8. And We shall provide you (every) facility and make things easy for you.
9. Therefore keep on reminding (the people), surely reminding does good.
10. He who stands in awe (of God) will heed,
11. But the person steeped in wickedness goes on avoiding it.
12. He who will enter the great Fire,
13. Then he shall neither die therein nor live.
14. Verily, that person who purifies himself truly will succeed (both in this life and in the Hereafter),
15. And remembers and extols the name of his Lord and offers Prayers.

سُورَةُ الْأَعْلَى مَكِّيَّةٌ

بِسْمِ اللَّهِ الرَّحْمَٰنِ الرَّحِيمِ

سَبِّحِ اسْمَ رَبِّكَ الْأَعْلَى ۝١ الَّذِي خَلَقَ
فَسَوَّى ۝٢ وَالَّذِي قَدَّرَ فَهَدَى ۝٣
وَالَّذِي أَخْرَجَ الْمَرْعَى ۝٤ فَجَعَلَهُ غُثَاءً
أَحْوَى ۝٥ سَنُقْرِئُكَ فَلَا تَنْسَى ۝٦ إِلَّا
مَا شَاءَ اللَّهُ إِنَّهُ يَعْلَمُ الْجَهْرَ وَمَا
يَخْفَى ۝٧ وَنُيَسِّرُكَ لِلْيُسْرَى ۝٨ فَذَكِّرْ
إِنْ نَفَعَتِ الذِّكْرَى ۝٩ سَيَذَّكَّرُ مَنْ
يَخْشَى ۝١٠ وَيَتَجَنَّبُهَا الْأَشْقَى ۝١١ الَّذِي
يَصْلَى النَّارَ الْكُبْرَى ۝١٢ ثُمَّ لَا يَمُوتُ
فِيهَا وَلَا يَحْيَى ۝١٣ قَدْ أَفْلَحَ مَنْ
تَزَكَّى ۝١٤ وَذَكَرَ اسْمَ رَبِّهِ فَصَلَّى ۝١٥

16. But the fact is that you people prefer the present life,
17. Though (the life in) the Hereafter is much better and more lasting.
18. These (teachings) are so stated in the earlier Scriptures;
19. The Scriptures of Abraham and Moses.

بَلْ تُؤْثِرُونَ الْحَيٰوةَ الدُّنْيَا ﴿١٦﴾ وَالْآخِرَةُ
خَيْرٌ وَّأَبْقَىٰ ﴿١٧﴾ إِنَّ هٰذَا لَفِي الصُّحُفِ
الْأُولَىٰ ﴿١٨﴾ صُحُفِ إِبْرٰهِيمَ وَمُوسَىٰ ﴿١٩﴾

CHAPTER
88

AL-GHÂSHIYAH
(The Overwhelming Event)
(Revealed before Hijrah)

سُورَةُ الْغٰشِيَةِ مَكِّيَّةٌ

With the name of Allâh,
the Most Gracious, the Ever Merciful
(I commence to read Sûrah Al-Ghâshiyah).

بِسْمِ اللّٰهِ الرَّحْمٰنِ الرَّحِيمِ

1. THERE has reached you the news of the overwhelming event (- the Resurrection).
2. Some persons shall be downcast and humble that day.
3. Toil-worn and weary.
4. They shall enter a blazing Fire.
5. They shall be made to drink from a spring of boiling hot water;
6. Dry, bitter and thorny herbage shall be their only food,
7. Which neither nourishes nor satisfies hunger.
8. On that day some (other) persons will be fresh and joyful,
9. Well-satisfied with (the fruit of) their (pious) strivings.
10. (They will live) in a sublime Garden,
11. Wherein you will hear no vain talk.
12. It shall have a running spring,
13. It shall have thrones raised high,
14. And goblets properly set,
15. And cushions (beautifully) ranged in rows,

هَلْ أَتٰكَ حَدِيثُ الْغٰشِيَةِ ﴿١﴾ وُجُوهٌ
يَوْمَئِذٍ خٰشِعَةٌ ﴿٢﴾ عَامِلَةٌ نَّاصِبَةٌ ﴿٣﴾
تَصْلَىٰ نَارًا حَامِيَةً ﴿٤﴾ تُسْقَىٰ مِنْ عَيْنٍ
ءَانِيَةٍ ﴿٥﴾ لَيْسَ لَهُمْ طَعَامٌ إِلَّا مِنْ
ضَرِيعٍ ﴿٦﴾ لَّا يُسْمِنُ وَلَا يُغْنِي مِنْ جُوعٍ ﴿٧﴾
وُجُوهٌ يَوْمَئِذٍ نَّاعِمَةٌ ﴿٨﴾ لِّسَعْيِهَا رَاضِيَةٌ ﴿٩﴾
فِي جَنَّةٍ عَالِيَةٍ ﴿١٠﴾ لَّا تَسْمَعُ فِيهَا لٰغِيَةً ﴿١١﴾
فِيهَا عَيْنٌ جَارِيَةٌ ﴿١٢﴾ فِيهَا سُرُرٌ مَّرْفُوعَةٌ ﴿١٣﴾
وَأَكْوَابٌ مَّوْضُوعَةٌ ﴿١٤﴾ وَنَمَارِقُ مَصْفُوفَةٌ ﴿١٥﴾

16. And velvety carpets (tastefully) spread.
17. Do the people not then look at the clouds and the camels, how they are made,
18. And at the heaven, how it is raised high;
19. And at the mountains, how they are set up;
20. And at the earth, how it is spread out?
21. Keep on admonishing (them even if they insist on shutting their eyes), so your duty is one of an admonisher.
22. You are not (appointed) a keeper, stern and hard, to (compel) them.
23. But as to him who turns away and disbelieves,
24. Allâh shall punish him with the greatest punishment.
25. Verily, to Us is their ultimate return;
26. Then it is surely for Us to call them to account.

وَزَرَابِيُّ مَبْثُوثَةٌ ﴿١٦﴾ أَفَلَا يَنْظُرُونَ إِلَى
الْإِبِلِ كَيْفَ خُلِقَتْ ﴿١٧﴾ وَإِلَى السَّمَاءِ
كَيْفَ رُفِعَتْ ﴿١٨﴾ وَإِلَى الْجِبَالِ كَيْفَ
نُصِبَتْ ﴿١٩﴾ وَإِلَى الْأَرْضِ كَيْفَ سُطِحَتْ ﴿٢٠﴾
فَذَكِّرْ إِنَّمَا أَنْتَ مُذَكِّرٌ ﴿٢١﴾ لَسْتَ عَلَيْهِمْ
بِمُصَيْطِرٍ ﴿٢٢﴾ إِلَّا مَنْ تَوَلَّى وَكَفَرَ ﴿٢٣﴾ فَيُعَذِّبُهُ
اللَّهُ الْعَذَابَ الْأَكْبَرَ ﴿٢٤﴾ إِنَّ إِلَيْنَا إِيَابَهُمْ ﴿٢٥﴾
ثُمَّ إِنَّ عَلَيْنَا حِسَابَهُمْ ﴿٢٦﴾

CHAPTER
89

AL-FAJR
(The Dawn)
(Revealed before Hijrah)

سُورَةُ الْفَجْرِ مَكِّيَّةٌ

With the name of Allâh,
the Most Gracious, the Ever Merciful
(I commence to read Sûrah Al-Fajr).

بِسْمِ اللَّهِ الرَّحْمَٰنِ الرَّحِيمِ

1. **I** CALL to witness (all the times and places specially important for the acceptance of prayers including) the dawn (of the twentieth of *Ramadzân*),
2. And the (last) ten Nights (of *Ramadzân*),
3. And (the Prayers which consist of) the even and odd (number of *Rak'ats* performed during these nights).
4. And the Night (- *Lailatul-Qadr*, the Blessed Night), when it moves on (to its close).
5. In it there is surely a strong evidence for one

وَالْفَجْرِ ﴿١﴾ وَلَيَالٍ عَشْرٍ ﴿٢﴾ وَالشَّفْعِ
وَالْوَتْرِ ﴿٣﴾ وَاللَّيْلِ إِذَا يَسْرِ ﴿٤﴾ هَلْ فِي ذَٰلِكَ

who has sense and understanding.
6. Have you not considered how your Lord dealt with 'Âd
7. Of Iram, possessors of tall statures and lofty columns,
8. The like of whom have not been created in these parts of land?
9. And (how He dealt with the tribe of) Thamûd who hewed out huge rocks in the valley (to make their dwellings)?
10. And (how He dealt with) Pharaoh, lord of vast hosts?
11. (All these people were) those who committed (all sort of) excesses in the cities,
12. And they spread a lot of corruption and lawlessness therein,
13. (So much) so that your Lord let loose on them the scourge and various kinds of punishments.
14. Behold! Your God is always on the watch.
15. Moreover a human being is such that when his Lord disciplines him (by prosperity) and (thus) honours him and bestows favours on him, he says, 'My Lord has honoured me.'
16. And when He disciplines him (with affliction) and (thus) straitens for him his (means of) subsistence, he says, 'My Lord has (for no reason) disgraced me.'
17. Nay, (what you think is wrong,) but (the reason for this degradation is that) you (for your part) do not honour the orphan,
18. And you do not urge one another to feed the poor,
19. And you devour the heritage (of others) wholly and indiscriminately,
20. And you are exceedingly fond of wealth.
21. By no means (will it be so as you think). When the earth is completely crushed into pieces,
22. And when (the judgment of) your Lord comes (to pass), and the angels (descend also) ranged rank on rank (to execute His decree),
23. On that Day Gehenna shall be brought near.

قَسَمٌ لِّذِي حِجْرٍ ﴿٥﴾ أَلَمْ تَرَ كَيْفَ فَعَلَ
رَبُّكَ بِعَادٍ ﴿٦﴾ إِرَمَ ذَاتِ الْعِمَادِ ﴿٧﴾ الَّتِي لَمْ
يُخْلَقْ مِثْلُهَا فِي الْبِلَادِ ﴿٨﴾ وَثَمُودَ الَّذِينَ
جَابُوا الصَّخْرَ بِالْوَادِ ﴿٩﴾ وَفِرْعَوْنَ ذِي
الْأَوْتَادِ ﴿١٠﴾ الَّذِينَ طَغَوْا فِي الْبِلَادِ ﴿١١﴾ فَأَكْثَرُوا
فِيهَا الْفَسَادَ ﴿١٢﴾ فَصَبَّ عَلَيْهِمْ رَبُّكَ سَوْطَ
عَذَابٍ ﴿١٣﴾ إِنَّ رَبَّكَ لَبِالْمِرْصَادِ ﴿١٤﴾ فَأَمَّا
الْإِنسَانُ إِذَا مَا ابْتَلَاهُ رَبُّهُ فَأَكْرَمَهُ
وَنَعَّمَهُ فَيَقُولُ رَبِّي أَكْرَمَنِ ﴿١٥﴾ وَأَمَّا
إِذَا مَا ابْتَلَاهُ فَقَدَرَ عَلَيْهِ رِزْقَهُ
فَيَقُولُ رَبِّي أَهَانَنِ ﴿١٦﴾ كَلَّا بَل لَّا
تُكْرِمُونَ الْيَتِيمَ ﴿١٧﴾ وَلَا تَحَاضُّونَ عَلَى
طَعَامِ الْمِسْكِينِ ﴿١٨﴾ وَتَأْكُلُونَ التُّرَاثَ
أَكْلًا لَّمًّا ﴿١٩﴾ وَتُحِبُّونَ الْمَالَ حُبًّا جَمًّا ﴿٢٠﴾
كَلَّا إِذَا دُكَّتِ الْأَرْضُ دَكًّا دَكًّا ﴿٢١﴾
وَجَاءَ رَبُّكَ وَالْمَلَكُ صَفًّا صَفًّا ﴿٢٢﴾ وَجِيءَ

(It is) on that very Day that a person will remember (the admonition), but of what avail shall that remembrance be to him (at that time)?
24. He will say, 'O would that I had sent forward (some good deeds as a provision) for this my life here (on this side).'
25. So on that day none but He shall execute His punishment,
26. And no one but He shall bind like His binding.
27. (As for the person who has been blessed with a contented and peaceful mind He will say to him,) 'O you soul at peace!
28. 'Come back to your Lord well-pleased with Him and He well-pleased with you.
29. 'Enter the fold of My chosen servants,
30. 'And enter the Garden made by Me.'

يومئذ بجهنم يومئذ يتذكر الإنسن
وأنى له الذكرى ﴿٢٣﴾ يقول يليتني قدمت
لحياتي ﴿٢٤﴾ فيومئذ لا يعذب عذابه أحد ﴿٢٥﴾
ولا يوثق وثاقه أحد ﴿٢٦﴾ يأيتها النفس
المطمئنة ﴿٢٧﴾ ارجعي إلى ربك راضية
مرضية ﴿٢٨﴾ فادخلي في عبدي ﴿٢٩﴾
وادخلي جنتي ﴿٣٠﴾

CHAPTER
90

AL-BALAD
(The City)
(Revealed before Hijrah)

سورة البلد مكية

With the name of Allâh,
the Most Gracious, the Ever Merciful
(I commence to read Sûrah Al-Balad).

بسم الله الرحمن الرحيم

1. NAY, (it will never happen as the disbelievers desire.) I do swear by this city (of Makkah),
2. When you will surely alight (as a conqueror) in this city.
3. And (I cite as witness your) father (-Abraham) and (his exalted) son (- Ismâîl).
4. We have certainly created a human being (to face obstacles and) to struggle hard (to achieve a marvelous goal).
5. Does he think that no one will have power (to use) against him?
6. He will say, 'I have wasted enormous wealth.'

لا أقسم بهذا البلد ﴿١﴾ وأنت حل
بهذا البلد ﴿٢﴾ ووالد وما ولد ﴿٣﴾ لقد
خلقنا الإنسن في كبد ﴿٤﴾ أيحسب أن
لن يقدر عليه أحد ﴿٥﴾ يقول أهلكت

7. But does he think that no one sees him?
8. Have We not given him two eyes (to distinguish right from wrong);
9. And a tongue and two lips (so that he can ask if he cannot see for himself),
10. And We have pointed out to him the two conspicuous high ways (of right and wrong)?
11. Yet he would not attempt the uphill path of steep and difficult ascent.
12. And what should make you know what the uphill path of steep and difficult ascent is?
13. (It is) the freeing of a captive (from the bondage of slavery, debt and other afflictions),
14. Or feeding in the time of famine
15. An orphan, near of kin,
16. Or a downtrodden poor person.
17. And what is even more, then he is of those who believe and exhort one another to be patiently persevering and exhort one another to be compassionate (towards God's creation).
18. These (who follow this hard path) are the blessed ones (- the people of the right hand).
19. But those who denied Our Messages are the wretched ones (- the people of the left hand).
20. There shall envelop them the Fire closed over (- a Fire the heat of which is not allowed to escape and they themselves cannot get out of it).

مَالًا لُّبَدًا ﴿٦﴾ أَيَحْسَبُ أَن لَّمْ يَرَهُ أَحَدٌ ﴿٧﴾
أَلَمْ نَجْعَل لَّهُ عَيْنَيْنِ ﴿٨﴾ وَلِسَانًا وَشَفَتَيْنِ ﴿٩﴾
وَهَدَيْنَٰهُ النَّجْدَيْنِ ﴿١٠﴾ فَلَا اقْتَحَمَ الْعَقَبَةَ ﴿١١﴾
وَمَا أَدْرَىٰكَ مَا الْعَقَبَةُ ﴿١٢﴾ فَكُّ رَقَبَةٍ ﴿١٣﴾ أَوْ
إِطْعَٰمٌ فِي يَوْمٍ ذِي مَسْغَبَةٍ ﴿١٤﴾ يَتِيمًا ذَا
مَقْرَبَةٍ ﴿١٥﴾ أَوْ مِسْكِينًا ذَا مَتْرَبَةٍ ﴿١٦﴾ ثُمَّ
كَانَ مِنَ الَّذِينَ آمَنُوا وَتَوَاصَوْا بِالصَّبْرِ
وَتَوَاصَوْا بِالْمَرْحَمَةِ ﴿١٧﴾ أُولَٰئِكَ أَصْحَٰبُ
الْمَيْمَنَةِ ﴿١٨﴾ وَالَّذِينَ كَفَرُوا بِآيَٰتِنَا هُمْ
أَصْحَٰبُ الْمَشْـَٔمَةِ ﴿١٩﴾ عَلَيْهِمْ نَارٌ مُّؤْصَدَةٌ ﴿٢٠﴾

ع ١٥

CHAPTER
91

سُوْرَةُ الشَّمْسِ ٩١

AL-SHAMS
(The Sun)
(Revealed before Hijrah)

سُوْرَةُ الشَّمْسِ مَكِّيَّةٌ

With the name of Allâh,
the Most Gracious, the Ever Merciful
(I commence to read Sûrah Al-Shams).

بِسْمِ اللّٰهِ الرَّحْمٰنِ الرَّحِيْمِ

1. I CALL to witness the sun and its light and heat,
2. And the moon when it borrows light from it (- the sun),
3. And the day when it reveals its (- the sun's) glory,
4. And the night when it draws a veil over it,
5. And the heaven and That (Great Omnifice Divinity) Who made it,
6. And the earth and That (Great Being) Who expanded it,
7. And the (human) soul and That (Mighty Lord) Who made it perfect,
8. Then He revealed to it (- the soul, the ways of) its evil and its righteousness,
9. (All these are cited to witness that) one who purifies it (- his soul), certainly succeeds,
10. And he indeed is ruined who corrupts it.
11. (The tribe of) Thamûd belied (Sâlih) because of their rebelliousness.
12. (It was) when the wretched-most among them arose,
13. And Allâh's Messenger said to them, '(Do not interfere with) the she-camel (- a symbol appointed by the command) of Allâh and (do not obstruct) her (from) watering.'
14. But they belied (and disobeyed) him and hamstrung her. Then their Lord destroyed them completely for their sin, so much so that He leveled them (all to the ground).
15. And He did not care at all for their end (as to what an utterly miserable state they were reduced).

وَالشَّمْسِ وَضُحٰهَا ﴿١﴾ وَالْقَمَرِ إِذَا تَلٰهَا ﴿٢﴾
وَالنَّهَارِ إِذَا جَلّٰهَا ﴿٣﴾ وَالَّيْلِ إِذَا يَغْشٰهَا ﴿٤﴾
وَالسَّمَآءِ وَمَا بَنٰهَا ﴿٥﴾ وَالْأَرْضِ وَمَا
طَحٰهَا ﴿٦﴾ وَنَفْسٍ وَّمَا سَوّٰهَا ﴿٧﴾ فَأَلْهَمَهَا
فُجُوْرَهَا وَتَقْوٰهَا ﴿٨﴾ قَدْ أَفْلَحَ مَنْ
زَكّٰهَا ﴿٩﴾ وَقَدْ خَابَ مَنْ دَسّٰهَا ﴿١٠﴾
كَذَّبَتْ ثَمُوْدُ بِطَغْوٰهَآ ﴿١١﴾ إِذِ انْبَعَثَ
أَشْقٰهَا ﴿١٢﴾ فَقَالَ لَهُمْ رَسُوْلُ اللّٰهِ نَاقَةَ
اللّٰهِ وَسُقْيٰهَا ﴿١٣﴾ فَكَذَّبُوْهُ فَعَقَرُوْهَا
فَدَمْدَمَ عَلَيْهِمْ رَبُّهُمْ بِذَنْۢبِهِمْ فَسَوّٰهَا ﴿١٤﴾
وَلَا يَخَافُ عُقْبٰهَا ﴿١٥﴾

ع ١٥ ١٦

CHAPTER
92

سُوْرَةُ اللَّيْلِ ٩٢

AL-LAIL
(The Night)
(Revealed before Hijrah)

With the name of Allâh,
the Most Gracious, the Ever Merciful
(I commence to read Sûrah Al-Lail).

1. **I** CALL to witness the night when it spreads (its) veil,
2. And the day when it becomes bright,
3. And all the males and the females that He created;
4. (That) diverse are the ends you strive to achieve.
5. Then as for the person who devotes (all his resources and capacities in the cause of God), gives (to others) and guards against evil,
6. And declares his faith in all that is best and right,
7. We will, then, invariably provide for him every facility (for doing good).
8. But as for him who is niggardly (and cripples his capacities) and is (disdainfully) indifferent (to God and the Hereafter),
9. And belies all that is best,
10. We will, then, of course make easy for him (the downhill path to) a state of distress,
11. And his wealth shall not avail him when he dies.
12. It is for Us to provide guidance,
13. And to Us belong (all the blessings of) both, the next world and the present.
14. (O people!) Now I have warned you of a flaming Fire.
15. None shall enter it but the wretched (sinner),
16. Who belies (the Truth) and turns (his) back (on it).

سُوْرَةُ الَّيْلِ مَكِّيَّةٌ

بِسْمِ اللّٰهِ الرَّحْمٰنِ الرَّحِيْمِ

وَالَّيْلِ إِذَا يَغْشٰى ١ وَالنَّهَارِ إِذَا تَجَلّٰى ٢
وَمَا خَلَقَ الذَّكَرَ وَالْأُنْثٰى ٣ إِنَّ
سَعْيَكُمْ لَشَتّٰى ٤ فَأَمَّا مَنْ أَعْطٰى وَاتَّقٰى ٥
وَصَدَّقَ بِالْحُسْنٰى ٦ فَسَنُيَسِّرُهٗ لِلْيُسْرٰى ٧
وَأَمَّا مَنْ بَخِلَ وَاسْتَغْنٰى ٨ وَكَذَّبَ
بِالْحُسْنٰى ٩ فَسَنُيَسِّرُهٗ لِلْعُسْرٰى ١٠ وَمَا
يُغْنِيْ عَنْهُ مَالُهٗۤ إِذَا تَرَدّٰى ١١ إِنَّ عَلَيْنَا
لَلْهُدٰى ١٢ وَإِنَّ لَنَا لَلْاٰخِرَةَ وَالْأُوْلٰى ١٣
فَأَنْذَرْتُكُمْ نَارًا تَلَظّٰى ١٤ لَا يَصْلٰهَا
إِلَّا الْأَشْقَى ١٥ الَّذِيْ كَذَّبَ وَتَوَلّٰى ١٦

17. But the one who guards against evil and keeps his duty (to God and others), shall most carefully be kept away from it (- the Fire).
18. A person who spends his wealth (seeking) to purify himself,
19. And not because he is under an obligation to anyone which (- obligation) has to be repaid,
20. But (he spends) only to seek the pleasure of his Lord, the Most High,
21. Surely, He will be well-pleased (with such a one).

وَ سَيُجَنَّبُهَا الۡاَتۡقَى ﴿١٧﴾ الَّذِيۡ يُؤۡتِيۡ مَالَهٗ يَتَزَكّٰى ﴿١٨﴾ وَمَا لِاَحَدٍ عِنۡدَهٗ مِنۡ نِّعۡمَةٍ تُجۡزٰۤى ﴿١٩﴾ اِلَّا ابۡتِغَآءَ وَجۡهِ رَبِّهِ الۡاَعۡلٰى ﴿٢٠﴾ وَ لَسَوۡفَ يَرۡضٰى ﴿٢١﴾

CHAPTER
93

AL-DZUHÂ
(The Forenoon Brightness)
(Revealed before Hijrah)

سُوۡرَةُ الضُّحٰى مَكِّيَّةٌ

With the name of Allâh,
the Most Gracious, the Ever Merciful
(I commence to read Sûrah Al-Dzuhâ).

بِسۡمِ اللّٰهِ الرَّحۡمٰنِ الرَّحِيۡمِ

1. **I** CALL to witness the growing brightness of the forenoon,
2. And the night when it becomes still,
3. (O Prophet!) Your Lord has not forsaken you, nor is He displeased (with you).
4. Surely, (your) future is better for you than your past.
5. Your Lord will soon give you (what you desire), and you will be well pleased (with Him).
6. Did He not find you an orphan and take (you) under (His) care?
7. He found you lost in (His) love (and that of His people), and gave you guidance (so as to enable you help the people reach the goal),
8. And He found you having a large family to support, He freed you from want (of every kind).
9. Therefore as to the orphan, do not allow him

وَ الضُّحٰى ﴿١﴾ وَ الَّيۡلِ اِذَا سَجٰى ﴿٢﴾ مَا وَدَّعَكَ رَبُّكَ وَ مَا قَلٰى ﴿٣﴾ وَ لَلۡاٰخِرَةُ خَيۡرٌ لَّكَ مِنَ الۡاُوۡلٰى ﴿٤﴾ وَ لَسَوۡفَ يُعۡطِيۡكَ رَبُّكَ فَتَرۡضٰى ﴿٥﴾ اَلَمۡ يَجِدۡكَ يَتِيۡمًا فَاٰوٰى ﴿٦﴾ وَ وَجَدَكَ ضَآلًّا فَهَدٰى ﴿٧﴾ وَ وَجَدَكَ

to be an oppressed person.
10. And as for the person who seeks (your assistance) do not chide him away.
11. Then as to the blessings and favours of your Lord, keep on proclaiming (your gratitude by doing similar favours to your fellow beings).

عَآئِلًا فَأَغْنٰى ﴿٨﴾ فَأَمَّا الْيَتِيمَ فَلَا
تَقْهَرْ ﴿٩﴾ وَأَمَّا السَّآئِلَ فَلَا تَنْهَرْ ﴿١٠﴾
وَأَمَّا بِنِعْمَةِ رَبِّكَ فَحَدِّثْ ﴿١١﴾

ع ١١ ١٨

CHAPTER
94

AL-SHARHA
(The Expanding)
(Revealed before Hijrah)

سُورَةُ الشَّرْحِ مَكِّيَّةٌ

With the name of Allâh,
the Most Gracious the Ever Merciful
(I commence to read Sûrah Al-Sharha).

1. **H**AVE We not (in fulfillment of your vision in your boyhood and again when you were entrusted with the Divine Mission) opened, expanded (and illuminated) for you your bosom,
2. And (have We not) relieved you of your burden (of various responsibilities)
3. Which had weighed your back down?
4. And have (We not) exalted for you your name and given you fame?
5. So surely every hardship is followed by ease.
6. Yes, every hardship shall be followed by an ease.
7. When you are free (having finished one task) strive hard to do (the next).
8. And to your Lord you do attend (wholeheartedly) and humble yourself before Him.

بِسْمِ اللهِ الرَّحْمٰنِ الرَّحِيمِ

أَلَمْ نَشْرَحْ لَكَ صَدْرَكَ ﴿١﴾ وَوَضَعْنَا
عَنْكَ وِزْرَكَ ﴿٢﴾ الَّذِيٓ أَنْقَضَ ظَهْرَكَ ﴿٣﴾
وَرَفَعْنَا لَكَ ذِكْرَكَ ﴿٤﴾ فَإِنَّ مَعَ
الْعُسْرِ يُسْرًا ﴿٥﴾ إِنَّ مَعَ الْعُسْرِ يُسْرًا ﴿٦﴾
فَإِذَا فَرَغْتَ فَانْصَبْ ﴿٧﴾ وَإِلٰى رَبِّكَ
فَارْغَبْ ﴿٨﴾

ع ٨ ١٩

CHAPTER
95

سُوۡرَةُ التِّيۡنِ ٩٥

AL-TÎN
(The Fig)
(Revealed before Hijrah)

سُوۡرَةُ التِّيۡنِ مَكِّيَّةٌ

With the name of Allâh,
the Most Gracious, the Ever Merciful
(I commence to read Sûrah Al-Tîn).

بِسۡمِ اللّٰهِ الرَّحۡمٰنِ الرَّحِيۡمِ

1. **I** CALL to witness (four periods of human evolution including) the Fig (symbolic of the era of Adam when the foundations of the human civilization were laid), and the Olive (that of Noah, the founder of *sharî'at*),
2. And Mount Sinai (that of Moses when the details of the Sharî'at were revealed),
3. And this Town of security (of Makkah where with the advent of the Prophet Muhammad, the divine law was perfected and finalized),
4. (That) We have surely created the human being in the finest make and the best proportions (with enormous capabilities for an all round advancement through the process of evolution).
5. Then (according to Our law of cause and consequence) We degrade him to the lowest of the low (if he does evil deeds).
6. Different, however, is the case of those who believe and do deeds of righteousness. There awaits them a never-ending reward.
7. Who is there, after this to belie you (O Prophet!) with regard to (the day of) Requital?
8. Is (there still anyone to say that it is) not Allâh the Best of Judges.

وَالتِّيۡنِ وَالزَّيۡتُوۡنِ ۙ﴿۱﴾ وَطُوۡرِ سِيۡنِيۡنَ ۙ﴿۲﴾
وَهٰذَا الۡبَلَدِ الۡاَمِيۡنِ ۙ﴿۳﴾ لَقَدۡ خَلَقۡنَا
الۡاِنۡسٰنَ فِيۡۤ اَحۡسَنِ تَقۡوِيۡمٍ ۫﴿۴﴾ ثُمَّ رَدَدۡنٰهُ
اَسۡفَلَ سٰفِلِيۡنَ ۙ﴿۵﴾ اِلَّا الَّذِيۡنَ اٰمَنُوۡا
وَعَمِلُوا الصّٰلِحٰتِ فَلَهُمۡ اَجۡرٌ غَيۡرُ
مَمۡنُوۡنٍ ؕ﴿۶﴾ فَمَا يُكَذِّبُكَ بَعۡدُ بِالدِّيۡنِ ؕ﴿۷﴾
اَلَيۡسَ اللّٰهُ بِاَحۡكَمِ الۡحٰكِمِيۡنَ ﴿۸﴾ ع

CHAPTER
96

سُورَةُ الْعَلَقِ ٩٦

AL-'ALAQ

(The Clot)

(Revealed before Hijrah)

سُورَةُ الْعَلَقِ مَكِّيَّةٌ

With the name of Allâh,
the Most Gracious, the Ever Merciful
(I commence to read Sûrah Al-'Alaq).

بِسْمِ اللّٰهِ الرَّحْمٰنِ الرَّحِيْمِ

1. **R**ECITE with the name of your Lord Who created (all the universe),
2. Who (also) created human being from a clot (-germinating-cell).
3. Proclaim, for your Lord is the Most Benignant;
4. Who taught knowledge by means of the pen,
5. He taught human being what he did not know.
6. Nay! (It is not at all as these people think), this human being does indeed indulge in transgression,
7. Because he thinks himself to be independent (of God).
8. (O people!) Surely, to your Lord is the ultimate return (of you all to be accounted for your deeds).
9. Have you considered (the case of one) who forbids
10. A servant (of God) when he prays (to His Lord)?
11. (O people!) Do you ever consider if he (who prays to God) follows the right guidance,
12. Or enjoins guarding against evil. (How bad will be the end of that forbidder?)
13. Do you (also) consider if a person (- the rejecter of Divine commandments) belies (them) and turns his back (upon the truth, what his end will be like)?

إِقْرَأْ بِاسْمِ رَبِّكَ الَّذِي خَلَقَ ﴿١﴾
خَلَقَ الْإِنْسٰنَ مِنْ عَلَقٍ ﴿٢﴾ إِقْرَأْ
وَرَبُّكَ الْأَكْرَمُ ﴿٣﴾ الَّذِي عَلَّمَ بِالْقَلَمِ ﴿٤﴾
عَلَّمَ الْإِنْسٰنَ مَا لَمْ يَعْلَمْ ﴿٥﴾ كَلَّا إِنَّ
الْإِنْسٰنَ لَيَطْغَىٰ ﴿٦﴾ أَنْ رَّاٰهُ اسْتَغْنَىٰ ﴿٧﴾
إِنَّ إِلَىٰ رَبِّكَ الرُّجْعَىٰ ﴿٨﴾ أَرَءَيْتَ الَّذِي
يَنْهَىٰ ﴿٩﴾ عَبْدًا إِذَا صَلَّىٰ ﴿١٠﴾ أَرَءَيْتَ إِنْ
كَانَ عَلَى الْهُدَىٰ ﴿١١﴾ أَوْ أَمَرَ بِالتَّقْوَىٰ ﴿١٢﴾
أَرَءَيْتَ إِنْ كَذَّبَ وَتَوَلَّىٰ ﴿١٣﴾ أَلَمْ يَعْلَمْ
بِأَنَّ اللّٰهَ يَرَىٰ ﴿١٤﴾ كَلَّا لَئِنْ لَّمْ يَنْتَهِ ۵

14. Does He not know that Allâh indeed observes (all)?
15. Nay, (it will never be as the rejecter desires.) If he does not desist (from these wicked ways), We shall assuredly (seize him and) drag him by the forelock -
16. A lying, sinful forelock.
17. Then let him call members of his association.
18. We will call Our brave defending guards.
19. Nay, (he will never succeed in his evil designs.) Yield not to him, rather continue to prostrate yourself (before your Lord) and draw near (to Him).

[PROSTRATION]

لَنَسْفَعًا بِالنَّاصِيَةِ ﴿١٥﴾ نَاصِيَةٍ كَٰذِبَةٍ خَاطِئَةٍ ﴿١٦﴾ فَلْيَدْعُ نَادِيَهُ ﴿١٧﴾ سَنَدْعُ الزَّبَانِيَةَ ﴿١٨﴾ كَلَّا لَا تُطِعْهُ وَاسْجُدْ وَاقْتَرِب ﴿١٩﴾ السجدة

ع ٥ ٢٢

CHAPTER 97

سُورَةُ الْقَدْرِ مَكِّيَّةٌ

AL-QADR
(The Majesty)
(Revealed before Hijrah)

With the name of Allâh, the Most Gracious, the Ever Merciful (I commence to read Sûrah Al-Qadr).

1. **W**E began to reveal it (- the Qur'ân) during the Night of Majesty (- a Night usually in the last ten days of the month of *Ramadzân*).
2. And what shall make you know what the Night of Majesty is!
3. The Night of Majesty is better than a thousand months.
4. The angels and the Divine word come down therein, by the command of their Lord to (determine) each and every affair.
5. (That Night is all) peace. It lasts till the rise of the dawn.

بِسْمِ اللّٰهِ الرَّحْمٰنِ الرَّحِيْمِ

إِنَّا أَنْزَلْنَهُ فِي لَيْلَةِ الْقَدْرِ ﴿١﴾ وَمَا أَدْرَىٰكَ مَا لَيْلَةُ الْقَدْرِ ﴿٢﴾ لَيْلَةُ الْقَدْرِ خَيْرٌ مِّنْ أَلْفِ شَهْرٍ ﴿٣﴾ تَنَزَّلُ الْمَلَٰٓئِكَةُ وَالرُّوحُ فِيهَا بِإِذْنِ رَبِّهِم مِّن كُلِّ أَمْرٍ ﴿٤﴾ سَلَٰمٌ هِيَ حَتَّىٰ مَطْلَعِ الْفَجْرِ ﴿٥﴾

ع ٥ ٢٢

CHAPTER
98

AL-BAYYINAH
(The Manifest Proof)
(Revealed after Hijrah)

سُورَةُ الْبَيِّنَةِ مَدَنِيَّةٌ

With the name of Allâh,
the Most Gracious, the Ever Merciful
(I commence to read Sûrah Al-Bayyinah).

بِسْمِ اللّٰهِ الرَّحْمٰنِ الرَّحِيمِ

1. **T**HOSE who disbelieve from among the people of the Scripture and (from among) those who associate gods with God, would not be rid of their bigotry and rejection of Faith until there should come to them the manifest proof -
2. A great Messenger (- Muhammad) from Allâh reciting (to them) written leaves of the Book, free from all impurities,
3. Consisting of eternal laws and commandments.
4. Those to whom the Scripture was given became divided only after the manifest proof had come to them.
5. (They have done it) though (in Islam) they were enjoined nothing more than to serve Allâh, bearing true faith in Him, (and) being upright, and to observe Prayer and to keep on presenting the *Zakât*. That is the true and firm conduct of faith.
6. Verily, those who disbelieve from among the people of the Scripture and (from among) those who associate gods with God shall be consigned to the Fire of Gehenna. Therein they shall abide. It is they who are the worst of all creatures.
7. Verily, those who believe and do deeds of righteousness, it is they who are the noblest of all creatures.
8. Their reward is with their Lord - Gardens of Eternity served with running streams (to keep

لَمْ يَكُنِ الَّذِينَ كَفَرُوا مِنْ أَهْلِ
الْكِتٰبِ وَالْمُشْرِكِينَ مُنْفَكِّينَ حَتّٰى
تَأْتِيَهُمُ الْبَيِّنَةُ ﴿١﴾ رَسُولٌ مِّنَ اللّٰهِ
يَتْلُوا صُحُفًا مُّطَهَّرَةً ﴿٢﴾ فِيهَا كُتُبٌ
قَيِّمَةٌ ﴿٣﴾ وَمَا تَفَرَّقَ الَّذِينَ أُوتُوا
الْكِتٰبَ إِلَّا مِنْ بَعْدِ مَا جَآءَتْهُمُ
الْبَيِّنَةُ ﴿٤﴾ وَمَآ أُمِرُوٓا إِلَّا لِيَعْبُدُوا اللّٰهَ
مُخْلِصِينَ لَهُ الدِّينَ حُنَفَآءَ وَيُقِيمُوا
الصَّلٰوةَ وَيُؤْتُوا الزَّكٰوةَ وَذٰلِكَ
دِينُ الْقَيِّمَةِ ﴿٥﴾ إِنَّ الَّذِينَ كَفَرُوا
مِنْ أَهْلِ الْكِتٰبِ وَالْمُشْرِكِينَ فِي
نَارِ جَهَنَّمَ خٰلِدِينَ فِيهَآ أُولٰٓئِكَ
هُمْ شَرُّ الْبَرِيَّةِ ﴿٦﴾ إِنَّ الَّذِينَ ءَامَنُوا
وَعَمِلُوا الصّٰلِحٰتِ أُولٰٓئِكَ هُمْ خَيْرُ
الْبَرِيَّةِ ﴿٧﴾ جَزَآؤُهُمْ عِنْدَ رَبِّهِمْ جَنّٰتُ
عَدْنٍ تَجْرِي مِنْ تَحْتِهَا الْأَنْهٰرُ

them green and flourishing), they shall abide therein, forever and ever. Allâh is well-pleased with them and they are well-pleased with Him (in their state of highest bliss). Such is (the reward) for a person who stands in awe of his Lord.

خٰلِدِينَ فِيهَآ أَبَدًا ۖ رَضِيَ اللّٰهُ عَنْهُمْ
وَرَضُوا عَنْهُ ۚ ذٰلِكَ لِمَنْ خَشِيَ رَبَّهُ ۝٨

CHAPTER
99

AL-ZALZALAH
(The Shaking)
(Revealed after Hijrah)

With the name of Allâh,
the Most Gracious, the Ever Merciful
(I commence to read Sûrah Al-Zalzalah).

1. **W**HEN the earth is shaken with its violent shaking,
2. And when the earth shall throw up all her treasures,
3. And when a person will say (in bewilderment at the extraordinary happenings on the earth), 'What is the matter with her?'
4. That day she will relate all her news (pertaining to every action done in secret on it).
5. For your Lord will have inspired her (to do so).
6. On that day (of Reckoning) all people will come forth in various groups to be shown (the results of) their deeds.
7. Then whosoever has done so much as an atom's weight of good will see (the good result of) it.
8. Similarly whosoever has done so much as an atom's weight of evil shall also see it.

سُورَةُ الزَّلْزَلَةِ مَدَنِيَّةٌ

بِسْمِ اللّٰهِ الرَّحْمٰنِ الرَّحِيمِ

إِذَا زُلْزِلَتِ الْأَرْضُ زِلْزَالَهَا ۝١
وَأَخْرَجَتِ الْأَرْضُ أَثْقَالَهَا ۝٢ وَقَالَ
الْإِنْسٰنُ مَا لَهَا ۝٣ يَوْمَئِذٍ تُحَدِّثُ
أَخْبَارَهَا ۝٤ بِأَنَّ رَبَّكَ أَوْحٰى لَهَا ۝٥
يَوْمَئِذٍ يَصْدُرُ النَّاسُ أَشْتَاتًا لِّيُرَوْا
أَعْمٰلَهُمْ ۝٦ فَمَنْ يَعْمَلْ مِثْقَالَ ذَرَّةٍ
خَيْرًا يَرَهُ ۝٧ وَمَنْ يَعْمَلْ مِثْقَالَ
ذَرَّةٍ شَرًّا يَرَهُ ۝٨

CHAPTER
100

AL-'ÂDIYÂT
(The Chargers)
(Revealed before Hijrah)

With the name of Allâh,
the Most Gracious, the Ever Merciful
(I commence to read Sûrah Al-'Âdiyât).

1. **I** CALL to witness the panting and snorting chargers (of the warriors).
2. And those that strike sparks of fire dashing (their hoofs) against the stones,
3. And those that make raids at dawn,
4. And raising up clouds of dust therewith.
5. They penetrate thus right into the middle of the (enemy) ranks,
6. That (good for nothing) human being is indeed very ungrateful to his Lord.
7. And he himself bears witness to all this (by his conduct).
8. And he is, truly speaking, the extreme limit in (his) love for wealth.
9. Does not, then, such a one know (the time) when all those in the graves will be raised up (in the Hereafter);
10. And (the time when) what is (hidden) in the bosoms (of people) shall be made known.
11. Verily, their Lord is, of course, fully Aware of (all regarding) them that day.

سُوْرَةُ الْعٰدِيٰتِ مَكِّيَّةٌ

بِسْمِ اللّٰهِ الرَّحْمٰنِ الرَّحِيْمِ

وَ الْعٰدِيٰتِ ضَبْحًا ۙ﴿١﴾ فَالْمُوْرِيٰتِ قَدْحًا ۙ﴿٢﴾
فَالْمُغِيْرٰتِ صُبْحًا ۙ﴿٣﴾ فَاَثَرْنَ بِهٖ نَقْعًا ۙ﴿٤﴾
فَوَسَطْنَ بِهٖ جَمْعًا ۙ﴿٥﴾ اِنَّ الْاِنْسٰنَ لِرَبِّهٖ
لَكَنُوْدٌ ۚ﴿٦﴾ وَ اِنَّهٗ عَلٰى ذٰلِكَ لَشَهِيْدٌ ۚ﴿٧﴾
وَ اِنَّهٗ لِحُبِّ الْخَيْرِ لَشَدِيْدٌ ؕ﴿٨﴾ اَفَلَا يَعْلَمُ
اِذَا بُعْثِرَ مَا فِي الْقُبُوْرِ ۙ﴿٩﴾ وَ حُصِّلَ مَا فِي
الصُّدُوْرِ ۙ﴿١٠﴾ اِنَّ رَبَّهُمْ بِهِمْ يَوْمَئِذٍ لَّخَبِيْرٌ ﴿١١﴾ ع ١١ ٢٥

سُورَةُ الْقَارِعَةِ ١٠١

CHAPTER
101

AL-QÂRI'AH

(The Disastrous Rattling)
(Revealed before Hijrah)

With the name of Allâh,
the Most Gracious, the Ever Merciful
(I commence to read Sûrah Al-Qâri'ah).

1. THE Disastrous Rattling (of this life as seen in warfare is sure to visit the world).
2. How very terrible is the Disastrous Rattling!
3. What should make you know how very severe and destructive the Disastrous Rattling is!
4. On that day people shall be (in great confusion and distress) like moths scattered,
5. And the mountains shall look like carded wool.
6. Now as for the person whose scales (of virtues) are heavy (and good deeds are preponderant),
7. He shall have a pleasant life.
8. But as for the person whose scales (of good deeds) are light (and of no account),
9. The abyss (- Gehenna) shall then be a (nursing) mother to him (till the souls are completely cleansed of the taint of sin and they are reborn).
10. Ah! What should make you know what that (abyss) is!
11. It is a blazing Fire (for burning out all the dross that people collect by leading a sinful life in this world).

سُورَةُ الْقَارِعَةِ مَكِّيَّةٌ

بِسْمِ اللّٰهِ الرَّحْمٰنِ الرَّحِيْمِ

اَلْقَارِعَةُ ﴿١﴾ مَا الْقَارِعَةُ ﴿٢﴾ وَ مَآ
اَدْرٰىكَ مَا الْقَارِعَةُ ﴿٣﴾ يَوْمَ يَكُوْنُ
النَّاسُ كَالْفَرَاشِ الْمَبْثُوْثِ ﴿٤﴾ وَتَكُوْنُ
الْجِبَالُ كَالْعِهْنِ الْمَنْفُوْشِ ﴿٥﴾ فَاَمَّا
مَنْ ثَقُلَتْ مَوٰزِيْنُهٗ ﴿٦﴾ فَهُوَ فِيْ عِيْشَةٍ
رَّاضِيَةٍ ﴿٧﴾ وَ اَمَّا مَنْ خَفَّتْ مَوٰزِيْنُهٗ ﴿٨﴾
فَاُمُّهٗ هَاوِيَةٌ ﴿٩﴾ وَمَآ اَدْرٰىكَ مَا هِيَهْ ﴿١٠﴾
نَارٌ حَامِيَةٌ ﴿١١﴾

ع ٢٦

الجزء الثلاثون

CHAPTER
102

AL-TAKÂTHUR
(The Vying With One Another To Excel)
(Revealed before Hijrah)

With the name of Allâh,
the Most Gracious, the Ever Merciful
(I commence to read Sûrah Al-Takâthur).

1. (**O** PEOPLE! your) vying with one another to excel in multiplying worldly possessions diverts you (from God and true values of life),
2. Until (on your death) you embrace the graves.
3. Nay, (you should never hanker after worldly gains, power and position,) you shall come to know in time (that you have been chasing a shadow).
4. Nay, again (We repeat, never should you misuse your life of probation,) you shall come to know (the consequences of it) in time.
5. No, never! If you only knew the consequences thereof with sure and certain knowledge
6. You will certainly see the very Hell-Fire (in this present life by seeing the sad fate of the wicked).
7. Again, you shall most certainly see it (in the Hereafter) with the eye of certainty.
8. And then on that day (of Reckoning) you shall be called to account for the favours (bestowed upon you).

سُورَةُ التَّكَاثُرِ مَكِّيَّةٌ

أَلْهَىٰكُمُ التَّكَاثُرُ ۝١ حَتَّىٰ زُرْتُمُ الْمَقَابِرَ ۝٢ كَلَّا سَوْفَ تَعْلَمُونَ ۝٣ ثُمَّ كَلَّا سَوْفَ تَعْلَمُونَ ۝٤ كَلَّا لَوْ تَعْلَمُونَ عِلْمَ الْيَقِينِ ۝٥ لَتَرَوُنَّ الْجَحِيمَ ۝٦ ثُمَّ لَتَرَوُنَّهَا عَيْنَ الْيَقِينِ ۝٧ ثُمَّ لَتُسْأَلُنَّ يَوْمَئِذٍ عَنِ النَّعِيمِ ۝٨

ع ٨ ٢٧

CHAPTER
103

AL-‘ASR
(The Time)
(Revealed before Hijrah)

سُورَةُ الْعَصْرِ مَكِّيَّةٌ

With the name of Allâh,
the Most Gracious, the Ever Merciful
(I commence to read Sûrah Al-‘Asr).

بِسْمِ اللّٰهِ الرَّحْمٰنِ الرَّحِيمِ

1. **I** CITE as witness the Time.
2. Verily, a person (who is unmindful of God and higher values of his life) is pursuing a losing bargain.
3. Different, however, is the case of those who believe and do deeds of righteousness and (who) exhort one another to (accept and preach) the truth and exhort one another to (abide by it with) patience and perseverance.

وَالْعَصْرِ ۝١ إِنَّ الْإِنْسٰنَ لَفِي خُسْرٍ ۝٢ إِلَّا الَّذِينَ اٰمَنُوا وَعَمِلُوا الصّٰلِحٰتِ وَتَوَاصَوْا بِالْحَقِّ ۙ وَتَوَاصَوْا بِالصَّبْرِ ۝٣

CHAPTER
104

AL-HUMAZAH
(The Slanderer)
(Revealed before Hijrah)

سُورَةُ الْهُمَزَةِ مَكِّيَّةٌ

With the name of Allâh,
the Most Gracious, the Ever Merciful
(I commence to read Sûrah Al-Humazah).

بِسْمِ اللّٰهِ الرَّحْمٰنِ الرَّحِيمِ

1. **D**ISASTER is (decreed) for every slanderer, defamer,
2. Who amasses wealth (instead of spending it for the good of humanity), counts it over and over and depends upon it as a safeguard (against his future possible hardships).
3. He thinks that his wealth will make him immortal.

وَيْلٌ لِّكُلِّ هُمَزَةٍ لُّمَزَةٍ ۝١ الَّذِي جَمَعَ مَالًا وَّعَدَّدَهُ ۝٢ يَحْسَبُ أَنَّ مَالَهُ أَخْلَدَهُ ۝٣ كَلَّا لَيُنْبَذَنَّ فِي الْحُطَمَةِ ۝٤

4. No, never! He shall surely be cast into the crushing torment (of Hell).
5. And what should make you know what the crushing torment is?
6. (It is) the Fire set ablaze by Allâh,
7. And which rises over (the feelings of) the hearts (- the origin of a man's hell).
8. It (- Fire) will be closed in on them (so as not to let them escape from it and also increase for them the torture of heat).
9. (The flames of the Fire will rise) in (the form of) huge outstretched columns.

وَمَا أَدْرٰكَ مَا الْحُطَمَةُ ٥ نَارُ اللّٰهِ
الْمُوقَدَةُ ٦ الَّتِي تَطَّلِعُ عَلَى الْأَفْئِدَةِ ٧
إِنَّهَا عَلَيْهِم مُّؤْصَدَةٌ ٨ فِي عَمَدٍ مُّمَدَّدَةٍ ٩ ع ٢٩

CHAPTER
105

AL-FÎL
(The Elephant)
(Revealed before Hijrah)

سُورَةُ الْفِيلِ مَكِّيَّةٌ

With the name of Allâh,
the Most Gracious, the Ever Merciful
(I commence to read Sûrah Al-Fîl).

بِسْمِ اللّٰهِ الرَّحْمٰنِ الرَّحِيمِ

1. **H**AVE you not considered how your Lord dealt with the People of the Elephant (- the army of *Abrahah,* the viceroy of the Negus, king of Abyssînia at Yemen)?
2. Did He not (cause the war to end in confusion and) ruin their plan (to destroy the *Ka'bah* by making it revert to themselves)?
3. And He sent against them flocks of birds,
4. (Which tore off flesh from their bodies to eat by) striking them against stones of hardened and petrified clay.
5. And thus He reduced them to rotten chaff (and in a similar way will they be ruined who would ever make an attack to destroy the *Ka'bah*).

أَلَمْ تَرَ كَيْفَ فَعَلَ رَبُّكَ بِأَصْحٰبِ
الْفِيلِ ١ أَلَمْ يَجْعَلْ كَيْدَهُمْ فِي
تَضْلِيلٍ ٢ وَّأَرْسَلَ عَلَيْهِمْ طَيْرًا أَبَابِيلَ ٣
تَرْمِيهِم بِحِجَارَةٍ مِّن سِجِّيلٍ ٤ فَجَعَلَهُمْ
كَعَصْفٍ مَّأْكُولٍ ٥ ع ٣٠

CHAPTER
106

AL-QURAISH
(The Quraish)
(Revealed before Hijrah)

سُورَةُ قُرَيْشٍ مَكِّيَّةٌ

With the name of Allâh,
the Most Gracious, the Ever Merciful
(I commence to read Sûrah Al-Quraish).

بِسْمِ اللّٰهِ الرَّحْمٰنِ الرَّحِيمِ

1. (**THE LORD** destroyed the People of the Elephants which event proved helpful) for making covenants of the Quraish (with their contemporary kings for trade).
2. (And also) for their covenants of journeying (by taking caravans) in winter (to the south) and in summer (to the north).
3. (They should be ever grateful to God for this favour and) therefore they should worship the Lord of this House (*Ka'bah* at Makkah),
4. Who has fed them against hunger, and given them peace and security against all fear.

لِإِيلٰفِ قُرَيْشٍ ① إِلٰفِهِمْ رِحْلَةَ الشِّتَاءِ وَالصَّيْفِ ② فَلْيَعْبُدُوا رَبَّ هٰذَا الْبَيْتِ ③ الَّذِي أَطْعَمَهُمْ مِّنْ جُوعٍ وَّ ءَامَنَهُمْ مِّنْ خَوْفٍ ④

CHAPTER
107

AL-MÂ'ÛN
(The Acts of Kindness)
(Revealed before Hijrah)

سُورَةُ الْمَاعُونِ مَكِّيَّةٌ

With the name of Allâh,
the Most Gracious, the Ever Merciful
(I commence to read Sûrah Al-Mâ'ûn).

بِسْمِ اللّٰهِ الرَّحْمٰنِ الرَّحِيمِ

1. **HAVE** you considered the case of one who belies the Requital and Faith?
2. As a result of it this (despicable) fellow (instead of taking care of him with affection) repulses the orphan,
3. And does not urge in feeding of the needy.

أَرَءَيْتَ الَّذِي يُكَذِّبُ بِالدِّينِ ① فَذٰلِكَ الَّذِي يَدُعُّ الْيَتِيمَ ② وَلَا

4. So woe to those who Pray,
5. But are unmindful of their Prayer (and ignore the spirit and aim of it),
6. And they like (only) to be seen (of people while they make a show of their deeds),
7. And who withhold (legal) alms and other acts of kindness (starting from the *Zakât* to the lowest form of lending ordinary things of utility like a needle or a piece of thread to a neighbour).

يَحُضُّ عَلٰى طَعَامِ الْمِسْكِيْنِ ٣ فَوَيْلٌ لِّلْمُصَلِّيْنَ ٤ الَّذِيْنَ هُمْ عَنْ صَلَاتِهِمْ سَاهُوْنَ ٥ الَّذِيْنَ هُمْ يُرَآءُوْنَ ٦ وَ يَمْنَعُوْنَ الْمَاعُوْنَ ٧

CHAPTER
108

AL-KAUTHAR
(The Abundance Of Good)
(Revealed before Hijrah)

سُوْرَةُ الْكَوْثَرِ مَكِّيَّةٌ

With the name of Allâh,
the Most Gracious, the Ever Merciful
(I commence to read Sûrah Al-Kauthar).

بِسْمِ اللّٰهِ الرَّحْمٰنِ الرَّحِيْمِ

1. **V**ERILY, We have bestowed upon you (O Muhammad!) abundance of good (both of this life and of the Hereafter).
2. Therefore observe Prayer for the sake of your Lord and offer sacrifice (to Him).
3. Surely, it is your enemy who is cut off entirely (from all good and prosperity and is deprived of Spiritual issues).

إِنَّآ أَعْطَيْنٰكَ الْكَوْثَرَ ١ فَصَلِّ لِرَبِّكَ وَانْحَرْ ٢ إِنَّ شَانِئَكَ هُوَ الْأَبْتَرُ ٣

CHAPTER
109

AL-KÂFIRÛN
(The Disbelievers)
(Revealed before Hijrah)

سُورَةُ الكَافِرُونَ مَكِّيَّةٌ

With the name of Allâh,
the Most Gracious, the Ever Merciful
(I commence to read Sûrah Al-Kâfirûn).

بِسْمِ اللهِ الرَّحْمٰنِ الرَّحِيْمِ

1. **S**AY (plainly to those present and who are not), 'O you disbelievers!
2. 'I will not at all worship those (false deities) which you worship,
3. 'Nor are you worshippers of Him Whom I worship.
4. 'Neither have I ever been a worshipper of those (false ancestral customs, superstitions, and deities) which you worship,
5. 'Nor are you worshippers on the lines on which I worship.
6. 'For you is your recompense and for me is my recompense.'

قُلْ يَأَيُّهَا الْكٰفِرُوْنَ ① لَآ أَعْبُدُ مَا تَعْبُدُوْنَ ② وَلَآ أَنْتُمْ عٰبِدُوْنَ مَآ أَعْبُدُ ③ وَلَآ أَنَا عَابِدٌ مَّا عَبَدْتُّمْ ④ وَلَآ أَنْتُمْ عٰبِدُوْنَ مَآ أَعْبُدُ ⑤ لَكُمْ دِيْنُكُمْ وَلِيَ دِيْنِ ⑥

CHAPTER
110

AL-NASR
(The Help)
(Revealed after Hijrah)

سُورَةُ النَّصْرِ مَدَنِيَّةٌ

With the name of Allâh,
the Most Gracious, the Ever Merciful
(I commence to read Sûrah Al-Nasr).

بِسْمِ اللهِ الرَّحْمٰنِ الرَّحِيْمِ

1. **T**HE help of Allâh and the victory (over the Makkans) has indeed come (in fulfillment of the prophecies),
2. And you see people thronging to the fold of the Faith of Allâh.
3. So glorify your Lord with His praises and extol His name and ask His protection. Surely, He is Oft-Returning (with grace and mercy).

إِذَا جَآءَ نَصْرُ اللهِ وَالْفَتْحُ ① وَرَأَيْتَ النَّاسَ يَدْخُلُوْنَ فِيْ دِيْنِ اللهِ أَفْوَاجًا ② فَسَبِّحْ بِحَمْدِ رَبِّكَ وَاسْتَغْفِرْهُ إِنَّهٗ كَانَ تَوَّابًا ③

CHAPTER
111

AL-MASAD
(The Twisted Strands)
(Revealed before Hijrah)

With the name of Allâh,
the Most Gracious, the Ever Merciful
(I commence to read Sûrah Al-Masad).

1. LET the two hands of Abû Lahab (the Prophet's uncle, one of his most inveterate opponents and other fiery tempered enemies of Islam) perish, and let he himself (also) perish!
2. His wealth and what he has accomplished shall avail him naught.
3. He shall soon enter a Fire full of leaping flames (to burn others of his kind as well),
4. And his wife too, the carrier of fire wood and bearer of slanders and calumnies (will also be enveloped in the flames);
5. Having round her neck a halter of twisted strands.

سورة المسد مكية

بسم الله الرحمن الرحيم

تَبَّتْ يَدَآ أَبِي لَهَبٍ وَّتَبَّ ۝١ مَآ أَغْنٰى عَنْهُ مَالُهٗ وَمَا كَسَبَ ۝٢ سَيَصْلٰى نَارًا ذَاتَ لَهَبٍ ۝٣ وَّامْرَأَتُهٗ حَمَّالَةَ الْحَطَبِ ۝٤ فِي جِيدِهَا حَبْلٌ مِّنْ مَّسَدٍ ۝٥

ع ٣٦

CHAPTER
112

AL-IKHLÂS
(The Purification Of The Unity Of God)
(Revealed before Hijrah)

With the name of Allâh,
the Most Gracious, the Ever Merciful
(I commence to read Sûrah Al-Ikhlâs).

1. SAY, '(The fact is) He is Allâh, the One and Alone in His Being.
2. 'Allâh is that Supreme Being Who is the, Independent and Besought of all and Unique in all His attributes.
3. 'He begets none and is begotten by no one.
4. 'And there is none His equal.'

سورة الإخلاص مكية

بسم الله الرحمن الرحيم

قُلْ هُوَ اللّٰهُ أَحَدٌ ۝١ اَللّٰهُ الصَّمَدُ ۝٢ لَمْ يَلِدْ وَلَمْ يُولَدْ ۝٣ وَلَمْ يَكُنْ لَّهٗ كُفُوًا أَحَدٌ ۝٤

ع ٣٧

CHAPTER
113

AL-FALAQ
(The Daybreak)
(Revealed before Hijrah)

سُورَةُ الْفَلَقِ مَكِّيَّةٌ

With the name of Allâh,
the Most Gracious, the Ever Merciful
(I commence to read Sûrah Al-Falaq).

بِسْمِ اللّٰهِ الرَّحْمٰنِ الرَّحِيمِ

1. **S**AY, 'I seek refuge in the Lord of the day break, and the plain appearing and emergence of truth.
2. 'From the evil of that which He has created,
3. 'And from the evil (that usually prevails in the times) of darkness when it overspreads (at night),
4. 'And from the evil of those who try (and whisper evil suggestions) to deter (people) from doing their duty,
5. 'And from the evil of the envier when he envies.'

قُلْ أَعُوذُ بِرَبِّ الْفَلَقِ ﴿١﴾ مِنْ شَرِّ مَا خَلَقَ ﴿٢﴾ وَمِنْ شَرِّ غَاسِقٍ إِذَا وَقَبَ ﴿٣﴾ وَمِنْ شَرِّ النَّفّٰثٰتِ فِي الْعُقَدِ ﴿٤﴾ وَمِنْ شَرِّ حَاسِدٍ إِذَا حَسَدَ ﴿٥﴾

ع ٥ ٣٨

CHAPTER
114

AL-NÂS
(The People)
(Revealed before Hijrah)

سُورَةُ النَّاسِ مَكِّيَّةٌ

With the name of Allâh,
the Most Gracious, the Ever Merciful
(I commence to read Sûrah Al-Nâs).

بِسْمِ اللّٰهِ الرَّحْمٰنِ الرَّحِيمِ

1. **S**AY, 'I seek refuge in the Lord of People,
2. 'The Sovereign, the Controller of all affairs of People,
3. 'The God of People,
4. '(That He may protect me) from the evil (of the whisperings) of the whisperer, the sneaking one.
5. 'Who whispers evil suggestions into the hearts of People,
6. 'From among the *jinn* (- fiery natured, haughty) and the (ordinary) people.'

قُلْ أَعُوذُ بِرَبِّ النَّاسِ ﴿١﴾ مَلِكِ النَّاسِ ﴿٢﴾ إِلٰهِ النَّاسِ ﴿٣﴾ مِنْ شَرِّ الْوَسْوَاسِ الْخَنَّاسِ ﴿٤﴾ الَّذِي يُوَسْوِسُ فِي صُدُورِ النَّاسِ ﴿٥﴾ مِنَ الْجِنَّةِ وَالنَّاسِ ﴿٦﴾

ع ٦ ٣٩

دُعَاءُ

خَتْمِ الْقُرْآنِ الْعَظِيْمِ

PRAYER AFTER COMPLETING THE READING AND RECITATION OF THE HOLY QUR'ÂN

اَللّٰهُمَّ ، آنِسْ وَحْشَتِيْ فِيْ قَبْرِيْ -
اَللّٰهُمَّ ، ارْحَمْنِيْ بِالْقُرْآنِ الْعَظِيْمِ وَاجْعَلْهُ
لِيْ إِمَامًا وَّنُوْرًا وَّهُدًى وَّرَحْمَةً - اَللّٰهُمَّ
ذَكِّرْنِيْ مِنْهُ مَا نَسِيْتُ وَعَلِّمْنِيْ مِنْهُ مَا
جَهِلْتُ وَارْزُقْنِيْ تِلَاوَتَهُ آنَاءَ اللَّيْلِ
وَآنَاءَ النَّهَارِ وَاجْعَلْهُ لِيْ حُجَّةً ،
يَا رَبَّ الْعٰلَمِيْنَ -

O Allâh! Change into love any fear (I may have) in my grave. O Allâh! Have mercy on me because of the great Qur'ân. Make it my leader, my light, my (source) of guidance and mercy. O Allâh! Make me remember whatever of the Qur'ân I may forget; make me learn that which I have become ignorant of, make me recite it day and night and make it an argument and plea for me (on the Day of Judgement) O Lord of all the worlds!

APPENDICES

SOME QUR'ÂNIC WORDS AND EXPRESSIONS EXPLAINED

Each word will be found under its verbal root. Occasionally, words which seem likely to puzzle may be found in their alphabetical place or another more appropriate position. For convenience sake we have given the English of the infinitive instead of the third person singular or grammatical root of the verb.

(A) ا

Âdam آدم derived from *âdama:* To reconcile; to be brown; human skin; human being; man; person; intelligent person; brown man; brave man; human race; humankind; civilized person; a chief; honest person; kind and polite person; a person who is created from different substances; a person in possession of different powers; one who enjoys the comforts of life; one who is by nature social.

Âdam who lived about 6,000 years ago is generally taken by the followers of the Holy Bible to be the proper name for the first human being. But the Holy Qur'ân does not affirm that he was the first man, or that there was no creation before him. The Holy Qur'ân does not follow the Holy Bible in holding that the world began with the birth of this Âdam, about six thousand years ago, and that before this there was nothing. Neither does it claim that all human beings, who are now found in different parts of the earth, are the progeny of the selfsame Âdam or that the races which lived before this Âdam were entirely swept away before he was born. On the contrary it holds that this Âdam was not the first man and that the humankind existed even before him as the Holy Qur'ân says: 'I am about to place a *Khalîfah* in the earth' (2:30). *Khalîfah* means a successor, someone who comes after someone and stands in the place of someone, one who precedes someone and is followed by him. It also means a supreme religious head. By using the word *khalîfah* the Holy Qur'ân clarifies that human beings were already living on this earth and that this Âdam was a successor of the old race. In 7:10-11 addressing the human race Allâh says, 'We have indeed established you in the earth and provided for you therein means of subsistence. How little thanks you give. We did determine you, then We gave you shape, then said to the angels, "Make submission to Âdam," So they all submitted. But Iblîs (did not), he would not be of those who submitted'. These verses clearly point to the same conclusion that human beings were already living on this earth and it was after the creation of human beings and not just Âdam when 'angles' received the order of submission of the verse 2:34.

The word Âdam also stands for the children of Âdam (L.T.), and for human being who is the object, the crown and acme of all creations (17:70), and whose creation became complete after a long process of gradual development and evolution. His creation was the result of a predetermined plan and has been created to rule and dominate other creations as the Qur'ân says, 'And (recall) when your Lord said to the Angels, 'I am (according to my usual practice) going to appoint a *khalîfah* - a supreme religious head in the earth (to convey My Message to human beings and to execute My will in the universe) (2:30).' Again, as the verse continues, "the shedding of the blood" cannot be the work of one person. The reference here is to the "shedding of the blood" of man by man. The world has passed through different cycles of creation, aeons and civilizations, and this Âdam is only the first link in the present cycle and civilization and not the very first human being in Allâh's creation.

The garden which Âdam was bidden to leave (7:24) was not the Heaven or Paradise of the Hereafter, because the

Paradise is a place from where nobody will ever be turned out (15:48). Iraq is considered by Muslim scholars to be the place where this Âdam lived. The Holy Prophet ﷺ is reported to have described the Euphrates as the river of the garden referring to the Paradise of Âdam (Muslim, chapter *Jannat*). Great Muslim scholars were also of the view that there were hundreds of thousands of Âdams before this Âdam (Ma'ânî). Muhyuddin ibn Àrabî, the great Muslim mystic says, "I saw a ruin of a building which was erected thirty thousands years ago. Then I saw myself in a vision performing a circuit of Ka'bah with some other people. I inquired one of them who they were. He replied, 'We are from your ancestors'. I asked them how long is that they died. The man replied, 'More than forty thousand years.' But this period is much more than which separates us from Âdam, said I. The man replied, 'Of which Âdam are you speaking, about the Âdam who is nearest to you and the people of your generation?' Then I recollected the saying of the Holy Prophet ﷺ to the effect that Allâh has created hundred and thousands of Âdams and between each and every Âdam there is a period of seventeen thousand years. And I said to myself, perhaps these people who are said to be ancestors of mine were the previous Âdams." (Fatûhât al-Makkiyyah, 3:607).

Âyah آية: Pl. Âyât: Message; sign or mark; wonder; miracle; verse of the sacred Book; example (R.L.T.Kf.). This word is of very frequent occurrence in the Holy Qur'ân.

Ab اب : Father; any male ancestor; sire; uncle. In Arabic the word for real father is *wâlid*. **Abawain:** Father and mother; father and uncle (R.L.T.).

Abâbîl ابابيل: Flocks of birds; swarms; flock after flock; a company in a state of dispersion; dispersed flock following one another; birds in company from this or that quarter (L.T.R.).

Abad ابد: To be wild (an animal); for-ever; for a long time (to remain in a place); perpetuity (L.T.).

A<u>h</u>â<u>t</u>â احاط: Is derived from *<u>h</u>awâ<u>t</u>*: To surround; to destroy; to make the destruction near (L.T.R.).

As<u>h</u>âb al-Rass اصحاب الرس: The People of Rass. Rass means old well; first touch, beginning; name of a country in which part of the tribe of Thamûd resided. According to an opinion quoted in Tâj *Rass* رس was a town in Yamamah. Ibn Kat<u>h</u>îr says that Rass meant a well. It is said that they were a people who threw their prophet into a well. In the modern maps of Arabia Rass or Ras is placed in Wâdî Rummah in the district of Qasîm (latitude 26 N and longitude 43 E) (Ḷ.T.).

A<u>kh</u> اخ: Brother, friend, companion, match, fellow. **A<u>kh</u>iyyah:** Tie; bond (L.T.R.).

Al ال: The definite article. It is equivalent to 'the' in English, the most, all, complete, maximum, whole. It is used to denote comprehensiveness that is to say all aspects or categories of a subject or to denote perfection and includes all degrees and grades. It is also used to indicate something which has already been mentioned or a concept of which is present in the mind of the writer or reader (M.Ḷ.Kf.).

Alla الا: (*an-la*): Lest... that he... not.

Allâh الله: Is the proper noun applied to the Supreme Being Who is the sole possessor of all perfect attributes, Who is free from all defects and Who exists necessarily by Himself (L.T.). It is not a common noun. All Divine attributes mentioned in the Holy Qur'ân are qualities of the name Allâh. No other language has a distinctive name for the Divine Being. The names found in other languages are either attributive or descriptive and are often used in the plural form. But the word Allâh is never used for any other thing, being or deity. It is never used as a qualifying word. Sîbwaih and <u>K</u>halîl say, since 'Al' in the beginning of the word Allâh is inseparable from it so it is a simple substantive, not derived (M.L.). Al-ilâh is a different word. Allâh is not a contraction of *Al-ilâh*. The English word God, which is the common Tentonic word for a personal object of religious worship applied to all superhuman beings of heathen mythologies who exercise power over nature and human being, can hardly be even an approximate substitute. While pronouncing the word Allâh the stress is on the letter L ل. This being the proper name of the Supreme Being and having no parallel or equivalent in any other language, therefore the name 'Allâh' should be retained in the translations of the Holy Book.

Aliha اله: To adore; to worship. **Ilâh:** Allâh, deity, worthy of worship. ***La* ilâha:** There is no other, cannot be and will never be one worthy of Worship (but Allâh) (M.L.T.).

Am ام: Either; or; is (he, she, it)..... not; rather. It is not always used in the interrogative sense. Sometime it is an equivalent of *bal* بل (rather, may, but) and has no interrogative connotation. According to the great philologist Abû 'Ubaid Ma'mar bin Muthannâ this particle is also synonymous with the conjunction *Wâw* 'and'. (Baghawî).

Amana امَنَ: To believe; to have faith; to protect; to put under shelter; to shelter from danger. **Aman** امن: Safety; safe conduct; security; protection. **Amânat**: Loyalty; security; fidelity; faithfulness; deposit; thing entrusted to. **Amîn**: Faithful; loyal; steadfast. **Ma'man:** Place of safety. **Mu'min:** Believer. **Îmân:** Belief; faith. In the Holy Qur'ân Îmân is spoken of as light *(nûr)* and disbelief is likened to darkness (2:257; 57;12). The word *Islam* conveys the idea of accepting a certain principle as the truth, but when the truth is actually fulfilled then it becomes Îmân. The inner faith is always followed by a real outward change in the conduct of a believer. Thus faith without action is a dead letter. According to Râghib, the famous lexicologist of the Qur'ân, Îmân is sometimes nothing more than a confession with the tongue that one believes in Muhammad ﷺ as in 2:62. But Îmân also implies the condition in which a confession with the tongue is accompanied by an assent of heart (*tasdîq bil qalb*) and carrying into practice of what is believed as in 57:19. The word Îmân is derived from *amânat* which, when used intransitively means, became into peace or security; and when used transitively, he granted (him) peace or security. Hence the believer is called *mu'min* - one who has come into peace and security, because he has accepted the principles which bring about peace of mind and security from fear. Allâh is called *Mu'min* - the Granter of security (59:23). In the Traditions (Hadith) the word Îmân is frequently used as standing for good deeds. The Holy Prophet ﷺ said, Îmân has over sixty branches and modesty is a branch of Îmân (B. 2:3). In another Hadith the words are, 'Îmân has over seventy branches the highest of which is the belief that there is no other, cannot be and will not be One worthy of worship other than Allâh and the lowest of which is the removal from the way of a stone that which might cause injury to any one' (M. 1:12). According to one report, the Prophet ﷺ said, 'One has no Îmân unless he loves for his brother what he loves for himself.' (B. 2:7) Imâm Bukhârî has, as the heading of one of his chapters, 'He who says Îmân is nothing but the doing of good'. Îmân is not only a conviction of the truth but essentially the acceptance of a proposition as a basis for action (L.).

Anath انث: Soft; tender; sweet; effeminate (L. T.). **Anûthah**: To be safe; to be effeminate. **Unthâ:** Pl. Inâth. Female; lifeless thing. It includes inanimate things; anything that is passive (R.); idols (Ibn Jarîr, on the authority of 'Âishah); false deities whether living or dead. Hasan says that every one of the Arabian tribes had an idol which they called *unthâ* of such tribe (Râzî).

Athara اثر: To relate or narrate (a fact); to recite; to choose; to propose; **Athar** Pl. Âthâr: Trace; mark; print, footstep; tradition; remain; sunnah; memorials of antiquity; practices and sayings; a significance to which all the authorities agree (L. T.).

Aou او: Whether; unless; or; and

(L. T.).

Ayyim اَيِّم: Pl. Ayâmâ; who lives in celibacy; widower; widow; woman having no husband, whether she had married before or not (T.); a man having no wife (R.).

Ayyûb ايوب (Job): Some authorities say that he lived in Arabian Desert and Mesopotamia was his native place. He lived there before the Exodus of Israelites from Egypt. He was not an Israelite.

(ʻA) ع

ʻAbqarî عبقري: Great; excellent; strong; beautiful; fine; of finest quality; glittering; surpassing; extraordinary; superior; prominent; superseding; quick-witted; expert; vigorous; magnificent; grand; sublime; high; dignified; learned; perfect; accomplished; mighty; powerful; rigorous. There is no other word in Arabic to indicate fine of the finest qualities (L.T,R.).

ʻÂd عاد: The grand son of Aram, who was a grand son of Noah. The tribe of ʻÂd spoken of in the Holy Qur'ân is also called the first ʻÂd (53:50) to distinguish it from the tribe of Thamûd which is also called the second ʻÂd. The tribe of ʻÂd lived in the desert of Ahqâf (46:21) which extends from Oman to Hadzramût, Syria and Iraq. It was an ancient and potent tribe of Arabs. Hûd was the name of their Prophet. He was seventh in descent from Noah. Geographical works in Greek state that in the pre-Christian era Yemen was ruled by a tribe called Adramital, who were no other than the ʻÂd who have been called ʻÂdi Iram in the Holy Qur'ân (89:7). The termination of the Greek name is a noun-suffix, the real name being Adram which is a corruptions of Adi Iram. The Greek rendering for the place of Hadzramût is Adramot. In Arabic the verb ʻÂda means he returned. Their destruction was caused by the blowing of a violent wind which continued to rage over their territory for seven nights and eight days continuously, burying their chief cities under heaps of sand and dust (69:7). Adites were a powerful and cultured people. They built fortresses, palatial buildings and great reservoirs. They invented new weapons and implements of war. Their kingdom lasted up to 500 B.C. their language was Aramic which is akin to Hebrew. This kingdom included in its boundaries the whole of Mesopotamia, Palestine, Syria and Chaldea.

'Abada عبد: To worship; to serve; to accept the impression of a thing; to submit; to devote; **'Abbada:** To render submissive; to enslave; to open (a road). **Ta'bbada**: To apply to; to devote oneself to; to enslave; to treat a person like a slave; to invite to Allâh's obedience. **'Abd**: Human being; slave; servant; worshipper; Pl.. 'Abîd and 'Ibâd. **'Abdullâh**: Servant of Allâh who accepts the impression of Allâh's attributes. **'Âbid:** Worshipper; pious; godly. Pl. 'Abâdah, Ubbâd, Abîdûn. **M'abad**: Place of worship; sanctuary; temple. Pl. Ma'âbid. **Mu'abbad**: Beaten; trodden (road); honoured. **'Ibâdat:** Obedience; worship; piety; the impress of Divine attributes and imbibing and reflecting them on one's own person; complete and utmost humility; submissiveness; obedience and service (M. T.). The idea of 'ibâdat in the Qur'ân lies not in a mere declaration of the glory of Allâh and performance of certain rites of service, e.g. Prayer, Fasting etc., but it is in fact the imbibing of Divine morals and receiving their impress and imbibing His ways and complete obedience to Him (L. T. Kf.).

'Afallâhu 'anka عفي الله عنك Allâh set your affairs aright. It does not necessarily imply the committing of a sin on the part of a person about whom it is used. It is also used for a person who has committed no sin and even for him who is incapable of committing a sin. It is sometimes used to express love. An Arab would say this to one whom he holds in high esteem meaning Allâh set your affairs aright and bring honour and glory to you (L. Aqrab).

'Akafa عكف: To arrange; to set a thing in order; to confine; to withhold; to debar from; to apply one's self assiduously to; to stay in a place; to cleave;

to keep to. *I'tikâf* is one of the recommended acts of worship of high merit, and consists of retiring to the mosque during the last ten days of Ramadzân, devoting oneself exclusively to prayers and to remembering Allâh, and not leaving the mosque except for one's essential needs. It is not valid if one is not keeping the fast or if it is done out of the month of Ramadzân. It commences on the 20th of Ramadzân after the morning Prayer (L. R. T.).

'Alâ علىٰ: To become high; lofty; to go up; to rise in rank; dignity; to be advanced; to mount (a beast). **Ist'alâ**: to ascend higher; to mount upon a thing; **'Alâ** *fil ardzi* - he became proud. **Ta'âlâ**: To be lofty; to be proud; to be exalted; too high; *akhazhû* **'ala***wan* - he took him forcibly. **'Alî:** High; lofty; noble; illustrious; eminent; the most high (Allâh). **'Illîyûn**: The blessed; the highest place. **'Âlin:** High; lofty; sublime; first rate; of dignity; proud. **'A'lâ**: Higher; loftier; nobler. **Isti'lâ**: Superiority; high place; rank. **Muta'âl**: Lofty, high; Most high. **'Alâ**: On; upon; at; against; according to; for the sake of; above; inspite of; **'Alâ** *zahr al-dâbbati* - on horse back; **'Alâ** *hîni ghaflatin* - during a time of heedlessness; *jalasna* **'alal** *nâr* - we sat down near the fire; **'Alâ** *hudan* -on guidance. Here the word 'alâ is very significant which literally means, they are on guidance and this guidance becomes as it were a riding thing for them which they conveniently use in their march towards the Al-Mighty. The construction is in vogue in Arabic. The Arabs say of a person steeped in ignorance جعل الغواية مركبة such a one has made error and ignorance a riding beast for himself (Kf. L. T.).

'Amal عمل: Work; deed; action; a motion of the whole or of a portion of the body or even of the mind; the utterance of a saying, this word may also mean the doer of a deed. This construction is permissible in the Arabic language when an intensified sense is intended (Muhît; T.). In that case the infinitive is sometimes used in place of the active participle to impart emphasis. An Arab poet describing the restlessness of a she-camel who had lost her young ones says she is so restless that she has become the very act of moving forward and backward.

'Amaya عمي: To become blind; ignorant; without signs of the way; to stray from the right path. **'Amâ**: One mentally and physically blind. Pl. 'Umyun (L.).

'An عن: On account of; transitions; compensation; against. (L. T.).

'Aqaba عقب: To strike on the heel; to come at the heel of; to succeed; to take the place of; to follow any one closely. **'Aqqaba**: To endeavor repeatedly; to return; to punish; to requite; **'Aqaba:** To die; to leave offspring; to give in exchange. **T'aqqaba:** To take careful information about; to follow step by step. **'Aqab**: Heel; son; grand son; offspring; pivot; axis. **'Uqbâ:** Requital; result; reward. **'Iqâb**: Pl. 'Aqûbât, punishment after sin. **Mu'aqqibât**: A double plural feminine of *mu'aqqib* which signifies some thing that comes immediately after another thing, or succeeds another thing without interruption. Most of the commentators understand by this; hosts and companions of guardian 'angels' of the night and day who attend on every human being succeeding each other by turns without interruption. The word *'aqqaba* also means he looked to the consequence or result of the affairs (T.). The plural feminine form is used because of the frequency of their doing so, since in Arabic the feminine form is sometimes employed to impart emphasis and frequency. (L. Kf.).

'Aradz عرض: A thing that is not permanent; paltry goods of the present world; worldly goods or commodities; an object of desire; compensation with (T.).

'Arafât عرفات: The name given to a valley east of K'abah, about nine miles from there. Here Pilgrims halt in the later part of the ninth day of Dhul Hijjah (the 12th. month of Islamic calendar). The halt at this place forms the principal factor of Hajj. *Mash'aral harâm* مَشْعَرالحَرام is the name given to a small hillock in

Muzdalifah, about midway between 'Arafât and Minâ which is six miles from Makkah. The name is a compound of *mash'ar*, meaning the place or means of perception and knowledge, and *harâm* meaning sacred. Here the Holy Prophet ﷺ said the evening (*maghrib*) and the night (*'ishâ'*) Prayers during Pilgrimage and offered a long prayer before the rising of the sun. It is thus a place specially meant for meditation and prayer during Hajj. Here the pilgrims stop for the night after their return from 'Arafât on the evening of the ninth of Dhul Hijjah.

'Asâ عسى: It may be; perhaps (with *'an*); a verb of proximity; to be near; about to; to be on the eve of; it might be that. It expresses eager desire or hope and fear, sometimes with reference to the person addressed and sometimes with reference to the speaker himself. It denotes hope in the case of that which is liked and fear in the case of that which is disliked. It also denotes opinion or doubt and certainty (L.T.R.).

'Asâ عصا: Stick; staff; rod; stay; support. *Shaqq al-***'Asâ**: To split the staff; to make a schism; *inshiqâq al-***'asâ** - they are disunited; *idzrib bi* **'asâ***ka*: - strike with your staff; go forth with your people, pitch a (tent).

'Asâ عصى: To rebel against; to disobey. **'Isyân:** rebellion disobedience (L.T.).

'Atabah عتبة Threshold; hold of a door; stair; step of a ladder; favour; blame; reproof (R.L.T.).

'Atîq عتيق: Excellent; noble; freed; old (R.L.T.).

(B) ب

Bâ ب: This particle conveys the following meanings: With the help of; during; for; by; on account of; according to (M.L.T.). According to Arabic usage the words as *'ashrau'* or *'aqrau'* or I begin or I recite would be taken to be understood before this (Kf.). Thus the phrase *bismallâh* is in fact equivalent to saying, 'I begin with the help and assistance of the name and attributes of Allâh and with establishing a communion with Him.' It is in accord with the commandment of 96:1. The English word 'in' is not the equivalent and appropriate for the Arabic particle *bâ* here. This particle is also used as a corroborative, to confirm, to make more certain (R. L.T.) as in 2:8.

Badhara بَذَرَ: To scatter; to waste. **Tabdhîr:** Wastefulness; squandering. It does not relate to the quantity, for which the Arabic word *Isrâf* is used but rather to the purpose of one's spending (R.T.). Thus Ibn Mas'ûd and Ibn 'Abbâs defined tabdhîr as spending without a righteous cause and purpose or in a frivolous cause (L.). Mujâhid says that if a person were to spend even a small amount in a frivolous cause it is tabdhîr, when a person spends more in quantity than is actually needed it is *isrâf*. Both imply an utter lack of gratitude for the gift of sustenance bestowed by Allâh.

Badî' بديع: Is derived from *bada*. To begin a thing; to produce; to find out a new thing; to be matchless; unequalled; to invent; to create; to excel in doing a thing; to contrive a new thing (L.R.).

Bahar بَحَرَ: To till (the earth); to cut open. **Bahr,** Pl. Abhur: Sea; land; any great river; a generous man; a man of extensive knowledge; swift horse; fruitful land.

Bahala بهل: To curse any one. **Ibtahala:** To implore; to beseech; to supplicate (Allâh); to call upon Allâh against; to imprecate upon; to humble and abase himself; to address with earnest and energetic supplication (T.). **Mubahalah:** Imprecation; a prayer contest.

Bakim بكم: To be dumb, mute. **Bakum:** To be silent. **Abkam:** Dumb; mute; who is unable to speak properly because of intellectual weakness; dull witted; stupid (L., T.).

Bal بل: A particle of digression signifying the cancellation of what precedes, as in 21:26. Transitions from one object of discourse to another as in 87:16; but; on the contrary; besides; much more; rather; no; nay (L. T.). It is used for confirmation. It must be followed by a clause in the affirmative, whether the question which it follows is in the negative or affirmative. Thus in English it may either be rendered as 'yes' or 'nay', as the case may be, but not as 'no' (L.T.R.).

Balâ'بلاء: To test; to try; to afflict; to take care of; to esteem; to honour; to bestow favour. And **Ibtalâ ابتلاء** is derived from *ballâ* which means it become old and worn out. Both means to try and test; a trial or test whether resulting in praise or disgrace (L. T.).

Balâ بَلي: Yes; no doubt; ay; yea; so; verily; nay but verily; on the contrary. It also denotes a connection between the verses and supplies the answer to the question. This particle is used after a negative proposition (interrogative or otherwise) and affirms the opposite to such proposition to be the truth hence it differs from *na'am* which asserts to the preceding proposition. (L. T.).

Balasa بلس and **Ablasa:** To remain disheartened and gloomy; mournful; to be desperate; stupefied; to remain speechless; to despair. The word **Iblîs** إبليس is also derived from *ablasa* and mean: The one who despaired; the one with whom good and virtue became less or decreased; who became broken in spirit; who was perplexed and was unable to see his ways; who became silent on account of grief or despair; who was cut short or silenced in argument; who became unable to prosecute his journey; who was prevented from attaining his wish (L. T.). The Greek word 'disa los', from which the English word devil is derived is a Hellenized form of the Arabic word Iblîs. It is a fact that the Greeks derived a good deal of their mythological concept from the much earlier Arabian civilization. There is not the slightest evidence that the pre-Islamic Arabs borrowed this or any other mythological term from the Greeks. Iblîs was not one of the 'angels'. He was one of the *Jinns* and transgressed (18:5). *Jinn* are from fire and 'angels' from that of light. In verse 2:36 he is called satan. Iblîs has been described in 2:34 as disobeying Allâh while the 'angels' have been described as ever submissive and obedient (16:49; 66:6). The fact of his rebellion is repeatedly stressed in the Holy Qur'ân. Hence Iblîs could not be an 'angel'. The theory of 'fallen angel' is un-Islamic.

Bâna بان: To be separated; far away; remote from; to be divorced (women); to be clear; obvious; to appear; to explain. **Tabayyana**: To be clear; easily understood; to appear. **Baina** *Yadaihi***:** Before him; in his presence. **Bayân**: Declaration; explanation; argument; rhetoric; clear meaning; intelligent and distinct speech; applies to both thought and speech, in as much as it comprises the faculty of making a thing or an idea apparent to the mind and conceptually distinct from other things or ideas, as well as the power to express the cognition in spoken or written language (T.). **Bayyinah:** Pl. bayyinât. Evidence; clear proof; argument; precise testimony; clearer. **Mubîn**: explaining clearly; clear; beyond doubt; obvious; parting; cutting (L.R.T.).

Banân بنان(collective noun): The tips of the fingers .Its verbal root is *banna* meaning to stand fast. (L.T.R.).

Bara'a برء: He was or became clear (of doubt); to absolve; to declare him free from the defect attributed to him; he acquitted him (T.); innocent. (L.R.). **Barâ'at:** A declaration of vindication; exemptions; absolution from a fault or responsibility; exemption or absolution from a demand (L.T.).

Barzakh برزخ: A thing that intervenes between two things; an obstacle; a hindrance (T.R.). The word has been used in three places in the Holy Qur'ân (25:53; 55:20; 23:99). The state between death and Resurrection. This intervening state is also known by the name of *qabr* which means grave (80:21,22). There is some kind of awakening in barzakh is evident from various Qur'ânic statements (40:45) The state of barzakh is a state similar to semi consciousness hence it is sometimes likened to a state of sleep (36:52). Again the 90th chapter of Sahîh Bukhârî has the following heading, 'The dead person is shown his abode morning and evening', under this heading a tradition is narrated on the authority of Ibn Omar reporting the Holy Prophet ﷺ as saying that 'When a person dies his abode in the Hereafter is brought before him morning and evening, in Paradise if he is one of the inmates of Paradise and of Fire if he is one of the inmates of Hell' (90:23). The very idea of time and space as relating to the Hereafter are quite different, therefore we cannot conceive of the duration of barzakh in term of this world's time.

Bidz'a بضع: Denotes a variety of numbers from three to nine (L. T.).

Binâ' بناء: Building; edifice; structure; construction; roof; means of protection for those living in or under it; any production or piece of work consisting of parts joined together in some definite manner (M.T.L.). The heaven is called a structure in reference to the order which prevails in heavenly bodies. It suggests also that just as a building or a roof is a source of protection similarly the remote parts of the universe are protection for our planet and the atmosphere is a shield from harmful rays of the sun.

(D) د

Dân دَان: To lend; to give a loan to; to requite; to be honoured; to be reviled; to comply; to rebel; to have a good or bad habit; to serve; to do good; to possess; to constrain; to judge; to reveal; to profess (a faith); to submit to. *Kamâ tadînu tudânu*: You shall be treated as you had treated. **Dayana**: To give to or to receive a loan from; to sell upon credit. **Dain**: Debt; loan; credit (T.).

Dîn دين: Requital; recompense; faith; custom; condition; affair; religion; law; sect; victory; government; power; authority; management; reckoning; obedience; institution (R.T.).

Danâ دنا: To be near or low; to draw near like fruit hanging low and near at hand as in 69:23 (L.R.).

Dunyah دنية: Nearer; nearest; easier; less; worse. **Adna**: nearest part; more or somewhat less; baser (L.T.R.).

Dûn دُون: To be mean; weak; despised beneath; below; before; besides; near; without;

against; opposite; between; important; vile (L. T.).

(DH) ذ

Dhâlika ذَلِكَ: Is primarily used in the sense of 'that'; but it is also used in the sense of 'this' indicating the high rank and dignity of the thing to which it refers (L.T.). **Kadhâlika**: So; too; also; thus; thus so; the fact is; in that way (L.T.R.).

Dhakâ ذكي: To slaughter; the infinitive noun *idhkiyaha* means causing the natural heat حرارت غريزي *(harârat-i-gharîzî)* to pass forth. Technically it indicates a particular mode of slaughtering from the side of jugular vein (R.T.).

Dhanb ذنب: Pl. Dhunûb. Tail; extremity of a whip; offense; crime; fault; sin; follower; every act of which the consequence is disagreeable or unwholesome; an act of disobedience (R.). It differs from *ithm* (see **Ithm**) which is particularly intentional, but dhanb is either intentional or committed through inadvertence (T.).

Dhikr ذكر:Fame; good report; admonition; commemoration; cause of good reputation; honour and status; means of exaltation and fame (L.T.R.).

(DZ) ض

Dza'fa ضعف**:** To exceed; two-fold; manifold. **Idz'âf:** double; triple; multiple. Words **adzâfan** *mudzâ'fah* are not used in 3:130 as a qualifying phrase to restrict the meaning of *ribâ'* (interest and usury) so as to confine it to a particular kind of *ribâ'*. They are used as a descriptive clause to point to the inherent nature of *ribâ'* which continually goes on increasing (R.L.T.).

Dzahikat ضحكت**:** She laughed; she wondered; she was frightened; she feared; she menstruated; **Dzahikat** *al-tarîq* ضحكت الطريق - the way became clear; **Dzahikat** *al-ardzu* ضحكتالارض - the land brought forth its herbage (R.L.T,).

Dziyâ ضياء: Light. **Adzâ'a**: It lighted up; he or it became bright or lit up. Thus it is used both transitively and intransitively (L.T.).

Dzalla ضل: To stray from the

right path; to deviate; to be misled; to disappear; to die; to forget; to lose. **Istad<u>z</u>alla**: To try to mislead any one. **D<u>z</u>alâl:** Confusion; mistake; lose; doom; love. **D<u>z</u>allatun**: Anxiety; uncertainty; absence. **D<u>z</u>illatun**: Error. **D<u>z</u>allun** Pl. **D<u>z</u>âllîn:** Misled; erring; astray. **Mud<u>z</u>ill**: Misleader; seducer; deluder; looming. **Yud<u>z</u>illu**: Many does he adjudge to be erring (Kf.). They say *a***d<u>z</u>all***anî sadîqî* to indicate that my friend pronounced me to be in error (R.T.). It is said of the Holy Prophet that he came to a people f*a* **ad<u>z</u>alla***hum* i.e. he found them to have gone astray. A similar use of the measure *ifâl a<u>h</u>madtuhû* means I found him praiseworthy. Similarly *Ab***d<u>z</u>al***tuhû* means I found him parsimonious or niggardly (N.).

D<u>z</u>araba ضرب**:** To strike any one with; to mix a thing with; to propound (a proverb); to pitch (a tent); to impose (a tax); to perform or act; to divide; to separate; to prevent any one (from hearing); to multiply; to incline towards; to swim; to make a journey; to go forth; to set up as an example (R.T.L.). All these meanings can be applied to in verse 2:60 and 4:34. **Ad<u>z</u>rib***ûhunna:* (4:34) Separate from them; incline towards them (by giving them more attention); try to prevent them by (giving a mild) punishment; take an action. It does not mean to beat someone physically (see 2:60; **'A<u>s</u>â** عصا)..

(F) ف

Fâ ف**:** Prefixed particle expressing:

i. Order, uninterrupted succession to mean: And; then; after. They say, *Jâ'a Zaidun* **fa***'Amrun* - Zaid came first then 'Amr, or *youman* **fa***youman, sanatan* **fa***sanatan* - day by day, year after year.

ii. Change of subject: They say, *s'alahû* **fa** *qâla* i.e. he questioned him and the latter answered.

iii. Causality, result of an action: *Inkuntum tu<u>h</u>ibbûnallâha* **fa**-*ttabi'unî* - if you love Allâh you must consequently follow me.

iv. In order to: *zurni* **fa**

ukrimuka - pay me a visit that I may honour you.

v. Therefore, after the interrogative *a'* ?: *A'* **fa***ra'aitahû*, - then you have seen him.

vi. When following *ammâ* it is explanative; *ammal mouta* **fa** *yaqûmûna* - as to the dead they shall rise.

vii. It is also a prefixed conjunction having less conjunctive power than *wâw* and hence principally employed in connecting sentences. It signifies: And; then; for; therefore; so that; in order that; in that case; in consequence; afterwards; atleast; lest; for fear that; truly (R.L.T.N.).

Fata<u>h</u>a فتح: To open; to explain or reveal; to grant; to adjudicate. **Fat<u>h</u>un**: victory; a decision or judgment. **Mifta<u>h</u>** Pl. Mafâtî<u>h</u>: A hoard; a treasure; a store; storeroom; magazine; buried properly. Mafâti<u>h</u> is also plural of *miftâ<u>h</u>* meaning a key (L.T.R.).

Fî في: Preposition meaning, in; into; amongst; in company with; to; during; with; in company of; for; for the sake of; upon; on concerning; after; in comparison, as they say: *maddunyah* **fi***l âkhirati* مالدُنيا فيالآخَرة - what is the present world in comparison with the Hereafter; in multiplication by, as they say, *<u>kh</u>amsatun* **fa'** *<u>th</u>lâ<u>th</u>atin* five multiplied by three (L.R.T.).

Fala<u>h</u>a فلح: To till (the earth); to cleave a thing. ***Afla<u>h</u>*:** To be successful; lucky; to live on. ***Falâ<u>h</u>*:** Prosperity; safety; success both in this life and in the Hereafter (T.); to unfold something in order to reveal its intrinsic properties; tilling and breaking open the surface of the earth to make its productive powers active. The English word 'plough' seems to have been derived from this Arabic word *fala<u>h</u>*. It is one of the striking beauties of the Arabic, which is the mother of all languages, that its words in their primary sense denote the state which when realized conveys the import of the same. This is well illustrated in this very word; *falâ<u>h</u>* which not only means success but also signifies what constitutes real and complete success. Success or *falâ<u>h</u>*, therefore, consists in the working out of our latent faculties to our best ability, whatever of noble and good hidden in us must come out and what ever is in the form of potentiality in human mind must be converted into actuality. So *falâ<u>h</u>* is really to work out our own evolution and to bring to realization what our Creator has placed in us. In Arabic '*falâ<u>h</u>*' is much higher stage than the attainment of *najah* (salvation). In Arabic there is no better word than *falâ<u>h</u>*, be it material or spiritual, of this world or of the Hereafter and attaining that what one desires and reaping the fruits of his labour and for such success and gains as others may envy (R. T.).

Fa<u>t</u>ara فطر : To cleave; to split; to find out; to begin; to create; to break the fast; **Fi<u>t</u>rat**: Natural disposition; religion of Islam; religious frame of mind. **Fâ<u>t</u>ir:** Creator from the beginning (R. L.).

Fauq فوق: Above; upon; over; more; on high; superior in rank or excellence; and signifies both greater and smaller (R. L.).

Fawâq فُواق: Time between two milkings; time between two suckings; turning of the milk into the udder after the milking; time between the opening of one's hand and grasping with it the udder or when the milker grasps the udder and then lets it go in milking (R.T.).

Fitnatun فتنةٌ: Persecution; trials; probation; bearings; assailing; seduction from faith by any means; confusion; temptation; burning someone with fire; hardship; punishment (L.T.R.).

Fuâd فؤاد: Heart and appendages of the esophagus; as the lungs; liver; heart; mind; soul; intellect; power of understanding and reflection (L. T.).

(<u>GH</u>) غ

<u>Gh</u>a<u>dz</u>ab غَضَبَ: Anger; wrath; passion; displeasure: indignation. **<u>Gh</u>a<u>dz</u>bân:** Hot tempered; angry. **Ma<u>ghdz</u>ûb**: Object of anger and displeasure (L.T.). Allâh's displeasure is but a reflection of a person's own attitude. Allâh treats every one according to his merit and every human action is followed by Divine reaction. So the expression Divine displeasure should not be construed to mean that

Allâh is ranged against people. It means that because of his sinfulness one is alienated from the mercy of the Lord of Holiness. One must not conceive the Divine displeasure in term of wrath of a human being. There is a world of difference between the action of Allâh and that of a human being. According to almost all the commentators Allâh's condemnation and displeasure is synonymous with the evil consequences which a human being brings upon himself by willfully rejecting Allâh's guidance so it is a kind of punishment (L.T.R.).

<u>Gh</u>afara غفر**:** To cover; to hide; to conceal; to forgive. **<u>Gh</u>afaral** *jalabu al-sûqa* - import has lowered the prices of the market. **Mig<u>h</u>far**: Shield; helmet. The word *<u>gh</u>afr* means as Barmâwî explains: protection of two kinds - 'protecting human being from committing the sin' or 'protecting him from the punishment of his sins'. The Divine attributes **<u>Gh</u>âfir, <u>Gh</u>affâr** and **<u>Gh</u>afûr**: Who protects us from committing of sins and faults and passes over our sins and faults (L.T.R.).

<u>Gh</u>aib غيب: To be remote; to be hidden from; to be absent; to disappear (sun, moon); to be concealed in; to render unapparent; unseen; to remove; to conceal; hidden reality;beyond ordinary human perception. **<u>Gh</u>ayyaba**: To learn by heart. **Ag<u>h</u>âba**: To have her husband absent (woman). **<u>Gh</u>aibah**: Depressed ground. 'Âlim *al*-**<u>gh</u>aib**: The knower of secrets and hidden realities. **<u>Gh</u>iyâb** *al- shajar* غياب الشجر: Roots of the tree. **<u>Gh</u>yabah:** Cover; screen. **<u>Gh</u>ayâbah**: Pl. <u>Gh</u>iyâbât: Bottom (L.T.R.). So *<u>gh</u>aib* does not mean imaginary and unreal things simply because they are unseen though still beyond the reach of perception through ordinary human senses and cognizance. They are real but needs verification. There are things though unseen or undiscovered, are of intrinsic nature, and can be proven by experiment or reason. This Islamic belief in the existence of *<u>gh</u>aib* -the unseen hidden realities conferred a great boom and stimilus to the new discoveries in material sciences. And the world saw an upsurge in the discovery of new laws of nature, which were undiscovered before. Thus, Muslim scientists became the forerunners of modern material sciences.

Gharaq غرق: To sink into water. **Istaghraqa:** To exceed (the bounds). **Aghraqa:** To brace a bowstring to the utmost. **Gharaqa:** To come near to any one. (L.T.N.).

Ghislîn غسلين: Extremely hot; which has washed off; refuse; filth (T.R.N.).

(H) ح

Habl حبل: Treaty; pact; covenant; cause of union; halter; cord; vein; cause of link and connection; bond of love; obligation; assurance of security or safety (L.T.R.Asâs)

Hadîd حديد: Iron; something that is sharp in both the concrete and abstract sense of the word (L.).

Hajara حجر: To prevent; hinder; resist; prohibit; to interdict; forbid; deprive any one of civil rights; hide a thing; harden. **Hajr:** Prohibition; protection; deprivation of civil rights. **Hajar,** Pl. Ahjâr and Hijârah: Stone. A stone is called hajar because it resists pressure owing to its hardness. It also means a rock;. The word also means a big mass of stone or a metal. It may also be used for a very sagacious, crafty and political man (T.), and metaphorically for idols (Kf.) and stone-hearted persons (L.). **Hujrah** Pl. Hujarât: Chamber; house; enclosure; cell; side; region (L.).

Hanjarah حنجره: Pl. Hanâjir: Throat,

Hajja حجّ: To repair; to undertake; to aim; to argue. **Hijjah**: Argument; protest. **Hajj** and Hijj: Pilgrimage. (See 2:196). The Hajj takes place once a year in the month of Dhul Hijjah, whereas *'Umrah* a pious visit may be performed at any time (see also **'Umrah**). In both Hajj and *'Umrah* the pilgrims are required to walk seven times around the Ka'bah and seven times between Safâ and Marwah. In the course of the Hajj they must, in addition, attend the gathering on the plain of 'Arafât on the 9th of Dhul Hijjah which constitutes the climax of the Hajj. The pilgrims are required to remain until sunset on that plain. The multitudes of pilgrims move back in the direction of Makkah, stopping overnight at a place called Muzdalifah and then at Minâ for two or three days. Irrespective of whether they are performing a Hajj or only an *'Umrah* the pilgrims must enter the state of pilgrimage, *Ihrâm* أحرام (see also **Harrama**) until the end of the pilgrimage, the pilgrims, irrespective of whether they are performing a Hajj or only an *'Umrah*, they must refrain from cutting or even trimming the hairs and nails from the time they enter the state of *Ihrâm* until the end of the pilgrimage. For those who have performed the Hajj it is expected - provided they can afford it - to sacrifice at Minâ a quadruped e.g. sheep, goat, cow or the like and to distribute most of its flesh any where in charity 'till the offering reaches its destination in time or place' (2:196). According to Râzî time of sacrifice is meant here the conclusion of the pilgrimage. *Tamattu'* is the interruption of the state of pilgrimage or *Ihrâm* during the time intervening between the completion of an *'Umrah* and the performance of the Hajj (see also **Tamattu'**). The pilgrim who takes the advantage is obliged to sacrifice an animal or to fast for ten days. In *tamattu'* after the performance of the Hajj, the pilgrim does not remain in the state of *Ihrâm,* but again enters into that state at the time of the Hajj. The month of the performing Hajj are well known (2:189). The well known months are Shawwal, Dhul Qa'dah and the first 9 days of Dhul Hijjah. It is in these days that a Muslim can enter into the state of *Ihrâm* for performing the Hajj. Since the Hajj culminates in one particular month, namely Dhul Hijjah, the plural (months) refers also to its annual recurrence.

Harab/Mihrâb: مْحراب The upper end of a house; first seat in a place; palace; private apartment; fortress; chamber (R. L. T.).

Haratha حرث: To till and sow (the earth); to cut a thing round; to study a thing thoroughly. **Harth**: Land prepared for sowing; tillage; track of a road; piece of land ploughed for sowing; or actually sown with some crop; produce of field crop or garden crop; gain; wife (T. Azharî).

H̲arrama حرم: To forbid; to declare a thing to be sacred; inviolable; to prevent. **Ih̲tarama**: To show regard to ; to hold a thing as sacred. **H̲aramain:** Makkah and Madînah. **H̲arâm**: Sin; unlawful; sacred; venerable. **Ih̲râm**: Rites of a pilgrimage; the state into which the pilgrim is required to put himself on the occasion of H̲ajj or *'Umrah*; entering upon a state in which a particular dress is put on and certain acts, ordinarily lawful are forbidden. The *Ih̲râm* dress for men consists of two seamless sheets, a sheet reaching from the navel to below the knees and a sheet which covers the upper part of the body. Both these sheets should preferably be white. Women can wear their ordinary clothes. They should not cover their face nor wear thin veils in *Ih̲râm* (B. 3:53; 25:23), but they must wear simple dress. Before wearing the *Ih̲ram* dress the pilgrim must take a bath and utter *talbiyah* facing the Qiblah. The practice is also to say two *rak'ats* of Prayer. During the state of *Ih̲ram* and even before that from the beginning of the journey to Makkah no amorous discourse or sexual intercourse is allowed (2:197), nor is the use of scent allowed in the state of *Ih̲râm*, nor shaving or cutting of hair nor the paring of nails. The cares of the body are sacrificed for a few days to devote greater attention to the cares of soul. (See also **H̲ajj** and **'Umrah**)

H̲asana حسن is the root of *muh̲sin:* To surpass any one in beauty; to treat any one kindly. **Muh̲sin:** Doer of excellent deeds; doer of good deeds to others; one who strives to be perfect in good deeds; the Holy Prophet ﷺ said, 'The *muh̲sin* is one who does a good deed as if he is actually seeing Allâh or that atleast Allâh is seeing him' (B.).

H̲ashr حشر: To gather people at a place and then send them toward another place. **Mah̲shar**: Syrian cities; place of gathering (T. L.).

Haqqa حقّ: To overcome any one in contending for a right; to strike any one on the back of the neck; to prove a thing; to realize the fear of; to be sure of; to ascertain; to be suitable; necessary and incumbent. **Istahaqqa:** To be due (payment); to deserve a punishment (culprit), to have claim to; to deserve a thing; to render a thing necessary. **Haqq** Pl. Huqûq: Right; truth; duty; justice; authentic; the true; suitableness; to the requirement of justice and wisdom and exigencies of the case (R. T.). Pointing out the right way in the differences which existed before it or as giving a correct account of the past or being true with respect to the promises and threats relating to the future (Râzî). Some commentators explain it with arguments and proofs (Bahr). **Haqîq**: Worthy of; reality; truth; essence (L.).

Hill حل: To make free from obligations; to be a target of every conceivable abuse; harm; injury; cruelty or violence against life, property or honour; to consider lawful to do any harm even to kill; to alight as a conqueror

Hamada حمد: This word not only embodies the idea of thankfulness but also has reference to the intrinsic qualities of the object of praise. *Hamd* is always true and used only about such acts as are volitional (R.). It also implies admiration, magnifying and honouring of the object of praise and humility and submissiveness in the person who offers it (T.). Thus *hamd* is the most appropriate word to be used where a reference to the intrinsic goodness of Allâh and extreme lowliness in the person who offers it is intended, instead of any other word which is used in varying significance in the sense of praise and thankfulness. So *hamd* is praise which is offered in appreciation of commendable action of one worthy of praise. It also includes lauding one who has done a favour of his own volition and according to his own choice. It is not only a true praise but also an admiration. The word *shukr* شكر (thanks) differs from *hamd* in the sense that its application is restricted to beneficent qualities and praise. The word *madha* مدح (gratitude) differs from *hamd* in the sense that it also applies to involuntary beneficence. The word *hamd* is much more comprehensive than *shukr*, *madha* and *thanâ* (R.L.T.). The word hamd also conveys that Allâh combines all kinds of glorification in His Being and is unique in all His beauties and bounties. He is sublime. His glory is free from any defect and is not subject to any change and is immune from every affliction and drawback. He is Perfect, the Glorious and subject to no limitation. To Him is due all praise in the beginning and in the end through eternity. It also declares that Allâh is the Being Whose attributes are beyond computation and Whose excellences cannot be numbered and Who combines in His Being all beauty, bounty and glory. Reason is not able to conceive of any good which is not comprehended among Divine attributes. It also connotes that all excellence belong to Him as a matter of right; and that every type of praise whether relating to external aspects or internal realities is due exclusively to Him. The word *hamd* is used in the Holy Qur'ân both in the active and the passive sense, that is, it is used both for the subject and the object, and signifies that Allâh receives perfect praise and also bestows it. In Surah al-Fâtihah the attribute *Rahmân* signifies that the word *hamd* is used in the active sense and the attribute *Rahîm* signifies that it is used in the passive sense.

Hamala حَمَلَ: To carry; to bear; to take upon himself. **Haml:** To be pregnant; to produce (fruit); to take responsibility; to know by heart (a book); to show anger; to relate; to rely upon; to charge (the enemy); to incite. **Himl**: Load; burden; to accept; to take upon himself; to betray the trust (L. T. R. Kf.).

Hanîf حنيف Pl. Hunafâ': Is derived from the root *hanafa* meaning to lean to one side; to incline; to turn away from error to guidance. Hence Hanif is one inclining towards a right state or tendency (R.T.). In pre-Islamic times this term had a definitely monotheistic connotation and was used to describe a person who turned away from sin and worldliness and from all dubious beliefs, especially idol worship. Many instances of this use of the term occur in the verses of pre-Islamic poets, e.g., Umayyah bin Abî Salt and Jarîr, al Oud (L.). The word Hanîf is of Arabic origin. It is wrong to say that it is not of Arabic origin but is derived from the Canaanite - Aramaic hanpâ, one who turns away.

Hunain حنين: A place on the road to Tâif from Makkah and about 14 miles to the South-East of it, This place was the scene of a battle between the Muslims and certain tribes of pagan Arabs in 8 A. H., the tribes of Hawâzin and Thaqîf were leading them.

Hûr حور: It is the plural of *ahwar* (masculine) and of *houra'* (feminine). The word *ahwar* signifies pure and clear intellect (L.) and it stand for purity (L. Râzî), and beauty (Kathîr). The word *hawâr* also denotes intense whiteness of the eyeballs and lustrous blackness of the iris (Qâmûs). As regards the word hûr in its feminine connotation quite a number of the earliest commentators among them al-Hasan of Basra understood it as signifying the righteous among the women of the humankind (I.). So the term applies to the righteous of both sexes (L.T.R.).

Hattâ حتي: To; till; until; included; even; in order that; even to; up to; down to; as far as. This particle is used in four different ways:

i. It is used as a preposition to indicate a certainty and governs the genitive case as in 97:5 - 'until the time of the rising of the dawn'.

ii. As a conjunction, or adverb meaning 'and even', or 'up to an extreme point inclusive', thus it differs from *ilâ* which signifies 'up to' or 'as far as' but not 'including'. But no instance of the use occurs in the Holy Qur'ân.

iii. As a conjunction serving to connect a proposition with that which precedes it. It than means 'until' and has grammatically no effect on the succeeding proposition, as at 6:149. In the Holy Qur'ân it is frequently followed by *idhâ*.

iv. It governs a verb in the subjective mood when that verb has a future significance it then means 'until' or 'in order that' as in 12:80. Sometimes it is used as a conjunction like *wâw* signifying 'and' (L.T.).

H̲aya' حياء: Repentance; prudency; bashfulness; modesty. **Istah̲yâ'**: To abstain from; to disdain; to feel ashamed; to shrink; to veil her face (woman); to make shameless; to deprive of chastity; to let anyone live (L.R.T.).

H̲ayya حي: To keep any one alive; to spare any one; to let any one live; to remove prudency, modesty and shamefulness. The order of Pharaoh was to spare the daughters of Israel who were thus allowed to grow to womanhood and become *nisâ*' (-women). The object was to demoralize them and make them immodest. This is the significance of the phrase in the text *yastahyuna nisa'hum* - sparing your women to make them immodest (2:49). **Ah̲yâ:** Those who are in paradise (R.L.T.).

H̲awârî حواري: This word is used by the Holy Qur'ân for the disciples of Jesus which means, one tried and found to be free from vice and faults; person of pure and unsullied character; one who advises or counsels or acts honestly and faithfully; a true and sincere friend or helper; a selected friend and helper of a Prophet (R. T.).

(H) ه

Hârût هاروت and Mârût ماروت: Are both descriptive names. Hârût means one who tears, Mârût means one who breaks (L.). These descriptive names signify that the object of these holy men was to tear asunder and break the glory and power of certain people. The word angels as applied to them is figurative. It means holy and good; men of knowledge, wisdom and power (Bag̲hawî; Râzî). The Holy Qur'ân says about Joseph, 'He is but a gracious angel'. (12:31) To denote him as handsome and pious youth.

Habat̲a هبط: To go from a place to another; to fall down; to descend; to come down; to go down into. **Habat̲** *al-wâdî* - he descended into the valley; also for change in condition (R. L.).

Hal هل: It is an interrogative particle which when followed by *Illâ*, may signify a negative statement. Whether? Is there? Does he? Some times it is used to express a positive statement as in 76:1 (L.T.).

Hidâyat هدايه: To show the right path; to lead on the right path; to keep on the right path till one reaches the goal (R. Baqâ'). **Hidâ:** To bring (the bride) to (the bridegroom). **Ihtidâ':** He has followed the true course for obtaining his want. **Hadiyyah**: Gift; present; offering; presentation (L.T.). **Yahiddî**: To find the way by himself. It is really *yahtadî*, the letter *'t'* having been merged into the letter *'d'* and is the intransitive form of *hada*, which means he directed him aright or caused him to take or follow the right path (L. T. R. Baqâ).

Haza'a هَزءَ: To make light of a person; sending down disgrace and contempt for the object which a mocker has in view and to hold him when he mocks in light estimation and to bring down disgrace on him (Kf. T.L.). **Yastahzi**: is derived from *haz'a*. In Arabic punishment for an evil deed is sometimes denoted by the word used for the evil itself. The famous Arab poet Amar bin Kul<u>th</u>ûm says,

Ala la tajhalan a<u>h</u>dun 'alaina
Fa-najhalu fouqa
jahalil jâhilina.

'Beware! none should dare imply ignorance against us, or we will show greater ignorance, i.e. we will punish him'; so yastahzi also means to punish the mockery (L.).

(I)

Ibil ابل: Camel; camels; a generic noun like sheep, a herd of camels; clouds that bear the rain-water; rope (R.T.L.).

Iblîs ابليس see **Balasa**

Ibrâhîm ابرهيم (Abraham): literally this word means the father of the nations (L.T.). Abraham was a native of Ur of the Chaldees. The people of Ur worshipped the stars and their chief god was the sun and their king was Nimrod

(Gen. 10:8,9). He was a Prophet. He preached against idolatry and worship of heavenly bodies. He is a progenitor of Arabs. He settled Ismâîl his son with his mother Hâjirah near the Ka'bah and prayed for a secure city to be raised there, for it to become the spiritual center of the world and for a great Messenger to be raised in it. He rebuilt the Ka'bah. He journeyed from Ur (Mesopotamia) to Harran and from there by Allâh's command to Cann'ân, accompanied by Lot, which Allâh had decreed to give to his posterity. All prophets have to emigrate from their homes.

Idrîs ادريس: literally means one who reads much or instructs much. It is the name of a Prophet mentioned in the Holy Qur'ân. Most commentators of the Qur'ân are of the opinion that Idrîs is Enoch of the Bible. The words Hanûk (Enoch) and Idrîs closely resemble each other in their meanings. Hanûk means instruction (Ibn Sikkît; L. Asma'î).

Idh اذ و اذا/ idhâ: Then; at that time; when; as; while; since; if. It is a time reference and is used as a corroborative particle meant to draw the reader's attention to a turn in the discourse (M. T.), and can be translated as 'remember the time'.

Illâ الا: If not; unless; except; some; otherwise; less; but. This word is used to signify the sense of exception. In Arabic this exception is of two kinds: i. An exception in which the thing excepted belongs to the same class or species to which the things from which an exception is sought to be made belongs; as they say *jâ alqaumu illâ Zaidan*, all the people came except Zaid (who was one of them). Here the person Zaid belongs to the same class to which the people belong. It is called *istithsnâ muttasil* استثناء متّصل.

ii. An exception in which the excepted thing belongs to a different class or species, as they say, جاء القوم الاحماراً *Jâ al- qaumu illâ himâran* all the people came but the donkey did not. Here the donkey does not belong to the class or species from which exception is sought to be made. In the verse 2:34 the word *illâ* (but) denotes the latter kind of exception, Iblîs not being one of the angels. Though not an angel yet he was also ordered to submit to Âdam (7:12). It is called استثناء منفصل *istithnâ munfasil*. It commonly governs the accusative. Illâ also means 'not even' (Qâmûs Mughnî).

Îlâ' ايلاء: literally means swearing and technically the taking of an oath that one shall not go into one's wife. In the pre-Islamic days the Arabs used to take such oaths. By this practice the wife remained as a deserted wife and she was kept in a state of suspense sometimes for the whole of her life. Just as *Zihâr,* it is also not allowed in Islam (2:226).

Îlâf ايلاف: Alliance; compact; agreement; friendship; to attach the heart; to stick to a thing; a covenant or an obligation involving responsibility for safety and protection; unifying together (L. T.).

Imâm امام: Leader; president; any object that is followed, whether a human being or a book (R.), or a highway (L.); model; example (T.).

In ان: If, different from *lou* لو in as much as the former is simply conditional, as if you are wise, while the latter supposes what is not the case, as if you were wise. This is made clear by 35:15. **In** ان sometimes gives a future signification to the verb in the preterite, unless where *kâna* كان is interposed. Sometimes signifies *idh* (when). It is a mistake to take it as referring to the future. It has sometimes a negative meaning as in 5:53. *Immâ* was really *inmâ*. This addition of *mâ* is technically called *zâidah,* which is used to emphasize or intensify the meaning of the word to which it is added. The change effected in the sense of the particle **in** by the addition of *mâ* is that whereas **in** alone expresses a greater contingency or possibility which is not necessarily accompanied by hope; the addition of *mâ* makes the contingency not only more emphatic but also expressive of hope (L.T.).

Innâ ان: Like *anna* is used with

almost every kind of prefix and affix. When without an affixed pronoun it governs nouns in the accusative. It has an affirmative meaning, and may generally be rendered verily, indeed.

Innanâ **اننا:** It is a particle of restriction, may be rendered 'only'. The word has the force of *inna.*

Injîl **انجيل:** Evangel, Just as the *Taurât* (see **Taurât**) is not the old testament or the Pentateuch so the Injîl mentioned in the Qur'ân is certainly not the New Testament, and it is not the four Gospels as now received by the Christian Church but the original one single Injîl which was revealed to and formulated by Jesus, as the Taurât (Torah) was formulated by Moses. Fragments of it survived in the Hebrew Canonicals, the New Testament and in some others, of which some traces survive e.g. the Gospel of Childhood and the Gospel of Barnabas. But all this body of immethodical literature is casual in its nature and an odd miscellanies. None of the Books of the New Testament was intended by its authors and writers to form one of the canons. They are all been put together side by side inharmoniously. The four Canonical Gospels were only four out of many and some others besides the four have survived. The final form of the New Testaments Canons for the west was filed in the fourth century A. D. by Athanasius and the Necene creed. Injîl from which the English word Evangel is derived literally means good tidings or gospels. The reason why Jesus' revelation was called Injîl is that it contained not only good news for those who accepted him but also because it gave the glad tidings of the advent of the greatest Prophet which is variously described in Jesus' metaphorical language as the coming of the kingdom of Allâh (Mk.I: 15), the coming of the Lord Himself (Mtt. 21:40), the advent of Paracalet or Periklutos (John. 14:16), or the spirit of Truth (John. 14:17) etc. The Holy Prophet said, the breasts of my Companions are like Gospel (L.). It sheds some light on the significance and position of Injîl. It means that the breasts of his Companions are repositories of his life history and teachings. It indicates that the position of the present Gospels is analogous to that of the collection of Hadîth. In short the Taurât and Injîl frequently mentioned in the Qur'ân are not identical with what is known today as the Bible or Old and New Testaments. The fact of their having been lost or forgotten or abandoned is alluded to in the Holy Qur'ân (5: 14). Thus the confirmation by the Holy Qur'ân refers only to the basic truths still described in Bible and not to its legislations or to its present text, a confirmation of whatever was extant in it of its basic teachings and prophecies at the time of the revelation of the Qur'ân, and it is this that the phrase 'which still remains' (2:106) expresses.

Ism اسم: The word is a derivative of *wsm* and *wasam* (a mark) and of *samow* (height). In Arabic means a mark of identification by which one is recognised. The Arabic word *wasmiyyun* is also derived from it. It means first spring rain. They call the earth *ardzun musawamatun* when the first spring rain falls on it and by its flowering pleases the heart of the cultivators. Also the word *mismun* is its derivative and means beauty and good-looks. **Wasama:** To brand; to stamp; to mark; to describe; to depict; to surpass in beauty. **Wasm**: To bear the impress of beauty. **Wasama**: To vie in beauty. **Wisâm**: Title of a book. **Wasamah:** Beauty of the face (M. L. T.). The Arabs used *wasm* and its derivatives generally in a neologistic sense, whether relating to worldly welfare or to spiritual well-being. In popular parlance the *ism* of a thing stands for its distinguishing mark but in the view of the learned it signifies its reality. In the verse *bismillah*, the name Allâh, the Most Gracious, the Ever Merciful, possess that characteristic and each one of them denotes its particular properties and nature. In the language of the Qur'ân Allâh is the very apex of beauty, love and beneficence. According to some authorities as Râg̲hib the word ism is a derivative of *smw* and means to be high, raised. **Sâma:** To vie in glory with. **Tasamma:** To claim relationship to. **Samâ'**: Sky; canopy of heaven, roof, cloud, rain, everything that is above. **Samâwah**: Figure seen from a far; good repute; fame. **Sâm**: High; lofty; sublime. The word *ism* means a name or attribute.

Ith̲m اثم: Sin; guilt; crime; lie; unlawful; harmful; anything that hinders from good deeds; anything which renders a person deserving of punishment; anything - words or deeds - that pricks the mind as something evil. It differs from *Dh̲anb* (see **Dh̲anb**)

Is̲r اصر: Burden; compact; crime; sin; a burden which restrains one from motion; burden of sin, (as sin also hampers the spiritual progress and restrains from advancing spiritually); a heavy responsibility the breaking of which renders one deserving of punishment; grievous punishment of a sin (R.T.).

Iyya ايّ: Particle prefixed to the objective case of pronouns to give the meanings of 'only' as *Iyyâka* - only you; *iyyaya* - only me (L.Kf.).

('I) ع

'Ibâdat عِبَادَتْ is the noun infinitive from **'Abada**: To adore; worship. It also means to accept the impress of a thing. The way is called *mu'abbad* when on account of constant travelling it becomes susceptible to the travellers footprints. With reference to Allâh the meaning would be receiving, the impress of His attributes. The word also signifies humility; submissiveness; obedience and service. The idea is not of simple humility but of complete humility. It is more intensive and more extensive in its significance than *'abûdiyat*. (See **'Abada**) (L.R.Ṭ.)

'Iddat عدت: Legal period of retirement assigned to a widow or divorced woman before she may marry again. The 'iddat of divorced women is three *qurû'* (2:228) - entering from the state of *t̲uhr* (cleanliness) into the state of menstruation (see also **Qurû'** قروء. In normal cases Qurû' takes about four weeks. In the case of women who do not menstruate as well as those whose courses have stopped, the 'iddat is three months (65:4), and in the case of pregnant women this waiting period is till delivery (65:4). The 'iddat serves the purpose of affording the parties a chance of reconciliation. Though they are divorced, they still live in the same house (65:1). This injunction aims at restoring revocable relations between the parties. If there is any life in the union, its pangs would assert themselves during the period of waiting. After the first and second divorce but not after the third, the parties have the right to reassert their conjugal relations within the period of waiting or iddat or to remarry after the waiting period is over.

'Ilm عِلم**:** Science; learning; firm belief. **'Allama**: To know; to distinguish; to mark; to learn; to be informed of; to be aware of; to teach; to assume a distinctive mark; to sign (a deed). **'Alam**: Book marker; target; aim. **'Alâmat** Pl. 'Alâmât: Mark; sign; token; symptoms; to distinguish; to know. **'Alam** Pl. A'lâm: Sign; mark; limit-stone; way-mark; elevated mountain, **'Âlam** Pl. 'Âlamîn: World; universe; several kinds of created beings and things. Primarily it means that by means of which one is able to know the Creator and hence signifies world or creation, because by it the Creator is known (T. M. L.). There are many worlds, spiritual, physical, astronomical, world of thought and wisdom, world knowable through the senses, invisible world of angels etc. **N'alama:** We might distinguish (Bahr). **'Ilm:** Is not followed by the particle *min* except when it is used in the sense of distinguishing one thing from the other (R. L. T.).

'Îsa عيسىٰ**:** Is the Arabic form of the Hebrew word Jasu or Jeshua and Joshua. In Arabic the word may be considered to have been derived from the root *Is* or *Ûs* which means white camels, the whiteness of whose hair is mixed with a dark shade and this is looked upon as particularly good animal. It also means to manage a property well, to improve and make better life (L.).

(J) ج

Jabal **جَبْل:** Mountain; metaphorically it signifies a big and proud person; the chief or leader of a people; lord; a great and mighty man (L. T.).

Jabbâr **جبار:** Is derived from *Jabara*. To set (a broken bone); to restore; to compel. **Jabara** *Khâtirahû*: To converse kindly. **Jabara**: To oblige. **Tajabbar**: To become green again (tree); to recover from (illness, destitution); to regain (wealth); to be reinstated in a former position. **Jabrût**: might; power; greatness (L.T,R.).

Jahada **جهد:** To toil; to exert strenuously; to over load (a camel). **Jahada** *hû al-'atshu*: He suffered from thirst; to struggle; to strive after; to meditate upon a thing; to struggle against (difficulties). **Juhd**: Ability; power; energy; **Juhadaka** *an taf'ala kadhâ*: Do so to the utmost of your ability. **Majhûd:** Zeal; exertion. **Jihâd** جهاد: The exerting of one's utmost power in contending with an object of disapprobation (T.). It is only in a secondary sense that the word signifies fighting; rather there is nothing in the word to indicate that this striving hard is to be effected by the sword (Râzî). Jihâd is of three kinds, viz., the carrying on of a struggle i. against a visible enemy, ii. against the devil, iii. against self (R.) Exerting one's self to the extent of one's ability and power whether it is by word (*qaul*) or deed (*fi'l*). Jihâd properly signifies the using or exerting of one's utmost power, efforts, endeavors or ability, in contending with an object of disapprobation (T.). Jihâd is, therefore, far from being synonymous with war. Its meaning as war undertaken for the propagation of religion is unknown to the Arabic language and the teachings of the Qur'ân. The 29th chapter of the Qur'ân (29:6,8,69) is one of the group which was undoubtedly revealed in the fifth and sixth years of the Call of the Prophet, and it is an admitted fact that permission to fight was given to the

Muslims after the twelfth year of the Call, when they had moved to Madînah, or at the earliest, when they were on the eve of leaving Makkah, yet the word *Jihâd* is freely used, without implying any war. Imâm Bukhârî in his Book of Jihâd has several chapters speaking of simple invitation to Islam (B. 56:99, 100, 102, 143, 145, 178). This fact indicates that up to the time of Bukhârî the word Jihâd was used in the sense on which it is used in the Qur'ân. Other books of tradition contain similar references. The correct rendering of the word Jîhâd is using one's utmost power in contending with an object of disapprobation and striving for it. There is nothing in the word to indicate that this striving is to be effected by sword. It can be by the tongue or by any other method (Râzî). Fighting in defense of religion received the name of Jihâd because under some circumstances it became necessary for the truth to live and prosper; if fighting had not been permitted, truth would have been uprooted. According to the Qur'ân the greatest jihâd which a Muslim must carry on is by means of the Qur'ân - its teachings and reasonings (25:52).

Jaham **جهم:** To meet any one with a frowning face; to have a stern look; to look at any one with a severe, morose and contracted face. **Jahamtun:** The darkest part of the night. **Juham**: Waterless cloud.

Jahannam جهنّم: Gehenna; Hell; a place of punishment which is dark and waterless and which makes the face of its inmates ugly and contracted (Muhît).

Jamal **جمل:** He-camel; full grown he-camel; camel; palm tree; large sea fish or whale; cable; ship's rope; twisted rope (L. T. Jawharî).

Jân **جان:** Harmless swift and small serpent.

Janna **جن:** to be dark; to cover; to wrap; to conceal; to be mad; to be covered with plants; to be mad with joy or anger; to be hidden; to be excited. **Junna**: Covering; shield; protective. **Janîn:** Embryo; fetus; anything hidden. **Junûn:** Madness; insanity; diabolical fury; passion. **Majnûn**: Mad, possessed; luxuriant (plant).

Jannat جنة: Garden; Paradise. The description of Paradise as given in the Holy Qur'ân is a parable (13:35; 47:15). It is beyond human mind to comprehend its nature (32:18). The Holy Prophet said, 'No eye has seen it, nor has any ear heard of it, nor can the imagination of human being conceive of it' (B.). While describing the blessings of Paradise the Holy Qur'ân uses names of things generally looked upon as good in this world, though in the Hereafter they will be there in a far better form. The life after death is spiritual, but not in the sense that it will consists of a mental state only. There the human soul will have a kind of body. It is a real and true gift of Allâh. The streams of the Paradise represent the good deeds, and gardens represent faith. Fruits of the deeds will be similar to the deeds and actions in this life will be mirrored in their fruits (2:25). The word *zauj*, of which *azwaj* is the plural signifies either of the two companions of a couple, that is, the male as well as the female. The Holy Qur'ân is full of clear statements that women shall enjoy the bliss of Paradise (13:23).

Jinn جن: A genius; whatever hides or conceals or covers; whatever remains hidden or becomes invisible. The word therefore signifies such beings that remain aloof from the people as if remaining concealed from the eyes of the common folk as kings and other potentates generally do. It is in this sense that the word is used by Zuhair. Technically speaking the word Jinn has been spoken of in the Holy Qur'ân as well as the traditions in diversified senses. The Jinn has been applied to evil spirits which inspire evil thoughts; various germs and insects etc.; the imaginary beings whom the infidels worshipped; people of different far flung countries living detached from other civilized human beings; people who inhabited the earth in prehistoric times, subject to no laws or rules of conduct; before the birth of Âdam who laid the foundation of the civilization; by the jinns are also meant the Jews of 'Nasîbîn'; the jinns were those stalwarts whom Solomon had taken into custody and having subjugated them made them work as constructors of huge buildings and who were expert divers for him. Ibn-Manzûr in his book Lisân al-'Arab has quoted a verse of an ancient poet in which he calls his beloved by the name of Jinnî. Zuhair ibn Abî Sulmâ has used the word Jinn for people who are peerless, having no match or equal. Tabrîzî writes in his book *Sharah-al-Hamâsah* that Jinn is a being who is highly potent, shrewd and possessed of great powers and abilities. The primary meaning of the word *ma'shar* in the verses; 6:128,130; 55:33 also reinforce this interpretation. *Ash'arahû* means he lived in close communion with him and was on intimate terms (L.T.). Thus by calling, Jinn and human beings a single community, the Holy Qur'ân clears that here jinn and human being are not two different kind of beings.

Jarama جرم: To cut; to lap off; to acquire a thing; to commit a crime against anyone; to commit a sin. ***Mujrim*** is derived from *jaram*: One who commits a crime; *la jarama* - certainly, without lap (L.T.).

Jidh'a جِذع: Palmtree; stock; trunk of a tree; branch of a tree (L.R.T.).

Jizyah جِزَيَة is derived from *Jazaya:* He or it paid or gave satisfaction; he paid such a one his right or due. Jizyah is the tax that is taken from the free non-Muslim subjects of a Muslim state in lieu of the protection it ensures them (T.), and because it is a compensation for the protection which is guaranteed them, the non-Muslim subjects being free from military service (AH.) and Zakât. But if they perform military service and pay Zakât their is no Jizyah on them (L. R. Rz.). The tax imposed on Muslims is called Zakât which is a heavier tax than Jizyah, and Muslims in addition to this tax have to perform military service as well.

(K) ك

Kafara كفر: To cover; to conceal; to become a disbeliever; to be ungrateful; to deny. **Kafr**: Darkness. **Kâfir**: Disbeliever; ungrateful; dark cloud; night; coat of mail; impious. Just as *îmân* is the acceptance of the truth so *kufr* is its rejection, and as the practical acceptance of the truth or doing of a good deed is called *îmân* or part of *îmân* so the practical rejection of truth or the doing of an evil deed is called *kufr* or part of *kufr*. The Holy Prophet ﷺ is reported to have warned his Companions in the following words, 'Beware! Do not become disbelievers *(kuffâr)* after me, so that some of you should strike off the necks of others (B. 25:132). Here the slaying of a Muslim by a Muslim is condemned as an act of disbelief. In another tradition it is said, 'Abusing a Muslim is transgression and fighting against him is *Kufr* - disbelief or a part of disbelief (B. 2:36). Ibn A<u>th</u>îr in his well known dictionary of traditions, the Nihâyah writes, '*Kufr* is of two kinds, one is denial of the faith itself and the other is denial of a *fra'* (branch) of the branches of Islam and on account of it a person does not get out of the faith of Islam: this is what is called *kufrun dûna kufrin*.

Kâffatan كافةً: All together; wholly and completely; repulsing the enemy of peace; restraining oneself and others from sin and digression.

Kahf كهف: Shelter; cavern; cave (L. T.); a place of refuge; a spacious cave; a cave excavated out of a mountain in the form of a house (L. T. R.).

Kalâlah كلالة: One who has no child (4:12); who has neither parents left nor a child (4:176).

Kalimah كلمة, Pl. Kalimât: Word; speech; prophecy; news (R.L.T.). The announcement of Jesus' advent had been made in the Books of the Prophets before him, so when he came it was said, 'This is the prophetic word', and so he was called a 'Word' (Râzî). Jesus had been called *Kalimat-Allâh* because his words were helpful to the cause of Allâh, just as a person who helps the cause of religion by his velour is called *Saif Allâh* (the sword of Allâh), or *Asad Allâh* (the lion of Allâh), so is the expression

Kalimat-Allâh (T.). Besides the above mentioned meanings the Holy Qur'ân has used this word Kalimah in the following senses also: A sign (66:12); punishment (10:96); plan and design (9:39); glad tiding (7:137); creation of Allâh (31:27).

Kallâ كلا: This particle signifies rejection, rebuke and reprimanding a person for what he has said being untrue. It also indicates that what has been said before is wrong and what follows after it is right. It is also used to reject the request of a person and to reprimand him for making it (L.T.R.).

Kamâ كما: This particle means because; as; just as; since (L. T. Muhît).

Kasaba كسب: Earned. **Iktasaba** اكتسب: Incurred: These are two words from the same root *ksb*. The word *kasaba* generally denotes the doing of good deeds and *iktasaba* the doing of evil deeds and denotes greater exertion on the part of the person who commits that evil deed (L.).

Kashafat an Sâqiha كشفت عن ساقها: She uncovered her shanks; she got ready to meet the situation; she became perturbed or perplexed or was taken aback (L.T.).

Kariha كره: He found it difficult; he disliked it; he did not desire; he disapproved; he hated and loathed; he did it unwillingly and against his wish or liking (L.T.R.).

Katama كتم: To conceal; to restrain (anger). **Kitmân**: It is used to denote a state of affairs without there being any attempt or desire on one's part to conceal or suppress anything. It may merely be the result of circumstances or outcome of nature (T.).

Kursî كرسي: learning; power; chair; throne. *Huwa min ahlil kursî*: He is a learned man. *Khairun nâsi alkrâsî*: خير الناس الاكراسي The best of men are men of learning. **Kursiyyohû**: His knowledge (L.T.). Râzî inclines to the view that it means 'Allâh's majesty, glory and power'. Zama<u>kh</u>sharî interprets it as 'His sovereignty and dominion'.

(<u>KH</u>) خ

<u>Kh</u>ada‘a خدع: He forsook; abandoned; refrained (L.T.).

Akhda'a: He sought or desired to deceive but did not succeed in his attempt, while Khada'a means he succeeded in his attempt to deceive (Baqâ'. T.).

Khafâ خفي, **Akhfâ** أخفي: To conceal a thing; to remove its covering, to manifest (T.). This word has contradictory meanings.

Khairan خيرا: To earn wealth; to prefer; to select; to give to anyone the option between. **Khair** Pl. Akhyâr and **Khiyâr**: Good; excellent; better; the best; moral or physical good; wealth; welfare; virtue. **Khair** Pl. Khairât: Good; the best; good deed. **Khair**: Considerable and much wealth (Kf.).

Khalada خلد: To last long; to remain; to live on; to retain a youthful appearance; to abide in a place; to live without change or deterioration, and does not necessarily convey the idea of perpetuity (R.L.T.). **Akhlada**: To lean towards; to stick faithfully to (a friend). **Khuld**: Paradise; continuity (L.T.R. Asâs).

Khalafa خلف: To succeed; to take the place of; to be the agent; substitute of. **Khalifa:** To be stupid. *Khalafa 'an khulqi abîhi*: He has not his father's worth. **Khalafa**: To be altered in; to be corrupt; to ascend a mountain; to remain behind; to repair (clothes); to seize any one from behind; to disobey; to transgress; to forfeit one's word; to disagree. **Akhlafa** mouidahû: To break a promise; to repair (a garment); to send behind; To replace. **Takhallafa**: To remain behind; to disagree. **Ikhtalafa**: To be diversified; to branch off; to succeed; to replace; to leave behind; to return repeatedly to. **Istakhlafa**: To appoint as successor; to substitute one for another. **Khalaf**: Good son; good substitute; good compensation. **Khalf:** Bad son; bad substitute; bad compensation. **Khawâlif**: Women. **Khilaf**: diversity; other; else; contrary. **Khilâf:** It is infinitive noun from Khalafa. He disagreed; he disobeyed or defied; he put a thing on opposite side or in opposite direction. **Khilâf**: Disobedience, defiance, the contrary or opposing of a thing; contrary or opposing side (L.T.R.). **Khalîfah**: supreme chief: successor; religious head (T.L.). Ibn Mas'ûd and Ibn 'Abbâs explain this word as one who judges among or rules the creatures of Allâh by His command (L.). The word *Khalîfah* in 2:30 refers to the children of Âdam, i.e. the whole of humankind. The correctness of this view is corroborated by the Holy Qur'ân itself (6:165) (see also **Âdam**آدم).

Khalaqa خلق: To measure; to proportion; to determine; to fashion; to create; to form a thing; to be fit; apt to a thing; to behave kindly with. **Khulq**: Moral; character; nature; temper; habit. **Mukhallaq**: Well proportioned (L.T.R.).

Khamṣa/Makhmaṣatun مخمصة: Emptiness caused by hunger; extreme hunger. It also covers other situations in which overwhelming extraneous forces beyond a person's control may compel against one's will to do some thing that is prohibited (L.T.R.).

Khamara خمر: To conceal; to hide; to withhold. **Khamira**: To be unaware of (news). **Khamara**: To mingle with. **Ikhtamara**: To be fermented. **Khamr**: Any thing that clouds or obscures and covers the intellect; grapes. **Khamira**: Intoxicated; giddy (T.). **Khimâr**, Pl. Khumur: Screen; muffler; head dress (women) (L.).

Khasafa خسف: To bring disgrace; to sink down; to be eclipsed; to humble and vex; to tear off; to cause a land to be swallowed up with its inhabitants; to bury one beneath the earth; cause the earth to swallow up. The infinitive noun *khasf* signifies being vile; abject; It also contains the sense of abasing or humbling others (L. T.).

Khasha'a خشع: To be submissive; humble; lowly; bow down; cast down (of eyes); faint (voice); to exercise restraint; throw himself completely at His mercy (2:46) (L.T.R.).

Khatama ختم: To seal; to put a signet upon; to stamp; to cicatrise (word). **Khatama** 'alâ qalbihi: To seal the heart; to harden it; to finish; to read over (a book); To complete a thing. **Khâtim**: Seal; signet-ring; stamp; last. **Khâtam**: Seal; the best; the Most Perfect; last; the embellishment and ornament (R. L. T.). The difference between *Khâtim* and *Khâtam* is that the meaning of *khâtim* is last part or portion but the word *khatâm* means that last part or portion of a thing that is the best. Thus it indicates finality combined with perfection and continuation of its blessings (L.T.R. Zurqânî, Asâs).

Khula'a خلع: To release; to take off; to disown; to depose; to throw off (all restrained); to divorce. The right of the wife to claim a divorce. The right of the wife to claim a divorce is recognized by Islam (2:229, B. 68: 3,11). The two parties are on a perfect level of equality in the matter of divorce. She has the right to claim divorce on those very grounds on which the husband could divorce his wife. The wife is also entitled to a divorce if the husband is missing.

Khinzîr خنزير: This word is a combination of two words **Khin** means 'bad' and **Arâ** means 'I see'. Khinzîr thus means I see bad or evil; It also means dirty, greedy and stubborn (L.T.R.)

(L) ل

Lâ لا: No; not. It is also used to impart emphasis to the oath, meaning that the thing which is going to be explained is so self-evident that it does not need calling anything to bear witness to its truth as in 4:65 and 56:75. But when the refutation of a certain hypothesis is intended *Lâ* is used to signify that the just said thing is incorrect and that the correct statement will follow immediately as in 75:1 (L.T. Kf.).

La'alla لعل: It is used to denote either a state of hope or fear whether that state pertains to the speaker or to the addressee or to someone else. Râzî says, 'It is used for a person when you intend to show his remoteness from a thing.'

La'allaka لعلّك: You may have power to do such a thing. In verse 11:12. this word has been used to signify that the people imagine that you are now perhaps going to abandon. It is also used to denote expectations or doubt combined with expectation. It also signifies not doubt but certainty, as in 2:21 (L.T.R.Rz.).

Lâm ل: The particle denotes purpose result; consequence; end; as it is said, *'Lidu lil mouti wabnû lil kharâbi'* bear children that they should die and, build houses that they should fall into ruins. The significance is not that you should bear children for death or you should build houses for ruin. Such Lâm is called *Lâm Âqbat.* It also denotes cause such Lâm is called *Lâm Ta'lîl*. This proposition is used in the sense of *fî* (-for); in the sense of *ba'd* (- after); in the sense of *ilâ* (- to); to express a right; in the sense of *ma* (-with or in spite of) (L.T.R.). This particle also used as a corroborative e.g. indeed; surely; verily; certainly etc. When used instead of *li* with the affixed pronoun such as *lî* (-to me), *laka* (-to you) as proposition; expressing possession. Before the aorist it is used as a conjunction to express the aim, intention, order. *Ji'tuka li akrimuka*: I have come to you in order to show you regard. When prefixed to the article *'al'* the latter loses its *hamza* as in 4:144. It denotes both the genetive and dative cases.

Lâna لَانَ: It was or it became tender smooth.

Lînah لينة: A palm tree of which the dates are of very inferior quality and are unfit for human consumption (L. T. Raudz al-Unaf).

La'nat لعنت: It is usually but inexactly translated as curse, in reality it denotes banishment or alienation from all that is good (L.). Whenever it is attributed in the Holy Qur'ân to Allâh with reference to a sinner, it signifies the latter's exclusion from Allâh's mercy and grace or his rejection and disapproval by Allâh (L. T.).

Lâqih لاقح Pl. Lawâqih: A she camel having just conceived or become pregnant. *Riyahun Lawaqihun*; - pregnant winds, impregnating or fecundating or fertilizing winds, winds which collect vapours and then form into the clouds and send down rain which make herbage and plants fruitful. *Harbun lawaqihun* - a war pregnant with great events. Laqihun also means a man to whom offspring is born (L.T.).

Laulâ لولا: Had not (sometimes synonymous with *halla);* could; therefore; why not. But its meaning becomes clear if we remember that it is one of the *hurûf at tashdîd* - particle denoting insistence. Whenever it is followed by a verb in the past tense, as in 10:98 it implies reproof for one's not having done something that should have been done (L.T.R.). We should admit that there is no idiomatic equivalent in modern English conveying this shade of meaning.

Lub لب Pl. Albâb: The best and choicest part of a thing; kernel; pith; heart; mind; pure understanding and intellect; the essence and substance of a thing. **Lub**: Something higher and purer than understanding or *'aql* (L.T.) **Labîb** لبيب: Gifted with sound judgment (L.T.R.).

(M) م

Mârût ماروت: See **Hârût.**

Ma'âd معاد: Makkah; is derived from *'aud*; to return; to come back to; to become beneficial to; to visit a place time after time; to repeat. **'Aidah**: Return; profit; advantage; benefit. **Ma'âd**: Place of return; meeting place; the pilgrimage to Makkah (M.L.T. Aqrab.).

Madda مد: To spread; to stretch; to pull; to put oil in a lamp; to lengthen; to take ink from (an ink stand); to grant a delay; to manure (a land); to draw forth from another thing; to make productive and fertile by means of particles of other things; to strain (L.T.R.). **Madd**: Ebb; rising of water; lengthening of the vowels. **Mudd**: Measure of various standards; bushel; two pints; dip of ink; length; space of time. **Madad**: Assistance. **Midâd**: Ink; manure; pattern. **Madiyyûn**: Material. **Mumaddadah:** Pitched.

Mafâtih مفاتيح plural of **Miftâh:** Keys; treasures; store; hoarded wealth; magazine (L.T.R.)

Mâidah مائده: Food; a table with food on it. A table without food is not called mâidah (R. T.). **Tamîda**: To be a source of benefit and provision of food; it sways; convulse or quake (R.T.).

Makar مكر: To plot and plan secretly with a view to circumventing the other; to practice device; to requite the machination of a person (R.

T.). It is of two kinds, a good plan by which a good objective is sought and an evil plan by which an evil objective is sought (R.).

Malaka مَلَكَ: To possess; to become the owner of; to conquer; to rule over; to control; to take (a wife); to supervise; to reign over; to get sovereignty; to get ownership. **Mallaka**: To give (a wife) to. **Umlika**: To take a wife; to marry. **Mâlik** Pl. Mulûk: Master; king; conqueror; ruler. **Malaka**: Habit; royalty; queen; faculty; treatment; custom. **Mâlik**: Owner; possessor; who possesses the right of ownership over a thing and has the power to deal with it as one desires (M. L.). According to the rules of Arabic increasing the number of letters added to a root, as the letter *Alif* in Mâlik, makes its meaning more extensive (Kf.); hence a *mâlik* is more than a *malak* i.e. king. The adoption of the word *mâlik* or owner and lord is to show that the *mâlik* is not unjust if he forgives his servants or gives more than their right, as he is not like a king or a judge who is bound to give his judgment strictly in accordance with a prescribed law, but being Mâlik or master he can forgive and show love and mercy wherever and in whatever manner he may like. The use of the word *Mâlik* for the Almighty Allâh as in 1:4 serves a twofold purpose. On the one hand it gives courage, hope and confidence to a person who has in a moment of weakness committed some wrong, not to lose hope as the beneficent and Gracious Allâh being his Mâlik and Master has the power to forgive. On the other hand it serves as a warning against taking undue advantage of the Merciful Allâh as he would hate to see His servants being degraded on account of sin. Both the things are essential for human progress. **Malakût**: Kingdom; empire; heaven; the invisible world. **Mâlik**: Owner; possessor, sovereign. **Milk**-*i-yamîn*: Wife; slave. **Malak** Pl. Malâikah: Angel. Angels are part of the system with which Allâh executes His will in both the physical and the spiritual worlds. They are message bearers and in the physical world they form the first link with a number of other links, descending downwards; but in the spiritual world they form a direct link between Allâh and human beings. They inspire people to do righteous deeds moving their mind to virtue. There is quite a large number of angels. They are divided into classes, each occupying a definite position and serving a definite purpose. Angels are not visible to the physical eye, yet they do sometimes appear in one form or another. Their appearance is not in any real shape but simply a sort of manifestation. The contact, however, is not imaginary. They exercise direct influence which is definitely felt and may even be tested through the results. When we speak of an angel appearing to us we do not mean his actual descending on the earth and leaving his actual station in the heavens. We simply mean his manifestation by means of which he assumes a form which becomes visible to human beings. An angel is not merely a force but can be a living being who executes the will of his Lord, whenever and in whatever manner He demands. There are several sayings of the Holy Prophet ﷺ to the effect that an 'angel' appeared to him a number of times in one form or another. The existence of the angels has been recognised by righteous people in all ages and all countries. The angels though holy, pure and cannot commit sin and are provided with some powers and abilities from Allâh yet can represent only one side of creation. We may imagine them without passion or emotion. They have no independent will of their own (16:50). But on the other hand a human being is endowed with emotion and passion. The power of will or choosing gave him to some extent a mastery over his own fortunes and over nature, thus bringing him nearer the Allâh-like nature which has supreme mastery and will. So the real vicegerent is he who has the power of initiative, but whose independent action always reflects perfecttly the will of his Lord. So the angels, because of their one-sidedness were not meant to be raised to the dignity of vicegerent of Allâh. This shows the high place that humanity was destined to hold in the whole of creation (17:62). According to the Holy Qur'ân for the existence, growth and development of the whole universe certain mediums are essential; and those pure beings, known as angels have distinctive functions in the running of this universe. All plants, minerals and animal life are constantly being influenced by these bodies. There is no discourtesy or disrespect in thinking that for the sake of Divine communication there should be a medium between the Almighty Allâh and His prophets, rather this is perfectly in accordance with Allâh's Laws of nature. These beings of splendour influence the growth of spiritual perfection and visions of heart and mind to their maximum limit of development. 'Angels' in their own form of existence do not descend to earth and walk about like human beings, in that case it would have been impossible for them to carry out any of their functions. Take for instance the angel of Death, **Izrail**. Every second of the day and night he 'visits' thousands of persons separated by thousands of miles in all parts of the world, if he were earthbound, his task would be impossible. In fact angels do not move from the place which Allâh has appointed for them in order to carry out their duty. In the Holy Qur'ân on behalf of the angels it is said, 'Each one of us has his assigned place. And verily we are the ones who stand ranged in rows' (37:164-165). Just as the sun remains within its orbit, its light and warmth spreading to the earth, in the same manner in the spiritual and physical spheres angels remain attached to their respective appointed places. It should also be borne in mind that according to the Islamic Shariah the best among 'angels' do not have a better rank than the best among the human beings; and the best among them are superior to the best angels. All the angels do not enjoy the same rank and honour, and they do not perform the same kind of duties. Every angel has a different set of duties to carry out. It does also happen that one angel influences properties in different ways. **Gabriel** is an outstanding 'angel' and he has many duties to perform in accordance with the sublime position he holds. He 'descends' on every such person who has been blessed with Divine revelation, but the scope of the effect of his influence is different on the various abilities, capacities and according to the condition of the soul (Taudzîh i-Marâm). Figuratively *Malaikah* means holy and good men of knowledge wisdom and power (Râzî. Baidzâwî), as the Holy Qur'ân says about Joseph, 'He is but a gracious angel' (12:31).

Manna من: To bestow a favour upon; to recall (benefits); to reproach any one for a gift. **Mann**: gift; favour; benefit. Any thing which comes without much effort; honey; dew. According to Zajjaj it includes all that Allâh bestowed on Israelites as a gift in the wilderness and granted to them freely without much exertion on their part (M.L.Bahr). Truffle is one of the things included in the manna (B.).

Maqâlîd مقاليد: Pl. of Iqlîd, Qalîd and Miqlâd: All that encircle; treasured; collected (L.T.R.).

Maridza مرض: To be diseased. **Maradz**: Disease; anything whereby a person loses his physical, moral or spiritual health; any physical, moral or spiritual weakness or defect in faith; anything that hinders a human being's physical, moral spiritual progress; hypocrisy (R. L.). The Holy Qur'ân is revealed for healing these diseases (10:57).

Masîh مسيح (Messiah): One anointed and wiped over with some such thing as oil; one who journeys or travels much; one beautiful in the face; one very truthful; one created blessed and goodly; a king (L.T.). It is the Arabic form of Messiah which represented the Hebrew Mashiah, and Aramic Messiah. Jesus

Christ is said to have been so called because he used to travel much (R. Râzî), or because he was anointed with a pure blessed ointment with which the Prophets are anointed (Râzî).

Mâta ماتَ: To die; to die away (fire); to be worn out (garment); to be forlorn (place); to become still (wind). **Amâta**: To soften (meat) by cooking; to cool (anger); to mortify (passions). Omit; to be obsolete (word). **Istamata**: To exert one's self to the utmost. **Maut**: Death; swoon; madness; deprived of sensation, intellect or understanding; stupor; sleep; lifelessness; slippage of the power of growth; to be as though dead with grief or sorrow or fear and pain. Motionlessness or stillness; being reduced to poverty; becoming worn out; becoming base, abject, vile and despised; any painful condition (R. L. T.). This word does not always denote physical death. Râghib explains the verb *mâta* as having the meaning - he became deprived of sensation; dead as to the senses. *Yuhyî wa yumîtu* -He fertilizes (the earth) and causes desolation. **Mayyit** (Pl. Amwât) also signifies one whose blood has not been avenged, one who leaves behind no good successor; one stricken with sorrow and grief (L. T.).

Ma<u>th</u>al مَثَلَ: To be excellent; eminent; to show a pattern; to liken; to relate a fact; to use a parable; to set up; to follow; to argue; to narrate. *<u>Dz</u>araba mathalan* - he cited a proverb, as an allegory. **Mi<u>th</u>âl** Pl. Mu<u>th</u>ul: Pattern; type; example; excellent; first rate thing (L. T.).

Mi<u>h</u>âl مِحال: This expression occurs in the Holy Qur'ân only in one place (13:13). It signifies: powerful in contriving; in a manner hidden from human eyes; that wherein wisdom lies. It also means, seizure; punishment; power; seniority; death; reveçaling of defects (M. L.).

Min مِن: A portion or a source of something; part of a whole; from; of; than; some; amongst; proposition used for expressing a starting point; proposition for determining time, origin, composition, explanation, commencement or separation; any; according to, mood of action; on; upon; out of; by reason of. *Mâta* **min** *youmihî* he died the very same day. *Ijtanibur rijsa* **min** *al ou<u>th</u>ân* - shun the abomination of idols. Proposition means separation; distinction. *Ya'lam al-mufsida* **min** *al- mu<u>s</u>li<u>h</u>i* - he knows the wicked from the righteous; means sometimes instead of. It is explanative before the subject of a negative or interrogative verb, *Mâ jâ'anî* **min** *rajulin* - no man came to me. It also means relation; likeness between; *Lastu* **min***hu wa laisa* **min***nî* - there is no relation between him and me (L. T. Râzî).

Mubârak مبارك: Passive participle derived from *baraka* signifying the continuance for ever of the blessings which a thing possesses and from which extensive good flows. It also possesses the sense of firmness, steadiness, abundance of good, exaltation, collection, blessings: Highly Exalted; far removed from every defect, impurity, imperfection and everything derogatory (L.T.R.).

Mudda<u>thth</u>ir مدّثّر: One who is adorned with the best natural powers and qualities and with the prophetic dignity (Rû<u>h</u> al-Ma'ânî); one who is entrusted with the heavy load of the responsibility of prophethood (Qadîr); One who adjusts or puts things in order; one who is about to leap upon a horse and ride; one who wrapped himself with a garment; Reformer; effacer; vanquisher (L.T.R.)

Mudhâmmatân مدهامتان: Dark green with foliage. This adjective is used in the Holy Qur'ân to indicate ever fresh (R. J.).

Muqa<u>tt</u>a'ât مَقَطّعات: The Abbreviations. Abbreviations are known to all nations. In the modern world the use of abbreviations is very widely spread. Nearly every dictionary forms a list of them along with their meaning. In the past when all writing was done by hand, abbreviations saved time and space. Today when so much is printed on so many subjects they serve the same purpose. In government, business, the armed forces, sports and so many other fields abbreviated forms make a sort of language within a language. There are various ways of abbreviating words, but there is no single set of rules of abbreviation. A part of the whole word may be used. It is often the first letter taken for the whole word as UN, USA etc. In other cases key letters are selected e.g. Dr. for doctor and Mr. for mister. Modern abbreviations often use initials and many omit periods. An acronym is a word formed from initial letters in a phrase or title. It is also a form of abbreviation but it is pronounced as a single word not as a series of letters e.g. NATO. The Christian and Jewish Scriptures have also made frequent use of abbreviations e.g. INRI. Compare the book of Psalms in Old Testament where the psalmist has arranged his meditation in an elaborate alphabetical form. It has been called the alphabet of Divine love. In every language they carry different meanings in different places, and the meanings are decided in each case by the context. Their use is not an extraordinary thing, or out of the usual order. The use of abbreviations was in vogue among the Arabs even before Islam. They used them in their poems and speeches and conversations as an Arab poet said: قلنا قفي لنافقالت ق "We said to our beloved stop for us for a while so she said lo I am stopping". Here the letter *qâf* stands for *waqaftu* (I am stopping) (see also Diwân al-Mutanabbî). There is also a saying of the Holy Prophet ﷺ *Kafa bisSaifi shâ* كفي بالسيف شا (Sufficient is the sword as a remedy). Here *sha* stands for *shafion* (Qurtubî). There are so many couplets in Arabic poetry in which this kind of abbreviation is used. Same is the interpretation that well-known philologists A<u>kh</u>fash, Zajjaj and Ibn al-Anbârî have given to such abbreviations. From the sayings of the Holy Prophet Qurtubî quotes some abbreviations. Abbreviations in the Holy Qur'ân like *Alif Lâm Mîm* or *Sâd* are shortened forms of words and phrases. They are not at all mystic symbols. The significance of the abbreviations used in the Holy Qur'ân can in most cases be traced to the Holy Prophet ﷺ and his Companions. So it is absolutely wrong to say that the meanings of these abbreviations were unknown even to the Holy Prophet ﷺ and his Companions. I must warn the reader that abbreviations like *Alif Lâm Mîm* are not acronyms. The Arabic name for these abbreviations is Muqatta'ât i.e., letters used and pronounced separately. So these abbreviations are not pronounced as single words but as series of letters. These letters are part of the text of the Holy Qur'ân, so it is wrong on the part of those translators who leave abbreviations untranslated. The letters of these abbreviations stand for words and they have not been placed at random in the beginning of different chapters nor are their letters combined arbitrarily. There exists a deep and far-reaching connection between their various sets. Much has been written about the significance of these letters of which two points are very important and authentic. One is that each abbreviation represents a specific attribute of Allâh and the chapter before which the abbreviations are placed and the subsequent chapter having no abbreviations is in its subject matter duly connected with the Divine attributes for which the abbreviation stands. The second is that they represent in numerical terms the period of rise and fall of every new community in Islamic world and their future history. Each letter of Arabic Alphabet, according to *Hisâb al-Jummal,* has a definite numerical value of its own. Thus *Alif* has the value of 1 (one), *Bâ* of 2 (two), *Jîm* of 3 (three) and so on. This system was known to the early Arabs and is mentioned in some of the well known books of Islamic traditions (e.g. Ibn Jarîr). From among the companions of the Holy Prophet ﷺ, 'Alî the fourth Caliph, Ibn-'Abbas, Ibn-Mas'ûd and Ubbayy bin Ka'b and their pupil Mujâhid, ibn Jubair, Qatâdah, Ikramah and Hasan and after them Suddî, Sh'abî and Akhfash agreed in interpreting the letters *Alif Lâm Mîm* prefixed to the second chapter of the

Holy Qur'ân and chapters 3, 29, 30, 31 and 32 (six in all) as meaning I am Allâh, the all-knowing. *Alif* standing for *anâ* and *Lâm* for *Allâh* and *Mîm* for *a'lamo* as being respectively the first , the middle and the last letters of the words they stand for. These abbreviations occur in the beginning of not less than 28 chapters and are made up of one or more, to a maximum of five letters of the Arabic alphabet, *Alif, Hâ, Ra, Sîn, Sâd, Tâ, Ain, Qâf, Kâf, Lâm, Mîm, Hâ, Yâ.*

Mûsâ (Moses) مُوسىٰ: It is a Hebrew-Arabic word. In Hebrew it is written and pronounced as Moshe and means a thing drawn out of water. He was an Israelite, who according to the Bible lived about 500 years after Abraham and about 1400 before Jesus Christ. It is wrong to say that Moses was not an Israelite by birth and did not belong to Hebrew stock (L.T.).

Muta' متْع **Istamta'** اِستمْتاع are derived from *mata'*: Explaining this word Lisânal-'Arab quotes Zajjaj as saying about the verse 4:24, 'This is a verse while interpreting of which some people have committed a great blunder owing to their ignorance of the Arabic. They have inferred from it the legality of Muta' (- temporary marriage which is unlawful in Islam)'. The Arabic idiom does not countenance this use of *istimta'* with regard to a woman in the sense of temporary connection. *Tamatta' bil mar'ati* means he benefited by the woman temporarily, but *istamta' bikadhâ* means he benefited by her for a long time (L.). It must also be noted that whenever the noun *tamattu'* is used to denote temporary connection, it is followed by the proposition *bâ* put before the word standing for woman as in the above example, but in the expression (4:24) the pronoun is preceded by the proposition *'min'*. **Tamattu'**: To profit. There are two ways in which Hajj may be combined with *'Umrah*, Tamattu' and *Qirân*. Tamattu' consists of combining the Hajj and the *'Umrah* in such a manner that the pilgrim should enter a state of *Ihrâm* with the intention of performing an *'Umrah* and get out of that state after the performance of the *'Umrah* and again entering into a state of *Ihrâm* in the days of Hajj, thus between the *'Umrah* and the Hajj the pilgrim profits by living in his ordinary condition and is not bound by the strict rules of *Ihrâm*. (See also **Hajj**, **'Umrah** and **Ihrâm**).

(N) ن

Nâziât نازعت Pl. of Nâziun: Who perform their duty vigorously; group of people who draw arrows and bows. The famous follower of the Companions 'Atâ has said that it alludes to bows which are drawn in a fight. **Nâzi':** Stranger; remote; out of the tribe; thus it indicates *Muhâjirîn*; who were not of the clan of Ansâr (L.Rûh.T.).

Naba'a نباء: News; information; a message or announcement of great utility which results either to great knowledge or predominance of opinion and which inspires awe and makes the heart tremble with fear. **Nabûwwat** نبوت Prophethood. **Nabû'at:** نبؤت Giving the news, information or prophecy (L.T.R. Baqâ').

Nabî نبئ (pronounced with *Hamza* ء**):** Prophet, who acquaints or informs others; who is informed respecting Allâh and things unseen. But if it is derived from *nabûw'at* it signifies prophethood, elevation, evidence and giving news. **Nabba'**: A bigger signification than *naba'* (L.T.R.). A person came to the Holy Prophet ﷺ addressing him يانبئ الله (with *hamzah* ء) 'O! The person who foretells things of Allâh'. He replied, 'Say يانبي الله -"O Prophet and Messenger of Allâh!"'. - (without *Hamza* ء but with *yâ* ي).

Nafasa نفس: To be tenacious of; to envy the good. **Nafîsa**: Precious. **Nafasa**: To aspire to a thing; to vie with any one in (the pursuit of). **Nafs** Pl. Nufûs and Anfûs: Soul; vital principle; blood; spirit; person; individual; self of a human being or thing; intentions; desire; pride; essence; precious; much sought; ring leader; dearer; relative, punishment. **Tanaffasa**: To breathe; to respire; to become long (day); to shine (dawn); to sprinkle; to draw a deep sigh. Râzî says that *faqtulû anfusakum* means mortify yourselves thus *anfusakum* means here your desires and passions (L.T,R.).

Nafl نفل Pl. Anfâl: Gift. It denotes in its purely linguistic sense some thing given in excess of ones obligation from which the term *Salâtun Nafl* (supererogatory Prayer) is derived (R.T. Miqyâs.).

Na<u>h</u>l نحل and Na<u>h</u>lah: Bee. **Ni<u>h</u>lah**: Giving a thing willingly, cheerfully and without expecting a return; a free gift (R.).

Najama نَجّمَ: To appear; to begin; to proceed; to ensure; to unfold a thing that comes or appears gradually as if by installments; to pay (a debt) by installments (L.T.). **Najm** Pl. Najûm: Star; appointed time; creeper; germinative plant; tree; origin; from the very beginning this word has also been applied to each of the gradually revealed parts of the Holy Qur'ân. This was the interpretation of the verse 53:1 by Ibn 'Abbâs (I.). This translation is regarded as fully justified by Râg<u>h</u>ib; Zamak<u>kh</u>shary, Râzî, Bai<u>dz</u>âwî, Ibn Ka<u>th</u>îr and other authorities. Râg<u>h</u>ib and Ibn Ka<u>th</u>îr in particular point to the phrase *mawâqiun nujûm* in 56:75 which undoubtedly refers to the step by step revelation of the Holy Qur'ân.

Najas نجس Unclean; dirty; filthy; impure (L.T.R.). **Najâsat**: Is of two kinds, one kind is perceived by senses and the other is perceived by the mind (R.).

Nasal نسل: Offspring; produce; fruit *Al-hartha wan* **nasla** - land and its produce; wife and her offspring (R. L. T.).

Nâs<u>h</u>i<u>t</u>ât نشطت: When its source is *nashtan* as in 79:2. It means those beings or groups of people who exert themselves vigorously in the discharge of their duties; those who travel from one place to another; those who tie as to form a knot, those who draw up (a bucket) at one pull; those who draw up quickly; those who pull out in a smooth and gentle manner. It is an act. But if the source is *nishâtan* then it means those who are lively or pleased or happy or cheerful (L.T.R.).

Nashûz نشوز: Rebellion; ill will; disobedience; deliberate bad behaviour; desertion; rising against; resisting; hating; ill conduct; perverseness; to rise up (Qâmûs, T.). Abû Hayyân explains it as leaving the husband's place and taking up an abode which he does not like (Bahr). It also includes what is now a days described as mental cruelty and persistent breach of one's marital obligations (L.T.).

Nid ند Pl. Andâd: Alike; rival; compeers. The rival and compeers to Allâh may be idols, great and glorious things, superstitions, poetry; things of art and sciences, pride of race, wealth, power, learning or even spiritual pride. The commentators of the Holy Qur'ân agree that the term andâd, which is always used in the Holy Qur'ân in plural form, implies any object of adoration to which some or all of Allâh's qualities are ascribed (R. L. T.).

Nisyân نسيان: Severing; ceasing to think of a person with feelings of love and affection; ceasing to think of a person or a thing either owing to loss of memory or negligence or doing it deliberately; forgetfulness; cutting of connection by way of punishment (L.T.R.).

Nutfah نطفة: Pure fluid; being applied to a very small quantity as well as a very large volume of it; any good drink; sea (T); small life germ; a sperm in the seminal fluid; drop of water. **Nutfatân**: Two seas; Mediterranean and the Red Sea (L. Aqrab).

Nûn ن: Large fish; ink pot; fig; science; **Dhun-nûn**: Jonah (-the prophet) (L. T.).

(O)

Ou أوْ: Or; either; whether; unless; and. It does not always indicate doubt but simply indicates the presentation of an alternative (M.L.).

(Q) ق

Qadam قَدم: The human foot; precedence; preference; rank; footing; foundations; example; strength. *Qadama sidqin* means going forward or advancement in excellence; footing of firmness (R.L.T.).

Qâla قَالَ: To say; to speak; to profess (a doctrine); to grasp a thing; to point out; to relate; to emit an opinion upon; to think; It is also used to describe the practical upshot of events without there being any actual speech or dialogue. An Arab poet says;

قالت لها العنين سمعا و طاعة

Qâlat láhal'ainaini sam'anwatâ 'atan both of my eyes said to her, 'I obey'.

It is also said:

امتلأ الحوض و قال قطني

Imt'alal houdzu wa qâla qatnî

the tank became full and said, 'That will suffice'. It does not mean that the tank actually said so, but simply that its condition implied that it was full (R.). The purpose of such narration being only to show the existing condition of things in a vivid and graphic form. To proclaim loudly, repeatedly and in clear and definite terms, deeds and actions (L.T.R.N.Kf.).

Qâma قَام: To rise; to stand up; to be lively; to appear in broad light (truth); to come back to life; to rise against; to superintend; to persevere in; to rise for honouring; to sustain. Qâma *bi amrin*-he undertook an affair. Qâma *bi wa'dihî* - he fulfilled his promise. **Qawwama**: To maintain; to erect; to set up; to set aright; to rectify; to make accurate; to awake. **Aqâma:** To perform (Prayer); to establish (a roof); to raise (the dead); to make one to stand up; to continue; to keep to; to remain in (a place); to straighten a thing; to render (a market) brisk; to appoint; to set up. **Istaqâma**: To get up; to rise; to be upright; to be in good state; to be straight forward; to return to. **Qaum:** Nation; tribe; party; some people. **Qauma**: Station; pause in Prayer; revolution. **Qawâm**: Livelihood; sustenance. **Qiwâm and Qiyâm**: Main stay; normal state. **Qawwâm**: Sustainer; guardian; who manages and maintains the affairs well; who undertakes the maintenance and protection of, maintainer (L.T.). **Qiyâm** *billâh* -worship of Allâh. **Qiyâmah**: Resurrection; Hereafter; Day of the last judgment. **Qâm** *al qiyâmah* -he raised an uproar. **Qîmat**: Value; price; stature of a person. **Qayyim** ***ul***

mar'at - the husband; guardian; sustainer. **Qayyimah**: True faith. **Qayyûm**: Self-Existing; All-Sustaining. **Maqâm**: Abode; place; time of abode; standing place; residence; rank; dignity. **Mustaqîm**: Straight; right; undeviating and without any crookedness (M.T.). **Aqâma**: He kept a thing or an affair in a right state (T.). **Aqâma** *al- salâta* - to observe Prayer; to perform the Prayer with all prescribed conditions. The perfect Prayer is that in which body and soul both play their part (R.L.T.).

Qatala قتل: He killed; put to death; slain; attempted to kill; rendered the person like the one killed; accursed (L.T.R. Zamakhsharî).

Qara' قرء: To read; to study; to convey; to make up (things); to collect.

Qaranقرن Pl. Qurûn: Generation; part or division of time; people of one time; a century; age; horn; edge; border of the rising sun; trumpet; noble man; ones equal in age; ray (R.L.T).

Qur'ân قرآن: Name of the Book which was revealed to the Holy Prophet of Islam - Muhammad ﷺ; a book which is meant to be read; a book or message which is meant to be conveyed and delivered to other people; a book which comprises of and has collected in itself all truth; a book which contains not only visible truth which may be seen and felt by all but it also contains truths that lie hidden from the eyes of most persons and come to light only as and when time ripens (R.L.T.).

Qurû'قروء: It is the plural of Qara'. Entering from the state of cleanliness and purity (*tuhr*) into the state of menstruation. Normally it is about four weeks but there are variations in the case of different women (R.L.). Menstruations; period or state of purity; preceding and following a menstrual discharge; that is the period between two menstruation; termination of a menstruation; the whole month (R.T.) (See also **'Iddat** عِدِت).

Qaradza قرض: To cut; to incline in walk. **Qarradza**: To requite; to praise or blame. **Miqrâdz:** Scissors.

Yuqridzu: He will offer a good action or gift or any thing for which a reward may be sought (Abû Ishâq). Akhfash another very famous grammarian says that *yuqridzullah* means who will do a good action by following and obeying the command of Allâh (L.T.). According to Zajjaj *qardz* signifies any thing done on which a reward may be expected (Râzî).

Qaub قوب: To draw near. **Qâb**: Space between middle and the end of a bow; space. **Qâb***a qousain* -one chord of two bows. The proverb reminds us of an ancient Arab custom, according to which when two persons pledged themselves to close and firm friendship they would join their bows in such a way that they appeared as one and then they would shoot an arrow from that combined bow; thus indicating that they had become as it were one person and that an attack on one would be considered as an attack on the other (T. L.). The two bows seem to indicate also the Holy Prophet's two fold perfection in his nearness to Allâh and his service to humanity.

(R) ر

Rabb رب**:** This word translated as Lord, means master; chief; determiner; provider; sustainer; rewarder; perfecter; ruler; creator; maintainer; reposer of properties in things of nature; developer; framer of rules and laws of the growth of things; regulariser; foster of things in such a manner as to make them attain one condition after another until they reach their goal of completion (R.L.T.). Thus this word Rabb conveys not only the idea of fostering, bringing up or nourishing but also that of regulating, completing, accomplishing, cherishing, sustaining and bringing to maturity by evolution from the earliest state to that of the highest perfection. Rabb also means the originator of things and their combiner to create new forms and it means the Lawgiver, who frames Laws under which he propounds the shapes which things must assume and the ratio and proportion in which various ingredients must combine with each other. He is the arranger of the different stages through which they have to pass on their way to completion. He sees to the necessary provision for them in their journey. He is the Lord Who puts things on the way to perfection. Thus the word Rabb signifies about two dozen processes which every entity passes through in its course of creation and evolution before it reaches its final development. These meanings have not been forced and thrust upon this word. The lexicons of Arabic language speaks of all of them when they give the meanings of the root *rabb*. This word points to a law of evolution in the physical and spiritual worlds and the principle of evolution is not inconsistent with the belief in Allâh. But we must warn the readers that the process of evolution referred to here is not identical with the theory of Darwin. The verse also points to the fact that a human being has been created for unlimited progress. We must admit that all other languages lack an equivalent of the word as they have no equivalent for the words *Rahmân, Rahîm, Hamd, Allâh.*

Rabwah ربوة: Fertile ground; elevated ground (R.L.T.).

Rafa'a رفع: To extol a thing; to lift; to take away; to put a noun in the native; to trace back (a tradition); to exalt; to raise; to elevate; to honour; to show regard to; to introduce any one to a king; to be raised to dignity. **Râfi'oka**: Will exalt you . It is the active participle from *rafa'* which signifies raising; elevating; exalting and making honourable (T.). When the rafa' of a human being to Allâh is spoken of in the Holy Qur'ân or in the religious literature of Islam it is always in the sense of making honourable. Raising a human being in his body to Allâh implies that the Divine Being is limited to a place. The Holy Qur'ân says, *fî buyûtin adhinallah an turfa'a* (24:36) - in houses which Allâh has commanded to be exalted. The Holy Prophet ﷺ said, *Man tawâdza'a lillâhi* **rafa'***a hullâho ilas samâis sâbia'*

- he who humbles himself for the sake of Allâh, Allâh will lift him up to the seventh heaven. In a prayer taught by the Holy Prophet we pray *Allâhumma* **rfa'***nî* O Allâh! Exalt me. No one supposes that in this place **rafa'a** means raising of the body to the heavens. Râzî writes that this shows that rafa' is the exalting in degree and in praise not in place and direction. **Rafa'a**: He took a report or complaint to a person or authority; to make a thing tower above another standing beside it. There is a saying of the Holy Prophet ﷺ, *'rufia' lanâ sakhratun tawîltatun lahâ zillun* (B. Chapter on Hijrah) - a big stone giving good shade was raised above us i.e. we found ourselves beside a high shady stone. Again the Holy Prophet ﷺ says, 'Allâh will, by means of this Qur'ân exalt some people and humble others' (Muslim). Of course no one supposes that in these places raf'a means raising of the body to the heavens. In fact when the raf'a of a person is spoken of as being to or toward Allâh the meaning is invariably his spiritual elevation (L.T.R.B.). Jesus himself has denied the possibility of his rising physically to heaven. Says he, 'And no man has ascended up to heaven but he that came down from heaven, even the Son of man which is in heaven'. (John, 3:13).

Rahmân رحمن: The Arabic words Rahmân and Rahîm are translated as 'Most Gracious' and 'Ever Merciful'. They are derived from the same root *rhm*. The word *rahm* signifies: love; tenderness; mercy; pity; forgiveness; goodness; favour; all that is required for exercising beneficence (M.L.T.). Rahmân and Rahîm are both active participle nouns of different measures denoting intensiveness of significance. Arabic intensive is more suited to express Allâh's attributes than the superlative degree. Rahmân is in the measure of *Fa'lân* which conveys the idea of fullness and extensiveness and indicates the greatest preponderance of the quality of love and mercy which comprehends the entire universe without regard to the effort and asking even before we are born. The creation of the sun, the moon, air and water etc. are all there because of this attribute.

Rahîm رحيم: Is in the measure of *Fa'îl.* This measure denotes the idea of constant repetition and giving of liberal reward to those who deserve it and seek it. The manifestation of this attribute is in response to and as a result of the action of the human beings (A.H.). So Rahîm means extremely and continuously Merciful and Dispenser of grace and love as a result of our deeds and supplications, and One in Whom the attribute is constantly and excessively repeated. The Holy Prophet ﷺ has explained the meaning of Rahmân and Rahîm رحمن الدنيا رحيم الاخرة The attribute Rahmân generally pertains to this life. His love and mercy is manifested in the creation of the universe. He is the bestower of gifts which precede our birth. While the attribute Rahîm generally pertains to the life to come and His love and mercy are manifested in the state that comes after. He causes good results to follow on good deeds and would not nullify and render void anyone's right works (H.A.). The measure of *fa'lân* conveys the idea of fullness and extensiveness while the measure of *Fa'îl* denotes the idea of repetitions (Muhît). The term Rahmân circumscribes the quality of abounding grace inherent in and inseparable from the concept of the Almighty; whereas Rahîm expresses the continuous manifestation of that grace in and its effect upon us and is an aspect of His activity (Ibn Qayyim). So Rahmân and Rahîm are not the repetition of one and the same attribute for the sake of emphasis but are two different attributes.

Raib ريب: Doubt; affliction or calamity; false charge; discomfort or uneasiness of mind; such doubt as is based on prejudice or suspicions and not the doubt which helps in research and promotion of knowledge (L.T. Ahmad).

Rajam رجم: To cast a stone at; to stone any one to death; to course; to revile any one; to expel; to speak conjecturally.

Marâjim: Foul speech (R.L.T.).

Raka'a رَكَعَ: To bow down in Prayer; to be bent (old man); to stoop the head to kneel; to Pray. **Rak'at** Pl. Rak'ât: The word is derived from *raka'a* meaning he bowed down and literally the Rak'at is an act of bowing down before Allâh in Prayer. The Prayer is made up of a number of *rak'ats*, varying from two to four. Technically it means one complete act of devotion which includes standing; bowing down; prostration and sitting reverentially in Prayer; and is thus a kind of one unit in Prayer. The worshipper first stands reverently, and recites *Surah Fâtihah* and certain prayers; then he bows down and glorifies Allâh; then he stands up again praising Allâh, then falls prostrate placing his forehead and nose on the ground and glorifying Allâh, then he sits down in a reverential position and makes a petition then again falls down in prostration then he sits down or stands reverently. This is a complete *rak'at* of a Prayer. Posture of *rukû'* in Prayer, the *qiyâm* is followed by *rukû'* which means bowing down. In this posture the worshipper while standing, bows forward and places both hands on his knees without bending his legs and arms.

Rahw رَهْو: Calm; motionless; depressed place where water collects; an elevated and plain place; dry tract of ground (R.L.T.).

Raja' رجاء: To be disappointed; to hope for; to fear, but in this sense it is always found with a negative (L.R.T.).

Rattala رتل: To put together and arrange nicely the component parts (of the speech) and make it distinct, and separate one from the other; to fairly arrange; to repeat with a slow and distinct enunciation (L.T.).

Ribâ رباء: Any fixed sum (money or commodity) stipulated to be received or given for lending or borrowing over and above what one advances or receives not in the way of legitimate and actual circulation and utilising labour and before fetching profit or loss, whether the dealing is with an individual or organisation, irrespective of the cause and aim of borrowing or lending is *riba* (interest or usury). The stress is on 'fixed' and 'before'. The debtor shall not be made to pay more which was fixed before lending. The word *riba* covers both usury and interest.

Rîh ريح: Wind; power; dominance; conquest; predominance; strength; victory. When it is used in the singular number it generally signifies Divine punishment (17:69; 54:19; 69:6), but when it is used in the plural number it generally signifies Divine blessings (27:63) (L.T.R.).

Rouh روح: Mercy. Linguistically it is related to the noun *Rûh* (breath of life) and has also the significance of *Râhat* (rest from grief and sadness) (T.). Thus the most appropriate translation would be life giving and soothing mercy. The word *rûh* is often used in the Holy Qur'ân in the sense of Divine inspiration and revelation (T.). Since it gives life to hearts that were dead in their ignorance and has in the spiritual world the same function as a soul has in the physical world (Kf. Râzî).

Rûh روح: Breath of life; soul; spirit; inspiration; revelation; essence (R.L.). The Holy Qur'ân; joy and happiness; mercy; life giving words of Allâh; Prophet's Divine Message because of its life-giving qualities; angel; archangel Gabriel (R.L.T).

(S) س

Sâda ساد: To be noble and glorious; to rule; to lead; to overcome any one in glory. **Sawida**: To be black; to be bold. **Sawwada** *Wajhuhû*: To disgrace any one. **Aswada**: To beget a black boy or a boy who is chief. **Sawâd**: Great number. **Assayyadah**: Our blessed lady. **Asswad** اسود: Black, greater. **Aswadda** *wajhuhu*: His face became expressive of grief or sorrow; he was in a bad condition, failure and sorrow; he became sorrowful or confounded; he became disgraced (R.L.T.).

Sâq ساق: Shank; difficulty; distress. **Kashafat** *'an sâqiha* كشفت عن ساقها is a well known idiom. It refers to a person when difficulty befalls him, meaning he prepared himself to meet the difficulty or to become perturbed or perplexed. It is a common place idiom of Arabic literature. Only gross ignorance of the Arabic idioms would make anyone adopt the literal significance of the words. **Kashfat** *'an sâqaihâ* - as she uncovered her shanks in 27:44. **Kashf** *'annissâq* is a proverb signifying the hardness of an afair and the severity of a calamity. The origin of it is in the fright and the flight and the tucking up of their garments by women from their shanks in fleeing and the disclosing of their anklets (Kf.). **Kashafal** *amru 'an sâqihi*: The affair became distressful. **Yukshafa** *'an sâqin* - the truth shall be laid bare. They say *qâmatil qoumu alâ sâqin* - the people were or became in a state of distress. **Kashaft***il harbo 'an sâqin* - the fight became vehement. Kashshaf says while explaining 68:42 that it means the day when the affair becomes hard and formidable and there is neither any laying bare nor a shank. Baidzâwî says it means the day when there is a severe affliction and when the truth of the matter is laid bare (L. T.Kf. Baidzâwî).

Saba' سبع: F. Sab'atun: Seven. **Sab'ûn**: Seventy. They are also used in a vague manner as meaning seven or more; several or many; a large number (L.T).

Sahara سحر: To fascinate; to bewitch; to wheedle; to turn any one from; to gild. **Sihr**: Witchcraft; sorcery; eloquence; seduction; falsehood; deception; anything the source of which is not quite visible; showing off falsehood in the form of truth; a crafty device; mischief; mesmerism; hypnotism. **Sâhir** Pl. sâhirûn and sâharah: Wizard; deluder; man of vast learning (L.T.R.). **Sahira**: To rise or act at day break. **Sahar** Pl. ashâr: Day break; end; edge. **Mashûr**: Bewitched; fudged; deceived, deluded; beguiled; circumvented; outwitted; *ashâr* is the plural and denotes the later part of the night and also signifies the core of the heart; the inner part of the heart or simply heart (L.T.).

Sahata سحت: To make unlawful profits; to destroy; doing of anything that leads to destruction; to devour all that is forbidden; to gain any property or thing that is prohibited; not lawful (L.). It is also applied to a bribe (R.).

Sajada سجد: To bow down; to lower the head; to cast down one's looks; to be lowly and submissive; to prostrate; to obey; to be humble; to bow down in adoration with the forehead touching the ground; to worship. **Sajada***til safînâtu lir riyâhi* - the boat bowed before the wind; it followed the direction of the wind. (R.T.). **Masjid**: A place of adoration and worship (17:1), as at that time there was no mosque there.

Sakar سكر: To fill a vessel; to dam (a stream); to shut (a door); to abate (wind); to be dim (sight); to be dazzled; to rage against; to become drunk. **Sakr**: Sugar; wine; vinegar; food; intoxicating thing. **Sakr***atul mout* - pangs of death. **Sukârâ** pl. *sukrân*: One intoxicated with drink or sleep (T.), confused of judgment; one who has no sense on account of extreme grief or in a fit of anger or in raptures of love; or had received a great and sudden shock or is stricken with fear or is overpowered by any disturbing element which may distract his attention or obscure his reason; who is in a dazed state of mind or is in any state of mental disequilibrium (R.L.T.).

Salâm سلام: Safety; security; immunity; freedom from fault or defects or imperfections or blemishes or vice; peace; obedience; heaven. Salâm is also one of the names of Allâh. **Islâm**: Obedience to Allâh; peace with Allâh; peace with other fellow beings; peace with oneself; peace of mind and soul; religion of Islam (L.T.R.).

Samâ' سماء: Sky; canopy of heaven; cloud; ram; roof; back of a horse. Any thing which hangs overhead and gives shade; above; visible sky; cosmic space in which the stars, the planets, the solar system and the galaxies pursue their course (T. L. Bahr). *Kullu mâ 'alâk fa huwa* **samâk***a* -every thing which is above you is your *samâ* (L.T.R.).

Sarafa سرف : To eat up; to suckle (a child); to excess. **Asrafa**:

To squander one's wealth; to act immoderately (L.). The word *musrif* denotes or commits excesses, who is wasteful who wastes his own self (Râzî) or destroys his moral and spiritual potentialities.

Sidrah سدرة: Lote-tree. **Sadîr**: Sea (T. L.). Explaining the expression Sidrah Râg<u>h</u>îb suggest that owing to the abundance of its leafy shade the Sidrah, the Arabian lote-tree, appears in the Qur'ân (53:14) as well as in the sayings of the Holy Prophet ﷺ relating to the Ascension, as a symbol of the shade of Paradise. It is a place for which the Holy Prophet ﷺ was chosen for Divine favours and great blessings. As the leaves of the Lote-tree possess the quality of safeguarding a dead body from decay the word also signifies that the revelation of the Holy Prophet ﷺ not only is itself immune to, but is eminently fitted to save and preserve humankind from becoming corrupt. The word occurs elsewhere in the Holy Qur'ân as indicating a tree in Paradise (53:16). The word may possess a symbolic allusion to the fact that the revelation of the Holy Prophet ﷺ would, like the lote-tree, gives comfort and shelter to the tired and jaded limbs of the spiritual wayfarer. **Sadîr** is derived from the same root means the sea. Thus the verse indicates that at that stage a sea of endless vistas of Divine knowledge and eternal realities opened out for the Holy Prophet ﷺ.

Sîn س: Prefixed to the aorist of a verb is the sign of the future; as a sign of must and certainty. It also indicates, leader; chief; noble; glorious; the perfect one (L.T.R.).

Sirr سر: Secret. Pl. Asârra: and Sarân: To conceal; to manifest a secret; to express. The word has contrary meanings (L.T.).

SH ش

<u>Sh</u>afâ'at شفاعت: Interceding or praying for a person that he may be shown favour as he is connected with the intercessor, the word has a significance of likeness and similarity, it is also implied that the petitioner or the intercessor is a person of higher position than the one for whom he pleads and that he has deep connection with the one with whom he intercedes (L.T.R.)

Shahida شهد: To witness a thing; to give evidence. **Shahida** *billâhi* -to swear by Allâh. **Shahida** *'alâ ahadin*: -he gave; to give testimony before a judge against anyone. **Tashahhada**: To say, 'There is no other, cannot be and will never be one worthy of worship but Allâh'. **Shahîd**: Martyr; trustworthy witness. According to Islamic terminology, Shahîd is an example of the practical life of the Prophet. His status is next to that of a *Siddique,* but above all other believers who are lower than he in ranks of virtue and righteousness.

Shai شيء: Which is willed or desired; thing (L. T.).

Shaitân شيطن Pl. Shiyâtîn: A being who is not only himself far from truth but also try to turn others away from it; who burns with hatred and anger and is lost (T. Kf.). Râghib says, 'Every insolent or rebellious one from among *jinn*, men and the beasts; Seducer; wicked, troublesome'. The Holy Prophet ﷺ is reported to have said, 'A single rider is a *shaitân* a pair of riders is also a pair of *shaitâns*, but three riders are a body of riders' (D.). The tradition lends support to the view that shaitân does not necessarily mean a devil. By shaitân is also meant the leaders (L.). **Shâtana**: To oppose; to enter; to be far from; to bind or hold with a rope. **Shaitâna**: To be wicked; rebellious; to be noisy and troublesome (L. T.).

Shajara شجر: To turn aside; to thrust (with a spear); to be disputed between. **Shajar***al amru bainahum*: The affair or case became complicated and confused so as to be a subject of disagreement and difference between them; so it means a quarrel. **Shajar** pl. *shajarah*: Tree; shrub; stock or origin of a person. They say, *'howa min shajaratin tayyibatin* - he is of a good stock or origin (L.T.).

Shira شري: To purchase; to sell; to conclude a sale. **Shara:** To refuse; to choose from a flock; to prefer and refuse; giving up any thing and taking another; laying hold on another (L.T.).

Shûra شُوري: Consultation; the process by which honey is extracted from the hives (L. T.). In matters of society it consists of a continuous dialogue between the participants till a consensus emerges. It is a more effective process, but essentially more complicated than one of simple majority vote (R.L.T.Kf.).

(S) ص

Sâbî صابي: One who forsakes his old religion and adopts a new one. The name was applied to the following religious sects that were found in parts of Arabia and countries bordering it.

1. The star worshipers. They lived in Mesopotamia (Mas'ûdî: Murûj-al Dhahab).
2. The faith which was a sort of patch work of Judaism, Christianity and Zoroastrianism.
3. A semi-Christian sect of Babylonia closely resembling the Christians of St. John the Baptist, known as al-Mughtasillah.
4. People who lived near Mousul in Iraq and believed in one Allâh. They claimed to follow the religion of Noah.
5. A people who professed belief in all the Prophets of Allâh and had a special system of prayer and fasting (K.).

None of the above mentioned peoples should be confused with Sabaens (not Sabian) mentioned by some commentators of the Bible as people inhabiting ancient Yemen.

Sabr صبر: Patiently preserver; bondage. According to Râghib it is keeping oneself constrained to which reason or law requires, or with holding from that from which it requires to withhold.

Sadaqa صدق: To speak voraciously; to tell the truth to; to fulfill (a promise); **Sadaqa** *fil qitâl*: To fight gallantly. **Saddaqa**: To hold anyone as trustworthy; to fulfill. **Tasaddaqa**: To give alms. **Sâdiqah**: Perfect (woman). **Sadaqa** Pl. Suduqât: Dowry. **Sâdiq**: Sincere; trustworthy; perfect. **Siddîque**: According to Islamic terminology Siddîque is a person who is trustworthy; sincere and occupies a position above all other believers (L.T.R.). He is in a way possessor of the spiritual capacities of a Prophet and to be followed as an example of a person of prophetic knowledge. He is looked upon as the spiritual descendant of the Prophet. After the decease of the Messenger of Allâh their missions are carried out by Siddiques as was Abû Bakr (see also **Shâhîd**). *Qadama* **Sidq:** A footing of firmness, precedence of truthfulness, going forward with truth in words and deeds with complete sincerity (L.T.R.). **Saddaqa:** To confirm; to verify; to fulfill; confirming the right as right and wrong as wrong. Confirming; verification and fulfilling of a previous scriptures signify three things:

1. The prophecies about the coming of some future Prophets;
2. Future revelations becoming true;
3. The teachings which they gave were true; the claims of those Books and their Prophets about their Divine origin were true.

When the Holy Qur'ân uses the word in the sense of 'confirming and fulfilling of the prophecies contained in them' it is followed by the proposition *lâm* as in verse 2:41. Therefore the translation, 'Confirming (the prophecies of the Scripture) which are (already with you)'.

Sadîd صديد: Is an infinite noun of Sadda which denotes he turned away, he cried out loudly. It signifies anything that is repulsive. It also means hot or boiling water (Qâmûs; Asâs: L.).

Safâ صفا: To be pure; to be clear; to be free from all dross; to choose; to distinguish any one by a gift; to take the best of. **Mustafâ**: one of the titles of the Holy Prophet; the purified and the chosen one (L.T.). **Safâ**: A hillock near Ka'bah at Makkah.

Salb صلب: Killing by crucifying or a certain well known manner (L. T.). **Salaba***hû* - he put him to death in a certain well known manner (T.).

Salât صلاة: Prayer; supplication; mosque; place of Prayer; place of worship. Its root is *Sâd, Lâm, Wâw* and not *Sâd, Lâm Yâ.*

Sibghah صبغة: Attribute; faith; kind or mode or nature of a thing; dyeing; colouring; dipping; immersing in water hence it indicates baptism which the Christians effect by immersing in water (L. T.). In the Holy Qur'ân (2:138) the attributes of Allâh and faith of Islam is called Allâh's colour or faith. This particular word has been adopted here as a hint to Christians that the baptism of water does not effect any change in a person. It is *takhalluq bi Akhlâq Allâh* that is, the adaptation of Allâh's attributes and broad principle of faith and accepting the Prophets of all nations that brings about the real change in the mind. It is through this baptism that the new birth takes place. According to the Arabic grammar sometimes when it is intended strongly to induce a person to do a certain thing the verb is omitted, as in this verse, and only the object is mentioned. Therefore in the translation we have added the verb *khudhû* - assume!

Sirâṯ صراط: A path which is even, wide, enough and can be trodden without difficulty (R.); a way that is straight so that all parts of it are in orderly array and are properly adjusted to one another (R.T.L.). *Tarîq* (a way or a path) is not a *Sirâṯ al-Mustaqîm* until it comprises the following prominent features:

1. rectitude;
2. leading surely to the objective;
3. being the shortest;
4. being broad in width for travellers;

Surr صر: When derived from *Sâd, Wâw, Râ* with *Wâw* as the central root letter means he attached, inclined and leaned a thing, particularly when it is used with the proposition *ilâ.* But when derived from *Sâd, Yâ, Râ* with *Yâ* as the central root letter it means he cut, he divided a thing. The Holy Qur'ân uses in verse 2:260 Surr with *waw* in the central root letters as the *dzamma* in Surr indicates. Moreover here the preposition *ilâ* is used. So it means inclining; attaching and not cutting. The lexicologists are all agreed that the word Surr used here is the imperative form of sûra; which means he made it to incline; to attach (L. T.). Cutting into pieces is not the significance of this word in 2:260 (Râzî; Zamakhsharî).

(T) ت

Tâ ت: Pronoun postfixed to the verb at the first, second as well as the third feminine person of the past as *fa'ltu, fa'lta; fa'lti*; particle prefixed to the verbs at the second person as well as the third feminine of the future, *taf'alu; taf'lâni; taf alîna*. It is used also at swearing; as a preposition prefixed; as a form of oath. *Tallâhi* -, by Allâh.

Tâbût تابوت: Heart which is the storehouse of knowledge; wisdom and peace (R.). Tâj quotes the proverb *Mâ au'adtu tâbûtî shaian faqaddtuhû* - I have not deposited in my bosom (- tâbût) anything of knowledge that I have lost. Râghib quotes Omar as speaking of Ibn Mas'ûd, 'A vessel filled up with knowledge,' referring to his heart. Tranquility from Allâh is not a thing which is placed in boxes; rather the heart is its real place. In no less than five other places in the Holy Qur'ân the coming down of tranquility is mentioned and every time it is the heart that is its recipient. An ark; box (R.L.T.).

Ta'wîll تأويل: Interpretation; true significance; consequence of the rejection of truth; ultimate state of the perfect manifestation of truth (M.L.T.).

Taha تہا: pl. Yatîhûna. To lose a way; to become unfounded or perplexed; to become confused and perished; to magnify himself or behave proudly or insolently (L.T.).

Tahajjud تہجّد: It is derived from *hujûd* which means sleep and Tahajjud literally signifies the giving up of sleep (R.). The voluntary Tahajjud Prayer is so called because it is performed after one has had some sleep at night and sleep is then given up for the sake of Allâh (73:1-6; 17:79). The Holy Prophet's practice was to go to sleep immediately after the *Ishâ'* Prayer and then he generally woke up after midnight and passed almost all this latter half of the night in Tahajjud Prayer. This practice he kept up to the last. It is related that he used to stand so long in this Prayer that his feet would get swollen (B.19:6). The Tahajjud Prayer consists of eight *rakats*; divided into a service of two at a time followed by three *rakats* of *witr*.

Taht تحت: Beneath; below or under; the lower part; the slope and declination of a mountain; in wedlock, figuratively it means subordination (L.T.R.).

Talâ تلي: To follow; to walk behind; to imitate; to read; to recite (L.R.).

Tariba ترب : To be full of earth; to have dust in the hands. **Tirb** Pl. Atrâb: Match; contemporary; companion; friend; equal in quality (R.L.T.).

Taurât توراة: This word is 18 times referred to in the Holy Qur'ân. To translate it by the words 'The Old Testament' is wrong. The Old Testament is a Christian term. The Catholics and Protestants are not agreed precisely as to the numbers of records to be included in the Cannon. Nor is it correct to translate Taurât as the Pentateuch; a Greek word meaning 'The Five Books.' These are the first five Books of the Old Testament. They contain a semi historical and legendary narrative of the history of the world beginning from Âdam to the time of the arrival of the Jews in the Promised Land. A great part of the Mosaic Law is embodied in it. The Books are ascribed to Moses but it is certain that they were not written by Moses or within an appreciable distance of the time from Moses. The Qur'ânic teaching is that Moses was an inspired man and Messenger of Allâh and gave a Message. The name of the Book revealed to him is Taurât, which was afterwards distorted or lost.

Tayammum تيمم: Is derived from *amma* meaning to propose a thing, to aim at; to repair to a thing; Prayer is the means for the purification of soul and purification is the key to Prayer and it is a portion of *Îmân* (Im. 1:5) and *Îmân* is built on cleanliness as outward purity is a necessary preparation. A pure mind in a pure body is the watch word of Islâm. The first condition of bodily purification is *wadzû'*. But if any one is unable to find water for *wadzû* or when the use of water is harmful still it is necessary to perform an act which diverts attention from bodily purification to the purity of the soul which is the aim of Prayer. That is the aim and purpose of Tayammum. So by Tayammum attention is drawn to the inner purpose underlying *wadzû'* and the bath. Tayammum consists in striking both hands on pure earth or anything containing pure dust, then blowing off the excess of dust from the hands and passing them over the face and the backs of the two hands, the left over the right and the right over the left (7;4,5) (R.L.T.).

Tubba' تبع: Was the royal title of the kings of Himyar in Yemen. They were known by this title when they also held sway over Himyar; Hadzramût and Saba. Tubba' ruled over these territories from 27 A.D. to 525 A.D. (L.T. Ibn Khaladûn).

(T) ط

Taraf طرف: Pl. Atrâf: Side; part; extremity; edge; fringe; end; outlying parts; high and low persons; leader; scholar; thinker; best of the fruits (T.M.L.).

Tarafa طرف: To wink (with eyes); to slap on the face; to hurt the eye; to make it water. *Mâ baqiyat min um 'ainun* **tatrifu**: - there is no one left amongst them to be hurt; to newly acquired (property); to descend from an ancient family; to attack the extremity of the enemy's lines; to choose a thing (L.T.R.).

Târa طار: He or it flew or moved in the air; he or it ran or moved quickly or fled; conceived. **Tâir** Pl. Tair: flying bird; insect; one who soars into the higher (spiritual) regions and is not bent low upon earthly things. Arab proverb and poetry bear witness to bird, being spoken of as attending a victorious army to feed upon the corpses of the enemy left on the battlefield. It also means horses (cavalry), flying thing; swift animal; a company of men; a person who is sharp and quick; cause of good and evil; the action of a person, good or bad; fortune or destiny (L.T. Qâmûs; Midâni; Râzî).

(Th) ث

Thâba ثَابَ: To gather people; to rise (dust); to return to; to recover; to requite; to reward; to call to prayer; to repay; to compensate. **Thoub**: Garment; morals; behaviour; heart. **Tahiruth thiyâb**: Pure-hearted; of good character.

Thawâb ثواب Reward; (especially for good works); honey; bees; rain (L.T.R.).

Thakhana ثخن: It was thick or coarse or hard. **Athkhana**: He made a great slaughter or a great wounding (T.).

Thamûd ثمود: This tribe lived in the western parts of Arabia, between Adan and Syria shortly before the time of Ismâîl. Their Prophet of Allâh was Sâlih. This tribe is mentioned by Greek historians as well. Hijr or Agra as they call it, is given as the home of these people whom they call *thamudeni*. They mention a place near Hijr, according to them, the Arabs called (Fajj al-Nâqah). Ptolemy calls it Badata. Some Muslims read a poetic inscription about this tribe during the reign of Amîr Muawiyyah which was rediscovered by Haines and Wellstedt in 1834 A.D.

Thana ثنا: To fold; to bend; to bind; to conceal (hatred). **Thana** *sadrahu* literally means he folded his bosom indicate that he concealed enmity or anything in his breast (T.), and they wrap themselves in their garments in order that they might not see nor hear (L.). According to Râghib the meaning is that they make their garments a covering over their ears and this signifies their holding back from lending an ear, or it is an allusion to their running away. It also means that they are allowing their hearts to remain making them impervious to spiritual perception. **Mathânî** derived from *thanaya*: To repeat; to praise; to bend. According to such eminent authorities as 'Omar, 'Alî, Ibn 'Abbâs and Ibn Mas'ûd the words *sab'am min al-mathânî* refer to the opening chapter of the Holy Qur'ân because it is repeated and recited in every *rak'at* of the Prayer. The Holy Prophet ﷺ is reported to have said that al-Sab'al Mathânî is the opening chapter of the Holy Qur'ân (B.). According to Zajjaj and Abû Hayyân the chapter is given this name because it contains the praises of Allâh. Mathânî also meaning a bend of the valley thus the first chapter fully explains the relationship of Allâh to human beings. The Holy Qur'ân is also called Mathânî (39:23) which signifies that it describes its basic beliefs and principles repeatedly and in different ways and forms. The word also signifies that some of the teachings of the Holy Qur'ân resemble those of other Scriptures.

Thumma ثُمَّ: Then; afterwards; moreover. This is mostly used as a conjunction indicating a sequence in time or order to be rendered as 'then', 'thereafter' or 'thereupon ', also occasionally as a simple conjunction equivalent to 'and'. In yet another usage of which there are frequent instances in the Qur'ân as well as the sayings of the Holy Prophet ﷺ, and in pre-Islamic Arabian poetry it has the significance of a repetitive stress; alluding to something that has already been stated and is now again emphasized to be rendered as "and once again". In cases where it is used to link parallel statements it has the function of the simple conjunction *wâw* 'and' (R.T.).

(U) أ

Umm أُم: Pl. Ummahât and Ummat. Mother; source; principle; prototype; **Umm***ul Qurâ* - mother of the towns; metropolis, Makkah. **Ummî**: motherly; ignorant; illiterate; idolater; belonging to Makkah; an Arab (R. L. T.). According to Râzî it also refers to the people who have no revealed Scripture of their own.

Ummah أُمّة: A group of living beings having certain characteristics or circumstances in common, thus it is synonymous with community, nation, generation. In as much as every such grouping is characterised by the basic fact that it constitutes, whether human or animal are endowed with life. It also signifies creation. It is derived from amma to repair or direct (his) course to a thing to sought or aim. Ummah is way; course or manner or mode of acting; faith; religion; nation; a generation; time or a period of time. A righteous person who is an object of imitation and who is known for goodness; a person combining all kinds of good qualities; one who has no equal; one who combines within himself all virtues (L. T.).

'Umrah عُمْرَه: Is derived from 'amara: To inhabit a place or pay a visit to it. In the terminology of Islam 'Umrah means a sacred visit to the K'abah. It consists of entering into a state of *Ihrâm* - circling around the K'abah seven times, running between Safa and Marwah. It differs from Hajj in three respects. i) Hajj cannot be performed except at the fixed time while 'Umrah may be performed at any time. ii) Going to Arafât, Muzdalifah and Minâ and the assembling there is dispensed with in the case of 'Umrah, while it is an essential part of Hajj. iii) The sacrifice of an animal is almost essential to Hajj but not in the case of 'Umrah. 'Umrah may be performed separately or along with Hajj as *Tamattu'* and *Qirân*. There is an expressed injunction to accomplish both Hajj and 'Umrah (2:196-199).

Umniyyah امنية: Pl. Amâniyyah. A desire; because desire leads to lies; repetitions of words without knowing their significance; wishful thinking or belief; false notion; object of desire. This word is derived from *manya* (R.L.T.).

'Urf عرف: Elevated place is derived from **'Arafa**: To know; to perceive by the senses or mind; to bear a thing patiently; to manage skilfully; to govern over people; to use perfume. The people on the elevated places (7:46) are men of high dignity and distinguished position. According to Hasan and Mujâhid they will be the elite and the most learned, according to Kirmâni they will be the Martyrs, some others think that they will be the Prophets (L. T. R.). The difference between *'Urf* and *'ilm* is that the former refers to distinct and specific knowledge while the latter is more general, hence the opposite of *'arafa* is *ankara* (to deny) and to *'ilm* is *Jahl* (to be ignorant). **'Arafât**: A place 9 miles east of Ka'bah. **M'arûf**: Known; recognized; honourable; good; befitting; a kindness (R.L.T.)

(W) و

Wâhid واحد: Matchless; pairless; unique; alone; unparalleled. Real source of all creation and everything point to him just as a second or a third thing necessarily points to the first. One; a single one; the only one. **Ahad**: Denotes the absolute unity without relation to any other being. Who is and has ever been one and alone; who has no second to share in his lordship nor in his essence (L.R.T.).

Wa'aza وعظ: To exhort; to warn; to preach. **Mau'izatan**: Sermon; warning; teaching which proceeds from a genuine desire to impart good council; teaching which is deeply effective and touches the human heart; which has set forth in a good manner; all those principles and rules of conduct which lead to moral reformation and success in life (R. T.).

Wafaya وفي: To fulfill (a promise); to pay (a debt): to be plentiful; complete. **Tawaffâ***hullâhu* - Allâh caused him to die. **Tawaffa** توفي: To die. **Wafât:** Death (L.T.); **Tawaffait***anî*-you caused me to die; **Tawaffa***hun* - those whom they cause to die; **Tawaffat***hu* - they take over his soul and cause him to die; **Matawaffi-***yannaka* - we cause you to die (R. Kf.). Ibn 'Abbâs has translated **Mutawaffi***ka* as *mumîtu-ka* - I will cause you to die (B. 65:12). Jarîullah Abû al-Qârî Mahmûd ibn Umar al-Zamakhsharî an Arab linguist of great repute says, **Mutawaffi***ka* means, I will protect you from being killed by the people and will grant thee full leave till you to die a natural death, not being killed (Kashshâf). Outstanding scholars and commentators like Imâm Mâlik, Imâm Bukhârî, Imâm ibn Hazm, Imâm ibn Qayyim, Qatâda, and others are of the same view (Bukhârî, chapter on Tafsîr and chapter in Bad ul Khalq; Majma' Bihar al-Anwâr by Shaikh Muhammad Tâhir of Gujrât; al-Muhatta, Cairo, 1:23; Zâd al-Ma'âd by Muhammad ibn Abû Bakr al-Dimashqî, Dur-al-Manthûr by Sayûtî; and commentary by Abu-al-Fidâ Ismâîl ibn al-Kathîr). The word has been used at no less than 25 different places of the Holy Qur'ân and in twenty three of them the meaning is to take away the soul at the time of death. Only at two places the meaning is to take the soul away at the time of sleep; but there the qualifying word sleep or night has been added (6:60; 39:42). According to Lisânal 'Arab, you say **twaffahu***llaho* when you mean 'Allâh took his soul or caused him to die'. Biblical idiom for causing to die is gathering and means Allâh took away the soul of someone, that is to say He caused him to die - when Allâh is the subject and a human being the object. In fact all Arab lexicographers agree on the point that the word as used in the aforesaid meaning can bear no other interpretation. Not a single instance from the Holy Qur'ân, the sayings of the Holy Prophet ﷺ and the whole of Arabic literature can be shown against this expression or can be used in another sense.

Wajha وجه: Attention; self; face; beginning of a day; century; reason; way; manner; point of view; object of speech; honour; regard; dignity; purpose; course; lucidity of mind; aim; end; result; chief of a party. The part of a thing visible to the sight of a on- looker; favour. **Wajaha**: To enjoy consideration; regard; to send someone for a purpose. *Ibydzdza* **wajhuhû** - he has illustrated himself; *li* **wajhihî** - for the sake of Allâh; direction; object and motive; desired way; deed or action to which a person directs his attention; part of a thing visible to the sight of a person desirous of a favour or countenance; that which is under the care and protection of a person; to which a person directs his attention (L.T.R.).

Walaya ولي: To be adjacent; to follow anyone or a thing

immediately; to have charge of; to rule; to be the friend of. **Walla**: To turn away from; to shun; to entrust anyone with the care of (R.L.T.). **Maula**: Master; Lord; Helper: Friend; companion; ally, **Walî** Pl. Auliya: near in respect of place, religion, belief; helper; friend; Lord (R.)

Waqaya وقي: Guarding; saving; preserving. *Ittaqâ bihî* - he took him or it as a shield. **Wiqâyah**: A shield (M.T.L.). **Muttaqî** is in the nominative case of *ittaqâ:* One who guards against evil and against that which harms and injures, and is regardful of his duty. Ubbayy bin Ka'b, a distinguished Companion of the Holy Prophet says, 'Muttaqî is a man who walks through thorny bushes, taking every care that his clothes are not caught in and be torn by their branches' (K.). Thus in Qur'ânic language the word means who guards himself against sins and harmful things and takes Allâh as a shield or shelter and is dutiful.

Wasamaوسم: To brand, to be known by its outward signs. In its full significance the word *mutawisim* Pl. mutawasimîn, denotes one who applies his mind to the study of the outward appearance of a thing with a view to understanding its real nature and its inner characteristics (Kf); and one who deliberates over a thing and examines it and does so repeatedly to obtain a clear knowledge of it (L.T.). **Ism**: name; attribute; by-name; surname (R,L.T.).

Wasaṯa وسط: To be seated in the middle; midst of; to be equally distant from the extremes: to become noble; distinguished. The best part of a thing; *ummat* **wusṯâ** - middle most community; a community that keeps an equitable balance between extreme; rejecting both licentiousness and exaggeration in any aspect of their life; good and exalted (L. T. Kf.). It refers to place and at the same time to a degree. *S̱alâtul* **wusṯâ** - the most excellent Prayer. The most excellent Prayer is that in which the external form and spirit of the Prayer is carefully observed. According to a saying of the Holy Prophet ﷺ the latter afternoon Prayer ('As̱r) is spoken of as the *s̱alâtul* wusṯâ (B.).

This name may have given to it because 'Asr is the busiest part of the day thus most difficult to observe in its most excellent form and spirit.

Wasîlah وسيلة: Favour; honourable rank; degree; affinity; tie; nearness. It does not mean the intermediary between Allâh and the human being. The short prayer after *Adhân* (a call to Prayer) include the words 'O Allâh! Give Muhammad wasîlah' mean that Allâh may vouchsafe to the Holy Prophet ﷺ increasing nearness to Himself and not that the Holy Prophet ﷺ may have someone to act as intermediary between him and Allâh.

Wated وتد Pl. Autâd: Pegs firmly driven into the ground. **Autâdul Ardz, Autâdul bilâd**: Chiefs of the towns, provinces or countries (L.). The number of poles supporting a Bedouin tent is determined by its size and the latter has always depended on the status and power of its owner. Thus a mighty chieftain is often alluded to as one of many tent poles. In classical Arabic this term is used idiomatically as a metonymic for mighty dominion; firmness of heavy responsibility, one who unites (L.T.).

Zanîm زنيم: Base; ignoble; mean; notoriously mischievous; the son of an adulteress or fornicatoress; of doubtful birth; one adopted among a people to whom he does not belong; one who is not needed; useless; redundant (L.T.R.).

Zanam زنم: Either of the two wattles or fleshy skin protuberances hanging below the ears of a goat (L.T.).

Zibr زبر: Pl. zubûr زبور. Book; a book full of wisdom; a Divine Book; a book which is hard in writing; Psalms. **Zabrah** Pl. Zubar and Zubrah: Fragment of iron; mane of iron; anvil: a big piece of iron (L. M. Râzî).

(Z) ظ

Zalla ظل: To remain; to last; to continue doing a thing. **Zalâl**: Anything providing shade; cloud; screen; state; any thing that shades one in the sense of protecting him. **Zill**: Shade; shadow; shelter (L.T.R.).

Zalama ظلم: To misuse; to act

wrongfully; to over flow (river); to harm; to act tyrannical towards; to deprive any one of a right; to misplace; to misuse a thing; to dig the ground in a wrong place; to drink (the milk) before it thickens. *Mâ* **azalma***hû***:** How mischievous he is! How dark it is! **Tazallam**: To act wrongly; to trespass upon any one's rights. **Mazlûm:** Vexed; oppressed; wronged. **Muzlim**: Dark; nefarious; bad (day). **Zalima**: To be dark; obscure. **Azlama**: To enter upon; to be in darkness. **Zulm**: Misuse; wickedness; oppression; tyranny; injustice associating partners with Allâh (31:13), obscurity. The word is also used figuratively to signify error or ignorance just as the word *nûr* (light) is sometimes used to signify guidance. In the Holy Qur'ân, the Prophet; the Islamic faith, the Prayer and the Qur'ân are also called light. In the Holy Qur'ân the word *zulum* is always used in plural form. **Zulumât**: Denotes different kinds of darkness; thick darkness; afflictions; hardship; dangers, spiritual; or moral or physical. In the moral and spiritual sense the plural form also signifies that sins and evil deeds do not stand alone but grow and multiply. One stumbling leading to another.

Zan ظَن: Conjecture; supposition; thought; strong presumption; preponderant belief with the admission that the contrary may be the case; knowledge; certainty (L.T.R.).

Zihâr ظهار: Was a practice of the pre-Islamic days by which the wife was kept in a state of suspense. Sometimes for the whole of her life, having neither the position of a wife nor that of a divorced woman free to marry elsewhere. The word Zihâr is derived from *zahr* means the back. An Arab in the days of ignorance would say to his wife *anti `alayya ka* **zahri** *ummî* i.e. you are to me as the back of my mother. No sooner were these words pronounced than the conjugal relations between husband and wife ended as by a divorce but the woman was not free to leave the husband's house and remained as a deserted wife (L.T.R.). Zihâr is not allowed in Islam. The Holy Qur'ân calls it a hateful word and a lie (58:1-4) (R..L.T.).

INDEX

INDEX

The figures in the reference are separated by a colon(:). The figures before the colon indicate the number of chapter (sûrah), and the subsequent number or numbers indicate the number or numbers of verse(s) (âyat) in that chapter. For example a reference as Aaron, 7:122,142. means that Aaron is mentioned in the 122nd and 142 verses of the 7th chapter of the Holy Qur'ân. The word between the brackets shows that the word itself is not in the Holy Qur'ân, but the reference is to that word as (Abû Bakr): 9:40; 24:22.

(A)

(B)

(I)

(J)

(M)

(S)

(Y)

(Z)